Canadian Edition

Financial Markets and Institutions

Canadian Edition

Financial Markets and Institutions

Frederic S. Mishkin
Graduate School of Business, Columbia University

Stanley G. Eakins
East Carolina University

Apostolos Serletis
University of Calgary

Toronto

National Library of Canada Cataloguing in Publication

Mishkin, Frederic S.
Financial markets and institutions / Frederic S. Mishkin, Stanley G. Eakins, Apostolos Serletis. — Canadian ed.

ISBN 0-321-12666-1

1. Finance—Canada. 2. Financial institutions—Canada.
I. Eakins, Stanley G. II. Serletis, Apostolos, 1954- . III. Title.

HG185.C2M58 2004 332'.0971 C2003-900894-0

0-321-12666-1

Vice President, Editorial Director: Michael J. Young
Acquisitions Editor: Gary Bennett
Marketing Manager: Deborah Meredith
Associate Editor: Rema Celio
Production Editor: Mary Ann McCutcheon
Copy Editor: Jennifer Therriault
Production Coordinator: Janette Lush
Page Layout: Nelson Gonzalez
Permissions Research: Amanda McCormick
Art Director: Mary Opper
Interior and Cover Design: Anthony Leung
Cover Image: GettyImages

1 2 3 4 5 08 07 06 05 04

Printed and bound in the United States.

To My Dad

— F. S. M.

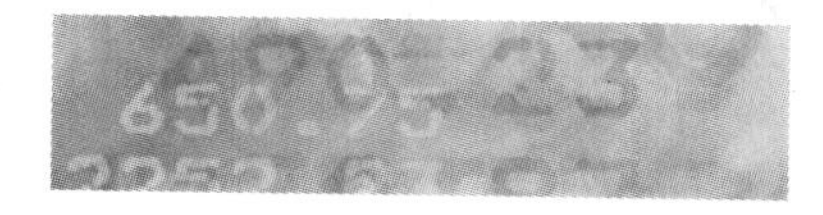

To My Wife, Laurie

— S. G. E.

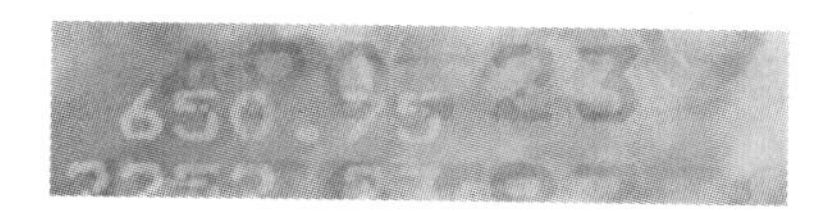

To My Mom and Dad

— A. S.

Brief Contents

Contents

Preface

In preparing the Canadian Edition of *Financial Markets and Institutions*, I retained the basic hallmarks that have made this text the best-selling textbook in this field in the past four U.S. editions. Other textbooks are almost entirely descriptive and so do not adequately prepare students either for jobs in the financial services industry or for successful interaction with financial institutions, whatever their jobs. In contrast, *Financial Markets and Institutions* provides the following features:

- A unifying analytic framework that uses a few basic principles to organize students' thinking, including:
  - asymmetric information (agency) problems
  - transaction costs
  - supply and demand
  - asset market equilibrium
  - efficient markets
  - measurement and management of risk
- A financial practitioner's approach to financial markets and institutions through emphasis of an applied managerial perspective that includes nearly 20 special applications called "The Practising Financial Institution Manager"
- A careful step-by-step development of models that enables students to master the material more easily
- A high degree of flexibility that allows professors to teach the course however they want
- Complete integration of an international perspective throughout the text
- Special features called "Following the Financial News" and "Reading the Financial Pages" to encourage the reading of a financial newspaper
- Numerous applications that increase students' interest by applying theory to real-world data and examples

THE CANADIAN PERSPECTIVE

The Canadian Edition of *Financial Markets and Institutions* is based on the fourth U.S. edition and offers features that make it highly distinctive from other textbooks in this field.

E-Focus

The incredible advances in electronic (computer and telecommunications) technology in recent years have had a major impact on the financial system. The book reflects these developments by having features with an electronic focus.

Web Enhancement The fourth edition embraces the exploding world of information now available over the World Wide Web. There are few areas where the Internet has been as valuable as in providing financial information. Data that were once difficult and tedious to collect are now readily available. To help students appreciate what they can access online we reflect these developments in the book.

1. **Web Exercises.** The book has a type of end-of-chapter problem called Web Exercises. These require that students collect information from online sources or use online resources to enhance their learning experience. The Web Exercises are designed to be relatively quick and easy to do, while still accomplishing the goal of familiarizing students with online sources of data.
2. **Web Sources.** Much of the data used to create the many tables and charts were collected from sources found online. Wherever a URL is available, it is exactly reported as the source. The interested student or instructor can use this URL to see what has happened since the chart or table was created.
3. **Marginal Web References.** In addition to listing the sources of data used to create the charts and graphs, we have also included in the margins URLs to websites that provide information or data that supplement the text material. These references include a brief description of what students will find at the site. The interested student can use these sites to extend their study, and instructors can use these sites to enhance their lecture notes. Because the URLs for web sources and references do sometimes change, the text resource site at www.pearsoned.ca/text/mishkin_fmi will provide the new URLs when they are needed.

E-Finance Boxes Since electronic technology is permeating financial markets in more and more ways, we included a type of special interest box. The E-Finance boxes relate how changes in technology have affected financial markets or institutions. The placement of these boxes throughout the text helps demonstrate the impact technology has had in a broad range of areas in finance.

Expanded Coverage of the Stock Market

With the wide swings in stock prices in recent years, students of financial markets and institutions have become increasingly interested in what drives the stock market. As a result, we provide an expanded discussion of this market by including simple valuation methods. These include using the Gordon Growth Model and the price/earnings ratio to determine stock prices.

Venture Capital

The book provides expanded coverage of venture capital because of its importance to the economy and especially to the technology sector. We discuss the process followed by venture capitalist firms in selecting companies to finance, and follow the life cycle of the typical venture capital deal in Chapter 20, Venture Capital Firms, Finance Companies, and Financial Conglomerates. We also discuss the role venture capital firms had in fueling the technology bubble and how they are affected by the recession that started in 2001.

Investment Banks and Mutual Funds

In Chapter 21, Investment Banks, Brokerage Firms, and Mutual Funds, we have an extended discussion of investment banks, which have also grown in importance because they have helped finance the technology sector, to include more details about how new securities are brought to the public. We also discuss in detail the various types of mutual funds available and how they may be used by investors.

Monetary Policy Strategy

Recent developments in the conduct of monetary policy around the world have prompted us to include the following material:

- Extensive treatment of the Large Value Transfer System (LVTS) framework within which the Bank of Canada conducts monetary policy (Chapter 7)
- A full discussion of the operating band for the overnight interest rate and the Bank of Canada's standing facilities (Chapter 7)
- A section on the market for settlement balances and the determination of the overnight interest rate (Chapter 7)
- A full discussion of monetary targeting and inflation targeting, two prominent monetary policy strategies used by central banks throughout the world (Chapter 7), and an extensive treatment of current Canadian monetary policy (Chapters 6 and 7)
- A discussion of exchange-rate strategies, including currency boards and dollarization, both of which have received a lot of attention lately, as well as a discussion of whether Canada should join a monetary union with the United States and perhaps Mexico (Chapter 13)

Material on Financial Markets and Institutions

Continuing changes in financial markets and institutions have prompted us to include the following material:

- Discussion of the rapid collapse of Enron and WorldCom, which resulted in the largest bankruptcies in U.S. history (Chapter 14)
- New material on the Basel Committee on Bank Supervision and where the Basel Accord is heading (Chapter 18)
- Discussion of the most recent developments regarding deposit insurance and risk management, including the modernization of the CDIC's *Standards of Sound Business and Financial Practices* (Chapter 18).
- Discussion of the spread of deposit insurance throughout the world (Chapter 18)
- A full discussion of the key elements of the new legislation based on the MacKay Report on the Future of the Canadian Financial Services Sector (Chapter 18). This legislation is regarded as one of the most significant revisions to the Bank Act in Canadian history.

Increased International Perspective

The growing importance of the global economy encouraged us to add material with an international perspective. Special-interest boxes with international material are designated as "Global." Material with an international perspective includes:

- Extensive treatment of the European Monetary Union and the introduction of the euro, including discussion of how it has fared in the currency markets in its first three years (Chapter 12), the birth of the European Monetary Union and the euro (Chapter 13), and whether the euro will challenge the dollar as a reserve currency (Chapter 13)
- Sections on capital controls and the role of the International Monetary Fund in preventing financial crises (Chapter 13)
- Discussion of dollarization and recent developments in Argentina's currency board (Chapter 13)

FLEXIBILITY

There are as many ways to teach financial markets and institutions as there are instructors. Thus, there is a great need to make a textbook flexible in order to satisfy the diverse needs of instructors, and that has been a primary objective in writing this book. This textbook achieves this flexibility in the following ways:

- Core chapters provide the basic analysis used throughout the book, and other chapters or sections of chapters can be assigned or omitted according to instructor preferences. For example, Chapter 2 introduces the financial system and basic concepts such as transaction costs, adverse selection, and moral hazard. After covering Chapter 2, an instructor can decide to teach a more detailed treatment of financial structure in Chapter 14, or can skip this chapter or take any of a number of different paths.
- The approach to internationalizing the text using separate, marked international sections within chapters and separate chapters on the foreign exchange market and the international monetary system is comprehensive yet flexible. Although many instructors will teach all the international material, others will choose not to. Instructors who want less emphasis on international topics can easily skip Chapter 12 (on the foreign exchange market) and Chapter 13 (on the international financial system).
- "The Practising Financial Institution Manager" applications, as well as Part VI on the management of financial institutions, are self-contained and so can be skipped without loss of continuity. Thus, an instructor wishing to teach a less managerially oriented course, who might want to focus more on public policy issues, will have no trouble doing so. Alternatively, Part VI can be taught earlier in the course, immediately after Chapter 15 on bank management.

The course outlines listed next for a semester teaching schedule illustrate how this book can be used for courses with a different emphasis. More detailed information about how the text can be used flexibly in your course is available in the *Instructor's Resource Manual.*

Financial markets and institutions emphasis: Chapters 1–5, 8–10, 14–16, 18, and six other chapters

Financial markets and institutions with international emphasis: Chapters 1–5, 8–10, 12–16, 18, and four other chapters

Managerial emphasis: Chapters 1–5, 15, 16, 18, 22, 23, and eight other chapters

Public policy emphasis: Chapters 1–7, 14, 15, 18, and eight other chapters

MAKING IT EASIER TO TEACH FINANCIAL MARKETS AND INSTITUTIONS

The demands for good teaching at business schools have increased dramatically in recent years. To meet these demands, we have provided the instructor with supplementary materials, unavailable with any competing text, that should make teaching the course substantially easier.

Along with the usual items in the *Instructor's Resource Manual*—sample course outlines, chapter outlines, overviews, teaching tips, and answers to the end-of-chapter problems that are not included in the text—this manual includes over 300 pages of lecture notes. The lecture notes are comprehensive and outline all the major points covered in the text. They have been class-tested successfully by the authors and should make it much easier for other instructors to prepare their lecture notes as well. The lecture notes are perforated so that they can be easily detached for class use or to make transparency masters.

SUPPLEMENTARY MATERIALS

Financial Markets and Institutions includes a comprehensive program of supplements. The following items are available to qualified adopters:

- **Instructor's Resource Manual** offers sample course outlines, chapter outlines, overviews, teaching tips, and answers to questions and problems in the text. In addition it has **Lecture Notes**, numbering over 300 in transparency master format, that comprehensively outline the major points covered in the text.
- **Test Item File** comprises more than 1700 multiple-choice, true-false, and essay test items, in a printed format.
- **Electronic Transparencies in PowerPoint** offer a chapter-by-chapter presentation highlighting key topics covered throughout the text.

PEDAGOGICAL AIDS

A textbook must be a solid motivational tool. To this end, we have incorporated a wide variety of pedagogical features.

1. **Chapter Previews** at the beginning of each chapter tell students where the chapter is heading, why specific topics are important, and how they relate to other topics in the book.
2. **Applications** demonstrate how the analysis in the book can be used to explain many important real-world situations. A special set of applications called "Reading the Financial Pages" shows students how to read daily columns in this leading financial newspaper.
3. **"The Practising Financial Institution Manager"** is a set of special applications that introduce students to real-world problems that managers of financial institutions have to solve.
4. **Numerical Examples** guide students through solutions to financial problems using formulas, time lines, and calculator key strokes.
5. **"Following the Financial News" Boxes** introduce students to relevant news articles and data that are reported daily in the press and explain how to read them.
6. **Global Boxes** include interesting material with an international focus.
7. **E-Finance Boxes** relate how changes in technology have affected financial markets and institutions.
8. **Special-Interest Boxes** highlight dramatic historical episodes, interesting ideas, and intriguing facts related to the subject matter.
9. **Study Guides** are highlighted statements scattered throughout the text that provide hints on how to think about or approach a topic as students work their way through it.
10. **Summary Tables** are useful study aids for reviewing material.
11. **Key Statements** are important points that are set in boldface type so that students can easily find them for later reference.

12. **Graphs** with captions, numbering over 60, help students understand the interrelationship of the variables plotted and the principles of analysis.
13. **Summaries** at the end of each chapter list the chapter's main points.
14. **Key Terms** are important words or phrases that appear in boldface type when they are defined for the first time and are listed at the ends of the chapters.
15. **End-of-Chapter Questions and Problems,** numbering 400, help students learn the subject matter by applying economic concepts, and feature a special class of problems that students find particularly relevant, titled "Predicting the Future."
16. **Web Exercises** encourage students to collect information from on-line sources or use on-line resources to enhance their learning experience.
17. **Web Sources** report the URL source of the data used to create the many tables and charts.
18. **Marginal Web References** point the student to websites that provide information or data that supplement the text material.
19. **Glossary** at the back of the book defines all the key terms.
20. **Solutions to Problems** at the back of the book provides the solutions to about half the questions and problems, indicated in the text by an asterisk (*).

ACKNOWLEDGMENTS

This book is the result of efforts by many people. First of all, I would like to thank Rick Mishkin and Stan Eakins for their excellent comments on my contributions. I am extremely grateful to Gary Bennett, Acquisitions Editor, Rema Celio, Associate Editor, Mary Ann McCutcheon, Editorial Manager, and many others at Pearson Education Canada who have contributed to the completion of this first Canadian edition.

I am also grateful to all of the many people who commented on various chapters of the book, made valuable suggestions, and kindly provided me with data. I would particularly like to thank Joseph Atta-Mensah, Doug Fisher, Jack Selody, Mark Zelmer, Bruce Palmer, Chris Graham, Donna Howard, Zisimos Koustas, Carmen Rakoz, Joey Chow, Ricardo Rangel-Ruiz, and Asghar Shahmoradi.

In addition, I would like to acknowledge the reviewers who provided thoughtful and constructive feedback. Their comments have made this a better book.

Roger Atindehou, University of Moncton
Edwin H. Neave, Queen's University
Brian Smith, Wilfrid Laurier University
Charles Schell, University of Northern British Columbia
Harjeet S. Bhabra, Concordia University
Susan Christoffersen, McGill University
Ebenezer Asem, University of Lethbridge
Saiful Huq, University of New Brunswick

Finally, I would like to dedicate this book to my mom and dad, who many years ago put me on the high road by endowing me with happiness and inspiration.

Although I have done my best to make the first Canadian edition as complete and error-free as possible, as most of you know, perfection is impossible. I would greatly appreciate any suggestions for improvement. Please send your comments to me at **serletis@ucalgary.ca**.

Apostolos Serletis

About the Authors

Frederic S. Mishkin is the Alfred Lerner Professor of Banking and Financial Institutions at the Graduate School of Business, Columbia University. He is also a research associate at the National Bureau of Economic Research. Since receiving his Ph.D. from the Massachusetts Institute of Technology in 1976, he has taught at the University of Chicago, Northwestern University, Princeton University, and Columbia. He has also received an honorary professorship from the People's University of China (Renmin). From 1994 to 1997 he was executive vice president and director of research at the Federal Reserve Bank of New York and an associate economist of the Federal Open Market Committee of the Federal Reserve System.

Professor Mishkin's research focuses on monetary policy and its impact on financial markets and the aggregate economy. He is the author of more than ten books, including *A Rational Expectations Approach to Macroeconometrics: Testing Policy Ineffectiveness and Efficient Markets Models* (University of Chicago Press, 1983); *Money, Interest Rates, and Inflation* (Edward Elgar, 1993); *Inflation Targeting: Lessons from the International Experience* (Princeton University Press, 1999); *The Economics of Money, Banking, and Financial Markets*, 6th edition (Addison-Wesley, 2001); and has published over 100 articles in professional journals and books.

Professor Mishkin has served on the editorial board of the *American Economic Review*, has been an associate editor at the *Journal of Business and Economic Statistics* and *Journal of Applied Econometrics*, and was the editor of the Federal Reserve Bank of New York's *Economic Policy Review*. He is currently an associate editor (member of the editorial board) at seven academic journals: the *Journal of Money, Credit and Banking; Macroeconomics and Monetary Economics Abstracts; Journal of International Money and Finance; International Finance; Finance India; Economic Policy Review;* and the *Journal of Economic Perspectives*. He has been a consultant to the Board of Governors of the Federal Reserve System, the World Bank, and the International Monetary Fund, as well as to many central banks throughout the world. He was also a member of the International Advisory Board to the Financial Supervisory Service of South Korea. He is currently an academic consultant to and serves on the Economic Advisory Panel of the Federal Reserve Bank of New York.

Stanley G. Eakins has notable experience as a financial practitioner, serving as vice president and comptroller at the First National Bank of Fairbanks and as a commercial and real estate loan officer. A founder of Denali title and escrow agency, a title insurance company in Fairbanks, Alaska, he also ran the operations side of a bank and was the chief finance officer for a multimillion-dollar construction and development company.

Professor Eakins received his Ph.D. from Arizona State University. He is the Chairman of the Finance Department at East Carolina University. His research is focused primarily on the role of institutions in corporate control and how they influence investment practices. He is also interested in integrating multimedia tools into the learning environment and has received grants from East Carolina University in support of this work.

A contributor to journals such as the *Quarterly Journal of Business and Economics,* the *Journal of Financial Research,* and the *International Review of Financial Analysis,* Professor Eakins is also the author of *Finance: Institutions, Investments, and Management* (Addison-Wesley, 2002).

Apostolos Serletis is Professor of Economics and Finance at the University of Calgary. Since receiving his Ph.D. from McMaster University in 1984, he has held visiting appointments at the University of Texas at Austin, the Athens University of Economics and Business, and the Research Department of the Federal Reserve Bank of St. Louis.

Professor Serletis' teaching and research focus on monetary and financial economics, macroeconometrics, and nonlinear and complex dynamics. He is the author of five books, including *The Theory of Monetary Aggregation*, co-edited with William A. Barnett (North-Holland, 2000), *The Demand for Money: Theoretical and Empirical Approaches* (Kluwer Academic Publishers, 2001), *The Economics of Money, Banking, and Financial Markets*, First Canadian Edition, with Frederic S. Mishkin (Addison Wesley Longman, 2002), and *Macroeconomic Policy in the Canadian Economy*, with Panos C. Afxentiou (Kluwer Academic Publishers, 2002).

In addition, he has published more than 100 articles in such journals as the *Journal of Economic Literature*, the *Journal of Monetary Economics*, the *Journal of Money, Credit and Banking*, the *Journal of Econometrics*, the *Canadian Journal of Economics*, the *Journal of Economic Dynamics and Control*, the *Journal of Business and Economic Statistics*, the *Journal of Applied Econometrics*, and *Economic Inquiry*.

Professor Serletis lives in Calgary, with his wife Aglaia and their son Demitre and daughter Anna.

Part 1
Introduction

Chapter 1 Why Study Financial Markets and Institutions?

Preview

On the evening news you have just heard that the bond market has been booming. Does this mean that interest rates will fall so that it is easier for you to finance the purchase of a new computer system for your small retail business? Will the economy improve in the future so that it is a good time to build a new building or add to the one you are in? Should you try to raise funds by issuing stocks or bonds or instead go to the bank for a loan? If you import goods from abroad, should you be concerned that they will become more expensive?

This book provides answers to these questions by examining how financial markets (such as those for bonds, stocks, and foreign exchange) and financial institutions (banks, insurance companies, mutual funds, and other institutions) work. Financial markets and institutions not only affect your everyday life but also involve huge flows of funds—trillions of dollars—throughout our economy, which in turn affect business profits, the production of goods and services, and even the economic well-being of countries other than Canada. What happens to financial markets and institutions is of great concern to our politicians and can even have a major impact on our elections. The study of financial markets and institutions will reward you with an understanding of many exciting issues. In this chapter we provide a road map of the book by outlining these exciting issues and exploring why they are worth studying.

WHY STUDY FINANCIAL MARKETS?

Parts 1 and 2 of this book focus on **financial markets**, markets in which funds are transferred from people who have an excess of available funds to people who have a shortage. Financial markets such as the bond and stock markets are important in channelling funds from people who do not have a productive use for them to those who do, resulting in greater economic efficiency. Activities in financial markets also have direct effects on personal wealth, the behaviour of businesses and consumers, and the overall performance of the economy.

Debt Markets and Interest Rates

A **security** (also called a *financial instrument*) is a claim on the issuer's future income or **assets** (any financial claim or piece of property that is subject to ownership). A **bond** is a debt security that promises to make payments periodically for a specified period.[1] Debt markets, also often referred to generically as the *bond market,* are especially important to economic activity because they enable corporations or governments to borrow to finance their activities and because the bond market is where interest rates are determined. The **interest rate** is the cost of borrowing or the price paid for the rental of funds (usually expressed as a percentage of the rental of $100 per year). There are many interest rates in the economy—mortgage interest rates, car loan rates, and interest rates on many different types of bonds.

Daily, weekly, monthly, quarterly, and annual releases as well as historical data for selected interest rates, foreign exchange rates, etc., are available at www.bankofcanada.ca

Interest rates are important on a number of levels. On a personal level, high interest rates could deter you from buying a house or a car because the cost of financing it would be high. Conversely, high interest rates could encourage you to save because you can earn more interest income by putting aside some of your earnings as savings. On a more general level, interest rates have an impact on the overall health of the economy because they affect not only consumers' willingness to spend or save but also businesses' investment decisions. High interest rates, for example, may cause a corporation to postpone building a new plant that would ensure more jobs.

The level of interest rates is especially important to financial institutions. A rise in interest rates raises the cost of acquiring funds for financial institutions such as banks and raises the income on assets such as loans. In addition, changes in interest rates affect the prices of securities such as stocks and bonds that are held by financial institutions. Changes in interest rates thus directly affect the profitability and value of financial institutions.

Because changes in interest rates have important effects on individuals, financial institutions, businesses, and the overall economy, it is important to explain fluctuations in interest rates, which have been substantial over the past 30 years. As a matter of fact, in no other 30-year period of Canadian history have interest-rate fluctuations been as great. For example, at the end of the 1970s, the interest rate on three-month treasury bills was around 13% and reached a peak of more than 20% in August 1981. This interest rate then fell to a low of less than 3% in 1997, rose to near 5% in 1998, and was less than 2% at the end of 2001.

Because different interest rates have a tendency to move in unison, economists frequently lump interest rates together and refer to "the" interest rate. As Figure 1 shows, however, interest rates on several types of bonds can differ substantially. The interest rate on three-month treasury bills, for example, fluctuates more than the other interest rates and is lower, on average. The interest rate on long-term corporate bonds is higher, on average, than the other interest rates, and the spread between it and the other rates fluctuates over time.

In Chapters 2, 8, 9, and 11 we study the role of debt markets in the economy, and in Chapters 3 through 5 we examine what an interest rate is, how the common movements in interest rates come about, and why interest rates on different securities vary.

---

[1]The definition of *bond* used throughout this book is the broad one in common use by academics, which covers short- as well as long-term debt instruments. However, some practitioners in financial markets use the word *bond* only to describe specific long-term debt instruments such as corporate bonds or Canada bonds.

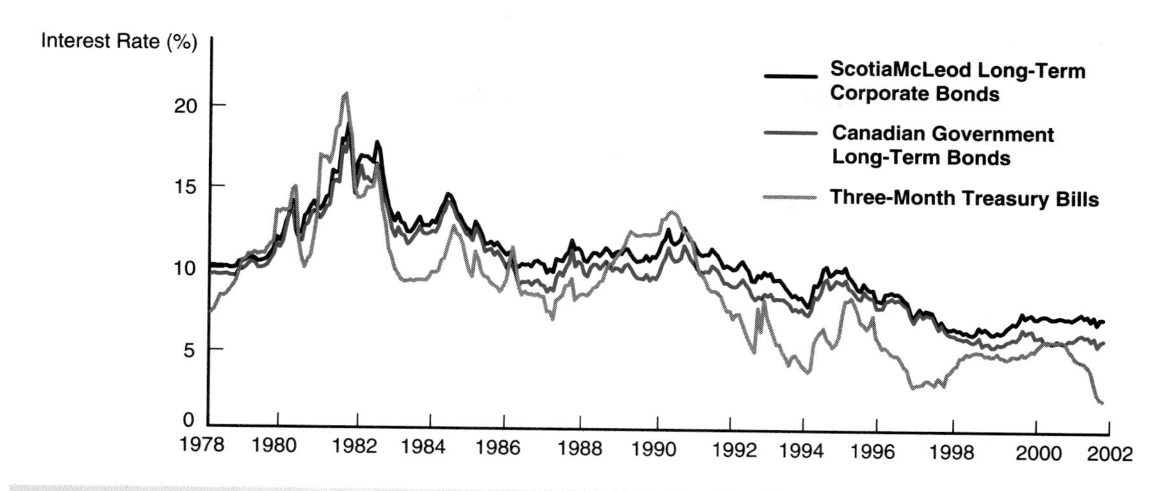

FIGURE 1 Interest Rates on Selected Bonds, 1978–2002

Source: Statistics Canada CANSIM II series V122531, V122544, and V122518

The Stock Market

A **stock** is a security that represents a share of ownership in a corporation. It is a claim on the earnings and assets of the corporation. Issuing stock and selling it to the public is a way for corporations to raise funds to finance their activities. The stock market, in which claims on the earnings of corporations (shares of stock) are traded, is the most widely followed financial market in Canada (that's why it is often called simply "the market"). A big swing in the prices of shares in the stock market is always a big story on the evening news. People often express their opinion on where the market is heading and will frequently tell you about their latest "big killing" (although you seldom hear about their latest big loss!). The attention that the market receives can probably be best explained by one simple fact: It is a place where people can get rich quickly.

As Figure 2 indicates, stock prices have been extremely volatile. They climbed steadily in the 1950s, reached a peak in 1966, and then fluctuated up and down until 1974, when they fell sharply. Stock prices had recovered substantially by the early 1980s when a major stock market boom began, sending the S&P/TSX Composite (formerly known as TSE 300) to a peak in August 1987. After a 12.5% decline over the next month and a half, the stock market experienced the worst one-day drop in its entire history on "Black Monday," October 19, 1987, when the S&P/TSX fell by more than 400 points, an 11% decline. The stock market then recovered, climbing above the 11,000 level in August 2000, but falling again below the 7000 level in September 2001. These considerable fluctuations in stock prices affect the size of people's wealth and as a result may affect their willingness to spend.

The stock market is also an important factor in business investment decisions because the price of shares affects the amount of funds that can be raised by selling newly issued stock to finance investment spending. A higher price for a firm's shares means that it can raise a larger amount of funds, which can be used to buy production facilities and equipment.

In Chapter 2 we examine the role that the stock market plays in the financial system, and we return to the issue of how stock prices behave and respond to information in the marketplace in Chapter 10. Stocks are also discussed in Chapter 9.

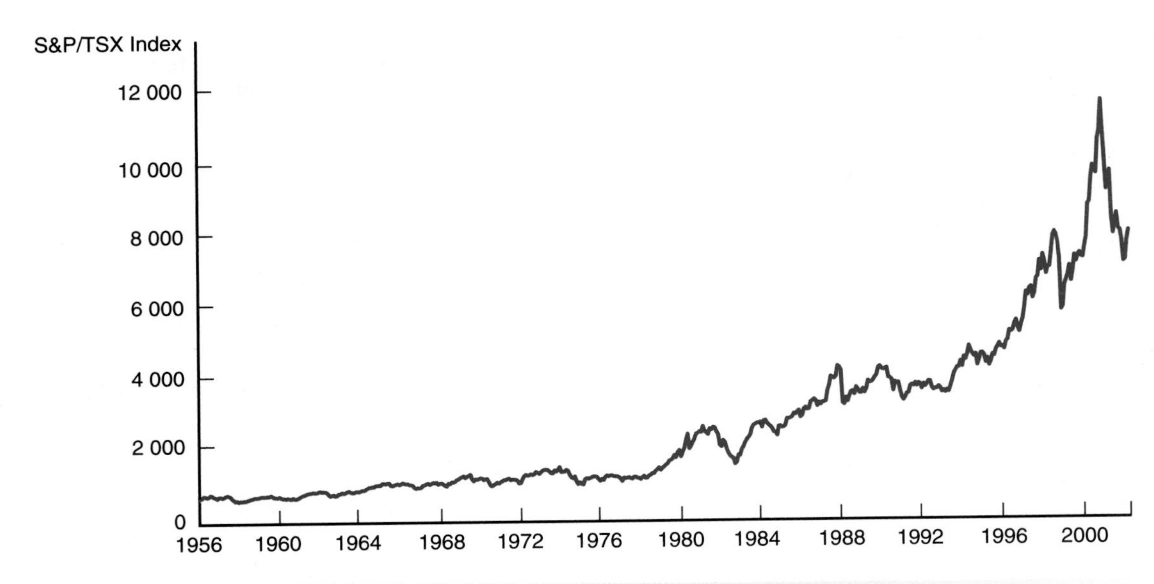

FIGURE 2 Stock Prices as Measured by the S&P/TSX Price Index, 1956–2002

Source: Statistics Canada CANSIM II series V122620

The Foreign Exchange Market

For funds to be transferred from one country to another, they have to be converted from the currency in the country of origin (say, dollars) into the currency of the country they are going to (say, euros). The **foreign exchange market** is where this conversion takes place, and so it is instrumental in moving funds between countries. It is also important because it is where the **foreign exchange rate,** the price of one country's currency in terms of another's, is determined.

Because the foreign exchange rate is the relative price of two national currencies, there are two ways of quoting an exchange rate: Either as the amount of domestic currency that can be purchased with a unit of foreign currency or as the amount of foreign currency that can be purchased with a unit of domestic currency. Throughout this book, we always use the latter quoting convention—that is, we express the exchange rate as units of foreign currency per Canadian dollar. In these terms, when the exchange rate increases so that a Canadian dollar buys more units of foreign currency, we say that the Canadian dollar has had an **appreciation**. A decline in the exchange rate is associated with a **depreciation** of the Canadian dollar.

Figure 3 shows exchange rates for the Canadian dollar from 1980 to 2001 in terms of the U.S. dollar and six major foreign currencies. The Canada-U.S. exchange rate is defined as the U.S. dollar price of one Canadian dollar. The G-6 Index line shows the Canadian dollar in terms of a basket of six currencies of major industrialized countries. It is expressed as an index, with the 1981 value set equal to 100.

Since the United States is Canada's major trading partner, the two exchange rates move closely together. In the early 1970s, the exchange rate was fixed, but in the 1980s and 1990s the fluctuations in the exchange rate have been substantial: The Canadian dollar weakened considerably in the early 1980s and reached a low point in 1986. From 1987 to the end of 1991, the dollar appreciated dramatically in value, but since then it has fallen substantially.

What have these fluctuations in the exchange rate meant to the Canadian public and businesses? A change in the exchange rate has a direct effect on Cana-

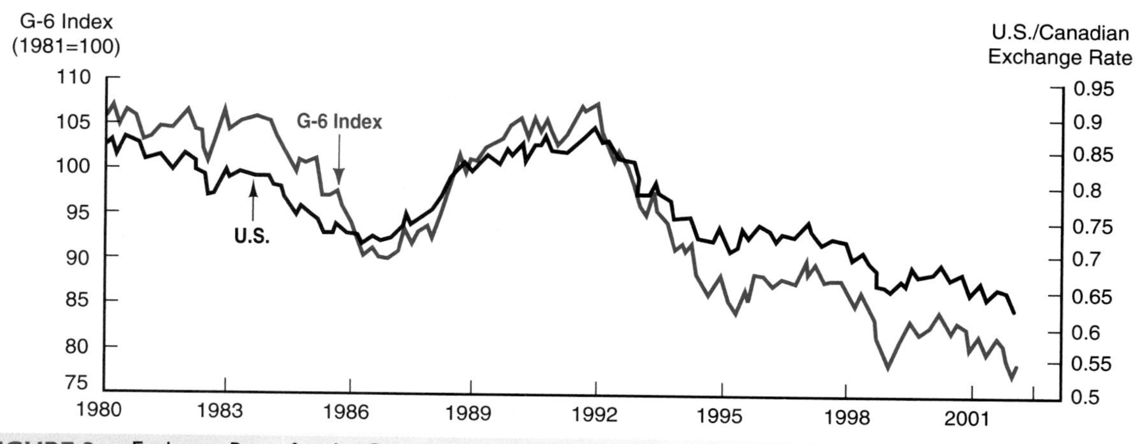

FIGURE 3 Exchange Rates for the Canadian Dollar, 1980–2002

Source: Statistics Canada CANSIM II series V37426 and V37451

dian consumers because it affects the cost of foreign goods. In 1984, when the British currency, the pound sterling, cost approximately $1.30, £100 of British goods (say, Shetland sweaters) would cost $130. When a weaker dollar raised the cost of a pound to $2.20 in 2000, the same £100 of Shetland sweaters cost $220. Thus a weaker dollar leads to more expensive foreign goods, makes vacationing abroad more expensive, and raises the cost of indulging your desire for imported delicacies. When the value of the dollar drops, Canadians will decrease their purchases of foreign goods and increase their consumption of domestic goods (such as travel in Canada or Canadian-made sweaters).

Conversely, a strong dollar means that Canadian goods exported abroad will cost more in foreign countries, and hence foreigners will buy fewer of them. Exports of steel, for example, declined sharply when the dollar strengthened in the late 1980s. A strong dollar benefited Canadian consumers by making foreign goods cheaper but hurt Canadian businesses and eliminated some jobs by cutting both domestic and foreign sales of their products. The decline in the value of the dollar since 1992 has had the opposite effect: It has made foreign goods more expensive, but it has made Canadian businesses more competitive. Fluctuations in the foreign exchange markets have major consequences for the Canadian economy.

In Chapters 12 and 13 we study how exchange rates are determined in the foreign exchange market in which dollars are bought and sold for foreign currencies.

WHY STUDY FINANCIAL INSTITUTIONS?

The second major focus of this book is financial institutions. Financial institutions are what make financial markets work. Without them, financial markets would not be able to move funds from people who save to people who have productive investment opportunities. They thus also have important effects on the performance of the economy as a whole.

Central Banks and the Conduct of Monetary Policy

The most important financial institution in the financial system is the **central bank,** the government agency responsible for the conduct of monetary policy, which in Canada is the **Bank of Canada** (also called simply **the Bank**). **Monetary policy** involves the management of interest rates and the quantity of **money**,

Access general information, monetary policy, the banking system, research, and economic data from the Bank of Canada at www.bankofcanada.ca

also referred to as the **money supply** (defined as anything that is generally accepted in payment for goods and services or in the repayment of debt). Because monetary policy affects interest rates, inflation, and business cycles, all of which have a major impact on financial markets and institutions, we study how monetary policy is conducted by central banks in both Canada and abroad in Chapters 6 and 7.

Structure of the Financial System

The financial system is complex, comprising many different types of private sector financial institutions, including banks, insurance companies, mutual funds, finance companies, and investment banks, all of which are heavily regulated by the government. If you wanted to make a loan to IBM or General Motors, for example, you would not go directly to the president of the company and offer a loan. Instead, you would lend to such companies indirectly through **financial intermediaries,** institutions such as commercial banks, trust and mortgage loan companies, credit unions, insurance companies, mutual funds, pension funds, and finance companies that borrow funds from people who have saved and in turn make loans to others.

Why are financial intermediaries so crucial to well-functioning financial markets? Why do they give credit to one party but not to another? Why do they usually write complicated legal documents when they extend loans? Why are they the most heavily regulated businesses in the economy?

We answer these questions by developing a coherent framework for analyzing financial structure both in Canada and in the rest of the world in Chapter 14.

Banks and Other Financial Institutions

Banks are financial institutions that accept deposits and make loans. Included under the term *banks* are firms such as commercial banks, trust and mortgage loan companies, and credit unions. Banks are the financial intermediaries that the average person interacts with most frequently. A person who needs a loan to buy a house or a car usually obtains it from a local bank. Most Canadians keep a large proportion of their financial wealth in banks in the form of chequing accounts, savings accounts, or other types of bank deposits. Because banks are the largest financial intermediaries in our economy, they deserve careful study. However, banks are not the only important financial institutions. Indeed, in recent years, other financial institutions such as insurance companies, finance companies, pension funds, mutual funds, and investment banks have been growing at the expense of banks, and so we need to study them as well. We study banks and all these other institutions in Parts 5 and 6.

Financial Innovation

In the good old days, when you took cash out of the bank or wanted to check your account balance, you got to say hello to the friendly teller. Nowadays you are more likely to interact with an automated teller machine when withdrawing cash and can get your account balance from your home computer. To see why these options have been developed, we study why and how financial innovation takes place in Chapters 15, 16, and 18. We also study financial innovation because it shows us how creative thinking on the part of financial institutions can lead to higher profits. By seeing how and why financial institutions have been creative in the past, we obtain a better grasp of how they may be creative in the future. This knowledge provides us with useful clues about how the financial system may change over time and will help keep our knowledge about banks and other financial institutions from becoming obsolete.

Managing Risk in Financial Institutions

In recent years, the economic environment has become an increasingly risky place. Interest rates fluctuate wildly, stock markets have crashed both here and abroad, speculative crises have occurred in the foreign exchange markets, and failures of financial institutions have reached levels unprecedented since the Great Depression. To avoid wild swings in profitability (and even possibly failure) resulting from this environment, financial institutions must be concerned with how to cope with increased risk. We look at techniques that these institutions use when they engage in risk management in Chapter 22. Then in Chapter 23, we look at how these institutions make use of new financial instruments, such as financial futures, options, and swaps, to manage risk.

APPLIED MANAGERIAL PERSPECTIVE

Another reason for studying financial institutions is that they are among the largest employers in the country and frequently pay very high salaries. Hence some of you have a very practical reason for studying financial institutions: It may help you get a good job in the financial sector. Even if your interests lie elsewhere, you should still care about how financial institutions are run because there will be many times in your life, as an individual, an employee, or the owner of a business, when you will interact with these institutions. Knowing how financial institutions are managed may help you get a better deal when you need to borrow from them or if you decide to supply them with funds.

This book emphasizes an applied managerial perspective in teaching you about financial markets and institutions by including special applications headed "The Practising Financial Institution Manager." These applications introduce you to the real-world problems that managers of financial institutions commonly face and need to solve in their day-to-day jobs. For example, how does the manager of a financial institution come up with a new financial product that will be profitable? How does a financial institution manager manage the risk that the institution faces from fluctuations in interest rates, stock prices, or foreign exchange rates? Should a manager hire an expert on Bank of Canada policymaking, referred to as a "Bank of Canada watcher," to help the institution discern where monetary policy might be going in the future?

Not only do "The Practising Financial Institution Manager" applications, which answer these questions and others like them, provide you with some special analytic tools that you will need if you make your career at a financial institution, but they also give you a feel for what a job as the manager of a financial institution is all about.

HOW WE WILL STUDY FINANCIAL MARKETS AND INSTITUTIONS

Instead of focusing on a mass of dull facts that will soon become obsolete, this textbook stresses a unifying, analytic framework to study financial markets and institutions. This framework uses a few basic concepts to help organize your thinking about the determination of asset prices, the structure of financial markets, bank management, and the role of monetary policy in the economy. The basic concepts are equilibrium, basic supply and demand analysis to explain behaviour in financial markets, the search for profits, and an approach to financial structure based on transaction costs and asymmetric information.

The unifying framework used in this book will not only keep your knowledge from becoming obsolete and make the material more interesting but also discourage you from memorizing a mass of facts that you will forget soon after the final exam. The framework also provides the tools you need to understand trends in the financial marketplace and in variables such as interest rates and exchange rates. To help you understand and apply the unifying analytic framework, simple models are constructed in which the variables held constant are carefully delineated, each step in the derivation of the model is clearly and carefully laid out, and the models are then used to explain various phenomena by focusing on changes in one variable at a time, holding all other variables constant. To reinforce the models' usefulness, this text emphasizes the interaction of theoretical analysis and empirical data in order to expose you to real-life events and data. To make the study of financial markets and institutions even more relevant and to help you learn the material, the book contains, besides "The Practising Financial Institution Manager" applications, numerous additional applications that demonstrate how the analysis in the book can be used to explain many real-world situations.

To function better in the real world outside the classroom, you must have the tools to follow the financial news that appears in leading financial publications such as the *Globe and Mail* and the *National Post*. To help and encourage you to read the financial section of the newspaper, this book contains two special features. The first is a set of special boxed inserts titled "Following the Financial News" that contain actual columns and data from the *Globe and Mail* and the *National Post* that typically appear daily or periodically. These boxes give you the detailed information and definitions you need to evaluate the data being presented. The second feature is a set of special applications titled "Reading the Financial News" that expand on the "Following the Financial News" boxes. These applications show you how the analytic framework in the book can be used directly to make sense of the daily columns in Canada's leading financial newspapers. In addition to these applications, this book also contains nearly 400 end-of-chapter problems that ask you to apply the analytic concepts you have learned to other real-world issues. Particularly relevant is a special class of problems headed "Predicting the Future." So that you can work on many of these problems on your own, answers to half of them are found at the end of the book. These give you an opportunity to review and apply many of the important financial concepts and tools presented throughout the book.

Exploring the Web

The World Wide Web has become an extremely valuable and convenient resource for financial research. We emphasize the importance of this tool in several ways. First, wherever we utilize the Web to find information to build the charts and tables that appear throughout the text, we include the source site's URL. These sites often contain additional information and are updated frequently. Second, in the margin of the text we have included the URLs of pertinent sites. Visit these sites to further explore a topic you find of particular interest. Finally, we have added Web exercises to the end of each chapter. These exercises prompt you to visit sites and to work with real-time data and information.

Website URLs are subject to frequent change. We have selected stable sites, but we realize that even government URLs change.

A sample Web exercise has been included in this chapter. This is an especially important example, since it demonstrates how to export data from a Website into Excel for further analysis. We suggest you work through this problem on your own so that you will be able to perform this activity when prompted in subsequent Web exercises.

Web Exercise

You have been hired by Risky Ventures Ltd. as a consultant to help them analyze interest rate trends. They are initially interested in determining the historical relationship between short-term interest rates. The biggest task you must immediately undertake is collecting market interest-rate data. You know the best source of this information is the Web.

1. You decide that your best indicators of short-term interest rates are the 3-month, 6-month, and 1-year treasury bill interest rates. Your first task is to gather historical data. Go to http://www.bankofcanada.ca and select "Rates and statistics" and then "Treasury Bill Yields."

2. Although you have located an accurate source of historical interest rate data, getting it onto a spreadsheet will be very tedious. You recall that Excel (Microsoft® Excel) will let you convert text data into columns. Begin by indicating that you want to display the data in CSV format, sorted by date. Under the monthly series frequency, click on "B14059," "B14061," and "B14062." Click on "PICK A DATE(S)" and choose the start and end dates. The site should look as follows:

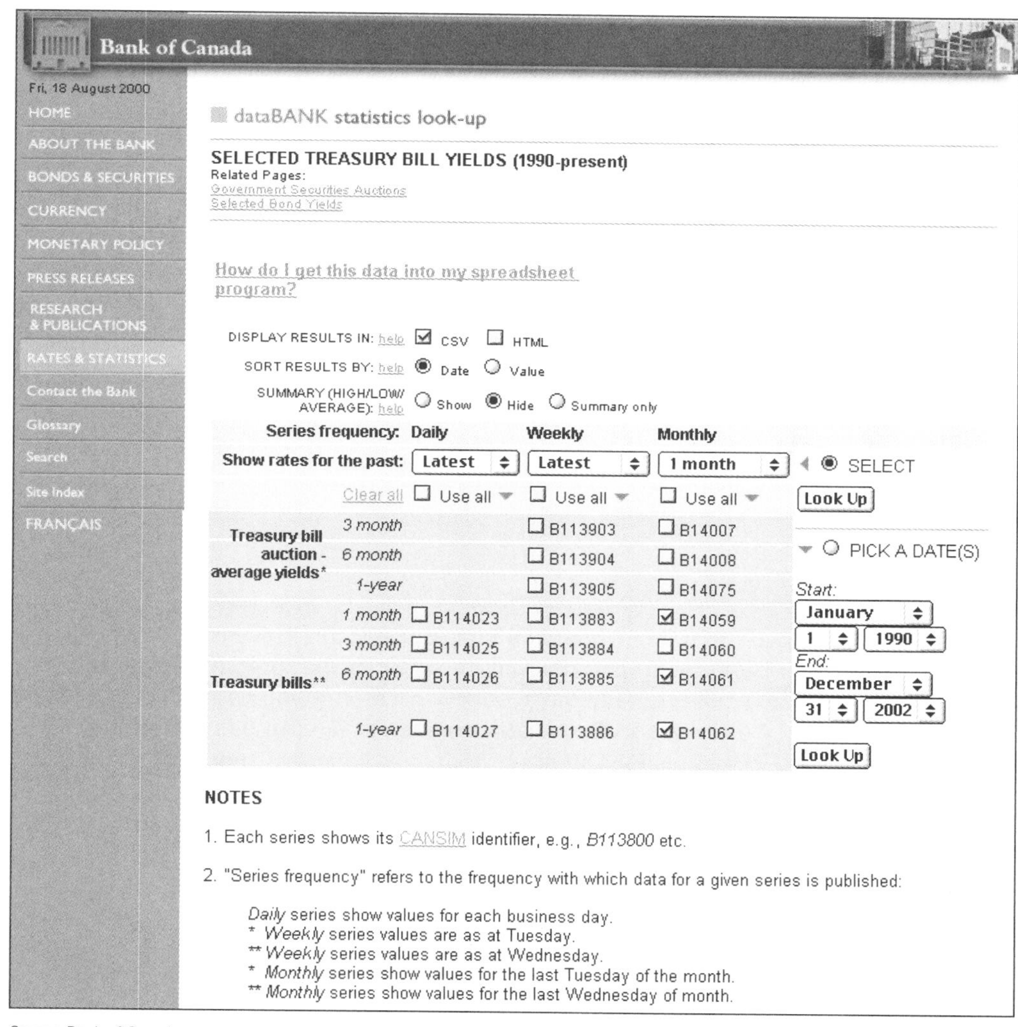

Source: Bank of Canada

3. You now want to analyze the interest rates by graphing them. Click on "Look Up" and then right-click to save the data to your hard drive. Now open Excel and then open the file with the interest rate series. Click on the charts icon on the tool bar (or INSERT/CHART). Select scatter diagram and choose any type of scatter diagram that connects the dots. Let the Excel wizard take you through the steps of completing the graph.

4. Now go back a page, and under "Exchange Rates," click on "Search monthly averages (1990-present)." Finally, click on "Australian dollar," "Euro," and "Russian ruble" and again repeat the instructions outlined in steps 2 and 3.

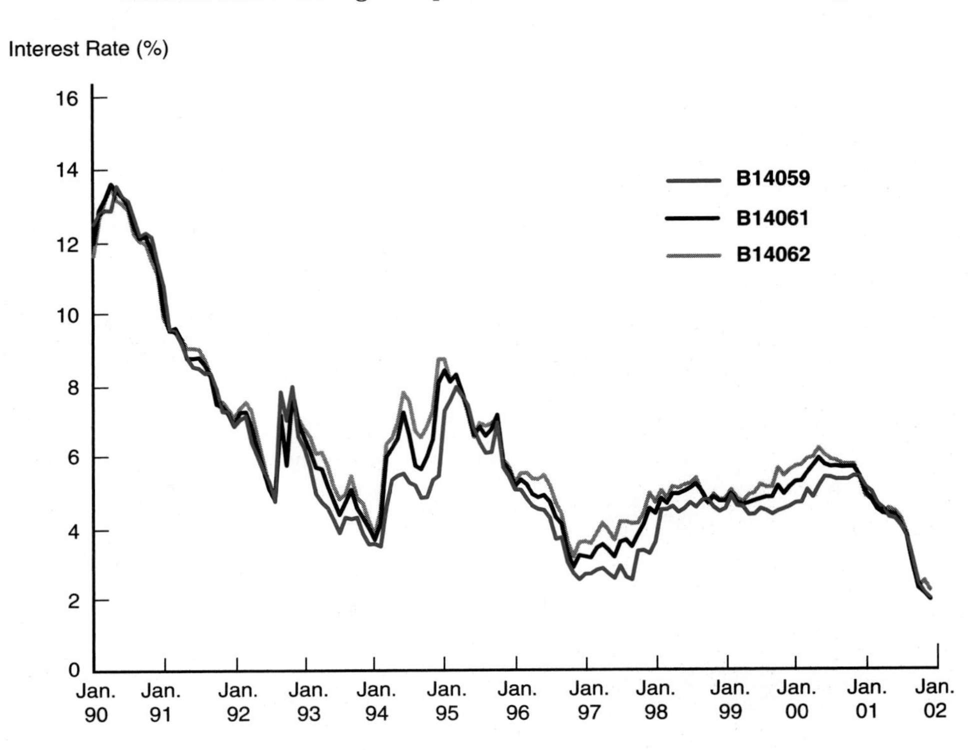

Source: Statistics Canada CANSIM II series, B14059, B14061, and B14062

CONCLUDING REMARKS

The field of financial markets and institutions is an exciting one. Not only will you learn material that affects your life directly—for example, gaining skills that would be valuable in your career—but you will also gain a clearer understanding of events in financial markets and institutions you frequently hear about in the news media. Our study of financial markets and institutions will also introduce you to many of the controversies that are currently the subject of hot debate in the political arena.

SUMMARY

1. Activities in financial markets have direct effects on individuals' wealth, the behaviour of businesses, and the efficiency of our economy. Three financial markets deserve particular attention: the bond market (debt markets), where interest rates are determined; the stock market, which has a major effect on people's wealth and on firms' investment decisions; and the foreign exchange market, because fluctuations in the foreign exchange rate have major consequences for the Canadian economy.
2. Because monetary policy affects interest rates, inflation, and business cycles, all of which have an important impact on financial markets and institutions, we need to understand how monetary policy is conducted by central banks in Canada and abroad.
3. Banks and other financial institutions channel funds from people who might not put them to productive use to people who can do so and thus play a crucial role in improving the efficiency of the economy.
4. Understanding how financial institutions are managed is important because there will be many times in your life, as an individual, an employee, or the owner of a business, when you will interact with them. "The Practising Financial Institution Manager" applications provide special analytic tools that are useful if you make your career at a financial institution and also give you a feel for what a job as the manager of a financial institution is all about.
5. This textbook stresses an analytic way of thinking by developing a unifying framework for the study of financial markets and institutions using a few basic principles. This textbook also emphasizes the interaction of theoretical analysis and empirical data.

KEY TERMS

appreciation, *p. 4*
asset, *p. 2*
Bank of Canada (the Bank), *p. 5*
banks, *p. 6*
bond, *p. 2*
central bank, *p. 5*
depreciation, *p. 4*
financial intermediaries, *p. 6*
financial markets, *p. 1*
foreign exchange market, *p. 4*
foreign exchange rate, *p. 4*
interest rate, *p. 2*
monetary policy, *p. 5*
money (money supply), *p. 5*
security, *p. 2*
stock, *p. 3*

QUESTIONS AND PROBLEMS

1. Why are financial markets important to the health of the economy?

*2. When interest rates rise, how might businesses and consumers change their economic behaviour?

3. How can a change in interest rates affect the profitability of financial institutions?

*4. Is everybody worse off when interest rates rise?

5. What effect might a fall in stock prices have on business investment?

*6. What effect might a rise in stock prices have on consumers' decisions to spend?

7. How does a decline in the value of the pound sterling affect British consumers?

*8. How does an increase in the value of the pound sterling affect Canadian businesses?

9. How can changes in foreign exchange rates affect the profitability of financial institutions?

*10. Looking at Figure 3, in what years would you have chosen to visit the Canadian Rockies rather than the Tower of London?

11. What is the basic activity of banks?

*12. What are the other important financial intermediaries in the economy besides banks?

13. Can you think of any financial innovation in the past ten years that has affected you personally? Has it made you better or worse off? In what way?

*14. What types of risks do financial institutions face?

15. Why do managers of financial institutions care so much about the activities of the Bank of Canada?

---

*Solutions to these problems are provided at the back of the book.

Chapter 2

Overview of the Financial System

Preview

Suppose that you want to start a business that manufactures a recently invented low-cost robot that cleans house (even does windows), mows the lawn, and washes the car, but you have no funds to put this wonderful invention into production. Walter has plenty of savings that he has inherited. If you and Walter could get together so that he could provide you with the funds, your company's robot would see the light of day, and you, Walter, and the economy would all be better off: Walter would earn a high return on his investment, you would get rich from producing the robot, and we would have cleaner houses, shinier cars, and more beautiful lawns.

Financial markets (bond and stock markets) and financial intermediaries (banks, insurance companies, pension funds) have the basic function of getting people such as you and Walter together by moving funds from those who have a surplus of funds (Walter) to those who have a shortage of funds (you). More realistically, when IBM invents a better computer, it may need funds to bring it to market, or a local government may need funds to build a road or a school. Well-functioning financial markets and financial intermediaries are needed to improve our economic well-being and are crucial to our economic health. Indeed, when the financial system breaks down, as it has in Russia and in East Asia recently, severe economic hardship results.

To study the effects of financial markets and financial intermediaries on the economy, we must first acquire an understanding of their general structure and operation. In this chapter we learn about the major financial intermediaries and the instruments that are traded in financial markets.

This chapter offers a preliminary overview of the fascinating study of financial markets and institutions. We will return to a more detailed treatment of the regulation, structure, and evolution of financial markets and institutions in Parts 3 through 5.

FUNCTION OF FINANCIAL MARKETS

Financial markets perform the essential economic function of channelling funds from people who have saved surplus funds by spending less than their income to people who have a shortage of funds because they wish to spend more than their income. This function is shown schematically in Figure 1. Those who have saved and are lending funds, the lender-savers, are at the left, and those who must borrow funds to finance their spending, the borrower-spenders, are at the right. The principal lender-savers are households, but business enterprises and the government (particularly provincial and local government), as well as foreigners and their governments, sometimes also find themselves with excess funds and so lend them out. The most important borrower-spenders are businesses and the government (particularly the federal government), but households and foreigners also borrow to finance their purchases of cars, furniture, and houses. The arrows show that funds flow from lender-savers to borrower-spenders via two routes.

In *direct finance* (the route at the bottom of Figure 1), borrowers borrow funds directly from lenders in financial markets by selling them *securities* (also called *financial instruments*), which are claims on the borrower's future income or assets. Securities are assets for the person who buys them but **liabilities** (IOUs or debts) for the individual or firm that sells (issues) them. For example, if Nortel Networks needs to borrow funds to pay for a new factory to manufacture telecommunications equipment, it might borrow the funds from a saver by selling the saver a *bond*, a debt security that promises to make payments periodically for a specified period.

For more information about Nortel Networks go to www.nortelnetworks.com

Why is this channelling of funds from savers to spenders so important to the economy? The answer is that the people who save are frequently not the same people who have profitable investment opportunities available to them, the entrepreneurs. Let's first think about this on a personal level. Suppose that you have saved $1000 this year, but no borrowing or lending is possible because there are

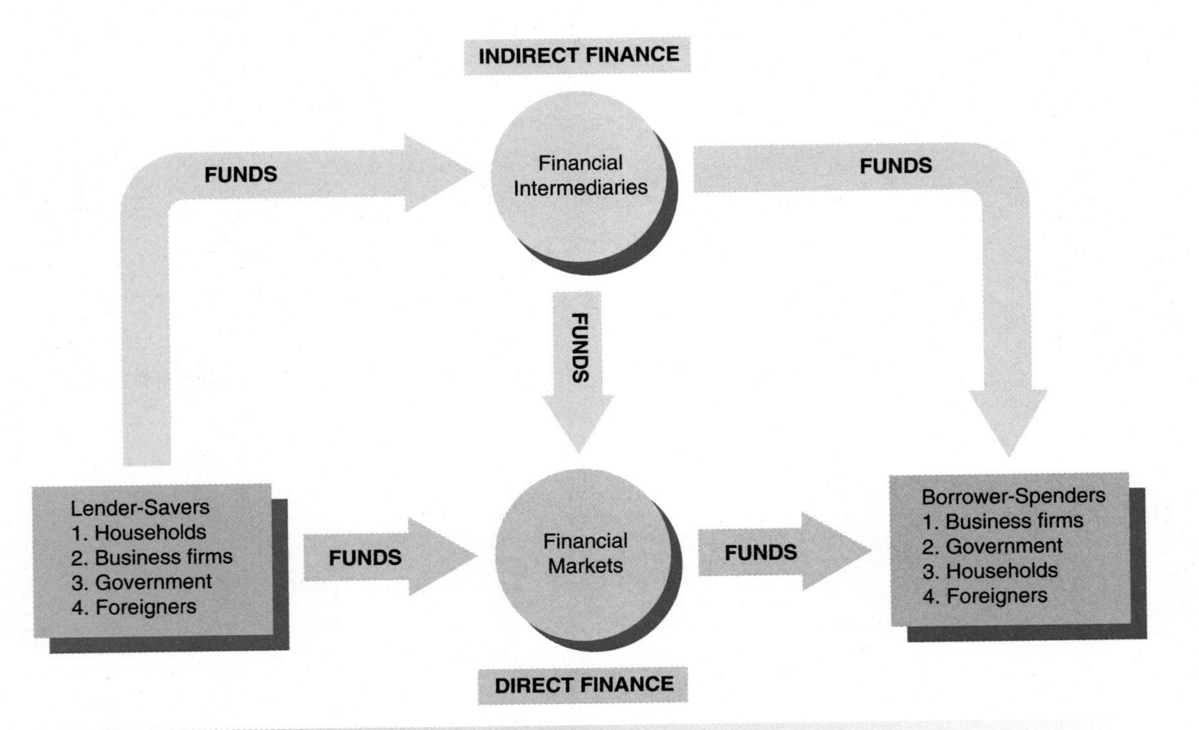

FIGURE 1 Flows of Funds Through the Financial System

no financial markets. If you do not have an investment opportunity that will permit you to earn income with your savings, you will just hold on to the $1000 and will earn no interest. However, Carl the Carpenter has a productive use for your $1000: He can use it to purchase a new tool that will shorten the time it takes him to build a house, thereby earning an extra $200 per year. If you could get in touch with Carl, you could lend him the $1000 at a rental fee (interest) of $100 per year, and both of you would be better off. You would earn $100 per year on your $1000, instead of the zero amount that you would earn otherwise, while Carl would earn $100 more income per year (the $200 extra earnings per year minus the $100 rental fee for the use of the funds).

In the absence of financial markets, you and Carl the Carpenter might never get together. Without financial markets, it is hard to transfer funds from a person who has no investment opportunities to one who has them; you would both be stuck with the status quo, and both of you would be worse off. Financial markets are thus essential to promoting economic efficiency.

The existence of financial markets is also beneficial even if someone borrows for a purpose other than increasing production in a business. Say that you are recently married, have a good job, and want to buy a house. You earn a good salary, but because you have just started to work, you have not yet saved much. Over time you would have no problem saving enough to buy the house of your dreams, but by then you would be too old to get full enjoyment from it. Without financial markets, you are stuck; you cannot buy the house and will continue to live in your tiny apartment.

If a financial market were set up so that people who had built up savings could lend you the money to buy the house, you would be more than happy to pay them some interest in order to own a home while you are still young enough to enjoy it. Then, when you had saved up enough funds, you would pay back your loan. The overall outcome would be such that you would be better off, as would the persons who made you the loan. They would now earn some interest, whereas they would not if the financial market did not exist.

Now we can see why financial markets have such an important function in the economy. They allow funds to move from people who lack productive investment opportunities to people who have such opportunities. By so doing, financial markets contribute to higher production and efficiency in the overall economy. They also directly improve the well-being of consumers by allowing them to time their purchases better. They provide funds to young people to buy what they need and can eventually afford without forcing them to wait until they have saved up the entire purchase price. Financial markets that are operating efficiently improve the economic welfare of everyone in the society.

STRUCTURE OF FINANCIAL MARKETS

Now that we understand the basic function of financial markets, let's look at their structure. The following descriptions of several categorizations of financial markets illustrate essential features of these markets.

Debt and Equity Markets

A firm or an individual can obtain funds in a financial market in two ways. The most common method is to issue a debt instrument, such as a bond or a mortgage, which is a contractual agreement by the borrower to pay the holder of the instrument fixed dollar amounts at regular intervals (interest and principal payments) until a specified date (the maturity date), when a final payment is made. The **maturity** of a debt instrument is the time (term) to that instrument's expiration date. A debt instrument is **short term** if its maturity is less than a year and **long term** if its maturity is ten years or longer. Debt instruments with a maturity between one and ten years are said to be **intermediate term.**

The second method of raising funds is by issuing **equities,** such as common stock, which are claims to share in the net income (income after expenses and taxes) and the assets of a business. If you own one share of common stock in a company that has issued one million shares, you are entitled to 1 one-millionth of the firm's net income and 1 one-millionth of the firm's assets. Equities usually make periodic payments (**dividends**) to their holders and are considered long-term securities because they have no maturity date. In addition, owning stock means that you own a portion of the firm and thus have the right to vote on issues important to the firm and to elect its directors.

The main disadvantage of owning a corporation's equities rather than its debt is that an equity holder is a *residual claimant;* that is, the corporation must pay all its debt holders before it pays its equity holders. The advantage of holding equities is that equity holders benefit directly from any increases in the corporation's profitability or asset value because equities confer ownership rights on the equity holders. Debt holders do not share in this benefit because their dollar payments are fixed. We examine the pros and cons of debt versus equity instruments in more detail in Chapter 14, which provides an analytical framework for understanding financial structure.

The total value of equities in Canada has typically fluctuated between $20 billion and $300 billion since the early 1970s, depending on the prices of shares. Although the average person is more aware of the stock market than any other financial market, the size of the debt market is almost on par with that of the equities market. The value of debt instruments was $183 billion at the end of 2000 while the value of equities was $242 billion at the end of 2000.

Primary and Secondary Markets

At www.tse.com and www.nyse.com, you'll find listed companies, quotes, company historical data, real-time market indices, and more.

A **primary market** is a financial market in which new issues of a security, such as a bond or a stock, are sold to initial buyers by the corporation or government agency borrowing the funds. A **secondary market** is a financial market in which securities that have been previously issued (and are thus secondhand) can be resold.

The primary markets for securities are not well known to the public because the selling of securities to initial buyers often takes place behind closed doors. An important financial institution that assists in the initial sale of securities in the primary market is the **investment bank.** It does this by **underwriting** securities: It guarantees a price for a corporation's securities and then sells them to the public.

The Toronto and Montreal stock exchanges, in which previously issued stocks are traded, are the best-known examples of secondary markets, although the bond markets, in which previously issued bonds of major corporations and the Canadian government are bought and sold, actually have a larger trading volume. Other examples of secondary markets are foreign exchange markets, futures markets, and options markets. Securities brokers and dealers are crucial to a well-functioning secondary market. **Brokers** are agents of investors who match buyers with sellers of securities; **dealers** link buyers and sellers by buying and selling securities at stated prices.

Find more details about the Toronto and Montreal exchanges by visiting www.tsx.ca and www.m-x.ca

When an individual buys a security in the secondary market, the person who has sold the security receives money in exchange for the security, but the corporation that issued the security acquires no new funds. A corporation acquires new funds only when its securities are first sold in the primary market. Nonetheless, secondary markets serve two important functions. First, they make it easier to sell these financial instruments to raise cash; that is, they make the financial instruments more **liquid.** The increased liquidity of these instruments then makes them more desirable and thus easier for the issuing firm to sell in the primary market. Second, they determine the price of the security that the issuing firm sells in the primary market. The firms that buy securities in the primary market will pay the issuing corporation no more than the price that they think the secondary market will set for this security. The higher the security's price in the secondary market, the higher the price that the issuing firm will receive for a new security in the primary market and hence the greater the amount of capital it can raise. Conditions in the secondary market are therefore the most relevant to corporations issuing securities. It is for this reason that books like this one, which deal with financial markets, focus on the behaviour of secondary markets rather than that of primary markets.

Exchanges and Over-the-Counter Markets

Secondary markets can be organized in two ways. One is to organize **exchanges**, where buyers and sellers of securities (or their agents or brokers) meet in one central location to conduct trades. The Toronto Stock Exchange for stocks; the Montreal Exchange for equity, interest rates, and index derivatives; and the Winnipeg Commodity Exchange for commodities (wheat, oats, barley, and other agricultural commodities) are examples of organized exchanges.

The other method of organizing a secondary market is to have an **over-the-counter (OTC) market**, in which dealers at different locations have an inventory of securities and stand ready to buy and sell securities "over the counter" to anyone who comes to them and is willing to accept their prices. Because over-the-counter dealers are in computer contact and know the prices set by one another, the OTC market is very competitive and not very different from a market with an organized exchange.

Visit the Winnipeg Commodity Exchange online at www.wce.mb.ca

The Canadian over-the-counter market has been patterned after the Nasdaq. In 1991, responsibility for the operation of this market was transferred to the Canadian Dealing Network Inc. (CDN), a subsidary of the Toronto Stock Exchange. Many common stocks are now traded over-the-counter, although the largest corporations have their shares traded at organized stock exchanges such as the Toronto Stock Exchange. The Canadian government bond market is set up as an over-the-counter market. Dealers establish a "market" in these securities by standing ready to buy and sell Canadian government bonds. Other over-the-counter markets include those that trade other types of financial instruments such as negotiable certificates of deposit, overnight funds, banker's acceptances, and foreign exchange.

Money and Capital Markets

Another way of distinguishing between markets is on the basis of the maturity of the securities traded in each market. The **money market** is a financial market in which only short-term debt instruments (original maturity of less than one year) are traded; the **capital market** is the market in which longer-term debt (original maturity of one year or greater) and equity instruments are traded. Money market securities are usually more widely traded than longer-term securities and so tend to be more liquid. In addition, as we will see in Chapter 3, short-term securities have smaller fluctuations in prices than long-term securities, making them safer investments. As a result, corporations and banks actively use this market to earn interest on surplus funds that they expect to have only temporarily. Capital market securities, such as stocks and long-term bonds, are often held by financial intermediaries such as insurance companies and pension funds, which have little uncertainty about the amount of funds they will have available in the future.

INTERNATIONALIZATION OF FINANCIAL MARKETS

The growing internationalization of financial markets has become an important trend. The extraordinary growth of foreign financial markets has been the result of both large increases in the pool of savings in foreign countries such as Japan and the deregulation of foreign financial markets, which has enabled them to expand their activities. Canadian corporations and banks are now more likely to tap international capital markets to raise needed funds, and Canadian investors often seek investment opportunities abroad. Similarly, foreign corporations and banks raise funds from Canadians, and foreigners are becoming important investors in Canada. A look at international bond markets and world stock markets will give us a picture of how this globalization of financial markets is taking place.

International Bond Market, Eurobonds, and Eurocurrencies

The traditional instruments in the international bond market are known as **foreign bonds**. Foreign bonds are sold in a foreign country and are denominated in that country's currency. For example, if the German automaker Porsche sells a bond in Canada denominated in Canadian dollars, it is classified as a foreign bond. Foreign bonds have been an important instrument in the international capital market for centuries.

A more recent innovation in the international bond market is the **Eurobond**, a bond denominated in a currency other than that of the country in which it is sold—for example, a bond issued by a Canadian corporation that is denominated in Canadian dollars sold in the United States.[1] Currently, more than 80% of the new issues in the international bond market are Eurobonds, and the market for these securities has grown very rapidly.

A variant of the Eurobond is **Eurocurrencies**, which are foreign currencies that are deposited in banks outside the home country. The most important of the Eurocurrencies is **Eurodollars**, which are U.S. dollars deposited in foreign banks outside the United States or in foreign branches of U.S. banks. These short-term deposits earn interest and so are similar to short-term Eurobonds. Canadian banks borrow EuroCan$ deposits from other banks or from their own foreign branches, and EuroCan$ are now an important source of funds for Canadian banks.

World Stock Markets

Until recently, the U.S. stock market was by far the largest in the world, but stock markets in other countries have been growing in importance (see Table 1). Now the United States is not always number one: In the 1980s, the value of stocks traded in Japan at times exceeded the value of stocks traded in the United States. The increased interest in foreign stocks has prompted the development in Canada of mutual funds specializing in trading in foreign stock markets. Canadian investors now pay attention not only to the Canadian stock markets (the Toronto and Montreal stock exchanges) but also to stock price indexes for foreign stock markets

[1]Note that the new currency, the euro, can create some confusion about the term *Eurobond.* A Eurobond does not mean a bond denominated in euros. A bond denominated in euros is only called a Eurobond *if it is sold outside the countries that have adopted the euro.*

TABLE 1 Top 10 Stock Exchanges in the World by Market Capitalization in 2000

Exchange	Billions of U.S. $	Rank in 2000
New York	11 534.6	1
Nasdaq	3 597.1	2
Tokyo	3 157.2	3
London	2 612.2	4
Euronext Paris	1 446.6	5
Deutsche Borse	1 270.2	6
Switzerland	792.3	7
Toronto	770.1	8
Italy	768.3	9
Euronext Amsterdam	640.5	10

Source: *Annual Report: World Exchanges Organization*, 2000, p. 73

such as the Dow Jones Industrial Average (New York), the Nikkei 225 Average (Tokyo) and the Financial Times–Stock Exchange 100-Share Index (London).

The internationalization of financial markets is having profound effects on Canada. Foreigners are not only providing funds to corporations in Canada but also helping to finance a significant portion of the federal government's budget deficits. Without these foreign funds, the Canadian economy would have grown far less rapidly in the past two decades. The internationalization of financial markets is also leading the way to a more integrated world economy in which flows of goods and technology between countries are more commonplace. In later chapters we will encounter many examples of the important roles that international factors play in our economy.

The home pages for the mentioned foreign stock markets can be found at www.nyse.com, www.londonstockexchange.com, and www.tse.or.jp

FUNCTION OF FINANCIAL INTERMEDIARIES

As shown in Figure 1, funds can move from lenders to borrowers by a second route, called *indirect finance* because it involves a financial intermediary that stands between the lender-savers and the borrower-spenders and helps transfer funds from one to the other. A financial intermediary does this by borrowing funds from the lender-savers and then using these funds to make loans to borrower-spenders. For example, a bank might acquire funds by issuing a liability to the public in the form of savings deposits. It might then use the funds to acquire an asset by making a loan to Canadian Pacific or by buying a Canadian Pacific bond in the financial market. The ultimate result is that funds have been transferred from the public (the lender-savers) to Canadian Pacific (the borrower-spender) with the help of the financial intermediary (the bank).

More information about Canadian Pacific can be found at www.canadianpacific.com

The process of indirect finance using financial intermediaries, called **financial intermediation**, is the primary route for moving funds from lenders to borrowers. Indeed, although the media focus much of their attention on securities markets, particularly the stock market, financial intermediaries are a far more important source of financing for corporations than securities markets are. This is true not only for Canada but for other industrialized countries as well (see Box 1). Why are financial intermediaries and indirect finance so important in financial markets? To answer this question, we need to understand the role of transaction costs and information costs in financial markets.

BOX 1: GLOBAL

The Importance of Financial Intermediaries to Securities Markets: An International Comparison

Patterns of financing corporations differ across countries, but one key fact emerges. Studies of the major developed countries, including Canada, the United States, Great Britain, Japan, Italy, Germany, and France, show that when businesses go looking for funds to finance their activities, they usually obtain them indirectly through financial intermediaries and not directly from securities markets.* Even in Canada and the United States, which have the most developed securities markets in the world, loans from financial intermediaries are far more important for corporate finance than securities markets are. The countries that have made the least use of securities markets are Germany and Japan; in these two countries, financing from financial intermediaries has been almost ten times greater than that from securities markets. However, with the deregulation of Japanese securities markets in recent years, the share of corporate financing by financial intermediaries has been declining relative to the use of securities markets.

Although the dominance of financial intermediaries over securities markets is clear in all countries, the relative importance of bond versus stock markets differs widely across countries. In the United States, the bond market is far more important as a source of corporate finance: On average, the amount of new financing raised using bonds is ten times the amount using stocks. By contrast, countries such as France and Italy make use of equities markets more than the bond market to raise capital.

*See, for example, Colin Mayer, "Financial Systems, Corporate Finance, and Economic Development," in *Asymmetric Information, Corporate Finance, and Investment*, ed. R. Glenn Hubbard (Chicago: University of Chicago Press, 1990), pp. 307–332.

Transaction Costs

Transaction costs, the time and money spent in carrying out financial transactions, are a major problem for people who have excess funds to lend. As we have seen, Carl the Carpenter needs $1000 for his new tool, and you know that it is an excellent investment opportunity. You have the cash and would like to lend him the money, but to protect your investment, you have to hire a lawyer to write up the loan contract that specifies how much interest Carl will pay you, when he will make these interest payments, and when he will repay you the $1000. Obtaining the contract will cost you $500. When you figure in this transaction cost for making the loan, you realize that you can't earn enough from the deal (you spend $500 to make perhaps $100) and reluctantly tell Carl that he will have to look elsewhere.

This example illustrates that small savers like you or potential borrowers like Carl might be frozen out of financial markets and thus be unable to benefit from them. Can anyone come to the rescue? Financial intermediaries can.

Financial intermediaries can substantially reduce transaction costs because they have developed expertise in lowering them and because their large size allows them to take advantage of **economies of scale,** the reduction in transaction costs per dollar of transactions as the size (scale) of transactions increases. For example, a bank knows how to find a good lawyer to produce an airtight loan contract, and this contract can be used over and over again in its loan transactions, thus lowering the legal cost per transaction. Instead of a loan contract (which may not be all that well written) costing $500, a bank can hire a topflight lawyer for $5000 to draw up an airtight loan contract that can be used for 2000 loans at a cost of $2.50 per loan. At a cost of $2.50 per loan, it now becomes profitable for the financial intermediary to loan Carl the $1000.

Because financial intermediaries are able to reduce transaction costs substantially, they make it possible for you to provide funds indirectly to people with productive investment opportunities like Carl. In addition, a financial intermediary's low transaction costs mean that it can provide its customers with liquidity services, services that make it easier for customers to conduct transactions. For example, banks

FOLLOWING THE FINANCIAL NEWS

Foreign Stock Market Indexes

— 52 week — high	low		Close	Net chg	% chg
Japan					
14176.8	9420.9	Nikkei	11336.95	-194.16	-1.68
1383.39	922.51	Topix	1074.79	-11.17	-1.03
Britain					
3340.80	2180.90	FT Ords	2537.00	-15.90	-0.62
5976.60	4433.70	FTSE 100	5204.80	33.60	0.65
2837.86	2110.47	FT 500	2396.67	6.27	0.26
2890.91	2128.10	FT All Shr	2529.60	13.00	0.51
3398.74	2268.36	FT EurTop	2708.02	26.11	0.97
Germany					
1901.08	1135.56	FAZ	1512.76	-12.74	-0.84
6278.90	3787.23	DAX	4975.48	103.78	2.13
Australia					
3440.00	2867.40	All Ords	3252.20	-26.90	-0.82
5881.00	4955.20	All Inds	5483.80	-45.40	-0.82
915.70	593.60	All Mng	914.50	9.80	1.09
Hong Kong					
13877.95	8934.20	HangSeng	11733.43	87.53	0.75
Taiwan					
6462.30	3446.26	Weighted	5742.66	-64.64	-1.11
China					
664.85	371.79	Shenzhen	475.11	-4.70	-0.98
2242.42	1358.69	Shanghai	1623.94	-14.26	-0.87

— 52 week — high	low		Close	Net chg	% chg
Indonesia					
551.61	367.07	JSX	537.14	-6.76	-1.24
Philippines					
1484.83	979.34	Comp	1353.50	2.73	0.20
Singapore					
1808.41	1241.29	Straits	1732.79	-3.16	-0.18
Thailand					
391.71	265.22	SET	380.67	-1.42	-0.37
France					
5693.47	3652.87	CAC 40	4375.39	45.55	1.05
Italy					
1761.42	1082.91	BancaCml	1418.70	-0.32	-0.02
40220	24234	MIB 30	31291	499.00	1.62
Switzerland					
7705.80	5110.20	SwissMkt	6568.30	35.20	0.54
Netherlands					
863.40	556.50	CBS Gen	696.70	4.20	0.61
Belgium					
18119.54	14382.31	General	17942.41	125.45	0.70
Sweden					
262.43	177.49	Affrsvldn	202.75	1.19	0.59
Spain					
935.52	648.57	Madrid	817.03	8.75	1.08

— 52 week — high	low		Close	Net chg	% chg
South Africa					
11205.60	6843.70	All Share	11149.00	-44.10	-0.39
Mexico					
7574.35	5081.92	Gen IPC	7307.16	3.59	0.05
Argentina					
471.34	200.86	BUSE	385.87	-1.67	-0.43
Brazil					
15464.06	10005.87	BRSP	12002.32	-127.83	-1.05
Venezuela					
8088.92	6070.09	IBC	clsd.	clsd.	clsd.
Chile					
115.58	93.53	IPSA	96.09	-0.41	-0.43
India					
3742.07	2600.12	Sensex	3442.49	11.17	0.33
Turkey					
14999.51	7306.38	ISE Natl	11669.23	30.33	0.26
Malaysia					
808.07	554.36	KLSE Cmp	786.03	-2.51	-0.32
Israel					
468.92	355.93	TA-100	372.83	-0.69	-0.18
Greece					
3222.45	2105.56	General	2325.04	4.23	0.18

Source: National Post: Financial Post, Tuesday, May 14, 2002, p. *IN*10

Foreign stock market indexes are published daily in *The Globe and Mail: Report on Business* and the *National Post: Financial Post*. In the *National Post: Financial Post* you can read the "International Indexes" column, which reports developments in foreign stock markets.

The third column identifies the market index of the country under consideration.

The first column, "high," gives the highest value of the index in the past 52 weeks, which was 14176.8 for the Nikkei 225 Average on May 14, 2002. The second column, "low," gives the lowest value of the index in the past 52 weeks, which was 9420.9 for the Nikkei 225 Average. The fourth column, "Close," gives the closing value of the index, which was 11336.95 for the Nikkei 225 Average on May 4. The "Net chg" column indicates the change in the index from the previous trading day, −194.16, and the "% chg" column indicates the percentage change in the index, −1.68.

provide depositors with chequing accounts that enable them to pay their bills easily. In addition, depositors can earn interest on chequing and savings accounts and yet still convert them into goods and services whenever necessary.

Asymmetric Information: Adverse Selection and Moral Hazard

The presence of transaction costs in financial markets explains, in part, why financial intermediaries and indirect finance play such an important role in financial markets. An additional reason is that in financial markets, one party often does not know enough about the other party to make accurate decisions. This inequality is called **asymmetric information.** For example, a borrower who takes out a loan usually has better information about the potential returns and risks associated with the investment projects for which the funds are earmarked than the lender does. Lack of information creates problems in the financial system on two fronts: before the transaction is entered into and after.

Adverse selection is the problem created by asymmetric information *before* the transaction occurs. Adverse selection in financial markets occurs when the potential borrowers who are the most likely to produce an undesirable *(adverse)* outcome—the bad credit risks—are the ones who most actively seek out a loan and are thus most likely to be selected. Because adverse selection makes it more likely that loans might be made to bad credit risks, lenders may decide not to make any loans even though there are good credit risks in the marketplace.

To understand why adverse selection occurs, suppose that you have two aunts to whom you might make a loan—Aunt Sheila and Aunt Louise. Aunt Louise is a conservative type who borrows only when she has an investment that she is quite sure will pay off. Aunt Sheila, by contrast, is an inveterate gambler who has just come across a get-rich-quick scheme that will make her a millionaire if she can just borrow $1000 to invest in it. Unfortunately, as with most get-rich-quick schemes, there is a high probability that the investment won't pay off and that Aunt Sheila will lose the $1000.

Which of your aunts is more likely to call you to ask for a loan? Aunt Sheila, of course, because she has so much to gain if the investment pays off. You, however, would not want to make a loan to her because there is a high probability that her investment will turn sour and she will be unable to pay you back.

If you knew both your aunts very well—that is, if information was not asymmetric—you wouldn't have a problem because you would know that Aunt Sheila is a bad risk and so you would not lend to her. Suppose, though, that you don't know your aunts well. You are more likely to lend to Aunt Sheila than to Aunt Louise because Aunt Sheila would be hounding you for the loan. Because of the possibility of adverse selection, you might decide not to lend to either of your aunts, even though there are times when Aunt Louise, who is an excellent credit risk, might need a loan for a worthwhile investment.

Moral hazard is the problem created by asymmetric information *after* the transaction occurs. Moral hazard in financial markets is the risk *(hazard)* that the borrower might engage in activities that are undesirable *(immoral)* from the lender's point of view because they make it less likely that the loan will be paid back. Because moral hazard lowers the probability that the loan will be repaid, lenders may decide that they would rather not make a loan.

As an example of moral hazard, suppose that you made a $1000 loan to another relative, Uncle Melvin, who needs the money to purchase a word processor so that he can set up a business typing students' term papers. Once you have made the loan, however, Uncle Melvin is more likely to slip off to the track and play the horses. If he bets on a 20-to-1 long shot and wins with your money, he is able to pay you back your $1000 and live high off the hog with the remaining $19 000. But if he loses, as is likely, you don't get paid back, and all he has lost is his reputation as a reliable, upstanding uncle. Uncle Melvin therefore has an incentive to go to the track because his gains ($19 000) if he bets correctly may be much greater than the cost to him (his reputation) if he bets incorrectly. If you knew what Uncle Melvin was up to, you would prevent him from going to the track, and he would not be able to increase the moral hazard. However, because it is hard for you to keep informed about his whereabouts—that is, because information is asymmetric—there is a good chance that Uncle Melvin will go to the track and you will not be paid back. The risk of moral hazard might therefore discourage you from making the $1000 loan to Uncle Melvin, even if you were sure that you would be paid back if he used it to set up his business.

Study Guide Because the concepts of adverse selection and moral hazard are extremely useful in understanding the behaviour we examine in this and many of the later chapters (and in life in general), you must understand them fully. One way to distinguish between them is to remember that adverse selection is a problem of asymmetric information *before* entering into a transaction, whereas moral hazard is a problem of asymmetric information *after* the transaction has occurred. A helpful way to nail down these concepts is to think of other examples, for financial or other types of transactions, in which adverse selection or moral hazard plays a role. Several problems at the end of the chapter provide additional examples of situations involving adverse selection and moral hazard.

The problems created by adverse selection and moral hazard are an important impediment to well-functioning financial markets. Again, financial intermediaries can alleviate these problems.

With financial intermediaries in the economy, small savers can provide their funds to the financial markets by lending these funds to a trustworthy intermediary, say, the Honest John Bank, which in turn lends the funds out either by making loans or by buying securities such as stocks or bonds. Successful financial intermediaries have higher earnings on their investments because they are better equipped than individuals to screen out good from bad credit risks, thereby reducing losses due to adverse selection. In addition, financial intermediaries have high earnings because they develop expertise in monitoring the parties they lend to, thus reducing losses due to moral hazard. The result is that financial intermediaries can afford to pay lender-savers interest or provide substantial services and still earn a profit.

The success of financial intermediaries is evidenced by the fact that most Canadians invest their savings with them and also obtain their loans from them. Financial intermediaries play a key role in improving economic efficiency because they help financial markets channel funds from lender-savers to people with productive investment opportunities. Without a well-functioning set of financial intermediaries, it is very hard for an economy to reach its full potential. We will explore further the role of financial intermediaries in the economy in Part 5.

FINANCIAL INTERMEDIARIES

We have seen why financial intermediaries play such an important role in the economy. Now we look at the principal financial intermediaries and how they perform the intermediation function. They fall into three categories: depository institutions (banks and near banks), contractual savings institutions, and investment intermediaries. Table 2 provides a guide to the discussion of the financial intermediaries that fit into these three categories by describing their primary liabilities (sources of funds) and assets (uses of funds). The relative size of these intermediaries, which are regulated by the Office of the Superintendent of Financial Institutions (OSFI), is indicated in Table 3.

Depository Institutions

Depository institutions (which for simplicity we refer to as *banks* throughout this text) are financial intermediaries that accept deposits from individuals and institutions and make loans. These institutions include chartered banks and the so-called **near banks:** trust and mortgage loan companies and credit unions and *caisses populaires*.

TABLE 2 Primary Assets and Liabilities of Financial Intermediaries

Type of Intermediary	Primary Liabilities (Sources of Funds)	Primary Assets (Uses of Funds)
Depository Institutions (Banks)		
Chartered banks	Deposits	Loans, mortgages, government bonds
Trust and mortgage loan companies	Deposits	Mortgages
Credit unions and *caisses populaires*	Deposits	Mortgages
Contractual Savings Institutions		
Life insurance companies	Premiums from policies	Corporate bonds and mortgages
P&C insurance companies	Premiums from policies	Corporate bonds and stocks
Pension funds	Retirement contributions	Corporate bonds and stocks
Investment Intermediaries		
Finance companies	Finance paper, stocks, bonds	Consumer and business loans
Mutual funds	Shares	Stocks and bonds
Money market mutual funds	Shares	Money market instruments

Chartered Banks These financial intermediaries raise funds primarily by issuing chequable deposits (deposits on which cheques can be written), savings deposits (deposits that are payable on demand but do not allow their owner to write cheques), and time deposits (deposits with fixed terms to maturity). They then use these funds to make commercial, consumer, and mortgage loans and to buy Canadian government securities and provincial and municipal bonds. There are 53 chartered banks in Canada, and as a group, they are the largest financial intermediary and have the most diversified portfolios (collections) of assets.

Trust and Mortgage Loan Companies Trust and mortgage loan companies (TMLs) obtain funds primarily through chequable and non-chequable savings deposits, term deposits, guaranteed investment certificates, and debentures. The acquired

TABLE 3 Financial Institutions and Pension Plans Regulated by OSFI (as at March 31, 2001)

Type of Intermediary	Number	Total Assets (in Millions)	Percent (%)
Depository Institutions			
Commercial banks			
Domestic	13	1 524 835	67.06
Foreign bank subsidiaries	37	97 340	4.28
Foreign bank branches	9	3 844	0.17
Trust and mortgage loan companies			
Bank-owned	36	197 330	8.68
Other	29	9 646	0.42
Cooperative credit associations	7	9 489	0.42
Insurance Companies			
Life insurance companies			
Canadian-incorporated	52	251 493	11.06
Foreign branches	67	23 546	1.04
Property & casualty insurance companies			
Canadian-incorporated	93	37 629	1.66
Foreign branches	111	17 092	0.75
Fraternal Benefit Societies			
Canadian-owned	13	7 067	0.31
Foreign branches	13	910	0.04
Pension Plans	1187	93 451	4.11
Total		2 273 672	100.00

Source: Adapted from OSFI Annual Report 1999–2000, page 2, Office of the Superintendent of Financial Institutions, 2000. Reproduced with the permission of the Minister of Public Works.

funds have traditionally been used to make loans. TMLs are the second group of depository institutions numbering around 65. In the 1950s and 1960s, TMLs grew much more rapidly than chartered banks, but when interest rates climbed sharply from the late 1960s to the early 1980s, TMLs encountered difficulties that slowed their rapid growth. Because most mortgages are long-term loans, with maturities in excess of 25 years, many were made years earlier when interest rates were substantially lower. When interest rates rose, TMLs frequently found that the income from their mortgages was well below the cost of acquiring funds. In the early 1980s, 30 TMLs suffered large losses and 15 went out of business.

Until 1954, Canadian chartered banks were restricted to making commercial loans and could not make mortgage loans. Following the 1954 revisions in the Bank Act and the National Housing Act (NHA), chartered banks were allowed for the first time to make residential mortgage loans, but under NHA terms. The Bank Act in 1967, however, extended the authority of chartered banks to issue mortgage loans, by allowing them to make conventional mortgage loans and thereby directly compete with TMLs. Also, until 1991, TMLs were restricted to making mortgage loans and could not make commercial loans. The Bank Act of 1991 opened new business opportunities for TMLs by permitting them to make commercial loans. The net result of these legislative changes is that the distinction between TMLs and chartered banks has blurred, and these intermediaries have become more alike and much more competitive with each other.

Credit Unions and *Caisses Populaires* Credit unions and *caisses populaires* (CUCPs), numbering about 2200, are very small cooperative lending institutions organized around a particular group: union members, employees of a particular firm, and so forth. Almost 10 million Canadians are members of CUCPs and more than 61 000 are employed in the credit union and *caisses populaire* system. CUCPs acquire funds from deposits and primarily make mortgage and consumer loans.

Contractual Savings Institutions

Contractual savings institutions, such as insurance companies and pension funds, are financial intermediaries that acquire funds at periodic intervals on a contractual basis. Because they can predict with reasonable accuracy how much they will have to pay out in benefits in the coming years, they do not have to worry as much as depository institutions about losing funds. As a result, the liquidity of assets is not as important a consideration for them as it is for depository institutions, and they tend to invest their funds primarily in long-term securities such as corporate bonds, stocks, and mortgages.

Life Insurance Companies Life insurance companies insure people against financial hazards following a death and sell annuities (annual income payments upon retirement). They acquire funds from the premiums that people pay to keep their policies in force and use them mainly to buy corporate bonds and mortgages. They also purchase stocks but are restricted in the amount that they can hold. Currently, with about $260 billion of assets, they are among the largest of the contractual savings institutions.

Property and Casualty (P&C) Insurance Companies These companies insure their policyholders against loss from theft, fire, and accidents. They are very much like life insurance companies, receiving funds through premiums for their policies, but they have a greater possibility of loss of funds if major disasters occur. For this reason, they use their funds to buy more liquid assets than life insurance companies do. Their largest holding of assets is government bonds and debentures; they also hold corporate bonds and stocks.

Pension Funds and Government Retirement Funds Private pension funds and provincial and municipal government retirement funds provide retirement income in the form of annuities to employees who are covered by a pension plan. Funds are acquired by contributions from employers or from employees, who either have a contribution automatically deducted from their paycheques or contribute voluntarily. The largest asset holdings of pension funds are corporate bonds and stocks. The establishment of pension funds has been actively encouraged by the federal government both through legislation requiring pension plans and through tax incentives to encourage contributions.

Investment Intermediaries

This category of financial intermediaries includes finance companies and mutual funds.

Finance Companies Finance companies raise funds by selling commercial paper (a short-term debt instrument) and by issuing stocks and bonds. They lend these funds to consumers, who make purchases of such items as furniture, automobiles, and home improvements, and to small businesses. Some finance companies are organized by a parent corporation to help sell its product. For example, Ford Credit makes loans to consumers who purchase Ford automobiles.

Mutual Funds These financial intermediaries acquire funds by selling shares to many individuals and use the proceeds to purchase diversified portfolios of stocks and bonds. Mutual funds allow shareholders to pool their resources so that they can take advantage of lower transaction costs when buying large blocks of stocks or bonds. In addition, mutual funds allow shareholders to hold more diversified portfolios than they otherwise would. Shareholders can sell (redeem) shares at any time, but the value of these shares will be determined by the value of the mutual fund's holdings of securities. Because these fluctuate greatly, the value of mutual fund shares will too; therefore, investments in mutual funds can be risky.

REGULATION OF THE FINANCIAL SYSTEM

The Ontario Securities Commission home page, www.osc.gov.on.ca, contains vast OSC resources, laws and regulations, investor information, and litigation updates.

The financial system is among the most heavily regulated sectors of the Canadian economy. The government regulates financial markets for three main reasons: to increase the information available to investors, to ensure the soundness of the financial system, and to improve control of monetary policy. We will examine how these three reasons have led to the present regulatory environment. As a study aid, the principal regulatory agencies of the Canadian financial system are listed in Table 4.

Increasing Information Available to Investors

Asymmetric information in financial markets means that investors may be subject to adverse selection and moral hazard problems that may hinder the efficient operation of financial markets. Risky firms or outright crooks may be the most eager to sell securities to unwary investors, and the resulting adverse selection problem may keep investors out of financial markets. Furthermore, once an investor has bought a security, thereby lending money to a firm, the borrower may

TABLE 4 Principal Regulatory Agencies of the Canadian Financial System

Regulatory Agency	Subject of Regulation	Nature of Regulations
Provincial securities and exchange commissions	Organized exchanges, financial markets, provincial banks and credit unions	Require disclosure of information and restrict insider trading.
Bank of Canada	Chartered banks, TMLs, and CUCPs	Examines the books of the deposit-taking institutions and coordinates with the federal agencies that are responsible for financial institution regulation: OSFI and CDIC. It also enforces the non-negative settlement balances requirement.
Office of the Superintendent of Financial Institutions (OSFI)	All federally regulated chartered banks, TMLs, CUCPs, life insurance companies, P&C insurance companies, and pension plans	Sets capital adequacy, accounting, and board-of-director responsibility standards. It conducts bank audits and coordinates with provincial securities commissions.
Canada Deposit Insurance Corporation (CDIC)	Chartered banks, TMLs, and CUCPs	Provides insurance of up to $60 000 for each depositor at a bank, examines the books of insured banks, imposes restrictions on assets they can hold, and deals with bank failures.
Quebec Deposit Insurance Board	TMLs and credit cooperatives in Quebec	Similar role as the CDIC.
Canadian Life and Health Insurance Compensation Corporation (CompCorp)	Life insurance companies	Compensates policyholders if the issuing life insurance company goes bankrupt.
Property and Casualty (P&C) Insurance Compensation Corporation (PACIC)	Property and casualty insurance companies	Compensates policyholders if the issuing P&C insurance company goes bankrupt.
Self-regulatory organizations (SROs) such as the Toronto Stock Exchange, the Montreal Exchange, and the Investment Dealers Association (IDA)	Securities industry	Regulation covers many areas such as, for example, trading regulation, listing requirements, and member regulation. The objective is the protection of investors and the promotion of efficient markets.

have incentives to engage in risky activities or to commit outright fraud. The presence of this moral hazard problem may also keep investors away from financial markets. Government regulation can reduce adverse selection and moral hazard problems in financial markets and increase their efficiency by increasing the amount of information available to investors.

Provincial securities commissions, the most significant being the Ontario Securities Commission (OSC), administer provincial acts requiring corporations issuing securities to disclose certain information about their sales, assets, and earnings to the public and restrict trading by the largest stockholders (known as insiders) in the corporation. By requiring disclosure of this information and by discouraging insider trading, which could be used to manipulate security prices, regulators hope that investors will be better informed and be protected from abuses in financial markets. Indeed, in recent years, the OSC has been particularly active in prosecuting people involved in insider trading in Canada's largest stock exchange, the Toronto Stock Exchange (TSX).

Moreover, a number of non-governmental organizations, such as the Toronto Stock Exchange (TSX), the Montreal Exchange, and the Investment Dealers

Association (IDA) are considered to be self-regulatory organizations (SROs), with regulatory power over their members. The role of the TSX and the Montreal Exchange in regulation covers many areas such as trading regulation, listing requirements, and member regulation. Top priority is the protection of investors and the promotion of equitable and ethical practices in the securities industry. Regulation is covered in detail in *The Conduct and Practices Handbook for Securities Industry Professionals* published by the Canadian Securities Institute (CSI), a not-for-profit educator of the securities industry in Canada.

The Investment Dealers Association of Canada was established in 1916 and is the trade association and self-regulatory organization of the Canadian securities industry. It has offices in Montreal, Toronto, Calgary, Vancouver, and Halifax and represents more than 190 investment dealer members across the country. The IDA monitors member firms in terms of their conduct of business and capital adequacy, with the ultimate objective of protecting investors and fostering competitive and efficient capital markets. Together with the Bank of Canada and the federal Department of Finance, the Association develops standards and practices for the primary and secondary fixed-income (t-bills, bonds, and debentures) and equity markets.

Go to www.csi.ca for details about the Canadian Securities Institute.

An electronic version of *The Conduct and Practices Handbook for Securities Industry Professionals* is available at www.ida.ca/Files/Regulation/CI_Bulletin/C135_en.pdf

An additional responsibility of the IDA is to express the views of the public and to offer advice to federal and provincial governments regarding public policy and industry issues that affect the Canadian capital markets. Moreover, the Association works closely with foreign securities regulators and SROs, promoting Canadian interests abroad and pursuing the international harmonization of capital markets regulation.

Ensuring the Soundness of Financial Intermediaries

Asymmetric information can also lead to widespread collapse of financial intermediaries, referred to as a **financial panic**. Because providers of funds to financial intermediaries may not be able to assess whether the institutions holding their funds are sound or not, if they have doubts about the overall health of financial intermediaries, they may want to pull their funds out of both sound and unsound institutions. The possible outcome is a financial panic that produces large losses for the public and causes serious damage to the economy. To protect the public and the economy from financial panics, the government has implemented six types of regulations.

The Investment Dealers Association of Canada Website at www.ida.ca provides further information about the IDA's responsibilities.

Restrictions on Entry Provincial banking and insurance commissions, the Bank of Canada, and the Office of the Superintendent of Financial Institutions (OSFI), an agency of the federal government, have created very tight regulations as to who is allowed to set up a financial intermediary. Individuals or groups that want to establish a financial intermediary, such as a bank or an insurance company, must obtain a charter from the provincial or federal government. Only if they are upstanding citizens with impeccable credentials and a large amount of initial funds will they be given a charter.

Examine the Office of the Superintendent of Financial Institutions home page at www.osfi-bsif.gc.ca

Disclosure There are stringent reporting requirements for financial intermediaries. Their bookkeeping must follow certain strict principles, their books are subject to periodic inspection, and they must make certain information available to the public.

Restrictions on Assets and Activities There are restrictions on what financial intermediaries are allowed to do and what assets they can hold. Before you put your funds into a chartered bank or some other such institution, you want to know that your funds are safe and that the bank or other financial intermediary will be able to meet its obligations to you. One way of doing this is to restrict the financial intermediary from engaging in certain risky activities. Another way is to restrict financial intermediaries from holding certain risky assets, or at least from holding a greater quantity of these risky assets than is prudent. For example, chartered banks and other depository institutions are not allowed to hold common stock because stock prices experience substantial fluctuations. Insurance companies are allowed to hold common stock, but their holdings cannot exceed a certain fraction of their total assets.

Deposit Insurance The most important government agency that provides this type of insurance is the Canada Deposit Insurance Corporation (CDIC), created by act of Parliament in 1967. It insures each depositor at a member deposit-taking financial institution up to a loss of $60 000 per account. Except for certain wholesale branches of foreign banks, credit unions, and some provincial institutions, all deposit-taking financial institutions in Canada are members of the CDIC. All CDIC members make contributions into the CDIC fund, which are used to payoff depositors in the case of a bank's failure. The Quebec Deposit Insurance Board, an organization similar to CDIC and set up at the same time as CDIC, provides insurance for TMLs and credit cooperatives in Quebec.

The Canada Deposit Insurance Corporation Website, www.cdic.ca, includes details about its role.

Limits on Competition Politicians have often declared that unbridled competition among financial intermediaries promotes failures that will harm the public. Although the evidence that competition does this is extremely weak, it has not stopped the provincial and federal governments from imposing many restrictive regulations. For example, from 1967 to 1980 the entry of foreign banks into Canadian banking was prohibited. Since 1980, the incorporation of foreign bank subsidiaries has been regulated, but according to the *World Competitiveness Survey*, Canada ranks 41st out of 53 countries surveyed with respect to the degree of competition from foreign banks.[2]

Improving Control of Monetary Policy

Because banks play a very important role in determining the supply of money (which in turn affects many aspects of the economy), much regulation of these financial intermediaries is intended to improve control over the money supply. One such regulation is **settlement balances**, which make it obligatory for depository institutions to keep money in accounts with the Bank of Canada (the Bank), the central bank in Canada. Settlement balances are held to facilitate the clearing of cheques and other transfers and help the Bank of Canada exercise more precise control over the money supply. Deposit insurance regulation can also be rationalized along these lines: The CDIC gives depositors confidence in the banking system and eliminates bank failures, which can in turn cause large, uncontrollable fluctuations in the quantity of money.

In later chapters, we will look more closely at government regulation of financial markets and will see whether it has improved the functioning of financial markets.

Financial Regulation Abroad

Not surprisingly, given the similarity of the economic system here and in the United States, Japan, and the nations of Western Europe, financial regulation in these

[2]Institute for International Management Development, *The World Competitiveness Yearbook* 1997, June 1997.

countries is similar to financial regulation in Canada. The provision of information is improved by requiring corporations issuing securities to report details about assets and liabilities, earnings, and sales of stock and by prohibiting insider trading. The soundness of intermediaries is ensured by licensing, periodic inspection of financial intermediaries' books, and the provision of deposit insurance (although its coverage is smaller and its existence is often intentionally not advertised).

The major differences between financial regulation in Canada and abroad relate to bank regulation. In the past, for example, the United States was the only industrialized country to subject banks to restrictions on branching, which limited banks' size and restricted them to certain geographic regions. These restrictions were abolished by legislation in 1994. Canadian and U.S. banks are the most restricted in the range of assets they may hold. Banks in other countries frequently hold shares in commercial firms; in Japan and Germany, those stakes can be sizable.

The Basel Accord Financial institutions are also required by regulatory authorities to hold capital to protect depositors, policyholders, and liability guarantors. This capital is known as **regulatory capital**. In recent years, regulators in different countries, under the sponsorship of the Bank of International Settlements, have developed a set of capital adequacy standards with the objective of levelling the playing field among international financial institutions and promoting global standards for financial institutions regulation. These capital adequacy standards are known as the Basel Accord and we will discuss it in detail in Chapter 18.

SUMMARY

1. The basic function of financial markets is to channel funds from savers who have an excess of funds to spenders who have a shortage of funds. Financial markets can do this either through direct finance, in which borrowers borrow funds directly from lenders by selling them securities, or through indirect finance, which involves a financial intermediary who stands between the lender-savers and the borrower-spenders and helps transfer funds from one to the other. This channelling of funds improves the economic welfare of everyone in the society because it allows funds to move from people who have no productive investment opportunities to those who have such opportunities, thereby contributing to increased efficiency in the economy. In addition, it directly benefits consumers by allowing them to make purchases when they need them most.
2. Financial markets can be classified as debt and equity markets, primary and secondary markets, exchanges and over-the-counter markets, and money and capital markets.
3. An important trend in recent years is the growing internationalization of financial markets. Eurobonds, which are denominated in a currency other than that of the country in which they are sold, are now the dominant security in the international bond market. Eurodollars, which are U.S. dollars deposited in foreign banks, are an important source of funds for Canadian banks.
4. Financial intermediaries are financial institutions that acquire funds by issuing liabilities and in turn use those funds to acquire assets by purchasing securities or making loans. Financial intermediaries play such an important role in the financial system because they reduce transaction costs and solve problems created by adverse selection and moral hazard. As a result, financial intermediaries allow small savers and borrowers to benefit from the existence of financial markets, thereby increasing the efficiency of the economy.
5. The principal financial intermediaries fall into three categories: (a) banks—chartered banks, trust and mortgage loan companies, and credit unions and *caisses populaires;* (b) contractual savings institutions—life insurance companies, property and casualty insurance companies, and pension funds; and (c) investment intermediaries—finance companies, mutual funds, and money market mutual funds.
6. The government regulates financial markets and financial intermediaries for three main reasons: to increase the information available to investors, to ensure the soundness of the financial system, and to improve control of monetary policy. Regulations include disclosure of information to the public, restrictions on who can set up a financial intermediary, restrictions on what assets financial intermediaries can hold, the provision of deposit insurance, reserve requirements, and the setting of maximum interest rates that can be paid on chequing accounts and savings deposits.

KEY TERMS

adverse selection, *p. 21*
asymmetric information, *p. 21*
brokers, *p. 16*
capital market, *p. 17*
dealers, *p. 16*
dividends, *p. 16*
economies of scale, *p. 21*
equities, *p. 16*
Eurobonds, *p. 18*
Eurocurrencies, *p. 18*
Eurodollars, *p. 18*
exchanges, *p. 17*
financial intermediation, *p. 19*
financial panic, *p. 28*
foreign bonds, *p. 18*
intermediate term, *p. 16*
investment bank, *p. 16*
liabilities, *p. 14*
liquid, *p. 17*
long term, *p. 16*
maturity, *p. 15*
money market, *p. 17*
moral hazard, *p. 21*
near banks, *p. 23*
over-the-counter (OTC) market, *p. 17*
primary market, *p. 16*
regulatory capital, *p. 30*
secondary market, *p. 16*
settlement balances, *p. 29*
short term, *p. 16*
transaction costs, *p. 20*
underwriting, *p. 16*

QUESTIONS AND PROBLEMS

***1.** Why is a share of IBM common stock an asset for its owner and a liability for IBM?

2. If I can buy a car today for $5000 and it is worth $10 000 next year in extra income to me because it enables me to get a job as a travelling anvil seller, should I take out a loan from Larry the Loan Shark at a 90% interest rate if no one else will give me a loan? Will I be better or worse off as a result of taking out this loan? Can you make a case for legalizing loan-sharking?

***3.** Some economists suspect that one of the reasons that economies in developing countries grow so slowly is that they do not have well-developed financial markets. Does this argument make sense?

4. Describe how authority over deposit-based financial intermediaries is split among the Bank of Canada, the OSFI, and the CDIC.

***5.** "Because corporations do not actually raise any funds in secondary markets, they are less important to the economy than primary markets." Comment.

6. If you suspect that a company will go bankrupt next year, which would you rather hold—bonds issued by the company or equities issued by the company? Why?

***7.** How can the adverse selection problem explain why you are more likely to make a loan to a family member than to a stranger?

8. Provide one example in which you have had to deal with the adverse selection problem.

***9.** Why do loan sharks worry less about moral hazard in connection with their borrowers than some other lenders do?

10. If you are an employer, what kinds of moral hazard problems might you worry about with your employees?

***11.** If there were no asymmetry in the information that a borrower and a lender had, could there still be a moral hazard problem?

12. "In a world without information and transaction costs, financial intermediaries would not exist." Is this statement true, false, or uncertain? Explain your answer.

***13.** Why might you be willing to make a loan to your neighbour by putting funds in a savings account earning a 5% interest rate at the bank and having the bank loan her the funds at a 10% interest rate, rather than loan her the funds yourself?

14. In two lists, rank the following money market instruments in terms of their liquidity and their safety:

a. Canadian treasury bills
b. Negotiable CDs
c. Repurchase agreements
d. Commercial paper

***15.** Discuss some of the manifestations of the globalization of world capital markets.

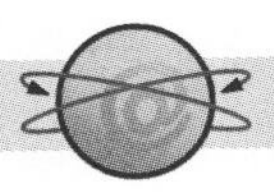

WEB EXERCISES

Overview of the Financial System

1. One of the single best sources of information about financial institutions is the "Financial Data" reported by the OSFI. To access the data, go to http://www.osfi-bsif.gc.ca. Click on the most current release and answer the following questions.
   a. What is the date of the most current release?
   b. What percentage of assets do commercial banks hold in loans? What percentage of assets are held in mortgage loans?
   c. What percentage of assets do trust and loan companies hold in mortgage loans?
   d. What percentage of assets do credit unions hold in mortgage loans and in consumer loans?
2. The most famous financial market in the world is the New York Stock Exchange. Check out their Website at http://www.nyse.com and answer the following questions.
   a. What is the mission of the NYSE?
   b. Firms must pay a fee to list their shares for sale on the NYSE. What would be the fee for a firm with 5 million common shares outstanding?

Part 2

Fundamentals of Interest Rates

Chapter 3 Understanding Interest Rates

Preview

At www.bankofcanada.ca/en click on "Other rates and statistics" and then on "Selected Historical Interest Rates," to access information on key Canadian and U.S. interest rates.

Interest rates are among the most closely watched variables in the economy. Their movements are reported almost daily by the news media because they directly affect our everyday lives and have important consequences for the health of the economy. They affect personal decisions such as whether to consume or save, whether to buy a house, and whether to purchase bonds or put funds into a savings account. Interest rates also affect the economic decisions of businesses and households, such as whether to use funds to invest in new equipment for factories or to save money in a bank.

Before we can go on with the study of financial markets, we must understand exactly what the phrase *interest rates* means. In this chapter we see that a concept known as the *yield to maturity* is the most accurate measure of interest rates; the yield to maturity is what financial economists mean when they use the term *interest rate.* We discuss how the yield to maturity is measured on credit market instruments and examine alternative (but less accurate) ways in which interest rates are quoted. We also see that a bond's interest rate does not necessarily indicate how good an investment the bond is because what it earns (its rate of return) can differ from its interest rate. Finally, we explore the distinction between real interest rates, which are adjusted for changes in the price level, and nominal interest rates, which are not.

Although learning definitions is not always the most exciting of pursuits, it is important to read carefully and understand the concepts presented in this chapter. Not only are they continually used throughout the remainder of this text, but a firm grasp of these terms will give you a clearer understanding of the role that interest rates play in your life as well as in the general economy.

MEASURING INTEREST RATES

Debt market instruments fall into four types:

1. A **simple loan** provides the borrower with an amount of funds (principal) that must be repaid to the lender at the maturity date along with an additional amount known as an *interest* payment. For example, if a bank made you a simple loan of $100 for one year, you would have to repay the principal of $100 in one year's time, along with an additional interest payment of, say, $10. Commercial loans to businesses are often of this type.
2. A **fixed-payment loan** provides a borrower with an amount of funds that is to be repaid by making the same payment every month, consisting of part of the principal and interest for a set number of years. For example, if you borrowed $1000, a fixed-payment loan might require you to pay $85.8 every year for 25 years. Installment loans (such as auto loans) and mortgages are frequently of the fixed-payment type.
3. A **coupon bond** pays the owner of the bond a fixed interest payment (coupon payment) every year until the maturity date, when a specified final amount **(face value** or **par value)** is repaid. The coupon payment is so named because the bondholder used to obtain payment by clipping a coupon off the bond and sending it to the bond issuer, who then sent the payment to the holder. Nowadays, for most coupon bonds it is no longer necessary to send in coupons to receive these payments. A coupon bond with $1000 face value, for example, might pay you a coupon payment of $100 per year for ten years and at the maturity date repay you the face value amount of $1000. (The face value of a bond is usually in $1000 increments.)

   A coupon bond is identified by three pieces of information. First is the corporation or government agency that issues the bond. Second is the maturity date of the bond. Third is the bond's **coupon rate**, the dollar amount of the yearly coupon payment expressed as a percentage of the face value of the bond. In our example, the coupon bond has a yearly coupon payment of $100 and a face value of $1000. The coupon rate is then $100/$1000 = 0.10, or 10%. Canada bonds and corporate bonds are examples of coupon bonds.
4. A **discount bond** (also called a **zero-coupon bond**) is bought at a price below its face value (at a discount), and the face value is repaid at the maturity date. Unlike a coupon bond, a discount bond does not make any interest payments; it just pays off the face value. For example, a discount bond with a face value of $1000 might be bought for $900 and in a year's time the owner would be repaid the face value of $1000. Canadian government treasury bills and long-term zero-coupon bonds are examples of discount bonds.

These four types of instruments require payments at different times: Simple loans and discount bonds make payment only at their maturity dates, whereas fixed-payment loans and coupon bonds have payments periodically until maturity. How would you decide which of these instruments provides you with more income? They all seem so different because they make payments at different times. To solve this problem, we use the concept of present value to provide us with a procedure for measuring interest rates on these different types of instruments.

Present Value

The concept of **present value** is based on the commonsense notion that a dollar paid to you one year from now is less valuable to you than a dollar paid to you today; this notion is true because you can deposit the dollar in a savings account that earns interest and have more than a dollar in one year. We will now define this concept more formally.

In the case of a simple loan, the interest payment divided by the amount of the loan is a natural and sensible way to measure the cost of borrowing funds: The measure of the cost is the *simple interest rate*. In the example we used to describe the simple loan, a loan of \$100 today requires the borrower to repay the \$100 a year from now and to make an additional interest payment of \$10. Hence, using the definition just given, the simple interest rate i is

$$i = \frac{\$10}{\$100} = 0.10 = 10\%$$

If you make this \$100 loan, at the end of the year you would receive \$110, which can be rewritten as

$$\$100 \times (1 + 0.10) = \$110$$

If you then loaned out the \$110, at the end of the second year you would receive

$$\$110 \times (1 + 0.10) = \$121$$

or, equivalently,

$$\$100 \times (1 + 0.10) \times (1 + 0.10) = \$100 \times (1 + 0.10)^2 = \$121$$

Continuing with the loan again, you would receive at the end of the third year

$$\$121 \times (1 + 0.10) = \$100 \times (1 + 0.10)^3 = \$133$$

The amounts you would have at the end of each year can be seen in the following time line:

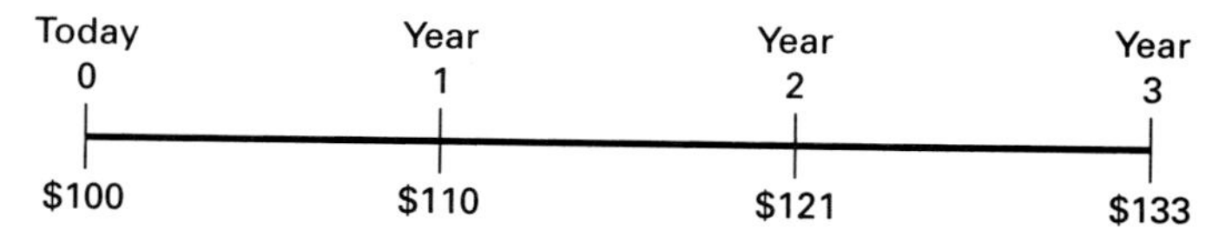

These calculations of the proceeds from a simple loan can be generalized as follows: If the simple interest rate i is expressed as a decimal fraction (such as 0.10 for the 10% interest rate in our example), then after making these loans for n years, you will receive a total payment of

$$\$100 \times (1 + i)^n$$

We can also work these calculations backward. Because \$100 today will turn into \$110 next year when the simple interest rate is 10%, we could say that \$110 next year is worth only \$100 today. Or we could say that no one would pay more than \$100 today to get \$110 next year. Similarly, we could say that \$121 two years from now or \$133 three years from now is worth \$100 today. This process of calculating what dollars received in the future are worth today is called *discounting the future*. We have been implicitly solving our forward-looking equations for today's value of a future dollar amount. For example, in the case of the \$133 received three years from now, when $i = 0.10$,

Today	Future
\$100	$\$100 \times (1 + i)^3 = \$133$

so that

$$\$100 = \frac{\$133}{(1 + i)^3}$$

More generally, we can solve this equation to tell us the present value *(PV)*, or **present discounted value**, of the future dollar amount—that is, the value *today* of a future payment *(FV)* received n years from now when the simple interest rate is i:

$$PV = \frac{FV}{(1 + i)^n} \tag{1}$$

Intuitively, what Equation 1 tells us is that if you are promised $1 for certain ten years from now, this dollar would not be as valuable to you as $1 is today because if you had the $1 today, you could invest it and end up with more than $1 in ten years.

EXAMPLE 1: Simple Present Value

What is the present value of $250 to be paid in two years if the interest rate is 15%?

Solution

The present value would be $189.04. Using Equation 1:

$$PV = \frac{FV}{(1 + i)^n}$$

where

FV = amount in two years = $250

i = annual interest rate = 0.15

n = number of years = 2

Thus

$$PV = \frac{\$250}{(1 + 0.15)^2} = \frac{\$250}{1.3225} = \$189.04$$

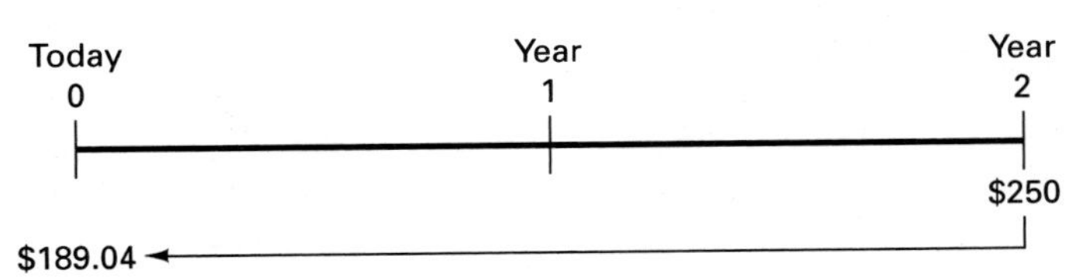

The concept of present value is extremely useful because it allows us to figure out today's value of a credit market instrument at a given simple interest rate i by just adding up the present value of all the future payments received. The present value concept allows us to compare the value of two instruments with very different timing of their payments, such as a discount bond and a coupon bond. As we will see, this concept also allows us to obtain an equivalent measure of the interest rate on all four types of credit market instruments discussed here.

Application **Cost of the Savings and Loan (S&L) Bailout: Was It Really $500 Billion?**

The U.S. government bailout of the savings and loan industry in 1989 was one of the major news stories of that decade. Statements frequently appeared in the press that the cost of the bailout to U.S. taxpayers would exceed $500 billion—more than $2000 for every man, woman, and child in the United States. The $500 billion-plus figure made for wonderful political rhetoric, but was the cost really this high?

The answer is no, and the concept of present value tells us why. The $500 billion figure includes bond payments over the next 40 years. The present value concept tells us that to figure out the cost of these payments in today's dollars, we have to discount them back to the present. When we do this, the present value of these payments is in the order of $150 billion, not $500 billion. It is still true that a present value of the bailout of $150 billion is nothing to sneeze at, but it is not quite as scary as a figure more than three times that size.

Yield to Maturity

Of the several common ways of calculating interest rates, the most important is the **yield to maturity**, the interest rate that equates the present value of payments received from a debt instrument with its value today. Because the concept behind the calculation of the yield to maturity makes good economic sense, financial economists consider it the most accurate measure of interest rates.

To understand the yield to maturity better, we now look at how it is calculated for the four types of credit market instruments.

Simple Loan Using the concept of present value, the yield to maturity on a simple loan is easy to calculate. For the one-year loan we discussed, today's value is $100, and the payments in one year's time would be $110 (the repayment of $100 plus the interest payment of $10). We can use this information to solve for the yield to maturity i by recognizing that the present value of the future payments must equal today's value of a loan.

EXAMPLE 2: Simple Loan

If Pete borrows $100 from his sister and next year she wants $110 back from him, what is the yield to maturity on this loan?

Solution

The yield to maturity on the loan is 10%.

$$PV = \frac{FV}{(1 + i)^n}$$

where

PV = amount borrowed = $100

FV = amount in one year = $110

n = number of years = 1

Thus

$$\$100 = \frac{\$110}{(1 + i)}$$

$$(1 + i)\$100 = \$110$$

$$(1 + i) = \frac{\$100}{\$110}$$

$$i = 1.10 - 1 = 0.10 = 10\%$$

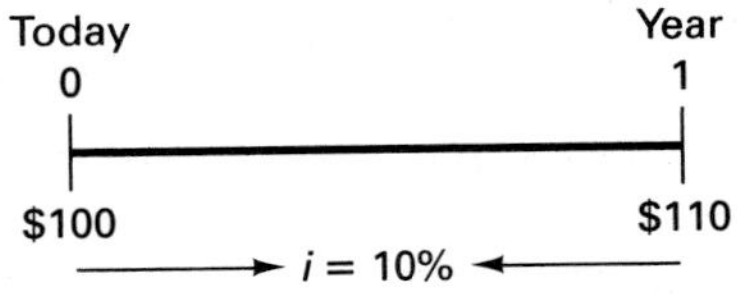

Today 0 — Year 1

\$100 → $i = 10\%$ ← \$110

This calculation of the yield to maturity should look familiar because it equals the interest payment of \$10 divided by the loan amount of \$100; that is, it equals the simple interest rate on the loan. An important point to recognize is that ***for simple loans, the simple interest rate equals the yield to maturity.*** Hence the same term i is used to denote both the yield to maturity and the simple interest rate.

Study Guide The key to understanding the calculation of the yield to maturity is equating today's value of the debt instrument with the present value of all of its future payments. The best way to learn this principle is to apply it to other specific examples of the four types of credit market instruments in addition to those we discuss here. See if you can develop the equations that would allow you to solve for the yield to maturity in each case.

Fixed-Payment Loan Recall that this type of loan has the same payment every year throughout the life of the loan. On a fixed-rate mortgage, for example, the borrower makes the same payment to the bank every month until the maturity date, when the loan will be completely paid off. To calculate the yield to maturity for a fixed-payment loan, we follow the same strategy we used for the simple loan—we equate today's value of the loan with its present value. Because the fixed-payment loan involves more than one payment, the present value of the fixed-payment loan is calculated as the sum of the present values of all payments (using Equation 1).

In the case of our earlier example, the loan is \$1000, and the yearly payment is \$85.81 for the next 25 years. The present value is calculated as follows: At the end of one year, there is an \$85.81 payment with a *PV* of $\$85.81/(1 + i)$; at the end of two years, there is another \$85.81 payment with a *PV* of $\$85.81/(1 + i)^2$; and so on until at the end of the twenty-fifth year, the last payment of \$85.81 with a *PV* of $\$85.81/(1 + i)^{25}$ is made. Making today's value of the loan (\$1000) equal to the sum of the present values of all the yearly payments gives us

$$\$1000 = \frac{\$85.81}{1 + i} + \frac{\$85.81}{(1 + i)^2} + \frac{\$85.81}{(1 + i)^3} + \cdots + \frac{\$85.81}{(1 + i)^{25}}$$

More generally, for any fixed-payment loan,

$$LV = \frac{FP}{1 + i} + \frac{FP}{(1 + i)^2} + \frac{FP}{(1 + i)^3} + \ldots + \frac{FP}{(1 + i)^n} \qquad (2)$$

where LV = loan value
FP = fixed yearly payment
n = number of years until maturity

For a fixed-payment loan amount, the fixed yearly payment and the number of years until maturity are known quantities, and only the yield to maturity is not. So we can solve this equation for the yield to maturity i. Because this calculation is not easy, tables have been created that allow you to find i given the loan's numbers for LV, FP, and n. For example, in the case of the 25-year loan with yearly payments of \$85.81, the yield to maturity from the table that solves Equation 2 is 7%. Real estate brokers always have such a table handy (or a pocket calculator that can solve such equations) so that they can immediately tell the prospective house buyer exactly what the yearly (or monthly) payments will be if the house purchase is financed by taking out a mortgage (see Figure 1).

EXAMPLE 3: Fixed-Payment Loan

You decide to purchase a new home and need a \$100 000 mortgage. You take out a loan from the bank that has an interest rate of 7%. What is the yearly payment to the bank to pay off the loan in 20 years?

Solution

The yearly payment to the bank is \$9439.29.

$$LV = \frac{FP}{1+i} + \frac{FP}{(1+i)^2} + \frac{FP}{(1+i)^3} + \cdots + \frac{FP}{(1+i)^n}$$

7% Monthly Payment Necessary to Amortize a Loan

	Term (years)						
Amount($)	5	10	15	17	20	25	30
25	.50	.29	.22	.21	.19	.18	.17
50	.99	.58	.45	.42	.39	.35	.33
75	1.49	.87	.67	.63	.58	.53	.50
100	1.98	1.16	.90	.84	.78	.71	.67
200	3.96	2.32	1.80	1.68	1.55	1.41	1.33
300	5.94	3.48	2.70	2.52	2.33	2.12	2.00
400	7.92	4.64	3.60	3.36	3.10	2.83	2.66
500	9.90	5.81	4.49	4.20	3.88	3.53	3.33
600	11.88	6.97	5.39	5.04	4.65	4.24	3.99
700	13.86	8.13	6.29	5.88	5.43	4.95	4.66
800	15.84	9.29	7.19	6.72	6.20	5.65	5.32
900	17.82	10.45	8.09	7.56	6.98	6.36	5.99
1000	19.80	11.61	8.99	8.40	7.75	7.07	6.65
2000	39.60	23.22	17.98	16.79	15.51	14.14	13.31
3000	59.40	34.83	26.96	25.19	23.26	21.20	19.96
4000	79.20	46.44	35.95	33.59	31.01	28.27	26.61
5000	99.01	58.05	44.94	41.98	38.76	35.34	33.27

FIGURE 1 A Mortgage Payment Table

This table is for loans with a 7% interest rate. To find the monthly payment for the loan, pick out the amount of the loan in the first column and then follow that row across to the entry in the column with the number of years to maturity of the loan. For a \$1000, 25-year fixed-payment loan with a 7% interest rate, following this procedure indicates that the monthly payment is \$7.07 (\$84.84 per year).

where

LV = loan value amount = \$100 000

i = annual interest rate = 0.07

n = number of years = 20

Thus

$$\$100{,}000 = \frac{FP}{1 + 0.07} + \frac{FP}{(1 + 0.07)^2} + \frac{FP}{(1 + 0.07)^3} + \ldots + \frac{FP}{(1 + 0.07)^{20}}$$

To find the monthly payment for the loan using the mortgage payment table in Figure 1, pick out the loan in the first column and then follow across to the entry in the column with the number of years to maturity of the loan. For a \$100 000, 20-year fixed-payment loan with a 7% interest rate, the yearly payment is \$9300 (7.75 × \$100 × 12). The monthly payment computed using the table is an approximation.

To solve using a financial calculator:

n = number of years = 20

PV = amount of the loan (LV) = −100 000

FV = amount of the loan after 20 years = 0

i = annual interest rate = 7%

Then push the *PMT* button = fixed yearly payment (*FP*) = \$9439.29.

Coupon Bond To calculate the yield to maturity for a coupon bond, follow the same strategy used for the fixed-payment loan: Equate today's value of the bond with its present value. Because coupon bonds have more than one payment, the present value of the bond is calculated as the sum of the present values of all the coupon payments plus the present value of the final payment of the face value of the bond.

The present value of a \$1000 face value bond with ten years to maturity and yearly coupon payments of \$100 (a 10% coupon rate) can be calculated as follows: At the end of one year, there is a \$100 coupon payment with a *PV* of $\$100/(1 + i)$; at the end of the second year, there is another \$100 coupon payment with a *PV* of $\$100/(1 + i)^2$; and so on, until at maturity, there is a \$100 coupon payment with a *PV* of $\$100/(1 + i)^{10}$ plus the repayment of the \$1000 face value with a *PV* of $\$1000/(1 + i)^{10}$. Setting today's value of the bond (its current price, denoted by *P*) equal to the sum of the present values of all the payments for this bond gives

$$P = \frac{\$100}{1 + i} + \frac{\$100}{(1 + i)^2} + \frac{\$100}{(1 + i)^3} + \cdots + \frac{\$100}{(1 + i)^{10}} + \frac{\$1000}{(1 + i)^{10}}$$

More generally, for any coupon bond,[1]

$$P = \frac{C}{1 + i} + \frac{C}{(1 + i)^2} + \frac{C}{(1 + i)^3} + \ldots + \frac{C}{(1 + i)^n} + \frac{F}{(1 + i)^n} \tag{3}$$

where
P = price of coupon bond
C = yearly coupon payment
F = face value of the bond
n = years to maturity date

[1]Most coupon bonds actually make coupon payments on a semiannual basis rather than once a year as assumed here. The effect on the calculations is only very slight and will be ignored here.

10.00%	Bond Values per $100 of Face Value									
	Years to Maturity									
Yield (%)	1	2	3	4	5	6	7	8	9	10
10.00	100.00	100.00	100.00	100.00	100.00	100.00	100.00	100.00	100.00	100.00
10.25	99.77	99.57	99.38	99.21	99.06	98.92	98.79	98.68	98.57	98.48
10.50	99.55	99.14	98.77	98.43	98.13	97.85	97.61	97.38	97.18	96.99
10.75	99.32	98.71	98.16	97.66	97.21	96.80	96.44	96.11	95.81	95.54
11.00	99.10	98.29	97.56	96.90	96.30	95.77	95.29	94.85	94.46	94.11
11.25	98.88	97.87	96.96	96.14	95.41	94.75	94.16	93.62	93.15	92.71
11.50	98.65	97.45	96.37	95.40	94.53	93.74	93.04	92.42	91.85	91.35
11.75	98.43	96.03	95.78	94.66	93.65	92.75	91.95	91.23	90.59	90.01
12.00	98.21	96.62	95.20	93.93	92.79	91.78	90.87	90.06	89.34	88.70
12.25	98.00	96.21	94.62	93.20	91.94	90.81	89.81	88.92	88.12	87.42
12.50	97.78	95.80	94.05	92.49	91.10	89.87	88.77	87.79	86.93	86.16
12.75	97.56	95.40	93.48	91.78	90.27	88.93	87.74	86.69	85.76	84.93

FIGURE 2 A Bond Table

This table is for bonds with a 10% coupon rate. To find the price of the bond, pick out its yield to maturity in the first column and then follow that row across to the entry in the column with the number of years to maturity for the bond. For an eight-year, 10% coupon rate bond with a yield to maturity of 12.25%, following this procedure indicates that the price of the bond is $88.92 per $100 of face value (which means that a $1000 face value bond sells for $889.20).

In Equation 3, the coupon payment, the face value, the years to maturity, and the price of the bond are known quantities, and only the yield to maturity is not. Hence we can solve this equation for the yield to maturity i.[2] Just as in the case of the fixed-payment loan, this calculation is not easy, so bond tables (see Figure 2) have been created that allow you to read the yield to maturity for a bond given its coupon rate, its years to maturity, and its price. Some business-oriented pocket calculators have built-in programs that solve this equation for you.

EXAMPLE 4: Coupon Bond

Find the price of a 10% coupon bond with a face value of $1000, a 12.25% yield to maturity, and eight years to maturity.

Solution

The price of the bond is $889.20. Using Figure 2, pick out its yield to maturity in the left-hand column, then follow the row across to the entry in the column with the number of years to maturity for the bond. Figure 2 indicates that the price of the bond is $88.92 per $100 of face value. Since the face value of the bond in the example is $1000, the bond price is $889.20 ($88.92 × 10).

To solve using a financial calculator:

n = years to maturity = 8
FV = face value of the bond = –1000
i = annual interest rate = 12.25%
PMT = yearly coupon payments = 100

Then push the *PV* button = price of the bond = $889.20.

[2]In other contexts, it is also called the *internal rate of return*.

Table 1 shows the yields to maturity calculated for several bond prices. Three interesting facts emerge:

1. When the coupon bond is priced at its face value, the yield to maturity equals the coupon rate.
2. The price of a coupon bond and the yield to maturity are negatively related; that is, as the yield to maturity rises, the price of the bond falls. If the yield to maturity falls, the price of the bond rises.
3. The yield to maturity is greater than the coupon rate when the bond price is below its face value.

These three facts are true for any coupon bond and are really not surprising if you think about the reasoning behind the calculation of the yield to maturity. When you put $1000 in a bank account with an interest rate of 10%, you can take out $100 every year and you will be left with the $1000 at the end of ten years. This is similar to buying the $1000 bond with a 10% coupon rate analyzed in Table 1, which pays a $100 coupon payment every year and then repays $1000 at the end of ten years. If the bond is purchased at the par value of $1000, its yield to maturity must equal the interest rate of 10%, which is also equal to the coupon rate of 10%. The same reasoning applied to any coupon bond demonstrates that if the coupon bond is purchased at its par value, the yield to maturity and the coupon rate must be equal.

It is straightforward to show that the bond price and the yield to maturity are negatively related. As i, the yield to maturity, rises, all denominators in the bond price formula must necessarily rise. Hence a rise in the interest rate as measured by the yield to maturity means that the price of the bond must fall. Another way to explain why the bond price falls when the interest rate rises is that a higher interest rate implies that the future coupon payments and final payment are worth less when discounted back to the present; hence the price of the bond must be lower.

Check out a review of the key financial concepts, time value of money, annuities, perpetuities, at www.teachmefinance.com

There is one special case of a coupon bond that is worth discussing because its yield to maturity is particularly easy to calculate. This bond is called a **perpetuity;** it is a perpetual bond with no maturity date and no repayment of principal that makes fixed coupon payments of $\$C$ forever. The formula in Equation 3 for the price of a perpetuity, P, simplifies to the following:[3]

$$P = \frac{C}{i} \tag{4}$$

where P = price of the perpetuity
C = yearly payment

[3]The bond price formula for a perpetuity is

$$P = \frac{C}{1+i} + \frac{C}{(1+i)^2} + \frac{C}{(1+i)^3} + \cdots$$

which can be written as

$$P = C(x + x^2 + x^3 + \ldots)$$

in which $x = 1/(1+i)$. From your high-school algebra you might remember the formula for an infinite sum:

$$1 + x + x^2 + x^3 + \ldots = \frac{1}{1-x} \quad \text{for} \quad x < 1$$

and so

$$P = C\left(\frac{1}{1-x} - 1\right) = C\left[\frac{1}{1 - 1/(1+i)} - 1\right]$$

which by suitable algebraic manipulation becomes

$$P = C\left(\frac{1+i}{i} - \frac{i}{i}\right) = \frac{C}{i}$$

TABLE 1 Yields to Maturity on a 10% Coupon Rate Bond Maturing in Ten Years (Face Value = $1000)

Price of Bond ($)	Yield to Maturity (%)
1200	7.13
1100	8.48
1000	10.00
900	11.75
800	13.81

One nice feature of perpetuities is that you can immediately see that as i goes up, the price of the bond falls. For example, if a perpetuity pays $100 per year forever and the interest rate is 10%, its price will be $1000 = $100/0.10. If the interest rate rises to 20%, its price will fall to $500 = $100/0.20. We can also rewrite this formula as

$$i = \frac{C}{P} \tag{5}$$

EXAMPLE 5: Perpetuity

What is the yield to maturity on a bond that has a price of $2000 and pays $100 annually forever?

Solution

The yield to maturity would be 5%.

$$i = \frac{C}{P}$$

where

C = yearly payment = $100

P = price of bond = $2000

Thus

$$i = \frac{\$100}{\$2000}$$

$$i = 0.05 = 5\%$$

Discount Bond The yield-to-maturity calculation for a discount bond is similar to that for the simple loan. Let us consider a discount bond such as a one-year Canadian treasury bill, which pays a face value of $1000 in one year's time. If the current purchase price of this bill is $900, then equating this price to the present value of the $1000 received in one year, using Equation 1, gives

$$\$900 = \frac{\$1000}{1 + i}$$

and solving for i,

$$(1 + i) \times \$900 = \$1000$$

$$\$900 + \$900i = \$1000$$

$$\$900i = \$1000 - \$900$$

$$i = \frac{\$1000 - \$900}{\$900} = 0.111 = 11.1\%$$

More generally, for any one-year discount bond, the yield to maturity can be written as

$$i = \frac{F - P}{P} \tag{6}$$

where F = face value of the discount bond
P = current price of the discount bond

In other words, the yield to maturity equals the increase in price over the year $F - P$ divided by the initial price P. In normal circumstances, investors earn positive returns from holding these securities and so they sell at a discount, meaning that the current price of the bond is below the face value. Therefore, $F - P$ should be positive, and the yield to maturity should be positive as well. However, this is not always the case, as recent extraordinary events in Japan indicate (see Box 1).

BOX 1: GLOBAL

Negative T-Bill Rates? Japan Shows the Way

We normally assume that interest rates must always be positive. Negative interest rates would imply that you are willing to pay more for a bond today than you will receive for it in the future (as our formula for yield to maturity on a discount bond demonstrates). Negative interest rates therefore seem like an impossibility because you would do better by holding cash that has the same value in the future as it does today.

The Japanese have demonstrated that this reasoning is not quite correct. In November 1998, interest rates on Japanese six-month treasury bills became negative, yielding an interest rate of –0.004%, with investors paying more for the bills than their face value. This is an extremely unusual event because no other country in the world has seen negative interest rates during the past 50 years. How could this happen?

As we will see in Chapter 4, the weakness of the Japanese economy and a negative inflation rate have driven Japanese interest rates to low levels, but they can't explain the negative rates. The answer is that large investors find it more convenient to hold these six-month bills as a store of value rather than holding cash because the bills are denominated in larger amounts and can be stored electronically. These advantages of the Japanese t-bills result in some investors being willing to hold them, given their negative rates, even though in monetary terms the investors would be better off holding cash. Clearly, the convenience of t-bills only goes so far, and thus their interest rates can go only a little bit below zero.

An important feature of this equation is that it indicates that for a discount bond, the yield to maturity is negatively related to the current bond price. This is the same conclusion that we reached for a coupon bond. For example, Equation 6 shows that a rise in the bond price from \$900 to \$950 means that the bond will have a smaller increase in its price over its lifetime, and the yield to maturity falls from 11.1% to 5.3%. Similarly, a fall in the yield to maturity means that the price of the discount bond has risen.

Summary The concept of present value tells you that a dollar in the future is not as valuable to you as a dollar today because you can earn interest on this dollar. Specifically, a dollar received n years from now is worth only $\$1/(1 + i)^n$ today. The present value of a set of future payments on a debt instrument equals the sum of the present values of each of the future payments. The yield to maturity for an instrument is the interest rate that equates the present value of the future payments on that instrument to its value today. Because the procedure for calculating the yield to maturity is based on sound economic principles, this is the measure that financial economists think most accurately describes the interest rate.

Our calculations of the yield to maturity for a variety of bonds reveal the important fact that ***current bond prices and interest rates are negatively related: When the interest rate rises, the price of the bond falls, and vice versa.***

OTHER MEASURES OF INTEREST RATES

The yield to maturity is the most accurate measure of interest rates and is what financial economists mean when they use the term *interest rate.* Unless otherwise specified, the terms *interest rate* and *yield to maturity* are used synonymously in this book. However, because the yield to maturity is sometimes difficult to calculate, other, less accurate measures of interest rates have come into common use in bond markets. You will frequently encounter two of these measures, the *current yield* and the *yield on a discount basis,* when reading the newspaper, and it is important for you to understand what they mean and how they differ from the more accurate measure of interest rates, the yield to maturity.

Current Yield

The **current yield** is an approximation of the yield to maturity on coupon bonds that is often reported because in contrast to the yield to maturity, it is easily calculated. It is defined as the yearly coupon payment divided by the price of the security,

$$i_c = \frac{C}{P} \tag{7}$$

where i_c = current yield
P = price of the coupon bond
C = yearly coupon payment

This formula is identical to the formula in Equation 5, which describes the calculation of the yield to maturity for a perpetuity. Hence, for a perpetuity, the current yield is an exact measure of the yield to maturity. When a coupon bond has a long term to maturity (say, 20 years or more), it is very much like a perpetuity, which pays coupon payments forever. Thus, you would expect the current yield to be a rather close approximation of the yield to maturity for a long-term coupon bond, and you can safely use the current yield calculation instead of looking up the yield to maturity in a bond table. However, as the time to maturity of the coupon bond shortens (say, it becomes less than five years), it behaves less and less like a perpetuity and so the approximation afforded by the current yield becomes worse and worse.

We have also seen that when the bond price equals the par value of the bond, the yield to maturity is equal to the coupon rate (the coupon payment divided by the par value of the bond). Because the current yield equals the coupon payment divided by the bond price, the current yield is also equal to the coupon rate when the bond price is at par. This logic leads us to the conclusion that when the bond price is at par, the current yield equals the yield to maturity. This means that the nearer the bond price is to the bond's par value, the better the current yield will approximate the yield to maturity.

The current yield is negatively related to the price of the bond. In the case of our 10% coupon rate bond, when the price rises from $1000 to $1100, the current yield falls from 10% (= $100/$1000) to 9.09% (= $100/$1100). As Table 1 indicates, the yield to maturity is also negatively related to the price of the bond; when the price rises from $1000 to $1100, the yield to maturity falls from 10% to 8.48%. In this we see an important fact: The current yield and the yield to maturity always move together; a rise in the current yield always signals that the yield to maturity has also risen.

EXAMPLE 6: Current Yield

What is the current yield for a bond that has a par value of $1000 and a coupon interest rate of 10.95%? The current market price for the bond is $921.01.

Solution

The current yield is 11.89%.

$$i_c = \frac{C}{P}$$

where

C = yearly payment $= 0.1095 \times \$1000 = \$109.50$

P = price of the bond $= \$921.01$

Thus

$$i_c = \frac{\$109.50}{\$921.01} = 0.1189 = 11.89\%$$

The general characteristics of the current yield (the yearly coupon payment divided by the bond price) can be summarized as follows: The current yield better approximates the yield to maturity when the bond's price is nearer to the bond's par value and the maturity of the bond is longer. It becomes a worse approximation when the bond's price is further from the bond's par value and the bond's maturity is shorter. Regardless of whether the current yield is a good approximation of the yield to maturity, a change in the current yield *always* signals a change in the same direction of the yield to maturity.

Yield on a Discount Basis

In calculating the yield to maturity on discount bonds, we assumed a maturity of one year. The typical treasury bill, however, has a maturity less than a year, perhaps 30 or 91 days. The interest rate on such bills with less than one year to maturity is quoted as a **yield on a discount basis** (or **discount yield**). Formally, the discount yield is defined, on an **annualized rate basis**, by the following formula:

$$i_{db} = \frac{F - P}{P} \times \frac{365}{\text{days to maturity}} \tag{8}$$

where i_{db} = yield on a discount basis
F = face value of the discount bond
P = purchase price of the discount bond

The discount yield understates the interest rate on bills as measured by the yield to maturity. For example, a 91-day treasury bill that is selling for $988 and has a face value of $1000, has a discount yield of

$$i_{db} = \frac{\$1000 - \$988}{\$988} \times \frac{365}{91} = 0.0487 \quad or \quad (4.87\%)$$

Over 91 days, however, the investor receives a rate of return of

$$\frac{\$1000 - \$988}{\$988} = 0.01215 \quad or \quad (1.215\%)$$

and if the proceeds were reinvested at the same rate four times over, the actual rate of return (i.e., the **annual percentage rate**) would have been $1.01215^4 - 1 = 0.0495$ (or 4.95%).

Even though the discount yield is a somewhat misleading measure of the interest rate, however, a change in the discount yield always indicates a change in the same direction for the yield to maturity.[4]

EXAMPLE 7: Yield on a Discount Basis

What is the discount yield (or yield on a discount basis) for a one-year bond that was purchased for $875 and has a face value of $1000?

Solution

The discount yield (or yield on a discount basis) is 14.29%.

$$i_{db} = \frac{F - P}{P} \times \frac{365}{\text{days to maturity}}$$

where

F = face value of the bond = $1000

P = purchase price of the bond = $875

days to maturity = one year = 365 days

Thus

$$i_{db} = \frac{\$1000 - \$875}{\$875} \times \frac{365}{365}$$

$$i_{db} = 0.1429 \times 1 = 0.1429 = 14.29\%$$

The characteristics of the yield on a discount basis can be summarized as follows: Yield on a discount basis understates the more accurate measure of the interest rate, the yield to maturity; and the longer the maturity of the discount bond, the greater this understatement becomes. Even though the discount yield is a somewhat misleading measure of the interest rates, however, a change in the discount yield always indicates a change in the same direction for the yield to maturity.

[4]The method used to calculate the yield on a discount basis in the U.S. is different from that used in Canada in two respects. First, the percentage gain on the face value of the bill $(F - P)/F$, rather than the percentage gain on the purchase price of the bill $(F - P)/P$, is used in calculating the discount yield. Moreover, it puts the yield on an annual basis by taking the year to be 360 days long rather than 365 days. Formally, the U.S. i_{db} is defined as

$$i_{db} = \frac{F - P}{F} \times \frac{360}{\text{days of maturity}}$$

Because of these peculiarities, the U.S. discount yield further understates the interest rate on bills as measured by the yield to maturity.

Application The Bond Page

READING THE FINANCIAL PAGES

Now that we understand the different interest-rate definitions, let's apply our knowledge and take a look at what kind of information appears on the bond page of a typical newspaper, in this case *The Globe and Mail: Report on Business*. The "Following the Financial News" boxes contain listings for government of Canada bonds, provincial and municipal bonds, corporate bonds, and real return bonds on Thursday, February 21, 2002.

The first box contains the information on Canada bonds. The information found in the "Coupon" and "Maturity" columns identifies the bonds by coupon rate and maturity date. For example, Bond 1 has a coupon rate of 5.25%, indicating that it pays out $52.50 per year on a $1000-face-value, and is a short-term bond maturing on September 1, 2003. In bond market parlance, it is referred to as the Canada 5.25% of 2003. The next column tells us about the bond's price. By convention, all prices in the bond market are quoted per $100 of face value. In the case of Bond 1, the price of 103.23 represents an actual price of $1032.30 for a $1000-face-value bond. Furthermore, this quoted price is the bid price. The bid price tells you what price you will receive if you sell the bond, and the asked price tells you what you must pay for the bond. (You might want to think of the bid price as the "wholesale" price and the asked price as the "retail" price.)

Further details about Hydro Québec and Ontario Hydro can be found at www.hydroquebec.com and www.ontariopowergeneration.com.

Notice that for all the bonds, the asked price is more than the bid price, with the bid-ask difference being generally $0.10 to $0.15 per $1000 of face value. Can you guess why this is so? The difference between the two (the *spread*) provides the bond dealer who trades these securities with a profit. This profit is what enables the dealer to make a living and provide the service of allowing you to buy and sell bonds at will.

The "Yield" column provides the yield to maturity, which is 3.06% for Bond 1. It is calculated with the method described earlier in this chapter using the asked price as the price of the bond. The asked price is used in the calculation because the yield to maturity is most relevant to a person who is going to buy and hold the security and thus earn the yield. The person selling the security is not going to be holding it and hence is less concerned with the yield. The "Price $ chg" column is the change in the closing price from the previous trading day.

FOLLOWING THE FINANCIAL NEWS

Government of Canada

Bond prices and interest rates are published weekly. In *The Globe and Mail: Report on Business*, the prices and yields on Canada bonds can be found in the "Canadian Bonds" section of the paper, under the general heading of "Government of Canada."

Government of Canada

	Issuer	Coupon	Maturity	Price	Yield	Price $ chg	
Bond 1	Canada	5.250	Sep 01/03	103.23	3.06	–0.05	Current yield = 5.08%
Bond 2	Canada	7.50	Dec 01/03	107.18	3.29	–0.07	Current yield = 6.99%
	Canada	10.000	Jun 01/08	126.74	4.98	–0.03	
	Canada	5.50	Jun 01/09	102.01	5.16	0.04	
	Canada	10.250	Mar 15/14	142.29	5.42	0.09	
	Canada	11.250	Jun 01/15	154.47	5.43	0.10	
Bond 3	Canada	9.000	Jun 01/25	140.39	5.81	0.11	Current yield = 6.41%
Bond 4	Canada	5.750	Jun 01/29	100.90	5.68	0.10	Current yield = 5.69%

Source: RBC Capital Market

The figure for the current yield is not usually included in the newspaper's quotations, but it has been added to give you some real-world examples of how well the current yield approximates the yield to maturity. Our previous discussion provided us with some rules for deciding when the current yield is likely to be a good approximation and when it is not.

Bonds 3 and 4 mature in more than 20 years, meaning that their characteristics are like those of a consol (perpetuity). The current yields should then be a good approximation of the yield to maturity, and they are: The current yield for the Canada 5.75% of 2029 is within one **basis point** of the value for the yield to maturity. This approximation is reasonable even for Bond 3, which has a price more than 40% above its face value. Notice that when financial analysts talk about differences in yields (or changes in the yield), they frequently describe it in terms of basis points, which are hundredths of a percentage point.

Now let's take a look at Bonds 1 and 2, which have a much shorter time to maturity. The current yield is a better approximation when the price is very near the par value of 100, as it is for Bond 1. However, the price of Bond 2 differs by more than 7% from the par value, and look how poor an approximation the current yield is for the yield to maturity; it overstates the yield to maturity by more than three percentage points. This bears out what we learned earlier about the current yield: It can be a very misleading guide to the value of the yield to maturity for a short-term bond if the bond price is not very close to par.

The second "Following the Financial News" box quotes yields on provincial and municipal bonds, in exactly the same way as for Canada bonds in the first "Following the Financial News" box. Provincial bonds include securities issued by the provinces and by provincial authorities, such as Hydro Quebec and Ontario Hydro. Municipal bonds include securities issued by large cities.

The third "Following the Financial News" box has quotations for corporate bonds, traded mostly in the over-the-counter market where about 100 dealers and a few banks and trust companies are active. These corporate bonds are reported in a similar manner: The first column identifies the bond by indicating the corporation that issued it. Bond 1 has been issued by Air Canada and Bond 2 has been issued by Union Gas. The next two columns tell the coupon rate and the maturity date (6.75% and February 2, 2004, for Bond 1). The "Price" column reports the last traded price that day per $100 of face value. The price of 75.00 represents

FOLLOWING THE FINANCIAL NEWS

Provincial and Municipal

In *The Globe and Mail: Report on Business*, the prices and yields on provincial and municipal bonds can be found in the "Canadian Bonds" section of the paper, under the general heading of "Provincial."

Provincial and Municipal

Issuer	Coupon	Maturity	Price	Yield	Price $ chg
Alberta	6.375	Jun 01/04	105.70	3.72	−0.08
BC	7.750	Jun 16/03	106.07	2.97	−0.11
Manitoba	7.875	Apr 07/03	105.50	2.81	−0.11
New Brunswick	8.000	Mar 17/03	105.42	2.75	−0.08
Newfoundland	6.150	Apr 17/28	96.73	6.41	0.11
Nova Scotia	5.250	Jun 02/03	102.84	2.94	−0.07
Ontario	8.000	Mar 11/03	105.42	2.67	−0.08
Ontario Hydro	9.000	Jun 24/02	102.23	2.13	−0.06
Quebec	7.500	Dec 01/03	107.00	3.37	−0.09
Saskatchewan	5.500	Jun 02/08	101.34	5.25	0.02
Toronto-Metro	6.100	Dec 12/17	100.01	6.10	0.10

Source: The Globe and Mail: Report on Business, Thursday, February 21, 2002, p. B30. Reprinted with permission.

FOLLOWING THE FINANCIAL NEWS

Corporate Bonds

In *The Globe and Mail: Report on Business*, the prices and yields on corporate bonds can be found in the "Canadian Bonds" section of the paper, under the general heading of "Corporate."

Corporate Bonds

	Issuer	Coupon	Maturity	Price	Yield	Price $ chg	
Bond 1	Air Canada	6.750	Feb 02/04	75.00	23.55	0.00	—Current yield = 9.0%
	Bank Of Mont	7.000	Jan 28/10	108.44	5.66	0.03	
	Bell Canada	6.250	Dec 01/03	104.41	3.64	–0.08	
	Coca-Cola	5.650	Mar 17/04	103.13	4.04	–0.08	
Bond 2	Union Gas	8.650	Nov 10/25	119.02	6.99	0.08	—Current yield = 7.27%

Source: Globe and Mail: Report on Business, Thursday, February 21, 2002, p. B30. Reprinted with permission.

$750 for a $1000-face-value bond. The "Yield" column reports the yield to maturity, calculated with the method described earlier in this chapter.

The current yield is also given for two bonds. This information is not provided in the newspaper, but it is included here because it shows how misleading the current yield can be for a bond with a short maturity such as the 6.75%, of February 2, 2004. The current yield of 9.0% is a misleading measure of the interest rate because the yield to maturity is actually 23.55 percent. By contrast, for the 8.65%, of November 10, 2025, with more than 20 years to maturity, the current yield is a reasonably good approximation of the yield to maturity despite the fact that the bond is traded at a price almost 20% above its face value.

THE DISTINCTION BETWEEN REAL AND NOMINAL INTEREST RATES

At www.martincapital.com/charts.htm, click on "Interest Rates and Yields" and then "Nominal versus Real Market Rates" to view 30 years of U.S. nominal interest rates compared with real rates for the 30-year T-Bond and 90-day T-Bill.

So far in our discussion of interest rates, we have ignored the effects of inflation on the cost of borrowing. What we have up to now been calling the interest rate makes no allowance for inflation, and it is more precisely referred to as the **nominal interest rate,** which is to distinguish it from the **real interest rate,** the interest rate that is adjusted by subtracting expected changes in the price level so that it more accurately reflects the true cost of borrowing.[5] The real interest rate is more accurately defined by the *Fisher equation,* named for Irving Fisher, one of the great monetary economists of the twentieth century. The Fisher equation states that the nominal interest rate i equals the real interest rate i_r plus the expected rate of inflation π^e.[6]

[5]The real interest rate defined in the text is more precisely referred to as the *ex ante real interest rate* because it is adjusted for *expected* changes in the price level. This is the real interest rate that is most important to economic decisions, and typically it is what financial economists mean when they make reference to the "real" interest rate. The interest rate that is adjusted for *actual* changes in the price level is called the *ex post real interest rate.* It describes how well a lender has done in real terms *after the fact.*

[6]A more precise formulation of the Fisher equation is

$$i = i_r + \pi^e + (i_r \times \pi^e)$$

because

$$1 + i = (1 + i_r)(1 + \pi^e) = 1 + i_r + \pi^e + (i_r \times \pi^e)$$

and subtracting 1 from both sides gives us the first equation. For small values of i_r and π^e, the term $i_r \times \pi^e$ is so small that we ignore it, as in the text.

$$i = i_r + \pi^e \tag{9}$$

Rearranging terms, we find that the real interest rate equals the nominal interest rate minus the expected inflation rate:

$$i_r = i - \pi^e \tag{10}$$

To see why this definition makes sense, let us first consider a situation in which you have made a one-year simple loan with a 5% interest rate (i = 5%) and you expect the price level to rise by 3% over the year (π^e = 3%). As a result of making the loan, at the end of the year you will have 2% more in **real terms,** that is, in terms of real goods and services you can buy.

In this case, the interest rate you have earned in terms of real goods and services is 2%; that is,

$$i_r = 5\% - 3\% = 2\%$$

as indicated by the Fisher definition.

EXAMPLE 8: Real and Nominal Interest Rates

What is the real interest rate if the nominal interest rate is 8% and the expected inflation rate is 10% over a year?

Solution

The real interest rate is −2%. Although you will be receiving 8% more dollars at the end of the year, you will be paying 10% more for goods. The result is that you will be able to buy 2% fewer goods at the end of the year, and you are 2% worse off in real terms.

$$i_r = i - \pi^e$$

where

i = nominal interest rate = 0.08

π^e = expected inflation rate = 0.10

Thus

$$i_r = 0.08 - 0.10 = -0.02 = -2\%$$

As a lender, you are clearly less eager to make a loan in Example 8 because in terms of real goods and services you have actually earned a negative interest rate of 2%. By contrast, as the borrower, you fare quite well because at the end of the year, the amounts you will have to pay back will be worth 2% less in terms of goods and services—you as the borrower will be ahead by 2% in real terms. ***When the real interest rate is low, there are greater incentives to borrow and fewer incentives to lend.***

The distinction between real and nominal interest rates is important because the real interest rate, which reflects the real cost of borrowing, is likely to be a better indicator of the incentives to borrow and lend. It appears to be a better guide to how people will be affected by what is happening in credit markets. Figure 3, which presents estimates from 1953 to 2001 of the real and nominal interest rates on three-month U.S. Treasury bills, shows us that nominal and real rates often do not move together. This is also true for nominal and real interest rates in other countries, including Canada. In particular, when nominal rates were high in the

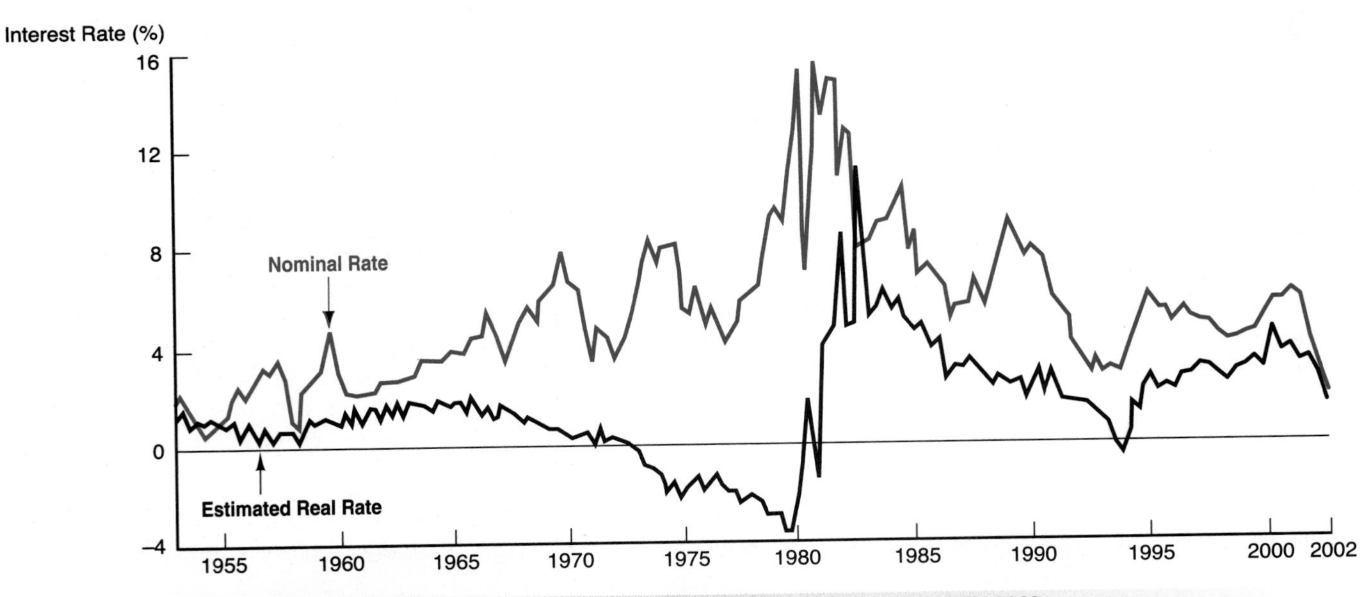

FIGURE 3 Real and Nominal Interest Rates (Three-Month Treasury Bill), 1953–2002

Sources: Nominal rates from the Citibase databank. The real rate is constructed using the procedure outlined in Frederic S. Mishkin, "The Real Interest Rate: An Empirical Investigation," *Carnegie–Rochester Conference Series on Public Policy* 15 (1981): 151–200. This involves estimating expected inflation as a function of past interest rates, inflation, and time trends and then subtracting the expected inflation measure from the nominal interest rate.

1970s, real rates were actually extremely low, often negative. By the standard of nominal interest rates, you would have thought that credit market conditions were tight in this period because it was expensive to borrow. However, the estimates of the real rates indicate that you would have been mistaken. In real terms, the cost of borrowing was actually quite low.[7]

Until recently, real interest rates in Canada were not observable, because only nominal rates were reported. This all changed when, on December 10, 1991, the government of Canada began to issue **indexed bonds,** bonds whose interest and principal payments are adjusted for changes in the price level (see Box 2 and the "Following the Financial News" box).

[7]Because most interest income in Canada is subject to income taxes, the true earnings in real terms from holding a debt instrument are not reflected by the real interest rate defined by the Fisher equation but rather by the *after-tax real interest rate,* which equals the nominal interest rate *after income tax payments have been subtracted,* minus the expected inflation rate. For a person facing a 30% tax rate, the after-tax interest rate earned on a bond yielding 10% is only 7% because 30% of the interest income must be paid to Canada Customs and Revenue Agency (CCRA). Thus the after-tax real interest rate on this bond when expected inflation is 20% equals –13% (= 7% – 20%). More generally, the after-tax real interest rate can be expressed as

$$i(1 - \tau) - \pi^e$$

where τ = the income tax rate.

This formula for the after-tax real interest rate also provides a better measure of the effective cost of borrowing for many corporations and individuals in Canada because in calculating income taxes, they can deduct interest payments on loans from their income. Thus if you face a 30% tax rate and take out a business loan with a 10% interest rate, you are able to deduct the 10% interest payment and thus lower your taxes by 30% of this amount. Your after-tax nominal cost of borrowing is then 7% (10% minus 30% of the 10% interest payment), and when the expected inflation rate is 20%, the effective cost of borrowing in real terms is again –13% (= 7% – 20%).

As the example (and the formula) indicates, after-tax real interest rates are always below the real interest rate defined by the Fisher equation. For a further discussion of measures of after-tax real interest rates, see Frederic S. Mishkin, "The Real Interest Rate: An Empirical Investigation," *Carnegie-Rochester Conference Series on Public Policy* 15 (1981): 151–200.

BOX 2

With Real Return Bonds, Real Interest Rates Have Become Observable in Canada

On December 10, 1991, the Canadian government issued coupon bonds whose coupon payment and face value are indexed to the Consumer Price Index (CPI). These securities are known as *real return bonds* and are designed to provide investors with a known real return if held to maturity. Other countries such as the United Kingdom, Australia, and Sweden also issue similar indexed securities and the U.S. Treasury recently joined the group (in September 1998) by issuing TIPS (Treasury Inflation Protection Securities).

These indexed securities have successfully acquired a niche in the bond market, enabling governments to raise more funds. In addition, because their interest and principal payments are adjusted for changes in the price level, the interest rate on these bonds provides a direct measure of a real interest rate. These indexed bonds are very useful to policymakers, especially monetary policymakers, because by subtracting their interest rate from a nominal interest rate on a nonindexed bond, they generate more insight into expected inflation, a valuable piece of information.

For example, on December 10, 1991, the interest rate on long-term Canada bonds (the Canada 5.75% of 2009) was 5.68%, while that on the long-term real return bond (the real return 4.0% of 2031) was 3.73%. Thus, the implied expected inflation rate, derived from the difference between these two rates, was 1.95%. The private sector finds the information provided by real return bonds very useful: Many financial institutions routinely publish the expected Canadian inflation rate derived from these bonds.

FOLLOWING THE FINANCIAL NEWS

Real Return Bonds

In *The Globe and Mail: Report on Business*, the prices and yields on real return bonds can be found in the "Canadian Bonds" section of the paper.

Real Return Bonds

Issuer	Coupon	Maturity	Price	Yield	Price $ chg
Real Return	4.250	Dec 01/21	106.81	3.76	0.00
Real Return	4.250	Dec 01/26	107.79	3.76	0.00
Real Return	4.000	Dec 01/31	104.85	3.73	0.00

Source: *The Globe and Mail: Report on Business*, Thursday, February 21, 2002, p. B30. Reprinted with permission.

THE DISTINCTION BETWEEN INTEREST RATES AND RETURNS

Many people think that the interest rate on a bond tells them all they need to know about how well off they are as a result of owning it. If Irving the Investor thinks he is better off when he owns a long-term bond yielding a 10% interest rate and the interest rate rises to 20%, he will have a rude awakening: As we will shortly see, Irving has lost his shirt! How well a person does by holding a bond or any other security over a particular period is accurately measured by the **return** or, in more precise terminology, the **rate of return.** For any security, the rate of return is defined as the payments to the owner plus the change in its value, expressed as a fraction of its purchase price. To make this definition clearer, let us see what the return would look like for a $1000-face-value coupon bond with a coupon rate of 10% that is bought for $1000, held for one year, and then sold for $1200. The payments to the owner are the yearly coupon payments of $100, and the change in its value is $1200 − $1000 = $200. Adding these together and expressing them as a fraction of the purchase price of $1000 gives us the one-year holding-period return for this bond:

$$\frac{\$100 + \$200}{\$1000} = \frac{\$300}{\$1000} = 0.30 = 30\%$$

You may have noticed something quite surprising about the return that we have just calculated: It equals 30%, yet as Table 1 indicates, initially the yield to maturity was only 10%. This demonstrates that ***the return on a bond will not necessarily equal the interest rate on that bond.*** We now see that the distinction between interest rate and return can be important, although for many securities the two may be closely related.

Study Guide The concept of return discussed here is extremely important because it is used continually throughout the book. Make sure that you understand how a return is calculated and why it can differ from the interest rate. This understanding will make the material presented later in the book easier to follow.

More generally, the return on a bond held from time t to time $t + 1$ can be written as

$$R = \frac{C + P_{t+1} - P_t}{P_t} \tag{11}$$

where R = return from holding the bond from time t to time $t + 1$
P_t = price of the bond at time t
P_{t+1} = price of the bond at time $t + 1$
C = coupon payment

EXAMPLE 9: Rate of Return

What would the rate of return be on a bond bought for $1000 and sold one year later for $800? The bond has a face value of $1000 and a coupon rate of 8%.

Solution

The rate of return on the bond for holding it one year is –12%.

$$R = \frac{C + P_{t+1} - P_t}{P_t}$$

where

C = coupon payment = $\$1000 \times 0.08$ = $80
P_{t+1} = price of the bond one year later = $800
P_t = price of the bond today = $1000

Thus

$$R = \frac{\$80 + (\$800 - \$1000)}{\$1000} = \frac{-\$120}{\$1000} = -0.12 = -12\%$$

A convenient way to rewrite the return formula in Equation 11 is to recognize that it can be split into two separate terms:

$$R = \frac{C}{P_t} + \frac{P_{t+1} - P_t}{P_t}$$

The first term is the current yield i_c (the coupon payment over the purchase price):

$$\frac{C}{P_t} = i_c$$

The second term is the **rate of capital gain**, or the change in the bond's price relative to the initial purchase price:

$$\frac{P_{t+1} - P_t}{P_t} = g$$

where g = rate of capital gain. Equation 11 can then be rewritten as

$$R = i_c + g \tag{12}$$

which shows that the return on a bond is the current yield i_c plus the rate of capital gain g. This rewritten formula illustrates the point we just discovered. Even for a bond for which the current yield i_c is an accurate measure of the yield to maturity, the return can differ substantially from the interest rate. Returns will differ from the interest rate especially if there are sizable fluctuations in the price of the bond that produce substantial capital gains or losses.

To explore this point even further, let's look at what happens to the returns on bonds of different maturities when interest rates rise. Table 2 calculates the one-year return on several 10% coupon rate bonds all purchased at par when interest rates on all these bonds rise from 10% to 20%. Several key findings in this table are generally true of all bonds:

- The only bond whose return equals the initial yield to maturity is one whose time to maturity is the same as the holding period (see the last bond in Table 2).
- A rise in interest rates is associated with a fall in bond prices, resulting in capital losses on bonds whose terms to maturity are longer than the holding period.
- The more distant a bond's maturity, the greater the size of the price change associated with an interest-rate change.
- The more distant a bond's maturity, the lower the rate of return that occurs as a result of the increase in the interest rate.
- Even though a bond has a substantial initial interest rate, its return can turn out to be negative if interest rates rise.

TABLE 2 One-Year Returns on Different-Maturity 10% Coupon Rate Bonds When Interest Rates Rise from 10% to 20%

(1)	(2)	(3)	(4)	(5)	(6)
Years to Maturity When Bond Is Purchased	Initial Current Yield (%)	Initial Price ($)	Price Next Year* ($)	Rate of Capital Gain (%)	Rate of Return (2 + 5) (%)
30	10	1000	503	−49.7	−39.7
20	10	1000	516	−48.4	−38.4
10	10	1000	597	−40.3	−30.3
5	10	1000	741	−25.9	−15.9
2	10	1000	917	− 8.3	+ 1.7
1	10	1000	1000	0.0	+10.0

*Calculated using Equation 3.

At first it frequently puzzles students that a rise in interest rates can mean that a bond has been a poor investment (as it puzzles poor Irving the Investor). The trick to understanding this is to recognize that a rise in the interest rate means that the price of a bond has fallen. A rise in interest rates therefore means that a capital loss has occurred, and if this loss is large enough, the bond can be a poor investment indeed. For example, we see in Table 2 that the bond that has 30 years to maturity when purchased has a capital loss of 49.7% when the interest rate rises from 10% to 20%. This loss is so large that it exceeds the current yield of 10%, resulting in a negative return (loss) of –39.7%. If Irving does not sell the bond, the capital loss is often referred to as a "paper loss." This is a loss nonetheless because if he had not bought this bond and had instead put his money in the bank, he would now be able to buy more bonds at their lower price than he presently owns.

Maturity and the Volatility of Bond Returns: Interest-Rate Risk

The finding that the prices of longer-maturity bonds respond more dramatically to changes in interest rates helps explain an important fact about the behaviour of bond markets: ***Prices and returns for long-term bonds are more volatile than those for shorter-term bonds.*** Price changes of +20% and –20% within a year, with corresponding variations in returns, are common for bonds more than 20 years away from maturity.

We now see that changes in interest rates make investments in long-term bonds quite risky. Indeed, the riskiness of an asset's return that results from interest-rate changes is so important that it has been given a special name, **interest-rate risk**. Dealing with interest-rate risk is a major concern of managers of financial institutions, as we will see in later chapters (see also Box 3).

Although long-term debt instruments have substantial interest-rate risk, short-term debt instruments do not. Indeed a bond with a maturity that is as short as the holding period has no interest-rate risk.[8] We see this for the coupon bond at

BOX 3

Helping Investors Select Desired Interest-Rate Risk

Because many investors want to know how much interest-rate risk they are exposed to, some mutual fund companies try to educate investors about the perils of interest-rate risk, as well as to offer investment alternatives that match their investors' preferences.

For example, one U.S. company, Vanguard Group, offers eight separate high-grade bond mutual funds. In its prospectus, Vanguard separates the funds by the average maturity of the bonds they hold and demonstrates the effect of interest-rate changes by computing the percentage change in bond value resulting from a 1% increase and decrease in interest rates. Three of the funds invest in bonds with average maturities of one to three years, which Vanguard rates as having the lowest interest-rate risk. Three other funds hold bonds with average maturities of five and ten years, which Vanguard rates as having medium interest-rate risk. Two funds hold long-term bonds with maturities of 15 to 30 years, which Vanguard rates as having high interest-rate risk.

By providing this information, Vanguard hopes to increase its market share in the sales of bond funds. Not surprisingly, Vanguard is one of the most successful mutual fund companies in the business.

[8]The statement that there is no interest-rate risk for any bond whose time to maturity matches the holding period is literally true only for discount bonds and zero-coupon bonds that make no intermediate cash payments before the holding period is over. A coupon bond that makes an intermediate cash payment before the holding period is over requires that this payment be reinvested at some future date. Because the interest rate at which this payment can be reinvested is uncertain, there is some uncertainty about the return on this coupon bond even when the time to maturity equals the holding period. However, the riskiness of the return on a coupon bond from reinvesting the coupon payments is typically quite small, and so the basic point that a coupon bond with a time to maturity equalling the holding period has very little risk still holds true.

the bottom of Table 2, which has no uncertainty about the rate of return because it equals the yield to maturity, which is known at the time the bond is purchased. The key to understanding why there is no interest-rate risk for *any* bond whose time to maturity matches the holding period is to recognize that (in this case) the price at the end of the holding period is already fixed at the face value. The change in interest rates can then have no effect on the price at the end of the holding period for these bonds, and the return will therefore be equal to the yield to maturity known at the time the bond is purchased.

Reinvestment Risk

Up to now, we have been assuming that all holding periods are short and equal to the maturity on short-term bonds and are thus not subject to interest-rate risk. However, if an investor's holding period is longer than the term to maturity of the bond, the investor is exposed to a type of interest-rate risk called **reinvestment risk.** Reinvestment risk occurs because the proceeds from the short-term bond need to be reinvested at a future interest rate that is uncertain.

To understand reinvestment risk, suppose that Irving the Investor has a holding period of two years and decides to purchase a $1000 one-year bond at face value and will then purchase another one at the end of the first year. If the initial interest rate is 10%, Irving will have $1100 at the end of the year. If the interest rate on one-year bonds rises to 20% at the end of the year, as in Table 2, Irving will find that buying $1100 worth of another one-year bond will leave him at the end of the second year with $\$1100 \times (1 + 0.20) = \$1320$. Thus Irving's two-year return will be $(\$1320 - \$1000)/\$1000 = 0.32 = 32\%$, which equals 14.9% at an annual rate. In this case, Irving has earned more by buying the one-year bonds than if he had initially purchased the two-year bond with an interest rate of 10%. Thus, when Irving has a holding period that is longer than the term to maturity of the bonds he purchases, he benefits from a rise in interest rates. Conversely, if interest rates on one-year bonds fall to 5% at the end of the year, Irving will have only $1155 at the end of two years: $\$1100 \times (1 + 0.05)$. Thus his two-year return will be $(\$1155 - \$1000)/\$1000 = 0.155 = 15.5\%$, which is 7.5% at an annual rate. With a holding period greater than the term to maturity of the bond, Irving now loses from a fall in interest rates.

We thus see that when the holding period is longer than the term to maturity of a bond, the return is uncertain because the future interest rate when reinvestment occurs is also uncertain—in short, there is reinvestment risk. We also see that if the holding period is longer than the term to maturity of the bond, the investor benefits from a rise in interest rates and is hurt by a fall in interest rates.

Summary

The return on a bond, which tells you how good an investment it has been over the holding period, is equal to the yield to maturity in only one special case: when the holding period and the maturity of the bond are identical. Bonds whose term to maturity is longer than the holding period are subject to interest-rate risk: Changes in interest rates lead to capital gains and losses that produce substantial differences between the return and the yield to maturity known at the time the bond is purchased. Interest-rate risk is especially important for long-term bonds, where the capital gains and losses can be substantial. This is why long-term bonds are not considered to be safe assets with a sure return over short holding periods. Bonds whose terms to maturity are shorter than the holding period are also subject to reinvestment risk. Reinvestment risk occurs because the proceeds from the short-term bond need to be reinvested at a future interest rate that is uncertain.

THE PRACTISING FINANCIAL INSTITUTION MANAGER

Calculating Duration to Measure Interest-Rate Risk

Earlier in our discussion of interest-rate risk, we saw that when interest rates change, a bond with a longer term to maturity has a larger change in its price and hence more interest-rate risk than a bond with a shorter term to maturity. Although this is a useful general fact, in order to measure interest-rate risk, the manager of a financial institution needs more precise information on the actual capital gain or loss that occurs when the interest rate changes by a certain amount. To do this, the manager needs to make use of the concept of **duration**, the average lifetime of a debt security's stream of payments.

The fact that two bonds have the same term to maturity does not mean that they have the same interest-rate risk. A long-term discount bond with ten years to maturity, a so-called zero-coupon bond, makes all of its payments at the end of the ten years, whereas a 10% coupon bond with ten years to maturity makes substantial cash payments before the maturity date. Since the coupon bond makes payments earlier than the zero-coupon bond, we might intuitively guess that the coupon bond's *effective maturity*, the term to maturity that accurately measures interest-rate risk, is shorter than it is for the zero-coupon discount bond.

Indeed, this is exactly what we find in example 10.

EXAMPLE 10: Rate of Capital Gain

Calculate the rate of capital gain or loss on a ten-year zero-coupon bond for which the interest rate has increased from 10% to 20%. The bond has a face value of $1000.

Solution

The rate of capital loss is 49.7%.

$$g = \frac{P_{t+1} - P_t}{P_t}$$

where

$$P_{t+1} = \text{price of the bond one year from now} = \frac{\$1000}{(1 + 0.20)^9} = \$193.81$$

$$P_t = \text{price of the bond today} = \frac{\$1000}{(1 + 0.10)^{10}} = \$385.54$$

Thus

$$g = \frac{\$193.81 - \$385.54}{\$385.54}$$

$$g = -0.497 = -49.7\%$$

But as we have already calculated in Table 2, the capital loss on the 10% ten-year coupon bond is 40.3%. We see that interest-rate risk for the ten-year coupon bond is less than for the ten-year zero-coupon bond, so the effective maturity on the coupon bond (which measures interest-rate risk) is, as expected, shorter than the effective maturity on the zero-coupon bond.

Calculating Duration

To calculate the duration or effective maturity on any debt security, Frederick Macaulay, a researcher at the U.S. National Bureau of Economic Research, invented the concept of duration more than half a century ago. Because a zero-coupon bond makes no cash payments before the bond matures, it makes sense to define its effective maturity as equal to its actual term to maturity. Macaulay then realized that he could measure the effective maturity of a coupon bond by recognizing that a coupon bond is equivalent to a set of zero-coupon discount bonds. A ten-year 10% coupon bond with \$1000 face value has cash payments identical to the following set of zero-coupon bonds: a \$100 one-year zero-coupon bond (which pays the equivalent of the \$100 coupon payment made by the \$1000 ten-year 10% coupon bond at the end of one year), a \$100 two-year zero-coupon bond (which pays the equivalent of the \$100 coupon payment at the end of two years),..., a \$100 ten-year zero-coupon bond (which pays the equivalent of the \$100 coupon payment at the end of ten years), and a \$1000 ten-year zero-coupon bond (which pays back the equivalent of the coupon bond's \$1000 face value). This set of coupon bonds is shown in the following time line:

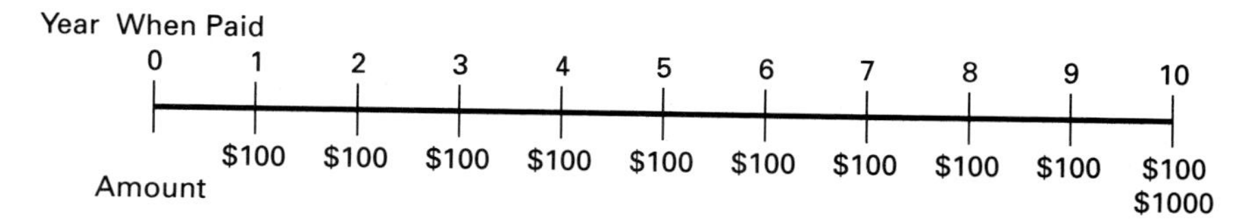

This same set of coupon bonds is listed in column (2) of Table 3, which calculates the duration on the ten-year coupon bond when its interest rate is 10%.

To get the effective maturity of this set of zero-coupon bonds, we would want to sum up the effective maturity of each zero-coupon bond, weighting it by the percentage of the total value of all the bonds that it represents. In other words, the duration of this set of zero-coupon bonds is the weighted average of the effective maturities of the individual zero-coupon bonds, with the weights equalling the proportion of the total value represented by each zero-coupon bond. We do this in several steps in Table 3. First we calculate the present value of each of the zero-coupon bonds when the interest rate is 10% in column (3). Then in column (4) we

TABLE 3 Calculating Duration on a \$1000 Ten-Year 10% Coupon Bond When Its Interest Rate Is 10%

(1)	(2)	(3)	(4)	(5)
Year	Cash Payments (Zero-Coupon Bonds) (\$)	Present Value (*PV*) of Cash Payments (i = 10%) (\$)	Weights (% of total *PV* = *PV*/\$1000) (%)	Weighted Maturity (1 × 4)/100 (years)
1	100	90.91	9.091	0.09091
2	100	82.64	8.264	0.16528
3	100	75.13	7.513	0.22539
4	100	68.30	6.830	0.27320
5	100	62.09	6.209	0.31045
6	100	56.44	5.644	0.33864
7	100	51.32	5.132	0.35924
8	100	46.65	4.665	0.37320
9	100	42.41	4.241	0.38169
10	100	38.55	3.855	0.38550
10	1000	385.54	38.554	3.85500
Total		1000.00	100.000	6.75850

divide each of these present values by $1000, the total present value of the set of zero-coupon bonds, to get the percentage of the total value of all the bonds that each bond represents. Note that the sum of the weights in column (4) must total 100%, as shown at the bottom of the column.

To get the effective maturity of the set of zero-coupon bonds, we add up the weighted maturities in column (5) and obtain the figure of 6.76 years. This figure for the effective maturity of the set of zero-coupon bonds is the duration of the 10% ten-year coupon bond because the bond is equivalent to this set of zero-coupon bonds. In short, we see that ***duration is a weighted average of the maturities of the cash payments.***

The duration calculation done in Table 3 can be written as follows:

$$DUR = \sum_{t=1}^{n} t \frac{CP_t}{(1+i)^t} \Big/ \sum_{t=1}^{n} \frac{CP_t}{(1+i)^t} \tag{13}$$

where DUR = duration
t = years until cash payment is made
CP_t = cash payment (interest plus principal) at time t
i = interest rate
n = years to maturity of the security

This formula is not as intuitive as the calculation done in Table 3, but it does have the advantage that it can easily be programmed into a calculator or computer, making duration calculations very easy.

If we calculate the duration for an 11-year 10% coupon bond when the interest rate is again 10%, we find that it equals 7.14 years, which is greater than the 6.76 years for the ten-year bond. Thus we have reached the expected conclusion: ***All else being equal, the longer the term to maturity of a bond, the longer its duration.***

You might think that knowing the maturity of a coupon bond is enough to tell you what its duration is. However, that is not the case. To see this and to give you more practice in calculating duration, in Table 4 we again calculate the duration for the ten-year 10% coupon bond, but when the current interest rate is 20% rather than 10% as in Table 3. The calculation in Table 4 reveals that the duration of the coupon bond at this higher interest rate has fallen from 6.76 years to 5.72 years. The explanation is fairly straightforward. When the interest rate is higher, the cash payments in the future are discounted more heavily and become less important in present-value terms relative to the total present value of all the payments. The relative weight for these cash payments drops as we see in Table 5, and so the effective maturity of the bond falls. We have come to an important conclusion: ***All else being equal, when interest rates rise, the duration of a coupon bond falls.***

The duration of a coupon bond is also affected by its coupon rate. For example, consider a ten-year 20% coupon bond when the interest rate is 10%. Using the same procedure, we find that its duration at the higher 20% coupon rate is 5.98 years versus 6.76 years when the coupon rate is 10%. The explanation is that a higher coupon rate means that a relatively greater amount of the cash payments are made earlier in the life of the bond, and so the effective maturity of the bond must fall. We have thus established a third fact about duration: ***All else being equal, the higher the coupon rate on the bond, the shorter the bond's duration.***

TABLE 4 Calculating Duration on a $1000 Ten-Year 10% Coupon Bond When Its Interest Rate Is 20%

(1) Year	(2) Cash Payments (Zero-Coupon Bonds) ($)	(3) Present Value (PV) of Cash Payments (i = 20%) ($)	(4) Weights (% of total PV = PV/$580.76) (%)	(5) Weighted Maturity (1 × 4)/100 (years)
1	100	83.33	14.348	0.143 48
2	100	69.44	11.957	0.239 14
3	100	57.87	9.965	0.298 95
4	100	48.23	8.305	0.332 20
5	100	40.19	6.920	0.346 00
6	100	33.49	5.767	0.346 02
7	100	27.91	4.806	0.33642
8	100	23.26	4.005	0.320 40
9	100	19.38	3.337	0.300 33
10	100	16.15	2.781	0.278 10
10	$1000	161.51	27.808	2.781 00
Total		580.76	100.000	5.722 04

Study Guide To make certain that you understand how to calculate duration, practise doing the calculations in Tables 3 and 4. Try to produce the tables for calculating duration in the case of an 11-year 10% coupon bond and also for the ten-year 20% coupon bond mentioned in the text when the current interest rate is 10%. Make sure your calculations produce the same results found in the text. You can get more practice by doing some of the problems involving duration calculations at the end of the chapter.

One additional fact about duration makes this concept useful when applied to a portfolio of securities. Our examples have shown that duration is equal to the weighted average of the durations of the cash payments (the effective maturities of the corresponding zero-coupon bonds). So if we calculate the duration for two different securities, it should be easy to see that the duration of a portfolio of the two securities is just the weighted average of the durations of the two securities, with the weights reflecting the proportion of the portfolio invested in each.

EXAMPLE 11: Duration

A manager of a financial institution is holding 25% of a portfolio in a bond with a five-year duration and 75% in a bond with a ten-year duration. What is the duration of the portfolio?

Solution

The duration of the portfolio is 8.75 years.

$$(0.25 \times 5) + (0.75 \times 10) = 1.25 + 7.5 = 8.75 \text{ years}$$

We now see that ***the duration of a portfolio of securities is the weighted average of the durations of the individual securities, with the weights reflecting the proportion of the portfolio invested in each.*** This fact about duration is often referred to as the *additive property of duration,* and it is extremely useful because it means that the duration of a portfolio of securities is easy to calculate from the durations of the individual securities.

To summarize, our calculations of duration for coupon bonds have revealed four facts:

1. The longer the term to maturity of a bond, everything else being equal, the greater its duration.
2. When interest rates rise, everything else being equal, the duration of a coupon bond falls.
3. The higher the coupon rate on the bond, everything else being equal, the shorter the bond's duration.
4. Duration is additive: The duration of a portfolio of securities is the weighted average of the durations of the individual securities, with the weights reflecting the proportion of the portfolio invested in each.

Duration and Interest-Rate Risk

Now that we understand how duration is calculated, we want to see how it can be used by the practising financial institution manager to measure interest-rate risk. Duration is a particularly useful concept because it provides a good approximation, particularly when interest-rate changes are small, for how much the security price changes for a given change in interest rates, as the following formula indicates:

$$\%\Delta P \approx -DUR \times \frac{\Delta i}{1 + i} \tag{14}$$

where $\%\Delta P = (P_{t+1} - P_t)/P_t$ = percent change in the price of the security from t to $t + 1$ = rate of capital gain
DUR = duration
i = interest rate

EXAMPLE 12: Duration and Interest-Rate Risk

A pension fund manager is holding a ten-year 10% coupon bond in the fund's portfolio and the interest rate is currently 10%. What loss would the fund be exposed to if the interest rate rises to 11% tomorrow?

Solution

The approximate percentage change in the price of the bond is –6.15%.

As the calulation in Table 3 shows, the duration of a ten-year 10% coupon bond is 6.76 years.

$$\%\Delta P \approx -DUR \times \frac{\Delta i}{1 + i}$$

where

DUR = duration = 6.76

Δi = change in interest rate = $0.11 - 0.10 = 0.01$

i = current interest rate = 0.10

Thus

$$\%\Delta P \approx -6.76 \times \frac{0.01}{1 + 0.10}$$

$$\%\Delta P \approx -0.0615 = -6.15\%$$

EXAMPLE 13: Duration and Interest-Rate Risk

Now the pension manager has the option to hold a ten-year coupon bond with a coupon rate of 20% instead of 10%. As mentioned earlier, the duration for this 20% coupon bond is 5.98 years when the interest rate is 10%. Find the approximate change in the bond price when the interest rate increases from 10% to 11%.

Solution

This time the approximate change in bond price is –5.4%. This change in bond price is much smaller than for the higher-duration coupon bond.

$$\%\Delta P \approx -DUR \times \frac{\Delta i}{1 + i}$$

where

DUR = duration = 5.98

Δi = change in interest rate = 0.11 − 0.10 = 0.01

i = current interest rate = 0.10

Thus

$$\%\Delta P \approx -5.98 \times \frac{0.01}{1 + 0.10}$$

$$\%\Delta P \approx -0.054 = -5.4\%$$

The pension fund manager realizes that the interest-rate risk on the 20% coupon bond is less than on the 10% coupon, so he switches the fund out of the 10% coupon bond and into the 20% coupon bond.

Examples 12 and 13 have led the pension fund manager to an important conclusion about the relationship of duration and interest-rate risk: ***The greater the duration of a security, the greater the percentage change in the market value of the security for a given change in interest rates. Therefore, the greater the duration of a security, the greater its interest-rate risk.***

Other Measures of Duration

Equation (14) can be rearranged, resulting in

$$\%\Delta P = -\frac{DUR}{1 + i} \times \Delta i$$

where the quantity $DUR/(1 + i)$ is referred to as **modified duration**. The modified duration gives the percentage change in the price of the security for a 1%

change in its yield and is a better measure of the interest-rate risk than Macaulay's duration, *DUR*.

Frequently, however, managers of banks and other financial institutions express the sensitivity of fixed income securities to changes in interest rates not in terms of percentage changes in the price of the security as above, but in terms of dollars gained or lost. In particular, rearranging Equation (14) yields

$$\Delta P = -DUR \times \frac{\Delta i}{1+i} \times P \tag{15}$$

where the quantity

$$DUR \times \frac{\Delta i}{1+i} \times P$$

is referred to as **dollar duration**. Equation (15) gives the change in price in terms of dollars, ΔP.

EXAMPLE 14: Modified Duration, Dollar Duration, and Interest-Rate Risk

A pension fund manager is holding a 10% coupon, $1000 face-value bond with a duration of 2. The interest rate is currently 10%. What is the modified duration? What is the dollar duration for a 100-basis point change in the interest rate?

Solution

The modified duration is

$$\text{Modified Duration} = \frac{DUR}{1+i}$$

where

DUR = duration = 2

i = current interest rate = 0.10

Thus

$$\text{Modified Duration} = \frac{2}{1+0.10} = 1.82$$

meaning that the percentage change in the price of the security will be 1.82 times the change in the interest rate.

The dollar duration is

$$\text{Dollar Duration} = DUR \times \frac{\Delta i}{1+i} \times P$$

where

DUR = duration = 2

i = current interest rate = 0.10

Δi = change in interest rate = 0.01

P = price of the security = \$1000

Thus

$$\text{Dollar Duration} = 2 \times \frac{0.01}{1+0.10} \times \$1000 = \$18.2$$

Duration analysis applies equally to a portfolio of securites. So by calculating the duration of the fund's portfolio of securities using the methods outlined here, a pension fund manager can easily ascertain the amount of interest-rate risk the entire fund is exposed to. As we will see in Chapter 22, duration is a highly useful concept for the management of interest-rate risk that is widely used by managers of banks and other financial institutions.

SUMMARY

1. The yield to maturity, which is the measure that most accurately reflects the interest rate, is the interest rate that equates the present value of future payments of a debt instrument with its value today. Application of this principle reveals that bond prices and interest rates are negatively related: When the interest rate rises, the price of the bond must fall, and vice versa.
2. Two less accurate measures of interest rates are commonly used to quote interest rates on coupon and discount bonds. The current yield, which equals the coupon payment divided by the price of a coupon bond, is a less accurate measure of the yield to maturity the shorter the maturity of the bond and the greater the gap between the price and the par value. The yield on a discount basis (also called the discount yield) understates the yield to maturity on a discount bond, and the understatement worsens the more distant the maturity of the discount security. Even though these measures are misleading guides to the size of the interest rate, a change in them always signals a change in the same direction for the yield to maturity.
3. The real interest rate is defined as the nominal interest rate minus the expected rate of inflation. It is a better measure of the incentives to borrow and lend than the nominal interest rate, and it is a more accurate indicator of the tightness of credit market conditions than the nominal interest rate.
4. The return on a security, which tells you how well you have done by holding this security over a stated period, can differ substantially from the interest rate as measured by the yield to maturity. Long-term bond prices have substantial fluctuations when interest rates change and thus bear interest-rate risk. The resulting capital gains and losses can be large, which is why long-term bonds are not considered to be safe assets with a sure return. Bonds whose maturity is shorter than the holding period are also subject to reinvestment risk, which occurs because the proceeds from the short-term bond need to be reinvested at a future interest rate that is uncertain.
5. Duration, the average lifetime of a debt security's stream of payments, is a measure of effective maturity, the term to maturity that accurately measures interest-rate risk. Everything else being equal, the duration of a bond is greater the longer the maturity of a bond, when interest rates fall, or when the coupon rate of a coupon bond falls. Duration is additive: The duration of a portfolio of securities is the weighted average of the durations of the individual securities, with the weights reflecting the proportion of the portfolio invested in each. The greater the duration of a security, the greater the percentage change in the market value of the security for a given change in interest rates. Therefore, the greater the duration of a security, the greater its interest-rate risk.

KEY TERMS

annual percentage rate, *p. 47*
annualized rate basis, *p. 46*
basis points, *p. 49*
coupon bond, *p. 34*
coupon rate, *p. 34*
current yield, *p. 45*
discount bond (zero-coupon bond), *p. 34*
dollar duration, *p. 64*
duration, *p. 58*
face value (par value), *p. 34*
fixed-payment loan, *p. 34*
indexed bonds, *p. 52*
interest-rate risk, *p. 56*
modified duration, *p. 63*
nominal interest rate, *p. 50*
perpetuity, *p. 42*
present discounted value, *p. 36*
present value, *p. 34*
rate of capital gain, *p. 55*
real interest rate, *p. 50*
real terms, *p. 51*
reinvestment risk, *p. 57*
return (rate of return), *p. 53*
simple loan, *p. 34*
yield on a discount basis (discount yield), *p. 46*
yield to maturity, *p. 37*

QUESTIONS AND PROBLEMS

*1. Would a dollar tomorrow be worth more to you today when the interest rate is 20% or when it is 10%?

2. You have just won $20 million in the provincial lottery, which promises to pay you $1 million (tax free) every year for the next 20 years. Have you really won $20 million?

*3. If the interest rate is 10%, what is the present value of a security that pays you $1100 next year, $1210 the year after, and $1331 the year after that?

4. If the security in Problem 3 sold for $3500, is the yield to maturity greater or less than 10%? Why?

*5. Write down the formula that is used to calculate the yield to maturity on a 20-year 10% coupon bond with $1000 face value that sells for $2000.

6. What is the yield to maturity on a $1000-face-value discount bond maturing in one year that sells for $800?

*7. What is the yield to maturity on a simple loan for $1 million that requires a repayment of $2 million in five years' time?

8. To pay for university, you have just taken out a $1000 government loan that makes you pay $126 per year for 25 years. However, you don't have to start making these payments until you graduate from university two years from now. Why is the yield to maturity necessarily less than 12%, the yield to maturity on a normal $1000 fixed-payment loan in which you pay $126 per year for 25 years?

*9. Which $1000 bond has the higher yield to maturity, a 20-year bond selling for $800 with a current yield of 15% or a one-year bond selling for $800 with a current yield of 5%?

10. Pick five Canada bonds from the bond page of the newspaper, and calculate the current yield. Note when the current yield is a good approximation of the yield to maturity.

*11. You are offered two bonds, a one-year Canada bond with a yield to maturity of 9% and a one-year treasury bill with a yield on a discount basis of 8.9%. Which would you rather own?

12. If there is a decline in interest rates, which would you rather be holding, long-term bonds or short-term bonds? Why? Which type of bond has the greater interest-rate risk?

*13. A financial adviser has just given you the following advice: "Long-term bonds are a great investment because their interest rate is over 20%." Is the financial adviser necessarily right?

14. If mortgage rates rise from 5% to 10% but the expected rate of increase in housing prices rises from 2% to 9%, are people more or less likely to buy houses?

*15. Interest rates were lower in the mid-1980s than they were in the late 1970s, yet many observers have commented that real interest rates were actually much higher in the mid-1980s than in the late 1970s. Does this make sense? Do you think that these observers are right?

16. When interest rates rise, would you rather be holding a ten-year coupon bond with a 5% coupon rate or one with a 10% coupon rate?

*17. Calculate the duration on a five-year 8% coupon bond when the interest rate is 3%.

18. Calculate the duration on a five-year 5% coupon bond when the interest rate is 3%. Compare your answer with the answer to Problem 17 given at the back of the book. What is the rationale behind the difference in the answers?

*19. If a bond has a duration of eight years and interest rates rise from 7% to 8%, what will be the approximate percentage change in the price of the bond?

20. Calculate the approximate price change of two bonds, one with a three-year duration and the other with a five-year duration, when interest rates rise from 4% to 5%. Which of the bonds would you rather hold? Does this accord with your intuition?

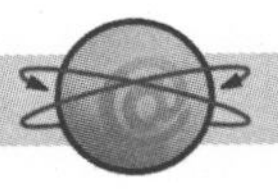

WEB EXERCISES

Understanding Interest Rates

1. Investigate the data available from the Bank of Canada at http://www.bankofcanada.ca/en/sel_hist.htm. Then answer the following questions.
   a. What is the difference in the interest rates on three-month treasury bills and long-term government of Canada bonds?
   b. What was the interest rate on the one-month banker's acceptances at the end of 1971?
   c. What was the interest rate on three-month euro-U.S. dollar deposits in London at the end of 2001?

2. Figure 3 in the chapter shows the estimated real and nominal rates for three-month U.S. Treasury bills. Go to http://www.martincapital.com/charts.htm. Click on "interest rates and yields" then on "Nominal versus Real Market Rates."
   a. Compare the three-month real rate to the long-term real rate. Which is greater?
   b. Compare the short-term nominal rate with the long-term nominal rate. Which appears most volatile?

Chapter 4

The Behaviour of Interest Rates

Preview

In the early 1950s, nominal interest rates on three-month treasury bills were about 1% at an annual rate; by 1981, they had reached more than 20%, then fell to 3% in 1997, and rose above 5% in 1998. What explains these substantial fluctuations in interest rates? One reason we study financial markets and institutions is to provide some answers to this question.

In this chapter we examine how the overall level of *nominal* interest rates (which we refer to simply as "interest rates") is determined and the factors that influence their behaviour. We learned in Chapter 3 that interest rates are negatively related to the price of bonds, so if we can explain why bond prices change, we can also explain why interest rates fluctuate. Here we will apply supply and demand analysis to examine how bond prices and interest rates change.

DETERMINANTS OF ASSET DEMAND

An **asset** is a piece of property that is a store of value. Items such as money, bonds, stocks, art, land, houses, farm equipment, and manufacturing machinery are all assets. Facing the question of whether to buy and hold an asset or whether to buy one asset rather than another, an individual must consider the following factors:

1. **Wealth,** the total resources owned by the individual, including all assets
2. **Expected return** (the return expected over the next period) on one asset relative to alternative assets
3. **Risk** (the degree of uncertainty associated with the return) on one asset relative to alternative assets
4. **Liquidity** (the ease and speed with which an asset can be turned into cash) relative to alternative assets

Study Guide As we discuss each factor that influences asset demand, remember that we are always holding all the other factors constant. Also, think of additional examples of how changes in each factor would influence your decision to purchase a particular asset, say, a house or a share of common stock. This intuitive approach will help you understand how the theory works in practice.

Wealth

When we find that our wealth has increased, we have more resources available with which to purchase assets and so, not surprisingly, the quantity of assets we demand increases.[1] Therefore, the effect of changes in wealth on the quantity demanded of an asset can be summarized as follows: ***Holding everything else constant, an increase in wealth raises the quantity demanded of an asset.***

Expected Returns

In Chapter 3 we saw that the return on an asset (such as a bond) measures how much we gain from holding that asset. When we make a decision to buy an asset, we are influenced by what we expect the return on that asset to be. If a Nortel Networks bond, for example, has a return of 15% half of the time and 5% the other half of the time, its expected return (which you can think of as the average return) is 10%. More formally, the expected return on an asset is the weighted average of all possible returns, where the weights are the probabilities of occurrence of that return:

$$R^e = p_1R_1 + p_2R_2 + \ldots + p_nR_n \tag{1}$$

where
R^e = expected return
n = number of possible outcomes (states of nature)
R_i = return in the ith state of nature
p_i = probability of occurrence of the return R_i

EXAMPLE 1: Expected Return

What is the expected return on the Nortel bond if the return is 12% two-thirds of the time and 8% one-third of the time?

Solution

The expected return is 10.68%.

$$R^e = p_1R_1 + p_2R_2$$

where

p_1 = probability of occurrence of return 1 $= \frac{2}{3} = .67$
R_1 = return in state 1 $= 12\% = 0.12$
p_2 = probability of occurrence of return 2 $= \frac{1}{3} = .33$
R_2 = return in state 2 $= 8\% = 0.08$

Thus

$$R^e = (.67)(0.12) + (.33)(0.08) = 0.1068 = 10.68\%$$

If the expected return on the Nortel bond rises relative to expected returns on alternative assets, holding everything else constant, then it becomes more desirable to purchase it, and the quantity demanded increases. This can occur

[1]Although it is possible that some assets (called *inferior assets*) might have the property that the quantity demanded does not increase as wealth increases, such assets are rare. Hence we will always assume that demand for an asset increases as wealth increases.

in either of two ways: (1) when the expected return on the Nortel bond rises while the return on an alternative asset—say, stock in IBM—remains unchanged or (2) when the return on the alternative asset, the IBM stock, falls while the return on the Nortel bond remains unchanged. To summarize, ***an increase in an asset's expected return relative to that of an alternative asset, holding everything else unchanged, raises the quantity demanded of the asset.***

Risk

The degree of risk or uncertainty of an asset's returns also affects the demand for the asset. Consider two assets, stock in Fly-by-Night Airlines and stock in Feet-on-the-Ground Bus Company. Suppose that Fly-by-Night stock has a return of 15% half of the time and 5% the other half of the time, making its expected return 10%, while stock in Feet-on-the-Ground has a fixed return of 10%. Fly-by-Night stock has uncertainty associated with its returns and so has greater risk than stock in Feet-on-the-Ground, whose return is a sure thing.

To see this more formally, we can use a measure of risk called the **standard deviation.** The standard deviation of returns on an asset is calculated as follows. First you need to calculate the expected return, R^e; then you subtract the expected return from each return to get a deviation; then you square each deviation and multiply it by the probability of occurrence of that outcome; finally, you add all these weighted squared deviations and take the square root. The formula for the standard deviation, σ, is thus:

$$\sigma = \sqrt{p_1(R_1 - R^e)^2 + p_2(R_2 - R^e)^2 + \ldots + p_n(R_n - R^e)^2} \qquad (2)$$

The higher the standard deviation, σ, the greater the risk of an asset.

EXAMPLE 2: Standard Deviation

What is the standard deviation of the returns on the Fly-by-Night Airlines stock and Feet-on-the Ground Bus Company, with the same return outcomes and probabilities described above? Of these two stocks, which is riskier?

Solution

Fly-by-Night Airlines has a standard deviation of returns of 5%.

$$\sigma = \sqrt{p_1(R_1 - R^e)^2 + p_2(R_2 - R^e)^2}$$

$$R^e = p_1R_1 + p_2R_2$$

where

p_1 = probability of occurrence of return 1 $= \frac{1}{2}$ $= .50$

R_1 = return in state 1 = 15% $= 0.15$

p_2 = probability of occurrence of return 2 $= \frac{1}{2}$ $= .50$

R_2 = return in state 2 = 5% $= 0.05$

R^e = expected return $= (.50)(0.15) + (.50)(0.05)$ $= 0.10$

Thus

$$\sigma = \sqrt{(.50)(0.15 - 0.10)^2 + (.50)(0.05 - 0.10)^2}$$

$$\sigma = \sqrt{(.50)(0.0025) + (.50)(0.0025)} = \sqrt{0.0025} = 0.05 = 5\%$$

Feet-on-the-Ground Bus Company has a standard deviation of returns of 0%.

$$\sigma = \sqrt{p_1(R_1 + R^e)^2}$$
$$R^e = p_1 R_1$$

where

p_1 = probability of occurrence of return 1 = 1.0

R_1 = return in state 1 = 10% = 0.10

R^e = expected return = (1.0)(0.10) = 0.10

Thus

$$\sigma = \sqrt{(1.0)(0.10 - 0.10)^2}$$
$$= \sqrt{(0)} = 0 = 0\%$$

Clearly, Fly-by-Night Airlines is a riskier stock because its standard deviation of returns of 5% is higher than the zero standard deviation of returns for Feet-on-the-Ground Bus Company, which has a certain return.

A *risk-averse* person prefers stock in the Feet-on-the-Ground (the sure thing) to Fly-by-Night stock (the riskier asset), even though the stocks have the same expected return, 10%. By contrast, a person who prefers risk is a *risk preferrer* or *risk lover*. Most people are risk-averse: Everything else being equal, they prefer to hold the less risky asset. Hence, ***holding everything else constant, if an asset's risk rises relative to that of alternative assets, its quantity demanded will fall.***

Liquidity

Another factor that affects the demand for an asset is how quickly it can be converted into cash without incurring large costs—its liquidity. An asset is liquid if the market in which it is traded has depth and breadth, that is, if the market has many buyers and sellers. A house is not a very liquid asset because it may be hard to find a buyer quickly; if a house must be sold to pay off bills, it might have to be sold for a much lower price. And the transaction costs in selling a house (broker's commissions, lawyer's fees, and so on) are substantial. A Canadian government treasury bill, by contrast, is a highly liquid asset. It can be sold in a well-organized market where there are many buyers, so it can be sold quickly at low cost. ***The more liquid an asset is relative to alternative assets, holding everything else unchanged, the more desirable it is, and the greater will be the quantity demanded.***

TABLE 1 SUMMARY Response of the Quantity of an Asset Demanded to Changes in Income or Wealth, Expected Returns, Risk, and Liquidity

Variable	Change in Variable	Change in Quantity Demanded
Income or wealth	↑	↑
Expected return relative to other assets	↑	↑
Risk relative to other assets	↑	↓
Liquidity relative to other assets	↑	↑

Note: Only increases (↑) in the variables are shown. The effect of decreases in the variables on the change in demand would be the opposite of those indicated in the righthand column.

Summary

All the determining factors we have just discussed can be summarized by stating that, holding all the other factors constant:

1. The quantity demanded of an asset is usually positively related to wealth, with the response being greater if the asset is a luxury than if it is a necessity.
2. The quantity demanded of an asset is positively related to its expected return relative to alternative assets.
3. The quantity demanded of an asset is negatively related to the risk of its returns relative to alternative assets.
4. The quantity demanded of an asset is positively related to its liquidity relative to alternative assets.

These results are summarized in Table 1.

BENEFITS OF DIVERSIFICATION

Our discussion of the determinants of asset demand indicates that most people like to avoid risk; that is, they are risk-averse. Why, then, do many investors hold many risky assets rather than just one? Doesn't holding many risky assets expose the investor to more risk?

The old warning about not putting all your eggs in one basket holds the key to the answer: Because holding a variety of risky assets (called **diversification**) reduces the overall risk an investor faces, diversification is beneficial. To see why this is so, let's look at some specific examples of how an investor fares when holding two risky securities.

Consider two assets, common stock of Frivolous Luxuries Ltd. and common stock of Bad Times Products, Unlimited. When the economy is strong, which we'll assume is half of the time, Frivolous Luxuries has high sales and the return on the stock is 15%; when the economy is weak, the other half of the time, sales are low and the return on the stock is 5%. In contrast, suppose that Bad Times Products thrives when the economy is weak so that its stock has a return of 15%, but it earns less when the economy is strong and has a return on the stock of 5%. Both stocks have a return of 15% half of the time and 5% the other half of the time, and both have an expected return of 10%. However, both stocks carry a fair amount of risk because there is uncertainty about their actual returns.

Suppose now that instead of buying one stock or the other, Irving the Investor puts half his savings in Frivolous Luxuries stock and the other half in Bad Times Products stock. When the economy is strong, Frivolous Luxuries stock has a return of 15% and Bad Times Products has a return of 5%. The result is that Irving earns a return of 10% (the average of 5% and 15%) on his holdings of the two stocks. When the economy is weak, Frivolous Luxuries has a return of only 5% and Bad Times Products has a return of 15%, so Irving still earns a return of 10%. If Irving diversifies by buying both stocks, he earns a return of 10% regardless of whether the economy is strong or weak. Irving is better off from this strategy of diversification because his expected return is 10%, the same as from holding either Frivolous Luxuries or Bad Times Products alone, yet he is not exposed to *any* risk.

Although the case we have described demonstrates the benefits of diversification, it is somewhat unrealistic. It is hard to find two securities with the characteristic that when the return of one is low, the return of the other is always high.[2] In the real world, we are more likely to find at best returns on securities that are

[2]Such a case is described by saying that the returns on the two securities are perfectly *negatively* correlated.

independent of each other; that is, when one is low, the other is just as likely to be high as to be low.

Suppose that both securities have an expected return of 10%, with a return of 5% half of the time and 15% the other half of the time. Sometimes both securities will earn the higher return, and sometimes both will earn the lower return. In this case, if Irving holds equal amounts of each security, he will on average earn the same return as if he had just put all his savings into one of the securities. However, because the returns on these two securities are independent, it is just as likely that when one earns the high 15% return, the other earns the low 5% return, and vice versa, giving Irving a return of 10% (equal to the expected return). Because Irving is more likely to earn what he expected to earn when he holds both securities instead of just one, we can see that Irving has again reduced his risk through diversification.

The one case in which Irving will not benefit from diversifying occurs when the returns on the two securities move perfectly together. In this case, when the first security has a return of 15%, the other also has a return of 15%, and holding both securities results in a return of 15%. When the first security has a return of 5%, the other has a return of 5%, and holding both results in a return of 5%. The result of diversifying by holding both securities is a return of 15% half of the time and 5% the other half of the time, which is exactly the same returns that are earned by holding only one of the securities. Consequently, diversification in this case does not lead to any reduction of risk.

The examples we have just examined illustrate the following important points about diversification:

1. Diversification is almost always beneficial to the risk-averse investor because it reduces risk except in the extremely rare case where returns on securities move perfectly together.

2. The less the returns on two securities move together, the more benefit (risk reduction) there is from diversification.

LOANABLE FUNDS FRAMEWORK: SUPPLY AND DEMAND IN THE BOND MARKET

We first approach the analysis of interest-rate determination by studying the supply of and demand for bonds. Because interest rates on different securities tend to move together, in this chapter we will act as if there is only one type of security and a single interest rate in the entire economy. In Chapter 5, we will expand our analysis to look at why interest rates on different securities differ.

The first step is to use the analysis of the determinants of asset demand to obtain a **demand curve,** which shows the relationship between the quantity demanded and the price when all other economic variables are held constant (that is, values of other variables are taken as given). You may recall from previous finance and economics courses that the assumption that all other economic variables are held constant is called *ceteris paribus,* which means "other things being equal" in Latin.

Demand Curve

To clarify our analysis, let us consider the demand for one-year discount bonds, which make no coupon payments but pay the owner the $1000 face value in a year. If the holding period is one year, then as we have seen in Chapter 3, the return on the bonds is known absolutely and is equal to the interest rate as measured by the yield to maturity. This means that the expected return on this bond is equal to the interest rate i, which, using Equation 6 in Chapter 3, is

$$i = R^e = \frac{F - P}{P}$$

where

i = interest rate = yield to maturity
R^e = expected return
F = face value of the discount bond
P = initial purchase price of the discount bond

This formula shows that a particular value of the interest rate corresponds to each bond price. If the bond sells for \$950, the interest rate and expected return is

$$\frac{(\$1000 - \$950)}{\$950} = 0.053 = 5.3\%$$

At this 5.3% interest rate and expected return corresponding to a bond price of \$950, let us assume that the quantity of bonds demanded is \$100 billion, which is plotted as point A in Figure 1. To display both the bond price and the corresponding interest rate, Figure 1 has two vertical axes. The left vertical axis shows the bond price, with the price of bonds increasing from \$750 near the bottom of the axis toward \$1000 at the top. The right vertical axis shows the interest rate, which increases in the *opposite* direction from 0% at the top of the axis to 33% near the bottom. The right and left vertical axes run in opposite directions

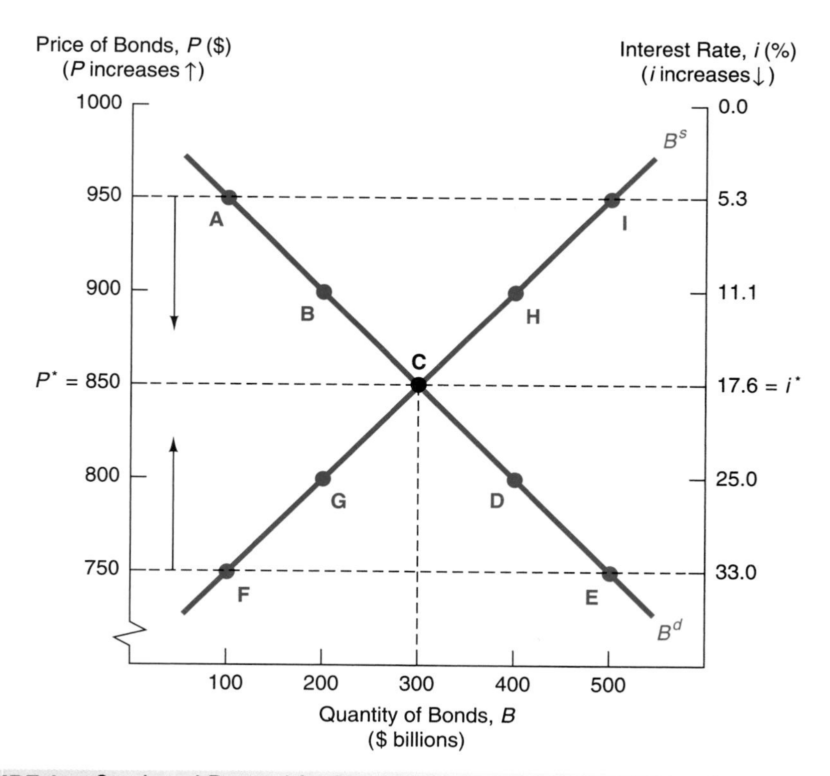

FIGURE 1 Supply and Demand for Bonds

Equilibrium in the bond market occurs at point C, the intersection of the bond demand curve B^d and the bond supply curve B^s. The equilibrium price is P^* = \$850, and the equilibrium interest rate is i^* = 17.6%. (*Note*: P and i increase in opposite directions. P on the left vertical axis increases as we go up the axis from \$750 near the bottom to \$1000 at the top, while i on the right vertical axis increases as we go down the axis from 0% at the top to 33% near the bottom.)

because, as we learned in Chapter 3, bond price and interest rate are always negatively related: As the price of the bond rises, the interest rate on the bond necessarily falls.

At a price of $900, the interest rate and expected return equals

$$\frac{(\$1000 - \$900)}{\$900} = 0.111 = 11.1\%$$

Because the expected return on these bonds is higher, with all other economic variables (such as income, expected returns on other assets, risk, and liquidity) held constant, the quantity demanded of bonds will be higher as predicted by our analysis of the determinants of asset demand. Point B in Figure 1 shows that the quantity of bonds demanded at the price of $900 has risen to $200 billion. Continuing with this reasoning, if the bond price is $850 (interest rate and expected return = 17.6%), the quantity of bonds demanded (point C) will be greater than at point B. Similarly, at the lower prices of $800 (interest rate = 25%) and $750 (interest rate = 33.3%), the quantity of bonds demanded will be even higher (points D and E). The curve B^d, which connects these points, is the demand curve for bonds. It has the usual downward slope, indicating that at lower prices of the bond (everything else being equal), the quantity demanded is higher.[3]

Supply Curve

An important assumption behind the demand curve for bonds in Figure 1 is that all other economic variables besides the bond's price and interest rate are held constant. We use the same assumption in deriving a **supply curve,** which shows the relationship between the quantity supplied and the price when all other economic variables are held constant.

When the price of the bonds is $750 (interest rate = 33.3%), point F shows that the quantity of bonds supplied is $100 billion for the example we are considering. If the price is $800, the interest rate is the lower rate of 25%. Because at this interest rate it is now less costly to borrow by issuing bonds, firms will be willing to borrow more through bond issues, and the quantity of bonds supplied is at the higher level of $200 billion (point G). An even higher price of $850, corresponding to a lower interest rate of 17.6%, results in a larger quantity of bonds supplied of $300 billion (point C). Higher prices of $900 and $950 result in even greater quantities of bonds supplied (points H and I). The B^s curve, which connects these points, is the supply curve for bonds. It has the usual upward slope found in supply curves, indicating that as the price increases (everything else being equal), the quantity supplied increases.

Market Equilibrium

In finance and economics, **market equilibrium** occurs when the amount that people are willing to buy (*demand*) equals the amount that people are willing to sell (*supply*) at a given price. In the bond market, this is achieved when the quantity of bonds demanded equals the quantity of bonds supplied:

$$B^d = B^s \tag{3}$$

In Figure 1, equilibrium occurs at point C, where the demand and supply curves intersect at a bond price of $850 (interest rate of 17.6%) and a quantity

[3]Note that although our analysis indicates that the demand curve is downward sloping, it does not imply that the curve is a straight line. For ease of exposition, however, we will draw demand curves and supply curves as straight lines.

of bonds of $300 billion. The price of $P^* = 850$, where the quantity demanded equals the quantity supplied, is called the *equilibrium* or *market-clearing* price. Similarly, the interest rate of $i^* = 17.6\%$ that corresponds to this price is called the equilibrium or market-clearing interest rate.

The concepts of market equilibrium and equilibrium price or interest rate are useful because there is a tendency for the market to head toward them. We can see that it does in Figure 1 by first looking at what happens when we have a bond price that is above the equilibrium price. When the price of bonds is set too high, at, say, $950, the quantity of bonds supplied at point I is greater than the quantity of bonds demanded at point A. A situation like this, in which the quantity of bonds supplied exceeds the quantity of bonds demanded, is called a condition of **excess supply.** Because people want to sell more bonds than others want to buy, the price of the bonds will fall, and this is why the downward arrow is drawn in the figure at the bond price of $950. As long as the bond price remains above the equilibrium price, there will continue to be an excess supply of bonds, and the price will continue to fall. This will stop only when the price has reached the equilibrium price of $850, where the excess supply of bonds has been eliminated.

Now let's look at what happens when the price of bonds is below the equilibrium price. If the price of the bonds is set too low, at, say, $750, the quantity demanded at point E is greater than the quantity supplied at point F. This is called a condition of **excess demand.** People now want to buy more bonds than others are willing to sell, and so the price of bonds will be driven up. This is illustrated by the upward arrow drawn in the figure at the bond price of $750. Only when the excess demand for bonds is eliminated by the price rising to the equilibrium level of $850 is there no further tendency for the price to rise.

We can see that the concept of equilibrium price is a useful one because it indicates where the market will settle. Because each price on the left vertical axis of Figure 1 corresponds to a value of the interest rate on the right vertical axis, the same diagram also shows that the interest rate will head toward the equilibrium interest rate of 17.6%. When the interest rate is below the equilibrium interest rate, as it is when it is at 5.3%, the price of the bond is above the equilibrium price, and there will be an excess supply of bonds. The price of the bond then falls, leading to a rise in the interest rate toward the equilibrium level. Similarly, when the interest rate is above the equilibrium level, as it is when it is at 33.3%, there is excess demand for bonds, and the bond price will rise, driving the interest rate back down to the equilibrium level of 17.6%.

Supply and Demand Analysis

Our Figure 1 is a conventional supply and demand diagram with price on the left vertical axis and quantity on the horizontal axis. Because the interest rate that corresponds to each bond price is also marked on the right vertical axis, this diagram allows us to read the equilibrium interest rate, giving us a model that describes the determination of interest rates. It is important to recognize that a supply and demand diagram like Figure 1 can be drawn for *any* type of bond because the interest rate and price of a bond are *always* negatively related for any type of bond, be it a discount bond or a coupon bond.

One disadvantage of the diagram in Figure 1 is that interest rates run in an unusual direction on the right vertical axis: As we go up the right axis, interest rates fall. Because financial economists are typically more concerned with the value of interest rates rather than the price of bonds, we could plot the supply of and demand for bonds on a diagram that has only a left vertical axis that provides the values of the interest rates running in the usual direction, rising as we go up the axis. Figure 2 is such a diagram, in which points A through I match the corresponding points in Figure 1.

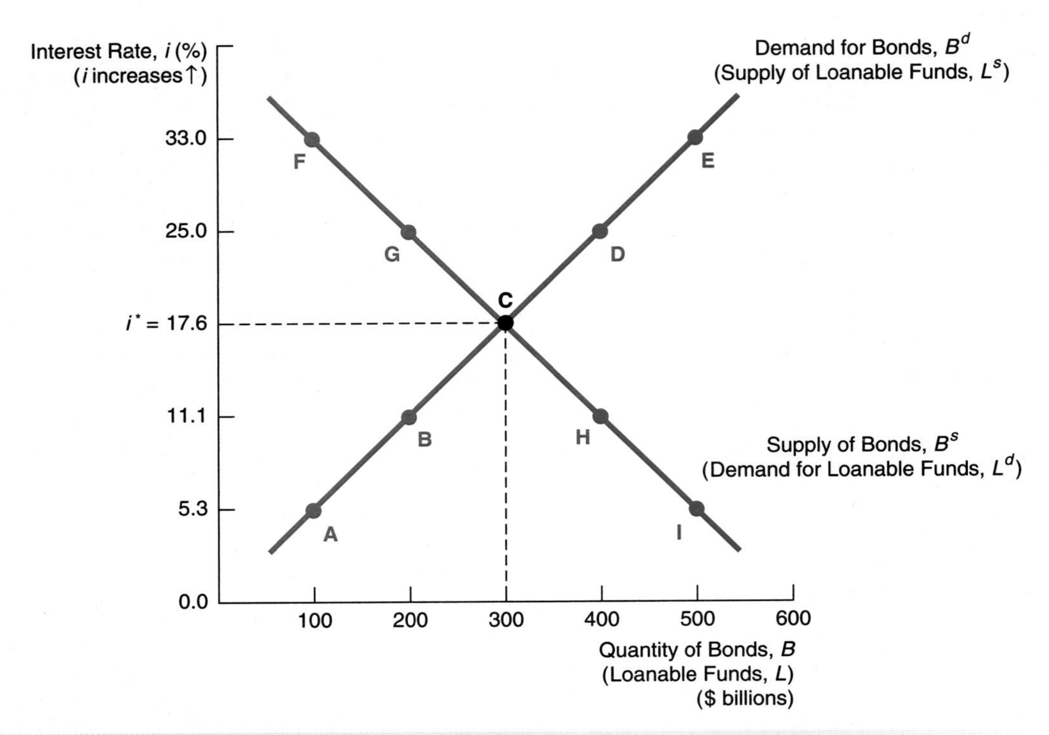

FIGURE 2 A Comparison of Terminology: Loanable Funds and Supply and Demand for Bonds

The demand for bonds is equivalent to the supply of loanable funds, and the supply of bonds is equivalent to the demand for loanable funds. (*Note*: i increases as we go up the vertical axis, in contrast to Figure 1, in which the opposite occurs.)

However, making interest rates run the "usual" direction on the vertical axis presents us with a problem. Our demand curve for bonds, points A through E, now looks peculiar because it has an upward slope. This upward slope is, however, completely consistent with our usual demand analysis, which produces a negative relationship between price and quantity. The inverse relationship between bond prices and interest rates means that in moving from point A to point B to point C, bond prices are falling and, consistent with usual demand analysis, the quantity demanded is rising. Similarly, our supply curve for bonds, points F through I, has an unusual-looking downward slope but is completely consistent with the usual view that price and the quantity supplied are positively related.

One way to give the demand curve the usual downward slope and the supply curve the usual upward slope is to rename the horizontal axis and the demand and supply curves. Because a firm supplying bonds is in fact taking out a loan from a person buying a bond, "supplying a bond" is equivalent to "demanding a loan." Thus the supply curve for bonds can be reinterpreted as indicating the *quantity of loans demanded* for each value of the interest rate. If we rename the horizontal axis **loanable funds,** defined as the quantity of loans, the supply of bonds can be reinterpreted as the *demand for loanable funds.* Similarly, the demand curve for bonds can be reidentified as the *supply of loanable funds* because buying (demanding) a bond is equivalent to supplying a loan. Figure 2 relabels the curves and the horizontal axis using the loanable funds terminology in parentheses, and now the renamed loanable funds demand curve has the usual downward slope and the renamed loanable funds supply curve the usual upward slope.

Because supply and demand diagrams that explain how interest rates are determined in the bond market most commonly use the loanable funds terminology, this analysis is frequently referred to as the **loanable funds framework.** However, because in later chapters describing the conduct of monetary policy we focus on how the demand for and supply of bonds is affected, we will continue to conduct supply and demand analysis in terms of bonds, as in Figure 1, rather than loanable funds. Whether the analysis is done in terms of loanable funds or in terms of the demand for and supply of bonds, the results are the same; the two ways of analyzing the determination of interest rates are equivalent.

An important feature of the analysis here is that supply and demand are always in terms of *stocks* (amounts at a given point in time) of assets, not in terms of *flows*. This approach is somewhat different from certain loanable funds analyses, which are conducted in terms of flows (loans per year). The **asset market approach** for understanding behaviour in financial markets—which emphasizes stocks of assets rather than flows in determining asset prices—is now the dominant methodology used by financial economists because correctly conducting analyses in terms of flows is very tricky, especially when we encounter inflation. (See the appendix to this chapter for an application of the asset market approach to another market.)

CHANGES IN EQUILIBRIUM INTEREST RATES

We will now use the supply and demand framework for bonds to analyze why interest rates change. To avoid confusion, it is important to make the distinction between *movements along* a demand (or supply) curve and *shifts in* a demand (or supply) curve. When quantity demanded (or supplied) changes as a result of a change in the price of the bond (or, equivalently, a change in the interest rate), we have a *movement along* the demand (or supply) curve. The change in the quantity demanded when we move from point A to B to C in Figure 1 or Figure 2, for example, is a movement along a demand curve. A *shift in* the demand (or supply) curve, by contrast, occurs when the quantity demanded (or supplied) changes *at each given price (or interest rate)* of the bond in response to a change in some other factor besides the bond's price or interest rate. When one of these factors changes, causing a shift in the demand or supply curve, there will be a new equilibrium value for the interest rate.

In the following pages we will look at how the supply and demand curves shift in response to changes in variables, such as expected inflation and wealth, and what effects these changes have on the equilibrium value of interest rates.

Shifts in the Demand for Bonds

Our analysis of the determinants of asset demand at the beginning of the chapter provides a framework for deciding what factors cause the demand curve for bonds to shift. These factors include changes in four parameters:

1. Wealth
2. Expected returns on bonds relative to alternative assets
3. Risk of bonds relative to alternative assets
4. Liquidity of bonds relative to alternative assets

To see how a change in each of these factors (holding all other factors constant) can shift the demand curve, let us look at some examples. (As a study aid, Table 2 summarizes the effects of changes in these factors on the bond demand curve.)

Wealth When the economy is growing rapidly in a business cycle expansion and wealth is increasing, the quantity of bonds demanded at each bond price (or interest rate) increases as shown in Figure 3. To see how this works, consider point B on the initial demand curve for bonds B^d_1. It tells us that at a bond price of \$900 and an interest rate of 11.1%, the quantity of bonds demanded is

TABLE 2 SUMMARY Factors That Shift the Demand Curve for Bonds

Variable	Change in Variable	Change in Quantity Demanded	Shift in Demand Curve
Wealth	↑	↑	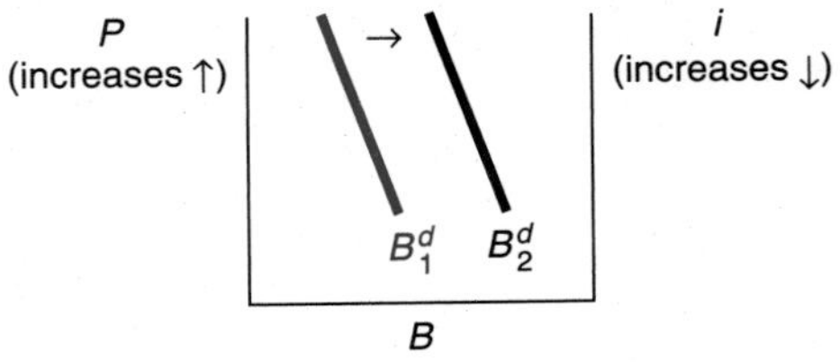 P (increases ↑) → B^d_1 B^d_2 B i (increases ↓)
Expected interest rate	↑	↓	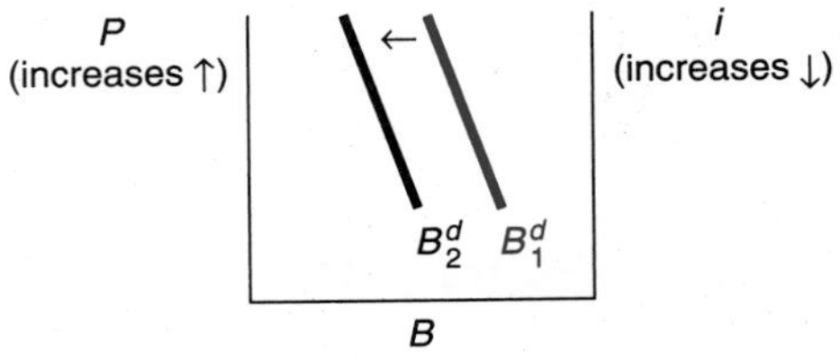 P (increases ↑) ← B^d_2 B^d_1 B i (increases ↓)
Expected inflation	↑	↓	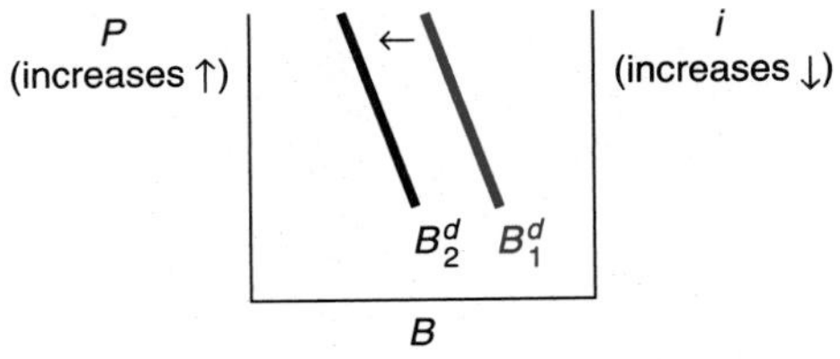 P (increases ↑) ← B^d_2 B^d_1 B i (increases ↓)
Riskiness of bonds relative to other assets	↑	↓	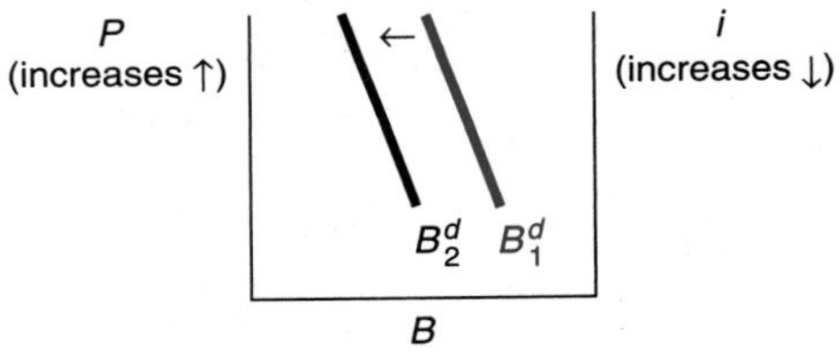 P (increases ↑) ← B^d_2 B^d_1 B i (increases ↓)
Liquidity of bonds relative to other assets	↑	↑	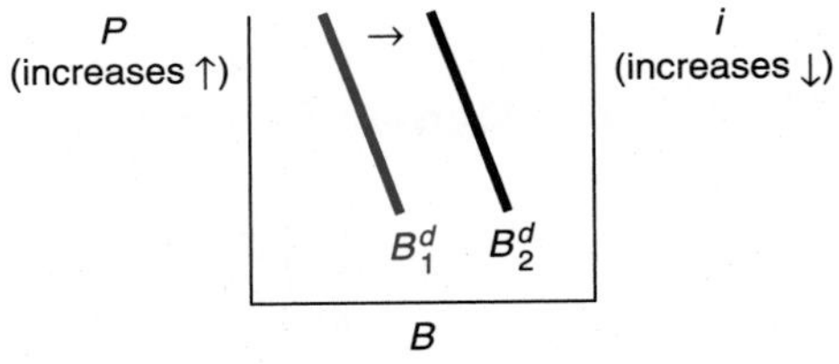 P (increases ↑) → B^d_1 B^d_2 B i (increases ↓)

Note: Only increases (↑) in the variables are shown. The effect of decreases in the variables on the change in demand would be the opposite of those indicated in the remaining columns.

$200 billion. With higher wealth, the quantity of bonds demanded at the same interest rate must rise, say, to $400 billion (point B′). Similarly, the higher wealth causes the quantity demanded at a bond price of $800 and an interest rate of 25% to rise from $400 billion to $600 billion (point D to D′). Continuing with this reasoning for every point on the initial demand curve B^d_1, we can see that the demand curve shifts to the right from B^d_1 to B^d_2 as is indicated by the arrows.

The conclusion we have reached is that ***in a business cycle expansion with growing wealth, the demand for bonds rises and the demand curve for bonds shifts to the right.*** Using the same reasoning, ***in a recession, when income and wealth are falling, the demand for bonds falls, and the demand curve shifts to the left.***

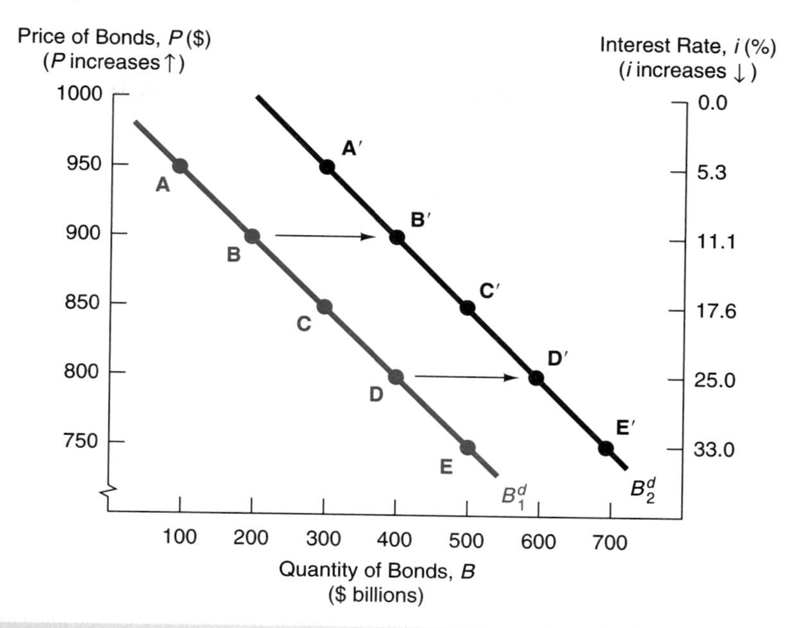

FIGURE 3 Shift in the Demand Curve for Bonds

When the demand for bonds increases, the demand curve shifts to the right as shown. (*Note*: P and i increase in opposite directions. P on the left vertical axis increases as we go up the axis, while i on the right vertical axis increases as we go down the axis.)

Another factor that affects wealth is the public's propensity to save. If households save more, wealth increases and, as we have seen, the demand for bonds rises and the demand curve for bonds shifts to the right. Conversely, if people save less, wealth and the demand for bonds will fall and the demand curve shifts to the left.

Expected Returns For a one-year discount bond and a one-year holding period, the expected return and the interest rate are identical. No component of the expected return is unrelated to the bond price or the interest rate.

For bonds with maturities of greater than one year, the expected return may differ from the interest rate. For example, we saw in Chapter 3, Table 2, that a rise in the interest rate on a long-term bond from 10% to 20% would lead to a sharp decline in price and a very negative return. Hence if people begin to think that interest rates will be higher next year than they had originally anticipated, the expected return today on long-term bonds would fall, and the quantity demanded would fall at each interest rate. ***Higher expected interest rates in the future decrease the demand for long-term bonds and shift the demand curve to the left.***

By contrast, a revision downward of expectations of future interest rates would mean that long-term bond prices would be expected to rise more than originally anticipated, and the resulting higher expected return today would raise the quantity demanded at each bond price and interest rate. ***Lower expected interest rates in the future increase the demand for long-term bonds and shift the demand curve to the right*** (as in Figure 3).

Changes in expected returns on other assets can also shift the demand curve for bonds. If people suddenly became more optimistic about the stock market and began to expect higher stock prices in the future, both expected capital gains and expected returns on stocks would rise. With the expected return on bonds held constant, the expected return on bonds today relative to stocks would fall, lowering the demand for bonds and shifting the demand curve to the left.

A change in expected inflation is likely to alter expected returns on physical assets (also called *real assets*) such as automobiles and houses, which affect the demand for bonds. An increase in expected inflation, say, from 5% to 10%, will lead to higher prices on cars and houses in the future and hence higher nominal capital gains. The resulting rise in the expected returns today on these real assets will lead to a fall in the expected return on bonds relative to the expected return on real assets today and thus cause the demand for bonds to fall. Alternatively, we can think of the rise in expected inflation as lowering the real interest rate on bonds, and the resulting decline in the relative expected return on bonds causes the demand for bonds to fall. ***An increase in the expected rate of inflation will cause the demand for bonds to decline and the demand curve to shift to the left.***

Risk If prices in the bond market become more volatile, the risk associated with bonds increases, and bonds become a less attractive asset. ***An increase in the riskiness of bonds causes the demand for bonds to fall and the demand curve to shift to the left.***

Conversely, an increase in the volatility of prices in another asset market, such as the stock market, would make bonds more attractive. ***An increase in the riskiness of alternative assets causes the demand for bonds to rise and the demand curve to shift to the right*** (as in Figure 3).

Liquidity If more people started trading in the bond market and as a result it became easier to sell bonds quickly, the increase in their liquidity would cause the quantity of bonds demanded at each interest rate to rise. ***Increased liquidity of bonds results in an increased demand for bonds, and the demand curve shifts to the right*** (see Figure 3). ***Similarly, increased liquidity of alternative assets lowers the demand for bonds and shifts the demand curve to the left.*** The reduction of brokerage commissions for trading common stocks that occurred when the fixed-rate commission structure was abolished in 1975, for example, increased the liquidity of stocks relative to bonds, and the resulting lower demand for bonds shifted the demand curve to the left.

Shifts in the Supply of Bonds

Certain factors can cause the supply curve for bonds to shift, among them these:

1. Expected profitability of investment opportunities
2. Expected inflation
3. Government activities

We will look at how the supply curve shifts when each of these factors changes (when all others remain constant). (As a study aid, Table 3 summarizes the effects of changes in these factors on the bond supply curve.)

Expected Profitability of Investment Opportunities The more profitable investments that a firm expects it can make, the more willing it will be to borrow and increase the amount of its outstanding debt in order to finance these investments. When the economy is growing rapidly, as in a business cycle expansion, investment opportunities that are expected to be profitable abound, and the quantity of bonds supplied at any given bond price and interest rate will increase (see Figure 4). Therefore, ***in a business cycle expansion, the supply of bonds increases, and the supply curve shifts to the right. Likewise, in a recession, when there are far fewer expected profitable investment opportunities, the supply of bonds falls, and the supply curve shifts to the left.***

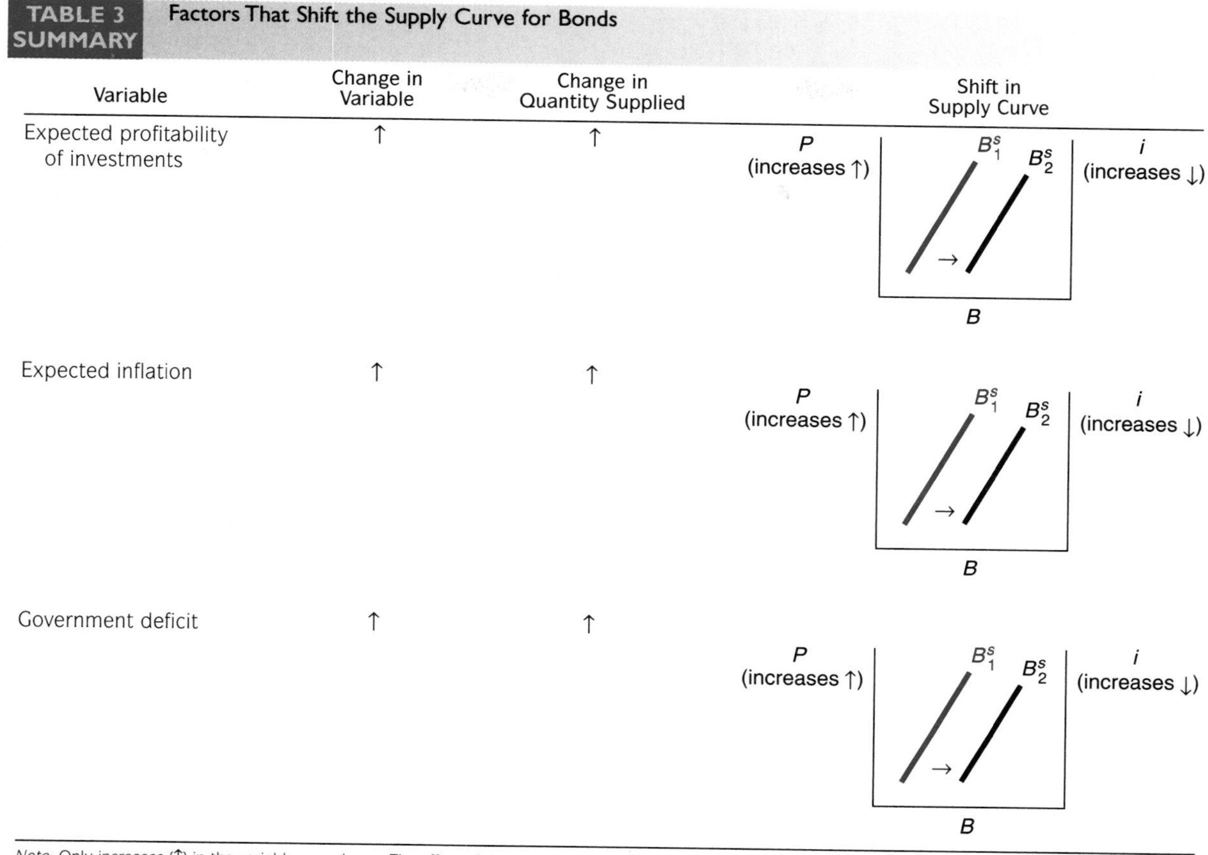

TABLE 3 SUMMARY Factors That Shift the Supply Curve for Bonds

Variable	Change in Variable	Change in Quantity Supplied	Shift in Supply Curve
Expected profitability of investments	↑	↑	P (increases ↑), B^s_1 → B^s_2, B, i (increases ↓)
Expected inflation	↑	↑	P (increases ↑), B^s_1 → B^s_2, B, i (increases ↓)
Government deficit	↑	↑	P (increases ↑), B^s_1 → B^s_2, B, i (increases ↓)

Note: Only increases (↑) in the variables are shown. The effect of decreases in the variables on the change in supply would be the opposite of those indicated in the remaining columns.

Weekly updates on global economic, monetary, and policy trends influencing inflation are available at www.forecasts.org/inflationwatch/index.htm

Expected Inflation As we saw in Chapter 3, the real cost of borrowing is more accurately measured by the real interest rate, which equals the (nominal) interest rate minus the expected inflation rate. For a given interest rate, when expected inflation increases, the real cost of borrowing falls; hence the quantity of bonds supplied increases at any given bond price and interest rate. ***An increase in expected inflation causes the supply of bonds to increase and the supply curve to shift to the right*** (see Figure 4).

Government Activities The activities of the government can influence the supply of bonds in several ways. The Canadian government issues bonds to finance government deficits, the gap between the government's expenditures and its revenues. When these deficits are large, as they have been recently, the government sells more bonds, and the quantity of bonds supplied at each bond price and interest rate increases. ***Higher government deficits increase the supply of bonds and shift the supply curve to the right*** (see Figure 4). ***On the other hand, government surpluses decrease the supply of bonds and shift the supply curve to the left.***

Provincial and municipal governments and other government agencies also issue bonds to finance their expenditures, and this can also affect the supply of bonds. We will see in later chapters that the conduct of monetary policy involves the purchase and sale of bonds, which in turn influences the supply of bonds.

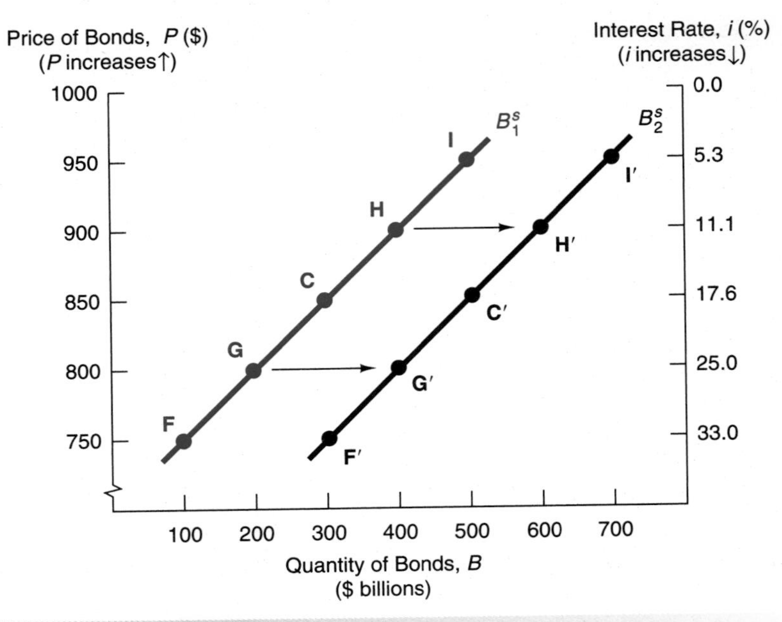

FIGURE 4 Shift in the Supply Curve for Bonds

When the supply of bonds increases, the supply curve shifts to the right. (*Note*: P and i increase in opposite directions. P on the left vertical axis increases as we go up the axis, while i on the right vertical axis increases as we go down the axis.)

Application Changes in the Equilibrium Interest Rate Due to Expected Inflation or Business Cycle Expansions

We can now use our knowledge of how supply and demand curves shift to analyze how the equilibrium interest rate can change. The best way to do this is to pursue several applications that are particularly relevant to our understanding of how monetary policy affects interest rates.

Study Guide Supply and demand analysis for the bond market is best learned by practising applications. When there is an application in the text and we look at how the interest rate changes because some economic variable increases, see whether you can draw the appropriate shifts in the supply and demand curves when this same economic variable decreases. While you are practising applications, keep two things in mind:

1. When you examine the effect of a variable change, remember that we are assuming that all other variables are unchanged; that is, we are making use of the *ceteris paribus* assumption.
2. Remember that the interest rate is negatively related to the bond price, so when the equilibrium bond price rises, the equilibrium interest rate falls. Conversely, if the equilibrium bond price moves downward, the equilibrium interest rate rises.

Changes in Expected Inflation: The Fisher Effect

We have already done most of the work to evaluate how a change in expected inflation affects the nominal interest rate in that we have already analyzed how a change in expected inflation shifts the supply and demand curves. Figure 5 shows the effect on the equilibrium interest rate of an increase in expected inflation.

Suppose that expected inflation is initially 5% and the initial supply and demand curves B_1^s and B_1^d intersect at point 1, where the equilibrium bond price is P_1 and the equilibrium interest rate is i_1. If expected inflation rises to 10%, the expected return on bonds relative to real assets falls for any given bond price and interest rate. As a result, the demand for bonds falls, and the demand curve shifts to the left from B_1^d to B_2^d. The rise in expected inflation also shifts the supply curve. At any given bond price and interest rate, the real cost of borrowing has declined, causing the quantity of bonds supplied to increase, and the supply curve shifts to the right from B_1^s to B_2^s.

When the demand and supply curves shift in response to the change in expected inflation, the equilibrium moves from point 1 to point 2, which is the intersection of B_2^d and B_2^s. The equilibrium bond price has fallen from P_1 to P_2, and because the bond price is negatively related to the interest rate (as is indicated by the interest rate rising as we go down the right vertical axis), this means that the interest rate has risen from i_1 to i_2. Note that Figure 5 has been drawn so that the equilibrium quantity of bonds remains the same for both point 1 and point 2. However, depending on the size of the shifts in the supply and demand curves, the equilibrium quantity of bonds could either rise or fall when expected inflation rises.

Our supply and demand analysis has led us to an important observation: ***When expected inflation rises, interest rates will rise.*** This result has been named the **Fisher effect,** after Irving Fisher, the economist who first pointed out the relationship of expected inflation to interest rates. The accuracy of this prediction is shown in Figure 6. The interest rate on U.S. three-month Treasury bills has

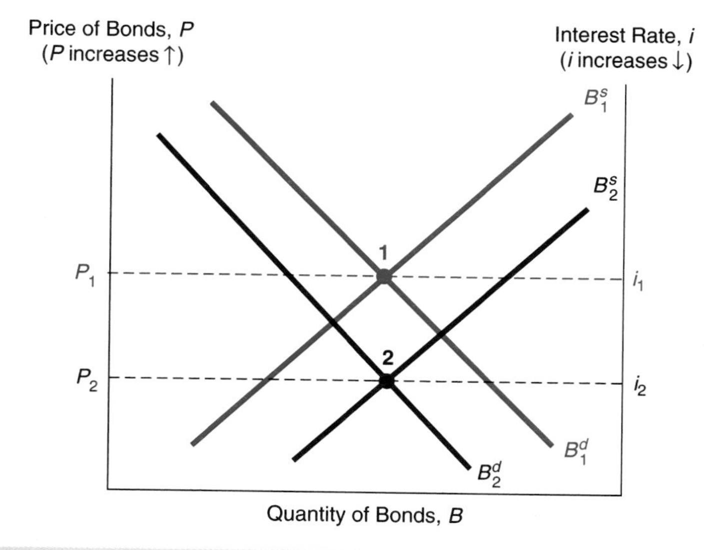

FIGURE 5 Response to a Change in Expected Inflation

When expected inflation rises, the supply curve shifts from B_1^s to B_2^s, and the demand curve shifts from B_1^d to B_2^d. The equilibrium moves from point 1 to point 2, with the result that the equilibrium bond price (left axis) falls from P_1 to P_2 and the equilibrium interest rate (right axis) rises from i_1 to i_2. (*Note:* P and i increase in opposite directions. P on the left vertical axis increases as we go up the axis, while i on the right vertical axis increases as we go down the axis.)

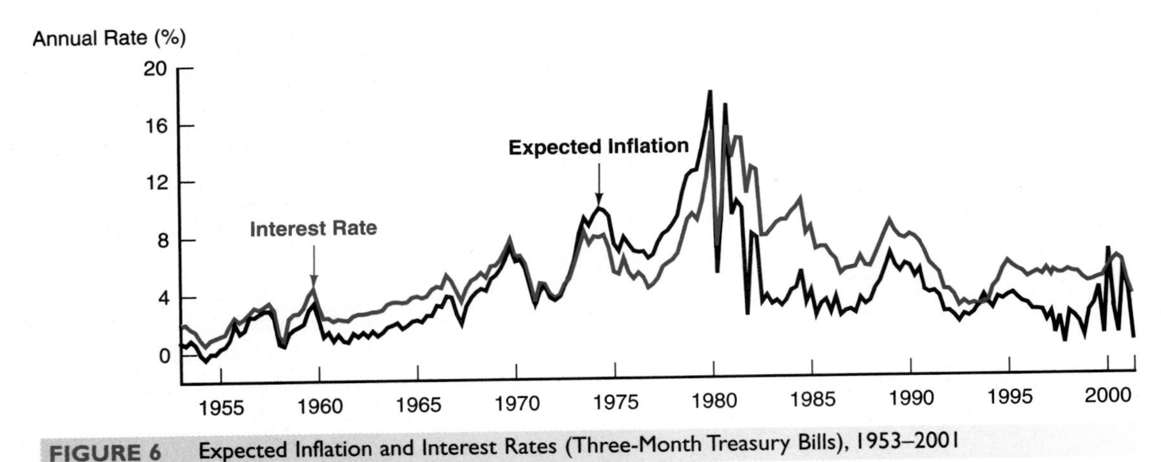

FIGURE 6 Expected Inflation and Interest Rates (Three-Month Treasury Bills), 1953–2001

Source: Expected inflation calculated using procedures outlined in Frederic S. Mishkin, "The Real Interest Rate: An Empirical Investigation," *Carnegie-Rochester Conference Series on Public Policy* 15 (1981): 151–200. This involves estimating expected inflation as a function of past interest rates, inflation, and time trends.

usually moved along with the expected inflation rate. Consequently, it is understandable that many economists recommend that the fight against inflation must be won if we want to lower interest rates.

Business Cycle Expansion

Figure 7 analyzes the effects of a business cycle expansion on interest rates. In a business cycle expansion, the amount of goods and services being produced in the economy rises, so national income increases. When this occurs, businesses will be more willing to borrow because they are likely to have many profitable investment opportunities for which they need financing. Hence, at a given bond price and interest rate, the quantity of bonds that firms want to sell (that is, the supply of bonds) will increase. This means that in a business cycle expansion, the supply curve for bonds shifts to the right (see Figure 7) from B_1^s to B_2^s.

The expanding economy will also affect the demand for bonds. Our discussion of the determinants of asset demand tells us that as the economy expands and wealth increases, the demand for bonds will rise as well. We see this in Figure 7, where the demand curve has shifted to the right from B_1^d to B_2^d.

Given that both the supply and demand curves have shifted to the right, we know that the new equilibrium reached at the intersection of B_2^d and B_2^s must also move to the right. However, depending on whether the supply curve shifts more than the demand curve or vice versa, the new equilibrium interest rate can either rise or fall.

The supply and demand analysis used here gives us an ambiguous answer to the question of what will happen to interest rates in a business cycle expansion. The figure has been drawn so that the shift in the supply curve is greater than the shift in the demand curve, causing the equilibrium bond price to fall to P_2, leading to a rise in the equilibrium interest rate to i_2. The reason the figure has been drawn so that a business cycle expansion and a rise in income lead to a higher interest rate is that this is the outcome we actually see in the data. Figure 8 plots the movement of the interest rate on three-month Canadian treasury bills from 1953 to 2001 and indicates when the business cycle is undergoing recessions (shaded areas). As you can see, the interest rate rises during business cycle expansions and falls during recessions, which is what the supply and demand diagram indicates.

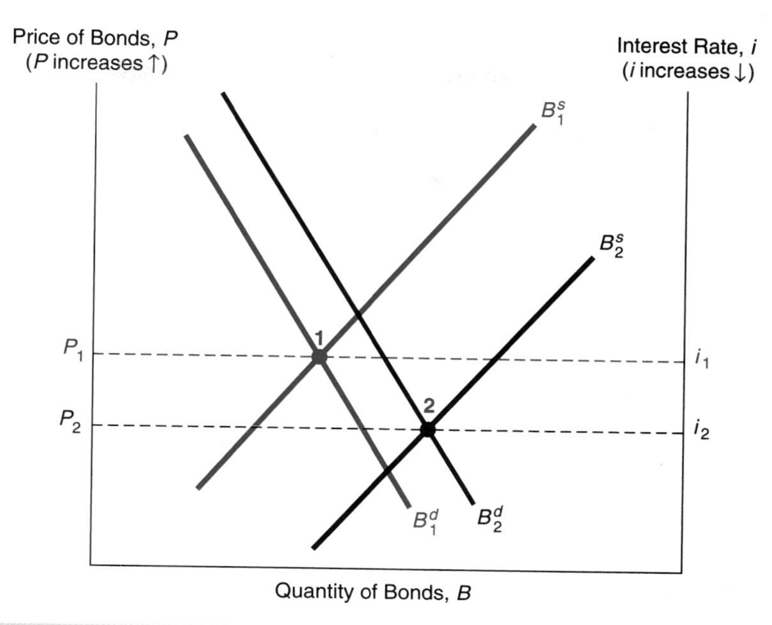

FIGURE 7 **Response to a Business Cycle Expansion**

In a business cycle expansion, when income and wealth are rising, the demand curve shifts rightward from B_1^d to B_2^d, and the supply curve shifts rightward from B_1^s to B_2^s. If the supply curve shifts to the right more than the demand curve, as in this figure, the equilibrium bond price (left axis) moves down from P_1 to P_2, and the equilibrium interest rate (right axis) rises from i_1 to i_2. (*Note*: P and i increase in opposite directions. P on the left vertical axis increases as we go up the axis, while i on the right vertical axis increases as we go down the axis.)

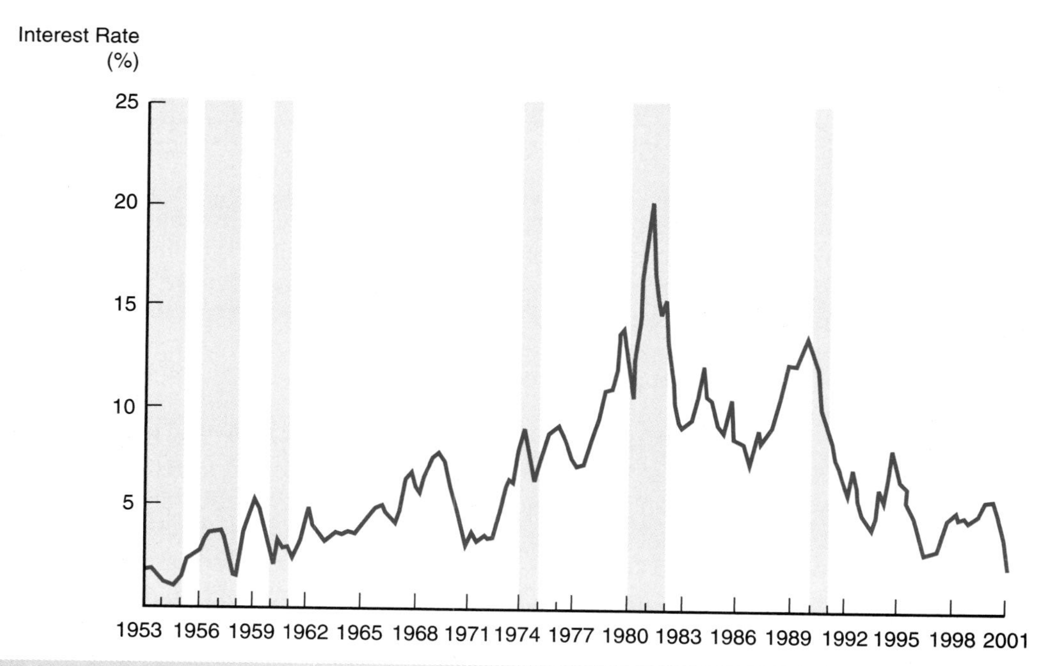

FIGURE 8 **Business Cycle and Interest Rates (Three-Month Treasury Bills), 1953–2001**

Source: Statistics Canada CANSIM II series V122531. Shaded areas indicate periods of recession. The figure shows that interest rates rise during business cycle expansions and fall during contractions, which is what Figure 7 suggests would happen.

Application Explaining Low Japanese Interest Rates

In the 1990s and early 2000s, Japanese interest rates became the lowest in the world. Indeed, in November 1998, an extraordinary event occurred: Interest rates on Japanese six-month treasury bills turned slightly negative (see Chapter 3). Why did Japanese rates drop to such low levels?

In the late 1990s, Japan had been experiencing a prolonged recession, accompanied by a negative inflation rate. Using these facts, analysis similar to that used in the preceding application explains the low Japanese interest rates.

Negative inflation causes the demand for bonds to rise because the expected return on real assets falls, thereby raising the relative expected return on bonds and in turn causing the demand curve to shift to the right. The negative inflation also raises the real interest rate and therefore the real cost of borrowing for any given nominal rate, thereby causing the supply of bonds to contract and the supply curve to shift to the left. The outcome is then exactly the opposite of that graphed in Figure 5: The rightward shift of the demand curve and leftward shift of the supply curve lead to a rise in the bond price and a fall in interest rates.

The business cycle contraction in Japan also leads to lower interest rates because the resulting lack of investment opportunities decreases the supply of bonds, shifting the supply curve to the left. Although the demand curve also shifts to the left because wealth decreases during the business cycle contraction, we have seen in the preceding application that the demand curve shifts less than the supply curve, so that we get exactly the opposite outcome as that in Figure 7: The bond price rises, and the interest rates fall.

Usually we think that low interest rates are a good thing because they make it cheap to borrow. But the Japanese example shows that just as there is a fallacy in the adage "You can never be too rich or too thin"—maybe you can't be too rich, but you certainly can be too thin and do damage to your health—there is a fallacy in always thinking that lower interest rates are better. In Japan, the low and even negative interest rates are a sign that the Japanese economy is in real trouble, with falling prices and a contracting economy. Only when the Japanese economy returns to health will interest rates rise back to more normal levels.

Application The "Credit Markets" Column

READING THE *WALL STREET JOURNAL*

Now that we have an understanding of how supply and demand determines prices and interest rates in the bond market, we can use our analysis to understand discussions about bond prices and interest rates appearing in the financial press. Every day, the *Wall Street Journal* reports on developments in the bond market on the previous business day in its "Credit Markets" column, an example of which is found in the "Following the Financial News" box on page 88. Let's see how statements in the "Credit Markets" column can be explained using our supply and demand framework.

Go to www.wsj.com to examine the *Wall Street Journal.*

The column featured in the "Following the Financial News" box begins by stating that Treasury prices fell sharply as the economy showed improvement. This is exactly what our supply and demand analysis predicts would happen.

A stronger economy raises the supply of bonds because of increased investment opportunities and thus shifts the supply curve out to the right, while it also increases the demand for bonds and shifts the demand curve out to the right because a stronger economy raises wealth and income. However, as illustrated in Figure 7, because the supply curve generally shifts by more than the demand curve when the economy get stronger, the price of bonds falls rather than rises.

The column also points out that prospects of a stronger economy raise the fear that the U.S. Federal Reserve will raise interest rates in the future. Higher future interest rates imply that the price of long-term bonds will be lower in the future, thus decreasing their expected return. The lower expected return causes the demand for bonds to decrease, the demand curve to shift to the left and the price of bonds to fall. The column also mentions that the outlook (expected return) for nongovernment bonds is improving as the economy improves, so that the relative expected returns for Treasury bonds falls, thus also causing the demand for Treasurys to fall and the demand curve to shift to the left. This provides an additional reason for weakness in the Treasury bond market.

Application Have Negative Savings Rates in Canada Led to Higher Interest Rates?

Since 1980, Canada has experienced a sharp drop in personal savings rates. Many commentators, including high officials of the Bank of Canada, have blamed the profligate behaviour of the Canadian public for high interest rates. Are they right?

Our supply and demand analysis of the bond market indicates that they could be. The decline in savings means that the wealth of Canadian households is lower than would otherwise be the case. This smaller amount of wealth decreases the demand for bonds and shifts the demand curve to the left from B^d_1 to B^d_2 in Figure 9. The result is that the equilibrium bond price drops from P_1 to P_2 and the interest rate rises from i_1 to i_2. Low savings can thus raise interest rates, and the higher rates may retard investment in capital goods. The low savings rate of Canadians may therefore lead to a less productive economy and is of serious concern to both economists and policymakers. Suggested remedies for the problem range from changing the tax code to encourage saving to forcing Canadians to save more by mandating increased contributions into retirement plans.

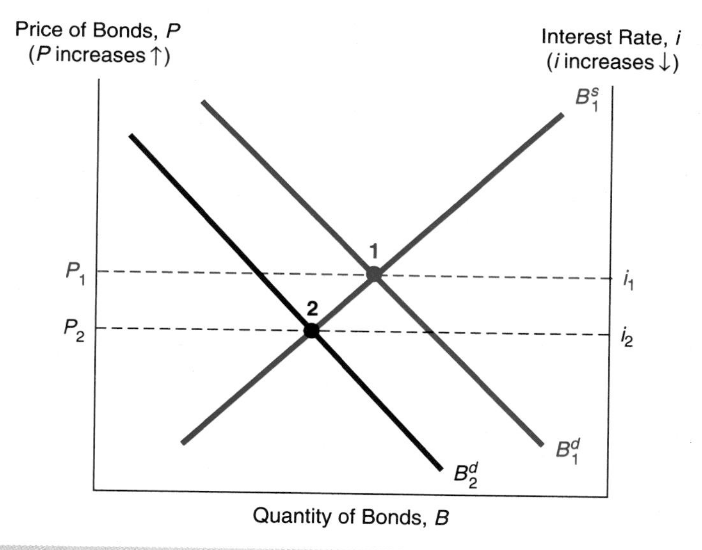

FIGURE 9 **Response to a Lower Savings Rate**

With a lower savings rate, wealth decreases, and the demand curve shifts from B^d_1 to B^d_2. The equilibrium moves from point 1 to point 2, with the result that the equilibrium bond price (left axis) drops from P_1 to P_2 and the equilibrium interest rate (right axis) rises from i_1 to i_2. (*Note*: P and i increase in opposite directions. P on the left vertical axis increases as we go up the axis, while i on the right vertical axis increases as we go down the axis.)

FOLLOWING THE FINANCIAL NEWS
The "Credit Markets" Column

The "Credit Markets" column appears daily in the *Wall Street Journal*; an example is presented here. It is found in the third section, "Money and Investing."

CREDIT MARKETS

Treasurys Drop on Signs Economy Is Improving As Funds Are Moved to Bonds With Higher Yields

BY STEVEN VAMES
Dow Jones Newswires

NEW YORK—Treasurys prices fell sharply in the first trading session of 2002, as the economy showed improvement and money managers shifted funds into higher-yielding bonds.

Declines came across the spectrum, but were especially heavy in short-dated securities. That reflected a belief that short-dated issues had become less attractive because of their relatively lower yields and a risk that their prices will fall further as the market continues to grapple with economic data that suggest the economy is improving.

Selling in longer-dated securities was said to be related to pending issuance of corporate bonds.

Trading was halted Tuesday for the New Year's holiday.

Compared with levels Monday, the benchmark 10-year Treasury note at 4 p.m. yesterday was down 1 1/32 points, or $10.3125 per $1,000 face value, at 98 26/32. Its yield rose to 5/157% from 5.020% Monday, as yields move inversely to prices.

The 30-year Treasury bond's price was down 1 12/32 points at 97 11/32 to yield 5.560%, up from 5.463% Monday.

People in the market said much of the weakness in Treasurys was driven by repositioning by funds managers into bonds that offer higher returns than Treasurys.

"Municipal bonds and corporate bonds are holding their ground," said Zane Brown, director of fixed income at Lord, Abbett in New York. "Investors see great value in (nongovernment bonds) because they are historically cheap relative to Treasurys, and they will continue to improve as the economy improves," he added.

Bond underwriters were also said to be selling Treasurys as they hedged coming bond offerings, using transactions known as rate locks to protect against interest rate moves. The transactions involve selling Treasurys or Treasury futures. When corporate deals are done, underwriters make offsetting purchases of Treasurys.

"When we see a major seller of bond futures like we did today, we can presume there is a rate-lock activity going on," said Gerald Lucas, senior government bond strategist at Merrill Lynch in New York.

Coming offerings include a $1.25 billion, 10-year deal from Goldman Sachs Group and a $3 billion three-year deal from the Federal Home Loan Bank, though it was unclear whether the rate-locks activity seen was related to those deals.

Many fund managers still entrenched in heavy positions in short-dated Treasurys may be fleeing because of what they see as a growing risk that the economy will recover sooner than many had expected. If coming data continue to suggest a quick start to economic recovery, that could spark fear that the Federal Reserve will start raising interest rates, which would likely result in more selling in Treasurys.

Signs of recovery came yesterday in a report indicating that conditions improved for the nation's manufacturers in December.

The Institute of Supply Management, formerly known as the National Association of Purchasing Management, said its index of manufacturing activity rose to 48.2 in December from 44.5 in November and 39.8 in October.

Readings above 50 indicate expansion of activity, while readings under 50 denote contraction. December's was the 17th straight month of contraction in manufacturing. Economists had expected the index to move to 46.0, but gains in orders for new goods helped push it higher.

"The data are positive for the economy and reinforce the notion for investors that the economy is bottoming out and is poised for a recovery some time this year," said Kevin Flanagan, fixed-income strategist at Morgan Stanley.

The next major economic signpost is today's Labor Department release of weekly initial claims for unemployment benefits. Economists expect to see a rise of about 6,000, according to a Dow Jones Newswires/CNBC survey.

Tomorrow, the Labor Department will release its December employment report. That report, which is widely watched, is seen by many economists as a make-or-break factor for expectations about whether Fed policymakers will continue to cut rates when they meet in late January.

Source: Wall Street Journal, January 3, 2002, p. C12. Republished by permission of Dow Jones, Inc. via Copyright Clearance Center, Inc.

LIQUIDITY PREFERENCE FRAMEWORK: SUPPLY AND DEMAND IN THE MARKET FOR MONEY

Whereas the loanable funds framework determines the equilibrium interest rate using the supply of and demand for bonds, an alternative model developed by John Maynard Keynes, known as the **liquidity preference framework,** determines the equilibrium interest rate in terms of the supply of and demand for money. Although the two frameworks look different, the liquidity preference analysis of the market for money is closely related to the loanable funds framework of the bond market.[4]

The starting point of Keynes's analysis is his assumption that there are two main categories of assets that people use to store their wealth: money and bonds. Therefore, total wealth in the economy must equal the total quantity of bonds plus money in the economy, which equals the quantity of bonds supplied B^s plus the quantity of money supplied M^s. The quantity of bonds B^d and money M^d that people want to hold and thus demand must also equal the total amount of wealth because people cannot purchase more assets than their available resources allow. The conclusion is that the quantity of bonds and money supplied must equal the quantity of bonds and money demanded:

$$B^s + M^s = B^d + M^d \tag{4}$$

Collecting the bond terms on one side of the equation and the money terms on the other, this equation can be rewritten as

$$B^s - B^d = M^d - M^s \tag{5}$$

The rewritten equation tells us that if the market for money is in equilibrium ($M^s = M^d$), the right-hand side of Equation 5 equals zero, implying that $B^s = B^d$, meaning that the bond market is also in equilibrium.

Thus, it is the same to think about determining the equilibrium interest rate by equating the supply and demand for bonds or by equating the supply and demand for money. In this sense, the liquidity preference framework, which analyzes the market for money, is equivalent to the loanable funds framework, which analyzes the bond market. In practice, the approaches differ because by assuming that there are only two kinds of assets, money and bonds, the liquidity preference approach implicitly ignores any effects on interest rates that arise from changes in the expected returns on real assets such as automobiles and houses. In most instances, both frameworks yield the same predictions.

The reason that we approach the determination of interest rates with both frameworks is that the loanable funds framework is easier to use when analyzing the effects from changes in expected inflation, whereas the liquidity preference framework provides a simpler analysis of the effects from changes in income, the price level, and the supply of money.

Because the definition of money that Keynes used includes currency (which earns no interest) and chequing account deposits (which in his time typically earned little or no interest), he assumed that money has a zero rate of return. Bonds, the only alternative asset to money in Keynes's framework, have an expected return equal to the interest rate i.[5] As this interest rate rises (holding

---

[4]Note that the term *market for money* refers to the market for the medium of exchange, money. This market differs from the *money market* referred to by finance practitioners, which is the financial market in which short-term debt instruments are traded.

[5]Keynes did not actually assume that the expected returns on bonds equalled the interest rate but rather argued that they were closely related. This distinction makes no appreciable difference in our analysis.

everything else unchanged), the expected return on money falls relative to the expected return on bonds, and this causes the demand for money to fall.

We can also see that the demand for money and the interest rate should be negatively related by using the concept of **opportunity cost,** the amount of interest (expected return) sacrificed by not holding the alternative asset—in this case, a bond. As the interest rate on bonds i rises, the opportunity cost of holding money rises, and so money is less desirable and the quantity of money demanded must fall.

Figure 10 shows the quantity of money demanded at a number of interest rates, with all other economic variables, such as income and the price level, held constant. At an interest rate of 25%, point A shows that the quantity of money demanded is $100 billion. If the interest rate is at the lower rate of 20%, the opportunity cost of money is lower, and the quantity of money demanded rises to $200 billion, as indicated by the move from point A to point B. If the interest rate is even lower, the quantity of money demanded is even higher, as is indicated by points C, D, and E. The curve M^d connecting these points is the demand curve for money, and it slopes downward.

At this point in our analysis, we will assume that a central bank controls the amount of money supplied at a fixed quantity of $300 billion, so the supply curve for money M^s in the figure is a vertical line at $300 billion. The equilibrium where the quantity of money demanded equals the quantity of money supplied occurs at the intersection of the supply and demand curves at point C, where

$$M^d = M^s \tag{6}$$

The resulting equilibrium interest rate is at $i^* = 15\%$.

We can again see that there is a tendency to approach this equilibrium by first looking at the relationship of money demand and supply when the interest rate is above the equilibrium interest rate. When the interest rate is 25%, the quantity of money demanded at point A is $100 billion, yet the quantity of money supplied is $300 billion. The excess supply of money means that people are holding more money than they desire, so they will try to get rid of their excess money

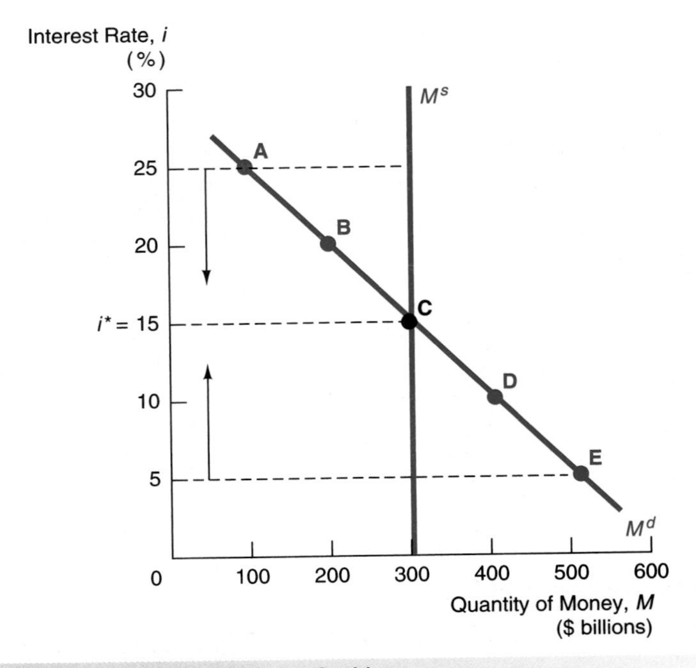

FIGURE 10 Equilibrium in the Market for Money

balances by trying to buy bonds. Accordingly, they will bid up the price of bonds, and as the bond price rises, the interest rate will fall toward the equilibrium interest rate of 15%. This tendency is shown by the downward arrow drawn at the interest rate of 25%.

Likewise, if the interest rate is 5%, the quantity of money demanded at point E is $500 billion, but the quantity of money supplied is only $300 billion. There is now an excess demand for money because people want to hold more money than they currently have. To try to get the money, they will sell their only other asset—bonds—and the price will fall. As the price of bonds falls, the interest rate will rise toward the equilibrium rate of 15%. Only when the interest rate is at its equilibrium value will there be no tendency for it to move further, and the interest rate will settle to its equilibrium value.

CHANGES IN EQUILIBRIUM INTEREST RATES

Analyzing how the equilibrium interest rate changes using the liquidity preference framework requires that we understand what causes the demand and supply curves for money to shift.

Study Guide Learning the liquidity preference framework also requires practising applications. When there is an application in the text to examine how the interest rate changes because some economic variable increases, see if you can draw the appropriate shifts in the supply and demand curves when this same economic variable decreases. And remember to use the *ceteris paribus* assumption: When examining the effect of a change in one variable, hold all other variables constant.

Shifts in the Demand for Money

In Keynes's liquidity preference analysis, two factors cause the demand curve for money to shift: income and the price level.

Income Effect In Keynes's view, there were two reasons why income would affect the demand for money. First, as an economy expands and income rises, wealth increases and people will want to hold more money as a store of value. Second, as the economy expands and income rises, people will want to carry out more transactions using money, with the result that they will also want to hold more money. The conclusion is that ***a higher level of income causes the demand for money to increase and the demand curve to shift to the right.***

Price-Level Effect Keynes took the view that people care about the amount of money they hold in real terms, that is, in terms of the goods and services that it can buy. When the price level rises, the same nominal quantity of money is no longer as valuable; it cannot be used to purchase as many real goods or services. To restore their holdings of money in real terms to its former level, people will want to hold a greater nominal quantity of money, so ***a rise in the price level causes the demand for money to increase and the demand curve to shift to the right.***

Shifts in the Supply of Money

We will assume that the supply of money is completely controlled by the central bank, which in Canada is the Bank of Canada. (Actually, the process that determines the money supply is substantially more complicated and involves banks, depositors, and borrowers from banks. We will study it in more detail later in the book.) For now, all we need to know is that ***an increase in the money supply engineered by the Bank of Canada will shift the supply curve for money to the right.***

Application: Changes in the Equilibrium Interest Rate Due to Changes in Income, the Price Level, or the Money Supply

To see how the liquidity preference framework can be used to analyze the movement of interest rates, we will again look at several applications that will be useful in evaluating the effect of monetary policy on interest rates. (As a study aid, Table 4 on page 94 summarizes the shifts in the demand and supply curves for money.)

Changes in Income

When income is rising during a business cycle expansion, we have seen that the demand for money will rise. It is shown in Figure 11 by the shift rightward in the demand curve from M_1^d to M_2^d. The new equilibrium is reached at point 2 at the intersection of the M_2^d curve with the money supply curve M^s. As you can see, the equilibrium interest rate rises from i_1 to i_2. The liquidity preference framework thus generates the conclusion that ***when income is rising during a business cycle expansion (holding other economic variables constant), interest rates will rise.*** This conclusion is unambiguous when contrasted to the conclusion reached about the effects of a change in income on interest rates using the loanable funds framework.

Changes in the Price Level

When the price level rises, the value of money in terms of what it can purchase is lower. To restore their purchasing power in real terms to its former level, peo-

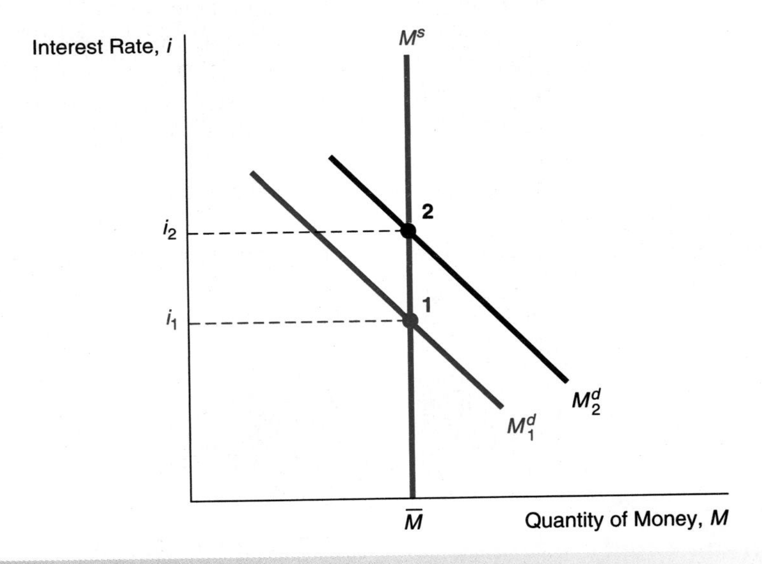

FIGURE 11 Response to a Change in Income

In a business cycle expansion, when income is rising, the demand curve shifts from M_1^d to M_2^d. The supply curve is fixed at $M^s = \overline{M}$. The equilibrium interest rate rises from i_1 to i_2.

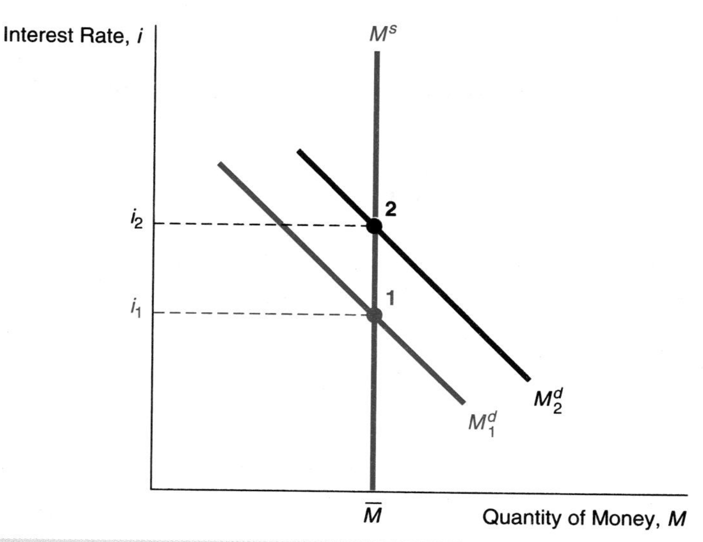

FIGURE 12 Response to a Change in the Price Level

An increase in price level shifts the money demand curve from M_1^d to M_2^d, and the equilibrium interest rate rises from i_1 to i_2.

ple will want to hold a greater nominal quantity of money. A higher price level shifts the demand curve for money to the right from M_1^d to M_2^d (see Figure 12). The equilibrium moves from point 1 to point 2, where the equilibrium interest rate has risen from i_1 to i_2, illustrating that ***when the price level increases, with the supply of money and other economic variables held constant, interest rates will rise.***

Changes in the Money Supply

Money supply data, which the Bank of Canada reports, are available online at www.bankofcanada.ca/en/graphs/a1-table.htm

An increase in the money supply due to expansionary monetary policy by the Bank of Canada implies that the supply curve for money shifts to the right. As is shown in Figure 13 (page 95) by the movement of the supply curve from M_1^s to M_2^s, the equilibrium moves from point 1 down to point 2, where the M_2^s supply curve intersects with the demand curve M^d and the equilibrium interest rate has fallen from i_1 to i_2. ***When the money supply increases (everything else remaining equal), interest rates will decline.***[6]

Application Money and Interest Rates

The liquidity preference analysis in Figure 13 seems to lead to the conclusion that an increase in the money supply will lower interest rates. This conclusion has important policy implications because it has frequently caused politicians to call for a more rapid growth of the money supply in order to drive down interest rates.

But is this conclusion that money and interest rates should be negatively related correct? Might there be other important factors left out of the liquidity preference analysis in Figure 13 that would reverse this conclusion? We will provide answers to these questions by applying the supply and demand analysis we

[6]This same result can be generated using the loanable funds framework. The primary way that a central bank produces an increase in the money supply is by buying bonds and thereby decreasing the supply of bonds to the public. The resulting shift to the left of the supply curve for bonds will lead to a decline in the equilibrium interest rate.

TABLE 4 SUMMARY Factors That Shift the Demand for and Supply of Money

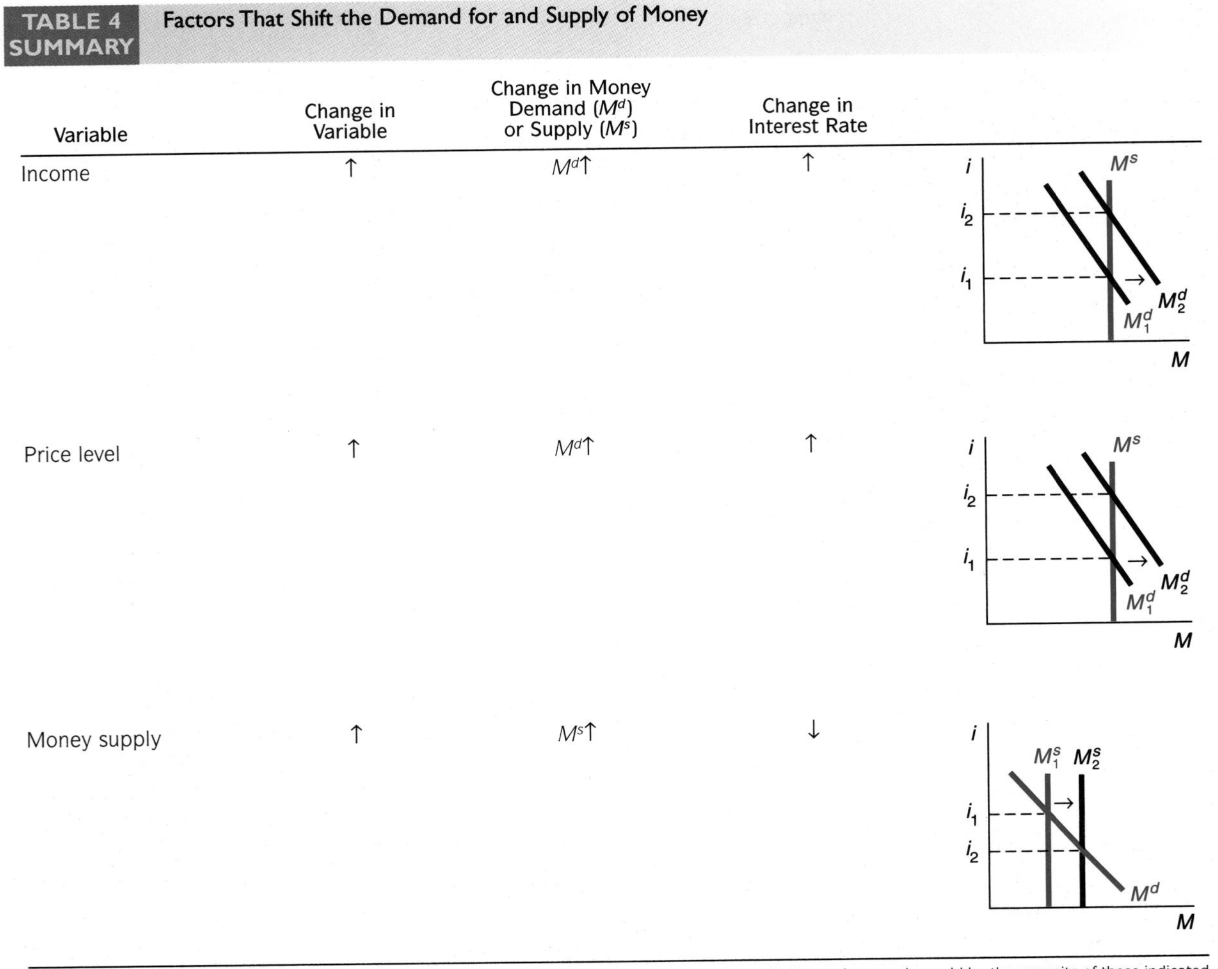

Variable	Change in Variable	Change in Money Demand (M^d) or Supply (M^s)	Change in Interest Rate
Income	↑	M^d↑	↑
Price level	↑	M^d↑	↑
Money supply	↑	M^s↑	↓

Note: Only increases (↑) in the variables are shown. The effect of decreases in the variables on the change in demand or supply would be the opposite of those indicated in the remaining columns.

have learned in this chapter to obtain a deeper understanding of the relationship between money and interest rates.

An important criticism of the conclusion that a rise in the money supply lowers interest rates has been raised by Milton Friedman, a Nobel laureate in economics. He acknowledges that the liquidity preference analysis is correct and calls the result—that an increase in the money supply (*everything else remaining equal*) lowers interest rates—the *liquidity effect.* However, he views the liquidity effect as merely part of the story: An increase in the money supply might not leave "everything else equal" and will have other effects on the economy that may make interest rates rise. If these effects are substantial, it is entirely possible that when the money supply rises, interest rates too may rise.

We have already laid the groundwork to discuss these other effects because we have shown how changes in income, the price level, and expected inflation affect the equilibrium interest rate.

Study Guide To get further practice with the loanable funds and liquidity preference frameworks, show how the effects discussed here work by drawing the supply and demand diagrams that explain each effect. This exercise will also improve your understanding of the effect of money on interest rates.

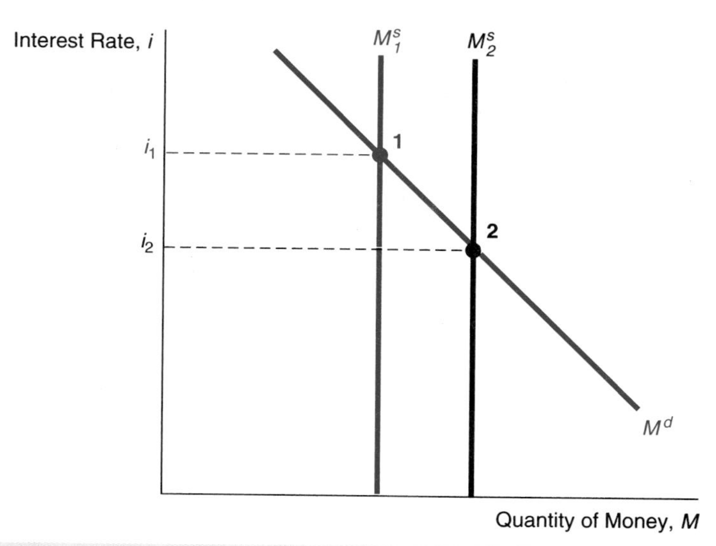

FIGURE 13 Response to a Change in the Money Supply

When the money supply increases, the supply curve shifts from M_1^s to M_2^s, and the equilibrium interest rate falls from i_1 to i_2.

1. *Income effect.* Because an increasing money supply is an expansionary influence on the economy, it should raise national income and wealth. Both the liquidity preference and loanable funds frameworks indicate that interest rates will then rise (see Figures 7 and 11). Thus ***the income effect of an increase in the money supply is a rise in interest rates in response to the higher level of income.***
2. *Price-level effect.* An increase in the money supply can also cause the overall price level in the economy to rise. The liquidity preference framework predicts that this will lead to a rise in interest rates. So ***the price-level effect from an increase in the money supply is a rise in interest rates in response to the rise in the price level.***
3. *Expected-inflation effect.* The rising price level (the higher inflation rate) that results from an increase in the money supply also affects interest rates by affecting the expected inflation rate. Specifically, an increase in the money supply may lead people to expect a higher price level in the future—hence the expected inflation rate will be higher. The loanable funds framework has shown us that this increase in expected inflation will lead to a higher level of interest rates. Therefore, ***the expected-inflation effect of an increase in the money supply is a rise in interest rates in response to the rise in the expected inflation rate.***

At first glance it might appear that the price-level effect and the expected-inflation effect are the same thing. They both indicate that increases in the price level induced by an increase in the money supply will raise interest rates. However, there is a subtle difference between the two, and this is why they are discussed as two separate effects.

Suppose that there is a onetime increase in the money supply today that leads to a rise in prices to a permanently higher level by next year. As the price level rises over this year, the interest rate will rise via the price-level effect. Only at the end of the year, when the price level has risen to its peak, will the price-level effect be at a maximum.

The rising price level will also raise interest rates via the expected-inflation effect because people will expect that inflation will be higher over the course of the year. However, when the price level stops rising next year, inflation and the expected inflation rate will fall back down to zero. Any rise in interest rates as a result of the earlier rise in expected inflation will then be reversed. We thus see that in contrast to the price-level effect, which reaches its greatest impact next year, the expected-inflation effect will have its smallest impact (zero impact) next year. The basic difference between the two effects, then, is that the price-level effect remains even after prices have stopped rising, whereas the expected-inflation effect disappears.

An important point is that the expected-inflation effect will persist only as long as the price level continues to rise. A onetime increase in the money supply will not produce a continually rising price level; only a higher rate of money supply growth will. Thus a higher rate of money supply growth is needed if the expected-inflation effect is to persist.

Does a Higher Rate of Growth of the Money Supply Lower Interest Rates?

We can now put together all the effects we have discussed to help us decide whether our analysis supports the politicians who advocate a greater rate of growth of the money supply when they feel that interest rates are too high. Of all the effects, only the liquidity effect indicates that a higher rate of money growth will cause a decline in interest rates. In contrast, the income, price-level, and expected-inflation effects indicate that interest rates will rise when money growth is higher. Which of these effects are largest, and how quickly do they take effect? The answers are critical in determining whether interest rates will rise or fall when money supply growth is increased.

Generally, the liquidity effect from the greater money growth takes effect immediately because the rising money supply leads to an immediate decline in the equilibrium interest rate. The income and price-level effects take time to work because the increasing money supply takes time to raise the price level and income, which in turn raise interest rates. The expected-inflation effect, which also raises interest rates, can be slow or fast, depending on whether people adjust their expectations of inflation slowly or quickly when the money growth rate is increased.

Three possibilities are outlined in Figure 14; each shows how interest rates respond over time to an increased rate of money supply growth starting at time T. Panel (a) shows a case in which the liquidity effect dominates the other effects so that the interest rate falls from i_1 at time T to a final level of i_2. The liquidity effect operates quickly to lower the interest rate, but as time goes by, the other effects start to reverse some of the decline. Because the liquidity effect is larger than the others, however, the interest rate never rises back to its initial level.

Panel (b) has a lesser liquidity effect than the other effects, with the expected-inflation effect operating slowly because expectations of inflation are slow to adjust upward. Initially, the liquidity effect drives down the interest rate. Then the income, price-level, and expected-inflation effects begin to raise it. Because these effects are dominant, the interest rate eventually rises above its initial level to i_2. In the short run, lower interest rates result from increased money growth, but eventually they end up climbing above the initial level.

Panel (c) has the expected-inflation effect dominating as well as operating rapidly because people quickly raise their expectation of inflation when the rate of money growth increases. The expected-inflation effect begins immediately to overpower the liquidity effect, and the interest rate immediately starts to climb. Over time, as the income and price-level effects start to take hold, the interest rate rises even higher, and the eventual outcome is an interest rate that is substantially above the initial interest rate. The result shows clearly that increasing money sup-

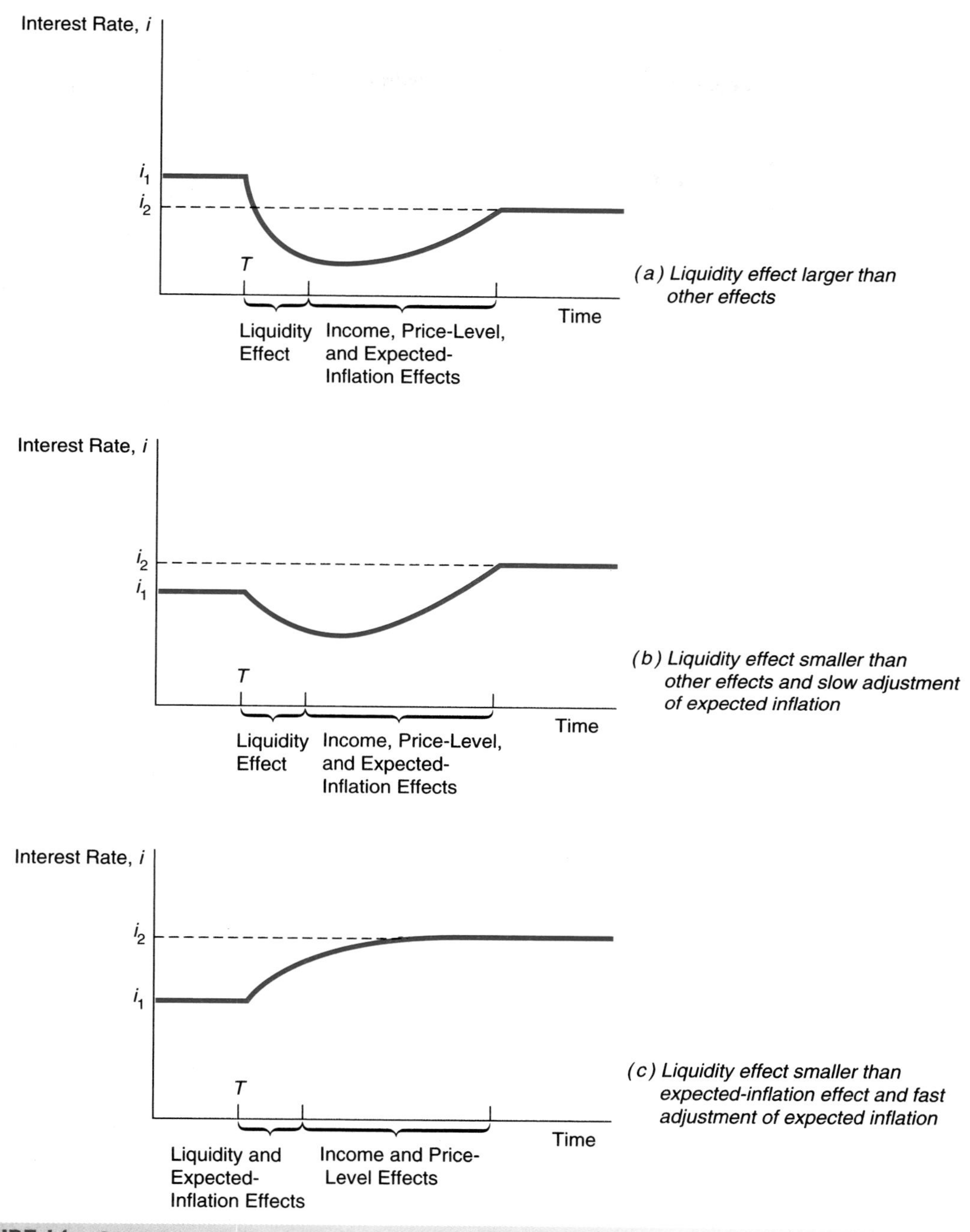

FIGURE 14 Response over Time to an Increase in Money Supply Growth

ply growth is not the answer to reducing interest rates but rather that money growth should be reduced in order to lower interest rates!

An important issue for economic policymakers is which of these three scenarios is closest to reality. If a decline in interest rates is desired, then an increase in money supply growth is called for when the liquidity effect dominates the other effects, as in panel (a). A decrease in money growth is appropriate if the other effects dominate the liquidity effect and expectations of inflation adjust rapidly, as in panel (c). If the other effects dominate the liquidity effect but expectations of inflation adjust only slowly, as in panel (b), then whether you want to increase or decrease money growth depends on whether you care more about what happens in the short run or the long run.

Which scenario is supported by the evidence? The relationship of interest rates and money growth from 1950 to 2001 is plotted in Figure 15. When the rate of money supply growth began to climb in the mid-1960s, interest rates rose, indicating that the liquidity effect was dominated by the price-level, income, and expected-inflation effects. By the 1970s, interest rates reached levels unprecedented in the period after World War II, as did the rate of money supply growth.

The scenario depicted in panel (a) of Figure 14 seems doubtful, and the case for lowering interest rates by raising the rate of money growth is much weakened. Looking back at Figure 6, which shows the relationship between interest rates and expected inflation, you should not find this too surprising. The rise in the rate of money supply growth in the 1960s and 1970s is matched by a large rise in expected inflation, which would lead us to predict that the expected-inflation effect would be dominant. It is the most plausible explanation for why interest rates rose in the face of higher money growth. However, Figure 15 does not really tell us which one of the two scenarios, panel (b) or panel (c) of Figure 14, is more accurate. It depends critically on how fast people's expectations about inflation adjust. However, recent research using more sophisticated methods than just looking at a graph like Figure 15 does indicate that increased money growth temporarily lowers short-term interest rates.[7]

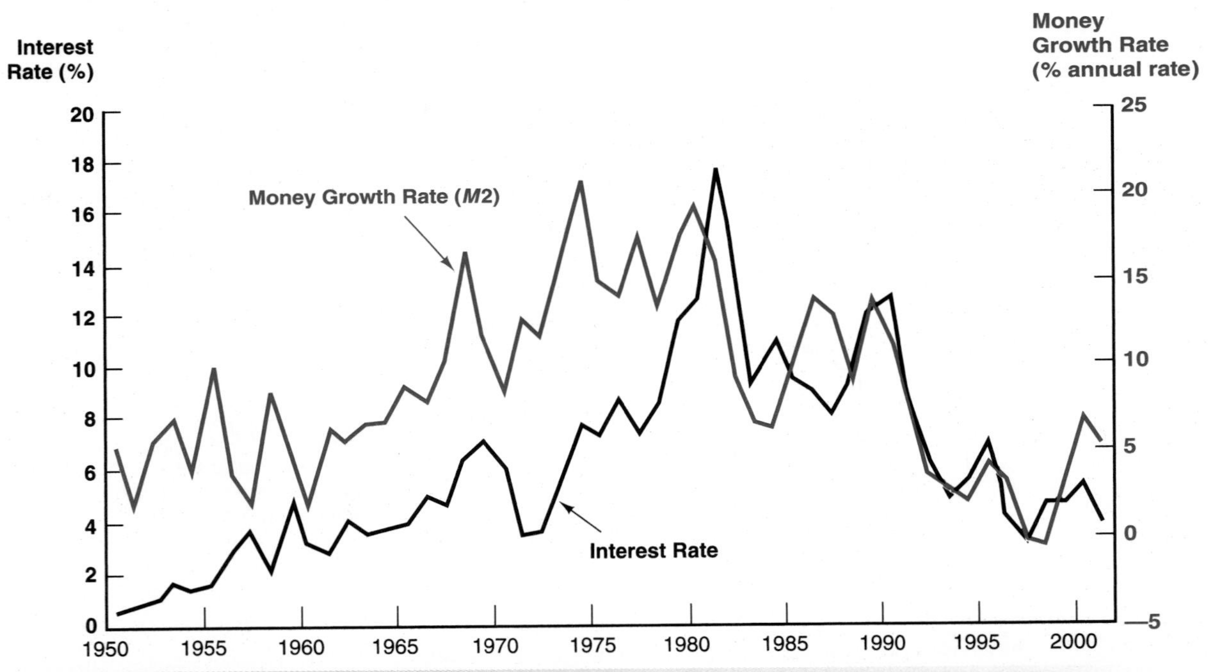

FIGURE 15 Money Growth (M2, Annual Rate) and Interest Rates (Three-Month Treasury Bills), 1950–2001

Source: Statistics Canada CANSIM II series V37128. From 1950 to 1967 the *M2* series is from Cherie Metcalf, Angela Redish, and Ronald Shearer, "New Estimates of the Canadian Money Stock: 1871–1967," The University of British Columbia, Discussion Paper No.: 96-17. From 1968 to 2001 it is Statistics Canada CANSIM II series V37128.

[7]See Lawrence J. Christiano and Martin Eichenbaum, "Identification and the Liquidity Effect of a Monetary Policy Shock," in *Business Cycles, Growth, and Political Economy,* ed. Alex Cukierman, Zvi Hercowitz, and Leonardo Leiderman (Cambridge, MA: MIT Press, 1992), pp. 335–370; Eric M. Leeper and David B. Gordon, "In Search of the Liquidity Effect," *Journal of Monetary Economics* 29 (1992): 341–370; Steven Strongin, "The Identification of Monetary Policy Disturbances: Explaining the Liquidity Puzzle," *Journal of Monetary Economics* 35 (1995): 463–497; and Adrian Pagan and John C. Robertson, "Resolving the Liquidity Effect," *Federal Reserve Bank of St. Louis Review* 77 (May–June 1995): 33–54.

THE PRACTISING FINANCIAL INSTITUTION MANAGER

Profiting from Interest-Rate Forecasts

Given the importance of interest rates, the media frequently report interest-rate forecasts, as the "Following the Financial News" box indicates. Because changes in interest rates have a major impact on the profitability of financial institutions, financial managers care a great deal about the path of future interest rates. Managers of financial institutions obtain interest-rate forecasts either by hiring their own staff economists to generate forecasts or by purchasing forecasts from other financial institutions or economic forecasting firms.

Several methods are used to produce interest-rate forecasts. One of the most popular is based on the loanable funds framework described earlier in the chapter, and it is used by many financial institutions. Using the loanable funds framework, analysts predict what will happen to the factors that affect the supply of and demand for bonds—factors such as the strength of the economy, the profitability of investment opportunities, the expected inflation rate, and the size of government deficits and borrowing. They then use the supply and demand analysis outlined in the chapter to come up with their interest-rate forecasts.

Forecasting done with the loanable funds framework often does not make use of formal economic models but rather depends on the judgment or "feel" of the forecaster. An alternative method of forecasting interest rates makes use of **econometric models**, models whose equations are estimated with statistical procedures using past data. These models involve interlocking equations that, once input variables such as the behaviour of government spending and monetary policy are plugged in, produce simultaneous forecasts of many variables including interest rates. The basic assumption of these forecasting models is that the estimated relationships among variables will continue to hold up in the future. Given this assumption, the forecaster makes predictions of the expected path of the input variables and then lets the model generate forecasts of variables such as interest rates.

Many of these econometric models are quite large, involving hundreds of and sometimes more than a thousand equations, and consequently require computers to produce their forecasts. In addition, many of these models rely heavily on the liquidity preference framework to produce their interest-rate forecasts and so are particularly concerned with developments in the market for money along lines we have discussed in the text. Prominent examples of these large-scale econometric models used by the private sector include those developed by Wharton Econometric Forecasting Associates, Chase Econometric Associates, and Data Resources, Inc. To generate its interest-rate forecasts, the Bank of Canada makes use of its own large-scale econometric model, although it makes use of judgmental forecasts as well.

Managers of financial institutions rely on these forecasts to make decisions about which assets they should hold. A manager who believes the forecast that long-term interest rates will fall in the future is reliable would seek to purchase long-term bonds for the asset account because, as we have seen in Chapter 3, the drop in interest rates will produce large capital gains. Conversely, if forecasts say that interest rates are likely to rise in the future, the manager will prefer to hold short-term bonds or loans in the portfolio in order to avoid potential capital losses on long-term securities.

Forecasts of interest rates also help managers decide whether to borrow long term or short term. If interest rates are forecast to rise in the future, the financial institution manager will want to lock in the low interest rates by borrowing long-term; if the forecasts say that interest rates will fall, the manager will seek to borrow short term in order to take advantage of low interest-rate costs in the future.

FOLLOWING THE FINANCIAL NEWS

Forecasting Interest Rates

Forecasting interest rates is a time-honoured profession. Financial economists are hired (sometimes at very high salaries) to forecast interest rates because businesses need to know what the rates will be in order to plan their future spending, and banks and investors require interest-rate forecasts in order to decide which assets to buy. The media frequently report interest rate forecasts by leading prognosticators. These forecasts are produced using a wide range of statistical models and a number of different sources of information. One of the most popular methods is based on the loanable funds framework described earlier in the chapter. Using this framework, analysts predict what will happen to the factors that affect the supply of and demand for bonds and then use the supply and demand analysis outlined in the chapter to come up with their interest-rate forecasts.

An alternative method of forecasting interest rates makes use of econometric models, models whose equations are estimated with statistical procedures using past data. Many of these econometric models are quite large, involving hundreds of and sometimes more than a thousand interlocking equations. They produce simultaneous forecasts for many variables, including interest rates, under the assumption that the estimated relationships between variables do not change over time.

Forecasting interest rates is a perilous business. To their embarrassment, even the top experts are frequently far off in their forecasts.

Clearly, good forecasts of future interest rates are extremely valuable to the financial institution manager, who, not surprisingly, would be willing to pay a lot for accurate forecasts. Unfortunately, interest-rate forecasting is a perilous business, and even the top forecasters, to their embarrassment, are frequently far off in their forecasts.

SUMMARY

1. The quantity demanded of an asset is (a) positively related to wealth, (b) positively related to the expected return on the asset relative to alternative assets, (c) negatively related to the riskiness of the asset relative to alternative assets, and (d) positively related to the liquidity of the asset relative to alternative assets.
2. Diversification (the holding of more than one asset) benefits investors because it reduces the risk they face, and the benefits are greater the less returns on securities move together.
3. The supply and demand analysis for bonds, known as the loanable funds framework, provides one theory of how interest rates are determined. It predicts that interest rates will change when there is a change in demand because of changes in income (or wealth), expected returns, risk, or liquidity, or when there is a change in supply because of changes in the attractiveness of investment opportunities, the real cost of borrowing, or government activities.
4. An alternative theory of how interest rates are determined is provided by the liquidity preference framework, which analyzes the supply of and demand for money. It shows that interest rates will change when there is a change in the demand for money because of changes in income or the price level or when there is a change in the supply of money.
5. There are four possible effects of an increase in the money supply on interest rates: the liquidity effect, the income effect, the price-level effect, and the expected-inflation effect. The liquidity effect indicates that a rise in money supply growth will lead to a decline in interest rates; the other effects work in the opposite direction. The evidence seems to indicate that the income, price-level, and expected-inflation effects dominate the liquidity effect such that an increase in money supply growth leads to higher rather than lower interest rates.

KEY TERMS

asset, *p. 67*
asset market approach, *p. 77*
demand curve, *p. 72*
diversification, *p. 71*
econometric model, *p. 99*
excess demand, *p. 75*
excess supply, *p. 75*
expected return, *p. 67*
Fisher effect, *p. 83*
liquidity, *p. 67*
liquidity preference framework, *p. 89*
loanable funds, *p. 76*
loanable funds framework, *p. 76*
market equilibrium, *p. 74*
opportunity cost, *p. 96*
risk, *p. 67*
standard deviation, *p. 69*
supply curve, *p. 74*
wealth, *p. 67*

QUESTIONS AND PROBLEMS

1. Explain why you would be more or less willing to buy a share of Air Canada stock in the following situations:
a. Your wealth falls.
b. You expect it to appreciate in value.
c. The bond market becomes more liquid.
d. You expect gold to appreciate in value.
e. Prices in the bond market become more volatile.

***2.** Explain why you would be more or less willing to buy a house under the following circumstances:
a. You just inherited $100 000.
b. Real estate commissions fall from 6% of the sales price to 4% of the sales price.
c. You expect Air Canada stock to double in value next year.
d. Prices in the stock market become more volatile.
e. You expect housing prices to fall.

3. "The more risk-averse people are, the more likely they are to diversify." Is this statement true, false, or uncertain? Explain your answer.

***4.** I own a professional football team, and I plan to diversify by purchasing shares in either a company that owns a pro basketball team or a pharmaceutical company. Which of these two investments is more likely to reduce the overall risk I face? Why?

5. "No one who is risk-averse will ever buy a security that has a lower expected return, more risk, and less liquidity than another security." Is this statement true, false, or uncertain? Explain your answer.

For items 6–15, answer each question by drawing the appropriate supply and demand diagrams.

***6.** An important way in which the Bank of Canada decreases the money supply is by selling bonds to the public. Using the loanable funds framework, show what effect this action has on interest rates. Is your answer consistent with what you would expect to find with the liquidity preference framework?

7. Using both the liquidity preference and loanable funds frameworks, show why interest rates are procyclical (rising when the economy is expanding and falling during recessions).

***8.** Why should a rise in the price level (but not in expected inflation) cause interest rates to rise when the nominal money supply is fixed?

9. What effect will a sharp increase in personal savings rates have on Canadian interest rates?

10. What effect will a sudden increase in the volatility of gold prices have on interest rates?

***11.** How might a sudden increase in people's expectations of future real estate prices affect interest rates?

12. Explain what effect a large federal deficit might have on interest rates.

***13.** Using both the loanable funds and liquidity preference frameworks, show what the effect is on interest rates when the riskiness of bonds rises. Are the results the same in the two frameworks?

14. If the price level falls next year, remaining fixed thereafter, and the money supply is fixed, what is likely to happen to interest rates over the next two years? (Hint: Consider both the price-level effect and the expected-inflation effect.)

***15.** Will there be an effect on interest rates if brokerage commissions on stocks fall? Explain your answer.

Predicting the Future

16. The governor of the Bank of Canada announces in a press conference that he will fight the higher inflation rate with a new anti-inflation program. Predict what will happen to interest rates if the public believes him.

***17.** The governor of the Bank of Canada announces that interest rates will rise sharply next year, and the market believes him. What will happen to today's interest rate on long-term corporate bonds?

18. Predict what will happen to interest rates if the public suddenly expects a large increase in stock prices.

***19.** Predict what will happen to interest rates if prices in the bond market become more volatile.

20. If the next governor of the Bank of Canada has a reputation for advocating an even slower rate of money growth than the current governor, what will happen to interest rates? Discuss the possible resulting situations.

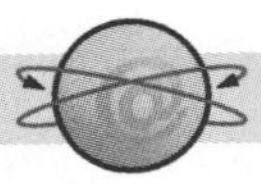

WEB EXERCISES

The Behaviour of Interest Rates

1. One of the largest single influences on the level of interest rates is inflation. There are a number of sites that report inflation over time. Go to www.bankofcanada.ca/en/cpi.htm and review the data available. Insert these data into an Excel spreadsheet using the method in Chapter 1. What has the average rate of inflation been since 1995? What year had the lowest level of inflation? What year had the highest level of inflation?
2. Increasing prices erode the purchasing power of the dollar. It is interesting to compute what goods would have cost at some point in the past after adjusting for inflation. Go to www.bankofcanada.ca/en/inflation_calc.htm. What would something that cost $10 000 when you were born cost you today?
3. One of the points made in this chapter is that inflation erodes investment returns. Go to http://www.src-net.com/InvestmentMultiplier/iminflation.htm and review how changes in inflation alter your real return. What happens to the difference between the adjusted value of an investment compared to its inflation-adjusted value as
   - **a.** Inflation increases?
   - **b.** The investment horizon lengthens?
   - **c.** Expected return increases?

CHAPTER 4

Appendix: Applying the Asset Market Approach to a Commodity Market: The Case of Gold

Both models of interest-rate determination in Chapter 4 make use of an asset market approach in which supply and demand are always considered in terms of stocks of assets (amounts at a given point in time). The asset market approach is useful in understanding not only why interest rates fluctuate but also how any asset's price is determined.

One asset that has fascinated people for thousands of years is gold. It has been a driving force in history: The conquest of the Americas by Europeans was to a great extent the result of the quest for gold, to cite just one example. The fascination with gold continues to the present day, and developments in the gold market are followed closely by financial analysts and the media. This appendix shows how the asset market approach can be applied to understanding the behaviour of commodity markets, in particular the gold market. (The analysis in this appendix can also be used to understand behaviour in many other asset markets.)

SUPPLY AND DEMAND IN THE GOLD MARKET

The analysis of a commodity market, such as the gold market, proceeds in a similar fashion to the analysis of the bond market by examining the supply of and demand for the commodity. We again use our analysis of the determinants of asset demand to obtain a demand curve for gold, which shows the relationship between the quantity of gold demanded and the price when all other economic variables are held constant.

Demand Curve

To derive the relationship between the quantity of gold demanded and its price, we again recognize that an important determinant of the quantity demanded is its expected return:

$$R^e = \frac{P^e_{t+1} - P_t}{P_t} = g^e$$

where
R^e = expected return
P_t = price of gold today
P^e_{t+1} = expected price of gold next year
g^e = expected capital gain

In deriving the demand curve, we hold all other variables constant, particularly the expected price of gold next year P^e_{t+1}. With a given value of the expected price of gold next year P^e_{t+1}, a lower price of gold today P_t means that there will be a greater appreciation in the price of gold over the coming year. The result is that a lower price of gold today implies a higher expected capital gain over the coming year and hence a higher expected return: $R^e = (P^e_{t+1} - P_t)/P_t$. Thus because the price of gold today (which for simplicity we will denote as P) is lower, the expected return on gold is higher, and the quantity demanded is higher. Consequently, the demand curve G^d_1 slopes downward in Figure A1.

Supply Curve

To derive the supply curve, expressing the relationship between the quantity supplied and the price, we again assume that all other economic variables are held constant. A higher price of gold will induce producers to mine for extra gold and also possibly induce governments to sell some of their gold stocks to the public, thus increasing the quantity supplied. Hence the supply curve G^s_1 in Figure A1 slopes upward. Notice that the supply curve in the figure is drawn to be very steep. The reason for this is that the actual amount of gold produced in any year is only a tiny fraction of the outstanding stock of gold that has been accumulated over hundreds of years. Thus the increase in the quantity of the gold supplied in response to a higher price is only a small fraction of the stock of gold, resulting in a very steep supply curve.

Market Equilibrium

Market equilibrium in the gold market occurs when the quantity of gold demanded equals the quantity of gold supplied:

$$G^d = G^s$$

With the initial demand and supply curves of G^d_1 and G^s_1, equilibrium occurs at point 1, where these curves intersect at a gold price of P_1. At a price above this equilibrium, the amount of gold supplied exceeds the amount demanded, and this condition of excess supply leads to a decline in the gold price until it

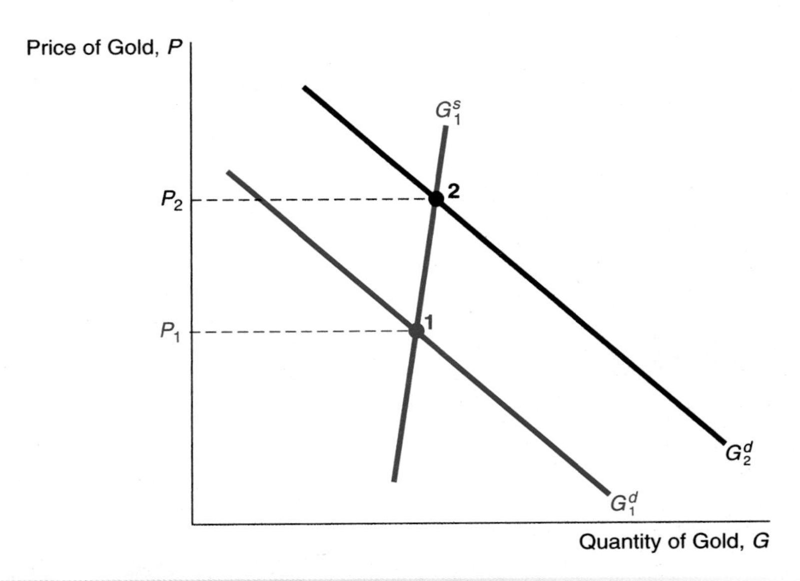

FIGURE A1 A Change in the Equilibrium Price of Gold

When the demand curve shifts rightward from G^d_1 to G^d_2, say, because expected inflation rises, equilibrium moves from point 1 to point 2, and the equilibrium price of gold rises from P_1 to P_2.

reaches P_1, the equilibrium price. Similarly, if the price is below P_1, there is excess demand for gold, which drives the price upward until it settles at the equilibrium price P_1.

CHANGES IN THE EQUILIBRIUM PRICE OF GOLD

Changes in the equilibrium price of gold occur when there is a shift in either the supply curve or the demand curve, that is, when the quantity demanded or supplied changes at each given price of gold in response to a change in some factor other than today's gold price.

Shift in the Demand Curve for Gold

Our analysis of the determinants of asset demand in the chapter provides the factors that shift the demand curve for gold: wealth, expected return on gold relative to alternative assets, riskiness of gold relative to alternative assets, and liquidity of gold relative to alternative assets. The analysis of how changes in each of these factors shift the demand curve for gold is the same as that found in the chapter.

When wealth rises, at a given price of gold, the quantity demanded increases, and the demand curve shifts to the right, as in Figure A1. When the expected return on gold relative to other assets rises—either because speculators think that the future price of gold will be higher or because the expected return on other assets declines—gold becomes more desirable; the quantity demanded therefore increases at any given price of gold, and the demand curve shifts to the right, as in Figure A1. When the relative riskiness of gold declines, either because gold prices become less volatile or because returns on other assets become more volatile, gold becomes more desirable, the quantity demanded at every given price rises, and the demand curve again shifts to the right. When the gold market becomes relatively more liquid and gold therefore becomes more desirable, the quantity demanded at any given price rises, and the demand curve also shifts to the right, as in Figure A1.

Shifts in the Supply Curve for Gold

The supply curve for gold shifts when there are changes in technology that make gold mining more efficient or when governments at any given price of gold decide to increase sales of their holdings of gold. In these cases, the quantity of gold supplied at any given price increases, and the supply curve shifts to the right.

Application Changes in the Equilibrium Price of Gold Due to a Rise in Expected Inflation

To illustrate how changes in the equilibrium price of gold occur when supply and demand curves shift, let's look at what happens when there is a change in expected inflation.

Suppose that expected inflation is 5% and the initial supply and demand curves are at G_1^s and G_1^d so that the equilibrium price of gold is at P_1 in Figure A1. If expected inflation now rises to 10%, prices of goods and commodities next year will be expected to be higher than they otherwise would have been, and the price of gold next year P_{t+1}^e will also be expected to be higher than otherwise. Now at any given price of gold today, gold is expected to have a greater rate of appreciation over the coming year and hence a higher expected capital gain and return. The greater expected return means that the quantity of gold demanded increases at any given price, thus shifting the demand curve from G_1^d to G_2^d. Equilibrium therefore moves from point 1 to point 2, and the price of gold rises from P_1 to P_2.

By using a supply and demand diagram like that in Figure A1, you should be able to see that if the expected rate of inflation falls, the price of gold today will also fall. We thus reach the following conclusion: ***The price of gold should be positively related to the expected inflation rate.***

Because the gold market responds immediately to any changes in expected inflation, it is considered a good barometer of the trend of inflation in the future. Indeed, Alan Greenspan, the chairman of the Board of Governors of the U.S. Federal Reserve System, has advocated using the price of gold as an indicator of inflationary pressures in the U.S. economy. Not surprisingly, then, the gold market is followed closely by financial analysts and monetary policymakers.

Study Guide To give yourself practice with supply and demand analysis in the gold market, see if you can analyze what happens to the price of gold for the following situations, remembering that all other things are held constant: (1) interest rates rise, (2) the gold market becomes more liquid, (3) the volatility of gold prices increases, (4) the stock market is expected to turn bullish in the near future, (5) investors suddenly become fearful that there will be a collapse in real estate prices, and (6) Russia sells a lot of gold in the open market to raise hard currency to feed its people.

The analysis in this appendix can also be applied to many other asset markets. See if you can apply the analysis here to understand fluctuations in the prices of classic comic books, old baseball cards, oil, Rembrandt paintings, or other commodities mentioned in the following application.

Application The "Commodities" Column

READING THE *WALL STREET JOURNAL*

The supply and demand analysis in this appendix can help you evaluate events in commodity markets that are reported in the media. Every day, the *Wall Street Journal* reports on developments in the commodities markets on the previous business day in its "Commodities" column, an example of which is found in the "Following the Financial News" box.

The column points out that soybean prices fell to new contract lows with fears of a bumper crop of soybeans in South America. Our supply and demand analysis explains why these fears would cause soybean prices to fall.

The column discusses why the soybean crop is likely to be so good in the near future. The resulting expanded supply will cause the supply curve for soybeans to shift out to the right, thus causing soybean prices to fall in the future. This will cause soybean prices in today's market to fall because the lower future prices means that the expected return on soybeans has declined, thus shifting the demand curve for soybeans today to the left.

FOLLOWING THE FINANCIAL NEWS

The "Commodities" Column

The "Commodities" column appears daily in the *Wall Street Journal;* an example is presented here. It is typically found in the third section, "Money and Investing."

FUTURES PRICES

Soybean Prices Drop on Fears of a Bumper Crop

COMMODITIES

By DYANNA DECOLA
Dow Jones Newswires

CHICAGO—Chicago Board of Trade soybean prices tumbled yesterday within four cents of making new contract lows as speculators sold aggressively and fears circulated about a huge South American soybean crop.

Tuesday's monthly report from the U.S. Department of Agriculture included a raised estimate for Argentine production, while analysts also pointed to favorable weather for the Brazilian and Argentine crops.

The January contract fell five cents to $4.3250 per bushel.

Traders said the selloff was mostly technical in nature, with sell stops—pre-placed sales orders—triggered as the market fell through what were seen as key levels on price charts.

Many traders said the price performance yesterday suggested more losses are ahead. Some believe that by week's end, January soybeans could test and possibly break the contract low of $4.2625.

"We could get there this week if we keep doing this," said Victor Lespinasse, a grain trader with A.G. Edwards, Chicago. "We were going down in fairly good volume today."

Market watchers said ideal planting and growing conditions in the Southern Hemisphere continue to weigh on the market. "Favorable South American weather has hung over the soy complex for most of the past month," said Dan Basse, executive vice president of consulting firm AgResource Co. in Chicago.

The U.S. is the world's largest producer of soybeans. Brazil and Argentina trail the U.S.

Brazilian farmers are in the final stages of the planting season, and Argentina is roughly two-thirds finished with planting.

"We're just now entering the real critical stage for yields in South America," said Jim Bower of Bower Trading, a brokerage firm in Lafayette, Ind. "As we enter this stage, it's important the trade focuses on the weather down there over the next five to six weeks."

On Tuesday, the Agriculture Department pegged Argentina's crop at 28.8 million metric tons, up 800,000 metric tons from its November estimate.

"Evidence of higher Argentine bean production has bolstered talk of impending competition and kept buying interests limited," said Professional Farmers of America, an agricultural-consulting firm in Ceder Falls, Iowa.

Brazil's 2001-02 soybean crop is projected by the Agriculture Department at 41.5 million metric tons, unchanged from the previous month's estimate and above the 38.8 million tons projected for 2000-01.

Also in the background, talk of economic woes in Argentina remains a bearish factor in the marketplace, some brokers said.

In other commodity markets:

CRUDE OIL: Prices gained moderately at the New York Mercantile Exchange on inventory data from the Department of Energy. The January contract rose 28 cents to $18.36 a barrel. The department said inventories shrank by 2.4 million barrels to 309.1 million barrels in the week ended Dec. 7, as imports dropped.

COPPER: Prices fell on the Comex division of the New York Mercantile Exchange as speculative funds sold and after another large rise in warehouse stocks overnight. The March contract dropped a penny to 67.90 cents a pound.

Another Hill of Beans?

Soybean-futures prices fell on talk of a possible bumper crop in Argentina; settle price in dollars per bushel

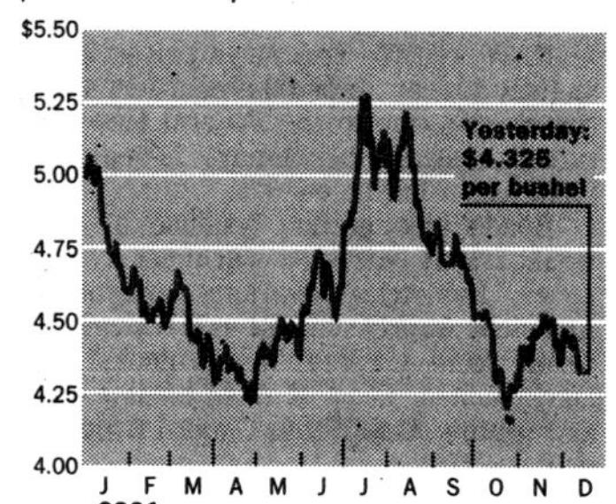

Source: Chicago Board of Trade via Thomson Financial/Datastream

COMMODITY INDEXES

Wednesday, December 12, 2001

	CLOSE		NET CHG.	YR. AGO
Dow Jones-AIG Futures..	87.557	–	0.331	111.417
Dow Jones Spot...........	95.82	–	0.69	113.81
Reuter U.K....................	1177.74	+	1.55	1404.50
C R B Bridge Futures...	188.15	–	0.76	227.32

Chapter 5

The Risk and Term Structure of Interest Rates

Preview

In our supply and demand analysis of interest-rate behaviour in Chapter 4, we examined the determination of just one interest rate. Yet we saw earlier that there are enormous numbers of bonds on which the interest rates can and do differ. In this chapter we complete the interest-rate picture by examining the relationship of the various interest rates to one another. Understanding why they differ from bond to bond can help businesses, banks, insurance companies, and private investors decide which bonds to purchase as investments or which ones to sell.

We first look at why bonds with the same term to maturity have different interest rates. The relationship among these interest rates is called the **risk structure of interest rates**, although risk, liquidity, and income tax rules all play a role in determining the risk structure. A bond's term to maturity also affects its interest rate, and the relationship among interest rates on bonds with different terms to maturity is called the **term structure of interest rates**. In this chapter we examine the sources and causes of fluctuations in interest rates relative to one another and look at a number of theories that explain these fluctuations.

RISK STRUCTURE OF INTEREST RATES

Figure 1 shows the yields to maturity for several categories of long-term bonds from 1980 to 2001. It shows us two important features of interest-rate behaviour for bonds of the same maturity: Interest rates on different categories of bonds differ from one another in any given year, and the spread (or difference) among the interest rates varies over time. The interest rates on corporate bonds, for example, are higher than those on Canada bonds and provincial bonds. In addition, the spread between the interest rates on corporate bonds and Canada bonds was very large during the 1980–1982 and 1990–1991 recessions, was smaller during the mid-1990s, and then widened again in the late 1990s (see also Figure 3). What factors are responsible for these phenomena?

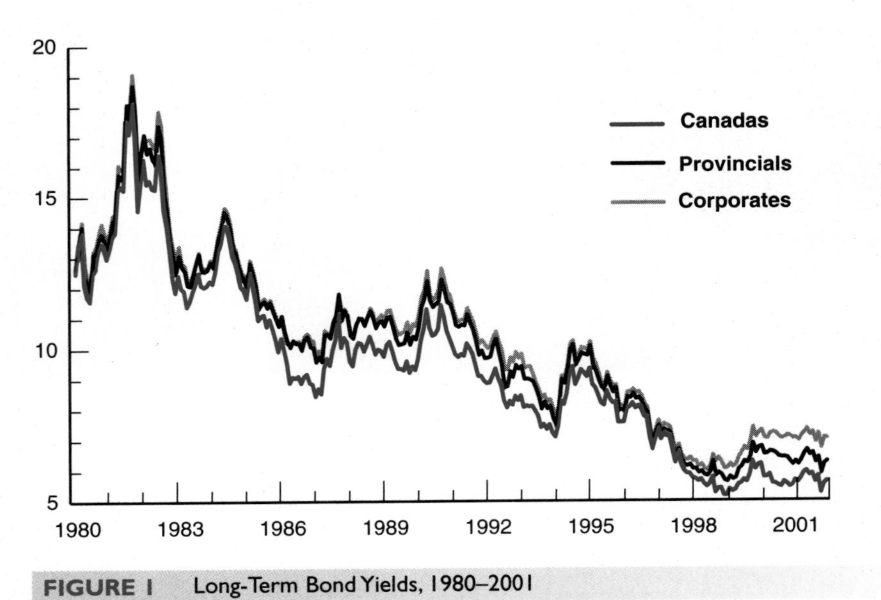

FIGURE 1 Long-Term Bond Yields, 1980–2001

Source: Statistics Canada CANSIM II series V122544, V122517, and V122518

Default Risk

One attribute of a bond that influences its interest rate is its **default risk**, the chance that the issuer of the bond will **default**, that is, be unable to make interest payments or pay off the face value when the bond matures. A corporation suffering big losses, such as Canadian Airlines did in the 1990s, might be more likely to suspend interest payments on its bonds.[1] The default risk on its bonds would therefore be quite high. By contrast, Canada bonds have usually been considered to have no default risk because the federal government can always increase taxes or even print money to pay off its obligations. Bonds like these with no default risk are called **default-free bonds**. The spread between the interest rates on bonds with default risk and default-free bonds, called the **risk premium**, indicates how much additional interest people must earn to be willing to hold a risky bond. Our supply and demand analysis of the bond market in Chapter 4 can be used to explain why a bond with default risk always has a positive risk premium and why the higher the default risk is, the larger the risk premium will be.

Study Guide Two exercises will help you gain a better understanding of the risk structure:

1. Put yourself in the shoes of an investor—see how your purchase decision would be affected by changes in risk and liquidity.
2. Practise drawing the appropriate shifts in the supply and demand curves when risk and liquidity change. For example, see if you can draw the appropriate shifts in the supply and demand curves when, in contrast to the examples in the text, a corporate bond has a decline in default risk or an improvement in its liquidity.

[1]Canadian Airlines did not default on its loans in this period. It would have were it not for a government bailout plan intended to preserve jobs that in effect provided Canadian Airlines with funds that it used to pay off creditors.

To examine the effect of default risk on interest rates, let us look at the supply and demand diagrams for the default-free (Canada) and corporate long-term bond markets in Figure 2. To make the diagrams somewhat easier to read, let's assume that initially there is no possibility of default on the corporate bonds, so they are default-free, like Canada bonds. In this case, these two bonds have the same attributes (identical risk and maturity); their equilibrium prices and interest rates will initially be equal ($P_1^c = P_1^T$ and $i_1^c = i_1^T$), and the risk premium on corporate bonds ($i_1^c - i_1^T$) will be zero.

If the possibility of a default increases because a corporation begins to suffer large losses, the default risk on corporate bonds will increase, and the expected return on these bonds will decrease. In addition, the corporate bond's return will be more uncertain as well. Our analysis of the determinants of asset demand predicts that because the expected return on the corporate bond falls relative to the expected return on the default-free Canada bond but its relative riskiness rises, the corporate bond is less desirable (holding everything else equal), and demand for it will fall. The demand curve for corporate bonds in panel (a) of Figure 2 then shifts to the left from D_1^c to D_2^c.

At the same time, the expected return on the default-free Canada bonds increases relative to the expected return on corporate bonds as their relative riskiness declines. The Canada bonds thus become more desirable and demand rises, as shown in panel (b) by the rightward shift in the demand curve for these bonds from D_1^T to D_2^T.

As we can see in Figure 2, the equilibrium price for corporate bonds (left axis) falls from P_1^c to P_2^c, and since the bond price is negatively related to the interest rate, the equilibrium interest rate on corporate bonds (right axis) rises from i_1^c to i_2^c. At the same time, however, the equilibrium price for the Canada bonds rises from P_1^T to P_2^T, and the equilibrium interest rate falls from i_1^T to i_2^T. The spread between the interest rates on corporate and default-free bonds—that is, the risk premium on corporate bonds—has risen from zero to $i_2^c - i_2^T$. We can now

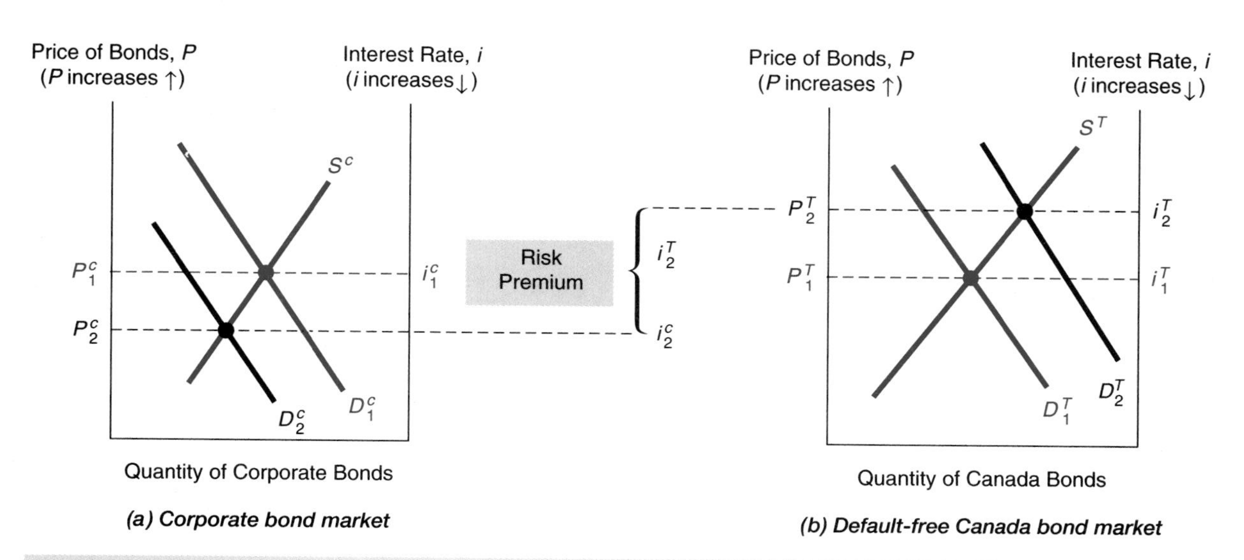

FIGURE 2 **Response to an Increase in Default Risk on Corporate Bonds**

An increase in the default risk on corporate bonds shifts the demand curve from D_1^c to D_2^c. Simultaneously, it shifts the demand curve for Canada bonds from D_1^T to D_2^T. The equilibrium price for corporate bonds (left axis) falls from P_1^c to P_2^c, and the equilibrium interest rate on corporate bonds (right axis) rises from i_1^c to i_2^c. In the Canada bond market, the equilibrium bond price rises from P_1^T to P_2^T, and the equilibrium interest rate falls from i_1^T to i_2^T. The brace indicates the difference between i_2^c and i_2^T, the risk premium on corporate bonds. (*Note:* P and i increase in opposite directions. P on the left vertical axis increases as we go up the axis, while i on the right vertical axis increases as we go down the axis.)

conclude that ***a bond with default risk will always have a positive risk premium, and an increase in its default risk will raise the risk premium.***

For information on the investment advisory firms in Canada and the U.S., visit the firms' Websites at www.dbrs.com, www.moodys.com, www.standardpoor.com

Because default risk is so important to the size of the risk premium, purchasers of bonds need to know whether a corporation is likely to default on its bonds. Two main investment advisory firms, Standard & Poor's Canada and the Dominion Bond Rating Service (DBRS), provide default risk information by rating the quality of the majority of corporate bonds in terms of their probability of default—in the United States, Moody's Investor Service and Standard and Poor's Corporation provide similar information.[2] The ratings and their descriptions are contained in Table 1. Bonds with relatively low risk of default are called *investment-grade* securities and have a rating of BBB and above. Bonds with ratings below BBB have higher default risk and have been aptly dubbed speculative-grade or **junk bonds**. Because these bonds always have higher interest rates than investment-grade securities, they are also referred to as high-yield bonds. Investment-grade securities whose rating has fallen to junk levels are referred to as **fallen angels**.

Next let's look back at Figure 1 and see if we can explain the relationship between interest rates on corporate and Canada bonds. Corporate bonds always have higher interest rates than Canada bonds because they always have some risk of default, whereas Canada bonds do not. Because BBB-rated corporate bonds have a greater default risk than the higher-rated AAA bonds, their risk premium is greater, and the BBB rate therefore always exceeds the AAA rate.

We can use the same analysis to explain the huge jump in the risk premium on BBB corporate bond rates during the 1980–1982 and 1990–1991 recessions (Figure 3). The recession periods saw a very high rate of business failures and defaults. As we would expect, these factors led to a substantial increase in default risk for bonds issued by vulnerable corporations, and the risk premium for BBB bonds reached unprecedentedly high levels.

Access ratings of various bonds and institutions at www.standardandpoors.com/RatingsActions/index.html

TABLE 1 Bond Ratings by Standard & Poor's Canada and DBRS

Standard and Poor's Canada	DBRS	Description	Examples of Corporations with Bonds Outstanding in 2002
AAA	AAA	Highest quality	Government of Canada, Exxon Mobil
AA	AA	Superior quality	Imperial Oil, Shell Canada, DuPont
A	A	Good quality	Dofasco, Ford, H&R Block
BBB	BBB	Medium quality	Noranda, Nova Chemicals
BB	BB	Lower medium quality	Nortel, Xerox Canada
B	B	Moderately speculative	Air Canada, Saskatchewan Wheat Pool, Scott Paper
CCC	CCC	Highly speculative	Imax Corp., International Utilities Structures
CC	CC	Default	Telesystem International Wireless
D	C	In default	Algoma Steel, Laidlaw

[2]Since October 31, 2000, Standard and Poor's and the Canadian Bond Rating Service have combined operations in Canada.

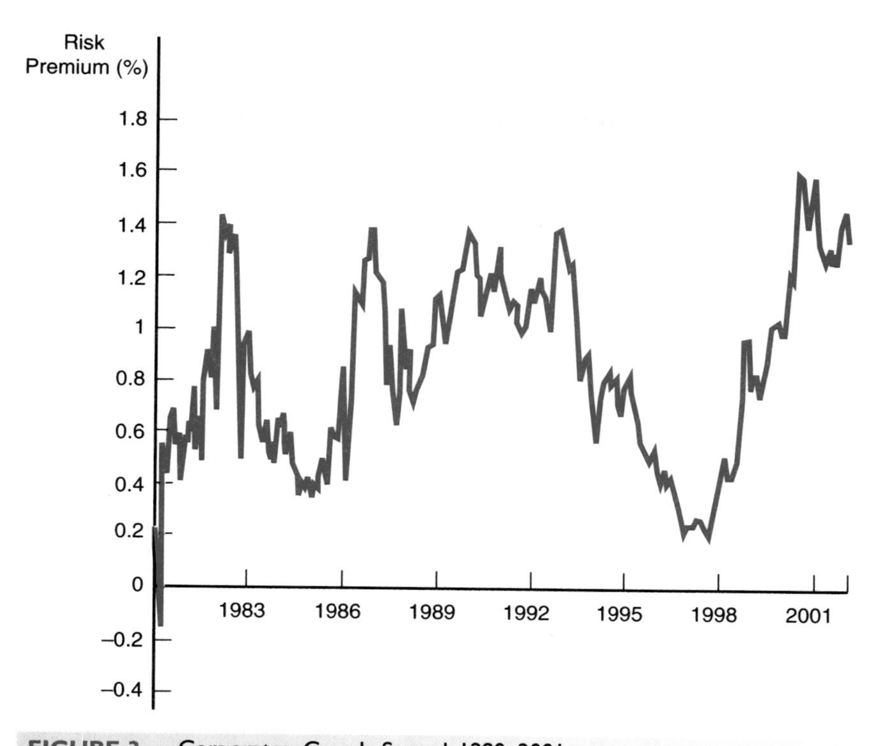

FIGURE 3 Corporates–Canada Spread, 1980–2001

Source: Statistics Canada CANSIM II series V122544 and V122518

Application The Stock Market Crash of 1987 and the Junk Bond–Canada Spread

The stock market crash on "Black Monday," October 19, 1987, when the S&P/TSX Composite fell more than 400 points, an 11% decline, had a major impact not only on prices of stocks but also on the bond market. Let's see how our supply and demand analysis explains the behaviour of the spread between interest rates on junk bonds and Canada securities in the aftermath of the crash using Figure 2.

As a consequence of the Black Monday crash, many investors began to doubt the financial health of corporations with lower credit ratings that had issued junk bonds. The increase in default risk for junk bonds made them less desirable at any given interest rate, decreased the quantity demanded, and shifted the demand curve for junk bonds to the left. As shown in panel (a) of Figure 2, the interest rate on junk bonds should have risen, which is indeed what happened: Interest rates on junk bonds shot up by about one percentage point. But the increase in the perceived default risk for junk bonds after the crash made default-free Canada bonds relatively more attractive and shifted the demand curve for these securities to the right—an outcome described by some analysts as a "flight to quality." Just as our analysis predicts in Figure 2, interest rates on Canada securities fell by about one percentage point. The overall outcome was that the spread between interest rates on junk bonds and government bonds rose by two percentage points, from 4% before the crash to 6% immediately after.

Application What If Canada Bonds Were No Longer Default-Risk Free?

Throughout our history, the Canadian government has never defaulted on its securities. In the early 1990s, however, because of government overspending and a lower average growth rate for real GDP, the federal government's debt/GDP ratio climbed to 75%. Because of this and an international concern about political instability in Canada (for example, Quebec separation), U.S. bond rating agencies such as S&P's and Moody's (which have also been in the practice of rating Canadian government bonds) threatened to lower their rating of the federal government's debt. What would have been the impact of a lower rating?

Our analysis in Figure 2 provides the answer. A lower rating on Canada bonds would mean that they would no longer be considered default-risk free and would now have the attributes of corporate bonds in panel (a) of Figure 2. The increase in default risk would decrease the quantity of Canada bonds demanded at any given interest rate and would thus cause their demand curve to shift to the left. As we see in panel (a), this would result in a fall in their bond price and a rise in their interest rate.

Liquidity

Another attribute of a bond that influences its interest rate is its liquidity. As we learned in Chapter 4, a liquid asset is one that can be quickly and cheaply converted into cash if the need arises. The more liquid an asset is, the more desirable it is (holding everything else constant). Canada bonds are the most liquid of all long-term bonds because they are so widely traded that they are the easiest to sell quickly and the cost of selling them is low. Corporate bonds are not as liquid because fewer bonds for any one corporation are traded; thus it can be costly to sell these bonds in an emergency because it may be hard to find buyers quickly.

How does the reduced liquidity of corporate bonds affect their interest rates relative to the interest rate on Canada bonds? We can use supply and demand analysis to show that the lower liquidity of corporate bonds relative to Canada bonds increases the spread between the interest rates on these two bonds. Let us start the analysis by assuming that, initially, corporate and Canada bonds are equally liquid and all their other attributes are the same. As shown in Figure 4, their equilibrium prices and interest rates will initially be equal: $P_1^c = P_1^T$ and $i_1^c = i_1^T$. If the corporate bond becomes less liquid than the Canada bond because it is less widely traded, then as our analysis of the determinants of asset demand indicates, its demand will fall, shifting its demand curve from D_1^c to D_2^c as in panel (a). The Canada bond now becomes relatively more liquid in comparison with the corporate bond, so its demand curve shifts rightward from D_1^T to D_2^T as in panel (b). The shifts in the curves in Figure 4 show that the price of the less liquid corporate bond falls and its interest rate rises, while the price of the more liquid Canada bond rises and its interest rate falls.

The result is that the spread between the interest rates on the two bond types has risen. Therefore, the differences between interest rates on corporate bonds and Canada bonds (that is, the risk premiums) reflect not only the corporate bond's default risk but its liquidity too. This is why a risk premium is sometimes called a *liquidity premium*. Most accurately, it should be called a "risk and liquidity premium," but convention dictates that it be called a *risk premium*.

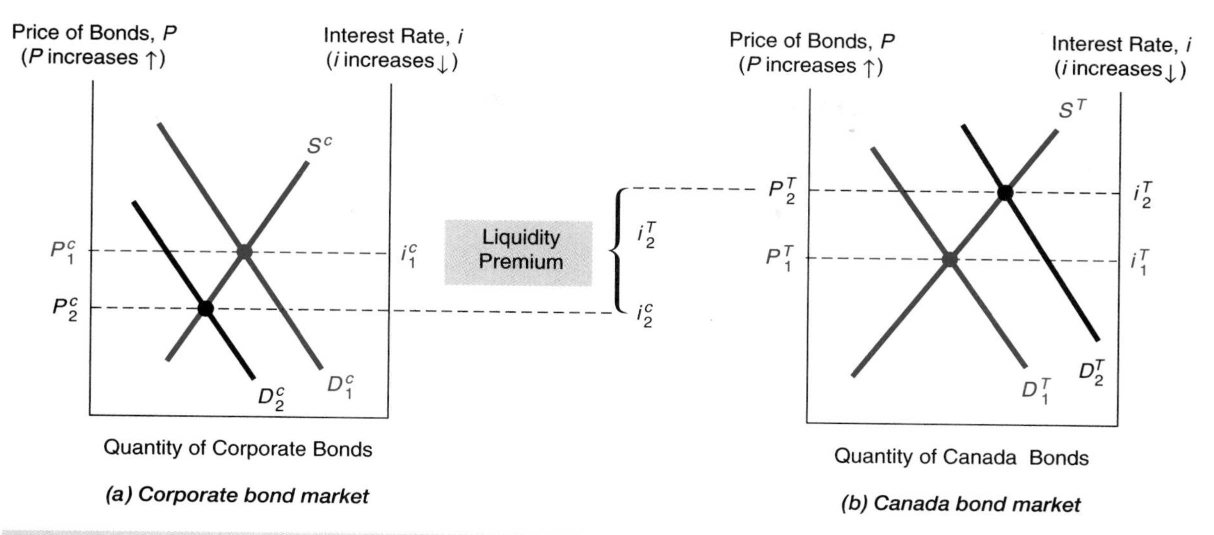

FIGURE 4 Response to a Decrease in the Liquidity of Corporate Bonds

A decrease in the liquidity of corporate bonds shifts the demand curve from D_1^C to D_2^C. Simultaneously, it shifts the demand curve for Canada bonds from D_1^T to D_2^T. The equilibrium price for corporate bonds (left axis) falls from P_1^C to P_2^C, and the equilibrium interest rate on corporate bonds (right axis) rises from i_1^C to i_2^C. In the Canada bond market, the equilibrium bond price rises from P_1^T to P_2^T, and the equilibrium interest rate falls from i_1^T to i_2^T. The brace indicates the difference between i_2^C and i_2^T, the liquidity premium on corporate bonds. (*Note:* P and i increase in opposite directions. P on the left vertical axis increases as we go up the axis, while i on the right vertical axis increases as we go down the axis.)

Income Tax Considerations

In Canada, coupon payments on fixed-income securities are taxed as ordinary income in the year they are received. In some other countries, however, certain government bonds are not taxable. In the United States, for example, interest payments on municipal bonds are exempt from federal income taxes, and these bonds have had lower interest rates than U.S. Treasury bonds for at least 40 years. How does taxation affect the interest rate on bonds?

Let us imagine that you have a high enough income to put you in the 40% income tax bracket, where for every extra dollar of income, you have to pay 40 cents to the government. If you own a $1000 face value taxable bond that sells for $1000 and has a coupon payment of $100, you get to keep only $60 of the payment after taxes. Although the bond has a 10% interest rate, you actually earn only 6% after taxes.

Suppose, however, that you put your savings into a $1000 face value tax-exempt bond that sells for $1000 and pays only $80 in coupon payments. Its interest rate is only 8%, but because it is a tax-exempt security, you pay no taxes on the $80 coupon payment, so you earn 8% after taxes. Clearly, you earn more on the tax-exempt bond after taxes, so you are willing to hold the riskier and less liquid tax-exempt bond even though it has a lower interest rate than the taxable bond. Notice that the tax-exempt status of a bond becomes a significant advantage when income tax rates are very high.

EXAMPLE 1: Income Tax Considerations

Suppose you had the opportunity to buy either a tax-exempt bond or a taxable bond, both of which have a face value and purchase price of $1000. Assume both bonds have identical risk. The tax-exempt bond has coupon payments of $60 and a coupon rate of 6%. The taxable bond has coupon payments of $80 and an interest rate of 8%. Which bond would you choose to purchase, assuming a 40% tax rate?

Solution

You would choose to purchase the tax-exempt bond because it will earn you $60 in coupon payments and an interest rate after taxes of 6%. In this case, you pay no taxes on the $60 coupon payments and earn 6% after taxes. However, you have to pay taxes on taxable bonds. You will keep only 60% of the $80 coupon payment because the other 40% goes to taxes. Therefore, you receive $48 of the coupon payment and have an interest rate of 4.8% after taxes. Buying the tax-exempt bond would yield you higher earnings.

Summary

The risk structure of interest rates (the relationship among interest rates on bonds with the same maturity) is explained by three factors: default risk, liquidity, and the income tax treatment of the bond's interest payments. As a bond's default risk increases, the risk premium on that bond (the spread between its interest rate and the interest rate on a default-free Canada bond) rises. The greater liquidity of Canada bonds also explains why their interest rates are lower than interest rates on less liquid bonds. If a bond has a favourable tax treatment, as do municipal bonds, whose interest payments are exempt from federal income taxes, its interest rate will be lower.

TERM STRUCTURE OF INTEREST RATES

We have seen how risk, liquidity, and tax considerations (collectively embedded in the risk structure) can influence interest rates. Another factor that influences the interest rate on a bond is its term to maturity: Bonds with identical risk, liquidity, and tax characteristics may have different interest rates because the time remaining to maturity is different. A plot of the yields on bonds with differing terms to maturity but the same risk, liquidity, and tax considerations is called a **yield curve**, and it describes the term structure of interest rates for particular types of bonds, such as government bonds. The "Following the Financial News" box shows several yield curves for Canada bonds that were published in *The Globe and Mail: Report on Business.* Yield curves can be classified as upward-sloping, flat, and downward-sloping (the last sort is often referred to as an **inverted yield curve**). When yield curves slope upward, as in the "Following the Financial News" box, the long-term interest rates are above the short-term interest rates; when yield curves are flat, short- and long-term interest rates are the same; and when yield curves are inverted, long-term interest rates are below short-term interest rates. Yield curves can also have more complicated shapes in which they first slope up and then down, or vice versa. Why do we usually see upward slopes of the yield curve as in the "Following the Financial News" box but sometimes other shapes?

Besides explaining why yield curves take on different shapes at different times, a good theory of the term structure of interest rates must explain the following three important empirical facts:

FOLLOWING THE FINANCIAL NEWS

Yield Curves

The Globe and Mail: Report on Business publishes a weekly plot of the yield curve for government of Canada securities (in the same way that the *Wall Street Journal* publishes a daily plot of the yield curve for U.S. Treasury securities), an example of which is presented here. It is typically found in the "Canadian Bonds" column.

The numbers on the vertical axis indicate the interest rate for the government of Canada security, with the maturity given by the numbers on the horizontal axis. For example, the yield curve marked "Last Friday" indicates that the interest rate on the three-month treasury bill last Friday was 2.3%, while the one-year bill had an interest rate of 3.5% and the ten-year bond had an interest rate of 5.75%. As you can see, the yield curves in the plot have an upward slope.

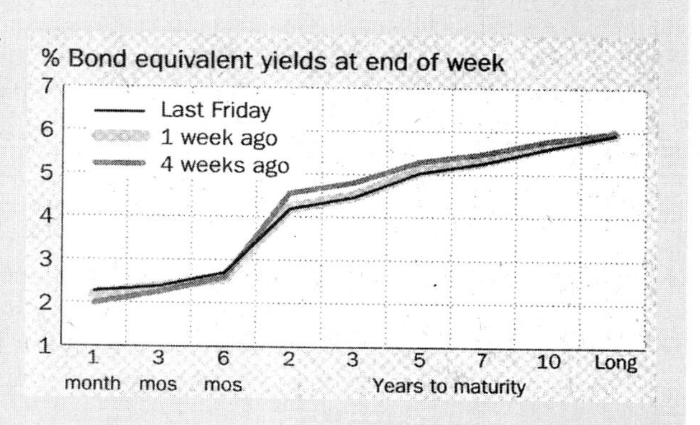

Source: RBC Capital Markets

1. As we see in Figure 5, interest rates on bonds of different maturities move together over time.
2. When short-term interest rates are low, yield curves are more likely to have an upward slope; when short-term interest rates are high, yield curves are more likely to slope downward and be inverted.
3. Yield curves almost always slope upward, as in the "Following the Financial News" box.

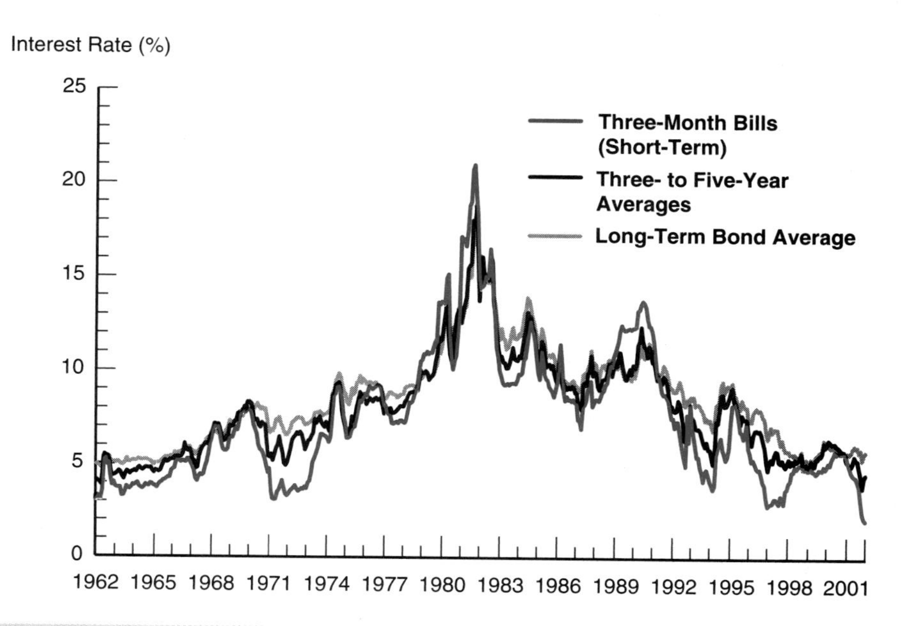

FIGURE 5 Movements over Time of Interest Rates on Government of Canada Bonds with Different Maturities, 1962–2001

Sources: Statistics Canada CANSIM II series V122531, V122485, and V122487

Three theories have been put forward to explain the term structure of interest rates, that is, the relationship among interest rates on bonds of different maturities reflected in yield curve patterns: (1) pure expectations theory, (2) market segmentation theory, and (3) liquidity premium theory. The pure expectations theory does a good job of explaining the first two facts on our list but not the third. The market segmentation theory can explain fact 3 but not the other two facts, which are well explained by the pure expectations theory. Because each theory explains facts that the other cannot, a natural way to seek a better understanding of the term structure is to combine features of both theories, which leads us to the liquidity premium theory, which can explain all three facts.

If the liquidity premium theory does a better job of explaining the facts and is consequently widely accepted, why do we spend time discussing the other two theories? There are two reasons. First, the ideas in these two theories provide the groundwork for the liquidity premium theory. Second, it is important to see how financial economists modify theories to improve them when they find that the predicted results are inconsistent with the empirical evidence.

Pure Expectations Theory

The **pure expectations theory** of the term structure states the following commonsense proposition: The interest rate on a long-term bond will equal an average of short-term interest rates that people expect to occur over the life of the long-term bond. For example, if people expect that short-term interest rates will be 10% on average over the coming five years, the expectations hypothesis predicts that the interest rate on bonds with five years to maturity will be 10% too. If short-term interest rates were expected to rise even higher after this five-year period so that the average short-term interest rate over the coming 20 years is 11%, then the interest rate on 20-year bonds would equal 11% and would be higher than the interest rate on five-year bonds. We can see that the explanation provided by the pure expectations theory for why interest rates on bonds of different maturities differ is that short-term interest rates are expected to have different values at future dates.

The key assumption behind this theory is that buyers of bonds do not prefer bonds of one maturity over another, so they will not hold any quantity of a bond if its expected return is less than that of another bond with a different maturity. Bonds that have this characteristic are said to be *perfect substitutes*. What this means in practice is that if bonds with different maturities are perfect substitutes, the expected return on these bonds must be equal.

To see how the assumption that bonds with different maturities are perfect substitutes leads to the pure expectations theory, let us consider the following two investment strategies:

1. Purchase a one-year bond, and when it matures in one year, purchase another one-year bond.
2. Purchase a two-year bond and hold it until maturity.

Because both strategies must have the same expected return if people are holding both one- and two-year bonds, the interest rate on the two-year bond must equal the average of the two one-year interest rates.

EXAMPLE 2: Pure Expectations Theory

The current interest rate on a one-year bond is 9%, and you expect the interest rate on the one-year bond next year to be 11%. What is the expected return over the two years? What interest rate must a two-year bond have to equal the two one-year bonds?

Solution

The expected return over the two years will average 10% per year ([9% + 11%]/2 = 10%). The bondholder will be willing to hold both the one- and two-year bonds only if the expected return per year of the two-year bond equals 10%. Therefore, the interest rate on the two-year bond must equal 10%, the average interest rate on the two one-year bonds. Graphically, we have:

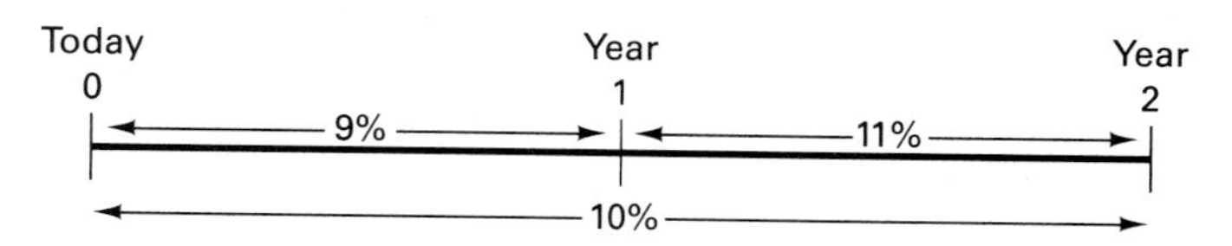

We can make this argument more general. For an investment of $1, consider the choice of holding, for two periods, a two-period bond or two one-period bonds. Using the definitions

i_t = today's (time t) interest rate on a one-period bond
i^e_{t+1} = interest rate on a one-period bond expected for next period (time $t + 1$)
i_{2t} = today's (time t) interest rate on the two-period bond

the expected return over the two periods from investing $1 in the two-period bond and holding it for the two periods can be calculated as

$$(1 + i_{2t})(1 + i_{2t}) - 1 = 1 + 2i_{2t} + (i_{2t})^2 - 1$$

This calculation is derived by recognizing that after the second period, the $1 investment is worth $(1 + i_{2t})(1 + i_{2t})$. Then subtracting the $1 initial investment from this amount and dividing by the initial $1 investment gives the rate of return calculated in the previous equation. Because $(i_{2t})^2$ is extremely small—if $i_{2t} = 10\% = 0.10$, then $(i_{2t})^2 = 0.01$—we can simplify the expected return for holding the two-period bond for the two periods to

$$2i_{2t}$$

With the other strategy, in which one-period bonds are bought, the expected return on the $1 investment over the two periods is

$$(1 + i_t)(1 + i^e_{t+1}) - 1$$
$$= 1 + i_t + i^e_{t+1} + i_t(i^e_{t+1}) - 1$$

After the first period, the $1 investment becomes $1 + i_t$, and this is reinvested in the one-period bond for the next period, yielding an amount $(1 + i_t)(1 + i^e_{t+1})$. Subtracting the $1 initial investment from this amount and dividing by the initial investment of $1 gives the expected return for the strategy of holding one-period bonds for the two periods. Because $i_t(i^e_{t+1})$ is also extremely small—if $i_t = i^e_{t+1} = 0.10$, then $i_t(i^e_{t+1}) = 0.01$—we can simplify this to

$$i_t + i^e_{t+1}$$

Both bonds will be held only if these expected returns are equal, that is, when

$$2i_{2t} = i_t + i^e_{t+1}$$

Solving for i_{2t} in terms of the one-period rates, we have

$$i_{2t} = \frac{i_t + i^e_{t+1}}{2} \qquad (1)$$

which tells us that the two-period rate must equal the average of the two one-period rates. Graphically, we have

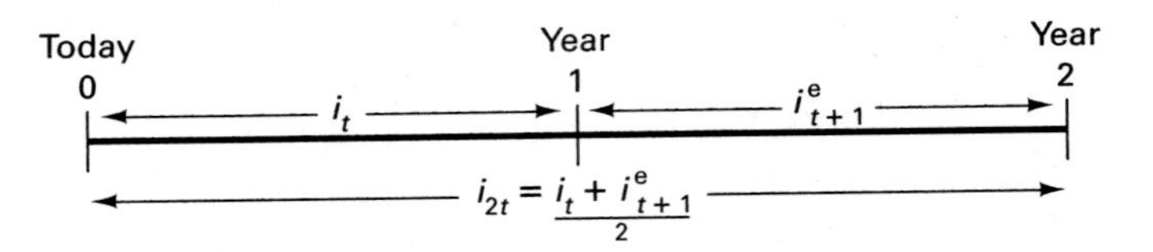

We can follow the same steps for bonds with a longer maturity so that we can examine the whole term structure of interest rates. Doing so, we will find that the interest rate of i_{nt} on an n-period bond must equal

$$i_{nt} = \frac{i_t + i^e_{t+1} + i^e_{t+2} + \cdots + i^e_{t+(n-1)}}{n} \tag{2}$$

Equation 2 states that the n-period interest rate equals the average of the one-period interest rates expected to occur over the n-period life of the bond. This is a restatement of the pure expectations theory in more precise terms.[3]

EXAMPLE 3: Pure Expectations Theory

The one-year interest rate over the next five years is expected to be 5%, 6%, 7%, 8%, and 9%. Given this information, what are the interest rates on a two-year bond and a five-year bond? Explain what is happening to the yield curve.

Solution

The interest rate on the two-year bond would be 5.5%.

$$i_{nt} = \frac{i_t + i^e_{t+1} + i^e_{t+2} + \cdots + i^e_{t+(n-1)}}{n}$$

where

i_t = year 1 interest rate = 5%
i^e_{t+1} = year 2 interest rate = 6%
n = number of years = 2

Thus

$$i_{2t} = \frac{5\% + 6\%}{2} = 5.5\%$$

The interest rate on the five-year bond would be 7%.

$$i_{nt} = \frac{i_t + i^e_{t+1} + i^e_{t+2} + \cdots + i^e_{t+(n-1)}}{n}$$

where

i_t = year 1 interest rate = 5%
i^e_{t+1} = year 2 interest rate = 6%
i^e_{t+2} = year 3 interest rate = 7%

[3] The analysis here has been conducted for discount bonds. Formulas for interest rates on coupon bonds would differ slightly from those used here but would convey the same principle.

i^e_{t+3} = year 4 interest rate = 8%

i^e_{t+4} = year 5 interest rate = 9%

n = number of years = 5

Thus

$$i_{5t} = \frac{5\% + 6\% + 7\% + 8\% + 9\%}{5} = 7.0\%$$

Using the same equation for the one-, three-, and four-year interest rates, you will be able to verify the one-year to five-year rates as 5.0%, 5.5%, 6.0%, 6.5%, and 7.0%, respectively. The rising trend in short-term interest rates produces an upward-sloping yield curve along which interest rates rise as maturity lengthens.

The pure expectations theory provides an elegant explanation of why the term structure of interest rates (as represented by yield curves) changes at different times. When the yield curve is upward-sloping, the pure expectations theory suggests that short-term interest rates are expected to rise in the future, as we have seen in our numerical example. In this situation, in which the long-term rate is currently above the short-term rate, the average of future short-term rates is expected to be higher than the current short-term rate, which can occur only if short-term interest rates are expected to rise. This is what we see in our numerical example. When the yield curve slopes downward and is inverted, the average of future short-term interest rates is expected to be below the current short-term rate, implying that short-term interest rates are expected to fall, on average, in the future. Only when the yield curve is flat does the pure expectations theory suggest that short-term interest rates are not expected to change, on average, in the future.

The pure expectations theory also explains fact 1—that interest rates on bonds with different maturities move together over time. Historically, short-term interest rates have had the characteristic that if they increase today, they will tend to be higher in the future. Hence, a rise in short-term rates will raise people's expectations of future short-term rates. Because long-term rates are related to the average of expected future short-term rates, a rise in short-term rates will also raise long-term rates, causing short- and long-term rates to move together.

The pure expectations theory also explains fact 2—that yield curves tend to have an upward slope when short-term interest rates are low and are inverted when short-term rates are high. When short-term rates are low, people generally expect them to rise to some normal level in the future, and the average of future expected short-term rates is high relative to the current short-term rate. Therefore, long-term interest rates will be substantially above current short-term rates, and the yield curve would then have an upward slope. Conversely, if short-term rates are high, people usually expect them to come back down. Long-term rates would then drop below short-term rates because the average of expected future short-term rates would be below current short-term rates and the yield curve would slope downward and become inverted.[4]

[4]The pure expectations theory explains another important fact about the relationship between short-term and long-term interest rates. As you can see by looking back at Figure 5, short-term interest rates are more volatile than long-term rates. If interest rates are mean-reverting—that is, if they tend to head back down after they are at unusually high levels or go back up when they are at unusually low levels—then an average of these short-term rates must necessarily have lower volatility than the short-term rates themselves. Because the pure expectations theory suggests that the long-term rate will be an average of future short-term rates, it implies that the long-term rate will have lower volatility than short-term rates.

The pure expectations theory is an attractive theory because it provides a simple explanation of the behaviour of the term structure, but unfortunately it has a major shortcoming: It cannot explain fact 3—that yield curves usually slope upward. The typical upward slope of yield curves implies that short-term interest rates are usually expected to rise in the future. In practice, short-term interest rates are just as likely to fall as they are to rise, and so the pure expectations theory suggests that the typical yield curve should be flat rather than upward-sloping.

Market Segmentation Theory

As the name suggests, the **market segmentation theory** of the term structure sees markets for different-maturity bonds as completely separate and segmented. The interest rate for each bond with a different maturity is then determined by the supply of and demand for that bond with no effects from expected returns on other bonds with other maturities.

The key assumption in market segmentation theory is that bonds of different maturities are not substitutes at all, so the expected return from holding a bond of one maturity has no effect on the demand for a bond of another maturity. This theory of the term structure is at the opposite extreme to the pure expectations theory, which assumes that bonds of different maturities are perfect substitutes.

The argument for why bonds of different maturities are not substitutes is that investors have strong preferences for bonds of one maturity but not for another, so they will be concerned with the expected returns only for bonds of the maturity they prefer. This might occur because they have a particular holding period in mind, and if they match the maturity of the bond to the desired holding period, they can obtain a certain return with no risk at all.[5] (We have seen in Chapter 3 that if the term to maturity equals the holding period, the return is known for certain because it equals the yield exactly, and there is no interest-rate risk.) For example, people who have a short holding period would prefer to hold short-term bonds. Conversely, if you were putting funds away for your young child to go to college, your desired holding period might be much longer, and you would want to hold longer-term bonds.

In market segmentation theory, differing yield curve patterns are accounted for by supply and demand differences associated with bonds of different maturities. If, as seems sensible, investors generally prefer bonds with shorter maturities that have less interest-rate risk, market segmentation theory can explain fact 3, that yield curves typically slope upward. Because the demand for long-term bonds is relatively lower than that for short-term bonds in the typical situation, long-term bonds will have lower prices and higher interest rates, and hence the yield curve will typically slope upward.

Although market segmentation theory can explain why yield curves usually tend to slope upward, it has a major flaw in that it cannot explain facts 1 and 2. Because it views the market for bonds of different maturities as completely segmented, there is no reason for a rise in interest rates on a bond of one maturity to affect the interest rate on a bond of another maturity. Therefore, it can-

[5]The statement that there is no uncertainty about the return if the term to maturity equals the holding period is literally true only for a discount bond. For a coupon bond with a long holding period, there is some risk because coupon payments must be reinvested before the bond matures. Our analysis here is thus being conducted for discount bonds. However, the gist of the analysis remains the same for coupon bonds because the amount of this risk from reinvestment is small when coupon bonds have the same term to maturity as the holding period.

not explain why interest rates on bonds of different maturities tend to move together (fact 1). Second, because it is not clear how demand and supply for short- versus long-term bonds change with the level of short-term interest rates, the theory cannot explain why yield curves tend to slope upward when short-term interest rates are low and to be inverted when short-term interest rates are high (fact 2).

Because each of our two theories explains empirical facts that the other cannot, a logical step is to combine the theories, which leads us to the liquidity premium theory.

Liquidity Premium Theory

The **liquidity premium theory** of term structure states that the interest rate on a long-term bond will equal an average of short-term interest rates expected to occur over the life of the long-term bond plus a liquidity premium that responds to supply and demand conditions for that bond.

The liquidity premium theory's key assumption is that bonds of different maturities are substitutes, which means that the expected return on one bond *does* influence the expected return on a bond of a different maturity, but it allows investors to prefer one bond maturity over another. In other words, bonds of different maturities are assumed to be substitutes but not perfect substitutes. Investors tend to prefer shorter-term bonds because these bonds bear less interest-rate risk. For this reason, investors must be offered a positive liquidity premium to induce them to hold longer-term bonds. Such an outcome would modify the pure expectations theory by adding a positive liquidity premium to the equation that describes the relationship between long- and short-term interest rates. The liquidity premium theory is thus written

$$i_{nt} = \frac{i_t + i^e_{t+1} + i^e_{t+2} + \cdots + i^e_{t+(n-1)}}{n} + \ell_{nt} \tag{3}$$

where ℓ_{nt} = the liquidity premium for the n-period bond at time t, which is always positive and rises with the term to maturity of the bond, n.

The relationship between the pure expectations theory and the liquidity premium theory is shown in Figure 6. There we see that because the liquidity premium is always positive and grows as the term to maturity increases, the yield curve implied by the liquidity premium theory is always above the yield curve implied by the pure expectations theory and has a steeper slope.

EXAMPLE 4: Liquidity Premium Theory

As in Example 3, let's suppose that the one-year interest rate over the next five years is expected to be 5%, 6%, 7%, 8%, and 9%. Investors' preferences for holding short-term bonds have the liquidity premiums for one-year to five-year bonds as 0%, 0.25%, 0.5%, 0.75%, and 1.0%, respectively. What is the interest rate on a two-year bond and a five-year bond? Compare these findings with the answer from Example 3 dealing with the pure expectations theory.

Solution

The interest rate on the two-year bond would be 5.75%.

$$i_{nt} = \frac{i_t + i^e_{t+1} + i^e_{t+2} + \ldots + i^e_{t+(n-1)}}{n} + \ell_{nt}$$

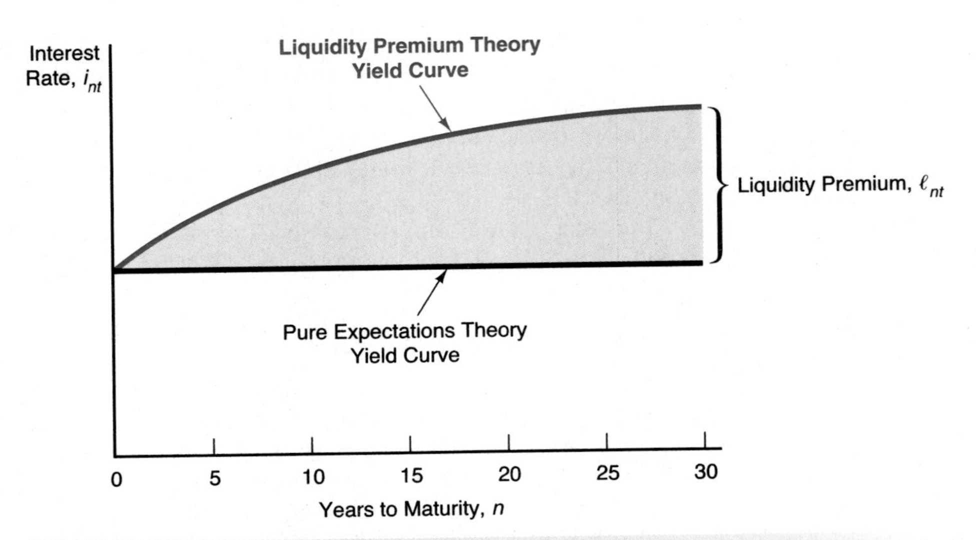

FIGURE 6 The Relationship Between the Liquidity Premium and Pure Expectations Theories

Because the liquidity premium is always positive and grows as the term to maturity increases, the yield curve implied by the liquidity premium theory is always above the yield curve implied by the pure expectations theory and has a steeper slope.

where

i_t = year 1 interest rate = 5%
i^e_{t+1} = year 2 interest rate = 6%
ℓ_{2t} = liquidity premium = 0.25%
n = number of years = 2

Thus

$$i_{2t} = \frac{5\% + 6\%}{2} + 0.25\% = 5.75\%$$

The interest rate on the five-year bond would be 8%.

$$i_{nt} = \frac{i_t + i^e_{t+1} + i^e_{t+2} + \ldots + i^e_{t+(n-1)}}{n} + \ell_{nt}$$

where

i_t = year 1 interest rate = 5%
i^e_{t+1} = year 2 interest rate = 6%
i^e_{t+2} = year 3 interest rate = 7%
i^e_{t+3} = year 4 interest rate = 8%
i^e_{t+4} = year 5 interest rate = 9%
ℓ_{5t} = liquidity premium = 1%
n = number of years = 5

Thus

$$i_{5t} = \frac{5\% + 6\% + 7\% + 8\% + 9\%}{5} + 1\% = 8.0\%$$

If you did similar calculations for the one-, three-, and four-year interest rates, the one-year to five-year interest rates would be as follows: 5.0%, 5.75%, 6.5%, 7.25%, and 8.0%, respectively. Comparing these findings with those for the pure expectations theory, we can see that the liquidity preference theory produces yield curves that slope more steeply upward because of investors' preferences for short-term bonds.

Let's see if the liquidity premium theory is consistent with all three empirical facts we have discussed. It explains fact 1 that interest rates on different-maturity bonds move together over time: A rise in short-term interest rates indicates that short-term interest rates will, on average, be higher in the future, and the first term in Equation 3 then implies that long-term interest rates will rise along with them.

It also explains why yield curves tend to have an especially steep upward slope when short-term interest rates are low and to be inverted when short-term rates are high (fact 2). Because investors generally expect short-term interest rates to rise to some normal level when they are low, the average of future expected short-term rates will be high relative to the current short-term rate. With the additional boost of a positive liquidity premium, long-term interest rates will be substantially above current short-term rates, and the yield curve would then have a steep upward slope. Conversely, if short-term rates are high, people usually expect them to come back down. Long-term rates would then drop below short-term rates because the average of expected future short-term rates would be so far below current short-term rates that despite positive liquidity premiums, the yield curve would slope downward.

The liquidity premium theory explains fact 3 that yield curves typically slope upward by recognizing that the liquidity premium rises with a bond's maturity because of investors' preferences for short-term bonds. Even if short-term interest rates are expected to stay the same on average in the future, long-term interest rates will be above short-term interest rates, and yield curves will typically slope upward.

How can the liquidity premium theory explain the occasional appearance of inverted yield curves if the liquidity premium is positive? It must be that at times short-term interest rates are expected to fall so much in the future that the average of the expected short-term rates is well below the current short-term rate. Even when the positive liquidity premium is added to this average, the resulting long-term rate will still be below the current short-term interest rate.

As our discussion indicates, a particularly attractive feature of the liquidity premium theory is that it tells you what the market is predicting about future short-term interest rates just by looking at the slope of the yield curve. A steeply rising yield curve, as in panel (a) of Figure 7, indicates that short-term interest rates are expected to rise in the future. A moderately steep yield curve, as in panel (b), indicates that short-term interest rates are not expected to rise or fall much in the future. A flat yield curve, as in panel (c), indicates that short-term rates are expected to fall moderately in the future. Finally, an inverted yield curve, as in panel (d), indicates that short-term interest rates are expected to fall sharply in the future.

The Predictive Power of the Yield Curve

People often think that the slope of the yield curve can be used to forecast future short-term interest rates. The yield curve has this practical use only if it is determined by the expectations theory of the term structure that views long-term interest rates as equalling the average of future short-term interest rates. If, however,

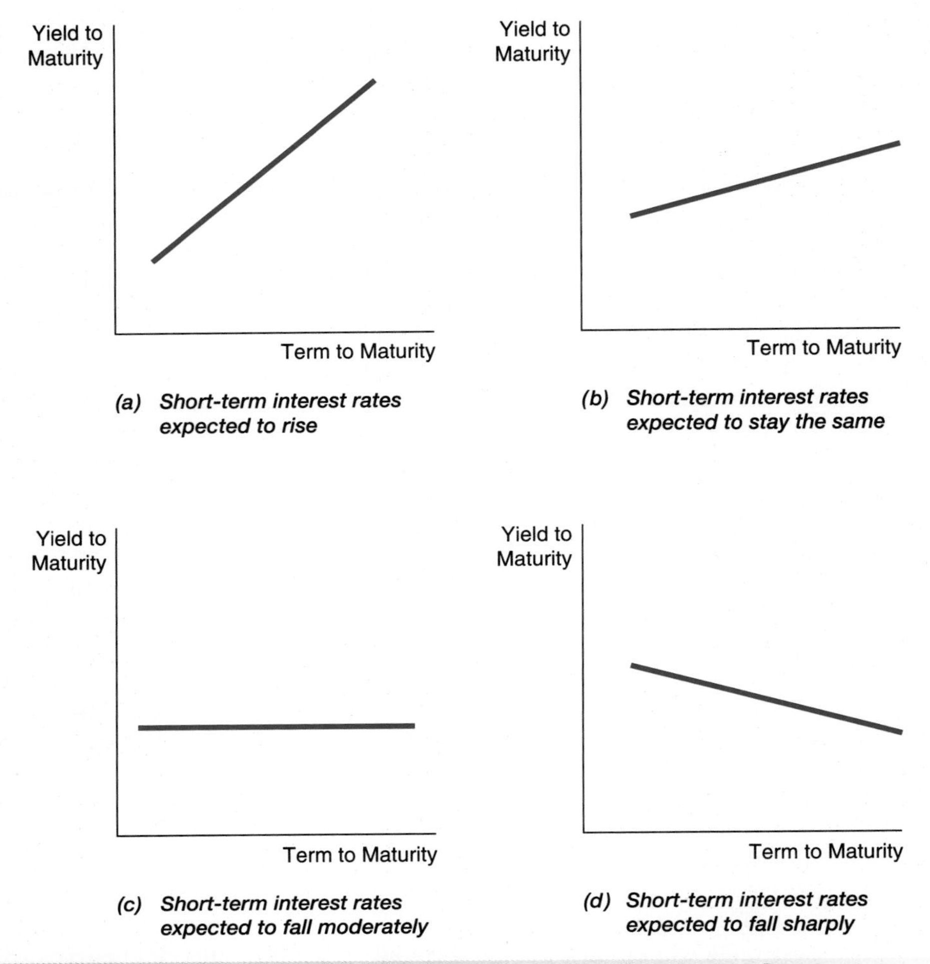

FIGURE 7 Yield Curves and the Market's Expectations of Future Short-Term Interest Rates

there are liquidity (term) premiums in the term structure, then it will be difficult to extract a reliable forecast of future short-term interest rates without good measures of these premiums.

In the 1980s, researchers examining the term structure of interest rates questioned whether the slope of the yield curve provides information about movements of future short-term interest rates.[6] They found that the spread between long- and short-term interest rates does not always help predict future short-term interest rates, a finding that may stem from substantial fluctuations in the liquidity premium for long-term bonds. More recent research using more discriminating tests now favours a different view. It shows that the term structure contains quite a bit of information for the very short run, over the next several months, and the

[6]Robert J. Shiller, John Y. Campbell, and Kermit L. Schoenholtz, "Forward Rates and Future Policy: Interpreting the Term Structure of Interest Rates," *Brookings Papers on Economic Activity* 1 (1983): 173–217; N. Gregory Mankiw and Lawrence H. Summers, "Do Long-Term Interest Rates Overreact to Short-Term Interest Rates?" *Brookings Papers on Economic Activity* 1 (1984): 243–247.

long run, over several years, but is unreliable at predicting movements in interest rates over the intermediate term, the time in between.[7]

Summary

The liquidity premium theory is the most widely accepted theory of the term structure of interest rates because it explains the major empirical facts about the term structure so well. It combines the features of both the pure expectations theory and the market segmentation theory by asserting that a long-term interest rate will be the sum of a liquidity premium and the average of the short-term interest rates that are expected to occur over the life of the bond.

The liquidity premium theory explains the following facts: (1) Interest rates on bonds of different maturities tend to move together over time, (2) yield curves usually slope upward, and (3) when short-term interest rates are low, yield curves are more likely to have a steep upward slope, whereas when short-term interest rates are high, yield curves are more likely to be inverted.

The theory also helps us predict the movement of short-term interest rates in the future. A steep upward slope of the yield curve means that short-term rates are expected to rise, a mild upward slope means that short-term rates are expected to remain the same, a flat slope means that short-term rates are expected to fall moderately, and an inverted yield curve means that short-term rates are expected to fall sharply.

Application Interpreting Yield Curves, 1980–2002

Figure 8 illustrates several yield curves that have appeared for U.S. government bonds in recent years. What do these yield curves tell us about the public's expectations of future movements of short-term interest rates?

Study Guide Try to answer the Application question before reading further in the text. If you have trouble answering it with the liquidity premium theory, first try answering it with the pure expectations theory (which is simpler because you don't have to worry about the liquidity premium). When you understand what the expectations of future interest rates are in this case, modify your analysis by taking the liquidity premium into account.

The steep inverted yield curve that occurred on January 15, 1981, indicated that short-term interest rates were expected to decline sharply in the future. In order for longer-term interest rates with their positive liquidity premium to be well below the short-term interest rate, short-term interest rates must be expected to decline so sharply that their average is far below the current short-term rate. Indeed, the public's expectations of sharply lower short-term interest rates evident in the yield curve were realized soon after January 15; by March, three-month U.S. Treasury bill rates had declined from the 16% level to 13%.

[7]Eugene Fama, "The Information in the Term Structure," *Journal of Financial Economics* 13 (1984): 509–528; Eugene Fama and Robert Bliss, "The Information in Long-Maturity Forward Rates," *American Economic Review* 77 (1987): 680–692; John Y. Campbell and Robert J. Shiller, "Cointegration and Tests of the Present Value Models," *Journal of Political Economy* 95 (1987): 1062–1088; John Y. Campbell and Robert J. Shiller, "Yield Spreads and Interest Rate Movements: A Bird's Eye View," *Review of Economic Studies* 58 (1991): 495–514.

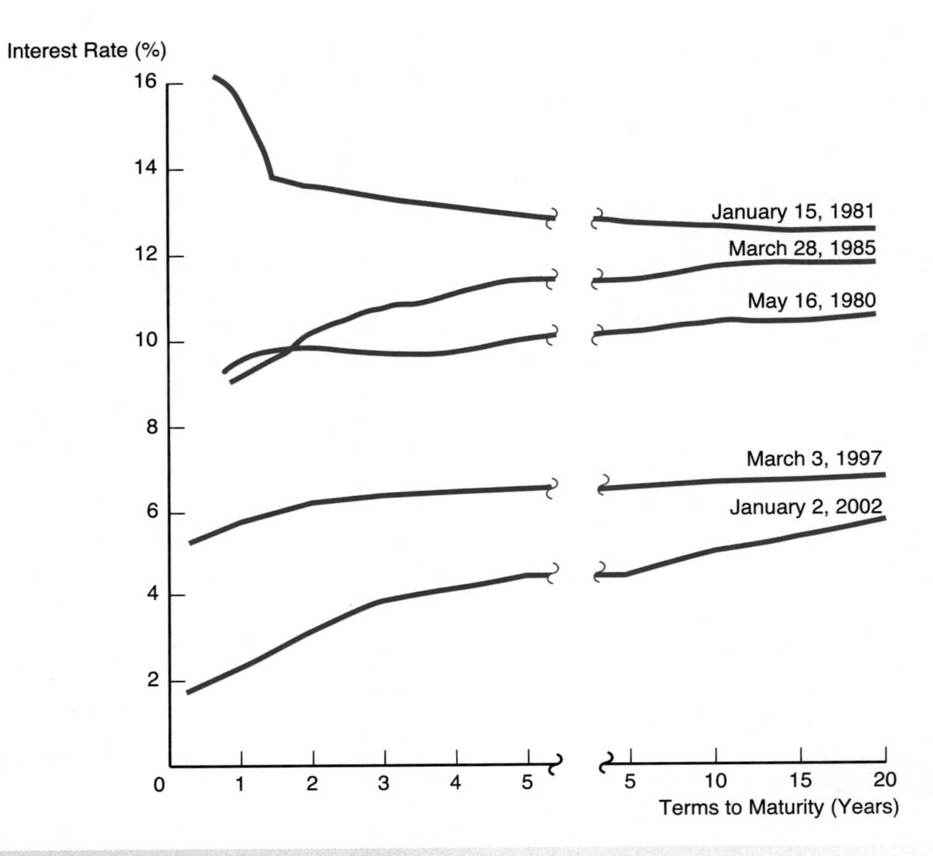

FIGURE 8 Yield Curves for U.S. Government Bonds

Sources: Federal Reserve Bank of St. Louis; *U.S. Financial Data*, various issues; *Wall Street Journal*, various dates.

The steep upward-sloping yield curves on March 28, 1985, and especially January 2, 2002, indicated that short-term interest rates would climb in the future. The long-term interest rate is above the short-term interest rate when short-term interest rates are expected to rise because their average plus the liquidity premium will be above the current short-term rate. The moderately upward-sloping yield curves on May 16, 1980, and March 3, 1997, indicated that short-term interest rates were expected neither to rise nor to fall in the near future. In this case, their average remains the same as the current short-term rate, and the positive liquidity premium for longer-term bonds explains the moderate upward slope of the yield curve.

THE PRACTISING FINANCIAL INSTITUTION MANAGER

Using the Term Structure to Forecast Interest Rates

As was discussed in Chapter 4, interest-rate forecasts are extremely important to managers of financial institutions because future changes in interest rates have a significant impact on the profitability of their institutions. Furthermore, interest-rate forecasts are needed when managers of financial institutions have to set interest rates on loans that are promised to customers in the future. Our discussion of the term structure of interest rates has indicated that the slope of the yield curve provides general information about the market's prediction of the future path of interest rates. For example, a steeply upward-sloping yield curve indicates that short-term interest rates are predicted to rise in the future, and a downward-sloping yield curve indicates that short-term interest rates are predicted to fall. However, a financial institution manager needs much more specific information on interest-rate forecasts than this. Here we show how the manager of a financial institution can generate specific forecasts of interest rates using the term structure.

To see how this is done, let's start the analysis using the approach we took in developing the pure expectations theory. Recall that because bonds of different maturities are perfect substitutes, we assumed that the expected return over two periods from investing $1 in a two-period bond, which is $(1 + i_{2t})(1 + i_{2t}) - 1$, must equal the expected return from investing $1 in one-period bonds, which is $(1 + i_t)(1 + i^e_{t+1}) - 1$. This is shown graphically as follows:

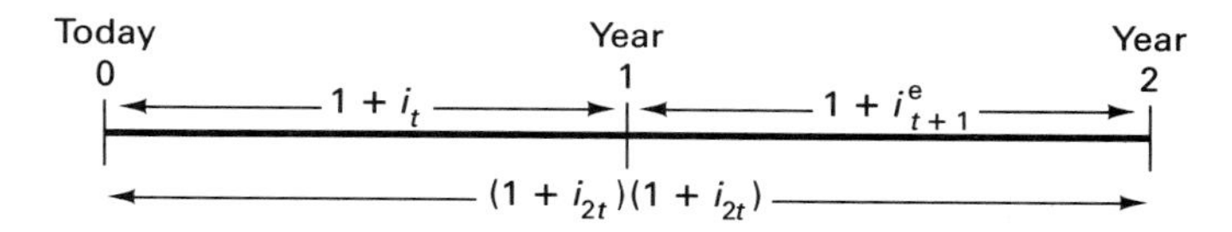

In other words,

$$(1 + i_t)(1 + i^e_{t+1}) - 1 = (1 + i_{2t})(1 + i_{2t}) - 1$$

Through some tedious algebra we can solve for i^e_{t+1}:

$$i^e_{t+1} = \frac{(1 + i_{2t})^2}{1 + i_t} - 1 \qquad (4)$$

This measure of i^e_{t+1} is called the **forward rate** because it is the one-period interest rate that the pure expectations theory of the term structure indicates is expected to prevail one period in the future. To differentiate forward rates derived from the term structure from actual interest rates that are observed at time *t*, we call these observed interest rates **spot rates**.

Going back to Example 3, which we used to discuss the pure expectations theory earlier in this chapter, at time *t* the one-year interest rate is 5% and the two-year rate is 5.5%. Plugging these numbers into Equation 4 yields the following estimate of the forward rate one period in the future:

$$i^e_{t+1} = \frac{(1 + 0.055)^2}{1 + 0.05} - 1 = 0.06 = 6\%$$

Not surprisingly, this 6% forward rate is identical to the expected one-year interest rate one year in the future that we used in Example 3. This is exactly what we should find, as our calculation here is just another way of looking at the pure expectations theory.

We can also compare holding the three-year bond against holding a sequence of one-year bonds, which reveals the following relationship:

$$(1 + i_t)(1 + i^e_{t+1})(1 + i^e_{t+2}) - 1 = (1 + i_{3t})(1 + i_{3t})(1 + i_{3t}) - 1$$

and plugging in the estimate for i^e_{t+1} derived in Equation 4, we can solve for i^e_{t+2}:

$$i^e_{t+2} = \frac{(1 + i_{3t})^3}{(1 + i_{2t})^2} - 1$$

Continuing with these calculations, we obtain the general solution for the forward rate n periods into the future:

$$i^e_{t+n} = \frac{(1 + i_{n+1t})^{n+1}}{(1 + i_{nt})^n} - 1 \tag{5}$$

Our discussion indicated that the pure expectations theory is not entirely satisfactory because investors must be compensated with liquidity premiums to induce them to hold longer-term bonds. Hence, we need to modify our analysis, as we did when discussing the liquidity premium theory, by allowing for these liquidity premiums in estimating predictions of future interest rates.

Recall from the discussion of those theories that because investors prefer to hold short-term rather than long-term bonds, the n-period interest rate differs from that indicated by the pure expectations theory by a liquidity premium of ℓ_{nt}. So to allow for liquidity premiums, we need merely subtract ℓ_{nt} from i_{nt} in our formula to derive i^e_{t+n}:

$$i^e_{t+n} = \frac{(1 + i_{n+1t} - \ell_{n+1t})^{n+1}}{(1 + i_{nt} - \ell_{nt})^n} - 1 \tag{6}$$

This measure of i^e_{t+n} is referred to, naturally enough, as the *adjusted forward-rate forecast.*

In the case of i^e_{t+1}, Equation 6 produces the following estimate:

$$i^e_{t+1} = \frac{(1 + i_{2t} - \ell_{2t})^2}{1 + i_t} - 1$$

Using Example 4 in our discussion of the liquidity premium theory, at time t the ℓ_{2t} liquidity premium is 0.25%, $\ell_{1t} = 0$, the one-year interest rate is 5%, and the two-year interest rate is 5.75%. Plugging these numbers into our equation yields the following adjusted forward-rate forecast for one period in the future:

$$i^e_{t+1} = \frac{(1 + 0.0575 - 0.0025)^2}{1 + 0.05} - 1 = 0.06 = 6\%$$

which is the same as the expected interest rate used in Example 3, as it should be.

Our analysis of the term structure thus provides managers of financial institutions with a fairly straightforward procedure for producing interest-rate forecasts. First they need to estimate ℓ_{nt}, the values of the liquidity premiums for various n. Then they need merely apply the formula in Equation 6 to derive the market's forecasts of future interest rates.

EXAMPLE 5: Forward Rate

A customer asks a bank if it would be willing to commit to making the customer a one-year loan at an interest rate of 8% one year from now. To compensate for the costs of making the loan, the bank needs to charge one percentage point more than the expected interest rate on a Canada bond with the same maturity if it is to make a profit. If the bank manager estimates the liquidity premium to be 0.4%, and the one-year Canada bond rate is 6% and the two-year bond rate is 7%, should the manager be willing to make the commitment?

Solution

The bank manager is unable to make the loan because at an interest rate of 8%, the loan is likely to be unprofitable to the bank.

$$i^e_{t+n} = \frac{(1 + i_{n+1t} - \ell_{n+1t})^{n+1}}{(1 + i_{nt} - \ell_{nt})^n} - 1$$

where

i_{n+1t} = two-year bond rate = 0.07

ℓ_{n+1t} = liquidity premium = 0.004

i_{nt} = one-year bond rate = 0.06

ℓ_{1t} = liquidity premium = 0

n = number of years = 1

Thus

$$i^e_{t+1} = \frac{(1 + 0.07 - 0.004)^2}{1 + 0.06} - 1 = 0.072 = 7.2\%$$

The market's forecast of the one-year Canada bond rate one year in the future is therefore 7.2%. Adding the 1% necessary to make a profit on the one-year loan means that the loan is expected to be profitable only if it has an interest rate of 8.2% or higher.

As we will see in Chapter 10, the bond market's forecasts of interest rates may be the most accurate ones possible. If this is the case, the estimates of the market's forecasts of future interest rates using the simple procedure outlined here may be the best interest-rate forecasts that a financial institution manager can obtain.

Study Guide To make sure you understand how to generate interest-rate forecasts from the term structure, calculate the forecasts of the one-year interest rates using Equation 6 for two, three, and four years in the future using the liquidity premiums and one-year through five-year interest rates in Example 4. The resulting forecasts should equal the expected future interest rates found in the example. Problems 14 and 15 at the end of the chapter will give you more practice in generating interest-rate forecasts from the term structure.

SUMMARY

1. Bonds with the same maturity will have different interest rates because of three factors: default risk, liquidity, and tax considerations. The greater a bond's default risk, the higher its interest rate relative to other bonds; the greater a bond's liquidity, the lower its interest rate; and tax-exempt bonds will have lower interest rates than they otherwise would. The relationship among interest rates on bonds with the same maturity that arise because of these three factors is known as the risk structure of interest rates.
2. Several theories of the term structure provide explanations of how interest rates on bonds with different terms to maturity are related. The pure expectations theory views long-term interest rates as equalling the average of future short-term interest rates expected to occur over the life of the bond; by contrast, market segmentation theory treats the determination of interest rates for each bond's maturity as the outcome of supply and demand in that market only. Neither of these theories by itself can explain both the fact that interest rates on bonds of different maturities move together over time and the fact that yield curves usually slope upward.

3. The liquidity premium theory combines the features of the other two theories and by so doing is able to explain the facts just mentioned. It views long-term interest rates as equalling the average of future short-term interest rates expected to occur over the life of the bond plus a liquidity premium that reflects the supply of and demand for bonds of different maturities.
4. These theories allow us to infer the market's expectations about the movement of future short-term interest rates from the yield curve. A steeply upward-sloping curve indicates that future short-term rates are expected to rise, a mildly upward-sloping curve indicates that short-term rates are expected to stay the same, a flat curve indicates that short-term rates are expected to decline slightly, and an inverted yield curve indicates that a substantial decline in short-term rates is expected in the future.

KEY TERMS

default, *p. 110*
default-free bonds, *p. 110*
default risk, *p. 110*
fallen angels, *p. 112*
forward rate, *p. 129*
inverted yield curve, *p. 116*
junk bonds, *p. 112*
liquidity premium theory, *p. 123*
market segmentation theory, *p. 112*
pure expectations theory, *p. 118*
risk premium, *p. 110*
risk structure of interest rates, *p. 109*
spot rate, *p. 129*
term structure of interest rates, *p. 109*
yield curve, *p. 116*

QUESTIONS AND PROBLEMS

1. Which should have the higher risk premium on its interest rates, a corporate bond with a BBB rating or a corporate bond with a C rating? Why?

***2.** Why do Canadian treasury bills have lower interest rates than large-denomination negotiable bank CDs?

3. Risk premiums on corporate bonds are usually anticyclical; that is, they decrease during business cycle expansions and increase during recessions. Why is this so?

***4.** "If bonds of different maturities are close substitutes, their interest rates are more likely to move together." Is this statement true, false, or uncertain? Explain your answer.

5. If yield curves, on average, were flat, what would this say about the liquidity premiums in the term structure? Would you be more or less willing to accept the pure expectations theory?

***6.** Assuming that the pure expectations theory is the correct theory of the term structure, calculate the interest rates in the term structure for maturities of one to five years, and plot the resulting yield curves for the following series of one-year interest rates over the next five years:

a. 5%, 7%, 7%, 7%, 7%
b. 5%, 4%, 4%, 4%, 4%

How would your yield curves change if people preferred shorter-term bonds over longer-term bonds?

7. Assuming that the pure expectations theory is the correct theory of the term structure, calculate the interest rates in the term structure for maturities of one to five years, and plot the resulting yield curves for the following path of one-year interest rates over the next five years:

a. 5%, 6%, 7%, 6%, 5%
b. 5%, 4%, 3%, 4%, 5%

How would your yield curves change if people preferred shorter-term bonds over longer-term bonds?

***8.** If a yield curve looks like the one shown below, what is the market predicting about the movement of future short-term interest rates? What might the yield curve indicate about the market's predictions about the inflation rate in the future?

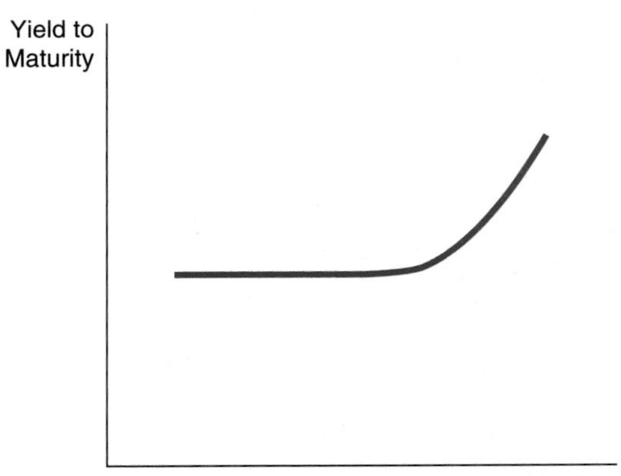

9. If a yield curve looks like the one shown at the top of the next column, what is the market predicting about the movement of future short-term interest rates? What might the yield curve indicate about the market's predictions about the inflation rate in the future?

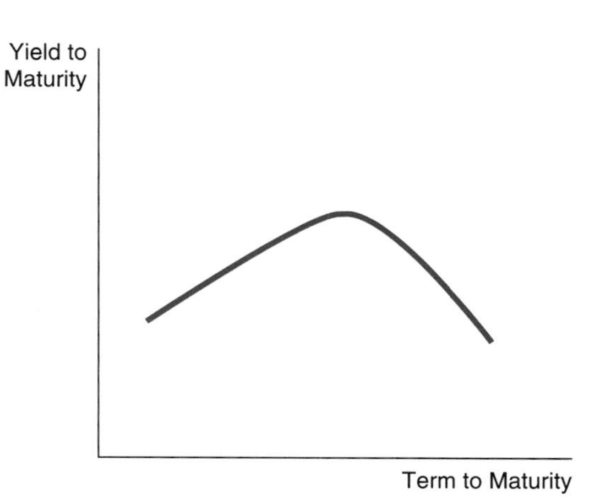

*10. What are the financial implications of a firm with a high default risk?

Predicting the Future

11. Predict what will happen to interest rates on a corporation's bonds if the federal government guarantees today that it will pay creditors if the corporation goes bankrupt in the future. What will happen to the interest rates on Canada bonds?

*12. Predict what would happen to the risk premiums on corporate bonds if brokerage commissions were lowered in the corporate bond market.

13. Predict what would happen to yield spreads in response to the following macroeconomic events: recession, high inflation, and stock market increase.

*14. If the interest rates on one- to five-year bonds are currently 4%, 5%, 6%, 7%, and 8% and the term premiums for one- to five-year bonds are 0%, 0.25%, 0.35%, 0.40%, and 0.50%, predict what the one-year interest rate will be two years from now.

15. If the interest rates on one- to five-year bonds are currently 7%, 6%, 5%, 6%, and 7% and the term premiums for one- to five-year bonds are 0%, 0.15%, 0.25%, 0.30%, and 0.60%, predict what the one-year interest rate will be four years from now.

WEB EXERCISES

The Risk and Term Structure of Interest Rates

1. The amount of additional interest investors receive from the various premiums changes over time. Sometimes the risk premiums are much larger than at other times. For example, the default risk premium was very small in the late 1990s, when the economy was healthy and business failures were rare. It follows that this risk premium increases during recessions.

   Go to http://www.bankofcanada.ca (Selected Historical Interest Rates) and find the interest rate listings for long-term government and corporate bonds at three points in time: the most recent, June 1, 1995, and June 1, 1992. Prepare a graph that shows these three periods (see Figure 1 in this chapter for an example). Are the risk premiums stable, or do they change over time?

2. Figure 8 in this chapter shows a number of U.S. yield curves at various points in time. Go to http://www.bloomberg.com and click on "Markets" at the top of the page. Find the U.S. Treasury yield curve. Does the current U.S. yield curve fall above or below the most recent one listed in Figure 8? Is the current U.S. yield curve flatter or steeper than the most recent one reported in Figure 8?

3. Investment companies attempt to explain to investors the nature of the risk the investor incurs when buying shares in their mutual funds. For example, Vanguard carefully explains interest-rate risk and offers alternative funds with different interest-rate risks. Go to www.majestic.vanguard.com/FP/DA.
   a. Select the bond fund you would recommend to an investor who has very low tolerance for risk and a short investment horizon. Justify your answer.
   b. Select the bond fund you would recommend to an investor who has very high tolerance for risk and a long investment horizon. Justify your answer.

Chapter 6 Structure of Central Banks and the Bank of Canada

Preview

The most important players in financial markets throughout the world are central banks, the government authorities in charge of monetary policy. Central banks' actions affect interest rates, the amount of credit, and the money supply, all of which have direct impacts not only on financial markets but also on aggregate output and inflation. To understand the role that central banks play in financial markets and the overall economy, we need to understand how these organizations work. Who controls central banks and determines their actions? What motivates their behaviour? Who holds the reins of power?

In this chapter we look at the institutional structure of major central banks and particularly focus on the Bank of Canada, Canada's central bank, often just called the **Bank**. We start by focusing on the formal institutional structure of the Bank and then examine the more relevant informal structure that determines who has the ultimate responsibility for monetary policy in Canada. By understanding who makes the decisions, we will have a better idea of how they are made. We then look at several other major central banks and see how they are organized. With this information, we will be better able to comprehend the actual conduct of monetary policy described in the following chapters.

The Bank of Canada's home page is www.bankofcanada.ca

ORIGINS OF THE BANK OF CANADA

Scattered agricultural settlements over vast geographical areas in Canada were for years individually served by local banks that, influenced by the British tradition, depended on a small number of banks with multiple branches. As long as the needs of the rural economy were satisfied by the evolution of a branch-banking system, the imperative for a central bank was downgraded and early attempts to establish such an institution in Canada were unsuccessful. As the central government's needs for funding of its debt and managing fiat money (the notes and coins used in the country) became more important and as the worth of monetary policy came to be more appreciated, the creation of a central bank proved inevitable.

The devastation of the Great Depression was of fundamental importance in the creation of the Bank of Canada. From 1929 to 1933, Canadian real GDP fell by almost 30% and the unemployment rate increased sevenfold from less than 3%

to close to 20%. The Great Depression involved not only the largest decline in the level of economic activity in the history of Canada, but was also followed by an extremely slow recovery. Being such a cataclysmic event, the Great Depression contributed to significant changes in government policy, including fiscal policy, monetary policy, banking policy, and international policy.

In particular, as the depth of the Great Depression was blamed on the operation of the monetary system, in 1933 the federal Conservative government established a royal commission to study the problems of the Great Depression. Based on a recommendation of the royal commission, Parliament passed the Bank of Canada Act in 1934 and the newly founded Bank of Canada started operations on March 11, 1935. By this time, most other countries already had central banks (see Box 1). Although the primary motivation for the formation of the Bank of Canada was economic (or monetary), other motives within the government were the need for Canada to reflect its growing political independence from Britain and the need to coordinate its international economic policy.

Initially the Bank of Canada was a private institution. It was nationalized in 1938, so it is now a national institution with headquarters in Ottawa. The Bank also has regional offices in Toronto, Vancouver, Calgary, Montreal, and Halifax. Unlike a private bank that operates in pursuit of profit, the Bank of Canada is responsible for the country's monetary policy and for the regulation of Canada's deposit-based financial institutions.

FORMAL STRUCTURE OF THE BANK OF CANADA

The overall responsibility for the operation of the Bank of Canada rests with a **Board of Directors**, which consists of fifteen members—the governor, the senior deputy governor, the deputy minister of finance, and twelve outside directors. The Board appoints the governor and senior deputy governor with the government's approval, for a renewable term of seven years. The outside directors are appointed by the minister of finance, with cabinet approval, for a three-year term, and they are required to come from all regions of Canada and represent a variety of occupations with the exception of banking. The governor of the Bank is the chief executive officer and chairman of the Board of Directors. Currently, the governor of the Bank of Canada is David Dodge (see Box 2).

BOX 1
Establishment of Selected Central Banks

Canada did not have a central bank for almost the first 70 years after Confederation. By the time the Bank of Canada began operations in 1935, most other countries already had central banks. In fact, as you can see in the table, Sweden and the United Kingdom created their central banks in the seventeenth century. These early central banks, however, were initially privately owned and gradually evolved into modern, publicly owned central banks.

Country	Year of Central Bank's Establishment
Sweden	1656
United Kingdom	1694
France	1800
Belgium	1850
Germany	1875
Japan	1882
Italy	1893
Switzerland	1905
United States	1913
Canada	1935

Source: Forrest H. Capie, Terence C. Mills, and Geoffrey E. Wood, "Central Bank Dependence and Inflation Performance: An Exploratory Data Analysis," in *Varieties of Monetary Reform: Lessons and Experiences on the Road to Monetary Union*, ed. Pierre L. Siklos (Dordrecht, The Netherlands: Kluwer Academic Publishers, 1994), pp. 95–132. © Kluwer Plenum.

BOX 2

The Political Environment and the Bank of Canada

Since the inception of the Bank of Canada, there have been seven governors:

1935–1954, Graham Towers
1955–1961, James Coyne
1961–1973, Louis Rasminsky
1973–1987, Gerald Bouey
1987–1994, John Crow
1994–2000, Gordon Thiessen
2001–present, David Dodge

It is interesting to note that during the same period Canadians went to the polls 20 times to elect a federal government. The Bank of Canada is not completely independent from the government. For example, the government can directly influence the Bank by not renewing the governor's appointment when it expires. In 1994, the Liberal government did not renew the appointment of John Crow, who was appointed by the Conservative government in 1987.

In 1994 the Board of Directors made some changes in the internal organization of the Bank. The most prominent was the establishment of a new senior decision-making authority within the Bank called the **Governing Council**. The Council is chaired by the governor and is composed of the senior deputy governor and the four deputy governors. Since this change, the six members of the Governing Council of the Bank collectively assume responsibility for the Bank's new semiannual *Monetary Policy Report*, and its *Update*, published in January and July. This system of collective responsibility ensures that the Bank's governor is not personally identified with the Bank's policy.

THE FUNCTIONS OF THE BANK OF CANADA

In the words of the preamble of the Bank of Canada Act, the functions of the Bank of Canada are

> to regulate credit and currency in the best interests of the economic life of the nation, to control and protect the external value of the national monetary unit and to mitigate by its influence fluctuations in the general level of production, trade, prices and employment, so far as may be possible within the scope of monetary action, and generally to promote the economic and financial welfare of Canada.

This is a vague mandate, leaving a lot of room for interpretation. To explore this subject, we discuss four functions of the Bank of Canada as they are mentioned in the Bank's Website:

1. bank note issue
2. government debt and asset management services
3. central banking services
4. monetary policy management

Bank Note Issue

Before the creation of the Bank of Canada, the federal government and the early banks issued notes designed to circulate as currency. The day it began operations, the Bank replaced the outstanding issue of federal government notes and provision was also made for the gradual removal of notes issued by banks. By 1945 the Bank had a monopoly over note issue. Although the original Bank Act required the Bank to redeem its notes in gold, this provision was never used. In fact, it was removed with the 1967 revision of the Bank Act, thereby providing the Bank with unlimited powers to issue legal tender.

The Bank also conducts ongoing research, working closely with private sector partnerships and note-issuing authorities in other countries, in order to improve cost-effectiveness, increase the durability of bank notes, and reduce counterfeiting. In its role as provider of paper money, the Bank's overall objective is to preserve the integrity and safety of Canadian currency in the most economical and efficient manner possible.

Government Debt and Asset Management Services

Go to the Department of Finance's Website at www.fin.gc.ca to examine the department's interactions with the Bank of Canada.

In its role as the federal government's fiscal agent, the Bank of Canada provides debt-management services for the federal government, such as advising on borrowings, managing new debt offerings, and servicing outstanding debt. Before 1995 these services were provided for all the federal government's debt. In 1995, however, a special agency of the Department of Finance was created, known as Canada Investment and Savings, to be responsible for the federal government's debt held by individuals, commonly known as retail debt.

Canada Investment and Savings handles government of Canada securities such as Canada Savings Bonds, treasury bills, and marketable bonds, and is also responsible for the development of new investment products and marketing initiatives. The Bank of Canada, however, continues to be responsible for all the government's securities after they are issued, administering millions of bondholder accounts and making payments on behalf of the federal government for interest and debt redemption.

In its role as fiscal agent, the Bank of Canada also manages the government's foreign exchange reserves held by the **Exchange Fund Account** of the Department of Finance. In particular, the Bank assists the Department of Finance in investing these foreign reserves and in borrowing when necessary to maintain an adequate level of reserves. The Bank also engages in international financial transactions, on behalf of the government, in order to influence exchange rates. (We discuss the Bank's foreign exchange interventions more formally in Chapter 13.)

Central Banking Services

The Bank of Canada serves as the lender of last resort if a deposit-taking financial institution faces a liquidity crisis. Because of its unique power to create base money, the Bank can ease the liquidity problems of any financial institution, by extending advances, and therefore deter bank runs and panics. **Base money** (also called **monetary base**) consists of the monetary liabilities of the central bank and, as you will see in the next chapter, is an important part of the money supply, because changes in it lead to multiple changes in the money supply. Of course, lender-of-last-resort lending is closely coordinated with the two federal agencies that are set up specifically to regulate financial institutions—the Office of the Superintendent of Financial Institutions and the Canada Deposit Insurance Corporation.[1] Moreover, such lending is done judiciously, explicitly considering the effects on other financial institutions, the money supply, and government policy.

The Websites www.osfi-bsif.gc.ca and www.cdic.ca provide more information about the roles of the OSFI and the CDIC.

[1]The Office of the Superintendent of Financial Institutions was created in 1987 to succeed the Department of Insurance and the Inspector General of Banks, whereas the Canada Deposit Insurance Corporation was created by act of Parliament in 1967 to insure deposits, up to $60 000 per account, of member deposit-taking institutions.

Go to www.cdnpay.ca to look at the Canadian Payments Association's home page.

The Bank also plays a central role in Canada's national payments system (to be discussed in some detail in Chapter 7). This is essentially an electronic system that clears and settles payments and transactions involving securities and foreign exchange, currently handling 15 times our gross domestic product per year. Although the Canadian Payments Association operates this system, federal legislation that came into force in 1996 gave the Bank explicit responsibility for the regulatory oversight of this system. The Bank's main concern is preventing problems that affect one participant in the clearing and settlement system from spreading to other participants.

The International Monetary Fund's Website, www.imf.org, provides details about the organization's activities.

Finally, the Bank acts as the holder of deposit accounts of the federal government, the directly clearing members of the Canadian Payments Association, international organizations such as the International Monetary Fund, and other central banks. As the federal government's banker, the Bank is also responsible for the government's operating accounts. In this role, as you will see in Chapter 7, the Bank shifts government balances between the government's transactions account with the Bank and the government's nontransactions accounts with the direct clearers.

Monetary Policy

The Bank of Canada employs such tools as **open market operations** (the purchase and sale of government securities that affect both interest rates and the amount of reserves in the banking system) and, to a lesser extent, the shifting of government balances between it and the directly clearing members of the Canadian Payments Association to implement changes in the money supply. The Bank's ultimate objective is to keep inflation low. The Bank has a staff of professional economists that provides economic analysis that the Board of Directors uses in making its decisions. (Box 3 discusses the role of the research staff.)

The Bank's goal of low inflation is closely related to the goal of steady economic growth, because businesses are more likely to invest in capital equipment to increase productivity and economic growth when inflation is low. Low

BOX 3

Role of the Bank's Research Staff

The Bank of Canada is the largest employer of economists in Canada. What do all these economists do?

The most important task of the Bank's economists is to follow the incoming data from government agencies and private sector organizations on the economy and provide guidance to the policymakers on where the economy may be heading and what the impact of monetary policy actions on the economy might be. Moreover, the Bank's economists maintain large econometric models (models whose equations are estimated with statistical procedures) that help them produce forecasts of the national economy and brief the governor and the senior management of the Bank on their forecasts for the Canadian economy.

Because of the increased influence of developments in foreign countries on the Canadian economy, the research staff produces reports on the major foreign economies. They also conduct research on developments in the foreign exchange market because of its growing importance in the monetary policy process and to support the activities of the Bank's foreign exchange desk.

Staff economists also engage in basic research on the effects of monetary policy on output and inflation, developments in the labour markets, international trade, international capital markets, banking and other financial institutions, financial markets, and the regional economy, among other topics. This research is published widely in academic journals and in Bank of Canada publications. (Bank of Canada publications, such as the *Bank of Canada Review*, the *Bank of Canada Banking and Financial Statistics*, the *Monetary Policy Report*, and the *Monetary Policy Report Update* are a good source of supplemental material for money and banking students.)

Another important activity of the research staff is in the public education area. Staff economists are called on frequently to make presentations to the public.

inflation is also desirable because it protects the purchasing power of pensioners and those on fixed incomes.

Although the Bank determines monetary policy, in the following section you will learn that the ultimate responsibility for policy rests with the government, since it is the government that must answer to Parliament. This system of joint responsibility dates back to 1967, when the Bank of Canada Act was amended to give responsibility for monetary policy to the government.

HOW INDEPENDENT IS THE BANK OF CANADA?

When we look, in the next chapter, at how the Bank of Canada conducts monetary policy, we will want to know why it decides to take certain policy actions but not others. To understand its actions, we must understand the incentives that motivate the Bank's behaviour. How free is the Bank from the whims of the government? Do economic, bureaucratic, or political considerations guide it? Is the Bank truly independent of outside pressures?

The Bank's degree of independence has evolved over time, in part because of changing circumstances, in part because a clear division of authority was not established in the original Bank of Canada Act. Initially the Bank of Canada was privately owned, with about 12 000 individual shareholders, and so was largely free of political pressures. It was also free of private interference, because of regulations regarding who could hold how much stock in the Bank. The Conservative government in office at the time of the Bank's creation believed that the Bank should possess a large share of the responsibility for the development of monetary policy.

Significant changes in the balance of power occurred with the election of a majority Liberal government in the fall of 1935. The Liberals moved the Bank in the direction of public ownership, culminating in its complete nationalization by 1938. This was done to further isolate the Bank from the pressures of the private system. However, the nationalization of the Bank did tilt the balance of authority for monetary policy back toward the federal cabinet and the Parliament. The Liberals believed that the Bank should have discretion in internal management and in implementing monetary policy but that the policies being implemented should be in harmony with the views of the government.

In June 1954, the first governor of the Bank of Canada, Graham Towers, retired after 19 years of service. Graham Towers was replaced by James Coyne (see Box 2). Like many Canadians at the time, James Coyne was concerned about the level of foreign ownership and the increase in consumer prices during the Korean War. He was convinced that the solution to these problems was a tighter monetary policy stance. A decline in the supply of bank reserves would increase interest rates, thereby raising national savings and reducing Canada's dependence on foreign capital inflows. The tighter monetary policy led to rising unemployment and weak output growth. As a result, the Bank's policies were criticized by commentary in the popular press and by most of the academic community. In fact, 30 economists signed a letter to the minister of finance calling for Coyne's dismissal.[2]

James Coyne, however, did not change his mind. He was convinced that there was no long-run relationship between inflation and unemployment, despite the publication of a famous paper in 1958 by the British economist A. W. Phillips, showing that higher inflation was typically associated with a lower unemployment rate.[3]

---

[2]See H. S. Gordon, *The Economists versus the Bank of Canada* (Toronto: The Ryerson Press, 1961): v–vi.

[3]A. W. Phillips, "The Relation between Unemployment and the Rate of Change of Money Wages in the United Kingdom," *Economica* 24 (1958): 283–299.

Although the Phillips hypothesis attracted widespread support in Canada and was replicated with Canadian data, Coyne was anticipating the pathbreaking work by Milton Friedman and Edmund Phelps on the vertical Phillips curve, to be published 10 years later in 1968.[4] But as the former governor of the Bank of Canada, Gordon Thiessen, put it in a recent speech[5]

> [t]here was one critical area, however, where Coyne and many other policy analysts, both within and outside the Bank, appear to have been misguided. Those who had questioned the effectiveness of monetary policy in earlier years had failed to appreciate that it was likely to be much stronger than fiscal policy under a flexible exchange rate system, especially when capital was highly mobile. The large capital movements triggered by any change in interest rates would put significant pressure on the exchange rate, amplifying the effects of monetary policy while undercutting the effects of any opposing fiscal policy. Coyne did not realize that, for similar reasons, it was unlikely that a tighter monetary policy would ever raise national savings or reduce foreign investment inflows.

To avoid accepting blame for this state of affairs, the Liberal government in office reversed its previous stand and disavowed its position that the government was responsible for monetary policy. The government was criticized for this reversal and the new hands-off approach to monetary policy. When the government changed hands on June 10, 1957, and Donald Fleming became the federal minister of finance, the stage was set for a confrontation with the governor of the Bank, James Coyne. After a long and acrimonious debate, the so-called Coyne Affair was resolved in 1961 with the resignation of Governor Coyne.

On July 24, 1961, Louis Rasminsky accepted the position as the third governor of the Bank of Canada on the condition that the relationship between the government and the Bank be clearly defined. Soon after he assumed office, he issued a public statement containing two main principles reflecting his views on that relationship[6]

> ... (1) in the ordinary course of events, the Bank has the responsibility for monetary policy, and (2) if the government disapproves of the monetary policy being carried out by the Bank, it has the right and the responsibility to direct the Bank as to the policy which the Bank is to carry out.

A royal commission, whose appointment was partly initiated by the Coyne Affair, accepted governor Rasminsky's views regarding the relationship between the Bank and the government. The commission recommended a system of joint responsibility under which the Bank has considerable autonomy in the conduct of day-to-day monetary policy but the government must accept full responsibility for the policy being followed.

The Bank of Canada Act was amended in 1967 to confirm the joint responsibility system, and this state of affairs regarding monetary policy has generally remained in order to this day. Under this joint responsibility system, the governor of the Bank of Canada and the minister of finance, acting on behalf of the government, consult regularly, and in the event of a serious disagreement over the conduct of monetary policy, the government has the right to override the Bank's decisions. In particular, the minister of finance can issue a directive to the Bank

---

[4]Milton Friedman, "The Role of Monetary Policy," *American Economic Review* 58 (1968): 1–17; Edmund Phelps, "Money-Wage Dynamics and Labour Market Equilibrium," *Journal of Political Economy* 76 (1968): 678–711.

[5]Gordon Thiessen, "Can a Bank Change? The Evolution of Monetary Policy at the Bank of Canada 1935–2000," Lecture to the Faculty of Social Science, University of Western Ontario.

[6]Bank of Canada, *Annual Report*, 1961, p. 3.

indicating the specific policy changes that the Bank must follow. The directive, however, must be published indicating not only the new policy that the Bank is supposed to undertake but also the period during which it is to apply.

Hence, ultimate responsibility for monetary policy rests with the democratically elected government. However, because of the consequences of issuing a directive, it is unlikely that such a directive would be issued, and none has been issued to date.

THE CHANGING FACE OF THE BANK OF CANADA

The legislation governing the Bank of Canada's responsibility for monetary policy has remained relatively unchanged since the Bank Act of 1967. Over the past decade, however, the Bank has undertaken a broad range of initiatives and made significant institutional changes to the way it operates. The impetus for change came from the interaction of experience and economic theory, the desire to explain and build confidence in the Bank's actions, and (to a smaller extent) from technological change and globalization.

Clarifying objectives is an important starting point for any successful monetary policy framework. The legislation by which the Bank of Canada is governed does not facilitate a clear understanding of objectives. For example, the preamble to legislation governing the Bank refers to multiple, and potentially inconsistent, policy objectives. Over the past few decades, however, the performance of the Canadian economy, together with the evolution of economic theory, led to the view that price stability is the most important goal of monetary policy. As John Crow put it, in his January 1988 Hanson Memorial Lecture at the University of Alberta,[7]

> [t]heory and experience—much of this experience not overly cheerful but certainly instructive—both point to a very clear answer. Monetary policy should be conducted so as to achieve a pace of monetary expansion that promotes stability in the value of money. This means pursuing a policy aimed at achieving and maintaining stable prices.

The Hanson lecture was designed to explicitly identify price stability as the objective of Bank of Canada policy. This message was reinforced on February 26, 1991, through a joint announcement by the governor of the Bank and the minister of finance regarding the establishment of formal inflation targets (to be discussed in detail in Chapter 7). Clearly defined targets can be applied as an institutional way of improving the macroeconomic outcomes of monetary policy.

The effectiveness of such an institutional framework, however, depends on two fundamental requirements: independence and accountability. Although the Bank of Canada has not been given *goal independence*—the goal of price stability has been set jointly by the Bank and the Department of Finance—over the last decade the Bank placed increased emphasis on its responsibility to achieve the goal of price stability and its greater freedom to take whatever action is needed to do so. This freedom is referred to as *operational* (or *instrument*) *independence* and although it hasn't been explicitly legislated, it exists in practice. Increased operational independence has also raised the standards for accountability. As already noted, for example, the governor of the Bank has delegated the authority for monetary policy decisions to a committee—the six-member internal Governing Council. Moreover, it has become a de facto standard for the governor to appear before a parliamentary committee following the release of the Bank's *Monetary Policy Report*.

[7]John Crow, "The Work of Canadian Monetary Policy," The Eric J. Hanson Memorial Lecture, University of Alberta, Edmonton, Alberta. *Bank of Canada Review* (1988): 3–17.

The Bank has also improved its communications activities by moving toward greater transparency in its operations and objectives. In 1999, for example, the Bank started a twice-yearly *Update* to the *Monetary Policy Report*, both published by the Bank's Governing Council. The *Monetary Policy Report* is published every May and November while the *Update* is published every January and July giving an account of the Bank's management of monetary policy. Moreover, the Bank has noticeably increased the number of press conferences, press releases, and speeches, and also reorganized its regional offices in 1996–1997 with the objective of improving communication, transparency, and its assessment of economic conditions across Canada. For example, the Bank's regional offices, by maintaining contact with provincial governments, industries, and the general public, present quarterly grassroots assessments of current and prospective economic developments to the Bank's Governing Council—information that complements economic projections prepared by the Bank's staff. Finally, the Bank maintains a comprehensive Website to disseminate information regarding financial statistics, publications, the transmission of monetary policy, and Bank-related material.

Visit the Bank of Canada's Website at www.bankofcanada.ca

The direction taken in the recent evolution of the monetary policy framework in Canada has been heavily influenced by the role that the institutional monetary structure plays in influencing the monetary conduct.[8] As the Bank's former governor, Gordon Thiessen, put it in his October 17, 2000, speech to the Faculty of Social Science of the University of Western Ontario[9]

> [t]he Bank tries to work with the markets, rather than against them, to avoid surprising them with unexpected actions. Greater transparency facilitates the policy-transmission process by conditioning market expectations, and helps avoid unnecessary confusion about the reasons for our actions.

STRUCTURE AND INDEPENDENCE OF FOREIGN CENTRAL BANKS

In contrast to the Bank of Canada, which is a centralized unit owned by the government, central banks in other industrialized countries have a more decentralized structure. Here we examine the structure and degree of independence of four of the most important foreign central banks: the Bank of England, the Bank of Japan, the European Central Bank, and the Federal Reserve System of the United States.

Bank of England

Founded in 1694, the Bank of England is one of the oldest central banks. The Bank Act of 1946 gave the government statutory authority over the Bank of England. The Court (equivalent to a board of directors) of the Bank of England is made up of the governor and two deputy governors, who are appointed for five-year terms, and 16 nonexecutive directors, who are appointed for three-year terms.

Go to www.bankofengland.co.uk **for details about the Bank of England.**

Until 1997, the Bank of England was the least independent of the central banks examined in this chapter because the decision to raise or lower interest rates resided not within the Bank of England but with the chancellor of the Exchequer (the equivalent of the Canadian minister of finance). All this changed when the new Labour government came to power in May 1997. At this time, the new chancellor of the Exchequer, Gordon Brown, made a surprise announcement that

[8]For a discussion of similar changes implemented by other central banks around the world, see Graydon Paulin, "The Changing Face of Central Banking in the 1990s," *Bank of Canada Review* (Summer 2000): 3–13.

[9]Gordon Thiessen, "Can a Bank Change? The Evolution of Monetary Policy at the Bank of Canada 1935–2000," Lecture to the Faculty of Social Science, University of Western Ontario.

the Bank of England would henceforth have the power to set interest rates. However, the Bank was not granted total independence: The government can overrule the Bank and set rates "in extreme economic circumstances" and "for a limited period." Nonetheless, as in Canada, because overruling the Bank would be so public and is supposed to occur only in highly unusual circumstances and for a limited time, it is unlikely that the government will ever overrule the Bank.

The decision to set interest rates resides in the Monetary Policy Committee, made up of the governor, four other central bank officials (two deputy governors and two other central bank officials chosen by the governor), plus four outside economic experts appointed by the chancellor. (Surprisingly, two of the four outside experts initially appointed to this committee were not British citizens—one was Dutch and the other American, although both were residents of the United Kingdom.)

Bank of Japan

The Bank of Japan's homepage is www.boj.or.jp/en

The Bank of Japan (Nippon Ginko) was founded in 1882 during the Meiji Restoration. Monetary policy is determined by the Policy Board, which is composed of the governor, two vice governors, and six outside members appointed by the cabinet and approved by Parliament, all of whom serve for five-year terms.

Until recently, the Bank of Japan was not formally independent of the government, with ultimate power residing with the ministry of finance. However, the new Bank of Japan Law, which took effect in April 1998—the first major change in the powers of the Bank of Japan in 55 years—has changed this. In addition to stipulating that the objective of monetary policy is to attain price stability, the law granted greater independence to the Bank of Japan. Before this, the government had two voting members on the Policy Board, one from the ministry of finance and the other from the Economic Planning Agency. Now the government may send two representatives from these agencies to board meetings, but they no longer have voting rights, although they do have the ability to request delays in monetary policy decisions. In addition, the ministry of finance lost its authority to oversee many of the operations of the Bank of Japan, particularly the right to dismiss senior officials. However, the ministry of finance continues to have control over the part of the Bank's budget that is unrelated to monetary policy. Some critics of the new law argue that giving the ministry veto power over most of the Bank's budget may substantially limit the independence of the Bank of Japan.

European Central Bank

Gather general information about the organizational structure of ECB, its history and goals, its monetary policy strategy, and operational framework by clicking on "About the ECB" at www.ecb.int

The Maasricht Treaty established the European Central Bank (ECB) and the European System of Central Banks (ESCB), which began operation in January 1999. The structure of the central bank is patterned after the U.S. Federal Reserve System in that central banks for each country have a role similar to that of the Federal Reserve banks. The executive board of the ECB is made up of the president, a vice president, and four other members, who are appointed for eight-year terms. The monetary policymaking body of the bank includes the six members of the executive board and the central bank governors from the 11 euro countries, all of whom must have five-year terms at a minimum.

At the Swiss National Bank's Website, www.snb.ch, you can get more information about its activities.

The European Central Bank will be the most independent in the world, even more independent than the German central bank, the Bundesbank, which, before the establishment of the ECB, was considered the world's most independent central bank, along with the Swiss National Bank. The ECB is independent of both the European Union and the national governments and has complete control over monetary policy. In addition, the ECB's mandated mission is the pursuit of price stability. The ECB is far more independent than any other central bank in the world because its charter cannot be changed by legislation: It can be changed only by revision of the Maasricht Treaty, a difficult process because all signatories to the treaty would have to agree.

Federal Reserve System

Check out information on the structure of the Federal Reserve System at www.federalreserve.gov/pubs/frseries/frseri.htm

Of all the central banks in the world, the United States' **Federal Reserve System** (also called simply **the Fed**) probably has the most unusual structure. It includes the following entities: the **Board of Governors**, the 12 **Federal Reserve banks**, the **Federal Open Market Committee (FOMC)**, the Federal Advisory Council, and around 3000 member commercial banks.

At the head of the Federal Reserve System is the seven-member Board of Governors, headquartered in Washington, D.C. Each governor is appointed by the president of the United States and confirmed by the Senate. To limit the president's control over the Fed and insulate the Fed from other political pressures, the governors serve one nonrenewable 14-year term, with one governor's term expiring every other January. The chairman of the Board of Governors is chosen from among the seven governors and serves a four-year term. It is expected that once a new chairman is chosen, the old chairman resigns from the Board of Governors, even if there are many years left to his or her term as a governor.

Find addresses and phone numbers of Federal Reserve banks and branches as well as links to the main pages of the 12 reserve banks and Board of Governors at www.federalreserve.gov/otherfrb.htm

Each of the 12 Federal Reserve banks is a quasi-public (part private, part government) institution owned by the private commercial banks in the district, which are members of the Federal Reserve System.[10] The three largest Federal Reserve banks in terms of assets are those of New York, Chicago, and San Francisco—combined they hold 50% of the assets (discount loans, securities, and other holdings) of the Federal Reserve System. The New York bank, with around one-quarter of the assets, is the most important of the Federal Reserve banks. The 12 Federal Reserve banks and the Board of Governors are actively involved in decisions concerning the conduct of monetary policy. In particular, all seven governors are voting members of the FOMC together with the president of the Federal Reserve Bank of New York and presidents of four other Federal Reserve banks. The FOMC usually meets eight times a year (about every six weeks) and makes decisions regarding the conduct of monetary policy in the United States.

Find general information on the FOMC, including its schedule of meetings, statements, minutes, and transcripts, information on its members, and the beige book at www.federalreserve.gov/fomc

The Federal Reserve appears to be remarkably free of the political pressures that influence other government agencies in the United States. Yet it is still subject to the influence of the president of the United States, since the president appoints members to the Board of Governors. The power of the United States president in appointing members to the Board of Governors is limited, however. Because the term of the chairman of the Board of Governors is not necessarily concurrent with that of the president of the United States, a president may have to deal with a chairman of the Board of Governors appointed by a previous administration. Alan Greenspan, for example, was appointed chairman in 1987 by President Ronald Reagan and was reappointed to another term by another Republican president, George Bush. When Bill Clinton, a Democrat, became president in 1993, Greenspan had several years left to his term. Clinton was put under tremendous

Go to the Websites of the Federal Reserve Banks of New York, Chicago, and San Francisco at www.ny.frb.org, www.chicagofed.org, and www.frbsf.org to examine their set-ups.

[10]Currently, around one-third of the commercial banks in the United States are members of the Federal Reserve System. However, there is no distinction between member and nonmember banks, as they all are on equal footing in terms of reserve requirements and access to the Federal Reserve facilities, such as the discount window and Fed cheque clearing.

pressure to reappoint Greenspan when his term expired and did so in 1996, even though Greenspan is a Republican.[11]

You can see that the Federal Reserve has extraordinary independence for a government agency and is one of the most independent central banks in the world. Moreover, the Fed's independence is reinforced by the fact that it faces less constraint than any other central bank from the behaviour of other central banks; other central banks, including the Bank of Canada, have to pay considerable attention to the behaviour of the U.S. Federal Reserve.

The Trend Toward Greater Independence

Go to www.rbnz.govt.nz, and www.riksbank.se for details about the central banks of New Zealand and Sweden.

As our survey of the structure and independence of the major central banks indicates, in recent years we have been seeing a remarkable trend toward increasing independence. It used to be that the Federal Reserve was substantially more independent than almost all other central banks, with the exception of those in Germany and Switzerland. Now the newly established European Central Bank is far more independent than the Fed, and greater independence has been granted to central banks such as the Bank of England and the Bank of Japan, putting them more on a par with the Fed, as well as to central banks in such diverse countries as New Zealand, Sweden, and the euro nations. Both theory and experience suggest that more independent central banks produce better monetary policy, thus providing an impetus for this trend.

EXPLAINING CENTRAL BANK BEHAVIOUR

One view of government bureaucratic behaviour is that bureaucracies serve the public interest (this is the *public interest view*). Yet some economists have developed a theory of bureaucratic behaviour that suggests other factors that influence how bureaucracies operate. The *theory of bureaucratic behaviour* suggests that the objective of a bureaucracy is to maximize its own welfare, just as a consumer's behaviour is motivated by the maximization of personal welfare and a firm's behaviour is motivated by the maximization of profits. The welfare of a bureaucracy is related to its power and prestige. Thus, this theory suggests that an important factor affecting a central bank's behaviour is its attempt to increase its power and prestige.

What predictions does this view of a central bank like the Bank of Canada suggest? One is that the Bank will fight vigorously to preserve its autonomy, a prediction verified time and time again as the Bank has continually counterattacked attempts to control its functions. Another prediction is that the Bank of Canada will try to avoid conflict with powerful groups that may threaten to curtail its power and reduce its autonomy. The Bank's behaviour may take several forms. One possible factor explaining why the Bank is sometimes slow to increase interest rates and so smoothes out their fluctuations is that it wants to avoid a conflict with the government over increases in interest rates. The desire to avoid conflict may also explain why some central banks devised clever stratagems to avoid blame for their mistakes (see Box 4).

The theory of bureaucratic behaviour seems applicable to the Bank of Canada's actions, but we must recognize that this view of the Bank as being solely concerned with its own self-interest is too extreme. Maximizing one's welfare does not rule

[11]Similarly, William McChesney Martin Jr., the chairman from 1951 to 1970, was appointed by President Truman (Dem.) but was reappointed by Presidents Eisenhower (Rep.), Kennedy (Dem.), and Nixon (Rep.). Also Paul Volcker, the chairman from 1979 to 1987, was appointed by President Carter (Dem.) but was reappointed by President Reagan (Rep.).

BOX 4

Games the Central Banks Play

As the theory of bureaucratic behaviour predicts, central banks may play games to obscure their actions in order to avoid governmental interference in their activities. For example, in 1975 the U.S. Congress passed a resolution that instructed the Fed to report quarterly target ranges for the growth in the monetary aggregates over the next 12 months and how successful it had been in achieving previous targets. One game that the Fed played was to report on several monetary aggregates (such as M1, M2, and M3) rather than on one: When the Fed testified to Congress on its success in achieving its past targets, it would focus on the particular monetary aggregate whose growth rate was closest to the target range.

In addition to this clever tactic, the Fed devised a procedure for setting its target for monetary aggregates (called *base drift*) that made it more likely that it would hit its targets, thereby avoiding conflict with Congress. Every quarter, the Fed would revise the target values for monetary aggregates by applying target growth rates to the amount at which the aggregate had ended up (a new base). When the Fed overshot its targets, as frequently occurred after 1975, it revised future target values upward, making it less likely that the monetary aggregates would exceed target ranges in the future. Similarly, if the Fed undershot its targets, it revised future target values downward, making it less likely that the monetary aggregates would fall below the target ranges in the future. Subsequent legislation now restricts the Fed to changing the base for its target ranges only once a year, reducing the extent of base drift.

out altruism. (You might give generously to a charity because it makes you feel good about yourself, but in the process you are helping a worthy cause.) The Bank is surely concerned that it conduct monetary policy in the public interest. However, much uncertainty and disagreement exist over what monetary policy should be. When it is unclear what is in the public interest, other motives may influence the Bank's behaviour. In these situations, the theory of bureaucratic behaviour may be a useful guide to predicting what motivates the Bank.

SHOULD THE BANK OF CANADA BE INDEPENDENT?

As we have seen, the Bank of Canada is probably the most independent government agency in Canada. Every few years, the question arises as to whether the independence of the Bank of Canada should be curtailed. Politicians who strongly oppose a Bank policy often want to bring it under their supervision in order to impose a policy more to their liking. Should the Bank of Canada be independent, or would we be better off with a central bank under the control of the government?

The Case for Independence

The strongest argument for an independent Bank of Canada rests on the view that subjecting the Bank to more political pressures would impart an inflationary bias to monetary policy. In the view of many observers, politicians in a democratic society are shortsighted because they are driven by the need to win their next election. With this as the primary goal, they are unlikely to focus on long-run objectives, such as promoting a stable price level. Instead, they will seek short-run solutions to problems, like high unemployment and high interest rates, even if the short-run solutions have undesirable long-run consequences. For example, we saw in Chapter 4 that high money growth might lead initially to a drop in interest rates but might cause an increase later as inflation heats up. Would a Bank of Canada under the control of the government be more likely to pursue a policy of excessive money growth when interest rates are high, even though it would eventually lead to inflation and even higher interest rates in the future? The advocates of an independent central bank say yes. They believe that a politically insulated central bank is more likely to be concerned with long-run objectives and thus be a defender of a sound dollar and a stable price level.

A variation on the preceding argument is that the political process in Canada leads to the so-called **political business cycle**, in which just before an election, expansionary policies are pursued to lower unemployment and interest rates. After the election, the bad effects of these policies—high inflation and high interest rates—come home to roost, requiring contractionary policies that politicians hope the public will forget before the next election. Although the issue has not been completely settled, recent work by Serletis and Afxentiou of the University of Calgary indicates that there is no credible evidence that such a political business cycle exists in Canada (see Box 5).

Putting the Bank of Canada under the control of the government is also considered dangerous because the Bank can be used to facilitate government financing of large budget deficits by its purchases of government bonds in the open market. Such open-market purchases by the Bank increase the money supply and lead to inflation. Government pressure on the Bank to "help out" might lead to a more inflationary bias in the economy. An independent Bank of Canada is better able to resist this pressure from the government.

Another argument for Bank of Canada independence is that control of monetary policy is too important to leave to politicians, a group that has repeatedly demonstrated a lack of expertise at making hard decisions on issues of great economic importance, such as reducing the budget deficit or reforming the banking system. Another way to state this argument is in terms of the principal-agent problem discussed in Chapters 14 and 17. Both the Bank of Canada and politicians are agents of the public (the principals), and as we have seen, both politicians and the Bank have incentives to act in their own interest rather than in the interest of the public. The argument supporting Bank of Canada independence is that

BOX 5

Electoral and Partisan Cycle Regularities

Recent politico-institutional approaches to the theory of economic policy emphasize the incentives of rational and maximizing policymakers in explaining movements in macroeconomic variables. Central to this perspective is the general assumption that policymakers respond to incentives and constraints just like the rest of the economic agents. As a consequence, the actual policies of government give rise to political cycles, which on the basis of the primary motivational force involved are distinguished into opportunistic and partisan cycles.

In opportunistic (or electoral) business cycle models, politicians maximize their popularity or their probability of re-election by following pre-election expansionary fiscal policies in order to please the fiscally illuded voters. As a consequence, their actual policies give rise to electoral cycles, that is, persistent cyclical patterns of key policy and target variables across electoral terms, regardless of the political orientation of the incumbent government. In particular, models of opportunistic cycles predict pre-election high growth and low unemployment, increasing inflation around the election time, and a post-election contraction, regardless of the political party in power. In the more accepted partisan cycle models, politicians are ideological, that is, they represent the interests of different pressure groups and, when in office, follow policies that are favourable to their supporting groups. For example, the left-wing parties pursue expansionary policies in order to reduce unemployment, while the right-wing parties tend to induce post-election contractions in economic performance in order to reduce inflation. The outcome, therefore, is partisan cycles, that is, systematic and permanent differences in macroeconomic outcomes that differ by political party.

Recent work by Apostolos Serletis and Panos Afxentiou of the University of Calgary indicates that there is no credible evidence that such a political business cycle exists in Canada.[12]

[12]Apostolos Serletis and Panos C. Afxentiou, "Electoral and Partisan Cycle Regularities in Canada," *Canadian Journal of Economics* 31 (1998): 28-46.

the principal-agent problem is worse for politicians than for the Bank because politicians have fewer incentives to act in the public interest.

Indeed, some politicians may prefer to have an independent Bank of Canada, which can be used as a public scapegoat to take some of the heat off their shoulders. It is possible that a politician who in private opposes an inflationary monetary policy will be forced to support such a policy in public for fear of not being re-elected. An independent Bank of Canada can pursue policies that are politically unpopular yet in the public interest.

The Case Against Independence

Proponents of a Bank of Canada under the control of the goverment argue that it is undemocratic to have monetary policy (which affects almost everyone in the economy) controlled by an elite group responsible to no one. The current lack of de facto accountability of the Bank of Canada has serious consequences: If the Bank performs badly, there is no provision for replacing members (as there is with politicians). True, the Bank of Canada needs to pursue long-run objectives, but elected government officials vote on long-run issues also (foreign policy, for example). If we push the argument further that policy is always performed better by elite groups such as the Bank of Canada, we end up with such conclusions as Canada Customs and Revenue Agency (CCRA), formerly Revenue Canada, should set tax policies with no oversight from the government. Would you advocate this degree of independence for the CCRA?

The public holds government responsible for the economic well-being of the country, yet it lacks control over the government agency that may well be the most important factor in determining the health of the economy. In addition, to achieve a cohesive program that will promote economic stability, monetary policy must be coordinated with fiscal policy (management of government spending and taxation). Only by placing monetary policy under the control of the politicians who also control fiscal policy can these two policies be prevented from working at cross-purposes.

There is yet no consensus on whether Bank of Canada independence is a good thing, although public support for independence of the central bank seems to have been growing both in Canada and abroad. As you might expect, people who like the Bank's policies are more likely to support its independence, while those who dislike its policies advocate a less independent Bank of Canada.

CENTRAL BANK INDEPENDENCE AND MACROECONOMIC PERFORMANCE IN SEVENTEEN COUNTRIES

We have seen that advocates of an independent central bank believe that macroeconomic performance will be improved by making the central bank more independent. Recent research seems to support this conjecture: When central banks are ranked from 1 (least independent) to 4 (most independent), inflation performance is found to be the best for countries with the most independent central banks.[13] As you can see in Figure 1, Germany and Switzerland, with the two most independent central banks, were also the countries with the lowest infla-

[13]Alberto Alesina and Lawrence H. Summers, "Central Bank Independence and Macroeconomic Performance: Some Comparative Evidence," *Journal of Money, Credit and Banking* 25 (1993): 151–162. However, Adam Posen, "Central Bank Independence and Disinflationary Credibility: A Missing Link," *Oxford Economic Papers* 50 (1998): 335–359, has cast some doubt on whether the casuality runs from central bank independence to improved inflation perfomance.

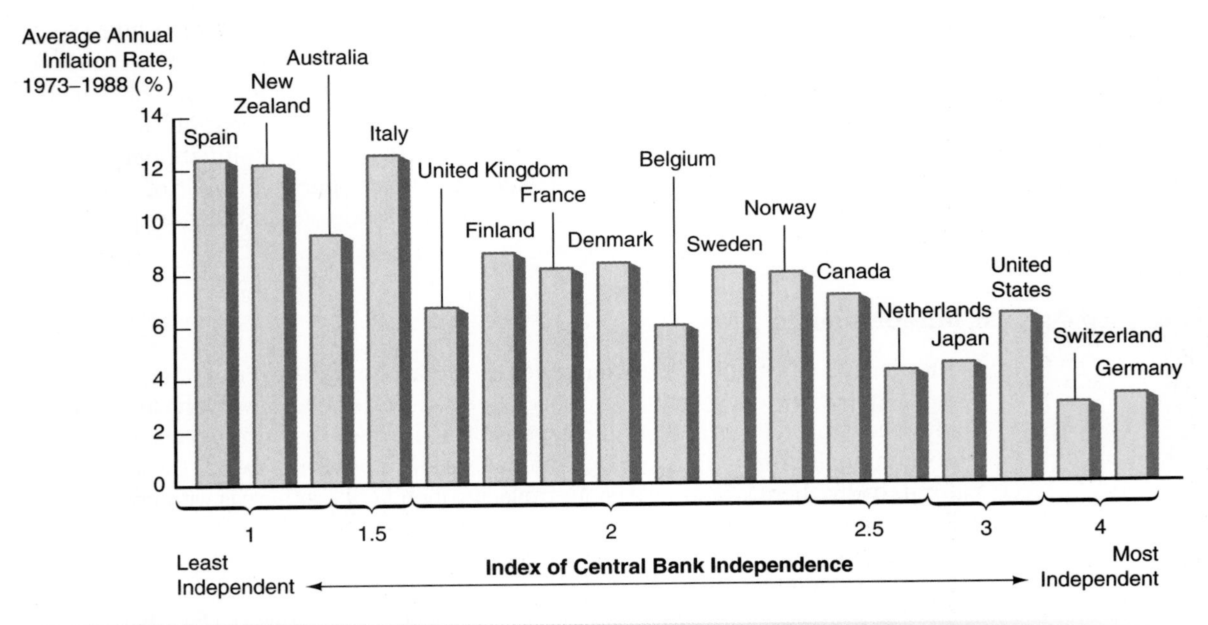

FIGURE 1 Central Bank Independence and Macroeconomic Performance in Seventeen Countries

On the horizontal axis, the 17 central banks are rated from least independent, 1, to most independent, 4. More independent banks have generally produced lower inflation than less independent central banks.

Source: Alberto Alesina and Lawrence H. Summers, "Central Bank Independence and Macroeconomic Performance: Some Comparative Evidence," *Journal of Money, Credit and Banking* 25 (1993): 151–162.

The central bank of Spain's Website is www.bde.es

tion rates in the 1973–1988 period. By contrast, the countries with the highest inflation in those years—Spain, New Zealand, Australia, and Italy—were also the countries with the least independent central banks. (The Spanish and New Zealand central banks have since gained greater independence.) Although a more independent central bank appears to lead to a lower inflation rate, this is not achieved at the expense of poorer real economic performance. Countries with independent central banks are no more likely to have high unemployment or greater output fluctuations than countries with less independent central banks.

SUMMARY

1. The Bank of Canada was created by act of Parliament in 1934 and began operations on March 11, 1935. Initially it was privately owned but became a crown corporation in 1938.
2. The overall responsibility for the operation of the Bank of Canada rests with a Board of Directors, consisting of the governor, the senior deputy governor, the deputy minister of finance, and 12 outside directors. The Bank's governor (currently David Dodge) is the chief executive officer and chairman of the Board of Directors.
3. Although on paper the Bank of Canada is an arm of the government, in practice the Bank has more independence than the Bank of Canada Act suggests.
4. The Bank of Canada is more independent than most agencies of the Canadian government, but it is still subject to political pressures. The theory of bureaucratic behaviour indicates that one factor driving the Bank's behaviour is its attempt to increase its power and prestige. This view explains many of the Bank's actions, although the agency may also try to act in the public interest.
5. The case for an independent Bank of Canada rests on the view that curtailing the Bank's independence and subjecting it to more political pressures would impart an inflationary bias to monetary policy. An independent Bank of Canada can afford to take the long view and not respond to short-run problems that will result in expansionary monetary policy

and a political business cycle. The case against an independent Bank of Canada holds that it is undemocratic to have monetary policy (so important to the public) controlled by an elite group that is not accountable to the public. An independent Bank of Canada also makes the coordination of monetary and fiscal policy difficult.

KEY TERMS

Bank, *p. 135*
Base money, *p. 138*
Board of Directors, *p. 136*
Board of Governors (of the Fed), *p. 145*
Exchange Fund Account, *p. 138*
Federal Open Market Committee (FOMC), *p. 145*
Federal Reserve banks, *p. 145*
Federal Reserve System (the Fed), *p. 145*
Governing Council, *p. 137*
monetary base, *p. 138*
open market operations, *p. 139*
political business cycle, *p. 148*

QUESTIONS AND PROBLEMS

***1.** What political realities might explain the creation of the Bank of Canada in 1934?

2. In what ways can the government influence the conduct of monetary policy?

3. Who is responsible for monetary policy in Canada?

4. Do you think that the seven-year renewable term for the governor of the Bank of Canada effectively insulates the Bank from political pressure?

***5.** How did the Coyne Affair motivate the current system of joint responsibility for monetary policy?

6. Over time, which entities have gained power in the conduct of monetary policy in Canada and which have lost power? Why do you think this has happened?

***7.** "The strongest argument for an independent Bank of Canada rests on the view that subjecting the Bank to more political pressures would impart an inflationary bias to monetary policy." Is this statement true, false, or uncertain? Explain your answer.

8. The Bank of Canada is the most independent of all Canadian government agencies. What is the main difference between it and other government agencies that explains its greater independence?

***9.** How can the government directly influence the Bank of Canada?

10. How is the responsibility for monetary policy shared in the Eurosystem?

***11.** "The theory of bureaucratic behaviour indicates that the Bank of Canada never operates in the public interest." Is this statement true, false, or uncertain? Explain your answer.

12. Why might eliminating the Bank's independence lead to a more pronounced political business cycle?

***13.** "The independence of the Bank of Canada leaves it completely unaccountable for its actions." Is this statement true, false, or uncertain? Explain your answer.

14. "The independence of the Bank of Canada has meant that it takes the long view and not the short view." Is this statement true, false, or uncertain? Explain your answer.

***15.** Why did Canada show little interest in the establishment of a central bank during the first 60 or so years of Confederation?

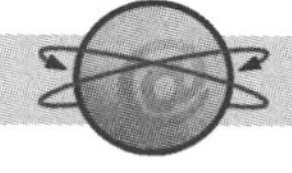

WEB EXERCISES

Structure of Central Banks and the Bank of Canada

1. Go to http://www.bankofcanada.ca and click on the link "About the Bank." Choose "Management Structure." What is the most important responsibility of the Governing Council?

2. Go to the previously mentioned site and click on "Monetary Policy." According to the information provided, what is the objective of the Bank of Canada's monetary policy?

Chapter 7

Conduct of Monetary Policy: Tools, Goals, and Targets

Preview

Understanding the conduct of monetary policy is important because it affects not only the money supply and interest rates but also the level of economic activity and hence our well-being. To explore this subject, we look first at the Bank of Canada's balance sheet and how the tools of monetary policy affect the money supply and interest rates. Then we examine in more detail the institutional framework within which the Bank of Canada conducts monetary policy, how the Bank of Canada uses the tools of monetary policy, and what goals the Bank and other countries' central banks establish for monetary policy. After examining strategies for conducting monetary policy, we can evaluate central banks' conduct of monetary policy in the past, with the hope that it will give us some clues as to where monetary policy may head in the future.

THE BANK OF CANADA'S BALANCE SHEET

The conduct of monetary policy by the Bank of Canada involves actions that affect its balance sheet (holdings of assets and liabilities). Here we discuss the following simplified balance sheet:

Bank of Canada	
Assets	Liabilities
Government securities	Notes in circulation
Advances to banks	Settlement balances

Liabilities

The two liabilities on the balance sheet, Bank of Canada notes in circulation and settlement balances, are often referred to as the *monetary liabilities* of the Bank of Canada. They are an important part of the money supply story because increases in either or both will lead to an increase in the money supply (everything else being constant). The sum of the Bank's monetary liabilities (notes in circulation and settlement balances) and the Canadian Mint's monetary liabilities (coins in circulation) is called the **monetary base.** When discussing the monetary base, we will

Historic and current data on the aggregate settlement balances of depository institutions and the monetary base is available at www.cba.ca and www.osfi.gc.ca

focus only on the monetary liabilities of the Bank of Canada because the monetary liabilities of the Canadian Mint account for a small fraction of the base.[1]

1. *Bank of Canada notes outstanding.* The Bank of Canada issues notes (those blue, purple, green, red, and brown pieces of paper in your wallet that say "Bank of Canada"). The Bank of Canada notes outstanding is the amount of these notes that is in the hands of the public and the depository institutions. Coins issued by the Canadian Mint are not a liability of the Bank of Canada. The coins and Bank of Canada notes that we use in Canada today are collectively known as **currency**.

   Bank of Canada notes are IOUs from the Bank to the bearer and are also liabilities, but unlike most, they promise to pay back the bearer solely with Bank of Canada notes; that is, they pay off IOUs with other IOUs. Accordingly, if you bring a $100 bill to the Bank of Canada and demand payment, you will receive two $50s, five $20s, ten $10s, or twenty $5 bills.

   People are more willing to accept IOUs from the Bank of Canada than from you or me because Bank of Canada notes are a recognized medium of exchange; that is, they are accepted as a means of payment and so function as money. Unfortunately, neither you nor I can convince people that our own IOUs are worth anything more than the paper they are written on.[2]

2. *Reserves.* All the direct Large Value Transfer System (LVTS) and Automated Clearing Settlement System (ACSS) participants (to be discussed in detail later in this chapter) have accounts at the Bank of Canada in which they hold settlement deposits. As of January 2002, there were 13 direct LVTS and ACSS participants in addition to the Bank of Canada: the Big Six, Alberta Treasury Branches, Bank of America Canada, La Caisse centrale Desjardins du Quebec, Canada Trustco Mortgage Company, Credit Union Central of Canada, HSBC Bank Canada, and the Laurentian Bank of Canada.

   Reserves consist of **settlement balances** at the Bank of Canada plus currency that is physically held by banks (called *vault cash* because it is held in bank vaults, cash tills, and automated teller machines). Under the LVTS, positive settlement balances held by direct clearers earn the bank rate less 50 basis points. **Reserves** are assets for the banks but liabilities for the Bank of Canada because the banks can demand payment on them at any time and the Bank of Canada is required to satisfy its obligation by paying Bank of Canada notes. As you will see, an increase in reserves leads to an increase in the level of deposits and hence in the money supply.

   As you will learn in Chapter 15, Canadian banks are no longer required to hold reserves. Banks, however, hold some reserves in order to manage their own short-term liquidity requirements and respond to predictable clearing drains and across-the-counter and automated teller machine drains. We call these reserves desired excess reserves or simply **desired reserves**. For

The following are links to some of the LVTS and ACSS participants' Websites: www.lbcdirect.laurentianbank.ca, www.atb.com, www.hsbc.ca, www.cucentral.ca, www.trustcorp.com

[1]It is also safe to ignore the Canadian Mint's monetary liabilities when discussing the monetary base because the Canadian Mint cannot actively supply its monetary liabilities to the economy because of legal restrictions.

[2]The notes item on the Bank of Canada's balance sheet refers only to notes in circulation, that is, the amount in the hands of the public. Currency that has been printed is not automatically a liability of the Bank of Canada. For example, consider the importance of having $1 million of your own IOUs printed up. You give out $100 worth to other people and keep the other $999 900 in your pocket. The $999 900 of IOUs does not make you richer or poorer and does not affect your indebtedness. You care only about the $100 of liabilities from the $100 of circulated IOUs. The same reasoning applies for the Bank of Canada in regard to its Bank of Canada notes.

For similar reasons, the currency component of the money supply, no matter how it is defined, includes only currency in circulation. It does not include any additional currency that is not yet in the hands of the public. The fact that currency has been printed but is not circulating means that it is not anyone's asset or liability and thus cannot affect anyone's behaviour. Therefore, it makes sense not to include it in the money supply.

example, banks might desire that for every dollar of deposits, a certain fraction (say, 5 cents) must be held as reserves. This fraction (5 percent) is called the **desired reserve ratio**. Reserves in excess of the desired amounts are called unwanted or **excess reserves**.

Assets

The two assets on the Bank of Canada's balance sheet are important for two reasons. First, changes in the asset items lead to changes in reserves and consequently to changes in the money supply. Second, because these assets (government securities and advances to banks) earn interest while the liabilities (notes in circulation and settlement balances) do not, the Bank makes millions of dollars every year—its assets earn income, and its liabilities cost little. Although it returns most of its earnings to the federal government, the Bank does spend some of it on "worthy causes," such as supporting economic research.

1. *Government of Canada securities*. These are the Bank's holdings of government of Canada securities. The total amount of securities is controlled by open market operations (the Bank's purchase and sale of these securities). Government of Canada securities is by far the Bank's largest category of assets, accounting for over 80% of the balance sheet.
2. *Advances*. These are loans the Bank of Canada makes to members of the Canadian Payments Association. There is a big difference between normal advances and extraordinary advances (to be discussed in detail later) lent by the Bank of Canada to troubled banks to prevent bank and financial panics. Normal advances are fully collateralized and generally overnight in duration.

The Canadian Payments Association Website, www.cdnpay.ca, provides more details about its members and loans they receive.

Open Market Operations

Open market operations, the central bank's purchase or sale of bonds in the open market, are the most important monetary policy tool because they are the primary determinant of changes in settlement balances in the banking system and interest rates. To see how they work, let's use T-accounts to examine what happens when the Bank of Canada conducts an open market purchase in which $100 of bonds are bought from the public.

When the person or corporation that sells the $100 of bonds to the Bank of Canada deposits the Bank's cheque in the local bank, the nonbank public's T-account after this transaction is

Nonbank Public

Assets		Liabilities	
Securities	−$100		
Chequable deposits	+$100		

When the bank receives the cheque, it credits the depositor's account with the $100 and then deposits the cheque in its account with the Bank of Canada, thereby adding to its settlement balances. The banking system's T-account becomes

Banking System

Assets		Liabilities	
Settlement balances	+$100	Chequable deposits	+$100

The effect on the Bank of Canada's balance sheet is that it has gained $100 of securities in its assets column, while settlement balances have increased by $100, as shown in its liabilities column:

Bank of Canada			
Assets		Liabilities	
Securities	+$100	Settlement balances	+$100

As you can see, the result of the Bank of Canada's open market purchase is an expansion of settlement balances and deposits in the banking system. Another way of seeing this is to recognize that open market purchases of bonds expand settlement balances because the central bank pays for the bonds with settlement balances. Because the monetary base equals currency plus settlement balances, we have shown that an open market purchase increases the monetary base by an equal amount. Also because deposits are an important component of the money supply, another result of the open market purchase is an increase in the money supply. This leads to the following important conclusion: ***An open market purchase leads to an expansion of settlement balances and deposits in the banking system and hence to an expansion of the monetary base and the money supply.***

Similar reasoning indicates that when a central bank conducts an open market sale, the public pays for the bonds by writing a cheque that causes deposits and settlement balances in the banking system to fall. Thus ***an open market sale leads to a contraction of settlement balances and deposits in the banking system and hence to a decline in the monetary base and the money supply.***

Although open market operations are the most important monetary policy tool for most central banks around the world, in 1994 the Bank of Canada stopped conducting open market operations in government of Canada bills and bonds. Since then, the Bank's most common open market operations have involved repurchase transactions, either SPRAs or SRAs (see page 167). As we will discuss in detail later in this chapter, the Bank of Canada is currently conducting repurchase transactions to reinforce its operating target—the midpoint of the operating band for the overnight interest rate.

Bank of Canada Lending

Open market operations are not the only way the Bank of Canada can affect the amount of settlement balances. Settlement balances are also changed when the Bank of Canada makes a loan to a bank. For example, suppose that the Bank of Canada makes a $100 discount loan to the First Bank. The Bank of Canada then credits $100 to the bank's settlement balances account. The effects on the balance sheets of the banking system and the Bank of Canada are illustrated by the following T-accounts:

Banking System		**Bank of Canada**	
Assets	Liabilities	Assets	Liabilities
Settlement balances +$100	Advances +$100	Advances +$100	Settlement balances +$100

We thus see that ***a Bank of Canada advance leads to an expansion of settlement balances, which can be lent out as deposits, thereby leading to an expansion of the monetary base and the money supply.*** Similar reasoning indicates that ***when a bank repays its Bank of Canada loans and so reduces the total amount of Bank of Canada lending, the amount of settlement balances decreases along with the monetary base and the money supply.***

THE FRAMEWORK FOR THE IMPLEMENTATION OF MONETARY POLICY

The tools used by the Bank of Canada to implement monetary policy are closely linked to the institutional arrangements regarding the clearing and settlement systems in the Canadian economy. Understanding the tools of monetary policy therefore requires that we know the key features of the framework for the implementation of monetary policy. As you will see, this framework has been designed to encourage deposit-taking financial institutions to deal directly with the market, rather than with the Bank of Canada.[3]

The Large Value Transfer System (LVTS)

Go to www.cdnpay.ca for more information about the Canadian Payments Association.

The core of the Canadian payments system is the **Large Value Transfer System (LVTS)**, introduced by the Canadian Payments Association on February 4, 1999. The LVTS is an electronic, real-time net settlement network, designed to provide immediate finality and settlement to time-critical transactions. As of January 2002, in addition to the Bank of Canada, there were 13 **LVTS participants**. All other members of the Canadian Payments Association are able to arrange LVTS payments for their clients through the LVTS participants.

The LVTS has been put in place in order to eliminate **systemic risk**—the risk to the entire payments system due to the inability of one financial institution to fulfill its payment obligations in a timely fashion. In particular, each LVTS payment is backed by collateral pledged to the Bank of Canada by the LVTS participant, is subject to real-time risk-control tests to confirm that sufficient collateral is available, and is final and irrevocable in real time. Of course, it is not just Canada that is concerned about systemic risk. The United States was the first country to initiate a real-time settlement system, the Fedwire system, in 1918. More recently, real-time settlement systems have been implemented by Sweden in 1986, Germany and Switzerland in 1987, Japan in 1988, Italy in 1989, Belgium and the United Kingdom in 1996, and France, Hong Kong, and the Netherlands in 1997. Moreover, the central banks of the G-10 countries, through the Bank for International Settlements, have developed minimum standards for the operation of the global payment network for large-value funds transfers.

At www.bis.org you can get more details about the Bank for International Settlements.

In Canada's LVTS, participants know in real time their large-value, wholesale transactions (over $50 000).[4] Although these transactions account for less than 1% of the total number of transactions, they account for about 94% of the value of transactions in Canada. This information eliminates most of the uncertainty from settlement balance prediction—the largest reason for financial institutions not being able to hit their target settlement balances with the Bank of Canada in the pre-LVTS system. Settlement of payment obligations among LVTS participants

---

[3]For more details, see Donna Howard, "A Primer on the Implementation of Monetary Policy in the LVTS Environment," *Bank of Canada Review* (Autumn, 1998): 57–66; Kevin Clinton, "Implementation of Monetary Policy in a Regime with Zero Reserve Requirements," Bank of Canada Working Paper 97-8; and "The Framework for the Implementation of Monetary Policy in the Large Value Transfer System Environment," Bank of Canada *Release*, March 31, 1999.

[4]Although the LVTS is suitable for large-value transactions, almost half of the transmitted payments are for amounts less than $50 000. On average the LVTS handles 13 000 transactions each day, totalling about $100 billion.

takes place, at the end of each banking day, through the transfer of funds in their settlement accounts at the Bank of Canada. The LVTS uses **multilateral netting**, in which only the net credit or debit position of each participant vis-à-vis all other participants is calculated for settlement, thereby reducing the need for a large amount of settlement balances.

Non-LVTS Transactions

Although the LVTS eliminates the uncertainty from daily wholesale settlement balances prediction, there is still a residual stochastic element in settlement balances from non-LVTS paper-based payments items (such as cheques, travellers' cheques, gift certificates, and money orders) and electronic payments items (such as pre-authorized debits and fund transfers, direct deposit items, and debits and credits initiated at the point of sale for goods or services). Those items are cleared through the Automated Clearing Settlement System (ACSS), an electronic payments system also operated by the Canadian Payments Association. The ACSS aggregates interbank payments and calculates the net amounts to be transferred from and to each participant's settlement account with the Bank of Canada. The Bank retroactively completes the settlement the next day (at midday) through the LVTS.

All LVTS participants also participate directly in the ACSS and are known as **direct clearers**. However, many deposit-taking financial institutions that are members of the Canadian Payments Association do not have a clearing account with the Bank of Canada. These institutions, known as **indirect clearers**, hold deposits in direct clearers in exchange for a variety of services, including cheque clearing, foreign exchange transactions, and help with securities purchases. This is an aspect of a system called correspondent banking.

The Operating Band for the Overnight Interest Rate

The overnight market in Canada is the key market for finance and monetary policy. This market is very liquid, with an estimated $50 billion traded per day by a broad range of participants, the most active of which are deposit-taking institutions and their investment dealer affiliates.[5] The interest rate at which participants borrow and lend overnight funds to each other in the money market is called the **overnight interest rate**. This rate is the shortest-term rate available and forms the base of any term structure of interest rates relation.

The Bank of Canada implements monetary policy by changing the overnight interest rate. In fact, the Bank's operational objective is to keep the overnight rate within a band (or channel) of 50 basis points. This channel system of monetary control is also used by other central banks that no longer have reserve requirements such as, for example, the Reserve Bank of Australia and the Reserve Bank of New Zealand. Since December 2000, the Bank of Canada has operated under a system of eight "fixed" dates throughout the year for announcing any changes to the **operating band** for the overnight rate, keeping the option of acting between the fixed dates in "extraordinary circumstances." Early in the morning (at 9 A.M.) on each of those specified announcement dates, the Bank of Canada announces an operating band of 50 basis points ($\frac{1}{2}$ of 1%) for the overnight rate (see Box 1).

---

[5]See Eugene Lundrigan and Sari Toll, "The Overnight Market in Canada," *Bank of Canada Review* (Winter 1997–1998): 27–42, for details regarding the evolution of the overnight market.

BOX 1

Monetary Policy Implementation in the LVTS Environment

The Market Timetable

9:00 A.M.	Bank of Canada announces changes (if any) to the operating band
9:15 A.M.	Cutoff time for bids for Receiver General term deposit auction
9:30 A.M.	Release of Receiver General term deposit auction results
11:45 A.M.	Special Purchase and Resale Agreements (SPRAs) or Sale and Repurchase Agreements (SRAs) transacted (if any)
3:00 P.M.	Cutoff time for presentation of government items to Bank of Canada
4:00 P.M.	Payment exchange for Debt Clearing Services (DCS)
4:15 P.M.	Cutoff time for bids for Receiver General term deposit auction
4:30 P.M.	Release of Receiver General auction results
6:00 P.M.	Close of LVTS for client (third-party) transactions
6:00–6:30 P.M.	Pre-settlement trading
8:00 P.M. or earlier	Settlement of LVTS balances at the Bank of Canada

Source: Donna Howard, "A Primer on the Implementation of Monetary Policy in the LVTS Environment," *Bank of Canada Review* (Autumn, 1998): 57–66; Kevin Clinton, "Implementation of Monetary Policy in a Regime with Zero Reserve Requirements," Bank of Canada Working Paper 97-8; and "The Framework for the Implementation of Monetary Policy in the Large Value Transfer System Environment," Bank of Canada *Release*, March 31, 1999.

In the LVTS environment, the Bank of Canada operates under a system of eight fixed dates throughout the year for announcing, via a press release (at 9 A.M.), any changes to the operating band for the overnight interest rate. The upper limit of the operating band defines the bank rate and the lower limit is the rate the Bank pays to LVTS participants with positive settlement balances at the end of the day.

The operating band for the overnight interest rate, reinforced by the Bank of Canada's standing facilities, and a target level of settlement balances of roughly $50 million are currently the framework within which the Bank of Canada implements monetary policy. The midpoint of the operating band is the operating target of the Bank's monetary policy.

In targeting the midpoint of the operating band, the Bank uses two rounds of repurchase transactions, either SPRAs or SRAs, although effective April 2, 2001, the Bank discontinued the second round of repurchase transactions, except in extraordinary circumstances.

To maintain the target level of settlement balances, the Bank neutralizes the effects of repurchase transactions and those of certain federal government and Bank of Canada flows that potentially affect settlement balances. The neutralization is effected through the shifting of federal government deposits between the government's account at the Bank of Canada and the government's accounts with LVTS participants. The shifting is made through twice-daily auctions of government term deposits (the first at 9:15 A.M. and the second at 4:15 P.M.).

The LVTS has a pre-settlement trading period of half an hour, at the end of the banking day (6–6:30 P.M.), to permit participating financial institutions to adjust positions with each other at a better return than can be achieved at the Bank of Canada's standing facilities. LVTS participants with settlement imbalances at the end of the banking day use the Bank of Canada's standing facilities to bring their settlement balances to the target level. That is, LVTS participants that require an overdraft loan to cover negative settlement balances on the books of the Bank borrow from the Bank at the bank rate. LVTS participants with positive settlement balances at the end of the day earn the bank rate less 50 basis points.

As Figure 1 shows, the upper limit of the operating band defines the bank rate. The **bank rate** is the interest rate the Bank charges LVTS participants that require an overdraft loan to cover negative settlement balances on the books of the Bank at the end of the banking day. The lower limit of the operating band is the rate the Bank pays to LVTS participants with positive settlement balances at the end of the day. The midpoint of the operating band is the operating target of the Bank of Canada's monetary policy. When, for example, the operating band is from 3.5% to 4.0%, the bank rate is 4.0%, the rate the Bank pays on deposits to LVTS participants is 3.5%, and the Bank's operating target is an overnight interest rate of 3.75%.

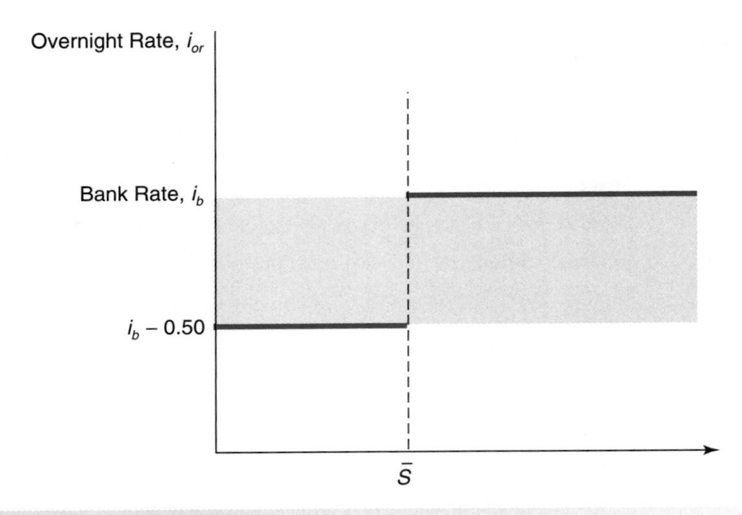

FIGURE 1 Operating Band for the Overnight Interest Rate

The Bank of Canada's Standing Facilities

LVTS participants can make a payment only if they have, in real time (right now), either positive settlement balances in their accounts with the Bank of Canada, or posted collateral (such as government of Canada treasury bills and bonds), or explicit lines of credit with other participants. As a result, the large-value clearing and settlement systems will settle at the end of each day even in the face of risk and liquidity problems. Moreover, at the end of each banking day, each participant must bring its settlement balance with the Bank of Canada close to zero. Of course, it can scarcely be expected that LVTS participants will always be successful in ending up with near-zero settlement balances. The Bank of Canada therefore stands ready (we call this **standing facilities**) to lend to or borrow from a participant to bring their settlement balances to zero at the end of the banking day. As already noted, participants also know with certainty the rates applicable to positive and negative settlement balances with the Bank of Canada (see Box 1).

To permit participating financial institutions to adjust positions with each other (i.e., reduce the costs of either positive or negative positions), the LVTS has a pre-settlement trading period of half an hour, at the end of the banking day (6:00–6:30 P.M.)—see Box 1. The purpose of the pre-settlement trading period is to provide a window for those participants with excess positions to trade with those in deficit, at a better return than can be achieved at the Bank's facilities, to the advantage of both. In fact, the typical bid-ask spread on overnight funds in the interbank market has been less than 1/8 percent. This is significantly less than the spread of 50 basis points between the rate charged on overdrafts and that paid on deposits by the Bank of Canada at the end of the LVTS day.

In general, pre-settlement trading among participants will achieve a zero settlement balance for each participant on wholesale transactions. However, if at the end of the settlement day a participant has a negative balance on the books of the Bank of Canada, the deficit will be financed by a collateralized advance at the bank rate. Participants with positive settlement balances at the end of the day are paid interest at the bank rate less 50 basis points (i.e., the bottom of the operating band). Hence, as long as the bank rate is set so that the market bid-ask spread is within the operating band, participants will resolve their nonzero settlement balances among themselves rather than through the Bank of Canada's standing facilities. In fact, in a fully competitive market, participants would be expected to trade at the midpoint of the operating band for the overnight interest rate.

Regarding ACSS settlement, the Bank of Canada charges the bank rate plus 150 basis points on ACSS collateralized advances and pays the bank rate less 150 basis points on ACSS positive balances. There is, however, an overnight interbank market in retroactive ACSS balances that allows participating financial institutions to resolve their nonzero retail clearing balances among themselves. In fact, since the rate spread at the Bank of Canada for ACSS balances is 300 basis points (250 basis points wider than that for LVTS balances), participants find that they can resolve their nonzero retail clearing balances at more favourable rates among themselves. This market, however, is thin and the Bank of Canada does not regard the interest rates that are formed in this market as a good indicator of the banking system's supply of overnight funds.

Clearly, the LVTS and the Bank of Canada's standing facilities have been set up in such a way as to ensure a determinate demand for settlement balances, treating the costs of deficits and surpluses symmetrically. That is, the cost of holding excess settlement balances (an opportunity cost of 25 basis points) equals the cost of holding deficit levels of settlement balances (a premium of 25 basis points for an overdraft borrowing). These cost incentives are very important in the absence of reserve requirements; they encourage banks to target zero settlement balances at the Bank of Canada and in doing so to deal directly with the market rather than to rely on the Bank's automatic standing facilities. Most days banks are within $25 million from zero and, in aggregate, $500 million to $700 million away from target.

The Bank's Implementation of the Operating Band

It is through its lending and taking deposits from LVTS participants that the Bank of Canada implements its operating band for the overnight interest rate. ***If the overnight rate increases toward the upper limit of the operating band, then the Bank will lend at the bank rate to put a ceiling on the overnight rate.*** The bank rate is the ceiling on the overnight rate in the money market for LVTS participants, because they are unlikely to borrow overnight funds at a higher interest rate, since they can borrow at the bank rate from the Bank of Canada.

If the overnight rate declines toward the lower limit of the operating band, then the Bank will accept deposits from LVTS participants at the bank rate less 50 basis points, to put a floor on the overnight rate. The bank rate less 50 basis points is the floor on the overnight rate because LVTS participants are unlikely to lend overnight funds at a lower rate, since they can leave funds on deposit at this rate at the Bank of Canada.

THE MARKET FOR SETTLEMENT BALANCES AND THE OVERNIGHT RATE

The market for settlement balances is where the overnight interest rate is determined, and this is why we turn to a supply and demand analysis of this market to analyze how the tools of monetary policy affect the overnight rate. Our analysis of the market for settlement balances proceeds in a similar fashion to the analysis of the bond market we conducted in Chapter 4 and describes determination of the overnight interest rate in a channel system of interest-rate control such as that in Canada, Australia, and New Zealand.

We derive a demand and supply curve for settlement balances. When the market equilibrium in which the quantity of settlement balances demanded equals the quantity of settlement balances supplied determines the overnight rate, the interest rate charged on the loans of these settlement balances.

Supply Curve

As already noted, the Bank of Canada targets the overnight interest rate at the midpoint of the operating band of 50 basis points. The target overnight interest rate is denoted by i^*_{or} in Figure 2. In addition, the Bank of Canada offers a lending facility, standing ready to lend (upon presentation of suitable collateral) overnight settlement balances to LVTS participants with negative clearing balances at the end of the business day. The lending rate is the bank rate, denoted by i_b in Figure 2, and is 25 basis points higher than the target overnight interest rate, so as to penalize participants for not using the overnight interbank market. Moreover, those participants with excess end-of-day clearing balances have the right to maintain these balances with the Bank of Canada at the deposit rate 25 basis points lower than the target overnight interest rate, again so as to penalize participants for not dealing directly with the market. The deposit rate is denoted by $i_b - 0.50$ in Figure 2. LVTS participants know with certainty the rates applicable to positive and negative settlement balances with the Bank of Canada.

The Bank of Canada's two standing liquidity facilities define an effective supply curve for settlement balances, shown in Figure 2. In particular, at i_b the supply curve of overnight settlement balances from the bank's lending facility is perfectly elastic, indicating that the equilibrium overnight interest rate cannot exceed the bank rate, no matter how high the demand for settlement balances may be. At i_b less 50 basis points, the supply curve is also perfectly elastic, indicating that the equilibrium overnight interest rate cannot fall below the lower limit of the operating channel. The vertical segment of the supply curve for settlement balances indicates the net supply of settlement balances other than those obtained through the Bank of Canada's standing liquidity facilities. Initially, the Bank targeted a daily level of settlement balances of zero, although effective April 2, 2001, the Bank is targeting a minimum of $50 million for LVTS clearing balances, to reduce frictions in the system; the Bank's target level of balances for a given day is always announced the previous day. Assuming here that the Bank is targeting a level of settlement balances of $\bar{S}$, the supply of settlement balances is represented by the supply curve shown in Figure 2.

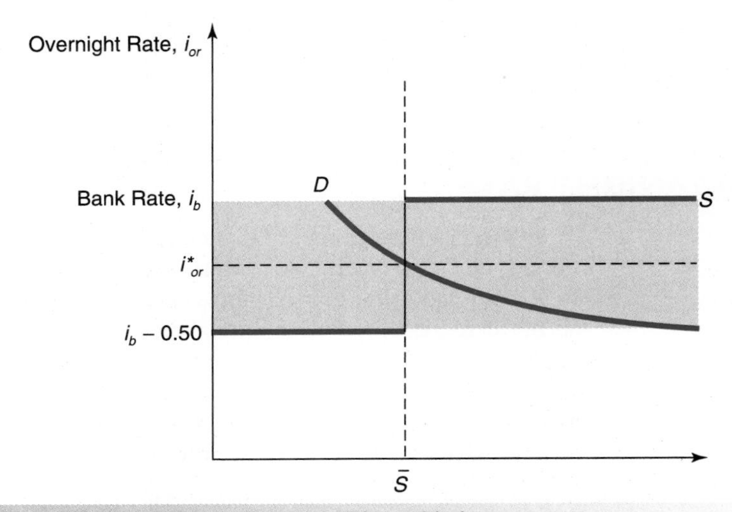

FIGURE 2 Equilibrium in the Overnight Money Market

Demand Curve

Assuming that the overnight interbank market is a perfectly competitive market held at a point in time (during the pre-settlement trading period), but before LVTS participants are able to determine with certainty their settlement balances at the end of the business day, the demand for settlement balances is decreasing in the overnight interest rate, as shown in Figure 2.[6] As shown in the figure, as the overnight interest rate approaches the lower limit of the operating band (and therefore as the opportunity cost of holding positive end-of-day settlement balances with the Bank of Canada declines), desired clearing balances increase significantly.

This happens because of the existence of residual uncertainty; that is, even after banks adjust positions with each other in the overnight interbank market, there is still a small but positive probability that they will have negative clearing balances on the books of the Bank of Canada at the end of the day. When the opportunity cost of holding positive end-of-day clearing balances with the Bank of Canada is small, LVTS participants ensure against this possibility by increasing desired clearing balances.

Equilibrium in the Market for Settlement Balances

Market equilibrium occurs where the quantity of settlement balances demanded equals the quantity supplied. In terms of Figure 2, equilibrium occurs at the intersection of the vertical supply curve and the demand curve at the Bank of Canada's target level of settlement balances (here assumed to be zero). The equilibrium overnight interest rate is necessarily within the operating band. However, i^*_{or} is indeterminate and could be anywhere within the operating band. As Kevin Clinton of the Bank of Canada puts it, "[t]he actual rate will be affected by a variety of technical factors, such as the size and distribution of clearing imbalances among banks. This implies that the realized rate will generally differ somewhat from the target indicated at the start of the day by the Bank of Canada."[7]

The degree to which the Bank of Canada succeeds in targeting the overnight rate at the midpoint of the band is shown in Figure 3, which plots the spread between the overnight rate and the target overnight rate, since the introduction of the LVTS. Although in the early months after the introduction of the LVTS the overnight rate was higher than the target rate, the figure shows that since early in 2000 the overnight interest rate has usually been within about one basis point of the target overnight rate.

It is to be noted that, in the model sketched here, the demand for clearing balances is a function of the overnight interest rate relative to the bank rate and the lower limit of the operating band; it is independent of the absolute level of any of these rates. As Michael Woodford puts it,

> [t]his means that an adjustment of the level of overnight rates by the central bank need not require any change in the supply of clearing balances, as long as the location of the lending and deposit rates relative to the tar-

[6]Models of the determinants of the demand for clearing balances in banking systems without reserve requirements can be found in Kevin Clinton, "Implementation of Monetary Policy in a Regime with Zero Reserve Requirements," Bank of Canada Working Paper 97-8; Timo Henckel, Alain Ize, and Arto Kovanen, "Central Banking without Central Bank Money," IMF Working Paper 99-92; Graeme Guthrie and Julian Wright, "Open Mouth Operations," *Journal of Monetary Economics* 24 (2000): 489–516; Graig H. Furfine, "Interbank Payments and the Daily Federal Funds Rate," *Journal of Monetary Economics* 46 (2000): 535–553; and Michael Woodford, "Monetary Policy in the Information Economy," Princeton University Working Paper, September 2001.

[7]Kevin Clinton, "Implementation of Monetary Policy in a Regime with Zero Reserve Requirements," Bank of Canada Working Paper 97-8.

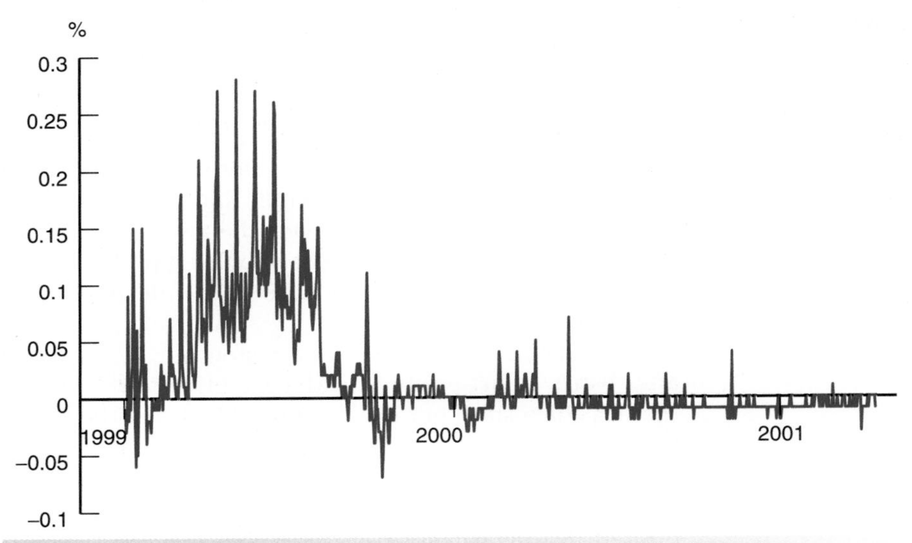

FIGURE 3 Spread Between the Overnight Interest Rate and the Target Rate

Source: Statistics Canada CANSIM II series V122514

get overnight rate do not change. Thus under a channel system, changes in the level of overnight interest rates are brought about by simply announcing a change in the target rate, which has the implication of changing the lending and deposit rates at the central bank's standing facilities; no quantity adjustments in the target supply of clearing balances are required.[8]

THE BANK OF CANADA'S APPROACH TO MONETARY POLICY

The goal of the Bank of Canada's current monetary policy is to keep the inflation rate within a target range of 1% to 3%, with the midpoint of the inflation target range, 2%, being the most desirable outcome. In setting its inflation targets, the Bank of Canada uses the rate of change in the consumer price index (CPI), because it is the most commonly used and understood price measure in Canada. Although the Bank's targets are specified in terms of "headline CPI" (all items), the Bank uses "core CPI," which excludes volatile components such as food, energy, and the effect of indirect taxes. Core CPI inflation is useful in assessing whether trend inflation is on track for the medium term. Also, defining the inflation targets in terms of ranges provides the Bank of Canada sufficient flexibility to deal with supply shocks, beyond those already taken care of by the exclusion of volatile components from core inflation.

Figure 4 shows what has happened to the Canadian inflation rate since February 1991, when the Bank's governor and the minister of finance jointly announced a series of declining inflation targets, with a band of plus and minus one percentage point around them. In what follows, we examine the tools used by the Bank of Canada to implement monetary policy.

How Monetary Policy Affects the Economy

The Bank of Canada affects interest rates and the level of economic activity by changing the operating band for the overnight interest rate. As we saw in Chapter 5, interest rates on different assets tend to move together over time. Hence,

[8]Michael Woodford, "Monetary Policy in the Information Economy," Princeton University Working Paper, September 2001.

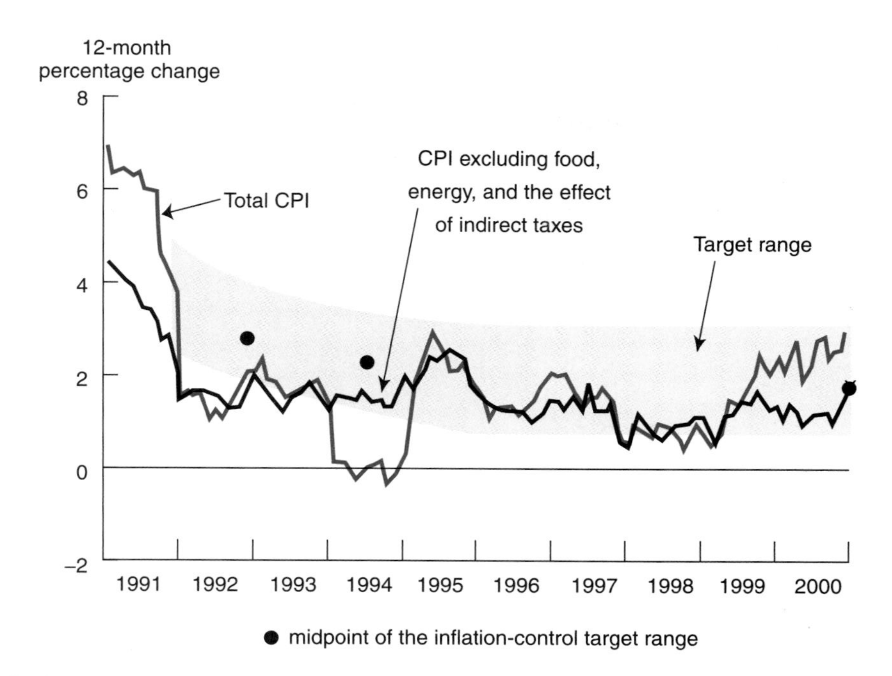

FIGURE 4 Inflation Rates and Inflation Targets for Canada, 1991–2000

Source: Bank of Canada *Annual Report,* 2000. Reprinted with permission.

changes in the operating band and thus the bank rate influence other rates, such as, for example, the prime rate (the interest rate banks charge to their best customers) and the interest rates on bank deposits and mortgages. These changes in interest rates may also lead to changes in the exchange rate. The level of short-term interest rates and the exchange rate of the Canadian dollar determine the **monetary conditions** in which the economy operates.

The concept of monetary conditions, introduced by the Bank in its conduct of monetary policy in the early 1990s, focuses on the effect on the economy of both short-term interest rates and the exchange rate. Changes in monetary conditions affect the economy and the Bank's ultimate objective, the inflation rate, only indirectly and are usually felt over a period of several months to several years. This means that the Bank of Canada must always be forward looking in its conduct of monetary policy, anticipating the level of monetary conditions needed today to achieve its ultimate goal of low and stable inflation in the future.

As an example, suppose that the Bank of Canada expects the economy to slow down and wants to ease monetary conditions. It lowers the operating band for the overnight interest rate, thereby encouraging banks to borrow settlement balances either from each other at the overnight rate or from the Bank of Canada at the bank rate.[9] As you can see in Figure 5, this reduces interest rates and the value of the dollar and leads to an increase in the supply of money, aggregate demand, and the price level, thereby preventing the inflation rate from falling below the target range of 1% to 3%.

In the opposite case, if the Bank expects the economy to be exceeding its capacity at some point in the future, it raises the operating band in order to prevent inflationary pressures from building. The consequent increase in interest rates and the value of the dollar lead to a decline in the supply of money, aggregate demand, and the price level, thereby preventing the inflation rate from moving above the Bank's target range of 1% to 3%—see Figure 6.

[9] For example, the Bank might lower the operating band by 25 basis points from 3.5% to 4.0% to 3.25% to 3.75%.

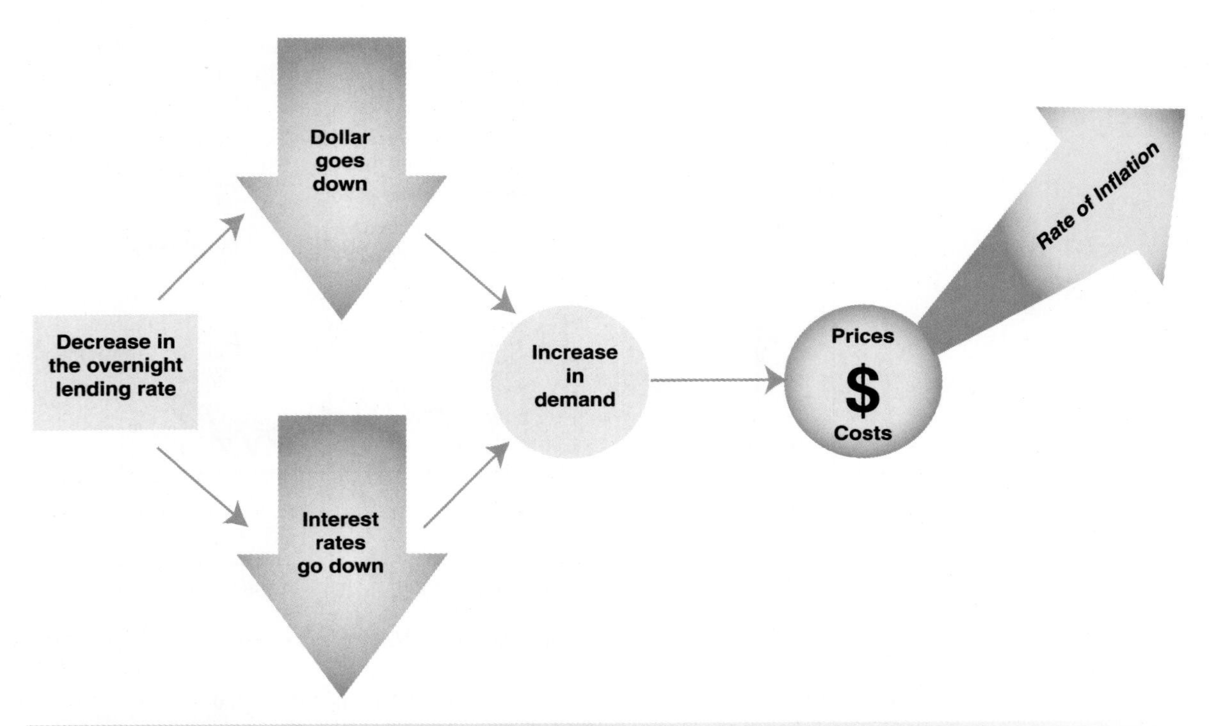

FIGURE 5 How the Bank of Canada Keeps the Rate of Inflation From Falling Below the Target Range

Source: Bank of Canada Website: www.bankofcanada.ca. Reprinted with permission.

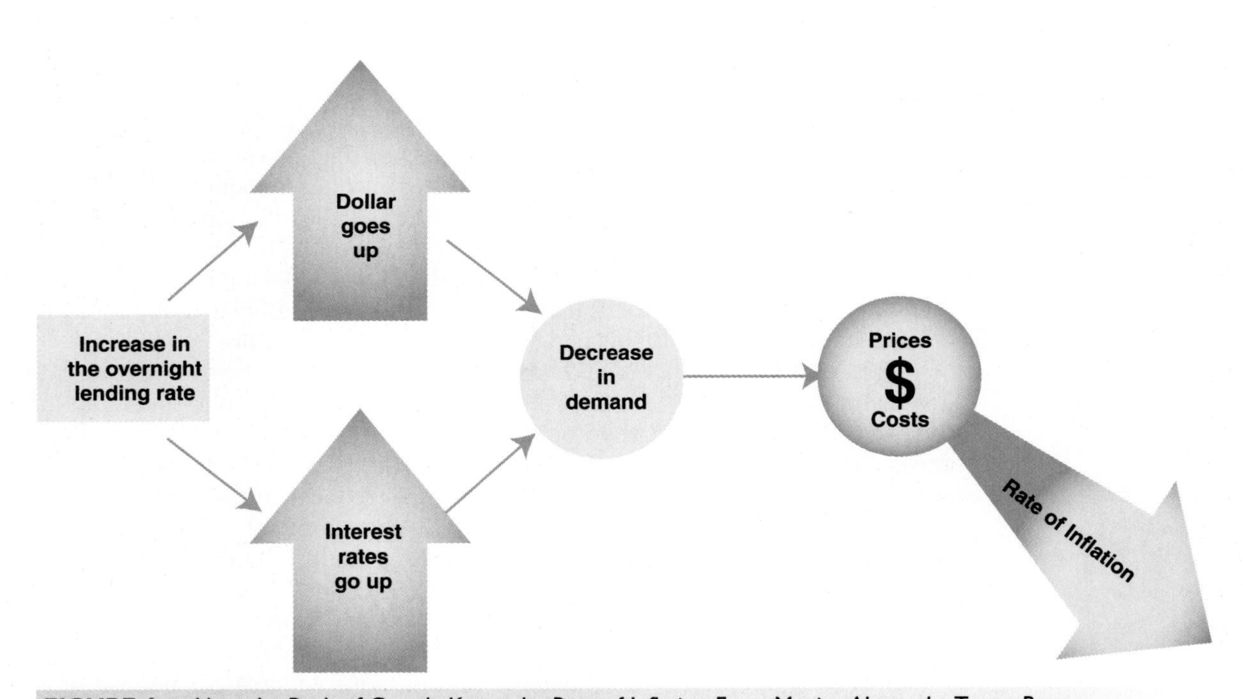

FIGURE 6 How the Bank of Canada Keeps the Rate of Inflation From Moving Above the Target Range

Source: Bank of Canada Website: www.bankofcanada.ca. Reprinted with permission.

Hence, by changing the operating band for the overnight rate, the Bank of Canada sends a signal regarding the direction that it would like interest rates and the money supply to take. A rise in the operating band and thus the bank rate is a signal that the Bank would like to see higher interest rates and less money in the economy. A fall in the operating band is a signal that the Bank would like lower interest rates and more money.

However, the Bank of Canada's direct influence on long-term interest rates diminishes as the time period increases. Long-term interest rates can be either higher or lower than short-term rates depending on expectations about the inflation rate and the level of short-term interest rates in the future, the relative balance between the demand for and supply of loanable funds, the level of interest rates in the Unites States, and the relative stance of monetary policies in the two countries. The Bank of Canada typically changes the operating band for the overnight rate to ratify movements in the general level of interest rates that have already taken place in the market. The Bank, however, wouldn't ratify interest rate movements in the opposite direction to what it feels is required by the fundamentals.

TOOLS OF MONETARY POLICY

Now that we understand how the tools of monetary policy can be used by the Bank of Canada to manipulate the money supply and interest rates, we will examine each of them in turn to see how the Bank wields them in practice and how relatively useful each tool is.

Open Market Operations

Open market operations are an important monetary policy tool for many central banks around the world, because they are the primary determinants of changes in interest rates and the monetary base, the main source of fluctuations in the money supply. **Open market purchases** expand bank settlement balances and the monetary base, thereby lowering short-term interest rates and raising the money supply. **Open market sales** shrink bank settlement balances and the monetary base, raising short-term interest rates and lowering the money supply.

There are two types of open market operations. **Dynamic open market operations** are intended to change the level of bank settlement balances and the monetary base. **Defensive open market operations** are intended to offset movements in other factors that affect bank settlement balances, such as changes in government deposits with the central bank. To avoid conflicts of interest, central banks do not conduct open market operations in privately issued securities.[10] They conduct open market operations in government bills and bonds, because the markets for these securities are the most liquid and have the largest trading volume; these markets have the capacity to absorb the central bank's substantial volume of transactions without experiencing excessive price fluctuations that would disrupt the market.

Over the years, the Bank of Canada has introduced additional tools in its conduct of monetary policy. In 1985, the Bank of Canada introduced **repos**, which in Canada are known as Special Purchase and Resale Agreements (SPRAs), as a tool to reduce undesired upward pressure on the overnight interest rate. In 1986, the Bank introduced **reverse repos**, known in Canada as Sale and Repurchase Agreements (SRAs), as a tool to reduce undesired downward pressure on the overnight rate. By 1994, the Bank of Canada has stopped conducting open mar-

[10] For example, think of the conflict if the Bank of Canada purchased bonds issued by a company owned by the governor's brother-in-law.

ket operations in government of Canada treasury bills and bonds and its most common operations since then have been repurchase transactions, either SPRAs or SRAs, with **primary dealers** (formerly known as jobbers)—the Big Six and the major investment dealers.

SPRAs and SRAs

The operating band for the overnight interest rate, reinforced by the Bank of Canada's standing facilities, and a target level of settlement balances of roughly $50 million are currently the framework within which the Bank of Canada implements monetary policy. As already noted, the Bank's current operation to support the management of settlement balances in targeting the overnight interest rate around the midpoint of the operating band involves repurchase transactions, either SPRAs or SRAs. Between 1994 and the implementation of the LVTS on February 4, 1999, **SPRAs** were used to reinforce the upper end of the operating band and **SRAs** the lower end. Since the LVTS, two rounds of SPRAs and SRAs are used to reinforce the target rate in the middle of the operating band, although effective April 2, 2001, the Bank discontinued the second round of repurchase transactions, except in extraordinary circumstances.

Let's see how the Bank of Canada uses SPRAs and SRAs in order to support the management of settlement balances in achieving the desired impact on the overnight rate. Assume that the operating band for the overnight interest rate is 3.5% to 4% and that the Bank of Canada is targeting the overnight rate at the midpoint of the band, at 3.75%. If overnight funds are traded at a rate higher than the target rate of 3.75%, then the Bank of Canada enters into SPRAs, at a price that works out to a 3.75% interest rate, the midpoint of the operating band. That is, the Bank purchases government of Canada t-bills or bonds, with an agreement that the seller will repurchase them one business day later.

Since the securities are placed with the Canadian Depository for Securities (CDS), Canada's central securities depository owned and operated by the financial community, the title of the securities changes hands by electronic instruction. The balance sheets of the Bank of Canada and the direct clearers look like this:

Bank of Canada				**Direct Clearers**			
Assets		Liabilities		Assets		Liabilities	
SPRAs	+100	Settlement balances	+100	Settlement balances	+100	SPRAs	+100

Hence, ***repos, also known as Special Purchase and Resale Agreements (SPRAs), relieve undesired upward pressure on the overnight interest rate***.

If on the other hand overnight funds are traded at a rate below the target rate of 3.75%, then the Bank of Canada enters into SRAs, in which the Bank sells government securities and the buyer agrees to sell them back to the Bank one business day later. The balance sheets of the Bank of Canada and the direct clearers now look like this:

Bank of Canada				**Direct Clearers**			
Assets		Liabilities		Assets		Liabilities	
		Settlement balances	−100	Settlement balances	−100		
		SRAs	+100	SRAs	+100		

Hence, ***reverse repos, also known as Sale and Repurchase Agreements (SRAs), alleviate undesired downward pressure on the overnight financing rate.***

Because the effects on settlement balances of SPRAs and SRAs are reversed on the day the agreement matures, SPRAs and SRAs are actually temporary open market operations. Moreover, ***because the effects on settlement balances of SPRAs and SRAs are neutralized by the end of the day by the Bank of Canada, there is no change at the end of the day in the level of settlement balances in the system***; the end-of-day level of settlement balances equals exactly the quantity announced the previous day.

Bank of Canada Lending

In addition to its use as a standing liquidity facility to reinforce the operating band for the overnight interest rate, Bank of Canada lending is also important in preventing financial panics. In fact, one of the Bank's most important roles is to be the **lender of last resort** in the Canadian economy; it provides settlement balances to solvent banks in order to prevent bank failures from spinning out of control, thereby preventing bank and financial panics. In doing so, the Bank always makes a judgment with respect to the trade-off between morally hazardous behaviour and the costs in terms of financial stability. Last-resort lending is a particularly effective way to provide settlement balances to the banking system during a banking crisis because settlement balances are immediately channelled to the banks that need them most.

Avoiding financial panics by performing the role of lender of last resort is an extremely important requirement of successful monetary policymaking. For example, the bank panics in the United States in the 1930–1933 period were the cause of the sharpest decline in the money supply in U.S. history, which many economists see as the driving force behind the collapse of the world economy during the Great Depression (see Box 2). Financial panics can also severely damage the economy because they interfere with the ability of financial intermediaries and mar-

BOX 2

Bank Panics of 1930–1933: Why Did the Fed Let Them Happen?

The U.S. Federal Reserve System was totally passive during the bank panics of the Great Depression period and did not perform its intended role of lender of last resort to prevent them. In retrospect, the Fed's behaviour seems quite extraordinary, but hindsight is always clearer than foresight.

The primary reason for the Fed's inaction was that Federal Reserve officials did not understand the negative impact bank failures could have on the money supply and economic activity. Friedman and Schwartz report that the Federal Reserve officials "tended to regard bank failures as regrettable consequences of bank management or bad banking practices, or as inevitable reactions to prior speculative excesses, or as a consequence but hardly a cause of the financial and economic collapse in process." In addition, bank failures in the early stages of the bank panics "were concentrated among smaller banks and, since the most influential figures in the system were big-city bankers who deplored the existence of smaller banks, their disappearance may have been viewed with complacency."*

Friedman and Schwartz also point out that political infighting may have played an important role in the passivity of the Fed during this period. The Federal Reserve Bank of New York, which until 1928 was the dominant force in the Federal Reserve System, strongly advocated an active program of open market purchases to provide settlement balances to the banking system during the bank panics. However, other powerful figures in the Federal Reserve System opposed the New York bank's position, and the bank was outvoted. (Friedman and Schwartz's discussion of the politics of the Federal Reserve System during this period makes for fascinating reading, and you might enjoy their highly readable book.)

*Milton Friedman and Anna Jacobson Schwartz, *A Monetary History of the United States, 1867–1960* (Princeton, N.J.: Princeton University Press, 1963), p. 358.

kets to move funds to people with productive investment opportunities (see Chapter 14).

Go to www.cdic.ca to learn more about the CDIC.

At first glance, it might appear as though the presence of the Canada Deposit Insurance Corporation (CDIC), which insures depositors from losses due to a bank's failure up to a limit of $60 000 per account, would make the lender-of-last resort function of the Bank of Canada superfluous. (The CDIC is described in detail in Chapter 18). There are two reasons why this is not the case. First, it is important to recognize that the CDIC's insurance fund amounts to a small fraction of the amount of these deposits outstanding. If a large number of bank failures occurred, the CDIC would not be able to cover all the depositors' losses. Indeed, the failures of deposit-based financial institutions in the 1980s and early 1990s in Canada led to large losses and a shrinkage in the CDIC's insurance fund, which reduced the CDIC's ability to cover depositors' losses. This fact has not weakened the confidence of small depositors in the banking system because the Bank of Canada has been ready to stand behind the banks to provide whatever settlement balances are needed to prevent bank panics. Second, the large-denomination deposits in the banking system are not guaranteed by the CDIC because they exceed the $60 000 limit. A loss of confidence in the banking system could still lead to runs on banks from the large-denomination depositors, and bank panics could still occur despite the existence of the CDIC.

The FDIC's Website, www.fdic.gov, has information about its activities.

The importance of the Bank of Canada's role as lender of last resort is, if anything, more important today because of the bank failures experienced in Canada in the 1980s and early 1990s. In fact, the Bank of Canada advanced considerable funds in the recent past to financial institutions facing liquidity crises. Unfortunately, the Bank of Canada's lending policy has not always been successful in preventing financial crises. Two examples of the use of the Bank's lending weapon to avoid bank panics are the provisions of huge loans to the Canadian Commercial Bank and the Northland Bank in 1985 (see Box 3).

BOX 3

Advances to Troubled Banks

Canadian Commercial and Northland. In 1985, there was public concern over the quality of the assets of two small Alberta-based banks—the Canadian Commercial Bank and the Northland Bank—who had made many bad loans. Large depositors, whose accounts exceeded the $60 000 limit insured by the CDIC, began to withdraw their deposits, and the failure of the banks was imminent. Because the immediate failure of Canadian Commercial and Northland would have had repercussions on other vulnerable banks, the Bank of Canada, under the advice of the Inspector General of Banks (the predecessor of the Office of the Superintendent of Financial Institutions) made extraordinary advances. Total advances amounted to $1.8 billion so that depositors, including the largest, would not suffer any losses.

In doing this, the Bank of Canada was following the precedent established in 1984 by the Federal Reserve's rescue of Continental Illinois National Bank. Continental Illinois had made bad loans (primarily to business in the energy industry and to foreign countries), and rumours of financial trouble in early May 1984 caused large depositors to withdraw more than $10 billion of deposits from the bank. The Federal Deposit Insurance Corporation (FDIC) arranged a rescue effort in July 1984 that culminated in a $4.5 billion commitment of funds to save the bank. Still the Fed had to lend Continental Illinois more than $5 billion—making the Bank of Canada's $1.8 billion advances to Canadian Commercial and Northland look like small potatoes! Although Continental Illinois was taken over by the FDIC, the Fed's action prevented further bank failures, and a potential bank panic was averted.

The Bank of Canada, however, was not as successful in preventing a bank crisis. With the failure of Canadian Commercial and Northland, rumours of financial trouble caused many large depositors to withdraw large deposits from the Bank of British Columbia, Mercantile Bank, and Continental Bank. By the time Mercantile was acquired by the National Bank of Canada, Bank of British Columbia by the Hongkong Bank of Canada, and Continental by Lloyds Bank of Canada, the Bank of Canada had lent more than $5 billion. The loss of public confidence in the Canadian banking system led to the financial reforms of 1987–1992 and the consolidating of financial institution supervision under the Office of the Superintendent of Financial Institutions.

Not only can the central bank be a lender of last resort to banks, but it can also play the same role for the financial system as a whole. The existence of the advances mechanism can help prevent financial panics that are not triggered by bank failures, as was the case in the United States during the Black Monday stock market crash of 1987 and the terrorist destruction of the World Trade Center in September 2001 (see Box 4).

Although the Bank of Canada's role as the lender of last resort has the benefit of preventing bank and financial panics, it does have a cost. If a bank expects that the Bank of Canada will provide it with advances when it gets into trouble, it will be willing to take on more risk knowing that the Bank of Canada will come to the rescue. The Bank of Canada's lender-of-last-resort role has thus created a

BOX 4

Last-Resort Lending to Prevent a Financial Panic: The Black Monday Stock Market Crash of October 1987 and the Terrorist Destruction of the World Trade Center in September 2001

Although October 19, 1987, dubbed "Black Monday," will go down in the history books as the largest one-day percentage decline in stock prices to date (the Dow Jones Industrial Average declined by more than 20%), it was on Tuesday, October 20, 1987, that financial markets almost stopped functioning. Felix Rohatyn, one of the most prominent men on Wall Street, stated flatly: "Tuesday was the most dangerous day we had in 50 years."* Much of the credit for prevention of a market meltdown after Black Monday must be given to the U.S. Federal Reserve System and the chairman of the Board of Governors, Alan Greenspan.

The stress of keeping markets functioning during the sharp decline in stock prices on Monday, October 19, meant that many brokerage houses and specialists (dealer-brokers who maintain orderly trading on the stock exchanges) were severely in need of additional funds to finance their activities. However, understandably enough, New York banks, as well as foreign and regional U.S. banks, growing very nervous about the financial health of securities firms, began to cut back credit to the securities industry at the very time when it was most needed. Panic was in the air. One chairman of a large specialist firm commented that on Monday, "from 2 P.M. on, there was total despair. The entire investment community fled the market. We were left alone on the field." It was time for the Fed, like the cavalry, to come to the rescue.

Upon learning of the plight of the securities industry, Alan Greenspan and E. Gerald Corrigan, then president of the Federal Reserve Bank of New York and the Fed official most closely in touch with Wall Street, became fearful of a spreading collapse of securities firms. To prevent this from occurring, Greenspan announced before the market opened on Tuesday, October 20, the Federal Reserve System's "readiness to serve as a source of liquidity to support the economic and financial system." In addition to this extraordinary announcement, the Fed made it clear that it would provide discount loans to any bank that would make loans to the securities industry, although this did not prove to be necessary. As one New York banker said, the Fed's message was, "We're here. Whatever you need, we'll give you."

The outcome of the Fed's timely action was that a financial panic was averted. The markets kept functioning on Tuesday, and a market rally ensued that day, with the Dow Jones Industrial Average climbing more than 100 points.

A similar lender-of-last resort operation was carried out in the aftermath of the destruction of the World Trade Center on Tuesday, September 11, 2001, in the worst terrorist incident in U.S. history. Because of the disruption of the most important financial center in the world, the liquidity needs of the financial system skyrocketed. To satisfy this need and so keep the financial system from seizing up, within a few hours of the incident, the Fed made a similar announcement to that made after the crash of 1987, stating, "The Federal Reserve System is open and operating. The discount window is available to meet liquidity needs."† The Fed then proceeded to provide $45 billion to banks through the discount window, a 200-fold increase over the previous week. As a result of this action, along with as much as $80 billion of reserves injected into the banking system through open market operations, the financial system kept functioning. When the stock market reopened on Monday, September 17, trading was orderly, although the Dow Jones average did decline 7%.

The terrorists were able to bring down the twin towers of the World Trade Center and kill more than 3000 people. However, they were unable to bring down the U.S. financial system because of the timely actions of the Federal Reserve.

*"Terrible Tuesday: How the Stock Market Almost Disintegrated a Day After the Crash," *Wall Street Journal,* November 20, 1987, p. 1. This article provides a fascinating and more detailed view of the events described here and is the source of all the quotations cited on this event.

† "Economic Front: How Policy Makers Regrouped to Defend the Financial System," *Wall Street Journal,* Tuesday, September 18, 2001, p. A1, provides more detail on this episode.

moral hazard problem similar to the one created by deposit insurance (to be discussed in Chapter 18): Banks take on more risk, thus exposing the deposit insurance agency, and hence taxpayers, to greater losses. The moral hazard problem is most severe for large banks, which may believe that the Bank of Canada and the CDIC view them as "too big to fail"; that is, they will always receive Bank of Canada advances when they are in trouble because their failure would be likely to precipitate a bank panic.

Similarly, Bank of Canada actions to prevent financial panic may encourage financial institutions other than banks to take on greater risk. They, too, expect the Bank of Canada to ensure that they will get loans if a financial panic seemed imminent. When the Bank of Canada considers using the lending weapon to prevent panics, it therefore needs to consider the trade-off between the moral hazard cost of its role as lender of last resort and the benefit of preventing financial panics. This trade-off explains why the Bank of Canada must be careful not to perform its role as lender of last resort too frequently.

Government Deposit Shifting

Before the introduction of the LVTS, the management of settlement balances (**cash setting**) was the main mechanism by which the Bank of Canada implemented monetary policy. By shifting federal government deposits between the government's account at the Bank and the government's accounts at the direct clearers, the Bank was essentially implementing its target band for the overnight interest rate.[11] It was also neutralizing certain federal government and Bank of Canada transactions that affect the financial system. With the introduction of the LVTS, however, the Bank introduced a new framework for implementing monetary policy. This involves lending to and taking deposits from LVTS participants, as we discussed earlier.

However, in aiming at an almost zero level of settlement balances for the financial system each day, the Bank of Canada continues to use government deposit shifting in order to neutralize certain federal government and Bank of Canada flows that potentially affect settlement balances. These flows (such as federal government receipts and disbursements) affect settlement balances, because the Bank of Canada acts as the fiscal agent for the federal government. In particular, net government disbursements would increase the direct clearers' settlement balances at the Bank, while net government receipts would reduce them.

In the pre-LVTS system, **government deposit transfers** between the government's accounts at financial institutions and its account at the Bank of Canada were effected by the Bank's daily **drawdowns** (transfers of government deposits from the direct clearers to the Bank of Canada) and **redeposits** (transfers of government deposits from the Bank of Canada to the direct clearers). However, with the instantaneous transfer of funds allowed by the LVTS environment, the drawdown/redeposit mechanism is not a practical tool for government deposit shifting; the Bank of Canada is not able to debit the government's account with a direct clearer on a day with a net disbursement by the government. ***In the LVTS environment, twice-daily auctions of government term deposits (the first at 9:15 A.M. and the second at 4:15 P.M.) are used to effect the transfer*** (see Box 1).[12]

[11]For detailed descriptions of the process, see the discussion in Kevin Clinton, "Bank of Canada Cash Management: The Main Technique for Implementing Monetary Policy," *Bank of Canada Review*, (1991): 3–25; or Bruce Montador, "The Implementation of Monetary Policy in Canada," *Canadian Public Policy* (1995): 107–120.

[12]For more details, see "The Framework for the Implementation of Monetary Policy in the Large Value Transfer System Environment," Bank of Canada *Release*, March 31, 1999.

To illustrate the process for neutralizing federal government flows using government deposit shifting, suppose that there is a net government receipt of $100 (i.e., the government's receipts from the public exceed its payments to the public by $100). Net receipts are drawn on the government's deposits at the direct clearers, creating claims on the direct clearers in favour of the Bank of Canada and ultimately reducing settlement balances by an amount equal to the government's net receipts. In the absence of any offsetting transactions by the Bank of Canada, through the workings of supply and demand, a decline in settlement balances will normally cause an increase in the overnight interest rate, as many direct clearers would have to borrow more to meet their settlement obligations.

However, in targeting the overnight interest rate, the Bank of Canada will neutralize the net government receipt by morning and afternoon auctions of government term deposits. This procedure results in the following balance sheets for the Bank and the direct clearers:

Bank of Canada		Direct Clearers	
Assets	**Liabilities**	**Assets**	**Liabilities**
	Government deposits −100	Settlement balances +100	Government deposits +100
	Settlement balances +100		

Note that government deposits at the Bank of Canada are reduced by $100 and at the same time the settlement balances of the direct clearers are increased by $100.

If instead of a net receipt by the government, there were a net disbursement of $100 (i.e., the government's payments to the public exceed its receipts from the public by $100), then the financial system's settlement balances would increase by the same amount. This would prompt a fall in the overnight interest rate, as many direct clearers would have to borrow less to meet their settlement obligations. The Bank's neutralization process would prevent a decline in the overnight rate by reducing the banking system's settlement balances. This would involve LVTS transfers of $100 from the government's accounts at the LVTS participating institutions to the government's account at the Bank. This procedure results in the following T-accounts

Bank of Canada		Direct Clearers	
Assets	**Liabilities**	**Assets**	**Liabilities**
	Government deposits +100	Settlement balances −100	Government deposits −100
	Settlement balances −100		

In this case government deposits at the Bank of Canada are increased by $100 and at the same time the clearing balances of the participants are reduced by $100.

Swaps With the Exchange Fund Account

When the Bank of Canada transfers government balances, it usually brings onto its balance sheet Exchange Fund Account assets to back its liabilities. It does so, by arranging a swap with the **Exchange Fund Account**, which holds the country's foreign exchange balances. This involves a spot purchase and a simultaneous forward sale of foreign exchange. To illustrate the operation, assume that the Bank temporarily buys $100 of foreign currency assets from the Exchange Fund Account. It credits the government's account on its own books and the operation results in the following balance sheets for the Bank and the government:

Bank of Canada		Government of Canada	
Assets	Liabilities	Assets	Liabilities
Foreign exchange +100	Government deposits +100	Exchange Fund Account −100	
		Deposits at the Bank of Canada +100	

We see that government deposit balances at the Bank of Canada increase and these balances can then be transferred to participants to increase settlement balances, as we saw earlier.

Although the spot transaction adds to the government deposits at the Bank of Canada and enables the Bank to auction government balances, the forward contract between the Bank and the Exchange Fund Account does not affect the settlement balances of participating financial institutions. The Bank simply sells foreign exchange to the Exchange Fund Account in the future at a price agreed upon today. The advantage to the Bank of Canada of using swap transactions with the Exchange Fund Account is that it can bring a temporary change in the level of settlement balances or respond to some event that the Bank thinks will have a significant but not long-lived effect.

As we will learn in Chapter 13, the foreign exchange balances held in the Exchange Fund Account can also be used by the Bank of Canada in international financial transactions to prevent undesirable movements in the exchange rate. For example, a Bank of Canada sale of domestic currency and corresponding purchase of foreign assets in the foreign exchange market leads to a gain in international reserves, an increase in the monetary base and the money supply, and a depreciation of the domestic currency. A Bank purchase of domestic currency and corresponding sale of foreign exchange leads to a loss of international reserves, a decline in the monetary base and the money supply, and an appreciation of the domestic currency. We discuss such foreign exchange interventions in detail in Chapter 13.

Advantages of SPRAs and SRAs over Other Tools

The Bank of Canada's repurchase transactions, either SPRAs or SRAs, have four advantages over other tools of monetary policy.

1. SPRAs and SRAs occur at the initiative of the Bank of Canada, which has complete control over their volume. This control is not found, for example, in lending operations, in which the Bank can encourage or discourage banks to take out loans by altering the bank rate but cannot directly control the volume of advances.
2. Repurchase transactions are flexible and precise; together with the Bank's standing facilities, they can be used to any extent. No matter how small a change in interest rates is desired, SPRAs or SRAs can achieve it with a small purchase or sale of securities. Conversely, if the desired change in interest rates is very large, the repurchase-transactions tool is strong enough to do the job through a very large purchase or sale of securities.
3. Repurchase transactions are easily reversed. If a mistake is made, the Bank of Canada can immediately reverse it. If, for example, the Bank decides that the overnight rate is too low because it has offered too many SPRAs, it can immediately make a correction by offering SRAs. Reversing, however, repurchase transactions too often will result in a loss of credibility.

4. Repurchase transactions can be implemented quickly; they involve no administrative delays. When the Bank of Canada decides to change interest rates on the fixed action dates, it makes the interest rate announcement at 9:00 A.M. and enters into SPRAs or SRAs.

GOALS OF MONETARY POLICY

Six basic goals are continually mentioned by personnel at the Bank of Canada and other central banks when they discuss the objectives of monetary policy: (1) high employment, (2) economic growth, (3) price stability, (4) interest-rate stability, (5) stability of financial markets, and (6) stability in foreign exchange markets. It is to be noticed that different countries and different regimes may give different weights to these goals. As we shall see, the current Canadian regime, and the regimes of most hard currency countries, is now strongly attached to the goals of price stability and financial markets stability.

High Employment

Statistics Canada's Website at www.statcan.ca contains statistics on employment level, a summary of the employment situation, and other useful information related to employment issues.

High employment is a worthy goal for two main reasons: (1) the alternative situation, high unemployment, causes much human misery, with families suffering financial distress, loss of personal self-respect, and increase in crime (though this last conclusion is highly controversial), and (2) when unemployment is high, the economy has not only idle workers but also idle resources (closed factories and unused equipment), resulting in a loss of output (lower GDP).

Although it is clear that high employment is desirable, how high should it be? At what point can we say that the economy is at full employment? At first, it might seem that full employment is the point at which no worker is out of a job, that is, when unemployment is zero. But this definition ignores the fact that some unemployment, called *frictional unemployment*, which involves searches by workers and firms to find suitable matchups, is beneficial to the economy. For example, a worker who decides to look for a better job might be unemployed for a while during the job search. Workers often decide to leave work temporarily to pursue other activities (raising a family, travel, returning to school), and when they decide to reenter the job market, it may take some time for them to find the right job. The benefit of having some unemployment is similar to the benefit of having a nonzero vacancy rate in the market for rental apartments. As many of you who have looked for an apartment have discovered, when the vacancy rate in the rental market is too low, you will have a difficult time finding the right apartment.

Another reason that unemployment is not zero when the economy is at full employment is due to what is called *structural unemployment*, a mismatch between job requirements and the skills or availability of local workers. Clearly, this kind of unemployment is undesirable. Nonetheless, it is something that monetary policy can do little about.

The goal for high employment should therefore not seek an unemployment level of zero but rather a level above zero consistent with full employment at which the demand for labour equals the supply of labour. This level is called the **natural rate of unemployment.**

Although this definition sounds neat and authoritative, it isn't, because it leaves a troublesome question unanswered: What unemployment rate is consistent with full employment? On the one hand, in some cases, it is obvious that the unemployment rate is too high: The unemployment rate in excess of 20% during the Great Depression, for example, was clearly far too high. In the early 1960s, on the other hand, policymakers thought that a reasonable goal was 4%, a level that was probably too low because it led to accelerating inflation. Current estimates of the natural rate of unemployment place it between 6% and 7%, but even this estimate is subject to a great deal of uncertainty and disagreement. In addition, it is possible that appropriate government policy, such as the provision of better information about job vacancies or job training programs, might decrease the natural rate of unemployment.

Economic Growth

The goal of steady economic growth is closely related to the high-employment goal because businesses are more likely to invest in capital equipment to increase productivity and economic growth when unemployment is low. Conversely, if unemployment is high and factories are idle, it does not pay for a firm to invest in additional plants and equipment. Although the two goals are closely related, policies can be specifically aimed at promoting economic growth by directly encouraging firms to invest or by encouraging people to save, which provides more funds for firms to invest. In fact, this is the stated purpose of so-called supply-side economics policies, which are intended to spur economic growth by providing tax incentives for businesses to invest in factories and equipment and for taxpayers to save more. There is also an active debate over what growth role monetary policy can play in boosting growth.

Price Stability

Over the past few decades, policymakers in Canada have become more aware of the social and economic costs of inflation and more concerned with a stable price level as a goal of economic policy. (The growing commitment to price stability is also evident in Europe—see Box 5.) Price stability is desirable because a rising price level (inflation) creates uncertainty in the economy, and that may hamper economic growth. For example, the information conveyed by the prices of goods and services is harder to interpret when the overall level of prices is changing, which complicates decision making for consumers, businesses, and government. Not only do public opinion surveys indicate that the public is very hostile to inflation, but also a growing body of evidence suggests that inflation leads to lower economic growth.[13] The most extreme example of

Go to www.ecb.int for more details about the European System of Central banks

BOX 5: GLOBAL

The Growing European Commitment to Price Stability

Not surprisingly, given Germany's experience with hyperinflation in the 1920s, its central bank has the strongest commitment to price stability. In contrast to statutes for the German central bank, the statutes of other central banks in Europe set various objectives for policy, including all the goals outlined here in the text. However, European policymakers have been coming around to the view that the primary objective for a central bank should be price stability. The increased importance of this goal is reflected in the December 1991 Treaty of European Union, known as the Maastricht Treaty, which proposed the creation of the European System of Central Banks, which would function very much like the Federal Reserve System. The statute of the European System of Central Banks sets price stability as the primary objective of this system and indicates that the general economic policies of the European Union are to be supported only if they are not in conflict with price stability.

---

[13]For example, see Stanley Fischer, "The Role of Macroeconomic Factors in Growth," *Journal of Monetary Economics* 32 (1993): 485–512.

unstable prices is *hyperinflation*, such as Argentina, Brazil, and Russia have experienced in the recent past. Many economists attribute the slower growth that these countries have experienced to their problems with hyperinflation.

Inflation also makes it hard to plan for the future. For example, it is more difficult to decide how much should be put aside to provide for a child's university education in an inflationary environment. Further, inflation may strain a country's social fabric: Conflict may result because each group in the society may compete with other groups to make sure that its income keeps up with the rising level of prices.

Interest-Rate Stability

Interest-rate stability is desirable because fluctuations in interest rates can create uncertainty in the economy and make it harder to plan for the future. Fluctuations in interest rates that affect consumers' willingness to buy houses, for example, make it more difficult for consumers to decide when to purchase a house and for construction firms to plan how many houses to build. A central bank may also want to reduce upward movements in interest rates for the reasons that we discussed in Chapter 6: Upward movements in interest rates generate hostility toward central banks such as the Bank of Canada and lead to demands that their power be curtailed.

Stability of Financial Markets

As our analysis in Chapter 14 will show, financial crises can interfere with the ability of financial markets to channel funds to people with productive investment opportunities, thereby leading to a sharp contraction in economic activity. The promotion of a more stable financial system in which financial crises are avoided is thus an important goal for a central bank. Indeed, as discussed in Chapter 6, the Bank of Canada was created in response to the problems of the Great Depression to promote financial stability.

The stability of financial markets is also fostered by interest-rate stability because fluctuations in interest rates create great uncertainty for financial institutions. An increase in interest rates produces large capital losses on long-term bonds and mortgages, losses that can cause the failure of the financial institutions holding them. In recent years, more pronounced interest-rate fluctuations have been a particularly severe problem for financial institutions, many of which got into serious financial trouble in the 1980s.

Stability in Foreign Exchange Markets

With the increasing importance of international trade to the Canadian economy, the value of the dollar relative to other currencies has become a major consideration for the Bank of Canada. As we will see in Chapter 12, a rise in the value of the dollar makes Canadian industries less competitive with those abroad, and declines in the value of the dollar stimulate inflation in Canada. In addition, preventing large changes in the value of the dollar makes it easier for firms and individuals purchasing or selling goods abroad to plan ahead. Stabilizing extreme movements in the value of the dollar in foreign exchange markets is thus viewed as a worthy goal of monetary policy. In other countries, which are even more dependent on foreign trade, stability in foreign exchange markets takes on even greater importance.

Conflict Among Goals

The IMF and the Bank for International Settlements Websites can be found at www.imf.org and www.bis.org

Although many of the goals mentioned are consistent with one another—high employment with economic growth, interest-rate stability with financial market stability—this is not always the case. The goal of price stability often conflicts with the goals of interest-rate stability and high employment in the short run (but probably not in the long run). For example, when the economy is expanding and unemployment is falling, both inflation and interest rates may start to rise. If the central bank tries to prevent a rise in interest rates, this may cause the economy to overheat and stimulate inflation. But if a central bank raises interest rates to prevent inflation, in the short run unemployment may rise. The conflict among goals may thus present central banks such as the Bank of Canada with some hard choices. Strictly speaking, it is not central banks that face hard choices, or at least not once their mandate has been narrowed in the way that it has been in Canada. It is rather the more defined monetary authorities, including the ministry of finance and, for all countries more or less, the International Monetary Fund (IMF) and the Bank for International Settlements, which face them.

CENTRAL BANK STRATEGY: USE OF TARGETS

The central bank's problem is that it wants to achieve certain goals, such as price stability with high employment, but it does not directly influence the goals. It has a set of tools to employ (open market operations, changes in the operating band for the overnight interest rate, etc.) that can affect the goals indirectly after a period of time (typically more than a year). If the central bank waits to see what the price level and employment will be one year later, it will be too late to make any corrections to its policy—mistakes will be irreversible.

All central banks consequently pursue a different strategy for conducting monetary policy by aiming at variables that lie between its tools and the achievement of its goals. The strategy is as follows: After deciding on its goals for employment and the price level, the central bank chooses a set of variables to aim for, called **intermediate targets,** such as the monetary aggregates (various measures of the money supply denoted by M1+, M2+, or M3) or interest rates (short or long term), which have a direct effect on employment and the price level. However, even these intermediate targets are not directly affected by the central bank's policy tools. Therefore, it chooses another set of variables to aim for, called **operating targets,** or alternatively called *instruments*, such as reserve aggregates (reserves or the monetary base) or interest rates (overnight rate or treasury bill rate), which are more responsive to its policy tools.[14]

The central bank pursues this strategy because it is easier to hit a goal by aiming at targets than by aiming at the goal directly. Specifically, by using intermediate and operating targets, it can more quickly judge whether its policies are on the right track, rather than waiting until it sees the final outcome of its policies on employment and the price level.[15] By analogy, a hot air balloon operator employs the strategy of using targets when trying to land the balloon on the ground. He will check to see whether the balloon is positioned correctly as it lands (we can think

[14]There is some ambiguity as to whether to call a particular variable an operating target or an intermediate target. The monetary base and the treasury bill rate are often viewed as possible intermediate targets, even though they may function as operating targets as well. In addition, if the Bank of Canada wants to pursue a goal of interest-rate stability, an interest rate can be both a goal and a target.

[15]This reasoning for the use of monetary targets has come under attack because information on employment and the price level can be useful in evaluating policy. See Benjamin M. Friedman, "The Inefficiency of Short-Run Monetary Targets for Monetary Policy," *Brookings Papers on Economic Activity* 2 (1977): 292–346.

of this as an "operating target"). If the balloon is off course at this stage, the operator will adjust its thrust (a policy tool) to get it back on target. The operator may check the position of the balloon again when it is halfway to the landing spot (we can think of this as the "intermediate target") and can make further midcourse corrections if necessary.

The central bank's strategy works in a similar way. Suppose that the central bank's employment and price-level goals are consistent with a nominal GDP growth rate of 5%. If the central bank feels that the 5% nominal GDP growth rate will be achieved by a 4% growth rate for M1+ (its intermediate target), which will in turn be achieved by a growth rate of 3.5% for the monetary base (its operating target), it will carry out open market operations (its tool) to achieve the 3.5% growth in the monetary base. After implementing this policy, the central bank may find that the monetary base is growing too slowly, say, at a 2% rate; then it can correct this too slow growth by increasing the amount of its open market purchases. Somewhat later, the central bank will begin to see how its policy is affecting the growth rate of the money supply. If M1+ is growing too fast, say, at a 7% rate, the central bank may decide to reduce its open market purchases or make open market sales to reduce the M1+ growth rate.

One way of thinking about this strategy (illustrated in Figure 7) is that the central bank is using its operating and intermediate targets to direct monetary policy (the hot air balloon) toward the achievement of its goals. After the initial setting of the policy tools, an operating target such as the monetary base, which the central bank can control fairly directly, is used to reset the tools so that monetary policy is channelled toward achieving the intermediate target of a certain rate of money supply growth. Midcourse corrections in the policy tools can be made again when the central bank sees what is happening to its intermediate target, thus directing monetary policy so that it will achieve its goals of high employment and price stability.

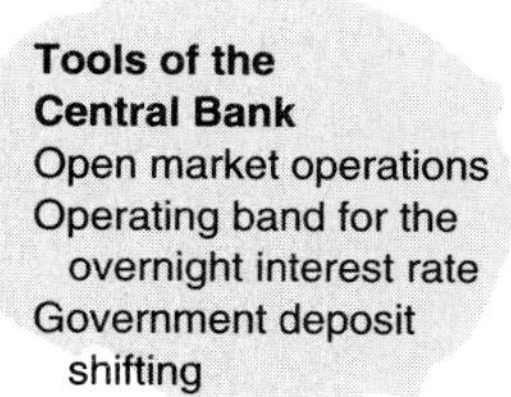

FIGURE 7 Central Bank Strategy

CHOOSING THE TARGETS

As we see in Figure 7, there are two different types of target variables: interest rates and aggregates (monetary aggregates and reserve aggregates). In our example, the central bank chose a 4% growth rate for M1+ to achieve a 5% rate of growth for nominal GDP. It could have chosen to lower the overnight rate to, say, 3% to achieve the same goal. Can the central bank choose to pursue both of these targets at the same time? The answer is no. The application of the supply and demand analysis of the market for money that we covered in Chapter 4 explains why a central bank must choose one or the other.

Let's first see why a monetary aggregate target involves losing control of the interest rate. Figure 8 contains a supply and demand diagram for the market for money. Although the central bank expects the demand curve for money to be at M^{d*}, it fluctuates between $M^{d'}$ and $M^{d''}$ because of unexpected increases or decreases in output or changes in the price level. The money demand curve might also shift unexpectedly because the public's preferences about holding bonds versus money may change. If the central bank's monetary aggregate target of a 4% growth rate in M1+ results in a money supply of M^*, it expects that the interest rate will be i^*. However, as the figure indicates, the fluctuations in the money demand curve between $M^{d'}$ and $M^{d''}$ will result in an interest rate fluctuating between i' and i''. ***Pursuing a monetary aggregate target implies that interest rates will fluctuate.***

The supply and demand diagram in Figure 9 shows the consequences of an interest-rate target set at i^*. Again, the central bank expects the money demand curve to be at M^{d*}, but it fluctuates between $M^{d'}$ and $M^{d''}$ due to unexpected changes in output, the price level, or the public's preferences toward holding money. If the demand curve rises to $M^{d''}$, the interest rate will begin to rise above i^*, and the price of bonds will fall. With an interest-rate target, the central bank will prevent the interest rate from rising by buying bonds to drive their price back up and the interest rate back down to its former level. The central bank open

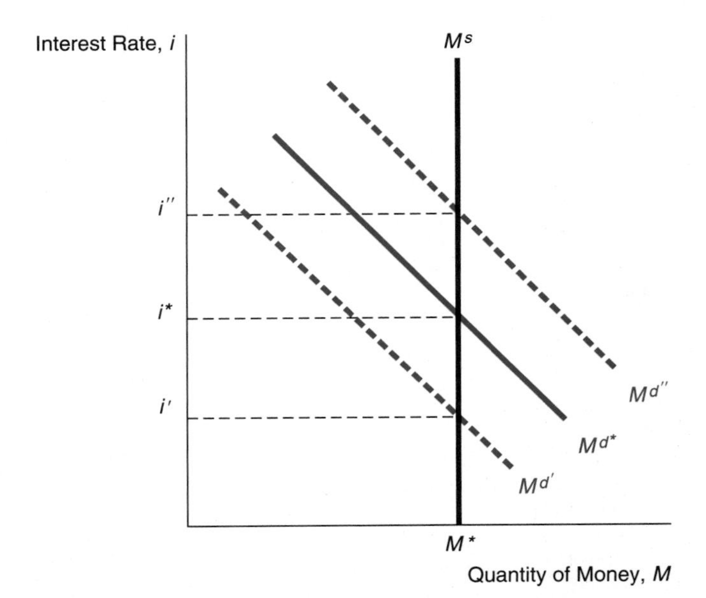

FIGURE 8 Result of Targeting on the Money Supply

Targeting on the money supply at M^* will lead to fluctuations in the interest rate between i' and i'' because of fluctuations in the money demand curve between $M^{d'}$ and $M^{d''}$.

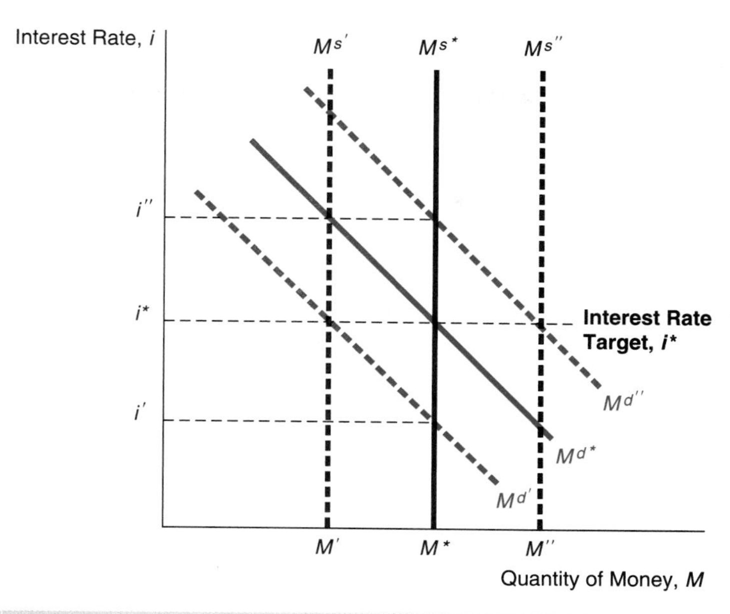

FIGURE 9 Result of Targeting on the Interest Rate

Targeting the interest rate at i^* will lead to fluctuations of the money supply between M' and M'' because of fluctuations in the money demand curve between $M^{d\prime}$ and $M^{d\prime\prime}$.

market purchase of bonds will mean that settlement balances and deposits in the banking system will rise because the central bank pays for these bonds with settlement balances, thus raising the money supply. The central bank will continue to make open market purchases until the money supply rises to $M^{s\prime\prime}$, at which point the equilibrium interest rate is again i^*. Conversely, if the demand curve falls to $M^{d\prime}$ and lowers the interest rate, the central bank would keep interest rates from falling by selling bonds to keep their prices from rising. The central bank will make open market sales until the money supply falls to $M^{s\prime}$ and the equilibrium interest rate is i^*. The central bank's adherence to the interest-rate target thus leads to a fluctuating money supply as well as to fluctuations in reserve aggregates.

The conclusion from the supply and demand analysis is that interest-rate and monetary aggregate targets are incompatible: A central bank can hit one or the other but not both. Because a choice between them has to be made, we need to examine what criteria should be used to decide on the target variable.

Criteria for Choosing Intermediate Targets

The rationale behind a central bank's strategy of using targets suggests three criteria for choosing an intermediate target: It must be measurable, it must be controllable by the central bank, and it must have a predictable effect on the goal.

Measurability Quick and accurate measurement of an intermediate-target variable is necessary because the intermediate target will be useful only if it signals when policy is off track more rapidly than the goal. What good does it do for the central bank to plan to hit a 4% growth rate for M1+ if it has no way of quickly and accurately measuring M1+? Data on the monetary aggregates are available with about a month's delay, and interest-rate data are available almost immediately. Data on a variable such as GDP that serves as a goal, by contrast, are compiled quarterly and are obtained after a two-month delay. In addition, the GDP data are less accurate than data on the monetary aggregates or interest rates. On these grounds alone, focusing on interest rates and monetary aggregates as intermediate targets rather than on a goal such as GDP can provide clearer signals about the status of the central bank's policy.

At first glance, interest rates seem to be more measurable than monetary aggregates and hence more useful as intermediate targets. Not only are the data on interest rates available more quickly than on monetary aggregates, but they are also measured more precisely and are rarely revised, in contrast to the monetary aggregates, which are subject to a fair amount of revision. However, as we learned in Chapter 3, the interest rate that is quickly and accurately measured, the nominal interest rate, is typically a poor measure of the real cost of borrowing, which indicates with more certainty what will happen to GDP. This real cost of borrowing is more accurately measured by the real interest rate—the interest rate adjusted for expected inflation ($i_r = i - \pi^e$).

Until recently, the real interest rate was extremely hard to measure because we didn't have a direct way to measure expected inflation. This all changed, however, when governments in countries such as Australia, Canada, Sweden, the United Kingdom, and the United States began to issue indexed bonds (discussed in Box 2 of Chapter 3) that make it possible to observe the real interest rate. Since the interest rate is now more measurable than monetary aggregates, it should be preferred to the monetary aggregates as an intermediate target.

Controllability A central bank must be able to exercise effective control over a variable if it is to function as a useful target. If the central bank cannot control an intermediate target, knowing that it is off track does little good because the bank has no way of getting back on track. Some economists have suggested that nominal GDP should be used as an intermediate target, but since the central bank has little direct control over nominal GDP, it will not provide much guidance on how the Bank of Canada should set its policy tools. A central bank does, however, have a good deal of control over the monetary aggregates and interest rates.

Our discussion of the money supply process and the central bank's policy tools indicates that a central bank does have the ability to exercise a powerful effect on the money supply, although its control is not perfect. We have also seen that open market operations can be used to set interest rates by directly affecting the price of bonds. Because a central bank can set interest rates directly whereas it cannot completely control the money supply, it might appear that interest rates dominate the monetary aggregates on the controllability criterion. However, a central bank cannot set real interest rates because it does not have control over expectations of inflation. So again, a clear-cut case cannot be made that interest rates are preferable to monetary aggregates as an intermediate target or vice versa.

Predictable Effect on Goals The most important characteristic a variable must have to be useful as an intermediate target is that it must have a predictable impact on a goal. If a central bank can accurately and quickly measure the price of tea in China and can completely control its price, what good will it do? The central bank cannot use the price of tea in China to affect unemployment or the price level in its country. Because the ability to affect goals is so critical to the usefulness of an intermediate-target variable, the linkage of the money supply and interest rates with the goals—output, employment, and the price level—is a matter of much debate.

Criteria for Choosing Operating Targets

The choice of an operating target can be based on the same criteria used to evaluate intermediate targets. Both the overnight rate and reserve aggregates are measured accurately and are available daily with almost no delay; both are easily controllable using the policy tools that we discussed earlier in the chapter. When we look at the third criterion, however, we can think of the intermediate target as the goal for the operating target. An operating target that has a more predictable impact on the most desirable intermediate target is preferred. If the desired intermediate target is an interest rate, the preferred operating target will be an interest-rate variable like the overnight rate because interest rates are closely tied to one another (as we saw in Chapter 5). However, if the desired intermediate target is a monetary aggregate, a reserve aggregate operating target such as the monetary base will be preferred. Because there does not seem to be much reason to choose an interest rate over a reserve aggregate on the basis of measurability or controllability, the choice of which operating target is better rests on the choice of the intermediate target (the goal of the operating target).

BANK OF CANADA POLICY PROCEDURES: HISTORICAL PERSPECTIVE

The well-known adage "The road to hell is paved with good intentions" applies as much to the Bank of Canada as it does to human beings. Understanding a central bank's goals and the strategies it can use to pursue them cannot tell us how monetary policy is actually conducted. To understand the practical results of the theoretical underpinnings, we have to look at how central banks have actually conducted policy in the past. First we will look at the Bank of Canada's past policy procedures: its choice of goals, policy tools, operating targets, and intermediate targets. This historical perspective will not only show us how our central bank carries out its duties but will also help us interpret the Bank's activities and see where Canadian monetary policy may be heading in the future. Once we finish studying the Bank of Canada, we will examine central banks' experiences in other countries.

The Early Years

From the end of World War II in 1945 until the early 1970s, the world economy operated under a system of fixed exchange rates, known as the Bretton Woods system (to be discussed in detail in Chapter 13). Initially, Canada opted out of this system, but joined in 1962 and participated with the exchange rate fixed at 92.5 U.S. cents. Even before 1962, Canadian monetary policy had been driven by the goal of maintaining a stable exchange rate with the United States, and the Bank of Canada therefore kept short-term interest rates more or less in step with U.S. interest rates. This meant that short-term interest rates, or the differential between U.S. and Canadian rates, were the intermediate target of monetary policy. As a result, inflation rates and interest rates followed generally similar patterns in the two countries (see Figures 10 and 11).

In 1971, Canada switched to a flexible exchange rate regime, but the Bank of Canada continued to adjust short-term interest rates to keep the foreign exchange and domestic bond markets functioning smoothly and paid no attention to the growth rate of money. As a result, monetary policy was quite expansionary in the early 1970s and the inflation rate increased to double digits—in fact, the price level increased by 11% in 1974 compared with only 3% in 1971. By the mid-1970s there was little doubt that one consequence of the policy of using interest rates as the intermediate target was that the Bank of Canada did not concern

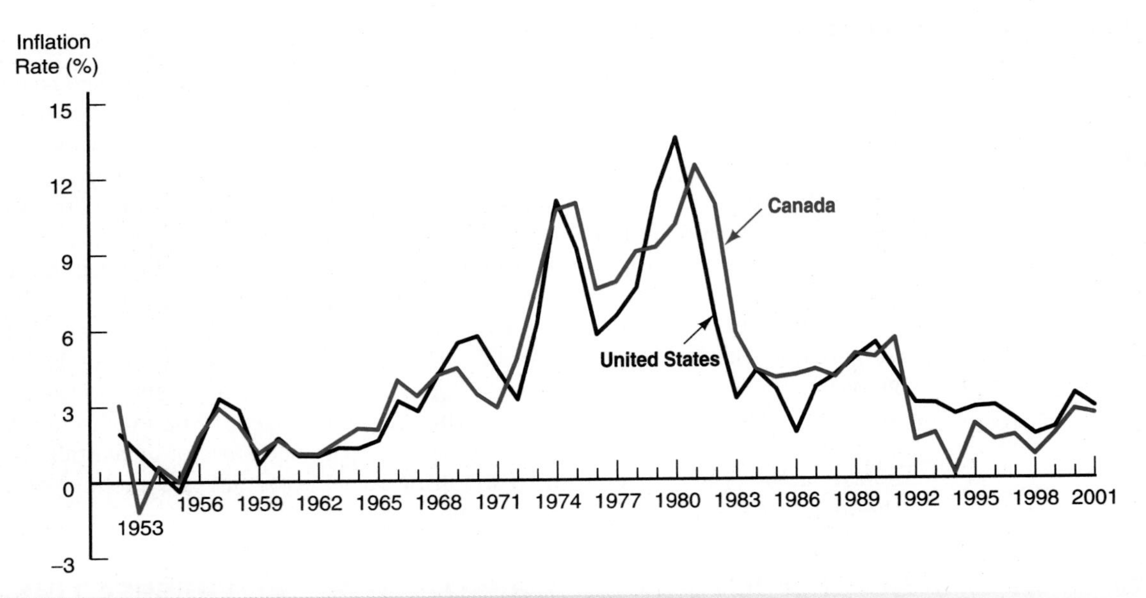

FIGURE 10 Inflation Rates, Canada and the United States, 1951–2001

Source: Statistics Canada CANSIM II series V735319 and V11123

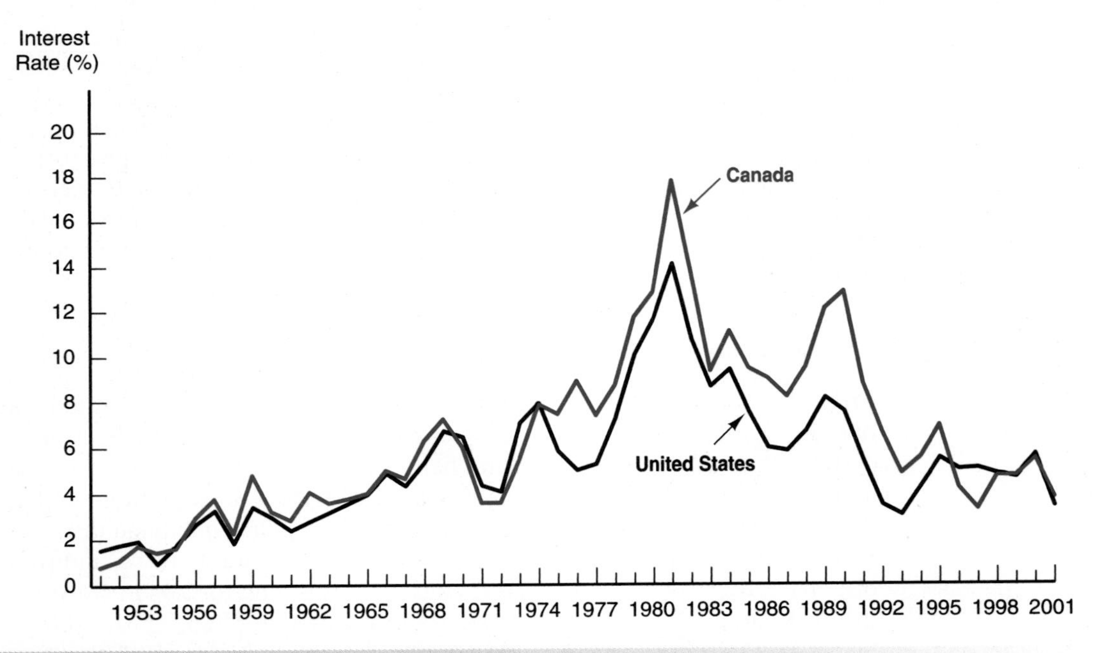

FIGURE 11 Inflation Rates (90-Day T-Bills), Canada and the United States, 1951–2001

Source: Statistics Canada CANSIM II series V122541 and V122139

itself with the rate of growth of the money supply, as measured by the monetary aggregates.

By the end of this period there was also a wide consensus among central banks around the world that fluctuations in money contained useful information about income and prices. This evidence contributed to the rise of **monetarism,** a theory that emphasizes a steady, predictable rate of growth in the monetary aggregates. It led the Bank of Canada and many other central banks, including the

Federal Reserve, the Bank of England, the Bundesbank, the Swiss National Bank, and the Bank of Japan, to adopt key monetary aggregates as the intermediate targets of monetary policy.

Monetary Targeting, 1975–1981

In response to rising inflation in the early 1970s, in 1975 the Bank of Canada introduced a program of "monetary gradualism," under which M1 growth would be controlled within a gradually falling target range (see Table 1). The change in monetary strategy did not extend to a change in operating procedures—the Bank continued to use an interest rate as its operating target. The idea was to announce about one year in advance the target path for the growth of M1 and then adjust policy during the course of the year to make the actual growth rate lie within the target range. The rationale for announcing the monetary policy targets in advance was to influence people's expectations, with the hope that this would help bring down actual inflation faster than otherwise. Moreover, the Bank decided to target M1 because it was the most prominent measure of money with a very stable demand.

As can be seen from Table 1, the Bank of Canada was successful at keeping actual M1 growth within the target range, and the goal of reducing M1 growth was achieved by the end of the decade. However, the inflation rate accelerated, and by the end of the 1970s, it was almost at the same level as when monetary gradualism was introduced in 1975. What went wrong? Why did the inflation rate remain high? The answers to these questions lie in a series of financial innovations that reduced the demand for M1 balances. In particular, the introduction of new kinds of bank deposit accounts, and the development of cash management techniques for corporate accounts, motivated individuals and firms to substitute out of demand deposits—part of M1—into new chequable savings deposits—part of M2. This increased the growth rate of M2 and reduced the growth rate of M1, at the same time that M1 growth was being targeted, thereby rendering what seemed like tight anti-inflationary policy into one that was in fact accommodating inflation.

By 1978, only three years after monetary targeting had begun, the Bank of Canada began to distance itself from this strategy out of concern for the nominal exchange rate, which had been depreciating. In particular, when interest rates in the United States increased sharply in late 1979, the Bank of Canada had to choose between allowing Canadian rates to increase to prevent an outflow of financial capital, and allowing the exchange rate to depreciate to accommodate the spread in interest rates between the two countries. The Bank responded with an extremely restrictive monetary policy to resist depreciation of the Canadian dollar and the possible inflationary shock from import prices. Not surprisingly, M1 growth was negative in 1981 even though the target range was for growth between

TABLE 1 Canadian M1 Target Ranges and Actual Growth Rates for 1975–1980

Announcement Date	Base Period	M1 Growth Target (%)	Outcome (%)
November 1975	April–June 1975	10–15	9.3
August 1976	February–April 1976	8–12	7.7
October 1977	June 1977	7–11	9.3
September 1978	June 1978	6–10	5.1
December 1979	April–June 1979	5–9	5.9
February 1981	August–October 1980	4–8	0.4

Source: Ben Bernanke and Frederic Mishkin, "Central Bank Behaviour and the Strategy of Monetary Policy: Observations from Six Industrialized Countries." *NBER Macroeconomics Annual* (1992): 183–228. Published by the MIT Press.

Notes: Outcomes are annualized growth rates (%) of seasonally adjusted M1 between the base period and the next announcement of new targets. For example, the outcome corresponding to the November 1975 announcement is the annualized growth rate of M1 between May and June 1975 and August 1976.

4% and 8% (see Table 1), and Canadian interest rates increased to unprecedented levels (see Figure 11). The cost was the very deep 1981–1982 recession, the most severe since the 1930s.

Because of the conflict with exchange rate goals, as well as the uncertainty about M1 as a reliable guide to monetary policy, monetary targeting was formally abandoned in November 1982.

The Checklist Approach, 1982–1988

The period following 1982 was one of groping. With the abandonment of M1 targets, the Bank of Canada switched its focus to a range of broader monetary aggregates, such as M2 and M2+, but no aggregate was found that would be suitable as a guide for conducting monetary policy. As a result, the Bank adopted what came to be called the "checklist" approach to policy, meaning that it looked at a list of factors in order to design and implement monetary policy. The Bank's checklist included the interest rate, the exchange rate, and with less weight attached to it, the money supply. The goal of monetary policy was inflation containment in the short term and price stability in the long term.

The Bank's anti-inflation policy during the 1982–1988 period can be viewed as one in which the interest rate became the operating target and the exchange rate was the intermediate target. Throughout most of the period the Bank targeted interest rates, resisting depreciation of the Canadian dollar (fearing that depreciation would worsen inflation). The Bank's policy, however, had been undertaken against the backdrop of a persistent federal budget deficit that led to higher interest rates, making it difficult for the Bank to control money growth and inflation. In fact inflation had begun to increase again and the Bank responded with a dramatic reversal of its ad hoc monetary strategy. It announced early in 1988 that short-term issues would henceforth less guide policy and that price stability would be the Bank's long-term objective of monetary policy.

Inflation Targeting, 1989–Present

The adoption of inflation targets in Canada followed a three-year campaign by the Bank of Canada to promote price stability as the long-term goal of monetary policy. Beginning with the Hanson Lecture at the University of Alberta in January 1988, the newly appointed Bank of Canada governor, John Crow, announced that the Bank would subsequently pursue an objective of price stability (or zero inflation).[16] Initially, the policy of zero inflation took the form of a return to the high interest rates of the early 1980s. For example, during 1987 through 1989, interest rates increased and the Canadian dollar appreciated by more than would have normally been expected under previous regimes. The idea was that higher interest rates and a stronger dollar would lower aggregate demand and eventually bring inflation down.

In this most recent attempt at lowering inflation, the Bank of Canada, however, followed a different strategy, by announcing explicit targets for its ultimate goal—the inflation rate—rather than for an intermediate variable such as money growth. In particular, in February 1991 the Bank's governor and the minister of finance jointly announced a series of declining inflation targets, with a band of plus and minus one percentage point around them. The targets were 3% by the end of 1992, falling to 2% by the end of 1995, to remain within a range of 1% to 3% thereafter. The 1% to 3% target range for inflation was renewed in December 1995,

[16] Zero inflation should be interpreted as a small positive rate of measured inflation.

in early 1998, and again in May 2001, to apply until the end of 2006.[17] The midpoint of the current inflation target range, 2%, is regarded as the most desirable outcome.

As already noted, in setting its inflation targets, the Bank uses the rate of change in the CPI because of its "headline" quality—it is the most commonly used and understood price measure in Canada. Moreover, the CPI comes out monthly and without revisions, whereas other price indexes, such as for example the GDP deflator, are frequently revised. However, because headline CPI (all items) includes volatile components such as food, energy, and the effect of indirect taxes, the Bank, in order to avoid responses to short-run fluctuations, prefers to use and report inflation in "core CPI" which excludes volatile components. A core inflation rate is useful in assessing whether trend inflation is on track for the medium term.

The move to targeting directly a goal of policy rather than an intermediate variable represented a significant shift in Bank of Canada policy procedures. An implication of this change was that the Bank had to broaden its information gathering to include variables containing significant information about future inflation. It has since used the overnight interest rate as the operating target and indicated that a range of monetary aggregates is useful in guiding policy along with an index of monetary conditions based on interest rates and exchange rates. The main purpose of this index is to capture the two key monetary policy transmission mechanisms in an open economy—the one operating through interest rates and the one operating through exchange rates.

What are the results of Canada's inflation-targeting monetary policy? Figure 4 plots headline CPI and core CPI (that is, with volatile food and energy prices excluded) inflation rates, for each year since 1990 and shows the Bank's target range since 1992. Clearly, inflation has fallen dramatically since the adoption of inflation targets, from more than 5% in 1991 to a 1% rate in 1998, being most of the time in the lower half of the target range. However, this decline was not without cost: Unemployment soared to above the 10% level from 1991 until 1994 but has since fallen. What is difficult to say is whether explicit inflation targets are the only way to achieve good macroeconomic outcomes. As the Bank's former governor, Gordon Thiessen, recently put it, "It is too early to draw very strong conclusions about the impact of inflation targets on actual economic performance in Canada. We really do require a longer period of time for targets to demonstrate their ability to deal successfully with the peak of an economic upturn without the trend of inflation moving persistently outside the target range."[18]

INTERNATIONAL CONSIDERATIONS

The growing integration and interdependence of national economies (a process known as **globalization**), has brought international considerations to the forefront of Bank of Canada policymaking in recent years. With integrated financial markets, the Bank of Canada's monetary policy is also influenced by developments

[17]The 1995 and 1998 inflation-control agreements between the Bank of Canada and the government had a three-year horizon. The 2001 agreement, however, has a five-year horizon, reflecting the wide acceptance of the targets after almost a decade of operation.

[18]Gordon G. Thiessen, "The Canadian Experience with Targets for Inflation Control," *Canadian Public Policy* 24 (1998): p. 425. For a more detailed discussion of Canada's experience with inflation targets see also Charles Freedman, "Inflation Targeting and the Economy: Lessons from Canada's First Decade," *Contemporary Economic Policy* 19 (2001): pp. 2–19; and Ben Bernanke, Thomas Laubach, Frederic Mishkin, and Adam Posen, *Inflation Targeting: Lessons from the International Experience*, Princeton, NJ: Princeton University Press, 1999.

outside Canada. This is not a bad thing, but it requires international policy cooperation to reduce potential disruptions to domestic policymaking and promote greater stability in financial markets. International cooperation has been encouraged by the process of **international policy coordination** (agreements among countries to enact policies cooperatively) that led to the Plaza Agreement in 1985 and the Louvre Accord in 1987 (see Box 6).

International considerations also played a role in the initiatives recently undertaken by the International Monetary Fund and the Bank for International Settlements, following the G-7 Halifax Summit in 1995, to improve the functioning of international financial markets. These initiatives seek to maximize the benefits of financial globalization, reduce the risks of financial instability that unrestrained capital flows may cause, and develop mechanisms for support in times of financial crisis. For example, the issue of international financial stability played a role in the Federal Reserve's decision to lower the federal funds rate by $\frac{3}{4}$ of a percentage point in the fall of 1998. Concerns about the potential for worldwide financial crisis in the wake of the collapse of the Russian financial system at that time and weakness in other economies, particularly in Asia, stimulated the bank to take a dramatic step to calm down markets.

International considerations, although not the primary focus of the Bank of Canada, are likely to also be a major factor in the conduct of Canadian monetary policy in the future.

MONETARY TARGETING IN OTHER COUNTRIES

To understand more about how monetary policy is conducted, we must compare our experiences with those of other nations. Here we examine how central banks in other countries have conducted monetary policy. Note that many of their experiences parallel those in Canada.

As we noted in our study of the conduct of Canadian monetary policy, the Bank of Canada has flirted with monetary targeting as its basic monetary policy strat-

BOX 6: GLOBAL

International Policy Coordination: The Plaza Agreement and the Louvre Accord

By 1985, the decrease in the competitiveness of American corporations as a result of the strong U.S. dollar was raising strong sentiment in the United States for restricting imports. This protectionist threat to the international trading system stimulated finance ministers and the heads of central banks from the Group of Five (G-5) industrial countries—the United States, the United Kingdom, France, West Germany, and Japan—to reach an agreement at New York's Plaza Hotel in September 1985 to bring down the value of the U.S. dollar. From September 1985 until the beginning of 1987, the value of the U.S. dollar did indeed undergo a substantial decline, falling by 35% on average relative to other currencies. At this point, there was growing controversy over the decline in the U.S. dollar, and another meeting of policymakers from the G-5 countries plus Canada took place in February 1987 at the Louvre Museum in Paris. There the policymakers agreed that exchange rates should be stabilized around the levels currently prevailing. Although the value of the U.S. dollar did continue to fluctuate relative to foreign currencies after the Louvre Accord, its downward trend had been checked as intended.

Because subsequent exchange rate movements were in line with the Plaza Agreement and the Louvre Accord, these attempts at international policy coordination have been considered successful. However, other aspects of the agreements were not adhered to by all signatories. For example, West German and Japanese policymakers agreed that their countries should pursue more expansionary policies by increasing government spending and cutting taxes, and the United States agreed to try to bring down its budget deficit. At that time, the United States was not particularly successful in lowering its deficit, and the Germans were reluctant to pursue expansionary policies because of their concerns about inflation.

egy. And the Bank was not alone in adopting a monetary targeting framework in the late 1970s; many other central banks did as well. Why did monetary targeting become so popular in the 1970s?[19]

The primary reason was the rise in inflation throughout the industrialized world. Central banks realized that using nominal interest rates as a target variable could lead to rising inflationary pressures. They believed that monetary aggregates could serve as a guidepost, or *nominal anchor,* that could promote a less inflationary monetary policy. Of probably even more importance, central banks believed that monetary targets could help send almost immediate signals to both the public and markets about the stance of monetary policy and the intentions of the policymakers to keep inflation in check. These signals might then help fix inflation expectations and help produce lower wage and price increases and thus less actual inflation.

We examine the experiences of four foreign countries—the United States, the United Kingdom,Germany, and Japan—to evaluate the extent to which monetary targeting has been a successful strategy for monetary policy.

United States

In response to concerns about inflation in the late 1960s, in 1970 the Federal Reserve committed itself to the use of monetary aggregates as intermediate targets. Every six weeks, the Federal Open Market Committee would set target ranges for the growth rate of various monetary aggregates and would determine what federal funds rate (the interest rate on funds loaned overnight between banks) it thought consistent with these aims. The target ranges for the growth in monetary aggregates were fairly broad—a typical range for the growth of M1 (a monetary aggregate that consists primarily of currency and chequable deposits) might be 3% to 6%; for M2 (a monetary aggregate that adds to M1 money market mutual funds and deposit accounts, small-denomination time deposits, savings deposits, and overnight repurchase agreements and eurodollars), 4% to 7%—while the range for the federal funds rate was a narrow band, say, from 7.5% to 8.25%. The trading desk at the Federal Reserve Bank of New York was then instructed to meet both sets of targets, but as we saw earlier, interest-rate targets and monetary aggregate targets might not be compatible. If the two targets were incompatible—say, the federal funds rate began to climb higher than the top of its target band when M1 was growing too rapidly—the trading desk was instructed to give precedence to the federal funds rate target. In the situation just described, this would mean that although M1 growth was too high, the trading desk would make open market purchases to keep the federal funds rate within its target range.

The Fed was actually using the federal funds rate as its operating target. During the six-week period between FOMC meetings, an unexpected rise in income (which would cause the federal funds rate to hit the top of its target band) would then induce open market purchases and a too rapid growth of the money supply. When the FOMC met again, it would try to bring money supply growth back on track by raising the target range on the federal funds rate. However, if income continued to rise unexpectedly, money growth would overshoot again. This is exactly what occurred from June 1972 to June 1973, when the economy boomed unexpectedly: M1 growth greatly exceeded its target, increasing at approximately an 8% rate, while the federal funds rate climbed from 4.5% to 8.5%. The economy soon became overheated, and inflationary pressures began to mount.

---

[19]The discussion here is based on Ben Bernanke and Frederic S. Mishkin, "Central Bank Behavior and the Strategy of Monetary Policy: Observations from Six Industrialized Countries," in *NBER Macroeconomics Annual, 1992,* ed. Oliver Blanchard and Stanley Fischer (Cambridge, MA: MIT Press, 1992), pp. 183–228.

The opposite chain of events occurred at the end of 1974, when the economic contraction was far more severe than anyone had predicted. The federal funds rate fell dramatically, from more than 12% to 5%, and persistently bumped against the bottom of its target range. The trading desk conducted open market sales to keep the federal funds rate from falling, and money growth dropped precipitously, actually turning negative by the beginning of 1975. Clearly, this sharp drop in money growth when the United States was experiencing one of the worst economic contractions of the postwar era was a serious mistake.

Using the federal funds rate as an operating target promoted a procyclical monetary policy despite the Fed's lip service to monetary aggregate targets. If the Federal Reserve really intended to pursue monetary aggregate targets, it seems peculiar that it would have chosen an interest rate for an operating target rather than a reserve aggregate. (However, as the discussion of the conduct of Japanese monetary policy later in this chapter makes clear, more effective monetary control can be achieved even when an interest rate is used as an operating target.) The explanation for why the Fed chose an interest rate as an operating target is that it was still very concerned with achieving interest-rate stability and was reluctant to relinquish control over interest-rate movements. The incompatibility of the Fed's policy procedure with its stated intent of targeting on the monetary aggregates had become very clear by October 1979, when the Fed's policy procedures underwent drastic revision.

In October 1979, two months after Paul Volcker became chairman of the Board of Governors, the Fed finally de-emphasized the federal funds rate as an operating target by widening its target range more than fivefold: A typical range might be from 10% to 15%. The primary operating target became nonborrowed reserves that the Fed would set after estimating the volume of discount loans the banks would borrow. Figure 12 shows what happened to the federal funds rate and the growth rate of the M1 money supply both before and after October 1979. Not surprisingly, the federal funds rate underwent much greater fluctuations after it was de-emphasized as an operating target. What is surprising, however, is that the de-emphasis of the federal funds target did not result in improved monetary control: After October 1979, the fluctuations in the rate of money supply growth *increased* rather than decreased as would have been expected. In addition, the Fed missed its M1 growth target ranges in all three years of the 1979–1982 period. What went wrong?

There are several possible answers to this question. The first is that the U.S. economy was exposed to several shocks during this period that made monetary control more difficult: the acceleration of financial innovation and deregulation, which added new categories of deposits such as NOW accounts to the measures of monetary aggregates; the imposition by the Fed of credit controls from March to July 1980, which restricted the growth of consumer and business loans; and the back-to-back recessions of 1980 and 1981–1982.

A more persuasive explanation for poor monetary control is that controlling the money supply was never really the intent of Volcker's policy shift. Despite Volcker's statements about the need to target monetary aggregates, he was not committed to these targets. Rather, he was far more concerned with using interest-rate movements to wring inflation out of the economy. Volcker's primary reason for changing the Fed's operating procedure was to free his hands to manipulate interest rates in order to fight inflation. It was necessary to abandon interest-rate targets if Volcker were to be able to raise interest rates sharply when a slowdown in the economy was required to dampen inflation. This view of Volcker's strategy suggests that the Fed's announced attachment to monetary aggregate targets may have been a smokescreen to keep the Fed from being blamed for the high interest rates that would result from the new policy.

The interest rate movements in Figure 12 support this interpretation of Fed strategy. After the October 1979 announcement, short-term interest rates were driven up by nearly 5%, until in March 1980 they exceeded 15%. With the imposition of credit controls in March 1980 and the rapid decline in real GDP in the second quarter of 1980, the Fed eased up on its policy and allowed interest rates to decline sharply. When recovery began in July 1980, inflation remained persistent, still exceeding 10%. Because the inflation fight was not yet won, the Fed tightened the screws again, sending short-term rates above the 15% level for a second time. The 1981–1982 recession and its large decline in output and high unemployment began to bring inflation down. The inflationary psychology apparently broken, interest rates were allowed to fall.

The Fed's anti-inflation strategy during the October 1979–October 1982 period was neither intended nor likely to produce smooth growth in the monetary aggregates. Indeed, the large fluctuations in interest rates and the business cycle, along with financial innovation, helped generate volatile money growth. In October 1982, with inflation in check, the Fed returned, in effect, to a policy of smoothing interest rates. It did this by placing less emphasis on monetary aggregate targets and shifting to borrowed reserves (discount loan borrowings) as an operating target.

United Kingdom

As in the United States, the British introduced monetary targeting in late 1973 in response to mounting concerns about inflation. The Bank of England targeted M3, a broader monetary target than the Fed used, but did not pursue it seriously: Announced targets were consistently overshot, and the Bank of England frequently revised its targets midstream or abandoned them entirely. The outcome was greater volatility of British monetary aggregates compared with American ones. After inflation accelerated in the late 1970s, Prime Minister Margaret Thatcher in 1980 introduced the Medium-Term Financial Strategy, which proposed a gradual deceleration of M3 growth. Unfortunately, the M3 targets ran into problems similar to those of the M1 targets in the United States: They were not reliable indicators of the tightness of monetary policy. After 1983, arguing that financial innovation was wreaking havoc with the relationship between M3 and national income, the Bank of England began to deemphasize M3 in favour of a narrower monetary aggregate, M0 (the monetary base). The target for M3 was temporarily suspended in October 1985 and was completely dropped in 1987, and monetary targets were abandoned altogether when the nation tied its exchange rate to the deutsche mark and became part of the European Monetary System (EMS) in October 1990.

Germany

Germany's central bank, the Bundesbank, also responded to rising inflation in the early 1970s by adopting monetary targets in 1975. The monetary aggregate chosen was a narrow one known as *central bank money*, the sum of currency in circulation and bank deposits weighted by the 1974 required reserve ratios. The Bundesbank has allowed growth outside its target ranges for periods of two to three years, and overshoots of its targets have subsequently been reversed. The primary reason for allowing deviations from its targets has been exchange rate considerations, which have been important to international agreements such as the European Monetary System, the Plaza Agreement, and the Louvre Accord. In 1988, the Bundesbank switched targets from central bank money to M3. German monetary policy using monetary targeting has been quite successful in maintaining a low and stable inflation rate.

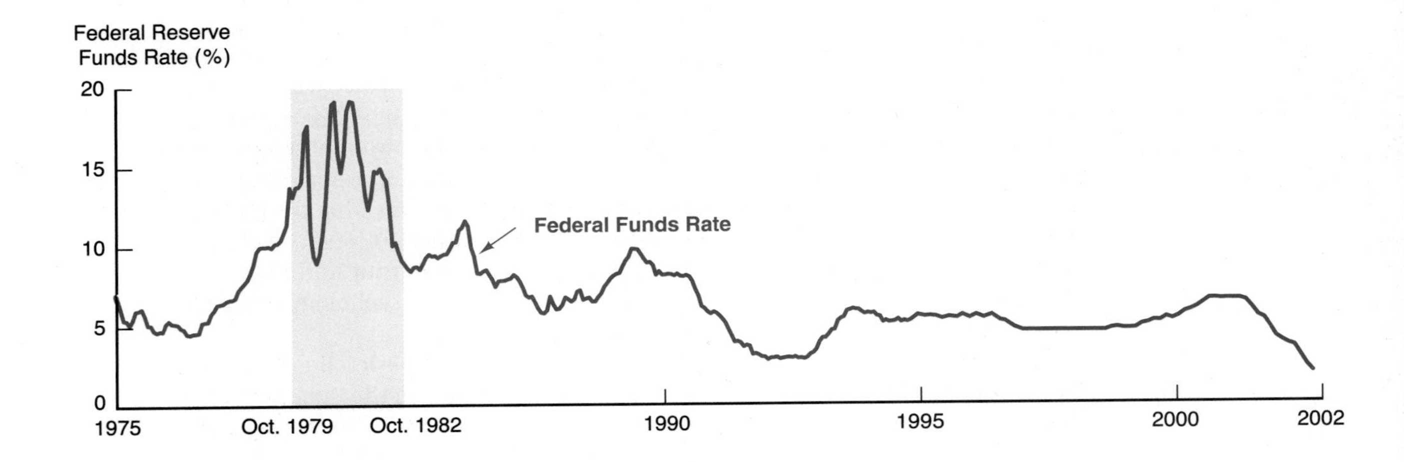

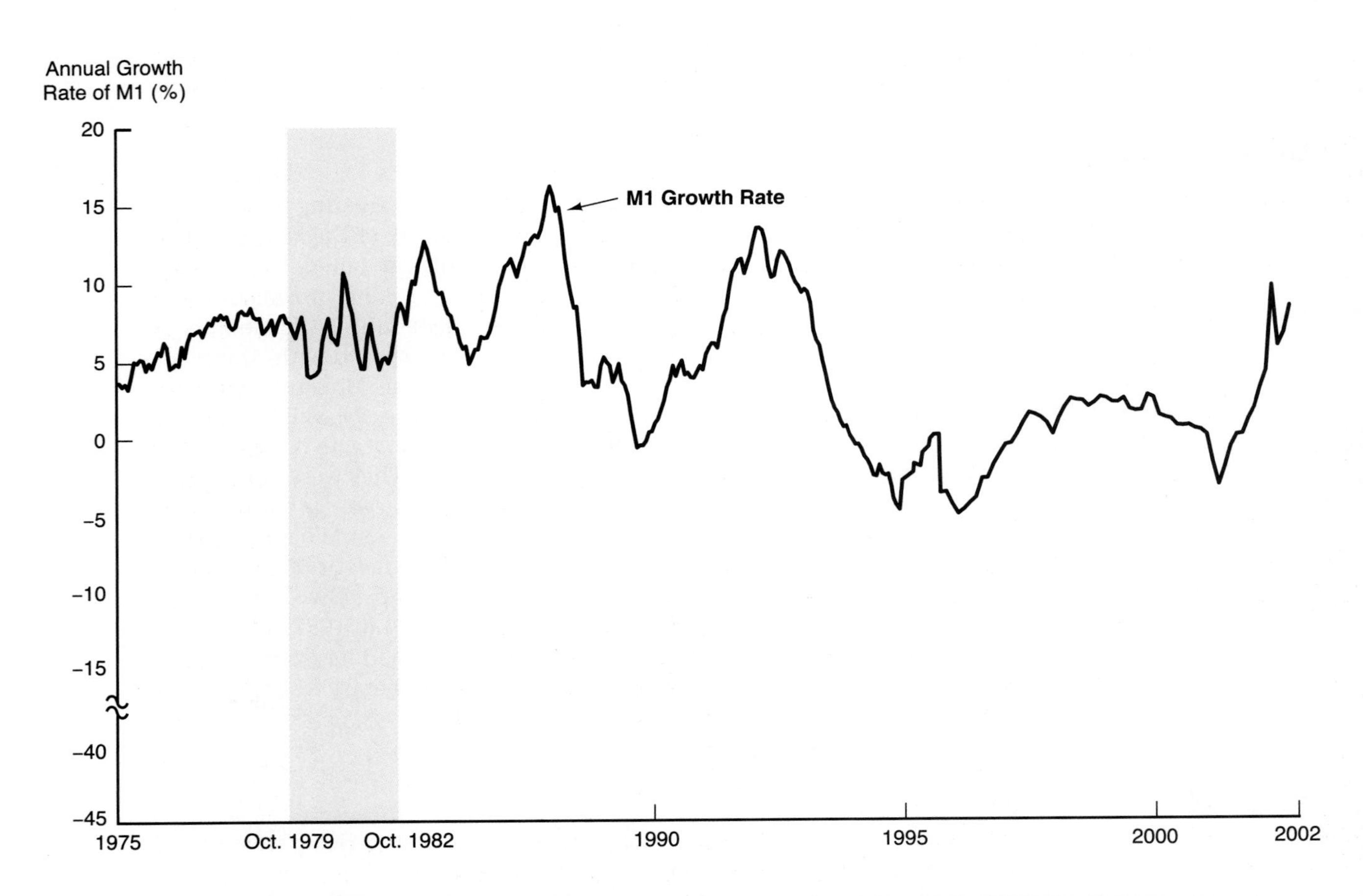

FIGURE 12 Federal Funds Rate and Growth Rate of the Money Supply: Before and After October 1979

Source: http://www.federalreserve.gov/releases/H6/hist/h6hist1.txt

The reunification of Germany in 1990 created some difficult problems for monetary policy. The Bundesbank was torn between trying to restrain the inflationary pressures created by reunification and keeping its exchange rate in line with those in other European countries. These strains contributed to an exchange rate crisis in Europe in September 1992, which will be discussed further in Chapter 13. The Bundesbank continued to subscribe to monetary targeting until it became part of the European System of Central Banks in January 1999, but recent research suggests that its commitment may have been weaker than its rhetoric suggested.[20]

Japan

The increase in oil prices in late 1973 was a major shock for Japan, which experienced a huge jump in the inflation rate to more than 20% in 1974—a surge facilitated by money growth in 1973 in excess of 20%. The Bank of Japan, like the other central banks discussed here, began to pay more attention to money growth rates. In 1978, the Bank of Japan began to announce "forecasts" at the beginning of each quarter for M2 + CDs. Although the Bank of Japan was not officially committed to monetary targeting, monetary policy appeared to be more money-focused after 1978. For example, after the second oil price shock in 1979, the Bank of Japan quickly reduced M2 + CDs growth, rather than allowing it to shoot up as had occurred after the first oil shock. The Bank of Japan conducted monetary policy with operating procedures that are similar in many ways to those that the Federal Reserve has used in the United States. The Bank of Japan uses the interest rate in the Japanese interbank market (which has a function similar to that of the federal funds market in the United States) as its daily operating target, just as the Fed has done.

The Bank of Japan's monetary policy performance during the 1978–1987 period was much better than the Fed's. Money growth in Japan slowed gradually, beginning in the mid-1970s, and was much less variable than in the United States. The outcome was a more rapid braking of inflation and an average inflation rate that was lower in Japan. In addition, these excellent results on inflation were achieved with lower variability in real output in Japan than in the United States. The success of Japanese monetary policy in the 1978–1987 period using an interest rate as an operating target, in contrast to the lack of success in the 1970–1979 period in the United States when the Fed used a similar operating procedure, suggests that using an interest rate as an operating target is not necessarily a barrier to successful monetary policy. More important might be a commitment to a low inflation rate, something that was true for the Bank of Japan in this period.

In parallel with the United States, financial innovation and deregulation in Japan began to reduce the usefulness of the M2 + CDs monetary aggregate as an indicator of monetary policy. Because of concerns about the appreciation of the yen, the Bank of Japan significantly increased the rate of money growth from 1987 to 1989. Many observers blamed speculation in Japanese land and stock prices (the so-called bubble economy) on the increase in money growth, and to reduce this speculation, in 1989 the Bank of Japan switched to a tighter monetary policy aimed at slower money growth. The aftermath has been a substantial decline in land and stock prices and the collapse of the bubble economy.

---

[20]See Richard Clarida and Mark Gertler, "How the Bundesbank Conducts Monetary Policy," National Bureau of Economic Research Working Paper No. 5581, May 1996.

Lessons from Monetary Targeting Experiences

There are several lessons to be drawn from the experience with monetary targeting in the four countries and Canada. First, successful use of monetary targeting seems to require that the central bank pursue its targeting strategy seriously. Countries like the United States, Canada, and especially the United Kingdom were unable to use monetary targeting to bring inflation under control because the procedures they used to implement the targets did not imply a strong commitment to the strategy and they consistently overshot their monetary targets. Germany and Japan, by contrast, were more successful in using monetary aggregates to keep inflation in check. This did not mean that the Bundesbank and the Bank of Japan always met their targets; more critical to their success was that they subsequently reversed overshoots of the targets. A further lesson from the Japanese experience is that the success of monetary targeting can be achieved with operating procedures that focus on interest rates as the operating target. The final lesson is that the breakdown in the relationship between monetary aggregates and the goal variables, nominal GDP and inflation, in many countries made the monetary targeting strategy untenable. As the former governor of the Bank of Canada, John Crow, is said to have stated, "We didn't abandon monetary aggregates; they abandoned us."

THE NEW INTERNATIONAL TREND IN MONETARY POLICY STRATEGY: INFLATION TARGETING

Although central banks have abandoned monetary targeting, the reasons they adopted it in the first place remain. Central banks still see the need to have a nominal anchor that will promote price stability. Another nominal anchor for monetary policy can be the foreign exchange rate. As we will see in Chapter 13, some countries have achieved low inflation by tying the value of their currency to the currency of a country with a good inflation record. However, the problem with this strategy is that, as shown in Chapter 13, with a fixed exchange rate, a country no longer exercises control over its own monetary policy and so cannot use monetary policy to respond to domestic shocks.

The search for a nominal anchor has led many countries to pursue inflation targeting as their basic monetary strategy. We discussed Canada's experience with inflation targeting earlier in this chapter. Now we look at inflation targeting in New Zealand because it was the first country to adopt it. We then go on to look at the experience of the United Kingdom.[21]

New Zealand

As part of a general reform of the government's role in the economy, the New Zealand Parliament in 1989 passed the Reserve Bank of New Zealand Act, which became effective on February 1, 1990. Besides increasing the independence of the central bank, the Reserve Bank of New Zealand, transforming it from one of the least independent to one of the most independent among the developed countries, the act also committed the Reserve Bank to the sole objective of price stability. The act stipulated that the minister of finance and the governor of the Reserve Bank should negotiate and make public a "policy targets agreement" that sets

[21]The discussion here is based on Frederic S. Mishkin and Adam S. Posen, "Inflation Targeting: Lessons from Four Countries," Federal Reserve Bank of New York, *Economic Policy Review* 3 (1997): 9–110; and Ben S. Bernanke, Thomas Laubach, Frederic S. Mishkin, and Adam S. Posen, *Inflation Targeting: Lessons from the International Experience* (Princeton, NJ: Princeton University Press, 1999).

out the targets against which monetary policy performance will be evaluated. These agreements have specified numerical target ranges for inflation and the dates by which they were to be reached. An unusual feature of the New Zealand legislation is that the governor of the Reserve Bank is held personally accountable for the success of monetary policy. If the goals set forth in the policy targets agreement are not met, the governor is subject to dismissal.

The first policy that targeted agreement, signed by the minister of finance and the governor of the Reserve Bank on March 2, 1990, directed the Reserve Bank to achieve an annual inflation rate within the 0% to 2% range, and subsequent agreements stuck with this range until November 1996, when the upper limit was increased to 3%. As a result of tight monetary policy, the inflation rate was brought down from more than 5% to less than 2% by the end of 1992, but at the cost of a deep recession and a sharp rise in unemployment. Through 1998, inflation typically remained within the 0% to 2% range, with the exception of a brief period in 1995, when it exceeded the upper limit by a few tenths of a percentage point. (Under the Reserve Bank Act, the governor, Don Brash, could have been dismissed, but after parliamentary debate, he retained his job.) Since 1992, New Zealand's growth rate has on average been strong, with some years exceeding 5%, and unemployment has come down significantly.

United Kingdom

When the United Kingdom left the European Monetary System after the speculative attack on the pound in September 1992 (more on this in Chapter 13), the British decided to turn to inflation targets to replace the exchange rate as the nominal anchor. As you may recall from Chapter 6, the central bank in the United Kingdom, the Bank of England, at that time did not have statutory authority over monetary policy; it could only make recommendations. Thus, it was the chancellor of the Exchequer (the equivalent of the Canadian minister of finance) who announced an inflation target for the nation on October 8, 1992. Three weeks later, he "invited" the governor of the Bank of England to issue on a quarterly basis a report on the progress being made in achieving the target—an invitation that the governor accepted. The inflation target range was set at 1% to 4% until the next election (May 1997), with the intent that the inflation rate should settle down to the lower half of the range (below 2.5%). In 1997, the range was changed to a point target of 2.5%. Along with this inflation target, the government implemented the institutional changes mentioned in Chapter 6, which, along with the governor's report, gave the Bank of England a more independent voice on monetary policy, culminating in the granting of the power to set interest rates to the Bank in May 1997.

Before the adoption of inflation targets, inflation had already been falling in the United Kingdom, from a peak of 9% at the beginning of 1991 to 4% at the time of adoption. After a small upward movement in early 1993, inflation continued to fall until by the third quarter of 1994, it was at 2.2%, within the intended range articulated by the chancellor. Subsequently inflation rose, climbing above the 2.5% level by 1996, but has remained close to 2.5% since then. Meanwhile, growth of the U.K. economy has been strong, causing a reduction in the unemployment rate.

Lessons from Inflation Targeting Experiences

Several lessons can be drawn from the inflation targeting experiences in Canada, New Zealand, and the United Kingdom. First, as the New Zealand and Canadian experience indicates, inflation targets have not been able to produce a decline in inflation without a substantial decline in output and a rise in unemployment. Hopes that inflation targets would lead to disinflation at a lower cost have not been realized. Second, inflation targets have so far worked well in keeping inflation at moderate levels. One important advantage of inflation targets is that they keep the goal of price stability in the public's eye, thus making the central bank more accountable for keeping inflation low, which can also help reduce political pressures on the central bank to pursue inflationary monetary policy.

How successful will inflation targeting be at keeping inflation low in the countries examined here? It is still too early to tell. Nonetheless, many other countries have followed New Zealand, Canada, and the United Kingdom in adopting inflation targets, including Australia, Israel, Sweden, Switzerland, Brazil, Chile, South Africa, Poland, and Thailand. The growing popularity of inflation targeting indicates that it might become the wave of the future for central bank strategy.

THE PRACTISING FINANCIAL INSTITUTION MANAGER

Using a Bank of Canada Watcher

As we have seen, the most important player in the determination of the Canadian money supply and interest rates is the Bank of Canada. When the Bank wants to inject reserves into the system, it conducts open market purchases of bonds, which cause their prices to increase and their interest rates to fall, at least in the short term. If the Bank withdraws reserves from the system, it sells bonds, thereby depressing their price and raising their interest rates. From a longer-run perspective, if the Bank pursues an expansionary monetary policy with high money growth, inflation will rise and, as we saw in Chapter 4, interest rates will rise as well. Contractionary monetary policy is likely to lower inflation in the long run and lead to lower interest rates.

Knowing what actions the Bank of Canada might be taking can thus help financial institution managers predict the future course of interest rates with greater accuracy. Because, as we have seen, changes in interest rates have a major impact on a financial institution's profitability, the managers of these institutions are particularly interested in scrutinizing the Bank of Canada's behaviour. To help in this task, managers hire so-called Bank of Canada watchers, experts on Bank of Canada behaviour who may have worked in the Bank of Canada and so have an insider's view of Bank of Canada operations.

Divining what the Bank of Canada is up to is by no means easy. Box 4 in Chapter 6 suggests that the central banks have a penchant for secrecy. For example, the Bank of Canada does not provide information on the amount of certain transactions and frequently tries to obscure from the market whether it is injecting reserves into the banking system by making open market purchases and sales simultaneously.

Bank of Canada watchers, with their specialized knowledge of the ins and outs of the Bank, scrutinize the public pronouncements of Bank officials to get a feel for where monetary policy is heading. They also carefully study the data on past Bank of Canada actions and current events in the bond markets to determine what the Bank is up to.

If a Bank of Canada watcher tells a financial institution manager that Bank of Canada concerns about inflation are high and the Bank will pursue a tight monetary policy and raise short-term interest rates in the near future, the manager may decide immediately to acquire funds at the currently low interest rates in order to keep the cost of funds from rising. If the financial institution trades foreign exchange, the rise in interest rates and the attempt by the Bank of Canada to keep inflation down might lead the manager to instruct traders to purchase dollars in the foreign exchange market. As we will see in Chapter 12, these actions by the Bank of Canada would be likely to cause the value of the dollar to appreciate, so the purchase of dollars by the financial institution should lead to substantial profits.

If, conversely, the Bank of Canada watcher thinks that the Bank is worried about a weak economy and will thus pursue an expansionary policy and lower interest rates, the financial institution manager will take very different actions. Now the manager might instruct loan officers to make as many loans as possible so as to lock in the higher interest rates that the financial institution can earn currently. Or the manager might buy bonds, anticipating that interest rates will fall and their prices will rise, giving the institution a nice profit. The more expansionary policy is also likely to lower the value of the dollar in the foreign exchange market, so the financial institution manager might tell foreign exchange traders to buy foreign currencies and sell dollars in order to make a profit when the dollar falls in the future.

A Bank of Canada watcher who is right is a very valuable commodity to a financial institution. Successful Bank of Canada watchers are actively sought out by financial institutions and often earn high salaries, well into the six-figure range.

SUMMARY

1. The conduct of monetary policy involves actions that affect the Bank of Canada's balance sheet. Open market purchases lead to an expansion of reserves and deposits in the banking system and hence to an expansion of the monetary base and the money supply. An increase in advances to banks leads to an expansion of reserves, thereby causing an expansion of the monetary base and the money supply.
2. The Bank of Canada views the overnight interest rate as the centrepiece of its monetary policy implementation. At 9 A.M. on the fixed action date, the Bank announces an operating band of 50 basis points for the overnight rate. The upper limit of the operating band is the bank rate—the rate the Bank charges LVTS participants that require an overdraft loan to cover negative settlement balances. The lower limit is the rate the Bank pays LVTS participants with positive settlement balances.
3. Before the introduction of the LVTS, the Bank reinforced the target band for the overnight rate by offering SPRAs at the upper end of the band and SRAs at the lower end of the band. With the introduction of the LVTS on February 4, 1999, however, the Bank introduced a new framework for implementing monetary policy. This involves the lending to and taking deposits from LVTS participants.
4. The Bank of Canada targets the value of the overnight interest rate within its operating band, at the midpoint of the band. In doing so, the Bank intervenes in the overnight market using open-market buyback operations at the target rate. If the overnight rate is trading above the target rate, the Bank uses repos in which it purchases government of Canada securities from primary dealers with an agreement to resell them on the next business day. If the overnight rate is too low relative to the target rate, the Bank uses reverse repos in which it sells government of Canada securities to primary dealers with an agreement to buy them back on the next business day.
5. The Bank continues to use government deposit shifting to neutralize public sector flows that affect LVTS participants' settlement balances—this in effect is a cash setting, a cash setting that is currently $50 million. Because its holdings of government of Canada securities is often much smaller than its monetary liabilities, the Bank brings onto its balance sheet Exchange Fund Account assets to back its liabilities. These amounts are adjusted daily, depending on factors such as the level of financial institution borrowings and deposits.
6. The six basic goals of monetary policy are high employment, economic growth, price stability, interest-rate stability, stability of financial markets, and stability in foreign exchange markets.
7. By using intermediate and operating targets, a central bank such as the Bank of Canada can more quickly judge whether its policies are on the right track and make midcourse corrections, rather than waiting to see the final outcome of its policies on such goals as employment and the price level. The Bank's policy tools directly affect its operating targets, which in turn affect the intermediate targets, which in turn affect the goals.
8. Because interest-rate and monetary aggregate targets are incompatible, a central bank must choose between them on the basis of three criteria: measurability, controllability, and the ability to affect goal variables predictably. Unfortunately, these criteria do not establish an overwhelming case for one set of targets over another.

9. The historical record of the Bank of Canada's conduct of monetary policy reveals that the Bank has switched its targets many times, pursuing inflation targeting in recent years.

10. In response to the rise in inflation in the early 1970s, central banks around the world also began to target monetary aggregates. Monetary targeting seems to have been most effective when it has been pursued seriously, which does not mean that targets are always met; more critical to success was a reversal of overshoots of the targets. Unfortunately, the breakdown in many countries of the relationship between monetary aggregates and the goal variables, nominal GDP and inflation, made the monetary targeting strategy untenable.

11. After disappointments with monetary targeting, the search for a nominal anchor has lead several countries to pursue inflation targeting as their basic monetary strategy. Although inflation targeting so far has been successful in keeping inflation rates low in countries that have adopted it, hopes that inflation targets would lead to disinflation at a lower cost have not been realized.

12. Because predicting the Bank of Canada's actions can help managers of financial institutions predict the course of future interest rates, which has a major impact on the financial institutions' profitability, such managers value the services of Bank of Canada watchers, experts on Bank of Canada behaviour.

KEY TERMS

QUESTIONS AND PROBLEMS

***1.** "Unemployment is a bad thing, and the government should make every effort to eliminate it." Do you agree or disagree? Explain your answer.

2. Which goals of the Bank of Canada frequently conflict?

***3.** "If the demand for money did not fluctuate, the Bank of Canada could pursue both a money supply target and an interest-rate target at the same time." Is this statement true, false, or uncertain? Explain your answer.

4. Classify each of the following as either an operating target or an intermediate target, and explain why.
   a. The three-month treasury bill rate
   b. The monetary base
   c. M2+

***5.** What procedures can the Bank of Canada use to control the three-month treasury bill rate? Why does control of this interest rate imply that the Bank of Canada will lose control of the money supply?

6. If the Bank of Canada has an interest-rate target, why will an increase in money demand lead to a rise in the money supply?

***7.** "Interest rates can be measured more accurately and more quickly than the money supply. Hence an interest rate is preferred over the money supply as an intermediate target." Do you agree or disagree? Explain your answer.

8. Compare the monetary base to M2+ on the grounds of controllability and measurability. Which do you prefer as an intermediate target? Why?

***9.** Explain why an inflation-targeting framework is sufficient to hold the Bank of Canada accountable to the public.

10. The benefits of using the Bank of Canada's standing liquidity facilities to prevent bank panics are straightforward. What are the costs?

*11. How does the Bank of Canada influence interest rates and the money supply by changing the operating band for the overnight interest rate?

12. Excess reserves are frequently called idle reserves, suggesting that they are not useful. Does the episode of the rise in reserve requirements in 1936–1937 bear out this view?

*13. Explain how repos and reserve repos affect the overnight rate.

14. Why is pegging the nominal interest rate problematic for a central bank?

*15. How have the Bank of Canada's concerns about the value of the Canadian exchange rate affected monetary policy?

16. "The failure of the Bank of Canada to control the money supply in the 1970s and 1980s suggests that the Bank is not able to control the money supply." Do you agree or disagree? Explain your answer.

*17. "When the economy enters a recession, either a reserve target or an interest-rate target will lead to a slower rate of growth for the money supply." Explain why this statement is true. What does it say about the use of reserves or interest rates as targets?

18. How can bank behaviour and the Bank of Canada's behaviour cause money supply growth to be procyclical (rising in booms and falling in recessions)?

*19. Why might the Bank of Canada say that it wants to control the money supply but in reality not be serious about doing so?

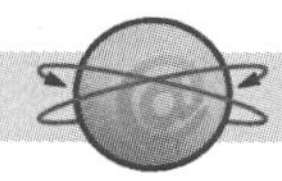

WEB EXERCISES

Conduct of Monetary Policy: Tools, Goals, and Targets

1. The Federal Open Market Committee (FOMC) meets about every six weeks to assess the state of the U.S. economy and to determine what actions the U.S. central bank should take. The minutes of these meetings are released after the next scheduled meeting. However, a brief press release is made available immediately. Find the schedule of minutes and press releases at http://www.federalreserve.gov/fomc/.
   a. When was the last scheduled meeting of the FOMC? When is the next meeting?
   b. Review the press release from the last meeting. What did the committee decide to do about short-term interest rates?
   c. Review the most recently published meeting minutes. What areas of the U.S. economy seemed to be of most concern to the committee members?

2. It is possible to access other central bank Websites to learn about their structure. One example is the European Central Bank (ECB). Go to http://www.ecb.int/. On the ECB home page, locate the link to the current exchange rate between the euro and the dollar. When the euro debuted in January 1999 it was valued at $1.18. What is it at now?

Chapter 8 The Money Markets

Preview

In April 2002, an interest-bearing chequing account paid less than 1% per year. This same money invested in a three-month treasury bill would have paid 2.2%. It is no wonder that individuals, as well as businesses, have aggressively pursued alternatives to low-interest-rate bank accounts. One such alternative is provided by the money markets, which we first introduced in Chapter 2. Recall that money market securities are short-term, low-risk, and very liquid. Because of the high degree of safety and liquidity these securities exhibit, they are close to being money, hence their name.

The money markets have been active since the early nineteenth century but have become much more important since 1970, when interest rates rose above historic levels. This chapter carefully reviews the money markets and the securities that are traded there. In addition, we discuss why the money markets are important to our financial system.

THE MONEY MARKETS DEFINED

The term *money market* is actually a misnomer. Money—currency—is not traded in the money markets. Because the securities that do trade there are short-term and highly liquid, however, they are close to being money. Money market securities, which are discussed in detail later in this chapter, have three basic characteristics in common:

1. They are usually sold in large denominations.
2. They have low default risk.
3. They mature in one year or less from their original issue date. Most money market instruments mature in fewer than 120 days.

Money market transactions do not take place in any one particular location or building. Instead, traders usually arrange purchases and sales between participants over the phone and complete them electronically. Because of this characteristic, money market securities usually have an active *secondary market.* This means that after the security has been sold initially, it is relatively easy to find buyers who will purchase it in the future. An active secondary market makes money market securities very flexible instruments to use to fill short-term financial needs.

Another characteristic of the money markets is that they are **wholesale markets.** This means that most transactions are very large, usually in excess of $1 million. The size of these transactions prevents most individual investors from participating directly in the money markets. Instead, dealers and brokers, operating in the trading rooms of large banks and brokerage houses, bring customers together. These traders will buy or sell $50 million or $100 million in mere seconds—certainly not a job for the faint of heart!

As you may recall from Chapter 2, flexibility and innovation are two important characteristics of any financial market, and the money markets are no exception. Despite the wholesale nature of the money market, innovative securities and trading methods have been developed to give small investors access to money market securities. We will discuss these securities and their characteristics later in the chapter.

Why Do We Need the Money Markets?

In theory, the money markets should not be necessary. The banking industry exists primarily to provide short-term loans and to accept short-term deposits. Banks should have an efficiency advantage in gathering information, an advantage that should eliminate the need for the money markets. Thanks to continuing relationships with customers, banks should be able to offer loans more cheaply than diversified markets, which must evaluate each borrower every time a new security is offered. Furthermore, short-term securities offered for sale in the money markets are neither as liquid nor as safe as deposits placed in banks and thrifts. Given the advantages that banks have, why do the money markets exist at all?

The banking industry exists primarily to mediate the asymmetric information problem between saver-lenders and borrower-spenders, and banks can earn profits by capturing economies of scale while providing this service. However, the banking industry is subject to more regulations and governmental costs than the money markets are. In situations where the asymmetric information problem is not severe, the money markets have a distinct cost advantage over banks in providing short-term funds.

Cost Advantages

Banks must put aside a portion of their deposits in the form of reserves that are held without earning interest. Thus, for every dollar deposited, the bank can invest only between 90 and 97 cents. This means that it must pay a lower interest rate to the depositor than if the full deposit could be reinvested. In doing so, banks provide valuable intermediation, as we will see in several later chapters. In some situations, however, the cost structure of the banking industry makes it unable to compete effectively in the market for short-term funds against the less restricted money markets.

THE PURPOSE OF THE MONEY MARKETS

The well-developed secondary market for money market instruments makes the money market an ideal place for a firm or financial institution to "warehouse" surplus funds for short periods until they are needed. Similarly, the money markets provide a low-cost source of funds to firms, the government, and intermediaries that need a short-term infusion of funds.

Most investors in the money market who are temporarily warehousing funds are ordinarily not trying to earn unusually high returns on their money market funds. Rather, they use the money market as an interim investment that provides a higher return than holding cash or money in banks. They may feel that market conditions are not right to warrant the purchase of additional stock, or they may expect interest rates to rise and hence not want to purchase bonds. It is important to keep in mind that holding idle surplus cash is expensive for an investor because cash balances earn no income for the owner. Idle cash represents an *opportunity cost* in terms of lost interest income. Recall from Chapter 4 that an asset's opportunity cost is the amount of interest sacrificed by not holding an alternative asset. The money markets provide a means to invest idle funds and to reduce this opportunity cost.

Investment advisers often hold some funds in the money market so that they will be able to act quickly to take advantage of investment opportunities they identify. Most investment funds and financial intermediaries also hold money market securities to meet investment or deposit outflows.

The sellers of money market securities find that the money market provides a low-cost source of temporary funds. Table 1 shows the interest rates available on a variety of money market instruments sold by a variety of firms and institutions. For example, banks may issue overnight funds (we will define the money market securities later in this chapter) to obtain funds in the money market to meet settlement balances shortages. The government funds a large portion of the Canadian debt with treasury bills. Finance companies such as GMAC (General Motors Acceptance Company, the financing division of General Motors) may enter the money market to raise the funds that it uses to make car loans.

Why do corporations and the Canadian government sometimes need to get their hands on funds quickly? The primary reason is that cash inflows and outflows are rarely synchronized. Government tax revenues, for example, usually come only at certain times of the year, but expenses are incurred all year long. The government can borrow short-term funds that it will pay back when it receives tax revenues. Businesses also face problems caused by revenues and expenses occurring at different times. The money markets provide an efficient, low-cost way of solving these problems.

WHO PARTICIPATES IN THE MONEY MARKETS?

An obvious way to discuss the players in the money market would be to list those who borrow and those who lend. The problem with this approach is that most money market participants operate on both sides of the market. For example, any large bank will borrow aggressively in the money market by selling large commercial CDs. At the same time, it will lend short-term funds to businesses through

TABLE 1 Sample Money Market Rates, May 17, 2002

Instrument	Interest Rate (%)
overnight money market financing	2.2453
overnight repo (CORRA)	2.2569
one-month commercial paper	2.4200
three-month commercial paper	2.6400
one-month treasury bill	2.1900
two-month treasury bill	2.4000
three-month treasury bill	2.5500
six-month treasury bill	2.8100
one-year treasury bill	3.4300

Source: Bank of Canada Website: www.bankofcanada.ca

its commercial lending departments. Nevertheless, we can identify the primary money market players—the government, the Bank of Canada, banks and near banks, businesses, investments and securities firms, and individuals—and discuss their roles (summarized in Table 2).

Government of Canada

The government of Canada is unique because it is always a demander of money market funds and never a supplier. The government is the largest of all money market borrowers worldwide. It issues treasury bills (often called T-bills) and other securities that are popular with other money market participants. Short-term issues enable the government to raise funds until tax revenues are received. The government also issues T-bills to replace maturing issues.

Bank of Canada

The Bank of Canada is the government's agent for the distribution of all government securities. The Bank holds vast quantities of government securities that it sells if it believes that the money supply should be reduced. Similarly, the Bank will purchase government securities if it believes that the money supply should be expanded. The Bank's responsibility for the money supply makes it the single most influential participant in the Canadian money market. The Bank of Canada's role in controlling the economy was discussed further in Chapters 6 and 7.

Banks and Near Banks

Banks and near banks hold a larger percentage of government securities than any other group of financial institutions. This is partly because of regulations that limit the investment opportunities available to banks. Specifically, banks are prohibited from owning risky securities, such as stocks or corporate bonds. There are no restrictions against holding government securities because of their low risk and liquidity.

TABLE 2 Money Market Participants

Participant	Role
Government of Canada	Sells securities to fund the national debt
Bank of Canada	Buys and sells government securities as its primary method of controlling the money supply
Banks and other deposit-taking institutions	Buy government securities; sell certificates of deposit and make short-term loans; offer individual investors accounts that invest in money market securities
Businesses	Buy and sell various short-term securities as a regular part of their cash management
Investment companies (brokerage firms)	Trade on behalf of commercial accounts
Finance companies (commercial leasing companies)	Lend funds to individuals
Insurance companies (property and casualty insurance companies)	Maintain liquidity needed to meet unexpected demands
Pension funds	Maintain funds in money market instruments in readiness for investment in stocks and bonds
Individuals	Buy money market mutual funds
Money market mutual funds	Allow small investors to participate in the money market by aggregating their funds to invest in large-denomination money market securities

Banks are also the major issuer of negotiable certificates of deposit (CDs), banker's acceptances, overnight funds, and repurchase agreements (we will discuss these securities in the next section). In addition to using money market securities to help manage their own liquidity, many banks trade on behalf of their customers.

Not all banks deal for their customers in the secondary money market. The ones that do are among the largest in the country and are often referred to as *money centre banks.* The biggest money centre banks are the **Big Six**—the Royal Bank of Canada, Canadian Imperial Bank of Commerce (CIBC), Bank of Montreal, Scotiabank, TD Canada Trust, and the National Bank of Canada.

Businesses

Many businesses buy and sell securities in the money markets. Such activity is usually limited to major corporations because of the large dollar amounts involved. As discussed earlier, the money markets are used extensively by businesses both to warehouse surplus funds and to raise short-term funds. We will discuss the specific money market securities that businesses issue later in this chapter.

Investment and Securities Firms

The other financial institutions that participate in the money markets are listed in Table 2.

Investment Companies Large diversified brokerage firms are active in the money markets. The largest of these include RBC Dominion Securities, BMO Nesbitt Burns, CIBC World Markets, ScotiaMcLeod, and TD Securities. The primary function of these dealers is to "make a market" for money market securities by maintaining an inventory from which to buy or sell. These firms are very important to the liquidity of the money market because they ensure that both buyers and sellers can readily market their securities. We discuss investment companies in Chapter 21.

Finance Companies Finance companies raise funds in the money markets primarily by selling commercial paper. They then lend the funds to consumers for the purchase of durable goods such as cars, boats, or home improvements. Finance companies and related firms are discussed in Chapter 20.

Insurance Companies Property and casualty insurance companies must maintain liquidity because of their unpredictable need for funds. For example, insurance companies paid out billions of dollars in benefits to policyholders after the ice storm of 1998. To meet this demand for funds, the insurance companies sold some of their money market securities to raise cash. Insurance companies are discussed in Chapter 19.

Pension Funds Pension funds invest a portion of their cash in the money markets so that they can take advantage of investment opportunities that they may identify in the stock or bond markets. Like insurance companies, pension funds must have sufficient liquidity to meet their obligations. However, because their obligations are reasonably predictable, large money market security holdings are unnecessary. Pension funds are discussed in Chapter 19.

Individuals

When inflation rose in the late 1970s, the interest rates that banks were offering on deposits became unattractive to individual investors. At this same time, brokerage houses began promoting money market mutual funds, which paid much higher rates. Banks quickly raised rates in an attempt to recapture individual investors' dollars. This halted the rapid movement of funds, but money market mutual funds remain a popular individual investment option. The advantage of mutual funds is that they give investors with relatively small amounts of cash to invest access to large-denomination securities. We will discuss money market mutual funds in more depth later in this chapter.

MONEY MARKET INSTRUMENTS

A variety of money market instruments are available to meet the diverse needs of market participants. One security will be perfect for one investor; a different security may be best for another. Here we gain a greater understanding of money market security characteristics and how money market participants use them to manage their cash.

Treasury Bills

To finance the national debt, the government of Canada issues a variety of debt securities. The most widely held liquid security is the treasury bill. Treasury bills have 1-, 3-, 6-, and 12-month maturities. The treasury bill had a minimum denomination of $10 000 but recently new $1000 T-bills became available in an attempt to make government securities more widely available.

The government does not actually pay interest on treasury bills. Instead they are issued at a discount from par (their value at maturity). The investor's yield comes from the increase in the value of the security between the time it was purchased and the time it matures.

Application **Discounting the Price of Canada Securities to Pay the Interest**

Most money market securities do not pay interest. Instead, the investor pays less for the security than it will be worth when it matures, and the increase in price provides a return. This is called **discounting** and is common to short-term securities because they often mature before the issuer can mail out interest cheques. (We discussed discounting in Chapter 3.)

The yield on an investment is found by computing the increase in value in the security during its holding period and dividing by the amount paid for the security. This yield is converted into an annual yield by multiplying by 365 divided by the number of days until maturity. This gives the following equation:

$$i_{yt} = \frac{F - P}{P} \times \frac{365}{n} \tag{1}$$

where
i_{yt} = annualized yield on the investment
F = face value (amount paid to the investor at maturity)
P = purchase price
n = number of days until maturity

EXAMPLE 1: Discounting

You decide to purchase a three-month treasury bill for $9850. When it matures, the bill will be worth $10 000. What is the bill's annualized yield?

Solution

You would earn 6.11% on the three-month investment in the treasury bill.

$$i_{yt} = \frac{F - P}{P} \times \frac{365}{n}$$

where

$F =$ face value (amount paid to investor at maturity) $= \$10\ 000$

$P =$ purchase price $= \$9850$

$n =$ number of days until maturity $= 91$

Thus

$$i_{yt} = \frac{\$10\ 000 - \$9850}{\$9850} \times \frac{365}{91} = 0.0611 = 6.11\%$$

EXAMPLE 2: Discounting

Now suppose that you decide to sell the treasury bill 31 days before it matures. By selling before it matures, you will receive $9948. What is the bill's annualized yield?

Solution

On this 60-day investment in the treasury bill, you would earn 6.05%.

$$i_{yt} = \frac{F - P}{P} \times \frac{365}{n}$$

where

$F =$ face value (in this case amount paid to investor before maturity) $= \$9948$

$P =$ purchase price $= \$9850$

$n =$ number of days security held $= 91 - 31$ $= 60$

Thus

$$i_{yt} = \frac{\$9948 - \$9850}{\$9850} \times \frac{365}{60} = 0.0605 = 6.05\%$$

Risk Treasury bills have virtually zero default risk because even if the government ran out of money, it could simply print more to pay them off when they mature. The risk of unexpected changes in inflation is also low because of the short term to maturity. The market for treasury bills is extremely deep and liquid. A **deep market** is one with many different buyers and sellers. A **liquid market** is one in which securities can be bought and sold quickly and with low transaction costs. Investors in markets that are deep and liquid have little risk that they will not be able to sell their securities when they want to.

Treasury Bill Auctions As of September 18, 1997, every two weeks the Bank of Canada, on behalf of the government of Canada, announces how many treasury bills it will offer for sale. Treasury bills are generally issued with maturities of 98 days, 168 or 182 days, and 350 or 364 days, although for cash management purposes the Bank of Canada often issues T-bills with a maturity of less than 91 days. T-bills are available in denominations of $1000, $5000, $25 000, $100 000, and $1 million, and in bearer form. Government securities distributors (see Box 1) submit bids, on their own behalf and on behalf of their customers, subject to

Find information about upcoming auctions, results, debt buyback operations, and historical information at www.bankofcanada.ca

BOX 1
Government Securities Distributors

On April 18, 2002, there were 23 government securities distributors (that is, investment banks and banks):

- Bank of Montreal (T-bills only)
- Beacon Securities Limited
- BMO Nesbitt Burns Inc. (marketable bonds only)
- Canaccord Capital Corp.
- Canadian Imperial Bank of Commerce (T-bills only)
- Casgrain & Company Limited
- CIBC World Markets Inc.
- CTI Capital Inc.
- Desjardins Securities
- Deutsche Bank Securities Limited
- Golden Capital Securities Limited
- HSBC Bank Canada
- Laurentian Bank Securities Inc.
- Merrill Lynch Canada Inc.
- J.P. Morgan Securities Canada Inc.
- National Bank Financial Inc.
- Ocean Securities Inc.
- Odlum Brown Limited
- RBC Dominion Securities Inc.
- Resolution Capital Inc.
- Scotia Capital Inc.
- Société Générale Valeurs Mobilièrs Inc.
- TD Canada Trust

Source: Bank of Canada Website: www.bankofcanada.ca

auction limits. The Bank of Canada accepts the bids offering the highest price and makes the awards. The highest bidder is satisfied first. Subsequent bidders are satisfied in the order of their bid amount until the total amount of securities is distributed. Note that this implies that not everyone at the auction pays the same price for the securities.

As an alternative to the **competitive bidding** procedure just outlined, the Bank of Canada also permits **noncompetitive bidding.** When competitive bids are offered, investors state both the amount of securities desired and the price they are willing to pay. By contrast, noncompetitive bids include only the amount of securities the investor wants. The price is set as the weighted average of the competitive bids accepted. For example, if 30% of the issue was sold for \$98 per \$100 of par value, 50% for \$97, and the remaining 20% for \$96, the weighted average would be

$$\text{Weighted average price} = 0.30(\$98) + 0.50(\$97) + 0.20(\$96) = \$97.10$$

Bidders submitting noncompetitive bids would pay \$97.10 per \$100 of treasury bills purchased.

In delivering the treasury bills to government securities distributors, the Bank of Canada uses the Debt Clearing Service (DCS) of the Canadian Depository for Securities (CDS). That is, the allocation of treasury bills to each government securities distributor is effected by crediting the DCS securities account designated by the government securities distributor and debiting the Bank of Canada's DCS securities account, in exchange for a DCS fund transfer in the amount of the purchase. This procedure reduces the cost of holding government securities as well as the cost of transferring them as they are bought and sold in the secondary market.

The Bank of Canada's auction of government of Canada T-bills is supposed to be highly competitive and fair. A number of government securities distributors and nine primary dealers (see Box 2) regularly participate in the auction. To ensure proper levels of competition, no one dealer is allowed to purchase, for its own behalf and on behalf of its customers, more than 40% of any one issue. Primary dealers face serious consequences if they are caught violating the limits on the percentage of one issue they may purchase. (See, for example, Box 3 on the Salomon Smith Barney scandal in the United States.)

BOX 2

Primary Dealers for Treasury Bills

On April 18, 2002, there were nine primary dealers* for government of Canada treasury bills:

Bank of Montreal
Canadian Imperial Bank of Commerce
Deutsche Bank Securities Limited
Laurentian Bank Securities Inc.
Merrill Lynch Canada Inc.
National Bank Financial Inc.
RBC Dominion Securities Inc.
Scotia Capital Inc.
TD Canada Trust

* Primary dealers are government securities distributors that maintain a certain threshold level of activity in the government securities market.

Source: Bank of Canada Website: www.bankofcanada.ca

Treasury Bill Interest Rates Treasury bills are very close to being risk-free. As expected for a risk-free security, the interest rate earned on treasury bill securities is among the lowest in the economy. Investors in treasury bills have found that in some years, their earnings did not even compensate them for changes in purchasing power due to inflation. Figure 1 shows the interest rate on treasury bills and the inflation rate over the period 1973–2001. As discussed in Chapter 3, the *real rate* of interest has occasionally been less than zero. For example, in 1973–1977 and again in 1977–1978, the inflation rate matched or exceeded the earnings on T-bills. Clearly, the T-bill is not an investment to be used for anything but temporary storage of excess funds, because it barely keeps up with inflation.

Overnight Funds

Overnight funds are short-term funds transferred (loaned or borrowed) among financial institutions, usually for a period of one day. In the United States these funds are called *federal funds*. The term *federal funds* (or *fed funds*) is misleading. Fed funds really have nothing to do with the U.S. federal government. The term is a holdover from when the fed funds market began in the 1920s and banks with excess reserves loaned them to banks that needed them.

BOX 3

U.S. Treasury Bill Auctions Go Haywire

Every Thursday, the U.S. Treasury announces how many 91-day and 182-day Treasury bills it will offer for sale. Buyers must submit bids by the following Monday, and awards are made the next morning. Fifty-two-week Treasury bills are offered similarly once a month. The Treasury accepts the bids offering the highest price.

The Treasury auction of securities is supposed to be highly competitive and fair. To ensure proper levels of competition, no one dealer is allowed to purchase more than 35% of any one issue. About 40 primary dealers regularly participate in the auction.

In 1991, the disclosure that Salomon Smith Barney had broken the rules to corner the market cast the fairness of the auction in doubt. Salomon Smith Barney purchased 35% of the Treasury securities in its own name by submitting a relatively high bid. It then bought additional securities in the names of its customers, often without their knowledge or consent. Salomon then bought the securities from the customers. As a result of these transactions, Salomon cornered the market and was able to charge a monopolylike premium. The investigation of Salomon Smith Barney revealed that during one auction in May 1991, the brokerage managed to gain control of 94% of an $11 billion issue. During the scandal that followed this disclosure, John Gutfreund, the firm's chairman, and several other top executives with Salomon retired. The Treasury has instituted new rules since then to ensure that the market remains competitive.

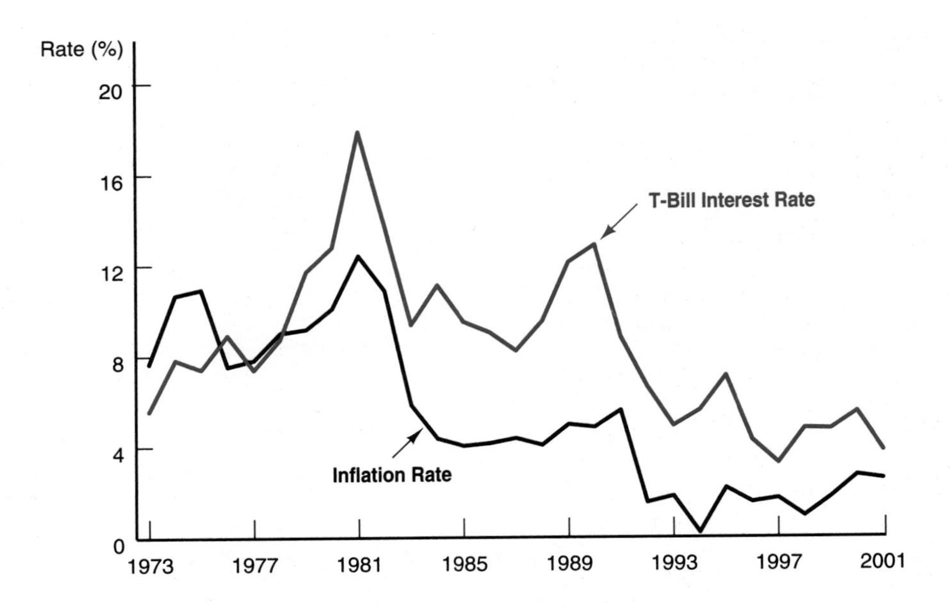

FIGURE 1 Treasury Bill Interest Rate and the Inflation Rate, 1973–2001

Source: Statistics Canada CANSIM II series V122531 and V73519

Purpose of Overnight Funds One reason why a bank might borrow in the overnight funds market is that it might find it does not have enough settlement balances at the Bank of Canada. It can then borrow these balances from another bank with excess settlement balances. The main purpose for the overnight funds is to provide depository institutions with an immediate infusion of reserves should they be short.[1] As noted in Chapter 7, depository institutions can borrow directly from the Bank of Canada, but they prefer to borrow from other institutions so that they do not pay the bank rate when they borrow from the Bank of Canada. Similarly, the reason that banks like to lend in the overnight funds market is that money at the Bank of Canada's standing liquidity facility earns a lower interest rate than in the overnight money market.

Terms for Overnight Funds Overnight funds are usually overnight investments. Banks analyze their reserve position on a daily basis and either borrow or invest in overnight funds, depending on whether they have excess or deficit settlement balances with the Bank of Canada at the end of the day. Suppose that a bank finds that it has $50 million in excess settlement balances. It will call its correspondent banks (banks that have reciprocal accounts) to see whether they need reserves that day. The bank will sell its excess funds to the bank that offers the highest rate. Once an agreement has been reached, the bank with excess funds will wire the funds to the borrowing bank. This involves telecommunicating to the Bank of Canada instructions to take funds out of the seller's account at the Bank and deposit the funds in the borrower's account. The next day, the funds are transferred back, and the process begins again.

Most overnight funds borrowings are unsecured. Typically, the entire agreement is supported only by oral communication between buyer and seller.

[1]See Eugene Lundrigan and Sari Toll, "The Overnight Market in Canada," *Bank of Canada Review* (Winter 1997–1998): 27–42, for details regarding the evolution of the overnight market.

Overnight Interest Rate The overnight market is very sensitive to the credit needs of the deposit-taking institutions, so the interest rate on overnight loans, called the **overnight interest rate**, is a closely watched barometer of the tightness of credit market conditions in the banking system and the stance of monetary policy. When it is high, it indicates that the banks are strapped for funds, whereas when it is low, banks' credit needs are low.

As you learned in Chapter 7, the overnight interest rate is the operating target of the Bank of Canada's monetary policy. That is, the Bank implements monetary policy by changing the overnight interest rate. Since December 2000, the Bank of Canada has operated under a system of eight "fixed" dates throughout the year for announcing any changes to the operating band of 50 basis points for the overnight rate, keeping the option of acting between the fixed dates in "extraordinary circumstances." Moreover, the Bank targets the overnight interest rate at the midpoint of the band using repurchase transactions, either SPRAs or SRAs.

Though changes in the overnight interest rate directly affect few businesses or consumers, they are an important indicator of the direction in which the Bank of Canada wants the economy to move. Figure 2 compares the overnight rate with the T-bill rate. Clearly, the two track together.

Repurchase Agreements

Repurchase agreements (repos) work much the same way as overnight funds except that nonbanks can participate. A firm can sell Canada securities in a repurchase agreement whereby the firm agrees to buy back the securities at a specified future date. Most repos have a very short term, the most common being for 3 to 14 days. There is a market, however, for one- to three-month repos.

The Use of Repurchase Agreements Government securities dealers frequently engage in repos. The dealer may sell the securities to a bank with the promise to buy the securities back the next day. This makes the repo essentially a

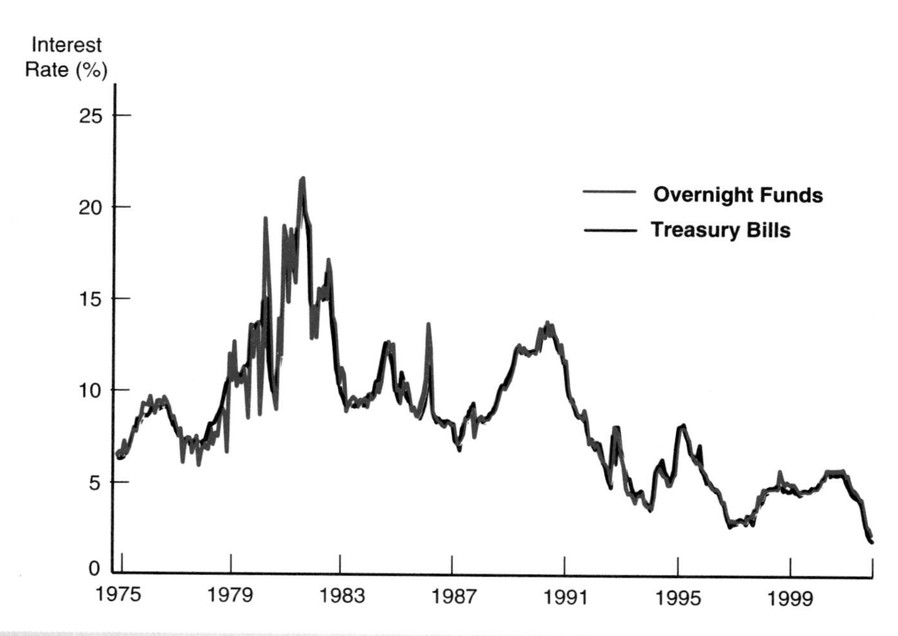

FIGURE 2 Overnight Funds and Treasury Bill Interest Rates, 1975–2001

Source: Statistics Canada CANSIM II series V122514 and V122531

short-term collateralized loan. Securities dealers use the repo to manage their liquidity and to take advantage of anticipated changes in interest rates.

The Bank of Canada also uses repos in conducting monetary policy. We presented the details of monetary policy in Chapter 7. Recall that the conduct of monetary policy typically requires that the Bank adjust bank reserves on a temporary basis. To accomplish this adjustment, the Bank will buy or sell Canada securities in the repo market. The maturities of Bank of Canada repos are typically one business day. However, the Bank of Canada also uses longer-term repos (i.e., with maturities between one and three weeks) when there are seasonal factors affecting a need to increase assets on its balance sheet.

Interest Rate on Repos Because repos are collateralized with Canada securities, they are usually low-risk investments and therefore have low interest rates.

Certificates of Deposit

A *certificate of deposit* (*CD*) is a bank-issued security that documents a deposit and specifies the interest rate and the maturity date. Because a maturity date is specified, a CD is a **term security** as opposed to a **demand deposit**: term securities have a specified maturity date; demand deposits can be withdrawn at any time. Similar term deposits issued by trust and mortgage loan companies are known as **guaranteed investment certificates (GICs)**. CDs and GICs are often negotiable, meaning that they can be traded, and in bearer form (called **bearer deposit notes**). This means that whoever holds the instrument at maturity receives the principal and interest. The CD can be bought and sold until maturity.

Terms of Certificates of Deposit The denominations of negotiable certificates of deposit range from $100 000 to $10 million. Few negotiable CDs are denominated less than $1 million. The reason that these instruments are so large is that dealers have established the round lot size to be $1 million. A round lot is the minimum quantity that can be traded without incurring higher than normal brokerage fees. Negotiable CDs typically have a maturity of one to four months. Some have six-month maturities, but there is little demand for ones with longer maturities.

Chartered banks also issue non-negotiable CDs. That is, they cannot be sold to someone else and cannot be redeemed from the bank before maturity without paying a substantial penalty. Non-negotiable CDs are issued in denominations ranging from $5000 to $100 000 and with maturities of one day to five years. They are also known as **term deposit receipts** or **term notes**.

CDs are also an extremely important source of funds for trust and mortgage loan companies (to be discussed later in this chapter). These institutions issue CDs under a variety of names such as, for example, DRs (Deposit Receipts), GTCs (Guaranteed Trust Certificates), GICs (Guaranteed Investment Certificates), and GIRs (Guaranteed Investment Receipts).

History of the CD Citibank issued the first large certificates of deposit in the U.S. in 1961. The bank offered the CD to counter the long-term trend of declining demand deposits at large banks. Corporate treasurers were minimizing their cash balances and investing their excess funds in safe, income-generating money market instruments such as T-bills. The attraction of the CD was that it paid a market interest rate. There was a problem, however. The rate of interest that U.S. banks could pay on CDs was restricted by Regulation Q. As long as interest rates on most securities were low, this regulation did not affect demand. But when interest rates rose above the level permitted by Regulation Q, the market for these certificates of deposit evaporated. In response, banks in the United States began offering the certificates overseas, where they were exempt from Regulation Q limits. In 1970, the U.S. Congress amended Regulation Q to exempt certificates of deposit over $100 000. By 1972, the CD represented approximately 40 percent of all U.S. bank deposits. The certificate of deposit is now the second most popular money market instrument worldwide, behind only the T-bill.

Interest Rate on CDs Figure 3 plots the interest rate on CDs along with that on T-bills. The rates paid on CDs are negotiated between the bank and the customer. They are similar to the rate paid on other money market instruments because the level of risk is relatively low. Large money centre banks can offer rates a little lower than other banks because many investors in the market believe that the government would never allow one of the nation's largest banks to fail. This belief makes these banks' obligations less risky. CD rates tend to be slightly above the T-bill rate because of the slightly greater chance of default.

Commercial Paper

The home pages of General Motors and DaimlerChrysler can be found at www.gmcanada.com and www.daimlerchrysler.ca

Commercial paper is an unsecured short-term debt instrument issued in either Canadian dollars or other currencies by large banks and well-known corporations such as General Motors and DaimlerChrysler. Because commercial paper is unsecured, only the largest and most creditworthy corporations issue commercial paper. The interest rate the corporation is charged reflects the firm's level of risk. The interest rate on commercial paper is low relative to those on other corporate fixed-income securities and slightly higher than rates on government of Canada treasury bills.

Find detailed information on commercial paper, banker's acceptances, and other money market rates at www.bankofcanada.ca

Terms and Issuance Finance and commercial paper are issued in minimum denominations of $50 000 and in maturities of 30 to 365 days for finance paper and 1 to 365 days for commercial paper. Most finance and commercial paper actually

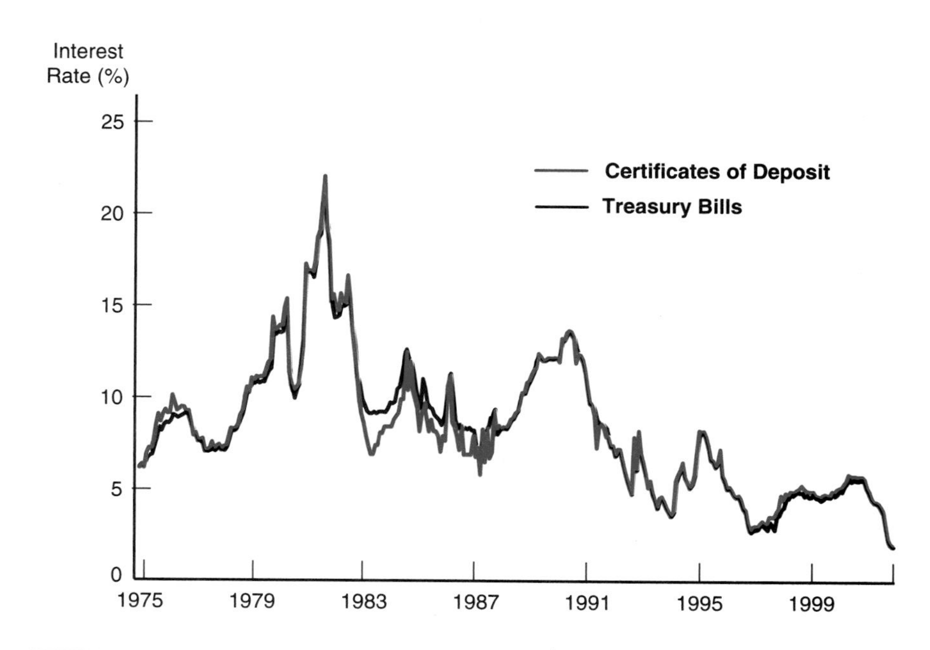

FIGURE 3 Interest Rates on Certificates of Deposit and Treasury Bills, 1975–2001

Source: Statistics Canada CANSIM II series V122513 and V122531

matures in 20 to 45 days. Like T-bills, most finance and commercial paper is issued on a discounted basis.

About 60% of commercial paper is sold directly by the issuer to the buyer. The balance is sold by dealers in the commercial paper market. A strong secondary market for commercial paper does not exist. A dealer will redeem commercial paper if a purchaser has a dire need for cash, though this is generally not necessary.

History of Commercial Paper Commercial paper has been used in various forms since the 1920s. In 1969, a tight-money environment caused bank holding companies in the United States to issue commercial paper to finance new loans. In response, to keep control over the money supply, the U.S. Federal Reserve imposed reserve requirements on bank-issued commercial paper in 1970. These reserve requirements removed the major advantage to banks of using commercial paper. Bank holding companies still use commercial paper to fund leasing and consumer finance.

In Canada, the use of commercial paper increased substantially in the early 1980s because of the rising cost of bank loans. Figure 4 graphs the interest rate on commercial paper against the bank prime rate for the period 1975–2001. Commercial paper has become an important alternative to bank loans primarily because of its lower cost.

Market for Commercial Paper Nonbank corporations use commercial paper extensively to finance the loans that they extend to their customers. For example, General Motors Acceptance Corporation (GMAC) borrows money by issuing commercial paper and uses the money to make loans to consumers buying General Motors cars. Most of these firms issuing commercial paper use commercial paper dealers who match up buyers and sellers. The large money centre banks are very active in this market. Some of the larger issuers of commercial paper choose to distribute their securities with **direct placements.** In a direct placement, the issuer bypasses the dealer and sells directly to the end investor. The advantage of this method is that the issuer saves the 0.125% commission that the dealer charges.

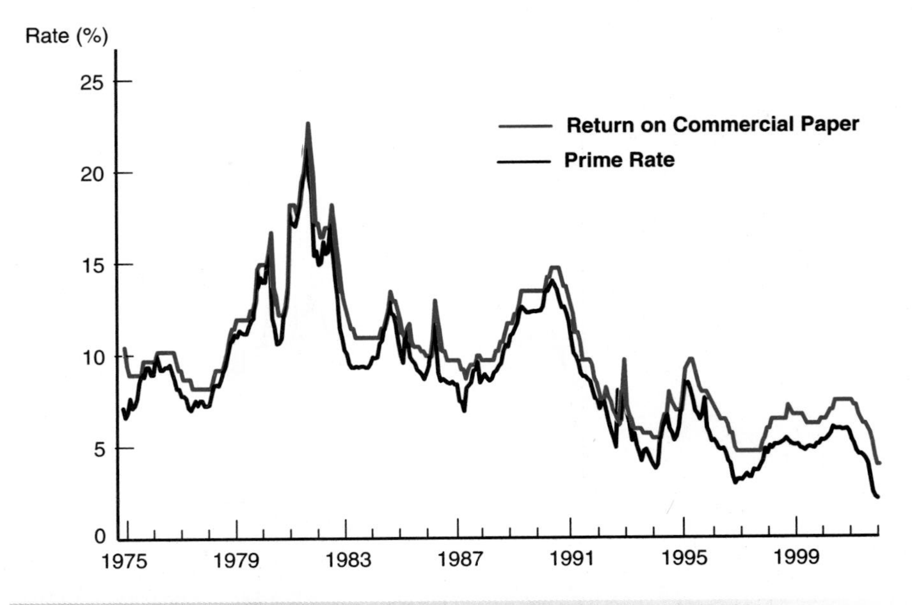

FIGURE 4 Return on Commercial Paper and the Prime Rate, 1975-2001

Source: Statistics Canada CANSIM II series V122495 and V122491.

Most issuers of commercial paper back up their paper with a line of credit at a bank. This means that in the event the issuer cannot pay off or roll over the maturing paper, the bank will lend the firm funds for this purpose. The line of credit reduces the risk to the purchasers of the paper and so lowers the interest rate. The bank that provides the backup line of credit agrees in advance to make a loan to the issuer if needed to pay off the outstanding paper. The bank charges a fee of 0.5% to 1% for this commitment. Issuers pay this fee because they are able to save more than this in lowered interest costs by having the line.

Banks were the original purchasers of commercial paper. Today the market has greatly expanded to include large insurance companies, nonfinancial businesses, bank trust departments, and government pension funds. These firms are attracted by the relatively low default risk, short maturity, and high yields these securities offer. Currently, about $120 billion in commercial paper is outstanding in Canada (see Figure 5) and about $1.5 trillion in the United States.

Banker's Acceptances

A banker's acceptance is an order to pay a specified amount of money to the bearer on a given date. Banker's acceptances have been in use since the 12th century. However, they were not major money market securities until the volume of international trade ballooned in the 1960s. They are used to finance goods that have not yet been transferred from the seller to the buyer. For example, suppose that Builtwell Construction Company wants to buy a bulldozer from Komatsu in Japan. Komatsu does not want to ship the bulldozer without being paid because Komatsu has never heard of Builtwell and realizes that it would be difficult to collect if payment were not forthcoming. Similarly, Builtwell is reluctant to send money to Japan before receiving the equipment. A bank can intervene in this standoff by issuing a banker's acceptance.

Using a Banker's Acceptance The transaction would begin with Builtwell obtaining a letter of credit from its bank. A letter of credit simply says that if Builtwell

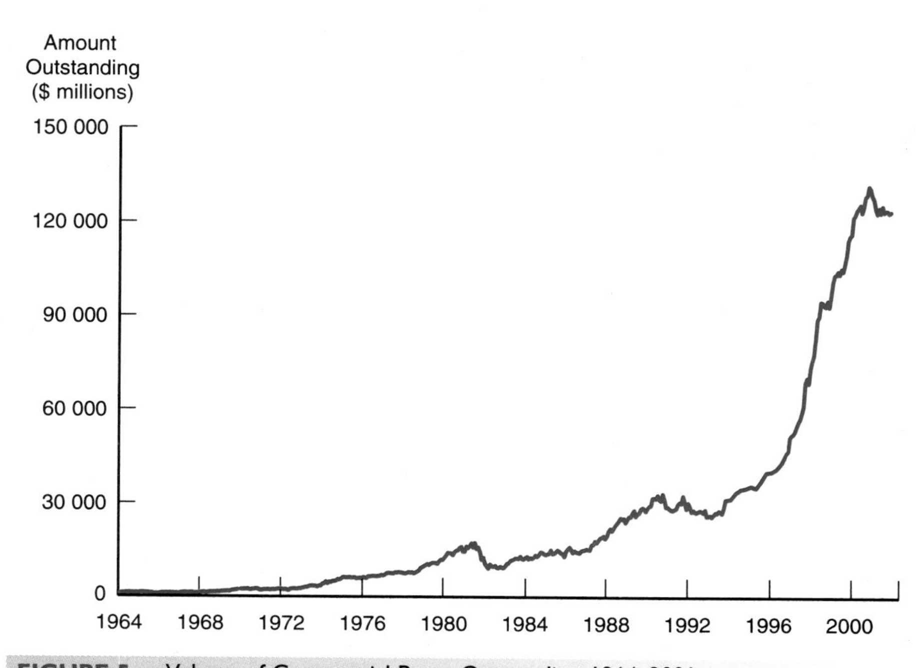

FIGURE 5 Volume of Commercial Paper Outstanding, 1964–2001

Source: Statistics Canada CANSIM II series V122246

has not paid its obligation by a certain time, the bank will make payment. This particular letter of credit will also authorize the exporter (Komatsu or its bank) to draw a time draft for the amount of the sale. A time draft is like a postdated cheque: It can be cashed only after a certain date. Builtwell sends the order for the bulldozer, along with the letter of credit, to Komatsu.

When Komatsu receives these documents, it is willing to ship the equipment because the bank's credit standing has been substituted for that of the actual buyer. Once the equipment has been shipped, Komatsu will present the letter of credit and the shipping documents to its own bank in Japan. This bank will create the time draft authorized by the letter of credit and send it to Builtwell's bank. When Builtwell's bank receives the time draft and the shipping documents, it will stamp the time draft "accepted" and return it to Komatsu's bank.

This accepted time draft is now a banker's acceptance. Because it is backed by the credit of a bank, it can be traded on the secondary market. Typically, the exporter's bank will sell it so that the exporter can receive funds before the maturity date. It will be sold at a discount so that the buyer can earn a fair return for holding it until its maturity date.

The transaction is completed when Builtwell deposits the funds in its bank to cover the amount of the time draft (now a banker's acceptance). When the banker's acceptance finally matures and is presented for payment, the issuing bank withdraws funds from Builtwell's account to make payment. Of course, if for some reason Builtwell was unable to make the required deposit, its bank would pay the acceptance anyway and attempt to collect from Builtwell later.

Let us summarize the steps for using banker's acceptances.

1. The importer requests its bank to send an irrevocable letter of credit to the exporter.
2. The exporter receives the letter, ships the goods, and is paid by presenting to its bank the letter along with proof that the merchandise was shipped.
3. The exporter's bank creates a time draft based on the letter of credit and sends it along with proof of shipment to the importer's bank.
4. The importer's bank stamps the time draft "accepted" and sends the banker's acceptance back to the exporter's bank so that the exporter's bank can sell it on the secondary market to collect payment.
5. The importer deposits funds at its bank sufficient to cover the banker's acceptance when it matures.

Advantages of Banker's Acceptances As the bulldozer example demonstrates, banker's acceptances are crucial to international trade. Without them, many transactions simply would not occur because the parties would not feel properly protected from losses. There are other advantages as well:

- The exporter is paid immediately. This is important when delivery times are long after shipment.
- The exporter is shielded from foreign exchange risk because the local bank pays in domestic funds.
- The exporter does not have to assess the creditworthiness of the importer because the importer's bank guarantees payment.

The phenomenal growth in banker's acceptances in Canada is due to the growth of the Canadian money market and the fact that Canadian chartered banks enjoy stronger credit ratings than all but the largest corporations. Moreover, revisions in the Bank Act have removed certain restrictions regarding the issuance of banker's acceptances and the banks have reduced the stamping fees that they charge for banker's acceptances—these fees vary from 0.20% to 0.75%.

Secondary Market for Banker's Acceptances Because banker's acceptances are payable to the bearer, they can be bought and sold until they mature. They are sold on a discounted basis like commercial paper and T-bills. Dealers in this market match up firms that want to discount a banker's acceptance (sell it for immediate payment) with companies wanting to invest in banker's acceptances.

Interest rates on banker's acceptances are low because the risk of default is very low. For example, no investor in banker's acceptances in Canada and the United States has suffered a loss of principal in more than 60 years. The reason is that only large money centre banks are involved in this market.

Eurodollars

Many contracts around the world call for payment in U.S. dollars due to the U.S. dollar's stability. For this reason, many companies and governments choose to hold dollars. Before World War II, most of these deposits were held in New York money centre banks. However, as a result of the Cold War that followed, there was fear that deposits held on U.S. soil could be expropriated. Some large London banks responded to this opportunity by offering to hold U.S. dollar-denominated deposits in British banks. These deposits were dubbed Eurodollars (see Box 4).

The Eurodollar market has continued to grow rapidly. The primary reason is that depositors receive a higher rate of return on a dollar deposit in the Eurodollar market than in the domestic market. At the same time, the borrower is able to receive a more favourable rate in the Eurodollar market than in the domestic market. Multinational banks are not subject to the same regulations restricting U.S. banks and they are willing and able to accept narrower spreads between the interest paid on deposits and the interest earned on loans.

London Interbank Market Some large London banks act as brokers in the interbank Eurodollar market. Recall that overnight funds are used by banks to make up temporary shortfalls in their settlement balances. Eurodollars are an alternative to overnight funds. Banks from around the world buy and sell overnight funds in this market. The rate paid by banks buying funds is the **London interbank bid rate (LIBID).** Funds are offered for sale in this market at the **London interbank offer rate (LIBOR).** Because many banks participate in this market, it is extremely competitive. The spread between the bid and the offer rate seldom exceeds 0.125%. Eurodollar deposits are time deposits, which means that they cannot be withdrawn for a specified period. Although the most common time period is overnight, different maturities are available. Each maturity has a different rate.

BOX 4: GLOBAL

Ironic Birth of the Eurodollar Market

One of capitalism's great ironies is that the Eurodollar market, one of the most important financial markets used by capitalists, was created by the Soviet Union. In the early 1950s, during the height of the Cold War, the Soviets had accumulated a substantial amount of U.S. dollar balances held by banks in the United States. Because the Russians feared that the U.S. government might freeze these assets in the United States, they wanted to move the deposits to Europe, where they would be safe from expropriation. (This fear was not unjustified—consider the U.S. freeze on Iranian assets in 1979 and Iraqi assets in 1990.) However, they also wanted to keep the deposits in U.S. dollars so that they could be used in their international transactions. The solution was to transfer the deposits to European banks but to keep the deposits denominated in U.S. dollars. When the Soviets did this, the Eurodollar was born.

The overnight LIBOR, the overnight interest rate in Canada, and the fed funds rate in the United States, tend to move together. This is because they are near-perfect substitutes. Suppose that the overnight funds rate exceeded the overnight LIBOR. Banks that need to borrow funds will borrow overnight Eurodollars, thus tending to raise rates, and banks with funds to lend will lend overnight funds, thus tending to lower rates. The demand and supply pressure will cause a rapid adjustment that will drive the three rates together.

At one time, most short-term loans with adjustable interest rates were tied to the treasury bill rate. However, the market for Eurodollars is so broad and deep that it has recently become the standard rate against which others are compared. For example, the U.S. commercial paper market now quotes rates as a spread over LIBOR, rather than over the U.S. T-bill rate.

The Eurodollar market is not limited to London banks. The primary brokers in this market maintain offices in all of the major financial centres worldwide.

Eurodollar Certificates of Deposit Because Eurodollars are time deposits with fixed maturities, they are to a certain extent illiquid. As usual, the financial markets created new types of securities to combat this problem. These new securities were transferable negotiable certificates of deposit (negotiable CDs). Because most Eurodollar deposits have a short term to begin with, the market for Eurodollar negotiable CDs is relatively limited, comprising less than 10% of the amount of regular Eurodollar deposits. The market for the negotiable CDs is still thin.

Other Eurocurrencies The Eurodollar market is by far the largest short-term security market in the world because of the international popularity of the U.S. dollar for trade. However, the market is not limited to U.S. dollars. It is possible to have an account denominated in Japanese yen held in a London or New York bank. Such an account would be termed a Euroyen account. Similarly, you may also have Euromark or Europeso accounts denominated in marks and pesos, respectively, and held in various banks around the world. Keep in mind that if market participants have a need for a particular security and are willing to pay for it, the financial markets stand ready and willing to create it.

COMPARING MONEY MARKET SECURITIES

Although money market securities share many characteristics, such as liquidity, safety, and short maturities, they all differ in some aspects.

Interest Rates

Figure 6 compares the interest rates on many of the money market instruments we have discussed. The most notable feature of this graph is that all of the money market instruments appear to move very closely together over time. This is because all have a very low risk and a short term. They all have deep markets and so are priced competitively. In addition, because these instruments have so many of the same risk and term characteristics, they are close substitutes. Consequently, if one rate should temporarily depart from the others, market supply and demand forces would soon cause a correction.

The Globe and Mail: Report on Business reports money market rates in a table called "Money Rates," which appears daily. This table contains a brief description of each security and the most recent available interest rate. The "Following the Financial News" box shows a "Money Rates" table from *The Globe and Mail: Report on Business.*

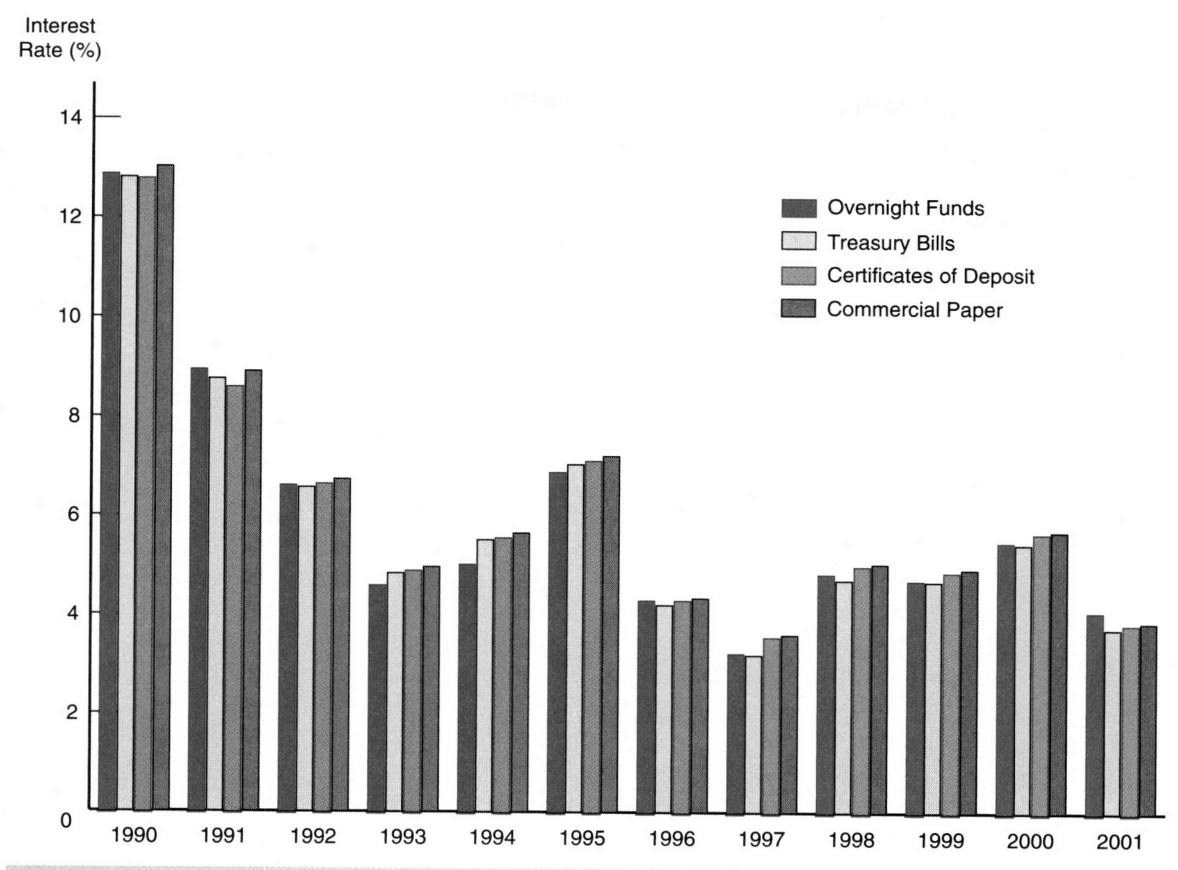

FIGURE 6 Interest Rates on Money Market Securities, 1990–2001

Source: Statistics Canada CANSIM II series V122514, V122531, V122513, and V122491

Liquidity

As we discussed in Chapter 3, the *liquidity* of a security refers to how quickly, easily, and cheaply it can be converted into cash. Typically, the depth of the secondary market where the security can be resold determines its liquidity. For example, the secondary market for treasury bills is extensive and well developed. As a result, treasury bills can be converted into cash quickly and with little cost. By contrast, there is no well-developed secondary market for commercial paper. Most holders of commercial paper hold the securities until maturity. In the event that a commercial paper investor needed to sell the securities to raise cash, it is likely that brokers would charge relatively high fees.

In some ways, the depth of the secondary market is not as critical for money market securities as it is for long-term securities such as stocks and bonds. This is because money market securities are short-term to start with. Nevertheless, many investors desire *liquidity intervention:* They seek an intermediary to provide liquidity where it did not previously exist. This is one function of money market mutual funds (discussed in the next section).

Table 3 summarizes the money market securities and the depth of the secondary market.

TABLE 3 Money Market Securities and Their Markets

Money Market Security	Issuer	Buyer	Usual Maturity	Secondary Market
Treasury bills	Canadian government	Consumers and companies	1, 3, 6, and 12 months	Excellent
Overnight funds	Banks	Banks	1 to 7 days	None
Repurchase agreements	Businesses and banks	Businesses and banks	1 to 15 days	Good
Negotiable certificates of deposit	Large money centre banks	Businesses	14 to 120 days	Good
Finance and commercial paper	Finance companies and businesses	Businesses	1 to 270 days	Poor
Banker's acceptance	Banks	Businesses	30 to 180 days	Good
Eurodollar deposits	Non-Canadian banks	Businesses, governments, and banks	1 day to 1 year	Poor

FOLLOWING THE FINANCIAL NEWS

Money Market Rates

The Globe and Mail and the *National Post* publish daily a listing of interest rates on many different financial instruments. In *The Globe and Mail: Report on Business*, this listing can be found in the "Money Rates" column.

The interest rates in the "Money Rates" column that are discussed most frequently in the media are as follows:

Bank rate: The interest rate charged by the Bank of Canada on loans made to members of the Canadian Payments Association.

Target overnight rate: The overnight interest rate that the Bank of Canada is targeting at the midpoint of the operating band for the overnight rate.

Prime rate: The base interest rate on corporate bank loans, an indicator of the cost of business borrowing from banks.

Treasury bill rates: The interest rates on government of Canada treasury bills, an indicator of general interest-rate movements.

Selected U.S. interest rates: Selected U.S. interest rates such as the federal funds rate, prime rate, and commercial paper rate. These are indicators of general interest-rate movements in the United States.

MONEY RATES

ADMINISTERED

Bank of Canada	2.50%
Target overnight rate	2.25%
Central bank call range	2.00-2.50%
Canadian prime	4.00%

MONEY MARKET

(for transactions of $1-million or more)	
3-month treasury bills	2.45%
6-month treasury bills	2.67%
1-year treasury bills	3.37%
10-year Canada bonds	5.69%
30-year Canada bonds	5.95%
1-month banker's accept.	2.41%
2-month banker's accept.	2.52%
3-month banker's accept.	2.65%
Commercial Paper (R-1 Low)	
1-month	2.41%
3-month	2.68%
Call money	2.25%

Bloomberg News

UNITED STATES

NEW YORK (AP) — Money rates for Thursday as reported by Moneyline Telerate as of 4 p.m.:

Prime Rate: 4.75

Discount Rate: 1.25

Broker call loan rate: 3.50

Federal funds market rate: High 1.8125; low 1.8125; last 1.8125

Dealers commercial paper: 30-180 days: 1.79-1.95

Commercial paper by finance company: 30-270 days: 1.90-2.09

Bankers acceptances dealer indications: 30 days, 1.84; 60 days, 1.85; 90 days, 1.86; 120 days, 1.91; 150 days, 1.99; 180 days, 2.04

Certificates of Deposit Primary: 30 days, 1.48; 90 days, 1.41; 180 days, 1.59

Certificates of Deposit by dealer: 30 days, 1.82; 60 days, 1.83; 90 days, 1.84; 120 days, 1.89; 150 days, 1.97; 180 days, 2.03

Eurodollar rates: Overnight, 1.75-1.81; 1 month, 1.75-1.88; 3 months, 1.75-1.88; 6 months, 2.00-2.13; 1 year, 2.56-2.69

London Interbank Offered Rate: 3 months, 1.91; 6 months, 2.12; 1 year, 2.71

Treasury Bill auction results: average discount rate: 3-month as of May. 13: 1.750; 6-month as of May. 13: 1.870

Treasury Bill annualized rate on weekly average basis, yield adjusted for constant maturity, 1-year, as of May. 13: 2.31

Treasury Bill market rate, 6 Mos: 1.85-1.84

Treasury Note market rate, 10-year: 5.18

Source: The Globe and Mail: Report on Business, May 17, 2002, p. B21. Reprinted with permission

MONEY MARKET MUTUAL FUNDS

Earlier in this chapter we pointed out that the money markets are wholesale markets where most securities trade in large denominations. This characteristic effectively blocks most individuals from investing directly in these securities. However, the markets usually find a way to correct for such deficiencies, especially when potential customers are available. Money market mutual funds represent one such correction.

Money market mutual funds (MMMFs) are funds that aggregate money from a group of small investors and invest it in money market instruments. They have grown enormously popular since their inception in the early 1970s because they provide a means for small investors to take advantage of the returns offered on money market securities. These securities would be out of reach to most small investors because of their large minimum denominations.

History of Money Market Mutual Funds

Money market mutual funds have existed since the early 1970s; however, the low market interest rates before 1977 kept them from being particularly advantageous relative to bank deposits. In 1978, Merrill Lynch in the United States recognized that it could provide better service to its customers if it offered an account that customers could use to warehouse money. Before the introduction of MMMFs as a small-investor account, customers had to bring cheques to the brokerage house when they wanted to invest and had to pick up cheques when they sold securities. Customers who had MMMF accounts, however, could simply direct the broker to take funds out of this account to buy stocks or to deposit funds in this account when they sold securities. Initially, Merrill Lynch did not look on the MMMF as a major source of income.

The most recent statistics on money market mutual funds can be found at www.ific.ca

In the early 1980s, inflation and interest rates skyrocketed. Regulation Q restricted U.S. banks from paying more than 5.25% in interest on savings accounts. With interest rates in the money market exceeding 15%, investors flocked to MMMFs. Figure 7 shows the growth in money market mutual funds between 1977 and 2001 in Canada.

The loss of deposits from banks and near banks to these MMMFs caused serious liquidity and profitability problems in both the banking and near banking industries. These problems are discussed further in Chapter 15.

Description of Money Market Mutual Funds

MMMFs are open-ended investment funds that invest only in money market securities. An *open-ended fund* is one that invests in securities and sells direct claims on the securities to investors. Most funds do not charge investors any fee for purchasing or redeeming shares. The funds usually have a minimum initial investment of $500 to $20 000. The funds yields depends entirely on the performance of the securities purchased.

An important feature of MMMFs in the United States is that many have cheque-writing privileges. They often do not charge a fee for writing cheques or have any minimum cheque amount as long as the balance in the account is above a stated level. This convenience, along with market interest rates, makes the accounts very popular with small investors. Canadian MMMFs do not yet have cheque-writing privileges.

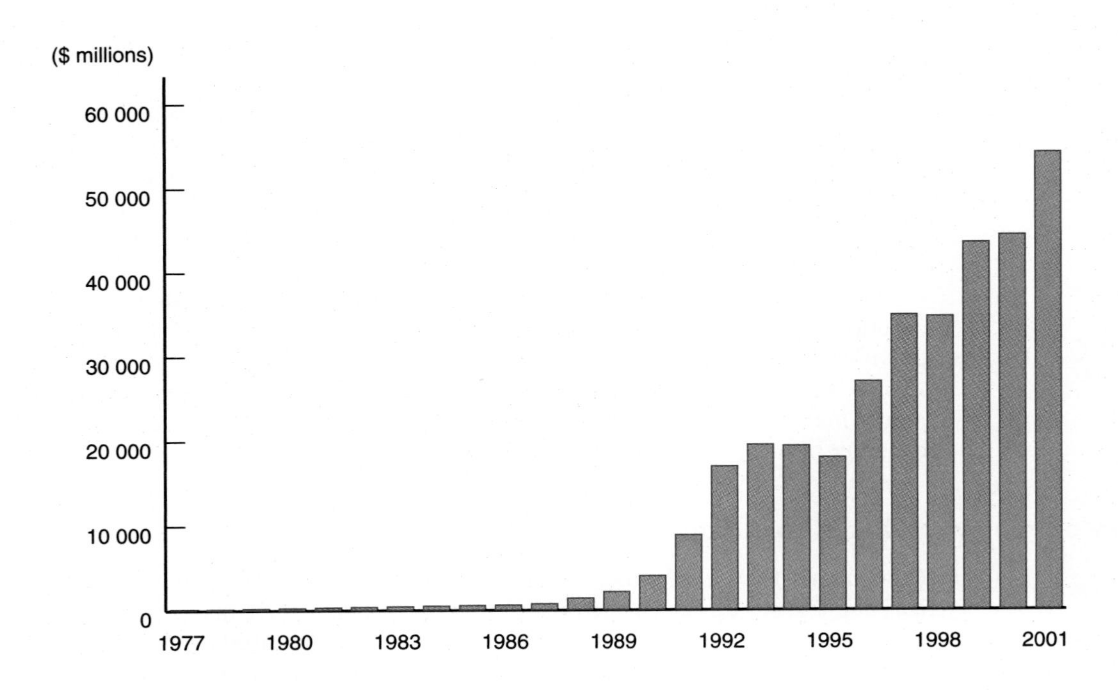

FIGURE 7 Money Market Mutual Funds, 1977–2001

Source: Statistics Canada CANSIM II series V37245

MMMF Risk

In the United States, investors took their money out of federally *insured* banks and thrifts and put it into *uninsured* MMMFs. An important question is why they were willing to take this extra level of risk. The reason is that the extra risk was really very small. The money invested in MMMFs was in turn invested in money market instruments. Commercial paper is by far the largest component of these funds, followed by certificates of deposit and repurchase agreements and then by banker's acceptances. Figure 8 shows the average distribution of U.S. money market fund assets (data on the average distribution of Canadian money market mutual fund assets are not available). Because the risk of default on these securities is very low, the risk of MMMFs is very low. Investors recognized this and so were willing to abandon the safety of their banks and near banks.

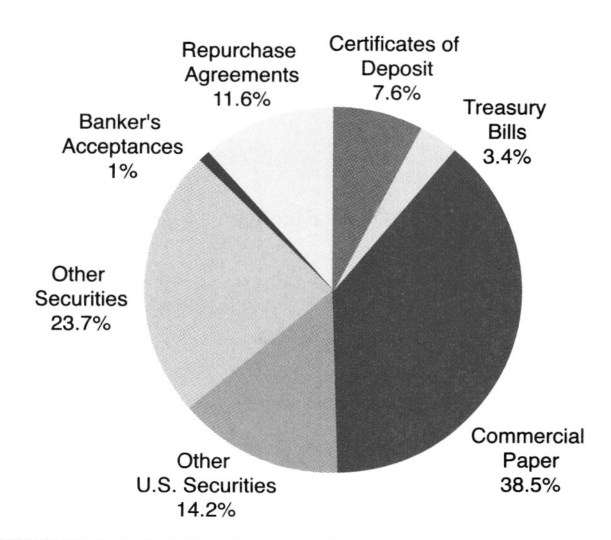

FIGURE 8 Average Distribution of U.S. Money Market Fund Assets, 2001

Source: Investment Company Institute, *Mutual Fund Fact Book*, 2001, p. 93

SUMMARY

1. Money market securities are short-term instruments with an original maturity of less than one year. These securities trade in the money markets. They include treasury bills, commercial paper, overnight funds, repurchase agreements, certificates of deposit, banker's acceptances, and Eurodollars.
2. Money market securities are used to "warehouse" funds until needed. The returns earned on these investments are low because of their low risk and high liquidity.
3. Many participants in the money markets both buy and sell money market securities. The government, commercial banks, businesses, and individuals all benefit by having access to low-risk short-term investments.
4. Interest rates on all money market securities tend to follow one another closely over time. Treasury bill returns are the lowest because they are virtually devoid of default risk. Banker's acceptances and negotiable certificates of deposit are next lowest because they are backed by the creditworthiness of large money centre banks.
5. Money market mutual funds aggregate the funds of many small investors and purchase money market instruments. The returns on these instruments are passed on to the investors. Money market mutual funds have grown rapidly since 1978.

KEY TERMS

bearer deposit notes, *p. 212*
Big Six, *p. 205*
competitive bidding, *p. 208*
deep market, *p. 207*
demand deposit, *p. 212*
direct placement, *p. 214*
discounting, *p. 206*
guaranteed investment certificates (GICs), *p. 212*
liquid market, *p. 207*
London interbank bid rate, (LIBID), *p. 217*
London interbank offer rate, (LIBOR), *p. 217*
noncompetitive bidding, *p. 208*
overnight interest rate, *p. 211*
term deposit receipts (term notes), *p. 212*
term security, *p. 212*
wholesale market, *p. 202*

QUESTIONS AND PROBLEMS

*1. What characteristics define the money markets?

2. Is a Canada bond issued 29 years ago with six months remaining before it matures a money market instrument?

*3. Why do banks not eliminate the need for money markets?

4. Distinguish between a term security and a demand security.

*5. What was the purpose motivating regulators to impose interest ceilings on bank savings accounts? What impact did this eventually have on the money markets?

6. Why does the government use the money markets?

*7. Why do businesses use the money markets?

8. What purpose initially motivated Merrill Lynch to offer money market mutual funds to its customers?

*9. Why are more funds from property and casualty insurance companies than funds from life insurance companies invested in the money markets?

10. Which of the money market securities is the most liquid and considered the most risk-free? Why?

*11. Distinguish between competitive bidding and non-competitive bidding for Canadian securities.

12. Who issues overnight funds, and what is the usual purpose of these funds?

*13. Does the Bank of Canada *directly* set the overnight funds interest rate?

14. Who issues commercial paper and for what purpose?

*15. Why are banker's acceptances so popular for international transactions?

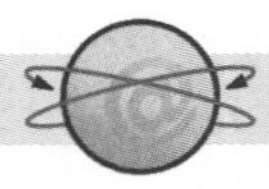

WEB EXERCISES

The Money Markets

1. Up-to-date interest rates are available from the Bank of Canada at www.bankofcanada.ca. Locate the current rate on the following securities:
   a. Overnight repos
   b. Overnight funds
   c. Commercial paper
   d. Treasury bills

   Compare these rates on (b), (c), and (d) to those reported in Table 1. Have short-term rates generally increased or decreased?

2. The Bank of Canada conducts auctions of money market government securities at regular intervals. Go to www.bankofcanada.ca and locate the schedule of auctions. When is the next auction of T-bills? When is the next auction of bonds? How often are these securities auctioned?

Chapter 9

The Capital Markets

Preview

In 1996, Netscape emerged as the leading software used for browsing the Internet. The firm needed additional cash to fund its explosive growth and to fight off efforts by Microsoft to capture the market. The managers of Netscape did not want to use short-term funds like those available in the money markets. Instead, they required long-term capital that could be used to fund long-term growth. Netscape's managers could have raised the funds using any number of long-term securities, but they decided to do it by offering stock for sale to the public in one of the decade's most closely watched stock offerings. The founders of Netscape became instant billionaires as a result.

This chapter discusses securities that have an original maturity that is *longer* than one year, such as the stock issued by Netscape. These securities trade in the capital markets. The best-known capital market securities are stocks and bonds. Mortgages, which also trade in the capital markets, are discussed in Chapter 11.

PURPOSE OF THE CAPITAL MARKET

Firms that issue capital market securities and the investors who buy them have very different motivations than they have when they operate in the money markets. Firms and individuals use the money markets primarily to warehouse funds for short periods until a more important need or a more productive use for the funds arises. By contrast, firms and individuals use the capital markets for long-term investments. The capital markets provide an alternative to investment in assets such as real estate or gold.

Suppose that after a careful financial analysis, your firm determines that it needs a new plant to meet the increased demand for its products. This analysis will be made using interest rates that reflect the *current* long-term cost of funds to the firm. Now suppose that your firm chooses to finance this plant by issuing money market securities, such as commercial paper. As long as interest rates do not rise, all is well: When these short-term securities mature, they can be reissued at the same interest rate. However, if interest rates rise, as they did in 1980, the firm may find that it does not have the cash flows or income to support the plant because when the short-term securities mature, the firm will have to reissue them at a higher interest rate. If long-term securities, such as bonds or stock, had been used, the increased interest rates would not have been as critical. The primary reason that individuals and firms choose to borrow long-term is to reduce the risk that interest rates will rise before they pay off their debt. This reduction in risk comes at a cost, however. As you may recall from Chapter 5, most long-term interest rates are higher than short-term rates because of risk premiums. Despite the need to pay higher interest rates to borrow in the capital markets, these markets remain very active.

CAPITAL MARKET PARTICIPANTS

The primary issuers of capital market securities are federal and local governments and corporations. The federal government issues long-term bonds to fund the national debt. Provincial and municipal governments also issue long-term bonds to finance capital projects, such as school and prison construction. Governments never issue stock, because they cannot sell ownership claims.

Corporations issue both bonds and stock. One of the most difficult decisions a firm faces can be whether it should finance its growth with debt or equity. The distribution of a firm's capital between debt and equity is its capital structure. (The factors that influence the capital structure decision are discussed in Chapter 14.) Corporations may enter the capital markets because they do not have sufficient capital to fund their investment opportunities. Alternatively, firms may choose to enter the capital markets because they want to preserve their capital to protect against unexpected needs. In either case, the availability of efficiently functioning capital markets is crucial to the continued health of the business sector.

The largest purchasers of capital market securities are households. Frequently, individuals and households deposit funds in financial institutions, such as mutual funds and pension funds, that use the funds to purchase capital market instruments such as bonds or stock.

CAPITAL MARKET TRADING

Capital market trading occurs in either the *primary market* or the *secondary market.* The primary market is where new issues of stocks and bonds are introduced. Investment funds, corporations, and individual investors can all purchase securities offered in the primary market. You can think of a primary market transaction as one where the issuer of the security actually receives the proceeds of the sale. When firms sell securities for the very first time, the issue is an **initial public offering (IPO)**. Subsequent sales of a firm's new stocks or bonds to the public are simply primary market transactions (as opposed to an initial one).

The capital markets have well-developed secondary markets. A secondary market is where the sale of previously issued securities takes place, and it is important because most investors plan to sell long-term bonds before they reach maturity and eventually to sell their holdings of stock as well. There are two types of exchanges in the secondary market for capital securities: *organized exchanges* and *over-the-counter exchanges.* Whereas most money market transactions originate over the phone, most capital market transactions, measured by volume, occur in organized exchanges.

Organized Securities Exchanges

An organized exchange has a building where securities (including stocks, bonds, options, and futures) trade. Exchange rules govern trading to ensure the efficient and legal operation of the exchange, and the exchange's board constantly reviews these rules to ensure that they result in competitive trading.

Stock Exchanges in Canada The largest of the organized stock exchanges in Canada is the Toronto Stock Exchange. It was established on October 25, 1861, as a nonprofit organization and now boasts the fourth most active stock exchange in North America, after the New York Stock Exchange, the American Stock Exchange, and the Nasdaq. The average trading volume on the Toronto Stock Exchange in 2001 was 148.8 million shares of stocks, with a total of 37.2 billion shares for the year. This translated into a $2.9 billion average daily value, or a 2001 total value of $712.5 billion.

Before 1999, the Canadian capital markets landscape consisted of the Toronto Stock Exchange and small regional exchanges in Vancouver, Calgary, and Montréal. In 1999, however, the Calgary and Vancouver exchanges consolidated to form the Canadian Dealing Network Exchange (CDNX), which dealt with emerging companies and the venture capital market. The Montreal Exchange (see Box 1) was left to provide for the derivatives market, and the Toronto Stock Exchange was the singular market left for senior stocks.

The Toronto Stock Exchange has undergone many significant changes in the last couple of years. It ditched the original initials TSE in favour of TSX, mainly in order to eliminate confusion with the Tokyo Stock Exchange. On May 1, 2001 the TSX bought the CDNX, forming the new joint venture called the TSX Group of Companies. The TSX Group of Companies encompasses the Toronto Stock Exchange, the TSX Venture Exchange, and its own regulatory arm, TSX Market Regulation Services.

To have a stock listed for trading on one of the organized exchanges, a firm must file an application and meet certain criteria set by the exchange designed to enhance trading. For example, to list on the TSX, a firm must meet the following minimum requirements:

- at least 300 investors
- at least 1 million freely tradable shares, with a market value of $4 million

BOX 1

The Montreal Exchange and the Canadian Derivatives Clearing Corporation (CDCC)

The Montreal Exchange was founded in 1874. In 1975 the Montreal Exchange became the first exchange in Canada to list equity derivatives (equity futures and options), and in December 2001 it became the first fully automated derivatives exchange in North America. Today, the Montreal Exchange is a world-class derivatives exchange, offering market participants a range of equity, interest rate, and index derivative products; in Canada all trading of stocks is done through the Toronto Stock Exchange (TSX).

For example, in addition to offering equity futures and options, the Montreal Exchange also offers a large number of interest rate futures such as the BAX (3-month Canadian Bankers' Acceptances futures), the CGB (10-year Government of Canada Bond futures), and the ONX (30-day Overnight Repo Rate futures), as well as options on BAX and options on CGB. The Exchange also offers index derivatives based on the S&P/TSX 60 index, such as the SXF (S&P Canada 60 Index futures) and the SXO (S&P Canada 60 Index options), as well as index derivatives based on a large number of sectorial indexes. Finally, the Montreal Exchange offers sponsored options—financial derivatives instruments issued by its wholly owned subsidiary, the Canadian Derivatives Clearing Corporation (CDCC), and sponsored by financial institutions. In 2001 the Montreal Exchange traded more than 5.2 million derivative contracts.

The CDCC is the issuer, clearinghouse, and guarantor of all exchange-traded derivative products traded in Canada. Until recently, the CDCC was a non-profit organization and therefore not subject to taxation by Canada Customs and Revenue Agency. Effective January 1, 2001, however, the CDCC changed its articles of association and is now a profit-oriented corporation and therefore subject to corporate income taxes.

You can learn more about the Montreal Exchange at www.m-x.ca.

- any shareholder with more than 10% of the stock must provide information on their experience in business
- a Participating Organization of the TSX must sponsor the company

The TSX Venture Exchange provides junior companies the venture capital needed to become more exposed, as well as a considerable range of investment opportunities for individuals. To become a listed company on the TSX Venture Exchange, there are three different routes to follow:

1. initial public offering (IPO)
2. reverse takeover (RTO)
3. the Capital Pool Company Program (CPC)

An initial public offering is the most common method for companies to obtain a listing, whereby the company compiles a prospectus for possible investors, and applies to become a listed company. There were 58 initial public offerings in 2001, accounting for more than half the newly listed companies. A merger or an issuance of shares in exchange for shares in the listed company can complete a reverse takeover. Finally, a capital pool company is created on the venture exchange through an IPO and then proceeds to acquire another company. Currently, the TSX Venture includes more than 2650 listed companies. There were 26 companies that graduated from the TSX Venture Exchange during 2001; this accounts for 28% of the new Toronto Stock Exchange listings.

Find listed companies, member information, real-time market indexes, and current stock quotes at www.nyse.com and www.tsx.com

Foreign Stock Exchanges There are also major organized stock exchanges around the world. The largest of the organized stock exchanges in North America is the New York Stock Exchange (NYSE). The NYSE occupies a building in downtown New York City, and only traders who are members of the exchange may engage in trading. To become a member, an individual or firm must buy a "seat." There are 1366 seats on the NYSE, most of them owned by brokerage houses. Today seats on the New York Stock Exchange can sell for as much as $1.2 million (see Box 2), depending on the market's perception of the profit potential in being a trader. Average daily volume on the NYSE in 2001 was 1.24 million shares of stocks, which was 19.2% higher than the record average daily trading volume of 1.04 billion shares achieved in 2000. By contrast, a total of about 10 million bonds were traded on organized exchanges during 1998.

The NYSE encourages only the largest firms to list so that transaction volume will be high. To list on the NYSE, a firm must meet the following minimum requirements:

- At least 2000 stockholders, each owning 100 shares or more
- A minimum of 1.1 million shares traded publicly

BOX 2

The Most Expensive Seat in North America

In October 2001 a seat on the NYSE sold for $2.2 million, a $100 000 decrease from the last sale that took place two weeks earlier. Owning one of the 1366 NYSE seats is the admission ticket to trading on the world's largest stock exchange. Membership gives the holders the right to trade stocks and vote at exchange meetings. The highest price ever paid for a Big Board seat was $2.65 million on August 23, 1999. As expensive as a seat on the exchange is, consider this: It doesn't even include a chair. If you want to sit down, you have to bring your own stool.

Source: www.NYSE.com/glossary/NT00011442.html

- Pretax earnings of $2.5 million at the time of listing plus at least $2 million in pretax earnings in each of the prior two years
- Market value of public shares of $100 million or more

The second-largest organized exchange in the Unites States is the American Stock Exchange (AMEX). About 700 firms trade on it. The American Stock Exchange has less restrictive listing requirements. Regional exchanges, such as the Philadelphia and Pacific Stock Exchanges, are even easier to list on. Some firms choose to list on more than one exchange, believing that more exposure will increase the demand for their stock and hence its price. Many firms also believe that there is a certain amount of prestige in being listed on one of the major exchanges. They may even include this fact in their advertising. There is little conclusive research to support this belief, however. Microsoft, for example, is not listed on any organized exchange, yet its stock had a total market value of more than US$320 billion in late 2001.

Other major organized exchanges around the world include the Nikkei in Tokyo, the London Stock Exchange in England, and the DAX in Germany.

Over-the-Counter Markets

If Microsoft's stock is not traded on any of the organized stock exchanges, where does it sell its stock? Securities not listed on one of the exchanges trade in the over-the-counter market. This market is not organized in the sense of having a building where trading takes place. Instead, trading occurs over a sophisticated telecommunications network, called the **National Association of Securities Dealers Automated Quotation System (Nasdaq).** This system, introduced in 1971, provides current bid and ask prices on about 4000 actively traded securities. Dealers "make a market" in these stocks by buying for inventory when investors want to sell and selling from inventory when investors want to buy. These dealers provide small stocks with the liquidity that is essential to their acceptance in the market. Total volume on the Nasdaq is usually slightly lower than on the NYSE; however, Nasdaq volume has been growing and occasionally exceeds NYSE volume. Figure 1 reports the number of firms listed on the Nasdaq, NYSE, AMEX, and TSX.

The Canadian over-the-counter market was patterned after the Nasdaq, but it is far less significant. In 1991, responsibility for the operation of this market was transferred to the Canadian Dealing Network Inc. (CDN), a subsidiary of the TSX. Of course, not all publicly traded stocks list on one of the organized exchanges or on the over-the-counter markets. Securities that trade very infrequently or trade primarily in one region of the country are usually handled by the regional offices of various brokerage houses. These offices often maintain small inventories of regionally popular securities. Dealers that make a market for stocks that trade in low volume are very important to the success of the over-the-counter market. Without these dealers standing ready to buy or sell shares, investors would be reluctant to buy shares of stock in regional or unknown firms, and it would be very difficult for start-up firms to raise needed capital. Recall from Chapter 4 that the more liquid an asset is, the greater the quantity demanded. By providing liquidity intervention, dealers increase demand for thinly traded securities.

CAPITAL MARKET SECURITIES: BONDS

The capital markets are where securities with original maturities of longer than one year trade. Capital market securities fall into three categories: bonds, stocks, and mortgages. In this section, we look at bonds.

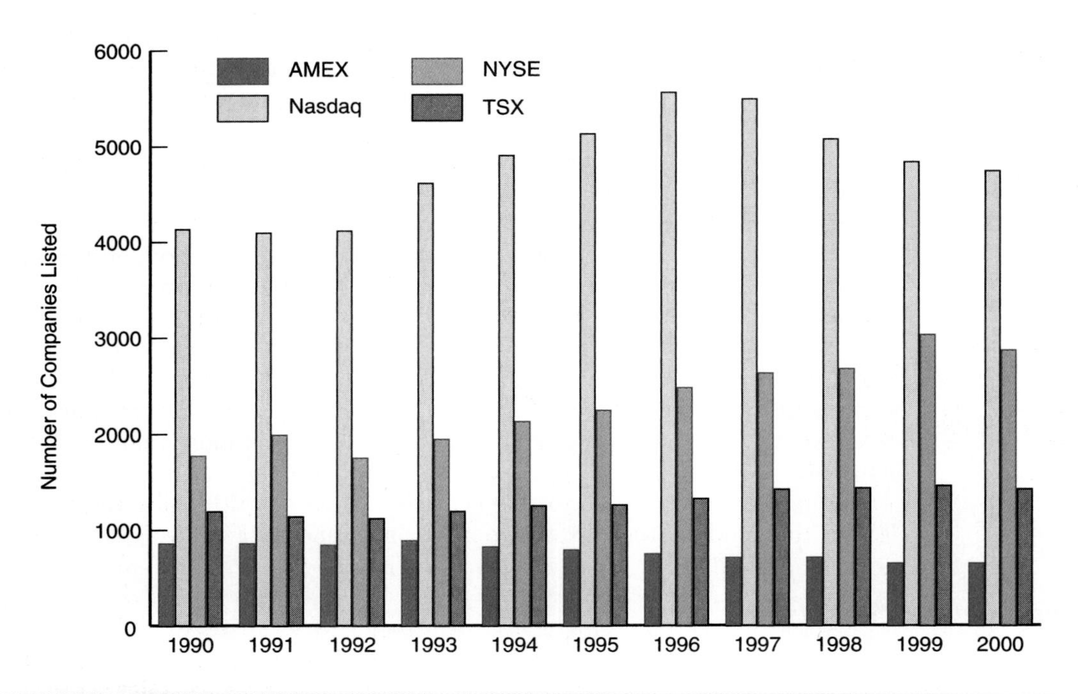

FIGURE 1 Number of Listed Companies Yearly Comparison with NYSE, AMEX, Nasdaq, and TSX

Source: World Federation of Exchanges Website: www.fibv.com

Bonds are securities that represent a debt owed by the issuer to the investor. Bonds obligate the issuer to pay a specified amount at a given date, generally with periodic interest payments. The par, face, or maturity value of the bond is the amount that the issuer must pay at maturity. The coupon rate is the rate of interest that the issuer must pay. This rate is usually fixed for the duration of the bond and does not fluctuate with market interest rates. If the repayment terms of a bond are not met, the holder of a bond has a claim on the assets of the issuer.

Long-term bonds traded in the capital market include long-term government bonds, municipal bonds, and corporate bonds.

CANADA BONDS

The government of Canada issues short-term bonds (those with initial maturities from 1 to 3 years), medium-term bonds (those with initial maturities from 3 to 10 years), and long-term bonds (those with initial maturities longer than 10 years) to finance the national debt. Because they are the most widely traded bonds in Canada, they are the most liquid security traded in the capital market. Canada bonds are held by the Bank of Canada, banks, and retail investors. Table 1 summarizes the maturity differences among government of Canada securities.

These debt instruments are issued in either bearer or registered form and in denominations of $1000, $5000, $25 000, $100 000, and $1 million. In the case of

TABLE 1 Government of Canada Securities

Type	Maturity
Treasury bill	Less than 1 year
Short-term bond	1 to 3 years
Medium-term bond	3 to 10 years
Long-term bond	10 years and longer

registered bonds, the name of the owner appears on the bond certificate and is also recorded at the Bank of Canada. Some issues have the additional **call** or **redemption** feature of allowing them to be "called" on specified notice (usually 30 to 60 days).

The prices of Canada bonds and treasury bills are quoted as a percentage of $100 face value. (Chapter 3 explains how newspaper bond quotes can be converted into market prices.)

Federal government bonds are free of default risk because the government can always print money to pay off the debt if necessary.[1] This does *not* mean that these securities are risk-free. There is still the possibility that market interest rates will rise, making the bonds fall in value.

Application **Interest-Rate Risk in Bond Investment**

The risk that the value of a bond will fall when market interest rates rise is called *interest-rate risk* (discussed in Chapter 3). Suppose that you wanted to sell a bond that pays 4.5% for $1000 when new ones that pay 5.5% are available. To sell an old bond when rates have risen, the holder will have to discount the bond until the yield to the buyer is the same as the market rate. In this example, if there were 20 years until the bond matured, the seller would have to drop the asking price to $879.61 to give the buyer a 5.5% yield. We did not discuss interest-rate risk in Chapter 8 because securities in the money market have short maturities and interest rates do not usually change greatly in the short run. When they do, the change does not influence the price of the security as much as when the security has a long time until maturity.

Canada Bond Interest Rates

Canada bonds have very low interest rates because they have no default risk. Although investors in Canada bonds have found themselves earning as little as the rate of inflation in some years (see Figure 2), most of the time, the interest rate on Canada bonds is above that on money market securities because of interest-rate risk.

Figure 3 plots the yield on long-term Canada bonds against the yield on 90-day treasury bills. Two things are noteworthy in this graph. First, in most years, the rate of return on the short-term bill is below that on the long-term bond. Second, short-term rates are more volatile than long-term rates. Short-term rates are more influenced by the current rate of inflation. Investors in long-term securities expect extremely high or low inflation rates to return to more normal levels, so long-term rates do not typically change as much as short-term rates.

Canada Savings Bonds

Canada Savings Bonds are non-marketable bonds issued by the government of Canada once a year, generally for about two weeks ending on November 1. *Canada Savings Bonds* (CSBs) are floating-rate bonds, available in denominations from $100 to $10 000, and offered exclusively to individuals, estates, and specified trusts. They are issued as registered bonds and can be purchased from financial institutions or through payroll savings plans. The sale of CSBs is restricted, to Canadian residents whereas treasury bills and marketable bonds may be purchased by foreigners.

[1]We noted in Chapter 8 that treasury bills were also considered default-risk-free.

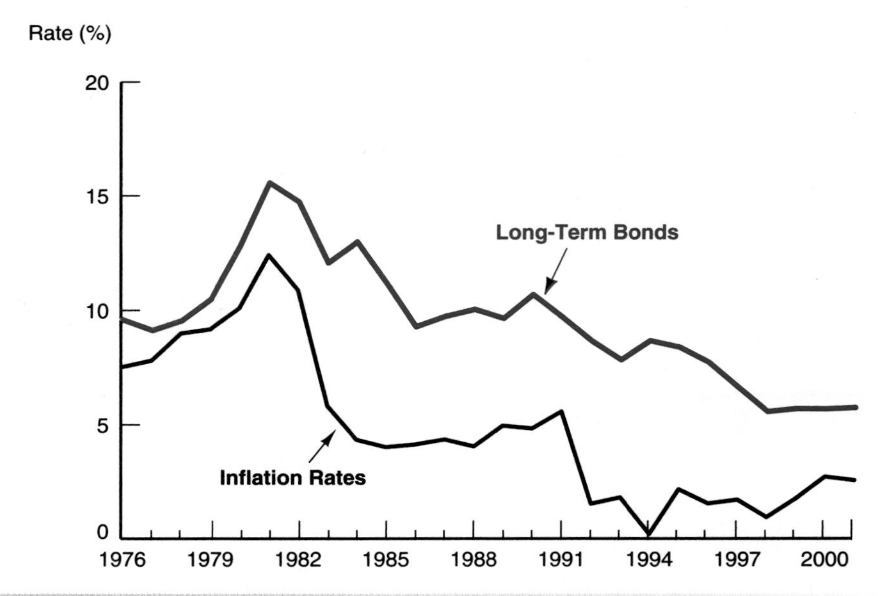

FIGURE 2 Interest Rate on Long-Term Canada Bonds and the Inflation Rate, 1976–2001

Source: Statistics Canada CANSIM II series V122544 and V735319

CSBs are different from all other bonds issued by the government of Canada in that they do not rise or fall in value, like other bonds do. They have the valuable option of being redeemable at face value plus accrued interest, at any time prior to maturity, by being presented at any financial institution. In October 1998 the government of Canada introduced another type of bond that is similar to CSBs—the Canada Premium Bond (CPB). CPBs offer a slightly higher coupon rate than the CSBs, but can be redeemed only once a year, on the anniversary of the issue date and during the month after that date.

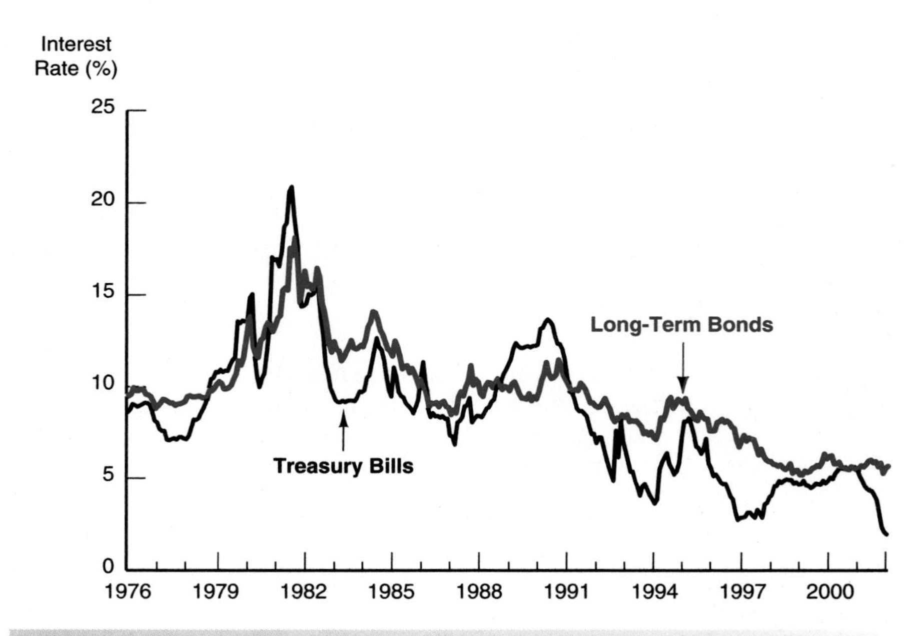

FIGURE 3 Interest Rate on Treasury Bills and Long-Term Canada Bonds, 1976–2002

Source: Statistics Canada CANSIM II series V122544 and V122531

Real Return Bonds

In 1991, the government of Canada began offering an innovative bond designed to remove inflation risk from holding Canada bonds. The new inflation-indexed bonds have an interest rate that does not change throughout the term of the security. However, the principal amount used to compute the interest payment does change based on the consumer price index. For example, if CPI inflation is 2%, the value of a $1000 Real Return Bond will be $1020 at the end of the year, and the interest payment will be based on the inflation-adjusted principal of $1020 rather than the original par value of $1000. At maturity, the securities are redeemed at the greater of their inflation-adjusted principal or par amount at original issue.

The advantage of inflation-indexed securities is that they give both individual and institutional investors a chance to buy a security whose value won't be eroded by inflation. These securities can be used by retirees who want to hold a very low-risk portfolio.

Canada STRIPS

Several investment-banking firms buy coupon-paying Canada bonds and create zero-coupon bonds by separating the principal from the coupon payments and selling them separately. These bonds are issued in book entry form and are called **separate trading of registered interest and principal securities**, more commonly **STRIPS.** Recall from Chapter 8 that to be sold in book entry form means that no physical document exists; instead, the security is issued and accounted for electronically. A STRIP separates the periodic interest payments from the final principal repayment. When a Canada fixed-principal or inflation-indexed bond is stripped, each interest payment and the principal payment becomes a separate zero-coupon security. Each component has its own identifying number and can be held or traded separately. For example, a Canada bond with five years remaining to maturity consists of a single principal payment at maturity and ten interest payments, one every six months for five years. When this note is stripped, each of the ten interest payments and the principal payment becomes a separate security. Thus, the single Canada bond becomes 11 separate securities that can be traded individually. STRIPS are also called **zero-coupon securities** because the only time an investor receives a payment during the life of a STRIP is when it matures.

Canada STRIPS are collateralized by the original Canada bonds and therefore are free of default risk. They sell at a discount from par and their price increases over time and approaches par value on the maturity date. To illustrate this point, consider a zero-coupon bond with a face value of $1000 and 20 years to maturity. If the market interest rate is 5%, the price of the bond today will be $\$1000/(1 + 0.05)^{20} = \$376.88$. Next year, the bond will have 19 years to maturity and its price will be $\$1000/(1 + 0.05)^{19} = \$395.73$. The price keeps on increasing exponentially and approaches par value on the maturity date.

STRIPS were introduced in the early 1980s in the United States when Merrill Lynch created the Treasury Investment Growth Fund (TIGRs, pronounced "tigers"), in which it purchased U.S. Treasury securities and then stripped them to create principal-only securities and interest-only securities. In addition, in 1985 the U.S. Treasury began issuing STRIPS to depository institutions. Currently, more than US$50 billion in stripped U.S. Treasury securities are outstanding.

Agency Bonds

These are long-term bonds issued by various government agencies. Issuers of agency bonds include Crown corporations such as the Ontario Municipal

Improvements Corporation, Hydro Quebec, the Alberta Municipal Financing Corporation, and the New Brunswick Electric Power Commission. These agencies issue bonds to finance such items as mortgages, farm loans, or power-generating equipment. Agency bonds function much like Canadas, provincials, and municipals and are held by similar parties.

The risk on agency bonds is actually very low. They are usually secured by the loans that are made with the funds raised by the bond sales. In addition, the agencies may use their lines of credit with the government should they have trouble meeting their obligations. Finally, it is unlikely that the government would permit its agencies to default on their obligations.

Despite this low level of risk, agency bonds offer interest rates that are significantly higher than those available on Canada bonds. A portion of the higher yield available on agencies may be due to their lower liquidity: Though a secondary market in agency securities exists, it is not as well developed or as deep as the market for government of Canada securities. (Chapter 5 discusses the effect liquidity has on interest rates.) Many investors feel that agency bonds represent an attractive alternative to low-interest-rate government of Canada bonds.

PROVINCIAL BONDS

The provincial governments also issue bonds to finance expenditures on schools, roads, and other large programs. Although the British North America Act of 1867 and the Constitution Act of 1982 gave certain powers and revenues to the provinces, the financing of provincial public interest projects is shared with federal and/or local governments. When large provincial projects are planned and/or provincial revenues fall short of provincial spending, provinces borrow by issuing securities.

The securities issued by provincial governments are referred to as **provincial bonds** or **provincials** and those issued by municipal governments (to be discussed later in this chapter) as **municipal bonds** or **municipals**—the securities issued by the federal government are referred to as **Canadas**. Provincials are denominated in either domestic currency or foreign currencies, mostly U.S. dollars, Swiss francs, and Japanese yen, and are mainly held by trusteed pension plans, social security funds (predominantly the Canada Pension Plan), financial institutions, and retail investors.

Risk in the Provincial Bond Market

Provincial bonds, like Canadas, are in fact debentures since they are not insured by any specific provincial assets. As a result, their value depends solely on the province's ability to make the promised coupon payments and repay the principal. In terms of default risk, provincial bonds rank second, after the government of Canada bonds. However, different provincial bonds trade at differing prices, since the credit rating of provincial governments depends on the wealth of the province, the amount of per capita debt that the province owes, the level of federal government transfers, and the stability of the provincial government.

MUNICIPAL BONDS

www.bloomberg.com/markets/munibondyield.html **supplies the latest municipal bond events in the United States, experts' insights and analyses, and a municipal bond yields table.**

Municipal bonds are securities issued by municipalities. The proceeds from these bonds are used to finance public interest projects such as schools, utilities, and transportation systems. In the United States, municipal bonds that are issued to pay for essential public projects are exempt from federal taxation. As we saw in Chapter 5, this allows the municipality to borrow at a lower cost because investors will be satisfied with lower interest rates on tax-exempt bonds. You can use the following equation to determine what tax-free rate of interest is equivalent to a taxable rate:

$$\text{Equivalent tax-free rate} = \text{taxable interest rate} \times (1 - \text{marginal tax rate})$$

EXAMPLE 1: Municipal Bonds in the United States

Suppose that the interest rate on a taxable corporate bond is 9% and that the marginal tax is 28%. Suppose a tax-free municipal bond with a rate of 6.75% were available. Which security would you choose if you were an American citizen?

Solution

The tax-free municipal interest rate is 6.75%.

$$\text{Equivalent tax-free rate} = \text{taxable interest rate} \times (1 - \text{marginal tax rate})$$

where

Taxable interest rate $= 0.09$

Marginal tax rate $= 0.28$

Thus

$$\text{Equivalent tax-free rate} = 0.09 \times (1 - 0.28) = 0.0648 = 6.48\%$$

Since the tax-free municipal bond rate is higher than the equivalent tax-free rate, choose the municipal bond.

There are two types of municipal bonds: general obligation bonds and revenue bonds. **General obligation bonds** do not have specific assets pledged as security or a specific source of revenue allocated for their repayment. Instead, they are backed by the "full faith and credit" of the municipality. This phrase means that the municipality promises to use every resource available to repay the bond as promised. Most general obligation bond issues must be approved by the taxpayers because the taxing authority of the government is pledged for their repayment.

Revenue bonds, by contrast, are backed by the cash flow of a particular revenue-generating project. For example, revenue bonds may be issued to build a toll bridge, with the tolls being pledged as repayment. If the revenues are not sufficient to repay the bonds, they may go into default, and investors may suffer losses. This occurred, for example, on a large scale in 1983 in the United States, when the Washington Public Power Supply System (since called "WHOOPS") used revenue bonds to finance the construction of two nuclear power plants. As a result of falling energy costs and tremendous cost overruns, the plants never became operational, and buyers of these bonds lost their investments.

Risk in the Municipal Bond Market

Municipal bonds are not default-free, since local governments are not exempt from financial distress. Unlike the federal government, local governments cannot print money, and there are real limits on how high they can raise taxes without driving the population away.[2] Although municipal bonds rank after federal and

[2] Review Chapter 4 for a complete discussion on the determinants of interest rates for securities.

provincial bonds in terms of default risk, it is possible for investors to favour securities issued by some large municipalities. Moreover, large municipalities with good credit records and many different types of industries have better credit ratings than new municipalities built around a few major industries.

CORPORATE BONDS

When large corporations need to borrow funds for long periods, they may issue bonds. Most corporate bonds have a face value of $1000 and pay interest semiannually (twice per year). Most are also callable, meaning that the issuer may redeem the bonds after a specified date.

The **bond indenture** is a contract that states the lender's rights and privileges and the borrower's obligations. Any collateral offered as security to the bondholders will also be described in the indenture.

The degree of risk varies widely among issues because the risk of default depends on the company's health, which can be affected by a number of variables. The interest rate on corporate bonds varies with the level of risk, as we discussed in Chapter 5. As Figure 4 shows, bonds with lower risk and a higher rating (AA being the highest) have lower interest rates than more risky bonds (BBB). A bond's interest rate will depend on its features and characteristics, which are described in the following sections.

Characteristics of Corporate Bonds

At one time bonds were sold with attached coupons that the owner of the bond clipped and mailed to the firm to receive interest payments. These were called *bearer bonds* because payments were made to whoever had physical possession of the bonds. Bearer bonds have now been largely replaced by registered bonds, which do not have coupons. Instead, the owner must register with the firm to receive interest payments. The firms are required to report to Canada Customs

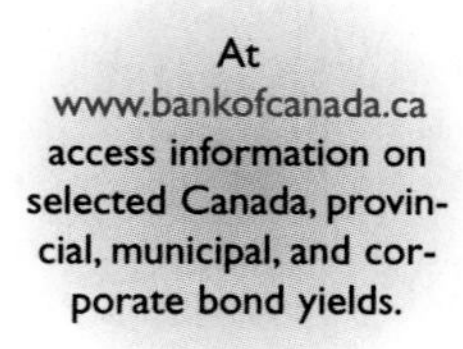

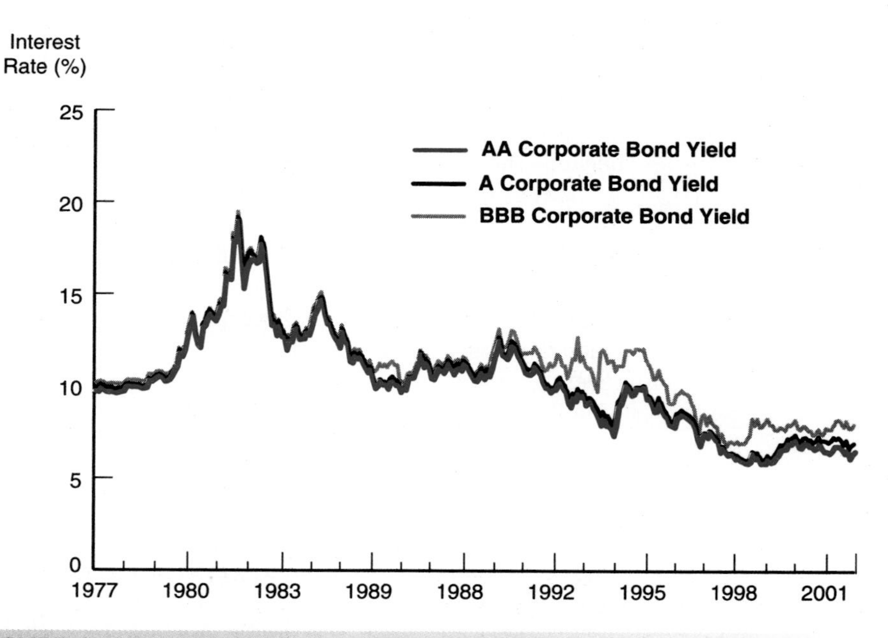

FIGURE 4 Corporate Bond Interest Rates, 1977–2002

Source: Statistics Canada CANSIM II series V35736, V35728, and V35744

and Revenue Agency (CCRA) the name of the person who receives interest income. Despite the fact that bearer bonds with attached coupons have been phased out, the interest paid on bonds is still called the "coupon interest payment," and the interest rate on bonds is the coupon interest rate.

Restrictive Covenants A corporation's financial managers are hired, fired, and compensated at the direction of the board of directors, which represents the corporation's *stockholders*. This arrangement implies that the managers will be more interested in protecting stockholders than they are in protecting bondholders. You should recognize this as an example of the moral hazard problem introduced in Chapter 2 and discussed further in Chapter 14. Managers may not use the funds provided by the bonds as the bondholders might prefer. Since bondholders cannot look to managers for protection when the firm gets into trouble, they must include rules and restrictions on managers designed to protect the bondholders' interests. These are known as **restrictive covenants**. They usually limit the amount of dividends the firm can pay and the ability of the firm to issue additional debt. Other financial policies, such as the firm's involvement in mergers, may also be restricted. Restrictive covenants are included in the bond indenture. Typically, the interest rate will be lower the more restrictions are placed on management through restrictive covenants because the bonds will be considered safer by buyers.

Call Provisions Most corporate indentures include a **call provision**, which states that the issuer has the right to force the holder to sell the bond back. The call provision usually requires a waiting period between the time the bond is initially issued and the time when it can be called. The price bondholders are paid for the bond is usually set at the bond's par price or slightly higher (usually by one year's interest cost). For example, a 10% coupon rate $1000 bond may have a call price of $1100.

If interest rates fall, the price of the bond will rise. If rates fall enough, the price will rise above the call price, and the firm will call the bond. Because call provisions put a limit on the amount that bondholders can earn from the appreciation of a bond's price, investors do not like call provisions.

A second reason that issuers of bonds include call provisions is to make it possible for them to buy back their bonds according to the terms of the **sinking fund**. A sinking fund is a requirement in the bond indenture that the firm pay off a portion of the bond issue each year. This provision is attractive to bondholders because it reduces the probability of default when the issue matures. Because a sinking fund provision makes the issue more attractive, the firm can reduce the bond's interest rate.

A third reason firms usually issue only callable bonds is that firms may have to retire a bond issue if the covenants of the issue restrict the firm from some activity that it feels is in the best interest of stockholders. Suppose that a firm needed to borrow additional funds to expand its storage facilities. If the firm's bonds carried a restriction against adding debt, the firm would have to retire its existing bonds before issuing new bonds or taking out a loan to build the new warehouse.

Finally, a firm may choose to call bonds if it wants to alter its capital structure. A maturing firm with excess cash flow may want to reduce its debt load if few attractive investment opportunities are available.

Because bondholders do not generally like call provisions, callable bonds must have a higher yield than comparable noncallable bonds. Despite the higher cost, firms still typically issue callable bonds because of the flexibility this feature provides the firm.

Conversion Some bonds can be converted into shares of common stock. This feature permits bondholders to share in the firm's good fortunes if the stock price rises. Most convertible bonds will state that the bond can be converted into a certain number of common shares at the discretion of the bondholder. The conversion ratio will be such that the price of the stock must rise substantially before conversion is likely to occur.

Issuing convertible bonds is one way firms avoid sending a negative signal to the market. If a firm chooses to issue stock, the market usually interprets this action as indicating that the stock price is relatively high or that it is going to fall in the future. The market makes this interpretation because it believes that managers are most concerned with looking out for the interests of existing stockholders and will not issue stock when it is undervalued. If managers believe that the firm will perform well in the future, they can, instead, issue convertible bonds. If the managers are correct and the stock price rises, the bondholders will convert to stock at a relatively high price that managers believe is fair. Alternatively, bondholders have the option not to convert if managers turn out to be wrong about the company's future.

Bondholders like a conversion feature. It is very similar to buying just a bond but receiving both a bond and a stock option (stock options are discussed fully in Chapter 23). The price of the bond will reflect the value of this option and so will be higher than the price of comparable nonconvertible bonds. The higher price received for the bond by the firm implies a lower interest rate.

Types of Corporate Bonds

A variety of corporate bonds is available. They are usually distinguished by the type of collateral that secures the bond and by the order in which the bond is paid off if the firm defaults.

Secured Bonds Secured bonds are ones with collateral attached. *Mortgage bonds* are used to finance a specific project. For example, a building may be the collateral for bonds issued for its construction. In the event that the firm fails to make payments as promised, mortgage bondholders have the right to liquidate the property in order to be paid. Because these bonds have specific property pledged as collateral, they are less risky than comparable unsecured bonds. As a result, they will have a lower interest rate.

Equipment trust certificates are bonds secured by tangible non-real estate property, such as heavy equipment or airplanes. Typically, the collateral backing these bonds is more easily marketed than the real property backing mortgage bonds. As with mortgage bonds, the presence of collateral reduces the risk of the bonds and so lowers their interest rates.

Unsecured Bonds *Debentures* are long-term unsecured bonds that are backed only by the general creditworthiness of the issuer. No specific collateral is pledged to repay the debt. In the event of default, the bondholders must go to court to seize assets. Collateral that has been pledged to other debtors is not available to the holders of debentures. *Debentures* usually have attached to them a contract that spells out the terms of the bond and the responsibilities of management. The contract attached to the debenture is called an *indenture.* (Be careful not to confuse the terms *debenture* and *indenture.*) Debentures have lower priority than secured bonds if the firm defaults. As a result, they will have a higher interest rate than otherwise comparable secured bonds.

Subordinated debentures are similar to debentures except that they have a lower priority claim. This means that in the event of a default, subordinated debenture holders are paid only after nonsubordinated bondholders have been paid in full. As a result, subordinated debenture holders are at greater risk of loss.

Variable-rate bonds (which may be secured or unsecured) are a financial innovation spurred by increased interest-rate variability in the 1980s and 1990s. The interest rate on these securities is tied to another market interest rate, such as the rate on Canada bonds, and is adjusted periodically. The interest rate on the bonds will change over time as market rates change.

Junk Bonds Recall from Chapter 5 that all bonds are rated by various companies according to their default risk. These companies study the issuer's financial characteristics and make a judgment about the issuer's possibility of default. A bond with a rating of AAA has the highest grade possible. Bonds *above* DBRS's or Standard and Poor's BBB rating are considered of investment grade. Those rated *below* this level are usually considered speculative (see Table 2). Speculative-grade bonds are often called **junk bonds**. Before the late 1970s, primary issues of speculative-grade securities were very rare; almost all new bond issues consisted of investment-grade bonds. However, when companies ran into financial difficulties, their bond ratings would fall. Holders of these downgraded bonds found that they were difficult to sell because no well-developed secondary market existed. It is easy to understand why investors would be leery of these securities, as they were usually unsecured.

TABLE 2 DBRS Bond and Long-Term Debt Rating Scale

Rating	Description
AAA	**Highest credit quality**, with exceptionally strong protection for the timely repayment of principal and interest. Earnings are considered stable, the structure of the industry in which the entity operates is strong, and the outlook for future profitability is favourable. There are few qualifying factors present that would detract from the performance of the entity, the strength of liquidity and coverage ratios is unquestioned and the entity has established a creditable track record of superior performance. Given the extremely tough definition that DBRS has established for this category, few entities are able to achieve an AAA rating.
AA	**Superior credit quality**, and protection of interest and principal is considered high. In many cases, they differ from bonds rated AAA only to a small degree. Given the extremely tough definition that DBRS has for the AAA category (which few companies are able to achieve), entities rated AA are also considered to be strong credits that typically exemplify above-average strength in key areas of consideration and are unlikely to be significantly affected by reasonably foreseeable events.
A	**Satisfactory credit quality**. Protection of interest and principal is still substantial, but the degree of strength is less than with AA rated entities. Although a respectable rating, entities in the "A" category are considered more susceptible to adverse economic conditions and have greater cyclical tendencies than higher rated companies.
BBB	**Adequate credit quality**. Protection of interest and principal is considered adequate, but the entity is more susceptible to adverse changes in financial and economic conditions, or there may be other adversities present that reduce the strength of the entity and its rated securities.
BB	**Speculative**, where the degree of protection afforded interest and principal is uncertain, particularly during periods of economic recession. Entities in the BB area typically have limited access to capital markets and additional liquidity support and, in many cases, small size or lack of competitive strength may be additional negative considerations.
B	**Highly speculative** and there is a reasonably high level of uncertainty as to the ability of the entity to pay interest and principal on a continuing basis in the future, especially in periods of economic recession or industry adversity.
CCC/CC/C	**Very highly speculative** and are in danger of default of interest and principal. The degree of adverse elements present is more severe than bonds rated "B." Bonds rated below "B" often have characteristics that, if not remedied, may lead to default. In practice, there is little difference between the "C" to "CCC" categories, with "CC" and "C" normally used to lower ranking debt of companies where the senior debt is rated in the "CCC" to "B" range.
D	This category indicates bonds in default of either interest or principal.

Source: www.dbrs.com/web/jsp/pubratingscale bond.jsp. Used with permission of Dominion Bond Rating Service.

In 1977, Michael Milken, at the U.S. investment banking firm of Drexel Burnham Lambert, recognized that there were many investors who would be willing to take on greater risk if they were compensated with greater returns. First, however, Milken had to address two problems that hindered the market for low-grade bonds. The first was that they suffered from poor liquidity. Whereas underwriters of investment-grade bonds continued to make a market after the bonds were issued, no such market maker existed for junk bonds. Drexel agreed to assume this role as market maker for junk bonds. That assured that a secondary market existed, an important consideration for investors, who seldom want to hold the bonds to maturity.

The second problem with the junk bond market was that there was a very real chance that the issuing firms would default on their bond payments. By comparison, the default risk on investment-grade securities was negligible. To reduce the probability of losses, Milken acted much as a commercial bank for junk bond issuers. He would renegotiate the firm's debt or advance additional funds if needed to prevent the firm from defaulting. Milken's efforts substantially reduced the default risk, and the demand for junk bonds soared.

During the early and mid-1980s, many firms took advantage of junk bonds to finance the takeover of other firms. When a firm greatly increases its debt level (by issuing junk bonds) to finance the purchase of another firm's stock, the increase in leverage makes the bonds high-risk. Frequently, part of the acquired firm is eventually sold to pay down the debt incurred by issuing the junk bonds. Some 1800 U.S. firms accessed the junk bond market during the 1980s.

Milken and his brokerage firm were very well compensated for their efforts. Milken earned a fee of 2% to 3% of each junk bond issue, which made Drexel the most profitable firm on Wall Street in 1987. Milken's personal income between 1983 and 1987 was in excess of $1 billion.

Unfortunately for holders of junk bonds, both Milken and Drexel were caught and convicted of insider trading. With Drexel unable to support the junk bond market, 250 companies defaulted between 1989 and 1991. Drexel itself filed for bankruptcy in 1990 due to losses on its own holdings of junk bonds. Milken was sentenced to three years in prison for his part in the scandal. *Fortune* magazine reported that Milken's personal fortune still exceeded $400 million.[3]

The junk bond market has recovered since its low in 1990 and now continues to permit medium-sized firms to obtain financing that might otherwise be unavailable to them because of the relatively high risk.

FINANCIAL GUARANTEES FOR BONDS

Financially weaker security issuers frequently purchase **financial guarantees** to lower the risk of their bonds. A financial guarantee ensures that the lender (bond purchaser) will be paid both principal and interest in the event the issuer defaults. Large, well-known insurance companies write what are actually insurance policies to back bond issues. With such a financial guarantee, bond buyers no longer have to be concerned with the financial health of the bond issuer. Instead, they are interested only in the strength of the insurer. Essentially, the credit rating of the insurer is substituted for the credit rating of the issuer. The resulting reduction in risk lowers the interest rate demanded by bond buyers. Of course, issuers must pay a fee to the insurance company for the guarantee. Financial guarantees make sense only when the cost of the insurance is less than the interest savings that result.

[3]A complete history of Milken was reported in *Fortune,* September 30, 1996, pp. 80–105.

Financial guarantees were developed in the early 1970s to insure municipal bonds. More recently, their use has been expanded to cover a variety of corporate bonds as well.

TRENDS IN THE BOND MARKET

During the first half of the 1980s, interest rates were very high, and firms were reluctant to borrow in the long-term market. In the second half of the 1980s, declining interest rates and a healthy economy combined to encourage bond issuance. Issuance again fell in 1990 when the economy entered a recession, and interest rates rose. Falling interest rates and a rebounding economy contributed toward record-breaking volumes in the bond markets in the late 1990s.[4]

CAPITAL MARKET SECURITIES: STOCK

A share of stock in a firm represents ownership. A stockholder owns a percentage interest in a firm, consistent with the percentage of outstanding stock held. This ownership is in contrast to a bondholder, who holds no ownership interest but is rather a creditor of the firm.

Investors can earn a return from stock in one of two ways. Either the price of the stock rises over time, or the firm pays the stockholder dividends. Frequently, investors earn a return from both sources. Stock is riskier than bonds because stockholders have a lower priority than bondholders when the firm is in trouble, the returns to investors are less assured because dividends can be easily changed, and stock price increases are not guaranteed. Despite these risks, it is possible to make a great deal of money by investing in stock, whereas that is very unlikely by investing in bonds. Another distinction between stock and bonds is that stock does not mature.

Ownership of stock gives the stockholder certain rights regarding the firm. One is the right of a *residual claimant:* Stockholders have a claim on all assets and income left over after all other claimants have been satisfied. If nothing is left over, they get nothing. As noted, however, it is possible to get rich as a stockholder if the firm does well.

Most stockholders have the *right to vote* for directors and on certain issues, such as amendments to the corporate charter and whether new shares should be issued.

Common Stock Versus Preferred Stock

There are two types of stock, common and preferred. A share of **common stock** in a firm represents an ownership interest in that firm. Common stockholders vote, receive dividends, and hope that the price of their stock will rise. There are various classes of common stock, usually denoted as type A, type B, and so on. Unfortunately, the type does not have any meaning that is standard across all companies. The differences among the types usually involve either the distribution of dividends or voting rights. It is important for an investor in stocks to know exactly what rights go along with the shares of stock being contemplated.

Preferred stock is a form of equity from a legal and tax standpoint. However, it differs from common stock in several important ways. First, because preferred

[4]For more details regarding recent developments in Canada's fixed-income market, see Éric Chouinard and Zahir Lalani, "The Canadian Fixed-Income Market: Recent Developments and Outlook," *Bank of Canada Review* (Winter 2001-2002): 15–25; Nancy Harvey, "Recent Initiatives in the Market for Government of Canada Securities," *Bank of Canada Review* (Summer 1999): 27–35; and Martin Miville and André Bernier, "The Corporate Bond Market in Canada," *Bank of Canada Review* (Autumn 1999): 3–8.

stockholders receive a fixed dividend that never changes, a share of preferred stock is as much like a bond as it is like common stock. Second, because the dividend does not change, the price of preferred stock is relatively stable. Third, preferred stockholders do not usually vote unless the firm has failed to pay the promised dividend. Finally, preferred stockholders hold a claim on assets that has priority over the claims of common shareholders but after that of creditors such as bondholders.

Less than 25% of new equity issues are preferred stock, and only about 5% of all capital is raised using preferred stock. This may be because preferred dividends are not tax deductible to the firm but bond interest payments are. Consequently, issuing preferred stock usually costs the firm more than issuing debt, even though it shares many of the characteristics of a bond.

Stock Value

Get detailed stock quotes, charts, and historical stock data at www.tsx.ca and www.stocks.tradingcharts.com

The price of a share of stock is the present value of expected future cash flows, which consist of dividends plus a final selling price. (The "Following the Financial News" box shows how stock market prices are reported each day.) Investors are willing to pay a price for stock that reflects the sum of all of the future cash flows the security will generate, after adjusting for the time value of money. The

FOLLOWING THE FINANCIAL NEWS

Stock Prices

Stock prices are published daily in most daily newspapers. *The Globe and Mail: Report on Business* provides quotations for companies listed on the Toronto Stock Exchange and the TSX Venture Exchange in Canada as well as for companies listed on the New York, Nasdaq, and American stock exchanges in the United States. The stocks' prices are quoted in the following format (companies listed on the Toronto exchange are used as an example):

365-day high	365-day low	Stock	Sym	Div	High	Low	Close	Chg	Vol (100s)	Yield	P/E ratio
20.16	13.33	Noranda	NRD	0.80	19.30	18.76	19.17	+0.45	3504	4.2	
21.50	8.40	Normandy	NDY		21.00	21.00	21.00	–0.50	11		
24.22	3.56	Nortel Netwk	NT		4.11	3.80	4.01	+0.06	81804		
57.33	41.60	♣Royal Bank	RY	1.52	57.33	55.35	56.99	+1.99	28052	2.7	15.8

Source: The Globe and Mail: Report on Business, May 24, 2002, p. B17. Reprinted with permission

The following information is included in each column. Royal Bank common stock is used as an example.

365-day high: Highest price of a share in the past 52 weeks: 57.33 for Royal Bank stock

365-day low: Lowest price of a share in the past 52 weeks: 41.60 for Royal Bank stock

Stock: Company name: Royal Bank for Royal Bank of Canada

Sym: Symbol that identifies company: RY

Div: Annual dividends (excluding special dividends): 1.52 for Royal Bank stock

High: Highest price of a share that day: 57.33

Low: Lowest price of a share that day: 55.35

Close: Closing price (last price) that day: 56.99

Chg: Change in the closing price from the previous day: +1.99

Vol (100s): Number of shares (in hundreds) traded that day: 28 052

Yield %: Yield expressed as a percentage, calculated by dividing annual dividends by today's closing price: 2.7% (= 1.52/56.99) for Royal Bank stock.

P/E ratio: Price-earnings ratio; the stock price divided by the amount the corporation earned per share over the past year. The P/E ratio is not shown if greater than 100 and cannot be calculated if the company has losses rather than earnings.

♣ indicates that free annual or quarterly reports are available

problem, of course, is predicting the future cash flows of the firm. If a firm does well, the residual cash flows available for dividends can be large, and a high share price is justified. If a firm does poorly, there may not be any cash flows available to pay any dividend at all.

We discuss the theory and mechanics of stock valuation in the next chapter.

Stock Market Indexes

A stock market index is used to monitor the behaviour of a group of stocks. By reviewing the average behaviour of a group of stocks, investors are able to gain some insight into how a broad group of stocks may have performed. Various stock market indexes are reported to give investors an indication of the performance of different groups of stocks. The most commonly quoted index in Canada is the TSE 300 Composite Index, reformulated on May 1, 2002, by Standard & Poor's Corp. to S&P/TSX Composite Index. The S&P/TSX Composite initially included the same 300 companies as the old TSE 300 but, during quarterly revisions, is allowed to float, in the sense that companies that do not meet size and liquidity requirements are turfed. Box 3 provides more background on Canada's stock market indices and Figure 5 shows the S&P/TSX since 1989.

At www.spglobal.com/TSX_method.pdf you can find details about the S&P/TSX Composite Index.

The most commonly quoted index in the world is the Dow Jones Industrial Average (DJIA), an index based on the performance of the stocks of 30 large companies in the United States. Box 4 on page 245 provides more background on this famous index, Table 3 lists the 30 stocks that made up the index in August 2001, and Figure 6 on page 246 shows the DJIA since 1990.

Other famous U.S. indexes are the Standard and Poor's 500 Index, the Nasdaq composite, and the NYSE composite. These indexes are more helpful for following the performance of different groups of stocks. The *Wall Street Journal* reports on 23 different indexes in its "Stock Market Daily Data Bank."

BOX 3

Canadian Stock Market Indexes

Over the years, several different stock market indexes have been developed for the Toronto Stock Exchange, including the most common TSE 300, as well as the TSE 35, 60, 100, and 200. Until recently, the TSE 300 had an industry classification system comprising 14 sectors, distinct to the Canadian market system. In March 2002, however, Standard and Poor's (S&P) introduced the Global Industry Classification Standard (GICS), which divides the stocks into 13 different sectors, in order to accommodate the need for global standardization in the stock exchanges. These 13 sectors include information technology, energy, financials, gold, consumer discretionary, consumer staples, health care, industrials, materials, telecommunication services, utilities, metals and mining, and real estate.

On May 1, 2002, the old TSE 300 and TSE 60 indixes were renamed the S&P/TSX Composite and S&P/TSX 60, respectively. The number of companies included in the S&P/TSX Composite is now allowed to float, rather than being fixed at 300. The S&P/TSX 60 is the Canadian counterpart for the S&P 500 in the United States. It represents the 60 largest companies that incorporate all sectors of the GICS. In addition, the CDNX Composite was renamed the S&P/TSX Venture Composite. This index is updated quarterly, based on the criteria for inclusion. The remaining composites (that is, the TSE 35, 100, and 200) have been discontinued. The addition of a MidCap index, a composite for mid-sized companies, as well as a Sector Index, complete the changes for composite indexes.

To be included in an index, a new company must represent at least 0.05% of the total index, meet various liquidity requirements, been public for 12 months, and have a share price of at least $1. Standard and Poor's reviews each company that is included in each index, to make sure that each section of the criteria is being met. This maintenance criteria includes that the company must represent 0.025% of the total index, trading volume must be at least 0.02% of the TSX's total trading volume, the share price must remain above $1, and the stock must not have more than 50 non-trading days. If a company is removed from an index, it will not be eligible for inclusion again for 12 months.

FIGURE 5 S&P/TSX Composite, 1989–2002

Source: Bank of Canada

TABLE 3 The Thirty Companies That Make Up the Dow Jones Industrial Average (August 2001)

Alcoa Inc.	General Electric Co.	McDonald's Corp.
American Express Co.	General Motors Corp.	Merck & Co. Inc.
AT&T Corp.	Hewlett-Packard Co.	Microsoft Corp.
Boeing Co.	Home Depot Inc.	Minnesota Mining & Manufacturing Co.
Caterpillar Inc.	Honeywell International Inc.	Philip Morris Cos.
Citigroup Inc.	Intel Corp.	Procter & Gamble Co.
Coca-Cola Co.	International Business Machines Corp.	SBC Communications Inc.
E. I. DuPont de Nemours & Co.	International Paper Co.	United Technologies Corp.
Eastman Kodak Co.	J. P. Morgan Chase & Co.	Wal-Mart Stores Inc.
Exxon Mobil Corp.	Johnson & Johnson	Walt Disney Co.

Buying Foreign Stocks

In Chapter 4 we learned that diversification of a portfolio reduces risk. In recent years, investors have come to realize that some risk can also be eliminated by diversifying across different countries. When one country is suffering from a recession, others may be booming. If inflationary concerns in Canada cause stock prices to drop, falling inflation in Japan may cause Japanese stocks to rise.

Buying foreign stocks is no more difficult than buying Canadian stocks, since Canadians can buy U.S. securities on U.S. exchanges through Canadian brokers. Moreover, a large number of foreign companies are cross-listed on Canadian stock markets and also a number of the largest European, Japanese, and Mexican companies trade in the United States in the form of **American depository receipts (ADRs)**. In particular, a U.S. bank buys the shares of a foreign company and places them in its vault. The bank then issues receipts against these shares, and these receipts can be traded domestically, usually on the Nasdaq. Trade in ADRs is conducted entirely in U.S. dollars, and the bank converts stock dividends into U.S. cur-

BOX 4

History of the Dow Jones Industrial Average

The Dow Jones Industrial Average (DJIA) is an index comprising 30 "blue chip" industrial firms in the United States. On May 26, 1896, Charles H. Dow added up the prices of 12 of the best-known stocks and created an average by dividing by the number of stocks. In 1916, eight more stocks were added, and in 1928, the 30-stock average made its debut.

Today the editors of the *Wall Street Journal* select the firms that make up the DJIA. They take a broad view of the type of firm that is considered "industrial": In essence, it is almost any company that is not in the transportation or utility business (because there are also Dow Jones averages for those kinds of stocks). In choosing a new company for the DJIA, they look at substantial industrial companies with a history of successful growth and wide interest among investors. The components of the DJIA are changed periodically. For example, in 1997, Bethlehem Steel, Texaco, Westinghouse, and Woolworth were replaced with Hewlett-Packard, Johnson & Johnson, Travelers Group, and Wal-Mart. In 1999, Home Depot, Intel, Microsoft, and SBC Communications joined the average, replacing Union Carbide, Goodyear Tire & Rubber, Sears, and Chevron.

Most market watchers agree that the DJIA is not the best indicator of the market's overall day-to-day performance. Indeed, it varies substantially from broader-based stock indexes in the short run. It continues to be followed so closely primarily because it is the oldest index and was the first to be quoted by other publications. But it tracks the performance of the market reasonably well over the long run.

Table 4 shows the greatest one-day gains and losses since the initiation of the DJIA.

TABLE 4 Greatest One-Day Changes in the Dow Jones Industrial Average

Rank	Date	Percent Gain	Date	Percent Loss
1	October 6, 1931	14.87	October 19, 1987	−22.61
2	October 30, 1929	12.34	October 28, 1929	−12.82
3	September 21, 1932	11.36	October 29, 1929	−11.73
4	October 21, 1987	10.15	November 6, 1929	−9.92
5	August 3, 1932	9.52	December 18, 1899	−8.72
6	February 11, 1932	9.47	August 12, 1932	−8.40
7	November 14, 1929	9.36	March 14, 1907	−8.29
8	December 18, 1931	9.35	October 26, 1987	−8.04
9	February 13, 1932	9.19	July 21, 1933	−7.84
10	May 6, 1932	9.08	October 18, 1937	−7.75

Source: Dow Jones Corp., www.djindexes.com provides a wealth of information about the current DJIA and its history.

rency. One advantage of the ADR is that it allows foreign firms to trade in the United States without having to meet the disclosure rules required by the SEC.

Foreign stock trading has been growing rapidly. Interest in firms in emerging economies such as Mexico, Brazil, and South Korea is particularly keen.

PUBLIC ISSUES OF STOCKS AND BONDS

Once a firm determines that it should issue stocks or bonds, it must somehow get them into the public's hands at the highest price possible. The more the public pays for either the stocks or the bonds of a firm, the lower the cost of capital to that firm, all other things being equal.

There are two principal ways for a firm to sell securities to the public: through a public sale organized by investment bankers who are underwriting the issue or through a private placement. **Underwriting** means that the investment bankers handle the details of placing the securities in the public's hands. The role of investment bankers in security distribution is discussed in Chapter 21.

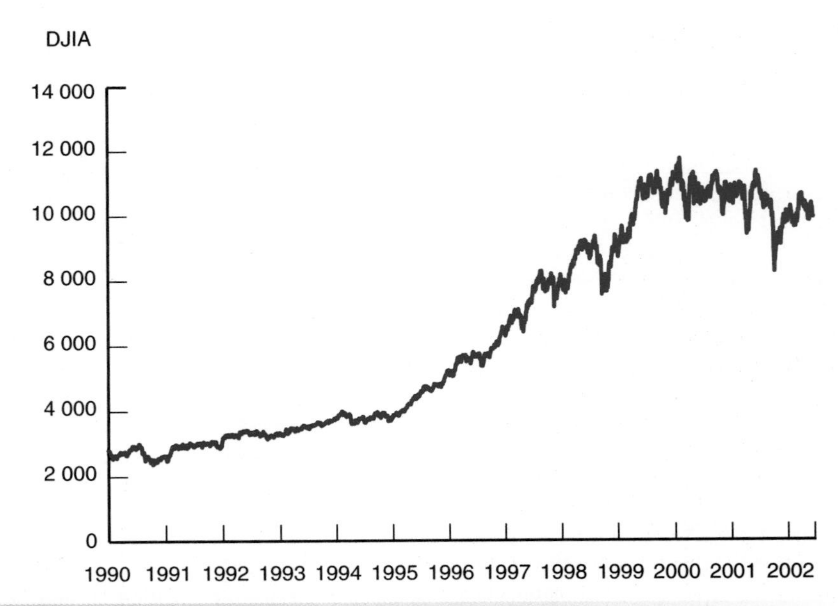

FIGURE 6 Dow Jones Industrial Average, 1990–2002

Source: Bank of Canada

SUMMARY

1. The capital markets exist to provide financing for long-term capital assets. Households, often through investments in pension and mutual funds, are net investors in the capital markets. Corporations and the federal and provincial governments are net users of these funds.
2. The three main capital market instruments are bonds, stocks, and mortgages. Bonds represent borrowing by the issuing firm. Stock represents ownership in the issuing firm. Mortgages are long-term loans secured by real property. Only corporations can issue stock. Corporations and governments can issue bonds. In any given year, far more funds are raised with bonds than with stock.
3. There are both organized and over-the-counter exchanges. Organized exchanges are distinguished by a physical building where trading takes place. The over-the-counter market operates primarily over phone lines and computer links. Typically, larger firms trade on organized exchanges and smaller firms in the over-the-counter market, though there are exceptions to this rule.
4. Firm managers are hired by stockholders to protect and increase their wealth. Bondholders must rely on a contract called an indenture to protect their interests. Bond indentures contain covenants that restrict the firm from activities that increase risk and hence the chance of default on the bonds. Bond indentures also contain many provisions that make them more or less attractive to investors, such as a call option, convertibility, or a sinking fund.

KEY TERMS

American depository receipts (ADRs), *p. 244*
bond indenture, *p. 236*
call (redemption), *p. 231*
call provision, *p. 237*
Canadas, *p. 234*
common stock, *p. 241*
financial guarantee, *p. 240*
general obligation bonds, *p. 235*
initial public offering (IPO), *p. 226*
junk bond, *p. 239*
municipal bonds (municipals), *p. 234*
National Association of Securities Dealers Automated Quotation System (Nasdaq), *p. 229*
preferred stock, *p. 241*
provincial bonds (provincials), *p. 234*
registered bonds, *p. 231*
restrictive covenants, *p. 237*
revenue bonds, *p. 235*
separate trading of registered interest and principal securities (STRIPS), *p. 233*
sinking fund, *p. 237*
underwriting, *p. 245*
zero-coupon securities, *p. 233*

QUESTIONS AND PROBLEMS

*1. Contrast investors' use of capital markets with their use of money markets.

2. What are the primary capital market securities, and who are the primary purchasers of these securities?

*3. Distinguish between the primary market and the secondary market for securities.

4. Discuss the features that differentiate organized exchanges from the over-the-counter market.

*5. What is the National Association of Securities Dealers Automated Quotation System (Nasdaq)?

6. A bond provides information about its par value, coupon interest rate, and maturity date. Define each of these.

*7. The government of Canada issues bills and bonds. How do these two securities differ?

8. As interest rates in the market change over time, the market price of bonds rises and falls. The change in the value of bonds due to changes in interest rates is a risk incurred by bond investors. What is this risk called?

*9. In addition to Canada securities, some agencies of the government issue bonds. List three such agencies, and state what the funds raised by the bond issues are used for.

10. A call provision on a bond allows the issuer to redeem the bond at will. Investors do not like call provisions and so require higher interest on callable bonds. Why do issuers continue to issue callable bonds anyway?

*11. What is a sinking fund? Do investors like bonds that contain this feature?

12. What is the document called that lists the terms of a bond?

*13. What distinguishes stocks from bonds?

14. Describe the two ways whereby capital market securities pass from the issuer to the public.

*15. Review the firms now included in the Dow Jones Industrial Average listed in Table 3. How many firms appear to be technology related? Discuss what this means in terms of the risk of the index.

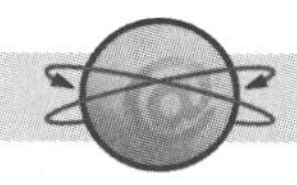

WEB EXERCISES

The Capital Markets

1. Stocks tend to get more publicity than bonds, but many investors, especially those nearing or in retirement, find that bonds are more consistent with their risk preferences. One site that will help an investor choose among bonds can be found at http://bonds.yahoo.com. Click on the calculators tab and choose the calculator titled, "Which bond is better?" Look at the example provided. Do the results change if you assume a 28% tax bracket and that you will sell the bond in two years?

2. There are a number of indexes that track the performance of the stock market. It is interesting to review how well they track along with each other. Go to http://bloomberg.com. Click on the "Charts" tab at the top of the screen. Put checks in the boxes to display the DJIA, S&P 500, Nasdaq, and the S&P/TSX Composite. Set the time frame to five years. Click on "Get Chart." You may want to add one index to the chart at a time to keep track of which colour corresponds to each index.
   a. Which index has been most volatile over the past five years?
   b. Which index has posted the greatest gains over the last five years?
   c. Now adjust the time frame to intraday. Which index has performed the best today? Which has been most volatile?

3. The capital markets are where individuals go to invest for their long-term retirement needs. These markets provide a variety of securities to meet different risk tolerances with different expected rates of return. An excellent site for computing your retirement needs and showing a possible distribution of investment assets can be found at http://www.quicken.com/retirement/planner/js/notemplates/intronn.dcg?partner=cnnfn. After responding to the questions posed on this site, discuss how you will save for your retirement.

Chapter 10

The Stock Market and the Efficient Market Hypothesis

Preview

The market for stocks is undoubtedly the financial market that receives the most attention and scrutiny. Great fortunes are made and lost as investors attempt to anticipate the market's ups and downs. We have witnessed an unprecedented period of volatility over the past decade. Stock indexes hit record highs in the late 1990s, largely led by technology companies, and then fell precipitously in 2000. In this chapter we begin looking at how this important market works.

We begin by discussing the fundamental theories that underlie the valuation of stocks. These theories are critical to an understanding of the forces that cause the value of stocks to rise and fall minute by minute and day by day. We will learn that determining a value for a common stock is very difficult and that it is this difficulty that leads to so much volatility in the stock markets.

Once we have learned the methods required for stock valuation, we will explore how good a job the markets do in establishing fair prices for securities. The idea that markets do a good job so that security prices fully reflect all available information is referred to as the *efficient market hypothesis*. We will examine whether the evidence supports this hypothesis.

COMPUTING THE PRICE OF COMMON STOCK

At www.stocks.tradingcharts.com, access detailed stock quotes, charts, and historical stock data.

Common stock is the principal way that corporations raise equity capital. Holders of common stock own an interest in the corporation consistent with the percentage of outstanding shares owned. This ownership interest gives **stockholders**—those who hold stock in a corporation—a bundle of rights. The most important are the right to vote and to be the **residual claimant** of all funds flowing into the firm (known as **cash flows**), meaning that the stockholder receives whatever remains after all other claims against the firm's assets have been satisfied. Stockholders are paid dividends from the net earnings of the corporation. **Dividends** are payments made periodically, usually every quarter, to stockholders. The board of directors of the firm sets the level of the dividend, usually upon the recommendation of management. In addition, the stockholder has the right to sell the stock.

One basic principle of finance is that the value of any investment is found by computing the value today of all cash flows the investment will generate over its life. For example, a commercial building will sell for a price that reflects the net cash flows (rents – expenses) it is projected to have over its useful life. Similarly, we value common stock as the value in today's dollars of all future cash flows. As noted above, the cash flows a stockholder may earn from stock are dividends, the sales price, or both.

To develop the theory of stock valuation, we begin with the simplest possible scenario: You buy the stock, hold it for one period to get a dividend, then sell the stock. We call this the *one-period valuation model.*

The One-Period Valuation Model

Suppose that you have some extra money to invest for one year. After a year you will need to sell your investment to pay tuition. After watching the financial news on TV, you decide that you want to buy Royal Bank stock. You call your broker and find that Royal Bank is currently selling for \$50 per share and pays \$0.16 per year in dividends. The analyst on the financial news predicts that the stock will be selling for \$60 in one year. Should you buy this stock?

To answer this question you need to determine whether the current price accurately reflects the analyst's forecast. To value the stock today, you need to find the present discounted value of the expected cash flows (future payments) using the formula in Equation 1 of Chapter 3 in which the discount factor used to discount the cash flows is the required return on investments in equity rather than the interest rate. The cash flows consist of one dividend payment plus a final sales price, which, when discounted back to the present, leads to the following equation which computes the current price of the stock.

$$P_0 = \frac{Div_1}{(1 + k_e)} + \frac{P_1}{(1 + k_e)} \tag{1}$$

where

P_0 = the current price of the stock. The zero subscript refers to time period zero, or the present.
Div_1 = the dividend paid at the end of year 1.
k_e = the required return on investments in equity.
P_1 = the price at the end of the first period. This is the assumed sale price of the stock.

EXAMPLE 1: Stock Valuation

Find the price of the Royal Bank stock given the figures reported above. You will need to know the required return on equity to find the present value of the cash flows. Since a stock is more risky than a bond, you will require a higher return than that offered in the bond market. Assume that after careful consideration you decide that you would be satisfied to earn 12% on the investment.

Solution

Putting the numbers into Equation 1 yields the following:

$$P_0 = \frac{0.16}{1 + 0.12} + \frac{\$60}{1 + 0.12} = \$0.14 + \$53.57 = \$53.71$$

Based on your analysis you find that the stock is worth \$53.71. Since the stock is currently available for \$50 per share, you would choose to buy it. Why is the stock selling for less than \$53.71? It may be because other investors place a different risk on the cash flows or estimate the cash flows to be less than you do.

The Generalized Dividend Valuation Model

The one-period dividend valuation model can be extended to any number of periods. The concept remains the same. The value of stock is the present value of all future cash flows. The only cash flows that an investor will receive are dividends and a final sales price when the stock is ultimately sold. The generalized formula for stock can be written as in Equation 2.

$$P_0 = \frac{D_1}{(1 + k_e)^1} + \frac{D_2}{(1 + k_e)^2} + \ldots + \frac{D_n}{(1 + k_e)^n} + \frac{P_n}{(1 + k_e)^n} \tag{2}$$

If you were to attempt to use Equation 2 to find the value of a share of stock, you would soon realize that you must first estimate the value the stock will have at some point in the future before you can estimate its value today. In other words, you must find P_n in order to find P_0. However, if P_n is far in the future, it will not affect P_0. For example, the present value of a share of stock that sells for \$50 seventy-five years from now using a 12% discount rate is just one cent [$\$50/(1.12^{75}) = \$0.01$]. This means that the current value of a share of stock can be found as simply the present value of the future dividend stream. The **generalized dividend model** is rewritten in Equation 3 without the final sales price.

$$P_0 = \sum_{t=1}^{\infty} \frac{D_t}{(1 + k_e)^t} \tag{3}$$

Consider the implications of Equation 3 for a moment. The generalized dividend model says that the price of stock is determined only by the present value of the dividends and that nothing else matters. Many stocks do not pay dividends, so how is it that these stocks have value? *Buyers of the stock expect that the firm will pay dividends someday.* Most of the time a firm institutes dividends as soon as it has completed the rapid growth phase of its life cycle. The stock price increases as the time approaches for the dividend stream to begin.

The generalized dividend valuation model requires that we compute the present value of an infinite stream of dividends, a process that could be difficult, to say the least. Therefore, simplified models have been developed to make the calculations easier. One such model is the **Gordon growth model** that assumes constant dividend growth.

The Gordon Growth Model

Many firms strive to increase their dividends at a constant rate each year. Equation 4 rewrites Equation 3 to reflect this constant growth in dividends.

$$P_0 = \frac{D_0 \times (1 + g)^1}{(1 + k_e)^1} + \frac{D_0 \times (1 + g)^2}{(1 + k_e)^2} + \ldots + \frac{D_0 \times (1 + g)^\infty}{(1 + k_e)^\infty} \tag{4}$$

where
D_0 = the most recent dividend paid
g = the expected constant growth rate in dividends
k_e = the required return on an investment in equity

Equation 4 has been simplified using algebra to obtain Equation 5.[1]

$$P_0 = \frac{D_0 \times (1 + g)}{(k_e - g)} = \frac{D_1}{(k_e - g)} \tag{5}$$

This model is useful for finding the value of stock, given a few assumptions:

1. *Dividends are assumed to continue growing at a constant rate forever.* Actually, as long as they are expected to grow at a constant rate for an extended period, the model should yield reasonable results. This is because errors about distant cash flows become small when discounted to the present.
2. *The growth rate is assumed to be less than the required return on equity, k_e.* Myron Gordon, in his development of the model, demonstrated that this is a reasonable assumption. In theory, if the growth rate were faster than the rate demanded by holders of the firm's equity, in the long run the firm would grow impossibly large.

EXAMPLE 2: Stock Valuation, Constant Growth

Find the current market price of Coca-Cola stock assuming dividends grow at a constant rate of 10.95%, D_0 = \$1.00, and the required return is 13%.

Solution

$$P_0 = \frac{D_0 \times (1 + g)}{k_e - g}$$

$$P_0 = \frac{\$1.00 \times (1.1095)}{0.13 - 0.1095}$$

$$P_0 = \frac{\$1.1095}{0.0205} = \$54.12$$

Coca-Cola stock should sell for \$54.12 if the assumptions regarding the constant growth rate and required return are correct.

[1]To generate Equation 5 from Equation 4, first multiply both sides of Equation 4 by $(1 + k_e)/(1 + g)$ and subtract Equation 4 from the result. This yields

$$\frac{P_0 \times (1 + k_e)}{(1 + g)} - P_0 = D_0 - \frac{D_0 \times (1 + g)^\infty}{(1 + k_e)^\infty}$$

Assuming that k_e is greater than g, the term on the far right will approach zero and can be dropped. Thus, after factoring P_0 out of the left hand side

$$P_0 \times \left[\frac{1 + k_e}{1 + g} - 1\right] = D_0$$

Next simplify by combining terms to

$$P_0 \times \frac{(1 + k_e) - (1 + g)}{1 + g} = D_0$$

$$P_0 = \frac{D_0 \times (1 + g)}{k_e - g} = \frac{D_1}{k_e - g}$$

Price Earnings Valuation Method

Theoretically, the best method of stock valuation is the dividend valuation approach. Sometimes, however, it is difficult to apply. If a firm is not paying dividends or has a very erratic growth rate, the results may not be satisfactory. Other approaches to stock valuation are sometimes applied. Among the more popular is the price/earnings multiple.

The **price earnings ratio (PE)** is a widely watched measure of how much the market is willing to pay for $1 of earnings from a firm. A high PE has two interpretations.

1. A higher than average PE may mean that the market expects earnings to rise in the future. This would return the PE to a more normal level.
2. A high PE may alternatively indicate that the market feels the firm's earnings are very low risk and is therefore willing to pay a premium for them.

The PE ratio can be used to estimate the value of a firm's stock. Note that algebraically the product of the PE ratio times expected earnings is the firm's stock price.

$$\frac{P}{E} \times E = P \tag{6}$$

Firms in the same industry are expected to have similar PE ratios in the long run. The value of a firm's stock can be found by multiplying the average industry PE times the expected earnings per share.

EXAMPLE 3: Stock Valuation, PE Ratio Approach

The average industry PE ratio for restaurants similar to Applebee's, a pub restaurant chain, is 23. What is the current price of Applebee's if earnings per share are projected to be $1.13?

Solution

Using Equation 6 and the data given we find:

$$P_0 = P/E \times E$$

$$P_0 = 23 \times \$1.13 = \$26$$

The PE ratio approach is especially useful for valuing privately held firms and firms that do not pay dividends. The weakness of the PE approach to valuation is that by using an industry average PE ratio, firm-specific factors that might contribute to a long-term PE ratio above or below the average are ignored in the analysis. A skilled analyst will adjust the PE ratio up or down to reflect unique characteristics of a firm when estimating its stock price.

HOW THE MARKET SETS SECURITY PRICES

Suppose you went to an auto auction. The cars are available for inspection before the auction begins, and you find a little Mazda Miata that you like. You test-drive it in the parking lot and notice that it makes a few strange noises, but you decide that you would still like the car. You decide $5000 would be a fair price that would allow you to pay some repair bills should the noises turn out to be serious. You see that the auction is ready to begin, so you go in and wait for the Miata to enter.

Suppose there is another buyer who also spots the Miata. He test-drives the car and recognizes that the noises are simply the result of worn brake pads that he can fix himself at a nominal cost. He decides that the car is worth $7000. He also goes in and waits for the Miata to enter.

Who will buy the car and for how much? Suppose only the two of you are interested in the Miata. You begin the bidding at $4000. He ups your bid to $4500. You bid your top price of $5000. He counters with $5100. The price is now higher than you are willing to pay, so you stop bidding. The car is sold to the more informed buyer for $5100.

This simple example raises a number of points. First, the price is set by the buyer willing to pay the highest price. The price is not necessarily the highest price the asset could fetch, but it is incrementally greater than what any other buyer is willing to pay.

Second, the market price will be set by the buyer who can take best advantage of the asset. The buyer who purchased the car knew that he could fix the noise easily and cheaply. Because of this he was willing to pay more for the car than you were. The same concept holds for other assets. For example, a piece of property or a building will sell to the buyer who can put the asset to the most productive use. Consider why one company often pays a substantial premium over current market prices to acquire ownership of another (target) company. The acquiring firm may believe that it can put the target firm's assets to work better than they are currently and that this justifies the premium price.

Finally, the example shows the role played by information in asset pricing. Superior information about an asset can increase its value by reducing its risk. When you consider buying a stock, there are many unknowns about the future cash flows. The buyer who has the best information about these cash flows will discount them at a lower interest rate than will a buyer who is very uncertain.

Now let us apply these ideas to stock valuation. Suppose that you are considering the purchase of stock expected to pay dividends of $2 next year. The firm is expected to grow at 3% indefinitely. You are quite *uncertain* about both the constancy of the dividend stream and the accuracy of the estimated growth rate. To compensate yourself for this risk, you require a return of 15%.

Now suppose Jennifer, another investor, has spoken with industry insiders and feels more confident about the projected cash flows. Jennifer only requires a 12% return because her perceived risk is lower than yours. Syed, on the other hand, is dating the CEO of the company. He knows with near certainty what the future of the firm actually is. He thinks that both the estimated growth rate and the estimated cash flows are lower than what they will *actually* be in the future. Because he sees almost no risk in this investment, he only requires a 7% return.

What are the values each investor will give to the stock? Applying the Gordon growth model yields the following stock prices.

Investor	Discount Rate	Stock Price
You	15%	$16.67
Jennifer	12%	$22.22
Syed	7%	$50.00

You are willing to pay $16.67 for the stock. Jennifer would pay up to $22.22, and Syed would pay $50. The investor with the lowest perceived risk is willing to pay the most for the stock. If there were no other traders, the market price would be just above $22.22. If you already held the stock, you would sell it to Syed.

The point of this section is that the players in the market, bidding against each other, establish the market price. When new information is released about a firm, expectations change and with them, prices change. New information can cause changes in expectations about the level of future dividends or the risk of those dividends. Since market participants are constantly receiving new information and constantly revising their expectations, it is reasonable that stock prices are constantly changing as well.

ERRORS IN VALUATION

In this chapter, we learned about several asset valuation models. An interesting exercise is to apply these models to real firms. Students who do this find that computed stock prices do not match market prices much of the time. Students often question whether the models are wrong or incomplete or whether they are simply being used incorrectly. There are many opportunities for errors in applying the models. These include problems estimating growth, estimating risk, and forecasting dividends.

Problems with Estimating Growth

The constant growth model requires the analyst to estimate the constant rate of growth the firm will experience. You may estimate future growth by computing the historical growth rate in dividends, sales, or net profits. This approach fails to consider any changes in the firm or economy that may affect the growth rate. Robert Haugen, a professor of finance at the University of California, writes in his book *The New Finance* that competition will prevent high-growth firms from being able to maintain their historical growth rate. He demonstrates that, despite this, the stock prices of historically high-growth firms tend to reflect a continuation of the high growth rate. The result is that investors in these firms receive lower returns than they would by investing in mature firms. This just points out that even the experts have trouble estimating future growth rates. Table 1 shows the stock price for a firm with a 15% required return, a $2 dividend, and a range of different growth rates. The stock price varies from $14.43 at 1% growth to $228 at a 14% growth rate. Estimating growth at 13% instead of 12% results in a $38.33 price difference.

Problems with Estimating Risk

The dividend valuation model requires the analyst to estimate the required return for the firm's equity. Table 2 shows how the price of a share of stock offering a $2 dividend and a 5% growth rate changes with different estimates of the required return. Clearly, stock price is highly dependent on the required return, despite our uncertainty regarding how it is found.

TABLE 1 Stock Prices for a Security with D_0 = $2.00, k_e = 15%, and Constant Growth Rates as Listed

Growth (%)	Price
1	$ 14.43
3	17.17
5	21.00
10	44.00
11	55.50
12	74.67
13	113.00
14	228.00

TABLE 2 Stock Prices for a Security with $D_0 = \$2.00, g = 5\%$, and Required Returns as Listed

Required Return (%)	Price
10	$42.00
11	35.00
12	30.00
13	26.25
14	23.33
15	21.00

Problems with Forecasting Dividends

Even if we are able to accurately estimate a firm's growth rate and its required return, we are still faced with the problem of determining how much of the firm's earnings will be paid as dividends. Clearly, many factors can influence the dividend payout ratio. These will include the firm's future growth opportunities and management's concern over future cash flows.

Putting all these concerns together, we see that stock analysts are seldom very certain that their stock price projections are accurate. This is why stock prices fluctuate so widely on news reports. For example, information that the economy is slowing can cause analysts to revise their growth expectations. When this happens across a broad spectrum of stocks, major market indexes can change.

Does all this mean that you should not invest in the market? No, it only means that short-term fluctuations in stock prices are expected and natural. Over the long term, the stock price will adjust to reflect the true earnings of the firm. If high-quality firms are chosen for your portfolio, they should provide fair returns over time. We investigate this issue further in the next section.

THE EFFICIENT MARKET HYPOTHESIS

To learn more about the efficient market hypothesis, go to www.investorhome.com/emh.htm

To more fully understand what determines stock prices, we need to look at how information in the market affects these prices. To do this we examine the **efficient market hypothesis** (also referred to as the **theory of efficient capital markets**), which states that prices of securities in financial markets fully reflect all available information. But what does this mean?

You may recall from Chapter 3 that the rate of return from holding a security equals the sum of the capital gain on the security (the change in the price) plus any cash payments, divided by the initial purchase price of the security:

$$R = \frac{P_{t+1} - P_t + C}{P_t} \tag{7}$$

where

R = rate of return on the security held from time t to time $t + 1$ (say, the end of 2002 to the end of 2003)

P_{t+1} = price of the security at time $t + 1$, the end of the holding period

P_t = the price of the security at time t, the beginning of the holding period

C = cash payment (coupon or dividend payments) made in the period t to $t + 1$

Let's look at the expectation of this return at time t, the beginning of the holding period. Because the current price and the cash payment C are known at the beginning, the only variable in the definition of the return that is uncertain is the price next period P_{t+1}.[2] Denoting the expectation of the security's price at the end of the holding period as P^e_{t+1}, the expected return R^e is

$$R^e = \frac{P^e_{t+1} - P_t + C}{P_t}$$

The efficient market hypothesis views expectations as equal to optimal forecasts using all available information. What exactly does this mean? An optimal forecast is the best guess of the future using all available information. This does not mean that the forecast is perfectly accurate, but only that it is the *best possible* given the available information. This can be written more formally as

$$P^e_{t+1} = P^{of}_{t+1}$$

which in turn implies that the expected return on the security will equal the optimal forecast of the return:

$$R^e = R^{of} \tag{8}$$

Unfortunately, we cannot observe either R^e or P^e_{t+1}, so the equations above by themselves do not tell us much about how the financial market behaves. However, if we can devise some way to measure the value of R^e, these equations will have important implications for how prices of securities change in financial markets.

The supply and demand analysis of the bond market developed in Chapter 4 shows us that the expected return on a security (the interest rate in the case of the bond examined) will have a tendency to head toward the equilibrium return that equates the quantity demanded to the quantity supplied. Supply and demand analysis enables us to determine the expected return on a security with the following equilibrium condition: The expected return on a security R^e equals the equilibrium return R^*, which equates the quantity of the security demanded to the quantity supplied; that is,

$$R^e = R^* \tag{9}$$

The academic field of finance explores the factors (risk and liquidity, for example) that influence the equilibrium returns on securities. For our purposes, it is sufficient to know that we can determine the equilibrium return and thus determine the expected return with the equilibrium condition.

We can derive an equation to describe pricing behaviour in an efficient market by using the equilibrium condition to replace R^e with R^* in Equation 8. In this way we obtain

$$R^{of} = R^* \tag{10}$$

This equation tells us that ***current prices in a financial market will be set so that the optimal forecast of a security's return using all available information equals the security's equilibrium return.*** Financial economists state it more simply: A security's price fully reflects all available information in an efficient market.

---

[2] There are cases where C might not be known at the beginning of the period, but that does not make a substantial difference to the analysis. We would in that case assume that not only price expectations but also the expectations of C are optimal forecasts using all available information.

EXAMPLE 4: The Efficient Market Hypothesis

Suppose that a share of Microsoft had a closing price yesterday of \$90, but new information was announced after the market closed that caused a revision in the forecast of price next year to go to \$120. If the annual equilibrium return on Microsoft is 15%, what does the efficient market hypothesis indicate the price will go to today when the market opens? (Assume that Microsoft pays no dividends.)

Solution

The price would rise to \$104.35 after the opening.

$$R^{of} = \frac{P^{of}_{t+1} - P_t + C}{P_t} = R^*$$

where

R^{of} = optimal forecast of the return = 15% = 0.15

R^* = equilibrium return = 15% = 0.15

P^{of}_{t+1} = optimal forecast of price next year = \$120

P_t = price today after opening

C = cash (dividend) payment = 0

Thus

$$0.15 = \frac{\$120 - P_t}{P_t}$$

$$P_t \times 0.15 = \$120 - P_t$$

$$P_t(1.15) = \$120$$

$$P_t = \$104.35$$

Rationale Behind the Hypothesis

Let's see what the efficient market condition means in practice and why it is a sensible characterization of pricing behaviour. Suppose that the equilibrium return on a security, say, Nortel common stock, is 10% at an annual rate, and its current price P_t is lower than the optimal forecast of tomorrow's price P^{of}_{t+1} so that the optimal forecast of the return at an annual rate is 50%, which is greater than the equilibrium return of 10%. We are now able to predict that, on average, Nortel's return would be abnormally high. This situation is called an **unexploited profit opportunity** because, on average, people would be earning more than they should, given the characteristics of that security. Knowing that, on average, you can earn such an abnormally high rate of return on Nortel because $R^{of} > R^*$, you would buy more, which would in turn drive up its current price relative to the expected future price P^{of}_{t+1}, thereby lowering R^{of}. When the current price had risen sufficiently so that R^{of} equals R^* and the efficient market condition (Equation 10) is satisfied, the buying of Nortel will stop, and the unexploited profit opportunity will have disappeared.

Learn more about Nortel Networks by visiting their Website at www.nortel.com

Similarly, a security for which the optimal forecast of the return is –5% while the equilibrium return is 10% ($R^{of} < R^*$) would be a poor investment because, on average, it earns less than the equilibrium return. In such a case, you would sell the security and drive down its current price relative to the expected future price until R^{of} rose to the level of R^* and the efficient market condition is again satisfied. What we have shown can be summarized as follows:

$$\left.\begin{array}{l} R^{of} > R^* \rightarrow P_t\uparrow \rightarrow R^{of}\downarrow \\ R^{of} < R^* \rightarrow P_t\downarrow \rightarrow R^{of}\uparrow \end{array}\right\} \quad \text{until} \quad R^{of} = R^*$$

Another way to state the efficient market condition is this: ***In an efficient market, all unexploited profit opportunities will be eliminated.***

An extremely important factor in this reasoning is that ***not everyone in a financial market must be well informed about a security or have rational expectations for its price to be driven to the point at which the efficient market condition holds.*** Financial markets are structured so that many participants can play. As long as a few keep their eyes open for unexploited profit opportunities, they will eliminate the profit opportunities that appear because in so doing, they make a profit. The efficient market hypothesis makes sense because it does not require everyone in a market to be cognizant of what is happening to every security.

Stronger Version of the Efficient Market Hypothesis

Many financial economists take the efficient market hypothesis one step further in their analysis of financial markets. Not only do they define an efficient market as one in which expectations are optimal forecasts using all available information, but they also add the condition that an efficient market is one in which prices reflect the true fundamental (intrinsic) value of the securities. Thus, in an efficient market, all prices are always correct and reflect **market fundamentals** (items that have a direct impact on future income streams of the securities). This stronger view of market efficiency has several important implications in the academic field of finance. First, it implies that in an efficient capital market, one investment is as good as any other because the securities' prices are correct. Second, it implies that a security's price reflects all available information about the intrinsic value of the security. Third, it implies that security prices can be used by managers of both financial and nonfinancial firms to assess their cost of capital (cost of financing their investments) accurately and hence that security prices can be used to help them make the correct decisions about whether a specific investment is worth making or not. The stronger version of market efficiency is a basic tenet of much analysis in the finance field.

EVIDENCE ON THE EFFICIENT MARKET HYPOTHESIS

Early evidence on the efficient market hypothesis was quite favourable to it, but in recent years, deeper analysis of the evidence suggests that the hypothesis may not always be entirely correct. Let's first look at the earlier evidence in favour of the hypothesis and then examine some of the more recent evidence that casts some doubt on it.

Evidence in Favour of Market Efficiency

Evidence in favour of market efficiency has examined the performance of investment analysts and mutual funds, whether stock prices reflect publicly available information, the random-walk behaviour of stock prices, and the success of so-called technical analysis.

Performance of Investment Analysts and Mutual Funds We have seen that one implication of the efficient market hypothesis is that when purchasing a security, you cannot expect to earn an abnormally high return, a return greater than the equilibrium return. This implies that it is impossible to beat the market. Many studies shed light on whether investment advisers and mutual funds (some of which charge steep sales commissions to people who purchase them) beat the market. One common test that has been performed is to take buy and sell recommendations from a group of advisers or mutual funds and compare the performance of the resulting selection of stocks with the market as a whole. Sometimes the advisers' choices have even been compared to a group of stocks chosen by putting a copy of the financial page of the newspaper on a dartboard and throwing darts. The *Wall Street Journal,* for example, has a regular feature called "Investment Dartboard" that compares how well stocks picked by investment advisers do relative to stocks picked by throwing darts. Do the advisers win? To their embarrassment, the dartboard beats them as often as they beat the dartboard. Furthermore, even when the comparison includes only advisers who have been successful in the past in predicting the stock market, the advisers still don't regularly beat the dartboard.

Consistent with the efficient market hypothesis, mutual funds are also not found to beat the market. Mutual funds not only do not outperform the market on average, but also when they are separated into groups according to whether they had the highest or lowest profits in a chosen period, the mutual funds that did well in the first period do not beat the market in the second period.[3]

The conclusion from the study of investment advisers and mutual fund performance is this: ***Having performed well in the past does not indicate that an investment adviser or a mutual fund will perform well in the future.*** This is not pleasing news to investment advisers, but it is exactly what the efficient market hypothesis predicts. It says that some advisers will be lucky and some will be unlucky. Being lucky does not mean that a forecaster actually has the ability to beat the market. (An exception that proves the rule is discussed in Box 1.)

Do Stock Prices Reflect Publicly Available Information? The efficient market hypothesis predicts that stock prices will reflect all publicly available information. Thus, if information is already publicly available, a positive announcement about a company will not, on average, raise the price of its stock because this information is already reflected in the stock price. Early empirical evidence also confirmed this conjecture from the efficient market hypothesis: Favourable earnings announcements or announcements of stock splits (a division of a share of stock into multiple shares, which is usually followed by higher earnings) do not, on average, cause stock prices to rise.[4]

Random-Walk Behaviour of Stock Prices The term **random walk** describes the movements of a variable whose future changes cannot be predicted (are random) because, given today's value, the variable is just as likely to fall as to rise.

[3]An early study that found that mutual funds do not outperform the market is Michael C. Jensen, "The Performance of Mutual Funds in the Period 1945–64," *Journal of Finance* 23 (1968): 389–416. More recent studies on mutual fund performance are Mark Grimblatt and Sheridan Titman, "Mutual Fund Performance: An Analysis of Quarterly Portfolio Holdings," *Journal of Business* 62 (1989): 393–416, R. A. Ippolito, "Efficiency with Costly Information: A Study of Mutual Fund Performance, 1965–84," *Quarterly Journal of Economics* 104 (1989): 1–23, J. Lakonishok, A. Shleifer, and R. Vishny, "The Structure and Performance of the Money Management Industry," *Brookings Papers on Economic Activity, Microeconomics* (1992), B. Malkiel, "Returns from Investing in Equity Mutual Funds, 1971–1991," *Journal of Finance* 50: 549–72.

[4]Ray Ball and Philip Brown, "An Empirical Evaluation of Accounting Income Numbers," *Journal of Accounting Research* 6 (1968): 159–178; Eugene F. Fama, Lawrence Fisher, Michael C. Jensen, and Richard Roll, "The Adjustment of Stock Prices to New Information," *International Economic Review* 10 (1969): 1–21.

BOX 1

An Exception That Proves the Rule: Ivan Boesky

The efficient market hypothesis indicates that investment advisers should not have the ability to beat the market. Yet that is exactly what Ivan Boesky was able to do until 1986, when he was charged by the U.S. Securities and Exchange Commission with making unfair profits (rumoured to be in the hundreds of millions of dollars) by trading on inside information. In an out-of-court settlement, Boesky was banned from the securities business, fined $100 million, and sentenced to three years in jail. (After serving his sentence, Boesky was released from jail in 1990.) If the stock market is efficient, can the SEC legitimately claim that Boesky was able to beat the market? The answer is yes.

Ivan Boesky was the most successful of the so-called *arbs* (short for *arbitrageurs*) who made hundreds of millions in profits for himself and his clients by investing in the stocks of firms that were about to be taken over by other firms at an above-market price. Boesky's continuing success was assured by an arrangement whereby he paid cash (sometimes in a suitcase) to Dennis Levine, an investment banker who had inside information about when a takeover was to take place because his firm was arranging the financing of the deal. When Levine found out that a firm was planning a takeover, he would inform Boesky, who would then buy the stock of the company being taken over and sell it after the stock had risen.

Boesky's ability to make millions year after year in the 1980s is an exception that proves the rule that financial analysts cannot continually outperform the market; yet it supports the efficient markets claim that only information *unavailable to the market* enables an investor to do so. Boesky profited from knowing about takeovers before the rest of the market; this information was known to him but unavailable to the market.

An important implication of the efficient market hypothesis is that stock prices should approximately follow a random walk; that is, ***future changes in stock prices should, for all practical purposes, be unpredictable.*** The random-walk implication of the efficient market hypothesis is the one most commonly mentioned in the press because it is the most readily comprehensible to the public. In fact, when people mention the "random-walk theory of stock prices," they are in reality referring to the efficient market hypothesis.

The case for random-walk stock prices can be demonstrated. Suppose that people could predict that the price of Happy Feet Corporation (HFC) stock would rise 1% in the coming week. The predicted rate of capital gains and rate of return on HFC stock would then be over 50% at an annual rate. Since this is very likely to be far higher than the equilibrium rate of return on HFC stock ($R^{of} > R^*$), the efficient market hypothesis indicates that people would immediately buy this stock and bid up its current price. The action would stop only when the predictable change in the price dropped to near zero so that $R^{of} = R^*$.

Similarly, if people could predict that the price of HFC stock would fall by 1%, the predicted rate of return would be negative ($R^{of} < R^*$), and people would immediately sell. The current price would fall until the predictable change in the price rose back to near zero, where the efficient market condition again holds. The efficient market hypothesis suggests that the predictable change in stock prices will be near zero, leading to the conclusion that stock prices will generally follow a random walk.[5]

Financial economists have used two types of tests to explore the hypothesis that stock prices follow a random walk. In the first, they examine stock market records to see whether changes in stock prices are systematically related to past changes and hence could have been predicted on that basis. The second type of

[5]Note that the random-walk behaviour of stock prices is only an *approximation* derived from the efficient market hypothesis. It would hold exactly only for a stock for which an unchanged price leads to its having the equilibrium return. Then, when the predictable change in the stock price is exactly zero, $R^{of} = R^*$.

test examines the data to see whether publicly available information other than past stock prices could have been used to predict changes. These tests are somewhat more stringent because additional information (money supply growth, government spending, interest rates, corporate profits) might be used to help forecast stock returns. Early results from both types of tests generally confirmed the efficient market view that stock prices are not predictable and do follow a random walk.[6]

Technical Analysis A popular technique used to predict stock prices, called *technical analysis,* is to study past stock price data and search for patterns such as trends and regular cycles. Rules for when to buy and sell stocks are then established on the basis of the patterns that emerge. The efficient market hypothesis suggests that technical analysis is a waste of time. The simplest way to understand why is to use the random-walk result derived from the efficient market hypothesis that holds that past stock price data cannot help predict changes. Therefore, technical analysis, which relies on such data to produce its forecasts, cannot successfully predict changes in stock prices.

Two types of tests bear directly on the value of technical analysis. The first performs the empirical analysis described earlier to evaluate the performance of any financial analyst, technical or otherwise. The results are exactly what the efficient market hypothesis predicts: Technical analysts fare no better than other financial analysts; on average, they do not outperform the market, and successful past forecasting does not imply that their forecasts will outperform the market in the future. The second type of test (first performed by Sidney Alexander) takes the rules developed in technical analysis for when to buy and sell stocks and applies them to new data.[7] The performance of these rules is then evaluated by the profits that would have been made using them. These tests also discredit technical analysis: It does not outperform the overall market.

Application Should Foreign Exchange Rates Follow a Random Walk?

Although the efficient market hypothesis is usually applied to the stock market, it can also be used to show that foreign exchange rates, like stock prices, should generally follow a random walk. To see why this is the case, consider what would happen if people could predict that a currency would appreciate by 1% in the coming week. By buying this currency, they could earn a greater than 50% return at an annual rate, which is likely to be far above the equilibrium return for holding a currency. As a result, people would immediately buy the currency and bid up

[6]The first type of test, using only stock market data, is referred to as a test of *weak-form efficiency* because the information that can be used to predict stock prices is restricted solely to past price data. The second type of test is referred to as a test of *semistrong-form efficiency* because the information set is expanded to include all publicly available information, not just past stock prices. A third type of test is called a test of *strong-form efficiency* because the information set includes insider information, known only to the owners of the corporation, as when they plan to declare a high dividend. Strong-form tests do sometimes indicate that insider information can be used to predict changes in stock prices. This finding does not contradict efficient markets theory because the information is not available to the market and hence cannot be reflected in market prices. In fact, there are strict laws against using insider information to trade in financial markets. For an early survey on the three forms of tests, see Eugene F. Fama, "Efficient Capital Markets: A Review of Theory and Empirical Work," *Journal of Finance* 25 (1970): 383–416.

[7]Sidney Alexander, "Price Movements in Speculative Markets: Trends or Random Walks?" *Industrial Management Review,* May 1961, pp. 7–26; and Sidney Alexander, "Price Movements in Speculative Markets: Trends or Random Walks? No. 2" in *The Random Character of Stock Prices,* ed. Paul Cootner (Cambridge, Mass.: MIT Press, 1964), pp. 338–372. More recent evidence also seems to discredit technical analysis, for example, F. Allen and R. Karjalainen, "Using Genetic Algorithms to Find Technical Trading Rules," *Journal of Financial Economics* (1999) 51: 245–71. However, some other research is more favourable to technical analysis, e.g., R. Sullivan, A. Timmerman, and H. White, "Data-Snooping, Technical Trading Rule Performance and the Bootstrap," Centre for Economic Policy Research Discussion Paper No. 1976, 1998.

its current price, thereby reducing the expected return. The process would stop only when the predictable change in the exchange rate dropped to near zero so that the optimal forecast of the return no longer differed from the equilibrium return. Likewise, if people could predict that the currency would depreciate by 1% in the coming week, they would sell it until the predictable change in the exchange rate was again near zero. The efficient market hypothesis therefore implies that future changes in exchange rates should, for all practical purposes, be unpredictable; in other words, exchange rates should follow random walks. This is exactly what empirical evidence finds.[8]

Evidence Against Market Efficiency

All the early evidence supporting the efficient market hypothesis appeared to be overwhelming, causing Eugene Fama, a prominent financial economist, to state in his famous 1970 survey of the empirical evidence on the efficient market hypothesis, "The evidence in support of the efficient markets model is extensive, and (somewhat uniquely in economics) contradictory evidence is sparse."[9] However, in recent years, the theory has begun to show a few cracks, referred to as *anomalies,* and empirical evidence indicates that the efficient market hypothesis may not always be generally applicable.

Small-Firm Effect One of the earliest reported anomalies in which the stock market did not appear to be efficient is called the *small-firm effect.* Many empirical studies have shown that small firms have earned abnormally high returns over long periods, even when the greater risk for these firms has been taken into account.[10] The small-firm effect seems to have diminished in recent years but is still a challenge to the theory of efficient markets. Various theories have been developed to explain the small-firm effect, suggesting that it may be due to rebalancing of portfolios by institutional investors, tax issues, low liquidity of small-firm stocks, large information costs in evaluating small firms, or an inappropriate measurement of risk for small-firm stocks.

January Effect Over long periods, stock prices have tended to experience an abnormal price rise from December to January that is predictable and hence inconsistent with random-walk behaviour. This so-called **January effect** seems to have diminished in recent years for shares of large companies but still occurs for shares of small companies.[11] Some financial economists argue that the January effect is due to tax issues. Investors have an incentive to sell stocks before the end of the year in December because they can then take capital losses on their tax return and reduce their tax liability. Then when the new year starts in January, they can repurchase the stocks, driving up their prices and producing abnormally high returns. Although this explanation seems sensible, it does not explain why institutional investors such as private pension funds, which are not subject to income taxes, do not take advantage of the abnormal returns

---

[8]See Richard A. Meese and Kenneth Rogoff, "Empirical Exchange Rate Models of the Seventies: Do They Fit out of Sample?" *Journal of International Economics* 14 (1983): 3–24.

[9]Eugene F. Fama, "Efficient Capital Markets: A Review of Theory and Empirical Work," *Journal of Finance* 25 (1970): 383–416.

[10]For example, see Marc R. Reinganum, "The Anomalous Stock Market Behavior of Small Firms in January: Empirical Tests of Tax Loss Selling Effects," *Journal of Financial Economics* 12 (1983): 89–104; Jay R. Ritter, "The Buying and Selling Behavior of Individual Investors at the Turn of the Year," *Journal of Finance* 43 (1988): 701–17; and Richard Roll, "Vas Ist Das? The Turn-of-the-Year Effect: Anomaly or Risk Mismeasurement?" *Journal of Portfolio Management* 9 (1988): 18–28.

[11]For example, see Donald B. Keim, "The CAPM and Equity Return Regularities," *Financial Analysts Journal* 42 (May–June 1986): 19–34.

in January and buy stocks in December, thus bidding up their price and eliminating the abnormal returns.[12]

Market Overreaction Recent research suggests that stock prices may overreact to news announcements and that the pricing errors are corrected only slowly.[13] When corporations announce a major change in earnings, say, a large decline, the stock price may overshoot, and after an initial large decline, it may rise back to more normal levels over several weeks. This violates the efficient market hypothesis because an investor could earn abnormally high returns, on average, by buying a stock immediately after a poor earnings announcement and then selling it after a couple of weeks when it has risen back to normal levels.

Excessive Volatility A closely related phenomenon to market overreaction is that the stock market appears to display excessive volatility; that is, fluctuations in stock prices may be much greater than is warranted by fluctuations in their fundamental value. In an important paper, Robert Shiller of Yale University found that fluctuations in the S&P 500 stock index could not be justified by the subsequent fluctuations in the dividends of the stocks making up this index. There has been much subsequent technical work criticizing these results, but Shiller's work, along with research that finds that there are smaller fluctuations in stock prices when stock markets are closed, has produced a consensus that stock market prices appear to be driven by factors other than fundamentals.[14]

Mean Reversion Some researchers have also found that stock returns display **mean reversion**: Stocks with low returns today tend to have high returns in the future, and vice versa. Hence stocks that have done poorly in the past are more likely to do well in the future because mean reversion indicates that there will be a predictable positive change in the future price, suggesting that stock prices are not a random walk. Other researchers have found that mean reversion is not nearly as strong in data after World War II and so have raised doubts about whether it is currently an important phenomenon. The evidence on mean reversion remains controversial.[15]

---

[12]Another anomaly that makes the stock market seem less than efficient is the fact that the *Value Line Survey,* one of the most prominent investment advice newsletters, has produced stock recommendations that have yielded abnormally high returns on average. See Fischer Black, "Yes, Virginia, There Is Hope: Tests of the Value Line Ranking System," *Financial Analysts Journal* 29 (September–October 1973): 10–14, and Gur Huberman and Shmuel Kandel, "Market Efficiency and Value Line's Record," *Journal of Business* 63 (1990): 187–216. Whether the excellent performance of the *Value Line Survey* will continue in the future is, of course, a question mark.

[13]Werner F. M. De Bondt and Richard Thaler, "Further Evidence on Investor Overreaction and Stock Market Seasonality," *Journal of Finance* 62 (1987): 557–580.

[14]Robert Shiller, "Do Stock Prices Move Too Much to Be Justified by Subsequent Changes in Dividends?" *American Economic Review* 71 (1981): 421–36, and Kenneth R. French and Richard Roll, "Stock Return Variances: The Arrival of Information and the Reaction of Traders," *Journal of Financial Economics* 17 (1986): 5–26.

[15]Evidence for mean reversion has been reported by James M. Poterba and Lawrence H. Summers, "Mean Reversion in Stock Prices: Evidence and Implications," *Journal of Financial Economics* 22 (1988): 27–59; Eugene F. Fama and Kenneth R. French, "Permanent and Temporary Components of Stock Prices," *Journal of Political Economy* 96 (1988): 246–73; and Andrew W. Lo and A. Craig MacKinlay, "Stock Market Prices Do Not Follow Random Walks: Evidence from a Simple Specification Test," *Review of Financial Studies* 1 (1988): 41–66. However, Myung Jig Kim, Charles R. Nelson, and Richard Startz, "Mean Reversion in Stock Prices? A Reappraisal of the Evidence," *Review of Economic Studies* 58 (1991): 515–28, question whether some of these findings are valid. For an excellent summary of this evidence, see Charles Engel and Charles S. Morris, "Challenges to Stock Market Efficiency: Evidence from Mean Reversion Studies," Federal Reserve Bank of Kansas City *Economic Review,* September–October 1991, pp. 21–35. See also N. Jegadeesh and Sheridan Titman, "Returns to Buying Winners and Selling Losers: Implications for Stock Market Efficiency," *Journal of Finance* 48 (1993): 65–92, which shows that mean reversion also occurs for individual stocks.

New Information Is Not Always Immediately Incorporated Into Stock Prices Although it is generally found that stock prices adjust rapidly to new information, as is suggested by the efficient market hypothesis, recent evidence suggests that, inconsistent with the efficient market hypothesis, stock prices do not instantaneously adjust to profit announcements. Instead, on average stock prices continue to rise for some time after the announcement of unexpectedly high profits, and they continue to fall after surprisingly low profit announcements.[16]

Chaos and Fractals Some researchers have also found evidence of chaotic dynamics in asset prices. The possible existence of **chaos** could be exploitable and even invaluable, as it implies that profitable, nonlinearity-based trading rules exist at least in the short run and provided the actual generating mechanism is known. Prediction, however, over long periods is all but impossible, because of a property of chaos known as sensitive dependence on initial conditions.[17]

In related literature, the famous mathematician Benoit Mandelbrot of Yale University has introduced complex geometric patterns in the description of financial markets, similar to those that describe the shapes of coastlines, ferns, and galaxies throughout the cosmos. Mandelbrot argues that charts of asset prices are **fractal curves** and applies many powerful tools of mathematical and computer analysis to explain how such prices soar and plummet.[18]

Go to www.washu.edu and www.ucalgary.ca to find out about the work of faculty at Washington University and the University of Calgary.

Recently there has been considerable criticism of the existing research on nonlinear dynamics in economics and finance. However, as William Barnett of Washington University in St. Louis and Apostolos Serletis of the University of Calgary report, "in the field of economics, it is especially unwise to take a strong opinion (either pro or con) in that area of research. Contrary to popular opinion within the profession, there have been no published tests of chaos 'within the structure of the economic system,' and there is very little chance that any such tests will be available in this field for a very long time. Such tests are simply beyond the state of the art."[19]

Overview of the Evidence on the Efficient Market Hypothesis

As you can see, the debate on the efficient market hypothesis is far from over. The evidence seems to suggest that the efficient market hypothesis may be a reasonable starting point for evaluating behaviour in financial markets. However, there do seem to be important violations of market efficiency that suggest that the efficient market hypothesis may not be the whole story and so may not be generalizable to all behaviour in financial markets.

---

[16]For example, see R. Ball and P. Brown, "An Empirical Evaluation of Accounting Income Numbers," *Journal of Accounting Research* (1968) 6: 159–78, L. Chan, N. Jegadeesh, and J. Lakonishok, "Momentum Strategies," *Journal of Finance* (1996) 51: 1681–713, and Eugene Fama, "Market Efficiency, Long-Term Returns and Behavioral Finance," *Journal of Financial Economics* (1998) 49: 283–306.

[17]Evidence for chaotic dynamics on financial data has been reported by José A. Scheinkman and Blake Lebaron, "Nonlinear Dynamics and Stock Returns," *Journal of Business* 62 (1989): 311–37; Murray Frank and Thanasis Stengos, "Measuring the Strangeness of Gold and Silver Rates of Return," *Review of Economic Studies* 56 (1989): 553–67; and Apostolos Serletis and Periklis Gogas, "Chaos in East European Black-Market Exchange Rates," *Research in Economics* 51 (1997): 359–85.

[18]See, for example, Benoit B. Mandelbrot, "A Multifractal Walk down Wall Street," *Scientific American* February (1999): 70-73.

[19]William A. Barnett and Apostolos Serletis, "Martingales, Nonlinearity, and Chaos," *Journal of Economic Dynamics and Control* 24 (2000): 703–24.

THE PRACTISING FINANCIAL INSTITUTION MANAGER

Practical Guide to Investing in the Stock Market

The efficient market hypothesis has numerous applications to the real world. It is especially valuable because it can be applied directly to an issue that concerns managers of financial institutions (and the general public as well): how to make profits in the stock market. A practical guide to investing in the stock market, which we develop here, provides a better understanding of the use and implications of the efficient market hypothesis.

HOW VALUABLE ARE PUBLISHED REPORTS BY INVESTMENT ADVISERS?

Suppose that you have just read in *The Globe and Mail: Report on Business* that investment advisers are predicting a boom in oil stocks because an oil shortage is developing. Should you proceed to withdraw all your hard-earned savings from the bank and invest it in oil stocks?

The efficient market hypothesis tells us that when purchasing a security, we cannot expect to earn an abnormally high return, a return greater than the equilibrium return. Information in newspapers and in the published reports of investment advisers is readily available to many market participants and is already reflected in market prices. So acting on this information will not yield abnormally high returns, on average. As we have seen, the empirical evidence for the most part confirms that recommendations from investment advisers cannot help us outperform the general market. Indeed, as Box 2 suggests, human investment advisers in San Francisco do not on average even outperform an orangutan!

Probably no other conclusion is met with more skepticism by students than this one when they first hear it. We all know or have heard of somebody who has been successful in the stock market for many years. We wonder, how could someone be so consistently successful if he or she did not really know how to predict when returns would be abnormally high? The following story, reported in the press, illustrates why such anecdotal evidence is not reliable.

A get-rich-quick artist invented a clever scam. Every week, he wrote two letters. In letter A, he would pick team A to win a particular football game, and in letter B, he would pick the opponent, team B. A mailing list would then be separated into two groups, and he would send letter A to the people in one group and letter B to the people in the other. The following week he would do the same thing but would send these letters only to the group who had received the first letter with the correct prediction. After doing this for ten games, he had a small cluster of people who had received letters predicting the correct winning team for every game. He then mailed a final letter to them, declaring that since he was obviously an expert predictor of the outcome of football games (he had picked win-

BOX 2

Should You Hire an Ape as Your Investment Adviser?

The *San Francisco Chronicle* came up with an amusing way of evaluating how successful investment advisers are at picking stocks. They asked eight analysts to pick five stocks at the beginning of the year and then compared the performance of their stock picks with those chosen by Jolyn, an orangutan living at Marine World/Africa USA in Vallejo, California. Consistent with the results found in the "Investment Dartboard" feature of the *Wall Street Journal*, Jolyn beat the investment advisers as often as they beat her. Given this result, you might be just as well off hiring an orangutan as your investment adviser as you would hiring a human being!

ners ten weeks in a row) and since his predictions were profitable for the recipients who bet on the games, he would continue to send his predictions only if he were paid a substantial amount of money. When one of his clients figured out what he was up to, the con man was prosecuted and thrown in jail!

What is the lesson of the story? Even if no forecaster is an accurate predictor of the market, there will always be a group of consistent winners. A person who has done well regularly in the past cannot guarantee that he or she will do well in the future. Note that there will also be a group of persistent losers, but you rarely hear about them because no one brags about a poor forecasting record.

SHOULD YOU BE SKEPTICAL OF HOT TIPS?

Suppose that your broker phones you with a hot tip to buy stock in the Happy Feet Corporation (HFC) because it has just developed a product that is completely effective in curing athlete's foot. The stock price is sure to go up. Should you follow this advice and buy HFC stock?

The efficient market hypothesis indicates that you should be skeptical of such news. If the stock market is efficient, it has already priced HFC stock so that its expected return will equal the equilibrium return. The hot tip is not particularly valuable and will not enable you to earn an abnormally high return.

You might wonder, though, if the hot tip is based on new information and would give you an edge on the rest of the market. If other market participants have received this information before you, the answer is no. As soon as the information hits the street, the unexploited profit opportunity it creates will be quickly eliminated. The stock's price will already reflect the information, and you should expect to realize only the equilibrium return. But if you are one of the first to know the new information (as Ivan Boesky was—see Box 1), it can do you some good. Only then can you be one of the lucky ones who, on average, will earn an abnormally high return by helping eliminate the profit opportunity by buying HFC stock.

DO STOCK PRICES ALWAYS RISE WHEN THERE IS GOOD NEWS?

If you follow the stock market, you might have noticed a puzzling phenomenon: When good news about a stock, such as a particularly favourable earnings report, is announced, the price of the stock frequently does not rise. The efficient market hypothesis and the random-walk behaviour of stock prices explain this phenomenon.

Because changes in stock prices are unpredictable, when information is announced that has already been expected by the market, the stock price will remain unchanged. The announcement does not contain any new information that should lead to a change in stock prices. If this were not the case and the announcement led to a change in stock prices, it would mean that the change was predictable. Because that is ruled out in an efficient market, ***stock prices will respond to announcements only when the information being announced is new and unexpected.*** If the news is expected, there will be no stock price response. This is exactly what the evidence that we described earlier suggests will occur—that stock prices reflect publicly available information.

Sometimes a stock price declines when good news is announced. Although this seems somewhat peculiar, it is completely consistent with the workings of an efficient market. Suppose that although the announced news is good, it is not as good as expected. HFC's earnings may have risen 15%, but if the market expected earnings to rise by 20%, the new information is actually unfavourable, and the stock price declines.

EFFICIENT MARKETS PRESCRIPTION FOR THE INVESTOR

What does the efficient market hypothesis recommend for investing in the stock market? It tells us that hot tips, investment advisers' published recommendations, and technical analysis—all of which make use of publicly available information—cannot help an investor outperform the market. Indeed, it indicates that anyone without better information than other market participants cannot expect to beat the market. So what is an investor to do?

The efficient market hypothesis leads to the conclusion that such an investor (and almost all of us fit into this category) should not try to outguess the market by constantly buying and selling securities. This process does nothing but boost the income of brokers, who earn commissions on each trade.[20] Instead, the investor should pursue a "buy-and-hold" strategy—purchase stocks and hold them for long periods. This will lead to the same returns, on average, but the investor's net profits will be higher because fewer brokerage commissions will have to be paid.[21]

It is frequently a sensible strategy for a small investor, whose costs of managing a portfolio may be high relative to its size, to buy into a mutual fund rather than individual stocks. Because the efficient market hypothesis indicates that no mutual fund can consistently outperform the market, an investor should not buy into one that has high management fees or that pays sales commissions to brokers but rather should purchase a no-load (commission-free) mutual fund that has low management fees.

As we have seen, the evidence indicates that it will not be easy to beat the prescription suggested here, although some of the anomalies to the efficient market hypothesis suggest that an extremely clever investor (which rules out most of us) may be able to outperform a buy-and-hold strategy.

Application What Does the Stock Market Crash of 1987 Tell Us About the Efficient Market Hypothesis?

Some observers have suggested that the October 19, 1987, stock market crash should make us question the validity of the efficient market hypothesis. They do not believe that an efficient market could have produced such a massive swing in share prices. To what degree should the stock market crash make us doubt the validity of the efficient market hypothesis?

Nothing in the efficient market hypothesis rules out large one-day changes in stock prices. A large change in stock prices can result from new information that produces a dramatic change in optimal forecasts of the future valuation of firms. Some financial economists have pointed out that there are many possible explanations for why optimal forecasts of the future value of firms might have dropped dramatically on October 19, 1987: moves in the U.S. Congress to restrict corporate takeovers, the disappointing performance of the U.S. trade deficit, failure to reduce the budget deficit substantially, increased fears of inflation, the decline of the U.S. dollar, and increased fears of financial distress in the banking industry. Other financial economists doubt whether these explanations are enough to explain the stock market drop because none of these market fundamentals seems important enough.

[20]The investor may also have to pay capital gains taxes on any profits that are realized when a security is sold—an additional reason why continual buying and selling does not make sense.

[21]As we saw in Chapter 4, the investor can also minimize risk by holding a diversified portfolio. The investor will be better off by pursuing a buy-and-hold strategy with a diversified portfolio or with a mutual fund that has a diversified portfolio.

One lesson from the Black Monday stock market crash appears to be that factors other than market fundamentals may have had an effect on stock prices. The crash of 1987 has therefore convinced many financial economists that the stronger version of the efficient market hypothesis, which states that asset prices reflect the true fundamental (intrinsic) value of securities, is incorrect. They attribute a large role in the determination of stock prices to market psychology and to the institutional structure of the marketplace. However, nothing in this view contradicts the basic reasoning behind the weaker version of the efficient market hypothesis—that market participants eliminate unexploited profit opportunities. Even though stock market prices may not always solely reflect market fundamentals, as long as the stock market crash was unpredictable, many of the basic lessons of the efficient market hypothesis hold.

Some financial economists have come up with theories of what they call *rational bubbles* to explain events such as the stock market crash. A **bubble** is a situation in which the price of an asset differs from its fundamental market value. In a rational bubble, investors can have expectations that a bubble is occurring because the asset price is above its fundamental value but continue to hold the asset anyway. They might do this because they believe that someone else will buy the asset for a higher price in the future. In a rational bubble, asset prices can therefore deviate from their fundamental value for a long time because the bursting of the bubble cannot be predicted and so there are no unexploited profit opportunities.

However, other financial economists believe that the stock market crash of 1987 suggests that there may be unexploited profit opportunities and that even the weaker version of the efficient market hypothesis may be fundamentally flawed. The controversy over whether capital markets are efficient continues.

SUMMARY

1. Stocks are valued as the present value of the dividends. Unfortunately, we do not know very precisely what these dividends will be. This introduces a great deal of error to the valuation process. The Gordon growth model is a simplified method of computing stock value that depends on the assumption that the dividends are growing at a constant rate forever. Given our uncertainty regarding future dividends, this assumption is often the best we can do.
2. An alternative method for estimating stock price is to multiply the firm's earnings per share times the industry price earnings ratio. This ratio can be adjusted up or down to reflect specific characteristics of the firm.
3. The interaction among traders in the market is what actually sets prices on a day-to-day basis. The trader who values the security the most either because of less uncertainty about the cash flows or because of greater estimated cash flows will be willing to pay the most. As new information is released, investors will revise their estimates of the true value of the security and will either buy or sell it depending upon how the market price compares with their estimated valuation. Because small changes in estimated growth rates or required return result in large changes in price, it is not surprising that the markets are often volatile.
4. The efficient market hypothesis states that current security prices will fully reflect all available information because in an efficient market, all unexploited profit opportunities are eliminated. The elimination of unexploited profit opportunities necessary for a financial market to be efficient does not require that all market participants be well informed.
5. The evidence on the efficient market hypothesis is quite mixed. Early evidence on the performance of investment analysts and mutual funds, whether stock prices reflect publicly available information, the random-walk behaviour of stock prices, and the success of so-called technical analysis was quite favourable to the efficient market hypothesis. However, in recent years, evidence on the small-firm effect, the January effect, market overreaction, excessive volatility, mean reversion, and new information is not always immediately incorporated into stock prices, and chaotic dynamics suggest that the hypothesis may not always be entirely correct. The evidence seems to suggest that the efficient market hypothesis may be a reasonable starting point for evaluating

behaviour in financial markets but may not be generalizable to all behaviour in financial markets.

6. The efficient market hypothesis indicates that hot tips, investment advisers' published recommendations, and technical analysis cannot help an investor out-perform the market. The prescription for investors is to pursue a buy-and-hold strategy—purchase stocks and hold them for long periods. Empirical evidence generally supports these implications of the efficient market hypothesis in the stock market.

7. The stock market crash of 1987 has convinced many financial economists that the stronger version of the efficient market hypothesis, which states that asset prices reflect the true fundamental (intrinsic) value of securities, is incorrect. It is less clear that the stock market crash shows that the weaker version of the efficient market hypothesis is wrong. Even if the stock market were driven by factors other than fundamentals, the crash does not clearly demonstrate that many of the basic lessons of the efficient market hypothesis are no longer valid as long as the crash could not have been predicted.

KEY TERMS

QUESTIONS AND PROBLEMS

1. What basic principle of finance can be applied to the valuation of any investment asset?

*2. Identify the cash flows available to an investor in stock. How reliably can these cash flows be estimated? Compare the problem of estimating stock cash flows with estimating bond cash flows. Which security would you predict to be more volatile?

3. Compute the price of a share of stock that pays a $1 per year dividend and that you expect to be able to sell in one year for $20, assuming you require a 15% return.

*4. After careful analysis, you have determined that a firm's dividends should grow at 7% on average in the foreseeable future. Its last dividend was $3. Compute the current price of this stock, assuming the required return is 18%.

5. The projected earnings per share for Risky Ventures Ltd. is $3.50. The average PE ratio for the industry comprising Risky Ventures' closest competitors is 21. After careful analysis, you decide that Risky Ventures is a little more risky than average, so decide a PE ratio of 23 better reflects the market's perception of the firm. Estimate the current price of the firm's stock.

*6. "Forecasters' predictions of inflation are notoriously inaccurate, so their expectations of inflation cannot be rational." Is this statement true, false, or uncertain? Explain your answer.

7. "Whenever it is snowing when Joe Commuter gets up in the morning, he misjudges how long it will take him to drive to work. Otherwise, his expectations of the driving time are perfectly accurate. Considering that it snows only once every ten years where Joe lives, Joe's expectations are almost always perfectly accurate." Are Joe's expectations rational? Why or why not?

*8. If a forecaster spends hours every day studying data to forecast interest rates but his expectations are not as accurate as predicting that tomorrow's interest rates will be identical to today's interest rate, are his expectations rational?

9. "If stock prices did not follow a random walk, there would be unexploited profit opportunities in the market." Is this statement true, false, or uncertain? Explain your answer.

*10. Suppose that increases in the money supply lead to a rise in stock prices. Does this mean that when you see that the money supply has had a sharp rise in the past week, you should go out and buy stocks? Why or why not?

11. If the public expects a corporation to lose $5 a share this quarter and it actually loses $4, which is still the

largest loss in the history of the company, what does the efficient market hypothesis say will happen to the price of the stock when the $4 loss is announced?

***12.** If I read in *The Globe and Mail: Report on Business* that the "smart money" on Bay Street expects stock prices to fall, should I follow that lead and sell all my stocks?

13. If my broker has been right in her five previous buy and sell recommendations, should I continue listening to her advice?

***14.** Can a person with rational expectations expect the price of IBM to rise by 10% in the next month?

15. "If most participants in the stock market do not follow what is happening to the monetary aggregates, prices of common stocks will not fully reflect information about them." Is this statement true, false, or uncertain? Explain your answer.

***16.** "An efficient market is one in which no one ever profits from having better information than the rest." Is this statement true, false, or uncertain? Explain your answer.

17. If higher money growth is associated with higher future inflation and if announced money growth turns out to be extremely high but is still less than the market expected, what do you think would happen to long-term bond prices?

***18.** "Foreign exchange rates, like stock prices, should follow a random walk." Is this statement true, false, or uncertain? Explain your answer.

19. Can we expect the value of the dollar to rise by 2% next week if our expectations are rational?

***20.** "Human fear is the source of stock market crashes, so these crashes indicate that expectations in the stock market cannot be rational." Is this statement true, false, or uncertain? Explain your answer.

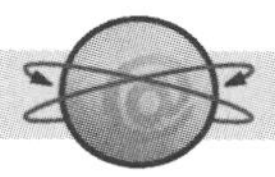

WEB EXERCISES

The Stock Market and the Efficient Market Hypothesis

1. Visit http://www.forecasts.org/data/index.htm. Click on "Stock Index Data" at the very top of the page. Now choose "International Stock Indices-Monthly." Review the indices for the Nikkei 225, DAX, Hang Seng, FTSE 100, and S&P/TSX Composite. Which index appears most volatile? In which index would you have rather invested in 1990 if the investment had been allowed to compound until now?
2. The Internet is a great source of information on stock prices and stock price movements. There are many sites that provide up-to-the minute data on stock market indices. One of the best is found at http://finance.lycos.com/home/livecharts. This site provides free real-time streaming of stock market data. Click on the $indu to have the chart display the Dow Jones Industrial Average. Look at the stock trend over various intervals by adjusting the update frequency (click on INT at the top of the chart). Have stock prices been going up or down over the last day, week, month, and year?

Chapter 11 The Mortgage Markets

Preview

Part of the classic Canadian dream is to own your own home. With the price of the average house now close to $200 000, few of us could hope to do this until late in life if we were not able to borrow the bulk of the purchase price. Similarly, businesses rely on borrowed capital far more than on equity investment to finance their growth. Many small firms do not have access to the bond market and must find alternative sources of funds. Consider the state of the mortgage loan markets 100 years ago. They were organized mostly to accommodate the needs of businesses and the very wealthy. Much has changed since then. The purpose of this chapter is to discuss these changes.

Chapter 8 discussed the *money markets,* the markets for short-term funds. Chapter 9 discussed the *capital markets,* the markets for long-term funds. This chapter discusses the *mortgage markets,* where borrowers—individuals, businesses, and governments—can obtain long-term collateralized loans. From one perspective, the mortgage markets form a subcategory of the capital markets because mortgages involve long-term funds. But the mortgage markets differ from the stock and bond markets in important ways. First, the usual borrowers in the capital markets are government entities and businesses, whereas the usual borrowers in the mortgage markets are individuals. Second, mortgage loans are made for varying amounts and maturities, depending on the borrowers' needs, features that cause problems for developing a secondary market.

In this chapter we will identify the characteristics of typical residential mortgages, discuss the usual term and types of mortgages available, and review who provides and services these loans. We will also discuss the growth of the mortgage-backed security market.

WHAT ARE MORTGAGES?

A **mortgage** is a long-term loan secured by real estate. A developer may obtain a mortgage loan to finance the construction of an office building, or a family may obtain a mortgage loan to finance the purchase of a home. In either case, the loan is

amortized: The borrower pays it off over time in some combination of principal and interest payments that result in full payment of the debt by maturity. Because most mortgage loans finance residential home purchases, that will be the primary focus of this chapter.

One way to understand the modern mortgage is to review its history. Originally, banks were prevented from funding mortgages so that they wouldn't tie up their funds in long-term loans. As a result, most mortgage contracts were arranged between individuals, usually with the help of a lawyer who brought the parties together and drew up the papers. Such loans were generally available only to the wealthy and socially connected. As the demand for long-term funds increased, however, more mortgage brokers surfaced.

The mortgage market was devastated by the Great Depression in the 1930s. Millions of borrowers were without work and were unable to make their loan payments. This led to foreclosures and land sales that caused property values to collapse. Mortgage-lending institutions were hit hard, and many failed. One reason that so many borrowers defaulted on their loans was the type of mortgage loan they had. Most mortgages in this period were **balloon loans**: The borrower paid only interest for three to five years, at which time the entire loan amount became due. The lender was usually willing to renew the debt with some reduction in principal. However, if the borrower were unemployed, the lender would not renew, and the borrower would default.

As part of the recovery program from the Depression, the federal government stepped in and restructured the mortgage market, by introducing the Dominion Housing Act in 1935, to be administered on behalf of the federal government by the National Housing Administration, a responsibility of the department of finance. The Act, considered to be one of the most important pieces of housing legislation in Canada, introduced joint mortgage lending by the government and approved private institutional lenders (mainly trust and mortgage loan companies and credit unions and *caisses populaires*). In particular, the government provided 20% of the loan and the private lenders provided between 50% and 60%, for a maximum loan-to-value ratio between 70% and 80%. Moreover, the Dominion Housing Act introduced the now standard amortization plan, which allowed borrowers to repay their loans over long periods by making equal monthly payments. It is no surprise that these new types of loans were very popular and the high demand helped restore the health of the mortgage industry.

The next significant piece of Canadian housing legislation was the National Housing Act of 1938. This Act restated the Dominion Housing Act of 1935 with one exception; it fixed the government's portion of the loan at 25%, irrespective of the level of the total loan, in an attempt to prevent private lenders from promoting loans with low loan-to-value ratios. The outbreak of World War II, however, changed the economic priorities of the federal government and restricted the use of the Act's provisions. To deal with this problem and the low level of lending activity before and during World War II, the government introduced the National Housing Act of 1944 and established the Canada Mortgage and Housing Corporation (CMHC) in 1945 to administer the new Act on behalf of the federal government. As stated in the National Housing Act, the mandate of the CMHC is "[t]o promote the construction of new houses, the repair and modernization of existing houses, and the improvement of housing and living conditions."

During this period, the primary lenders in the residential mortgage market were trust and mortgage loan companies and credit unions and *caisses populaires*. It was the revisions in the National Housing Act and the Bank Act in 1954 that allowed chartered banks to make insured mortgage loans. Moreover, the 1967 revision of the Bank Act extended the authority of chartered banks to make conventional residential mortgage loans (to be discussed in detail later in this chapter) and banks have entered this market very aggressively in the last two to three decades. In fact, their market share of residential mortgages has increased from about 50% in 1989 to about 75% in 2002.

CHARACTERISTICS OF THE RESIDENTIAL MORTGAGE

The modern mortgage lender has continued to refine the long-term loan to make it more desirable to borrowers. Even in the past 20 years, both the nature of the lenders and the instruments have undergone substantial changes. One of the biggest changes is the development of an active secondary market for mortgage contracts. We will examine the nature of mortgage loan contracts and then look at their secondary market.

The mortgage market has become very competitive in recent years. Twenty years ago, trust and mortgage loan companies, credit unions, and *caisses populaires* originated most mortgage loans. Currently, there are many loan production offices that compete in real estate financing. Some of these offices are subsidiaries of banks, and others are independently owned. As a result of the competition for mortgage loans, borrowers can choose from a variety of terms and options.

Mortgage Interest Rates

Track mortgage rates and shop for mortgage rates in different financial institutions at www.canadamortgage.com

The interest rate borrowers pay on their mortgages is probably the most important factor in their decision of how much and from whom to borrow. The interest rate on the loan is determined by three factors: current long-term market rates, the life (term) of the mortgage, and the number of discount points paid.

1. *Market rates.* Long-term market rates are determined by the supply of and demand for long-term funds, which are in turn influenced by a number of global, national, and regional factors. As Figure 1 shows, mortgage rates tend to stay above the less risky Canada bonds most of the time but tend to track along with them.

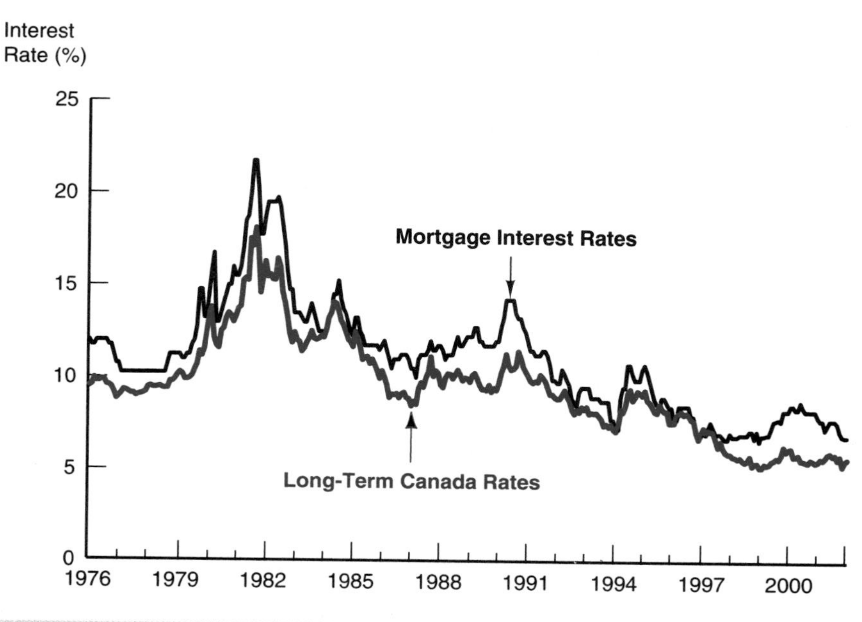

FIGURE 1 Mortgage Rates and Long-Term Canada Bond Interest Rates, 1976–2002

Source: Statistics Canada CANSIM II series V122544 and V122521

2. *Term.* Longer-term mortgages have higher interest rates than shorter-term mortgages. The usual mortgage lifetime is 25 years. Because interest-rate risk falls as the term to maturity decreases, the interest rate on short-term loans will be substantially less than on the 25-year loan.
3. *Incentives and rate discounting.* The competition among mortgage lenders has resulted in incentive offerings and rate discounting in order to attract borrowers. For example, some mortgage lenders may reduce the interest rate on the loan, some may be offering cash back based on the principal amount, and others may offer to pay the closing costs such as legal, appraisal, and inspection fees. In comparing the alternative incentives, borrowers must determine whether the reduced interest rate over the life of the loan fully compensates for the up-front cash back. To make this determination, borrowers must take into account how long they will hold on to the loan.

Application — Getting the Best Deal

Suppose that you are offered two loan alternatives. In the first, you are offered one percentage point off the current posted interest rate of 11%. In the second, you are offered no rate discounting but cash back of 2% of your mortgage amount. Which alternative do you choose?

To answer this question you must compute the actual interest rate on the loan, known as the **effective interest rate**. Assuming that the loan is compounded semi-annually (which is the case with fixed-rate loans in Canada), you pay 5% per six months on the reduced-rate loan. Because of the compounding, the effective annual rate is greater than the simple annual rate of 10%. The effective annual rate on the reduced-rate loan can be calculated as

$$\begin{aligned} \text{Effective annual rate} &= [1 + i/m]^n - 1 \\ &= (1 + 0.10/2]^2 - 1 \\ &= 1.1025 - 1 \\ &= 0.1025 \text{ or } 10.25\% \end{aligned}$$

Because of semi-annual compounding, a 10% annual percentage rate has an effective annual rate of 10.25%.[1] The application on page 278 discusses how mortgage loan payments are computed.

Now compute the effective annual rate on the 2% cash back loan. Assuming that this is a $100 000 loan, the cash back offer results in $2000 in your pocket. However, your payment is computed on the $100 000 and at the higher interest rate of 11%. In fact, in this case the effective annual rate is 11.30%. As a result of the 2% cash back, the effective annual rate has increased from 10.25% to 11.30%. On the surface, it would seem like a good idea to choose the reduced-rate loan. The problem is that these calculations were made assuming the loan will be held for 25 years. What happens if you sell the house before the loan matures? If the loan is paid off early, the borrower will benefit from the lower interest rate for a shorter time, and the cash back is spread over a shorter period of time.

Loan Terms

Mortgage loan contracts contain many legal and financial terms, most of which protect the lender from financial loss.

[1] Alternatively, the effective annual interest rate can be calculated using a financial calculator as follows: Input "10," "EFF," "2," and " =" to get 10.25.

Collateral One characteristic common to mortgage loans is the requirement that collateral, usually the real estate being financed, be pledged as security. The lending institution will place a **lien** against the property, and this remains in effect until the loan is paid off. A lien is a public record that attaches to the title of the property, advising that the property is security for a loan, and it gives the lender the right to sell the property if the underlying loan defaults.

No one can buy the property and obtain clear title to it without paying off this lien. For example, if you purchased a piece of property with a loan secured by a lien, the lender would file notice of this lien at the public recorder's office. The lien gives notice to the world that if there is a default on the loan, the lender has the right to seize the property. If you try to sell the property without paying off the loan, the lien would remain attached to the title or deed to the property. Since the lender can take the property away from whomever owns it, no one would buy it unless you paid off the loan. The existence of liens against real estate explains why a title search is an important part of any mortgage loan transaction. During the title search, a lawyer or title company searches the public record for any liens. Title insurance is then sold that guarantees the buyer that the property is free of *encumbrances,* any questions about the state of the title to the property, including the existence of liens.

Down Payments To obtain a mortgage loan, the lender also requires the borrower to make a **down payment** on the property, that is, to pay a portion of the purchase price. The balance of the purchase price is paid by the *loan proceeds.* Down payments (like liens) are intended to make the borrower less likely to default on the loan. A borrower who does not make a down payment could walk away from the house and the loan and lose nothing. Furthermore, if real estate prices drop even a small amount, the balance due on the loan will exceed the value of the collateral. As we discussed in Chapter 2, the down payment reduces *moral hazard* for the borrower. The amount of the down payment depends on the type of mortgage loan. Many lenders require that the borrower pay 5% of the purchase price; in other situations, up to 25% may be required.

Mortgage Default Insurance Another way that lenders protect themselves against default is by requiring the borrower to purchase **mortgage default insurance**. In fact, if the amount of the loan is more than 75% of the purchase price, the mortgage must be insured against default by CMHC or an approved private insurer. Mortgage default insurance is an insurance policy that guarantees to make up any discrepancy between the value of the property and the loan amount, should a default occur.

For example, if the balance on your loan was $120 000 at the time of default and the property was worth only $100 000, mortgage default insurance would pay the lending institution $20 000. The default still appears on the credit record of the borrower, but the lender avoids sustaining the loss. As already noted, mortgage default insurance is usually required on loans that have less than a 25% down payment and is added to the principal of the loan. If the loan-to-value ratio falls because of payments being made or because the value of the property increases, the borrower can request that the mortgage default insurance requirement be dropped. Mortgage default insurance usually costs between $20 and $30 per month for a $100 000 loan.

Borrower Qualification Before granting a mortgage loan, the lender will determine whether the borrower qualifies for it. Qualifying for a mortgage loan is different from qualifying for a bank loan because most lenders sell their mortgage loans to one of the government agencies in the secondary mortgage market. These agencies establish very precise guidelines that must be followed before they will accept the loan. If the lender gives a mortgage loan to a borrower who does not fit these guidelines, the lender may not be able to resell the loan. That ties up the lender's funds. Banks can be more flexible with loans that will be kept on the bank's own books.

The rules for qualifying a borrower are complex and constantly changing, but a rule of thumb is that the **gross debt service ratio (GDS)** should not exceed 32%. That is, the mortgage loan payment, including taxes, insurance, and heating costs, should not exceed 32% of gross (before tax) monthly income. For example, if gross monthly income is $5000, then the monthly housing expenses should not exceed $1600 (= $5000 × 0.32). Furthermore, the **total debt service ratio (TDS)** should not exceed 40%—the sum of the monthly payments on all loans to the borrower, including car loans and credit cards, cannot exceed 40% of gross monthly income. A borrower who fails this income test can pay off some of the outstanding debt, increase the down payment, or find a less expensive house to buy.

Mortgage Loan Amortization

Mortgage loan borrowers agree to pay a monthly amount of principal and interest that will fully amortize the loan by its maturity. "Fully amortize" means that the payments will pay off the outstanding indebtedness by the time the loan matures. During the early years of the loan, the lender applies most of the payment to the interest on the loan and a small amount to the outstanding principal balance. Many borrowers are surprised to find that after years of making payments, their loan balance has not dropped appreciably.

Table 1 shows the distribution of principal and interest for a 30-year, $130 000 loan at 8.5% interest. Only $78.75 of the first payment is applied to reduce the loan balance. At the end of two years, the balance due is $127 947, and at the end of five years, the balance due is $124 137. Put another way, of $59 975.40 in loan payments made during the first five years, only $5862.69 is applied to the principal. Over the life of the $130 000 loan, a total of $229 850 in interest will be paid.

If the loan in Table 1 had been financed for 15 years instead of for 30, the payment would have increased by about $280 per month to $1279.59, but the interest savings over the life of the loan would be nearly $130 000. It is no wonder why so many borrowers prefer the shorter-term loans.

Application **Computing the Payment on Mortgage Loans**

We can apply the techniques for computing loan payments introduced in Chapter 3 to computing the payment on mortgage loans. Suppose that you have graduated and want to buy a condominium instead of renting an apartment. The condo

TABLE 1 Amortization of a 30-Year, $130 000 Loan at 8.5%

Payment Number	Beginning Balance of Loan	Monthly Payment	Amount Applied to Interest	Amount Applied to Principal	Ending Balance of Loan
1	130 000.00	999.59	920.83	78.76	129 921.24
24	128 040.25	999.59	906.95	92.64	127 947.62
60	124 256.74	999.59	880.15	119.44	124 137.31
120	115 365.63	999.59	817.17	182.42	115 183.22
180	101 786.23	999.59	720.99	278.60	101 507.63
240	81 046.41	999.59	574.08	425.51	80 620.90
360	991.77	999.59	7.82	991.77	0

costs \$100 000, and a 5% down payment is required by your mortgage lender. How much will your monthly loan payment be?

To compute fixed-amount loan payments, we recognize that the lender must equate the present value of the stream of payments you will pay to the amount of the loan. In equation form,

$$\text{Loan amount} = \frac{P}{1+i} + \frac{P}{(1+i)^2} + \frac{P}{(1+i)^3} + \cdots + \frac{P}{(1+i)^n} \tag{1}$$

where

P = fixed payment
i = interest rate on the loan
n = term of the loan

Since the present value of having payments for n years in the amount of P equals the present value of a consol bond with its first payment in year 1 minus the present value of a consol bond with its first payment in year n +1, Equation 1 can be written as

$$\text{Loan amount} = \frac{P}{i} - \frac{P/i}{(i+1)^n} \tag{2}$$

where

$\frac{P}{i}$ = present value of a consol bond (perpetuity) with its first payment in year 1

$\frac{P/i}{(i+1)^n}$ = present value of a consol bond with its first payment in year $n + 1$

Equation 2 can also be written as

$$\text{Loan amount} = P\left[\frac{1}{i} - \frac{1}{i(1+i)^n}\right] \tag{3}$$

which can be solved for P to find the fixed payment.

An alternative form of Equation 3, which takes advantage of present value tables included at the end of most introductory finance texts, is

$$\text{Loan amount} = P\,(PVIFA_{i,n}) \tag{4}$$

where

$$PVIFA_{i,n} = \left[\frac{1}{i} - \frac{1}{i(1+i)^n}\right]$$

is the present value interest factor with an interest rate of i for n periods.

The fixed payment P can then be found either by using Equation 3 and doing the calculations or by looking up the factor for the term and interest rate on the loan in which you are interested and using Equation 4. However, most factor tables include only 50 or 60 periods, so we cannot use Equation 4 to compute the payment on 30-year loans with monthly payments ($30 \times 12 = 360$ periods). Instead, a close approximation of the monthly payment can be found by computing the annual payment and dividing by 12.

EXAMPLE 1: Mortgage Loans

You obtain a 30-year loan at 8% on the \$95 000 you need to finance your new condo. The price of the condo is \$100 000 minus a \$5000 down payment. Use Table 2 and Equation 4 to calculate the fixed payment on the loan.

TABLE 2 Present Value Interest Factor at Various Rates of Interest

Payment Periods	Interest Rate 5%	6%	7%	8%	9%	10%
15	10.3797	9.7122	9.1079	8.5595	8.0607	7.6061
20	12.4622	11.4699	10.5940	9.8181	9.1285	8.5136
25	14.0939	12.7834	11.6536	10.6748	9.8226	9.0770
30	15.3725	13.7648	12.4090	11.2578	9.8226	9.0770

Solution

The fixed payment on the loan would be $8439 per year.

$$\text{Loan amount} = P\ (PVIFA_{i,n})$$

where

$$\text{Loan amount} = \text{amount loaned by the bank} = \$95\ 000$$
$$i = \text{interest rate on the loan} = 0.08$$
$$n = \text{term of the loan} = 30$$

Thus

$$\$95\ 000 = P(PVIFA_{8\%,30})$$
$$\$95\ 000 = P(11.2578)$$
$$P = \frac{\$95\ 000}{11.2578}$$
$$P = \$8439$$

To find the present value interest factor in Table 2, pick out the payment period in the left-hand column and then move across the row to the entry in the column for the interest rate on the loan. For a 30-year loan at 8%, the present value interest factor is 11.2578.

To solve using a financial calculator:

$$N = \text{number of periods} = 30\text{ years} = 30$$
$$PV = \text{amount of the loan (LV)} = -95\ 000$$
$$FV = \text{amount of the loan after 30 years} = 0$$
$$\%i = \text{stated interest rate} = 8$$

Then push the CPT and PMT buttons = fixed payment (P) = $8439.

To find the fixed monthly payment on the loan, divide the fixed annual payment by 12,

$$\frac{\$8439}{12\text{ months}} = \$703\text{ per month}$$

Alternatively, solve using the financial calculator:

$$N = \text{number of periods} = 30\text{ years} \times 12\text{ months} = 360$$
$$PV = \text{amount of the loan (LV)} = -95\ 000$$
$$FV = \text{amount of the loan after 30 years} = 0$$
$$\%i = \text{monthly interest rate} = 8/12\text{ months} = 0.6667$$

Then push the CPT and PMT buttons to get the fixed monthly payment of $697.

(Note: small differences between the table solution and the calculator solution are due to rounding.)

Mortgage Calculations in Canada

To understand mortgage calculations in Canada, you have to keep in mind that Canadian cost-of-borrowing disclosure regulations require financial institutions to quote mortgage rates with semi-annual compounding on fixed-rate mortgage loans and with monthly compounding on variable-rate loans.

We already discussed mortgage loans compounded monthly in example 1. Let us now consider a 30-year, $95 000 fixed-rate loan at 8% with semi-annual compounding. To find the fixed monthly payment, we first calculate the effective annual interest rate. As already noted, since the loan is compounded semi-annually, you pay 4% per six months. Because of the compounding this semi-annual rate corresponds to an effective annual rate that is greater than the stated annual rate of 8%. We convert the stated annual rate of 8% to an effective annual rate as follows:

$$\begin{aligned}\text{Effective annual rate} &= [1 + i/m]^m - 1\\ &= (1 + 0.08/2]^2 - 1\\ &= 1.0816 - 1\\ &= 0.0816 \text{ or } 8.16\%\end{aligned}$$

To find the fixed monthly payment, we need to find the effective monthly rate, also known as the annual percentage rate (APR), and then use a financial calculator. The effective monthly rate can be found as[2]

$$\begin{aligned}\text{Effective monthly rate} &= [1 + \text{effective annual rate}]^{1/m} - 1\\ &= [1 + 0.0816]^{1/12} - 1\\ &= 1.006558 - 1\\ &= 0.006558 \text{ or } 0.6558\%\end{aligned}$$

The fixed monthly payment then is, using a financial calculator:

N = number of periods = 30 years × 12 months = 360

PV = amount of the loan (LV) = −95 000

FV = amount of the loan after 30 years = 0

$\%i$ = effective monthly interest rate = 0.6558

Push the CPT and PMT buttons to get P = $688.46 per month.

In the case of weekly payments, the fixed weekly payment can be found by first finding the effective weekly rate as

$$\begin{aligned}\text{Effective monthly rate} &= [1 + \text{effective annual rate}]^{1/m} - 1\\ &= [1 + 0.0816]^{1/52} - 1\\ &= 1.0015096 - 1\\ &= 0.001509 \text{ or } 0.1509\%\end{aligned}$$

[2] Alternatively, the effective monthly interest rate can be calculated using a financial calculator as follows: Input "8.16," "APR," "12," "=," and divide the result by 12.

The fixed weekly payment then is, using a financial calculator:

N = number of periods = 30 years × 52 weeks = 1560

PV = amount of the loan (LV) = −95 000

FV = amount of the loan after 30 years = 0

$\%i$ = effective weekly interest rate = 0.1509

Push the CPT and PMT buttons to get P = \$158.43 per week.

TYPES OF MORTGAGE LOANS

A number of types of mortgage loans are available in the market. Different borrowers may qualify for different ones. A skilled mortgage banker can help find the best type of mortgage loan for each particular situation.

Insured and Conventional Mortgages

Mortgages are classified as either *insured* or *conventional*. **Insured mortgages** (also known as **high-ratio mortgages**) are originated by banks or other mortgage lenders but are insured against default by the federal government through the CMHC or an approved private insurer. Those issuing high-ratio mortgages pay a one-time insurance premium to the insurer that is usually added to the principal amount of the mortgage loan; the insurance premium ranges between 0.5% and 3.75% of the principal amount of the mortgage loan, depending on the size of the loan. The insurer guarantees that it will pay off the lender if the borrower defaults. One important advantage to a borrower who qualifies for an insured mortgage loan is that a very low down payment is required.

Conventional mortgages are originated by the same sources as high-ratio mortgages but are not guaranteed. They require a down payment of 25% of the appraised value or purchase price of the property.

Fixed- and Variable-Rate Mortgages

In standard mortgage contracts, borrowers agree to make regular payments on the principal and interest they owe to lenders. As we saw earlier, the interest rate significantly affects the size of this monthly payment. In **fixed-rate mortgages**, the interest rate and the monthly payment do not vary over the term of the mortgage. The benefit of choosing a fixed-rate mortgage is that it protects the borrower if interest rates rise. However, the borrower loses if interest rates fall.

The interest rate on **variable-rate mortgages** is tied to some market interest rate and therefore changes over time as market conditions change. Variable-rate mortgages have terms of one or two years. Moreover, in a variable-rate mortgage, although the interest rate may change from month to month, the monthly payments can be fixed for up to two years in advance. In this case, if interest rates go down, more of the fixed monthly payment is applied toward the principal. If interest rates go up, more is applied toward the interest.

Variable-rate mortgages usually have limits, called caps, on how high (or low) the interest rate can move in one year and during the term of the loan. A typical variable-rate mortgage might tie the interest rate to the prime rate plus 2%, with caps of 2% per year and 6% over the term of the mortgage. Caps make variable-rate mortgages more palatable to borrowers.

Borrowers tend to prefer fixed-rate loans to variable-rate loans because variable-rate loans may cause financial hardship if interest rates rise. However, fixed-rate borrowers do not benefit if rates fall unless they are willing to **refinance** their mortgage (pay it off by obtaining a new mortgage at a lower interest rate). The fact that individuals are risk-averse means that fear of hardship most often overwhelms anticipation of savings.

Lenders, by contrast, prefer variable-rate loans because variable-rate loans lessen interest-rate risk. Recall from Chapter 3 that interest-rate risk is the risk that rising interest rates will cause the value of debt instruments to fall. The effect on the value of the debt is greatest when the debt has a long term to maturity. Since mortgages are usually long-term, their value is very sensitive to interest-rate movements. Lending institutions can reduce the sensitivity of their portfolios by making variable-rate loans instead of standard fixed-rate loans.

Seeing that lenders prefer variable-rate mortgages and borrowers prefer fixed-rate mortgages, lenders must entice borrowers by offering lower initial interest rates on variable-rate mortgages than on fixed-rate loans. For example, on June 4, 2002, the reported interest rate for 30-year fixed-rate mortgage loans was 9.3%. The rate at that time for adjustable-rate mortgages was 4.25%. The rate on the variable-rate mortgage would have to rise 5.05% before the borrower of the variable-rate mortgage would be in a worse position than the fixed-rate borrower.

Other Types of Mortgages

As the market for mortgage loans becomes more competitive, lenders are offering more innovative mortgage contracts in an effort to attract borrowers. We discuss some of these mortgages here.

Open and Closed Mortgages Variable-rate mortgages are open, in the sense that you can pay off as much of the principal as you want, or convert to a fixed-rate mortgage, at any time, without penalty. Fixed-rate mortgages can be either open or closed. A closed mortgage is for a fixed term and with fixed conditions. Open fixed-rate mortgages usually have terms of 6 months and 1 year whereas closed fixed-rate mortgages have terms of 6 months to 25 years. In Canada, most closed fixed-rate mortgages also offer some cost-free, partial prepayment privileges.

Second Mortgages Second mortgages are loans that are secured by the same real estate that is used to secure the first mortgage. The second mortgage is junior to the original loan. This means that should a default occur, the second mortgage holder will be paid only after the original loan has been paid off, if sufficient funds remain. Because second mortgages are riskier than first mortgages, higher interest rates are usually charged for second mortgages.

Second mortgages give borrowers a way to use the equity they have in their homes as security for another loan. An alternative to the second mortgage would be to refinance the home at a higher loan amount than is currently owed. The cost of obtaining a second mortgage is often much lower than refinancing. Second mortgages have all but been replaced by home equity lines of credit, which allow borrowers to pay interest only on the amount of money they are actually using.

In the United States, second mortgages also take advantage of one of the few remaining tax deductions available to the middle class. The interest on loans secured by residential real estate is tax deductible (the tax laws allow borrowers to deduct the interest on the primary residence and one vacation home). No other kind of consumer loan has this tax deduction. Many banks in the United States now offer lines of credit secured by second mortgages. In most cases, the value of the security is not of great interest to the bank. Consumers prefer that the line of credit be secured so that they can deduct the interest on the loan from their taxes.

Go to www.chip.ca for further information about the CHIP.

Reverse Mortgages The **reverse mortgage** is an innovative method for retired people to live on the equity they have in their homes. The reverse mortgage was introduced in Canada in 1986, when the Canadian Home Income Plan (CHIP) was founded to allow Canadian homeowners age 62 and older to unlock up to 40% of the equity in their homes. Reverse mortgages have been around for more than 50 years in the United Kingdom and more than 25 years in the United States.

The contract for a reverse mortgage has the bank advancing funds as a cash lump sum, on a guaranteed monthly schedule, or a combination of the two. The increasing-balance loan is secured by the real estate. The borrower does not make any payments against the loan and continues to own the property and therefore benefit from any future appreciation in its value. When the borrower dies, the borrower's estate sells the property to retire the debt. In Canada, the CHIP reverse mortgage has a ruling from Canada Customs and Revenue Agency (formerly Revenue Canada) that considers the income received from the reverse mortgage taxable but the accumulated interest on the mortgage loan deductible.

The advantage of the reverse mortgage is that it allows retired people to use the equity in their homes without the necessity of selling it. For retirees in need of supplemental funds to meet living expenses, the reverse mortgage can be a desirable option.

The various mortgage types are summarized in Table 3.

TABLE 3 Summary of Mortgage Types

Conventional mortgage	Loan is not guaranteed; 25% or more down payment
Insured mortgage	Loan is guaranteed by CMHC or an approved private insurer; low down payment
Variable-rate mortgage	Interest rate is tied to some other rate and is adjusted periodically; size of adjustment could be subject to annual limits
Open mortgage	Allows the borrower to pay off some or all of the loan at any time, at no cost
Closed mortgage	Provides the security of locking in the rate of interest for a longer term
Second mortgage	Loan is secured by a second lien against the real estate; often used for lines of credit or home improvement loans
Reverse mortgage	Lender disburses a monthly payment to the borrower on an increasing-balance loan; loan comes due when the real estate is sold

Looking Ahead

To fully appreciate the forces at work in the mortgage market, in this section we discuss some mortgage loans available in the United States. Given recent trends, and the presence of global players in Canadian financial markets, it is possible that some of these types of mortgage loans will soon be available in Canada.

Graduated-Payment Mortgages Graduated-payment mortgages are useful for homebuyers who expect their incomes to rise. The graduated-payment mortgage has lower payments in the first few years; then the payments rise. The early payments may not even be sufficient to cover the interest due, in which case the principal balance increases. As time passes, the borrower expects income to increase so that the higher payment will not be a burden.

The advantage of the graduated-payment mortgage is that borrowers will qualify for a larger loan than if they requested a conventional mortgage. This may help buyers purchase adequate housing now and avoid the need to move to more expensive homes as their family size increases. The disadvantage is that the payments escalate whether the borrower's income does or not.

Growing-Equity Mortgages Lenders designed the growing-equity mortgage loan to help the borrower pay off the loan in a shorter time. With a growing-equity mortgage, the payments will initially be the same as on a conventional mortgage. However, over time the payment will increase. This increase will reduce the principal more quickly than the conventional payment stream would. For example, a typical contract may call for level payments for the first two years. The payments may increase by 5% per year for the next five years, and then remain the same until maturity. The result is to reduce the life of the loan from 30 years to about 17.

Growing-equity mortgages are popular among borrowers who expect their incomes to rise in the future. It gives them the benefit of a small payment at the beginning while still retiring the debt early. Although the increase in payments is *required* in growing-equity mortgages, most mortgage loans have no prepayment penalty. This means that a borrower with a 30-year loan could create a growing-equity mortgage by simply increasing the monthly payments beyond what is required and designating that the excess be applied entirely to the principal.

The growing-equity mortgage is similar to the graduated-payment mortgage; the difference is that the goal of the graduated-payment mortgage is to help the borrower qualify by reducing the first few years' payments. The loan still pays off in 30 years. The goal of the growing-equity mortgage is to let the borrower pay off early.

Shared-Appreciation Mortgages When interest rates are high, the monthly payments on mortgage loans are also high. That prevents many borrowers from qualifying for loans. To help borrowers qualify and to keep loan volume high, lenders created the shared-appreciation mortgage. In a shared-appreciation mortgage, the lender lowers the interest rate on the mortgage in exchange for a share of any appreciation in the real estate (if the property sells for more than a stated amount, the lender is entitled to a portion of the gain). As interest rates and inflation fell in the United States in the late 1980s and into the 1990s, the popularity of these loans also diminished.

Equity Participation Mortgages In a shared-appreciation mortgage, the lender shares in the appreciation of the property. In an equity participation mortgage, an outside investor rather than the lender shares in the appreciation of the property. This investor will either provide a portion of the purchase price of the property or supplement the monthly payments. In return, the investor receives a portion of any appreciation in the property. As with shared-appreciation mortgages, the borrower benefits by being able to qualify for a larger loan than without such help.

MORTGAGE-LENDING INSTITUTIONS

As already noted, trust and mortgage loan companies and credit unions and *caisses populaires* were the primary lenders in the residential mortgage market until 1967. The 1967 revision of the Bank Act, however, extended the authority of chartered banks to make residential mortgage loans. This has led to intense competition in the residential mortgage market, with the chartered banks gaining ground over other mortgage-lending financial firms.

Figure 2 shows the share of the total residential mortgage market held by the major mortgage-lending institutions in Canada.

LOAN SERVICING

Many of the institutions making mortgage loans do not want to hold large portfolios of long-term securities. Commercial banks, for example, obtain their funds from short-term sources. Investing in long-term loans would subject them to unacceptably high interest-rate risk. Commercial banks, trust and mortgage loan companies, credit unions and *caisses populaires*, and most other loan originators

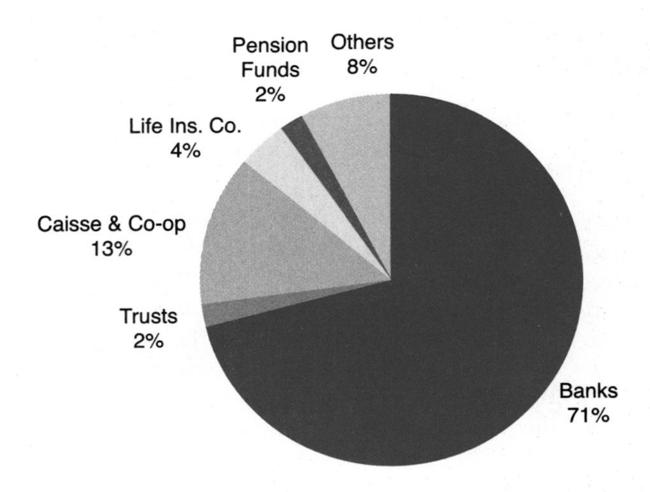

FIGURE 2 Share of the Mortgage Market Held by Major Mortgage-Lending Institutions, 2000:Q3

Source: CMHC Mortgage Trends, Fourth Quarter, 2000

do, however, make money through the fees that they earn for packaging loans for other investors to hold. Loan origination fees are typically 1% of the loan amount, though this varies with the market.

Once a loan has been made, many lenders immediately sell the loan to another investor. The borrower may not even be aware that the original lender transferred the loan. By selling the loan, the originator frees up funds that can be lent to another borrower, thereby generating additional fee income.

Some of the originators also provide servicing of the loan. The loan-servicing agent collects payments from the borrower, passes the principal and interest on to the investor, keeps required records of the transaction, and maintains **reserve accounts**. Reserve accounts are established for most mortgage loans to permit the lender to make tax and insurance payments for the borrower. Lenders prefer to make these payments because they protect the security of the loan. Loan-servicing agents usually earn 0.5% per year of the total loan amount for their efforts.

In summary, there are three distinct elements to most mortgage loans:

1. The originator packages the loan for an investor.
2. The investor holds the loan.
3. The servicing agent handles the paperwork.

One, two, or three different intermediaries may provide these functions.

Mortgage loans are increasingly obtained from the Web. Box 1 discusses this new source of mortgage loans.

SECURITIZATION OF MORTGAGES

Intermediaries still faced several problems when trying to sell mortgages. The first was that mortgages are usually too small to be wholesale instruments. The average mortgage loan is now about $130 000. This is far below the $5 million round lot established for commercial paper, for example. Many institutional investors do not want to deal in such small denominations.

BOX 1: E-FINANCE

Borrowers Shop the Web for Mortgages

One business area that has been significantly affected by the Web is mortgage banking. Historically, borrowers went to local banks, trust and mortgage loan companies, credit unions and *caisses populaires*, and mortgage banking companies to obtain mortgage loans. These offices packaged the loans and resold them. In recent years, hundreds of new Web-based mortgage banking companies have emerged.

The mortgage market is well suited to providing on-line service for several reasons. First, it is information-based and no products have to be shipped or inventoried. Second, the product (a loan) is homogeneous across providers. A borrower does not really care who provides the money as long as it is provided efficiently. Third, because home buyers tend not to obtain mortgage loans very often, they have little loyalty to any local lender. Finally, on-line lenders can often offer loans at lower cost because they can operate with lower overhead than firms that must greet the public.

The on-line mortgage market makes it much easier for borrowers to shop interest rates and terms. By filling out one application, Web service companies will provide a number of alternative loan options. Borrowers can then select the option that best suits their requirements.

On-line mortgage firms have made mortgage lending more competitive. This may lead to lower rates and better service. It has also led lenders to offer an often confusing array of loan alternatives that most borrowers have difficulty interpreting. This makes comparison shopping more difficult than simply comparing interest rates.

The second problem with selling mortgages in the secondary market was that they were not standardized. They have different times to maturity, interest rates, and contract terms. That makes it difficult to bundle a large number of mortgages together.

Third, mortgage loans are relatively costly to service. Compare the servicing a mortgage loan requires with that of a corporate bond. The lender must collect monthly payments, often pay property taxes and insurance premiums, and service reserve accounts. None of this is required if a bond is purchased.

Finally, mortgages have unknown default risk. Investors in mortgages do not want to spend a lot of time evaluating the credit of borrowers. These problems inspired the creation of the **mortgage-backed security.**

What Is a Mortgage-Backed Security?

An alternative to selling mortgages directly to investors is to create a new security backed by (secured by) a large number of mortgages assembled into what is called a *mortgage pool.* A trustee, such as a bank or a government agency, holds the mortgage pool, which serves as collateral for the new security. This process is called securitization. The most common type of mortgage-backed security is the **mortgage pass-through,** a security that has the borrower's mortgage payments pass through the trustee before being disbursed to the investors in the mortgage pass-through. If borrowers prepay their loans, investors receive more principal than expected. For example, investors may buy mortgage-backed securities on which the average interest rate is 9%. If interest rates fall and borrowers refinance at lower rates, the securities will pay off early. The possibility that mortgages will prepay and force investors to seek alternative investments, usually with lower returns, is called *prepayment risk.*

As is evident in Figure 3, the dollar volume of outstanding mortgage pools increased steadily since 1986. The reason that mortgage pools have become so popular is that they permit the creation of new securities (like mortgage pass-throughs) that make investing in mortgage loans much more efficient. For example, an institutional investor can invest in one large mortgage pass-through secured by a mortgage pool rather than investing in many small and dissimilar mortgage contracts.

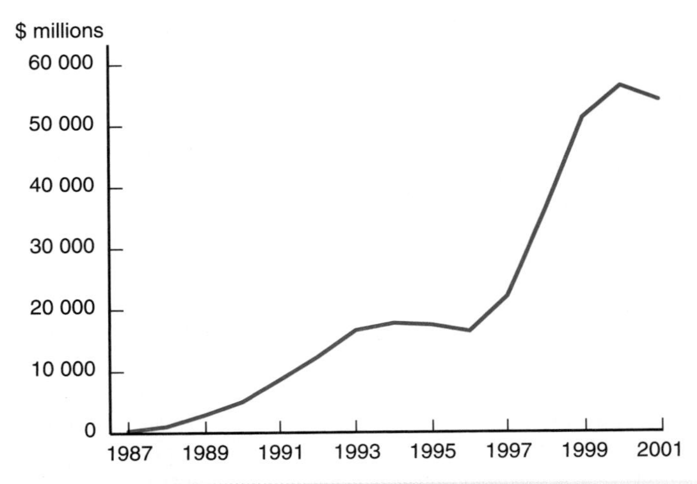

FIGURE 3 Value of Mortgage-Backed Securities, 1987–2001

Source: Statistics Canada CANSIM II series V33194

Types of Pass-Through Securities

There are several types of mortgage pass-through securities: NHA MBS pass-throughs, collateralized mortgage obligations, and private pass-throughs.

NHA MBS Pass-Throughs To stimulate mortgage lending, in late 1986, the government of Canada introduced a pass-through mortgage-backed security, patterned after the U.S. Government National Mortgage Association (GNMA, or "Ginnie Mae") and the Federal Home Loan Mortgage Corporation (FHLMC, or Freddie Mac). In particular, the Canada Mortgage and Housing Corporation (CMHC) created a new financial instrument called National Housing Act Mortgage-Backed Security (NHA MBS, or "Cannie Mae," as it is called in the investment community, after its U.S. cousins). NHA MBSs are not government of Canada securities, but they are guaranteed by the CMHC, a Crown corporation owned by the federal government. As a result, they have a very low default risk and have been very popular.

Learn more about NHA MBSs at www.cmhc.ca

Under this program, a variety of approved lenders of NHA-insured mortgages, including banks, trust and mortgage loan companies, and credit unions and *caisses populaires*, gather a group of residential first mortgages with similar interest rates and terms to maturity (usually five years) into a bundle (of, say, $1 million). These mortgages must be individually guaranteed by the CMHC under the National Housing Act. This bundle is then sold as a security to a third party, usually a large institutional investor such as a pension fund; the securities can also be bought by foreign investors and Canadians living outside Canada. When borrowers make their mortgage payments to the financial institution, the financial institution passes the payments through to the owners of the NHA MBSs by sending a cheque for the total of all payments.

Suppose, for example, that a financial institution groups together ten 25-year mortgages, each with a principal value of $100 000, into a pool of $1 million. If the interest rate on each mortgage is 8%, then the first month's payment for all of these mortgages will be $771.81, so that the financial institution will receive a payment of $7718.10 for all ten mortgages in the pool, which passes on to the holders of the pass-through securities. Moreover, if any of these mortgages is paid off, the holder of the pass-through will also receive that payment of principal. The timely payment of principal and interest is guaranteed by the federal government under the National Housing Act, even if individual borrowers default on their mortgages.

The usual minimum denomination for NHA MBSs pass-throughs is $5000. The minimum pool size is $2 million. One pool may back up many pass-through securities. The *National Post: Financial Post* reports prices and yields on various mortgage-backed securities (see "Following the Financial News").

Collateralized Mortgage Obligations (CMOs) A relatively recent innovation in the pass-through mortgage-backed securities market has been the **collateralized mortgage obligation (CMO)**. CMOs are securities classified by when prepayment is likely to occur. These differ from traditional mortgage-backed securities in that they are offered in different maturity groups. These securities help reduce prepayment risk, which is a problem with other types of pass-through securities.

CMOs backed by a particular mortgage pool are divided into classes. When principal is repaid, the investors in the first class are paid first, then those in the second class, and so on. Investors choose a class that matches their maturity requirements. For example, if they will need cash from their investment in a few years, they purchase class 1 or 2 CMOs. If they want the investment to be long-term, they can purchase CMOs from the last class.

Even when an investor purchases a CMO, there are no guarantees about how long the investment will last. If interest rates fall significantly, many borrowers will pay off their mortgages early by refinancing at lower rates.

Private Pass-Throughs In addition to the agency pass-throughs, intermediaries in the private sector have offered privately issued pass-through securities. One mortgage market opportunity available to private institutions is for mortgages larger than the maximum size set by the government. These so-called *jumbo mortgages* are often bundled into pools to back private pass-throughs.

Central Payor and Transfer Agent

Computershare Trust Company is currently the **Central Payor and Transfer Agent (CPTA)** for all NHA MBSs. The CPTA maintains the registry of NHA MBS investors, issues ownership certificates (and replaces certificates when sold or lost), collects payments of principal and interest from the MBS issuers (banks, trust and mortgage loan companies, and credit unions and *caisses populaires*), and makes payments to the registered NHA MBS investors. Moreover, the CPTA assists the CMHC in monitoring the performance of MBS issuers and maintains information useful in supporting secondary market pricing.

Mortgage-Backed Mutual Funds

Mortgage-backed mutual funds offer individual investors an opportunity to invest in mortgage-backed securities despite their large denomination. Since mortgage-backed securities offer a higher return than Canada bonds but are considered only slightly riskier, investors like them. A typical mortgage-backed mutual fund will hold a combination of pass-throughs, CMOs, and Canada bonds. Investors in these funds must be aware that when interest rates fall, many of the loans will pay off and be replaced with lower interest mortgages. As a result the fund's return will fall.

Pass-Throughs in the United States

We already mentioned the GNMA and FHLMC pass-throughs in the United States. Here we discuss these securities in a bit more detail.

GNMA Pass-Throughs Ginnie Mae began guaranteeing pass-through securities in 1968. Since then, the popularity of these instruments has increased dramatically.

In the United States, a variety of financial intermediaries, including commercial banks and mortgage companies, originate Ginnie Mae mortgages. Ginnie Mae aggregates these mortgages into a pool and issues pass-through securities that are collateralized by the interest and principal payments from the mortgages. Ginnie Mae also guarantees the pass-through securities against default. The usual minimum denomination for pass-throughs is $25 000. The minimum pool size is $1 million. One pool may back up many pass-through securities.

FHLMC Pass-Throughs Freddie Mac was created to assist savings and loan associations in the United States, which are not eligible to originate Ginnie Mae–guaranteed loans. Freddie Mac purchases mortgages for its own account and also issues pass-through securities similar to those issued by Ginnie Mae. Pass-through securities issued by Freddie Mac are called *participation certificates (PCs)*. Freddie Mac pools are distinct from Ginnie Mae pools in that they contain conventional (nonguaranteed) mortgages, are not federally insured, contain mortgages with different rates, are larger (ranging up to several hundred million dollars), and have a minimum denomination of $100 000.

THE IMPACT OF SECURITIZED MORTGAGES ON THE MORTGAGE MARKET

Mortgage-backed securities (also called **securitized mortgages**) have been a very important development in the financial markets in recent years. These new debt instruments compete for funds with government bonds, corporate bonds, and stocks. Securitized mortgages are low-risk securities that have higher yields than comparable government bonds and attract funds from around the world.

One benefit of the securitized mortgage is that it reduces the problems caused by regional lending institutions' sensitivity to local economic fluctuations. Because the loans are sold nationally and internationally, regional variations are no longer as great a source of risk to lenders.

A second benefit of the securitized mortgage is that borrowers now have access to a national capital market. In the early twentieth century, borrowers could choose among mortgages offered by only a few local lenders. The new securitized mortgages function much more like the rest of the capital markets. As a result, rates in the mortgage market follow other capital market rates much more closely.

Another benefit of the securitized mortgages is that an investor can enjoy the low-risk and long-term nature of investing in mortgages without having to service the loan.

A side effect of the development of securitized mortgages has been that mortgage rates are now more open to national and international influences. As a result, mortgage rates are more volatile than they were in the past.

FOLLOWING THE FINANCIAL NEWS

Mortgage-Backed Securities

MORTGAGE BACKED

Supplied by RBC Dominion Securities Inc. Bid side levels on minimum $1 million. Indicated yields assume no prepayments. All those NHA Mortgage backed securities are priced to their weighted average maturity date.

Pool #	Issuer	Coupon	Maturity	Price	Yield
NON-PREPAYABLE					
99007635	TD Bank	4.750	Nov 01/02	100.49	3.13
99007452	Peoples Trst	5.750	May 01/03	101.73	3.54
99007932	Bank of Mntl	4.875	Feb 01/04	100.95	4.15
99008088	TD Bank	5.625	Sep 01/04	102.05	4.52
99008237	TD Bank	5.750	May 01/05	102.22	4.81
99008443	TD Bank	5.000	Sep 01/06	99.34	5.13
99008005	Bank of Mntl	5.375	Apr 01/09	98.45	5.63
99007817	Peoples Trst	5.375	May 01/11	96.79	5.91
99007981	TD Bank	5.500	Apr 01/24	92.29	6.31
PREPAYABLE					
99007783	TD Bank	5.375	Jul 01/28	91.05	6.31
97000269	Canada Trust	5.400	Aug 01/02	100.10	2.88
97000608	Royal Bank	5.375	Oct 01/02	100.25	2.98
97000657	Royal Bank	5.125	Jan 01/03	100.68	3.28
97001267	Canada Trust	5.000	Jun 01/03	101.03	3.47
97001556	Canada Trust	5.000	Feb 01/04	101.04	4.07
96413364	TD Bank	4.875	Apr 01/04	100.87	4.13
97001713	Canada Trust	5.000	Jul 01/04	100.92	4.34
97001952	Bank of Mntl	6.250	Apr 01/05	103.19	4.51
97002414	Bank of Mntl	5.500	Sep 01/05	101.81	4.60
97002745	Bank of Mntl	5.375	Jun 01/06	101.36	4.82

Source: National Post: Financial Post, Friday, June 7, 2002, *p. IN11*. Reprinted with permission.

SUMMARY

1. Mortgages are long-term loans secured by real estate. Both individuals and businesses obtain mortgage loans to finance real estate purchases.
2. Mortgage interest rates are relatively low because of competition among various institutions that want to make mortgage loans. In addition to keeping interest rates low, the competition has resulted in a variety of terms and options for mortgage loans. For example, borrowers may choose to obtain a fixed-rate loan or a variable-rate loan that has its interest rate tied to the prime rate.
3. Several features of mortgage loans are designed to reduce the likelihood that the borrower will default. For example, a down payment is usually required so that the borrower will suffer a loss if the lender repossesses the property. Most lenders also require that the borrower purchase mortgage default insurance unless the loan-to-value ratio drops below 75%.
4. More types of mortgage loans are available in the United States and are likely to be introduced in Canada. Some of these are the graduated-payment mortgage, the growing-equity mortgage, and the shared-appreciation mortgage. The graduated-payment mortgage has low initial payments that increase over time. The growing-equity mortgage has increasing payments that cause the loan to be paid off in a shorter period than a level-payment loan. Shared-appreciation loans were used when interest rates and inflation were high. The lender shared in the increase in the real estate's value in exchange for lower interest rates.
5. Securitized mortgages have been growing in popularity in recent years as institutional investors look for attractive investment opportunities. Securitized mortgages are securities collateralized by a pool of mortgages. The payments on the pool are passed through to the investors. The Canada Mortgage and Housing Corporation (CMHC) in Canada, Ginnie Mae and Freddie Mac in the United States, and private banks issue pass-through securities.

KEY TERMS

amortized, *p. 274*
balloon loan, *p. 274*
Central Payor and Transfer Agent (CPTA), *p. 289*
collateralized mortgage obligation (CMO), *p. 289*
conventional mortgage, *p. 282*
down payment, *p. 277*
effective interest rate, *p. 276*
fixed-rate mortgage, *p. 282*
gross debt service ratio (GDS), *p. 278*
insured mortgage (high-ratio mortgage), *p. 282*
lien, *p. 277*
mortgage, *p. 273*
mortgage-backed security, *p. 287*
mortgage default insurance, *p. 277*
mortgage pass-through, *p. 287*
refinance, *p. 282*
reserve account, *p. 286*
reverse mortgage, *p. 283*
securitized mortgage, *p. 290*
total debt service ratio (TDS), *p. 278*
variable-rate mortgage, *p. 282*

QUESTIONS AND PROBLEMS

***1.** What distinguishes the mortgage markets from other capital markets?

2. Most mortgage loans once had balloon payments; now most current mortgage loans fully amortize. What is the difference between a balloon loan and an amortizing loan?

***3.** What features contribute to keeping long-term mortgage interest rates low?

4. What is the difference between open and closed mortgages?

***5.** What is a lien, and when is it used in mortgage lending?

6. What is the purpose of requiring that a borrower make a down payment before receiving a loan?

***7.** What kind of insurance do lenders usually require of borrowers who have less than a 75% loan-to-value ratio?

8. Lenders tend not to be as flexible about the qualifications required of mortgage customers as they can be for other types of bank loans. Why is this so?

***9.** Distinguish between conventional mortgage loans and insured mortgage loans.

10. Interpret what is meant when a lender quotes the terms on a loan as "floating at prime plus 2 with caps of 2 and 6"?

***11.** The monthly payments on both graduated-payment loans and growing-equity loans increase over time. Despite this similarity, the two types of loans have different purposes. What is the motivation behind each type of loan?

12. Many banks offer lines of credit that are secured by a second mortgage (or lien) on real property. These loans have been very popular among bank customers. Why are homeowners so willing to pledge their homes as security for these lines of credit?

***13.** The reverse mortgage allows retired people to live off the equity they have in their homes without having to sell the home. Explain how a reverse mortgage works.

14. What is a securitized mortgage?

***15.** Describe how a mortgage pass-through works.

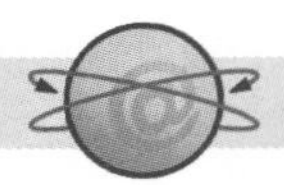

WEB EXERCISES

The Mortgage Market

1. You may be looking into acquiring a home in the near future. One common question you may have is how large a mortgage loan you can afford. Go to http://www.royalbank.com/products/mortgages/index.html and click on "Tools and Calculators." Choose the calculator labelled "How much can I afford?" Input your expected future salary data. How large a mortgage can you afford according to the calculator? Increase your debt to see the impact on the amount of mortgage loan you will qualify for.

2. One of the more difficult decisions faced by homeowners is whether it pays to refinance a mortgage loan when rates have dropped. Go to http://interest.com and click on "Mortgage Calculators." Choose the calculator that computes how long it will take to recoup the costs of refinancing your mortgage loan. Assume you obtained a 30-year $130 000 loan four years ago at 7%. Now rates have dropped and your income is higher. Determine how much you will save if you get a new loan for 15 years at 6.25%.

Chapter 12 The Foreign Exchange Market

Preview

In the early 1980s, Canadian businesses became less competitive with their foreign counterparts; in the 1990s, their competitiveness had increased. Was this swing in competitiveness primarily the result of Canadian management falling down on the job in the early 1980s, then getting its act together in the 1990s? Not really. Canadian businesses became less competitive in the early 1980s because Canadian dollars became worth more in terms of foreign currencies, making Canadian goods more expensive relative to foreign goods. By the 1990s, the value of the Canadian dollar had fallen appreciably from its highs in the mid-1980s, making Canadian goods cheaper and enabling Canadian businesses to be more competitive.

The price of one currency in terms of another is called the **exchange rate**. It affects the economy because when the Canadian dollar becomes more valuable relative to foreign currencies, Canadian goods become more expensive for foreigners and foreign goods become cheaper for Canadians. When the Canadian dollar falls in value, Canadian goods become cheaper for foreigners and foreign goods become more expensive for Canadians. In addition, changes in the exchange rate have a major impact on financial institutions because many of their assets are denominated in foreign currencies; when the value of foreign currencies changes, the market value of financial institutions changes as well. To understand why exchange rates change, we need to examine the market in which they are determined, the **foreign exchange market.**

As you can see in Figure 1, exchange rates have been highly volatile, with the dollar generally increasing in value relative to foreign currencies from 1980 to 1985 and falling in value since the early 1990s. What factors explain the dollar's former strength and later weakness, which caused major swings in the competitiveness of Canadian businesses? Why are exchange rates so volatile from day to day?

To answer these questions, we develop a modern view of exchange rate determination that explains recent behaviour in the foreign exchange market.

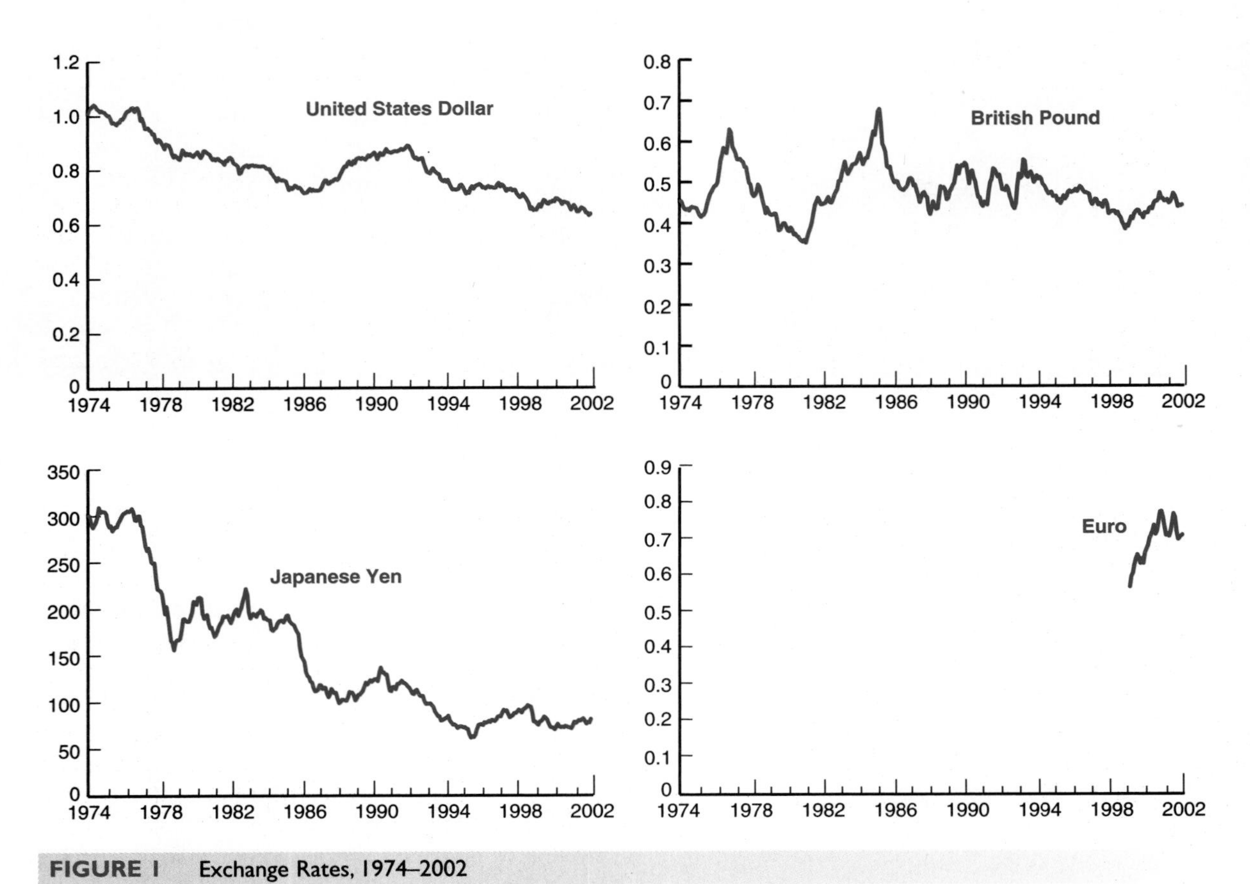

FIGURE 1 Exchange Rates, 1974–2002

The exchange rate between the Canadian dollar and selected foreign currencies. Note that the decline in these plots means a weakening of the Canadian dollar, and an increase indicates a strengthening of the Canadian dollar.

Source: Statistics Canada CANSIM series B3400, B3412, B3407, and B100032

FOREIGN EXCHANGE MARKET

At www.bankofcanada.ca/en/exchange.htm you can obtain information about exchange rates and access to academic papers.

Most countries of the world have their own currencies: Canada has its dollar; France, the euro; Brazil, its real; and India, its rupee. Trade between countries involves the mutual exchange of different currencies (or, more usually, bank deposits denominated in different currencies). When a Canadian firm buys foreign goods, services, or financial assets, for example, Canadian dollars (typically, bank deposits denominated in Canadian dollars) must be exchanged for foreign currency (bank deposits denominated in the foreign currency).

The trading of currency and bank deposits denominated in particular currencies takes place in the foreign exchange market. The volume of these transactions worldwide averages more than $1.5 trillion daily. Transactions conducted in the foreign exchange market determine the rates at which currencies are exchanged, which in turn determine the cost of purchasing foreign goods and financial assets.

What Are Foreign Exchange Rates?

There are two kinds of exchange rate transactions. The predominant ones, called **spot transactions**, involve the immediate (two-day) exchange of bank deposits.

Forward transactions involve the exchange of bank deposits at some specified future date. The **spot exchange rate** is the exchange rate for the spot transaction, and the **forward exchange rate** is the exchange rate for the forward transaction.

When a currency increases in value, it experiences **appreciation**; when it falls in value and is worth fewer Canadian dollars, it undergoes **depreciation**. At the beginning of 1999, for example, the euro was valued at $1.76, and, as indicated in the "Following the Financial News" box, on April 26, 2002, it was valued at $1.40. The euro *depreciated* by 20.4%: (1.40 – 1.76)/1.76 = –0.204 = –20.4%. Conversely, we could say that the Canadian dollar, which went from a value of 0.56 euros per dollar in 1999 to a value of 0.71 euros per dollar by April 2002, *appreciated* by 26.7%: (0.71 – 0.56)/0.56 = 0.268 = 26.8%.

Why Are Exchange Rates Important?

Exchange rates are important because they affect the relative price of domestic and foreign goods. The dollar price of French goods to a Canadian is determined by the interaction of two factors: the price of French goods in euros and the euro/dollar exchange rate.

Suppose that Wanda the Winetaster, a Canadian, decides to buy a bottle of 1961 (a very good year) Château Lafite Rothschild to complete her wine cellar. If the price of the wine in France is 1000 euros and the exchange rate is $1.40 to the euro, the wine will cost Wanda $1400 (= 1000 euros × $1.40/euro). Now suppose that Wanda delays her purchase by two months, at which time the euro has appreciated to $1.50 per euro. If the domestic price of the bottle of Lafite Rothschild remains 1000 euros, its dollar cost will have risen from $1400 to $1500.

The same currency appreciation, however, makes the price of foreign goods in France less expensive. At an exchange rate of $1.40 per euro, a Dell computer priced at $2000 costs Claude the Programmer 1428.6 euros; if the exchange rate increases to $1.50 per euro, the computer will cost only 1333.3 euros.

A depreciation of the euro lowers the cost of French goods in Canada but raises the cost of Canadian goods in France. If the euro drops in value to $1.20, Wanda's bottle of Lafite Rothschild will cost her only $1200 instead of $1400, and the Dell computer will cost Claude 1667 euros rather than 1428.6.

Such reasoning leads to the following conclusion: ***When a country's currency appreciates (rises in value relative to other currencies), the country's goods abroad become more expensive and foreign goods in that country become cheaper (holding domestic prices constant in the two countries). Conversely, when a country's currency depreciates, its goods abroad become cheaper and foreign goods in that country become more expensive.***

At http://quotes.ino.com/chart/, click on "Foreign Exchange" to get market rates and time charts for major world currencies.

Appreciation of a currency can make it harder for domestic manufacturers to sell their goods abroad and can increase competition at home from foreign goods because they cost less. From early 1986 to early 1992, the appreciating Canadian dollar against the U.S. dollar hurt Canadian industries. For instance, the Canadian steel industry was hurt because sales in the United States of the more expensive Canadian steel declined but also because sales of relatively cheap steel from other countries increased. Although appreciation of the Canadian dollar hurt some domestic businesses, consumers benefited because U.S. goods were less expensive. Canadian consumers also benefited in the 1980–1985 period when the cost of vacationing in Europe and the United States fell in price as a result of the stormy Canadian dollar against the major European currencies and the U.S. dollar.

FOLLOWING THE FINANCIAL NEWS

Foreign Exchange Rates

Foreign exchange rates are published daily and appear in the "Foreign Exchange" column of the *Globe and Mail: Report on Business*. The entries from one such column, shown here, are explained in the text.

Panel (a) gives the cross rates for several currencies in Toronto on April 25, 2002. For example, we find that U.S $/Can $ = 0.6396 by looking across the U.S dollar row for the Canadian dollar column. To find the U.S dollar price of euros, we look across the U.S dollar row for the euro column and see that $/euro = 0.8983. By dividing $/euro by $/Can $, we find the implied cross rate for Can $/euro = 1.4044, which is the same as the rate that we find by looking across the Canadian dollar column for the euro column.

In panel (b), the first entry for the euro lists the exchange rate for the spot transaction (the spot exchange rate) on April 25, 2002, and is quoted in two ways: Cdn.$ 1.4044 per euro and U.S.$ 0.8983 per euro. The entries immediately after the spot exchange rate for some currencies give the rates for forward transactions (the forward exchange rates) that will take place 1 month, 2 months, and so on, in the future.

FOREIGN EXCHANGE

Cross rates

	Canadian dollar	U.S. dollar	British pound	Japanese yen	Swiss franc	Euro
Canadian dollar	—	1.5634	2.2735	0.012180	0.9588	1.4044
U.S. dollar	0.6396	—	1.4542	0.007791	0.6133	0.8983
British pound	0.4399	0.6877	—	0.005357	0.4217	0.6177
Japanese yen	82.10	128.36	186.66	—	78.72	115.30
Swiss franc	1.0430	1.6306	2.3712	0.012703	—	1.4647
Euro	0.7120	1.1132	1.6188	0.008673	0.6827	—

Mid-market rates in Toronto at noon, April 25, 2002. Prepared by BMO Nesbitt Burns, Capital Markets.

	$1 U.S. in Cdn. $ =	$1 Cdn. in U.S. $ =
U.S./Canada spot	1.5634	0.6396
1 month forward	1.5641	0.6393
2 months forward	1.5648	0.6391
3 months forward	1.5657	0.6387
6 months forward	1.5685	0.6376
12 months forward	1.5742	0.6352
3 years forward	1.5834	0.6316
5 years forward	1.5889	0.6294
7 years forward	1.5924	0.6280
10 years forward	1.5984	0.6256
Canadian dollar in 2002: High	1.5740	0.6353
Low	1.6183	0.6179
Average	1.5921	0.6281

country	currency	Cdn. $ per unit	U.S. $ per unit
Britain	Pound	2.2735	1.4542
1 month forward		2.2705	1.4516
2 months forward		2.2672	1.4489
3 months forward		2.2645	1.4463
6 months forward		2.2564	1.4386
12 months forward		2.2445	1.4258
Europe	Euro	1.4044	0.8983
1 month forward		1.4033	0.8972
3 months forward		1.4011	0.8949
6 months forward		1.3991	0.8920
12 months forward		1.3985	0.8884
Japan	Yen	0.012180	0.007791
1 month forward		0.012206	0.007804
3 months forward		0.012256	0.007828
6 months forward		0.012349	0.007873
12 months forward		0.012588	0.007996
Algeria	Dinar	0.02021	0.0129
Antigua, Grenada & St. Lucia	E.C.Dollar	0.5855	0.3745
Argentina	Peso	0.50109	0.32051
Australia	Dollar	0.8517	0.5448
Austria	Euro	1.4044	0.8983
Bahamas	Dollar	1.5634	1.0000
Barbados	Dollar	0.7856	0.5025
Belgium	Euro	1.4044	0.8983
Bermuda	Dollar	1.5634	1.0000
Brazil	Real	0.6588	0.4214
Bulgaria	Lev	0.720461	0.4608
Chile	Peso	0.002381	0.001523
China	Renminbi	0.1889	0.1208
Cyprus	Pound	2.4344	1.5571
Czech Rep	Koruna	0.0462	0.0296
Denmark	Krone	0.1889	0.1208
Egypt	Pound	0.3384	0.2165
Fiji	Dollar	0.7106	0.4545
Finland	Euro	1.4044	0.8983
France	Euro	1.4044	0.8983
Germany	Euro	1.4044	0.8983
Greece	Euro	1.4044	0.8983
Hong Kong	Dollar	0.2005	0.1282
Hungary	Forint	0.00578	0.00370
Iceland	Krona	0.01663	0.01064
India	Rupee	0.03197	0.02045
Indonesia	Rupiah	0.000167	0.000107
Ireland	Euro	1.4044	0.8983
Israel	N Shekel	0.3206	0.2050
Italy	Euro	1.404400	0.898299
Jamaica	Dollar	0.03284	0.02101
Jordan	Dinar	2.2082	1.4124
Lebanon	Pound	0.001033	0.000661
Luxembourg	Euro	1.40440	0.89830
Malaysia	Ringgit	0.4114	0.2632
Mexico	N Peso	0.1671	0.1069
Netherlands	Euro	1.4044	0.8983
New Zealand	Dollar	0.7054	0.4512
Norway	Krone	0.1849	0.1183
Pakistan	Rupee	0.02612	0.01671
Panama	Balboa	1.5634	1.0000
Philippines	Peso	0.03081	0.01970
Poland	Zloty	0.3885	0.2485
Portugal	Euro	1.40440	0.89830
Romania	Leu	0.000047	0.000030
Russia	Ruble	0.050090	0.032039
Saudi Arabia	Riyal	0.4169	0.2667
Singapore	Dollar	0.8633	0.5522
Slovakia	Koruna	0.0335	0.0214
South Africa	Rand	0.1437	0.0919
South Korea	Won	0.001214	0.000777
Spain	Euro	1.40440	0.89830
Sudan	Dinar	0.00604	0.0039
Sweden	Krona	0.1522	0.0973
Switzerland	Franc	0.9588	0.6133
Taiwan	Dollar	0.04508	0.0288
Thailand	Baht	0.03618	0.0231
Trinidad & T	Dollar	0.2555	0.1634
Turkey	Lira	.0000011	.0000007
Venezuela	Bolivar	0.001861	0.00119
Zambia	Kwacha	0.000399	0.000255
Sp Draw Rt	S.D.R	1.9788	1.2657

Closing rates

The U.S. dollar closed at $1.5648 in terms of Canadian funds, down $0.0030 from Wednesday. The pound sterling closed at $2.2782, up $0.0066.

In New York, the Canadian dollar closed up $0.0013 at $0.6391 in terms of U.S. funds. The pound sterling was up $0.0070 to $1.4559.

Source: The Globe and Mail: Report on Business, Thursday, April 25, 2002, p. B14. Reprinted with permission.

How Is Foreign Exchange Traded?

You cannot go to a centralized location to watch exchange rates being determined; currencies are not traded on exchanges such as the Toronto Stock Exchange. Instead, the foreign exchange market is organized as an over-the-counter market in which several hundred dealers (mostly banks) stand ready to buy and sell deposits denominated in foreign currencies. Because these dealers are in constant telephone and computer contact, the market is very competitive; in effect, it functions no differently from a centralized market.

An important point to note is that although banks, companies, and governments talk about buying and selling currencies in foreign exchange markets, they do not take a fistful of dollar bills and sell them for British pound notes. Rather, most trades involve the buying and selling of bank deposits denominated in different currencies. So when we say that a bank is buying dollars in the foreign exchange market, what we actually mean is that the bank is buying deposits *denominated in dollars.*

Trades in the foreign exchange market consist of transactions in excess of $1 million. The market that determines the exchange rates in the "Following the Financial News" box is not where one would buy foreign currency for a trip abroad. Instead, we buy foreign currency in the retail market from dealers such as Thomas Cook or from banks. Because retail prices are higher than wholesale, when we buy foreign exchange, we obtain fewer units of foreign currency per dollar than exchange rates in the box indicate.

EXCHANGE RATES IN THE LONG RUN

Like the price of any good or asset in a free market, exchange rates are determined by the interaction of supply and demand. To simplify our analysis of exchange rates in a free market, we divide it into two parts. First, we examine how exchange rates are determined in the long run; then we use our knowledge of the long-run determinants of the exchange rate to help us understand how they are determined in the short run.

Law of One Price

The starting point for understanding how exchange rates are determined is a simple idea called the **law of one price**: If two countries produce an identical good, the price of the good should be the same throughout the world no matter which country produces it. Suppose that Canadian steel costs $100 per ton and identical Japanese steel costs 10 000 yen per ton. The law of one price suggests that the exchange rate between the yen and the dollar must be 100 yen per dollar ($0.01 per yen) in order for one ton of Canadian steel to sell for 10 000 yen in Japan (the price of Japanese steel) and one ton of Japanese steel to sell for $100 in Canada (the price of Canadian steel). If the exchange rate were 200 yen to the dollar, Japanese steel would sell for $50 per ton in Canada, or half the price of Canadian steel, and Canadian steel would sell for 20 000 yen per ton in Japan, twice the price of the Japanese steel. Because Canadian steel would be more expensive than Japanese steel in both countries and is identical to Japanese steel, the demand for Canadian steel would go to zero. Given a fixed dollar price for Canadian steel, the resulting excess supply of Canadian steel will be eliminated only if the exchange rate falls to 100 yen per dollar, making the price of Canadian steel and Japanese steel the same in both countries.

EXAMPLE 1: Law of One Price

Recently, the yen price of Japanese steel has increased by 10% (to 11 000 yen) relative to the dollar price of Canadian steel (unchanged at $100). By what amount must the dollar increase or decrease in value for the law of one price to hold true?

Solution

For the law of one price to hold, the exchange rate must rise to 110 yen per dollar, which is a 10% appreciation of the dollar.

The exchange rate rises to 110 yen so that the price of Japanese steel in dollars remains unchanged at $100 (= 11 000 yen/110 yen per dollar). In other words, the 10% depreciation of the yen (10% appreciation of the dollar) just offsets the 10% increase in the yen price of the Japanese steel.

Theory of Purchasing Power Parity

The page at www.oecd.org/std/ppp/pps.htm includes a PPP program overview, statistics, research, publications, and OECD meetings on PPP.

One of the most prominent theories of how exchange rates are determined is the **theory of purchasing power parity (PPP).** It states that exchange rates between any two currencies will adjust to reflect changes in the price levels of the two countries. The theory of PPP is simply an application of the law of one price to national price levels.

As Example 1 illustrates, if the law of one price holds, a 10% rise in the yen price of Japanese steel results in a 10% appreciation of the dollar. Applying the law of one price to the price levels in the two countries produces the theory of purchasing power parity, which maintains that if the Japanese price level rises 10% relative to the Canadian price level, the dollar will appreciate by 10%. As our Canadian/Japanese example illustrates, ***the theory of PPP suggests that if one country's price level rises relative to another's, its currency should depreciate (the other country's currency should appreciate).***

As you can see in Figure 2, this prediction of the theory of PPP is borne out in the long run. From 1973 to 2001, the U.S. price level fell 5% relative to the Canadian price level, and as the theory of PPP predicts, the Canadian dollar depreciated against the U.S. dollar, though by 31%, an amount larger than the 5% decrease predicted by PPP.

Yet, as the same figure indicates, PPP theory often has little predictive power in the short run. From early 1985 to the end of 1992, for example, the U.S. price level rose relative to that of Canada. Instead of depreciating, as PPP theory predicts, the Canadian dollar actually appreciated by 7.2% against the U.S. dollar. So even though PPP theory provides some guidance to the long-run movement of exchange rates, it is not perfect and in the short run is a particularly poor predictor (see Box 1). What explains PPP theory's failure to predict well?

Why the Theory of Purchasing Power Parity Cannot Fully Explain Exchange Rates

The PPP conclusion that exchange rates are determined solely by changes in relative price levels rests on the assumption that all goods are identical in both countries. When this assumption is true, the law of one price states that the relative prices of all these goods (that is, the relative price level between the two countries) will determine the exchange rate. The assumption that goods are identical may not be too unreasonable for Canadian and Japanese steel, but is it a reasonable assumption for Canadian and Japanese cars? Is a Toyota the equivalent of a Chevrolet?

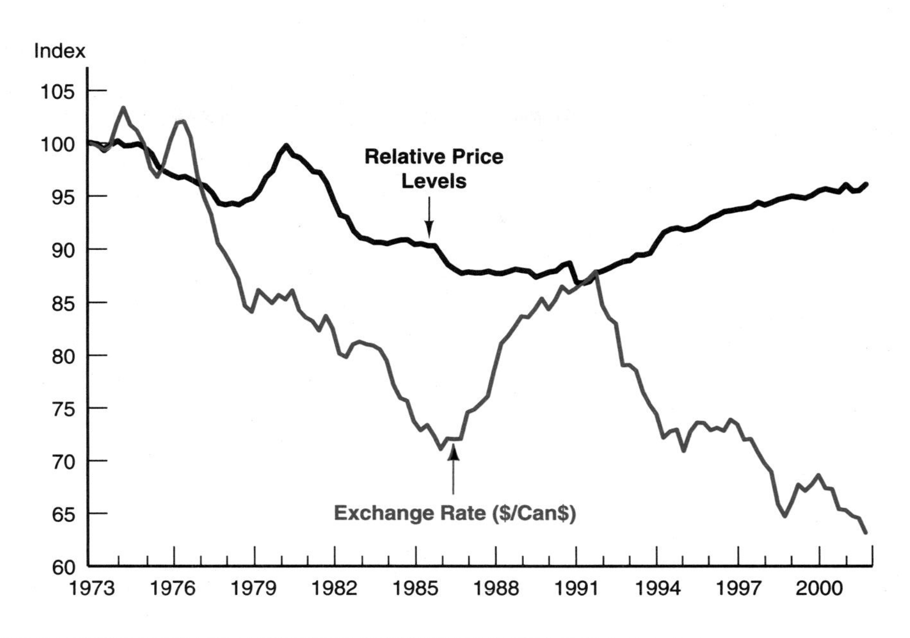

FIGURE 2 Purchasing Power Parity, Canada/United States, 1973–2002

Source: International Financial Statistics © International Monetary Fund, 2002.

BOX 1

The Purchasing Power Parity Puzzle

The theory of purchasing power parity has attracted a great deal of attention and has been explored extensively in the literature using recent advances in the field of applied econometrics. Based on the law of one price, the theory asserts that relative goods prices are not affected by exchange rates—or, equivalently, that exchange rate changes will be proportional to relative inflation. The relationship is important not only because it has been a cornerstone of exchange rate models in international economics, but also because of its policy implications—it provides a benchmark exchange rate and hence has some practical appeal for policymakers and exchange rate arbitragers.

Empirical studies generally fail to find support for long-run purchasing power parity, especially during the recent floating exchange rate period. In fact, the empirical consensus is that purchasing power parity does not hold over this period. But there are also studies covering different groups of countries, as well as studies covering periods of long duration or country pairs experiencing large differentials in price movements that report evidence consistent with the theory of purchasing power parity.

For an excellent discussion of this subject, see Kenneth Rogoff, "The Purchasing Power Parity Puzzle," *Journal of Economic Literature* 34 (1996): 647–68.

Because Toyotas and Chevys are obviously not identical, their prices do not have to be equal. Toyotas can be more expensive relative to Chevys and both Canadians and Japanese will still purchase Toyotas. Because the law of one price does not hold for all goods, a rise in the price of Toyotas relative to Chevys will not necessarily mean that the yen must depreciate by the amount of the relative price increase of Toyotas over Chevys.

PPP theory furthermore does not take into account that many goods and services (whose prices are included in a measure of a country's price level) are not traded across borders. Housing, land, and services such as restaurant meals, haircuts, and golf lessons are not traded goods. So even though the prices of these items might rise and lead to a higher price level relative to another country's, there would be little direct effect on the exchange rate.

Factors That Affect Exchange Rates in the Long Run

Our analysis indicates that relative price levels and additional factors affect the exchange rate. In the long run, there are four major factors: relative price levels, tariffs and quotas, preferences for domestic versus foreign goods, and productivity. We examine how each of these factors affects the exchange rate while holding the others constant.

The basic reasoning proceeds along the following lines: Anything that increases the demand for domestic goods relative to foreign goods tends to appreciate the domestic currency because domestic goods will continue to sell well even when the value of the domestic currency is higher. Similarly, anything that increases the demand for foreign goods relative to domestic goods tends to depreciate the domestic currency because domestic goods will continue to sell well only if the value of the domestic currency is lower.

Relative Price Levels In line with PPP theory, when prices of Canadian goods rise (holding prices of foreign goods constant), the demand for Canadian goods falls and the dollar tends to depreciate so that Canadian goods can still sell well. By contrast, if prices of Japanese goods rise so that the relative prices of Canadian goods fall, the demand for Canadian goods increases, and the dollar tends to appreciate because Canadian goods will continue to sell well even with a higher value of the domestic currency. ***In the long run, a rise in a country's price level (relative to the foreign price level) causes its currency to depreciate, and a fall in the country's relative price level causes its currency to appreciate.***

Trade Barriers Barriers to free trade such as **tariffs** (taxes on imported goods) and **quotas** (restrictions on the quantity of foreign goods that can be imported) can affect the exchange rate. Suppose that Canada imposes a tariff or a quota on Japanese steel. These trade barriers increase the demand for Canadian steel, and the dollar tends to appreciate because Canadian steel will still sell well even with a higher value of the dollar. ***Increasing trade barriers causes a country's currency to appreciate in the long run.***

Preferences for Domestic Versus Foreign Goods If the Japanese develop an appetite for Canadian goods—say, for Bombardier's high-speed trains and Canadian beef and pork—the increased demand for Canadian goods (exports) tends to appreciate the dollar because the Canadian goods will continue to sell well even at a higher value for the dollar. Likewise, if Canadians decide that they prefer Japanese cars to Canadian cars, the increased demand for Japanese goods (imports) tends to depreciate the dollar. ***Increased demand for a country's exports causes its currency to appreciate in the long run; conversely, increased demand for imports causes the domestic currency to depreciate.***

Productivity If one country becomes more productive than other countries, businesses in that country can lower the prices of domestic goods relative to foreign goods and still earn a profit. As a result, the demand for domestic goods rises, and the domestic currency tends to appreciate. If, however, its productivity lags behind that of other countries, its goods become relatively more expensive, and the currency tends to depreciate. ***In the long run, as a country becomes more productive relative to other countries, its currency appreciates.***[1]

Study Guide The trick to figuring out what long-run effect a factor has on the exchange rate is to remember the following: ***If a factor increases the demand for domestic goods relative to foreign goods, the domestic currency will appreciate, and if a factor decreases the relative demand for domestic goods, the domestic currency will depreciate.*** See how this works by explaining what happens to the exchange rate when any of the factors in Table 1 declines rather than increases.

Our long-run theory of exchange rate behaviour is summarized in Table 1. We use the convention that the exchange rate E is quoted so that an appreciation of the currency corresponds to a rise in the exchange rate. In the case of Canada, this means that we are quoting the exchange rate as units of foreign currency per dollar (say, yen per dollar).[2]

EXCHANGE RATES IN THE SHORT RUN

We have developed a theory of the long-run behaviour of exchange rates. However, if we are to understand why exchange rates exhibit such large changes (sometimes several percent) from day to day, we must develop a theory of how current exchange rates (spot exchange rates) are determined in the short run.

The key to understanding the short-run behaviour of exchange rates is to recognize that an exchange rate is the price of domestic bank deposits (those denominated in the domestic currency) in terms of foreign bank deposits (those denominated in the foreign currency). Because the exchange rate is the price of one asset in terms of another, the natural way to investigate the short-run determination of exchange rates is through an asset market approach that relies heavily on our analysis of the determinants of asset demand developed in Chapter 4. As you will see, however, the long-run determinants of the exchange

TABLE 1 SUMMARY **Factors That Affect Exchange Rates in the Long Run**

Factor	Change in Factor	Response of the Exchange Rate, E^*
Domestic price level†	↑	↓
Trade barriers†	↑	↑
Import demand	↑	↓
Export demand	↑	↑
Productivity†	↑	↑

Note: Only increases (↑) in the factors are shown; the effects of decreases in the variables on the exchange rate are the opposite of those indicated in the "Response" column.

*Units of foreign currency per dollar: ↑ indicates currency appreciation; ↓, depreciation.

†Relative to other countries.

[1]A country might be so small that a change in productivity or the preferences for domestic or foreign goods would have no effect on prices of these goods relative to foreign goods. In this case, changes in productivity or changes in preferences for domestic or foreign goods affect the country's income but will not necessarily affect the value of the currency. In our analysis, we are assuming that these factors can affect relative prices and consequently the exchange rate.

[2]In professional writing, many economists quote exchange rates as units of domestic currency per foreign currency so that an appreciation of the domestic currency is portrayed as a fall in the exchange rate. The opposite convention is used in the text here because it is more intuitive to think of an appreciation of the domestic currency as a rise in the exchange rate.

rate we have just outlined also play an important role in the short-run asset market approach.[3]

Earlier approaches to exchange rate determination emphasized the role of import and export demand. The more modern asset market approach used here does not emphasize the flows of purchases of exports and imports over short periods because these transactions are quite small relative to the amount of domestic and foreign bank deposits at any given time. For example, foreign exchange transactions in Canada each year are well over 25 times greater than the amount of Canadian exports and imports. Thus, over short periods such as a year, decisions to hold domestic or foreign assets play a much greater role in exchange rate determination than the demand for exports and imports does.

Comparing Expected Returns on Domestic and Foreign Deposits

In this analysis, we treat Canada as the home country, so domestic bank deposits are denominated in dollars. For simplicity, we use euros to stand for any foreign country's currency, so foreign bank deposits are denominated in euros. Our analysis of the determinants of asset demand suggests that the most important factor affecting the demand for domestic (dollar) deposits and foreign (euro) deposits is the expected return on these assets relative to each other. When Canadians or foreigners expect the return on dollar deposits to be high relative to the return on foreign deposits, there is a higher demand for dollar deposits and a correspondingly lower demand for euro deposits. To understand how the demands for dollar and foreign deposits change, we need to compare the expected returns on dollar deposits and foreign deposits.

To illustrate further, suppose that dollar deposits have an interest rate (expected return payable in dollars) of i^D, and foreign bank deposits have an interest rate (expected return payable in the foreign currency, euros) of i^F. To compare the expected returns on dollar deposits and foreign deposits, investors must convert the returns into the currency unit they use.

First let us examine how François the Foreigner compares the returns on dollar deposits and foreign deposits denominated in his currency, the euro. When he considers the expected return on dollar deposits in terms of euros, he recognizes that it does not equal i^D; instead, the expected return must be adjusted for any expected appreciation or depreciation of the dollar. If the dollar were expected to appreciate by 7%, for example, the expected return on dollar deposits in terms of euros would be 7% higher because the dollar has become worth 7% more in terms of euros. Thus, if the interest rate on dollar deposits is 10%, with an expected appreciation of the dollar of 7%, the expected return on dollar deposits in terms of euros is 17%: the 10% interest rate plus the 7% expected appreciation of the dollar. Conversely, if the dollar were expected to depreciate by 7% over the year, the expected return on dollar deposits in terms of euros would be only 3%: the 10% interest rate minus the 7% expected depreciation of the dollar.

Writing the currency exchange rate (the spot exchange rate) as E_t and the expected exchange rate for the next period as E^e_{t+1}, we can write the expected rate of appreciation of the dollar as $(E^e_{t+1} - E_t)/E_t$. Our reasoning indicates that the expected return on dollar deposits R^D in terms of foreign currency can be writ-

[3]For a further description of the modern asset market approach to exchange rate determination that we use here, see Paul Krugman and Maurice Obstfeld, *International Economics,* 4th ed. (Reading, MA: Addison Wesley Longman, 1997).

ten as the sum of the interest rate on dollar deposits plus the expected appreciation of the dollar:[4]

$$R^D \text{ in terms of euros} = i^D + \frac{E^e_{t+1} - E_t}{E_t}$$

However, François's expected return on foreign deposits R^F in terms of euros is just i^F. Thus, in terms of euros, the relative expected return on dollar deposits (that is, the difference between the expected return on dollar deposits and euro deposits) is calculated by subtracting i^F from the expression just given to yield

$$\text{Relative } R^D = i^D - i^F + \frac{E^e_{t+1} - E_t}{E_t} \tag{1}$$

As the relative expected return on dollar deposits increases, foreigners will want to hold more dollar deposits and fewer foreign deposits.

Next let us look at the decision to hold dollar deposits versus euro deposits from Al the Canadian's point of view. Following the same reasoning we used to evaluate the decision for François, we know that the expected return on foreign deposits R^F in terms of dollars is the interest rate on foreign deposits i^F plus the expected appreciation of the foreign currency, equal to minus the expected appreciation of the dollar, $-(E^e_{t+1} - E_t)/E_t$, that is,

$$R^F \text{ in terms of dollars} = i^F - \frac{E^e_{t+1} - E_t}{E_t}$$

If the interest rate on euro deposits is 5%, for example, and the dollar is expected to appreciate by 4%, then the expected return on euro deposits in terms of dollars is 1%. Al earns the 5% interest rate, but he expects to lose 4% because he expects the euro to be worth 4% less in terms of dollars as a result of the dollar's appreciation.

Al's expected return on the dollar deposits R^D in terms of dollars is just i^D. Hence, in terms of dollars, the relative expected return on dollar deposits is calculated by subtracting the expression just given from i^D to obtain

$$\text{Relative } R^D = i^D - \left(i^F - \frac{E^e_{t+1} - E_t}{E_t}\right) = i^D - i^F + \frac{E^e_{t+1} - E_t}{E_t}$$

This equation is the same as the one describing François's relative expected return on dollar deposits (calculated in terms of euros). The key point here is that

[4]This expression is actually an approximation of the expected return in terms of euros, which can be more precisely calculated by thinking how a foreigner invests in the dollar deposit. Suppose that François decides to put one euro into dollar deposits. First he buys $1/E_t$ of Canadian dollar deposits (recall that E_t, the exchange rate between dollar and euro deposits, is quoted in euros per dollar), and at the end of the period he is paid $(1 + i^D)(1/E_t)$ in dollars. To convert this amount into the number of euros he expects to receive at the end of the period, he multiplies this quantity by E^e_{t+1}. François's expected return on his initial investment of one euro can thus be written as $(1 + i^D)E^e_{t+1}/E_t)$ minus his initial investment of one euro:

$$(1 + i^D)\left(\frac{E^e_{t+1}}{E_t}\right) - 1$$

which can be rewritten as

$$i^D\left(\frac{E^e_{t+1}}{E_t}\right) + \frac{E^e_{t+1} - E_t}{E_t}$$

which is approximately equal to the expression in the text because E^e_{t+1}/E_t is typically close to 1.

the relative expected return on dollar deposits is the same whether it is calculated by François in terms of euros or by Al in terms of dollars. Thus as the relative expected return on dollar deposits increases, both foreigners and domestic residents respond in exactly the same way—both will want to hold more dollar deposits and fewer foreign deposits.

Interest Parity Condition

We currently live in a world in which there is **capital mobility**: Foreigners can easily purchase Canadian assets such as dollar deposits, and Canadians can easily purchase foreign assets such as euro deposits. Because foreign bank deposits and Canadian bank deposits have similar risk and liquidity and because there are few impediments to capital mobility, it is reasonable to assume that the deposits are perfect substitutes (that is, equally desirable). When capital is mobile and when bank deposits are perfect substitutes, if the expected return on dollar deposits is above that on foreign deposits, both foreigners and Canadians will want to hold only dollar deposits and will be unwilling to hold foreign deposits. Conversely, if the expected return on foreign deposits is higher than on dollar deposits, both foreigners and Canadians will not want to hold any dollar deposits and will want to hold only foreign deposits. For existing supplies of both dollar deposits and foreign deposits to be held, it must therefore be true that there is no difference in their expected returns; that is, the relative expected return in Equation 1 must equal zero. This condition can be rewritten as

$$i^D = i^F - \frac{E^e_{t+1} - E_t}{E_t} \tag{2}$$

This equation is called the **interest parity condition**, and it states that the domestic interest rate equals the foreign interest rate minus the expected appreciation of the domestic currency. Equivalently, this condition can be stated in a more intuitive way: The domestic interest rate equals the foreign interest rate plus the expected appreciation of the foreign currency. If the domestic interest rate is above the foreign interest rate, this means that there is a positive expected appreciation of the foreign currency, which compensates for the lower foreign interest rate.

EXAMPLE 2: Interest Parity Condition

If interest rates in Canada and Japan are 6% and 3%, respectively, what is the expected rate of appreciation of the foreign (Japanese) currency?

Solution

The expected appreciation of the foreign currency is 3%.

$$i^D = i^F - \frac{E^e_{t+1} - E_t}{E_t}$$

where

i^D = interest rate on dollars = 6%

i^F = interest rate on foreign currency = 3%

Thus

$$6\% = 3\% - \frac{E^e_{t+1} - E_t}{E_t}$$

$$-\frac{E^e_{t+1} - E_t}{E_t} = \text{rate of appreciation of the foreign currency} = 6\% - 3\% = 3\%$$

There are several ways to look at the interest parity condition. First, we should recognize that interest parity means simply that the expected returns are the same on both dollar deposits and foreign deposits. To see this, note that the left side of the interest parity condition (Equation 2) is the expected return on dollar deposits, while the right side is the expected return on foreign deposits, both calculated in terms of a single currency, the Canadian dollar. Given our assumption that domestic and foreign bank deposits are perfect substitutes (equally desirable), the interest parity condition is an equilibrium condition for the foreign exchange market. Only when the exchange rate is such that expected returns on domestic and foreign deposits are equal—that is, when interest parity holds—will the outstanding domestic and foreign deposits be willingly held.

Equilibrium in the Foreign Exchange Market

To see how the interest parity equilibrium condition works in determining the exchange rate, our first step is to examine how the expected returns on euro and dollar deposits change as the current exchange rate changes.

Expected Return on Euro Deposits As we demonstrated earlier, the expected return in terms of dollars on foreign deposits R^F is the foreign interest rate minus the expected appreciation of the domestic currency: $i^F - (E^e_{t+1} - E_t)/E_t$. Suppose that the foreign interest rate i^F is 10% and that the expected exchange rate next period E^e_{t+1} is 0.80 euros per dollar. When the current exchange rate E_t is 0.75 euros per dollar, the expected appreciation of the dollar is $(0.80 - 0.75)/0.75 = 0.066 = 6.6\%$, so the expected return on euro deposits R^F in terms of dollars is 3.4% (equal to the 10% foreign interest rate minus the 6.6% dollar appreciation). This expected return when $E_t = 0.75$ euros per dollar is plotted as point A in Figure 3. At a higher current exchange rate of $E_t = 0.80$ euros per dollar, the expected appreciation of the dollar is zero because E^e_{t+1} also equals 0.80 euros per dollar. Hence R^F, the expected dollar return on euro deposits, is now just $i^F = 10\%$. This expected return on euro deposits when $E_t = 0.80$ euros per dollar is plotted as point B. At an even higher exchange rate of $E_t = 0.85$ euros per dollar, the expected change in the value of the dollar is now -5.8% [$= (0.80 - 0.85)/0.85 = -0.058$], so the expected dollar return on foreign deposits R^F has now risen to 15.8% [$= 10\% - (-5.8\%)$]. This combination of exchange rate and expected return on euro deposits is plotted as point C.

The curve connecting these points is the schedule for the expected return on euro deposits in Figure 3, labelled R^F, and as you can see, it slopes upward; that is, as the exchange rate E_t rises, the expected return on euro deposits rises. The intuition for this upward slope is that because the expected next-period exchange rate is held constant as the current exchange rate rises, there is less expected appreciation of the dollar. Hence, a higher current exchange rate means a greater expected appreciation of the foreign currency in the future, which increases the expected return on foreign deposits in terms of dollars.

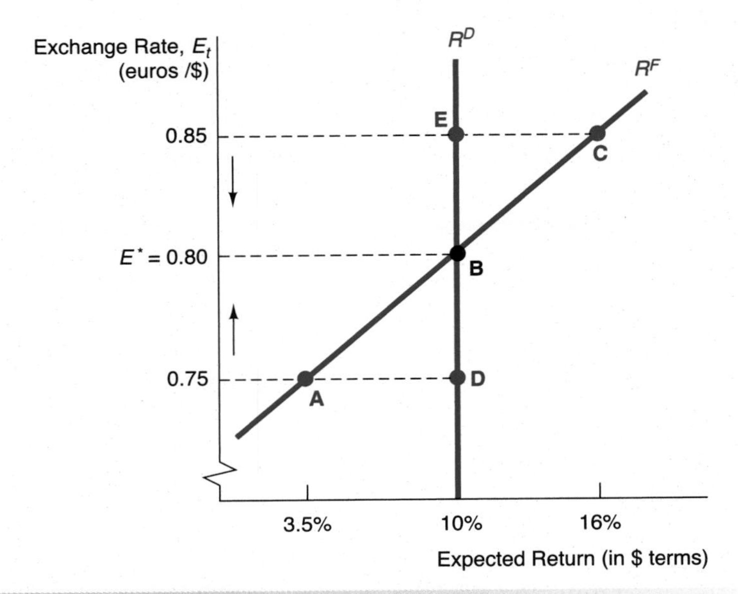

FIGURE 3 Equilibrium in the Foreign Exchange Market

Equilibrium in the foreign exchange market occurs at the intersection of the schedules for the expected return on euro deposits R^F and the expected return on dollar deposits R^D at point B. The equilibrium exchange rate is $E^* = 0.80$ euros per dollar.

Expected Return on Dollar Deposits The expected return on dollar deposits in terms of dollars R^D is always the interest rate on dollar deposits i^D no matter what the exchange rate is. Suppose that the interest rate on dollar deposits is 10%. The expected return on dollar deposits, whether at an exchange rate of 0.75, 0.80, or 0.85 euros per dollar, is always 10% (points D, B, and E). The line connecting these points is the schedule for the expected return on dollar deposits, labelled R^D in Figure 3.

Equilibrium The intersection of the schedules for the expected return on dollar deposits R^D and the expected return on euro deposits R^F is where equilibrium occurs in the foreign exchange market; in other words,

$$R^D = R^F$$

At the equilibrium point B where the exchange rate E^* is 0.80 euros per dollar, the interest parity condition is satisfied because the expected returns on dollar deposits and on euro deposits are equal.

To see that the exchange rate actually heads toward the equilibrium exchange rate E^*, let's see what happens if the exchange rate is 0.85 euros per dollar, a value above the equilibrium exchange rate. As we can see in Figure 3, the expected return on euro deposits at point C is greater than the expected return on dollar deposits at point E. Since dollar and euro deposits are perfect substitutes, people will not want to hold any dollar deposits, and holders of dollar deposits will try to sell them for euro deposits in the foreign exchange market (which is referred to as "selling dollars" and "buying euros"). However, because the expected return on these dollar deposits is below that on euro deposits, no one holding euros will be willing to exchange them for dollar deposits. The resulting excess supply of dollar deposits means that the price of the dollar deposits relative to euro deposits must fall; that is, the exchange rate (amount of euros per dollar) falls as is illustrated by the downward arrow drawn in the figure at the exchange rate of 0.85 euros per dollar. The decline in the exchange rate will continue until point B is reached at the equilibrium exchange rate of 0.80 euros per dollar, where the expected return on dollar and euro deposits is now equalized.

Now let us look at what happens when the exchange rate is 0.75 euros per dollar, a value below the equilibrium level. Here the expected return on dollar deposits is greater than that on euro deposits. No one will want to hold euro deposits, and everyone will try to sell them to buy dollar deposits ("sell euros" and "buy dollars"), thus driving up the exchange rate as illustrated by the upward arrow. As the exchange rate rises, there is a smaller expected appreciation of the dollar and so a higher expected appreciation of the euro, thereby increasing the expected return on euro deposits. Finally, when the exchange rate has risen to $E^* = 0.80$ euros per dollar, the expected return on euro deposits has risen enough so that it again equals the expected return on dollar deposits.

EXPLAINING CHANGES IN EXCHANGE RATES

To explain how an exchange rate changes over time, we have to understand the factors that shift the expected-return schedules for domestic (dollar) deposits and foreign (euro) deposits.

Shifts in the Expected-Return Schedule for Foreign Deposits

As we have seen, the expected return on foreign (euro) deposits depends on the foreign interest rate i^F minus the expected appreciation of the dollar $(E^e_{t+1} - E_t)/E_t$. Because a change in the current exchange rate E_t results in a movement along the expected-return schedule for euro deposits, factors that shift this schedule must work through the foreign interest rate i^F and the expected future exchange rate E^e_{t+1}. We examine the effect of changes in these factors on the expected-return schedule for euro deposits R^F, holding everything else constant.

Study Guide To grasp how the expected-return schedule for euro deposits shifts, just think of yourself as an investor who is considering putting funds into foreign deposits. When a variable changes (i^F, for example), decide whether at a given level of the current exchange rate, holding all other variables constant, you would earn a higher or lower expected return on euro deposits.

Changes in the Foreign Interest Rate If the interest rate on foreign deposits i^F increases, holding everything else constant, the expected return on these deposits must also increase. Hence at a given exchange rate, the increase in i^F leads to a rightward shift in the expected-return schedule for euro deposits from R^F_1 to R^F_2 in Figure 4. As you can see in the figure, the outcome is a depreciation of the dollar from E_1 to E_2. An alternative way to see this is to recognize that the increase in the expected return on euro deposits at the original equilibrium exchange rate resulting from the rise in i^F means that people will want to buy euros and sell dollars, so the value of the dollar must fall. Our analysis thus generates the following conclusion: ***An increase in the foreign interest rate i^F shifts the R^F schedule to the right and causes the domestic currency to depreciate (E↓).***

Conversely, if i^F falls, the expected return on euro deposits falls, the R^F schedule shifts to the left, and the exchange rate rises. This yields the following conclusion: ***A decrease in i^F shifts the R^F schedule to the left and causes the domestic currency to appreciate (E↑).***

Changes in the Expected Future Exchange Rate Any factor that causes the expected future exchange rate E^e_{t+1} to fall decreases the expected appreciation of

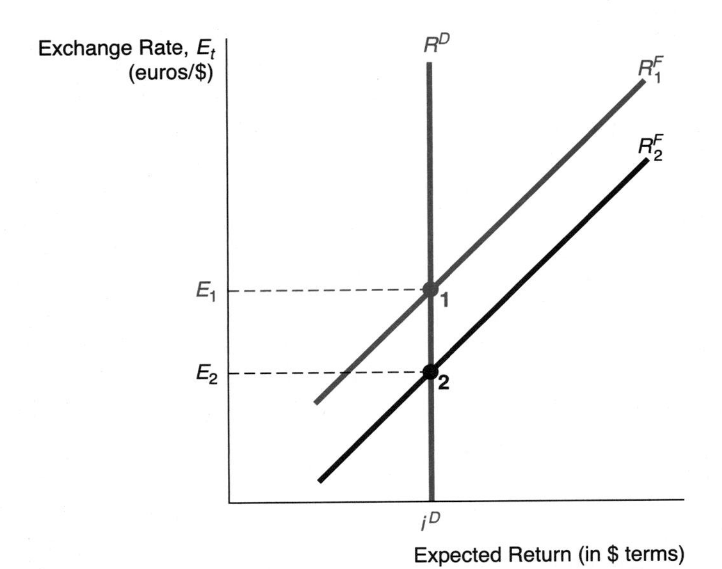

FIGURE 4 Shifts in the Schedule for the Expected Return on Foreign Deposits R^F

An increase in the expected return on foreign deposits, which occurs when either the foreign interest rate rises or the expected future exchange rate falls, shifts the schedule for the expected return on foreign deposits from R_1^F to R_2^F, and the exchange rate falls from E_1 to E_2.

the dollar and hence raises the expected appreciation of the euro. The result is a higher expected return on euro deposits, which shifts the schedule for the expected return on euro deposits to the right and leads to a decline in the exchange rate as in Figure 4. Conversely, a rise in E_{t+1}^e raises the expected appreciation of the dollar, lowers the expected return on foreign deposits, shifts the R^F schedule to the left, and raises the exchange rate. To summarize, ***a rise in the expected future exchange rate shifts the R^F schedule to the left and causes an appreciation of the domestic currency; a fall in the expected future exchange rate shifts the R^F schedule to the right and causes a depreciation of the domestic currency.***

Summary Our analysis of the long-run determinants of the exchange rate indicates the factors that influence the expected future exchange rate: the relative price level, relative trade barriers, import demand, export demand, and relative productivity (refer to Table 1). The theory of purchasing power parity suggests that if a higher Canadian price level relative to the foreign price level is expected to persist, the dollar will depreciate in the long run. A higher expected relative Canadian price level should thus have a tendency to raise the expected return on euro deposits, shift the R^F schedule to the right, and lower the current exchange rate.

Similarly, the other long-run determinants of the exchange rate we discussed earlier can also influence the expected return on euro deposits and the current exchange rate. Briefly, the following changes will increase the expected return on euro deposits, shift the R^F schedule to the right, and cause a depreciation of the domestic currency, the dollar: (1) expectations of a rise in the Canadian price level relative to the foreign price level, (2) expectations of lower Canadian trade barriers relative to foreign trade barriers, (3) expectations of higher Canadian import demand, (4) expectations of lower foreign demand for Canadian exports, and (5) expectations of lower Canadian productivity relative to foreign productivity.

Shifts in the Expected-Return Schedule for Domestic Deposits

Since the expected return on domestic (dollar) deposits is just the interest rate on these deposits i^D, this interest rate is the only factor that shifts the schedule for the expected return on dollar deposits.

Changes in the Domestic Interest Rate A rise in i^D raises the expected return on dollar deposits, shifts the R^D schedule to the right, and leads to a rise in the exchange rate, as is shown in Figure 5. Another way of seeing this is to recognize that a rise in i^D, which raises the expected return on dollar deposits, creates an excess demand for dollar deposits at the original equilibrium exchange rate, and the resulting purchases of dollar deposits cause an appreciation of the dollar. ***A rise in the domestic interest rate i^D shifts the R^D schedule to the right and causes an appreciation of the domestic currency; a fall in i^D shifts the R^D schedule to the left and causes a depreciation of the domestic currency.***

Study Guide As a study aid, the factors that shift the R^F and R^D schedules and lead to changes in the current exchange rate E_t are listed in Table 2. The table shows what happens to the exchange rate when there is an increase in each of these variables, holding everything else constant. To give yourself practice, see whether you can work out what happens to the R^F and R^D schedules and to the exchange rate if each of these factors falls rather than rises. Check your answers by seeing whether you get the opposite change in the exchange rate to those indicated in Table 2.

Application

Changes in the Equilibrium Exchange Rate: Two Examples

Our analysis has revealed the factors that affect the value of the equilibrium exchange rate. Now we use this analysis to take a close look at the response of the exchange rate to changes in interest rates and money growth.

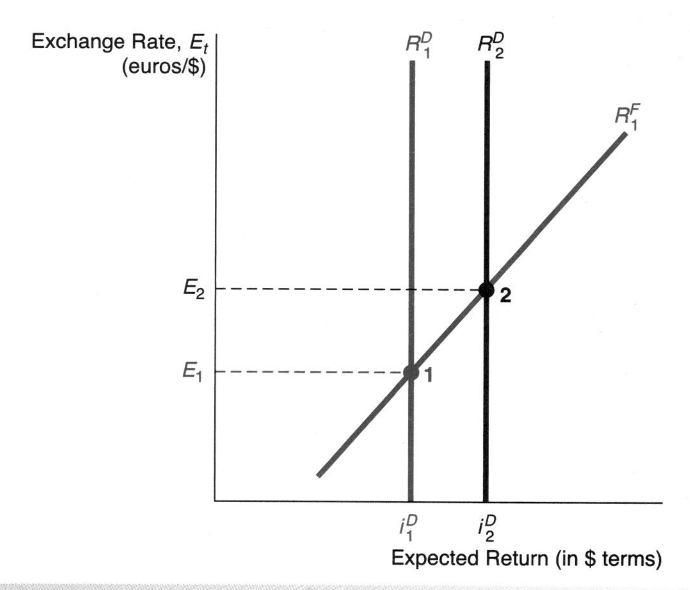

FIGURE 5 Shifts in the Schedule for the Expected Return on Domestic Deposits R^D

An increase in the expected return on dollar deposits i^D shifts the expected return on domestic (dollar) deposits from R^D_1 to R^D_2 and the exchange rate rises from E_1 to E_2.

TABLE 2 SUMMARY Factors That Shift the R^F and R^D Schedules and Affect the Exchange Rate

Factor	Change in Factor	Response of the Exchange Rate, E_t
Domestic interest rate, i^D 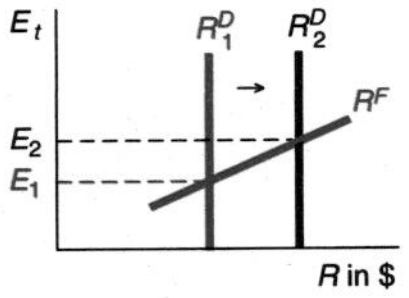	↑	↑
Foreign interest rate, i^F 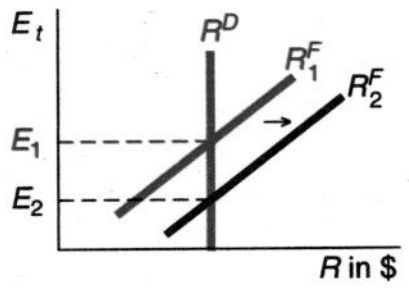	↑	↓
Expected domestic price level* 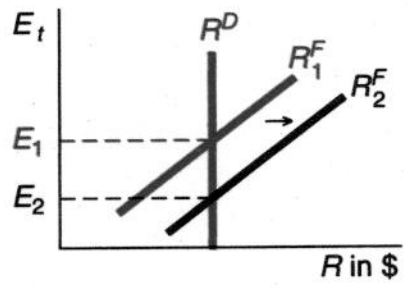	↑	↓
Expected trade barriers* 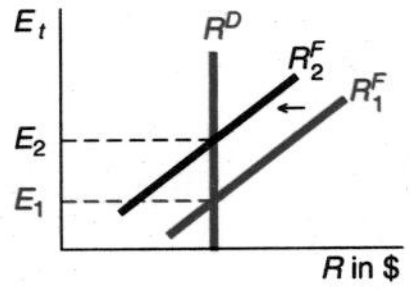	↑	↑
Expected import demand 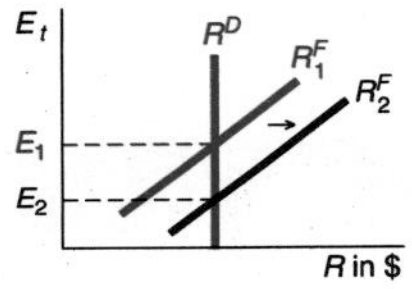	↑	↓
Expected export demand 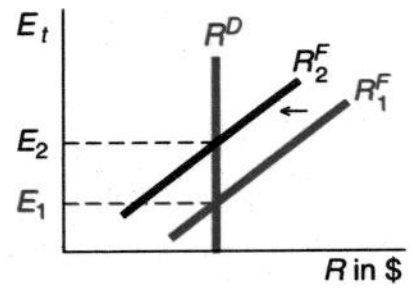	↑	↑
Productivity* 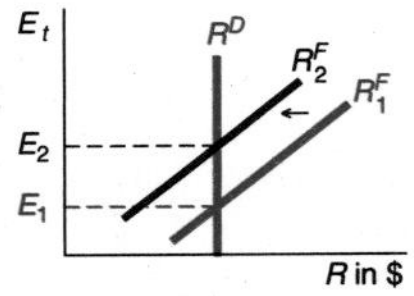	↑	↑

Note: Only increases (↑) in the factors are shown; the effects of decreases in the variables on the exchange rate are the opposite of those indicated in the "Response" column.

*Relative to other countries.

Changes in Domestic Interest Rates

Changes in domestic interest rates i^D are often cited as a major factor affecting exchange rates. For example, we see headlines in the financial press like this one: "Dollar Recovers As Interest Rates Edge Upward." But is the view presented in this headline always correct?

Not necessarily, because to analyze the effects of interest rate changes, we must carefully distinguish the sources of the changes. The Fisher equation (Chapter 3) states that a (nominal) interest rate equals the *real* interest rate plus expected inflation: $i = i_r + \pi^e$. The Fisher equation indicates that an interest rate i can change for two reasons: Either the real interest rate i_r changes or the expected inflation rate π^e changes. The effect on the exchange rate is quite different, depending on which of these two factors is the source of the change in the nominal interest rate.

Suppose that the domestic real interest rate increases so that the nominal interest rate i^D rises while expected inflation remains unchanged. In this case, it is reasonable to assume that the expected appreciation of the dollar will be unchanged because expected inflation is unchanged, and so the expected return on foreign deposits will remain unchanged for any given exchange rate. The result is that the R^F schedule stays put, the R^D schedule shifts to the right, and we end up with the situation depicted in Figure 5, which analyzes an increase in i^D, holding everything else constant. Our model of the foreign exchange market produces the following result: ***When domestic real interest rates rise, the domestic currency appreciates.***

When the nominal interest rate rises because of an increase in expected inflation, we get a different result from the one shown in Figure 5. The rise in expected domestic inflation leads to an expected depreciation of the dollar (an appreciation of the euro), which is typically thought to be larger than the increase in the domestic interest rate i^D.[5] As a result, at any given exchange rate, the expected return on foreign deposits rises more than the expected return on dollar deposits. Thus, as we see in Figure 6, the R^F schedule shifts to the right more than the R^D sched-

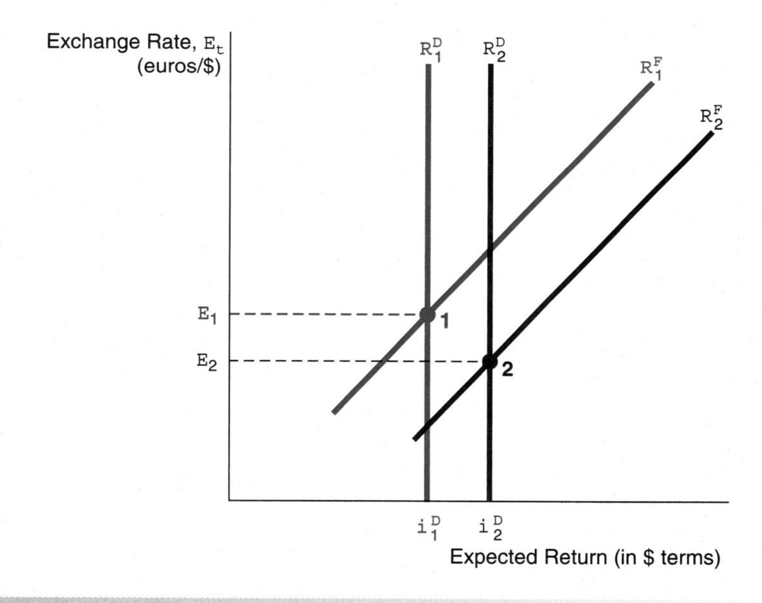

FIGURE 6 Effect of a Rise in the Domestic Nominal Interest Rate as a Result of an Increase in Expected Inflation

Because a rise in domestic expected inflation leads to an expected dollar depreciation that is larger than the resulting increase in the domestic interest rate, the expected return on foreign deposits rises by more than the expected return on domestic (dollar) deposits. R^F shifts to the right more than R^D, and the equilibrium exchange rate falls from E_1 to E_2.

[5]This conclusion is standard in asset market models of exchange rate determination; see Rudiger Dornbusch, "Expectations and Exchange Rate Dynamics," *Journal of Political Economy* 84 (1976): 1061–76. It is also consistent with empirical evidence that suggests that nominal interest rates do not rise one-for-one with increases in expected inflation. See Frederic S. Mishkin, "The Real Interest Rate: An Empirical Investigation," *Carnegie-Rochester Conference Series on Public Policy* 15 (1981): 151–200; and Lawrence Summers, "The Nonadjustment of Nominal Interest Rates: A Study of the Fisher Effect," in *Macroeconomics, Prices and Quantities*, ed. James Tobin (Washington, D.C.: Brookings Institution, 1983), pp. 201–40.

ule, and the exchange rate falls. Our analysis leads to this conclusion: ***When domestic interest rates rise due to an expected increase in inflation, the domestic currency depreciates.***

Because this conclusion is completely different from the one reached when the rise in the domestic interest rate is associated with a higher real interest rate, we must always distinguish between *real* and *nominal* measures when analyzing the effects of interest rates on exchange rates.

Changes in the Money Supply

Suppose that the Bank of Canada decides to increase the level of the money supply in order to reduce unemployment, which it believes to be excessive. The higher money supply will lead to a higher Canadian price level in the long run and hence to a lower expected future exchange rate. The resulting expected depreciation of the dollar increases the expected return on foreign deposits at any given current exchange rate and so shifts the R^F schedule rightward from R_1^F to R_2^F in Figure 7. In addition, the higher money supply will lead to a higher real money supply M/P because the price level does not immediately increase in the short run. As suggested in Chapter 4, the resulting rise in the real money supply causes the domestic interest rate to fall from i_1^D to i_2^D, which lowers the expected return on domestic (dollar) deposits, shifting the R^D schedule in from R_1^D to R_2^D. As we can see in Figure 7, the result is a decline in the exchange rate from E_1 to E_2. The conclusion is this: ***A higher domestic money supply causes the domestic currency to depreciate.***

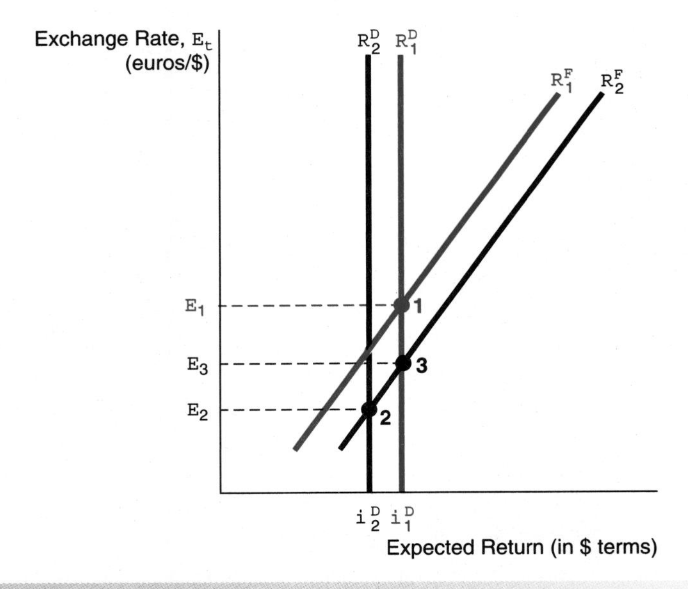

FIGURE 7 Effect of a Rise in the Money Supply

A rise in the money supply leads to a higher domestic price level in the long run, which in turn leads to a lower expected future exchange rate. The resulting decline in the expected appreciation of the dollar raises the expected return on foreign deposits, shifting the R^F schedule rightward from R_1^F to R_2^F. In the short run, the domestic interest rate i^D falls, shifting R^D from R_1^D to R_2^D. The short-run outcome is that the exchange rate falls from E_1 to E_2. In the long run, however, the interest rate returns to i_1^D and R^D returns to R_1^D. The exchange rate thus rises from E_2 to E_3 in the long run.

Exchange Rate Overshooting

Our analysis of the effect of a money supply increase on the exchange rate is not yet over—we still need to look at what happens to the exchange rate in the long run. A basic proposition in monetary theory, called **monetary neutrality,** states that in the long run, a one-time percentage rise in the money supply is matched by the same one-time percentage rise in the price level, leaving unchanged the real money supply and all other economic variables such as interest rates. An intuitive way to understand this proposition is to think of what would happen if our government announced overnight that an old dollar would now be worth 100 new dollars. The money supply in new dollars would be 100 times its old value and the price level would also be 100 times higher, but nothing in the economy would really have changed; interest rates and the real money supply would remain the same. Monetary neutrality tells us that in the long run, the rise in the money supply would not lead to a change in the domestic interest rate and so it would return to i_1^D in the long run, and the schedule for the expected return on domestic deposits would return to R_1^D. As we can see in Figure 7, this means that the exchange rate would rise from E_2 to E_3 in the long run.

The phenomenon we have described here in which the exchange rate falls by more in the short run than it does in the long run when the money supply increases is called **exchange rate overshooting.** It is important because, as we will see in the following application, it can help explain why exchange rates exhibit so much volatility.

Another way of thinking about why exchange rate overshooting occurs is to recognize that when the domestic interest rate falls in the short run, equilibrium in the foreign exchange market means that the expected return on foreign deposits must be lower. With the foreign interest rate given, this lower expected return on foreign deposits means that there must be an expected appreciation of the dollar (depreciation of the euro) in order for the expected return on foreign deposits to decline when the domestic interest rate falls. This can occur only if the current exchange rate falls below its long-run value.

Application Why Are Exchange Rates So Volatile?

The high volatility of foreign exchange rates surprises many people. Thirty or so years ago, economists generally believed that allowing exchange rates to be determined in the free market would not lead to large fluctuations in their values. Recent experience has proved them wrong. If we return to Figure 1, we see that exchange rates over the 1980–2001 period have been very volatile.

The asset market approach to exchange rate determination that we have outlined in this chapter gives a straightforward explanation of volatile exchange rates. Because expected appreciation of the domestic currency affects the expected return on foreign deposits, expectations about the price level, inflation, trade barriers, productivity, import demand, export demand, and the money supply play important roles in determining the exchange rate. When expectations about any of these variables change, our model indicates that there will be an immediate effect on the expected return on foreign deposits and therefore on the exchange rate. Since expectations on all these variables change with just about every bit of news that appears, it is not surprising that the exchange rate is volatile. In addition, we have seen that our exchange rate analysis produces exchange rate overshooting when the money supply increases. Exchange rate overshooting is an additional reason for the high volatility of exchange rates.

Because earlier models of exchange rate behaviour focused on goods markets rather than asset markets, they did not emphasize changing expectations as a source of exchange rate movements, and so these earlier models could not predict substantial fluctuations in exchange rates. The failure of earlier models to explain volatility is one reason why they are no longer so popular. The more modern approach developed here emphasizes that the foreign exchange market is like any other asset market in which expectations of the future matter. The foreign exchange market, like other asset markets such as the stock market, displays substantial price volatility, and foreign exchange rates are notoriously hard to forecast.

Application The Euro's First Three Years

With much fanfare, the euro debuted on January 1, 1999, at an exchange rate of 1.18 U.S. dollars per euro. Despite initial hopes that the euro would be a strong currency, it has actually proved to be weak, declining 30% to a low of 83 U.S. cents per euro in October 2000, only to recover slightly to 89 U.S. cents by the beginning of 2002. What explains the weakness of the euro in its first two years, and the meager recovery in its third year?

The previous application has shown how changes in real interest rates are an important factor determining the exchange rate. When the domestic real interest rate falls relative to the foreign real interest rate, then the domestic currency declines in value. Indeed, this is exactly what has happened to the euro. While the euro was coming into existence, European economies were experiencing only a slow recovery from recession, thus causing both real and nominal interest rates to fall. In contrast, in 1999 and 2000, the United States experienced very rapid growth, substantially higher than Europe, which kept real and nominal interest rates high and substantially above their European counterparts. As in the analysis of the previous application, the falling, low real interest rates in Europe relative to those in the United States led to a decline in the value of the euro.

With the slowing of the U.S. economy, which entered into recession in the spring of 2001, the process above reversed. The U.S. growth rate fell slightly behind Europe's, lowering its relative real and nominal interest rates, setting the stage for a limited recovery in the euro.

Application The "Foreign Exchange" Column

READING THE ***WALL STREET JOURNAL***

Now that we have an understanding of how exchange rates are determined, we can use our analysis to understand discussions about developments in the foreign exchange market reported in the financial press.

Every day, the *Wall Street Journal* reports on developments in the foreign exchange market on the previous business day in its "Foreign Exchange" column, an example of which is presented in the "Following the Financial News" box.

The column indicates that the introduction of the euro notes and coins in 2002 started well (and is the euro's second honeymoon given its initial introduction as a unit of account in January 1999). Our analysis of the foreign exchange market explains why this development has led to an appreciation of the euro against both the dollar and the yen.

The successful introduction of euro notes and coins has led to "euphoria," which brightens the prospects for the euro's value in the future. The higher expected value of the euro means that the yen and the dollar are expected to have a lower value in the future. In an analysis with the euro as the domestic currency, the R^F curve will shift to the left because the lower future value of the dollar and the yen imply a lower expected return on deposits denominated in these currencies. The improved prospects for the euro thus lead to the sharp appreciation of the euro. However, the column does caution that a similar phenomenon occurred when the euro was introduced in 1999, and so euphoria about the euro could fade.

The column also points out that another factor that may have caused the euro to appreciate was the U.S. Congress's failure to approve a fiscal stimulus program that could have stimulated the U.S. economy. A possibly weaker U.S. economy would mean lower U.S. interest rates in the future. These lower rates would then lower the expected return for dollar denominated deposits, also shifting the R^F curve to the left and lead to an appreciation of the euro.

THE PRACTISING FINANCIAL INSTITUTION MANAGER

Profiting from Foreign Exchange Forecasts

Managers of financial institutions care a great deal about what foreign exchange rates will be in the future because these rates affect the value of assets on their balance sheet that are denominated in foreign currencies. In addition, financial institutions often engage in trading foreign exchange, both for their own account and for their customers. Forecasts of future foreign exchange rates can thus have a big impact on the profits that financial institutions make on their foreign exchange trading operations.

Managers of financial institutions obtain foreign exchange forecasts either by hiring their own staff economists to generate them or by purchasing forecasts from other financial institutions or economic forecasting firms. In predicting exchange rate movements, forecasters look at the factors mentioned in this chapter. For example, if they expect domestic real interest rates to rise, they will predict, in line with our analysis, that the domestic currency will appreciate; conversely, if they expect domestic inflation to increase, they will predict that the domestic currency will depreciate.

Managers of financial institutions, particularly those engaged in international banking, rely on foreign exchange forecasts to make decisions about which assets denominated in foreign currencies they should hold. For example, if a financial institution manager has a reliable forecast that the euro will appreciate in the future but the yen will depreciate, the manager will want to sell off assets denominated in yen and instead purchase assets denominated in euros. Alternatively, the manager might instruct loan officers to make more loans denominated in euros and fewer loans denominated in yen. Likewise, if the yen is forecast to appreciate and the euro to depreciate, the manager would want to switch out of euro-denominated assets into yen-denominated assets and would want to make more loans in yen and fewer in euros.

If the financial institution has a foreign exchange trading operation, a forecast of an appreciation of the yen means that the financial institution manager should tell foreign exchange traders to buy yen. If the forecast turns out to be correct, the higher value of the yen means that the trader can sell the yen in the future and pocket a tidy profit. If the euro is forecast to depreciate, the trader can sell euros and buy them back in the future at a lower price if the forecast turns out to be correct, and again the financial institution will make a profit.

Accurate foreign exchange rate forecasts can thus help a financial institution manager generate substantial profits for the institution. Unfortunately, exchange rate forecasters are no more or less accurate than other economic forecasters, and they often make large errors. Reports on foreign exchange rate forecasts and how well forecasters are doing appear from time to time in the *Wall Street Journal* and in the trade magazine *Euromoney*.

FOLLOWING THE FINANCIAL NEWS

The "Foreign Exchange" Column

The "Foreign Exchange" column appears daily in the *Wall Street Journal;* an example is presented here. It is found in the third section, "Money and Investing."

Euro's Second Honeymoon Starts Well, But Traders Warn Euphoria Could Fade

FOREIGN EXCHANGE

By Michael R. Sesit
Staff Reporter of The Wall Street Journal

LONDON—The euro's second honeymoon began swimmingly, but traders cautioned that the euphoria could quickly fade as it did following the currency's creation three years ago.

The euro rose sharply against the dollar and yen on the first trading day since the smooth introduction of euro notes and coins, bringing relief to officials throughout the 12-nation euro zone.

"I think it was very important that the first day would be a good day, which is the case," European Central Bank governing-council member and Bank of France Governor Jean-Claude Trichet said in an interview on CNN. "It's extraordinary to see what I would call enthusiasm, which has not been foreseen."

With a rally that began in Asian trading, accelerated during European trading and picked up even more steam as New York opened, Europe's common currency at its peak yesterday stood at a two-week high against the dollar and a 28-month high against the yen. Traders attributed the currency's climb to the relatively trouble-free issue of euro-denominated bank notes and coins, coupled with signs of recovery in euro-zone manufacturing and continued disenchantment with Japan's economic prospects.

In late London trading, the euro stood at 90.30 U.S. cents and 119.24 yen, compared with 89.15 cents and 117.38 yen late in New York on Dec. 31. At one point in intraday activity, the common currency rose to a 16-day high of 90.69 cents and 119.91 yen, its highest level since Aug. 18, 1999. Late yesterday in New York, the euro was at 90.36 cents, up from 89.15 cents late Monday. The dollar was at 132.14 yen, up from 131.67 yen on Monday. The dollar was at 1.6444 Swiss francs, down from 1.6582 francs. Sterling was at $1.4461, down from $1.4560.

"The reason [the euro] is up really is a reflection of a psychological boost on the back of a successful notes and coins introduction on Jan. 1," said Shahab Jalinoos, a currency strategist at UBS Warburg, adding that the euro could climb to back toward 92 cents in the current environment.

That said, Mr. Jalinoos advised not to read too much into the initial trading enthusiasm. "We would caution that we saw a similar euro rally on the back of its introduction in January 1999, which broke down in spectacular fashion as the inadequacies of the euro-zone economy became apparent," he said.

What's more, UBS Warburg strategists don't discount this happening again. "At the moment, people are focused on the sheer fact that European policy makers have brought the [euro] project to a conclusion without a crisis," said Mr. Jalinoos. "But the cold reality of a weak European economy could come back to haunt euro bulls."

Besides the introduction of notes and coins, another factor that may have boosted the euro yesterday was the U.S. Congress's recent failure to approve a fiscal stimulus program that many had been counting on to ignite a U.S. economic recovery. Although somewhat old news, Paul Meggyesi, director of foreign-exchange strategy at Deutsche Bank, said that the holidays may have kept many investors from focusing on its impact.

Flowing from the congressional inaction, Deutsche Bank's economists have cut their forecast of U.S. growth for the second half of this year by a full percentage point to 3.5% from 4.5%. The absence of additional government spending has also prompted them to reduce their projections of Federal Reserve interest-rate increases.

In Sweden, which isn't part of the common currency, talk of possible participation helped to drive the Swedish currency to a 20-week high of 9.2 kronor to the euro, before it retreated on profit taking. "Public opinion has swung in Sweden, and is now euro-supportive," which should strengthen the krona against the euro, BNP Paribas strategists told clients in a memorandum.

Source: Wall Street Journal, January 3, 2002, p. C15. Republished by permission of Dow Jones, Inc. via Copyright Clearance Center, Inc.

SUMMARY

1. Foreign exchange rates (the price of one country's currency in terms of another's) are important because they affect the price of domestically produced goods sold abroad and the cost of foreign goods bought domestically.
2. The theory of purchasing power parity suggests that long-run changes in the exchange rate between two countries are determined by changes in the relative price levels of the two countries. Other factors that affect exchange rates in the long run are tariffs and quotas, import demand, export demand, and productivity.
3. Exchange rates are determined in the short run by the interest parity condition, which states that the expected return on domestic deposits is equal to the expected return on foreign deposits.
4. Any factor that changes the expected returns on domestic or foreign deposits will lead to changes in the exchange rate. Such factors include changes in the interest rates on domestic and foreign deposits as well as changes in any of the factors that affect the long-run exchange rate and hence the expected future exchange rate. Changes in the money supply lead to exchange rate overshooting, causing the exchange rate to change by more in the short run than in the long run.
5. The asset market approach to exchange rate determination can explain both the volatility of exchange rates and the rise of the dollar in the 1980–1985 period and its subsequent fall.
6. Forecasts of foreign exchange rates are very valuable to managers of financial institutions because these rates influence decisions about which assets denominated in foreign currencies the institutions should hold and what kinds of trades should be made by their traders in the foreign exchange market.

KEY TERMS

appreciation, *p. 295*
capital mobility, *p. 322*
depreciation, *p. 295*
exchange rate, *p. 293*
exchange rate overshooting, *p. 313*
foreign exchange market, *p. 293*
forward exchange rate, *p. 295*
forward transaction, *p. 295*
interest parity condition, *p. 304*
law of one price, *p. 297*
monetary neutrality, *p. 313*
quotas, *p. 300*
spot exchange rate, *p. 295*
spot transaction, *p. 294*
tariffs, *p. 300*
theory of purchasing power parity (PPP), *p. 298*

QUESTIONS AND PROBLEMS

1. When the euro appreciates, are you more likely to drink Canadian or French wine?

*2. "A country is always worse off when its currency is weak (falls in value)." Is this statement true, false, or uncertain? Explain your answer.

3. Check in a newspaper the exchange rates for the foreign currencies listed in the "Following the Financial News" box on page 296. Which of these currencies have appreciated and which have depreciated since December 31, 2001?

*4. If the European price level rises by 5% relative to the price level in Canada, what does the theory of purchasing power parity predict will happen to the value of the euro in terms of dollars?

5. If the demand for a country's exports falls at the same time that tariffs on imports are raised, will the country's currency tend to appreciate or depreciate in the long run?

*6. In the mid- to late 1970s, the yen appreciated relative to the U.S. dollar even though Japan's inflation rate was higher than America's. How can this be explained by an improvement in the productivity of Japanese industry relative to Canadian industry?

Predicting the Future

Answer the remaining problems by drawing the appropriate exchange market diagrams.

7. The governor of the Bank of Canada announces that he will reduce inflation with a new anti-inflation program. If the public believes him, predict what will happen to the Canadian exchange rate.

*8. If the British central bank prints money to reduce unemployment, what will happen to the value of the pound in the short run and the long run?

9. If the European government unexpectedly announces that it will be imposing higher tariffs on foreign goods one year from now, what will happen to the value of the euro today?

*10. If nominal interest rates in Canada rise but real interest rates fall, predict what will happen to the Canadian exchange rate.

11. If Canadian auto companies make a breakthrough in automobile technology and are able to produce a car that gets 90 km to the litre, what will happen to the Canadian exchange rate?

*12. If Canadians go on a spending spree and buy twice as much French perfume, Japanese TVs, English sweaters, Swiss watches, and Italian wine, what will happen to the value of the Canadian dollar?

13. If expected inflation drops in Europe so that interest rates fall there, predict what will happen to the Canadian exchange rate.

*14. If the European central bank decides to contract the money supply in order to fight inflation, what will happen to the value of the Canadian dollar?

15. If there is a strike in France, making it harder to buy French goods, what will happen to the value of the euro?

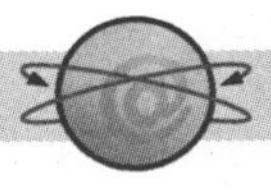

WEB EXERCISES

The Foreign Exchange Market

1. The U.S. Federal Reserve maintains a Website that lists the exchange rate between the United States and many other currencies. Go to http://www.federalreserve.gov/releases/H10/hist/. Go to the historical data from 1990 on and find the euro. What has the percentage change in the euro–U.S. dollar exchange rate been between introduction and now? What has been the annual percentage change in the euro–U.S. dollar exchange rate for each year since the euro's introduction?

2. International travellers and businesspeople frequently need to accurately convert from one currency to another. It is often easy to find the rate needed to convert the Canadian dollar into another currency. It can be more difficult to find cross-conversion rates. Go to http://www.bankofcanada.ca/en/rates.htm and click on "Currency Converter" under Exchange Rates. The currency converter lets you convert from any currency into any other currency. How many Polish zlotys can you currently buy with one Chilean peso?

Chapter 13 The International Financial System

Preview

Thanks to the growing interdependence between the Canadian economy and the economies of the rest of the world, the international financial system now plays a more prominent role in economic events in Canada. In this chapter we examine the evolution of the international financial system during the past half century and where it may be heading in the future. In addition, we see how international financial transactions and the structure of the international financial system affect monetary policy in Canada and provide substantial profit opportunities for financial institutions.

INTERVENTION IN THE FOREIGN EXCHANGE MARKET

In Chapter 12 we analyzed the foreign exchange market as if it were a completely free market that responds to all market pressures. However, the foreign exchange market, like many others, is not free of government intervention; central banks regularly engage in international financial transactions called **foreign exchange interventions** in order to influence exchange rates. In our current international financial arrangement, called a **managed float regime** (or a dirty float), exchange rates fluctuate from day to day, but central banks attempt to influence their countries' exchange rates by buying and selling currencies. The exchange rate analysis we developed in Chapter 12 is used here to explain the impact that central bank intervention has on the foreign exchange market.

Foreign Exchange Intervention and the Money Supply

The first step in understanding how central bank intervention in the foreign exchange market affects exchange rates is to see the impact on the monetary base and the money supply from a central bank sale in the foreign exchange market of some of its holdings of assets denominated in a foreign currency (called **international reserves**). Suppose that the Bank of Canada decides to sell $1 billion of its foreign assets in exchange for $1 billion of Canadian currency. The Bank's purchase of dollars has two effects. First, it reduces the Bank's holding of international reserves by $1 billion. Second, because its purchase of currency removes it from the hands of the public, currency in circulation falls by $1 billion. To see this we make use of a simplified balance sheet called a **T-account,** with lines in the form of a T, that lists only the changes that occur in balance sheet items starting from an initial balance sheet position. The T-account for the Bank of Canada illustrating this transaction is as follows:

Bank of Canada			
Assets		Liabilities	
Foreign assets (international reserves)	−$1 billion	Currency in circulation	−$1 billion

Because the monetary base is made up of currency in circulation plus reserves, this decline in currency implies that the monetary base has fallen by $1 billion.

If instead of paying for the foreign assets sold by the Bank of Canada with currency, the persons buying the foreign assets pay for them by cheques written on accounts at domestic banks, then the Bank of Canada deducts the $1 billion from the deposit accounts these banks have with the Bank. The result is that deposits with the Bank (reserves) decline by $1 billion, as shown in the following T-account:

Bank of Canada			
Assets		Liabilities	
Foreign assets (international reserves)	−$1 billion	Deposits with the Bank of Canada (reserves)	−$1 billion

In this case, the outcome of the Bank of Canada sale of foreign assets and the purchase of dollar deposits is a $1 billion decline in reserves and a $1 billion decline in the monetary base because reserves are also a component of the monetary base.

We now see that the outcome for the monetary base is exactly the same when a central bank sells foreign assets to purchase domestic bank deposits or domestic currency. This is why when we say that a central bank has purchased its domestic currency, we do not have to distinguish whether it actually purchased currency or bank deposits denominated in the domestic currency. We have thus reached an important conclusion: ***A central bank's purchase of domestic currency and corresponding sale of foreign assets in the foreign exchange market leads to an equal decline in its international reserves and the monetary base.***

We could have reached the same conclusion by a more direct route. A central bank sale of a foreign asset is no different from an open market sale of a government bond. We learned in Chapter 7 that an open market sale leads to an equal decline in the monetary base; therefore, a sale of foreign assets also leads to an equal decline in the monetary base. By similar reasoning, a central bank purchase of foreign assets paid for by selling domestic currency, like an open market purchase, leads to an equal rise in the monetary base. Thus we reach the following conclusion: ***A central bank's sale of domestic currency to purchase foreign assets in the foreign exchange market results in an equal rise in its international reserves and the monetary base.***

The intervention we have just described, in which a central bank allows the purchase or sale of domestic currency to have an effect on the monetary base and hence on the money supply, is called an **unsterilized foreign exchange intervention**. But what if the central bank does not want the purchase or sale of domestic currency to affect the monetary base and the money supply? All it has to do is to counter the effect of the foreign exchange intervention by conducting an offsetting open market operation in the government bond market. For example, in the case of a $1 billion purchase of dollars by the Bank of Canada and a corresponding $1 billion sale of foreign assets, which we have seen would decrease the monetary base by $1 billion, the Bank can conduct an open market purchase of $1 billion of government bonds, which would increase the monetary base by

$1 billion. The resulting T-account for the foreign exchange intervention and the offsetting open market operation leaves the monetary base unchanged:

Bank of Canada			
Assets		Liabilities	
Foreign assets (international reserves)	−$1 billion	Monetary base (currency in circulation plus reserves)	0
Government bonds	+$1 billion		

A foreign exchange intervention with an offsetting open market operation that leaves the monetary base unchanged is called a **sterilized foreign exchange intervention.**

Now that we understand that there are two types of foreign exchange interventions, unsterilized and sterilized, let's look at how each affects the exchange rate.

Unsterilized Intervention

Your intuition might lead you to suspect that if a central bank wants to lower the value of the domestic currency, it should sell its currency in the foreign exchange market and purchase foreign assets. Indeed, this intuition is correct for the case of an unsterilized intervention.

Recall that in an unsterilized intervention, if the Bank of Canada decides to sell dollars in order to buy foreign assets in the foreign exchange market, this works just like an open market purchase of bonds that increases the monetary base and the money supply. Hence we find ourselves analyzing exactly the situation described in Figure 7 of Chapter 12, which is reproduced here as Figure 1. The

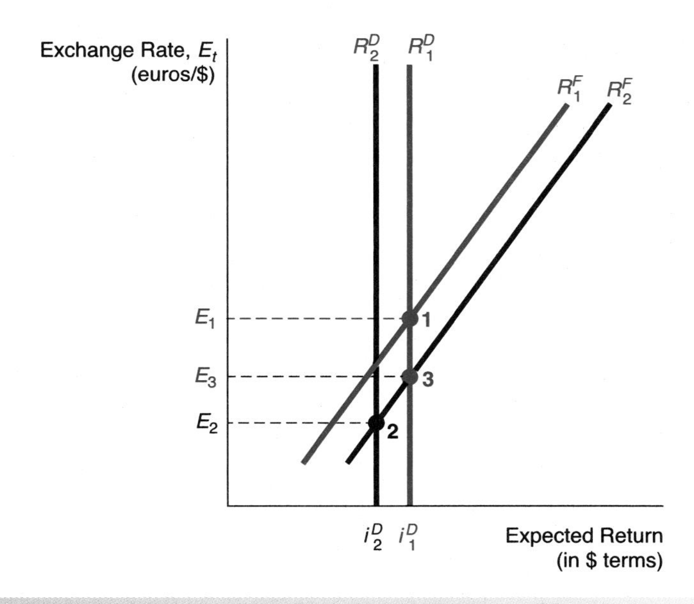

FIGURE 1 Effect of a Sale of Canadian Dollars and a Purchase of Foreign Assets

A sale of Canadian dollars and the consequent open market purchase of foreign assets increase the monetary base. The resulting rise in the money supply leads to a higher domestic price level in the long run, which leads to a lower expected future exchange rate. The resulting decline in the expected appreciation of the dollar raises the expected return on foreign deposits, shifting the R^F schedule rightward from R_1^F to R_2^F. In the short run, the domestic interest rate i^D falls, shifting R^D from R_1^D to R_2^D. The short-run outcome is that the exchange rate falls from E_1 to E_2. In the long run, however, the interest rate returns to i_1^D, and R^D returns to R_1^D. The exchange rate therefore rises from E_2 to E_3 in the long run.

higher money supply leads to a higher Canadian price level in the long run and so to a lower expected future exchange rate. The resulting decline in the expected appreciation of the dollar increases the expected return on foreign deposits and shifts the R^F schedule to the right. In addition, the increase in the money supply will lead to a higher real money supply in the short run, which causes the interest rate on dollar deposits to fall. The resulting lower expected return on dollar deposits translates as a leftward shift in the R^D schedule. The fall in the expected return on dollar deposits and the increase in the expected return on foreign deposits means that foreign assets have a higher expected return than dollar deposits at the old equilibrium exchange rate. Hence people will try to sell their dollar deposits, and the exchange rate will fall.

Our analysis leads us to the following conclusion about unsterilized interventions in the foreign exchange market: ***An unsterilized intervention in which domestic currency is sold to purchase foreign assets leads to a gain in international reserves, an increase in the money supply, and a depreciation of the domestic currency.***

The reverse result is found for an unsterilized intervention in which domestic currency is purchased by selling foreign assets. The purchase of domestic currency by selling foreign assets (reducing international reserves) works like an open market sale to reduce the monetary base and the money supply. The decrease in the money supply raises the interest rate on dollar deposits and shifts R^D rightward while causing R^F to shift leftward, because it leads to a lower Canadian price level in the long run and thus to a higher expected appreciation of the dollar and a lower expected return on foreign deposits. The increase in the expected return on dollar deposits relative to foreign deposits will mean that people will want to buy more dollar deposits, and the exchange rate will rise. ***An unsterilized intervention in which domestic currency is purchased by selling foreign assets leads to a drop in international reserves, a decrease in the money supply, and an appreciation of the domestic currency.***

Sterilized Intervention

The key point to remember about a sterilized intervention is that the central bank engages in offsetting open market operations so that there is no impact on the monetary base and the money supply. In the context of the model of exchange rate determination we have developed here, it is straightforward to show that a sterilized intervention has *no effect* on the exchange rate. Remember that in our model, foreign and domestic deposits are perfect substitutes, so equilibrium in the foreign exchange market occurs when the expected returns on foreign and domestic deposits are equal. A sterilized intervention leaves the money supply unchanged and so has no way of directly affecting interest rates or the expected future exchange rate.[1] Because the expected returns on dollar and foreign deposits are unaffected, the expected return schedules remain at R_1^D and R_1^F in Figure 1, and the exchange rate remains unchanged at E_1.

[1]Note that a sterilized intervention could indicate what central banks want to happen to the future exchange rate and so might provide a signal about the course of future monetary policy. In this way, a sterilized intervention could lead to shifts in the R^F schedule, but in reality it is the future change in monetary policy, not the sterilized intervention, that is the ultimate source of exchange rate effects. For a discussion of the signaling effect, see Maurice Obstfeld, "The Effectiveness of Foreign Exchange Intervention: Recent Experience, 1985–1988," in *International Policy Coordination and Exchange Rate Fluctuations,* ed. William H. Branson, Jacob A. Frenkel, and Morris Goldstein (Chicago: University of Chicago Press, 1990), pp. 197–237.

At first it might seem puzzling that a central bank purchase or sale of domestic currency that is sterilized does not lead to a change in the exchange rate. A central bank purchase of domestic currency cannot raise the exchange rate because with no effect on the domestic money supply or interest rates, any resulting rise in the exchange rate would mean that the expected return on foreign deposits would be greater than the expected return on domestic deposits. Given our assumption that foreign and domestic deposits are perfect substitutes (equally desirable), this would mean that no one would want to hold domestic deposits.[2] So the exchange rate would have to fall back to its previous level, where the expected returns on domestic and foreign deposits were equal.

BALANCE OF PAYMENTS

The site www.statcan.ca contains exchange rates, balance of payments, and trade data.

Because international financial transactions such as foreign exchange interventions have considerable effect on monetary policy, it is worth knowing how these transactions are measured. The **balance of payments** is a bookkeeping system for recording all payments that have a direct bearing on the movement of funds between a nation (private sector and government) and foreign countries.

The balance-of-payments account in the accompanying "Following the Financial News" box uses a standard double-entry bookkeeping system much like one that you or I might use to keep a record of payments and receipts. All transactions involving payments from foreigners to Canadians are entered in the "Receipts" column with a plus sign (+) to reflect that they are credits; that is, they result in a flow of funds to Canadians. Receipts include foreign purchases of Canadian products such as computers and wheat (exports), purchases by foreign tourists (services), income earned from Canadian investment abroad (investment income), foreign aid and gifts and pensions paid to Canadians (unilateral transfers), and foreign payments for Canadian assets (capital inflows).

All payments to foreigners are entered in the "Payments" column with a minus sign (–) to reflect that they are debits because they result in flows of funds to other countries. Payments include Canadian purchases of foreign products such as French wine and Japanese cars (imports), Canadian travel abroad (services), income earned by foreigners from investments in Canada (investment income), foreign aid and gifts and pensions paid to foreigners (unilateral transfers), and Canadian payments for foreign assets (capital outflows).

Current Account

The **current account** shows international transactions that involve currently produced goods and services. The difference between exports (line 1) and imports (line 2) is called the **trade balance**. When exports are greater than imports (here by $54.7 billion), we have a trade balance surplus; if imports are greater than exports, we have a trade balance deficit.

The next two items in the current account are the net payments or receipts that arise from investment income and unilateral transfers (gifts, pensions, and foreign aid). In 2001, for example, net investment income was −$27.4 billion (in line 3) for Canada because Canadians received less investment income from abroad than they paid out. Since Canadians made fewer unilateral transfers to

[2]If domestic and foreign deposits are not perfect substitutes, a sterilized intervention can affect the exchange rate. However, most studies find little evidence to support the position that sterilized intervention has a significant impact on foreign exchange rates. For a further discussion of the effects of sterilized versus unsterilized intervention, see Paul Krugman and Maurice Obstfeld, *International Economics,* 5th ed. (Reading, MA: Addison Wesley Longman, 2000).

FOLLOWING THE FINANCIAL NEWS

The Balance of Payments

The balance of payments summarizes a country's transactions with the rest of the world. The complete set of items in the balance of payments is published on a quarterly basis by Statistics Canada, with the figures released about two months after the end of the quarter to which they apply. An example of the balance-of-payments accounts for Canada appears here.

Canadian Balance of Payments, 2001 ($ billions)

	Receipts (+)	Payments (−)	Balance
Current Account			
(1) Exports	467.6		
(2) Imports		−412.9	
Trade balance			54.7
(3) Net investment income		−27.4	
(4) Net unilateral transfers	1.9		
Current account balance: (1) + (2) + (3) + (4)			29.2
Capital Account			
(5) Capital outflows		−91.8	
(6) Capital inflows	72.8		
(7) Statistical discrepancy		−8.3	
Official reserve transactions balance: (1) + (2) + (3) + (4) + (5) + (6) + (7)			1.9
Method of Financing			
(8) Increase in Canadian official reserve assets		−3.34	
(9) Increase in foreign official assets	1.44		
Total financing of surplus (8) + (9)			−1.9
Balance of Payments			
Sum (1) through (9)			0.0

Source: Statistics Canada CANSIM II Table 3760001. By convention, an increase in official reserve assets is recorded with a minus sign (debit).

Go to www.statcan.ca for more information about Statistics Canada.

foreign countries than foreigners made to Canada, a $1.9 billion receipt is shown in line 4.

The sum of the items in lines 1 through 4 is the current account balance, which in 2001 showed a surplus of $29.2 billion. The current account balance is an important balance-of-payments concept for several reasons. As we can see from the balance-of-payments account, any surplus or deficit in the current account must be balanced either by capital account transactions (lending or borrowing abroad) or by changes in government reserve asset items:

Current account + capital account = change in government reserve assets

The current account balance tells us whether Canada (private sector and government combined) is increasing or decreasing its claims on foreign wealth. A surplus indicates that Canada is increasing its claims on foreign wealth, as in 2001, and a deficit indicates that the country is reducing its claims on foreign wealth.[3]

[3]The current account balance can also be viewed as showing by how much total saving exceeds private sector and government investment in Canada. We can see this by noting that total Canadian saving equals the increase in total wealth held by the Canadian private sector and government. Total investment equals the increase in the Canadian capital stock (wealth physically in Canada). The difference between them is the increase in Canadian claims on foreign wealth.

Financial analysts follow the current account balance closely because they believe that it can provide information on the future movement of exchange rates. The current account balance provides some indication of what is happening to the demand for imports and exports, which, as we saw in Chapter 12, can affect the exchange rate. In addition, the current account balance provides information about what will be happening to Canadian claims on foreign wealth in the long run. Because a movement of foreign wealth to Canadian residents can affect the demand for dollar assets, changes in Canadian claims on foreign wealth, reflected in the current account balance, can affect the exchange rate over time.[4]

Capital Account

The **capital account** describes the flow of capital between Canada and other countries. Capital outflows are Canadian purchases of foreign assets (a "Payments" item), and capital inflows are foreign purchases of Canadian assets (a "Receipts" item). The capital outflows (line 5) are more than the capital inflows (line 6), resulting in a net outflow of $1.9 billion.

The statistical discrepancy (line 7) represents errors due to unrecorded transactions involving smuggling and other capital flows. The statistical discrepancy, which keeps the balance-of-payments account in balance, is –$8.3 billion, which suggests that some of the other items in the balance of payments may not be measured very accurately. Many experts believe that the statistical discrepancy is primarily the result of large hidden capital flows, and so the item has been placed in the capital account part of the balance of payments.

Official Reserve Transactions Balance

The sum of lines 1 through 7, called the **official reserve transactions balance**, equals the current account balance plus the items in the capital account. When we refer to a surplus or a deficit in the balance of payments, we actually mean a surplus or deficit in the official reserve transactions balance. Because the balance-of-payments account must balance, the official reserve transactions balance tells us the net amount of international reserves that must move between central banks to finance international transactions. One reason we are particularly interested in the movements of international reserves is that, as we saw earlier in the chapter, these movements can have an important impact on the money supply and exchange rates.

Methods of Financing the Balance of Payments

Because most countries' currencies are not held by other countries as international reserves, these countries must finance an excess of payments over receipts (a deficit in the balance of payments) by providing international reserves to foreign governments and central banks. A balance-of-payments deficit is associated with a loss of international reserves; likewise, a balance-of-payments surplus is associated with a gain.

Unlike the Canadian dollar, the U.S. dollar and U.S. dollar-denominated assets are the major component of international reserves held by other countries. Thus a U.S. balance-of-payments deficit can be financed by a decrease in U.S. international reserves, an increase in foreign central banks' holdings of international

[4]If Canadian residents have a greater preference for dollar assets than foreigners do, a movement of foreign wealth to Canadian residents when there is a balance-of-payments surplus will increase the demand for dollar assets over time and will cause the Canadian dollar to appreciate.

reserves (U.S. dollar assets), or both. Conversely, a U.S. balance-of-payments surplus can be financed by an increase in U.S. international reserves, a decrease in foreign central banks' international reserves, or both.

For Canada in 2001, the official reserve transactions surplus of $1.9 billion resulted in a $3.34 billion increase in Canadian international reserves (−3.34 in the "Payments" column of line 8) and a $1.44 billion increase of foreign holdings of Canadian dollars (1.44 in the "Receipts" column of line 9).[5] On net, Canada's international reserves increased by $1.9 billion (the $3.34 billion increase in Canadian holdings of international reserves minus the $1.44 billion foreign increase in holdings of Canadian dollars). This $1.9 billion increase in Canadian international reserves just matches the $1.9 billion official reserve transactions surplus, so the sum of lines 1 through 9 is zero, and the account balances.

EVOLUTION OF THE INTERNATIONAL FINANCIAL SYSTEM

Before examining the impact of international financial transactions on monetary policy, we need to understand the past and current structure of the international financial system.

Gold Standard

Before World War I, the world economy operated under the **gold standard**, meaning that the currency of most countries was convertible directly into gold. Canadian dollar bills, for example, could be exchanged for approximately $\frac{1}{20}$ ounce of gold. Likewise, the British Treasury would exchange $\frac{1}{4}$ ounce of gold for £1 sterling. Because a Canadian could convert $20 into 1 ounce of gold, which could be used to buy £4, the exchange rate between the pound and the Canadian dollar was effectively fixed at approximately $5 to the pound. Tying currencies to gold resulted in an international financial system with fixed exchange rates between currencies. The fixed exchange rates under the gold standard had the important advantage of encouraging world trade by eliminating the uncertainty that occurs when exchange rates fluctuate.

To see how the gold standard operated in practice, let us see what occurs if, under the gold standard, the British pound begins to appreciate above the $5 par value. If a Canadian importer of £100 of English tweed tries to pay for the tweed with dollars, it costs more than the $500 it cost before. Nevertheless, the importer has another option involving the purchase of gold that can reduce the cost of the tweed. Instead of using dollars to pay for the tweed, the Canadian importer can exchange the $500 for gold, ship the gold to Britain, and convert it into £100. The shipment of gold to Britain is cheaper as long as the British pound is above the $5 par value (plus a small amount to pay for the cost of shipping the gold).

The appreciation of the pound leads to a British gain of international reserves (gold) and an equal Canadian loss. Because a change in a country's holdings of international reserves (gold) leads to an equal change in its monetary base, the movement of gold from Canada to Britain causes the British monetary base to rise and the Canadian monetary base to fall. The resulting rise in the British money supply raises the British price level, while the fall in the Canadian money supply lowers the Canadian price level. The resulting increase in the British price level

[5]At first it may seem strange that when Canada gains $3.34 billion of international reserves, it is entered in the balance of payments as a payment with a negative sign. Recall, however, that when a central bank gains international reserves, it has purchased foreign assets. Thus, an increase in international reserves is just like an outflow of capital in the capital account and appears as a payment with a negative sign.

relative to Canada then causes the pound to depreciate. This process will continue until the value of the pound falls back down to its $5 par value.

A depreciation of the pound below the $5 par value, on the contrary, stimulates gold shipments from Britain to Canada. These shipments raise the Canadian money supply and lower the British money supply, causing the pound to appreciate back toward the $5 par value. We thus see that under the gold standard, a rise or fall in the exchange rate sets in motion forces that return the exchange rate to the par value.

As long as countries abided by the rules under the gold standard and kept their currencies backed by and convertible into gold, exchange rates remained fixed. However, adherence to the gold standard meant that a country had no control over its monetary policy because its money supply was determined by gold flows between countries. Furthermore, monetary policy throughout the world was greatly influenced by the production of gold and gold discoveries. When gold production was low in the 1870s and 1880s, the money supply throughout the world grew slowly and did not keep pace with the growth of the world economy. The result was deflation (falling price levels). Gold discoveries in Alaska and South Africa in the 1890s then greatly expanded gold production, which caused money supplies to increase rapidly and price levels to rise (inflation) until World War I.

Bretton Woods System and the IMF

World War I caused massive trade disruptions. Countries could no longer convert their currencies into gold, and the gold standard collapsed. Despite attempts to revive it in the interwar period, the worldwide depression, beginning in 1929, led to its permanent demise. As the Allied victory in World War II was becoming certain in 1944, the Allies met in Bretton Woods, New Hampshire, to develop a new international monetary system to promote world trade and prosperity after the war. In the agreement worked out among the Allies, central banks bought and sold their own currencies to keep their exchange rates fixed at a certain level (called a **fixed exchange rate regime**). The agreement lasted from 1945 to 1971 and was known as the **Bretton Woods system**.

The Bretton Woods agreement created the **International Monetary Fund (IMF)**, headquartered in Washington, D.C., which had 30 original member countries in 1945 and currently has more than 150. The IMF was given the task of promoting the growth of world trade by setting rules for the maintenance of fixed exchange rates and by making loans to countries that were experiencing balance-of-payments difficulties.[6] As part of its role of monitoring the compliance of member countries with its rules, the IMF also took on the job of collecting and standardizing international economic data.

Visit www.imf.org to learn more about the IMF.

The Bretton Woods agreement also set up the International Bank for Reconstruction and Development, commonly referred to as the **World Bank**, also headquartered in Washington, which provides long-term loans to help developing countries build dams, roads, and other physical capital that will contribute to their economic development. The funds for these loans are obtained primarily by issuing World Bank bonds, which are sold in the capital markets of the developed countries.[7]

The World Bank's home page, www.worldbank.org, provides further information about its activities.

[6]Rules for the conduct of trade between countries (the setting of tariffs and quotas) were given to the General Agreement on Tariffs and Trade (GATT), headquartered in Geneva. For a discussion of how this agency operates, see John Williamson, *The Open Economy and the World Economy* (New York: Basic Books, 1983).

[7]In 1960, the World Bank established an affiliate, the International Development Association (IDA), which provides particularly attractive loans to developing countries (with 50-year maturities and zero interest rates, for example). Funds for these loans are obtained by direct contributions of member countries.

Because the United States emerged from World War II as the world's largest economic power, with more than half of the world's manufacturing capacity and the greater part of the world's gold, the Bretton Woods system of fixed exchange rates was based on the convertibility of U.S. dollars into gold (for foreign governments and central banks only) at $35 per ounce. The fixed exchange rates were to be maintained by intervention in the foreign exchange market by central banks in countries besides the United States who bought and sold dollar assets, which they held as international reserves. The U.S. dollar, which was used by other countries to denominate the assets that they held as international reserves, was called the **reserve currency**. Thus, an important feature of the Bretton Woods system was the establishment of the United States as the reserve currency country. Even after the breakup of the Bretton Woods system, the U.S. dollar has kept its position as the reserve currency in which most international financial transactions are conducted. However, with the creation of the euro in 1999, the U.S. dollar may be subject to a serious challenge to its supremacy (see Box 1).

How a Fixed Exchange Rate Regime Works The most important feature of the Bretton Woods system was that it set up a fixed exchange rate regime. Figure 2 shows how a fixed exchange rate regime works in practice using the model of exchange rate determination we learned in Chapter 12. Panel (a) describes a situation in which the domestic currency is initially overvalued: The schedule for the expected return on foreign deposits R^F_1 intersects the schedule for the expected return on domestic deposits R^D_1 at exchange rate E_1, which is lower than the par (fixed) value of the exchange rate E_{par}. To keep the exchange rate at E_{par}, the central bank must intervene in the foreign exchange market to purchase domestic currency by selling foreign assets, and this action, like an open market sale, means that the monetary base and the money supply decline. Because the exchange rate will continue to be fixed at E_{par}, the expected future exchange rate remains unchanged, and so the schedule for the expected return on foreign deposits remains at R^F_1. However, the purchase of domestic currency, which leads to a fall in the money supply, also causes the interest rate on domestic deposits i^D to rise. This increase in turn shifts the expected return on domestic deposits R^D to the right. The central bank will continue purchasing domestic currency and selling foreign assets until the R^D curve reaches R^D_2 and the equilibrium exchange rate is at E_{par} at point 2 in panel (a).

BOX 1: GLOBAL

The Euro's Challenge to the U.S. Dollar

With the adoption of the euro by countries in the European Monetary System, in the future the U.S. dollar may face a challenge to its position as the key reserve currency in international financial transactions. Adoption of the euro has increased integration of Europe's financial markets, which could help them rival those in the United States. The resulting increase in the use of euros in financial markets is making it more likely that international transactions will be carried out in the euro. The economic clout of the European Union rivals that of the United States: Both have a similar share of world GDP (around 20%) and world exports (around 15%). If the European Central Bank can make sure that inflation remains low so that the euro becomes a sound currency, this should bode well for the euro.

However, for the euro to eat significantly into the dollar's position as a reserve currency, the European Union must function as a cohesive political entity that is able to exert its influence on the world stage. There are serious doubts on this score, and most analysts think that it will be a long time before the euro beats out the dollar in international financial transactions.

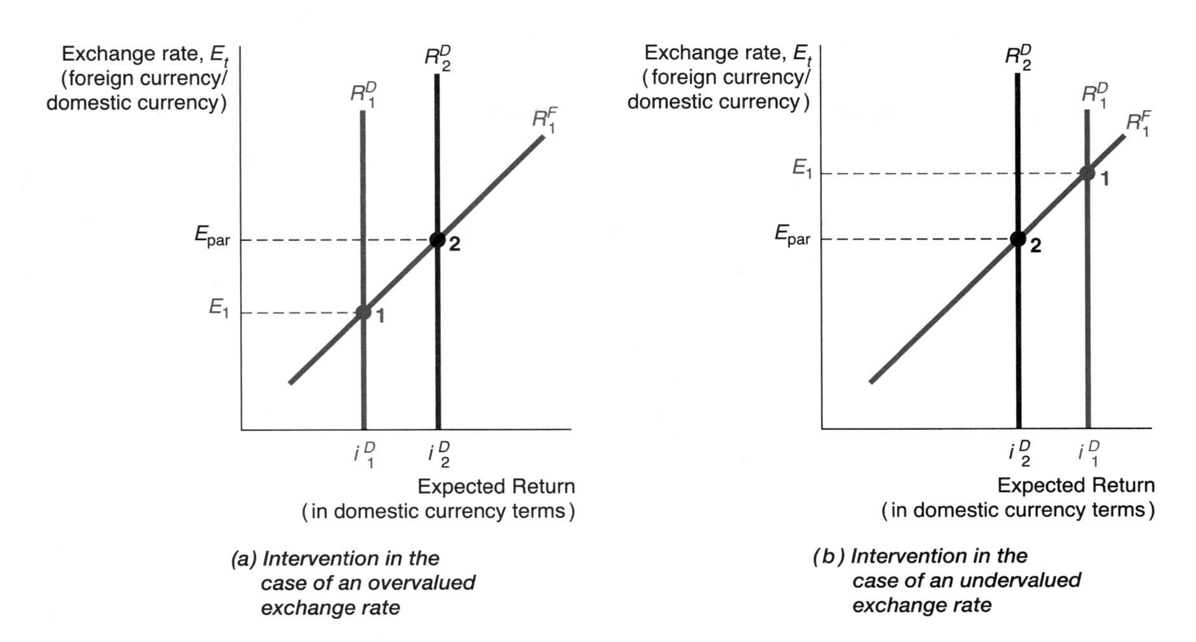

FIGURE 2 Intervention in the Foreign Exchange Market Under a Fixed Exchange Rate Regime

In panel (a), the exchange rate at E_{par} is overvalued. To keep the exchange rate at E_{par} (point 2), the central bank must purchase domestic currency to shift the schedule for the expected return on domestic deposits to R_2^D. In panel (b), the exchange rate at E_{par} is undervalued, so a central bank sale of domestic currency is needed to shift R^D to R_2^D to keep the exchange rate at E_{par} (point 2).

We have thus come to the conclusion that ***when the domestic currency is overvalued, the central bank must purchase domestic currency to keep the exchange rate fixed, but as a result it loses international reserves.***

Panel (b) in Figure 2 shows how a central bank intervention keeps the exchange rate fixed at E_{par} when the exchange rate is initially undervalued, that is, when R_1^F and the initial R_1^D intersect at exchange rate E_1, which is above E_{par}. Here the central bank must sell domestic currency and purchase foreign assets, and this works like an open market purchase to raise the money supply and to lower the interest rate on domestic deposits i^D. The central bank keeps selling domestic currency and lowers i^D until R^D shifts all the way to R_2^D, where the equilibrium exchange rate is at E_{par}—point 2 in panel (b). Our analysis thus leads us to the following result: ***When the domestic currency is undervalued, the central bank must sell domestic currency to keep the exchange rate fixed, but as a result it gains international reserves.***

As we have seen, if a country's currency has an overvalued exchange rate, its central bank's attempts to keep the currency from depreciating will result in a loss of international reserves. If the country's central bank eventually runs out of international reserves, it cannot keep its currency from depreciating, and a **devaluation** must occur, meaning that the par exchange rate is reset at a lower level.

If, by contrast, a country's currency has an undervalued exchange rate, its central bank's intervention to keep the currency from appreciating leads to a gain of international reserves. Because, as we will see shortly, the central bank might not want to acquire these international reserves, it might want to reset the par value of its exchange rate at a higher level (a **revaluation**).

Note that if domestic and foreign deposits are perfect substitutes, as is assumed in the model of exchange rate determination used here, a sterilized exchange rate intervention would not be able to keep the exchange rate at E_{par} because, as we saw in Chapter 12, neither R^F nor R^D will shift. For example, if the exchange rate is overvalued, a sterilized purchase of domestic currency will still leave the expected return on domestic deposits below the expected return on foreign deposits at the par exchange rate—so pressure for a depreciation of the domestic currency is not removed. If the central bank keeps purchasing its domestic currency but continues to sterilize, it will just keep losing international reserves until it finally runs out of them and is forced to let the value of the currency seek a lower level.

One implication of the foregoing analysis is that a country that ties its exchange rate to a larger country's currency loses control of its monetary policy. If the larger country pursues a more contractionary monetary policy and decreases its money supply, this would lead to lower expected inflation in the larger country, thus causing an appreciation of the larger country's currency and a depreciation of the smaller country's currency. The smaller country, having locked its exchange rate, will now find its currency overvalued and will therefore have to sell the larger country's currency and buy its own to keep its currency from depreciating. The result of this foreign exchange intervention will then be a decline in the smaller country's international reserves, a contraction of the monetary base, and thus a decline in its money supply. Sterilization of this foreign exchange intervention is not an option because this would just lead to a continuing loss of international reserves until the smaller country was forced to devalue. The smaller country no longer controls its monetary policy because movements in its money supply are completely determined by movements in the larger country's money supply.

Smaller countries are often willing to tie their exchange rate to that of a larger country in order to inherit the more disciplined monetary policy of their bigger neighbour, thus ensuring a lower inflation rate. An extreme example of such a strategy is the currency board, which has been used by Hong Kong and has recently been adopted by countries such as Argentina (see Box 2), Latvia, and Estonia. An even more extreme strategy is **dollarization**, in which a country abandons its currency altogether and adopts that of another country, typically the U.S. dollar (see Box 3 on page 332).

Bretton Woods System of Fixed Exchange Rates Under the Bretton Woods system, exchange rates were supposed to change only when a country was experiencing a "fundamental disequilibrium," that is, large persistent deficits or surpluses in its balance of payments. To maintain fixed exchange rates when countries had balance-of-payments deficits and were losing international reserves, the IMF would loan deficit countries international reserves contributed by other members. As a result of its power to dictate loan terms to borrowing countries, the IMF could encourage deficit countries to pursue contractionary monetary policies that would strengthen their currency or eliminate their balance-of-payment deficits. If the IMF loans were not sufficient to prevent depreciation of a currency, the country was allowed to devalue its currency by setting a new, lower exchange rate.

A notable weakness of the Bretton Woods system was that although deficit countries losing international reserves could be pressured into devaluing their currency or pursuing contractionary policies, the IMF had no way to force surplus countries to revise their exchange rates upward or pursue more expansionary policies. Particularly troublesome in this regard was the fact that the reserve currency country, the United States, could not devalue its currency under the Bretton Woods system even if the dollar was overvalued. When the United States attempted to reduce its unemployment in the 1960s by pursuing an inflationary monetary policy, a fundamental disequilibrium of an overvalued dollar developed. Because surplus countries were not willing to revise their exchange rates upward,

BOX 2: GLOBAL

Argentina's Currency Board

Argentina has a long history of monetary instability, with inflation rates fluctuating dramatically and sometimes surging beyond 1000% a year. To end this cycle of inflationary surges, Argentina decided to adopt a currency board in April 1991. A *currency board system* is one in which the domestic currency has 100% backing in foreign reserves and in which the note-issuing authority, whether the central bank or the government, adopts a fixed exchange rate against a particular foreign currency and then stands ready to exchange domestic currency for foreign currency at that rate whenever the public requests it.

The Argentine currency board worked as follows. Under Argentina's convertibility law, the peso/dollar exchange rate was fixed at one to one, and a member of the public could go to the Argentine central bank and exchange a peso for a dollar, or vice versa, at any time. A currency board is just a variant of a fixed exchange rate regime in which the commitment to the fixed exchange rate is especially strong because the conduct of monetary policy is in effect put on autopilot and is completely taken out of the hands of the central bank and the government. The money supply could expand only when dollars were exchanged for pesos at the central bank, meaning that the increased amount of pesos was matched by an equal increase in foreign exchange reserves. The central bank therefore no longer had the ability to print money and thereby cause inflation.

The early years of Argentina's currency board looked stunningly successful. Inflation, which had been running at an 800% rate in 1990, fell below 5% by the end of 1994, and economic growth was rapid, averaging almost 8% annually from 1991 to 1994. However, a currency board is not without problems. In the aftermath of the Mexican peso crisis, concern about the health of the Argentine economy resulted in the public's pulling money out of the banks (deposits fell by 18%) and exchanging pesos for dollars, thus causing a contraction of the Argentine money supply. The result was a sharp decline in Argentine economic activity, with real GDP down more than 5% in 1995 and the unemployment rate jumping above 15%. Only in 1996 did the economy begin to recover.

However, in 1998 Argentina entered another recession that has been both severe and very long lasting. By the end of 2001, unemployment had reached nearly 20%, a level comparable to that experienced in the United States during the Great Depression of the 1930s. The result had been civil unrest and the fall of the elected government, as well as a major banking crisis and a default on government debt. Because the Central Bank of Argentina had no control over monetary policy under the currency board system, it was unable to use monetary policy to expand the economy and get out of its recession. Furthermore, because the currency board did not allow the central bank to create pesos and lend them to banks, it had very little capability to act as a lender of last resort. Finally, in January 2002, Argentina abandoned its currency board.

adjustment in the Bretton Woods system did not take place, and the system collapsed in 1971. Attempts to patch up the Bretton Woods system with the Smithsonian Agreement in December 1971 proved unsuccessful, and by 1973, America and its trading partners had agreed to allow exchange rates to float.

Managed Float

Although exchange rates are currently allowed to change daily in response to market forces, central banks have not been willing to give up their option of intervening in the foreign exchange market. Preventing large changes in exchange rates makes it easier for firms and individuals purchasing or selling goods abroad to plan into the future. Furthermore, countries with surpluses in their balance of payments frequently do not want to see their currencies appreciate because it makes their goods more expensive abroad and foreign goods cheaper in their country. Because an appreciation might hurt sales for domestic businesses and increase unemployment, surplus countries have often sold their currency in the foreign exchange market and acquired international reserves.

Countries with balance-of-payments deficits do not want to see their currency lose value because it makes foreign goods more expensive for domestic consumers and can stimulate inflation. To keep the value of the domestic currency high, deficit

BOX 3: GLOBAL

Dollarization

Dollarization, which involves the adoption of another country's currency, usually the U.S. dollar (but other sound currencies like the euro or the yen are also possibilities), is a more extreme version of fixed exchange rate than is a currency board. A currency board can be abandoned, allowing a change in the value of the currency, but a change of value is impossible with dollarization: A dollar bill is always worth one dollar whether it is held in the United States or outside it. Panama has been dollarized since the inception of the country in the early twentieth century, while El Salvador and Ecuador have recently adopted dollarization.

Dollarization, like a currency board, prevents a central bank from creating inflation. Another key advantage is that it completely avoids the possibility of a speculative attack on the domestic currency (because there is none), which is still a danger even under a currency board arrangement. However, like a currency board, dollarization does not allow a country to pursue its own monetary policy or have a lender of last resort. Dollarization has one additional disadvantage not characteristic of a currency board: Because a country adopting dollarization no longer has its own currency, it loses the revenue that a government receives by issuing money, which is called *seigniorage*. Because governments (or their central banks) do not have to pay interest on their currency, they earn revenue (seigniorage) by using this currency to purchase income-earning assets such as bonds. In the case of the Federal Reserve in the United States, this revenue is on the order of $20 billion dollars per year. If an emerging-market country dollarizes and give up its currency, it needs to make up this loss of revenue somewhere, which is not always easy for a poor country.

countries have often bought their own currency in the foreign exchange market and given up international reserves.

The current international financial system is a hybrid of a fixed and a flexible exchange rate system. Rates fluctuate in response to market forces but are not determined solely by them. Furthermore, many countries continue to keep the value of their currency fixed against other currencies, as in the European Monetary System (to be described shortly).

The IMF continues to function as a data collector and international lender but does not attempt to encourage fixed exchange rates. The IMF's role of international lender has also become important recently because of situations like the third-world debt crisis of the 1980s and the more recent Mexican peso crisis (discussed later in the chapter). The IMF has been directly involved in helping developing countries with difficulties in repaying their loans and provided large loans to Mexico and other countries in the aftermath of the Mexican peso crisis.

At www.imf.org/external/np/exr/facts/sdr.htm, check out a special drawing rights fact sheet with information on allocation, valuation, and an SDR user's guide.

Another important feature of the current system is the continuing de-emphasis of gold in international financial transactions. Not only has the United States suspended convertibility of dollars into gold for foreign central banks, but since 1970 the IMF has been issuing a paper substitute for gold, called **special drawing rights (SDRs)**. Like gold in the Bretton Woods system, SDRs function as international reserves. Unlike gold, whose quantity is determined by gold discoveries and the rate of production, SDRs can be created by the IMF whenever it decides that there is a need for additional international reserves to promote world trade and economic growth.

The use of gold in international transactions was further de-emphasized by the IMF's elimination of the official gold price in 1975 and by the sale of gold by the U.S. Treasury and the IMF to private interests in order to demonetize it. Currently, the price of gold is determined in a free market. Investors who want to speculate in it are able to purchase and sell at will, as are jewellers and dentists, who use gold in their businesses.

European Monetary System (EMS)

In March 1979, eight members of the European Economic Community (Germany, France, Italy, the Netherlands, Belgium, Luxembourg, Denmark, and Ireland) set up an **exchange rate union**, the European Monetary System (EMS), in which they agreed to fix their exchange rates vis-à-vis one another and to float jointly against the U.S. dollar. Spain joined the EMS in June 1989, the United Kingdom in October 1990, and Portugal in April 1992.

The exchange rate mechanism (ERM) of the European Monetary System worked as follows. The exchange rate between every pair of currencies of the participating countries was not allowed to fluctuate outside narrow limits around a fixed exchange rate. (The limits were typically ± 2.25% but were raised to ± 15% in July 1993.) When the exchange rate between two countries' currencies moved outside these limits, the central banks of both countries were supposed to intervene in the foreign exchange market. If, for example, the French franc depreciated below its lower limit against the German mark, the Bank of France was required to buy francs and sell marks, thereby giving up international reserves. Similarly, the German central bank also was required to intervene to buy marks and sell francs and consequently increase its international reserves. The EMS thus required that intervention be symmetric when a currency fell outside the limits, with the central bank with the weak currency giving up international reserves and the one with the strong currency gaining them. Central bank intervention was also very common even when the exchange rate was within the limits, but in this case, if one central bank intervened, no others were required to intervene as well.

A serious shortcoming of fixed exchange rate systems such as the Bretton Woods system or the European Monetary System is that they can lead to foreign exchange crises involving a "speculative attack" on a currency—massive sales of a weak currency or purchases of a strong currency to cause a sharp change in the exchange rate. In the following application, we use our model of exchange rate determination to understand how the September 1992 exchange rate crisis that rocked the European Monetary System came about.

Application The Foreign Exchange Crisis of September 1992

In the aftermath of German reunification in October 1990, the German central bank, the Bundesbank, faced rising inflationary pressures, with inflation having accelerated from below 3% in 1990 to near 5% by 1992. To get monetary growth under control and to dampen inflation, the Bundesbank raised German interest rates to near double-digit levels. Figure 3 shows the consequences of these actions by the Bundesbank in the foreign exchange market for sterling. Note that in the diagram, the pound sterling is the domestic currency and R^D is the expected return on sterling deposits, while the foreign currency is the German mark (deutsche mark, DM), so R^F is the expected return on mark deposits.

The increase in German interest rates i^F shifted the R^F schedule rightward to R^F_2 in Figure 3, so that the intersection of the R^D_1 and the R^F_2 schedules at point 1′ was below the lower exchange rate limit (2.778 marks per pound, denoted E_{par}) under the exchange rate mechanism of the European Monetary System. To lower the value of the mark relative to the pound and restore the pound/mark exchange rate to within the ERM limits, either the Bank of England had to pursue a contractionary monetary policy, thereby raising British interest rates to i^D_2 and shifting the R^D_1 schedule to the right to point 2, or the Bundesbank could pursue an expansionary monetary policy, thereby lowering German interest rates, which would shift the R^F schedule to the left to move back to point 1. (The shifts in R^D to point 2 or R^F to point 1 are not shown in the figure.)

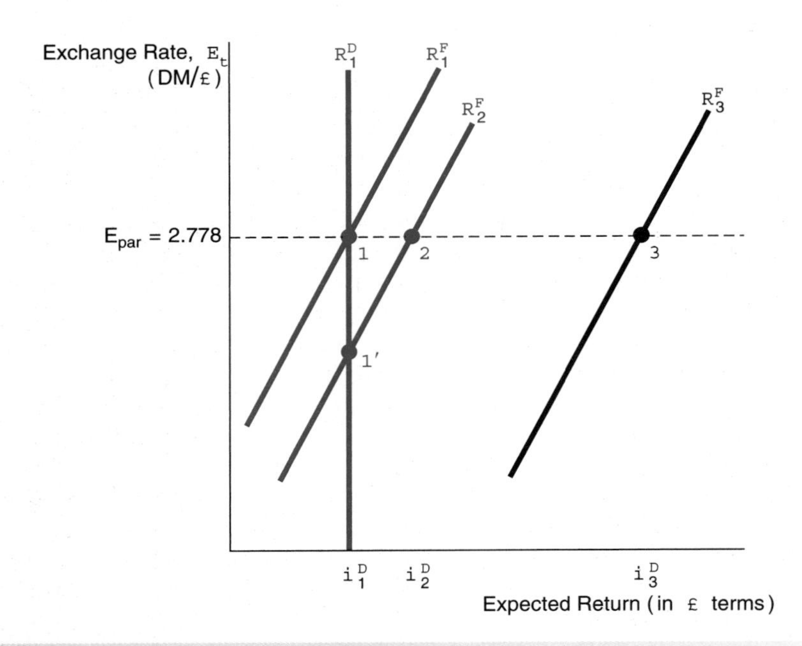

FIGURE 3 Foreign Exchange Market for British Pounds in 1992

The realization by speculators that the United Kingdom would soon devalue the pound increased the expected return on foreign (German mark, DM) deposits and shifted R_2^F rightward to R_3^F. The result was the need for a much greater purchase of pounds by the British central bank to raise the interest rate to i_3^D to keep the exchange rate at DM 2.778 per pound.

The catch was that the Bundesbank, whose primary goal is fighting inflation, was unwilling to pursue an expansionary monetary policy, while the British, who were facing their worst recession in the postwar period, were unwilling to pursue a contractionary monetary policy to prop up the pound. This impasse became clear when in response to great pressure from other members of the EMS, the Bundesbank was willing to lower its lending rates by only a token amount on September 14 after a speculative attack was mounted on the currencies of the Scandinavian countries. So at some point in the near future, the value of the pound would have to decline to point 1′. Speculators now knew that the appreciation of the mark was imminent and hence that the value of foreign (mark) deposits would rise in value relative to the pound. As a result, the expected return on mark deposits increased sharply, shifting the R^F schedule to R_3^F in Figure 3.

The Websites of the British, French, Italian, Spanish, and Swedish central banks can be found at www.bankofengland.co.uk, www.banque-france.fr, www.bancaditalia.it, www.bde.es and www.risksbank.se

The huge potential losses on pound deposits and potential gains on mark deposits caused a massive sell-off of pounds (and purchases of marks) by speculators. The need for the British central bank to intervene to raise the value of the pound now became much greater and required a huge rise in British interest rates all the way to i_3^D. After a major intervention effort on the part of the Bank of England, which included a rise in its lending rate from 10% to 15% that still wasn't enough, the British were finally forced to give up on September 16: They pulled out of the ERM indefinitely, allowing the pound to depreciate by 10% against the mark.

Speculative attacks on other currencies forced devaluation of the Spanish peseta by 5% and the Italian lira by 15%. To defend its currency, the Swedish central bank was forced to raise its daily lending rate to the astronomical level of 500%! By the time the crisis was over, the British, French, Italian, Spanish, and Swedish central banks had intervened to the tune of $100 billion; the Bundesbank alone had laid out $50 billion for foreign exchange intervention. Because foreign exchange crises lead to large changes in central banks' holdings of international reserves and thus affect the official reserve asset items in the balance of payments, these crises are also referred to as **balance-of-payments crises**.

The attempt to prop up the European Monetary System was not cheap for these central banks. It is estimated that they lost $4 billion to $6 billion as a result of exchange rate intervention during the crisis.

THE PRACTISING FINANCIAL INSTITUTION MANAGER

Profiting from a Foreign Exchange Crisis

Large banks and other financial institutions often conduct foreign exchange trading operations that generate substantial profits for their parent institution. When a foreign exchange crisis such as the one that occurred in September 1992 comes along, foreign exchange traders and speculators are presented with a golden opportunity. The foregoing analysis of this crisis helps explain why.

As we saw in Figure 3, the high German interest rates resulted in a situation in which the British pound was overvalued, in that the equilibrium exchange rate in the absence of intervention by the British and German central banks was below the lower exchange rate limit of 2.778 German marks per British pound. Once foreign exchange traders realized that the central banks would not be willing to intervene sufficiently or alter their policies to keep the value of the pound above the 2.778-mark-per-pound lower limit, the traders were presented with a "heads I win, tails you lose" bet. They knew that there was only one direction in which the exchange rate could go—down—and so they were almost sure to make money by buying marks and selling pounds. Our analysis of Figure 3 reflects this state of affairs; another way of looking at this one-sided bet is to recognize that it implies that the expected return on mark-denominated deposits increased sharply, shifting the R^F schedule to R^F_3 in Figure 3.

Savvy foreign exchange traders, who read the writing on the wall early in September 1992, sold pounds and bought marks. When the pound depreciated 10% against the mark after September 16, they made huge profits because the marks they had bought could now be sold at a price 10% higher. Foreign exchange traders at Citibank are reported to have made $200 million in the week of the September 1992 exchange rate crisis—not bad for a week's work! But these profits pale in comparison to those made by George Soros, an investment fund manager whose funds are reported to have run up profits of $1 billion during the crisis. (However, Soros gave some of these profits back in 1994 when he acknowledged that he had suffered a $600 million loss from trades on the yen.) Clearly, foreign exchange trading can be a highly profitable enterprise for financial institutions, particularly during foreign exchange rate crises.

At www.citibank.com you can find more information about Citibank.

Application The Mexican Peso Crisis of December 1994

As part of a reform plan initiated in 1987 to stabilize the Mexican economy, the Mexican government decided to put limits on the movements of the peso against the U.S. dollar. When the ruling party's presidential candidate was assassinated in March 1994, investors became concerned that the government might devalue the currency despite promises not to do so. The result was a speculative attack on the peso that not only brought down the peso but also threatened to bring down the currencies of other developing countries, particularly those in Latin America. Figure 3 can be used to understand the sequence of events during the Mexican peso crisis. We just need to recognize that R^D is now the expected return on peso deposits and, since the foreign currency is the U.S. dollar, R^F is the expected return on U.S. dollar deposits, with both denominated in the domestic currency, the peso.

Because of investors' concerns that the peso might be devalued after the March assassination, the expected return on dollar deposits rose, thus moving the R^F schedule from R^F_1 to R^F_2 in Figure 3. The result was that the intersection of R^D_1 and R^F_2 was below the lower exchange limit E_{par} of around 30 cents per peso. To keep the peso from falling through this limit, the Mexican authorities needed to buy pesos and sell dollars, to raise interest rates to i^D_2 by shifting the R^D curve to the right. This is exactly what they did, raising interest rates from around 10% to more than 20% and losing close to half their $30 billion in international reserves in the process. For the time being, the peso held, but more bad luck was to hit the Mexicans. An uprising in the southern state of Chiapas, the assassination of another high official in the ruling party, and concerns about the large current account deficit and particularly about the health of the banking system led to further rumours of devaluation. Now the R^F curve shifted even farther to the right, say, to R^F_3, and the Mexican authorities intervened further, doubling interest rates again and almost completely exhausting the nation's foreign exchange reserves. Once speculators guessed that the Mexicans were running out of reserves, the game was up. With near certainty that the new Mexican government installed on December 1 would be forced to devalue, the expected return on dollar deposits increased sharply, shifting R^F even farther to the right, making a devaluation inevitable. On December 20, Mexico's government had to devalue the peso; it had lost more than half its value by early 1995.

Application The East Asian Currency Crisis of 1997

The Bank of Thailand's Website can be found at www.bot.or.th

The East Asian currency crisis in 1997 started in Thailand. We use Figure 3 to demonstrate what happened during this crisis, again assuming that dollars are the foreign currency so that R^D is the expected return on deposits denominated in the Thai currency, the baht, and R^F is the expected return on U.S. dollar deposits. By May 1997, concerns about the large current account deficit in Thailand and the weakness in the Thai financial system made foreign creditors nervous and caused speculators to suspect that Thailand might be forced to devalue its currency. The result was a rise in the expected return on dollar deposits, which shifted the R^F schedule from R^F_1 to R^F_2, so that the intersection of the R^D_1 and R^F_2 curves was below the pegged value E_{par} of around 4 cents per baht. Intervention by the Thai central bank to purchase baht, which raised interest rates to i^D_2, was successful in containing this speculative attack. However, the failure of a major finance company, Finance One, imposed losses on creditors, causing foreign creditors to begin pulling out of the market in earnest and speculators to become even more confident that the Thais could not continue defending the baht. Thus, the expected return on dollar deposits shot up further, and R^F moved much farther to the right, to R^F_3. Given the weakness in the financial sector and the loss of reserves, the Thai monetary authorities could not continue to intervene and were forced to give up and let the baht depreciate on July 2.

Concerns that similar problems might be present in other East Asian countries generated speculative attacks against other currencies as well, leading to a scenario akin to that depicted in Figure 3. The result was that one by one, Indonesia, Malaysia, South Korea, and the Philippines were forced to devalue. The outcome was severe depreciations of all these currencies against the U.S. dollar: more than 30% for the Thai baht, the Malaysian ringgit, the South Korean won, and the Philippine peso, and more than 75% for the Indonesian rupiah. Even Hong Kong, Singapore, and Taiwan were subjected to speculative attacks, but because the financial systems in these countries were healthy, the attacks were successfully averted.

As we will see in Chapter 14, the sharp depreciation in Mexico and East Asia led to full-scale financial crises that severely damaged these countries' economies. The foreign exchange crisis that shocked the European Monetary System in September 1992 cost central banks a lot of money, but the public in European countries were not seriously affected. By contrast, the public in Mexico and the crisis countries of East Asia were not so lucky: The speculative attacks that triggered the collapse of those currencies produced severe depressions that caused hardship and political unrest.

European Monetary Union (EMU)

As part of the December 1991 Maastricht Treaty on European Union, the European Economic Commission outlined a plan to achieve the creation of a single European currency starting in 1999. Despite concerns that the plan might blow up, the European Monetary Union with its new common currency, the euro, came into existence right on schedule in January 1999, with 11 of the 15 European Union countries participating in the monetary union: Austria, Belgium, Finland, France, Germany, Italy, Ireland, Luxembourg, the Netherlands, Portugal and Spain. Denmark, Sweden and the United Kingdom chose not to participate initially, while Greece took some time to meet the economic criteria specified by the Maastricht Treaty (such as having a budget deficit less than 3% of GDP and total government debt less than 60% of GDP) and joined the European Monetary Union in January 2001.

Starting January 1, 1999, the exchange rates of countries entering the monetary union were fixed permanently to the euro (which became a unit of account), the European Central Bank took over monetary policy from the individual national central banks, and the governments of the member countries began to issue debt in euros. In January 2002 euro notes and coins began to circulate, and by June 2002 the old national currencies were phased out completely; now only euros are used in the member countries.

Advocates of monetary union point out the advantages that the single currency has in eliminating the transactions costs incurred in exchanging one currency for another. In addition, the use of a single currency may promote further integration of the European economies and enhance competition. Skeptics who think that monetary union may be bad for Europe suggest that, because labour will not be very mobile across national boundaries and because fiscal transfers (i.e., tax income from one region being spent on another) from better performing regions to worse performing regions will not take place as occurs in the United States, a single currency may lead to some regions of Europe being depressed for substantial periods of time while other regions are booming.

Whether the euro will be good for the economies of Europe and increase their GDP is an open question. However, the motive behind monetary union may be more political than economic. European monetary union may encourage political union, producing a unified Europe that can play a stronger economic and political role on the world stage.

CURRENCY BOARDS, DOLLARIZATION, AND CANADA'S EXCHANGE RATE REGIME

As the Bank of Canada's former governor, Gordon Thiessen, recently put it,[8]

> "[o]ne of the issues that has often surfaced over the years is the exchange rate for the Canadian dollar. Indeed, over the past couple of years, it has been a topic of considerable public discussion. That discussion has revolved around such questions as: Should we continue floating, or should we peg our currency to the U.S. dollar? In fact, should we even keep our own currency, or should we adopt the U.S. currency?"

The attention to alternative currency arrangements for Canada stems from the decline of the Canadian dollar against the U.S. dollar through the 1990s, and also from the recent creation of the single European currency, the euro, to replace the national currencies of 12 member countries of the European monetary union. The debate in Canada has revolved around exchange rate alternatives and particularly around the issue of whether a floating currency is the right exchange rate regime for Canada or whether we should fix the exchange rate between the Canadian and U.S. currencies, as we did from 1962 to 1970.

As already noted, an alternative exchange rate arrangement is the adoption of a "currency board," in which the domestic currency is backed 100% by a foreign (reserve) currency and the exchange rate between the two currencies is fixed. A currency board is thus a variant of a fixed exchange rate regime with an even stronger commitment mechanism, since domestic money can be issued only if it is fully backed by foreign reserves. In fact, a currency board arrangement is the modern day equivalent of a fully backed gold standard with foreign reserves taking the place of gold reserves. Currency boards have recently been adopted by countries such as Hong Kong (1983), Argentina (1991), and Lithuania (1994) with the U.S. dollar, and Estonia (1992), Bulgaria (1997), and Bosnia (1998) with the euro. In addition, several countries in Eastern Europe and the former Soviet Union are considering adopting a currency board with the euro.

Another possible exchange rate arrangement is dollarization. Dollarization is another variant of a fixed exchange rate regime, with an even better commitment device than a currency board. In particular, dollarization avoids the possibility of a speculative attack on the domestic currency and also eliminates the inflation-bias problem of discretionary policy (arising from attempts to stimulate the economy and incentives to monetize the public debt). However, dollarization is subject to the usual disadvantages of a fixed exchange rate regime—it implies the loss of an independent monetary policy, the inability of the central bank to act as a lender of last resort, and the loss of seigniorage (the revenue that the government receives by issuing money). Recently, Ecuador adopted full dollarization and El Salvador announced its determination to do the same.

Currency boards and dollarization, however, are strong measures that tend to be applied in extreme circumstances. They have been advocated as monetary policy strategies for emerging market countries, especially in parts of Latin America that have had a long history of monetary instability.

A floating exchange rate gives Canada the flexibility to have different monetary conditions from the United States. In particular, a floating currency acts as a shock absorber between the two economies, allowing us to respond differently to external economic shocks (such as, for example, fluctuations in world com-

[8]Gordon Thiessen, "Why a Floating Exchange Rate Regime Makes Sense for Canada," Bank of Canada *Review* (Winter 2000–2001): 47–51.

modity prices) and domestic policy requirements. The costs of a floating currency come in two forms. First and most obviously, there are certain transactions costs that are large when the amount of cross-border and financial transactions is large, as is Canada's case with the United States. A further cost is the fact that exchange rates fluctuate wildly in comparison with goods prices (in fact, almost as wildly as stock prices), although the effects of exchange rate volatility on macroeconomic quantities are difficult to demonstrate. In this regard, as the former First Deputy Managing Director of the International Monetary Fund (IMF), Stanley Fischer, recently said,[9]

> "... hard pegs are more attractive today, particularly when viewed from the asset markets, than had been thought some years ago. A small economy that depends heavily on a particular large economy for its trade and capital account transactions may wish to adopt that country's currency. But it will need to give careful consideration to the nature of the shocks that affect it before the choice is made."

The European developments, the trend toward **currency unions** and dollarization in Latin America and Eastern Europe, the international use of currencies (see Box 4), and Japan's recent interest in exploring alternative monetary arrangements, have spawned an interesting debate in Canada regarding the feasibility and potential advantages of alternative exchange rate regimes.[10] The issue

BOX 4

The Canadian Dollar in International Markets

Although the Canadian dollar has been used as an international currency, it has never approached the international use of other currencies, such as the Japanese yen, the German mark, and to a larger extent the U.S. dollar.

As you can see in the following table, in 1995 (before the introduction of the euro), the U.S. dollar was used as the invoice currency for 52% of world exports with an internationalization ratio of 3.9. An internationalization ratio greater than 1 (as with the U.S. dollar, the German mark, and the British pound), indicates that some (or all) of the exports of other countries are invoiced in that currency.

Trade Invoiced in Major Currencies (as of 1995)

Currency	Percent of World Exports	Internationalization Ratio
U.S. dollar	52.0	3.9
Euro-4	24.8	NA
Deutsche mark	13.2	1.4
French franc	5.5	1.0
British pound	5.4	1.1
Japanese yen	4.7	0.6
Italian lira	3.3	0.8
Netherlands guilder	2.8	0.9

Source: Patricia S. Pollard, "The Creation of the Euro and the Role of the Dollar in International Markets," Federal Reserve Bank of St. Louis *Review* (September/October 2001): 17–36. © 2001 by the Federal Reserve Bank of St. Louis.

Note: Euro-4 is the share of the four euro-area currencies listed in the table (deutsche mark, French franc, Italian lira, and Netherlands guilder). No data were available for the other euro-area currencies. World exports includes intra-euro-area trade. The internationalization ratio is the ratio of the share of world exports denominated in a currency to the share of the issuing country in world exports.

---

[9]Stanley Fischer, "Exchange Rate Regimes: Is the Bipolar View Correct?" *Finance & Development* 38 (2001): 18–21.

[10]See, for example, John Murray, "Why Canada Needs a Flexible Exchange Rate," Bank of Canada Working Paper 99-12, and John Murray and James Powell, "Dollarization in Canada: The Buck Stops There," Bank of Canada Technical Report No. 90.

is whether a floating currency is the right exchange rate regime for Canada or whether we should consider alternative monetary arrangements, such as a currency board, dollarization, or even membership in a currency union.

CAPITAL CONTROLS

Because capital flows have been an important element in the currency crises in Mexico and East Asia, politicians and some economists have advocated that capital mobility in emerging market countries should be restricted with capital controls in order to avoid financial instability. Are capital controls a good idea?

Controls on Capital Outflows

Capital outflows can promote financial instability in emerging market countries because when domestic residents and foreigners pull their capital out of a country, the resulting capital outflow forces a country to devalue its currency. This is why recently some politicians in emerging market countries have found capital controls particularly attractive. For example, Prime Minister Mahathir of Malaysia instituted capital controls in 1998 to restrict outflows in the aftermath of the East Asian crisis.

Although these controls sound like a good idea, they suffer from several disadvantages. First, empirical evidence indicates that controls on capital outflows are seldom effective during a crisis because the private sector finds ingenious ways to evade them and has little difficulty moving funds out of the country.[11] Second, the evidence suggests that capital flight may even increase after controls are put into place because confidence in the government is weakened. Third, controls on capital outflows often lead to corruption, as government officials get paid off to look the other way when domestic residents are trying to move funds abroad. Fourth, controls on capital outflows may lull governments into thinking they do not have to take the steps to reform their financial systems to deal with the crisis, with the result that opportunities are lost to improve the functioning of the economy.

Controls on Capital Inflows

Although most economists find the arguments against controls on capital outflows persuasive, controls on capital inflows receive more support. Supporters reason that if speculative capital cannot come in, then it cannot go out suddenly and create a crisis. Our analysis of the financial crises in East Asia in Chapter 7 provides support for this view by suggesting that capital inflows can lead to a lending boom and excessive risk taking on the part of banks, which then helps trigger a financial crisis.

However, controls on capital inflows have the undesirable feature that they may block from entering a country funds that would be used for productive investment opportunities. Although such controls may limit the fuel supplied to lending booms through capital flows, over time they produce substantial distortions and misallocation of resources as households and businesses try to get around them. Indeed, just as with controls on capital outflows, controls on capital inflows can lead to corruption. There are serious doubts whether capital controls can be effective in today's environment, in which trade is open and where there are many financial instruments that make it easier to get around these controls.

---

[11]See Sebastian Edwards, "How Effective are Capital Controls?" *Journal of Economic Perspectives*, Winter 2000; vol. 13, no. 4, pp. 65–84.

On the other hand, there is a strong case for improving bank regulation and supervision so that capital inflows are less likely to produce a lending boom and encourage excessive risk taking by banking institutions. For example, restricting banks in how fast their borrowing can grow might have the impact of substantially limiting capital inflows. Supervisory controls of this type, focusing on the sources of financial fragility rather than the symptoms, can enhance the efficiency of the financial system rather than hampering it.

THE ROLE OF THE IMF

The International Monetary Fund was originally set up under the Bretton Woods system to help countries deal with balance-of-payments problems and stay with the fixed exchange rate by lending to deficit countries. With the collapse of the Bretton Woods system of fixed exchange rates in 1971, the IMF has taken on new roles.

The IMF continues to function as a data collector and provides technical assistance to its member countries. Although the IMF no longer attempts to encourage fixed exchange rates, its role as an international lender has become more important recently. This role first came to the fore in the 1980s during the third-world debt crisis, in which the IMF assisted developing countries in repaying their loans. The financial crises in Mexico in 1994–1995 and in East Asia in 1997–1998 led to huge loans by the IMF to these and other affected countries to help them recover from their financial crises and to prevent the spread of these crises to other countries. This role, in which the IMF acts as an international lender of last resort to cope with financial instability, is indeed highly controversial.

The IMF's Website, www.imf.org, provides additional details about its functions.

Should the IMF Be an International Lender of Last Resort?

As we saw in Chapter 7, in industrialized countries when a financial crisis occurs and the financial system threatens to seize up, domestic central banks can address matters with a lender-of-last-resort operation to limit the degree of instability in the banking system. In emerging markets, however, where the credibility of the central bank as an inflation-fighter may be in doubt and debt contracts are typically short-term and in foreign currencies, a lender-of-last-resort operation becomes a two-edged sword—as likely to exacerbate the financial crisis as to alleviate it. For example, when the U.S. Federal Reserve engaged in a lender-of-last-resort operation during the 1987 stock market crash (Chapter 7), there was almost no sentiment in the markets that there would be substantially higher inflation. However, for a central bank having less inflation-fighting credibility than the Fed, central bank lending to the financial system in the wake of a financial crisis—even under the lender-of-last-resort rhetoric—may well arouse fears of inflation spiraling out of control, causing an even greater currency depreciation and still greater deterioration of balance sheets. The resulting increase in moral hazard and adverse selection problems in financial markets, along the lines we will discuss in Chapter 14, would only make the financial crisis worse.

Central banks in emerging market countries therefore have only a very limited ability to successfully engage in a lender-of-last-resort operation. However, liquidity provided by an international lender of last resort does not have these undesirable consequences, and in helping to stabilize the value of the domestic currency it strengthens domestic balance sheets. Moreover, an international lender of last resort may be able to prevent contagion, the situation in which a successful speculative attack on one emerging market currency leads to attacks on other emerging market currencies, spreading financial and economic disruption as it goes. Since a lender of last resort for emerging market countries is needed at times, and since it cannot be provided domestically, there is a strong rationale for an international institution to fill this role. Indeed, since Mexico's financial crisis in 1994, the International Monetary Fund and other international agencies have stepped into the lender-of-last-resort role and provided emergency lending to countries threatened by financial instability.

However, support from an international lender of last resort brings risks of its own, especially the risk that the perception it is standing ready to bail out irresponsible financial institutions may lead to excessive risk taking of the sort that makes financial crises more likely. In the Mexican and East Asian crises, governments in the crisis countries have used IMF support to protect depositors and other creditors of banking institutions from losses. This safety net creates a well-known moral hazard problem because the depositors and other creditors have less incentive to monitor these banking institutions and withdraw their deposits if the institutions are taking on too much risk. The result is that these institutions are encouraged to take on excessive risks. Indeed, critics of the IMF, most prominently the Congressional Commission headed by Professor Alan Meltzer of Carnegie-Mellon University, contend that its lending in the Mexican crisis, which was used to bail out foreign lenders, set the stage for the East Asian crisis because these lenders expected to be bailed out if things went wrong and thus provided funds that were used to fuel excessive risk taking.[12]

An international lender of last resort must find ways to limit this moral hazard problem, or it can actually make the situation worse. The international lender of last resort can make it clear that it will extend liquidity to governments that put the proper measures in place to prevent excessive risk taking. In addition, it can reduce the incentives for risk taking by restricting the ability of governments to bail out stockholders and large uninsured creditors of domestic financial institutions.

One problem that arises for international organizations such as the IMF engaged in lender-of-last-resort operations is that they know that if they don't come to the rescue, the emerging market country will suffer extreme hardship and possible political instability. Politicians in the crisis country may exploit these concerns and engage in a game of chicken with the international lender of last resort: they resist necessary reforms, hoping that the IMF will cave in. Elements of this game were present in the Mexico crisis of 1995 and were also a particularly important feature of the negotiations between the IMF and Indonesia during the Asian crisis.

The IMF would produce better outcomes if it makes it clear that it will not play this game. Just as giving in to ill-behaved children may be the easy way out in the short run, but supports a pattern of poor behaviour in the long run, some critics worry that the IMF may not be tough enough when confronted by short-run humanitarian concerns. For example, these people have been particularly critical of the IMF's lending to the Russian government, which has resisted adopting appropriate reforms to stabilize its financial system.

The IMF has also been criticized for imposing on the East Asian countries so-called austerity programs that focus on tight macroeconomic policies rather than on microeconomic policies to fix the crisis-causing problems in the financial sector. Such programs are likely to increase resistance to IMF recommendations, particularly in emerging market countries. Austerity programs allow these politicians to label institutions such as the IMF as being anti-growth, rhetoric that helps the politicians to mobilize the public against the IMF and avoid doing what they really need to do to reform the financial system in their country. IMF programs focused instead on microeconomic policies related to the financial sec-

[12]See International Financial Institution Advisory Commission, *Report* (IFIAC: Washington, D.C., 2000).

tor would increase the likelihood that the IMF will be seen as a helping hand in the creation of a more efficient financial system.

An important historical feature of successful lender-of-last-resort operations is that the faster the lending is done, the lower is the amount that actually has to be lent. An excellent example occurred in the aftermath of the stock market crash on October 19, 1987 (Chapter 7). At the end of that day, in order to service their customers' accounts, securities firms needed to borrow several billion dollars to maintain orderly trading. However, given the unprecedented developments, banks were very nervous about extending further loans to these firms. Upon learning this, the U.S. Federal Reserve engaged in an immediate lender-of-last-resort operation, with the Fed making it clear that it would provide liquidity to banks making loans to the securities industry. Indeed, what is striking about this episode is that the extremely quick intervention of the Fed resulted not only in a negligible impact of the stock market crash on the economy, but also meant that the amount of liquidity that the Fed needed to supply to the economy was not very large.

The ability of the Fed to engage in a lender-of-last-resort operation within a day of a substantial shock to the financial system is in sharp contrast to the amount of time it has taken the IMF to supply liquidity during the recent crises in Mexico and Asian countries, which exceeded $50 billion. Because IMF lending facilities were originally designed to provide funds after a country experienced a balance-of-payments crisis and because the conditions for the loan had to be negotiated, it took several months before the IMF made funds available. By this time, the crisis had gotten much worse—and much larger sums were needed to cope with the crisis, often stretching the resources of the IMF. One reason that central banks can lend so much more quickly than the IMF is that they have set up procedures in advance to provide loans, with the terms and conditions for this lending agreed upon beforehand. The need for quick provision of liquidity to keep the loan amount manageable argues for similar credit facilities at the international lender of last resort so that funds can be provided quickly as long as the borrower meets conditions such as properly supervising its banks or keeping budget deficits low. A step in this direction was made in 1999 when the IMF set up a new lending facility, the Contingent Credit Line, so it can provide liquidity faster during a crisis.

The debate on whether the world will be better off with the IMF operating as an international lender of last resort is currently a hot one. Much attention is being focused on making the IMF more effective in performing this role, and redesign of the IMF is at the centre of proposals for a new international financial architecture to help reduce international financial instability.

INTERNATIONAL CONSIDERATIONS AND MONETARY POLICY

Our analysis in this chapter so far has suggested several ways in which monetary policy can be affected by international events. And these occurrences can have significant implications for the way monetary policy is conducted.

Direct Effects of the Foreign Exchange Market on the Money Supply

When central banks intervene in the foreign exchange market, they acquire or sell off international reserves, and their monetary base is affected. When a central bank intervenes in the foreign exchange market, it gives up some control of its money supply. For example, in the early 1970s, the German central bank faced a dilemma. In attempting to keep the German mark from appreciating too much against the U.S. dollar, the Germans acquired huge quantities of international reserves, leading to a rapid rate of money growth that the German central bank considered inflationary.

The Bundesbank could have tried to halt the growth of the money supply by stopping its intervention in the foreign exchange market and reasserting control over its own money supply. Such a strategy has a major drawback when the central bank is under pressure not to allow its currency to appreciate: The lower price of imports and higher price of exports as a result of an appreciation in its currency will hurt domestic producers and increase unemployment.

The ability to conduct monetary policy is typically easier when a country's currency is a reserve currency. For example, because the U.S. dollar has been a reserve currency, the U.S. monetary base and money supply have been less affected by developments in the foreign exchange market. As long as other central banks, rather than the Fed, intervene to keep the value of the dollar from changing, U.S. holdings of international reserves are unaffected. However, the central bank of a reserve currency country must worry about a shift away from the use of its currency for international reserves.

Balance-of-Payments Considerations

Under the Bretton Woods system, balance-of-payments considerations were more important than they are under the current managed float regime. When a nonreserve currency country is running balance-of-payments deficits, it necessarily gives up international reserves. To keep from running out of these reserves, under the Bretton Woods system it had to implement contractionary monetary policy to strengthen its currency. Exactly that occurred in the United Kingdom before its devaluation of the pound in 1967. When policy became expansionary, the balance of payments deteriorated, and the British were forced to "slam on the brakes" by implementing a contractionary policy. Once the balance of payments improved, policy became more expansionary until the deteriorating balance of payments again forced the British to pursue a contractionary policy. Such on-again, off-again actions became known as a "stop-go" policy, and the domestic instability it created was criticized severely.

The situation is different with a major reserve currency country. The United States, for example, can run large balance-of-payments deficits without losing huge amounts of international reserves. This does not mean, however, that the Federal Reserve is never influenced by developments in the U.S. balance of payments. Current account deficits in the United States suggest that American businesses may be losing some of their ability to compete because the value of the dollar is too high. In addition, large U.S. balance-of-payments deficits lead to balance-of-payments surpluses in other countries, which can in turn lead to large increases in their holdings of international reserves (that was especially true under the Bretton Woods system). Because such increases put a strain on the international financial system and may stimulate world inflation, the Fed worries about U.S. balance-of-payments and current account deficits. To help shrink these deficits, the Fed might pursue a more contractionary monetary policy.

Exchange Rate Considerations

Unlike balance-of-payments considerations, which have become less important under the current managed float system, exchange rate considerations now play a greater role in the conduct of monetary policy. If a central bank does not want to see its currency fall in value, it may pursue a more contractionary monetary policy of reducing the money supply to raise the domestic interest rate, thereby strengthening its currency. Similarly, if a country experiences an appreciation in its currency, domestic industry may suffer from increased foreign competition and may pressure the central bank to pursue a higher rate of money growth in order to lower the exchange rate.

SUMMARY

1. An unsterilized central bank intervention in which the domestic currency is sold to purchase foreign assets leads to a gain in international reserves, an increase in the money supply, and a depreciation of the domestic currency. Available evidence suggests, however, that sterilized central bank interventions have little long-term effect on the exchange rate.
2. The balance of payments is a bookkeeping system for recording all payments between a country and foreign countries that have a direct bearing on the movement of funds between them. The official reserve transactions balance is the sum of the current account balance plus the items in the capital account. It indicates the amount of international reserves that must be moved between countries to finance international transactions.
3. Before World War I, the gold standard was predominant. Currencies were convertible into gold, thus fixing exchange rates between countries. After World War II, the Bretton Woods system and the IMF were established to promote a fixed exchange rate system in which the U.S. dollar was convertible into gold. The Bretton Woods system collapsed in 1971. We now have an international financial system that has elements of a managed float and a fixed exchange rate system. Some exchange rates fluctuate from day to day, although central banks intervene in the foreign exchange market, while other exchange rates are fixed, as in the European Monetary System.
4. Controls on capital outflows receive support because they might prevent domestic residents and foreigners from pulling capital out of a country during a crisis and make devaluation less likely. Controls on capital inflows make sense under the theory that if speculative capital cannot flow in, then it cannot go out suddenly and create a crisis. However, capital controls suffer from several disadvantages: They are seldom effective, they lead to corruption, and they may allow governments to avoid taking the steps to reform their financial systems to deal with the crisis.
5. The IMF has recently taken on the role of an international lender of last resort. Because central banks in emerging market countries are unlikely to be able to perform a lender-of-last-resort operation successfully, an international lender of last resort like the IMF is needed to prevent financial instability. However, the IMF's role as an international lender of last resort creates a serious moral hazard problem that can encourage excessive risk taking and make a financial crisis more likely. The IMF thus needs to limit the moral hazard created by its lender-of-last-resort role, but it may find this politically hard to do. In addition, it needs to be able to provide liquidity quickly during a crisis in order to keep manageable the amount of funds lent.
6. Three international considerations affect the conduct of monetary policy: direct effects of the foreign exchange market on the money supply, balance-of-payments considerations, and exchange rate considerations. A reserve currency country like the United States is less affected by developments in the foreign exchange market and its balance of payments than is true for other countries.

KEY TERMS

balance of payments, *p. 323*
balance-of-payments crises, *p. 334*
Bretton Woods system, *p. 327*
capital account, *p. 325*
currency union, *p. 339*
current account, *p. 323*
devaluation, *p. 329*
dollarization, *p. 330*
exchange rate union, *p. 333*
fixed exchange rate regime, *p. 327*
foreign exchange intervention, *p. 319*
gold standard, *p. 326*
International Monetary Fund (IMF), *p. 327*
international reserves, *p. 319*
managed float regime (dirty float), *p. 319*
official reserve transactions balance, *p. 325*
reserve currency, *p. 328*
revaluation, *p. 329*
special drawing rights (SDRs), *p. 332*
sterilized foreign exchange intervention, *p. 321*
T-account, *p. 319*
trade balance, *p. 323*
unsterilized foreign exchange intervention, *p. 320*
World Bank, *p. 327*

QUESTIONS AND PROBLEMS

1. If the Bank of Canada buys Canadian dollars in the foreign exchange market but conducts an offsetting open market operation to sterilize the intervention, what will be the impact on international reserves, the money supply, and the exchange rate?

*2. If the Bank of Canada buys Canadian dollars in the foreign exchange market but does not sterilize the intervention, what will be the impact on international reserves, the money supply, and the exchange rate?

3. For each of the following, identify in which part of the balance-of-payments account it appears (current account, capital account, or method of financing) and whether it is a receipt or a payment.
   a. A British subject's purchase of a share of Air Canada stock
   b. A Canadian's purchase of an airline ticket from Air France
   c. The Swiss government's purchase of Canadian treasury bills
   d. A Japanese's purchase of Canadian salmon
   e. $50 million of foreign aid to Honduras
   f. A loan by a Canadian bank to Mexico
   g. A Canadian bank's borrowing of Eurodollars

*4. Why does a balance-of-payments deficit for Canada have a different effect on its international reserves than a balance-of-payments deficit for the United States?

5. Under the gold standard, if Britain became more productive relative to Canada, what would happen to the money supply in the two countries? Why would the changes in the money supply help preserve a fixed exchange rate between Canada and Britain?

*6. What is the exchange rate between dollars and euros if one dollar is convertible into $\frac{1}{20}$ ounce of gold and one euro is convertible into $\frac{1}{40}$ ounce of gold?

7. If a country's par exchange rate was undervalued during the Bretton Woods fixed exchange rate regime, what kind of intervention would that country's central bank be forced to undertake, and what effect would it have on its international reserves and the money supply?

*8. How can a large balance-of-payments surplus contribute to the country's inflation rate?

9. "If a country wants to keep its exchange rate from changing, it must give up some control over its money supply." Is this statement true, false, or uncertain? Explain your answer.

*10. Why can balance-of-payments deficits force some countries to implement a contractionary monetary policy?

11. "Balance-of-payments deficits always cause a country to lose international reserves." Is this statement true, false, or uncertain? Explain your answer.

*12. How can persistent U.S. balance-of-payments deficits stimulate world inflation?

13. "Inflation is not possible under the gold standard." Is this statement true, false, or uncertain? Explain your answer.

*14. Why is it that in a pure flexible exchange rate system, the foreign exchange market has no direct effects on the money supply? Does this mean that the foreign exchange market has no effect on monetary policy?

15. "The abandonment of fixed exchange rates after 1973 has meant that countries have pursued more independent monetary policies." Is this statement true, false, or uncertain? Explain your answer.

*16. Are capital controls on capital outflows a good idea? Why or why not?

17. Discuss the pros and cons of capital controls on capital inflows.

*18. Why might central banks in emerging-market countries find that engaging in a lender-of-last resort operation might be counterproductive? Does this provide a rationale for having an international lender of last resort like the IMF?

19. Has the IMF done a good job in performing the role of the international lender of last resort?

*20. What steps should an international lender of last resort take to limit moral hazard?

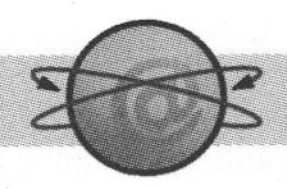

WEB EXERCISES

The International Financial System and Monetary Policy

1. The U.S. Federal Reserve publishes information online that explains the workings of the foreign exchange market. One such publication can be found at http://www.ny.frb.org/pihome/addpub/usfxm/. Review the table of contents and open Chapter 10, "The Evolution of the International Monetary System." Read this chapter and write a one-page summary that discusses why each monetary standard was dropped in favour of the succeeding one.

2. The International Monetary Fund stands ready to help nations facing monetary crises. Go to http://www.imf.org. Click on the tab labelled "About IMF." What is the stated purpose of the IMF? How many nations participate, and when was it established?

Part 5

The Financial Institutions Industry

Chapter 14 Theory of Financial Structure

Preview

A healthy and vibrant economy requires a financial system that moves funds from people who save to people who have productive investment opportunities. But how does the financial system make sure that your hard-earned savings get channelled to those with productive investment opportunities?

This chapter answers that question by providing a theory for understanding how our financial structure is designed to promote economic efficiency. The theoretical analysis focuses on a few simple but powerful economic concepts that enable us to explain features of our financial markets such as why financial contracts are written as they are, why financial intermediaries are more important than securities markets for getting funds to borrowers, and why financial crises occur and have such severe consequences for the health of the economy.

BASIC FACTS ABOUT FINANCIAL STRUCTURE THROUGHOUT THE WORLD

The financial system is complex in structure and function throughout the world. There are many different types of institutions: banks, insurance companies, mutual funds, stock and bond markets, and so on—all of which are regulated by government. The financial system channels billions of dollars per year from savers to people with productive investment opportunities. If we take a close look at financial structure all over the world, we need to explain eight basic (and sometimes surprising) facts in order to understand how the financial system works.

The pie charts in Figure 1 indicate how Canadian and American businesses financed their activities using external funds (those obtained from outside the business itself) in the period 1970–1985. The *Bank loans* category is made up primarily of bank loans; *nonbank loans* is made up primarily of loans by other financial intermediaries. The *bonds* category includes marketable debt securities such as corporate bonds and commercial paper. *Stock* consists of issues of new equity (stock market shares). Figure 2 uses the same classifications as Figure 1, and compares the Canadian and U.S. data with those of four other industrialized countries: France, Germany, Japan, and the United Kingdom.

Now let us explore the eight basic facts.

1. ***Stocks are not the most important source of external financing for businesses.*** Because so much attention in the media is focused on the

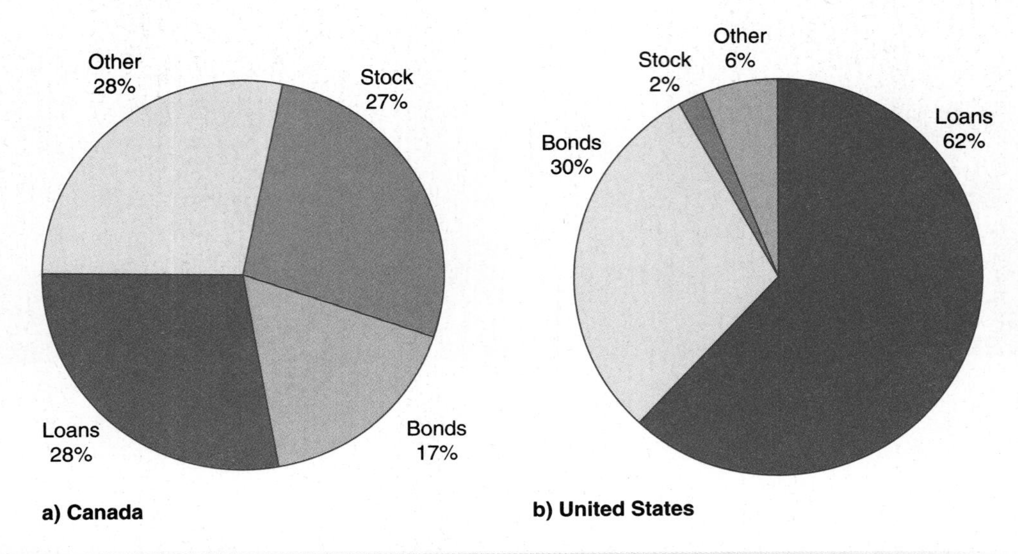

FIGURE 1 Sources of External Funds for Non-Financial Businesses in Canada and the United States

Source: Colin Mayer, "Financial Systems, Corporate Finance, and Economic Development." in *Assymetric Information, Corporate Finance, and Investment,* ed. R. Glenn Hubbard (Chicago: University of Chicago Press, 1990), p. 312.

stock market, many people have the impression that stocks are the most important sources of financing for corporations. However, as we can see from the pie charts in Figure 1 and from Figure 2, the stock markets accounted for only a small fraction of the external financing of business in the 1970-1985 period (2.1% in the United States, 14.2% in the United Kingdom, 17.9% in France, 5.5% in Germany, 5.3% in Japan, and 26.5% in Canada).[1] Only in Canada, France, and the United Kingdom do stock markets raise a significant proportion of external finance for businesses. Why is the stock market less important than other sources of financing?

2. ***Issuing marketable debt and equity securities is not the primary way in which businesses finance their operations.*** Figure 1 shows that for the United States bonds are a far more important source of financing than stocks (30% versus 2%). However, as you can see in Figure 2, bonds are less important than stocks in each of the other countries (9% versus 14.2% in the United Kingdom, 3.9% versus 17.9% in France, 1.8% versus 5.5% in Germany, 4.7% versus 5.3% in Japan, and 16.7% versus 26.5% in Canada). But stocks and bonds combined, which make up the total share of marketable securities, are still not the dominant source of external finance in all countries (31.9% in the United States, 23.2% in the United Kingdom, 21.8% in France, 7.3% in Germany, 10% in Japan, and 43.2% in Canada). Why don't businesses use marketable securities to finance their activities?

[1]The figures for the percentage of external financing provided by stocks are based on the flows of external funds to corporations. However, this flow figure is somewhat misleading because when a share of stock is issued, it raises funds permanently, whereas when a bond is issued, it raises funds only temporarily until they are paid back at maturity. To see this, suppose that a firm raises $1000 by selling a share of stock and another $1000 by selling a $1000 one-year bond. In the case of the stock issue, the firm can hold on to the $1000 it raised this way, but to hold on to the $1000 it raised through debt, it has to issue a new $1000 bond every year. If we look at the flow of funds to corporations over a 15-year period, as in Figures 1 and 2, the firm will have raised $1000 with a stock issue only once in the 15-year period, while it will have raised $1000 with debt 15 times, once in each of the 15 years. Thus it will look like debt is 15 times more important than stocks in raising funds, even though our example indicates that they are actually equally important for the firm.

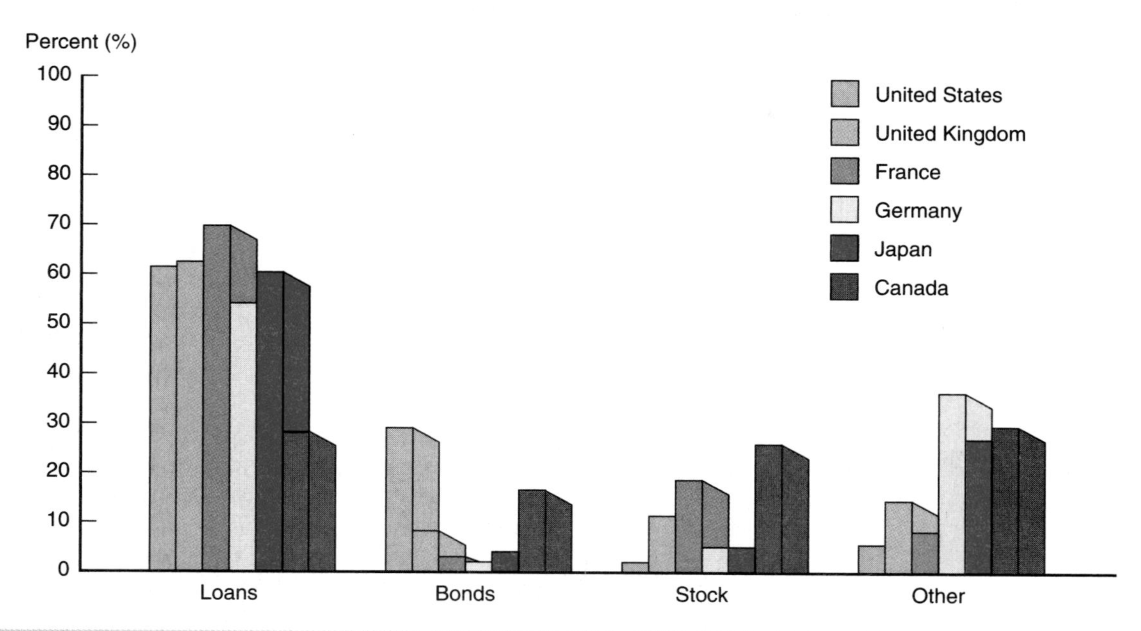

FIGURE 2 Sources of External Funds for Non-Financial Businesses: A Comparison of Canada, the United States, and Four Other Industrialized Countries

The categories of external funds are the same as in Figure 1.

Source: Colin Mayer, "Financial Systems, Corporate Finance, and Economic Development," in *Assymetric Information, Corporate Finance, and Investment*, ed. R. Glenn Hubbard (Chicago: University of Chicago Press, 1990), p. 312.

3. ***Indirect finance, which involves the activities of financial intermediaries, is many times more important than direct finance, in which businesses raise funds directly from lenders in financial markets.*** Direct finance involves the sale to households of marketable securities such as stocks and bonds. The shares of stocks and bonds that we mentioned as a source of external financing for businesses actually greatly overstate the importance of direct finance in the financial system throughout the world. In general, only a small fraction of newly issued corporate bonds and commercial paper and around 50% of stocks are sold directly to households. The rest of these securities are bought primarily by financial intermediaries such as insurance companies, pension funds, and mutual funds. This strengthens the argument that direct finance is a far less important source of finance than indirect finance. Why are financial intermediaries and indirect finance so important in financial markets throughout the world?
4. ***Banks are the most important source of external funds used to finance businesses.*** As we can see in Figures 1 and 2, the primary sources of external funds for businesses throughout the world are loans (61.9% in the United States, 62.2% in the United Kingdom, 70.2% in France, 55% in Germany, 61.3% in Japan, and 28.5% in Canada). Most of these loans are bank loans, so the data suggest that banks have the most important role in financing business activities throughout the world. Banks are more important in countries such as France, the United Kingdom, the United States, and Japan, but less important in countries such as Germany and Canada. Moreover, banks play an even more important role in the financial system of developing countries than they do in the industrialized countries. What makes banks so important to the working of the financial system?

5. ***The financial system is among the most heavily regulated sectors of the economy.*** You learned in Chapter 2 that the financial system is heavily regulated, not only in Canada but in all other developed countries as well. Governments regulate financial markets primarily to promote the provision of information in part to protect consumers, and to ensure the soundness (stability) of the financial system. Why are financial markets so extensively regulated throughout the world?
6. ***Only large, well-established corporations have easy access to securities markets to finance their activities.*** Individuals and smaller businesses that are not well established are less likely to raise funds by issuing marketable securities. Instead, they most often obtain their financing from banks. Why do only large, well-known corporations find it easier to raise funds in securities markets?
7. ***Collateral is a prevalent feature of debt contracts for both households and businesses.*** **Collateral** is property that is pledged to the lender to guarantee payment in the event that the borrower should be unable to make debt payments. Collateralized debt (which is also known as **secured debt** to contrast it with **unsecured debt**, such as credit card debt, which is not collateralized) is the predominant form of household debt and is widely used in business borrowing as well. The majority of household debt in Canada consists of collateralized loans: Your automobile is collateral for your auto loan, and your house is collateral for your mortgage. Commercial and farm mortgages, for which property is pledged as collateral, make up one-quarter of borrowing by non-financial businesses; corporate bonds and other bank loans also often involve pledges of collateral. Why is collateral such an important feature of debt contracts?
8. ***Debt contracts are typically extremely complicated legal documents that place substantial restrictions on the behaviour of the borrower.*** Many students think about a debt contract as a simple IOU that can be written on a single piece of paper. The reality of debt contracts is far different, however. In all countries, bond or loan contracts are typically long legal documents with provisions (called **restrictive covenants**) that restrict and specify certain activities that the borrower can engage in. Restrictive covenants are not just a feature of debt contracts for businesses; for example, personal automobile loan and home mortgage contracts have restrictive covenants that require the borrower to maintain sufficient insurance on the automobile or house purchased with the loan. Why are debt contracts so complex and restrictive?

As you may recall from Chapter 2, an important feature of financial markets is that they have substantial transaction and information costs. A theoretical analysis of how these costs affect financial markets provides us with solutions to the eight basic facts, which in turn provide us with a much deeper understanding of how our financial system works. In the next section we examine the impact of transaction costs on the structure of our financial system. Then we turn to how information costs affect financial structure.

TRANSACTION COSTS

Transaction costs are a major problem in financial markets. An example will make this problem clear.

How Transaction Costs Influence Financial Structure

Say you have $5000 you would like to invest, and you think about investing in the stock market. Because you have only $5000, you can buy only a small number of shares. The stockbroker tells you that your purchase is so small that the brokerage commission for buying the stock you picked will be a large percentage of the purchase price of the shares. If instead you decide to buy a bond, the problem is even worse because the smallest denomination for some bonds you might want to buy is as much as $10 000 and you do not have that much to invest. Indeed, the broker may not even be interested in your business at all because the small size of your account doesn't make spending time on it worthwhile. You are disappointed and realize that you will not be able to use financial markets to earn a return on your hard-earned savings. You can take some consolation, however, in the fact that you are not alone in being stymied by high transaction costs. This is a fact of life for most of us.

You also face another problem because of transaction costs. Because you have only a small amount of funds available, you can make only a restricted number of investments. That is, you have to put all your eggs in one basket, and your inability to diversify will subject you to a lot of risk.

How Financial Intermediaries Reduce Transaction Costs

This example of the problems posed by transaction costs and the example outlined in Chapter 2 when legal costs kept you from making a loan to Carl the Carpenter illustrate that small savers like you are frozen out of financial markets and are unable to benefit from them. Fortunately, financial intermediaries, an important part of the financial structure, have evolved to reduce transaction costs and allow small savers and borrowers to benefit from the existence of financial markets.

Economies of Scale One solution to the problem of high transaction costs is to bundle the funds of many investors together so that they can take advantage of *economies of scale,* the reduction in transaction costs per dollar of investment as the size (scale) of transactions increases. By bundling investors' funds together, transaction costs for each individual investor are far smaller. Economies of scale exist because the total cost of carrying out a transaction in financial markets increases only a little as the size of the transaction grows. For example, the cost of arranging a purchase of 10 000 shares of stock is not much greater than the cost of arranging a purchase of 50 shares of stock.

The presence of economies of scale in financial markets helps explain why financial intermediaries developed and are such an important part of our financial structure. The clearest example of a financial intermediary that arose because of economies of scale is a mutual fund. A *mutual fund* is a financial intermediary that sells shares to individuals and then invests the proceeds in bonds or stocks. Because it buys large blocks of stocks or bonds, a mutual fund can take advantage of lower transaction costs. These cost savings are then passed on to individual investors after the mutual fund has taken its cut in the form of management fees for administering their accounts. An additional benefit for individual investors is that a mutual fund is large enough to purchase a widely diversified portfolio of securities. The increased diversification for individual investors reduces their risk, thus making them better off.

Economies of scale are also important in lowering the costs of things, such as computer technology, that financial institutions need to accomplish their tasks. Once a large mutual fund has invested a lot of money in setting up a telecommunications system, for example, it can be used for a huge number of transactions at a low cost per transaction.

Expertise Financial intermediaries also arise because they are better able to develop expertise to lower transaction costs. Mutual funds, banks, and other financial intermediaries develop expertise in computer technology so that they can cheaply provide convenient services such as toll-free numbers that allow you to check on how well your investments are doing or the ability to write cheques on your account.

An important outcome of a financial intermediary's low transaction costs is that they allow a financial intermediary to provide its customers with *liquidity services,* services that make it easier for customers to conduct transactions. Money market mutual funds, for example, allow shareholders to write cheques that enable them to pay their bills easily while at the same time paying them high interest rates.

ASYMMETRIC INFORMATION: ADVERSE SELECTION AND MORAL HAZARD

The presence of transaction costs in financial markets explains in part why financial intermediaries and indirect finance play such an important role in financial markets (fact 3). To understand financial structure more fully, however, we turn to the role of information in financial markets.[2]

Asymmetric information—one party having insufficient knowledge about the other party involved in a transaction to make accurate decisions—is an important aspect of financial markets. For example, managers of a corporation know whether they are honest or have better information about how well their business is doing than the stockholders do. The presence of asymmetric information leads to adverse selection and moral hazard problems, which were introduced in Chapter 2.

Adverse selection is an asymmetric information problem that occurs *before* the transaction occurs: Potential bad credit risks are the ones who most actively seek out loans. Thus, the parties who are the most likely to produce an undesirable outcome are most likely to want to engage in the transaction. For example, big risk takers or outright crooks might be the most eager to take out a loan because they know that they are unlikely to pay it back. Because adverse selection increases the chances that a loan might be made to a bad credit risk, lenders may decide not to make any loans even though there are good credit risks in the marketplace.

Moral hazard arises *after* the transaction occurs: The lender runs the risk that the borrower will engage in activities that are undesirable from the lender's point of view because they make it less likely that the loan will be paid back. For example, once borrowers have obtained a loan, they may take on big risks (which have possible high returns but also run a greater risk of default) because they are playing with someone else's money. Because moral hazard lowers the probability that the loan will be repaid, lenders may decide that they would rather not make a loan.

THE LEMONS PROBLEM: HOW ADVERSE SELECTION INFLUENCES FINANCIAL STRUCTURE

A particular characterization of the adverse selection problem and how it interferes with the efficient functioning of a market was outlined in a famous article

[2]An excellent survey of the literature on information and financial structure that expands on the topics discussed in the rest of this chapter is contained in Mark Gertler, "Financial Structure and Aggregate Economic Activity: An Overview," *Journal of Money, Credit and Banking* 20 (1988): 559–88.

by George Akerlof, a Nobel prize-winner. It is referred to as the "lemons problem" because it resembles the problem created by lemons in the used-car market.[3] Potential buyers of used cars are frequently unable to assess the quality of the car; that is, they can't tell whether a particular used car is a good car that will run well or a lemon that will continually give them grief. The price that a buyer pays must therefore reflect the *average* quality of the cars in the market, somewhere between the low value of a lemon and the high value of a good car.

The owner of a used car, by contrast, is more likely to know whether the car is a peach or a lemon. If the car is a lemon, the owner is more than happy to sell it at the price the buyer is willing to pay, which, being somewhere between the value of a lemon and a good car, is greater than the lemon's value. However, if the car is a peach, the owner knows that the car is undervalued by the price the buyer is willing to pay, and so the owner may not want to sell it. As a result of this adverse selection, very few good used cars will come to the market. Because the average quality of a used car available in the market will be low and because very few people want to buy a lemon, there will be few sales. The used-car market will then function poorly, if at all.

Lemons in the Stock and Bond Markets

A similar lemons problem arises in securities markets, that is, the debt (bond) and equity (stock) markets. Suppose that our friend Irving the Investor, a potential buyer of securities such as common stock, can't distinguish between good firms with high expected profits and low risk and bad firms with low expected profits and high risk. In this situation, Irving will be willing to pay only a price that reflects the *average* quality of firms issuing securities—a price that lies between the value of securities from bad firms and the value of those from good firms. If the owners or managers of a good firm have better information than Irving and *know* that they are a good firm, they know that their securities are undervalued and will not want to sell them to Irving at the price he is willing to pay. The only firms willing to sell Irving securities will be bad firms (because the price is higher than the securities are worth). Our friend Irving is not stupid; he does not want to hold securities in bad firms, and hence he will decide not to purchase securities in the market. In an outcome similar to that in the used-car market, this securities market will not work very well because few firms will sell securities in it to raise capital.

The analysis is similar if Irving considers purchasing a corporate debt instrument in the bond market rather than an equity share. Irving will buy a bond only if its interest rate is high enough to compensate him for the average default risk of the good and bad firms trying to sell the debt. The knowledgeable owners of a good firm realize that they will be paying a higher interest rate than they should, and so they are unlikely to want to borrow in this market. Only the bad firms will be willing to borrow, and because investors like Irving are not eager to buy bonds issued by bad firms, they will probably not buy any bonds at all. Few bonds are likely to sell in this market, and so it will not be a good source of financing.

The analysis we have just conducted explains fact 2—why marketable securities are not the primary source of financing for businesses in any country in

[3]George Akerlof, "The Market for 'Lemons': Quality, Uncertainty and the Market Mechanism," *Quarterly Journal of Economics* 84 (1970): 488–500. Two important papers that have applied the lemons problem analysis to financial markets are Stewart Myers and N. S. Majluf, "Corporate Financing and Investment Decisions When Firms Have Information That Investors Do Not Have," *Journal of Financial Economics* 13 (1984): 187–221, and Bruce Greenwald, Joseph E. Stiglitz, and Andrew Weiss, "Information Imperfections in the Capital Market and Macroeconomic Fluctuations," *American Economic Review* 74 (1984): 194–9.

the world. It also partly explains fact 1—why stocks are not the most important source of financing for Canadian businesses. The presence of the lemons problem keeps securities markets such as the stock and bond markets from being effective in channelling funds from savers to borrowers.

Tools to Help Solve Adverse Selection Problems

In the absence of asymmetric information, the lemons problem goes away. If buyers know as much about the quality of used cars as sellers so that all involved can tell a good car from a bad one, buyers will be willing to pay full value for good used cars. Because the owners of good used cars can now get a fair price, they will be willing to sell them in the market. The market will have many transactions and will do its intended job of channelling good cars to people who want them.

Similarly, if purchasers of securities can distinguish good firms from bad, they will pay the full value of securities issued by good firms, and good firms will sell their securities in the market. The securities market will then be able to move funds to the good firms that have the most productive investment opportunities.

Private Production and Sale of Information The solution to the adverse selection problem in financial markets is to eliminate asymmetric information by furnishing people supplying funds with full details about the individuals or firms seeking to finance their investment activities. One way to get this material to saver-lenders is to have private companies collect and produce information that distinguishes good from bad firms and then sell it to purchasers of securities. In Canada, companies such as Standard & Poor's and the Dominion Bond Rating Service gather information on firms' balance sheet positions and investment activities, publish these data, and sell them to subscribers (individuals, libraries, and financial intermediaries involved in purchasing securities).

The system of private production and sale of information does not completely solve the adverse selection problem in securities markets, however, because of the so-called **free-rider problem.** The free-rider problem occurs when people who do not pay for information take advantage of the information that other people have paid for. The free-rider problem suggests that the private sale of information will be only a partial solution to the lemons problem. To see why, suppose that you have just purchased information that tells you which firms are good and which are bad. You believe that this purchase is worthwhile because you can make up the cost of acquiring this information, and then some, by purchasing the securities of good firms that are undervalued. However, when our savvy (free-riding) investor Irving sees you buying certain securities, he buys right along with you, even though he has not paid for any information. If many other investors act as Irving does, the increased demand for the undervalued good securities will cause their low price to be bid up immediately to reflect the securities' true value. As a result of all these free riders, you can no longer buy the securities for less than their true value. Now because you will not gain any profits from purchasing the information, you realize that you never should have paid for this information in the first place. If other investors come to the same realization, private firms and individuals may not be able to sell enough of this information to make it worth their while to gather and produce it. The weakened ability of private firms to profit from selling information will mean that less information is produced in the marketplace, and so adverse selection (the lemons problem) will still interfere with the efficient functioning of securities markets.

Government Regulation The free-rider problem prevents the private market from producing enough information to eliminate all the asymmetric information that leads to adverse selection. Could financial markets benefit from government intervention? The government could, for instance, produce information to help investors distinguish good from bad firms and provide it to the public free. This solution, however, would involve the government in releasing negative information about firms, a practice that might be politically difficult. A second possibility (and one followed by Canada and most governments throughout the world) is for the government to regulate securities markets in a way that encourages firms to reveal honest information about themselves so that investors can determine how good or bad the firms are. In Canada, government regulation exists that requires firms selling their securities in public markets to adhere to standard accounting principles and to disclose information about their sales, assets, and earnings. Similar regulations are found in other countries. However, disclosure requirements do not work well, as shown by recent accounting frauds or "mistakes" discovered in many U.S. companies such as Enron and WorldCom (see Box 1 on the Enron collapse).

The asymmetric information problem of adverse selection in financial markets helps explain why financial markets are among the most heavily regulated sectors in the economy (fact 5). Government regulation to increase information for investors is needed to reduce the adverse selection problem, which interferes with the efficient functioning of securities (stock and bond) markets.

Although government regulation lessens the adverse selection problem, it does not eliminate it. Even when firms provide information to the public about their sales, assets, or earnings, they still have more information than investors: There is a lot more to knowing the quality of a firm than statistics can provide. Furthermore, bad firms have an incentive to make themselves look like good firms because this would enable them to fetch a higher price for their securities. Bad firms will slant the information they are required to transmit to the public, thus making it harder for investors to sort out the good firms from the bad.

Financial Intermediation So far we have seen that private production of information and government regulation to encourage provision of information lessen but do not eliminate the adverse selection problem in financial markets. How, then, can the financial structure help promote the flow of funds to people with productive investment opportunities when there is asymmetric information? A clue is provided by the structure of the used-car market.

BOX 1

The Enron Implosion

Until 2001, Enron Corporation, a U.S. firm that specialized in trading in the energy market, appeared to be spectacularly successful. It had a quarter of the energy-trading market and was valued as high as $77 billion in August 2000, just a little over a year before its collapse, making it the seventh largest corporation in the United States at that time. However, toward the end of 2001, Enron came crashing down. In October 2001 Enron announced a big third-quarter loss of $618 million and disclosed accounting "mistakes." The U.S. SEC then engaged in a formal investigation of Enron's financial dealings with partnerships led by its former finance chief. It then became clear that Enron was engaged in a complex set of transactions that enabled it to keep substantial amounts of debt and financial contracts off its balance sheet, thus enabling it to hide its financial difficulties. Despite securing as much as $1.5 billion of new financing from J.P. Morgan Chase and Citigroup in December, the company was forced to declare bankruptcy, making it the largest one in U.S. history.

Enron's incredibly rapid collapse has raised concerns that disclosure and accounting regulations may be inadequate for firms that are involved in complicated financial transactions. The Enron collapse also illustrates that although government regulation lessens asymmetric information problems, it cannot eliminate them. When a firm is in trouble, its management has tremendous incentives to hide its problems, making it hard for investors to know the true value of the firm.

At www.consumerreports.org you can gather further information about *Consumer Reports*.

An important feature of the used-car market is that most used cars are not sold directly by one individual to another. An individual considering buying a used car might pay for privately produced information by subscribing to a magazine like *Consumer Reports* to find out whether a particular make of car has a good repair record. Nevertheless, reading *Consumer Reports* does not solve the adverse selection problem because even if a particular make of car has a good reputation, the specific car someone is trying to sell could be a lemon. The prospective buyer might also bring the used car to a mechanic for a once-over. But what if the prospective buyer doesn't know a mechanic who can be trusted or if the mechanic would charge a high fee to evaluate the car?

Because these roadblocks make it hard for individuals to acquire enough information about used cars, most used cars are not sold directly by one individual to another. Instead, they are sold by an intermediary, a used-car dealer who purchases used cars from individuals and resells them to other individuals. Used-car dealers produce information in the market by becoming experts in determining whether a car is a peach or a lemon. Once they know that a car is good, they can sell it with some form of a guarantee: either a guarantee that is explicit, such as a warranty, or an implicit guarantee in which they stand by their reputation for honesty. People are more likely to purchase a used car because of a dealer's guarantee, and the dealer is able to make a profit on the production of information about automobile quality by being able to sell the used car at a higher price than the dealer paid for it. If dealers purchase and then resell cars on which they have produced information, they avoid the problem of other people free-riding on the information they produced.

Just as used-car dealers help solve adverse selection problems in the automobile market, financial intermediaries play a similar role in financial markets. A financial intermediary such as a bank becomes an expert in the production of information about firms so that it can sort out good credit risks from bad ones. Then it can acquire funds from depositors and lend them to the good firms. Because the bank is able to lend mostly to good firms, it is able to earn a higher return on its loans than the interest it has to pay to its depositors. As a result, the bank earns a profit, which allows it to engage in this information production activity.

An important element in the ability of the bank to profit from the information it produces is that it avoids the free-rider problem by primarily making private loans rather than by purchasing securities that are traded in the open market. Because a private loan is not traded, other investors cannot watch what the bank is doing and bid up the loan's price to the point that the bank receives no compensation for the information it has produced. The bank's role as an intermediary that holds mostly non-traded loans is the key to its success in reducing asymmetric information in financial markets.

Our theoretical analysis of adverse selection indicates that financial intermediaries in general, and banks in particular because they hold a large fraction of non-traded loans, should play a greater role in moving funds to corporations than securities markets do. Our analysis thus explains facts 3 and 4: why indirect finance is so much more important than direct finance and why banks are the most important source of external funds for financing businesses.

Another important fact that is explained by the analysis here is the greater importance of banks in the financial systems of developing countries. As we have seen, when the quality of information about firms is better, asymmetric information problems will be less severe, and it will be easier for firms to issue securities. Information about private firms is even harder to collect in developing countries than in industrialized countries; therefore, the smaller role played by securities markets leaves a greater role for financial intermediaries such as banks. A corollary of this analysis is that as information about firms becomes easier to acquire, the role of banks should decline. A major development in the past 20 years has been huge improvements in information technology. Thus the analysis here suggests that the lending role of financial institutions such as banks should have declined, and this is exactly what has occurred (see Chapter 16).

Our analysis of adverse selection also explains which firms are more likely to obtain funds from banks and financial intermediaries, an indirect route, rather than directly from the securities markets. The better known a corporation is, the more information about its activities is available in the marketplace. Thus it is easier for investors to evaluate the quality of the corporation and determine whether it is a good firm or a bad one. Because investors have fewer worries about adverse selection with well-known corporations, they will be willing to invest directly in their securities. Hence we have an explanation for fact 6: The larger and more mature a corporation is, the more information investors have about it, and the more likely it is that the corporation can raise funds in securities markets.

Collateral and Net Worth Adverse selection interferes with the functioning of financial markets only if a lender suffers a loss when a borrower is unable to make loan payments and thereby defaults. Collateral, property promised to the lender if the borrower defaults, reduces the consequences of adverse selection because it reduces the lender's losses in the event of a default. If a borrower defaults on a loan, the lender can sell the collateral and use the proceeds to make up for the losses on the loan. For example, if you fail to make your mortgage payments, the lender can take title to your house, auction it off, and use the receipts to pay off the loan. Lenders are thus more willing to make loans secured by collateral, and borrowers are willing to supply collateral because the reduced risk for the lender makes it more likely they will get the loan in the first place and perhaps at a better loan rate. The presence of adverse selection in credit markets thus provides an explanation for why collateral is an important feature of debt contracts (fact 7).

Net worth (also called **equity capital**), the difference between a firm's assets (what it owns or is owed) and its liabilities (what it owes), can perform a similar role to collateral. If a firm has a high net worth, then even if it engages in investments that cause it to have negative profits and so defaults on its debt payments, the lender can take title to the firm's net worth, sell it off, and use the proceeds to recoup some of the losses from the loan. In addition, the more net worth a firm has in the first place, the less likely it is to default because the firm has a cushion of assets that it can use to pay off its loans. Hence when firms seeking credit have high net worth, the consequences of adverse selection are less important and lenders are more willing to make loans. This analysis lies behind the often-heard lament, "Only the people who don't need money can borrow it!"

Summary So far we have used the concept of adverse selection to explain seven of the eight basic facts about financial structure introduced earlier: The first four emphasize the importance of financial intermediaries and the relative unimportance of securities markets for the financing of corporations; the fifth, that financial markets are among the most heavily regulated sectors of the economy; the sixth, that only large, well-established corporations have access to securities markets; and the seventh, that collateral is an important feature of debt contracts. In the next section we will see that the other asymmetric information concept of moral hazard provides additional reasons for the importance of financial intermediaries and the relative unimportance of securities markets for the financing of corporations, the prevalence of government regulation, and the importance of collateral in debt contracts. In addition, the concept of moral hazard can be used to explain our final basic fact (fact 8) of why debt contracts are complicated legal documents that place substantial restrictions on the behaviour of the borrower.

HOW MORAL HAZARD AFFECTS THE CHOICE BETWEEN DEBT AND EQUITY CONTRACTS

Moral hazard is the asymmetric information problem that occurs after the financial transaction takes place, when the seller of a security may have incentives to hide information and engage in activities that are undesirable for the purchaser of the security. Moral hazard has important consequences for whether a firm finds it easier to raise funds with debt rather than with equity contracts.

Moral Hazard in Equity Contracts: The Principal-Agent Problem

Equity contracts, such as common stock, are claims to a share in the profits and assets of a business. Equity contracts are subject to a particular type of moral hazard called the **principal-agent problem.** When managers own only a small fraction of the firm they work for, the stockholders who own most of the firm's equity (called the *principals*) are not the same people as the managers of the firm, who are the *agents* of the owners. This separation of ownership and control involves moral hazard in that the managers in control (the agents) may act in their own interest rather than in the interest of the stockholder-owners (the principals) because the managers have less incentive to maximize profits than the stockholder-owners do.

To understand the principal-agent problem more fully, suppose that your friend Steve asks you to become a silent partner in his ice-cream store. The store requires an investment of $10 000 to set up, but Steve has only $1000. So you purchase an equity stake (stock shares) for $9000, which entitles you to 90% of the ownership of the firm, while Steve owns only 10%. If Steve works hard to make tasty ice cream, keeps the store clean, smiles at all the customers, and hustles to wait on tables quickly, after all expenses (including Steve's salary), the store will have $50 000 in profits per year, of which Steve receives 10% ($5000) and you receive 90% ($45 000).

But if Steve doesn't provide quick and friendly service to his customers, uses the $50 000 in income to buy artwork for his office, and even sneaks off to the beach while he should be at the store, the store will not earn any profit. Steve can only earn the additional $5000 (his 10% share of the profits) over his salary if he works hard and forgoes unproductive investments (such as art for his office). Steve might decide that the extra $5000 just isn't enough to make him want to expend the effort to be a good manager; he might decide that it would be worth his while only if he earned an extra $10 000. If Steve feels this way, he does not have enough incentive to be a good manager and will end up with a beautiful office, a good tan, and a store that doesn't show any profits. Because the store won't show any profits, Steve's decision not to act in your interest will cost you $45 000 (your 90% of the profits if he had chosen to be a good manager instead).

The moral hazard arising from the principal-agent problem might be even worse if Steve were not totally honest. Because his ice-cream store is a cash business, Steve has the incentive to pocket $50 000 in cash and tell you that the profits were zero. He now gets a return of $50 000, but you get nothing. The moral hazard incentive to underreport profits is illustrated by the experience with accounting practices in the movie industry described in Box 2.

Further indications that the principal-agent problem created by equity contracts can be severe are provided by examples of managers who build luxurious offices for themselves or drive high-priced corporate automobiles. Besides pursuing personal benefits, managers might also pursue corporate strategies (such as the acquisition of other firms) that enhance their personal power but do not increase the corporation's profitability.

BOX 2

"Hollywood Accounting": Was *Forrest Gump* a Money Loser?

Accounting practices in the movie industry are notorious, giving the phrase "Hollywood accounting" a dubious reputation. A standard practice at movie studios is to keep two sets of books, a practice that might not be tolerated in other businesses but is in the movie business, where standards of morality are not always the highest. One set is maintained according to the generally accepted accounting principles in other industries; that set is used to report profits to management and to shareholders. The second set of books, referred to as "contractual accounting," is used when a studio commits to paying out percentages of a movie's "net profits" among actors, directors, writers, and other parties as part of contractual arrangements. Given that the movie studios have a moral hazard incentive to minimize these "net profits," not surprisingly they are rarely positive. For example, *Forrest Gump*, which took in more than $600 million at the box office, did not show any profits according to Paramount, the filmmaker. The same has also been the case for other blockbusters such as the first *Batman* movie, *J.F.K.*, and *Coming to America*. Can we really believe that *Forrest Gump*, one of the most successful movies of all time, was a money loser, or is this just an example of the principal-agent problem at work?

The dubious accounting practices of the movie industry have been coming under attack as a result of numerous lawsuits. In addition, the squeaky-clean Walt Disney Company is trying to change industry practices by going on record that it will not use contractual accounting and a second set of books when it compensates movie actors, directors, and writers.

The principal-agent problem would not arise if the owners of a firm had complete information about what the managers were up to and could prevent wasteful expenditures or fraud. The principal-agent problem, which is an example of moral hazard, arises only because a manager, like Steve, has more information about his activities than the stockholder does—that is, there is asymmetric information. The principal-agent problem would also not arise if Steve alone owned the store and there was no separation of ownership and control. If this were the case, Steve's hard work and avoidance of unproductive investments would yield him a profit (and extra income) of $50 000, an amount that would make it worth his while to be a good manager.

Tools to Help Solve the Principal-Agent Problem

Production of Information: Monitoring You have seen that the principal-agent problem arises because managers have more information about their activities and actual profits than stockholders do. One way for stockholders to reduce this moral hazard problem is for them to engage in a particular type of information production, the monitoring of the firm's activities: auditing the firm frequently and checking on what the management is doing. The problem is that the monitoring process can be expensive in terms of time and money, as reflected in the name financial economists give it, **costly state verification**. Costly state verification makes the equity contract less desirable, and it explains, in part, why equity is not a more important element in our financial structure.

As with adverse selection, the free-rider problem decreases the amount of information production that would reduce the moral hazard (principal-agent) problem. In this example, the free-rider problem decreases monitoring. If you know that other stockholders are paying to monitor the activities of the company you hold shares in, you can take a free ride on their activities. Then you can use the money you save by not engaging in monitoring to vacation on a Caribbean island. If you can do this, though, so can other stockholders. Perhaps all the stockholders will go to the islands, and no one will spend any resources on monitoring the firm. The moral hazard problem for shares of common stock will then be severe, making it hard for firms to issue them to raise capital.

Government Regulation to Increase Information As with adverse selection, the government has an incentive to try to reduce the moral hazard problem created by asymmetric information. Governments everywhere have laws to force firms to adhere to standard accounting principles that make profit verification easier. They also pass laws to impose stiff criminal penalties on people who commit the fraud of hiding and stealing profits. However, these measures can only be partly effective. Catching this kind of fraud is not easy; fraudulent managers have the incentive to make it very hard for government agencies to find or prove fraud.

Financial Intermediation Financial intermediaries have the ability to avoid the free-rider problem in the face of moral hazard. One financial intermediary that helps reduce the moral hazard arising from the principal-agent problem is the **venture capital firm**. Venture capital firms pool the resources of their partners and use the funds to help budding entrepreneurs start new businesses. In exchange for the use of the venture capital, the firm receives an equity share in the new business. Because verification of earnings and profits is so important in eliminating moral hazard, venture capital firms usually insist on having several of their own people participate as members of the managing body of the firm, the board of directors, so that they can keep a close watch on the firm's activities. When a venture capital firm supplies start-up funds, the equity in the firm is not marketable to anyone *but* the venture capital firm. Thus other investors are unable to take a free ride on the venture capital firm's verification activities. As a result of this arrangement, the venture capital firm is able to garner the full benefits of its verification activities and is given the appropriate incentives to reduce the moral hazard problem.

Debt Contracts Moral hazard arises with an equity contract, which is a claim on profits in all situations, whether the firm is making or losing money. If a contract could be structured so that moral hazard would exist only in certain situations, there would be a reduced need to monitor managers, and the contract would be more attractive than the equity contract. The debt contract has exactly these attributes because it is a contractual agreement by the borrower to pay the lender *fixed* dollar amounts at periodic intervals. When the firm has high profits, the lender receives the contractual payments and does not need to know the exact profits of the firm. If the managers are hiding profits or are pursuing activities that are personally beneficial but don't increase profitability, the lender doesn't care as long as these activities do not interfere with the ability of the firm to make its debt payments on time. Only when the firm cannot meet its debt payments, thereby being in a state of default, is there a need for the lender to verify the state of the firm's profits. Only in this situation do lenders involved in debt contracts need to act more like equity holders; now they need to know how much income the firm has in order to get their fair share.

The advantage of a less frequent need to monitor the firm, and thus a lower cost of state verification, helps explain why debt contracts are used more frequently than equity contracts to raise capital. The concept of moral hazard thus helps explain fact 1, why stocks are not the most important source of financing for businesses.[4]

[4]Another factor that encourages the use of debt contracts rather than equity contracts is our tax code. Debt interest payments are a deductible expense for Canadian firms, whereas dividend payments to equity shareholders are not.

HOW MORAL HAZARD INFLUENCES FINANCIAL STRUCTURE IN DEBT MARKETS

Even with the advantages just described, debt contracts are still subject to moral hazard. Because a debt contract requires the borrowers to pay out a fixed amount and lets them keep any profits above this amount, the borrowers have an incentive to take on investment projects that are riskier than the lenders would like.

For example, suppose that because you are concerned about the problem of verifying the profits of Steve's ice-cream store, you decide not to become an equity partner. Instead, you lend Steve the $9000 he needs to set up his business and have a debt contract that pays you an interest rate of 10%. As far as you are concerned, this is a surefire investment because there is a strong and steady demand for ice cream in your neighbourhood. However, once you give Steve the funds, he might use them for purposes other than you intended. Instead of opening up the ice-cream store, Steve might use your $9000 loan to invest in chemical research equipment because he thinks he has a 1-in-10 chance of inventing a diet ice cream that tastes every bit as good as the premium brands but has no fat or calories.

Obviously, this is a very risky investment, but if Steve is successful, he will become a multimillionaire. He has a strong incentive to undertake the riskier investment with your money because the gains to him would be so large if he succeeded. You would clearly be very unhappy if Steve used your loan for the riskier investment because if he were unsuccessful, which is highly likely, you would lose most, if not all, of the money you gave him. And if he were successful, you wouldn't share in his success—you would still get only a 10% return on the loan because the principal and interest payments are fixed. Because of the potential moral hazard (Steve might use your money to finance a very risky venture), you would probably not make the loan to Steve, even though an ice-cream store in the neighbourhood is a good investment that would provide benefits for everyone.

Tools to Help Solve Moral Hazard in Debt Contracts

Net Worth When borrowers have more at stake because their *net worth* (the difference between their assets and their liabilities) is high, the risk of moral hazard—the temptation to act in a manner that lenders find objectionable—will be greatly reduced because the borrowers themselves have a lot to lose. Let's return to Steve and his ice-cream business. Suppose that the cost of setting up either the ice-cream store or the research equipment is $100 000 instead of $10 000. So Steve needs to put $91 000 of his own money into the business (instead of $1000) in addition to the $9000 supplied by your loan. Now if Steve is unsuccessful in inventing the no-calorie nonfat ice cream, he has a lot to lose, the $91 000 of net worth ($100 000 in assets minus the $9000 loan from you). He will think twice about undertaking the riskier investment and is more likely to invest in the ice-cream store, which is more of a sure thing. Hence, when Steve has more of his own money (net worth) in the business, you are more likely to make the loan to him.

One way of describing the solution that high net worth provides to the moral hazard problem is to say that it makes the debt contract **incentive-compatible**; that is, it aligns the incentives of the borrower with those of the lender. The greater the borrower's net worth, the greater the borrower's incentive to behave in the way that the lender expects and desires, the smaller the moral hazard problem in the debt contract is, and the easier it is for the firm to borrow. Conversely, when the borrower's net worth is lower, the moral hazard problem is greater, and it is harder for the firm to borrow.

Monitoring and Enforcement of Restrictive Covenants As the example of Steve and his ice-cream store shows, if you could make sure that Steve doesn't invest in anything riskier than the ice-cream store, it would be worth your while to make him the loan. You can ensure that Steve uses your money for the purpose *you* want it to be used for by writing provisions (restrictive covenants) into the debt contract that restrict his firm's activities. By monitoring Steve's activities to see whether he is complying with the restrictive covenants and enforcing the covenants if he is not, you can make sure that he will not take on risks at your expense.

Restrictive covenants are directed at reducing moral hazard either by ruling out undesirable behaviour or by encouraging desirable behaviour. There are four types of restrictive covenants that achieve this objective:

1. *Covenants to discourage undesirable behaviour.* Covenants can be designed to lower moral hazard by keeping the borrower from engaging in the undesirable behaviour of undertaking risky investment projects. Some such covenants mandate that a loan can be used only to finance specific activities, such as the purchase of particular equipment or inventories. Others restrict the borrowing firm from engaging in certain risky business activities, such as purchasing other businesses.
2. *Covenant to encourage desirable behaviour.* Restrictive covenants can encourage the borrower to engage in desirable activities that make it more likely that the loan will be paid off. One restrictive covenant of this type requires the breadwinner in a household to carry life insurance that pays off the mortgage upon that person's death. Restrictive covenants of this type for businesses focus on encouraging the borrowing firm to keep its net worth high because higher borrower net worth reduces moral hazard and makes it less likely that the lender will suffer losses. These restrictive covenants typically specify that the firm must maintain minimum holdings of certain assets relative to the firm's size.
3. *Covenants to keep collateral valuable.* Because collateral is an important protection for the lender, restrictive covenants can encourage the borrower to keep the collateral in good condition and make sure that it stays in the possession of the borrower. This is the type of covenant ordinary people encounter most often. Automobile loan contracts, for example, require the car owner to maintain a minimum amount of collision and theft insurance and prevent the sale of the car unless the loan is paid off. Similarly, the recipient of a home mortgage must have adequate insurance on the home and must pay off the mortgage when the property is sold.
4. *Covenants to provide information.* Restrictive covenants also require a borrowing firm to provide information about its activities periodically in the form of quarterly accounting and income reports, thereby making it easier for the lender to monitor the firm and reduce moral hazard. This type of covenant may also stipulate that the lender has the right to audit and inspect the firm's books at any time.

We now see why debt contracts are often complicated legal documents with numerous restrictions on the borrower's behaviour (fact 8): Debt contracts require complicated restrictive covenants to lower moral hazard.

Financial Intermediation Although restrictive covenants help reduce the moral hazard problem, they do not eliminate it completely. It is almost impossible to write covenants that rule out *every* risky activity. Furthermore, borrowers may be clever enough to find loopholes in restrictive covenants that make them ineffective.

Another problem with restrictive covenants is that they must be monitored and enforced. A restrictive covenant is meaningless if the borrower can violate it knowing that the lender won't check up or is unwilling to pay for legal recourse. Because monitoring and enforcement of restrictive covenants are costly, the free-rider problem arises in the debt securities (bond) market just as it does in the stock market. If you know that other bondholders are monitoring and enforcing the restrictive covenants, you can free-ride on their monitoring and enforcement. But other bondholders can do the same thing, so the likely outcome is that not enough resources are devoted to monitoring and enforcing the restrictive covenants. Moral hazard therefore continues to be a severe problem for marketable debt.

As we have seen before, financial intermediaries, particularly banks, have the ability to avoid the free-rider problem as long as they primarily make private loans. Private loans are not traded, so no one else can free-ride on the intermediary's monitoring and enforcement of the restrictive covenants. The intermediary making private loans thus receives the benefits of monitoring and enforcement and will work to shrink the moral hazard problem inherent in debt contracts. The concept of moral hazard has provided us with additional reasons why financial intermediaries play a more important role in channelling funds from savers to borrowers than marketable securities do, as described in facts 1 through 4.

Summary

The presence of asymmetric information in financial markets leads to adverse selection and moral hazard problems that interfere with the efficient functioning of those markets. Tools to help solve these problems involve the private production and sale of information, government regulation to increase information in financial markets, the importance of collateral and net worth to debt contracts, and the use of monitoring and restrictive covenants. A key finding from our theoretical analysis is that the existence of the free-rider problem for traded securities such as stocks and bonds indicates that financial intermediaries, particularly banks, should play a greater role than securities markets in financing the activities of businesses. Theoretical analysis of the consequences of adverse selection and moral hazard has helped elucidate the basic features of our financial system and has provided explanations for the eight basic facts about our financial structure outlined at the beginning of this chapter.

Application Financial Development and Economic Growth

Recent research has found that an important reason why many developing countries or ex-communist countries like Russia experience very low rates of growth is that their financial systems are underdeveloped (a situation referred to as *financial repression*).[5] The theoretical analysis of financial structure helps explain how an underdeveloped financial system leads to a low state of economic development and economic growth.

The financial systems in developing and ex-communist countries face several difficulties that keep them from operating efficiently. As we have seen, two important tools used to help solve adverse selection and moral hazard problems in credit markets are collateral and restrictive covenants. In many developing countries, the legal system functions poorly, making it hard to make effective use of these two tools. In these countries, bankruptcy procedures are often extremely slow and cumbersome. For example, in many countries, **creditors** (holders of debt) must first sue the defaulting debtor for payment, which can take several

[5] World Bank, *Finance for Growth: Policy Choices in a Volatile World* (World Bank and Oxford University Press, Oxford: 2001) for a survey of this literature and a list of further references.

years, and then once a favourable judgment has been obtained, the creditor has to sue again to obtain title to the collateral. The process can take in excess of five years, and by the time the lender acquires the collateral, it well may have been neglected and thus have little value. In addition, governments often block lenders from foreclosing on borrowers in politically powerful sectors such as agriculture. Where the market is unable to use collateral effectively, the adverse selection problem will be worse because the lender will need even more information about the quality of the borrower in order to screen out a good loan from a bad one. The result is that it will be harder for lenders to channel funds to borrowers with the most productive investment opportunities, thereby leading to less productive investment and hence a slower-growing economy. Similarly, a poorly developed legal system may make it extremely difficult for borrowers to enforce restrictive covenants. Thus they may have a much more limited ability to reduce moral hazard on the part of borrowers and so will be less willing to lend. Again, the outcome will be less productive investment and a lower growth rate for the economy.

Governments in developing and ex-communist countries have also often decided to use their financial systems to direct credit to themselves or to favoured sectors of the economy by setting interest rates at artificially low levels for certain types of loans, by creating so-called development finance institutions to make specific types of loans, or by directing existing institutions to lend to certain entities. As we have seen, private institutions have an incentive to solve adverse selection and moral hazard problems and lend to borrowers with the most productive investment opportunities. Governments have less incentive to do so because they are not driven by the profit motive and so their directed credit programs may not channel funds to sectors that will produce high growth for the economy. The outcome is again likely to result in less efficient investment and slower growth.

In addition, banks in many developing and ex-communist countries have been nationalized by their governments. Again because of the absence of the profit motive, these nationalized banks have little incentive to allocate their capital to the most productive uses. Indeed, the primary loan customer of these nationalized banks is often the government, which does not always use the funds wisely.

We have seen that government regulation can increase the amount of information in financial markets to make them work more efficiently. Many developing and ex-communist countries have an underdeveloped regulatory apparatus that retards the provision of adequate information to the marketplace. For example, these countries often have weak accounting standards, making it very hard to ascertain the quality of a borrower's balance sheet. As a result, asymmetric information problems are more severe, and the financial system is severely hampered in channelling funds to the most productive uses.

The institutional environment of a poor legal system, weak accounting standards, inadequate government regulation, and government intervention through directed credit programs and nationalization of banks all help explain why many countries stay poor while others grow richer.

FINANCIAL CRISES AND AGGREGATE ECONOMIC ACTIVITY

Our theoretical analysis of the effects of adverse selection and moral hazard can help us understand **financial crises**, major disruptions in financial markets that are characterized by sharp declines in asset prices and the failures of many financial and nonfinancial firms. Financial crises have been common in most countries throughout modern history. Canada experienced major financial crises in 1866, 1879, 1923, 1930–1933, and 1985 but has not had full-scale financial crises since then.[6] Studying financial crises is worthwhile because they have led to severe economic downturns in the past and have the potential for doing so in the future.

Financial crises occur when there is a disruption in the financial system that causes such a sharp increase in adverse selection and moral hazard problems in financial markets that the markets are unable to channel funds efficiently from savers to people with productive investment opportunities. As a result of this inability of financial markets to function efficiently, economic activity contracts sharply.

Factors Causing Financial Crises

To understand why banking and financial crises occur and more specifically how they lead to contractions in economic activity, we need to examine the factors that cause them. Four categories of factors can trigger financial crises: increases in interest rates, increases in uncertainty, asset market effects on balance sheets, and bank panics.

Increases in Interest Rates As we saw earlier, individuals and firms with the riskiest investment projects are exactly those who are willing to pay the highest interest rates. If market interest rates are driven up sufficiently because of increased demand for credit or because of a decline in the money supply, good credit risks are less likely to want to borrow while bad credit risks are still willing to borrow. Because of the resulting increase in adverse selection, lenders will no longer want to make loans. The substantial decline in lending will lead to a substantial decline in investment and aggregate economic activity.

Increases in Uncertainty A dramatic increase in uncertainty in financial markets, due perhaps to the failure of a prominent financial or nonfinancial institution, a recession, or a stock market crash, makes it harder for lenders to screen good from bad credit risks. The resulting inability of lenders to solve the adverse selection problem makes them less willing to lend, which leads to a decline in lending, investment, and aggregate economic activity.

Asset Market Effects on Balance Sheets The state of firms' balance sheets has important implications for the severity of asymmetric information problems in the financial system. A sharp decline in the stock market is one factor that can cause a serious deterioration in firms' balance sheets that can increase adverse selection and moral hazard problems in financial markets and provoke a financial crisis. A decline in the stock market means that the net worth of corporations has fallen because share prices are the valuation of a corporation's net worth. The decline in net worth as a result of a stock market decline makes lenders less willing to lend because, as we have seen, the net worth of a firm plays a role similar to that of collateral. When the value of collateral declines, it provides less protection to lenders, meaning that losses on loans are likely to be more severe. Because lenders are now less protected against the consequences of adverse selection, they decrease their lending, which in turn causes investment and aggregate output to decline. In addition, the decline in corporate net worth as a result of a stock market decline increases moral hazard by providing incentives for borrowing firms to make risky investments, as they now have less to lose if their investments go sour. The resulting increase in moral hazard makes lending less attractive—another reason why

[6]Although we in Canada have not experienced any financial crises since the Great Depression, we have had several close calls—the October 1987 stock market crash, for example. An important reason why we have escaped financial crises is the timely action of the Bank of Canada to prevent them during episodes like that of October 1987. The Bank's role in preventing financial crises was discussed in Chapter 7.

a stock market decline and hence a decline in net worth leads to decreased lending and economic activity.

In economies in which inflation has been moderate, which characterizes most industrialized countries, many debt contracts are typically of fairly long maturity with fixed interest rates. In this institutional environment, unanticipated declines in the aggregate price level also decrease the net worth of firms. Because debt payments are contractually fixed in nominal terms, an unanticipated decline in the price level raises the value of firms' liabilities in *real* terms (increases the burden of the debt) but does not raise the real value of firms' assets. The result is that net worth in *real* terms (the difference between assets and liabilities in *real* terms) declines. A sharp drop in the price level therefore causes a substantial decline in real net worth and an increase in adverse selection and moral hazard problems facing lenders. An unanticipated decline in the aggregate price level thus leads to a drop in lending and economic activity.

Because of uncertainty about the future value of the domestic currency in developing countries (and in some industrialized countries), many nonfinancial firms, banks, and governments in these countries find it easier to issue debt denominated in foreign currencies. This can lead to a financial crisis in a fashion similar to an unanticipated decline in inflation. With debt contracts denominated in foreign currency, when there is an unanticipated depreciation or devaluation of the domestic currency, the debt burden of domestic firms increases. Since assets are typically denominated in domestic currency, there is a resulting deterioration in firms' balance sheets and a decline in net worth, which then increases adverse selection and moral hazard problems along the lines just described. The increase in asymmetric information problems leads to a decline in investment and economic activity.

Although we have seen that increases in interest rates have a direct effect on increasing adverse selection problems, increases in interest rates also play a role in promoting a financial crisis through their effect on both firms' and households' balance sheets. A rise in interest rates and therefore in households' and firms' interest payments decreases firms' **cash flow**, the difference between cash receipts and cash expenditures. The decline in cash flow causes a deterioration in the balance sheet because it decreases the liquidity of the household or firm and thus makes it harder for lenders to know whether the firm or household will be able to pay its bills. As a result, adverse selection and moral hazard problems become more severe for potential lenders to these firms and households, leading to a decline in lending and economic activity. There is thus an additional reason why sharp increases in interest rates can be an important factor leading to financial crises.

Problems in the Banking Sector Banks play a major role in financial markets since they are well positioned to engage in information-producing activities that facilitate productive investment for the economy. The state of banks' balance sheets has an important effect on bank lending. If banks suffer a deterioration in their balance sheets and so have a substantial contraction in their capital, they will have fewer resources to lend, and bank lending will decline. The contraction in lending then leads to a decline in investment spending, which slows economic activity.

If the deterioration in bank balance sheets is severe enough, banks will start to fail, and fear can spread from one bank to another, causing even healthy banks to go under. The multiple bank failures that result are known as a **bank panic**. The source of the contagion is again asymmetric information. In a panic, depositors, fearing the safety of their deposits (in the absence of deposit insurance) and not knowing the quality of banks' loan portfolios, withdraw their deposits from other banks to the point that the banks fail. The disappearance of a large number of banks in a short period of time means that there is a loss of information production in financial markets and hence a direct loss of financial intermediation by the banking sector. The decrease in bank lending during a financial crisis also decreases the supply of funds to borrowers, which leads to higher interest rates. The outcome is an increase in adverse selection and moral hazard problems in credit markets; this produces an even sharper decline in lending to facilitate productive investments and a strong contraction in economic activity.

Application

Financial Crises in Canada

As mentioned, Canada had a number of banking and financial crises in the nineteenth and twentieth centuries—in 1866, 1879, 1923, 1930–1933, and 1985. Our analysis of the factors that lead to a financial crisis can explain why these crises took place and why they were so damaging to the Canadian economy.

Study Guide To understand fully what took place in a Canadian financial crisis, make sure that you can state the reasons why each of the factors—increases in interest rates, increases in uncertainty, asset market effects on balance sheets, and bank panics—increases adverse selection and moral hazard problems, which in turn lead to a decline in economic activity. To help you understand these crises, you might want to refer to Figure 3, a diagram that traces the sequence of events in a Canadian financial crisis.

As shown in Figure 3, most financial crises in Canada have begun with a deterioration in banks' balance sheets, a sharp rise in interest rates (frequently stemming from increases in interest rates in the United States), a steep stock market decline, and an increase in uncertainty resulting from a failure of major financial or nonfinancial firms (the Bank of Upper Canada in 1866 and the Home Bank in 1923) or from a bank panic (the panic of 1879). During these crises, deterioration in banks' balance sheets, the increase in uncertainty, the rise in interest rates, and the stock market decline increased the severity of adverse selection problems in credit markets; the stock market decline, the deterioration in banks' balance sheets, and the rise in interest rates, which decreases firms' cash flow, also increased moral hazard problems. The rise in adverse selection and moral hazard problems then made it less attractive for lenders to lend and led to a decline in investment and aggregate economic activity.

Because of the worsening business conditions and uncertainty about their bank's health (perhaps banks would go broke), depositors began to withdraw their funds from banks, and the massive withdrawal of deposits led to bank failures, which, if they snowballed, led to a full-scale bank panic. The resulting decline in the number of banks raised interest rates even further and decreased the amount of financial intermediation by banks. Worsening of the problems created by adverse selection and moral hazard led to further economic contraction.

Finally, there was a sorting out of firms that were **insolvent** (that had a negative net worth and hence were bankrupt) from healthy firms by bankruptcy proceedings. The same process occurred for banks, often with the help of public and private authorities. Once this sorting out was complete, uncertainty in financial markets declined, the stock market underwent a recovery, and interest rates fell. The overall result was that adverse selection and moral hazard problems diminished and the financial crisis subsided. With the financial markets able to operate well again, the stage was set for the recovery of the economy.

If, however, the economic downturn led to a sharp decline in prices, the recovery process was short-circuited. In this situation, shown in Figure 3, a process

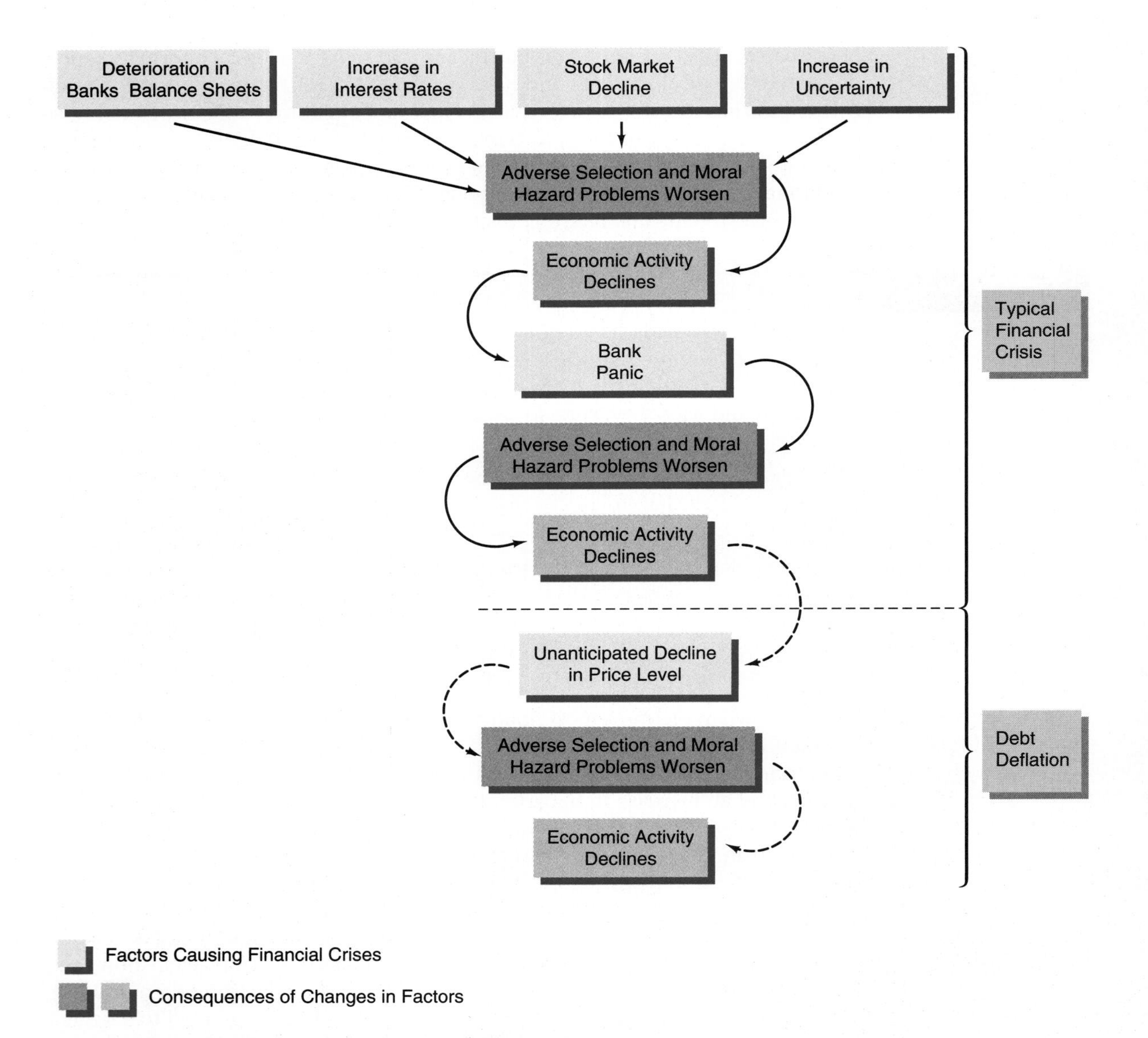

FIGURE 3 Sequence of Events in Canadian Financial Crises

The solid arrows trace the sequence of events in a typical financial crisis; the dotted arrows show the additional set of events that occurs if the crisis develops into a debt deflation.

called **debt deflation** occurred, in which a substantial decline in the price level set in, leading to a further deterioration in firms' net worth because of the increased burden of indebtedness. When debt deflation set in, the adverse selection and moral hazard problems continued to increase so that lending, investment spending, and aggregate economic activity remained depressed for a long time. The most significant financial crisis that included debt deflation was the Great Depression, the worst economic contraction in Canadian history (see Box 2).

BOX 3

Case Study of a Financial Crisis: The Great Depression

U.S. Federal Reserve officials viewed the stock market boom of 1928 and 1929, during which stock prices doubled, as excessive speculation. To curb it, they pursued a tight monetary policy to raise interest rates. The Fed got more than it bargained for when the stock market crashed in October 1929.

Although the 1929 crash had a great impact on the minds of a whole generation, most people forget that by the middle of 1930, more than half of the stock market decline had been reversed. What might have been a normal recession turned into something far different, however, with adverse shocks to the agricultural sector, a continuing decline in the stock market after the middle of 1930, and a sequence of bank collapses from October 1930 until March 1933 in which more than one-third of the banks in the United States went out of business. It is worth noting, however, that no Canadian banks failed during this period (there is some debate as to whether some Canadian banks were actually saved through government intervention or whether they survived because of their diversified loan portfolios).

The continuing decline in stock prices after mid-1930s (by mid-1932 stocks had declined to 10% of their value at the 1929 peak) and the increase in uncertainty from the unsettled business conditions created by the economic contraction made adverse selection and moral hazard problems worse in the credit markets. The loss of one-third of the banks reduced the amount of financial intermediation. This intensified adverse selection and moral hazard problems, thereby decreasing the ability of financial markets to channel funds to firms with productive investment opportunities. As our analysis predicts, the amount of outstanding commercial loans fell by half from 1929 to 1933, and investment spending collapsed, declining by 90% from its 1929 level.

The short-circuiting of the process that kept the economy from recovering quickly, which it does in most recessions, occurred because of a fall in the price level by 25% in the 1930–1933 period. This huge decline in prices triggered a debt deflation in which net worth fell because of the increased burden of indebtedness borne by firms. The decline in net worth and the resulting increase in adverse selection and moral hazard problems in the credit markets led to a prolonged economic contraction in which unemployment rose to 25% of the labour force. The financial crisis in the Great Depression was the worst ever experienced in the United States, and it explains why this economic contraction was also the most severe one ever experienced by the nation.*

*See Ben Bernanke, "Nonmonetary Effects of the Financial Crisis in the Propagation of the Great Depression," *American Economic Review* 73 (1983): 257–76, for a discussion of the role of asymmetric information problems in the Great Depression period.

Application

Financial Crises in Emerging-Market Countries: Mexico, 1994–1995, and East Asia, 1997–1998

Find out about the East Asian financial crisis at www.worldbank.org, which provides background information, speeches, articles, and press releases.

In recent years, many emerging-market countries have experienced financial crises, the most dramatic of which were the Mexican crisis, which started in December 1994, and the East Asian crisis, which started in July 1997. An important fact is how a developing country can shift dramatically from a path of high growth before a financial crisis—as was true for Mexico and particularly the East Asian countries of Thailand, Malaysia, Indonesia, the Philippines, and South Korea—to a sharp decline in economic activity, damaging both the economy and the social fabric of the country. We can again apply our asymmetric information analysis of financial crises to explain this fact and to understand the Mexican and East Asian situations.

Because of the different institutional features of emerging-market countries' debt markets, the sequence of events in the Mexican and East Asian crises is different from what occurred in Canada and the United States in the nineteenth and early twentieth centuries. Figure 4 diagrams the sequence of events that occurred in Mexico and East Asia.

An important factor leading up to both financial crises was the deterioration in banks' balance sheets because of increasing loan losses. When financial markets were deregulated, a lending boom ensued in which bank credit to the private nonfinancial business sector accelerated sharply. Because of weak supervision by bank

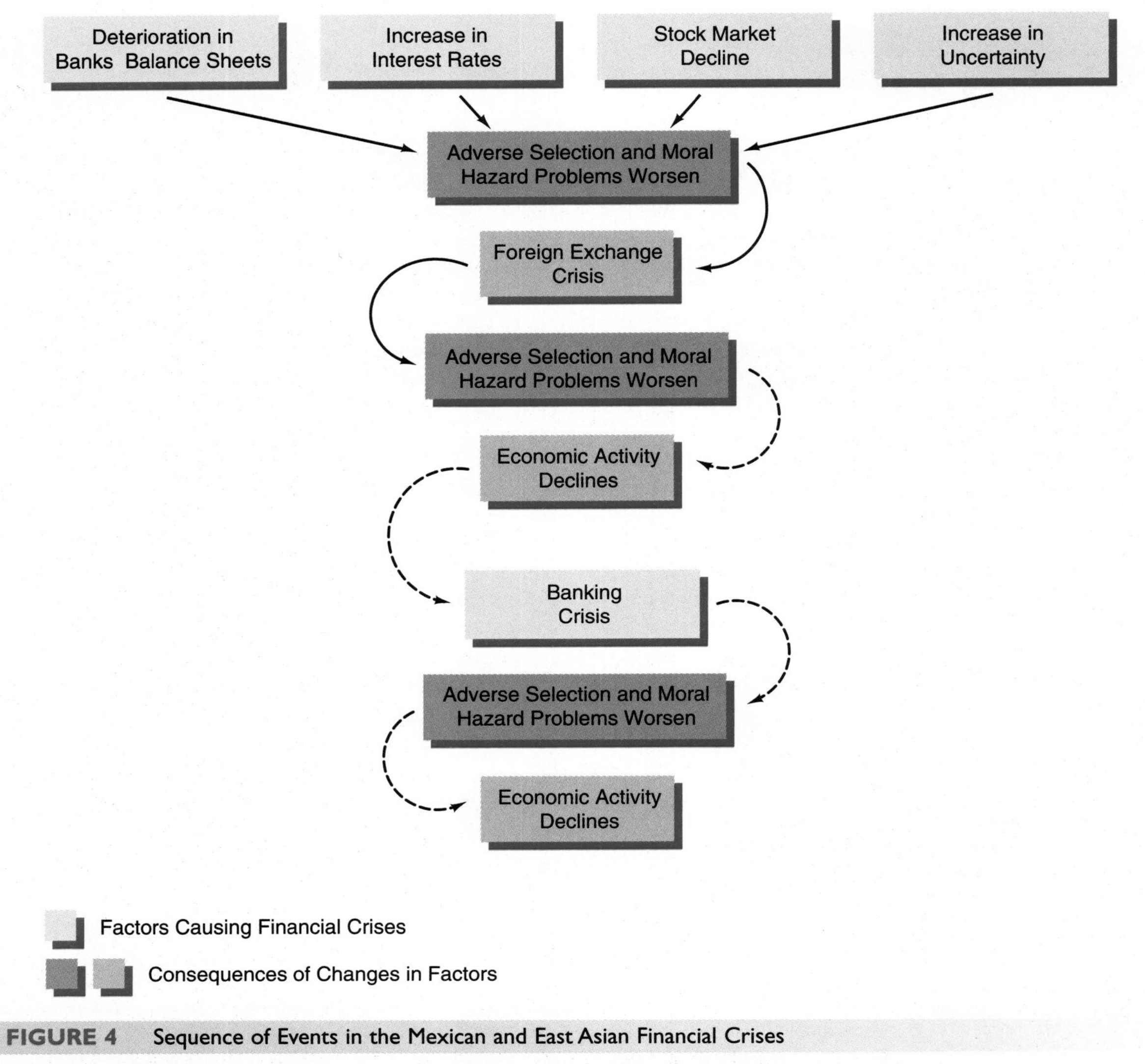

FIGURE 4 Sequence of Events in the Mexican and East Asian Financial Crises

The arrows trace the sequence of events during the Mexican and East Asian financial crises.

regulators and a lack of expertise in screening and monitoring borrowers at banking institutions, losses on the loans began to mount, causing an erosion of banks' net worth (capital). As we have seen, this would mean that the banks would have fewer resources to lend, and this lack of lending would eventually lead to a contraction in economic activity.

Another precipitating factor to the Mexican (but not East Asian) financial crisis was a rise in interest rates abroad. Beginning in February 1994, the Federal Reserve in the United States began to raise the federal funds rate to head off inflationary pressures. Although the policy was quite successful in keeping inflation in check in the United States, it put upward pressure on Mexican interest rates, thereby increasing asymmetric information problems in the Mexican financial system. Furthermore, the Mexican central bank, the Banco de Mexico, raised interest rates to protect the value of the peso in the foreign exchange market. The rise in interest rates directly added to increased adverse selection in Mexican financial markets because, as discussed earlier, it made it more likely that the parties willing to take on the most risk would seek loans.

The Banco de Mexico's Website can be found at www.banxiro.org.mx

The stock exchange of Mexico, the Bolsa, can be found at www.bmr.org.mx.

Also, stock market declines and increases in uncertainty were additional factors precipitating the full-blown crises in Mexico, Thailand, and South Korea. (The stock market declines in Malaysia, Indonesia, and the Philippines occurred simultaneously with the onset of the crisis.) The Mexican economy in 1994 was hit by political shocks that created uncertainty, specifically the assassination of Luis Donaldo Colosio, the ruling party's presidential candidate, and an uprising in the southern state of Chiapas. By the middle of December 1994, stock prices on the Bolsa (stock exchange) had fallen nearly 20% from their September 1994 peak. In January 1997, a major Korean *chaebol* (conglomerate), Hanbo Steel, collapsed; it was the first bankruptcy of a *chaebol* in a decade. Shortly thereafter, Sammi Steel and Kia Motors also declared bankruptcy. In Thailand, Samprosong Land, a major real estate developer, defaulted on its foreign debt in early February 1997, and financial institutions that had lent heavily in the real estate market began to encounter serious difficulties, requiring over $8 billion of loans from the Thai central bank to prop them up. Finally, in June, the failure of a major Thai finance company, Finance One, imposed substantial losses on both domestic and foreign creditors. These events increased general uncertainty in the financial markets of Thailand and South Korea, and both experienced substantial declines in their securities markets. From peak values in early 1996, Korean stock prices fell by 25% and Thai stock prices fell by 50%.

The Thai central bank's Website is www.bot.org.th

As we have seen, an increase in uncertainty and a decrease in net worth as a result of a stock market decline increase asymmetric information problems. It becomes harder to screen out good from bad borrowers, and the decline in net worth decreases the value of firms' collateral and increases their incentives to make risky investments because there is less equity to lose if the investments are unsuccessful. The increase in uncertainty and stock market declines that occurred before the crisis, along with the deterioration in banks' balance sheets, worsened adverse selection and moral hazard problems (shown at the top of the diagram in Figure 4) and made the economies ripe for a serious financial crisis.

At this point, full-blown speculative attacks developed in the foreign exchange market, plunging these countries into a full-scale crisis. With the Colosio assassination, the Chiapas uprising, and the growing weakness in the banking sector, the Mexican peso came under attack. Even though the Mexican central bank intervened in the foreign exchange market and raised interest rates sharply, it was unable to stem the attack and was forced to devalue the peso on December 20, 1994. In the case of Thailand, concerns about the large current account deficit and weakness in the Thai financial system, culminating with the failure of Finance One, a large finance company, led to a successful speculative attack that forced the Thai central bank to allow the baht to float downward. Soon thereafter, speculative attacks developed against the other countries in the region, leading to the collapse of the Philippine peso, the Indonesian rupiah, the Malaysian ringgit, and the South Korean won.

The institutional structure of debt markets in Mexico and East Asia now interacted with the currency devaluations to propel the economies into full-fledged financial crises. Because so many firms in these countries had debt denominated in foreign currencies like the dollar and the yen, depreciation of their currencies resulted in increases in their indebtedness in domestic currency terms, even though the value of their assets remained unchanged. When the peso lost half its value by March 1995 and the Thai, Philippine, Malaysian, and South Korean currencies lost between a third and half of their value by the beginning of 1998, firms' balance sheets took a big negative hit, which caused a dramatic increase in adverse selection and moral hazard problems. This negative shock was most severe for Indonesia, which saw the value of its currency fall by an astronomical 80%, resulting in insolvency for any firm with substantial amounts of debt denominated in foreign currencies.

The collapse of currencies also led to a rise in actual and expected inflation in these countries, and market interest rates rose sky high (to over 100% in Mexico). The resulting increase in interest payments caused reductions in households' and firms' cash flow, which led to further deterioration in their balance sheets. A feature of debt markets in emerging-market countries, like those in Mexico and East Asia, is that debt contracts have very short durations, typically less than one month. Thus the rise in short-term interest rates in these countries meant that the effect on cash flow and hence on balance sheets was substantial. As our asymmetric information analysis suggests, this deterioration in households' and firms' balance sheets increased adverse selection and moral hazard problems in the credit markets, making lenders even less willing to lend.

In addition, in the aftermath of the currency crises, stock markets crashed. The Mexican market declined 50% from its peak value, and the Thai, Philippine, Malaysian, Indonesian, and South Korean markets declined 50% to 80%. The collapse of stock market values further worsened adverse selection and moral hazard problems.

These asymmetric information problems were severe not only for domestic lenders but for foreign lenders as well because they had difficulty obtaining information regarding these economies. Foreign lenders were thus eager to pull their funds out of Mexico and the East Asian crisis countries, and that is what they did. Foreign portfolio investment inflows to Mexico, which had been on the order of $20 billion a year in 1993, reversed course, and the outflows exceeded $10 billion a year by the fourth quarter of 1994. Similarly in East Asia, capital flows for Thailand, Malaysia, the Philippines, Indonesia, and South Korea reversed from an inflow of close to $100 billion in 1996 to an outflow of more than $10 billion in 1997. Consistent with the theory of financial crises outlined in this chapter, the sharp decline in lending helped lead to a collapse of economic activity, with real GDP growth falling sharply.

As shown in Figure 4, further deterioration in the economy occurred because the collapse in economic activity and the deterioration in the cash flow and balance sheets of both firms and households led to a worsening banking crisis. The problems of firms and households meant that many of them were no longer able to pay off their debts, resulting in substantial losses for the banks. Even more problematic for the banks was that they had many short-term liabilities denominated in foreign currencies, and the sharp increase in the value of these liabilities after the devaluation led to a further deterioration in the banks' balance sheets. Under these circumstances, the banking system would have collapsed in the absence of a government safety net—as it did in the United States during the Great Depression. But with the assistance of the International Monetary Fund, these countries were in some cases able to protect depositors and avoid a bank panic. However, given the loss of bank capital and the need for the government to intervene to prop up the banks, the banks' ability to lend was nevertheless sharply curtailed. As we have seen, a banking crisis of this type hinders the ability of the banks to lend and also makes adverse selection and moral hazard problems worse in financial markets because banks are less capable of playing their traditional financial intermediation role. The banking crisis, along with other factors that increased adverse selection and moral hazard problems in the credit markets of Mexico and East Asia, explains the collapse of lending and hence economic activity in the aftermath of the crisis.

In the aftermath of their crises, Mexico began to recover in 1996, while the crisis countries in East Asia saw the glimmer of recovery in 1999. In all these countries, the economic hardship caused by the financial crises was tremendous. Unemployment rose sharply, poverty increased substantially, and even the social fabric of the society was stretched thin. For example, Mexico City has become one of the most crime-ridden sites in the world, while Indonesia has experienced waves of ethnic violence.

SUMMARY

1. There are eight basic facts about financial structure throughout the world. The first four emphasize the importance of financial intermediaries and the relative unimportance of securities markets for the financing of corporations; the fifth recognizes that financial markets are among the most heavily regulated sectors of the economy; the sixth states that only large, well-established corporations have access to securities markets; the seventh indicates that collateral is an important feature of debt contracts; and the eighth presents debt contracts as complicated legal documents that place substantial restrictions on the behaviour of the borrower.
2. Transaction costs freeze many small savers and borrowers out of direct involvement with financial markets. Financial intermediaries can take advantage of economies of scale and are better able to develop expertise to lower transaction costs, thus enabling their savers and borrowers to benefit from the existence of financial markets.
3. Asymmetric information results in two problems: adverse selection, which occurs before the transaction, and moral hazard, which occurs after the transaction. Adverse selection refers to the fact that bad credit risks are the ones most likely to seek loans, and moral hazard refers to the risk of the borrower's engaging in activities that are undesirable from the lender's point of view.
4. Adverse selection interferes with the efficient functioning of financial markets. Tools to help reduce the adverse selection problem include private production and sale of information, government regulation to increase information, financial intermediation, and collateral and net worth. The free-rider problem occurs when people who do not pay for information take advantage of information that other people have paid for. This problem explains why financial intermediaries, particularly banks, play a more important role in financing the activities of businesses than securities markets do.
5. Moral hazard in equity contracts is known as the principal-agent problem because managers (the agents) have less incentive to maximize profits than stockholders (the principals). The principal-agent problem explains why debt contracts are so much more prevalent in financial markets than equity contracts. Tools to help reduce the principal-agent problem include monitoring, government regulation to increase information, and financial intermediation.
6. Tools to reduce the moral hazard problem in debt contracts include net worth, monitoring and enforcement of restrictive covenants, and financial intermediaries.
7. Financial crises are major disruptions in financial markets. They are caused by increases in adverse selection and moral hazard problems that prevent financial markets from channelling funds to people with productive investment opportunities, leading to a sharp contraction in economic activity. The four types of factors that lead to financial crises are increases in interest rates, increases in uncertainty, asset market effects on balance sheets, and bank panics.

KEY TERMS

bank panic, *p. 366*
cash flow, *p. 366*
collateral, *p. 350*
costly state verification, *p. 359*
creditor, *p. 363*
debt deflation, *p. 368*
equity capital, *p. 357*
financial crisis, *p. 364*
free-rider problem, *p. 354*
incentive-compatible, *p. 361*
insolvent, *p. 367*
net worth, *p. 357*
principal-agent problem, *p. 358*
restrictive covenants, *p. 350*
secured debt, *p. 350*
unsecured debt, *p. 350*
venture capital firm, *p. 360*

QUESTIONS AND PROBLEMS

1. How can economies of scale help explain the existence of financial intermediaries?

*2. Describe two ways in which financial intermediaries help lower transaction costs in the economy.

3. Would moral hazard and adverse selection still arise in financial markets if information were not asymmetric? Explain your answer.

*4. How do standard accounting principles required by the government help financial markets work more efficiently?

5. Do you think the lemons problem would be more severe for stocks traded on the Toronto Stock Exchange or for those traded over-the-counter? Explain your answer.

*6. Which firms are most likely to use bank financing rather than to issue bonds or stocks to finance their activities? Why?

7. How can the existence of asymmetric information provide a rationale for government regulation of financial markets?

*8. Would you be more willing to lend to a friend if she put all her life savings into her business than you would if she had not done so? Why?

9. Rich individuals often worry that people will seek to marry them only for their money. Is this a problem of adverse selection? Explain your answer.

*10. "The more collateral there is backing a loan, the less the lender has to worry about adverse selection." Is this statement true, false, or uncertain? Explain your answer.

11. How does the free-rider problem aggravate adverse selection and moral hazard problems in financial markets?

*12. Explain how the separation of ownership and control in Canadian corporations might lead to poor management.

13. Is a financial crisis more likely to occur when the economy is experiencing deflation or inflation? Explain your answer.

*14. How can a stock market crash provoke a financial crisis?

15. How can a sharp rise in interest rates provoke a financial crisis?

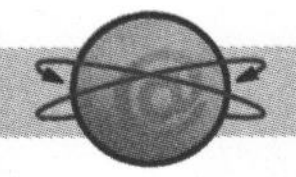

WEB EXERCISES

Theory of Financial Structure

1. In this chapter we discuss the lemons problem and its effect on the efficient functioning of a market. This theory was initially developed by George Akerlof. Go to http://www.nobel.se/economics/laureates/2001/public.html. This site reports that Akerlof, Michael Spence, and Joseph Stiglitz were awarded the Nobel Prize in Economics in 2001 for their work. Read this report down through the section on George Akerlof. Summarize his research ideas in a one-page report.

2. This chapter discusses how an understanding of adverse selection and moral hazard can help us better understand financial crises. The greatest financial crisis faced by the world economy was during The Great Depression from 1929 to 1933. Go to http://www.escape.com/~paulg53/politics/greatdepression.shtml. This site contains a brief discussion of the factors that led to this Depression. Write a one-page summary explaining how adverse selection and moral hazard were responsible for the Depression.

Chapter 15

The Banking Firm and Bank Management

Preview

Because banks (depository institutions) play such a major role in channelling funds to borrowers with productive investment opportunities, they are important in ensuring that the financial system and the economy run smoothly and efficiently. In Canada, banks provide loans to businesses, help us finance our college and university educations or the purchase of a new car or home, and provide us with services such as chequing and savings accounts.

In this chapter we examine how banks, the most important of all the financial intermediaries, operate to earn the highest profits possible: how and why they make loans, how they acquire funds and manage their assets and liabilities (debts), and how they earn income. Although we focus on commercial banks because they hold more than two-thirds of the assets in the banking system, the principles are equally applicable to other types of banking institutions, such as trust and mortgage loan companies, and credit unions and *caisses populaires*. Furthermore, many of the principles of bank management discussed here also apply to many other financial institutions.

THE BANK BALANCE SHEET

To understand how a bank operates, first we need to examine its **balance sheet**, a list of the bank's assets and liabilities. As the name implies, this list balances; that is, it has the characteristic that

$$\text{Total assets} = \text{total liabilities} + \text{capital}$$

A sample bank balance sheet is available at www.bankofmontreal.com (download the Consolidated balance Sheet from the latest Annual Report).

Furthermore, a bank's balance sheet lists *sources* of bank funds (liabilities) and *uses* to which they are put (assets). Banks obtain funds by borrowing and by issuing other liabilities such as deposits. They then use these funds to acquire assets such as securities and loans. Banks make profits by charging an interest rate on their holdings of securities and loans that is higher than the expenses on their liabilities. The balance sheet of all commercial banks as of February 28, 2002, appears in Table 1.

Liabilities

A bank acquires funds by issuing (selling) liabilities, which are consequently also referred to as *sources of funds.* The funds obtained from issuing liabilities are used to purchase income-earning assets. Chartered banks have three main sources of funds: deposits, borrowings, and equity. Table 1 shows that deposits make up 67% of bank liabilities, borrowings 27%, and equity 5%.

Demand and Notice Deposits Demand deposits are payable on demand; that is, if a depositor shows up at the bank and requests payment by making a withdrawal, the bank must pay the depositor immediately. Similarly, if a person who receives a cheque written on an account from a bank, presents that cheque at the bank, the bank must pay the funds out immediately (or credit them to that person's account).

Notice deposits are more important as a source of funds for the banks than are demand deposits (12.74% versus 8.96% in Table 1). Although notice deposits have a notice requirement in the contractual agreement with the client, the banks

TABLE 1 Balance Sheet of All Banks in Canada, in Millions (as of February 28, 2002)

Assets (Uses of Funds)	Amount ($)	Percent (%)	Liabilities (Sources of Funds)	Amount ($)	Percent (%)
Coins and bank notes	6 671	0.39	Demand deposits	153 101	8.96
Deposits with the Bank of Canada	729	0.04	Notice deposits	217 677	12.74
Deposits with other financial institutions	88 286	5.17	Fixed-term deposits	771 960	45.18
Cheques and other items in transit	1255	0.07	Total deposits	1 142 738	66.87
Total cash reserves	96 941	5.67			
Securities			Nondeposit liabilities		
Issued by the government of Canada	104 417	6.11	Cheques and other items in transit	3 960	0.23
Issued by provinces and municipalities	20 826	1.22	Advances from the Bank of Canada	1 092	0.06
Issued by other entities	291 967	17.09	Banker's acceptances	48 730	2.85
			Nondeposit liabilities of subsidiaries	12 160	0.71
			Insurance related liabilities	4 638	0.27
Total securities	417 210	24.42	Accrued interest payable	11 352	0.66
			Obligations related to borrowed securities	80 422	4.71
Loans			Obligations related to assets sold under repos	128 333	7.51
			Derivative contract obligations	108 832	6.37
To investment dealers and brokers	10 084	0.59	Other liabilities	50 613	2.96
To regulated financial institutions	16 270	0.95	Noncontrolling interest in subsidiaries	6 155	0.36
Other loans	602 801	35.28			
			Total nondeposit liabilities	456 287	26.70
Mortgage loans	330 133	19.32	Subordinated debt	28 393	1.66
Total loans	959 288	56.14	Bank capital	81 375	4.76
Fixed and other assets					
Customer liabilities under acceptances	48 730	2.85			
Other assets	186 624	10.92			
Total fixed and other assets	235 354	13.77			
Total assets	1 708 793	100.00	Total liabilities and bank capital	1 708 793	100.00

Source: OSFI Website, www.osfi-bsif.gc.ca

never enforce this clause, and so in fact, most notice deposits are really just like demand deposits in this sense.

Demand deposits and notice deposits are bank accounts that allow the owner to write cheques to third parties. Table 1 shows that this category of chequable deposits is an important low-cost source of bank funds, making up 22% of bank liabilities. Once, chequable deposits were the most important source of bank funds, but with the appearance of new, more attractive financial instruments, the share of chequable deposits in total bank liabilities has shrunk over time.

A chequable deposit is an asset for the depositor because it is part of his or her wealth. Conversely, because the depositor can withdraw funds from an account that the bank is obligated to pay, chequable deposits are a liability for the bank. They are usually the lowest-cost source of bank funds because depositors are willing to forgo some interest in order to have access to a liquid asset that can be used to make purchases. The bank's costs of maintaining chequable deposits include interest payments and the costs incurred in servicing these accounts—processing and storing cancelled cheques, preparing and sending out monthly statements, providing efficient tellers (human or otherwise), maintaining an impressive building and conveniently located branches, and advertising and marketing to entice customers to deposit their funds with a given bank. In recent years, interest paid on deposits (chequable and time) has accounted for around 56% of total bank operating expenses, while the costs involved in servicing accounts (employee salaries, building rent, and so on) have been approximately 35% of operating expenses.

Fixed-Term Deposits Fixed-term deposits are the primary source of bank funds (more than 45% of bank liabilities in Table 1). Owners (retail customers, small- and medium-sized businesses, large corporations, governments, and other financial institutions) cannot write cheques on fixed-term deposits, but the interest rates are usually higher than those on chequable deposits. There are two main types of fixed-term deposits: savings accounts and time deposits (also called certificates of deposit, or CDs).

Savings accounts were once the most common type of fixed-term deposit. In these accounts, to which funds can be added or from which funds can be withdrawn at any time, transactions and interest payments are recorded in a monthly statement or in a small book (the passbook) held by the owner of the account.

Time deposits have a fixed maturity length, ranging from several months to more than five years, and have substantial penalties for early withdrawal (the forfeiture of several months' interest). Small-denomination time deposits (deposits of less than $100 000) are less liquid for the depositor than passbook savings, earn higher interest rates, and are a more costly source of funds for the banks.

Large-denomination time deposits (CDs) are available in denominations of $100 000 or more and are typically bought by corporations or other banks. Large-denomination CDs are negotiable; like bonds, they can be resold in a secondary market before they mature. For this reason, negotiable CDs are held by corporations, money market mutual funds, and other financial institutions as alternative assets to treasury bills and other short-term bonds. Since 1964, when they first appeared in Canada, negotiable CDs have become an important source of bank funds.

Borrowings Banks obtain funds by borrowing from the Bank of Canada, other banks, and corporations. Borrowings from the Bank of Canada are called **overdrafts loans** (also known as **advances**). Banks also borrow reserves overnight in the overnight market from other Canadian banks and financial institutions. Banks borrow funds overnight in order to have enough **settlement balances** at the Bank of Canada to facilitate the clearing of cheques and other transfers.

Banks also have liabilities under banker's acceptances (BAs). These liabilities are very similar to negotiable CDs in that both are short-term bank promises to pay a specified amount on a specified date. In particular, upon the maturity of a banker's acceptance, the bank makes payment of its face amount, but at the same time the client reimburses the bank in the amount of the banker's acceptance. It is for this reason that banker's acceptances are also treated like corporate short-term assets of the bank and they appear on both sides of the balance sheet (in Table 1), in the same amount.

Other major sources of borrowed funds are loan arrangements with corporations, such as short sales and repurchase agreements; they exceed 15% of bank liabilities, reflecting banks' increasing investment banking activities. A **short sale** involves borrowing a security from an investor or another financial institution for a fixed time period and selling it in the market with the intention of repurchasing it when it is due to be returned to the lender. When an investment bank short sells a security, it generates cash for itself and shows the obligation to repay the loan as "Obligations related to borrowed securities" on the liabilities side of the balance sheet, as in Table 1.

Borrowings have become a more important source of bank funds over time: In 1960, they made up only a small fraction of bank liabilities; currently, they are about 27% of bank liabilities.

Bank Capital The final category on the liabilities side of the balance sheet is bank capital, the bank's net worth, which equals the difference between total assets and liabilities (5% of total bank assets in Table 1). The funds are raised by selling new equity (stock) or from retained earnings. Bank capital is a cushion against a drop in the value of its assets, which could force the bank into insolvency (when the value of bank assets falls below its liabilities, meaning that the bank can be forced into liquidation). One important component of bank capital is *loan loss reserves,* which are described in Box 1.

BOX 1

Understanding Loan Loss Reserves

Perhaps you have seen headlines in the press about a bank's large increase in loan loss (bad debt) reserves. Often there is confusion about loan loss reserves, perhaps because they have a similar-sounding name to the "reserves" item on a bank's balance sheet. Actually, loan loss reserves have nothing to do with the reserves shown on the assets side of the balance sheet; rather, they are a component of the liabilities item known as bank capital.

To see how loan loss reserves work, suppose that a bank suspects that some of its loans, say, $1 million worth, might prove to be bad debts that will have to be written off (valued at zero) in the future. The bank can set aside $1 million of its earnings and put it into its loan loss reserves account. Because the $1 million is now retained earnings, it adds to the difference between the bank's assets and liabilities and so increases bank capital. The fact that adding to loan loss reserves increases bank capital explains why loan loss reserves are counted as a component of capital. As a result of adding to loan loss reserves, the bank reduces its reported earnings by $1 million, even though it has not yet actually lost the $1 million—in effect, taking its lumps even before the bad debt is written off.

If the bank eventually determines that the $1 million loan will never be paid back and formally writes it off, it reduces the value of its assets by $1 million. The resulting $1 million decline in bank capital is reflected as a decrease in the loan loss reserves account by $1 million. At this time, however, reported earnings are unaffected by the loan write-off because they were reduced earlier when the bank set aside $1 million of earnings as loan loss reserves.

Banks add to loan loss reserves before some loans have to be written off because it is better for them to allow for potential losses when they have plenty of earnings rather than to wait and find that they must take the loss when they have little in earnings to write the loan off against. In addition, adding to loan loss reserves, which reduces reported earnings, can reduce the amount of taxes a bank has to pay and is also a way of informing the bank's stockholders, depositors, and regulators of potential future losses on loans.

Assets

A bank uses the funds that it has acquired by issuing liabilities to purchase income-earning assets. Bank assets are thus naturally referred to as *uses of funds,* and the interest payments earned on them are what enable banks to make profits.

Cash Reserves All banks hold some of the funds they acquire as deposits in an account at the Bank of Canada, in the form of settlement balances. **Cash reserves** are these settlement balances plus currency that is physically held by banks (called **vault cash** because it is stored in bank vaults overnight). Although Canadian banks are not required to hold reserves in proportion to their deposits (Canada removed all such legal requirements in June 1994), banks hold cash reserves in order to facilitate the clearing of cheques and to keep the automated teller machines with adequate amounts. Currently, cash reserves do not pay any interest and account for only 0.4% of bank assets.

Deposits at Other Banks These deposits are known as **interbank deposits** and account for about 5% of bank assets. About 85% of these interbank deposits are in foreign currencies and are connected to the large banks' extensive Eurocurrency operations and correspondent banking relationships. The main advantage of interbank deposits is the flexibility they provide banks to manage their own short-term liquidity requirements and respond to the liquidity needs of their clients.

Cash Items in Process of Collection Suppose that a cheque written on an account at another bank is deposited in your bank and the funds for this cheque have not yet been received (collected) from the other bank. The cheque is classified as a cash item in process of collection, and it is an asset for your bank because it is a claim on another bank for funds that will be paid within a few days. Items in process of collection are also called **items in transit** or **bank float**.

Collectively, cash reserves, cash items in process of collection, and deposits at other banks are often referred to as **total cash reserves** or simply **reserves**. In Table 1 they constitute only about 6% of total assets, and their importance has been shrinking over time: In 1960, for example, they accounted for more than 20% of total assets. Although Canadian banks are not required to hold reserves and there is a requirement of zero settlement balances with the Bank of Canada at the end of each banking day, banks hold some reserves, which we call **desired excess reserves** or simply **desired reserves**.

Banks hold reserves because of their desire to manage their own short-term liquidity requirements and respond to predictable clearing drains and predictable across-the-counter and automated teller machine drains. Moreover, banks hold reserves in order to meet unpredictable and potentially large withdrawals by their liability holders. The risk that net cash withdrawals might be negative is known as **banker's risk**, and from the perspective of this risk, banks hold reserves to meet unpredictable cash and clearing drains. We will refer to the fraction of deposits banks hold in the form of reserves (5%, for example) as the **desired reserve ratio.**

Securities A bank's holdings of securities are an important income-earning asset: Securities (made up entirely of debt instruments for commercial banks because banks are not allowed to hold stock) account for 24% of bank assets in Table 1, and they provide commercial banks with about 10% of their revenue. These securities can be classified into three categories: government of Canada, provincial and municipal securities, and other securities. The government of

Canada securities are the most liquid because they can be easily traded and converted into cash with low transaction costs.

Provincial and municipal securities are desirable for banks to hold primarily because provincial and municipal governments are more likely to do business with banks that hold their securities. Provincial and municipal government and other securities are less marketable (hence less liquid) and are also riskier than government of Canada securities, primarily because of default risk: There is some possibility that the issuer of the securities may not be able to make its interest payments or pay back the face value of the securities when they mature.

Loans Banks make their profits primarily by issuing loans. In Table 1, some 56% of bank assets are in the form of loans, and in recent years they have generally produced more than half of bank revenues. A loan is a liability for the individual or corporation receiving it but an asset for a bank because it provides income to the bank. Loans are typically less liquid than other assets because they cannot be turned into cash until the loan matures. If the bank makes a one-year loan, for example, it cannot get its funds back until the loan comes due in one year. Loans also have a higher probability of default than other assets. Because of the lack of liquidity and higher default risk, the bank earns its highest return on loans.

The largest categories of loans for commercial banks are commercial and industrial loans made to businesses and real estate loans. Commercial banks also make consumer loans and lend to each other. The bulk of these interbank loans are overnight loans lent in the overnight market. As the balance sheet in Table 1 considers both foreign and domestic assets of both Canadian and Canadian foreign-owned banks, it shows that corporate loans exceed mortgage loans (36.82% versus 19.3% of bank assets). This is so because a larger portion of the foreign activities of Canadian banks is in corporate loans rather than mortgages. In fact, the major difference in the balance sheets of the various depository institutions is primarily in the type of loan in which they specialize. Trust and mortgage loan companies and credit unions and *caisses populaires*, for example, specialize in residential mortgages.

Fixed and Other Assets The physical capital (bank buildings, computers, and other equipment) owned by the banks is included in this category.

BASIC OPERATION OF A BANK

Before proceeding to more detailed study of how a bank manages its assets and liabilities in order to make the highest profit, you should understand the basic operation of a bank.

In general terms, banks make profits by selling liabilities with one set of characteristics (a particular combination of liquidity, risk, size, and return) and using the proceeds to buy assets with a different set of characteristics. This process is often referred to as *asset transformation.* Instead of making a mortgage loan directly to a neighbour, a person can hold a savings deposit that enables a bank to use the funds provided by the deposit to make the loan to the neighbour. The bank has, in effect, transformed the savings deposit (an asset held by the depositor) into a mortgage loan (an asset held by the bank). Another way this process of asset transformation is described is to say that the bank "borrows short and lends long" because it makes long-term loans and funds them by issuing short-dated deposits.

The process of transforming assets and providing a set of services (cheque clearing, record keeping, credit analysis, and so forth) is like any other production process in a firm. If the bank produces desirable services at low cost and earns substantial income on its assets, it earns profits; if not, the bank suffers losses.

The key characteristic of banks is their ability to buy assets by issuing their own deposit liabilities. Suppose that the First Bank has found some profitable loans that it wants to add to its portfolio. It makes a loan in the amount of $100 to a business and credits the business's chequable deposit in that amount. The business accepts the First Bank's deposit liabilities because they have the characteristic of being the medium of exchange and are accepted as money by others. The T-accounts for the First Bank and the business look like these:

First Bank				**Business**			
Assets		Liabilities		Assets		Liabilities	
Loans	+100	Chequable deposits	+100	Chequable deposits	+100	Bank loans	+100

Note that the transaction is simply an exchange of assets and liabilities, with no change in the net worth of both the First Bank and the business. The bank's act of making a new loan to the business increases chequable deposits and thus the money supply, by the amount of the loan. Note, however, that the bank's objective is not to create deposits and increase the money supply; ***the bank is in the business of making a profit for its shareholders and the creation of deposits occurs as a byproduct of the bank's financing decisions.***

Acquiring income-producing assets is not the only way in which the First Bank can create new chequable deposits. Let's say that Jane Batohi has heard that the First Bank provides excellent service, so she opens a chequing account with a $100 bill. She now has a $100 chequable deposit at the bank, which shows up as a $100 liability on the bank's balance sheet. The bank now puts her $100 bill into its vault so that the bank's assets rise by the $100 increase in vault cash. The T-account for the bank looks like this:

First Bank			
Assets		Liabilities	
Vault cash	+$100	Chequable deposits	+$100

Since vault cash is also part of the bank's reserves, we can rewrite the T-account as follows:

Assets		Liabilities	
Reserves	+$100	Chequable deposits	+$100

Note that Jane Batohi's opening of a chequing account leads to *an increase in the bank's reserves equal to the increase in chequable deposits.*

If Jane had opened her account with a $100 cheque written on an account at another bank, say, the Second Bank, we would get the same result. The initial effect on the T-account of the First Bank is as follows:

Assets		Liabilities	
Cash items in process of collection	+$100	Chequable deposits	+$100

Chequable deposits increase by $100 as before, but now the First Bank is owed $100 by the Second Bank. This asset for the First Bank is entered in the T-account as $100 of cash items in process of collection because the First Bank will now try to collect the funds that it is owed. It could go directly to the Second Bank and ask for payment of the funds, but if the two banks are in separate provinces, that would be a time-consuming and costly process. Instead, the First Bank deposits the cheque in its account at the Bank of Canada, and the Bank of Canada collects the funds from the Second Bank. The result is that the Fed transfers $100 of reserves from the Second Bank to the First Bank, and the final balance sheet positions of the two banks are as follows:

First Bank		**Second Bank**	
Assets	Liabilities	Assets	Liabilities
Reserves +$100	Chequable deposits +$100	Reserves −$100	Chequable deposits −$100

The process initiated by Jane Batohi can be summarized as follows: When a cheque written on an account at one bank is deposited in another, the bank receiving the deposit gains reserves equal to the amount of the cheque, while the bank on which the cheque is written sees its reserves fall by the same amount. Therefore, ***when a bank receives additional deposits, it gains an equal amount of reserves; when it loses deposits, it loses an equal amount of reserves.***

Study Guide T-accounts are used to study various topics throughout this text. Whenever you see a T-account, try to analyze what would happen if the opposite action were taken; for example, what would happen if Jane Batohi decided to close her $100 account at the First Bank by writing a $100 cheque and depositing it in a new chequing account at the Second Bank?

Now that you understand how banks gain and lose reserves, we can examine how a bank rearranges its balance sheet to make a profit when it experiences a change in its deposits. Let's return to the situation when the First Bank has just received the extra $100 of chequable deposits. As you know, the bank wants to keep a certain fraction of its chequable deposits as desired reserves. If the fraction (the desired reserve ratio) is 10%, the First Bank's desired reserves have increased by $10, and we can rewrite its T-account as follows:

First Bank			
Assets		Liabilities	
Desired reserves	+$10	Chequable deposits	+$100
Excess reserves	+$90		

Let's see how well the bank is doing as a result of the additional chequable deposits. Because reserves pay no interest, it has no income from the additional $100 of assets. But servicing the extra $100 of chequable deposits is costly because the bank must keep records, pay tellers, return cancelled cheques, pay for cheque clearing, and so forth. The bank is making a loss! The situation is even worse if the bank makes interest payments on the deposits. If it is to make a profit, the bank must put to productive use all or part of the $90 of excess reserves it has available.

Let us assume that the bank chooses not to hold any excess reserves but to make loans instead. Assuming that the bank gives up its cash directly, the T-account then looks like this:

Assets		Liabilities	
Desired reserves	+$10	Chequable deposits	+$100
Loans	+$90		

The bank is now making a profit because it holds short-term liabilities such as chequable deposits and uses the proceeds to buy longer-term assets such as loans with higher interest rates. As mentioned earlier, this process of asset transformation is frequently described by saying that banks are in the business of "borrowing short and lending long." For example, if the loans have an interest rate of 10% per year, the bank earns $9 in income from its loans over the year. If the $100 of chequable deposits is in an account with a 5% interest rate and it costs another $3 per year to service the account, the cost per year of these deposits is $8. The bank's profit on the new deposits is then $1 per year (a 1% return on assets).

GENERAL PRINCIPLES OF BANK MANAGEMENT

Now that you have some idea of how a bank operates, let's look at how a bank manages its assets and liabilities in order to earn the highest possible profit. The bank manager has four primary concerns. The first is to make sure that the bank has enough ready cash to pay its depositors when there are **deposit outflows**, that is, when deposits are lost because depositors make withdrawals and demand payment. To keep enough cash on hand, the bank must engage in **liquidity management**, the acquisition of sufficiently liquid assets to meet the bank's obligations to depositors. Second, the bank manager must pursue an acceptably low level of risk by acquiring assets that have a low rate of default and by diversifying asset holdings (**asset management**). The third concern is to acquire funds at low cost (**liability management**). Finally, the manager must decide the amount of capital the bank should maintain and then acquire the needed capital (**capital adequacy management**).

To understand bank management fully, we must go beyond the general principles of bank asset and liability management described next and look in more detail at how a bank manages its assets. In Chapter 22 we look at how managers of financial institutions such as banks manage risk, specifically, **credit risk**, the risk arising because borrowers may default, and **interest-rate risk**, the riskiness of earnings and returns on bank assets that results from fluctuations in interest rates.

Liquidity Management and the Role of Reserves

Let us see how a typical bank, the First Bank, can deal with deposit outflows that occur when its depositors withdraw cash from chequing or savings accounts or write cheques that are deposited in other banks. In the example that follows, we assume that the bank has ample excess reserves and that all deposits have the same desired reserve ratio of 10% (the bank wants to keep 10% of its deposits as reserves). Suppose that the First Bank's initial balance sheet is as follows:

Assets		Liabilities	
Reserves	$20 million	Deposits	$100 million
Loans	$80 million	Bank capital	$ 10 million
Securities	$10 million		

The bank's desired reserves are 10% of $100 million, or $10 million. Since it holds $20 million of reserves, the First Bank has excess reserves of $10 million. If a deposit outflow of $10 million occurs, the bank's balance sheet becomes

Assets		Liabilities	
Reserves	$10 million	Deposits	$90 million
Loans	$80 million	Bank capital	$10 million
Securities	$10 million		

The bank loses $10 million of deposits *and* $10 million of reserves, but since its desired reserves are now 10% of only $90 million ($9 million), its reserves still exceed this amount by $1 million. In short, ***if a bank has ample reserves, a deposit outflow does not necessitate changes in other parts of its balance sheet.***

The situation is quite different when a bank holds insufficient excess reserves. Let's assume that instead of initially holding $10 million in excess reserves, the First Bank makes loans of $10 million, so that it holds no excess reserves. Its initial balance sheet would be

Assets		Liabilities	
Reserves	$10 million	Deposits	$100 million
Loans	$90 million	Bank capital	$ 10 million
Securities	$10 million		

When it suffers the $10 million deposit outflow, its balance sheet becomes

Assets		Liabilities	
Reserves	$ 0	Deposits	$90 million
Loans	$90 million	Bank capital	$10 million
Securities	$10 million		

After $10 million has been withdrawn from deposits and hence reserves, the bank has a problem: Its desired reserves are 10% of $90 million, or $9 million, but it has no reserves! To eliminate this shortfall, the bank has four basic options. One is to acquire reserves to meet a deposit outflow by borrowing them from other banks in the overnight market or by borrowing from corporations.[1] If the First Bank acquires the $9 million shortfall in reserves by borrowing it from other banks or corporations, its balance sheet becomes

Assets		Liabilities	
Reserves	$ 9 million	Deposits	$90 million
Loans	$90 million	Borrowings from other banks or corporations	$ 9 million
Securities	$10 million	Bank capital	$10 million

[1]One way that the First Bank can borrow from other banks and corporations is by selling negotiable certificates of deposit. This method for obtaining funds is discussed in the section on liability management.

The cost of this activity is the interest rate on these loans, such as the overnight interest rate.

A second alternative is for the bank to sell some of its securities to help cover the deposit outflow. For example, it might sell $9 million of its securities and deposit the proceeds with the Bank of Canada, resulting in the following balance sheet:

Assets		Liabilities	
Reserves	$ 9 million	Deposits	$90 million
Loans	$90 million	Bank capital	$10 million
Securities	$ 1 million		

The bank incurs some brokerage and other transaction costs when it sells these securities. The government of Canada securities that the bank holds are very liquid, so the transaction costs of selling them are quite modest. However, the other securities the bank holds are less liquid and the transaction costs can be appreciably higher.

A third way that the bank can meet a deposit outflow is to acquire reserves by borrowing from the Bank of Canada. In our example, the First Bank could leave its security and loan holdings the same and borrow $9 million in loans from the Bank of Canada. Its balance sheet would be

Assets		Liabilities	
Reserves	$ 9 million	Deposits	$90 million
Loans	$90 million	Advances from the Bank of Canada	$ 9 million
Securities	$10 million	Bank capital	$10 million

There are two costs associated with advances from the Bank of Canada. First is the interest rate that must be paid to the Bank of Canada (called the **bank rate**). The second is a nonexplicit cost resulting from the increased scrutiny of the bank by the Bank of Canada.

Finally, a bank can acquire the $9 million of reserves to meet the deposit outflow by reducing its loans by this amount and depositing the $9 million it then receives with the Bank of Canada, thereby increasing its reserves by $9 million. This transaction changes the balance sheet as follows:

Assets		Liabilities	
Reserves	$ 9 million	Deposits	$90 million
Loans	$81 million	Bank capital	$10 million
Securities	$10 million		

The First Bank is once again in good shape because its $9 million of reserves satisfies the reserve requirement.

However, this process of reducing its loans is the bank's costliest way of acquiring reserves when there is a deposit outflow. If the First Bank has numerous short-term loans renewed at fairly short intervals, it can reduce its total amount of loans outstanding fairly quickly by *calling in* loans—that is, by not renewing some loans when they come due. Unfortunately for the bank, this is likely to antagonize the customers whose loans are not being renewed because they have not done anything to deserve such treatment. Indeed, they are likely to take their business elsewhere in the future, a very costly consequence for the bank.

A second method for reducing its loans is for the bank to sell them off to other banks. Again, this is very costly because other banks do not personally know the customers who have taken out the loans and so may not be willing to buy the loans at their full value.

The foregoing discussion explains why banks hold excess reserves even though loans or securities earn a higher return. When a deposit outflow occurs, holding excess reserves allows the bank to escape the costs of (1) borrowing from other banks or corporations, (2) selling securities, (3) borrowing from the Bank of Canada, or (4) calling in or selling off loans. ***Excess reserves are insurance against the costs associated with deposit outflows. The higher the costs associated with deposit outflows, the more excess reserves banks will want to hold.***

Just as you and I would be willing to pay an insurance company to insure us against a casualty loss such as the theft of a car, a bank is willing to pay the cost of holding excess reserves (the opportunity cost, which is the earnings forgone by not holding income-earning assets such as loans or securities) in order to insure against losses due to deposit outflows. Because excess reserves, like insurance, have a cost, banks also take other steps to protect themselves; for example, they might shift their holdings of assets to more liquid securities.

Study Guide Bank management is easier to grasp if you put yourself in the banker's shoes and imagine what you would do in the situations described. To understand a bank's possible responses to deposit outflows, imagine how you as a banker might respond to two successive deposit outflows of $10 million.

Asset Management

Now that you understand why a bank has a need for liquidity, we can examine the basic strategy a bank pursues in managing its assets. To maximize its profits, a bank must simultaneously seek the highest returns possible on loans and securities, reduce risk, and make adequate provisions for liquidity by holding liquid assets. Banks try to accomplish these three goals in four basic ways.

First, banks try to find borrowers who will pay high interest rates and are unlikely to default on their loans. They seek out loan business by advertising their borrowing rates and by approaching corporations directly to solicit loans. It is up to the bank's loan officer to decide if potential borrowers are good credit risks who will make interest and principal payments on time. Typically, banks are conservative in their loan policies; the default rate is usually less than 1%. It is important, however, that banks not be so conservative that they miss out on attractive lending opportunities that earn high interest rates.

Second, banks try to purchase securities with high returns and low risk. Third, in managing their assets, banks must attempt to lower risk by diversifying. They accomplish this by purchasing many different types of assets (short- and long-term, government of Canada, and provincial and municipal bonds) and approving many types of loans to a number of customers. Banks that have not sufficiently sought the benefits of diversification often come to regret it later. For example, banks that had overspecialized in making loans to energy companies, real estate developers, or farmers suffered huge losses in the 1980s with the slump in energy, property, and farm prices. Indeed, some of these banks (i.e., the Canadian Commercial Bank and the Northland Bank) went broke because they had "put too many eggs in one basket."

Finally, the bank must manage the liquidity of its assets so that it can pay depositors when there are deposit outflows without bearing huge costs. This means that it will hold liquid securities even if they earn a somewhat lower return than other assets. In addition, it will want to hold short-term government securities so that even if a deposit outflow forces some costs on the bank, these will not be terribly high. Again, it is not wise for a bank to be too conservative. If it avoids all costs associated with deposit outflows by holding only excess reserves, losses are suffered because reserves earn no interest, while the bank's liabilities are costly to maintain. The bank must balance its desire for liquidity against the increased earnings that can be obtained from less liquid assets such as loans.

Liability Management

Before the 1960s, liability management was a staid affair: For the most part, banks took their liabilities as fixed and spent their time trying to achieve an optimal mix of assets. There were two main reasons for the emphasis on asset management. First, a large part of the sources of bank funds was obtained through chequable (demand) deposits that did not pay any interest. Thus banks could not actively compete with one another for these deposits, and so their amount was effectively a given for an individual bank. Second, because the markets for making overnight loans between banks were not well developed, banks rarely borrowed from other banks to meet their reserve needs.

Starting in the 1960s, however, large banks (called **money centre banks**) began to explore ways in which the liabilities on their balance sheets could provide them with reserves and liquidity. This led to an expansion of overnight loans markets, such as the federal funds market in the United States and the overnight funds market in Canada, and the development of new financial instruments such as negotiable CDs (first developed in 1961), which enabled money centre banks to acquire funds quickly.[2]

This new flexibility in liability management meant that banks could take a different approach to bank management. They no longer needed to depend on chequable deposits as the primary source of bank funds and as a result no longer treated their sources of funds (liabilities) as given. Instead, they aggressively set target goals for their asset growth and tried to acquire funds (by issuing liabilities) as they were needed.

For example, today, when a money centre bank finds an attractive loan opportunity, it can acquire funds by selling a negotiable CD. Or if it has a reserve shortfall, funds can be borrowed from another bank in the overnight market without incurring high transaction costs. The overnight market can also be used to finance loans.

The emphasis on liability management explains some of the important changes over the past three decades in the composition of banks' balance sheets. While negotiable CDs and bank borrowings have greatly increased in importance as a source of bank funds in recent years, chequable deposits have decreased in importance. Newfound flexibility in liability management and the search for higher profits have also stimulated banks to increase the proportion of their assets held in loans, which earn higher income.

Capital Adequacy Management

Banks have to make decisions about the amount of capital they need to hold for three reasons. First, bank capital helps prevent *bank failure,* a situation in which the bank cannot satisfy its obligations to pay its depositors and other creditors and so goes out of business. Second, the amount of capital affects returns for the

[2]Because small banks are not as well known as money centre banks and so might be a higher credit risk, they find it harder to raise funds in the negotiable CD market. Hence, they do not engage nearly as actively in liability management.

owners (equity holders) of the bank. And third, a minimum amount of bank capital (bank capital requirements) is required by regulatory authorities.

How Bank Capital Helps Prevent Bank Failure Let's consider two banks with identical balance sheets, except that the High Capital Bank has a ratio of capital to assets of 10% while the Low Capital Bank has a ratio of 4%.

High Capital Bank				**Low Capital Bank**			
Assets		Liabilities		Assets		Liabilities	
Reserves	$10 million	Deposits	$90 million	Reserves	$10 million	Deposits	$96 million
Loans	$90 million	Bank capital	$10 million	Loans	$90 million	Bank capital	$ 4 million

Suppose that both banks got caught up in the euphoria of the real estate market in the 1980s, only to find that $5 million of their real estate loans became worthless in the 1990s. When these bad loans are written off (valued at zero), the total value of assets declines by $5 million, and so bank capital, which equals total assets minus liabilities, also declines by $5 million. The balance sheets of the two banks now look like this:

High Capital Bank				**Low Capital Bank**			
Assets		Liabilities		Assets		Liabilities	
Reserves	$10 million	Deposits	$90 million	Reserves	$10 million	Deposits	$96 million
Loans	$85 million	Bank capital	$ 5 million	Loans	$85 million	Bank capital	−$1 million

The High Capital Bank takes the $5 million loss in stride because its initial cushion of $10 million in capital means that it still has a positive net worth (bank capital) of $5 million after the loss. The Low Capital Bank, however, is in big trouble. Now the value of its assets has fallen below its liabilities, and its net worth is now −$1 million. Because the bank has a negative net worth, it is insolvent: It does not have sufficient assets to pay off all holders of its liabilities (creditors). When a bank becomes insolvent, government regulators close the bank, its assets are sold off, and its managers are fired. Since the owners of the Low Capital Bank will find their investment wiped out, they would clearly have preferred the bank to have had a larger cushion of bank capital to absorb the losses, as was the case for the High Capital Bank. We therefore see an important rationale for a bank to maintain a high level of capital: ***A bank maintains bank capital to lessen the chance that it will become insolvent.***

How the Amount of Bank Capital Affects Returns to Equity Holders Because owners of a bank must know whether their bank is being managed well, they need good measures of bank profitability. A basic measure of bank profitability is the **return on assets (ROA)**, the net profit after taxes per dollar of assets:

$$ROA = \frac{\text{net profit after taxes}}{\text{assets}}$$

The return on assets provides information on how efficiently a bank is being run because it indicates how much profits are generated on average by each dollar of assets.

However, what the bank's owners (equity holders) care about most is how much the bank is earning on their equity investment. This information is provided by the other basic measure of bank profitability, the **return on equity (ROE)**, the net profit after taxes per dollar of equity capital:

$$ROE = \frac{\text{net profit after taxes}}{\text{equity capital}}$$

There is a direct relationship between the return on assets (which measures how efficiently the bank is run) and the return on equity (which measures how well the owners are doing on their investment). This relationship is determined by the so-called **equity multiplier (EM)**, which is the amount of assets per dollar of equity capital:

$$EM = \frac{\text{assets}}{\text{equity capital}}$$

To see this, we note that

$$\frac{\text{Net profit after taxes}}{\text{Equity capital}} = \frac{\text{net profit after taxes}}{\text{assets}} \times \frac{\text{assets}}{\text{equity capital}}$$

which, using our definitions, yields

$$ROE = ROA \times EM \tag{1}$$

The formula in Equation 1 tells us what happens to the return on equity when a bank holds a smaller amount of capital (equity) for a given amount of assets. As we have seen, the High Capital Bank initially has $100 million of assets and $10 million of equity, which gives it an equity multiplier of 10 (= $100 million/$10 million). The Low Capital Bank, by contrast, has only $4 million of equity, so its equity multiplier is higher, equaling 25 (= $100 million/$4 million). Suppose that these banks have been equally well run so that they both have the same returns on assets of 1%. The return on equity for the High Capital Bank equals 1% × 10 = 10%, while the return on equity for the Low Capital Bank equals 1% × 25 = 25%. The equity holders in the Low Capital Bank are clearly a lot happier than the equity holders in the High Capital Bank because they are earning more than twice as high a return. We now see why owners of a bank may not want it to hold a lot of capital. ***Given the return on assets, the lower the bank capital, the higher the return for the owners of the bank.***

Trade-Off Between Safety and Returns to Equity Holders We now see that bank capital has benefits and costs. Bank capital benefits the owners of a bank in that it makes their investment safer by reducing the likelihood of bankruptcy. But bank capital is costly because the higher it is, the lower will be the return on equity for a given return on assets. In determining the amount of bank capital, managers must decide how much of the increased safety that comes with higher capital (the benefit) they are willing to trade off against the lower return on equity that comes with higher capital (the cost).

In more uncertain times, when the possibility of large losses on loans increases, bank managers might want to hold more capital to protect the equity holders. Conversely, if they have confidence that loan losses won't occur, they might want to reduce the amount of bank capital, have a high equity multiplier, and thereby increase the return on equity.

Bank Capital Requirements Banks also hold capital because they are required to do so by regulatory authorities. Because of the high costs of holding capital for the reasons just described, bank managers often want to hold less bank capital than is required by the regulatory authorities. In this case, the amount of bank capital is determined by the bank capital requirements. We discuss the details of bank capital requirements and why they are such an important part of bank regulation in Chapter 18.

THE PRACTISING FINANCIAL INSTITUTION MANAGER

Strategies for Managing Bank Capital

Mona, the manager of the First Bank, has to make decisions about the appropriate amount of bank capital. Looking at the balance sheet of the bank, which has a ratio of bank capital to assets of 10% ($10 million of capital and $100 million of assets), Mona is concerned that the large amount of bank capital is causing the return on equity to be too low. She concludes that the bank has a capital surplus and should increase the equity multiplier to increase the return on equity. To lower the amount of capital relative to assets and raise the equity multiplier, she can do any of three things: (1) She can reduce the amount of bank capital by buying back some of the bank's stock. (2) She can reduce the bank's capital by paying out higher dividends to its stockholders, thereby reducing the bank's retained earnings. (3) She can keep bank capital constant but increase the bank's assets by acquiring new funds, say, by issuing CDs, and then seeking out loan business or purchasing more securities with these new funds. Because the bank manager feels that she will enhance her position with the stockholders, she decides to pursue the second alternative and raises the dividends on First Bank stock.

Now suppose that the First Bank is in a situation similar to that of the Low Capital Bank and has a ratio of bank capital to assets of 3%. The bank manager now might worry that the bank is short on capital relative to assets because it does not have a sufficient cushion to prevent bank failure. To raise the amount of capital relative to assets, she now has the following three choices: (1) She can raise capital for the bank by having it issue equity (common stock). (2) She can raise capital by reducing the bank's dividends to shareholders, thereby increasing retained earnings that it can put into its capital account. (3) She can keep capital at the same level but reduce the bank's assets by making fewer loans or by selling off securities and then using the proceeds to reduce its liabilities. Suppose that raising bank capital is not easy to do at the current time because capital markets are tight or because shareholders will protest if their dividends are cut. Then Mona might have to choose the third alternative and decide to shrink the size of the bank.

In recent years, many banks have experienced capital shortfalls and have had to restrict asset growth, as Mona did, when the bank is short of capital. The important consequences of this for the credit markets are discussed in the application that follows.

Application Did the Capital Crunch Cause a Credit Crunch in the Early 1990s?

During the 1990–1991 recession and the year following, there occurred a slowdown in the growth of credit that was unprecedented in the post–World War II era. Many economists and politicians have claimed that there was a "credit crunch" during this period in which credit was hard to get, and as a result the performance of the economy in 1990–1992 was very weak. Was the slowdown in credit growth a manifestation of a credit crunch, and if so, what caused it?

Our analysis of how a bank manages bank capital suggests that a credit crunch was likely to have occurred in 1990–1992 and that it was caused at least in part by the so-called capital crunch in which shortfalls of bank capital led to slower credit growth.

The period of the late 1980s saw a boom and then a major bust in the real estate market that led to huge losses for banks on their real estate loans. As our example on how bank capital helps prevent bank failures demonstrates, the loan losses caused a substantial fall in the amount of bank capital. At the same time, regulators were raising capital requirements (a subject we will discuss in Chapter 18). The resulting capital shortfalls meant that banks had either to raise new capital or to restrict their asset growth by cutting back on lending. Because of the weak economy at the time, raising new capital was extremely difficult for banks, so they chose the latter course. Banks did restrict their lending, and borrowers found it harder to obtain loans, leading to complaints from banks' customers.[3] Only with the stronger recovery of the economy in 1993, helped by a low-interest-rate policy at the Bank of Canada, did these complaints subside.

OFF-BALANCE-SHEET ACTIVITIES

Although asset and liability management has traditionally been the major concern of banks, in the more competitive environment of recent years banks have been aggressively seeking out profits by engaging in off-balance-sheet activities. **Off-balance-sheet activities** involve trading financial instruments and generating income from fees and loan sales, activities that affect bank profits but do not appear on bank balance sheets. Indeed, off-balance-sheet activities have been growing in importance for banks: The income from these activities as a percentage of assets has nearly doubled since 1980.

Loan Sales

One type of off-balance-sheet activity that has grown in importance in recent years involves income generated by loan sales. A **loan sale**, also called a *secondary loan participation,* involves a contract that sells all or part of the cash stream from a specific loan and thereby removes the loan from the bank's balance sheet. Banks earn profits by selling loans for an amount slightly greater than the amount of the original loan. Because the high interest rate on these loans makes them attractive, institutions are willing to buy them even though the higher price means that they earn a slightly lower interest rate than the original interest rate on the loan, usually on the order of 0.15 percentage point.

Generation of Fee Income

Another type of off-balance-sheet activity involves the generation of income from fees that banks receive for providing specialized services to their customers, such as making foreign exchange trades on a customer's behalf, servicing a mortgage-backed security by collecting interest and principal payments and then paying them out, guaranteeing debt securities such as banker's acceptances (the bank promises to make interest and principal payments if the party issuing the security cannot), and providing backup lines of credit. There are several types of backup lines of credit. The most important is the **loan commitment**, under which for a fee the bank agrees to provide a loan at the customer's request, up to a given dollar amount, over a specified period of time. Credit lines are also now available to bank depositors with "overdraft privileges"—these bank customers can write cheques in excess of their deposit balances and, in effect, write themselves a loan. Other lines of credit for which banks get fees include standby letters of credit to back up issues of

[3]As we will see in Chapter 18, not only were capital requirements raised, but also risk-based capital requirements were imposed that required even more capital if loans were made but not if banks bought government securities. The risk-based capital requirements thus encouraged banks to switch out of loans and into government securities, and this was an additional factor that led to a decline in bank lending. For a discussion of the evidence on how the capital crunch caused the credit crunch of 1990–1992, see "The Role of the Credit Slowdown in the Recent Recession," *Federal Reserve Bank of New York Quarterly Review,* Spring 1993.

commercial paper and other securities, and credit lines—called **note issuance facilities (NIFs)** and **revolving underwriting facilities (RUFs)**—for underwriting Euronotes, which are medium-term Eurobonds.

Off-balance-sheet activities involving guarantees of securities and backup credit lines increase the risk a bank faces. Even though a guaranteed security does not appear on a bank balance sheet, it still exposes the bank to default risk: If the issuer of the security defaults, the bank is left holding the bag and must pay off the security's owner. Backup credit lines also expose the bank to risk because the bank may be forced to provide loans when it does not have sufficient liquidity or when the borrower is a very poor credit risk.

Trading Activities and Risk Management Techniques

Available at www.federalreserve.gov/boarddocs/SupManual/default.htm#trading, the Federal Reserve Bank "Trading and Capital Market Activities Manual" offers an in-depth discussion of a wide range of risk management issues encountered in trading operations.

Banks' attempts to manage interest-rate risk led them to trading in financial futures, options for debt instruments, and interest-rate swaps. Banks engaged in international banking also conduct transactions in the foreign exchange market. All transactions in these markets are off-balance-sheet activities because they do not have a direct effect on the bank's balance sheet. Although bank trading in these markets is often directed toward reducing risk or facilitating other bank business, banks also try to outguess the markets and engage in speculation. This speculation can be a very risky business and indeed has led to bank insolvencies, the most dramatic being the failure of Barings, a British bank, in 1995.

Trading activities, although often highly profitable, are dangerous because they make it easy for financial institutions and their employees to make huge bets both easily and quickly. A particular problem for management of trading activities is that the principal-agent problem, discussed in Chapter 14, is especially severe. Given the ability to place large bets, a trader (the agent), whether she trades in bond markets, in foreign exchange markets, or in financial derivatives, has an incentive to take on excessive risks: If her trading strategy leads to large profits, she is likely to receive a high salary and bonuses, but if she takes large losses, the financial institution (the principal) will have to cover them. As the Barings Bank failure in 1995 so forcefully demonstrated, a trader subject to the principal-agent problem can take a bank that is quite healthy and drive it into insolvency very fast (see Box 2).

To reduce the principal-agent problem, bank management must set up internal controls to prevent debacles like the one at Barings. Such controls include the complete separation of the people in charge of trading activities and those in charge of the bookkeeping for trades. In addition, bank management must set limits on the total amount of traders' transactions and on the bank's risk exposure. Bank management must also scrutinize risk assessment procedures using the latest computer technology. One such method involves the so-called value-at-risk approach. In this approach, the bank develops a statistical model with which it can calculate the maximum loss that its portfolio is likely to sustain over a given time interval, dubbed the value at risk, or VAR. For example, a bank might estimate that the maximum loss that it would be likely to sustain over one day with a probability of 1 in 100 is \$1 million; the \$1 million figure is the bank's calculated value at risk. Another approach is called "stress testing." In this approach, the bank asks what would happen if a doomsday scenario occurs; that is, it looks at the losses it would sustain if an unusual combination of bad events occurred. With the value-at-risk approach and stress testing, a bank can assess its risk exposure and take steps to reduce it.

Because of the increased risk that banks are facing from their off-balance-sheet activities, Canadian bank regulators have become concerned about increased risk from banks' off-balance-sheet activities and, as we will see in Chapter 18,

BOX 2

Barings, Daiwa, and Sumitomo: Rogue Traders and the Principal-Agent Problem

The demise of Barings, a venerable British bank over a century old, is a sad morality tale of how the principal-agent problem operating through a rogue trader can take a financial institution that has a healthy balance sheet one month and turn it into an insolvent tragedy the next.

In July 1992, Nick Leeson, Barings's new head clerk at its Singapore branch, began to speculate on the Nikkei, the Japanese version of the Dow Jones index. By late 1992, Leeson had suffered losses of $3 million, which he hid from his superiors by stashing the losses in a secret account. He even fooled his superiors into thinking he was generating large profits, thanks to a failure of internal controls at his firm, which allowed him to execute trades on the Singapore exchange *and* oversee the bookkeeping of those trades. (As anyone who runs a cash business, such as a bar, knows, there is always a lower likelihood of fraud if more than one person handles the cash. Similarly for trading operations, you never mix management of the back room with management of the front room; this principle was grossly violated by Barings management.) Things didn't get better for Leeson, who by late 1994 had losses exceeding $250 million. In January and February 1995, he bet the bank. On January 17, 1995, the day of the Kobe earthquake, he lost $75 million, and by the end of the week had lost more than $150 million. When the stock market declined on February 23, leaving him with a further loss of $250 million, he called it quits and fled Singapore. Three days later, he turned himself in at the Frankfurt airport. By the end of his wild ride, Leeson's losses, $1.3 billion in all, ate up Barings's capital and caused the bank to fail.

Our asymmetric information analysis of the principal-agent problem explains Leeson's behaviour and the danger of Barings's management lapse. By letting Leeson control both his own trades and the back room, it increased asymmetric information because it reduced the principal's (Barings's) knowledge about Leeson's trading activities. This lapse increased the moral hazard incentive for him to take risks at the bank's expense, as he was now less likely to be caught. Furthermore, once he had experienced large losses, he had even greater incentives to take on even higher risk because if his bets worked out, he could reverse his losses and keep in good standing with the company, whereas if his bets soured, he had little to lose since he was out of a job anyway. Indeed, the bigger his losses, the more he had to gain by bigger bets, which explains the escalation of the amount of his trades as his losses mounted. If Barings's managers had understood the principal-agent problem, they would have been more vigilant in learning what Leeson was up to, and the bank might still be here today.

Unfortunately, Nick Leeson is no longer a rarity in the rogue traders' billionaire club, those who have lost more than $1 billion. Over 11 years, Toshihide Iguchi, an officer in the New York branch of Daiwa Bank, also had control of both the bond-trading operation and the back room, and he racked up $1.1 billion in losses over the period. In July 1995, Iguchi disclosed his losses to his superiors, but the management of the bank did not disclose them to its regulators. The result was that Daiwa was slapped with a $340 million fine and the bank was thrown out of the country by U.S. bank regulators. Yasuo Hamanaka is the latest member of the billionaire club. In July 1996, he topped Leeson's and Iguchi's record, losing $2.6 billion for his employer, the Sumitomo Corporation, one of Japan's top trading companies. The moral of these stories is that management of firms engaged in trading activities must reduce the principal-agent problem by closely monitoring their traders' activities.

are encouraging banks to pay increased attention to risk management. In addition, the Bank for International Settlements is developing additional bank capital requirements based on value-at-risk calculations for a bank's trading activities.

MEASURING BANK PERFORMANCE

To understand how well a bank is doing, we need to start by looking at a bank's income statement, the description of the sources of income and expenses that affect the bank's profitability.

Bank's Income Statement

The end of year 2001 income statement for the Big Six (Bank of Montreal, CIBC, National Bank, Royal Bank of Canada, Scotiabank, and TD Canada Trust) plus the Laurentian Bank of Canada and the Canadian Western Bank appears in Table 2.

Operating Income **Operating income** is the income that comes from a bank's ongoing operations. Most of a bank's operating income is generated by interest on its assets, particularly loans. As we see in Table 2, in 2001 interest income represented 72% of commercial banks' operating income. Interest income fluctuates with the level of interest rates, and so its percentage of operating income is highest when interest rates are at peak levels. That is exactly what happened in 1981, when interest rates rose above 20% and interest income rose to more than 90% of total bank operating income.

Noninterest income, which made up 28% of operating income in 2001, is generated partly by service charges on deposit accounts, but the bulk of it comes from the off-balance-sheet activities mentioned earlier, which generate fees or trading profits for the bank. The importance of these off-balance-sheet activities to bank profits has been growing in recent years. Whereas in 1980 other noninterest income from off-balance-sheet activities represented only 5% of operating income, it reached 20% in 2001.

Operating Expenses **Operating expenses** are the expenses incurred in conducting the bank's ongoing operations. An important component of a bank's operating expenses is the interest payments that it must make on its liabilities, particularly on its deposits. Just as interest income varies with the level of interest rates, so do interest expenses. Interest expenses as a percentage of total operating expenses reached a peak in 1981, when interest rates were at their highest, and fell in recent years as interest rates moved lower. Noninterest expenses include the costs of running a banking business: salaries for tellers and officers,

TABLE 2 Income Statement for Eight Domestic Banks (as at Fiscal Year-End 2001)

	Amount ($ millions)		Share of Operating Income or Expenses (%)	
Operating Income				
Interest income		81 473		72.01
Interest on loans	60 856		53.79	
Interest on securities	16 898		14.94	
Deposits with other banks	3 719		3.29	
Noninterest income		31 665		27.99
Total operating income		113 138		100.00
Operating expenses				
Interest expenses		53 451		53.72
Interest on deposits	41 994		42.21	
Bank debentures	1 804		1.81	
Other liabilities	9 653		9.70	
Noninterest expenses		40 168		40.37
Salaries and employee benefits	21 931		22.04	
Premises and equipment	8 712		8.76	
Other	9 525		9.57	
Provision for credit losses		5 873		5.90
Total operating expenses		99 492		100.00
Net operating income		13 646		
Provisions for income taxes		–3 842		
Net Income		9 804		

Source: Canadian Bankers Association Website, www.cba.ca

Note: The eight domestic banks are: Bank of Montreal, Canadian Western Bank, CIBC, Laurentian Bank, National Bank, RBC Financial Group, Scotiabank, and TD Bank Financial Group.

rent on bank buildings, purchases of equipment such as desks and vaults, and servicing costs of equipment such as computers.

The final item listed under operating expenses is provisions for credit losses. When a bank has a bad debt or anticipates that a loan might become a bad debt in the future, it can write up the loss as a current expense in its income statement under the "provision for credit losses" heading. Provisions for loan losses are directly related to loan loss reserves (discussed in Box 1 on page 378). When a bank wants to increase its loan loss reserves account by, say, $1 million, it does this by adding $1 million to its provisions for loan losses. Loan loss reserves rise when this is done because by increasing expenses when losses have not yet occurred, earnings are being set aside to deal with the losses in the future.

Provisions for loan losses have been a major element in fluctuating bank profits in recent years. The 1980s brought the third-world debt crisis mentioned in Chapter 18; a sharp decline in energy prices in 1986, which caused substantial losses on loans to energy producers; and a collapse in the real estate market. As a result, provisions for loan losses were particularly high in the late 1980s. Since then, losses on loans have begun to subside, and in 2001 provisions for loan losses dropped to only 5.9% of operating expenses.

Income Subtracting the $99 492 million in operating expenses from the $113 138 million of operating income in 2001 yields net operating income of $14 066 million. Net operating income is closely watched by bank managers, bank shareholders, and bank regulators because it indicates how well the bank is doing on an ongoing basis.

One item, net extraordinary items, which are events or transactions that are both unusual and infrequent, is added or deducted to the net operating income figure to get the figure for net income before taxes. Net income before taxes is more commonly referred to as profits before taxes. Subtracting the $3842 million of provisions for income taxes then results in $9804 million of net income. Net income, more commonly referred to as profits after taxes, is the figure that tells us most directly how well the bank is doing because it is the amount that the bank has available to keep as retained earnings or to pay out to stockholders as dividends.

Measures of Bank Performance

Although net income gives us an idea of how well a bank is doing, it suffers from one major drawback: It does not adjust for the bank's size, thus making it hard to compare how well one bank is doing relative to another. A basic measure of bank profitability that corrects for the size of the bank is the return on assets *(ROA)*, mentioned earlier in the chapter, which divides the net income of the bank by the amount of its assets. *ROA* is a useful measure of how well a bank manager is doing on the job because it indicates how well a bank's assets are being used to generate profits. At the end of 2002, the assets of the **Big Eight** banks amounted to $1485.5 billion, so using the $9.8 billion net income figure from Table 2 gives us a return on assets of

$$ROA = \frac{\text{net income}}{\text{assets}} = \frac{9.8}{1485.5} = 0.0066 = 0.66\%$$

Although *ROA* provides useful information about bank profitability, we have already seen that it is not what the bank's owners (equity holders) care about most. They are more concerned about how much the bank is earning on their equity investment, an amount that is measured by the return on equity (*ROE*), the net income per dollar of equity capital. At the end of 2001, equity capital for all the Big 8 banks was $70.6 billion, so the *ROE* was therefore

$$ROE = \frac{\text{net income}}{\text{assets}} = \frac{9.8}{70.6} = 0.1388 = 13.88\%$$

Another commonly watched measure of bank performance is called the **net interest margin** (*NIM*), the difference between interest income and interest expenses as a percentage of total assets:

$$NIM = \frac{\text{interest income} - \text{interest expenses}}{\text{assets}}$$

As we have seen earlier in the chapter, one of a bank's primary intermediation functions is to issue liabilities and use the proceeds to purchase income-earning assets. If a bank manager has done a good job of asset and liability management such that the bank earns substantial income on its assets and has low costs on its liabilities, profits will be high. How well a bank manages its assets and liabilities is affected by the spread between the interest earned on the bank's assets and the interest costs on its liabilities. This spread is exactly what the net interest margin measures. If the bank is able to raise funds with liabilities that have low interest costs and is able to acquire assets with high interest income, the net interest margin will be high, and the bank is likely to be highly profitable. If the interest cost of its liabilities rises relative to the interest earned on its assets, the net interest margin will fall, and bank profitability will suffer.

Recent Trends in Bank Performance Measures

Table 3 provides measures of return on assets (*ROA*), return on equity (*ROE*), and the net interest margin (*NIM*) for the Big 6 plus the Laurentian Bank of Canada and the Canadian Western Bank from 1991 to 2001. Because the relationship between bank equity capital and total assets for those eight domestic banks remained fairly stable in the 1990s, both the *ROA* and *ROE* measures of bank performance move closely together and indicate that in the early 1990s, there was an increase in bank profitability. The right most column, net interest margin, indicates that the spread between interest income and interest expenses declined throughout the 1990s.

TABLE 3 Measures of Eight Domestic Banks Performance (as at Fiscal Year-End), 1991–2001

Year	Return on Assets (ROA)(%)	Return on Equity (ROE)(%)	Net Interest Margin (NIM)(%)
1991	0.68	13.08	2.86
1992	0.32	5.92	2.79
1993	0.47	8.72	2.65
1994	0.59	11.62	2.53
1995	0.67	13.2	2.34
1996	0.71	14.93	2.07
1997	0.71	16.37	1.92
1998	0.57	13.39	1.75
1999	0.71	15.69	1.81
2000	0.71	15.25	1.73
2001	0.66	13.89	1.80

Source: Canadian Bankers Association Website, www.cba.ca, and authors' calculations

Note: The eight domestic banks are: Bank of Montreal, Canadian Western Bank, CIBC, Laurentian Bank, National Bank, RBC Financial Group, Scotiabank, and TD Bank Financial Group.

The explanation of the weak performance of the eight domestic banks in the early 1990s is that they had made many risky loans in the late 1980s that turned sour. The resulting huge increase in loan loss provisions in that period directly decreased net income and hence caused the fall in *ROA* and *ROE*. (Why bank profitability deteriorated and the consequences for the economy are discussed in Chapters 16 and 18.)

Beginning in 1994, bank performance improved substantially. The return on equity rose to nearly 12% in 1994 and remained above 13% in the 1995–2001 period. Similarly, the return on assets rose from the 0.5% level in the 1991–1993 period to around the 0.66% level in 1994–2001.

FINANCIAL INNOVATION

Center for the Study of Financial Innovation, www.csfi.fsnet.co.uk, is an independent think tank formed in 1993 to stimulate research into the future of the financial services industry.

Like other industries, the financial industry is in business to earn profits by selling its products. If a soap company perceives that there is a need in the marketplace for a laundry detergent with fabric softener, it develops a product to fit the need. Similarly, in order to maximize their profits, financial institutions develop new products to satisfy their own needs as well as those of their customers; in other words, innovation—which can be extremely beneficial to the economy—is driven by the desire to get (or stay) rich. This view of the innovation process leads to the following simple analysis: ***A change in the financial environment will stimulate a search by financial institutions for innovations that are likely to be profitable.***

Starting in the 1960s, individuals and financial institutions operating in financial markets were confronted with drastic changes in the economic environment: Inflation and interest rates climbed sharply and became harder to predict, a situation that changed demand conditions in financial markets. Computer technology advanced rapidly, which changed supply conditions. In addition, financial regulations became more burdensome. Financial institutions found that many of the old ways of doing business were no longer profitable; the financial services and products they had been offering to the public were not selling. Many financial intermediaries found that they were no longer able to acquire funds with their traditional financial instruments, and without these funds they would soon be out of business. To survive in the new economic environment, financial institutions had to research and develop new products and services that would meet customer needs and prove profitable, a process referred to as **financial engineering**. In their case, necessity was the mother of innovation.

Our discussion of why financial innovation occurs suggests that there are three basic types of financial innovations: responses to changes in demand conditions, responses to changes in supply conditions, and avoidance of regulations. Now that we have a framework for understanding why financial institutions such as banks produce innovations, let's look at examples of how financial institutions in their search for profits have produced financial innovations of the three basic types.

Responses to Changes in Demand Conditions

The most significant change in the economic environment that altered the demand for financial products in recent years has been the dramatic increase in the volatility of interest rates. In the 1950s, the interest rate on three-month treasury bills fluctuated between 1.0% and 5.5%; in the 1970s, it fluctuated between 3.0% and 14%. This volatility became even more pronounced in the 1980s, during which the three-month T-bill rate ranged from 7% to over 20%. We have seen in Chapter 3 (Table 2) that a rise in the interest rate from 10% to 20% would result in a capital loss of nearly 50% on a 30-year bond and a negative return of almost 40%. Large fluctuations in interest rates lead to substantial capital gains or losses and greater uncertainty about returns on investments. Recall that the risk that is related to the uncertainty about interest-rate movements and returns is called *interest-rate risk,* and high volatility of interest rates, such as we saw in the 1970s and 1980s, leads to a higher level of interest-rate risk.

We would expect the increase in interest-rate risk to increase the demand for financial products and services that could reduce that risk. This change in the economic environment would thus stimulate a search for profitable innovations by financial institutions that meet this new demand and would spur the creation of new financial instruments that help lower interest-rate risk. One financial innovation in the banking industry that appeared in the 1970s confirms this prediction: the development of adjustable-rate mortgages.

Adjustable-Rate Mortgages Like other investors, financial institutions find that lending is more attractive if interest-rate risk is lower. They would not want to make a mortgage loan at a 10% interest rate and two months later find that they could obtain a 12% interest rate on the same mortgage. To reduce interest-rate risk, financial institutions began to issue adjustable-rate mortgages, mortgage loans on which the interest rate changes when a market interest rate (usually the treasury bill rate) changes. Initially, an adjustable-rate mortgage might have a 5% interest rate. In six months, this interest rate might increase or decrease by the amount of the increase or decrease in, say, the six-month treasury bill rate, and the mortgage payment would change. Because adjustable-rate mortgages allow mortgage-issuing institutions to earn higher interest rates on mortgages when rates rise, profits are kept higher during these periods. This was the case in the early 1980s when the three-month T-bill rate exceeded 20%.

This attractive feature of adjustable-rate mortgages has encouraged mortgage-issuing institutions to issue adjustable-rate mortgages with lower initial interest rates than on conventional fixed-rate mortgages, making them popular with many households. However, because the mortgage payment on a variable-rate mortgage can increase, many households continue to prefer fixed-rate mortgages. Hence both types of mortgages are widespread.

Responses to Changes in Supply Conditions

The most important source of the changes in supply conditions that stimulate financial innovation has been the improvement in computer and telecommunications technology. These changes have made it profitable for financial institutions to create new financial products and services to supply to the public. When computer technology that substantially lowered the cost of processing financial transactions became available, financial institutions conceived new financial products and instruments dependent on this technology that might appeal to the public, including the bank credit card and electronic banking facilities.

The Websites for American Express and Diners Club can be found at www.americanexpress.com and www.dinersclub.com

Bank Credit and Debit Cards Credit cards have been around since well before World War II. Many individual stores (Sears, Eaton's, the Bay) institutionalized charge accounts by providing customers with credit cards that allowed them to make purchases at these stores without cash. Nationwide credit cards were not established until after World War II, when Diners Club developed one to be used in restaurants. Similar credit card programs were started by American Express and Carte Blanche, but because of the high cost of operating these programs, cards were issued only to selected persons and businesses who could afford expensive purchases.

A firm issuing credit cards earns income from loans it makes to credit card holders and from payments made by stores on credit card purchases (a percentage of the purchase price, say, 5%). A credit card program's costs arise from loan defaults, stolen cards, and the expense involved in processing credit card transactions.

Bankers saw the success of Diners Club, American Express, and Carte Blanche and wanted to share in the profitable credit card business. Several banks attempted to expand the credit card business to a wider market in the 1950s, but the cost per transaction when running these programs was so high that their early attempts failed.

In the late 1960s, improved computer technology, which lowered the transaction costs for providing credit card services, made it more likely that bank credit card programs would be profitable. The banks tried to enter this business again, and this time their efforts led to the creation of two successful bank credit card programs: Visa and MasterCard. These programs have become phenomenally successful; more than 1.1 million merchants in Canada accepted Visa and MasterCard in 1999. Indeed, bank credit cards have been so profitable that nonfinancial institutions such as Sears, General Motors, Canadian Tire, and Wal-Mart have also entered the credit card business. Consumers have benefited because credit cards are more widely accepted than cheques when paying for purchases (particularly abroad), and they allow consumers to take out loans more easily.

You can access Wal-Mart's Website at www.walmart.com

The success of bank credit cards has led these institutions to come up with a new financial innovation, *debit cards*. Debit cards often look just like credit cards and can be used to make purchases in an identical fashion. However, in contrast to credit cards, which extend the purchaser a loan that does not have to be paid off immediately, a debit card purchase is immediately deducted from the card holder's bank account. Debit cards depend even more on low costs of processing transactions, since their profits are generated entirely from the fees paid by merchants on debit card purchases at their stores. Debit cards have been growing increasingly popular in recent years. In fact, today more than 57% of payment transactions in Canada are made by debit or credit card.

Electronic Banking The wonders of modern computer technology have also enabled banks to lower the cost of bank transactions by having the customer interact with an electronic banking facility rather than with a human being. One important form of an e-banking facility is the **automated teller machine (ATM)**, an electronic machine that allows customers to get cash, make deposits, transfer funds from one account to another, and check balances. The ATM has the advantage that it does not have to be paid overtime and never sleeps, thus being available for use 24 hours a day. Not only does this result in cheaper transactions for the bank, but it also provides more convenience for the customer. Furthermore, because of its low cost, ATMs can be put at locations other than a bank or its branches, further increasing customer convenience. The low cost of ATMs has meant that they have sprung up everywhere and now number 17 000 in Canada alone (and more than 250 000 in the United States). Furthermore, it is now as easy to get foreign currency from an ATM when you are travelling in Europe as it is to get cash from your local bank. In addition, transactions with ATMs are so much cheaper for the bank than ones conducted with human tellers that some banks charge customers less if they use the ATM than if they use a human teller.

With the drop in the cost of telecommunications, banks have developed another financial innovation, home banking. It is now cost-effective for banks to set up an electronic banking facility in which the bank's customer is linked up with the bank's computer to carry out transactions by using either a telephone or a personal computer. Now a bank's customers can conduct many of their bank transactions without ever leaving the comfort of home. The advantage for the customer is the convenience of home banking, while banks find that the cost of transactions is substantially less than having the customer come to the bank. The success of ATMs and home banking has led to another innovation, the **automated banking machine (ABM)**, which combines in one location an ATM, an Internet connection to the bank's website, and a telephone link to customer service.

With the decline in the price of personal computers and their increasing presence in the home, we have seen a further innovation in the home banking area, the appearance of a new type of banking institution, the **virtual bank,** a bank that has no physical location but rather exists only in cyberspace. In 1995, Security First Network Bank, based in Atlanta but now owned by Royal Bank of Canada, became the first virtual bank, planning to offer an array of banking services on the Internet—accepting chequing account and savings deposits, selling certificates of deposits, issuing ATM cards, providing bill-paying facilities, and so on. The virtual bank thus takes home banking one step further, enabling the customer to have a full set of banking services at home 24 hours a day. In 1996, Bank of America and Wells Fargo entered the virtual banking market, to be followed by many others, with Bank of America now being the largest Internet bank in the United States. Will virtual banking be the predominant form of banking in the future (see Box 3)?

Electronic Payment The development of inexpensive computers and the spread of the Internet now makes it very cheap for banks to allow their customers to make bill payments electronically. Where in the past you had to pay your bills by mailing a cheque, now banks provide a Website in which you just log on, make a few clicks, and your payment is transmitted electronically. You not only save the cost of the stamp, but paying bills now becomes (almost) a pleasure, requiring little effort. Electronic payment systems provided by banks now even allow you to avoid the step of having to log on to pay the bill. Instead, recurring bills can be automatically deducted from your bank account without your having to do a thing. Providing these services increases profitability for banks in two ways. First, payment of a bill electronically means that banks don't need people to process what would

BOX 3: E-FINANCE

Will "Clicks" Dominate "Bricks" in the Banking Industry?

With the advent of virtual banks ("clicks") and the convenience they provide, a key question is whether they will become the primary form in which banks do their business, eliminating the need for physical bank branches ("bricks") as the main delivery mechanism for banking services. Indeed, will stand-alone Internet banks be the wave of the future?

The answer seems to be no. Internet-only banks such as Wingspan (owned by Bank One), First-e (Dublin-based), and Egg (a British Internet-only bank owned by Prudential) have had disappointing revenue growth and profits. The result is that pure on-line banking has not been the success that proponents had hoped for. Why has Internet banking been a disappointment?

There have been several strikes against Internet banking. First, bank depositors want to know that their savings are secure, so are reluctant to put their money into new institutions without a long track record. Second, customers worry about the security of their on-line transactions and whether their transactions will truly be kept private. Traditional banks are viewed as being more secure and trustworthy in terms of releasing private information. Third, customers may prefer services provided by physical branches. For example, banking customers seem to prefer to purchase long-term savings products face-to-face. Fourth, Internet banking still has run into technical problems—server crashes, slow connections over phone lines, mistakes in conducting transactions—that will probably diminish over time as technology improves.

The wave of the future thus does not appear to be pure Internet banks. Instead it looks like "clicks and bricks" will be the predominant form of banking, in which on-line banking is used to complement the services provided by traditional banks. Nonetheless, the delivery of banking services is undergoing massive changes, with more and more banking services delivered over the Internet and the number of physical bank branches likely to decline in the future.

have otherwise been a paper transaction. Estimates of the cost savings for banks when a bill is paid electronically rather than by a cheque exceed one dollar. Second, the extra convenience for you, the customer, means that you are more likely to open an account with the bank. Electronic payment is thus becoming far more common in Canada and the United States, but North Americans are far behind Europeans, particularly Scandinavians, in their use of electronic payments (see Box 4).

E-Money Electronic payments technology can not only substitute for cheques but can, in the form of **electronic money** (or **e-money**), money that exists only in electronic form, substitute for cash as well. The first form of e-money is a stored-value card. The simplest form of stored-value card is purchased for a preset dollar amount that the consumer spends down. The more sophisticated stored-value card is known as a **smart card**. It contains its own computer chip so that it can be loaded with digital cash from the owner's bank account whenever needed. Smart cards can be loaded either from ATM machines, personal computers with a smart card reader, or from specially equipped telephones.

A second form of electronic money is often referred to as **e-cash**, and it is used on the Internet to purchase goods or services. A consumer gets e-cash by setting up an account with a bank that has links to the Internet and then has the e-cash transferred to her PC. When she wants to buy something with e-cash, she surfs to a store on the Web, clicks the "buy" option for a particular item, whereupon the e-cash is automatically transferred from her computer to the merchant's

BOX 4: E-FINANCE

Why Are Scandinavians So Far Ahead of North Americans in Using Electronic Payments and Online Banking?

North Americans are the biggest users of cheques in the world. Close to 100 billion cheques are written every year in the United States alone, and more than three-quarters of noncash transactions are conducted with paper. In contrast, in most countries of Europe, more than two-thirds of noncash transactions are electronic, with Finland and Sweden having the greatest proportion of online banking customers of any countries in the world. Indeed, if you were Finnish or Swedish, instead of writing a cheque, you would be far more likely to pay your bills online, not only through a personal computer, but even with your mobile phone. Why are Europeans and especially Scandinavians so far ahead of North Americans in the use of electronic payments and online banking?

First, Europeans got used to making payments without cheques, even before the advent of the personal computer. Europeans have made use of so-called *giro* payments for a long time, in which banks and post offices transfer funds for customers to pay bills. Second, Europeans, and particularly Scandinavians, are much greater users of mobile phones and the Internet than are North Americans. Finland has the highest per capita use of mobile phones in the world, while Finland and Sweden lead the world in the percentage of the population that accesses the Internet. Maybe this is because of the low population densities of their countries and the fact that it is so cold and dark during the winter that Scandinavians prefer to stay inside at their PCs. Scandinavians would rather take the view that the reason for their being more high-tech is their good education systems and the resulting high degree of computer literacy, the presence of top technology companies such as Finland's Nokia and Sweden's Ericsson, and government policies to increase the use of personal computers, such as Sweden's giving companies tax incentives to provide their employees with home computers. The result of their wired population is that the Finns (and to a lesser extent Swedes) are percentagewise the biggest users of online banking in the world.

North Americans are clearly behind the curve in their use of electronic payments, and this has imposed a high cost on the economy. Switching from cheques to electronic payments might save the economy tens of billions of dollars per year, according to some estimates. Indeed, the federal government is trying to switch all its payments to electronic ones by directly depositing them into bank accounts in order to reduce its expenses. Can North Americans be weaned from paper cheques in the future and fully embrace the world of high-tech banking?

computer. The merchant can then have the funds transferred from the consumer's bank account to his before the goods are shipped.

Given the convenience of e-money, you might think that we would move quickly to the cashless society in which all payments were made electronically. However, this hasn't happened, as discussed in Box 5.

Avoidance of Existing Regulations

The process of financial innovation we have discussed so far is much like innovation in other areas of the economy: It occurs in response to changes in demand and supply conditions. However, because the financial industry is more heavily regulated than other industries, government regulation is a much greater spur to innovation in this industry. Government regulation leads to financial innovation by creating incentives for firms to skirt regulations that restrict their ability to earn profits. Edward Kane describes this process of avoiding regulations as "loophole mining."[4] The economic analysis of innovation suggests that when the economic environment changes such that regulatory constraints are so burdensome that large profits can be made by avoiding them, loophole mining and innovation are more likely to occur.

Because banking is one of the most heavily regulated industries, loophole mining is especially likely to occur. The rise in inflation and interest rates from the late 1960s to 1980 made the regulatory constraints imposed on this industry even more burdensome. Under these circumstances, we would expect the pace of financial innovation in banking to be rapid, and, indeed, it has been.

BOX 5: E-FINANCE

Are We Headed for a Cashless Society?

Predictions of a cashless society have been around for decades, but they have not come to fruition. For example, *Business Week* predicted in 1975 that electronic means of payment "would soon revolutionize the very concept of money itself," only to reverse itself several years later. Pilot projects in recent years with smart cards to convert consumers to the use of e-money have not been a success. Mondex, one of the widely touted, early stored-value cards that was launched in Britain in 1995, is only used on a few British university campuses. In Germany and Belgium, millions of people carry bank cards with computer chips embedded in them that enable them to make use of e-money, but very few use them. Why has the movement to a cashless society been so slow in coming?

Although e-money might be more convenient and may be more efficient than a payments system based on paper, several factors work against the disappearance of the paper system. First, it is very expensive to set up the computer, card reader, and telecommunications networks necessary to make electronic money the dominant form of payment. Second, electronic means of payment may raise security and privacy concerns. We often hear media reports that an unauthorized hacker has been able to access a computer database and to alter information stored there. The fact that this is not an uncommon occurrence means that unscrupulous persons might be able to access bank accounts in electronic payments systems and steal funds by moving them from someone else's accounts into their own. The prevention of this type of fraud is no easy task, and a whole new field of computer science is developing to cope with security issues. A further concern is that the use of electronic means of payment leaves an electronic trail that contains a large amount of personal data on buying habits. There are worries that government, employers, and marketers might be able to access these data, thereby encroaching on our privacy.

The conclusion from this discussion is that although the use of e-money will surely increase in the future, to paraphrase Mark Twain, "the reports of cash's death are greatly exaggerated."

---

[4]"Banking Takes a Beating," *Time,* December 3, 1984, p. 49.

Most examples of loophole mining and financial innovation are responses to taxation and regulation in the United States, reflecting the dominance of the U.S. financial markets. However, the innovative instruments that have been developed have left behind their U.S. origins and become international, now serving a much more diverse purpose than simply escaping U.S. banking regulations.

Two sets of regulations have seriously restricted the ability of U.S. banks to make profits: reserve requirements that force banks to keep a certain fraction of their deposits as reserves (deposits in the Federal Reserve System) and restrictions on the interest rates that can be paid on deposits. For the following reasons, these regulations have been among the major forces behind financial innovation in recent years.

Reserve Requirements The key to understanding why reserve requirements affect financial innovation is to recognize that they act, in effect, as a tax on deposits. Because the central bank does not pay interest on reserves, the opportunity cost of holding them is the interest that a bank could otherwise earn by lending the reserves out. For each dollar of deposits, reserve requirements therefore impose a cost on the bank equal to the interest rate i that could be earned if the reserves could be lent out times the fraction of deposits required as reserves r_D. The cost of $i \times r_D$ imposed on the bank is just like a tax on bank deposits of $i \times r_D$.

As you learned in Chapter 7, the current Canadian situation is that banks earn interest on positive settlement balances with the Bank of Canada. The interest rate is the bank rate less 50 basis points. There is still an opportunity cost for Canadian banks, but not of the order of magnitude when the central bank does not pay any interest on bank reserves.

It is a great tradition to avoid taxes if possible, and banks also play this game. Just as taxpayers look for loopholes to lower their tax bills, banks seek to increase their profits by mining loopholes and by producing new financial innovations that allow them to escape the tax on deposits imposed by reserve requirements.

Restrictions on Interest Paid on Deposits Although Canadian banks have never been subject to deposit rate ceilings, for decades after 1933, U.S. banks were prohibited from paying interest on chequing accounts. In addition, until 1986, the U.S. Federal Reserve had the power under **Regulation Q** to set maximum interest rates that banks could pay on time deposits. The desire to avoid these **deposit rate ceilings** also led to financial innovations.

If market interest rates rose above the maximum rates that banks paid on time deposits under Regulation Q, depositors withdrew funds from banks to put them into higher-yielding securities. This loss of deposits from the banking system restricted the amount of funds that banks could lend (called **disintermediation**) and thus limited bank profits. Banks had an incentive to get around deposit rate ceilings because by so doing, they could acquire more funds to make loans and earn higher profits.

We can now look at how the desire to avoid restrictions on interest payments and the tax effect of reserve requirements led to several important financial innovations.

Eurodollars and Bank Commercial Paper In the late 1960s, inflation was accelerating, and (as we would expect from our analysis of the Fisher effect in Chapter 4) interest rates began to rise. The tax on deposits from reserve requirements $i \times r_D$ also began to rise, and the incentives to avoid this tax increased. In addition, higher interest rates meant that market interest rates exceeded the maximum rate payable on time deposits under Regulation Q, and as market interest rates climbed to then record highs in 1969, investors reduced their time deposits to invest in higher-yielding securities. By the late 1960s, commercial banks had a strong incentive to search for new funds that would not be subject to reserve requirements and so escape the tax of $i \times r_D$ and not be subject to the interest rate ceiling set by Regulation Q.

As the economic analysis of innovation predicts, the banks began to mine loopholes and discovered two sources of funds that avoided both reserve requirements and deposit rate ceilings: Eurodollars and bank commercial paper. Because Eurodollars (deposits abroad denominated in dollars) were borrowed from banks outside the United States, they were not subject to reserve requirements or to Regulation Q. Similarly, commercial paper issued by a bank's parent holding company was not treated as deposits and so was also exempt from these regulations. Not surprisingly, the markets for Eurodollars and bank commercial paper have experienced phenomenal growth since then, even though the motivating U.S. regulations have changed.

Sweep Accounts and Overnight Repos Another innovation that enables banks to pay interest on corporate chequing accounts is the ATS (automatic transfer from savings) account. Balances above a certain amount in a chequing account are automatically transferred into a savings account that pays interest. When a cheque is written on the ATS account, the necessary funds to cover the cheque are automatically transferred from the savings account into the chequing account. Thus balances earning interest in a savings account are effectively part of the depositor's chequing account because they are available for writing cheques. Legally, however, it is the savings account and not the chequing account that pays interest to the depositor.

Commercial banks provide a variant of the ATS account to their corporate depositors, which involves the use of a so-called *sweep account* to engage in overnight repurchase agreements (repos). In this type of arrangement, any balances above a certain amount in a corporation's chequing account at the end of a business day are "swept out" of the account and invested in overnight repos that pay the corporation interest. (As you may recall from Chapter 2, the repo is an agreement whereby a corporation purchases treasury bills that the bank agrees to repurchase the next day at a slightly higher price.) Again, although the chequing account does not legally pay interest, in effect the corporation is receiving interest on balances that are available for writing cheques.

The financial innovations of ATS accounts and overnight repo arrangements were stimulated not only by deposit rate ceilings but also by new technology. Without low-cost computers to process inexpensively the additional transactions required by these accounts, neither of these innovations would be profitable and therefore would not have been developed. Technological factors often combine with other incentives, such as the desire to get around restrictions on deposit rates, to produce financial innovation.

Conclusion Our discussion of financial innovation and the challenges that are facing managers of banks indicates that banking is no longer the staid profession it once was, prompting one banker to state, "Despite all the dark suits worn by its leaders, banking is a very dynamic industry."[5]

[5]Ibid.

THE PRACTISING FINANCIAL INSTITUTION MANAGER

Profiting from a New Financial Product: A Case Study of Canada STRIPS

We have seen that the advent of high-speed computers, which lowered the cost of processing financial transactions, led to such financial innovations as bank credit and debit cards. Because there is money to be made from financial innovation, it is important for managers of financial institutions to understand the thinking that goes into producing new, highly profitable financial products that take advantage of computer technology. To illustrate how financial institution managers can figure out ways to increase profits through financial innovation, we look at Treasury strips, a financial instrument first developed in 1982 in the U.S. by Salomon Brothers and Merrill Lynch. (Indeed, this innovation was so successful that the Canadian government copied it when they issued STRIPS in 1982.)

One problem for investors in long-term coupon bonds, even when investors have a long holding period, is that there is some uncertainty in their returns arising from what is called *reinvestment risk.* Even if an investor holding a long-term coupon bond has a holding period of ten years, the return on the bond is not certain. The problem is that coupon payments are made before the bond matures in ten years, and these coupon payments must be reinvested. Because the interest rates at which the coupon payments will be reinvested fluctuate, the eventual return on the bond fluctuates as well. In contrast, long-term zero-coupon bonds have no reinvestment risk because they make no cash payments before the bond matures. The return on a zero-coupon bond if it is held to maturity is known at the time of purchase. The absence of reinvestment risk is an attractive feature of zero-coupon bonds, and as a result, investors are willing to accept a slightly lower interest rate on them than on coupon bonds, which do bear some reinvestment risk.

The fact that zero-coupon bonds have lower interest rates, along with the ability to use computers to create so-called hybrid securities, which are securities derived from other underlying securities, gave employees of Salomon Brothers and Merrill Lynch a brilliant idea for making profits. They could use computers to separate ("strip") a long-term Treasury coupon bond into a set of zero-coupon bonds. For example, a $1 million ten-year Treasury bond might be stripped into ten $100 000 zero-coupon bonds, which, naturally enough, are called *Treasury strips*. The lower interest rates on the more desirable Treasury strip zero-coupon bonds would mean that the value of these bonds would exceed the price of the underlying long-term Treasury bond, allowing Salomon Brothers and Merrill Lynch to make a profit by purchasing the long-term Treasury bond, separating it into Treasury strips, and selling them off as zero-coupon bonds.

To see in more detail how their thinking worked, let's look more closely at a $1 million ten-year Canada bond with a coupon rate of 10% whose yield to maturity is also 10%, so it is selling at par. The cash payments for this bond are listed in the second column of Table 4. To make things simple, let's assume that the yield curve is absolutely flat so that the interest rate used to discount all the future cash payments is the same. Because zero-coupon bonds, which have no reinvestment risk, are more desirable than the ten-year Canada coupon bond, the interest rate on the zero-coupon bonds is 9.75%, a little lower than the 10% interest rate on the coupon bond.

How would Fran, a smart and sophisticated financial institution manager, figure out if she could make a profit from creating and selling the Canada strips? Her first step is to figure out what the zero-coupon Canada strips would sell for. She would find this easy to do if she had read Chapter 3 of this book: Using Equation 1 in that chapter, she would figure out that each of the Canada strip zero-coupon bonds would sell for its present discounted value:

$$\frac{\text{Cash payment in year } n}{(1 + 0.0975)^n}$$

The results of this calculation for each year are listed in column (4) of Table 4. When Fran adds up the values of the collection of the Canada strip zero-coupon bonds, she gets a figure of $1 015 528, which is greater than the $1 million purchase price of the Canada bond. As long as it costs less than $15 528 to collect the payments from the Canada bonds and then pass them through to the owners of the zero-coupon strips, which is likely to be the case since computer technology makes the cost of conducting these financial transactions low, the zero-coupon strips will be profitable for her financial institution. Fran would thus recommend that her firm go ahead and market the new financial product. Because the financial institution can now generate much higher profits by selling substantial numbers of Canada strips, it would amply reward Fran with a spanking new red BMW and a $100 000 bonus!

TABLE 4 Market Value of Canada Strip Zero-Coupon Bonds Derived from a $1 Million Ten-Year Canada Bond with a 10% Coupon Rate and Selling at Par

(1) Year	(2) Cash Payment ($)	(3) Interest Rate on Zero-Coupon Bond (%)	(4) Present Discounted Value of Zero-Coupon Bond ($)
1	100 000	9.75	91 116
2	100 000	9.75	83 022
3	100 000	9.75	75 646
4	100 000	9.75	68 926
5	100 000	9.75	62 802
6	100 000	9.75	57 223
7	100 000	9.75	52 140
8	100 000	9.75	47 508
9	100 000	9.75	43 287
10	100 000	9.75	39 442
10	1 000 000	9.75	394 416
Total			$1 015 528

SUMMARY

1. The balance sheet of commercial banks can be thought of as a list of the sources and uses of bank funds. The bank's liabilities are its sources of funds, which include chequable deposits, time deposits, advances from the Bank of Canada, and borrowings from other banks and corporations. The bank's assets are its uses of funds, which include cash reserves, cash items in process of collection, deposits at other banks, securities, loans, and other assets (mostly physical capital).
2. Banks make profits through the process of asset transformation: They borrow short (accept deposits) and lend long (make loans). When a bank takes in additional deposits, it gains an equal amount of reserves; when it pays out deposits, it loses an equal amount of reserves.
3. Although more liquid assets tend to earn lower returns, banks still desire to hold them. Specifically, banks hold excess and secondary reserves because they provide insurance against the costs of a deposit outflow. Banks manage their assets to maximize profits by seeking the highest returns possible on loans and securities while at the same time trying to lower risk and making adequate provisions for liquidity. Although liability management was once a staid affair, large (money centre) banks now actively seek out sources of funds by issuing liabilities such as negotiable CDs or by actively borrowing from other banks and corporations. Banks manage the amount of capital they hold to prevent bank failure and to meet bank capital requirements set by the regulatory authorities. However, they do not want to hold too much capital because by so doing they will lower the returns to equity holders.
4. Off-balance-sheet activities consist of trading financial instruments and generating income from fees and loan sales, all of which affect bank profits but are not visible on bank balance sheets. Because these off-balance-sheet activities expose banks to

increased risk, bank management must pay particular attention to risk assessment procedures and internal controls to restrict employees from taking on too much risk.

5. A bank's net operating income equals operating income minus operating expenses. Adding or subtracting net extraordinary items to net operating income and then subtracting taxes yields net income (profits after taxes). Additional measures of bank performance include the return on assets *(ROA)*, the return on equity *(ROE)*, and the net interest margin *(NIM)*.
6. A change in the economic environment will stimulate financial institutions to search for financial innovations that are likely to be profitable. Changes in demand conditions, especially the rise in interest-rate risk, have stimulated a search for profits that has resulted in financial innovations such as adjustable-rate mortgages, while changes in supply conditions because of advances in computer technology have led to financial innovations such as bank credit cards and electronic banking facilities. Regulation leads to financial innovation at banks by encouraging loophole mining. Starting in the late 1960s, for example, higher interest rates (resulting from higher inflation) encouraged financial innovations including Eurodollars, bank commercial paper, and overnight repos.

KEY TERMS

asset management, *p. 383*
automated banking machine (ABM) *p. 400*
automated teller machine (ATM) *p. 399*
balance sheet, *p. 375*
bank rate, *p. 385*
banker's risk, *p. 379*
Big Eight, *p. 395*
capital adequacy management, *p. 383*
cash reserves, *p. 379*
credit risk, *p. 383*
deposit outflows, *p. 383*
deposit rate ceiling, *p. 403*
desired reserve ratio, *p. 379*
desired reserves (desired excess reserves), *p. 379*
disintermediation, *p. 403*
e-cash, *p. 401*
electronic money (e-money), *p. 401*
equity multiplier *(EM)*, *p. 389*
financial engineering, *p. 397*
interbank deposits, *p. 379*
interest-rate risk, *p. 383*
items in transit (bank float), *p. 379*
liability management, *p. 383*
liquidity management, *p. 383*
loan commitment, *p. 391*
loan sale, *p. 391*
money centre banks, *p. 387*
net interest margin (NIM), *p. 396*
note issuance facilities (NIFs), *p. 392*
off-balance-sheet activities, *p. 391*
operating expenses, *p. 394*
operating income, *p. 394*
overdraft loans (advances), *p. 377*
Regulation Q, *p. 403*
reserves (total cash reserves), *p. 379*
return on assets (ROA), *p. 388*
return on equity (ROE), *p. 388*
revolving underwriting facilities (RUFs), *p. 392*
settlement balances, *p. 378*
short sale, *p. 378*
smart card, *p. 401*
vault cash, *p. 379*
virtual bank, *p. 400*

QUESTIONS AND PROBLEMS

1. Why might a bank be willing to borrow funds from other banks at a higher rate than it can borrow from the Bank of Canada?

*2. Rank the following bank assets from most to least liquid:
 a. Commercial loans
 b. Securities
 c. Reserves
 d. Physical capital

3. Using the T-accounts of the First Bank and the Second Bank, describe what happens when Jane Bahoti writes a $50 cheque on her account at the First Bank to pay her friend Joe Green, who in turn deposits the cheque into his account at the Second Bank.

*4. What happens to reserves at the First Bank if one person withdraws $1000 cash and another person deposits $500 cash? Use T-accounts to explain your answer.

5. The bank you own has the following balance sheet:

Assets		Liabilities	
Reserves	$75 million	Deposits	$500 million
Loans	$525 million	Bank capital	$100 million

If the bank suffers a deposit outflow of $50 million with a desired reserve ratio on deposits of 10%, what actions must you take to make sure that your bank meets its reserve requirements?

***6.** If a deposit outflow of $50 million occurs, which balance sheet would a bank rather have initially, the balance sheet in Problem 5 or the following balance sheet? Why?

Assets		Liabilities	
Reserves	$100 million	Deposits	$500 million
Securities	$500 million	Bank capital	$100 million

7. If the president of a bank told you that the bank was so well run that it has never had to call in loans, sell securities, or borrow as a result of a deposit outflow, would you be willing to buy stock in that bank? Why or why not?

***8.** If the bank you own has no excess reserves and a sound customer comes in asking for a loan, should you automatically turn the customer down, explaining that you don't have any excess reserves to loan out? Why or why not? What options are available for you to provide the funds your customer needs?

9. Why has the development of overnight loan markets made it more likely that banks will hold fewer excess reserves?

***10.** If you are a banker and expect interest rates to rise in the future, would you want to make short-term or long-term loans?

11. "Bank managers should always seek the highest return possible on their assets." Is this statement true, false, or uncertain? Explain your answer.

***12.** "Banking has become a more dynamic industry because of more active liability management." Is this statement true, false, or uncertain? Explain your answer.

13. Why has noninterest income been growing as a source of bank operating income?

***14.** Which components of operating expenses experience the greatest fluctuations? Why?

15. Why do equity holders care more about *ROE* than about *ROA*?

***16.** What does the net interest margin measure, and why is it important to bank managers?

17. If a bank doubles the amount of its capital and *ROA* stays constant, what will happen to *ROE*?

***18.** If a bank finds that its *ROE* is too low because it has too much bank capital, what can it do to raise its *ROE*?

19. What are the benefits and costs for a bank when it decides to increase the amount of its bank capital?

***20.** If a bank is falling short of meeting its capital requirements by $1 million, what three things can it do to rectify the situation?

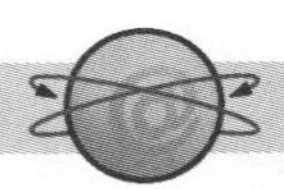

WEB EXERCISES

The Banking Firm and Bank Management

1. Table 1 on page 376 reports the balance sheet of all commercial banks based on aggregate data found in the OSFI Website. Compare this table with the balance sheet reported by the Bank of Montreal found at the same Website. Does the Bank of Montreal have more or less of its portfolio in loans than the average bank? What types of loans does it hold the most of?
2. It is relatively easy to find up-to-date information on banks because of their extensive reporting requirements. Go to http://www.cba.ca. Sponsored by the Canadian Bankers Association, this site offers summary data on banks. Go to "Bank Financial Results-Historical."
   a. Have banks' return on assets been increasing or decreasing over the last few years?
   b. Has the core capital been increasing, and how does it compare with the capital ratio reported in Table 1 in the text?
   c. How many institutions are currently reporting to the Canadian Deposit Insurance Corporation?

Chapter 16

Commercial Banking Industry: Structure and Competition

Preview

The operations of individual banks (how they acquire, use, and manage funds to make a profit) are roughly similar throughout the world. In all countries, banks are financial intermediaries in the business of earning profits. When you consider the structure and operation of the banking industry as a whole, however, Canada has a comparatively concentrated banking industry and small financial institutions. Unlike the United States, for example, which has more than 8100 commercial banks, 1200 savings and loan associations, 400 mutual savings banks, and 12 000 credit unions, Canada has six large commercial banks that dominate the banking industry.[1]

Is less better? Does it mean that the Canadian banking system is more stable and competitive and therefore more economically efficient and sound than banking systems in other countries? What in the Canadian economic and political system explains this small number of banking institutions? In this chapter we try to answer these questions by examining the historical trends in the banking industry and its overall structure.

We start by examining the commercial banking industry in detail and then in the next chapter go on to look at the near banking industry, which includes trust and mortgage loan companies and credit unions and *caisses populaires*. We spend more time on commercial banks because they are by far the largest depository institutions, accounting for more than two-thirds of the deposits in the banking system. In addition to looking at our domestic banking system, we also examine forces behind the growth in international banking to see how it has affected us in Canada. Finally, we examine how financial innovation has increased the competitive environment for the banking industry and is causing fundamental changes in it.

---

[1]Commercial banks in Canada are also called **chartered banks**, because they used to be established only by charter granted either in a special act of the federal Parliament or by the minister of finance. Today, however, banks are established under the authority of the Bank Act, rather than through obtaining a special charter from Parliament. In particular, approval for a new bank must be obtained from the minister of finance, but the establishment of the bank is not independent of the terms specified in the Bank Act.

HISTORICAL DEVELOPMENT OF THE CANADIAN BANKING SYSTEM

The modern Canadian banking industry began with the creation of the Bank of Montreal in 1817, by nine merchants in Montreal. Initially, the Bank of Montreal was without statutory authority, but a charter was approved by the legislature of Lower Canada and confirmed by royal assent in 1822. Meanwhile, other banks opened for business, and the Canadian banking industry was off and running; the Bank of New Brunswick received royal assent in 1820 and the Chartered Bank of Upper Canada in York (Toronto) in 1821. (As a study aid, Figure 1 provides a time line of the most important dates in the history of Canadian commercial banking before World War II.)

All these banks were authorized to issue notes (redeemable in specie, essentially British or American gold or silver coins, on demand), receive deposits, and lend for commercial purposes only; no bank was allowed to lend funds on mortgages, land, or real property. There were, however, some differences among the charters of these banks. For example, the terms of the charter of the Bank of New Brunswick followed the banking tradition of New England. The charter of the Bank of Montreal almost duplicated the terms governing the Bank of the United States (see Box 1), which had elements of both a private and a **central bank**, a government institution that has responsibility for the amount of money and credit supplied in the economy as a whole. Also, the Bank of New Brunswick had to submit regular annual statements to the government and was not allowed to open branches whereas the Bank of Montreal had to provide statements only on request and was allowed to open branches in any part of Upper or Lower Canada.

Information about the Bank of Montreal can be found at www.bankofmontreal.com

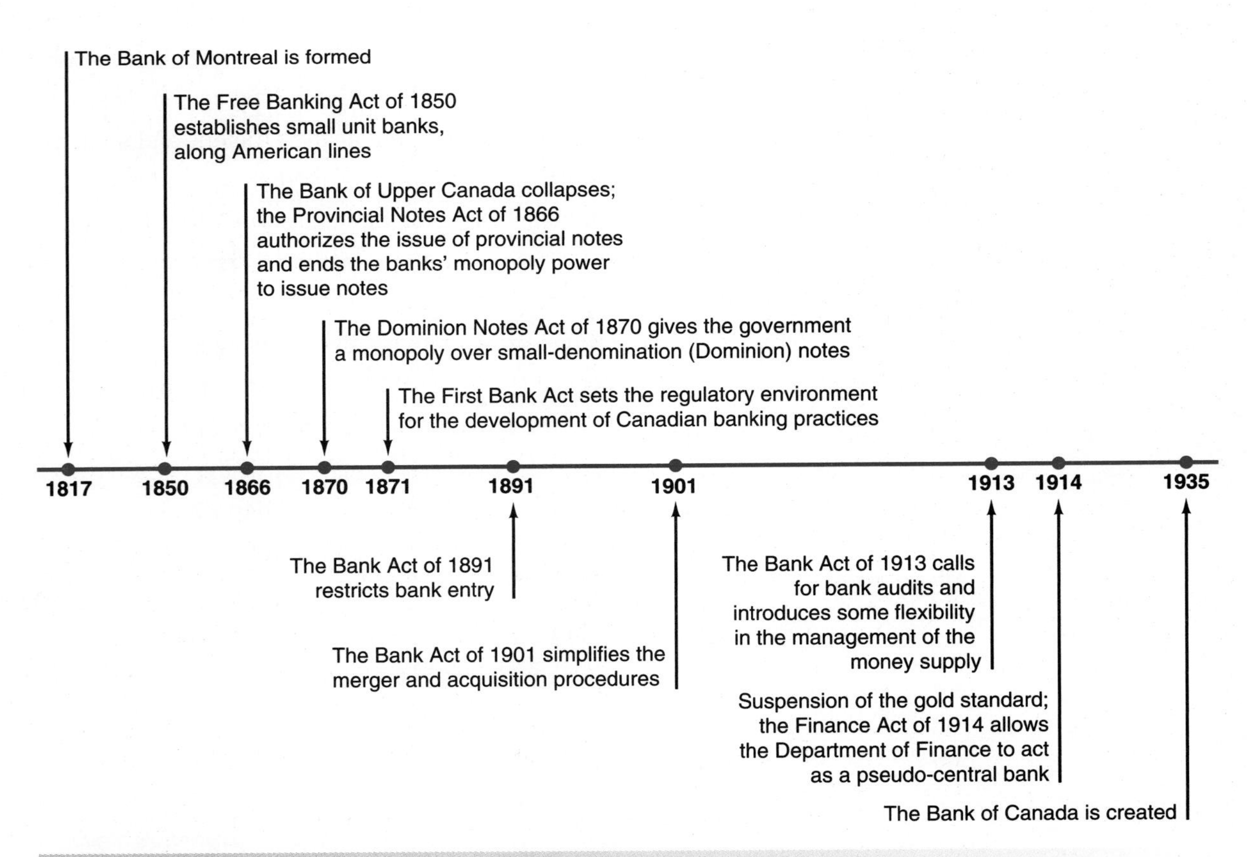

FIGURE 1 Time Line of the Early History of Commercial Banking in Canada

BOX 1

The Dual Banking System in the United States

The banking industry in the United States began when the Bank of North America was chartered in Philadelphia in 1782. A major controversy involving the U.S. banking industry in its early years was whether the federal government or the states should charter banks. The Federalists, particularly Alexander Hamilton, advocated greater centralized control of banking and federal chartering of banks. Their efforts led to the creation in 1791 of the Bank of the United States.

Until 1863, all commercial banks in the United States were chartered by the banking commission of the state in which they operated. No national currency existed, and banks obtained funds primarily by issuing banknotes. Because banking regulations were extremely lax in many states, banks regularly failed due to fraud or lack of sufficient bank capital; their banknotes became worthless.

To eliminate the abuses of the state-chartered banks (called **state banks**), the National Bank Act of 1863 (and subsequent amendments to it) created a new banking system of federally chartered banks (called **national banks**). This legislation was originally intended to dry up sources of funds to state banks by imposing a prohibitive tax on their banknotes while leaving the banknotes of the federally chartered banks untaxed. The state banks cleverly escaped extinction by acquiring funds through deposits. As a result, today the United States has a **dual banking system** in which banks supervised by the federal government and banks supervised by the states operate side by side.

The Free Banking Experiment

Until 1850, no national currency existed in Canada, and banks obtained funds primarily by issuing *banknotes* (currency circulated by the banks that could be redeemed for gold). Although no banks failed, banking regulations were extremely lax, and banks regularly experienced substantial declines in bank capital due to business failures; their banknotes tended to become scarce. The government tried various schemes to guarantee the provision of stable money, including the issuing of its own notes, but it was significantly influenced by the concept of **free banking**, implemented in New York in 1837. This system, as the name suggests, permitted the organization of a bank by any group that met certain established criteria concerning the amount of equity capital and maintenance of reserves.

The Free Banking Act was passed in Canada in 1850, with the purpose of facilitating the entry of small unit banks along American lines. It allowed the establishment of a bank, without a legislative charter, by any group that met the lax requirements set out in the free banking legislation. Under this legislation, the minimum amount of net worth to organize a bank was $100 000, branching was not allowed, and although the banknotes of the free banks were untaxed, the amount of note issue was limited to the amount of government debt held by the banks. The move to free banking was a step in the right direction, but Canada's experience with free banking was a failure. It did not lead to the establishment of a large number of new banks; only five new banks were established, two of which soon failed, and the other three converted to legislative charters.

The restriction on branching and the issue of banknotes based on government debt, rather than on commercial loans, were blamed for the failure of Canada's free banking experiment. The most important factor, however, was the fact that the option of a legislative charter was still available, unlike the situation in the United States where the provision of a legislative charter was simultaneously abolished in those states where free banking was established. In Canada, free banking with its restrictive provisions, particularly the restriction on branches and the less liberal provision for note issue, proved to be less profitable than banking under legislative charters.

In 1850, there were 15 chartered banks in Canada; 8 in Central Canada and 7 in what was to become Atlantic Canada. From 1850 until Confederation in 1867, and except for a short period after 1857, the Canadian provinces experienced an economic expansion and 30 new banks were established. However, 11 of these failed or closed their doors for other reasons, leaving 34 chartered banks with a total of 127 branches at the end of 1867.

The Provincial Notes Act, 1866

In the years before Confederation, governments were anxious about the commercial banks' control of the note issue. They believed that the best way to protect the public from some of the consequences of bank failures would be to separate the currency of the country from the banking interests. In 1860, Alexander Galt, finance minister of the Province of Canada, proposed the substitution of a government-issued paper currency for banknotes. His proposal, however, was defeated by his critics, especially the chartered banks, for obvious reasons; the substitution of interest-free government debt for interest-free bank debt would have directly reduced their profits.

In the midst of a minor financial crisis in 1866, with the collapse of the Bank of Upper Canada (Canada's first chartered bank failure), the proponents of government-issued paper money finally achieved their objective with the enactment of the Provincial Notes Act. The Act authorized the issue of provincial notes, which because of their legal reserve status could be substituted for specie. With the cooperation of the Bank of Montreal, which had become the government's fiscal agent in 1864 by replacing the Bank of Upper Canada, the banks began to hold the new currency, thereby surrendering their power to issue notes.

The Dominion Notes Act, 1870

Canada was created by the British North America Act in 1867. The Act granted the new federal government of Canada exclusive jurisdiction over all matters pertaining to currency and banking, and the first problem to be tackled was the issue of paper money. With the failure in 1867 of the Chartered Bank of Canada (the second chartered bank failure in Canadian history), the Dominion Notes Act was passed in 1870. The Act confirmed the rights of banks to issue banknotes on their own credit, but restricted to large-denomination (over $5) notes, thereby giving the government a monopoly over small-denomination ($1 and $2) notes, the Dominion notes.

Although the Dominion Notes Act of 1870 did not set any reserve requirements, it required banks to hold at least half of their reserves in Dominion notes, thereby giving the government a share of the profits from the issuance of money, which is called **seigniorage**. The Dominion notes themselves were fractionally backed by gold, and in this sense the Dominion Notes Act of 1870 confirmed that Canada would operate under the **gold standard**, meaning that its currency was convertible directly into gold.

Canada operated under the gold standard, keeping its currency backed by and convertible into gold, until World War I. During the years 1870 to 1935, Dominion notes increased in importance, but they never accounted for a major fraction of currency in circulation. They were superseded, together with the banknotes, by Bank of Canada notes, soon after the creation of the Bank of Canada (Canada's central bank) in 1935.

The First Bank Act, 1871

The first Bank Act came into effect in 1871. It was to be revised every 10 years, in light of experience and changing conditions; this "sunset" clause has effectively ensured that governments over the years paid periodic attention to banking reform. The Bank Act set the regulatory environment for Canadian chartered banks and for the future development of Canadian banking practices.

The Act continued the legislative chartering of banks, with each charter running for a 10-year period, then to be reviewed and renewed. New banks had to meet minimum capital requirements: $100 000 paid up before they opened for business against a total of $500 000. The banks' note issue continued to be restricted to large-denomination (over $5) notes and limited to the amount of their paid-up capital plus reserves. There were no reserve requirements, but one-third of a bank's cash reserves was required to be in the form of Dominion notes.

The Act continued the prohibition against mortgage lending and real estate loans, but it reinforced the commercial nature of banking, by allowing banks to make loans on the security of most kinds of merchandise. Also, for the greater security of the public, bank shareholders were liable for double the amount of their subscription. Finally, each bank was required to submit a detailed statement to the government each month, but there was no provision for government inspection or audit.

Revisions of the Bank Act, 1881–1913

A depression followed Confederation and lasted from 1873–1879. During the depression years, the banks were hard hit and 13 bank failures (4 in 1878, 5 in 1887, and another 4 in 1890) wiped out the savings of many noteholders. To prevent future losses from such failures, the early decennial revisions of the Bank Act, in 1881, 1891, 1901, and 1913 (postponed since 1911), were intended to provide better protection for the holders of banknotes, but the Act was not substantially changed.

In particular, in the Bank Act revision of 1891, the capital requirement was increased to $250 000 paid-up, thereby restricting entry into the industry. The proportion of Dominion notes in bank cash reserves was increased to 40%, and the notes of a failed bank were made a first charge against its assets in the event of liquidation. Moreover, in the Bank Act revision of 1891, a Bank Circulation Redemption Fund was created, each bank contributing an amount equal to 5% of its average note circulation, to insure noteholders against loss.

Between mid-1890 and the outbreak of World War I, the Canadian economy experienced a phenomenal economic expansion. Although bank entry was restrained (due to the increase in capital requirements in the Bank Act of 1891), the Bank Act revision of 1901 simplified the merger and acquisition procedures, by requiring only approval of Cabinet; previously a special Act of Parliament was required for all mergers. As a result of these legislative changes, 13 mergers took place before the end of 1914, relative to only 6 in the previous 33 years, and the number of banks declined from 41 in 1890 to 22 in 1914. Over the same period, however, the number of bank branches increased from 426 to more than 3000.

Another important legislative change occurred in the 1913 revision of the Bank Act. The Act called for a *bank audit*; annual, independent verification of the financial statements of the banks, with the results distributed to the shareholders and the minister of finance. The objective was to limit adverse selection and moral hazard problems that had increased over the years and been found to be the cause of a number of bank failures, particularly the failure of the Farmers Bank in 1910.

An additional noteworthy change was the excess circulation provision that introduced some flexibility in the management of the money supply. The economic expansion in the period after mid-1890 caused banknote issues to reach the ceiling that the Bank Act of 1871 had fixed at the amount of paid-up capital plus reserves. The banks did not increase their capital (and thus their note-issuing capacity), producing a shortage of currency. In order to achieve expansion in the money supply with the growth of economic activity, the Bank Act of 1913 allowed for the issuing of banknotes in excess of a bank's paid-up capital plus reserves.

The Finance Act, 1914

At the end of July 1914, less than a year after the revision of the Bank Act in 1913, World War I looked more and more inescapable. Canada's established banking legislation appeared to be inadequate and the immediate problem was to preserve the stability and liquidity of the financial system. Panic had taken hold, with depositors converting their money into gold for hoarding, and the banks and the government being concerned about their ability to convert money into gold on demand, since their gold reserves were a small fraction of their combined monetary liabilities. In light of these developments, on August 3, 1914, the government suspended the convertibility of Dominion notes and banknotes into gold, thereby ending the gold standard that had emerged over 40 years earlier in 1870. The gold standard was re-established in 1926 and suspended again in 1929, when the Great Depression hit the world.

A major legislative change, following the suspension of the gold standard, was the Finance Act of 1914. Patterned on the episode of 1907, during which banks could obtain cash reserves from the Department of Finance to prevent bank runs (which were triggered by bank failures in the United States), the Finance Act allowed the Department of Finance to act as a **lender of last resort**. That is, to provide Dominion notes to banks (on the pledge of approved securities) when no one else would, thereby preventing bank and financial panics. The Finance Act foreshadowed the increased flexibility in the management of the money supply that was provided by the Bank of Canada in 1935.

The Government of Canada's Department of Finance Website is www.fin.gc.ca.

STRUCTURE OF THE CANADIAN COMMERCIAL BANKING INDUSTRY

As of June 2000, there were 49 commercial banks in Canada (11 domestic and 38 foreign) with about 8400 branches and more than 222 000 employees (see Figure 2). As Table 1 indicates, however, the six largest commercial banks, the Royal Bank of Canada, Canadian Imperial Bank of Commerce (CIBC), Bank of Montreal, Bank of Nova Scotia, TD Canada Trust, and the National Bank of Canada, together hold more than 92% of the assets in the industry. These banks are often called the **Big Six**.

Schedule I, Schedule II, and Schedule III Banks

The Websites of the Big Six are www.cibc.com, www.tdcanadatrust.com, www.royalbank.com, www.bnc.ca, www.scotiabank.com, and www.bankofmontreal.com

The Big Six, together with the Laurentian Bank of Canada and the Canadian Western Bank, are Canada's **Schedule I** banks. Of the remaining 41 banks, 39 are **Schedule II** banks; they include three domestic banks, Citizen Bank (owned by VanCity Savings), First Nations Bank (owned by TD Canada Trust), and Manulife Bank (owned by Manulife Insurance), and 36 subsidiaries (i.e., separate Canadian legal entities) of foreign banks.

Before 1981, foreign banks operated in Canada as capital corporations, incorporated under provincial companies acts. However, they were not allowed to take deposits, to branch, or to call themselves banks. What they mostly did was to book banking business for their own countries' firms; for example, the Bank of Tokyo in Toronto would accept deposits in Canada to be booked in Tokyo. It was for this reason that Canadian regulatory authorities allowed foreign banks to use the word "bank" in their business name, despite the absence of a charter, because they thought the word referred to what they did abroad and not to what they did in Canada. The 1981 revisions to the Bank Act, however, focused on introducing more

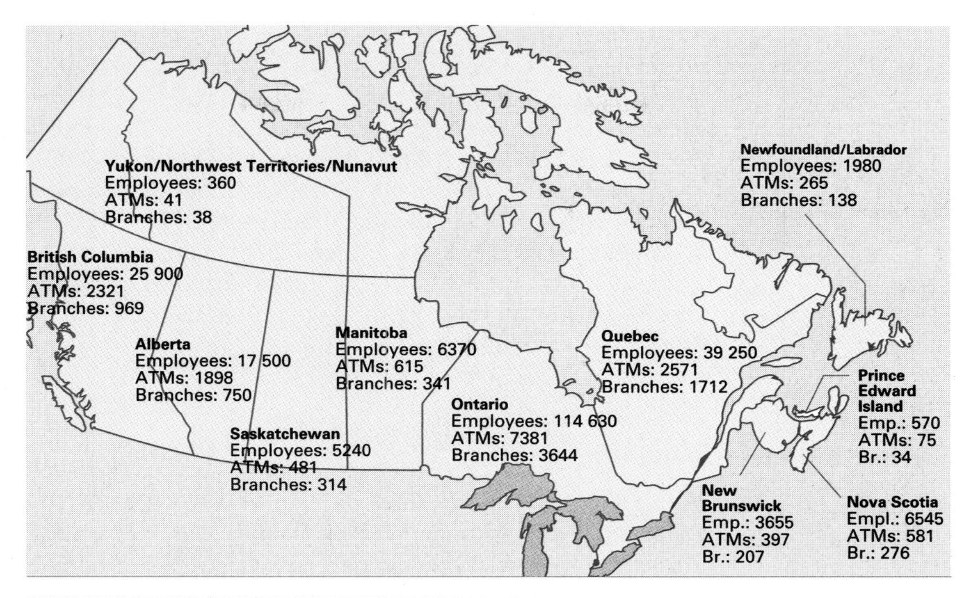

FIGURE 2 Banking Coast to Coast

Source: Canadian Bankers Association website: http://www.cba.ca

TABLE 1 Canadian Banks as of January 31, 2002

Bank	Date of Establishment	Assets (in millions)	Percent (%) of Bank Assets
The Big Six			
Royal Bank of Canada	1869	354 894.0	20.95
Canadian Imperial Bank of Commerce	1961	291 294.3	17.20
Bank of Montreal	1822	239 440.5	14.14
The Bank of Nova Scotia	1832	294 508.0	17.39
The Toronto Dominion Bank	1955	310 427.7	18.33
National Bank of Canada	1980	75 766.7	4.47
Big Six Subtotal		1 566 331.2	92.47
Laurentian Bank of Canada	1987	18 013.0	1.06
Canadian Western Bank	1988	3 452.6	0.20
Eight Domestic Banks Subtotal		1 587 796.8	93.74
Other Banks			
Domestic Banks		2 259.0	0.13
Foreign Banks		103 759.0	6.13
Total		1 693 814.8	100.00

Source: Canadian Bankers Association Website: http:/www.cba.ca

competition into the Canadian financial services industry by making a distinction between Schedule I and Schedule II banks.

Schedule I and Schedule II banks have identical powers; the only difference between them being the ownership structure permitted. In particular, according to current ownership policy, all Schedule I banks must be widely held: no individual can own more than 10% of any class of shares. Schedule II banks, however, are exceptions to this rule if small. In fact, there are three categories of exception. The first exception is that widely held foreign banks can own 100% of a Canadian bank subsidiary. The second exception is that a Schedule II bank may have a significant shareholder (more than 10%) for up to 10 years after establishment, as a transition measure to becoming a Schedule I bank. The third exception, introduced in the 1991 revision of the Bank Act, is that any widely held and regulated Canadian financial institution, other than a bank, may own 100% of a bank. In the case of big Schedule II banks (those with more than $5 billion in equity capital), the same widely held ownership rule that applies to Schedule I banks applies.

With the passage of Bill C-67 in June 1999, a foreign bank may enter the Canadian banking industry as either a Schedule II or a **Schedule III** bank. The difference between Schedule II and Schedule III banks is that a Schedule II bank is a Canadian subsidiary of a foreign bank whereas a Schedule III bank is a foreign bank allowed to branch directly into Canada, under certain restrictions (to be discussed later in the chapter). As of June 2000, there were only two Schedule III banks in Canada, but recently the OSFI has approved branching for a large number of foreign banks.

Go to www.vancity.com and www.manulifebank.com for more details about VanCity Savings or Manulife Bank.

Competition and Technology

Although Canada has a small number of banks relative to other countries, Canadians enjoy one of the most dynamic and competitive financial services industry. Besides commercial banks, there are more than 3000 financial institutions providing financial services. These include trust and mortgage loan companies, credit unions and *caisses populaires*, government savings institutions, insurance companies, pension funds, mutual funds, and investment dealers.

New technology and the Internet have also helped in the development of a more competitive and innovative banking system in Canada. They have enabled new entrants to enter the Canadian financial services market and provide increased competition to the Big Six. For example, ING Canada, a new Canadian banking subsidiary of a major Netherlands banking and insurance conglomerate, and Citizen Bank, a subsidiary of Vancouver City Savings Credit Union, are virtual banks offering an array of banking services on the Internet. Moreover, U.S. credit card banks, such as MBNA and Capital One Financial Corporation, are now offering specialized credit card products in Canada, and Wells Fargo, one of the largest banks in the United States, provides loans to Canadian small businesses from the United States.

The Websites of the new entrants to the Canadian financial services market listed in this section can be found at www.ing.com, www.mbna.com, www.wellsfargo.com, and www.capitalone.com

COMPETITION ACROSS ALL FOUR PILLARS

Another important feature of the structure of the banking industry in Canada until recently was the separation of the banking and other financial services industries—such as securities, insurance, and real estate. Regulations enforced the separation of institutions according to their core financial services, and only four distinct types of financial services were identified: banking, brokerage, trusts, and insurance. This approach to regulation by institution (versus regulation by function) has been known as the **four-pillar approach**. The separation of the four pillars prohibited commercial banks from engaging in insurance and real estate activities. In turn, it prevented investment banks and insurance companies from engaging in commercial banking activities and thus protected banks from competition.

Convergence

In recent years, however, financial markets have opened up and Canada's traditional four-pillar system has changed. Despite the prohibitions in the legislation, the pursuit of profits and financial innovation stimulated both banks and other financial institutions to bypass the intent of the legislation and encroach on each other's traditional territory. For example, credit unions long offered insurance to their members and brokerage firms engaged in the traditional banking business of issuing deposit instruments with the development of money market mutual funds and cash management accounts.

Not surprisingly, the regulatory barriers between banking and other financial services markets have been coming down, in response to these forces. Before the 1950s, for example, legislation allowed commercial banks to make loans for commercial purposes only and prohibited them from making residential mortgage loans. It was only after the 1967 revision of the Bank Act that banks were allowed to make conventional residential mortgage loans, thereby directly competing with trust and mortgage loan companies and credit unions and *caisses populaires*, to be discussed in detail in Chapter 17.

In the 1980s, the Bank Act was amended to allow Canadian and foreign financial institutions to own up to 100% of securities firms. Moreover, the 1990s revisions to the Bank Act allowed cross-ownership via subsidiaries between financial institutions. Commercial banks, for example, can either buy independent investment dealers or expand on their own into capital raising, brokerage, and other securities activities. As a result, the Big Six now dominate the investment banking industry through their investment brokerage subsidiaries; they hold a 70% share in the business. Investment banking is discussed in Chapter 21.

As a result of these recent legislative changes, Canada's traditional four pillars of financial services—banking, brokerage, trusts, and insurance—have now converged into a single financial services marketplace. Similar trends are also appearing in the United States as old rules and laws are overturned. With the Citicorp-Travelers merger in 1998 (see Box 2), the Gramm-Leach-Bliley Financial Services Modernization Act of 1999 overturned the Glass-Steagall separation of the banking and securities industries and allows securities firms and insurance companies to purchase banks and banks to underwrite insurance and securities and engage in real estate activities.

Implications for Financial Consolidation

Go to www.citibank.com, www.bankofamerica.com, and www.salomonsmithbarney.com, for more information about these groups.

As we have seen, recent legislation has stimulated consolidation of the banking industry. The financial consolidation process will be even further speeded up in the future, because the way is now open to consolidation in terms not only of the number of banking institutions, but also across financial service activities. Mergers of banks with other financial service firms like that of Citicorp and Travelers in the United States should become increasingly common, and more

BOX 2

The Citicorp-Travelers Merger

On April 6, 1998, the financial world was rocked by the announcement of what was expected to be the largest corporate merger ever, between Citicorp, the second-largest bank in the United States, and the Travelers Group, which was in the insurance business and also owned the third-largest securities firm in the country, Salomon Smith Barney. (Because of a decline in the value of Citicorp by the time the merger actually took place, it turned out only to be the second-largest corporate merger in history; the Bank of America and NationsBank merger around the same time edged it out slightly.) The merged bank holding company, called Citigroup, would be one of the largest financial services firms in the world, with 100 million customers in 100 countries, more than 150 000 employees, and $700 billion in assets.

The merger was remarkable not only for its size but also because under the Glass-Steagall Act of 1933 and the Bank Holding Company Act of 1956, the combination of these two corporations would be illegal. However, the marriage was approved by the Federal Reserve in September 1998 and was consummated in early October. As part of the approval process, the Federal Reserve produced a waiver giving Citigroup two to five years to sell off prohibited businesses like insurance underwriting. However, Citicorp and Travelers were betting that by the time the five-year period was up, Congress would pass legislation eliminating the restrictions imposed by Glass-Steagall and the Bank Holding Company Act, thereby enabling Citigroup to engage in all financial service activities. The Citigroup and Travelers bet was a good one—Congress finally did pass the Gramm-Leach-Bliley Act overturning Glass-Steagall in 1999.

mega-mergers are likely to be on the way. The move to larger banking organizations is also being driven by advances in computer technology (see Box 3), and it also means that there will be some increase in efficiency because of economies of scale. Banking institutions will become not only larger, but increasingly complex organizations, engaging in the full gamut of financial service activities.

Separation of Banking and Other Financial Services Industries Throughout the World

Not many other countries in the aftermath of the Great Depression followed the lead of Canada and the United States in separating the banking and other financial services industries. In fact, in the past this separation was the most prominent difference between banking regulation in Canada and the United States, and in other countries. Around the world there are three basic frameworks for the banking and securities industries.

The first framework is *universal banking*, which exists in Germany, the Netherlands, and Switzerland. It provides no separation at all between the banking and securities industries. In a universal banking system, commercial banks provide a full range of banking, securities, real estate, and insurance services, all within a single legal entity. Banks are allowed to own sizable equity shares in commercial firms, and often they do.

The British-style universal banking system, the second framework, is found in the United Kingdom and countries with close ties to it, such as Australia, Canada, and now the United States. The British-style universal bank engages in securities underwriting, but it differs from the German-style universal bank in three ways: Separate legal subsidiaries are more common, bank equity holdings of commercial firms are less common, and combinations of banking and insurance firms are less common.

The third framework features some legal separation of the banking and other financial services industries, as in Japan. A major difference between British-style and Japanese banking systems is that Japanese banks are allowed to hold substantial equity stakes in commercial firms, whereas British-style universal banks cannot. Although the banking and securities industries are legally separated in Japan under Section 65 of the Japanese Securities Act, commercial banks are increasingly being allowed to engage in securities activities and are thus becoming more like British-style universal banks.

BOX 3: E-FINANCE

Technology and Bank Consolidation

The advent of the Web and improved computer technology is another factor driving bank consolidation. To achieve low costs, huge investments in technology are necessary, requiring that a business line be of very large scale. This has been particularly true in the credit card business in recent years. Huge technology investments have been made to provide customers with convenient websites and to develop better systems to handle processing and risk analysis for both credit and fraud risk. The result has been substantial consolidation: As recently as 1995, the top five banking institutions issuing credit cards held less than 40% of total credit card debt, while today this number is above 60%.

Technology has also led to increasing consolidation of the bank custody business. Banks hold the actual certificate for investors when they purchase a stock or bond and provide data on the value of these securities and how much risk an investor is facing. Because this business is also computer intensive, it also requires very large scale investments in computer technology in order for the bank to offer these services at competitive rates. The percentage of assets at the top 10 custody banks has therefore risen from 40% in 1990 to more than 90% today.

The increasing importance of e-finance, in which the computer is becoming more important in delivering financial services, is leading to tremendous changes in the structure of the banking industry. Although banks are more than willing to offer a full range of products to their customers, they no longer find it profitable to produce all of them. Instead, they are contracting out the business, which will lead to further consolidation of technology-intensive banking businesses in the future.

COMPARISON WITH THE UNITED STATES

The structure of the commercial banking industry in Canada, although similar to that in many other industrialized countries, is radically different from that in the United States. There are around 8100 commercial banks in the United States, whereas every other industrialized country in the world has well under 1000 commercial banks. Japan, for example, has fewer than 100 commercial banks—a mere fraction of the number of banks in the United States, even though its economy and population are half the size of the United States—and, as already noted, Canada has 49 commercial banks. Moreover, as Table 2 indicates, banks in the United States tend to be much smaller than banks in other countries; 21.6% of the commercial banks in the United States have less than $50 million in assets, and the 10 largest U.S. banks (listed in Table 3) together hold just 59.8% of the assets in the industry.

The presence of so many commercial banks in the United States reflects past regulations that restricted the ability of these financial institutions to open branches. The result was that many small banks stayed in existence because a large bank capable of driving them out of business was often restricted from opening a branch nearby. Indeed, it was often easier for a U.S. bank to open a branch in a foreign country than to open one in another state in the United States! In fact, most industries in the United States have far fewer firms than the commercial banking industry. For example, Microsoft dominates the computer software industry and General Motors, Ford, DaimlerChrysler, Toyota, and Honda dominate the automobile industry.

Go to www.microsoft.com, www.ford.com, or www.toyota.com for more details about the companies described here.

TABLE 2 Size Distribution of Insured U.S. Commercial Banks, June 30, 2001

Assets	Number of Banks	Share of Banks (%)	Share of Assets Held (%)
Less than $25 million	967	11.8	0.3
$25 million–$50 million	1 620	19.8	1.0
$50 million–$100 million	2 098	25.6	2.3
$100 million–$300 million	2 303	28.2	6.1
$300 million–$500 million	474	5.8	2.8
$500 million–$1 billion	324	4.0	3.5
$1 billion–$3 billion	220	2.7	5.8
$3 billion–$10 billion	93	1.1	8.3
$10 billion or more	79	1.0	69.9
Total	8 178	100.0	100.0

Source: http://www.fdic.gov/bank/statistical/statistics/0109/allstru.html

The U.S. FDIC gathers data about individual U.S. financial institutions and the banking industry that you can access at www.fdic.gov/bank.

TABLE 3 Ten Largest U.S. Banks, 2001

Bank	Assets (U.S. $ billions)	Share of All Commercial Bank Assets (%)
1. Citicorp, New York	902.20	14.2
2. Chase, New York	715.30	11.2
3. Bank of America, Charlotte, NC	642.20	10.1
4. Wachovia/First Union, Charlotte, NC	328.20	5.2
5. Wells Fargo, San Francisco	272.40	4.3
6. Bank One, Columbus, OH	269.30	4.2
7. FleetBoston Financial Corp., Boston, MA	219.20	3.4
8. Washington Mutual, Seattle, WA	188.60	3.0
9. U.S. Bancorp/Firstar, Minneapolis, MN	164.90	2.6
10. Sun Trust Bank, Atlanta, GA	103.50	1.6
Total	3 805.80	59.8

Source: http://www.onlinebankingreport.com/resources/100.html

Does the large number of banks in the commercial banking industry in the United States and the absence of a few dominant firms suggest that commercial banking is more competitive than other industries? Advocates of restrictive state branching regulations in the United States argued that regulations foster competition by keeping so many banks in business. But the existence of large numbers of banks in the United States should be seen as an indication of a *lack* of competition, *not* the presence of vigorous competition. Inefficient banks were able to remain in business because their customers could not find a conveniently located branch of another bank.

Response to Branching Restrictions in the United States

An important feature of the U.S. banking industry is that competition can be repressed by regulation but not completely quashed. The existence of restrictive regulation will stimulate banking institutions to go "loophole mining," coming up with financial innovations that get around these regulations in the banks' search for profits. Regulations restricting branching have stimulated similar economic forces and have promoted the development of three financial innovations: bank holding companies, nonbank banks, and automated teller machines.

Bank Holding Companies A holding company is a corporation that owns several different companies. This form of corporate ownership has important advantages for banks. First, it has allowed them to circumvent restrictive branching regulations, because the holding company can own a controlling interest in several banks even if branching is not permitted. Second, a bank holding company can engage in other activities related to banking, such as the provision of investment advice, data processing and transmission services, leasing, credit card services, and servicing of loans in other states. Finally, the holding company can issue commercial paper, allowing the bank to tap into nondeposit sources of funds.

Bank holding companies also have the advantage that many states would allow bank holding companies headquartered in other states to purchase banks in their state. In addition, starting in 1982, banks were permitted to purchase out-of-state banks that were failing. For example, bank holding companies headquartered in New York, Ohio, North Carolina, Michigan, and California gained entry into the Texas market by purchasing failing institutions in that state.

The growth of the bank holding companies in the United States has been dramatic over the past three decades. Today bank holding companies own almost all large banks, and more than 90% of all commercial bank deposits are held in banks owned by holding companies.

Nonbank Banks Another way banks could avoid branching restrictions was through a loophole in the Bank Holding Act of 1956, which defined a bank as a financial institution that accepts deposits *and* makes loans. Once bank holding companies recognized this loophole, they realized that if they opened limited-service banks that either took deposits but did not make commercial loans or did not take deposits but made commercial loans, these so-called **nonbank banks** would not be subject to branching regulations. Thus, the bank holding companies discovered a way of branching across state lines. However, the Competitive Equality Act passed in 1987 placed a moratorium on new nonbank banks, thus closing this loophole.

Automated Teller Machines Another financial innovation that avoided the restrictions on branching is the electronic banking facility known as the automated teller machine (ATM). Banks realized that if they did not own or rent the ATM, but instead let it be owned by someone else and paid for each transaction with a fee, the ATM would probably not be considered a branch of the bank and thus would not be subject to branching regulations. This is exactly what the regulatory agencies and courts in most states in the United States concluded. Because they enable banks to widen their markets, a number of these shared facilities (such as Cirrus and NYCE) have been established nationwide. Furthermore, even when an ATM is owned by a bank, states typically have special provisions that allow wider establishment of ATMs than is permissible for traditional "brick and mortar" branches.

As we saw in Chapter 15, avoiding regulation was not the only reason for the development of the ATM. The advent of cheaper computer and telecommunications technology enabled banks to provide ATMs at low cost, making them a profitable innovation. This further illustrates that technological factors often combine with incentives such as the desire to avoid restrictive regulations like branching restrictions to produce financial innovations.

INTERNATIONAL BANKING

Canadian banks have a well-developed presence in the global financial services marketplace, which varies among the individual institutions. From its inception, for example, the Bank of Montreal found some of its best opportunities in international operations and was soon joined by the Canadian Imperial Bank of Commerce and the Bank of Nova Scotia. Currently, around 37% of the assets of the Big Six are employed in international operations (see Table 4 and Figure 3), generating 35% of their net income, which varies from 58% for the Bank of Montreal, to 49% for the Bank of Nova Scotia, to 28% for the Royal Bank of Canada. The spectacular growth in international banking can be explained by three factors.

First is the rapid growth in international trade and multinational (worldwide) corporations that has occurred in recent years. When Canadian firms operate abroad, they need banking services in foreign countries to help finance international trade, investment, and other activities. For example, they might need a loan in a foreign currency to operate a factory abroad. And when they sell goods abroad, they need to have a bank exchange the foreign currency they have received for

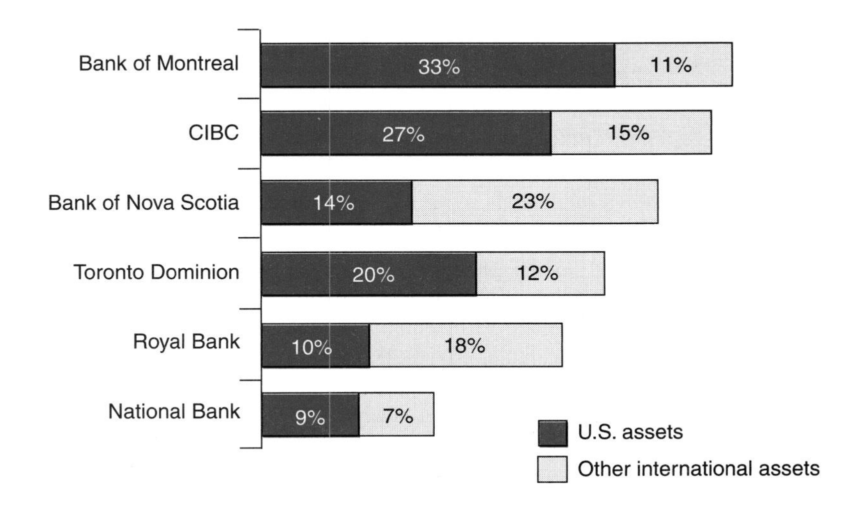

FIGURE 3 International Focus of the Big Six

Source: Mckinsey, *The Changing Landscape for Canadian Financial Services: New Forces, New Competitors, New Choices. Final Report for the Task Force on the Future of the Canadian Financial Services Sector* (Ottawa, September 1998), Exhibit 5-24.

TABLE 4 International Activity of the Big Six

Bank	Primary focus	International Assets (Cdn $ billions)	Percent of International Assets in Total Assets
Bank of Montreal	United States, Mexico	87.3	44%
CIBC	Unites States	99.4	42%
Bank of Nova Scotia	South America, Mexico	62.8	37%
Toronto Dominion	United States	51.9	32%
Royal Bank	Europe, Asia	60.1	28%
National Bank	No significant international presence	8.6	16%

Source: McKinsey, *The Changing Landscape for Canadian Financial Services: New Forces, New Competitors, New Choices. Final Report for the Task Force on the Future of the Canadian Financial Services Sector* (Ottawa, September 1998), Exhibits 5-24 and 2-12.

their goods into Canadian dollars. Although these firms could use foreign banks to provide them with these international banking services, many of them prefer to do business with the Canadian banks with which they have established long-term relationships and which understand Canadian business customs and practices. As international trade has grown, international banking has grown with it.

Second, Canadian banks have been able to earn substantial profits by being very active in global investment banking, in which they underwrite foreign securities. They also sell insurance abroad, and they derive substantial profits from these investment banking and insurance activities.

Third, Canadian banks have wanted to tap into the large pool of Eurocurrencies—currencies deposited in banks outside the home country. To understand the structure of Canadian banking overseas, let us first look at the Eurocurrencies market, an important source for international banking.

Eurocurrencies Market

The most important of the Eurocurrencies are Eurodollars, originated after World War II with U.S. dollar deposits in European banks. They were created when deposits in accounts in the United States were transferred to a bank outside the United States and were kept in the form of U. S. dollars. For example, if Rolls Royce PLC deposits a $1 million cheque, written on an account at an American bank, in its bank in London—specifying that the deposit be payable in U.S. dollars—$1 million in Eurodollars is created.[2] More than 90% of Eurodollar deposits are time deposits, more than half of them certificates of deposit with maturities of 30 days or more. The total amount of Eurodollars outstanding is US$2 trillion, making the Eurodollar market one of the most important financial markets in the world economy.

Although most offshore deposits are denominated in U.S. dollars, some are also denominated in other currencies. Collectively, these offshore deposits are referred to as Eurocurrencies. A Canadian dollar-denominated deposit held in London, for example, is called a Euro Canadian dollar, and a French franc-denominated deposit held in London is called a Eurofranc. Why would companies like Rolls Royce want to hold Eurocurrencies? First, some currencies are widely used in international trade, so Rolls Royce might want to hold deposits in these currencies to conduct its international transactions. Second, Eurocurrencies are "offshore" deposits—they are held in countries that will not subject them to regulations such as reserve requirements or restrictions (called *capital controls*) on taking the deposits outside the country.

[2]Note that the bank in London keeps the $1 million on deposits at the American bank, so the creation of Eurodollars has not caused a reduction in the amount of bank deposits in the United States.

The main centre of the Eurocurrencies market is London, a major international financial centre for hundreds of years. Eurocurrencies are also held outside Europe in locations that provide offshore status to these deposits—for example, Singapore, the Bahamas, and the Cayman Islands.

The minimum transaction in the Eurocurrencies market is typically $1 million, and banks hold approximately 75% of Eurocurrencies deposits. Plainly, you and I are unlikely to come into direct contact with Eurocurrencies. The Eurocurrencies market is, however, an important source of funds to Canadian banks. Rather than using an intermediary and borrowing all the deposits from foreign banks, Canadian banks decided that they could earn higher profits by opening their own branches abroad to attract these deposits. Consequently, the Eurocurrencies market has been an important stimulus to Canadian banking overseas.

Canadian Banking Overseas

Canadian banks have been present in international financial markets for more than 100 years, providing services to Canadians and multinational businesses. As Table 4 shows, the international presence of the Big Six varies among the individual institutions. In particular, the Bank of Montreal, the Canadian Imperial Bank of Commerce, and TD Canada Trust have significant presence in the United States, whereas the Bank of Nova Scotia has established a presence in South America, and the Royal Bank in Europe and Asia.

During the 1970s and early 1980s a large proportion of the banks' foreign lending was in **sovereign loans**; loans to foreign governments and their agencies in the less developed countries (LDCs), particularly Mexico, Brazil, Venezuela, Argentina, and Chile. Most of this activity in international lending was unregulated, with near disastrous consequences. One example is the international debt crisis, which had its origin in the oil price shocks of the 1970s. In particular, the 1973-1974 increase in the price of oil was a bonanza for some oil-exporting countries like Mexico, but a disaster for oil-importing countries like Brazil, which had to either cut their living standards or borrow massively abroad in order to pay their higher oil bills. At the time, real interest rates were very low (in fact negative) and the oil importers couldn't resist the temptation to borrow abroad.

At the same time the oil exporters were depositing huge sums in banks and as a result the banks were lending not only to the oil-importing countries but also to the oil-exporting countries, because the latter had large oil reserves and seemed like good credit risks. The banks underestimated the **indebtedness** of these countries—the total amount these countries had borrowed from banks—and, as a result, were severely punished in the early 1980s when the recession hit and real interest rates increased significantly. With Argentina, Brazil, Mexico, and Peru threatening to default on their loans, the banks had two choices: to reschedule their loans and make more loans to these countries (to enable them to pay the interest on the debt), or to declare these countries in default and acknowledge large losses on their balance sheets. The banks chose to make more loans, because in many cases the losses would have been large enough to destroy them.

Today, the LDC debt is no longer a significant threat to the international banking system, because of other arrangements as well. In recent years, for example, a variety of debt conversion schemes have been proposed to alleviate the debt service obligations of the major indebted LDCs. There are three main forms of debt conversion: **debt-debt swaps** (where banks holding the debt of one LDC exchange it for the debt of another LDC), **debt-currency swaps** (where the debt denominated in foreign currency is converted into domestic currency), and **debt-equity swaps** (where the debt is converted into the equity of public and private domestic enterprises). The main impetus of all these debt conversion schemes has been the recognition that the true value of the sovereign debt is well below its face value.

As a result of their lending experience in Latin America, the Big Six have withdrawn from certain countries and focused more of their international activities in the United States (see Figure 3 on page 421). Moreover, the international activities of Canadian banking organizations are now regulated, primarily by the Office of the Superintendent of Financial Institutions (OSFI), created in 1987 to succeed two separate regulatory bodies: the Inspector General of Banks and the Department of Insurance. In particular, in 1991, the OSFI asked the commercial banks to set up special reserves of 35% to 45% of their exposure to a number of LDCs.

Foreign Banks in Canada

The Website of HSBC Bank Canada is www.hsbc.ca.

The growth in international trade has not only encouraged Canadian banks to open offices overseas but has also encouraged foreign banks to establish offices in Canada. Foreign banks have been extremely successful in Canada. Over the past 20 years, since the 1981 revision to the Bank Act, globally prominent foreign banks have set up and expanded banking subsidiaries in Canada. Foreign banks are a highly fragmented group and as shown in Table 5 they currently hold about 12% of total Canadian bank assets, with the HSBC Bank Canada (the former Hongkong and Shanghai Banking Corp.) enjoying a national market share of 3.1%. It should be noted, however, that these institutions target specific groups, achieving a higher representation within their target groups than their national share would suggest. For example, HSBC, the largest of the Schedule II banks, enjoys a strong presence and success in the Chinese communities of British Columbia and Ontario.

Foreign banks may enter the Canadian financial services industry as either Schedule II or Schedule III banks. As already noted, Schedule II banks don't have to be widely held if small. If, however, their equity capital exceeds $1 billion then at least 35% of it must be widely held. In the case that their equity capital exceeds $5 billion then the same widely held ownership rule applies as for Schedule I banks. The major difference between Schedule II and Schedule III banks is that Schedule III banks can branch directly into Canada, following authorization by the minister of finance, whereas Schedule II banks can add branches to their initial branch only with ministerial approval. However, Schedule III banks cannot take retail deposits (i.e., deposits less that $150 000) and, as a result, have the advantage

TABLE 5 Schedule II Banks in Canada

Institution	Cdn $ Billions	Domestic assets Share (%)
Hongkong Bank	23.9	3.1
Deutsche Bank	8.7	1.1
Citibank	7.2	0.9
Bank of America	5.0	0.6
Sociētē Gēnērale	4.5	0.6
ABN Amro Bank	3.9	0.5
BT Bank of Canada	3.8	0.5
Bank of Tokyo-Mitsubishi	3.1	0.4
Crēdit Lyonnais	2.7	0.3
Bank Nationale de Paris	2.6	0.3
Union Bank of Switzerland	2.6	0.3
Crēdit Suisse First Boston	2.6	0.3
Banca Commerciale Italiana	2.0	0.2
Other	20.8	2.7
Total	93.4	11.8

Source: Mckinsey, *The Changing Landscape for Canadian Financial Services: New Forces, New Competitors, New Choices. Final Report for the Task Force on the Future of the Canadian Financial Services Sector* (Ottawa, September 1998), Exhibits 5-24 and 2-12.

of not being subject to regulations that apply to full-service banks (such as requirements for CDIC insurance). Given that most Schedule II banks do little retail deposit gathering, it is likely that in the future many Schedule II banks will become Schedule III banks.

The internationalization of banking, both by Canadian banks going abroad and by foreign banks entering Canada, has meant that financial markets throughout the world have become more integrated. As a result, there is a growing trend toward international coordination of bank regulation, one example of which is the 1988 Basel agreement to standardize minimum capital requirements in industrialized countries, discussed in Chapter 18. Financial market integration has also encouraged bank consolidation abroad, culminating in the creation of the first trillion-dollar bank with the proposed merger of the Industrial Bank of Japan, Dai-Ichi Kangyo Bank, and Fuji Bank. Another development has been the importance of foreign banks in international banking. As shown in Table 6, in 2001, none of the ten largest banks in the world was Canadian. In fact at the end of 1999, Canada's largest bank (Royal Bank) ranked 55th in the world.

FTA, NAFTA, and Banking in North America

The Free Trade Agreement (FTA) signed in 1988 by the Unites States and Canada, and its successor, the North American Free Trade Agreement (NAFTA) signed in 1993 by the United States, Canada, and Mexico have attempted to increase the efficiency of the North American economy by eliminating trade barriers and ensuring that each country has access to the other countries' markets. The increasing closeness and integration of the economies of Canada, Mexico, and the United States has not yet led to any significant mergers and acquisitions of commercial banks and other financial institutions in North America. Banks from each country, however, have been expanding their interests in the other countries' markets.

FINANCIAL INNOVATION AND THE DECLINE OF TRADITIONAL BANKING

The traditional financial intermediation role of banking has been to make long-term loans and fund them by issuing short-dated deposits, a process of asset transformation commonly referred to as "borrowing short and lending long." Earlier in the chapter, we saw that changes in regulations have been increasing the competitive environment in the banking industry in Canada. Another source of increasing competition for this industry is coming from financial innovations. Here we examine how the same economic forces we examined in Chapter 15 have generated financial innovations that present the banking industry with competitive

TABLE 6 Ten Largest Banks in the World, 2001

Bank	Assets (US $ billions)
1. Deutsche Bank (Germany)	955 579
2. Bank of Tokyo-Mitsubishi (Japan)	726 286
3. Citigroup (U.S.)	716 937
4. BNP Paribas (France)	703 091
5. Bank of America (U.S.)	632 574
6. UBS (Switzerland)	616 798
7. HSBC Holdings (U.K./Hong Kong)	601 847
8. Fuji Bank (Japan)	561 345
9. Bayerische Hypo Bank (Germany)	559 860
10. Sumitomo Bank (Japan)	519 153

Source: http://interactive.wsj.com/public/resources/documents/wb00-100-fpublic-2000-09-25.htm

The world's 20 largest banks by assets as of 1998 and 1999 are listed at www.financialservicefacts.org/international/fr.html

challenges that are causing traditional banking business to decline. The decline in traditional banking has important implications for the future of the banking industry and creates new challenges for regulators.

Behind the Decline: Four Financial Innovations

Four financial innovations have played an important role in the decline of traditional banking: mutual funds, junk bonds, the rise of the commercial paper market, and securitization.

Visit www.ific.ca for the Investment Funds Institute of Canada.

Mutual Funds As already noted, the financial behaviours of Canadians have been evolving. People are relying less and less on bank branches for basic transactions, switching to automated banking machines, telephone banking, and Internet banking. Moreover, consumers are widening their investment choices, putting more of their wealth into the stock market and new financial innovations such as mutual funds. In fact, mutual funds have experienced extraordinary growth and already exceed personal deposits at commercial banks. As Figure 4 shows, industry experts expect that in the near future, mutual funds will exceed personal deposits at commercial banks, trust and mortgage loan companies, credit unions and *caisses populaires*, and government saving institutions.

More important has been the development of money market mutual funds. These relatively new financial institutions have the characteristics of a mutual fund but also function to some extent as a depository institution because they offer deposit-type accounts. In particular, money market mutual funds issue shares (also called units) that are redeemable at a fixed price (usually $1). For example, if you buy 5000 units for $5000, the money market fund uses these funds to invest in short-term money market securities (treasury bills, certificates of deposit, commercial paper) that provide you with interest payments. Although money mar-

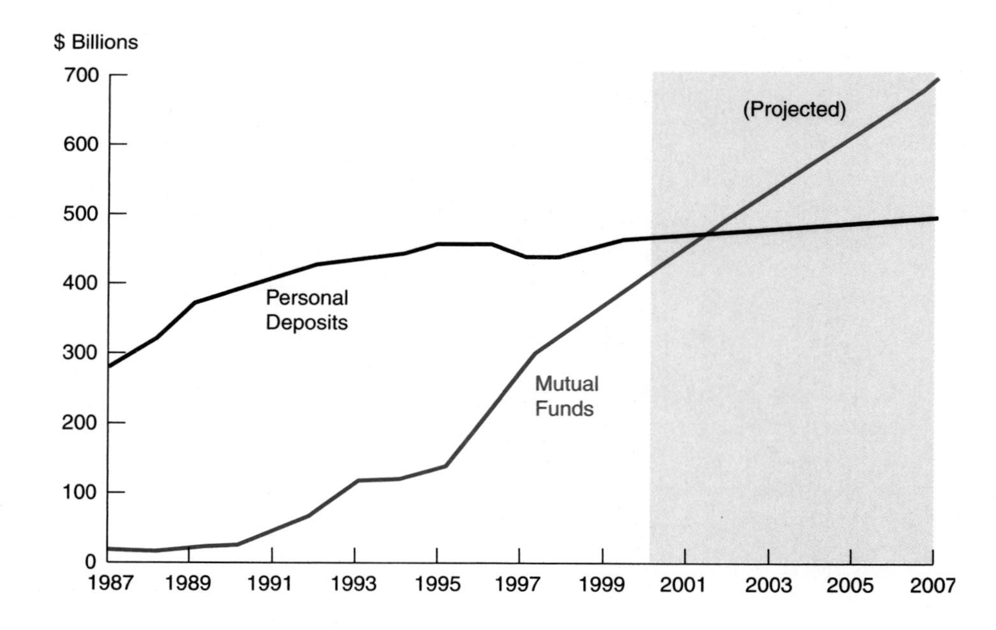

FIGURE 4 Personal Deposits Versus Mutual Funds

Source: Canadian Bankers Association website: http://www.cba.ca. Reproduced with the permission of the Minister of Public Works and Government Services Canada, 2001.

ket fund shares effectively function as deposits that earn interest, they are not legally deposits and so are not insured by the CDIC.

In the United States, money market mutual funds also offer chequing privileges, effectively functioning as chequing account deposits. For this reason, money market mutual funds in that country have experienced extraordinary growth since 1971, when they first appeared. By 1999, their assets had climbed to nearly $1500 billion. As consumers shift to mutual funds, deposit-taking financial institutions (throughout the world) risk losing a low-cost source of funds.

Junk Bonds Before the advent of computers and advanced telecommunications, it was difficult to acquire information about the financial situation of firms that might want to sell securities. Because of the difficulty in screening out bad from good credit risks, the only firms that were able to sell bonds were very well established corporations that had high credit ratings.[3] Before the 1980s, then, only corporations that could issue bonds with ratings of BBB or above could raise funds by selling newly issued bonds. Some firms that had fallen on bad times, so-called *fallen angels,* had previously issued long-term corporate bonds that now had ratings that had fallen below BBB, bonds that were pejoratively dubbed "junk bonds."

With the improvement in information technology in the 1970s, it became easier for investors to screen out bad from good credit risks, thus making it more likely that they would buy long-term debt securities from less well-known corporations with lower credit ratings. With this change in supply conditions, we would expect that some smart individual would pioneer the concept of selling new public issues of junk bonds, not for fallen angels but for companies that had not yet achieved investment-grade status. This is exactly what Michael Milken of Drexel Burnham, an investment banking firm, started to do in 1977. Junk bonds, discussed in Chapter 9, became an important factor in the corporate bond market. Although there was a sharp slowdown in activity in the junk bond market after Milken was indicted for securities law violations in 1989, it has heated up again in the 1990s.

The Website for Drexel Burnham is www.drexelburnham.com

Commercial Paper Market Recall that *commercial paper* is a short-term debt security issued by large banks and corporations. As we saw in Chapter 8, the commercial paper market has undergone tremendous growth since 1970. In fact, commercial paper has been one of the fastest-growing money market instruments.

Improvements in information technology also help provide an explanation for the rapid rise of the commercial paper market. We have seen that the improvement in information technology made it easier for investors to screen out bad from good credit risks, thus making it easier for corporations to issue debt securities. Not only did this make it easier for corporations to issue long-term debt securities as in the junk bond market, but it also meant that they could raise funds by issuing short-term debt securities like commercial paper more easily. Many corporations that used to do their short-term borrowing from banks now frequently raise short-term funds in the commercial paper market instead.

The development of money market mutual funds has been another factor in the rapid growth in the commercial paper market. Because money market mutual funds need to hold liquid, high-quality, short-term assets such as commercial paper, the growth of assets in these funds has created a ready market in commercial paper. The growth of pension and other large funds that invest in commercial paper has also stimulated the growth of this market.

[3]The discussion of adverse selection problems in Chapter 14 provides a more detailed analysis of why only well-established firms with high credit ratings were able to sell securities.

Securitization An important example of a financial innovation arising from improvements in both transaction and information technology is securitization, one of the most important financial innovations in the past two decades. **Securitization** is the process of transforming otherwise illiquid financial assets (such as residential mortgages), which have typically been the bread and butter of banking institutions, into marketable capital market securities. As we have seen, improvements in the ability to acquire information have made it easier to sell marketable capital market securities. In addition, with low transaction costs because of improvements in computer technology, financial institutions find that they can cheaply bundle together a portfolio of loans (such as mortgages) with varying small denominations (often less than $100 000), collect the interest and principal payments on the mortgages in the bundle, and then "pass them through" (pay them out) to third parties. By dividing the portfolio of loans into standardized amounts, the financial institution can then sell the claims to these interest and principal payments to third parties as securities. The standardized amounts of these securitized loans make them liquid securities, and the fact that they are made up of a bundle of loans helps diversify risk, making them desirable. The financial institution selling the securitized loans makes a profit by servicing the loans (collecting the interest and principal payments and paying them out) and charging a fee to the third party for this service.

Securitization first started in the United States in 1970 when the GNMA (now known as Ginnie Mae) began a program in which it guaranteed interest and principal payments on bundles of standardized mortgages, thereby encouraging the creation of a new financial instrument, the mortgage-backed security. The guarantee of the interest and principal payments makes it easy for private financial institutions to sell a bundle of guaranteed mortgages as a security and to pass through these payments to the owner of the security. Securitization, however, has not stopped with mortgages: Numerous types of assets are now routinely securitized, including residential mortgages, automobile loans, credit card receivables, and commercial and computer leases.

Computer technology has also enabled financial institutions to tailor securitization to produce securities that have payment streams considered especially desirable by the market. Collateralized mortgage obligations (CMOs), which are bonds that pass through the payments from a portfolio of mortgages, are a good example of such tailoring; they first appeared in 1983. Computerization enables a CMO to be split into several classes known as *tranches.* The first tranches receive interest payments according to the coupon rate on the CMO, with class 1 first receiving all principal payments and prepayments from the collateralized pool of mortgages. After the class 1 bonds have been paid off, the principal payments and prepayments are used to retire the remaining classes sequentially. The last class, called *accrual* or *Z bonds,* receives interest and principal payments only after the other classes have been paid off. The basic CMO described here has the advantage of containing bonds of both short maturity (class 1) and long maturity (the later classes or the accrual bond), thus increasing its potential market. Indeed, the financial innovation process has led to even more complicated CMOs that fit additional niches in the marketplace.

In Canada, securitization has not yet developed to the same degree as in the United States. Recently, however, the popularity of securitization is growing, primarily because of the benefits it provides to all stakeholders. For example, it benefits investors by increasing the variety of available instruments and offering a greater degree of liquidity than other investments. It benefits borrowers by offering greater flexibility in product choice and perhaps lower borrowing costs. It also allows financial institutions to move assets off their balance sheet, thereby reducing the need to hold regulatory capital.

Some of the first securitized transactions in Canada involved selling securities against blocks of Canada Mortgage and Housing Corporation (CMHC)-guaranteed mortgages; before that, blocks of CMHC mortgages were sold in a secondary market to other institutions. Recently, however, Canadian banks have securitized credit card debt as well as other forms of debt.

Decline of Traditional Banking

Clearly, the traditional financial intermediation role of banking, whereby banks make loans that are funded with deposits, is no longer as important in our financial system. However, the decline in the market share of banks in total lending and total financial intermediary assets does not indicate that the banking industry is in decline. If we look at bank profitability relative to GDP, there is no evidence of a declining trend. As we can see in Figure 5, after a dismal performance in the late 1980s and early 1990s, bank profits have rebounded sharply, with strong profits since 1992. In fact, in recent years the profit margins of Canadian banks have climbed close to those in the United States and the United Kingdom.

However, overall bank profitability is not a good indicator of the profitability of traditional banking because it includes an increasing amount of income from nontraditional off-balance-sheet activities discussed in Chapter 15. As you can see in Figure 6, noninterest income derived from off-balance-sheet activities, as a share of total bank income, increased from around 30% in 1988 to 60% of total bank income by 2000. Given that the overall profitability of banks has not risen, the increase in income from off-balance-sheet activities implies that the profitability of traditional banking business has declined. This decline in profitability then explains why banks have been reducing their traditional business.

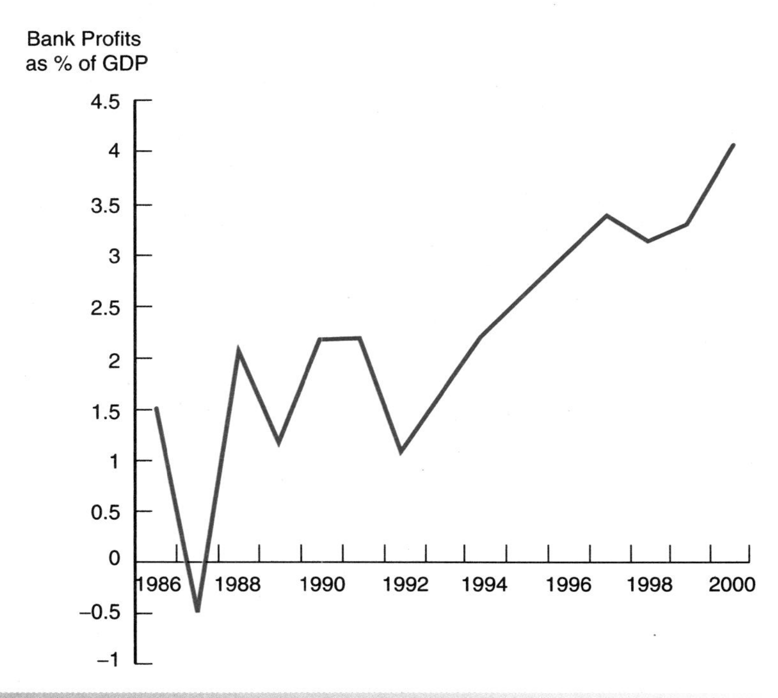

FIGURE 5 Commercial Bank Profitability, 1986–2000

Source: Bank of Canada and Statistics Canada CANSIM II series V498918

Reasons for the Decline

To understand why traditional banking business has declined in both size and profitability, we need to look at how the financial innovations described earlier have caused banks to suffer declines in their cost advantages in acquiring funds, that is, on the liabilities side of their balance sheet, while at the same time they have lost income advantages on the assets side of their balance sheet. The simultaneous decline of cost and income advantages has resulted in reduced profitability of traditional banking and an effort by banks to leave this business and engage in new and more profitable activities.

Decline in Cost Advantages in Acquiring Funds (Liabilities) Before the 1980s, banks were paying low interest rates on chequable deposits. This worked to the banks' advantage because their major source of funds was chequable deposits. Unfortunately, this cost advantage for banks did not last. The rise in inflation from the late 1960s on led to higher interest rates, which made investors more sensitive to yield differentials on different assets. The result was the so-called disintermediation process, in which people began to take their money out of banks, with their low interest rates on both chequable and time deposits, and began to seek out higher-yielding investments. Also, as we have seen, at the same time, financial innovation led to money market mutual funds, which put the banks at an even further disadvantage because depositors could now obtain deposit-like services while earning high interest on their money market mutual fund accounts. One manifestation of these changes in the financial system was that the low-cost source of funds declined dramatically in importance for banks.

Decline in Income Advantages on Uses of Funds (Assets) The loss of cost advantages on the liabilities side of the balance sheet for Canadian banks is one reason that they have become less competitive, but they have also been hit by a decline in income advantages on the assets side from the financial innovations we discussed earlier, junk bonds, securitization, and the rise of the commercial paper market.

We have seen that improvements in information technology have made it easier for firms to issue securities directly to the public. This has meant that instead of going to banks to finance short-term credit needs, many of the banks' best business customers now find it cheaper to go to the commercial paper market for funds instead. The loss of this competitive advantage for banks is evident in the fact that before 1970, nonfinancial commercial paper equalled 5% of commercial bank loans, whereas the figure has risen to close to 19% today.

The rise of the junk bond market has also eaten into banks' loan business. Improvements in information technology have made it easier for corporations to sell their bonds to the public directly, thereby bypassing banks. Although well-established companies started taking this route in the 1970s, now lower-quality corporate borrowers are using banks less often because they have access to the junk bond market.

We have also seen that improvements in computer technology have led to securitization, whereby illiquid financial assets such as bank loans or mortgages are transformed into marketable securities. Computers enable other financial institutions to originate loans because they can now accurately evaluate credit risk with statistical methods, while computers have lowered transaction costs, making it possible to bundle these loans and sell them as securities. As a result, banks no longer have an advantage in making loans when default risk can be easily evaluated with computers. Without their former advantages, banks have lost loan business to other financial institutions even though the banks themselves are involved in the process of securitization.

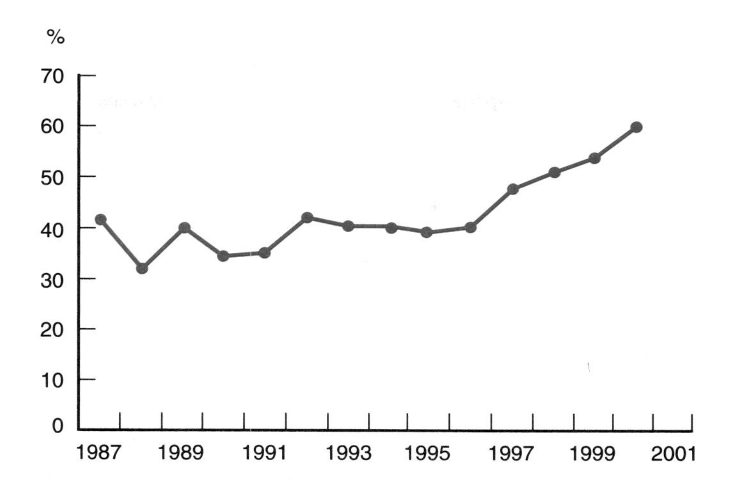

FIGURE 6 Share of Noninterest Income in Total Bank Income, 1987–2000

Source: Bank of Canada

Banks' Responses

Canadian banks have sought to maintain former profit levels by pursuing new off-balance-sheet activities that are more profitable. As we saw in Figure 6, commercial banks did this during the 1990s, significantly increasing the share of their income coming from off-balance-sheet, noninterest-income activities.[4] This strategy, however, has generated concerns about what are proper activities for banks and about whether nontraditional activities might be riskier and result in banks taking excessive risks.

The decline of banks' traditional business has thus meant that the banking industry has been driven to seek out new lines of business. This could be beneficial because by so doing, banks can stay vibrant and healthy. Indeed, bank profitability has been high in recent years, and nontraditional, off-balance-sheet activities have been playing an important role in the resurgence of bank profits. However, there is a danger that the new directions in banking could lead to increased risk taking, and thus the decline in traditional banking requires regulators to be more vigilant. It also poses new challenges for bank regulators, who, as we will see in Chapter 18, must now be far more concerned about banks' off-balance-sheet activities.

Decline of Traditional Banking in Other Industrialized Countries

Forces similar to those in Canada have been leading to the decline of traditional banking in other industrialized countries. The loss of banks' monopoly power over depositors has occurred outside Canada as well. For example, with the high savings by the Japanese public, Japanese banks were able to tap a large savings pool and thus had access to a cheaper source of funds than banks in the United States. This cost advantage of Japanese banks meant that they could more aggressively seek out loan business in the United States, which is exactly what they did. As a result, they grew at the expense of American banks. This explains why only two of the top ten banks are U.S. (see Table 6 on page 425).

[4]Note that some off-balance-sheet activities, such as loan commitments and letters of credit, which produce fee income, can be classified as being in the category of traditional banking business. The data in Figure 6 overstate somewhat the importance of nontraditional banking business.

Financial innovation and deregulation are occurring worldwide and have created attractive alternatives for both depositors and borrowers. In the United States, for example, the importance of commercial banks as a source of funds to nonfinancial borrowers has shrunk dramatically. In 1974, commercial banks provided close to 40% of these funds; by 1999, their market share was down to below 30%. The decline in market share for thrift institutions has been even more precipitous: from more than 20% in the late 1970s to below 10% today. In Japan, deregulation has opened a wide array of new financial instruments to the public, causing a disintermediation process similar to that in Canada and the United States. In European countries, innovations have steadily eroded the barriers that have traditionally protected banks from competition.

In other countries, banks have also faced increased competition from the expansion of securities markets. Both financial deregulation and fundamental economic forces in other countries have improved the availability of information in securities markets, making it easier and less costly for firms to finance their activities by issuing securities rather than going to banks. Further, even in countries where securities markets have not grown, banks have still lost loan business because their best corporate customers have had increasing access to foreign and offshore capital markets, such as the Eurobond market. In smaller economies, like Australia, which still do not have well-developed corporate bond or commercial paper markets, banks have lost loan business to international securities markets.

The increase in the competitive environment for foreign banks has meant that some of them have found themselves in financial difficulties. Return on assets and return on equity have fallen in Japan and many European countries, and banks in these countries have sometimes been finding themselves in financial difficulties. One of France's largest bank, Crédit Lyonnais, required a $10 billion bailout in 1995, with additional infusions of over $1 billion in 1996 and 1997, and in 1996, the Italian government injected over $1 billion to help keep the Banco di Napoli afloat. Even in countries like Switzerland and Germany, banks have been running into trouble. For example, in January 1993, BfG Bank, a German bank, needed a capital infusion from its parent company, Crédit Lyonnais, because it suffered huge losses in 1992. In Chapter 18, we will discuss the extensive problems in the Japanese banking industry. Canada is not unique in seeing its banks face a more difficult competitive environment.

SUMMARY

1. The history of banking in Canada has left us with a small number of banks chartered by the federal government. Multiple agencies regulate commercial banks: the Office of the Superintendent of Financial Institutions (OSFI), the Bank of Canada, and the Canada Deposit Insurance Corporation (CDIC).
2. The Big Six (the Royal Bank of Canada, Canadian Imperial Bank of Commerce, Bank of Montreal, Bank of Nova Scotia, TD Canada Trust, and the National Bank of Canada) together with the *Mouvement Desjardins* (to be discussed in Chapter 17) dominate the deposit-taking industry in Canada.
3. In the United States they have a dual banking system, with commercial banks chartered by the states and the federal government. Restrictive state branching regulations which prohibited branching across state lines, led to a large number of small commercial banks in the United States. The large number of commercial banks in the United States reflects the past *lack* of competition, not the presence of vigorous competition.
4. With the rapid growth of world trade since 1960, international banking has grown dramatically. Canadian banks engage in international banking activities by opening branches abroad and owning controlling interests in foreign banks. Foreign banks operate in Canada by owning a subsidiary Canadian bank or by operating branches or agency offices in Canada.
5. Until 1981, foreign banks were not allowed to operate in Canada. Today, we have about 40 foreign bank subsidiaries, operating as Schedule II and III banks. They have the same powers as the domestic banks but differ in the ownership structure permitted. That is, all Schedule I banks must be widely

held whereas Schedule II banks can be closely held if small.

6. Financial innovation has caused banks to suffer declines in cost advantages in acquiring funds and in income advantages on their assets. The resulting squeeze has hurt profitability in banks' traditional lines of business and has led to a decline in traditional banking.

KEY TERMS

Big Six, *p. 414*
central bank, *p. 410*
chartered banks, *p. 409*
debt-currency swaps, *p. 423*
debt-debt swaps, *p. 423*
debt-equity swaps, *p. 423*
dual-banking system, *p. 411*
four-pillar approach, *p. 416*
free banking, *p. 411*
gold standard, *p. 412*
indebtedness, *p. 423*
lender of last resort, *p. 414*
nonbank banks, *p. 420*
Schedule I banks, *p. 414*
Schedule II banks, *p. 414*
Schedule III banks, *p. 416*
securitization, *p. 428*
seigniorage, *p. 412*
sovereign loans, *p. 423*
state banks, *p. 411*

QUESTIONS AND PROBLEMS

1. Describe how early revisions to the Bank Act attempted to introduce more flexibility in the management of the money supply.

***2.** Which regulatory agency has the primary responsibility for supervising the following categories of financial institutions?
 a. commercial banks
 b. trust and mortgage loans companies
 c. credit unions and *caisses populaires*

3. "The commercial banking industry in Canada is less competitive than the commercial banking industry in the United States because in Canada only a few large banks dominate the industry, while in the United States there are around 8100 commercial banks." Is this statement true, false, or uncertain? Explain your answer.

***4.** How did new technology cause banks' traditional lending activities to decline in balance-sheet importance?

5. Contrast the activities of a Schedule I bank, a Schedule II bank, and a Schedule III bank.

***6.** Explain how sovereign loans in the 1970s and early 1980s caused problems for the Big Six.

7. Explain how the early development of chartered banks in Canada differed from the development of commercial banks in the United States.

***8.** If the bank at which you keep your chequing account is owned by Saudi Arabians, should you worry that your deposits are less safe than if the bank were owned by Canadians?

9. Explain how securitization can be used to change illiquid assets into liquid assets.

***10.** Why have banks been losing cost advantages in acquiring funds in recent years?

11. "If inflation had not risen in the 1960s and 1970s, the banking industry might be healthier today." Is this statement true, false, or uncertain? Explain your answer.

***12.** Why have banks been losing income advantages on their assets in recent years?

13. "The invention of the computer is the major factor behind the decline of the banking industry." Is this statement true, false, or uncertain? Explain your answer.

***14.** What incentives do Canadian regulatory agencies have to encourage the establishment of foreign banks in Canada?

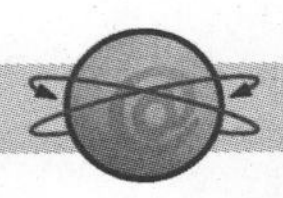

WEB EXERCISES

Commercial Banking Industry: Structure and Competition

1. Go to http://www.cba.ca. Select "Statistics." Choose "Bank Branches." Looking at the trend in bank branches, does the public appear to have more or less access to banking facilities? Now choose "ABMs [ATMs] in Canada." How many ATMs were there in 1982, and how many are there now? Which province has the most bank branches and ATMs?
2. Go to http://www.cba.ca. Look under "Quick Facts." How many Canadians are estimated to be shareholders in banks? Do Canadian banks pay taxes? If yes, how much did they pay in 2000?

Chapter 17

The Near Banks

Preview

Suppose that you are a typical middle-class worker in Toronto in 1820. You work hard and earn fair wages as a craftsperson. You are married and about to have a child, so you decide that you would like to own your own home. There are many commercial banks in the city, but as their name implies, these institutions exist to serve commerce, not the working class, because that is where the profits are. Where could you go to borrow the money to buy a home? Your options are very limited. Later in the century, however, a new institution emerged that opened the possibility of home ownership to more than the very wealthy. That institution was the mortgage loan company.

The middle class also had problems finding financial institutions willing to offer small consumer-type loans. Again, banks had determined that loans to these customers were not profitable. Another type of institution, the credit union, emerged at about the same time as mortgage loan companies to service the borrowing needs of this segment of the economy.

In Chapters 15 and 16 we discussed commercial banks, the largest of the depository institutions. Though smaller, trust and mortgage loan companies and credit unions and *caisses populaires* (people's banks), collectively called **near banks** (because they perform slightly different roles than commercial banks do), are important to the servicing of consumer borrowing needs. Near banks are primarily concerned with lending to individuals and households, as opposed to banks, which still tend to be more concerned with lending to businesses. We begin our discussion by reviewing the history of the near-banking industry. We then describe the nature of the industry today and project where it might be in the future. We also provide a brief discussion of American near banks.

TRUST AND MORTGAGE LOAN COMPANIES

Trust Companies

Over the years, the Bank Acts have denied to chartered banks the power to function as corporate **trustees** (or fiduciaries). Unlike the situation in the United States, legislators in Canada reasoned that deposit-taking financial institutions might face a conflict of interest if they were to act as both financial fiduciaries and banks. So beginning in 1843, trust companies were established, under a variety of provincial and federal laws, and specialized in the provision of fiduciary services. As financial fiduciaries, trust companies administer estates, trusts, and agencies (i.e., assets that belong to someone else), for a fee, and under conditions prescribed in a contract.

Over the years, the structure of the trust industry has changed significantly and the trust companies became closely associated with the chartered banks. In the early 1900s, the trust companies were also allowed to act as financial intermediaries. In this role, trust companies borrow funds by issuing deposit liabilities and then use these funds to make loans and purchase assets. Moreover, over the years the Bank Acts have allowed regulated federal financial institutions (domestic chartered banks and life insurance companies) to own trust companies. As a result, and with the acquisition of Canada Trust (Canada's largest trust company) by the TD Bank Financial Group in early 2000, trust companies now constitute a relatively small market segment.

Mortgage Loan Companies

History and Organization The development of trust companies was paralleled by the growth of mortgage loan companies. The concept of mortgage loan companies came from the building societies in the United Kingdom (during the early part of the nineteenth century), whose purpose was to enable members to acquire land, build homes, or develop farms. Today's mortgage loan companies take deposits and primarily make residential mortgage loans. They do not act as trustees, unless they are licensed specifically for that purpose. Examples of mortgage loan companies in Canada include Victoria & Grey Mortgage Corporation and League Savings and Mortgage Company.

Over the years, the mortgage loan companies together with the trust companies formed the second pillar of the traditional financial services industry in Canada. Although many had collapsed during the 1970s, trust and mortgage loan companies were widely held until the 1980s, when amendments to the Bank Act allowed commercial banks to diversify their financial practices and acquire subsidiaries. As you will see later in Chapter 18, financial innovation, competition, and regulatory evolution significantly changed the competitive position of financial institutions in recent years.

Regulation Trust and mortgage loan companies (TMLs) operate under a charter issued by either the federal government or one of the provincial governments. The majority of the TMLs are federally incorporated and come under the federal Trust and Loan Companies Act and are regulated and supervised by the Office of the Superintendent of Financial Institutions (OSFI). They must also register in all the provinces in which they operate and must conform to the regulations of those provinces. In the case of trust companies, the fiduciary component of their business is only subject to provincial legislation, even if the company is federally incorporated.

The legislation requirements by the federal and provincial governments consist of several components. First, there is the prudent person approach. This involves the TML company adhering to "investment and lending policies, standards and procedures that a reasonable and prudent person would apply in respect of a portfolio of investments and loans to avoid undue risk of loss and obtain a reasonable return." This indicates that the activities set out by the institution must not exceed risk limitations on lending. By complying with these rules, deposit-taking institutions will also follow the *Standards of Sound Business and Financial Practices* issued by the Canada Deposit Insurance Corporation, including the *Standard on Securities Portfolio Management*. The board of directors of an institution should decide on limits on the exposure to lending, including the interest rate and associated risks. This investment policy sets out proper ranges for different ventures, including lending, equity, and real property. For TMLs, the restriction on commercial lending requires it to be only 5% of assets if regulatory capital base is less than $25 million. If regulatory capital exceeds $25 million, the Superintendent can approve the adequate percentage of commercial lending allowed. There is no restriction on consumer lending. The laws regulating investments in real estate or equities limit them to 70% of regulatory capital.

Liquidity is another important aspect of regulation that the board of directors establish for TMLs. Financial institutions must have

- records of liquidity standards issued by the Board of Directors
- an administration system that is suitable to manage liquidity sufficiently
- a system set up to monitor liquid assets
- a contingency plan in place for funding requirements under alternative scenarios

In order to manage liquidity, a company must maintain an adequate amount of liquid assets that is associated with that company's cash flow and lending practices. The limitations set out by the Board of Directors are different among companies since they depend on the quality and diversification of assets. In addition, there are limits on large exposures to individual consumers and other financial institutions. The Board of Directors again decides upon the policies associated with large exposure for TMLs. The aggregate exposure of a consolidated company or foreign bank must not exceed 25% of total capital.

The OSFI is also responsible for the evaluation of the soundness of federally regulated TMLs, offering feedback and mediation. In particular, the OSFI will intervene in a TML's business if the proper practices are not adhered to in order to maintain the protection for depositors, policyholders, and pension plan members from losses. In 1999, the OSFI introduced a new supervisory agenda, which is consistent with international supervisory practices, in order to standardize the system of markets. This new policy strategy is concentrated on assessing the risk management practices and documentation of each institution, rather than periodic on-site visits:

- Sound judgment in evaluating risks in an institution is central to efficiency.
- The risk assessment of the TML will determine the level and occurrence of supervisory inspection.
- Supervision includes five major risk management functions: financial analysis, compliance, internal audit, risk management, and senior management and board oversight.
- Timely statement of risk assessment results and suggestions are sent to institutions.

- Each institution will be given a rating after a review, which is associated with the stages of involvement in compliance with the *Guide to Intervention for Federal Financial Institutions.*

The OSFI website, www.osfi-bsif.gc.ca, contains industry information, statistical reports, and laws and regulations for TMLs.

The *Guide to Intervention for Federal Financial Institutions* was developed jointly by the OSFI and the CDIC. This guide was introduced to reduce the possibility of a TML failure by setting out rules on when a supervisory institution should intervene. It lists the directives available to the OSFI and the CDIC to deal with the TML's source of instability, whether it is associated with liquidity constraints or risk management.

Deposit Insurance Deposit insurance for TMLs outside Quebec is provided by the CDIC (up to $60 000 per account). The Quebec Deposit Insurance Board (QDIB) insures deposits for Quebec TMLs, on terms similar to the CDIC's.

To be eligible for insurance, deposits must be

- in Canadian currency and payable in Canada
- held at a CDIC member institution
- repaid in a term of less than five years from the date of deposit

The CDIC insures savings and chequing deposits, term deposits, and debentures issued by loan companies. Stocks, bonds, foreign currency deposits, investments in mortgages, mutual funds, accounts held in foreign currency, and term deposits that mature in more than five years from the date of deposit are ineligible for deposit insurance. Qualified deposits held with an insolvent member institution are automatically protected and require no application.

The Balance Sheet Table 1 shows the aggregate balance sheet of trust and mortgage loan companies, excluding those that are subsidiaries of chartered banks. They are funded almost entirely by chequable and nonchequable savings deposits, term deposits, guaranteed investment certificates, and debentures; together, they account for 84% of the balance sheet. Their risk asset portfolio is made up mostly by residential mortgages and personal loans; together they account for 61.58% of assets. The low-risk assets are largely in short-term paper (7.7%) and Canadian bonds (more than 8%).

TABLE 1 Balance Sheet of All Trust and Mortgage Loan Companies (in millions, as of 2001:Q3)

Assets	Amount ($)	Percent (%)	Liabilities	Amount ($)	Percent(%)
Cash, items in transit, and gross demand and notice deposits	189	1.97	Savings deposits		
			Chequable	175	1.82
			Nonchequable	573	5.96
Term deposits	464	4.82			
			Term deposits, GICs, and debentures	7 333	76.25
Short-term paper	737	7.66			
Canadian bonds					
Government of Canada	243	2.53	Other liabilities	777	8.08
Provincial and municipal	226	2.35			
Corporate	328	3.41	Shareholders' equity	759	7.89
			Total liabilities	9 617	100.00
Loans and leases					
Residential mortgages	5 379	55.93			
Personal loans	543	5.65			
Nonresidential mortgages	494	5.14			
Other loans and assets	1 014	10.54			
Total assets	9 617	100.00			

Source: Bank of Canada *Banking and Financial Statistics,* March 2002.

COOPERATIVE BANKS: CREDIT UNIONS AND *CAISSES POPULAIRES*

The second type of near bank in Canada is the **cooperative bank**, a financial institution that focuses on servicing the banking and lending needs of its members. These institutions are also designed to service the needs of consumers, not businesses, and are distinguished by their ownership structure and their "common bond" membership requirement. Most cooperative banks are relatively small.

History and Organization

The concept behind credit unions originated in Germany in the nineteenth century. A group of consumers would pool their assets as collateral for a loan from a bank. The funds so raised were then loaned to the members of the group, and each member of the group was personally liable for repayment of the loan. Defaults were very rare because members knew one another well.

The cooperative banks in Canada are small lending institutions organized around a particular group of individuals with a common bond (union members or employees of a particular firm, although in recent years the bonds have been changing from employment to community linkages). Alphonse Desjardins formed Canada's first cooperative bank in 1900 in Quebec, and it was based on the cooperative movements in Europe, which, among other things, encouraged savings and stressed the provision of credit to the "little person." Today, there are two cooperative financial systems in Canada: the *caisses populaires* (people's bank) system in Quebec and the credit union system in other parts of the country.

Mutual Ownership Credit unions are organized as mutuals; that is, they are owned by their depositors. A customer receives shares when a deposit is made. Rather than earning interest on deposited funds, the customer earns dividends. The amount of the dividend is not guaranteed, like the interest rate earned on accounts at banks. Instead, the amount of the dividend is estimated in advance and is paid if at all possible.

Each depositor has one vote, regardless how much money he or she may have with the institution. Depositors vote for directors, who in turn hire managers to run the credit union.

Because credit unions are cooperative businesses, they are managed somewhat differently from other businesses. For example, many credit unions make extensive use of volunteer help to reduce their costs. Since any cost reductions are passed on to the depositors, volunteers feel that they are working for the common good. Similarly, as noted, operating facilities may be donated.

The mutual form of ownership has both advantages and disadvantages. On the one hand, since the capital of the institution is contributed by the depositors, more capital is available because all deposits represent equity. This leads to greater safety in that mutuals have far fewer liabilities than other banking organizations. On the other hand, the mutual form of ownership accentuates the principal-agent problem that exists in corporations. In corporations, managers are hired by the board of directors, who are in turn elected by the shareholders. Because most shareholders do not own a very large percentage of the firm, when there is a disagreement with management, it makes more sense to sell shares than to try to change policy. This problem also exists for the mutual form of ownership. Most depositors do not have a large enough stake in the firm to make it cost-effective for them to monitor the firm's managers closely.

The corporation, however, has alternative methods of aligning managers' goals with those of shareholders. For example, managers can be offered a stake in the firm, or stock options can be part of their compensation package. Similarly, managers of corporations are always under the threat of takeover by another firm if they fail to manage effectively. These alternatives are not available in the mutual form of ownership. As a result, there may be less control over management.

An advantage to the mutual form of ownership is that managers are more risk-averse than in the corporate form. This is because mutual managers gain nothing if the firm does very well, since they do not own a stake in the firm, but they lose everything if the firm fails. This incentive arrangement appeals to the very risk-averse investor, but its importance has diminished now that the government provides deposit insurance.

Common Bond Membership The single most important feature of credit unions that distinguishes them from other depository institutions is the common bond member rule. The idea behind **common bond membership** is that only members of a particular association, occupation, or geographic region are permitted to join the credit union. A credit union's common bonds define its field of membership. The most frequent type of common bond applies to employees of a single occupation or employer, although, as already noted, the bonds have been changing from employment to community linkages (as in the case, for example, of VanCity).

Go to www.vancity.com for more information about VanCity.

One problem with the common bond membership rule is that it prevents credit unions from diversifying their risk. If most of a credit union's members are employed by one business and that business is forced to lay off workers, it is likely that the credit union will have high default rates on loans. A recent trend among credit unions has been for several to merge, a move that helps reduce the risk of having all members linked by a single bond. To make mergers easier, regulators have interpreted the common bond requirement less strictly. For example, most credit unions now let members of the immediate family of an eligible member join, and many credit unions have adopted a "once a member, always a member" policy.

Non-Profit, Tax-Exempt Status Credit unions and *caisses populaires* are treated by Canada Customs and Revenue Agency as non-profit and consequently exempt from federal taxation. All of the income earned by the institutions is to be spent on their members. Credit unions and *caisses populaires* are currently the only financial institutions that are tax exempt. This makes it easier for them to accumulate retained earnings than it is for other institutions. Banks and other near banks are questioning this tax-exempt status as credit unions become larger and more significant competitors. It remains a question how long the favourable tax treatment of credit unions can be maintained. Partly as a result of being non-profit and partly due to the cost advantage of being tax exempt, credit union fees tend to be lower than those of banks.

Central Credit Unions Because many credit unions are small and have very little diversification, they are often susceptible to seasonal cash flow problems. Most credit unions also lack the size needed to support large administrative staffs. One way they overcome these problems is with "central" credit unions, which service the credit unions in their area by providing computer and financial assistance. Each province has a central credit union. Central credit unions provide a number of valuable services:

- They may help with member institutions' credit needs. The provincial Centrals can invest excess funds and make loans to cover short-term shortages.
- They can invest excess funds with the Credit Union Central of Canada, which in turn can invest in the financial markets.
- They can hold clearing balances.
- They can provide educational services.

In addition to using the Credit Union Central of Canada, many credit unions contract with commercial banks for data processing services. Cheques written by credit union customers are automatically routed to the bank, which takes the funds out of a credit union account. The bank then provides a transaction history in electronic form that is given to the credit union. The tie-in with the servicing bank may be so close that the credit union's teller terminals are linked to the bank's computer system, just like the bank's own teller terminals. The credit union customer may never be aware that a bank is involved in the process.

The Website of the Credit Union Central of Canada is www.cucentral.ca

Organizational Structure As member-owned, independent financial firms, credit unions and *caisses populaires* constitute an alternative financial system, different from the profit-seeking banking system. They have also developed their own set of institutions, including central banking and deposit insurance arrangements. As already noted, each province has a central credit union, owned by the member credit unions, which provides financial services to individual credit unions. All the provincial Centrals outside Quebec are members of the **Credit Union Central of Canada (CUCC)**, also known as **Canadian Central**, which acts as a central bank for credit unions.[1] The Canadian Central serves as the third tier for the credit union movement; it coordinates various functions and provides cheque-clearing services for all provincial Centrals.

Go to www.desjardins.com, the Website for the *Desjardins*.

In Quebec, *caisses populaires* are organized into eleven regional federations that in turn belong to *the Confédération des caisses populaires et d'économie Desjardins du Quebec*, which has a similar structure as the provincial Centrals in the rest of Canada but with considerably broader regulatory responsibilities. The confederation dominates retail and corporate financial intermediation in Quebec. It owns a property and casualty insurance company, *Assurances Générales*, a life insurance company, Desjardins Laurentian Life, an American banking subsidiary, Desjardins Federal Savings Bank, an investment dealer and discount brokerage, Desjardins Securities Inc. and Disnat, and an industrial investment subsidiary, *Investissement Desjardins*. It also owns *Caisse centrale Desjardins*, which functions as a central bank, as the CUCC does for the rest of Canada.

Deposit Insurance Credit unions and *caisses populaires* are not directly covered by the CDIC. However, each provincial government has an agency, commonly called a stabilization fund, which has a line of credit with the provincial treasury and provides deposit guarantees for credit unions. Deposits in New Brunswick and Prince Edward Island are insured up to $60 000 per account; in Ontario and British Columbia up to $100 000; in Nova Scotia and Newfoundland and Labrador up to $250 000; and in Alberta, Saskatchewan, and Manitoba there are no limits on the amount of coverage provided. In Quebec, the Quebec Deposit Insurance Board, the same provincial government agency that insures deposits in other deposit-taking financial institutions in Quebec, also provides deposit guarantees for *caisses populaires*, on terms similar to the CDIC's.

Credit Unions Across Canada The business importance of the cooperative banks in Canada varies significantly from province to province. In Quebec, the *Mouvement Desjardins*, named after its founder, accounts for more than 36% of the assets of all deposit-taking institutions, with strong presence in many financial product lines. For example, it accounts for 44% of deposits, 39% of residential

[1] The Canadian Central was incorporated by Act of Parliament in 1953. Its primary shareholders are the nine provincial Centrals.

mortgages, and almost 45% of agricultural credit in the province. In Saskatchewan and Manitoba the credit union movement accounts for about 35% and 25%, respectively, of the assets of deposit-taking institutions. In other provinces, the cooperative banks have a much less significant presence.

Credit Union Size Because their members share a common goal, credit unions and *caisses populaires* are typically quite small; most are about the size of a single bank branch and hold less than $10 million of assets, with the largest being Vancouver City Savings (VanCity) with assets close to $6 billion. Table 2 lists the largest credit unions.

TABLE 2 Largest Credit Unions, 2001:Q2

Rank	Credit Union	Province	Assets ($ millions)
1	Vancouver City Savings	BC	6 074
2	Coast Capital Savings	BC	3 224
3	Surrey Metro Savings	BC	2 350
4	First Heritage Delta Savings	BC	1 636
5	Capital City Savings	AB	1 379
6	Niagara Credit Union	ON	1 176
7	Community Credit Union	AB	1 129
8	Civil Service Co-op	ON	1 071
9	Hepcoe Credit Union	ON	1 046
10	Steinbach Credit Union	MB	995

Source: www.cucentral.ca. © Canadian Credit Union of Canada

As discussed earlier, mergers between credit unions help them capture economies of scale and diversify their risk. This trend has resulted in fewer but larger credit unions. As of the first quarter of 2001, there were 703 credit unions and 1069 *caisses populaires* (a total of 1772 credit unions and *caisses populaires*, down from about 2700 ten years earlier). Figure 1 reports the number of credit unions and *caisses populaires*, as well as the number of members and locations, from 1970 to 2000. The number has fallen steadily since 1970 as credit unions and *caisses populaires* merged.

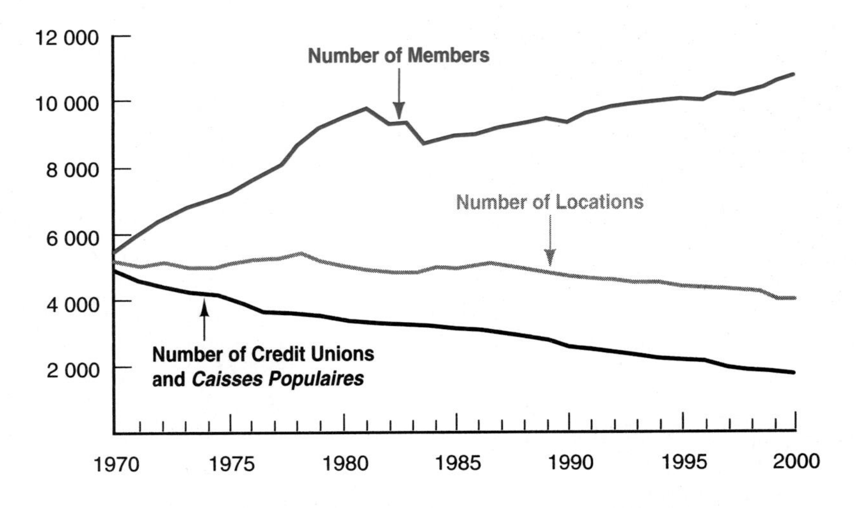

FIGURE 1 Consolidation Trend, Credit Unions and *Caisses Populaires* in Canada

Source: http://www.fin.gc.ca/toce/2002/ccu_e.html

Sources of Funds

Table 3 shows the aggregate balance sheet of credit unions and *caisses populaires*. More than 87% of credit union and *caisses populaires* funds come from customer deposit accounts. Unlike commercial banks, credit unions seldom purchase funds in the capital or money markets. Three main types of accounts are offered by credit unions and *caisses populaires*: chequable, non-chequable, and term deposit accounts. Note also that members' equity accounts for 7.17% of liabilities.

Uses of Funds

In the third quarter of 2001, 82% of credit union and *caisses populaires* assets were invested in loans. Most credit union and *caisses populaires* loans are relatively small. This is in keeping with the mission of credit unions to provide loans to small borrowers. Credit union loan losses are also usually quite small.

The loan portfolio is made up largely by residential and non-residential mortgages (53.8% of the balance sheet) and cash loans to members (12.82%). Figure 2 shows the loan distribution of the industry.

Low-risk assets, such as cash and deposits (primarily with central credit unions) also represent a significant proportion of the balance sheet (close to 16%). The balance of credit union and *caisses populaires* assets are in government securities, deposits at other institutions, and fixed assets. Credit unions and *caisses populaires* tend not to make risky investments and are limited by regulations to certain types of investment securities that assure low risk.

Advantages and Disadvantages of Credit Unions

Figure 1 shows the membership in credit unions from 1970 to 2000. The steady increase is expected to continue because credit unions enjoy several advantages over other depository institutions. These advantages have contributed toward their growth and popularity.

- *Employer support.* Many employers recognize that it is in their own best interest to help their employees manage their funds. This motivates the

TABLE 3 Balance Sheet of All Credit Unions and *Caisses Populaires* (in millions, as of 2001:Q3)

Assets	Amount ($)	Percent (%)	Liabilities	Amount ($)	Percent(%)
Cash and demand and notice deposits	9 219	7.03	Deposits		
			Chequable	29 449	22.45
			Nonchequable	8 594	6.55
Term deposits	11 872	9.05	Term	76 813	58.56
Short-term paper	540	0.41			
Canadian bonds			Loans	4 485	3.42
Government of Canada	535	0.41			
Provincial and municipal	207	0.16	Other liabilities	2 423	1.85
Other	467	0.36			
			Members' equity	9 404	7.17
Shares central credit unions	616	0.47			
Loans and other assets			Total liabilities	131 168	100.00
Personal loans	16 821	12.82			
Residential mortgages	60 613	46.21			
Nonresidential mortgages	9 972	7.60			
Other loans and assets	20 306	15.48			
Total assets	131 168	100.00			

Source: Bank of Canada *Banking and Financial Statistics*, March 2002.

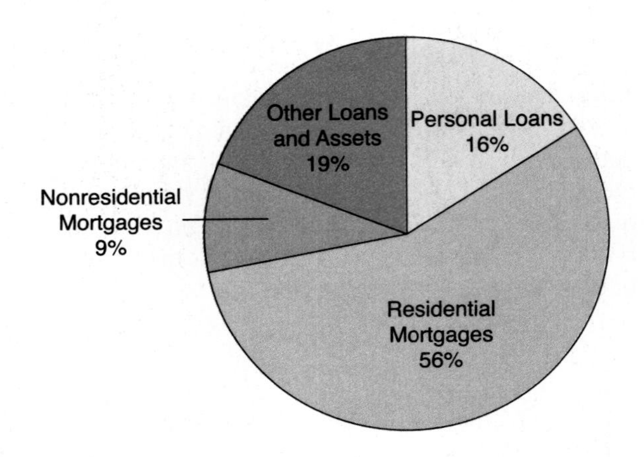

FIGURE 2 Loan Distribution of Credit Unions and *Caisses Populaires*, 2001:Q3

Source: Bank of Canada *Banking and Financial Statistics*, March 2002

firm to support the employee credit union. Businesses will frequently provide free office space, utilities, and other help to the credit unions.

- *Strong trade associations.* Credit unions have formed many trade associations, which lower their costs and provide the means to offer services the institutions could not otherwise offer.

The main disadvantage of credit unions is that the common bond requirement keeps many of them very small. The cost disadvantage can prevent them from offering the range of services available from larger institutions. This disadvantage is not entirely equalized by the use of trade associations.

The Future of Credit Unions

Credit unions are well positioned to continue their growth as a significant provider of financial services to consumers. Figure 3 shows that credit union and *caisses populaires* assets increased from $3 billion to about $134 billion over a 35-year

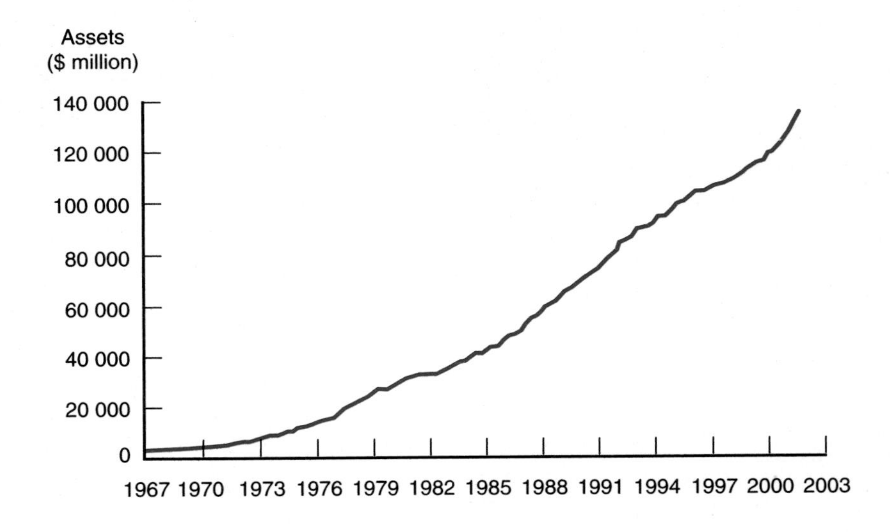

FIGURE 3 Credit Union and *Caisses Populaires* Assets, 1967–2001

Source: Statistics Canada CANSIM II series V122571.

period. Though credit unions and *caisses populaires* are likely to remain small compared to other financial institutions, their cost advantages give them a competitive edge that will continue to attract consumer business.

GOVERNMENT SAVINGS INSTITUTIONS

In addition to the near banks (trust and mortgage loans companies and credit unions and *caisses populaires*), there are some government-operated deposit-taking institutions such as the Province of Ontario Savings Office and the Alberta Treasury branches.

The Province of Ontario Savings Office was established in 1921 with the objective of gathering funds from the public to lend to farmers. Today, however, the Savings Office only lends funds to the treasurer of Ontario for provincial government purposes. In fact, its deposit liabilities are a debt of the province of Ontario and are guaranteed by the province.

Information about Alberta Treasury branches can be found at www.atb.com

Alberta established treasury branches back in 1938 in response to Albertans' needs in remote areas. Today, there are 278 branches in 109 communities across the province operating in three target markets: individual financial services, agricultural operations, and independent business. Alberta Treasury branches are funded almost entirely by demand, notice, and fixed-term deposits, and their risk asset portfolio is made up largely of residential mortgages, and personal, commercial, and agricultural loans.

NEAR BANKS IN THE UNITED STATES

The Office of Thrift Supervision's Website, www.ots.treas.gov, contains quarterly industry information, statistical reports, and laws and regulations. The OTS 2000 Fact Book, www.ots.treas.gov/docs/48080.pdf, offers a statistical profile of the thrift industry.

Given the importance of the financial system in the United States to economic activity in Canada, in this section we briefly discuss American near banks, in the same way that we discussed American commercial banks in Chapter 16.

There are three types of near banks in the United States, known as thrift institutions (or thrifts): mutual savings banks, credit unions, and savings and loan (S&L) associations. Though smaller than commercial banks, thrifts are important to the servicing of consumer borrowing needs in the United States, in the same way that trust and mortgage loan companies and credit unions and *caisses populaires* are important to consumers in Canada.

Mutual Savings Banks

Information about U.S. savings institutions is available on-line; for example, the Wisconsin Department of Financial Institutions Website, www.wdfi.org/fi/saving_institutions, gives lists of savings institutions, statutes, rules, and financial data of the institutions.

The first pure savings banks were established by philanthropists in Scotland and England to encourage saving by the poor. The founders of the institutions would often provide subsidies that allowed the institution to pay interest rates above the current market level. Because of the nature of the savings banks' customers, the institutions were very conservative with their funds and placed most of them in commercial banks. The first savings banks in the United States were chartered by Congress and founded in the Northeast in 1816. These institutions quickly lost their distinction of being strictly for the poor and instead became a popular place for members of the middle class to store their excess money.

Savings banks were originally organized as mutual banks, like credit unions and *caisses populaires* in Canada, meaning that the depositors were the owners of the firm. This form of ownership led to a conservative investment posture, which prevented many of the mutual savings banks from failing during the recession at the end of the nineteenth century or during the Great Depression in the 1930s. In fact, between 1930 and 1937, deposits in mutual savings banks grew while those in commercial banks actually shrank. Following World War II, savings banks made mortgage lending their primary business. This focus made them similar to savings and loans (to be discussed shortly).

Mutual ownership means that no stock in the bank is issued or sold; the depositors own a share of the bank in proportion to their deposits. There are currently 815 mutual savings banks operating in 17 states, primarily concentrated on the eastern seaboard. Most are state chartered (federal chartering of savings banks did not begin until 1978.) Because they are state chartered, they are regulated and supervised by the state as well as the U.S. federal government.

Credit Unions in the United States

The second type of thrift institution in the United States is the credit union. In the early 1900s, commercial banks in the United States focused most of their attention on the business borrower. This left the small consumer without a ready source of funds. Because the U.S. Congress was concerned that commercial banks were not meeting the needs of consumers, it established savings banks and savings and loan associations to help consumers obtain mortgage loans. In the early 1900s, the credit union was also established to help consumers with other types of loans. A secondary purpose was to provide a place for small investors to place their savings.

The first two credit unions in the United States were established in Massachusetts. The Massachusetts Credit Union (MCU) was organized in 1914 as a functioning credit union but with the additional purpose of encouraging the formation of additional credit unions. The MCU evolved into a kind of central credit union facility. In 1921, the MCU was reorganized as the **Credit Union National Extension Bureau (CUNEB)**, which worked to have credit unions established in every state. In 1935, CUNEB was replaced by the **Credit Union National Association (CUNA)**.

In 1934, the U.S. Congress passed the **Federal Credit Union Act**, which allowed federal chartering of credit unions in all states. Prior to this, most credit unions were chartered by the state in which they operated. Currently, about 40% of credit unions have state charters and 60% have federal charters.

One reason for the growth of credit unions has been the support they received from employers. They realized that employee morale could be raised and time saved if banking-type facilities were readily available. In many cases, employers donated space on business property for the credit union to operate. The convenience of this institution soon attracted a large number of customers.

Non-Profit, Tax-Exempt Status The Federal Credit Union Act of 1934 contained the provision that credit unions in the United States were to be non-profit and consequently exempt from federal taxation. All of the income earned by the institutions is to be spent on their members. Credit unions are currently the only financial institutions in the United States that are tax exempt. This makes it easier for them to accumulate retained earnings than it is for other institutions. Banks and S&Ls are questioning this tax-exempt status as credit unions become larger and more significant competitors. Savings and loans lost their tax-exempt status in 1951. The American Bankers Association estimates that the subsidy reduces the cost of funds to credit unions by almost 2.5% and gives them a cost advantage of $1 billion per year. The credit unions themselves dispute this number and assign their cost advantage to their use of volunteer help. It remains a question how long the favourable tax treatment for credit unions can be maintained.

Partly as a result of being non-profit and partly due to the cost advantage of being tax exempt, credit union fees in the United States tend to be lower than those of commercial banks.

The National Credit Union Administration Website, www.ncua.gov, includes general information about credit unions and credit union data in the United States.

Regulation and Insurance The **National Credit Union Act of 1970** established the **National Credit Union Administration (NCUA)**. This independent federal agency is charged with the task of regulating and supervising federally chartered credit unions and state-chartered credit unions that receive federal deposit insurance. The remaining credit unions are regulated by state credit union or banking departments, which generally follow federal practices.

The National Credit Union Act of 1970 also established the **National Credit Union Share Insurance Fund (NCUSIF)**, to be controlled by the NCUA. This fund insures the deposits of all nationally chartered credit unions and most state-chartered credit unions for up to $100 000 per account. The remaining state-chartered credit unions are insured by one of the state insurance systems. Since the savings and loan crisis, most states are eager to get out of the insurance business. It is likely that in the future, all credit union deposit insurance will be provided by the NCUSIF.

U.S. Central Credit Unions There are currently 44 state central credit unions in the United States. Moreover, the **U.S. Central Credit Union** was organized in 1974 to act as a central bank for credit unions. It is chartered as a commercial bank in Kansas, and its primary function is to provide banking services to the 44 state central credit unions. It allows these institutions access to the money markets and to long-term capital markets. Most individual credit unions and even most state central credit unions lack sufficient size and transaction volume to operate efficiently in these wholesale markets.

In 1978, the **Financial Institutions Reform Act** created the **Central Liquidity Facility (CLF)** as the lender of last resort for credit unions. This agency provides many of the same functions for credit unions that the Federal Reserve provides for commercial banks. Although most day-to-day liquidity needs of credit unions are met by the state central organizations, in the event of a national liquidity crisis, a federal agency can raise far more funds. For example, in a crisis, the CLF can borrow directly from the Federal Reserve.

Membership in the CLF is voluntary, and any state or federally chartered credit union may join the CLF by pledging 0.5% of capital. Most of the funds in the CLF are borrowed from the federal government.

Credit Union Size The U.S. credit union industry accounts for only about 10% of all consumer deposits and about 15% of all consumer loans. Nevertheless, some credit unions have grown quite large. The Navy Credit Union, for example, dwarfs the others, with nearly US$14 billion in total assets. However, most credit unions have less than US$1 billion in assets, and many have less than US$5 million.

Savings and Loan (S&L) Associations

The most important type of thrift institution in the United States is the saving and loan. The savings and loan industry suffered huge losses in the 1970s and the 1980s (to be discussed in more detail in Chapter 18), but managed to survive, although somewhat changed. In this section we review the current state of the industry.

Savings and loan associations are in many ways similar to mutual savings banks and credit unions; however, they do differ in ways other than ownership structure.

The FDIC's Website, www.fdic.gov/qbp, provides a source of tools and charts related to savings and loans. Most current data in this chapter comes from this source.

- Mutual savings banks are concentrated in the northeastern United States; savings and loans are located throughout the country.
- Mutual savings banks may insure their deposits with the state or with the Federal Deposit Insurance Corporation (FDIC); S&Ls may not.

- Mutual savings banks are not as heavily concentrated in mortgages and have had more flexibility in their investing practices than savings and loans.

Number of Institutions The savings and loan industry has witnessed a substantial reduction in the number of institutions. Many failed or were taken over by the **Resolution Trust Corporation (RTC)** that was established to manage and resolve insolvent thrifts placed in conservatorship or receivership; others merged with stronger institutions to avoid failure. The number of S&Ls declined by more than half between the end of 1986, when there were 3600 of them, and 2001, when there were only 1584. Although new S&Ls continue to open, existing ones convert to commercial banks or credit unions or merge with other savings banks. It is interesting to note that consolidation in the savings industry has not been as dramatic as in commercial banking in the United States in recent years.

S&L Size Between 1988 and 1991, the average size of S&Ls fell. This was likely due to the 1989 passage of **Financial Institutions Reform, Recovery, and Enforcement Act (FIRREA)**, which required S&Ls to increase their capital-to-asset ratio. Many institutions met the new standard by decreasing their assets rather than by increasing their capital. From 1992 to 2001, total S&L assets increased, even though the number of institutions decreased. The result is fewer but larger institutions.

A second point to note is that the average size of savings and loans is substantially greater than that of commercial banks. Recall from Chapter 16 that the growth of commercial banks in the United States was often constrained by restrictive banking regulations. As a result, the average size of commercial banks at the end of 2001 was about U.S.$800 million in assets. Thus, the size of the average commercial bank is less than that of the average savings and loan. Now that Congress has removed most of the restrictions on interstate branching by commercial banks, many industry observers expect a period of rapid consolidation in that industry.

S&L Assets Table 4 provides a consolidated balance sheet for the savings and loan industry. Let us first discuss the assets side.

The 1982 reforms allowed S&Ls to make consumer and commercial loans. The intent of this legislation was to give S&Ls a source of assets with short maturities. The problem was that commercial loans are far riskier and require lending expertise that many S&Ls did not possess. FIRREA severely curtailed S&Ls' commercial lending. In the four years following passage of the law, the number of loans made for commercial purposes dropped by about 50%. Currently, nearly 90% of

TABLE 4 Consolidated Balance Sheet for Savings and Loan Associations (U.S.$ billions, 2001:Q2)

Savings and Loan Associations

Assets		Liabilities	
Cash and reserves	47.1	Deposits	755.5
Securities	255.3	Other borrowed funds	289.7
Mortgage loans	751.7	All other liabilities	121.7
Commercial loans	43.8	Equity	107.0
Consumer credit	65.3	Total liabilities and equities	1 273.9
Corporate equities	25.6		
Miscellaneous	85.1		
Total assets	1 273.9		

Sources: Flow of Funds, Table L114 and www.federalreserve.gov/releases/z1

all S&L loans are secured by real estate, and 69% are for residential mortgages. Clearly, the industry has returned to its original mandate of financing home ownership.

Savings and loans are subject to reserve requirements, just as banks are in the United States. Reserve requirements are cash deposits that must be held in the vault or at the Federal Reserve in non-interest-bearing accounts. The purpose of reserve requirements is to limit the expansion of the money supply and to ensure adequate liquidity for the institutions. About 4% of total S&L assets are kept in cash.

In addition to cash, savings and loans hold securities, such as corporate, Treasury, and government agency bonds. Unlike reserve deposits, these assets earn interest. The 1982 legislation allowed savings and loans to hold up to 11% of their assets in junk bonds. S&Ls were a major source of funds during the mid-1980s for corporations looking for capital to use in acquiring other firms. In 1989, the FIRREA required that savings and loans divest themselves of these high-risk securities. Currently, only relatively safe securities can be purchased.

S&L Liabilities and Net Worth Now let's look at the right-hand side of the balance sheet in Table 4. The primary liabilities of savings and loans are deposits and borrowed funds.

The largest liability of savings and loans are customer funds held on deposit. In the past, the bulk of the deposits were from **passbook savings accounts**, interest-bearing savings accounts. In the past, banks issued small books to savers to use for keeping track of their savings balances. The customer would present this book to the teller every time a deposit or withdrawal was made, and the teller would validate the entry. The physical passbook has almost been phased out over the years and replaced with computerized record keeping.

The second major liability is borrowings, funds obtained in either the money or capital markets. Since savings and loan deposits are typically short-term, one way to lengthen their average maturity is to borrow long-term funds. Borrowed funds have become a major source of funds for savings and loans, now accounting for about 23% of total assets, up from 11% in 1990.

Capital As already noted, the capital of financial institutions is often measured by the net worth ratio, total equity (also known as net worth) divided by total assets. This figure is closely watched by regulators for indications that a financial institution may be undercapitalized. The average net worth-to-assets ratio was about 3% in 1984. Many institutions had a negative net worth at this time. Since 1989, the average net worth ratio has improved. At the end of 2000, it stood at 8.4%. This is now about the same as the 8.5% average net worth ratio for commercial banks in the United States. One reason for the improvement in the capital of savings and loans is that FIRREA mandated that it be increased.

The accounting for savings and loans permitted extensive use of goodwill, an asset account on the balance sheet that supposedly reflects the value of a firm's good name and reputation. For example, in 1987, goodwill accounted for $29.6 billion of savings and loan assets. This represented more than half of the $53.8 billion in total capital. If we removed goodwill from capital before calculating the net worth-to-assets ratio in 1987, we find that the ratio is only 1.6%, not the 3.7% it was when including goodwill. The value of goodwill fell steadily since its high that year. Listing large amounts of goodwill as an asset was another way that savings and loans were able to hide the fact that they were insolvent.

Profitability and Health One indication that the health of savings and loans has improved in recent years is that their earnings have increased. From 1987 through

1990, the industry suffered net losses. But in 1991, net after-tax income for the industry was $859 million, and by 2000, it had reached $10.7 billion.

A better measure of a firm's health than net income is its return on equity (ROE). There was a steady increase in S&Ls' ROE from 1993 to 2001, when it was nearly 12%. S&L profits for 1999 were the highest ever reported by the industry. Over 94% of all S&Ls were profitable. Part of this income was due to the sale of mortgage loans that had increased in value when interest rates fell.

Only four S&Ls have failed since 1995. Furthermore, the number of "problem" thrifts is down to 13, compared with 146 in 1993. The percentage of loans being charged off as losses is also at a low 0.25%.

In summary, savings institutions, which were in grave condition a decade ago, have returned to robust health. They are providing fair returns to their shareholders and are not in any danger of causing additional taxpayer losses. The industry's equity-to-capital ratio is now the highest it has ever been.

The Future of the Savings and Loan Industry One issue that has received considerable attention in recent years is whether the U.S. savings and loan industry is still needed. Observers who favour eliminating S&L charters altogether point out that there is now a large number of alternative mortgage loan outlets available for homebuyers. In Chapter 11 we introduced the securitized mortgage. This new instrument has provided the majority of the funds needed by the U.S. mortgage market. A reasonable question to ask is whether there is a need for an industry dedicated exclusively to providing a service efficiently provided elsewhere in the financial system.

Let us review the history of the savings and loan industry for a moment. S&Ls were established to provide mortgages to homebuyers. The industry was healthy until interest rates increased and they were stuck holding low-interest fixed-rate mortgages financed with high-cost funds. The U.S. Congress attempted to provide relief by giving S&Ls a great deal of flexibility in their capital structure and lending functions. Due to abuses, poor market conditions, inadequate supervision by **Federal Savings and Loan Insurance Corporation (FSLIC)**, and fraud, tremendous losses accrued. Finally, the U.S. Congress reregulated the industry and again required that its primary business be mortgage lending. The only trouble now is that mortgage loans are available from many other sources.

Just as efficient markets develop new securities and services when the need for them arises, efficient markets should eliminate unneeded institutions when they are no longer required. Many industry analysts expect the savings and loan industry to disappear, perhaps by existing savings and loans being acquired by other institutions or by commercial banks. We can examine the evidence to see if this is beginning to happen.

We noted earlier that the number of savings and loans has decreased by 56% since its high in 1986. There were fewer S&Ls in 2001 than in 1994. However, the drop in the number of institutions could be due to consolidation within the industry, much like what is happening in commercial banking in the United States. A better indication of the future of the industry may be provided by the trend in total assets. In fact, the total assets of savings and loans have increased since 1993. This suggests that there is at least not a rapid trend to eliminate these institutions. It may be that they will continue to be a provider of mortgage loans along with a number of other sources.

The U.S. Congress will be pressured again to deregulate the industry to allow S&Ls to perform more of the functions allowed by commercial banks. Although this may happen, the losses sustained as a result of the last attempt at deregulation are still fresh in the minds of regulators. It is unlikely that we will again witness an attempt at rapid deregulation. Instead, we can expect to see gradual changes in the industry that will continue to blur the distinction between savings and loans and commercial banks.

SUMMARY

1. The regulation and structure of the near banks (trust and mortgage loan companies and credit unions and *caisses populaires*) parallel closely the regulation and structure of the chartered banks. Federally incorporated near banks are regulated and supervised by the OSFI. They must also register in all the provinces in which they do business and must conform to the regulations of those provinces.
2. Credit unions were established to serve the public's demand for consumer-type loans. They are unique because members must satisfy a common bond requirement to join. This common bond requirement has restricted the growth of credit unions. Most are small compared to commercial banks.
3. Because of their small size, credit unions have benefited by forming cooperative organizations. These co-ops provide technical, liquidity, mortgage, and insurance services that would be impossible for the individual credit unions to have otherwise.
4. Credit unions enjoy several advantages that should keep them viable in the future. First, many have strong support from a sponsoring company or business, which lowers the operating cost of the institution. Second, the use of volunteers also helps keep costs low.
5. The U.S. Congress mandated that savings and loans and mutual savings banks in the Unites States provide mortgage loan opportunities for consumers. For most of the twentieth century, savings and loans and mutual savings banks profitably satisfied this need.
6. In the late 1970s and the 1980s, savings and loans in the United States lost money because interest rates on their deposits rose while the return on their mortgage portfolios was fixed. These losses initially led to deregulation. Savings and loans continued to lose money despite regulatory reform.
7. Due to mounting losses among savings and loans the industry was reregulated in 1987. It has since recovered in terms of both profitability and net worth. The industry continues to consolidate, though total assets are remaining about constant. It is too early to determine whether the industry will simply merge with commercial banks or remain independent.

KEY TERMS

Central Liquidity Facility (CLF), *p. 447*
common bond membership, *p. 440*
cooperative bank, *p. 439*
Credit Union Central of Canada (CUCC) or Canadian Central, *p. 441*
Credit Union National Association (CUNA), *p. 446*
Credit Union National Extension Bureau (CUNEB), *p. 446*
Federal Credit Union Act, *p. 446*
Federal Savings and Loan Insurance Corporation (FSLIC), *p. 450*
Financial Institutions Reform Act, *p. 447*
Financial Institutions Reform, Recovery, and Enforcement Act (FIRREA), *p. 448*
National Credit Union Act of 1970, *p. 447*
National Credit Union Administration (NCUA), *p. 447*
National Credit Union Share Insurance Fund (NCUSIF), *p. 447*
near banks, *p. 435*
passbook savings account, *p. 449*
Resolution Trust Corporation (RTC), *p. 448*
trustees, *p. 436*
U.S. Central Credit Union, *p. 447*

QUESTIONS AND PROBLEMS

*1. How does the mutual form of ownership differ from the typical corporate form of ownership?

2. What is the primary disadvantage of the mutual form of ownership?

*3. What are the primary assets of trust and mortgage loan companies?

4. What are the primary assets of credit unions and *caisses populaires*?

*5. What has been the trend in credit unions and *caisses populaires* assets since 1967?

6. What are the essential differences between credit unions and commercial banks?

*7. What is the most common measure of the capital adequacy of a financial institution?

8. What has been the trend in S&L net income since the mid-1990s?

*9. What types of customers are credit unions focused on servicing?

10. What is the purpose of the Credit Union Central of Canada (CUCC)?

*11. Describe the common bond membership rule.

12. Why does the commercial banking lobby object to the non-profit, tax-exempt status enjoyed by credit unions in the United States?

*13. Are most credit unions larger or smaller than commercial banks? Why?

14. Which regulatory agencies have the primary responsibility for supervising trust and mortgage loan companies and credit unions and *caisses populaires*?

*15. What are the primary advantages enjoyed by credit unions?

16. Why is regulatory forbearance a dangerous strategy for a deposit insurance agency?

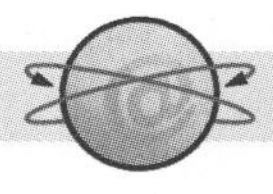

WEB EXERCISES

1. Go to http://www.osfi-bsif.ca. This is the home page of the Office of the Superintendent of Financial Institutions (OSFI). Click on "Deposit-Taking Institutions."
   - **a.** According to the Trust and Loan Companies Act, what features define trust and mortgage loan companies?
   - **b.** According to the Cooperatives Credit Associations Act, what features define a cooperative credit association?
   - **c.** What kind of financial data are available for trust and loan companies?

2. Like commercial banks, thrift institutions in the United States provide a great deal of summary information to the public. One of the most extensive sites for thrift information is at http://www.ots.treas.gov. Select "Industry Performance" under "Data and Research" on the left margin of the site. Now go to "Select Indicator" on the site to answer the following questions.
   - **a.** What is the return on average assets for the most recent period?
   - **b.** What is the return on average equity for the most recent period?
   - **c.** How many thrift institutions are reporting to the OTS during the most recent period?

Chapter 18 Banking Regulation

Preview

As we have seen in earlier chapters, the financial system is among the most heavily regulated sectors of the economy, and banks are among the most heavily regulated of financial institutions. In this chapter we develop an economic analysis of why regulation of banking takes the form it does.

Unfortunately, the regulatory process may not always work very well, as evidenced by recent crises in the banking systems, not only in Canada but in many countries throughout the world. Here we also use our analysis of banking regulation to explain the worldwide crises in banking and how the regulatory system can be reformed to prevent future disasters.

ASYMMETRIC INFORMATION AND BANK REGULATION

In earlier chapters we have seen how asymmetric information, the fact that different parties in a financial contract do not have the same information, leads to adverse selection and moral hazard problems that have an important impact on our financial system. The concepts of asymmetric information, adverse selection, and moral hazard are especially useful in understanding why government has chosen the form of banking regulation we see in Canada and in other countries. There are seven basic categories of banking regulation: the government safety net, restrictions on bank asset holdings and capital requirements, chartering and bank examination, disclosure requirements, consumer protection, restrictions on competition, and separation of the banking and securities industries.

Bank regulation information is available at www.osfi-bsif.gc.ca

Government Safety Net: Deposit Insurance and the CDIC

As we saw in Chapter 14, banks are particularly well suited to solving adverse selection and moral hazard problems because they make private loans that help avoid the free-rider problem. However, this solution to the free-rider problem creates another asymmetric information problem because depositors lack information about the quality of these private loans. This asymmetric information problem leads to two reasons why the banking system might not function well.

First, before the CDIC started operations in 1967, a bank failure (in which a bank is unable to meet its obligations to pay its depositors and other creditors and so must go out of business) meant that depositors would have to wait to get their deposit funds until the bank was liquidated (until its assets had been turned into cash); at that time, they would be paid only a fraction of the value of their deposits. Unable to learn if bank managers were taking on too much risk or were outright crooks, depositors would be reluctant to put money in the bank, thus making banking institutions less viable. Second is that depositors' lack of information about the quality of bank assets can lead to bank panics, which, as we saw in Chapter 14, can have serious harmful consequences for the economy. To see this, consider the following situation. There is no deposit insurance, and an adverse shock hits the economy. As a result of the shock, 5% of the banks have such large losses on loans that they become insolvent (have a negative net worth and so are bankrupt). Because of asymmetric information, depositors are unable to tell whether their bank is a good bank or one of the 5% that are insolvent. Depositors at bad *and* good banks recognize that they may not get back 100 cents on the dollar for their deposits and will want to withdraw them. Indeed, because banks operate on a "sequential service constraint" (a first-come, first-served basis), depositors have a very strong incentive to show up at the bank first because if they are last in line, the bank may run out of funds and they will get nothing. Uncertainty about the health of the banking system in general can lead to runs on banks both good and bad, and the failure of one bank can hasten the failure of others (referred to as the *contagion effect*). If nothing is done to restore the public's confidence, a bank panic can ensue.

A government safety net for depositors can short-circuit runs on banks and bank panics, and by providing protection for the depositor, it can overcome reluctance to put funds in the banking system. One form of the safety net is deposit insurance, a guarantee such as that provided by the Canada Deposit Insurance Corporation (CDIC) in Canada in which depositors are paid off in full on the first $60 000 they have deposited in the bank no matter what happens to the bank. With fully insured deposits, depositors don't need to run to the bank to make withdrawals—even if they are worried about the bank's health—because their deposits will be worth 100 cents on the dollar no matter what.

The CDIC uses two primary methods to handle a failed bank. In the first, called the *payoff method,* the CDIC allows the bank to fail and pays off deposits up to the $60 000 insurance limit (with funds acquired from the insurance premiums paid by the banks that have bought CDIC insurance). After the bank has been liquidated, the CDIC lines up with other creditors of the bank and is paid its share of the proceeds from the liquidated assets. Typically, when the payoff method is used, account holders with deposits in excess of the $60 000 limit get back more than 90 cents on the dollar, although the process can take several years to complete.

In the second method, called the *purchase and assumption method,* the CDIC reorganizes the bank, typically by finding a willing merger partner who assumes (takes over) all of the failed bank's deposits so that no depositor loses a penny. The CDIC may help the merger partner by providing it with subsidized loans or by buying some of the failed bank's weaker loans. The net effect of the purchase and assumption method is that the CDIC has guaranteed *all* deposits, not just those under the $60 000 limit.

Deposit insurance is not the only way in which governments provide a safety net for depositors.Governments have often stood ready to provide support to domestic banks when they face runs even in the absence of explicit deposit insurance. This support is sometimes provided by lending from the central bank to troubled institutions and is often referred to as the "lender of last resort" role of the central bank. In other cases, funds are provided directly by the government to troubled institutions, or these institutions are taken over by the government and the government then guarantees that depositors will receive their money in full. However, in recent years, government deposit insurance has been growing in popularity and has spread to many countries throughout the world. Whether this trend is desirable is discussed in Box 1.

Moral Hazard and the Government Safety Net Although a government safety net has been successful at protecting depositors and preventing bank panics, it is a mixed blessing. The most serious drawback of the government safety net stems from moral hazard, the incentives of one party to a transaction to engage in activities detrimental to the other party. Moral hazard is an important concern in insurance arrangements in general because the existence of insurance provides increased incentives for taking risks that might result in an insurance payoff. For example, some drivers with automobile collision insurance that has a low deductible might be more likely to drive recklessly because if they get into an accident, the insurance company pays most of the costs for damage and repairs.

Moral hazard is a prominent concern in government arrangements to provide a safety net. Because with a safety net depositors know that they will not suffer losses if a bank fails, they do not impose the discipline of the marketplace on banks by withdrawing deposits when they suspect that the bank is taking on too much risk. Consequently, banks with a government safety net have an incentive to take on greater risks than they otherwise would.

Adverse Selection and the Government Safety Net A further problem with a government safety net like deposit insurance arises because of adverse selection, the fact that the people who are most likely to produce the adverse outcome insured against (bank failure) are those who most want to take advantage of the insurance. For example, bad drivers are more likely than good drivers to take out automobile collision insurance with a low deductible. Because depositors protected by a government safety net have little reason to impose discipline on the bank, risk-loving entrepreneurs might find the banking industry a particularly attractive one to enter—they know that they will be able to engage in highly risky activities. Even worse, because protected depositors have so little reason to monitor the bank's activities, without government intervention outright crooks might also find banking an attractive industry for their activities because it is easy for them to get away with fraud and embezzlement.

BOX 1: GLOBAL

The Spread of Government Deposit Insurance Throughout the World: Is This a Good Thing?

Government deposit insurance has taken off throughout the world because of growing concern about the health of banking systems, particularly after the increasing number of banking crises in recent years (documented at the end of the chapter). Has this spread of deposit insurance been a good thing? Has it helped improve the performance of the financial system and prevent banking crises?

The answer seems to be no under many circumstances. Research at the World Bank has found that on average, the adoption of explicit government deposit insurance is associated with less banking sector stability and a higher incidence of banking crises.* Furthermore, on average it seems to retard financial development. However, the negative effects of deposit insurance appear only in countries with weak institutional environments: an absence of rule of law, ineffective regulation and supervision of the financial sector, and high corruption. This is exactly what might be expected because, as we will see later in this chapter, a strong institutional environment is needed to limit the incentives for banks to engage in excessively risky behaviour created by deposit insurance. The problem is that developing a strong institutional environment may be very difficult to achieve in many emerging market countries. This leaves us with the following conclusion: Adoption of deposit insurance may be exactly the wrong medicine for promoting stability and efficiency of banking systems in emerging market countries.

*See World Bank, *Finance for Growth: Policy Choices in a Volatile World* (World Bank and Oxford University Press: Oxford 2001).

"Too Big to Fail" The moral hazard created by a government safety net and the desire to prevent bank failures have presented bank regulators with a particular quandary. Because the failure of a very large bank makes it more likely that a major financial disruption will occur, bank regulators are naturally reluctant to allow a big bank to fail and cause losses to its depositors.

One problem with the too-big-to-fail policy is that it increases the moral hazard incentives for big banks. If the CDIC were willing to close a bank using the alternative payoff method, paying depositors only up to the $60 000 limit, large depositors with more than $60 000 would suffer losses if the bank failed. Thus they would have an incentive to monitor the bank by examining the bank's activities closely and pulling their money out if the bank was taking on too much risk. To prevent such a loss of deposits, the bank would be more likely to engage in less risky activities. However, once large depositors know that a bank is too big to fail, they have no incentive to monitor the bank and pull out their deposits when it takes on too much risk: No matter what the bank does, large depositors will not suffer any losses. The result of the too-big-to-fail policy is that big banks might take on even greater risks, thereby making bank failures more likely.[1]

Another serious problem with the too-big-to-fail policy is that it is basically unfair. Small banks are put at a competitive disadvantage because they will be allowed to fail, creating potential losses for their large depositors, while big banks' large depositors are immune from losses. The unfairness of the too-big-to-fail doctrine came to a head with the different treatment by the Federal Deposit Insurace Corporation (FDIC) in the United States of two insolvent banks in late 1990 and early 1991 described in Box 2. (Note that the FDIC insures deposits up to US$100 000 per account).

Financial Consolidation and the Government Safety Net As we have seen in Chapter 16, financial consolidation has been proceeding at a rapid pace, leading to both larger and more complex banking organizations. Financial consolidation poses two challenges to banking regulation because of the existence of the government safety net. First, the increased size of banks as a result of financial consolidation increases the too-big-to-fail problem because there will now be more large institutions whose failure exposes the financial system to systemic (systemwide) risk. Thus, more banking institutions are likely to be treated as too big to fail, and the increased moral hazard incentives for these large institutions to take on greater risk can then increase the fragility of the financial system. Second, financial consolidation of banks with other financial service firms means that the government safety net may be extended to new activities such as securities underwriting, insurance, or real estate activities, thereby increasing incentives for greater risk taking in these activities, which can also weaken the fabric of the financial system. Limiting the moral hazard incentives for larger, more complex, financial organizations that are resulting from recent changes in legislation will be one of the key issues facing banking regulators in the future.

Restrictions on Asset Holdings and Bank Capital Requirements

As we have seen, the moral hazard associated with a government safety net encourages too much risk taking on the part of banks. Bank regulations that restrict asset holdings and bank capital requirements are directed at minimizing this moral hazard, which can cost the taxpayers dearly.

---

[1]Recent evidence reveals, as our analysis predicts, that large banks have taken on riskier loans than smaller banks and that this has led to higher loan losses for big banks; see John Boyd and Mark Gertler, "U.S. Commercial Banking: Trends, Cycles and Policy," *NBER Macroeconomics Annual,* 1993, pp. 319–68.

BOX 2

A Tale of Two Bank Collapses in the United States: Bank of New England and Freedom National Bank

The FDIC's procedures for handling two bank collapses, those of the Bank of New England and Freedom National Bank, illustrate how the too-big-to-fail policy works.

The Bank of New England, based in Boston, was the 33rd-largest bank holding company in the United States, with more than $20 billion of assets. In the 1980s, it was the region's most aggressive real estate lender; more than 30% of its loan portfolio was in commercial real estate. With the collapse of real estate prices in New England beginning in the late 1980s (commercial real estate values dropped by more than 25%), many of the bank's loans went sour. On Friday, January 4, 1991, the bank announced a projected $450 million fourth-quarter loss that exceeded the bank's capital of $255 million. Expecting the failure of the bank, in the next 48 hours depositors lined up at the bank and withdrew more than $1 billion in funds, much of it from automated teller machines.

The chairman of the FDIC, William Seidman, expressed his concern over the ramifications of the potential failure: "Given the condition of the financial system in New England, it would be unwise to send a signal that large depositors weren't going to be protected."* The FDIC invoked its too-big-to-fail policy. Sunday night, January 6, the FDIC moved in to stop the run on the bank and agreed to guarantee all Bank of New England deposits, including those in excess of the $100 000 insurance limit. To keep the bank in operation until a buyer could be found and the purchase and assumption method could be used to make sure that no depositors would suffer any loss, the FDIC created what is called a *bridge bank*. In this arrangement, the FDIC creates a new corporation to run the bank and immediately injects capital ($750 million in the case of the Bank of New England). The FDIC and the buyer of the bank then put additional capital into the bank over time, and eventually the acquirer buys out the FDIC's share. The net result of these transactions was that the FDIC spent $2.3 billion bailing out the Bank of New England, the third-costliest bailout in the FDIC's history. However, when all was said and done and spent, none of the depositors lost a penny.

The very different FDIC treatment of a small insolvent bank in Harlem several months earlier raised serious questions of fairness. The Freedom National Bank was founded in 1964 by baseball great Jackie Robinson and other minority investors. Despite its small size (under $100 million of deposits), it was one of the most prominent black-owned banks.

As a result of numerous speculative loans that went bad, the bank became insolvent in November 1990. Because of the bank's small size, the FDIC was not concerned that the failure of the bank would have serious repercussions for the rest of the banking system, so it decided to close the bank on November 9 using the payoff method. The Freedom National Bank was liquidated, and large depositors were paid only 50 cents on the dollar for deposits in excess of $100 000. Not only fat cats suffered losses when this bank failed. Charitable organizations like the United Negro College Fund, the National Urban League, and several churches were among the large depositors at the bank. Seidman described the unfairness of the treatment of the Freedom National Bank to Congress: "My first testimony when I came to this job was that it's unfair to treat big banks in a way that covers all depositors but not small banks. I promised to do my best to change that. Five years later, I can report that my best wasn't good enough."**

*Quoted in John Meehan, "A Shock to the System: How Far Will Banking's Crisis of Confidence Spread?" *Business Week*, January 21, 1991, p. 26.

**Quoted in Kenneth H. Bacon, "Failures of a Big Bank and a Little Bank Bring Fairness of Deposit-Security Policy into Question," *Wall Street Journal*, December 5, 1990, p. A18.

Source: Reprinted from January 24, 1991 issue of *Business Week* by special permission, Copyright © 1991 by the McGraw-Hill Companies, Inc.

Even in the absence of a government safety net, banks still have the incentive to take on too much risk. Risky assets may provide the bank with higher earnings when they pay off; but if they do not pay off and the bank fails, depositors are left holding the bag. If depositors were able to monitor the bank easily by acquiring information on its risk-taking activities, they would immediately withdraw their deposits if the bank was taking on too much risk. To prevent such a loss of deposits, the bank would be more likely to reduce its risk-taking activities. Unfortunately, acquiring information on a bank's activities to learn how much risk the bank is taking can be a difficult task. Hence, most depositors are incapable of imposing discipline that might prevent banks from engaging in risky activities. A strong rationale for government regulation to reduce risk taking on the part of banks therefore existed even before the establishment of federal deposit insurance.

Bank regulations that restrict banks from holding risky assets such as common stock are a direct means of making banks avoid too much risk. Bank regulations also promote diversification, which reduces risk by limiting the amount of loans in particular categories or to individual borrowers. Requirements that banks have sufficient bank capital are another way to change the bank's incentives to take on less risk. When a bank is forced to hold a large amount of equity capital, the bank has more to lose if it fails and is thus more likely to pursue less risky activities.

Bank capital requirements take three forms. The first type is based on the so-called **leverage ratio**, the amount of capital divided by the bank's total assets. To be classified as well capitalized, a bank's leverage ratio must exceed 5%; a lower leverage ratio, especially one below 3%, triggers increased regulatory restrictions on the bank.

In the past decade, regulators in Canada and the rest of the world have become increasingly worried about banks' holdings of risky assets and about the increase in banks' **off-balance-sheet activities**, activities that involve trading financial instruments and generating income from fees, which do not appear on bank balance sheets but nevertheless expose banks to risk. An agreement among banking officials from industrialized nations has set up the **Basel Committee on Banking Supervision** (because it meets under the auspices of the Bank for International Settlements in Basel, Switzerland), which has implemented the so-called **Basel Accord** on risk-based capital requirements. The Basel Accord, which required that banks hold as capital at least 8% of their risk-weighted assets, has been adopted by more than 100 countries, including Canada. Assets and off-balance-sheet activities were allocated into four categories, each with a different weight to reflect the degree of credit risk. The first category carried a zero weight and included items that have little default risk, such as reserves and government securities in the OECD (industrialized) countries. The second category had a 20% weight and included claims on banks in OECD countries. The third category had a weight of 50% and included municipal bonds and residential mortgages. The fourth category had the maximum weight of 100% and included debts to consumers and corporations. Off-balance-sheet activities are treated in a similar manner by assigning a credit-equivalent percentage that converts them to on-balance-sheet items to which the appropriate risk weight applies. The 1996 Market Risk Amendment to the Accord set minimum capital requirements for risks in banks' trading accounts.

Over time, limitations of the Accord have become apparent because the regulatory measure of bank risk as stipulated by the risk weights can differ substantially from the actual risk the bank faces. This has resulted in what is known as **regulatory arbitrage**, in which banks keep on their books assets that have the same risk-based capital requirement but are relatively risky, such as a loan to a company with a very low credit rating, while taking off their books low-risk assets such as a loan to a company with a very high credit rating. The Basel Accord could thus lead to increased risk taking, the opposite of its intent. To address these limitations, the Basel Committee on Bank Supervision has released proposals for a new capital accord, often referred to as Basel 2, but it is not clear if it is workable and when it will be implemented (see Box 3).

The Basel Committee's work on bank capital requirements is never ending. As the banking industry changes, the regulation of bank capital must change with it to ensure the safety and soundness of the banking institutions.

Bank Supervision: Chartering and Examination

Overseeing who operates banks and how they are operated, referred to as **bank supervision** or more generally as **prudential supervision,** is an important method for reducing adverse selection and moral hazard in the banking business. Because banks can be used by crooks or overambitious entrepreneurs to engage in highly speculative activities, such undesirable people would be eager to run a

BOX 3

Basel 2: Is It Spinning Out of Control?

Starting in June 1999, the Basel Committee on Banking Supervision has released several proposals to reform the original 1988 Basel Accord. Basel 2 is based on three pillars.

Pillar 1 intends to link capital requirements more closely to actual risk. It does this by specifying many more categories of risk with different weights in its so-called standardized approach and allows sophisticated banks to instead pursue an internal ratings-based approach that allows banks to use their own models of credit risk. Pillar 2 focuses on strengthening the supervisory process, particularly in assessing the quality of risk management in banking institutions and whether these institutions have adequate procedures to determine how much capital they need. Pillar 3 focuses on improving market discipline by increased disclosure such as details about the bank's credit exposures, its amount of reserves and capital, who controls the bank, and how well a bank's internal ratings system operates.

Although Basel 2 makes great strides in the direction of limiting excessive risk taking by banking institutions, it has come at a cost of greatly increasing the complexity of the Accord. The document describing the original Basel Accord was 26 pages, while the second draft of Basel 2 issued in January 2001 is more than 500 pages long. The original timetable called for the completion of the final round of consultation by the end of May 2001, with the new rules taking effect by 2004. However, criticism from banks, trade associations, and national regulators has led to several postponements, with the final draft now scheduled to be published in the last quarter of 2003 and the Accord to be implemented by 2006. Will the increasing complexity of the Basel Accord lead to further postponements? Will Basel 2 eventually be put into operation? As of this writing, these questions remain unanswered.

bank. Chartering banks is one method for preventing this adverse selection problem; through chartering, proposals for new banks are screened to prevent undesirable people from controlling them.

Regular on-site bank examinations, which allow regulators to monitor whether the bank is complying with capital requirements and restrictions on asset holdings, also function to limit moral hazard. Bank examiners give banks a so-called *CAMELS rating* (the acronym is based on the six areas assessed: capital adequacy, asset quality, management, earnings, liquidity, and sensitivity to market risk). With this information about a bank's activities, regulators can enforce regulations by taking such formal actions as *cease and desist orders* to alter the bank's behaviour or even close a bank if its CAMELS rating is sufficiently low. Actions taken to reduce moral hazard by restricting banks from taking on too much risk help reduce the adverse selection problem further because with less opportunity for risk taking, risk-loving entrepreneurs will be less likely to be attracted to the banking industry.

Note that the methods regulators use to cope with adverse selection and moral hazard have their counterparts in private financial markets (see Chapter 14). Chartering is similar to the screening of potential borrowers, regulations restricting risky asset holdings are similar to restrictive covenants that prevent borrowing firms from engaging in risky investment activities, bank capital requirements act like restrictive covenants that require minimum amounts of net worth for borrowing firms, and regular bank examinations are similar to the monitoring of borrowers by lending institutions.

A chartered bank obtains a charter either by an Act of Parliament or through application to the minister of finance, who has the authority to issue a charter. To obtain a charter, the people planning to organize the bank must submit an application that shows how they plan to operate the bank. In evaluating the application, the regulatory authority looks at whether the bank is likely to be sound by examining the quality of the bank's intended management, the likely earnings of the bank, and the amount of the bank's initial capital. Moreover, the chartering agency typically explores the issue of whether the community needs a new bank. Often a new bank charter would not be granted if existing banks in a community would be severely hurt by its presence. Today this anticompetitive stance (justified by the desire to prevent bank failures of existing banks) is no longer as strong.

Once a bank has been chartered, it is required to file periodic (usually quarterly) *call reports* that reveal the bank's assets and liabilities, income and dividends, ownership, foreign exchange operations, and other details. The bank is also subject to examination by the bank regulatory agencies to ascertain its financial condition at least once a year. To avoid duplication of effort, the three federal agencies work together and usually accept each other's examinations. This means that, typically, chartered banks are examined by the Bank of Canada, the CDIC, and the OSFI.

Bank examinations are conducted by bank examiners, who study a bank's books to see whether it is complying with the rules and regulations that apply to its holdings of assets. If a bank is holding securities or loans that are too risky, the bank examiner can force the bank to get rid of them. If a bank examiner decides that a loan is unlikely to be repaid, the examiner can force the bank to declare the loan worthless (to write off the loan). If, after examining the bank, the examiner feels that it does not have sufficient capital or has engaged in dishonest practices, the bank can be declared a "problem bank" and will be subject to more frequent examinations.

A New Trend in Bank Supervision: Assessment of Risk Management

Traditionally, on-site bank examinations have focused primarily on assessment of the quality of the bank's balance sheet at a point in time and whether it complies with capital requirements and restrictions on asset holdings. Although the traditional focus is important for reducing excessive risk taking by banks, it is no longer felt to be adequate in today's world in which financial innovation has produced new markets and instruments that make it easy for banks and their employees to make huge bets easily and quickly. In this new financial environment, a bank that is quite healthy at a particular point in time can be driven into insolvency extremely rapidly from trading losses, as forcefully demonstrated by the failure of Barings in 1995 (discussed in Chapter 15). Thus, an examination that focuses only on a bank's position at a point in time, may not be effective in indicating whether a bank will in fact be taking on excessive risk in the near future.

This change in the financial environment for banking institutions has resulted in a major shift in thinking about the bank supervisory process throughout the world. Bank examiners are now placing far greater emphasis on evaluating the soundness of a bank's management processes with regard to controlling risk. This shift in thinking is now reflected in a new focus on risk management in the guidelines to examiners on trading and derivatives activities. Now bank examiners focus on four elements of sound risk management: (1) The quality of oversight provided by the board of directors and senior management, (2) the adequacy of policies and limits for all activities that present significant risks, (3) the quality of the risk measurement and monitoring systems, and (4) the adequacy of internal controls to prevent fraud or unauthorized activities on the part of employees.

This shift toward focusing on management processes is also reflected in recent guidelines adopted by the Canadian bank regulatory authorities to deal with interest-rate risk. At one point, Canadian regulators were contemplating requiring banks to use a standard model to calculate the amount of capital a bank would need to have to allow for the interest-rate risk it bears. Because coming up with a one-size-fits-all model that would work for all banks has proved difficult, the regulatory agencies have instead decided to adopt guidelines for the management of interest-rate risk, although bank examiners will continue to consider interest-rate risk in deciding on the bank's capital requirements. These guidelines require the bank's board of directors to establish interest-rate risk limits, appoint officials of the bank to manage this risk, and monitor the bank's risk exposure. The guidelines also require that senior management of a bank develop formal risk management policies and procedures, to ensure that the board of directors' risk limits are not violated and to implement internal controls to monitor interest-rate risk and compliance with the board's directives.

Disclosure Requirements

The free-rider problem described in Chapter 14 indicates that individual depositors and other bank creditors will not have enough incentive to produce private information about the quality of a bank's assets. To ensure that there is better information for depositors and the marketplace, regulators can require that banks adhere to certain standard accounting principles and disclose a wide range of information that helps the market assess the quality of a bank's portfolio and the amount of the bank's exposure to risk. More public information about the risks incurred by banks and the quality of their portfolio can better enable stockholders, creditors, and depositors to evaluate and monitor banks and so act as a deterrent to excessive risk taking. This view is consistent with a recent position paper issued by the Eurocurrency Standing Committee of the G-10 Central Banks, which recommends that estimates of financial risk generated by firms' own internal risk management systems be adapted for public disclosure purposes.[2] Such information would supplement disclosures based on traditional accounting conventions by providing information about risk exposure and risk management that is not normally included in conventional balance sheet and income statement reports. Disclosure requirements can also be the primary focus of a bank regulatory system, as with a new approach recently implemented in New Zealand (see Box 4).

Consumer Protection

The existence of asymmetric information also suggests that consumers may not have enough information to protect themselves fully. Consumer protection regulation has taken several forms. First is "truth in lending," which requires all lenders, not just banks, to provide information to consumers about the cost of borrowing including a standardized interest rate (called the annual percentage rate, or APR) and the total finance charges on the loan. Legislation also requires creditors, especially credit card issuers, to provide information on the method of assessing finance charges and requires that billing complaints be handled quickly.

Restrictions on Competition

Increased competition can also increase moral hazard incentives for banks to take on more risk. Declining profitability as a result of increased competition could tip the incentives of bankers toward assuming greater risk in an effort to maintain former profit levels. Thus governments in many countries have instituted regulations to protect banks from competition. These regulations have taken different forms in the past, preventing nonbank institutions from competing with banks by engaging in banking business.

---

[2]See Eurocurrency Standing Committee of Central Banks of Group of Ten Countries (Fisher Group), "Discussion Paper on Public Disclosure of Markets and Credit Risks by Financial Intermediaries," September 1994, and a companion piece to this report, Federal Reserve Bank of New York, "A Discussion Paper on Public Disclosure of Risks Related to Market Activity," September 1994.

BOX 4: GLOBAL

New Zealand's Disclosure-Based Experiment in Bank Regulation

Until 1995, New Zealand took a conventional approach to bank regulation that relied on regular examinations by the central bank to ensure that the banks complied with capital requirements and asset restrictions and followed good management practices. At the start of 1996, this system was scrapped for one based on disclosure requirements that uses the market to police the behaviour of the banks.

As part of this new system, every bank in New Zealand must supply a comprehensive, quarterly financial statement that provides information on the quality of its assets, its lending activities, and its ratings from private credit-rating agencies, among other things. These financial statements must be audited two times a year, and not only must they be provided to the central bank, which will monitor them, but they must also be made public, with a two-page summary posted in all bank branches. In addition, bank directors are required to validate these statements and state publicly that their bank's risk management systems are adequate and being properly implemented. A most unusual feature of this system is that a bank's directors now face unlimited liability—that is, they can lose all their assets, not just their holdings in the bank—if they are found to have made false or misleading statements. Directors are thus in the dangerous position that they can be sued by creditors for everything they are worth if the bank goes bust.

The rationale for this approach is that the market will now provide the necessary discipline to prevent bankers from taking excessive risks because it will have sufficient information about banks' activities—depositors have the incentive to monitor the banks because there is no deposit insurance in New Zealand. Furthermore, banks will now have the incentive to improve their financial health in order to acquire good credit ratings. The system also has the advantage that it reduces regulatory costs for the banks because it will eliminate examination fees and burdensome rules on management procedures.

Critics of New Zealand's new approach point out that even with the new disclosure requirements, the asymmetric information problem may still not be solved. Banks may be less willing to admit to problems if the information has to be made public. In addition, depositors may not have the sophistication to understand the information provided and thus may not impose the necessary discipline on the banks. Furthermore, unlimited liability for directors might discourage top people from taking these positions, thereby weakening the management of the banks.

Although advocates of the New Zealand system think that it may prove to be a model for the rest of the world, skeptics point out that it might work only because of the peculiar features of the New Zealand banking system. Almost all New Zealand banks are foreign-owned, and around 90% of deposits are at foreign-owned banks. Thus these skeptics contend that in effect, bank regulation has been outsourced to the regulators of the foreign banks that own the New Zealand banks—central banks such as the Bank of England and the Reserve Bank of Australia that supervise the banks with subsidiaries in New Zealand.

Although restricting competition may prop up the health of banks, restrictions on competition can also have serious disadvantages: They can lead to higher charges to consumers and can decrease the efficiency of banking institutions, which do not have to compete as hard. Thus although the existence of asymmetric information provides a rationale for anticompetitive regulations, it does not mean that they will be beneficial. Indeed, in recent years, the impulse of governments in industrialized countries to restrict competition has been waning. Electronic banking has raised a new set of concerns for regulators to deal with. See Box 5 for a discussion of this challenge.

Study Guide Because so many laws regulating banking have been passed in Canada, it is hard to keep track of them all. As a study aid, Table 1 lists the major banking legislation in the twentieth century and its key provisions.

TABLE 1 Major Banking Legislation in Canada in the Twentieth Century

Bank of Canada Act (1934)
Created the Bank of Canada following the recommendations of the Macmillan Commission

Bank Act of 1935
Prohibited banks from issuing banknotes
Imposed reserve requirements on depository institutions to be held with the Bank of Canada

Bank Act of 1954
Increased reserve requirements on depository institutions
Allowed chartered banks to offer mortgages issued under the National Housing Act

Canada Deposit Insurance Corporation Act (1967)
Created the CDIC to insure deposits with all federally chartered banks and near banks

Bank Act of 1967
Removed the 6% loan interest rate ceiling
Restricted foreign competition
Imposed secondary reserve requirements on depository institutions
Put chartered banks and near banks on equal footing regarding mortgage lending

Bank Act of 1981
Created the Canadian Payments Association to operate the national payments system and plan its development
Lowered reserve requirements on Canadian dollar deposits
Introduced new reserve requirements on some foreign currency deposits
Increased competition by introducing a less complicated procedure for obtaining a licence to operate as a bank
Allowed foreign banks to establish subsidiaries in Canada, subject to reciprocal treatment of Canadian banks
Extended banks' business powers to include financial leasing, factoring, and data-processing
Redesigned corporate clauses to ensure consistency between the Bank Act and the Canada Business Corporations Act
Provided a simpler incorporation method for new banks (letters patent) while retaining incorporation through a special Act of Parliament

Office of the Superintendent of Financial Institutions Act (1987)
Created the OSFI to succeed two separate federal regulatory bodies (the Department of Insurance and the Inspector General of Banks) in the supervision of financial institutions

Financial Institutions and Deposit Insurance System Amendment Act (1987)
Allowed chartered banks to own investment banking subsidiaries, thereby initiating the merging of the four pillars

Savings and Credit Union Act of the Province of Quebec (1988)
Sets rules for credit unions, federations, and confederations, with specific reference to the *Mouvement Desjardins*

Bank Act of 1992
Comprehensive banking law
Allowed chartered banks to own trust companies
Allowed trust companies to make commercial loans
Made provisions for the phasing out of reserve requirements
Set rules regarding the supervisory role of the Bank of Canada and the OSFI with respect to chartered banks
Reset the sunset clause from 10 years to 5 years to address the changing Canadian financial services marketplace

Cooperative Credit Associations Act (1992)
Replaced the Cooperative Credit Associations Act of 1952–1953 and set rules for federally chartered credit unions
Followed the same format as the Bank Act

Insurance Companies Act (1992)
Replaced the Canadian and British Insurance Companies Act and the Foreign Insurance Companies Act, both passed in 1932
Set rules for life insurance companies and property and casualty (P&C) insurance companies
Allowed insurance companies to own Schedule II chartered banks
Followed the same format as the Bank Act

Trust and Loan Companies Act (1992)
Replaced the Trust Companies Act and the Loan Companies Act, both passed in 1914
Set rules for federally incorporated TMLs and provincially incorporated TMLs reporting to the OSFI
Required large, formerly closely held TMLs to become 35% widely held
Followed the same format as the Bank Act

Bank Act of 1997
Yielded minor changes because the government was waiting for the recommendations of the Mackay Task Force

Bank Act of 2001
Set new ownership rules
Established a process for reviewing mergers involving large banks
Allowed bank financial groups to organize under a holding company structure
Allowed greater flexibility for bank involvement in the information technology area
Allowed nondeposit taking financial institutions access to the payments and clearance systems

BOX 5: E-FINANCE

Electronic Banking: New Challenges for Bank Regulation

The advent of electronic banking has raised new concerns for banking regulation, specifically about security and privacy.

Worries about the security of electronic banking and e-money are an important barrier to their increased use. With electronic banking, you might worry that criminals might access your bank account and steal your money by moving your balances to someone else's account. Indeed, a notorious case of this happened in 1995, when a Russian computer programmer got access to Citibank's computers and moved funds electronically into his and his conspirators' accounts. Private solutions to deal with this problem have arisen with the development of more secure encryption technologies to prevent this kind of fraud. However, because bank customers are not knowledgeable about computer security issues, there is a role for the government to regulate electronic banking to make sure that encryption procedures are adequate. Similar encryption issues apply to e-money, so requirements that banks make it difficult for criminals to engage in digital counterfeiting make sense. To meet these challenges, bank examiners assess how a bank deals with the special security issues raised by electronic banking and also oversee third-party providers of electronic banking platforms. Also, because consumers want to know that electronic banking transactions are executed correctly, bank examiners also assess the technical skills of banks in setting up electronic banking services and the bank's capabilities for dealing with problems.

Electronic banking also raises serious privacy concerns. Because electronic transactions can be stored on databases, banks are able to collect a huge amount of information about their customers—their assets, creditworthiness, what they purchase, and so on—that can be sold to other financial institutions and businesses. This potential invasion of our privacy rightfully makes us very nervous. To protect customers' privacy, legislation has limited the distribution of these data, but it does not go as far as the European Data Protection Directive, which prohibits the transfer of information about on-line transactions. How to protect consumers' privacy in our electronic age is one of the great challenges our society faces, so privacy regulations for electronic banking are likely to evolve over time.

INTERNATIONAL BANKING REGULATION

Because asymmetric information problems in the banking industry are a fact of life throughout the world, bank regulation in other countries is similar to that in Canada. Banks are chartered and supervised by government regulators, just as they are in Canada. Deposit insurance is also a feature of the regulatory systems in most other developed countries, although its coverage is often different from Canada's. We have also seen that bank capital requirements are in the process of being standardized across countries with agreements like the Basel accord.

Problems in Regulating International Banking

Particular problems in bank regulation occur when banks are engaged in international banking and thus can readily shift their business from one country to another. Bank regulators closely examine the domestic operations of banks in their country, but they often do not have the knowledge or ability to keep a close watch on bank operations in other countries, either by domestic banks' foreign affiliates or by foreign banks with domestic branches. In addition, when a bank operates in many countries, it is not always clear which national regulatory authority should have primary responsibility for keeping the bank from engaging in overly risky activities. The difficulties inherent in regulating international banking were highlighted by the BCCI scandal discussed in Box 6. Cooperation among regulators in different countries and standardization of regulatory requirements provide potential solutions to the problems of regulating international banking. The world has been moving in this direction through agreements like the Basel accord on capital requirements in 1988 and the new regulatory oversight procedures announced by the Basel Committee in July 1992.

BOX 6: GLOBAL

The BCCI Scandal

The Bank of Credit and Commerce International (BCCI) was chartered in Luxembourg in 1972 by a Pakistani businessman, Agha Hasan Abedi. The bank grew rapidly to $20 billion in assets and by 1991 was operating in more than 70 countries. Unfortunately, the bank was siphoning off funds to secret accounts in the Cayman Islands, where much of this money was stolen. Indeed, estimates suggest that nearly half of the bank's assets may have "disappeared." Fraud was not the only shady activity BCCI engaged in. BCCI supposedly helped dictators such as Saddam Hussein of Iraq, Manuel Noriega of Panama, and Ferdinand Marcos of the Philippines steal huge sums from their countries, helped the CIA channel funds to the *contra* rebels in Nicaragua, and acted as a banker for the notorious Abu Nidal terrorist group. Not surprisingly, BCCI has been dubbed the "Bank of Crooks and Criminals, Inc."

How did BCCI get away with these fraudulent activities for so long? The answer illustrates the difficulties of regulating banks with operations in many countries. Although BCCI's headquarters were in London, regulatory oversight fell to the chartering country, Luxembourg, whose tiny bank regulator, the Institut Monétaire Luxembourgeois (IML), was not up to the task. As a result, BCCI effectively operated free of government regulatory oversight for 15 years. In 1987, the IML reached an agreement with seven other countries' regulators to oversee BCCI jointly, but even this larger group was unable to keep track of the bank's activities. Only in spring 1990 did these regulators uncover some evidence of fraud, and not until July 1991 did the Price Waterhouse accounting firm document the pervasiveness of the fraud to the Bank of England, which then closed BCCI down.

The losses to depositors and stockholders from the BCCI collapse were immense, and national regulators, particularly the Bank of England, have been severely criticized for their slowness in uncovering the scandal. A year after the BCCI collapse, in July 1992, the Basel Committee announced an agreement to standardize further the regulation of international banks. Now a bank's worldwide operations will be under the scrutiny of a single home-country regulator with enhanced powers to acquire information on the bank's activities. Furthermore, regulators in other countries will have the right to restrict operations of a foreign bank if they feel that it lacks effective oversight. Despite this improvement in the regulation of international banks, fears remain that a BCCI-like scandal could happen again.

However, whether agreements of this type will solve the problem of regulating international banking in the future is an open question.

Summary

Asymmetric information analysis explains what types of banking regulations are needed to reduce moral hazard and adverse selection problems in the banking system. However, understanding the theory behind regulation does not mean that regulation and supervision of the banking system are easy in practice. Getting bank regulators and supervisors to do their job properly is difficult for several reasons. First, as we learned in the discussion of financial innovation in Chapter 15, in their search for profits, financial institutions have strong incentives to avoid existing regulations by loophole mining. Thus, regulation applies to a moving target: Regulators are continually playing cat and mouse with financial institutions—financial institutions think up clever ways to avoid regulations, which then causes regulators to modify their regulation activities. Regulators continually face new challenges in a dynamically changing financial system, and unless they can respond rapidly to change, they may not be able to keep financial institutions from taking on excessive risk. This problem can be exacerbated if regulators and supervisors do not have the resources or expertise to keep up with clever people in financial institutions who think up ways to hide what they are doing or ways to get around the existing regulations.

Bank regulation and supervision are difficult for two other reasons. In the regulation and supervision game, the devil is in the details. Subtle differences in the details may have unintended consequences; unless regulators get the regulation and supervision just right, they may be unable to prevent excessive risk taking. In addition, regulators and supervisors may be subject to political pressure not to do their jobs properly. For all these reasons, there is no guarantee that bank regulators and supervisors will be successful in promoting a healthy financial system. Indeed, as we will see, bank regulation and supervision have not always worked well, leading to banking crises in Canada and throughout the world.

THE 1980S' CANADIAN BANKING CRISIS

The period from 1923 (when the Home Bank failed) to 1985 was one in which the failure of Canadian chartered banks was thought to be impossible. During the same period, failures of deposit-taking financial institutions in the United States were averaging about 20 a year. In the mid-1980s, however, the situation in Canada changed dramatically with the failure of two chartered banks and the financial difficulties of a large number of other financial institutions. Why did this happen? How did a stable banking system that seemed to be working well find itself in trouble?

Early Stages of the Crisis

The story starts with the oil boom in western Canada in the 1970s. It led to the creation of several western banks, including two Alberta-based Schedule I banks, the Canadian Commercial Bank and the Northland Bank, both formed in 1975. Unfortunately, the managers of these banks did not have the expertise that would have enabled them to manage risk appropriately; they excessively concentrated in a few borrowers in western Canada and placed a large percentage of their total loans in real estate.

The existence of deposit insurance increased moral hazard for the Canadian Commercial and Northland banks, because insured depositors had little incentive to keep the banks from taking on too much risk. Regardless of how much risk the banks were taking, deposit insurance guaranteed that depositors would not suffer any losses.

Canadian Commercial and Northland pursued rapid growth and took on risky projects, attracting the necessary funds by issuing large denomination certificates of deposit with high interest rates. Without deposit insurance, high interest rates would not have induced depositors to provide the high-rolling banks with funds because of the realistic expectation that they might not get the funds back. But with deposit insurance, the government was guaranteeing that the deposits were safe, so depositors were more than happy to make deposits in the Canadian Commercial and Northland banks with the higher interest rates.

As already noted, the managers of Canadian Commercial and Northland did not have the required expertise to manage risk in the permissive atmosphere of western Canada. Even if the required expertise was available initially, rapid credit growth may outstrip the available information resources of the banking institution, resulting in excessive risk taking. Also, the lending boom meant that the activities of Canadian Commercial and Northland were expanding in scope and were becoming more complicated, requiring an expansion of regulatory resources to monitor these activities appropriately. Unfortunately, regulators at the Office of the Inspector General of Banks (the predecessor of the Office of the Superintendent of Financial Institutions) had neither the expertise nor the resources that would have enabled them to sufficiently monitor the activities of Canadian Commercial and Northland. Given the lack of expertise in both the banks and the Inspector General of Banks, the weakening of the regulatory apparatus, and the moral hazard incentives provided by deposit insurance, it is no surprise that Canadian Commercial and Northland took on excessive risks, which led to huge losses on bad loans.

In addition, the incentives of moral hazard were increased dramatically by a historical accident: the combination of sharp increases in interest rates from late 1979 until 1981 and a severe recession in 1981-1982, both of which were engineered by the Federal Reserve in the United States to bring down inflation. The sharp rise in interest rates produced rapidly rising costs of funds for the banks that were not matched by higher earnings on their principal asset, long-term residential mortgages (whose rates had been fixed at a time when interest rates were far lower). The 1981–1982 recession and a collapse in the prices of energy and farm products hit the economy of Alberta very hard. As a result, there were defaults on many loans. Losses for Canadian Commercial and Northland mounted and the banks had a negative net worth and were thus insolvent by the beginning of 1985.

Later Stages of the Crisis: Regulatory Forbearance

At this point, a logical step might have been for the regulators—the Bank of Canada and the Inspector General of Banks—to close the insolvent banks. Instead, the regulators adopted a stance of **regulatory forbearance**: They refrained from exercising their regulatory right to put the insolvent Canadian Commercial Bank and Northland Bank out of business.

There were two main reasons why the Bank of Canada and the Inspector General of Banks opted for regulatory forbearance. First, the CDIC did not have sufficient funds in its insurance fund to close the insolvent banks and pay off their deposits. Second, because bureaucrats do not like to admit that their own agency is in trouble, the regulators preferred to sweep their problems under the rug in the hope that they would go away.

When Canadian Commercial and Northland were declared insolvent in September of 1985, rumours of financial trouble caused many large depositors to withdraw large deposits from the Bank of British Columbia, Mercantile Bank, and Continental Bank. By the time Mercantile was acquired by the National Bank of Canada, Bank of British Columbia by the Hongkong Bank of Canada, and Continental by Lloyds Bank of Canada (a subsidiary of a UK-based banking powerhouse), the Bank of Canada had lent more than $5 billion.

The loss of public confidence in the Canadian banking system led to the financial reforms of 1987–1992 (see Table 1) and the consolidating of financial institution supervision under the Office of the Superintendent of Financial Institutions. Moreover, in the 2001 revision of the Bank Act legislation was introduced to reform the regulatory framework governing Canada's financial services marketplaces. We will discuss this new legislation later in this chapter.

POLITICAL ECONOMY OF THE BANKING CRISIS

Although we now have a grasp of the regulatory and economic forces that created the 1980s Canadian banking crisis, we still need to understand the political forces that produced the regulatory structure and activities that led to it. The key to understand the political economy of the crisis is to recognize that the relationship between voter-taxpayers and the regulators and politicians creates a particular type of moral hazard problem, discussed in Chapter 14: the *principal-agent problem*, which occurs when representatives (agents) such as managers have incentives that differ from those of their employer (the principal) and so act in their own interest rather than in the interest of the employer.

Principal-Agent Problem for Regulators and Politicians

Regulators and politicians are ultimately agents for voter-taxpayers (principals) because in the final analysis, taxpayers bear the cost of any losses by the deposit insurance agency. The principal-agent problem occurs because the agent (a politician or regulator) does not have the same incentives to minimize costs to the economy as the principal (the taxpayer).

To act in the taxpayers' interest and lower costs to the deposit insurance agency, regulators have several tasks, as we have seen. They must set tight restrictions on holding assets that are too risky, must impose high capital requirements, and must not adopt a stance of regulatory forbearance, which allows insolvent institutions to continue to operate. However, because of the principal-agent problem, regulators have incentives to do the opposite. Indeed, as our sad saga of the Canadian Commercial and Northland debacle indicates, they have at times loosened capital requirements and restrictions on risky asset holdings and pursued regulatory forbearance. One important incentive for regulators that explains this phenomenon is their desire to escape blame for poor performance by their agency. By loosening capital requirements and pursuing regulatory forbearance, regulators can hide the problem of an insolvent bank and hope that the situation will improve. Edward Kane characterizes such behaviour on the part of regulators as "bureaucratic gambling."

CDIC DEVELOPMENTS

The CDIC's Website at www.cdic.ca provides a list of CDIC members, information on how deposit insurance works, and the most important recent laws that have affected the deposit insurance business.

The Canada Deposit Insurance Corporation (CDIC) insures each depositor at member institutions up to a loss of $60 000 per account. All federally incorporated financial institutions and all provincially incorporated trust and mortgage loan companies are members of the CDIC. Insurance companies, credit unions, *caisses populaires*, and investment dealers are not eligible for CDIC membership; the Quebec Deposit Insurance Board (QDIB) insures provincially incorporated financial institutions in Québec and the other provinces have deposit insurance corporations that insure the deposits of credit unions in their jurisdiction, on terms similar to the CDIC's.

The CDIC is allowed to insure only deposits in Canadian currency and payable in Canada; foreign currency deposits, such as for example accounts in U.S. dollars, are not insured. Moreover, not all deposits and investments offered by CDIC member institutions are insurable. Insurable deposits include savings and chequing accounts, term deposits with a maturity date of less than five years, money orders and drafts, certified drafts and cheques, and travellers' cheques. The CDIC does not insure term deposits with an initial maturity date of more than five years, treasury bills, bonds and debentures issued by governments and corporations (including the chartered banks), and investments in stocks, mutual funds, and mortgages.

The primary rationale for deposit insurance is protecting depositors from bank insolvency and thus ensuring financial stability. Deposit insurance could also promote competition among financial institutions by removing barriers to entry for new deposit-taking institutions. In the absence of deposit insurance it is difficult for new banks to attract deposits. Most depositors, for example, are not capable of making appropriate risk calculations to assess the risk of a new bank. Those depositors would tend to place their deposits in banks that are considered as too big to fail, thereby producing significant barriers to entry and unfair disadvantages for small new entrants. By insuring deposits at all deposit-taking financial institutions, the CDIC effectively removes barriers to entry for new deposit takers.

Differential Premiums

Until recently, CDIC premium revenue was not tied to the risk profile of the financial institutions; the premium rate was the same for all deposit-taking institutions, irrespective of their risk profile. For example, in the 1998/1999 fiscal year, the flat-rate insurance premium was 1/6 of 1%, or 0.1667%, meaning that each deposit-taking financial institution paid an insurance premium of close to 17 cents per $100 of insured deposits. This was one of the reasons that the Big Six, represented by the Canadian Bankers Association, vigorously opposed the establishment of the CDIC in 1967; it was argued that deposit insurance would be a subsidy to small banks paid by the big banks.

Over the years, the Canadian Bankers Association strongly promoted the reform of the Canadian deposit insurance system. As a result, the CDIC developed the Differential Premiums By-law, which came into force on March 31, 1999. The important feature of this legislation is its implicit, prompt corrective action provisions, which require the CDIC to intervene earlier and more vigorously when a bank gets into trouble. CDIC member institutions are now classified into four premium groups based on their risk profile. An institution's risk profile is determined using a variety of quantitative and qualitative criteria, including capital adequacy, profitability, asset concentration, income volatility, regulatory ratings, and adherence to CDIC's Standards of Sound Business and Financial Practices, with capital adequacy dominating the criteria accounting for 25% of the score.

Under the new system the premium rates for CDIC member institutions are those shown in Table 2; they vary from 4 cents to 33 cents per $100. Group 1, classified as "best," is well-capitalized banks that significantly exceed minimum requirements. On the other hand, banks in group 4, classified as "worst," are significantly (and perhaps critically) undercapitalized and the insurance premium that they pay is 33 basis points, the maximum allowed under the CDIC Act. In addition, for group 4 banks, the CDIC is required to take prompt corrective actions such as requiring them to submit a capital restoration plan, restrict their asset growth, and seek regulatory approval to open new branches or develop new lines of business. Today, over 90% of CDIC member institutions are classified in categories 1 and 2, but as in other countries, the premium category and related supervisory information applicable to individual CDIC members are confidential.

Opting-Out

Another interesting recent development is the Opting-Out By-law that came into effect on October 15, 1999. This legislation permits Schedule III banks that accept primarily wholesale deposits (defined as $150 000 or more) to opt out of CDIC membership and therefore to operate without deposit insurance. The new legislation, however, includes provisions to protect depositors who hold deposits eligible for CDIC protection. In particular, it requires an opted-out bank to inform all depositors, by posting notices in its branches, that their deposits will not be protected by the CDIC, and not to charge any early withdrawal penalties for depositors who choose to withdraw.

TABLE 2 New Premium Structure and Rates for CDIC Member Institutions

Premium category	Premium rate (as a % of insured deposits)
1	1/24th of 1%, or 0.0417%
2	1/12th of 1%, or 0.0833%
3	1/6th of 1%, or 0.1667%
4	1/3rd of 1%, or 0.3333%

Source: CDIC Website: www.cdic.ca

Probably the most important feature of the opting-out legislation is its minimization of CDIC exposure to uninsured deposits. This represents a significant departure from past practices when the CDIC showed generosity to uninsured depositors. For example, in the Canadian Commercial and Northland failures of the mid-1980s, the CDIC paid 100 cents on the dollar to all depositors, both insured and uninsured. By compensating only the insured depositors rather than all depositors, the opting-out legislation increases the incentives of uninsured depositors to monitor the risk-taking activities of banks, thereby reducing moral hazard risk.

Application

Evaluating CDIC and Other Proposed Reforms of the Banking Regulatory System

The new system of risk-based premiums and opting-out rules is a major step in reformulating the banking regulatory system. How well will it work to solve the adverse selection and moral hazard problems of the bank regulatory system? Let's use the analysis in the chapter to evaluate the new legislation to answer this question.

Study Guide Before looking at the evaluation for each set of provisions and proposals in this application, try to reason out how well they will solve the current problems with banking regulation. This exercise will help you develop a deeper understanding of the material in this chapter.

Limits on the Scope of Deposit Insurance

CDIC's reductions of the scope of deposit insurance by limiting insurance to insured deposits might have increased the incentives for uninsured depositors to monitor banks and to withdraw funds if the bank is taking on too much risk. Because banks might now fear the loss of deposits when they engage in risky activities, they might have less incentive to take on too much risk.

Although the cited new elements of deposit insurance strengthen the incentive of depositors to monitor banks, some critics would take these limitations on the scope of deposit insurance even further. Some suggest that deposit insurance should be eliminated entirely or should be reduced in amount from the current $60 000 limit to, say, $20 000 or $10 000. Another proposed reform would institute a system of **coinsurance** in which only a percentage of a deposit, say 90% would be covered by insurance. In this system, the insured depositor would suffer a percentage of the losses along with the deposit insurance agency. Because depositors facing a lower limit on deposit insurance or coinsurance would suffer losses if the bank goes broke, they will have an incentive to monitor the bank's activities.

However, other experts do not believe that depositors are capable of monitoring banks and imposing discipline on them. The basic problem with reducing the scope of deposit insurance even further as proposed is that banks would be subject to runs, sudden withdrawals by nervous investors. Such runs could by themselves lead to bank failures. In addition to protecting individual depositors, the purpose of deposit insurance is to prevent a large number of bank failures, which would lead to an unstable banking system and an unstable economy. From this perspective, deposit insurance has been a resounding success. Bank panics, in which there are simultaneous failures of many banks and consequent disruption of the financial system, have not occurred since deposit insurance was established.

Eliminating the too-big-to-fail policy altogether would also cause some of the same problems that would occur if deposit insurance were eliminated or reduced: The probability of bank panics would increase. If a bank were allowed to fail, the repercussions in the financial system might be immense. Other banks with a correspondent relationship with the failed bank (those that have deposits at the bank in exchange for services) would suffer large losses and might fail in turn, leading to full-scale panic. In addition, the problem of liquidating the big bank's loan portfolio might create a major disruption in the financial system.

Prompt Corrective Action

The prompt corrective action provisions of CDIC should also substantially reduce incentives for bank risk taking and reduce taxpayer losses. CDIC uses a carrot-and-stick approach to get banks to hold more capital. If they are well capitalized, they receive better ratings and are placed in a better premium rate category; if their capital ratio falls, they are subject to more and more onerous regulation. Increased bank capital reduces moral hazard for the bank because the bank now has more to lose if it fails and so is less likely to take on too much risk. In addition, encouraging banks to hold more capital reduces potential losses for the CDIC because increased bank capital is a cushion that makes bank failure less likely.

Prompt corrective action, which requires regulators to intervene early when bank capital begins to fall, is a serious attempt to reduce the principal-agent problem for politicians and regulators. With prompt corrective action provisions, regulators no longer have the option of regulatory forbearance, which, as we have seen, can greatly increase moral hazard incentives for banks.

Risk-Based Insurance Premiums

Under the Differential Premiums By-law, banks deemed to be taking on greater risk, in the form of lower capital or riskier assets, are subjected to higher insurance premiums. Risk-based insurance premiums consequently reduce the moral hazard incentives for banks to take on higher risk. In addition, the fact that risk-based premiums drop as the bank's capital increases encourages the banks to hold more capital, which has the benefits already mentioned.

One problem with risk-based premiums is that the scheme for determining the amount of risk the bank is taking may not be very accurate. For example, it might be hard for regulators to determine when a bank's loans are risky. Some critics have also pointed out that the classification of banks by such measures as the Basel risk-based capital standard solely reflects credit risk and does not take sufficient account of interest-rate risk. The regulatory authorities, however, are encouraged to modify existing risk-based standards to include interest-rate risk.

Other CDIC Provisions

CDIC's requirements that regulators perform frequent bank examinations and member institutions file a Standards report at least once a year are necessary for monitoring banks' compliance with bank capital requirements and asset restrictions. As the Canadian Commercial and Northland debacles illustrate, frequent supervisory examinations of banks are necessary to keep them from taking on too much risk or committing fraud. Similarly, beefing up the ability of the regulators to monitor foreign banks might help dissuade international banks from engaging in these undesirable activities.

The stricter and more burdensome reporting requirements for banks have the advantage of providing more information to regulators to help them monitor bank activities. However, these reporting requirements have been criticized by banks, which claim that the requirements make it harder to lend to small businesses. As a result, the CDIC recently developed the Modernized Standards By-law, adopted in early 2001, that enables the CDIC to determine the frequency of a member institution's reporting based on its categorization under the Differential Premiums By-law.

The new legislation allows CDIC discretion in examining the performance of problem member institutions. Under the new regime, well capitalized, category 1 banks will be required to file a Standards report every five years. However, banks in categories 3 and 4 may be subjected to special examination at any time, the cost of which will be chargeable to the institution. The Modernized Standards By-law, in addition to increasing the regulatory supervision of problem banks, also increases the accountability of the CDIC. Moreover, it decreases the incentives of banks to take on excessive risk and increases their incentives to hold capital.

Other Changes in Banking Regulations

Regulatory Consolidation The current bank regulatory system in Canada has banking institutions supervised by three federal agencies: the Bank of Canada, the Office of the Superintendent of Financial Institutions, and the CDIC. Critics of this system of multiple regulatory agencies with overlapping jurisdictions believe it creates a system that is too complex and too costly because it is rife with duplication. For example, although the CDIC has no direct supervisory role, its Standards of Sound Business and Financial Practices overlap with those of the OSFI.

The MacKay Task Force, named after its chairman Harold MacKay and set up by the government in 1996 to review the financial services sector and propose a framework for its future, considered whether the CDIC and the OSFI should be amalgamated. Although the task force recommended that the regulator (OSFI) and the insurer (CDIC) should not be combined in a single institution, it proposed that the CDIC's mandate be amended to remove the overlap with the OSFI's mandate.

The National Financial Services OmbudService Another recent significant achievement is the creation of a National Financial Services OmbudService (NFSO) that began operations on July 1, 2002. This service has been created, with the support of the federal and provincial governments, by the banking sector (through the Canadian Bankers Association), the insurance sector (through the Insurance Bureau of Canada and the Canadian Life and Health Insurance Association), and the securities sector (through the Investment Dealers Association of Canada, the Mutual Funds Dealers Association, and the Investment Funds Institute of Canada). The NFSO provides Canadian consumers and small businesses access to dispute resolution services regarding their dealings with financial institutions.

The creation of the NFSO has been viewed as a first step towards building a national regulatory system and eliminating the overlap between the many federal, provincial, and territorial departments and agencies that currently regulate the different industries of the Canadian financial services sector.

Market-Value Accounting for Capital Requirements We have seen that the requirement that a bank have substantial equity capital makes the bank less likely to fail. The requirement is also advantageous because a bank with high equity capital has more to lose if it takes on risky investments and so will have less incentive to hold risky assets. Unfortunately, capital requirements, including new risk-based measures, are calculated on a historical-cost (book value) basis in which the value of an asset is set at its initial purchase price. The problem with historical-cost accounting is that changes in the value of assets and liabilities because of changes in interest rates or default risk are not reflected in the calculation of the firm's equity capital. Yet changes in the market value of assets and liabilities and hence changes in the market value of equity capital are what indicate if a firm is truly insolvent. Furthermore, it is the market value of capital that determines the incentives for a bank to hold risky assets.

Market-value accounting when calculating capital requirements is another reform that receives substantial support. All assets and liabilities could be updated to market value periodically, say, every three months, to determine if a bank's capital is sufficient to meet the minimum requirements. This market-value accounting information would let the deposit insurance agency know quickly when a bank was falling below its capital requirement. The bank could then be closed down before its net worth fell below zero, thus preventing a loss to the deposit insurance agency. The market-value-based capital requirement would also ensure that banks would not be operating with negative capital, thereby preventing the bet-the-bank strategy of taking on excessive risk.

Objections to market-value-based capital requirements center on the difficulty of making accurate and straightforward market-value estimates of capital. Historical-cost accounting has an important advantage in that accounting rules are easier to define and standardize when the value of an asset is simply set at its purchase price. Market-value accounting, by contrast, requires estimates and approximations that are harder to standardize. For example, it might be hard to assess the market value of your friend Joe's car loan, whereas it would be quite easy to value a government bond. In addition, conducting market-value accounting would prove costly to banks because estimation of market values requires the collection of more information about the characteristics of assets and liabilities. Nevertheless, proponents of market-value accounting for capital requirements point out that although market-value accounting involves some estimates and approximations, it would still provide regulators with more accurate assessment of bank equity capital than historical-cost accounting does.

Overall Evaluation

The recent CDIC developments appear to be an important step in the right direction because they increase the incentives for banks to hold capital and decrease their incentives to take on excessive risk. However, more could be done to improve the incentives for banks to limit their risk taking. Yet eliminating deposit insurance and the too-big-to-fail policy altogether may be going too far because these proposals might make the banking system too prone to a banking panic.

FINANCIAL SERVICES REFORM FOR THE 21ST CENTURY

We have seen that fundamental structural changes make it possible for new financial products and services, increasing the competitive environment in the financial services industry and changing the financial intermediation role of banking at Internet speed. It is against this backdrop of phenomenal change that the federal government has recently introduced legislation reforming the policy framework of the Canadian financial services sector. This legislation is mostly based on the Report of the Task Force on the Future of the Canadian Financial Services Sector, also known as the MacKay Report, and it has been called one of the most significant revisions to the Bank Act in Canadian history.

In what follows we provide an overview of the key elements of this important legislation that has the potential to dramatically change the face of competition in Canada's financial services marketplace. As you will see, the new legislation establishes the regulatory framework to accelerate changes already taking place throughout the Canadian and world economies and introduces new opportunities for strategic alliances and partnerships, with the objective of fostering more competition and providing more innovative products and services to Canadians.

Bank Holding Companies

Until 2001 the organizational structure of Canada's bank financial groups was based on the "bank-as-parent" model, where all banking functions and all subsidiaries of the bank were subject to the same regulation. Under the new legislation, however, bank financial groups have the option of organizing themselves under a holding company. A holding company is a corporation that owns several different companies. Most developed countries permit bank holding company structures and the growth of bank holding companies has been dramatic over the past three decades. Today, in the United States, for example, bank holding companies own almost all large banks, and over 90% of all commercial bank deposits are held in banks owned by holding companies. In fact, the Gramm-Leach-Bliley Act of 1999 modernized the holding company rules in the United States (which have been in place since 1956) to allow a new and more flexible holding company model—the financial holding company.

The holding company form of corporate ownership has important advantages for bank financial groups in that (1) it allows them to engage in other activities related to banking, such as the provision of investment advice, data processing and transmission services, leasing, and credit card services; (2) a holding company structure allows for lighter regulation throughout the bank financial group because certain activities (those not involving retail deposit-taking and insurance) can be undertaken by less-regulated, non-bank affiliated companies held by the holding company parent rather than the regulated operating bank; and (3) the holding company model provides bank financial groups increased flexibility to achieve economies of scale and scope through strategic partnerships, alliances, and joint ventures.[3]

The big advantage of the new regime for establishing holding companies is that bank financial groups are now able to move parts of their heavily regulated business into less regulated affiliates under a common holding company. The holding company, however, would be a viable option for bank financial groups, if the transition to a holding company would be tax-neutral and without increased costs or regulatory burdens. If, for example, additional taxes or heavier regulation were to arise as a result of a restructuring into a holding company, then the holding company option wouldn't be feasible. For this reason, the new legislation provides a set of transitional rules to address unintended cost consequences that would be triggered by the transition to a holding company.

The Permitted Investment Regime

A second item of the new legislation pertains to the type of investments Canadian bank financial groups are allowed to make. There was a restrictive list of activities beyond banking that banks could get involved in. The new legislation, however, provides greater flexibility for bank involvement in the information technology area (and in particular the Internet and wireless technology). It permits bank financial groups to establish and operate information services entities uti-

[3]Recently, for example, the British-based banking group HSBC entered into a joint venture with the U.S.-based securities dealer Merrill Lynch, to create a global on-line banking and investment services company, called Merrill Lynch HSBC.

lizing recent advances in Internet and wireless banking and voice recognition technologies.

New information technologies are critical in the ability of Canadian bank financial groups to provide new financial products and services and adapt to the changing marketplace. Although bank involvement in the information technology area is subject to regulation, the new permitted investment regime will enhance the ability of banks to pursue strategic alliances and joint ventures and will further accelerate the technological advances that are already taking place and revolutionize the financial services sector.

New Ownership Rules

A third policy measure that can change significantly the face of competition in Canada's financial services marketplace is the new ownership regime that enables investors to take a greater equity interest in widely held bank financial groups. In particular, the new legislation increases the limit a single shareholder can own of a widely held financial institution (either a bank holding company or a bank subsidiary under the holding company) from 10% of any class of shares to 20% of voting shares and 30% of non-voting shares. The new legislation, however, does not permit a single shareholder to own more than 10% of both a bank holding company and a bank subsidiary under the holding company at the same time. Moreover, acquisitions of more than 10% are subject to approval by the Minister of Finance based on a "fit and proper person" test.

The new legislation also includes a three-tiered ownership regime. Small banks (those with equity capital under $1 billion) don't have to be widely held and can be wholly owned (have one particular investor own 100% of their shares). Medium sized banks (and bank holding companies) with shareholders' equity between $1 billion and $5 billion can be closely held provided that there is a 35% public float (that is, they could have a single shareholder own up to 65% of their shares). Large banks (and bank holding companies), those with shareholders' equity in excess of $5 billion, are required to be widely held.

The new ownership regime, together with other provisions in the legislation, such as the lowering of the capital needed to create a bank from $10 million to $5 million and the allowance of domestic and foreign commercial enterprises (such as department stores and grocery chains) to establish small and medium-sized banks, will fundamentally change Canada's financial sector.

Access to the Payments and Clearance System

Another regulatory change that will significantly affect Canada's financial services marketplace is the decision to allow nondeposit-taking financial institutions, such as life insurance companies, securities dealers, and money market mutual funds, access to the payments and clearance system. This will allow these organizations to provide bank-like services, such as chequing accounts and debit cards, without being banks, thereby directly competing with banks, trust and mortgage loan companies, and credit unions and *caisses populaires*.

Expanding access to the payments and clearance system, by allowing nondeposit taking financial institutions to participate, will further accelerate the process of the blurring of distinction among deposit taking and nondeposit taking financial institutions. As already noted, this process started in 1987, when securities dealers were allowed to own banks, and was reinforced by the 1992 federal financial reforms that permitted cross ownership of financial institutions.

Merger Review Policy

The government has also issued a statement establishing a process for reviewing mergers involving large banks—banks such as the Bank of Montreal and CIBC with shareholder equity in excess of $5 billion (see Box 7). By doing so, the government acknowledges that mergers are a legitimate business option that should be available to Canadian bank financial groups. The bank merger review process, however, unlike those in other countries such as the United States and the United Kingdom, is political having the Parliament directly involved in it.

The government has also indicated that it will not allow mergers between large banks and large demutualized life insurance companies such as Manulife and Clarica Life. We would note, however, that in other countries such as Australia, Germany, the Netherlands, Switzerland, the United Kingdom, and the United States, mergers of banks, insurance companies, and other financial services providers are not prohibited.

Implications for the Canadian Banking Industry

A bank holding company structure (as an alternative to the current "bank-as-parent" structure), new ownership rules, expanded permitted investments, expanded access to the payments and clearance system, and a transparent merger review policy, offer new opportunities for strategic alliances and joint ventures that have the potential to reshape the Canadian financial services marketplace. These developments, together with new information technologies, make possible new financial products and services and a more vibrant and dynamic market for financial services.

BOX 7

Bank Mergers in Canada

In early 1998 four of the largest Canadian commercial banks announced their intention to merge. In particular, the Royal Bank of Canada (the largest bank in the country) and the Bank of Montreal (the third-largest bank) made the announcement on January 23, 1998 while the Canadian Imperial Bank of Commerce (CIBC) and the Toronto Dominion (TD) Bank followed suit and made a similar announcement on April 17, 1998.

The Competition Bureau reviewed and assessed the proposed mergers at the same time and advised the minister of finance against the planned mergers. In fact, in its letter to the presidents of the Royal Bank and the Bank of Montreal on December 11, 1998, it was argued that the merger[4]

> ... is likely to lead to a substantial lessening or prevention of competition that would cause higher prices and lower levels of service and choice for several key banking services in Canada.

The minister of finance, based on this advice from the Competition Bureau, rejected the mergers in January 1999.

Recently, however, James McIntosh of Concordia University published a paper in the *Canadian Journal of Economics* and argues that the Competition Bureau's recommendations were probably based on results from studies of the banking system in the United States. By estimating a general equilibrium model of the Canadian banking system and using the estimates to determine the effects of the mergers, McIntosh argues that[5]

> ... [s]cale efficiency is sufficiently large to offset the consequences of reduced competition that might have arisen from a merger between Bank of Montreal and Royal Bank of Canada, Canadian Imperial Bank of Commerce and Toronto Dominion Bank, or both. The estimated model predicts that all the mergers proposed in 1998 would have led to slightly lower prices and, consequently, to an increase in consumer welfare.

---

[4]See www.fin.gc.ca/LINKS/mergers_e.html.

[5]James McIntosh, "A Welfare Analysis of Canadian Chartered Bank Mergers," *Canadian Journal of Economics* 35 (2002): 457–75.

As we have seen, the 1992 federal financial reforms have stimulated consolidation of the Canadian banking industry. The financial consolidation process will be even further speeded up by the proposed legislation, because the way is now open to mergers and acquisitions, and strategic alliances, partnerships, and joint ventures. As already noted, bank financial groups will become not only larger, but increasingly complex organizations, engaging in a full gamut of financial activities.

BANKING CRISES THROUGHOUT THE WORLD

Because misery likes company, it might make you feel better to know that Canada has by no means been alone in suffering a banking crisis. Indeed, as Figure 1 and Table 3 illustrate, banking crises have struck a large number of countries throughout the world, and many of them have been substantially worse than ours. We will examine what took place in several of these other countries and see that the same forces that produced a banking crisis in Canada have been at work elsewhere too.

United States

Go to www.fdic.gov for details about the U.S. Federal Deposit Insurance Corporation.

Before the establishment of the Federal Deposit Insurance Corporation (FDIC) in 1934, bank failures were a fact of American life, with major ones occurring every 20 years or so in 1819, 1837, 1857, 1873, 1884, 1893, 1907, and 1930-1933. Bank failures were a serious problem even during the boom years of the 1920s, when the number of bank failures averaged around 600 per year. In contrast to the pre-1934 period, the period from 1934 to 1980 was one in which bank failures were a rarity, averaging 15 a year for commercial banks and fewer than 5 a year for savings and loans. After 1981, however, this rosy picture changed dramatically. Failures in both commercial banks and savings and loans (S&Ls) climbed to levels more than ten times greater than in earlier years. Why did this happen? How did a deposit insurance system that seemed to be working well for half a century find itself in so much trouble?

The story starts with the burst of financial innovation in the 1960s, 1970s, and early 1980s: NOW accounts, money market mutual funds, junk bonds, securitization and the rise of the commercial paper market. Financial innovation decreased the profitability of certain traditional business for commercial banks. Banks now faced increased competition for their sources of funds from new financial institutions such as money market mutual funds while they were losing commercial lending business to the commercial paper market and securitization. With the decreasing profitability of their traditional business, by the mid-1980s commercial banks were forced to seek out new and potentially risky business to keep their profits up, by placing a greater percentage of their total loans in real estate and in credit extended to assist corporate takeovers and leveraged buyouts (called *highly leveraged transaction loans*).

The most important laws that have affected the banking industry in the United States are described at www.fdic.gov/regulations/laws/important.

Adding fuel to the fire, financial innovation produced new financial instruments that widened the scope for risk taking. New markets in financial futures, swaps, and other instruments made it easier for banks to take on extra risk—making the moral hazard problem more severe. New legislation that deregulated the banking industry in the early 1980s, the Depository Institutions Deregulation and Monetary Control Act (DIDMCA) of 1980 and the Depository Institutions (Garn-St. Germain) Act of 1982, gave expanded powers to the S&Ls and mutual savings banks to engage in new risky activities. In addition, DIDMCA increased the mandated amount of federal deposit insurance from $40 000 per account to $100 000, increasing moral hazard for banks because insured depositors had little incentive to keep the banks from taking on too much risk.

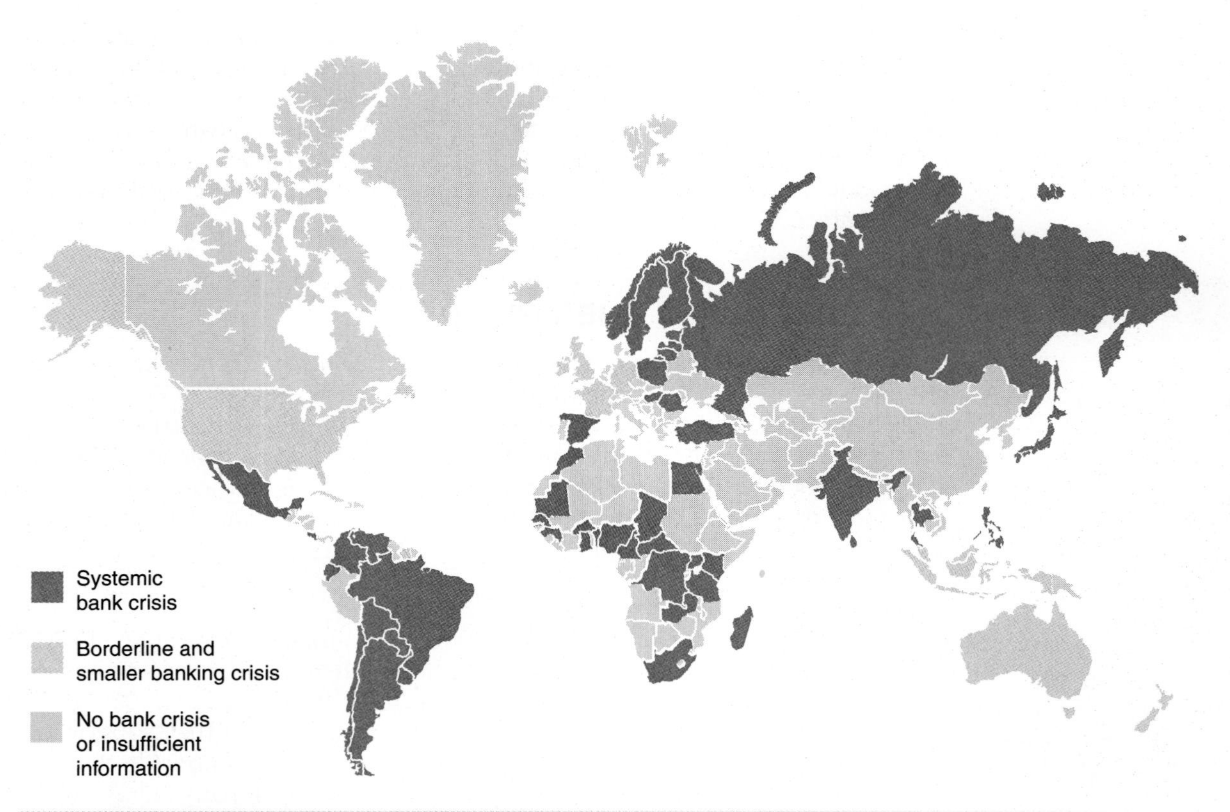

FIGURE 1 Banking Crises Throughout the World Since 1970

Source: Gerard Caprio Jr. and Daniela Klingbiel, "Bank Insolvency: Bad Luck, Bad Policy, or Bad Banking?" paper prepared for the World Bank's Annual Bank Conference on Development Economics, Washington, D.C., April 25–26, 1996.

TABLE 3 The Cost of Rescuing Banks in Several Countries

Date	Country	Cost as a Percentage of GDP
1980–1982	Argentina	55
1997–ongoing	Indonesia	50–55
1981–1983	Chile	41
1997–ongoing	Thailand	33
1997–ongoing	South Korea	27
1997–ongoing	Malaysia	21
1994–ongoing	Venezuela	20+
1995	Mexico	20
1990s	Japan	12+
1989–ongoing	Czech Republic	12+
1991–1994	Finland	11
1991–1995	Hungary	10
1994–1995	Brazil	5–10
1987–1993	Norway	8
1998	Russia	5–7
1991–1994	Sweden	4
1984–1991	United States	3

Source: Gerard Caprio Jr. and Daniela Klingbiel, "Episodes of Systemic and Borderline Financial Crises" mimeo., World Bank, October 1999.

Another financial innovation that made it even easier for high-rolling banks to raise funds is known as **brokered deposits**, which enable depositors to circumvent the $100 000 limit on deposit insurance. Brokered deposits work as follows: A large depositor with $10 million goes to a broker, who breaks the $10 million into 100 packages of $100 000 each and then buys $100 000 CDs at 100 different banks. Because the amount of each CD is within the $100 000 limit for deposits at each bank, the large depositor has in effect obtained deposit insurance on all $10 million.

Financial innovation and deregulation in the permissive atmosphere of the Reagan years led to expanded powers for the S&Ls industry that led to several problems. First, many S&Ls managers did not have the required expertise to manage risk appropriately in these new lines of business. Second, the new expanded powers meant that there was a rapid growth in new lending, particularly to the real estate sector. Third, regulators of the S&Ls at the Federal Savings and Loan Insurance Corporation (FSLIC) had neither the expertise nor the resources that would have enabled them to monitor these new activities sufficiently. It is no surprise then that the S&Ls took on excessive risks. As a result, when the 1981–1982 recession hit hard the economies of certain parts of the country such as Texas, there were defaults on many S&Ls' loans. Losses mounted to $10 billion in 1981-1982, and by some estimates over half of the S&Ls in the United States had a negative net worth and were thus insolvent by the end of 1982.

At that point, a logical step might have been for the S&L regulators to close the insolvent S&Ls. Instead, the regulators opted for regulatory forbearance, mainly because the FSLIC did not have sufficient funds in its insurance fund to close the insolvent S&Ls and pay off their depositors. Regulatory forbearance, however, increases moral hazard dramatically because an operating but insolvent S&L (nicknamed a "zombie S&L" by economist Edward Kane because it is the "living dead") has almost nothing to lose by taking on great risk and "betting the bank": If it gets lucky and its risky investments pay off, it gets out of insolvency. Unfortunately, if, as is likely, the risky investments don't pay off, the zombie S&L's losses will mount, and the deposit insurance agency will be left holding the bag.

Given the sequence of events we have discussed here, it should be no surprise that savings and loans began to take huge risks: They built shopping centres in the desert, bought manufacturing plants to convert manure to methane, and purchased billions of dollars of high-risk, high yield junk bonds. Consistent with our analysis, the situation deteriorated rapidly. Losses in the savings and loan industry surpassed $10 billion in 1988 and approached $20 billion in 1989. The crisis was reaching epidemic proportions. The collapse of the real estate market in the late 1980s led to additional huge loan losses that greatly exacerbated the problem.

The S&Ls problem was dealt with by the Bush administration immediately after taking office in 1989. The new legislation, the Financial Institutions Reform, Recovery, and Enforcement Act (FIRREA), was the most significant legislation to affect the thrift industry since the 1930s. The cost of the bailout ended up on the order of $150 billion. FIRREA eliminated the Federal Home Loan Bank Board and gave its regulatory role to the Office of Thrift Supervision. It also eliminated the FSLIC and turned its insurance role over to the FDIC. Moreover, FIRREA imposed new restrictions on thrift activities that in essence reregulated the S&L industry to the asset choices it had before 1982. S&Ls can no longer purchase junk bonds and had to sell their holdings by 1994. Commercial real estate loans are restricted to four times capital rather the previous limit of 40% of assets, and so this new restriction is a reduction for all institutions whose capital is less than 10% of assets. S&Ls must also hold at least 70%—up from 60%—of their assets in investments that are primarily housing-related. Troubled thrifts are not allowed to accept brokered deposits. FIRREA also enhanced the enforcement powers of thrift regulators by making it easier for them to remove managers, issue cease and desist orders, and impose civil money penalties.

FIRREA did not focus on the underlying adverse selection and moral hazard problems created by deposit insurance. FIRREA did, however, mandate that the U.S. Treasury produce a comprehensive study and plan for reform of the federal deposit insurance system. After this study appeared in 1991, Congress passed the Federal Deposit Insurance Corporation Improvement Act (FDICIA), which engendered major reforms in the U.S. bank regulatory system.

Scandinavia

As in the United States, an important factor in the banking crises in Norway, Sweden, and Finland was the financial liberalization that occurred in the 1980s. Before the 1980s, banks in the Scandinavian countries were highly regulated and subject to restrictions on the interest rates they could pay to depositors and on the interest rates they could earn on loans. In this noncompetitive environment, and with artificially low rates on both deposits and loans, these banks lent only to the best credit risks, and both banks and their regulators had little need to develop expertise in screening and monitoring borrowers. With the deregulated environment, a lending boom ensued, particularly in the real estate sector. Given the lack of expertise in both the banking industry and its regulatory authorities in keeping risk taking in check, banks engaged in risky lending. When real estate prices collapsed in the late 1980s, massive loan losses resulted. The outcome of this process was similar to what happened in the savings and loan industry in the United States. The government was forced to bail out almost the entire banking industry in these countries in the late 1980s and early 1990s on a scale that was even larger relative to GDP than in the United States (see Table 3).

Latin America

The Latin American banking crises show a similar pattern to those in Canada, the United States, and Scandinavia. Before the 1980s, banks in many Latin American countries were owned by the government and were subject to interest-rate restrictions as in Scandinavia. Their lending was restricted to the government and other low-risk borrowers. With the deregulation trend that was occurring worldwide, many of these countries liberalized their credit markets and privatized their banks. We then see the same pattern we saw in the United States and Scandinavia, a lending boom in the face of inadequate expertise on the part of both bankers and regulators. The result was again massive loan losses and the inevitable government bailout. What is particularly striking about the Latin American experience is the high cost of the bailout relative to GDP. For example, in the recent banking crises in Mexico and Venezuela, the cost to the taxpayer of the government bailouts exceeded 10% of GDP.

Russia and Eastern Europe

Before the end of the Cold War, in the communist countries of Eastern Europe and the Soviet Union, banks were owned by the state. When the downfall of communism occurred, banks in these countries had little expertise in screening and monitoring loans. Furthermore, bank regulatory and supervisory apparatus that could rein in the banks and keep them from taking on excessive risk barely existed. Given the lack of expertise on the part of regulators and banks, not surprisingly, substantial loan losses ensued, resulting in the failure or government bailout of many banks. For example, in the second half of 1993, eight banks in

Hungary with 25% of the financial system's assets were insolvent, and in Bulgaria, an estimated 75% of all loans in the banking system were estimated to be substandard in 1995. On August 24, 1995, a bank panic requiring government intervention occurred in Russia when the interbank loan market seized up and stopped functioning because of concern about the solvency of many new banks. This was not the end of troubles in the Russian banking system. On August 17, 1998, the Russian government announced that Russia would impose a moratorium on the repayment of foreign debt because of insolvencies in the banking system. In November, the Russian central bank announced that nearly half of the country's 1500 commercial banks were likely to go under and that the cost of the bailout would be around $15 billion.

Japan

Japan was a latecomer to the banking crisis game. Before 1990, the vaunted Japanese economy looked unstoppable. Unfortunately, it has recently experienced many of the same pathologies that we have seen in other countries. Before the 1980s, Japan's financial markets were among the most heavily regulated in the world, with very strict restrictions on the issuing of securities and interest rates. Financial deregulation and innovation produced a more competitive environment that set off a lending boom, with banks lending aggressively in the real estate sector. As in the other countries we have examined here, financial disclosure and monitoring by regulators did not keep pace with the new financial environment. The result was that banks could and did take on excessive risks, and when property values collapsed in the early 1990s, the banks were left holding massive amounts of bad loans. For example, Japanese banks decided to get into the mortgage lending market by setting up the so-called *jusen*, home mortgage lending companies that raised funds by borrowing from banks and then loaned these funds out to households. Seven of these *jusen* became insolvent, leaving banks with $60 billion or so of bad loans.

As a result, the Japanese have experienced their first bank failures since World War II. In July 1995, Tokyo-based Cosmo Credit Corporation, Japan's fifth-largest credit union, failed and on August 30, the Osaka authorities announced the imminent closing of Kizu Credit Cooperative, Japan's second-largest credit union. (Kizu's story is remarkably similar to that of many U.S. savings and loans. Kizu, like many American S&Ls, began offering high rates on large time deposits and grew at a blistering pace, with deposits rising from $2.2 billion in 1988 to $12 billion by 1995 and real estate loans growing by a similar amount. When the property market collapsed, so did Kizu.) On the same day, the ministry of finance announced that it was liquidating Hyogo Bank, a midsize Kobe bank that was the first commercial bank to fail. Larger banks now began to follow the same path. In late 1996, the Hanwa Bank, a large regional bank, was liquidated, and this was followed in 1997 by a government-assisted restructuring of the Nippon Credit Bank, Japan's seventeenth-largest bank. In November 1997, Hokkaido Takushoku Bank was forced to go out of business, making it the first city bank (a large commercial bank) to be closed during the crisis.

The Japanese have been going through the same cycle of regulatory forbearance as occurred in the United States in the 1980s. The Japanese regulators in the Ministry of Finance enabled banks to meet capital standards and to keep operating by allowing them to inflate the value of their assets. For example, they were allowed to value their large holdings of equities at historical value, rather than market value, which was much lower. Inadequate amounts were allocated for recapitalization of the banking system, and the extent of the problem was grossly underestimated by government officials. Furthermore, until the closing of the

Hokkaido Takushoku Bank, the bank regulators in the ministry of finance were unwilling to close down city banks and impose any losses on stockholders or uninsured creditors.

By the middle of 1998, the Japanese government began to take some steps to clean up the banking mess. In June, the supervision authority over financial institutions was taken away from the ministry of finance and transferred to the Financial Supervisory Agency (FSA), which reports directly to the prime minister. This was the first instance in half a century in which the all-powerful Ministry of Finance was stripped of some of its authority. In October, the parliament passed a bailout package of US$500 billion. However, disbursement of the funds depended on the voluntary cooperation of the banks: The law did not require insolvent banks to close or to accept the funds if they were insolvent. Indeed, acceptance of the funds required the bailed-out bank to open its books and reveal its true losses, and thus many banks remain very undercapitalized. The banking sector in Japan thus remains in very poor shape: It is burdened with bad loans and poor profitability. Indeed, in April 2001, new data from the Financial Supervisory Agency (FSA) indicates that bad loans had reached a level of 150 trillion yen (over US$1 trillion), almost double the previous amount estimated by the FSA.

There has been some progress in cleaning up the banking mess: Immediately after the 1998 banking law was passed, one of the ailing city banks, Long-Term Credit Bank of Japan, was taken over by the government and declared insolvent, and in December 1998, the Nippon Credit Bank was finally put out of its misery and closed down by the government. Since then, the cleanup process has stalled and the economy has remained weak, with a growth rate from 1991–2001 averaging an anemic 1%. However, the election in 2001 of a new, reform-oriented prime minister, Junichiro Koizumi, who has pledged to clean up the banking system, may lead to more progress in the future.

East Asia

The banking and financial crisis in the East Asian countries (Thailand, Malaysia, Indonesia, the Philippines, and South Korea) was discussed in Chapter 14. Due to inadequate supervision of the banking system, the lending booms that arose in the aftermath of financial liberalization led to substantial loan losses, which became huge after the currency collapses that occurred in the summer of 1997. An estimated 15% to 35% of all bank loans are now nonperforming in Thailand, Indonesia, and South Korea, and estimates of the cost of the bailout for the banking system in these countries is more than 20% of GDP. The cost of the bailout in Malaysia may also exceed 20%; the Philippines are expected to fare somewhat better.

"Déjà Vu All Over Again"

What we see in banking crises in these different countries is that history has kept on repeating itself. The parallels between the banking crisis episodes in all these countries are remarkably similar, leaving us with a feeling of déjà vu. Although financial liberalization is generally a good thing because it promotes competition and can make a financial system more efficient, as we have seen in the countries examined here, it can lead to an increase in moral hazard risk taking on the part of banks if there is lax regulation and supervision; the result can then be banking crises. However, these episodes do differ in that deposit insurance has not played an important role in many of the countries experiencing banking crises. For example, the size of the Japanese equivalent of the CDIC, the Deposit Insurance Corporation, was so tiny relative to the CDIC that it did not play a prominent role in the banking system and exhausted its resources almost immediately with the first bank failures. This means that deposit insurance is not to blame for some of these banking crises. However, what is common to all the countries discussed here is the existence of a government safety net, in which the government stands ready to bail out banks whether deposit insurance is an important feature of the regulatory environment or not. It is the existence of a government safety net, and not deposit insurance per se, that increases moral hazard incentives for excessive risk taking on the part of banks.

SUMMARY

1. The concepts of asymmetric information, adverse selection, and moral hazard help explain the seven types of banking regulation that we see in Canada and other countries: the government safety net, restrictions on bank asset holdings and capital requirements, bank supervision, disclosure requirements, consumer protection, restrictions on competition, and the separation of the banking and securities industries.
2. Because asymmetric information problems in the banking industry are a fact of life throughout the world, bank regulation in other countries is similar to that in Canada. It is particularly problematic to regulate banks engaged in international banking because they can readily shift their business from one country to another.
3. Because of financial innovation and deregulation, adverse selection and moral hazard problems increased in the 1980s and resulted in a banking crisis in Canada.
4. Recent CDIC legislation includes reforms for the deposit insurance and regulatory system so that taxpayer losses would be minimized. This legislation mandated prompt corrective action to deal with troubled deposit-taking financial institutions and instituted risk-based deposit insurance premiums. These provisions have helped reduce the incentives of banks to take on excessive risk and so should help reduce taxpayer exposure in the future.
5. Proposals for reforming the banking regulatory system include elimination of deposit insurance, lower limits on the amount of deposit insurance, outright elimination of the too-big-to-fail policy, coinsurance, risk-based insurance premiums, regulatory consolidation, and market-value accounting for capital requirements.
6. The parallels between the banking crisis episodes that have occurred in other countries are striking, indicating that similar forces are at work.

KEY TERMS

bank supervision, *p. 458*
Basel Accord, *p. 458*
Basel Committee on Banking Supervision, *p. 458*
brokered deposits, *p. 479*
coinsurance, *p. 470*
leverage ratio, *p. 458*
off-balance-sheet activities, *p. 458*
prudential supervision, *p. 458*
regulatory arbitrage, *p. 458*
regulatory forbearance, *p. 467*

QUESTIONS AND PROBLEMS

1. Give one example each of moral hazard and adverse selection in private insurance arrangements.

*2. If property and casualty insurance companies provided fire insurance without any restrictions, what kind of adverse selection and moral hazard problems might result?

3. What bank regulation is designed to reduce adverse selection problems for deposit insurance? Will it always work?

*4. What bank regulations are designed to reduce moral hazard problems created by deposit insurance? Will they completely eliminate the moral hazard problem?

5. What are the costs and benefits of a too-big-to-fail policy?

*6. What special problem do off-balance-sheet activities present to bank regulators, and what have they done about it?

7. Why does imposing bank capital requirements on banks help limit risk taking?

*8. What forms does bank supervision take, and how does it help promote a safe and sound banking system?

9. What steps were taken in recent CDIC legislation to improve the functioning of deposit insurance?

***10.** Why has the trend in bank supervision moved away from a focus on capital requirements to a focus on risk management?

11. How do disclosure requirements help limit excessive risk taking by banks?

***12.** Do you think that eliminating or limiting the amount of deposit insurance would be a good idea? Explain your answer.

13. Should the overlap between the OSFI and CDIC be eliminated? Why or why not?

***14.** How could higher deposit insurance premiums for banks with riskier assets benefit the economy?

15. How could market-value accounting for bank capital requirements benefit the economy? How difficult would it be to implement?

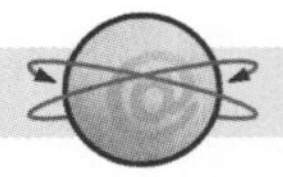

WEB EXERCISES

Banking Regulation

1. The Office of the Superintendent of Financial Institutions (OSFI) is responsible for many of the regulations affecting bank operations. Go to http://ww.osfi-bsif.gc.ca. Click on "Acts and Regulations." How many Acts does OSFI administer? What is the purpose of the Bank Act?

2. Go to http://www.fdic.gov/regulations/laws/important/. This site reports on the most significant pieces of legislation affecting banks in the United States since the 1800s. Summarize the most recently enacted bank regulation on this site.

Chapter 19

Insurance Companies and Pension Funds

Preview

In this chapter we continue our discussion of financial institutions by looking at two nonbank institutions: insurance companies and pension funds. Insurance is an important industry in Canada. Most people hold one or more types of insurance policies (health, life, homeowners, automobile, disability, and so on). Insurance companies are also a major employer, especially of business majors. Figure 1 shows the number of persons employed by the insurance industry. Currently, more than 210 000 Canadians are employed in the industry. In recent years, the rate of growth has slowed. There are a couple of possible explanations for this. First, technology has streamlined claims processing so that fewer back-office workers are needed. Second, competition by other financial institutions such as commercial banks and brokerage houses may be cutting into some of the business traditionally reserved for insurance companies.

One major competitor to insurance has been the private, company-sponsored pension plan. Better-educated and longer-lived workers are putting more money into pension funds than ever before. More than 5.3 million individuals now invest in a private pension fund. These plans are also reviewed in this chapter.

Insurance companies and pension funds are considered financial intermediaries for several reasons. First, they receive investment funds from their customers. For example, when a person buys a whole life insurance policy, the person receives a life insurance benefit and accumulates a cash balance. Many people use insurance companies as their primary investment avenue. Similarly, private pension funds also take in investment dollars from their customers. Second, both of these institutions place their money in a variety of money-earning investments. Insurance companies and pension funds make large commercial mortgage loans, invest in stocks, and buy bonds. Thus these institutions are financial intermediaries in that they take in funds from one sector and invest it in another.

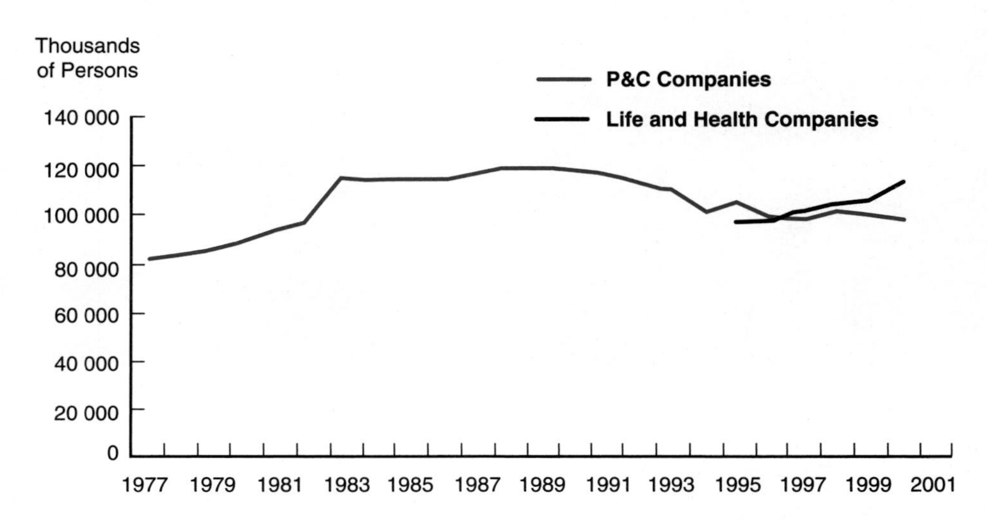

FIGURE 1 Number of Persons Employed in the Canadian Insurance Industry

Source: Canadian Life and Health Insurance Facts (1995–2000) and *Facts of the General Insurance Industry in Canada* (1977–2000) © Canadian Life and Health Insurance Association.

INSURANCE COMPANIES

Insurance companies are in the business of assuming risk on behalf of their customers in exchange for a fee, called a *premium.* Insurance companies make a profit by charging premiums that are sufficient to pay the expected claims to the company plus a profit. Why do people pay for insurance when they know that over the lifetime of their policy, they will probably pay more in premiums than the expected amount of any loss they will suffer? Because most people are risk averse: They would rather pay a **certainty equivalent** (the insurance premium) than accept the gamble that they will lose their house or their car. Thus it is because people are risk-averse that they prefer to buy insurance and know with certainty what their wealth will be (their current wealth minus the insurance premium) than to incur the risk and run the chance that their wealth may fall.

Consider how people's lives would change if insurance were not available. Instead of knowing that the insurance company would help if an emergency occurred, everyone would have to set aside reserves. These reserves could not be invested long-term but would have to be kept in an extremely liquid form. Furthermore, people would be constantly worried that their reserves would be inadequate to pay for catastrophic events such as the loss of their house to fire, the theft of their car, or the death of the family breadwinner. Insurance allows us the peace of mind that a single event can have only a limited impact on our lives.

FUNDAMENTALS OF INSURANCE

Although there are many types of insurance and insurance companies, all insurance is subject to several basic principles.

1. There must be a relationship between the *insured* (the party covered by insurance) and the *beneficiary* (the party who receives the payment should a loss occur). In addition, the beneficiary must be someone who may suffer potential harm. For example, you could not take out a policy on your neighbour's teenage driver because you are unlikely to suffer harm if the

teenager gets into an accident. The reason for this rule is that insurance companies do not want people to buy policies as a way of gambling.
2. The insured must provide full and accurate information to the insurance company.
3. The insured is not to profit as a result of insurance coverage.
4. If a third party compensates the insured for the loss, the insurance company's obligation is reduced by the amount of the compensation.
5. The insurance company must have a large number of insureds so that the risk can be spread out among many different policies.
6. The loss must be quantifiable. For example, an oil company could not buy a policy on an unexplored oil field.
7. The insurance company must be able to compute the probability of the loss occurring.

The purpose of these principles is to maintain the integrity of the insurance process. Without them, people may be tempted to use insurance companies to gamble or speculate on future events. Taken to an extreme, this behaviour could undermine the ability of insurance companies to protect persons in real need. In addition, these principles provide a way to spread the risk among many policies and to establish a price for each policy that will provide an expectation of a profitable return. Despite following these guidelines, insurance companies suffer greatly from the problems of asymmetric information that we first described in Chapter 2.

Adverse Selection and Moral Hazard in Insurance

Recall that adverse selection occurs when the individuals most likely to benefit from a transaction are the ones who most actively seek out the transaction and are thus most likely to be selected. In Chapter 2 we discussed adverse selection in the context of borrowers with the worst credit being the ones who most actively seek loans. The problem also occurs in the insurance market. Who is more likely to apply for health insurance, someone who is seldom sick or someone with chronic health problems? Who is more likely to buy flood insurance, someone who lives on a mountain or someone who lives in a river valley? In both cases, the party more likely to suffer a loss is the party likely to seek insurance. The implication of adverse selection is that loss probability statistics gathered for the entire population may not accurately reflect the loss potential for the persons who actually want to buy policies.

The adverse selection problem raises the issue of which policies an insurance company should accept. Because someone in poor health is more likely to buy a supplemental health insurance policy than someone in perfect health, we might predict that insurance companies should turn down anyone who applies. Since this does not happen, insurance companies must have found alternative solutions. For example, most insurance companies require physical exams and may examine previous medical records before issuing a health or life insurance policy. If some previous illness is found to be a factor in the person's health, the company may issue the policy but exclude this preexisting condition. Insurance firms often offer better rates to insure groups of people, such as everyone working at a particular business, because the adverse selection problem is then avoided.

In addition to the adverse selection problem, moral hazard plagues the insurance industry. Moral hazard occurs when the insured fails to take proper precautions to avoid losses because losses are covered by insurance. For example, moral hazard may cause you not to lock your car doors if you will be reimbursed by insurance if the car is stolen. When Hurricane Fran approached the North Carolina coast in 1996, many yacht owners did not take down their old canvas covers because they hoped the covers would be destroyed by the hurricane, in which case the owners could file a claim with the insurance company and get money to buy new covers.

One way that insurance companies combat moral hazard is by requiring a **deductible**. A deductible is the amount of any loss that must be paid by the insured before the insurance company will pay anything. For example, if new canvas yacht covers cost $5000 and the yacht owner has $1000 deductible, the owner will pay the first $1000 of the loss and the insurance company will pay $4000. In addition to deductibles, there may be other terms in the insurance contract aimed at reducing risk. For example, a business insured against fire may be required to install and maintain a sprinkler system on its premises to reduce the loss should a fire occur.

Although contract terms and deductibles help with the moral hazard problem, these issues remain a constant difficulty for insurance companies. The insurance industry's reaction to moral hazard and adverse selection are discussed in greater detail in "The Practising Financial Institutional Manager" later in this chapter.

Selling Insurance

Another problem common to insurance companies is that people often fail to seek as much insurance as they actually need. Human nature tends to cause people to ignore their mortality, for example. For this reason, insurance, unlike many banking services, does not sell itself. Instead, insurance companies must hire large sales forces to sell their products. The expense of marketing may account for up to 20% of the total cost of a policy. A good sales force can convince people to buy insurance coverage that they never would have pursued on their own yet may have a need for.

Insurance is unique in that agents sell a product that commits the company to a risk. The relationship between the agent and the company varies: *Independent agents* may sell insurance for a number of different companies. They do not have any particular loyalty to any one firm and simply try to find the best product for their customer. *Exclusive agents* sell the insurance products for only one insurance company.

Most agents, whether independent or exclusive, are compensated by being paid a commission. The agents themselves are usually not at all concerned with the level of risk of any one policy because they have little to lose if a loss occurs. (Rarely are commissions influenced by the claims submitted by an agent's customers.) To keep control of the risk that agents are incurring on behalf of the company, insurance companies employ **underwriters**, people who review and sign off on each policy an agent writes and who have the authority to turn down a policy if they deem the risk unacceptable. If underwriters have questions about the quality of customers, they may order an independent inspector to review the property being insured or request additional medical information. A final decision to accept the policy may depend on the inspector's report (see Box 1).

GROWTH AND ORGANIZATION OF INSURANCE COMPANIES

As of August 2001, there were 117 life insurance companies in Canada, down from 168 in 1990; Figure 2 shows the number of firms from 1984 to 2001. Insurance companies can be organized as either *stock* or *mutual* firms. A **stock company** is owned by stockholders and has the objective of making a profit.

Mutual insurance companies are owned by the policyholders. The objective of mutual insurance firms is to provide insurance at the lowest possible cost to the insured. Policyholders are paid dividends that reflect the surplus of pre-

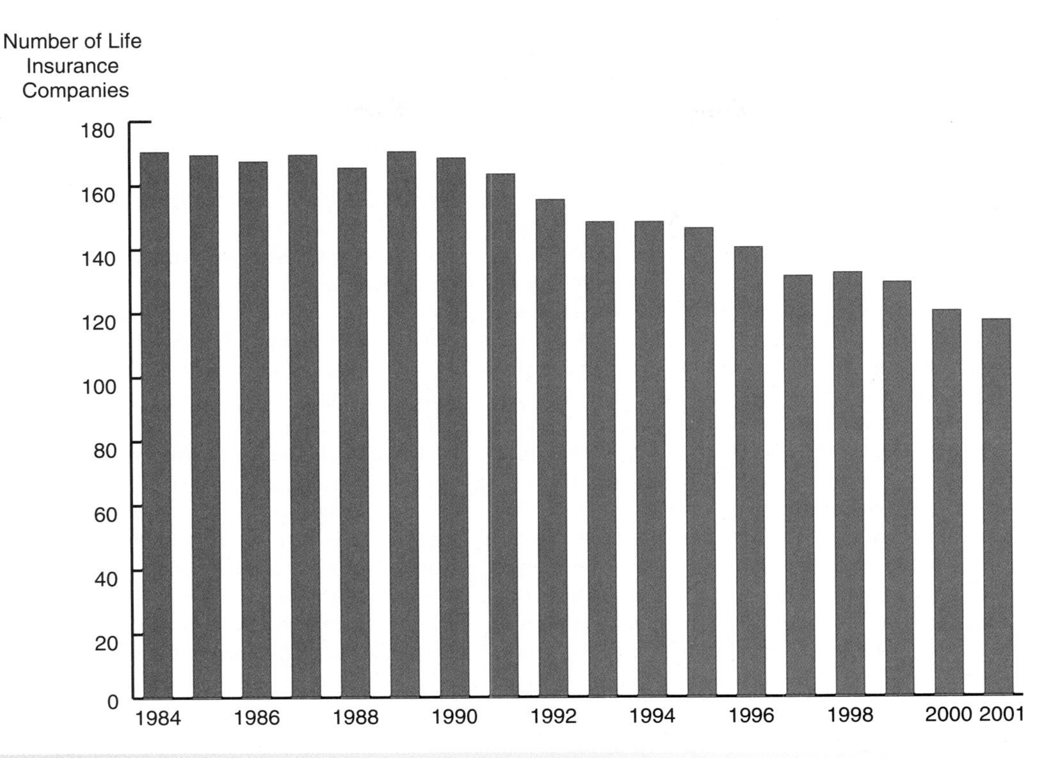

FIGURE 2 Number of Life Insurance Companies in Canada, 1984–2001

Source: Canadian Life and Health Insurance Facts (1984–2001) © Canadian Life and Health Insurance Association.

BOX 1

Insurance Agent: The Customer's Ally

An underwriter working for Prudential Insurance in the United States was responsible for a number of agents selling property insurance in Southern California in 1985. One agent sold a large number of fire insurance policies and was always careful to document clearly when a fire hydrant was on the property by including it in a photograph attached to the policy application. The agent made a mistake on one policy, however, when he included his car in a picture of a different view of the property. The picture showed a plastic fire hydrant lying in the open trunk of his car. He had been putting this fire hydrant on property for years when he needed to give a low quote to get business.

The agent was neither fired nor sued. He was simply advised to halt the practice, and his policies continued to be accepted by the company.

miums over costs. Because the policyholders share in reducing the cost of insurance, there may be some reduction in the moral hazard that most insurance companies face.

The Websites for the life insurance companies mentioned are www.canadalife.com, www.clarica.com, www.manulife.com, www.sunlife.com, and www.inalco.com.

Before 1999, half of the life insurance companies in Canada were organized as mutuals. In March 1999, however, the government passed legislation allowing mutual life insurance companies to convert to stock companies. This process is called **demutualization**, and most life insurance companies including some large ones, Canada Life, Clarica, Manulife Financial, Sun Life, and Industrial-Alliance, have now converted to stock companies; by August 2001 only 10 firms were organized as mutuals. (See Box 2 for a description of a unique form of insurance ownership.)

BOX 2: GLOBAL

The Woes of Lloyd's of London

In June 1993, Lloyd's of London announced the biggest loss in its history, US$4.33 billion for the year 1990 (Lloyd's waits three years to allow all claims to be processed before reporting profits or losses). The chairman of Lloyd's stated that the 1990 deficit "represents in every way the low point of Lloyd's history in the last 305 years."* Things continued to get worse for Lloyd's, with losses continuing until 1992, for a cumulative amount of more than US$12 billion over the five-year period 1988–1992.

Lloyd's began in 1688 in a London coffeehouse owned by Edward Lloyd, which was a meeting place for merchants, shipowners, and sea captains. Lloyd's became a marketplace in which members, known as "names," trade pieces of insurance policies in order to spread the risk, a process called *reinsurance*. An unusual feature of Lloyd's is that names are directly exposed to losses because they accept unlimited personal liability for any claims they have to pay. Many of those participating in Lloyd's have come to regret it in recent years, having lost their entire personal fortunes. Indeed, the average loss per name was over US$150 000 in 1990. The losses at Lloyd's have also resulted in a slew of lawsuits, with members suing each other right and left over who should be responsible for paying claims.

To survive, the basic structure of Lloyd's has had to change. Lloyd's has opened itself up to corporate capital with only limited liability, has taken measures to lower central spending by the organization, and has altered the way it is governed. In 1996, Lloyd's was able to announce record profits for the year 1993. However, to settle its lawsuits, Lloyd's offered a US$4.8 billion rescue package to its 34 000 names, including the creation of a new corporation called Equitas that took over Lloyd's liabilities incurred before 1993, and profits were high for the next few years.

Lloyd's is by no means out of the woods yet. It still has antiquated technology and high central operating costs and has experienced losses in recent years. While it had high profits in the mid-1990s, in March 2001, it announced that it lost over 1 billion pounds (US$1.4 billion) in 1999, after suffering a loss of over a billion pounds in 1998. Additionally, it may sustain losses exceeding US$1.5 billion in the aftermath of the terrorist attack on the World Trade Center in New York. A victim of the worldwide woes of the property and casualty insurance industry, Lloyd's of London, after three centuries, will never be the same.

*"Lloyd's of London Posts Big Loss, Raising Fears on Market's Viability," *Wall Street Journal*, June 23, 1993, p. A10.

TYPES OF INSURANCE

Information on Canada's insurance companies is available at www.fin.gc.ca

Insurance is classified by which type of undesirable event is insured. The most common types are life insurance and property and casualty insurance. In its simplest form, life insurance provides income for the heirs of the deceased. Many insurance companies offer policies that provide retirement benefits as well as life insurance. In this case, the premium combines the cost of the life insurance with a savings program. The cost of life insurance depends on such factors as the age of the insured, average life expectancies, the health and lifestyle of the insured (whether the insured smokes, engages in a dangerous hobby such as skydiving, and so on), and the insurance company's operating costs.

Access Lloyd's of London's Website at www.lloydsoflondon.com

Property and casualty insurance protects property (houses, cars, boats, and so on) against losses due to accidents, fire, disasters, and other calamities. Marine insurance, for example, which insures against the loss of a ship and its cargo, is the oldest form of insurance, predating even life insurance. Property and casualty policies tend to be short-term contracts subject to frequent renewal. Another significant distinction between life insurance policies and property and casualty policies is that the latter do not have a savings component. Property and casualty premiums are based simply on the probability of sustaining the loss. That is why car insurance premiums are higher if a driver has had speeding tickets, has caused accidents, or lives in a high-crime area. Each of these events increases the likelihood that the insurance company will have to pay a claim.

Life Insurance

Life is assumed to unfold in a predictable sequence: You work for a number of years while saving for retirement; then you retire, live off the fruits of your earlier labour, and die at a ripe old age. The problem is that you could die too young and not have time to provide for your loved ones, or you could live too long and run out of retirement assets. Either option is very unappealing to most people. The purpose of life insurance is to relieve some of the concern associated with either eventuality. Although insurance cannot make you comfortable with the idea of a premature death, it can at least allow you the peace of mind that comes with knowing that you have provided for your heirs. Life insurance companies also want to help people save for their retirement. In this way, the insurance company provides for the customer's whole life.

The basic products of life insurance companies are life insurance proper, disability insurance, annuities, and health insurance. Life insurance pays off if you die, protecting those who depend on your continued earnings. As mentioned, the person who receives the insurance payment after you die is called the *beneficiary* of the policy. Disability insurance replaces part of your income should you become unable to continue working because of illness or an accident. An **annuity** is an insurance product that will help if you live longer than you expect. For an initial fixed sum or stream of payments, the insurance company agrees to pay you a fixed amount for as long as you live. If you live a short life, the insurance company pays out less than expected. Conversely, if you live unusually long, the insurance company may pay out much more than expected.

Notice one curiosity among these various types of insurance: Although predicting any one individual's life expectancy or probability of being disabled is very difficult, when many people are insured, the actual amount to be paid out by the insurance company can be predicted very accurately. Insurance companies collect and analyze statistics on life expectancies, health claims, disability claims, and other relevant matters.

For example, a life insurance company can predict with a high degree of accuracy when death benefits must be paid by using *actuarial tables* that predict life expectancies. Table 1 lists the expected life of persons at various ages. A 25-year-old female can expect to live another 59.25 years; a 25-year-old male, however, can expect to live only another 53.02 years.

The **law of large numbers** says that when many people are insured, the probability distribution of the losses will assume a normal probability distribution, a distribution that allows accurate predictions. This distribution is important: Because insurance companies insure so many millions of people, the law of large numbers tends to make the company's predictions quite accurate and allows companies to price the policies so that they can earn a profit.

TABLE 1 Life Expectancy at Various Ages in Canada

Age	Male	Female
15	60	67
25	51	57
35	41	47
45	32	37
55	23	28
65	16	20
75	10	12
85	5	7

Source: With permission of life-insurance-canada.com and www.retireweb.com

Life insurance policies protect against an interruption in the family's stream of income. The broad categories of life insurance products are *term, whole life,* and *universal life.*

Term Life The simplest form of life insurance is the *term insurance policy,* which pays out if the insured dies while the policy is in force. This form of policy contains no savings element. Once the policy period expires, there are no residual benefits.

As the insured ages, the probability of death increases, so the cost of the policy rises. For example, Table 2 shows the estimated premiums for a 40-year-old male nonsmoker for $100 000 of term life insurance from a major insurance company. The premium for the first year is $155. This rises to $166 when the insured is 41 years old, $177 when the insured is 42, and so on. By the time the insured is 60 years old, $100 000 of life insurance costs $617 per year. Of course, rates vary among insurance companies, but these sample rates demonstrate how the annual cost of a term policy rises with the age of the insured.

Some term policies fix the premiums for a set number of years, usually five or ten. Alternatively, *decreasing term policies* have a constant premium, but the amount of the insurance coverage declines each year.

Term policies have been historically hard to sell because once they expire, the policyholder has nothing to show for the premium paid. This problem is solved with whole life policies.

Whole Life A *whole life insurance* policy pays a death benefit if the policyholder dies. Whole life policies usually require the insured to pay a level premium for the duration of the policy. In the beginning, the insured pays more than if a term policy had been purchased. This overpayment accumulates as a cash value that can be borrowed by the insured at reasonable rates.

Survivorship benefits also contribute to the accumulated cash values. When members of the insured pool die, any remaining cash values are divided among the survivors. If the policyholder lives until the policy matures, it can be surrendered for its cash value. This cash value can be used to purchase an annuity. In this way, the whole life policy is advertised as covering the insured for the duration of his or her life.

Universal Life In the late 1970s, whole life policies fell into disfavour because the rates of return earned on the policy premiums were well below rates available on other investments. For example, say that an investor bought a term policy instead of a whole life policy and invested the difference in the premiums. If she did this each year for the term of the whole life policy, she would be able to pay for term insurance and still have a much greater amount in her investment account than if she had initially purchased the whole life policy. Investment advisers and insurance agents began steering customers away from whole life policies. The sales pitch became "buy term and invest the difference." Because the

TABLE 2 Typical Annual Premiums on a $100 000 Term Policy for a Male Nonsmoker

Age of Insured	Cost ($)
40	155
41	166
42	177
45	209
50	282
55	422
60	617

Source: With permission of www.life-insurance-canada.com

agents were also selling other investments, they did not suffer from this change in insurance plans. To combat the flow of funds out of their companies, insurance firms introduced the *universal life policy.*

Universal life policies combine the benefits of the term policy with those of the whole life policy. The major benefit of the universal life policy is that the cash value accumulates at a much higher rate.

The universal life policy is structured to have two parts, one for the term life insurance and one for savings. One important advantage that universal life policies have over many alternative investment plans is that the interest earned on the savings portion of the account is tax-exempt until withdrawn. To keep this favourable tax treatment, the cash value of the policy cannot exceed the death benefit.

Universal life policies were introduced in the early 1980s when interest rates were at record high levels. They immediately became popular, but their popularity ebbed in the early 1990s as interest rates fell. In 2000, they accounted for 24% of the volume of life insurance sold.

Annuities If we think of term life insurance as insuring against death, the annuity can be viewed as insuring against life. As we noted earlier, one risk people have is outliving their retirement funds. If they live longer than they projected when they initially retired, they could spend all of their money and end up in poverty. One way to avoid this outcome is by purchasing annuities. Once an annuity has been purchased for a fixed amount, it makes payments as long as the beneficiary lives.

Annuities are particularly susceptible to the adverse selection problem. When people retire, they know more about their life expectancy than the insurance company knows. People who are in good health, have a family history of longevity, and have attended to their health all of their lives are more likely to live longer and hence to want to buy an annuity than people in poor or average health. To avoid this problem, insurance companies tend to price individual annuities expensively. Most annuities are sold to members of large groups where all employees covered by a particular pension plan automatically receive their benefit distribution by purchasing an annuity from the insurance company. Because the annuity is automatic, the adverse selection problem is eliminated.

Assets and Liabilities of Life Insurance Companies Life insurance companies derive funds from two sources. First, they receive premiums that represent future obligations that must be met when the insured dies. Second, they receive premiums paid into pension funds managed by the life insurance company. These funds are long-term in nature.

The Website www.osfi-bsfi.gc.ca provides a wide range of information, including financial data, on life insurance companies.

Since life insurance liabilities are predictable and long-term, life insurance companies can invest in long-term assets. Figure 3 shows the distribution of assets of the average life insurance company at the beginning of 2000. Most of the assets are in long-term investments such as corporate stocks and bonds.

Insurance companies have also invested heavily in mortgages and real estate over the years. In 2000, about 23% of life insurance assets were invested either in mortgage loans or directly in real estate. This percentage is down substantially from historic levels. Figure 4 displays the percentage of assets invested in mortgages from 1977 to 2001. The recent decline in mortgage investment, which represents a shift to lower-risk assets, has been offset by increased investment in corporate bonds and government securities.

The shift to less risky securities may be the result of losses suffered by some insurance companies in the late 1980s. As insurance companies competed against mutual funds and money market funds for retirement dollars, they found that they needed higher-return investments. This led some insurance companies to invest in real estate and junk bonds. Deteriorating real estate values brought on by overbuilding during the 1980s caused some firms to suffer large losses.

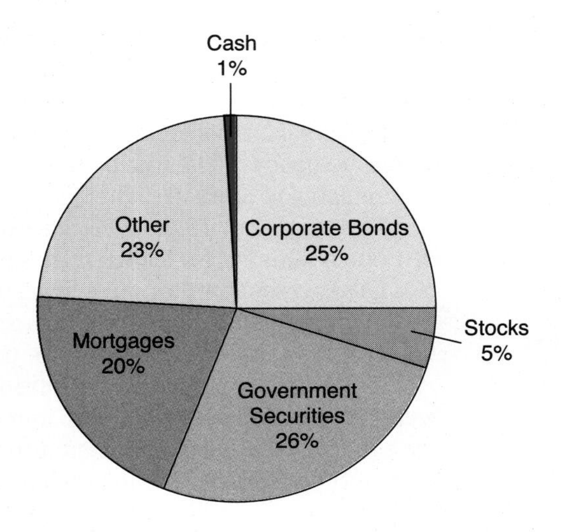

FIGURE 3 Distribution of Life Insurance Company Assets, 2001:Q3

Source: Bank of Canada *Banking and Financial Statistics,* Table D4

Health Insurance

Individual health insurance coverage is very vulnerable to adverse selection problems. People who know that they are likely to get ill are the most likely to seek health insurance coverage. This causes individual health insurance to be very expensive. Most policies are offered through company-sponsored programs in which the company pays all or part of the employee's policy premium.

Visit www.hc-sc.gc.ca, the site for Health Canada.

Most life insurance companies also offer health insurance. Health insurance premiums account for about 23% of total premium income. Life insurance companies compete with Blue Cross, a nonprofit firm that is sponsored by hospitals. Although the government is also involved in the provision of health services, most Canadians also purchase insurance for services not covered under government

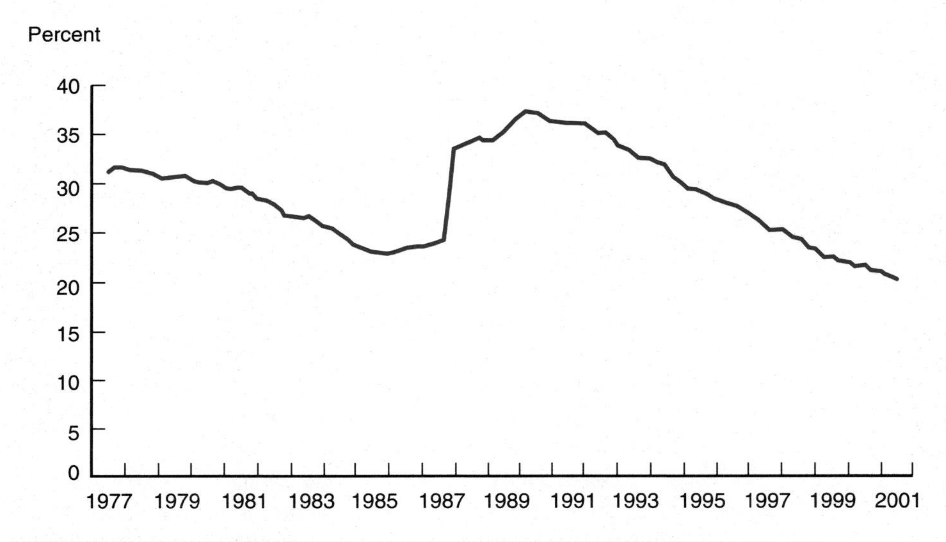

FIGURE 4 Percentage of Life Insurance Company Assets Invested in Mortgages, 1977–2001

Source: Statistics Canada CANSIM II series V37009 and V37000

programs; these services include travel insurance, dental insurance, disability income insurance, and extended health care benefits.

Health insurance has been a major political issue and continues to be the subject of regulation. One reason for the extensive debate over medical insurance has been the spiraling costs of health care. For most of the past decade, the cost of health care has risen much faster than the cost of living and real wages. One factor contributing to this increase is the more sophisticated and expensive treatments constantly being offered. For example, studies have shown that cholesterol-reducing drugs can reduce the likelihood of cardiovascular trouble across a broad portion of the population. These drugs cost about $3 per day and did not even exist 15 years ago. Insurance companies have dealt with these rising costs in a number of ways. For example, today the risk of most company-sponsored plans is borne by the company, with the insurance company administering the plan and covering catastrophic expenses. This increases the sponsoring company's incentive to maintain a healthy workforce and to encourage responsible use of medical facilities by its employees. For example, many large firms have found it cost-effective to employ physician assistants on site to reduce medical fees and absenteeism.

Property and Casualty Insurance

Financial data on property and casualty insurance companies can be found at www.osfi-bsif.gc.ca

Property and casualty insurance was the earliest form of insurance. It began in the Middle Ages when merchants sent ships off to foreign ports to trade. A merchant, though willing to accept the risk that the trading might not turn a profit, was often unwilling to accept the risk that the ship might sink or be captured by pirates. To reduce such risks, merchants began to band together and insure each other's ships against loss. The process became more sophisticated as time went on, and insurance policies were written that were then traded in the major commercial centers of the time.

In 1666, the Great Fire of London did much to advance the case for fire insurance. The first fire insurance company was founded in London in 1680. In the United States, the first fire insurance company was formed by a group led by Benjamin Franklin in 1752. In Canada, the first fire insurance company was formed by a group of Halifax businessmen in 1809. By the beginning of the nineteenth century, the assets of property and casualty insurance firms exceeded even those of commercial banks, making these firms the most important financial intermediary. The invention of the automobile did a great deal to spur the growth of property and casualty insurance companies during the twentieth century.

Property and Casualty Insurance Today There are about 230 property and casualty insurance companies in Canada, employing more than 90 000 people. Property and casualty insurance protects against losses from fire, theft, storm, explosion, and even neglect. **Property insurance** protects businesses and owners from the impact of risk associated with owning property. This includes replacement and loss of earnings from income-producing property as well as financial losses to owners of residential property. **Casualty insurance** (or **liability insurance**) protects against liability for harm the insured may cause to others as a result of product failure or accidents. For example, part of your car insurance is property insurance (which pays if your car is damaged), and part is casualty insurance (which pays if you cause an accident).

Property and casualty insurance is different from life insurance. First, policies tend to be short-term, usually for one year or less. Second, whereas life insurance is limited to insuring against one event, property and casualty companies insure against many different events. Finally, the amount of the potential loss is much more difficult to predict than for life insurance. For example, the

September 11, 2001, terrorist attacks in the United States will likely lead to one of the largest insurance payouts in U.S. history.

These characteristics cause property and casualty insurance companies to hold more liquid assets than those of life insurance companies; the wide range of losses means that these companies must maintain substantial liquidity. Figure 5 shows the distribution of assets of property and casualty insurance companies in Canada.

Property insurance can be provided in either **named-peril policies** or **open-peril policies**. Named-peril policies insure against loss only from perils that are specifically named in the policy, whereas open-peril policies insure against all perils except those specifically excluded by the policy. For example, many homeowners in low-lying areas are required to buy flood insurance. This insurance covers only losses due to flooding, so it is a named-peril policy. A homeowner's insurance policy, which protects the house from fire, hurricane, tornado, and other damage, is an example of an open-peril policy.

Casualty or liability insurance protects against financial losses because of a claim of negligence. Liability insurance is bought not only by manufacturers who might be sued because of product defects but also by many types of professionals, including physicians, lawyers, and building contractors. Whereas the risk exposure in property insurance policies is relatively easy to predict, since it is usually limited to the value of the property, liability risk exposure is much more difficult to determine.

Liability risk exposure can have long lag times (often referred to as "tails"). This means that a liability claim may be filed long after the policy expires. Consider liability claims filed against the manufacturers of light airplanes. In the 1950s, 1960s, and 1970s, Cessna and Piper produced airplanes that are still being used today. The companies often get sued when one of these 30- or 40-year-old planes crashes. Insurance premiums grew so large in the 1980s because of the extensive lag time that both Cessna and Piper had to stop producing private airplanes. The cost of the liability insurance put the price of the planes out of reach of most private pilots.

There has been extensive publicity about high liability awards given by juries. These awards have often been well above what the insurance companies could

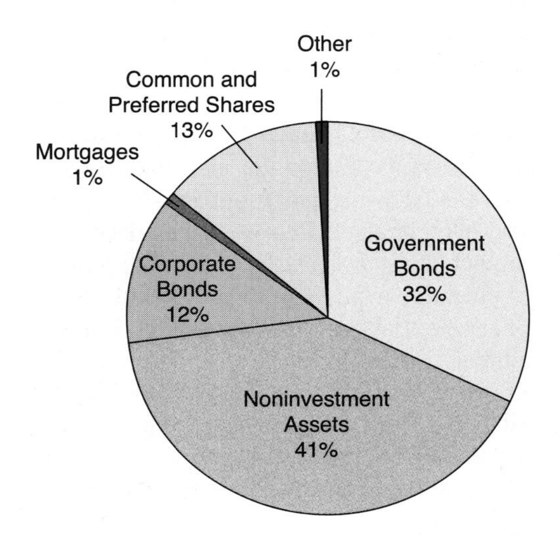

FIGURE 5 Distribution of Assets of Property and Casualty Insurance Companies in Canada, 2000

Source: Social Insurance Bureau of Canada Website: www.ibc.ca

have predicted. Liability insurance premiums continue to rise as a result. Some provinces have attempted to limit liability awards in an effort to contain these insurance costs.

The "Facts Book" at www.ibc.ca provides essential facts and statistics about the property and casualty insurance industry.

Reinsurance One way that insurance companies may reduce their risk exposure is to obtain **reinsurance**. Reinsurance allocates a portion of the risk to another company in exchange for a portion of the premium. Reinsurance allows insurance companies to write larger policies because a portion of the policy is actually held by another firm.

About 10% of all property and casualty insurance is reinsured. Smaller insurance firms obtain reinsurance more frequently than large firms. You can think of it as insurance for the insurance company.

Since the originator of the policy usually has more to lose than the reinsurer, the moral hazard and adverse selection problems are small. This means that little specific information about the risk being reinsured is required. As a result of the simplified information requirements, the reinsurance market consists of relatively standardized contracts. One problem with the market is the risk that the reinsurer can fail.

INSURANCE REGULATION AND SUPERVISION

The purpose of most regulations is to protect policyholders from losses due to the insolvency of the company. To accomplish this, insurance companies are restricted as to their asset composition and minimum capital ratio. All provinces also require that insurance agents and brokers obtain licences to sell each kind of insurance: life, property and casualty, and health. These licenses are to ensure that all agents have a minimum level of knowledge about the products they sell.

Life and Health Insurance Companies

Life and health insurance company regulation is the responsibility of the federal and provincial governments. In practice, the federal government regulates the sector as close to 80% of the life and health insurance companies are registered under federal laws. Moreover, all provinces, with the exception of Quebec, accept the laws that govern federally regulated firms and have agreements with the federal government to carry out supervision of provincially incorporated firms on their behalf.

Federal oversight is administered by the OSFI. In particular, OSFI regulation is directed at sales practices, the provision of adequate liquid assets to cover losses, and restrictions on the amount of risky assets (such as common stock) the companies can hold. In other words, OSFI performs the same oversight functions as it does for banks and near banks.

Go to www.compcorp.ca for more details about CompCorp.

Life and health insurance policies are guaranteed up to certain limits by the Canadian Life and Health Insurance Compensation Corporation (CompCorp). CompCorp has no regulatory role in overseeing individual life and health insurance companies. It is a federally incorporated private, not-for-profit corporation established and funded by the Canadian life and health insurance industry to provide liability insurance to policyholders: it compensates policyholders if the issuing company goes bankrupt.[1] Coverage is $200 000 for death benefits under life insur-

[1]Since the establishment of CompCorp in 1990, a large insurance company, Confederation Life, went bankrupt in 1994 and two smaller ones, Sovereign Life and Les Coopérants, in 1992—no life insurance company had failed in Canada before CompCorp's establishment.

ance policies, $2000 per month for disability benefits under disability income insurance policies, and $60 000 for health benefits.

Property and Casualty Insurance Companies

Most property and casualty insurance companies in Canada are incorporated federally and subject to federal regulation, administered by the OSFI. OSFI also looks after the regulation and supervision of the Canadian branch operations of foreign companies. Provincially incorporated companies are largely regulated by the provincial governments. Some lines of property and casualty insurance, such as, for example, auto insurance, are also subject to provincial laws and regulations.

Visit www.pacic.com for information about the PACIC.

Policyholder protection is provided by the Property and Casualty Insurance Compensation Corporation (PACIC), an industry-financed non-profit corporation. PACIC was set up in 1988 and performs the same role for property and casualty companies as CompCorp does for life insurance companies. In particular, it guarantees payments up to $250 000 per claim in the event of loss of policy benefits due to the insolvency of the property and casualty insurance company.

The New Legislative Framework

As already noted in Chapter 18, in June 2001 the government passed legislation allowing demutualized life and health insurance companies to restructure under a holding company structure, to enter into joint ventures and strategic alliances, and to access the Canadian payments and clearance systems, in an attempt to bring the sector in line with the banking sector. However, the new legislation does not allow mergers involving large banks and large demutualized life and health insurance companies. Moreover, the new legislation requires that large life and health insurance companies (those with equity over $5 billion) are widely held, in the sense that an individual or firm cannot own more than 20% of the voting shares. Small demutualized companies (those with equity under $1 billion) are eligible to be closely held.

THE PRACTISING FINANCIAL INSTITUTION MANAGER

Insurance Management

Insurance companies, like banks, are in the financial intermediation business of transforming one type of asset into another for the public. Insurance companies use the premiums paid on policies to invest in assets such as bonds, stocks, mortgages, and other loans; the earnings from these assets are then used to pay out claims on the policies. In effect, insurance companies transform assets such as bonds, stocks, and loans into insurance policies that provide a set of services (for example, claim adjustments, savings plans, friendly insurance agents). If the insurance company's production process of asset transformation efficiently provides its customers with adequate insurance services at low cost and if it can earn high returns on its investments, it will make profits; if not, it will suffer losses.

In Chapters 2 and 14 the concepts of adverse selection and moral hazard allowed us to understand why financial intermediaries like insurance companies are important in the economy. Here we use the adverse selection and moral hazard concepts to explain many management practices specific to the insurance industry.

In the case of an insurance policy, moral hazard arises when the existence of insurance encourages the insured party to take risks that increase the likelihood of an insurance payoff. For example, a person covered by burglary insurance might not take as many precautions to prevent a burglary because the insurance company will reimburse most of the losses if a theft occurs. Adverse selection holds that the people most likely to receive large insurance payoffs are the ones who will want to purchase insurance the most. For example, a person suffering from a terminal disease would want to take out the biggest life and medical insurance policies possible, thereby exposing the insurance company to potentially large losses. Both adverse selection and moral hazard can result in large losses to insurance companies because they lead to higher payouts on insurance claims. Minimizing adverse selection and moral hazard to reduce these payouts is therefore an extremely important goal for insurance companies, and this goal explains the insurance practices we discuss here.

Screening

To reduce adverse selection, insurance companies try to screen out poor insurance risks from good ones. Effective information collection procedures are therefore an important principle of insurance management.

When you apply for auto insurance, the first thing your insurance agent does is ask you questions about your driving record (number of speeding tickets and accidents), the type of car you are insuring, and certain personal matters (age, marital status). If you are applying for life insurance, you go through a similar grilling, but you are asked even more personal questions about such things as your health, smoking habits, and drug and alcohol use. The life insurance company even orders a medical evaluation (usually done by an independent company) that involves taking blood and urine samples. The insurance company uses the information you provide to allocate you to a risk class—a statistical estimate of how likely you are to have an insurance claim. Based on this information, the insurance company can decide whether to accept you for the insurance or to turn you down because you pose too high a risk and thus would be an unprofitable customer for the insurance company.

Risk-Based Premium

Charging insurance premiums on the basis of how much risk a policyholder poses for the insurance company is a time-honoured principle of insurance management. Adverse selection explains why this principle is so important to insurance company profitability.

To understand why an insurance company finds it necessary to have risk-based premiums, let's examine an example of risk-based insurance premiums that at first glance seems unfair. Harry and Sally, both college students with no accidents or speeding tickets, apply for auto insurance. Normally, Harry will be charged a much higher premium than Sally. Insurance companies do this because young males have a much higher accident rate than young females. Suppose, though, that one insurance company did not base its premiums on a risk classification but rather just charged a premium based on the average combined risk for males and females. Then Sally would be charged too much and Harry too little. Sally could go to another insurance company and get a lower rate, while Harry would sign up for the insurance. Because Harry's premium isn't high enough to cover the accidents he is likely to have, on average the company would lose money on Harry. Only with a premium based on a risk classification, so that Harry is charged more, can the insurance company make a profit.[2]

[2]You may recognize that the example here is in fact the lemons problem described in Chapter 14.

Restrictive Provisions

Restrictive provisions in policies are another insurance management tool for reducing moral hazard. Such provisions discourage policyholders from engaging in risky activities that make an insurance claim more likely. One type of restrictive provision keeps the policyholder from benefiting from behaviour that makes a claim more likely. For example, life insurance companies have provisions in their policies that eliminate death benefits if the insured person commits suicide. Restrictive provisions may also require certain behaviour on the part of the insured that makes a claim less likely. A company renting motor scooters may be required to provide helmets for renters in order to be covered for any liability associated with the rental. The role of restrictive provisions is not unlike that of restrictive covenants on debt contracts described in Chapter 14: Both serve to reduce moral hazard by ruling out undesirable behaviour.

Prevention of Fraud

Insurance companies also face moral hazard because an insured person has an incentive to lie to the company and seek a claim even if the claim is not valid. For example, a person who has not complied with the restrictive provisions of an insurance contract may still submit a claim. Even worse, a person may file claims for events that did not actually occur. Thus an important management principle for insurance companies is conducting investigations to prevent fraud so that only policyholders with valid claims receive compensation.

Cancellation of Insurance

Being prepared to cancel policies is another insurance management tool. Insurance companies can discourage moral hazard by threatening to cancel a policy when the insured person engages in activities that make a claim more likely. If your auto insurance company makes it clear that if a driver gets too many speeding tickets, coverage will be cancelled, you will be less likely to speed.

Deductibles

The deductible is the fixed amount by which the insured's loss is reduced when a claim is paid off. A $250 deductible on an auto policy, for example, means that if you suffer a loss of $1000 because of an accident, the insurance company will pay you only $750. Deductibles are an additional management tool that helps insurance companies reduce moral hazard. With a deductible, you experience a loss along with the insurance company when you make a claim. Because you also stand to lose when you have an accident, you have an incentive to drive more carefully. A deductible thus makes a policyholder act more in line with what is profitable for the insurance company; moral hazard has been reduced. And because moral hazard has been reduced, the insurance company can lower the premium by more than enough to compensate the policyholder for the existence of the deductible.

Another function of the deductible is to eliminate the administrative costs of small losses by forcing the insured to bear these losses.

Coinsurance

When a policyholder shares a percentage of the losses along with the insurance company, their arrangement is called **coinsurance**. For example, some medical insurance plans provide coverage for 80% of medical bills, and the insured person pays 20% after a certain deductible has been met. Coinsurance works to reduce moral hazard in exactly the same way that a deductible does. A policyholder who suffers a loss along with the insurance company has less incentive to take actions, such as going to the doctor unnecessarily, that involve higher claims. Coinsurance is thus another useful management tool for insurance companies.

Limits on the Amount of Insurance

Another important principle of insurance management is that there should be limits on the amount of insurance provided, even though a customer is willing to pay for more coverage. The higher the insurance coverage, the more the insured person can gain from risky activities that make an insurance payoff more likely and hence the greater the moral hazard. For example, if Zelda's car were insured for more than its true value, she might not take proper precautions to prevent its theft, such as making sure that the key is always removed or putting in an alarm system. If her car were stolen, she comes out ahead because the excessive insurance payoff would allow her to buy an even better car. By contrast, when the insurance payment is lower than the value of her car, she will suffer a loss if it is stolen and will thus take the proper precautions to prevent this from happening. Insurance companies must always make sure that their coverage is not so high that moral hazard leads to large losses.

Summary

Effective insurance management requires several practices: information collection and screening of potential policyholders, risk-based premiums, restrictive provisions, prevention of fraud, cancellation of insurance, deductibles, coinsurance, and limits on the amount of insurance. All of these practices reduce moral hazard and adverse selection by making it harder for policyholders to benefit from engaging in activities that increase the amount and likelihood of claims. With smaller benefits available, the poor insurance risks (those who are more likely to engage in the activities in the first place) see less benefit from the insurance and are thus less likely to seek it out.

PENSIONS

A **pension plan** is an asset pool that accumulates over an individual's working years and is paid out during the nonworking years. Pension plans represent the fastest-growing financial intermediary. There are a number of reasons for this rapid growth.

As Canada became more urban, people realized that they could not rely on their children to care for them in their retirement. In a rural culture, families tend to stay together on the farm. The property passes from generation to generation with an implicit understanding that the younger generations will care for the older ones. When families became more dispersed and moved off farms, both the opportunity for and the expectation of extensive financial support of the older generations declined.

A second factor contributing to the growth of pension plans is that people are living longer and retiring younger. Again, in the rural setting, people often remained productive well into their retirement years. Many companies in urban Canada, however, encourage older workers to retire. They are often earning high wages as a result of seniority, yet may be less productive than younger workers. The result of this trend toward younger retirement and longer lives is that the average person can expect to spend more years in retirement. These years must be funded somehow, and the pension plan is often the vehicle of choice.

TYPES OF PENSIONS

Pension plans can be categorized in several ways. They may be defined-benefit or defined-contribution plans, and they may be public or private.

Defined-Benefit Pension Plans

Under a **defined-benefit plan**, the plan sponsor promises the employees a specific benefit when they retire. The payout is usually determined with a formula that uses the number of years worked and the employee's final salary. For example, a pension benefit may be calculated by the following formula:

$$\text{Annual payment} = 2\% \times \text{average of final 3 years' income} \times \text{years of service}$$

In this case, if a worker had been employed for 35 years and the average wages during the last three years were $50 000, the annual pension benefit would be

$$0.02 \times \$50\ 000 \times 35 = \$35\ 000 \text{ per year}$$

The defined-benefit plan puts the burden on the employer to provide adequate funds to ensure that the agreed payments can be made. External audits of pension plans are required to determine whether sufficient funds have been contributed by the company. If sufficient funds are set aside by the firm for this purpose, the plan is **fully funded**. If more than enough funds are available, the plan is **overfunded**. Often, insufficient funds are available and the fund is **underfunded**. For example, if Kim Huang contributes $100 per year into her pension plan and the interest rate is 10%, after ten years, the contributions and their interest earnings would be worth $1753.[3] If the defined benefit on her pension plan is $1753 or less after ten years, the plan is fully funded because her contributions and earnings will cover this payment in full. But if the defined benefit is $2000, the plan is underfunded because her contributions and earnings do not cover this amount. Underfunding is most common when the employer fails to contribute adequately to the plan. Surprisingly, it is not illegal for a firm to sponsor an underfunded plan. The General Motors Corporation pension plan was underfunded by billions of dollars for most of the 1990s. The degree of funding does not affect the sponsor's responsibility to pay its obligations under the plan. Difficulties arise, however, when firms go bankrupt. If the pension fund is underfunded, retirees may not receive their benefits.

Defined-Contribution Pension Plans

As the name implies, instead of defining what the pension plan will pay, **defined-contribution plans** specify only what will be contributed into the fund. The retirement benefits are entirely dependent on the earnings of the fund. Corporate sponsors of defined-contribution plans usually put a fixed percentage of each employee's wages into the pension fund each pay period. In some instances, the employee also contributes to the plan. An insurance company or fund manager acts as trustee and invests the fund's assets. Frequently, employees are allowed to specify how the funds in their individual accounts will be invested. For example, an employee who is a conservative investor may prefer government securities, while one who is a more aggressive investor may prefer to have her retirement funds

[3]The $100 contributed in year 1 would become worth $\$100 \times (1 + 0.10)^{10} = \$259.37$ at the end of ten years; the $100 contributed in year 2 would become worth $\$100 \times (1 + 0.10)^{9} = 235.79$; and so on until the $100 contributed in year 10 would become worth $\$100 \times (1 + 0.10) = \$110$. Adding these together, we get the total value of these contributions and their earnings at the end of ten years as $1753.

invested in corporate stock. When the employee retires, the balance in the pension account can be transferred into an annuity or some other form of distribution.

Defined-contribution pension plans are becoming increasingly popular. Many existing defined-benefit plans are converting to this form, and virtually all new plans are established as defined-contribution. One reason the defined-contribution plan is becoming so popular is that the onus is put on the employee rather than the employer to look out for the pension plan's performance. This reduces the liability of the employer.

Another problem is that plan participants may not understand the need to diversify their holdings. For example, many firms actively encourage employees to invest in company stock. The firm's motivation is to better align employee interest with that of stockholders. The downside is that employees suffer twice should the firm fail. First, they lose their jobs, and second, their retirement portfolios evaporate. The recent collapse of Enron Inc. has brought this issue forcibly to public attention.

One problem with defined-contribution plans is that many employees are not familiar enough with investments to make wise long-term choices. For example, only a small fraction of plan participants choose to put any more than half of their investment in stocks, even though long-term growth potential is greatest in the stock market.

Private and Public Pension Plans

Private pension plans, sponsored by employers, groups, and individuals, have grown rapidly as people have become more concerned about the viability of Social Security and more sophisticated about preparing for retirement. As of 2000, there were more than 15 000 private pension plans in Canada, covering over 5.3 million members, with total accumulated assets close to $700 billion. Trusteed pension plans account for the majority of private pension plans in Canada. Typically, a pension plan sponsor (such as a government or private-sector employer) will hire a bank, a life insurance company, or a pension fund manager to manage the fund, for the benefit of the plan members. The largest trusteed pension funds in Canada are the Ontario Teachers' Pension Board and the Ontario Municipal Employees' Retirement Board. Among the largest pension fund managers are the *Caisse de dépôt et placement du Québec* and Royal Trust, a subsidiary of the Royal Bank.

Many private pension plans are underfunded because they plan to meet their pension obligations out of current earnings when the benefits come due. As long as companies have sufficient earnings, underfunding creates no problems, but if not, they may not be able to meet their pension obligations. Because of potential problems caused by corporate underfunding, mismanagement, fraudulent practices, and other abuses of private pension funds, these funds are heavily regulated.

In the past, private pension plans invested mostly in government securities and corporate bonds. Although these instruments are still important pension plan assets, corporate stocks, mortgages, open market paper, and time deposits now play a significant role. This makes pension plan managers a potentially powerful force if they choose to exercise control over firm management (see Box 3).

An alternative to privately sponsored pension plans is the public plans, though in many cases there is very little difference between the two. A **public pension plan** is one that is sponsored by a governmental body.

The most important government pension plan is Social Security—Old Age Security (OAS) and Guaranteed Income Supplement (GIS)—that covers all Canadians. It makes monthly flat payments (out of federal government revenues) to retired or disabled workers or their surviving spouses. Other government pen-

BOX 3

Power to the Pensions

One ramification of the growth of pension plans and other institutional investors is that the managers of these funds have the ability to exercise substantial control over corporate management. Clearly, when a pension fund manager, who controls many thousands of shares, calls a corporate officer, the officer is going to listen. Evidence suggests that fund managers actively apply the power they have to influence corporate management. In the United States, for example, pension funds recently defeated management-sponsored anti-takeover proxy proposals at Honeywell. And Texaco agreed to name a director from candidates submitted by the huge California Public Employees Retirement System. In addition, the stated mission of the U.S. Council of Institutional Investors is to "encourage trustees to take an active role in assuring that corporate actions are not taken at the expense of shareholders." It is possible that these actions will work to benefit shareholders, who do not individually wield enough clout to exert control. However, the clout shareholders wield when their shares are placed into a fund manager's hands may be sufficient to improve corporate management significantly.

This site reports the CPP contribution rates since 1966: www.cpp-rpc.gc.ca

sion plans are the Canada Pension Plan (CPP) and in Quebec, the Quebec Pension Plan (QPP), both supported by contributions from employees and their employers. The accumulated funds of the CPP are managed by an investment board, called the CPP Investment Board, and those of the QPP are managed by the *Caisse de dépôt et placement du Québec*.

The amount of CPP or QPP benefits a retiree receives is based on the person's earnings history. Workers contribute 4.3% of wages up to a current maximum of $38 300 (as of 2001). Employers contribute the same amount. Self-employed persons pay both portions, for a total contribution rate of 8.6%. There is a certain amount of redistribution in the benefits, with low-income workers receiving a relatively larger return on their investment than high-income workers. One way to evaluate the amount of benefits of a pension plan is to determine how the monthly benefits compare to preretirement income. This replacement ratio is about 25% of the inflation-adjusted average pensionable earnings during the contributory period.

When the government pension plans were established, the federal government intended to operate them like private pension plans. However, unlike private pension plans but like Old Age Security and Guaranteed Income Supplement plans, benefits are typically paid out from current contributions, not tied closely to a participant's past contributions. Future generations will be called on to pay benefits to the individuals who are currently contributing. Many people fear that the funds will be unable to meet their obligations by the time they retire. This fear is based on the realization that a large number of people from the baby boom generation (born between 1946 and 1964) will swell the ranks of retirees in the rapidly approaching future. In fact, nine million baby boomers will begin reaching their normal retirement ages in 2011. Meanwhile, the number of workers supporting each one of those retirees will fall from five to three by 2016.

The government has been grappling with the problems of the public pension plans for years (see Box 4), but the prospect of a huge bulge of new retirees has resulted in calls for radical surgery. Figure 6 shows that total assets in CPP and QPP decreased in the early 1990s at the same time that the number of insured people was increasing. This situation led to a restructuring that included raising program contributions. In particular, in 1999 the CPP was given authority to sharply increase contribution levels from $969 to a maximum of $1635 by the year 2003. It was also given the authority to invest its accumulated assets (estimated to rise to $100 billion by 2006 and to $300 billion by 2015) in the market in order to earn a higher return so that future increases in contribution levels will not be needed.

BOX 4

Should Public Pension Plans Be Privatized?

In recent years, public confidence in the public pension plans has reached a new low. Some surveys suggest that young people have more confidence in the existence of flying saucers than they do in the government's promise to pay them their public pension plan benefits. Without some overhaul of the system, public pension plans will not be able to meet their future obligations. The government has set up advisory commissions and has been holding hearings to address this problem.

Currently, the assets of the public pension plans, which reside in trust funds, are all invested in government securities. Because stocks and corporate bonds have higher returns than government securities, many proposals to save the public pension plans suggest investing part of the trust fund in corporate securities and thus partially privatizing the systems.

Suggestions for privatization take three basic forms:

1. *Government investment of trust fund assets in corporate securities.* This plan has the advantage of possibly improving the trust funds' overall return, while minimizing transactions costs because it exploits the economies of scale of the trust funds. Critics warn that government ownership of private assets could lead to increased government intervention in the private sector.
2. *Shift of trust fund assets to individual accounts that can be invested in private assets.* This option has the advantage of possibly increasing the return on investments and does not involve the government in the ownership of private assets. However, critics warn that it might expose individuals to greater risk and to transaction costs on individual accounts that might be very high because of the small size of many of these accounts.
3. *Individual accounts in addition to those in the trust funds.* This option has advantages and disadvantages similar to those of option 2 and may provide more funds to individuals at retirement. However, some increase in contributions would be required to fund these accounts.

Whether some privatization of the public pension plans occurs is an open question. In the short term public pension plan reform is likely to involve an increase in contributions, a reduction in benefits, or both. For example, under the 1997 changes to the CPP Act, the percentage of liabilities of CPP that are funded is expected to increase from the current 8% to 20% by 2018.

An alternative to both privately sponsored pension plans and public pension plans is **personal pension plans**. These are the Registered Retirement Savings Plans (RRSPs) that Canadians set up with financial institutions. They provide tax-sheltered, self-financed retirement funds. At the end of 1999, RRSP accumulated assets totalled about $260 billion. This is an increase of 273% over the $95 billion of total RRSP accumulated assets a decade ago. The recent declines in

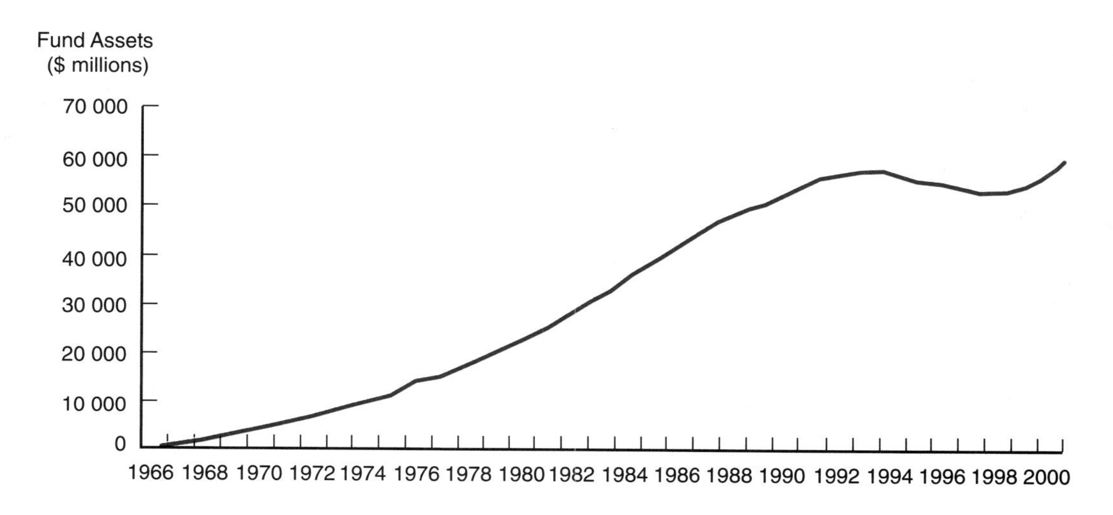

FIGURE 6 CPP and QPP Total Financial Assets, 1966–2001

Source: Statistics Canada CANSIM II series V12393360 and V12393370

the stock market, however, have significantly reduced RRSP accumulated assets. Upon retirement, an RRSP must be converted into an annuity or a Registered Retirement Income Fund (RRIF), which provides taxable annuity payments. Since RRIFs are less popular than annuities, which may only be offered by insurance companies, the insurance industry has benefited from the introduction of the RRSP.

REGULATION OF PENSION PLANS

For many years, pension plans were relatively free of government regulation. Many companies provided pension benefits as rewards for long years of good service and used the benefits as an incentive. Frequently, pension benefits were paid out of current income. When the firm failed or was acquired by another firm, the benefits ended. During the Great Depression, widespread pension plan failures led to increased regulation and to the establishment of public pension plans.

As with insurance companies, the regulatory system governing pension funds is split between OSFI and provincial superintendents of pensions. Pension funds administered for people working in business that are federal in scope (for example, railways, air transport, telecommunications, and banking) are the responsibility of OSFI. However, the regulation of private sector pension plans is a provincial responsibility. Provincial acts and regulations tend to be similar across provinces, with Ontario pension legislation setting the standard for the regulation of private sector pension plans. They establish minimum standards for the reporting and disclosure of information, set rules for vesting and the degree of underfunding, and place restrictions on investment practices. One difference among provincial acts is that Ontario provides default insurance on private sector plans while the other provinces generally do not.

Individual retirement plans are registered with Canada Customs and Revenue Agency (CCRA), which determines the maximum value of the annual RRSP contribution limit for every individual taxpayer. Currently, the maximum amount is 18% of annual income up to a maximum of $13 500, with the contribution limit being affected if an individual is covered by other pension plans. All Canadians are eligible to purchase RRSPs regardless of age. According to the Income Tax Act, financial institutions need to get approval from the CCRA in order to issue RRSPs. RRSP funds can be invested in a variety of products, as long as they are approved by the CCRA and have 70% Canadian content. The contribution and profits generated from the RRSP investments are not taxable until withdrawal.

THE FUTURE OF PENSION FUNDS

We can expect that pension funds will continue their growth and popularity as the population continues to grow and age. Workers in their early years of employment often find discussions of retirement investing creeping into their conversations. This heightened attention to providing for the future will result in an increased number of pension funds as well as a greater variety of pension fund options to choose among. We can also expect to see pension funds gain increased power over corporations as they control increasing amounts of stock.

SUMMARY

1. Insurance companies exist because people are risk-averse and prefer to transfer risk away from themselves. Insurance benefits people's lives by reducing the size of reserves they would have to maintain to cover possible loss of life or property.
2. Adverse selection and moral hazard are problems inherent to the insurance business. Many of the provisions of insurance policies—including deductibles, application screening, and risk-based premiums—are aimed at reducing their effects.
3. Insurance is usually divided into two primary types, life insurance and property and casualty insurance. Many life insurance products also serve as savings vehicles. Property and casualty insurance usually has a much shorter term than most life insurance.
4. Because life insurance liabilities are very predictable, these insurers are able to invest in long-term assets. Property and casualty insurance companies must keep their assets more liquid to pay out on unexpected losses.
5. Pension plans are rapidly growing as a longer-lived generation plans for early retirement.
6. There are two primary types of pension plans: defined-benefit and defined-contribution. Defined-benefit plans pay benefits according to a formula that is established in advance. Defined-contribution plans specify only how much is to be saved; benefits depend on the returns generated by the plans.
7. The largest public pension plan is Social Security, which is a pay-as-you-go system. Current retirees receive payments from current workers. Many people are concerned that as the number of retirees increases, the amount paid in to the Social Security system will not be sufficient to cover the sums being paid out.

KEY TERMS

annuity, *p. 491*
casualty (liability) insurance, *p. 495*
certainty equivalent, *p. 486*
coinsurance, *p. 500*
deductible, *p. 488*
defined-benefit plan, *p. 502*
defined-contribution plan, *p. 502*
demutualization, *p. 489*
fully funded, *p. 502*
law of large numbers, *p. 491*
mutual insurance company, *p. 488*
named-peril policy, *p. 496*
open-peril policy, *p. 496*
overfunded, *p. 502*
pension plan, *p. 501*
personal pension plan, *p. 505*
private pension plan, *p. 503*
property insurance, *p. 495*
public pension plan, *p. 503*
reinsurance, *p. 497*
stock company, *p. 488*
underfunded, *p. 502*
underwriter, *p. 488*

QUESTIONS AND PROBLEMS

*1. Why do people choose to buy insurance even if their expected loss is less than the payments they will make to the insurance company?

2. Why do insurance companies not allow people to buy insurance on personally unrelated risks?

*3. What is information asymmetry, and how does it affect insurance companies?

4. Distinguish between adverse selection and moral hazard as they relate to the insurance industry.

*5. How do insurance companies protect themselves against losses due to adverse selection and moral hazard?

6. Distinguish between independent agents and exclusive agents.

*7. Are most insurance companies organized as mutuals or stock companies?

8. How are insurance companies able to predict their losses from claims accurately enough to let them price their policies such that they will make a profit?

*9. What is the difference between term life insurance and whole life insurance?

10. What risk do property and casualty insurance policies protect against?

*11. What is the purpose behind reinsurance?

12. Distinguish between defined-benefit and defined-contribution pension plans.

*13. Why have private pension plans grown rapidly in recent years?

14. What is a pay-as-you-go pension plan?

*15. Why is Social Security in danger of eventually going bankrupt?

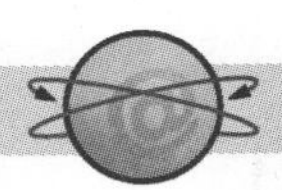

WEB EXERCISES

Insurance Companies and Pension Funds

1. There are many sites on the Web to help you compute whether you are properly preparing for your retirement. One of the better is offered by Quicken. You will find it at http://www.quicken.com/retirement/planner/.

   Have you set aside enough retirement money to last your lifetime? The earlier you start, the easier it will be.

   In general, your retirement funds will come from four sources:
   - Pension plans
   - Social Security
   - Tax-deferred savings
   - Basic (taxable) savings

   Use the Retirement Planner to predict the income from the first two, and to determine how much you will need to save to make up the balance for your retirement goals.

2. An alternative to the financial goals calculation in exercise 1 is sites that offer calculators that let you input figures to compute your goals. Go to http://library.thinkquest.org/10326/other_features/calc.html. Use the financial calculator provided to answer the following questions.

   Solve for the length of time and total gains in the following problems (do not input $) by plugging in each number in the following sequence:

   a. Your goals = $1 000 000; Initial capital = $1000; Monthly invested = $400; ROI = 12%.
   b. Your goals = $2 000 000; Initial capital = $1000; Monthly invested = $600; ROI = 15%.
   c. Your goals = $1 500 000; Initial capital = $10 000; Monthly invested = $0; ROI = 15%.

3. The Internet offers many calculators to help consumers estimate their needs for various financial services. When using these tools, you must remember that they are usually sponsored by financial intermediaries that hope to sell you products. Visit one such site at www.finaid.org/calculators/lifeinsuranceneeds.phtml and calculate how much life insurance you need. Are you the beneficiary of any life insurance policies? Use the calculator to see if that policy is large enough.

Chapter 20

Venture Capital Firms, Finance Companies, and Financial Conglomerates

Preview

Suppose that you are graduating from university and about to start work at that high-paying job you were offered. You may decide that your first purchase must be a car. If you are not mechanically inclined, you may opt to buy a new one. The problem, of course, is that you do not have the $20 000 needed for the purchase. A finance company may come to your rescue. Most automobile financing is provided by finance companies owned by the automobile companies.

Now suppose that you have gone to work and your first assignment is to acquire a new piece of equipment. After doing some math, you may decide that the company should lease the equipment. Again, you may find yourself dealing with another type of finance company.

Later, you are asked to see what you can do to increase your company's liquidity. You may again find that finance companies can help by purchasing your accounts receivable in a transaction called *factoring.*

Finally, you decide to develop and market a new process that you think has a great chance of being a success. However, since it is new and unproven, you cannot get funding from conventional sources. Instead you appeal to the venture capital industry for financial support.

It is clear that finance companies are an important intermediary to many segments of the economy. In this chapter we discuss the different types of finance companies and describe what they do. A specialized firm that provides start-up financing is the venture capital firm. We begin our discussion with this industry.

VENTURE CAPITAL FIRMS

Description of Industry

Venture capital is usually defined as money supplied to young, start-up firms. This money is most frequently raised by limited partnerships and invested by the general partner in firms showing promise of high returns in the future.

Since the mid 1940s venture capital firms have nurtured the growth of North America's high-technology and entrepreneurial communities. Their activities have resulted in job creation, economic growth, and international competitiveness. Venture capitalists backed many of the most successful high-technology companies during the 1980s and 1990s, including Apple Computer, Cisco Systems, Genetech, Microsoft, Netscape, and Sun Microsystems. A number of service firms, such as Staples and Starbucks, also benefited from venture financing. Indeed, much of the growth experienced through the 1980s and 1990s can be traced back to the funding provided by the venture capital industry.

Table 1 shows the explosive growth in venture capital funding witnessed during the late 1990s. As you can see, 2001 was the industry's second-best year, with investments totalling $4.9 billion, down 26% from 2000 (the industry's best year ever), but still well above 1999 disbursement levels. By comparison, the U.S. venture capital industry disbursed US$37.7 billion in 2001, as compared to US$102.3 billion in the record-breaking 2000.

Venture Capitalists Reduce Asymmetric Information

The Website for the Canadian Venture Capital Association is www.cvca.ca

Uncertainty and information asymmetries frequently accompany start-up firms, especially in high-technology communities. Managers of these firms may engage in wasteful expenditures, such as leasing expensive office space, since the manager may benefit disproportionately from them but does not bear their entire cost. The difficulty outside investors have of tracking early-stage high-technology companies leads to other types of costs. For example, a biotechnology company founder may invest in research that brings personal acclaim but little chance for significant returns to investors. As a result of these informational asymmetries, external financing may be costly, difficult, or even impossible to obtain.

Venture capital firms can alleviate the information gap and thus allow firms to receive financing they could not obtain elsewhere. First, as opposed to bank loans or bond financing, venture capital firms hold an equity interest in the firm. The firms are usually privately held, so the stock does not trade publicly. Equity interests in privately held firms are very illiquid. As a result, venture capital investment horizons are long-term. The partners do not expect to earn any return for a number of years, often as long as a decade. In contrast, most investors in stocks are anxious to see annual returns through either stock appreciation or dividend payouts. They are often unwilling to wait years to see if a new idea, process, innovation, or invention will yield profits. Similarly, most investors in bonds are not going to wait years for revenues to grow to a point where interest payments become available. Venture capital financing thus fills an important niche left vacant by alternative sources of capital.

As a second method of addressing the asymmetric information problem, venture capital usually comes with strings attached, the most noteworthy being that the partners in a venture capital firm take seats on the board of directors of the financed firm. Venture capital firms are not passive investors. They actively

TABLE 1 Venture Capital Investments in Canada and the United States, 1997–2001

	Canada		United States	
Year	Number of Companies Funded	Investment Total ($ millions)	Number of Companies Funded	Investment Total ($US millions)
1997	2 297	1 821	2 385	14 823
1998	2 603	1 655	2 821	19 843
1999	2 601	2 720	4 202	54 499
2000	4 173	6 629	5 608	102 308
2001	3 359	4 874	3 224	37 672

Source: www.NVCA.com/ffax.html and www.cvca.ca

attempt to add value to the firm through advice, assistance, and business contacts. Venture capitalists may bring together two firms that can complement each other's activities. Venture capital firms will apply their expertise to help the firm solve various financing and growth-related problems. The venture capital partners on the board of directors will carefully monitor expenditures and management to help safeguard the investment in the firm.

One of the most effective ways venture capitalists have of controlling managers is to disburse funds to the company in stages only as the firm demonstrates progress toward its ultimate goal. If development stalls or markets change, funds can be withheld to cut losses.

Implicit to venture capital financing is an expectation of high risk and large compensating returns. Venture capital firms will search very carefully among hundreds of companies to find a few that show real growth potential. Despite this exhaustive search effort, the selected firms usually have little to show initially other than a unique and promising idea. Venture capitalists mitigate the risk by developing a portfolio of young companies within a single fund. Additionally, many venture capital partnerships will manage multiple funds simultaneously. By diversifying the risk among a number of start-up firms, the risk of loss is significantly lowered.

Origins of Venture Capital

The first true venture capital firm was American Research and Development (ARD), established in 1946 in the United States by MIT president Karl Compton and local business leaders. The bulk of their success can be traced to one US$70 000 investment in a new firm, the Digital Equipment Company. This seed money grew in value to US$355 million over the next three decades.[1] In Canada, the first venture capital firm was Whitecap Venture Partners, a division of Whitecastle Investments Ltd., which was founded in 1959. It was established by A. Ephraim Diamond as an investment medium for his family. Although originating in real estate projects, in the late 1980s they focused on developing young technology firms.

Visit www.whitecapvp.com, the Website for Whitecap Venture Partners.

During the 1960s and 1970s most venture capital funding was for the development of real estate and oil fields. By the late 1980s a shift occurred toward financing technology start-ups. High technology remains the dominant area for venture capital funding. Table 2 shows the breakdown of the venture capital disbursements by industry. About 78% of venture dollars were spent on technology in 2001.

The source of venture capital funding has shifted from wealthy individuals to pension funds and corporations. In 1985, the Pension Benefits Standard Act (PBSA) was introduced, which restricted pension funds from making risky investments, to explicitly allow investment in some high-risk assets.[2] This resulted in a surge of pension fund dollars going into venture projects.

Corporate funding of venture capital projects increased when many companies reduced their investment in their own in-house R&D in favour of outside start-up companies. If the project was successful, the company could acquire the start-up. This change was fueled by evidence that many of the best ideas from in-house centralized R&D languished unused or were commercialized in new firms started by defecting employees. Salaried employees tend not to be as motivated as entrepreneurs who stand to capture a large portion of the profits a new idea may generate. By investing in start-up firms, corporations can benefit from new discoveries while supporting the entrepreneurial spirit.

---

[1]Part of this discussion is based on "The Venture Capital Revolution," by Paul Gompers and Josh Lerner, *Journal of Economic Perspectives,* Number 2, Spring 2001, pages 145–68.

[2]Source: www.acpm.com/ACPMenglish/asumbissiontocapsa.htm.

TABLE 2 Canadian Venture Capital Disbursements by Industry in 2001

Industry Group	Number of Companies	Sum Invested ($ millions)	Percent of Total
Biotechnology	467	842	17
Medical/Health related	248	249	5
Communications	462	1 223	25
Computer related	640	759	16
Internet related	398	586	12
Electronics	415	618	13
Other technology	203	245	5
Consumer related	248	199	4
Manufacturing	191	93	2
Miscellaneous	87	60	1
Total	3 359	4 874	100

Source: Macdonald & Associates.

Structure of Venture Capital Firms

Most early venture capital firms were organized as closed-end mutual funds. A closed-end mutual fund sells a fixed number of shares to investors. Once all of the shares have been sold, no additional money can be raised. Instead, a new venture fund is established. The advantage of this organizational structure is that it provides the long-term money required for venture investing. Investors cannot pull money out of the investment as they could from an open-end mutual fund.

In the 1980s venture capital firms began organizing as limited partnerships. This organizational structure is exempt from securities regulations, including the burdensome disclosure requirements of the provincial securities Acts. While both organizational forms continue to be used, currently most venture capital firms are limited partnerships.

Many of the largest venture capital firms have ties to established brokerage houses. Table 3 lists the top 10 venture deals made in 2001.

The Life of a Deal

Most venture capital deals follow a similar life cycle that begins when a limited partnership is formed and funds are raised. In the second phase, the funds are invested in start-up companies. Finally, the venture firm exits the investment.

Next, we take a more detailed look at this process.

TABLE 3 Top 10 Venture Capital Deals Made in 2001

Company Invested In	$ Invested (in millions)	City	Province
Ceyba Inc.	144.5	Ottawa	Ontario
SS8 Networks Inc.	96.1	Kanata	Ontario
Tropic Networks Inc.	93.0	Kanata	Ontario
Accelight Networks Inc.	93.0	Ottawa	Ontario
Q9 Networks	88.5	Toronto	Ontario
Mobile Satellite Ventures	85.2	Gloucester	Ontario
Celmed BioSciences Inc.	60.0	Saint-Laurent	Quebec
Xantrex Technology Inc.	58.5	Burnaby	B.C.
DWL Incorporated	48.1	Toronto	Ontario
Quake Technologies Inc.	46.5	Kanata	Ontario

Source: Macdonald & Associates.

Fundraising A venture firm begins by soliciting commitments of capital from investors. As discussed above, these investors are typically pension funds, corporations, and wealthy individuals. Venture capital firms usually have a portfolio target amount that they attempt to raise. The average venture fund will have from just a few investors up to 100 limited partners. Because the minimum commitment is usually so high, venture capital funding is generally out of reach of most average individual investors.

Once the venture fund begins investing, it will "call" its commitments from the limited partners. These capital calls from the limited partners to the venture fund are sometimes called "takedowns" or "paid-in-capital." Venture firms typically call their capital on an as-needed basis.

The limited partners understand that investments in venture funds are long-term. It may be several years before the first investment starts to pay. In many cases, the capital may be tied up for seven to ten years. The illiquidity of the investment must be carefully considered by the potential investor.

Investing Once commitments have been received, the venture fund can begin the investment phase. Venture funds may either specialize in one or two industry segments or may generalize, looking at all available opportunities. It is not uncommon for venture funds to focus investments in a limited geographical area to make it easier to review and monitor the firms' activities.

Frequently, venture capitalists invest in a firm before it has a real product or is even clearly organized as a company. This is called "seed investing." Investing in a firm that is a little further along in its life cycle is known as "early stage investing." Finally, some funds focus on "later stage investing" by providing funds to help the company grow to a critical mass to attract public financing.

In 2001, about 60% of venture capital funds went into seed investments and early-stage investments, and 40% went into later-stage investments.

Exiting The goal of a venture capital investment is to help nurture a firm until it can be funded with alternative capital. Venture firms hope that an exit can be made in no more than seven to ten years. Later-stage investments may take only a few years. Once an exit is made, the partners receive their share of the profits and the fund is dissolved.

There are a number of ways for a venture fund to successfully exit an investment. The most glamorous and visible is through an initial public offering. At the public stock offering, the venture firm is considered an insider and receives stock in the company, but the firm is regulated and restricted in how that stock can be sold or liquidated for several years. Once the stock is freely tradable, usually after two years, the venture fund distributes the stock to its limited partners, who may then hold the stock or sell it.

While not as visible, an equally common type of successful exit for venture investments is through mergers and acquisitions. In these cases, the venture firm receives stock or cash from the acquiring company. These proceeds are then distributed to the limited partners.

Venture Fund Profitability Venture investing is extremely high risk. Most start-up firms do not succeed. Despite the careful monitoring and advice provided by the venture capital firm, there are innumerable hurdles that must be jumped before a new concept or idea yields profits. If venture investing is high-risk then there must also be the possibility of a high return to induce investors to continue supplying funds.

Historically, venture capital firms have been very profitable, despite their high risk. The 20-year average return in the U.S. venture capital industry is 20.3%. Seed investing is the most profitable, with a 20-year average return of 24.5% compared with about 18% for later-stage investing. The 1990s were a wonderful time to be a venture capitalist. The ten-year average return was 30%. From 1995 to 2000, the average return soared to over 50%.

In the late 1990s, venture capital returns continued to be extraordinary. For example, in 1998, investors with Canadian venture capital firms earned an average return 3.77 times their original investment, when exiting through the initial public offering route. The deal of the year award for the year 2000 went to Celtic House International, who invested $2.7 million in Abatis Systems, and exited for a price of $17 million, a return of more than 500%. Unfortunately, as the market cooled to technology, so too did venture capital returns. By 2000, average returns were lower, and in 2001, many venture firms reported a loss. These losses are likely to extend for a number of years while venture capital firms recover from excessive investment in Web-based technology companies. Box 1 discusses possible explanations for the losses suffered by venture capital firms.

HISTORY OF FINANCE COMPANIES

The earliest examples of finance companies date back to the beginning of the 1800s when retailers offered **installment credit** to customers. With an installment credit agreement, a loan is made that requires the borrower to make a series of equal payments over some fixed length of time. Prior to installment credit agreements, loans were usually of the single-payment or balloon type. A **balloon loan** requires the borrower to make a single large payment at the loan's maturity to retire the debt. Installment loans appealed to consumers because they allowed them to make small payments on the loan out of current income.

Finance companies came into their own when automobile companies began mass marketing. In the early 1900s, banks did not offer car loans because cars were considered consumer purchases rather than productive assets. Many people wanted to buy cars but found it difficult to raise the purchase price. The automobile companies established subsidiaries, called *finance companies,* to provide installment loans to car buyers. Renamed in 1998, finance companies became known as *nondepository credit intermediaries,* under the industry classification system.

Soon many other retailers adopted the idea of providing financing for consumers who wanted to buy their goods. They found not only that sales increased but also the subsidiary finance company was profitable.

BOX 1: E-FINANCE

Venture Capitalists Lose Focus With Internet Companies

A tremendous surge in funds available for venture capitalists took place in the last half of the 1990s. Much of the investing focus was on the financing of dot-com companies. There are two serious ramifications that result. First, it is likely that there are only a certain number of worthy projects to finance at any one time. When too much money is chasing too few deals, firms are going to obtain financing that would be rejected at other times. As a result, the average quality of venture fund portfolios falls.

A second problem caused by the surge of money into venture funds is that the ability of the partners to provide quality monitoring is reduced. Consider, for example, the case of Webvan, a U.S. Internet grocer that received more than *$1 billion* in venture financing. Even though it was backed by a group of experienced financiers, including Goldman Sachs and Sequoia Capital, its business plan was fundamentally flawed. In its short life, Webvan spent more than $1 billion building automated warehouses and pricey tech gear. This high overhead made it impossible to compete in the grocery business, where average margins are about 1%. Had the investment bankers been actively monitoring the activities of Webvan, they might have balked at developing an infrastructure that required 4000 orders per day per warehouse just to break even. Not surprisingly, Webvan declared bankruptcy in July 2001.

Eventually, banks recognized the value of consumer loans and began offering them too. By offering lower interest rates, banks rapidly gained the larger part of the consumer credit market. By the end of 2001, banks in the United States held $129.7 billion in consumer loans, compared to $18.6 billion by finance companies.[3]

As the proportion of credit offered by finance companies to consumers declined, the proportion offered to businesses in the form of sales and leasing also decreased. At the end of 2001, for example, finance companies in Canada held $12.9 billion of business loans, a drop from $14 billion in 2000.[4]

PURPOSE OF FINANCE COMPANIES

Finance companies are money market intermediaries. Recall from Chapter 8 that the money markets are wholesale markets. This means that most securities that trade there have very large denominations. The minimum investment of $100 000 makes it impossible for individuals and most small companies to trade in this market. A second obstacle is that consumers and small companies lack the credit standing necessary to borrow in the money markets. These factors exclude consumers and small businesses from being able to take advantage of the low interest rates available on money market securities.

Finance companies allow smaller participants access to this market by selling commercial paper and using the proceeds to make loans. (In Chapter 8 we noted that finance companies were the largest sellers of commercial paper.)

The financial intermediation process of finance companies can be described by saying that they borrow in large amounts but often lend in small amounts—a process quite different from that of commercial banks, which collect deposits in small amounts and then often make large loans.

A key feature of finance companies is that although they lend to many of the same customers that borrow from banks, they are virtually unregulated compared to commercial banks and thrift institutions. Provinces regulate the maximum amount they can loan to individual consumers and the terms of the debt contract, but there are no restrictions on branching, the assets they hold, or how they raise their funds. The lack of restrictions enables finance companies to tailor their loans to customer needs better than banking institutions can.

Finance companies exist to service both individuals and businesses. Consumer finance companies that focus on loans to individuals differ from banks in significant ways. First, consumer finance companies often accept loans with much higher risk than banks would. These high-risk customers may not have any source of loans other than the consumer finance company. Second, consumer finance companies are often wholly owned by a manufacturer who uses the company to make loans to consumers interested in purchasing the manufacturer's products. For example, almost all automobile companies own consumer finance companies that fund auto loans. Often these loans are made on very favourable terms to encourage product sales.

Business finance companies exist to fill financing needs not served by banks, such as lease financing. Manufacturers of business products often own finance companies for the same reasons as automobile companies: Sales can be increased if attractive financing terms are available.

---

[3]*Source*: Statistics Canada CANSIM II series V800014.

[4]*Source*: Statistics Canada CANSIM II series V800019 and V122700.

RISK IN FINANCE COMPANIES

Like other financial institutions, finance companies face several types of risk. The greatest is **default risk**, the chance that customers will fail to repay their loans. As mentioned earlier, many consumer finance companies lend to borrowers who are unable to obtain credit from other sources. Naturally, these borrowers tend to default more frequently. Finance company delinquency rates are usually higher than those for banks or thrifts. Finance companies recoup the losses they suffer from bad loans by charging higher interest rates, often as much as twice that charged by banks. When economic conditions deteriorate, finance company customers are often the first to be unemployed, and defaults cause losses.

Another type of risk finance companies face is **liquidity risk**. Liquidity risk refers to problems that arise when a firm runs short of cash. For example, a bank may have a liquidity problem if many depositors withdraw their funds at once. Finance companies run the risk of liquidity problems because their assets, consumer and business loans, are not easily sold in the secondary financial markets. Thus if they are in need of cash, they must borrow. This is not difficult for larger finance companies because they have access to the money markets and can sell commercial paper, but borrowing may be more difficult for smaller firms.

Offsetting the lack of a secondary market for finance company assets is the fact that none of the firm's funds come from deposits, so unexpected withdrawals do not occur. The greater problem is that a change in the perceived risk of the finance company may make it difficult to **roll over** its short-term debt instruments. The term *roll over* means to renew the debt each time it matures.

Interest-rate risk is a major problem for banks and near banks but not of great concern to finance companies. Recall that interest-rate risk refers to a decline in value of fixed-rate loans when market interest rates rise. Banks and near banks hold more long-term loans than finance companies do and hence are subject to greater interest-rate risk. Finance companies can be affected by changing interest-rate levels because their assets (loans) are not as interest-rate sensitive as their liabilities (borrowings). We discuss risk management in financial institutions and in finance companies in particular in greater detail in Chapter 22.

TYPES OF FINANCE COMPANIES

There are three types of finance companies: business, sales, and consumer. Figure 1 shows the distribution of loans for finance companies. Real estate loans are the most common type. Note that loans secured by real estate can be made to both businesses and consumers but more often result when consumers obtain second mortgages on their homes. (Second mortgage loans are discussed in Chapter 11.)

Business (Commercial) Finance Companies

In the early 1900s, commercial banks were reluctant to lend money secured by a company's accounts receivable (funds owed to the company by other businesses and individuals) because central banks discounted or bought only promissory notes that were related to productive purposes, such as financing for a factory. Not until after the Great Depression did commercial banks begin competing for loans secured by accounts receivable. By this time, finance companies were offering to make loans that were secured by equipment and inventory to businesses as well. Finance companies gained the reputation of being more innovative than banks at finding ways to finance small businesses. One reason they could be more flexible was their near-total absence of regulation. Because there are no depositors to protect, the government has never found the need to restrict the activities of

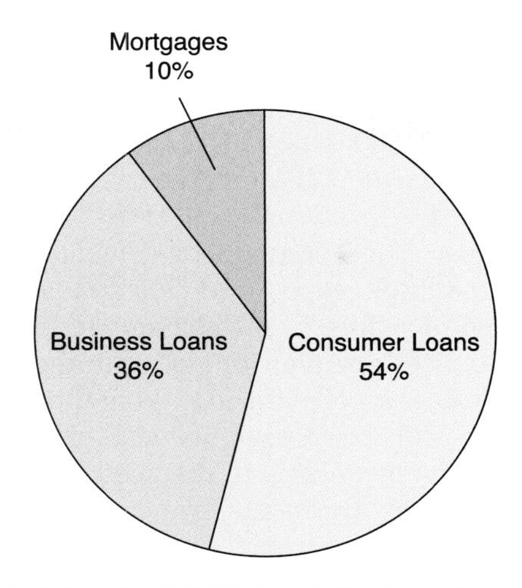

FIGURE 1 Types of Loans Made by Finance Companies, 2001

Source: Bank of Canada *Banking and Financial Statistics*, April 2002

these types of firms. Figure 2 reports the different types of business loans made by U.S. finance companies (data on the average distribution of business loans made by Canadian finance companies are not available). Equipment financing is the most prevalent. Loans secured by motor vehicles, which include loans to buy autos for business use and for resale, are also common.

Factoring Business finance companies provide specialized forms of credit to businesses by making loans and purchasing accounts receivable at a discount; this provision of credit is called **factoring**. For example, a dressmaking firm might have outstanding bills (accounts receivable) of $100 000, due from the retail stores that have bought its dresses. If this firm needs cash to buy 100 new sewing machines, it can sell its accounts receivable for, say, $90 000 to a finance company, which is now entitled to collect the $100 000 owed to the firm.

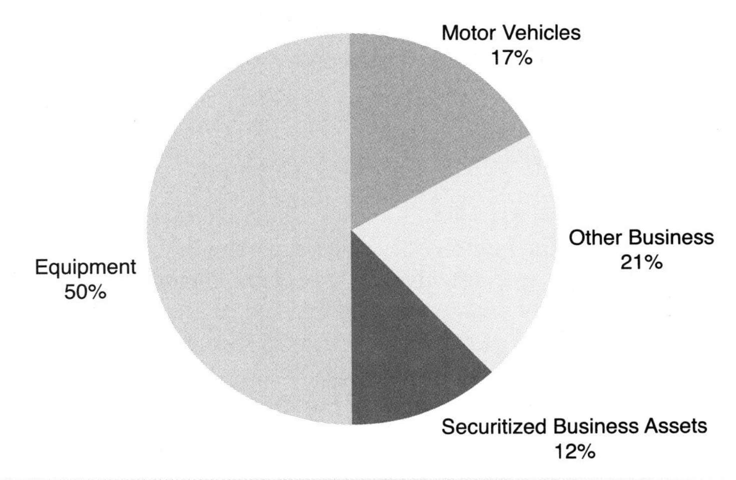

FIGURE 2 Types of Business Loans Made by U.S. Finance Companies (end of 2001)

Source: Federal Reserve Bulletin, Table 1.52

Factoring is a very common practice in the apparel industry. One advantage of factoring is that the finance company (called a *factor* in this situation) usually assumes responsibility for collecting the debt. If the debt becomes uncollectable, the factor suffers the loss. This removes the need for the apparel company to have a credit department or be involved in the collection effort.

Factors usually check the credit of the firm's receivables before accepting them. The factoring arrangement works well because the factor is able to specialize in bill processing and collections and to take advantage of economies of scale. Besides the cost savings from reduced salary expenses, many firms like to use factors because they do not want their relationship with their customers spoiled by having to collect money from them.

Finance companies also provide financing of accounts receivable without taking ownership of the accounts receivable. In this case, the finance company receives documents from the business giving it the right to collect and keep the accounts receivable should the business fail to pay its debt to the finance company. Many firms prefer this arrangement over factoring because it leaves them in control of their accounts receivable. They can work with their customers if special arrangements are required to assure payment.

Leasing Business finance companies also specialize in **leasing** equipment (such as railroad cars, jet planes, and computers), which they purchase and then lease to businesses for a set number of years. Indeed, much of the growth in finance companies in recent years has come from business leasing. Under a lease, the finance company buys the asset and then leases it back to the business. One advantage of leasing is that **repossession** of the asset is easier. Repossession occurs when the finance company takes the asset back when the lessee (the firm that is leasing the asset) fails to make the payments on time. Lenders can repossess an asset under loans and lease contracts, but it is easier under a lease because the finance company already owns the asset, so no transfer of title of ownership is required.

Finance companies that are subsidiaries of equipment manufacturers have an additional advantage over banks. When a piece of equipment must be repossessed, the manufacturer is in a better position to re-lease or resell the asset.

The owner of an asset is able to depreciate the asset over time and to capture a tax savings as a result. If the firm that plans to use the asset does not have income to offset with the depreciation, the tax saving may be more valuable to the finance company. Part of this tax benefit can be passed on to the lessee in the form of lower payments than on a straight loan. In effect, the government is supporting the equipment purchase in the amount of the tax savings. This support is lost unless a firm earning income actually owns the asset.

A final advantage to leasing is that the lessee is often not required to make as large an up-front payment as is usually required on a straight loan. This conserves valuable working capital and is often the critical factor in leasing decisions.

Floor Plan Loans Some auto manufacturers require that dealers accept auto deliveries throughout the year, even though sales tend to be seasonal. To help dealers pay for their inventories of cars, finance companies began offering **floor plans**. In a floor plan arrangement, the finance company pays for the car dealership's inventory of cars received from the manufacturer and puts a lien on each car on the showroom floor. When a car is sold, the dealer must pay off the debt owed on that car before the finance company will provide a clear title of ownership. The dealer must pay the finance company interest on the floor loans until the inventory has been sold. Floor plan financing is most common in the auto industry because cars have titles that the finance company can hold to secure its loans. Floor plan financing exists in other industries where assets with titles are involved, such as construction equipment and boats.

A close relationship usually evolves between the finance company and the dealer. Consider that each sale requires correspondence between the firms. As a result of the close relationship, it is common to find that the same finance company also provides retail financing for the dealer's customers. The help that an aggressive finance company can provide by financing weak credit customers also helps the finance company's floor loans get paid.

Note that banks also provide floor plan financing; however, such loans tend to be high-maintenance. The unregulated, lower-cost structure of finance companies often makes them the preferred intermediaries.

Finance companies have enjoyed continued growth in business loans (see Figure 3). This trend is likely to continue due to the regulatory advantages such loans enjoy.

Consumer Finance Companies

Consumer finance companies make loans to consumers to buy particular items such as furniture or home appliances, to make home improvements, or to help refinance small debts. Consumer finance companies are separate corporations (like Household Financial Corporation Canada) or are owned by banks. Typically, these companies make loans to consumers who cannot obtain credit from other sources due to low income or poor credit history. Finance companies will often accept items for security, such as old cars or old mobile homes, that would be unacceptable to banks. Because these loans are often high in both risk and maintenance, they usually carry high interest rates.

Another growth area for consumer finance companies is in retail credit cards. Many retailers like to offer their customers a "private label" credit card to increase sales. Many large retailers operate their own credit card programs either in-house

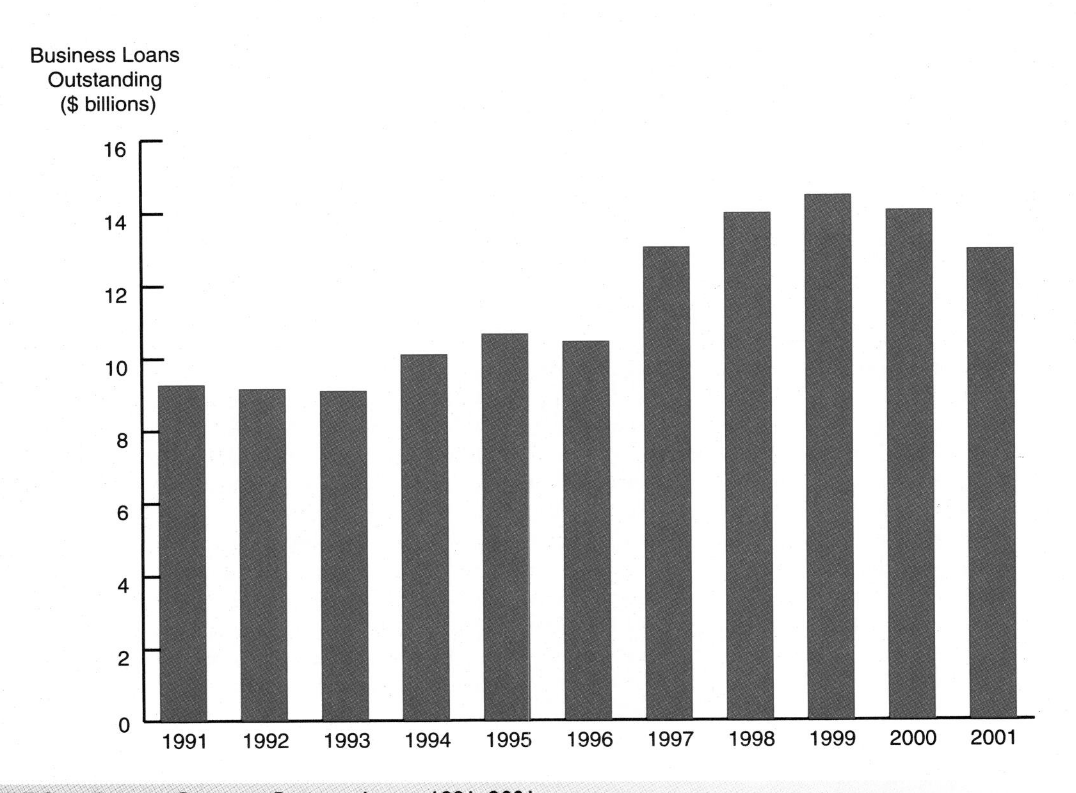

FIGURE 3 Finance Company Business Loans, 1991–2001

Source: Statistics Canada Cansim II series V800014.

or through finance subsidiaries, but smaller retailers may contract with a finance company. When the retailers accept applications for credit cards, they pass them on to the finance company for approval. The finance company then sends the retailer's card to the customer. The finance company provides billing and collection services for the account. The consumer may never be aware that a finance company is involved in these transactions. Finance companies allow smaller retailers to provide a service that only larger retailers could offer otherwise.

Sales Finance Companies

Sales finance companies make loans to consumers to purchase items from a particular retailer or manufacturer. Sears Acceptance Corporation, for example, finances consumer purchases of all goods and services at Sears stores, and General Motors Acceptance Corporation (GMAC) finances purchases of GM cars. Sales finance companies compete directly with banks for consumer loans and are used by consumers because loans can frequently be obtained faster and more conveniently at the location where an item is purchased.

A sales finance company, also called a **captive finance company**, is owned by the manufacturer to make loans to consumers to help finance the purchase of the manufacturer's products. These captive finance companies often offer interest rates below those of banks and other finance companies to increase sales. Profits made on the sale offset any losses made on the loans. Other major manufacturers also own captive finance companies (Box 2 profiles Ford Motor Credit, a major U.S. sales finance company).

REGULATION OF FINANCE COMPANIES

As noted, because there are no depositors to protect and no government deposit insurance is involved, finance companies are far less regulated than banks and near banks. The exception to this is when a finance company is acting as a bank hold-

BOX 2

The Expansion of Ford Motor Credit

In December 1996, Ford Motor Credit announced its intention to expand its lending operations to include subprime loans, loans to individuals with poor credit records. The lure to make these types of loans is that $100 billion is lent to people with flawed credit each year to buy new and used cars. Most of this business now goes to a number of smaller finance companies that specialize in high-risk lending, often charging very high rates to compensate for the risk. Ford Motor Credit thinks it can compete effectively for these loans.

Ford is very interested in the income generated by its finance operations. Its credit program began in 1923 when customers were permitted to pay $5 per week toward the purchase of a $265 Ford. Only when the full amount had been paid was the customer allowed to drive the car home. In 2000, credit operations had expanded to the point where Ford earned $442 million from financial services, compared to $1 billion from its automotive operations. Ford's financial service operations consists of the Ford Motor Credit Company, which is primarily an auto lender; the Associates, which is the second-biggest independent finance company in the United States; and International Businesses, which makes auto loans internationally.

Ford's entry into high-risk lending is a departure from the usual lending practices of the major automotive finance companies. Ford admits that it will be difficult to balance the need to protect its assets by repossessing cars while they can still be located against protecting Ford's reputation. The new subsidiary, to be named Fairlane Credit, hopes to identify customers who have once had problems but have recovered, such as college students who overextended on credit cards or people who unexpectedly lost their jobs but are now employed. Whereas a normal, high-credit loan is usually approved in less than an hour, Fairlane expects to spend several days evaluating its subprime customers. It hopes to be rewarded for its effort with loyal, long-term Ford customers and high profits due to the high interest rates these types of loans command.

ing company or is a subsidiary of a bank holding company. (Recall from Chapter 16 that bank holding companies are firms that own the stock of one or more banking institutions.) In these cases, federal regulations are imposed. Finance companies without a direct relationship to a bank are regulated by the province.

What regulations do affect finance companies are aimed at protecting unsophisticated customers. The Cost of Credit Disclosure Act (the "truth in lending" regulation) requires that banks and finance companies disclose the annual percentage rate charged on loans in a prominent and understandable fashion. The lender must also disclose what the total interest cost of the credit will be over the life of the loan.

The Bankruptcy Insolvency Act (BIA) allows for protection provided to consumers who declare bankruptcy.[5] The partial homestead exemption, which varies across provinces, allows consumers to declare bankruptcy, thereby eliminating their debts, while still retaining ownership of many of their assets. Because many finance company customers have few assets to begin with, they lose little if they declare bankruptcy. This is a serious concern for finance companies and is one reason they usually demand adequate security before making a loan.

The level of interest rates that finance companies can charge customers is limited by **usury** statutes, encompassed within the Small Loans Act. Usury is charging an excessive or inordinate interest rate on a loan. The permissible interest-rate ceiling depends on the size and maturity of the loan, with small, short-term loans having the highest rates. The usury limits vary by province, but most are sufficiently high not to be a limiting factor to reputable finance companies.[6]

Provincial and federal government regulations impose restrictions on finance companies' ability to collect on delinquent and defaulted loans. For example, many provinces restrict how aggressive a finance company can be when calling customers and prohibit them from calling late at night or at work. Regulations also require that certain legal procedures be followed and that the lender bear the expense of collecting on the bad debt.

In contrast to consumer lending, few regulations limit finance companies in the business loan market. Regulators feel that businesses should be financially sophisticated enough to protect themselves without government intervention.

FINANCE COMPANY BALANCE SHEET

Table 4 presents the aggregate balance sheet for finance companies.

Assets

The primary asset of finance companies is their loan portfolio, consisting of consumer and business loans and leasing contracts. The largest category of loans is personal loans, currently representing 22.3% of total assets and 41% of all loans made.

Because of the high risk of loans made to consumers, more loans default. To protect their income against these defaults, finance companies allocate a portion of income each period to an account to be used to offset losses, called the **reserve for loan losses**. The reason for having a reserve for loan losses is to smooth losses over time. By recognizing a set amount of loss each period, different losses in one period over another do not show up on the bottom line. Banks and near banks also maintain a reserve for loan losses; however, it does not need to be as large as that for finance companies.

[5]*Source:* www.insolvency.ca/papers/PICReport.doc

[6]Some critics of usury laws counter that these laws do not protect consumers but instead prevent marginal or high-risk borrowers from obtaining credit.

TABLE 4 Consolidated Balance Sheet of Nondepository Credit Intermediaries, in Millions (as of 2001)

Assets	Amount ($)	Percent (%)	Liabilities	Amount ($)	Percent (%)
Cash and deposits	3 580	4.17	Bankers' acceptances and paper	15 070	17.54
Investments with affiliates	21 341	24.83	Long-term debt	34 555	40.21
Portfolio investments	834	0.97	Loans and accounts with affiliates	16 680	19.41
Mortgages			Loans and overdrafts	3 542	4.12
Residential	2 040	2.37	Other liabilities	6 094	7.09
Non-residential	1 622	1.89			
Total mortgages	3 662	4.26			
Nonmortgage loans			Shareholders' equity	9 992	11.63
Personal loans	19 165	22.30			
Business loans	12 803	14.90	Total liabilities and equity	85 933	100.00
Leasing contracts	11 125	12.95			
Total nonmortgage loans	43 093	50.15			
Allowance for doubtful accounts	−993	−1.16			
Other assets	14 416	16.78			
Total assets	85 933	100.00			

Source: Bank of Canada *Banking and Financial Statistics*, April 2002

Liabilities

Because finance companies do not accept deposits, they must raise funds from other sources to fund their loans. An important source of funds is commercial paper (discussed in detail in Chapter 8). Recall that commercial paper is unsecured, short-term debt issued by low-risk companies. Its advantage over bank loans and other sources of funds is that it carries a low interest rate. Finance companies also obtain funds by borrowing from other money market sources and occasionally from banks (about 1% of assets). Captive finance companies have the option of borrowing directly from their parent corporation. Figure 4 shows that the use of commercial paper by finance companies has increased dramatically in recent years as this market has continued to develop.

On average, finance companies have a 12% capital-to-total-assets ratio. This is relatively strong when compared to the 9% to 10% usually observed for banks and near banks.

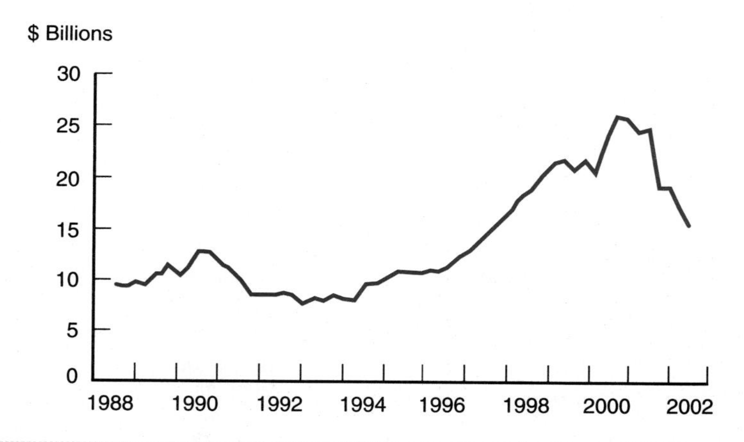

FIGURE 4 Commercial Paper Placed by Finance Companies, 1988–2001

Source: Statistics Canada CANSIM II series V636899

Income

Finance company income derives from several sources. The primary source, of course, is interest income from its loan portfolio. Finance companies also earn income from loan origination fees. These are fees they charge borrowers for making a loan. These fees cover the processing costs involved. Many finance companies also sell credit insurance, which pays off any balance due on a loan if the borrower should die or become disabled. Credit insurance tends to generate very high profits compared to other types of life insurance coverage. Some finance companies earn additional income from expanding their operations to include income tax preparation services.

Finance Company Growth

Finance companies grew rapidly in the late 1980s and, after a pause, the 1990s. This growth was fueled by the expansive economy, which caused the demand for finance company business loans to increase. The recession of the early 1990s caused a dip in the demand for business loans, as did the growth in assets, but growth soon resumed. Figure 5 traces the growth in finance company assets from 1988 to 2001.

FINANCIAL CONGLOMERATES

Go to www.tdcanadatrust.com, the Website for TD Canada Trust.

A **financial conglomerate** is a firm that owns and manages a number of different types of financial intermediaries. For example, the Toronto Dominion Financial Group, in addition to its banking activities, introduced TD Securities and TD Capital to incorporate the investment and venture capital markets.

Financial conglomerates began in the early 1970s in the United States when Merrill Lynch made a cash management account available to its customers. This account allowed investors to transfer money conveniently into and out of various securities. Many customers began using these accounts as substitutes for chequing accounts. Securities firms have historically offered margin loans, which are used to pay a portion of the cost of security purchases. Thus by the late 1970s, we saw securities firms offering the equivalent of chequing accounts, loans, and broker-

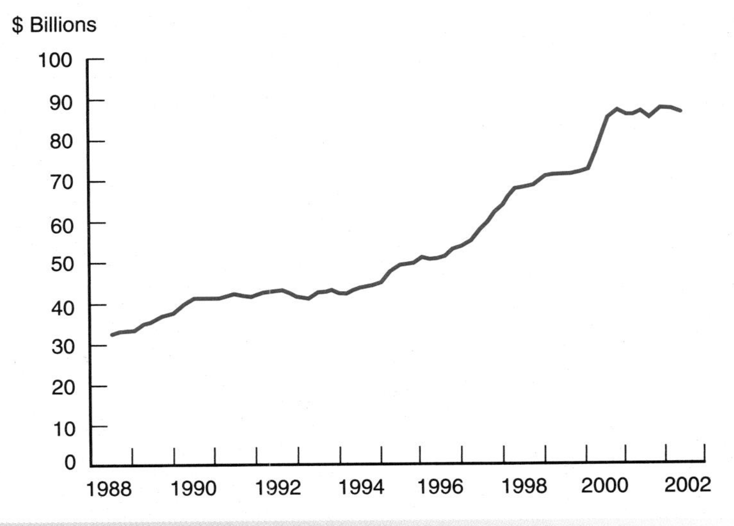

FIGURE 5 Growth of Finance Company Assets, 1988–2001

Source: Statistics Canada CANSIM II series V636852

age services. In Canada, financial conglomerates began as a result of the deregulating financial sector, from the 1987 and 1991 amendments to the Bank Act. Canadian banks are now allowed to become involved in other areas of financial markets such as the securities, insurance, and venture capital business.

The Website for Investor's Group is www.investorsgroup.com

Securities and mutual fund companies are other types of financial conglomerates that offer a wide range of investment options under one corporate umbrella. For example, Investors Group launched its Canadian investment operations in 1926, and offered its first mutual fund by 1950. Now, they offer several other forms of financial products including mortgages and insurance. We discuss securities firms more extensively in Chapter 21.

Find more details about Manulife at www.manulife.com

Insurance companies have also entered the financial conglomerate fray. Many of their customers were already trusting insurance agents to help them plan for retirement when they bought whole life policies (see Chapter 19 for a discussion of the different types of insurance policies offered). For example, Manulife Financial, which began as an insurance company in 1887, diversified into banking with the establishment of the Manulife Bank of Canada in 1993. The purchase of Confederation Life's group life and health plans in 1994 as well as North American Life Assurance Company in 1996 allowed Manulife to boast the largest earnings ever for an insurance company. In addition, Manulife created the Manulife one, which allowed personal bank deposits to act as credits against a mortgage account.

More recently, we have seen many banks combine with security firms, such as the 1998 merger in the United States of Citicorp with Travelers Group, the parent of Travelers Insurance and Salomon Smith Barney. This megafirm, now called Citigroup, employs 160 000 people and serves 100 million customers in 100 countries. The impetus for its formation was the desire to take advantage of the synergies of a financial superstore. Analysts expect the firm to trim expenses by at least $1 billion in two years. (The Citicorp-Travelers merger is discussed in Box 2 in Chapter 16.) In Canada, we have also seen many banks combine with securities firms, such as the 1988 merger of CIBC with Wood Gundy Inc., one of Canada's leading investment firms. After the 1992 amendment to the Bank Act, CIBC acquired Morgan Trust Company of Canada, which allowed them to introduce personal trust and estate planning. This new firm called CIBC Wood Gundy Securities Corp., became the megafirm CIBC World Markets in 1997, once they acquired Oppenheimer & Co., Inc., a securities firm in the United States.

By putting these businesses under one roof, the goal is to achieve economies of scale and scope. **Economies of scale** reflect the savings that can be achieved through increased size. For example, one computer system or warehouse could provide service to several different subsidiaries. Similarly, existing management could oversee operations for a number of similar firms. **Economies of scope** reflect increased business from offering many products in one easy-to-reach location. For example, a customer wanting auto insurance could also be sold a life insurance policy and shares in a mutual fund. Large retailers felt that customers would rather deal with one well-known and trusted business than with a variety of smaller firms.

Though the concept of a one-stop-shopping financial conglomerate may seem reasonable, it has often not been successful. The types of businesses tackled by these conglomerates are very competitive. Consumers generally do not perceive any great benefit from dealing with a single firm for all of their financial needs and instead continue to shop for the best deals available.

The Websites for Desjardins and VanCity can be found at www.desjardins.com and www.vancity.com

However, two major success stories emerged from the Canadian financial sector, namely the Desjardins Group and the VanCity Group. The Desjardins Group was established as a cooperative bank in 1900 and created the Desjardins Life Assurance Company in 1948, followed by the addition of securities brokerage and credit union subsidiaries during the 1970s. In 1994, it acquired the Laurentian Group, which enhanced their insurance business substantially. The Group expanded further with the introduction of the Desjardins Federal Savings Bank in Florida in 1992.

The Vancity Group is Canada's largest credit union, which was founded in 1946. It established insurance and securities subsidiaries, known as Vancity Insurance and Vancity Investment Management, respectively. Vancity incorporated banking in its wide range of financial services, with the launch of the Citizens Bank of Canada in 1997.

Despite the success of Canada's major banks and some large financial firms, the luster has apparently vanished from the conglomerate concept. Companies have learned that it is more important to be flexible than to be big and it is better to be an expert at one business than a dabbler in many. Although finance companies continue to grow and prosper, the future of financial conglomerates is not at all assured.

SUMMARY

1. Venture capital firms are intermediaries that typically invest in start-up firms with good prospects for growth. They are usually organized as limited partnerships or closed-end mutual funds. The investors are pension funds, corporations, and wealthy individuals.
2. Venture capital firms act as intermediaries to reduce asymmetric information between firm insiders and investors. They closely monitor firm management, often taking seats on the board of directors. They usually fund a firm in stages as progress is demonstrated.
3. Venture funds may invest in very new firms that have little more than a good idea to sell. These are called "seed investments." Alternatively, they may invest in firms that have made some progress or in firms that are nearly ready to go public but just need some help in getting to that level. These are called early stage investments and later-stage investments, respectively.
4. The goal of the venture fund is to successfully exit the company once the company has matured to a point where traditional financing is available. The exit is usually made through an initial public offering or through a merger or acquisition.
5. Finance companies were initially owned by manufacturers who wanted to provide easy financing to help the sales of their products. The concept rapidly expanded when automobile financing became more commonplace.
6. Finance companies sell short-term securities in the money markets and use the proceeds to make small consumer and business loans. In this way, they act as intermediaries in the money markets. They typically borrow in large amounts and lend in small.
7. Another purpose served by consumer finance companies is servicing higher-risk customers. As a result of making these high-risk loans, default is the primary risk finance companies face. Finance companies compensate for default risk by charging higher interest rates. Finance companies also make business loans and offer leases.
8. The three types of finance companies are business, consumer, and sales. Business finance companies finance accounts receivable (often through an arrangement called factoring) and provide inventory loans and leases. Consumer finance companies make loans to high-risk customers for the purchase of autos and appliances and to refinance other debt. Sales finance companies finance a firm's sales, often through in-house credit or credit cards.
9. Because there are no deposits at risk, finance companies are less regulated than banks and near banks. They are subject, however, to consumer regulations that limit interest rates and require disclosure of the cost of loans.
10. Financial conglomerates are firms offering a variety of financial services under one umbrella. These services may include consumer loans, credit cards, insurance, real estate sales, and brokerage services. Most of the efforts to provide a one-stop financial superstore have not fared well. Many early efforts are being dismantled.

KEY TERMS

balloon loan, *p. 514*
captive finance company, *p. 520*
default risk, *p. 516*
economies of scale, *p. 524*
economies of scope, *p. 524*
factoring, *p. 517*
financial conglomerate, *p. 523*
floor plan, *p. 518*
installment credit, *p. 514*
leasing, *p. 518*
liquidity risk, *p. 516*
repossession, *p. 518*
reserve for loan losses, *p. 521*
roll over, *p. 516*
usury, *p. 521*

QUESTIONS AND PROBLEMS

1. What factors distinguish venture capital financing from other types of capital market financing?

***2.** Why would a pension fund be more likely to invest in a venture capital fund than would a property and casualty insurance company?

3. Why is a start-up high-technology firm more subject to asymmetric information than a mature company?

***4.** How can venture capital firm intermediation reduce the asymmetric information problem?

5. How can a venture capital investment be exited?

***6.** What is the difference between an installment loan and a balloon loan?

7. What caused finance companies to grow rapidly in the early 1900s?

***8.** Who are the typical customers of consumer finance companies, and why do they not go to commercial banks, where interest rates are lower?

9. How do consumer finance companies maintain their income in the face of high default rates on their loans?

***10.** Do finance companies face liquidity risk? Why?

11. Do finance companies face interest-rate risk? Why?

***12.** What is factoring?

13. What is the advantage of leasing assets to the lessor? To the lessee?

***14.** Many auto dealers finance their inventory using floor plan loans advanced by finance companies. What is a floor plan loan?

15. Many manufacturers own finance companies that finance the purchase of the manufacturers' products. What are these finance companies called?

***16.** Why are home equity loans popular in the United States?

17. Why are finance companies so concerned that their customers may file bankruptcy?

***18.** Have financial conglomerates been successful at providing one-stop shopping for financial services?

19. What types of statutes limit the interest rates that finance companies can charge their customers?

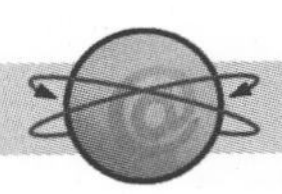

WEB EXERCISES

Venture Capital Firms Finance Companies and Financial Conglomerates

1. Initial Public Offerings (IPOs) are where securities are sold to the public for the very first time. Go to http://ipo.com. This site lists various statistics regarding the IPO market.

a. What is the largest IPO year-to-date ranked by amount raised?

b. What is the next IPO to be offered to the public?

c. How many IPOs were priced this year?

2. Cansim II maintains historical data on finance companies, also known as nondepository financial intermediaries. Go to your library site that comprises the CANSIM II data. Search for series V800014, V800023, V800019.

a. Do finance companies make more consumer, real estate, or business loans?

b. Which type of loan has grown the most rapidly over the past five years?

Chapter 21

Investment Banks, Brokerage Firms, and Mutual Funds

Preview

If you decide to take advantage of that hot stock tip you just heard about from your roommate or if you want to earn more than 1.5% on funds you have on deposit at your bank, you will need to interact with one of many securities companies. Similarly, as the new CFO of WWCF, a candy manufacturer, you may need a securities company if you are asked to coordinate a bond sale or issue additional stock. If your grandfather decides to sell his firm to the public, you may need to help him by working with investment bankers at that securities company. Finally, if you are looking for a high-paying job, your next stop may be a securities firm.

The smooth functioning of securities markets, in which bonds and stocks are traded, involves several financial institutions, including securities brokers and dealers, investment banks, and organized exchanges. None of these institutions were included in our list of financial intermediaries in Chapter 12 because they do not perform the intermediation function of acquiring funds by issuing liabilities and then using the funds to acquire financial assets. Nonetheless, they are important in the process of channelling funds from savers to spenders.

To begin our look at how securities markets work, recall the distinction between primary and secondary securities markets discussed in Chapter 2. In a **primary market**, new issues of a security are sold to buyers by the corporation or government agency ultimately using the funds. A **secondary market** then trades the securities that have been sold in the primary market (and so are secondhand). Investment banks assist in the initial sale of securities in the primary market; securities brokers and dealers assist in the trading of securities in the secondary markets, some of which are organized into exchanges.

INVESTMENT BANKS

Investment bankers were called "Masters of the Universe" in Tom Wolfe's *The Bonfire of the Vanities.* They are the elite on Bay Street and Wall Street. They have earned this reputation from the types of financial services they provide. Investment banks are best known as intermediaries that help corporations raise funds.

However, this definition is far too narrow to accurately explain the many valuable and sophisticated services these companies provide. (Despite its name, an investment bank is not a bank in the ordinary sense; that is, it is not a financial intermediary that takes in deposits and then lends them out.) In addition to underwriting the initial sale of stocks and bonds, **investment banks** also play a pivotal role as deal makers in the mergers and acquisitions area, as intemediaries in the buying and selling of companies, and as private brokers to the very wealthy. Some well-known Canadian investment banking firms are ScotiaMcLeod, RBC Dominion Securities, and BMO Nesbitt Burns. Well-known U.S. investment banking firms are Morgan Stanley, Merrill Lynch, Salomon Brothers, First Boston Corporation, and Goldman Sachs.

One feature of investment banks that distinguishes them from stockbrokers and dealers is that they usually earn their income from fees charged to clients rather than from commissions on stock trades. These fees are often set as a fixed percentage of the dollar size of the deal being worked. Because the deals frequently involve huge sums of money, the fees can be substantial. The percentage fee will be smaller for large deals, in the neighbourhood of 3%, and much larger for smaller deals, sometimes exceeding 10%.

Background

The securities industry in Canada began in 1832 when railroad shares were traded among investors in a Montreal café. The industry began with chartered banks as underwriters but by the 1900s, many independent securities firms were established.

Initially, the Bank Act allowed chartered banks in Canada to deal government bonds but prohibited them from underwriting corporate securities. The original reasoning behind this legislation was to insulate commercial banks from the greater risk inherent in the securities business. There were also concerns that conflicts of interest might arise that would subject commercial banks to increased risk. For example, suppose that an investment banker working at a commercial bank makes a mistake pricing a new stock offering. After promising the customer that he can sell the stock for $20, no sales materialize. The investment banker might be tempted to go down the hall to the commercial bank's investment department and talk them into bailing him out. This would subject depositors to the risk that the bank could lose money on poor investments.

Regulators thought another problem existed. Suppose the investment banker still cannot sell all of that $20 stock issue. He could call up bank customers and offer to loan them 100% of the funds needed to buy a portion of the stock issue. This would not cause a problem if the stock price rose in the future, but if it fell, the value of the securities would be less than the amount of the loan and the customer might not feel a great obligation to repay the loan.

When the Bank Act separated commercial banking from investment banking, new securities firms were created, many of which offer both investment banking services (selling new securities to the public) as well as brokerage services (selling existing securities to the public). The Bank Act revision of 1987, however, allowed chartered banks to own investment firms. Subsequently, national financial institutions now own the majority of full-service firms. The industry has since expanded to include over 190 investment firms either as institutional firms or retail brokerages. Table 1 summarizes the six largest full-service securities firms in Canada, measured by sales of preferred shares, common equity, and trust and corporate debt.

TABLE 1 Largest Full-Service Securities Firms in Canada (as of 1999)

Firm	Market Share (%)
RBC Dominion Securities	15.5
BMO Nesbitt Burns	13.8
CIBC World Markets	12.7
Scotia Capital	10.2
TD Securities	9.7
Merrill Lynch HSBC	6.8
Total for top six	68.7

Source: www.fin.gc.ca

Underwriting Stocks and Bonds

When a corporation wants to borrow or raise funds, it may decide to issue long-term debt or equity instruments. It then usually hires an investment bank to facilitate the issuance and subsequent sale of the securities. The investment bank may underwrite the issue. The process of underwriting a stock or bond issue requires that the securities firm *purchase* the entire issue at a predetermined price and then resell it in the market. There are a number of services provided in the process of underwriting.

Giving Advice Most firms do not issue capital market securities very frequently. More than 80% of all corporate expansion is financed using profits retained from prior-period earnings. As a result, the financial managers at most firms are not familiar with how to proceed with a new security offering. Investment bankers, since they participate in this market daily, can provide advice to firms contemplating a sale. For instance, a firm may not know if it should raise capital by selling stocks or by selling bonds. The investment bankers may be able to help by pointing out, for example, that the market is currently paying high prices for stocks in the firm's industry (historically high PE ratios), while bonds are currently carrying relatively high interest rates (and therefore low prices).

Firms may also need advice as to *when* securities should be offered. If, for example, competitors have recently released earnings reports that show poor profits, it may be better to wait before attempting a sale: Firms want to time the market to sell stock when it will obtain the highest possible price. Again, because of daily interaction with the securities markets, investment bankers should be able to advise firms on the timing of their offerings.

Possibly the most difficult advice an investment banker must give a customer concerns at what *price* the security should be sold. Here the investment banker and the issuing firm have somewhat differing motives. First, consider that the firm wants to sell the stock for the highest price possible. Suppose you started a firm and ran it well for 20 years. You now want to sell it to the public and retire to Tahiti. If 500 000 shares are to be offered and sold at $10 each, you will receive $5 million for your company. If you can sell the stock for $12, you will receive $6 million.

Investment bankers, however, do not want to overprice the stock because in most underwriting agreements, they will buy the entire issue at the agreed price and then resell it through their brokerage houses. They earn a profit by selling the stock at a slightly higher price than they paid the issuing firm. If the issue is priced too high, the investment bank will not be able to resell, and it will suffer a loss.

Pricing securities is not too hard if the firm has prior issues currently selling in the market, called **seasoned issues**. When a firm issues stock for the first time, called an **initial public offering (IPO)**, it is much more difficult to determine what the correct price should be. All of the skill and expertise of the investment banking firm will be used to determine the most appropriate price. If the issuing firm and the investment banking firm can come to agreement on a price, the investment banker can assist with the next stage, filing the required documents.

Filing Documents In addition to advising companies, investment bankers will assist with making the required provincial securities commission filings. The activities of investment banks and the operation of primary markets are heavily regulated by the securities commissions, which were created to ensure that adequate information reaches prospective investors. Issuers of new securities to the general public must file a **registration statement** with the securities commissions. This statement contains information about the firm's financial condition, management, competition, industry, and experience. The firm also discloses what the funds will be used for and management's assessment of the risk of the securities.

The securities commission review in no way represents an endorsement of the offering by the commission. Their approval merely means that all of the required statements and disclosures are included in the statement. Nor does the commission's approval mean that the information is accurate. Inaccuracies in the registration statement open the issuing firm's management up to lawsuits if it incurs a loss. In extreme cases, inaccuracies could result in criminal charges.

A portion of the registration statement is reproduced and made available to investors for review. This widely circulated document is called a **prospectus** (see Figure 1). By law, investors must be given a prospectus before they can invest in a new security.

While the registration document is in the process of being approved, the investment banker has other chores to attend to. For issues of debt, the investment banker must:

- Secure a credit rating from one or more of the credit review companies, such as Standard & Poor's or DBRS.
- Select a trustee who is responsible for seeing that the issuer fulfills its obligations as stated in the security's contract.
- Have the securities printed and prepared for distribution.

For equity issues, the investment banker may arrange for the securities to appear on one of the stock exchanges. Clearly, the investment banker can be of great assistance to an issuer well before any securities are actually offered for sale.

Underwriting Once all of the paperwork has been completed, the investment banker can proceed with the actual underwriting of the issue. At a prespecified time and date, the issuer will sell all of the stock or bond issue to the investment banking firm at the agreed price. The investment banker must now distribute this issue to the public at a greater price to earn its fee. (The ten largest underwriters in the United States are listed in Table 2.) In Canada, RBC Dominion Securities became the leading underwriter via merger with six other investment dealers and injection of capital by the Royal Bank.

By agreeing to underwrite an issue, the investment banking firm is certifying the qualify of the issue to the public. We again see how asymmetric information helps justify the need for an intermediary. Investors do not want to put in weeks and weeks of hard technical study of a firm before buying its stock. Nor can they trust the firm's insiders to accurately report its condition. Instead, they rely on the ability of the investment bank to collect information about the firm in order to accurately establish the firm's value. They trust the investment bank's assessment, since it is backing up its opinion by actually purchasing securities in the process of underwriting them. Investment bankers recognize the responsibility they have to report information accurately and honestly, since once they lose investors' confidence, they will no longer be able to market their deals.

No securities regulatory authority has expressed an opinion about these securities and it is an offence to claim otherwise.

This short form prospectus constitutes a public offering of these securities only in those jurisdictions where they may be lawfully offered for sale and therein only by persons permitted to sell such securities. Information has been incorporated by reference in this prospectus from information record in the Province of Quebec) filed with securities commissions or similar authorities in Can *information record in the Province of Quebec) incorporated herein by reference may be obtained on request without charge from the secretary of Atlas Cold Storage Holdings Inc. at 5255 Yonge Street, Suite 900, Toronto, Ontario M2N 5P8: telephone number: (416) 512-2352. These securities have not been and will not be registered under the United States Securities Act of 1933, as amended, and, subject to certain exceptions, may not be offered or sold within the United States of America or to, or for the account or benefit of, U.S. persons.*

SHORT FORM PROSPECTUS

New Issue August 29, 2002

ATLAS COLD STORAGE INCOME TRUST

$75 012 000

6 580 000 Trust Units

This offering (the Offering) consists of 6,580,000 trust units (Trust Units) of Atlas Cold Storage Income Trust (the T rust). The Trust is an open-end trust established under the laws of the Province of Ontario, which has been created to invest in the securities of Atlas Cold Storage Holdings Inc. (ACSHI).

Price: $11.40 per Trust Unit

	Price to the Public	Underwriters' Fee	Net Proceeds To the Trust[1]
Total per Trust Unit	$11.40[2]	$0.57	$10.83
Total under the Offering[3]	$75 012 000	$3 750 600	$71 261 400

Notes:

(1) Before deducting expenses of the Offering, estimated to be approximately $400,000 which, together with the Underwriters' Fee will be paid by the Trust. The aggregate net proceeds to the Trust after deducting expenses will be approximately $70,861,400.

(2) The price per Trust Unit was determined by negotiation between the Trust, ACSHI and the Underwriters.

(3) The Trust has granted the Underwriters an over-allotment option to purchase up to an additional 880,000 Trust Units exercisable at the offering price, in whole or in part, at any time up to 48 hours preceding the closing of this Offering. This short form prospectus also qualifies both the grant of the option and the distribution of any Trust Units issuable on the exercise of the option. If such option is exercised in full, the total Price to the Public relating to the Offering, the Underwriters' Fee and the Net Proceeds to the Trust, before expenses of the Offering, will be $85,044,000, $4,252,200 and $80,791,800, respectively.

FIGURE 1 Front Page of a Prospectus

Source: www.sedar.com

TABLE 2 Top Ten Underwriters of U.S. Debt and Equity Issues, 2001

Underwriter	Market Share (%)
1. Citigroup/Salomon Smith Barney	12.0
2. Merrill Lynch	10.6
3. Credit Suisse First Boston	8.5
4. J.P. Morgan Chase	7.7
5. Goldman Sachs	7.4
6. Morgan Stanley	6.8
7. Lehman Brothers	6.4
8. UBS Warburg	6.2
9. Deutsche Bank	5.5
10. Banc of America Securities	4.0
Total for top ten	75.1

Source: Wall Street Journal, January 2, 2002, p. R19

The investment banking firm is clearly taking a huge risk at this point. One way that they can reduce the risk is by forming a **syndicate**. A syndicate is a group of investment banking firms each of which buys a portion of the security issue. Each firm in the syndicate is then responsible for reselling its share of the securities. Most securities issues are sold by syndicates because it is such an effective way to spread the risk among many different firms.

Investment banks advertise upcoming securities offerings with ads in newspapers and on their Websites. These ads are called **tombstones** because of their shape and they list all of the investment banking firms included in the syndicate. Review the tombstone reproduced in the Following the Financial News box. Notice the prominent statement that this is neither an offer to sell nor a solicitation, but only an announcement. The actual offer to sell can only be made in the prospectus. Also note the number of different investment banking firms involved in the syndicate.

The longer the investment banker holds the securities before reselling them to the public, the greater the risk that a negative price change will cause losses. One way that the investment banking firm speeds the sale is to solicit offers to buy the securities from investors prior to the date the investment bankers actually take ownership. Then, when the securities are available, the orders are filled and the securities are quickly transferred to the final buyers.

Most investment bankers are attached to larger brokerage houses (multifunction securities firms) that have nationwide sales offices. Each of these offices will be contacted prior to the issue date, and the sales agents will contact their customers to see if they would like to review a prospectus on the new security. The goal is to **fully subscribe** the issue. A fully subscribed issue is one where all of the securities available for sale have been spoken for before the issue date. Security issues may also be **undersubscribed**. In this case, the sales agents have been unable to generate sufficient interest in the security among their customers to sell all of the securities by the issue date. An issue may also be **oversubscribed,** in which case there are more offers to buy than there are securities available.

It is tempting to assume that the best alternative is for an issue to be oversubscribed, but in fact this will alienate the investment banker's customers. Suppose you were issuing a security for the first time and had negotiated with your investment banker to sell the issue of 500 000 shares of stock at $20. Now you find out that the issue is oversubscribed. You would feel that the investment banker had set the price too low and that you had lost money as a result. Maybe the stock could have sold for $25 and you could have collected an extra $2.5 million ($\$25 - \$20 \times 500\,000 = \$2\,500\,000$). You, as well as other issuing firms, would be unlikely to use this investment banker in the future.

FOLLOWING THE FINANCIAL NEWS

New Securities Issues

Information about new securities being issued is presented in distinctive advertisements published in newspapers. These advertisements, called "tombstones" because of their appearance, are typically found in the financial section of the paper and the Websites of investment banks.

The tombstone shown here, from the Website of Harris Nesbitt (at www.harrisnesbitt.com), indicates that the deal was a private placement coordinated by Harris Nesbitt and the six listed companies were the ones that ended up taking the shares as part of the deal.

Hewitt

$100,000,000

Series A due 2007 and 2012
Series B due 2010
Series C due 2001
Series D due 2005
Series E due 2010

Funds Provided By:
Allstate Life Insurance Co.
Canada Life Assurance Co.
Massachusetts Mutual Life Insurance Co.
New York Life Insurance Co.
Pacific Life Insurance Co.
Phoenix Investment Partners

The undersigned acted as a financial advisor and placement agent in connection with the private placement of these securities

BMO Nesbitt Burns

Source: www.harrisnesbitt.com/deals/tombstones/default.asp

It is equally serious for an issue to be undersubscribed, since it may be necessary to lower the price below the price the investment bankers paid to the issuer in order to sell all of the securities to the public. The investment banking firm stands to lose extremely large amounts of money because of the volume of securities involved. For example, review the tombstone shown in the Following the Financial News box once more. There are 2.3 million shares being offered for sale.

If the price must be lowered by even $0.25 per share, $575 000 would be lost. The high risk taken by investment bankers explains why they tend to be the most elite and highest paid professionals on Bay Street and Wall Street, many earning in the millions of dollars per year.

Best Efforts An alternative to underwriting a securities offering is to offer the securities under a *best efforts agreement*. In a best efforts agreement the investment banker sells the securities on a commission basis with no guarantee regarding the price the issuing firm will receive. The advantage to the investment banker of a best efforts transaction is that there is no risk of mispricing the security. There is also no need for the time-consuming task of establishing the market value of the security. The investment banker simply markets the security at the price the customer asks. If the security fails to sell, the offering can be cancelled.

Private Placements In Chapter 10, we discussed an alternative method of selling securities called the *private placement*. In a private placement, securities are sold to a limited number of investors rather than to the public as a whole. The advantage of the private placement is that the security does not need to be registered with the Securities Commission (SC) as long as certain restrictive requirements are satisfied. Investment bankers are also often involved in private placement transactions. While investment bankers are not required for a private placement, they often facilitate the transaction by advising the issuing firm on the appropriate terms for the issue and by identifying potential purchasers.

The buyers of private placements must be large enough to purchase large amounts of securities at one time. This means that the usual buyers are insurance companies, commercial banks, pension funds, and mutual funds. Private placements are more common for the sale of bonds than for stocks. Goldman Sachs is the most active investment banking firm in the private placement market.

The process of taking a security public is summarized in Figure 2.

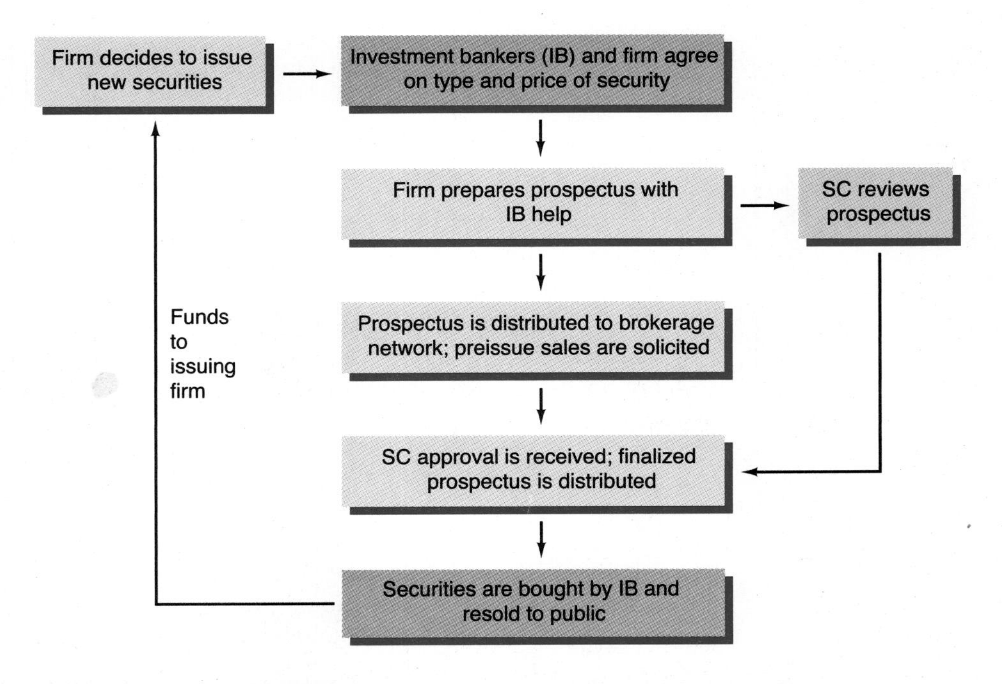

FIGURE 2 Using Investment Bankers to Distribute Securities to the Public

Equity Sales

Another service offered by investment banks is to help with the sale of companies or corporate divisions. For example, in the United States in 1984, Mattel was dangerously close to having its bank loans called when its electronics subsidiary incurred significant losses. Mattel enlisted the help of the investment banking firm Drexel Burnham Lambert. The first step in the firm's restructuring was to sell off all of its nontoy businesses. Mattel returned to health until it again ran into problems in 1999 due to the acquisition of a software company. In 2000, Mattel again used the services of investment bankers to sell this subsidiary.

The first step in any equity sale will be the seller's determination of the business's worth. The investment banker will provide a detailed analysis of the current market for similar companies and apply various sophisticated models to establish company value. Unlike a box of detergent or bar of candy, a going concern has no set price. The company value is based on the use the buyer intends to make of it. If a buyer is only interested in the physical assets, the firm will be worth one amount. A buyer who sees the firm as an opportunity to take advantage of synergies between this firm and another will have a very different price. Despite the elasticity of the metrestick, investment bankers have developed a number of tools to give business owners a range of values for their firms.

How much cash flows will have to be discounted depends very much on who will be bidding on the firm. Again, investment bankers help. They may make discreet inquiries to feel out who in the market may be interested. Additionally, they will prepare a **confidential memorandum** that presents the detailed financial information required by prospective buyers to make an offer for the company. All prospective buyers must sign a confidentiality agreement stipulating that they will not use the information to compete or share it with third parties. The investment bank will screen prospects to ensure that the information goes only to qualified buyers.

The next step in an equity sale will be the **letter of intent** issued by a prospective buyer. This document signals a desire to go forward with a purchase and outlines preliminary terms. The investment banker will negotiate the terms of the sale on the seller's behalf and will help to analyze and rank competing offers. The investment banker may even help structure financing in order to obtain a better offer.

Once the letter of intent has been accepted by the seller, the **due diligence** period begins. This 20- to 40-day period is used by the buyer to verify the accuracy of the information contained in the confidential memorandum. The findings shape the terms of the **definitive agreement**. This agreement converts information gathered during the due diligence period and the results of subsequent negotiations into a legally binding contract.

As this discussion demonstrates, a wide variety of skills are required to move a typical corporate sale forward. To meet these needs, investment banks often send in multidisciplined teams of experts to work with clients on their projects. These teams include attorneys, financial analysts, accountants, and industry experts.

Mergers and Acquisitions

Investment banks have been active in the **mergers and acquisitions** market since the 1960s. A merger occurs where two firms combine to form one new company. Both firms support the merger, and corporate officers are usually selected so that both companies contribute to the new management team. Stockholders turn in their stock for stock in the new firm. In an acquisition, one firm acquires ownership of another by buying its stock. Often this process is friendly, and the firms agree that certain economies can be captured by combining resources. At other times, the firm being purchased may resist. Resisted takeovers are called *hostile.* In these cases, the acquirer attempts to purchase sufficient shares of the target firm to gain a majority of the seats on the board of directors. Board members are then able to vote to merge the target firm with the acquiring firm.

Investment bankers serve both acquirers and target firms. Acquiring firms require help in locating attractive firms to pursue, soliciting shareholders to sell their shares in a process called a *tender offer* and raising the required capital to complete the transaction. Target firms may hire investment bankers to help ward off undesired takeover attempts.

The mergers and acquisitions market requires very specialized knowledge and expertise. Investment bankers involved in this market are highly trained (and, not incidentally, highly paid). The best known investment banker involved in mergers and acquisitions was Michael R. Milken who worked at the U.S. firm Drexel Burnham Lambert, Inc. Milken is credited with inventing the junk bond market which we discussed in Chapter 9. *Junk bonds* are high-risk, high-return debt securities that were used primarily to finance takeover attempts. By allowing companies to raise large amounts of capital, even small firms could pursue and take over large ones. During the 1980s, when Milken was most active in this market, merger and acquisition activity peaked. On February 13, 1990, Drexel Burnham Lambert filed for bankruptcy becuase of rising default rates on its portfolio of junk bonds, a slow economy, and regulations that forced the savings and loan industry out of the junk bond market. Milken pled guilty to securities fraud and was sent to prison.

As a result of the collapse of Drexel and the junk bond market, merger and acquisitions activity slowed during the early 1990s. A healthy economy and regulatory changes caused a resurgence, especially among commercial banks, in the mid and late 1990s. Mergers and acquisitions again receded during the slowdown in 2001.

SECURITIES BROKERS AND DEALERS

Securities brokers and dealers conduct trading in secondary markets. *Brokers* are pure middlemen who act as agents for investors in the purchase or sale of securities. Their function is to match buyers with sellers, a function for which they are paid brokerage commissions.

In contrast to brokers, dealers link buyers and sellers by standing ready to buy and sell securities at given prices. Therefore, dealers hold inventories of securities and make their living by selling these securities for a slightly higher price than they paid for them—that is, on the *spread* between the *bid price*, the price that the broker pays for securities they buy for their inventory, and the *ask price*, the price they receive when they sell the securities. This is a high-risk business because dealers hold securities that can rise or fall in price. Brokers, by contrast, are not as exposed to risk because they do not own the securities involved in their business dealings.[1]

Brokerage Services

Securities brokers offer several types of services.

[1]It is easy to remember the distinction between dealers and brokers if you relate to auto dealers and real estate brokers. Auto *dealers* take ownership of the cars and resell them to the public. Real estate *brokers* do not take ownership of the property; they just act as go-betweens.

Securities Orders If you call a securities brokerage house to buy a stock, you will speak with a broker who will take your order. You have three primary types of transactions available: market orders, limit orders, and short sells.

The two most common types of securities orders are the market order and the limit order. When you place a **market order**, you are instructing your agent to buy or sell the security at the current market price. When placing a market order, there is a risk that the price of the security may have changed significantly from what it was when you made your investment decision. If you are buying a stock and the price falls, no harm is done, but if the price goes up, you may regret your decision. The most notable occasion when prices changed between when orders were placed and when they were filled was during the October 19, 1987, stock market crash. Panicked investors told their brokers to sell their stocks, but the transaction volume was so great that day that many orders were not filled until hours after they were placed. By the time they were filled, the price of the stocks had often fallen far below what they were at the time the original orders were placed.

An alternative to the market order is the **limit order**. Here buy orders specify a *maximum* acceptable price and sell orders specify a *minimum* acceptable price. For example, you could place a limit order to sell your 100 shares of Nortel at $5. If the current market price of Nortel is less than $5, the order will not be filled. Unfilled limit orders are reported to the stock specialist who works that particular stock on the exchange. When the stock price moves in such a way that limit orders are activated, the stock specialist initiates the trade.

When investors believe that the price of a stock will rise in the future, they buy that stock and hold it until the increase occurs. They can then sell at a profit and capture a gain for their effort. What can be done if an investor is convinced that a stock will *fall* in the future? The solution is to sell short. A **short sell** requires that the investor borrow stocks from a brokerage house and sell them today, with the promise of replacing the borrowed stocks by buying them in the future. Suppose that you just tried out the new Apple notebook computer and decided that it would sell poorly (in fact, in 1995, Apple had to recall all of its Powerbook computers to fix problems). You might believe that as the rest of the market learned of the poor product, the price of Apple's stock could decline. To take advantage of this situation, you might instruct your broker to short Apple 100 shares. The broker would then borrow 100 shares from another investor on your behalf and sell them at current market prices. You do not own those shares, of course. They are borrowed and at some point in the future, you would be required to purchase those 100 shares at the new market price to replace them. If you were right and the price of Apple declined, you would buy the shares at a lower price than you received for their earlier sale and would earn a profit. Of course, if you are wrong and the price rises, you will suffer a loss.

Market and limit orders allow you to take advantage of stock price *increases,* and short sells allow you to take advantage of stock price *decreases.* Analysts track the number of short positions taken on a stock as an indicator of the number of investors who feel that a stock's price is likely to fall in the future. Box 1 presents an example of how a stock specialist responds to various types of orders.

Other Services In addition to trading in securities, stockbrokers provide a variety of other services. Investors typically leave their securities in storage with the broker for safekeeping. If the securities are left with the broker, they are insured against loss by Canadian Investor Protection Fund (CIPF), a national contingency fund created by the Canadian securities industry in 1969. The Fund protects investors in the event of the insolvency of a member of any of the self-regulatory organizations—the Toronto Stock Exchange, the Montreal Exchange, and the Investment Dealers Association of Canada. This guarantee is not against loss in value, only against loss of the securities themselves. The U.S. equivalent of the

The CIPF Website, www.cipf.ca, lists its members and its sponsoring self-regulatory organizations.

BOX 1

Using the Limit-Order Book

Suppose that an order trader on the Toronto Stock Exchange is a specialist responsible for Circuit City stock. The limit-order book might look like the following:

Unfilled Circuit City Limit Orders

Buy Orders		Sell Orders	
37	100		
37 1/8	300		
37 1/4	100		
		37 3/8	200
		37 1/2	500
		37 5/8	100

Listed under "Buy Orders" are the highest prices investors are willing to pay to buy the stock. Listed under "Sell Orders" are the lowest prices investors holding Circuit City stock are willing to accept to sell. Currently, no transactions occur because there are no crossover or common prices. In other words, no one is currently willing to sell Circuit City stock at a price anyone is willing to pay.

Now suppose that the specialist receives a new 200-share market order to buy, an order to be filled at the best market price currently available. The specialist consults the "Sell Orders" column and fills the order at 37 3/8.

Next the specialist receives a 300-share limit order to sell at 37 1/8. Again, the specialist consults the book but this time looks in the "Buy Orders" column. The limit order is filled with 100 shares at 37 1/4 and 200 shares at 37 1/8.

Next suppose that a limit order to buy 500 shares at 36 7/8 is received. Because there is no sell order for this amount, the order is added to the book, which now looks like this:

Unfilled Circuit City Limit Orders

Buy Orders		Sell Orders	
36 7/8	500		
37	100		
37 1/8	100		
		37 1/2	500
		37 5/8	100

CIPF is the Securities Investor Protection Corporation (SIPC), an agency of the federal government in the United States.

Brokers also provide **margin credit**. Margin credit refers to loans advanced by the brokerage house to help investors buy securities. For example, if you are certain that Air Canada stock is going to rise rapidly, you could increase the amount of stock you can buy by borrowing from the brokerage house. If you had $5000 and borrowed an additional $5000, you could buy $10 000 worth of stock. Then, if the price goes up as you predict, you could earn nearly twice as much as without the loan. Interest rates on margin loans are usually 1 or 2 percentage points above the prime interest rate (the rate charged large, creditworthy corporate borrowers).

As noted in Chapter 16, the forces of competition have led brokerage firms to offer services and engage in activities traditionally conducted by commercial banks. The merger of HSBC with Merrill Lynch Canada allowed for Merrill Lynch HSBC to develop the cash management account (CMA), which provides a package of financial services that includes credit cards, immediate loans, cheque-writing privileges, automatic investment of proceeds from the sale of securities in a money market mutual fund, and unified record keeping. CMAs were adopted by other brokerage firms and spread rapidly. Many of these accounts allow cheque-writing privileges and offer ATM and debit cards. In these ways, they compete directly with banks.

As a result of CMAs, the distinction between banking activities and the activities of nonbank financial institutions has become blurred. The advantage of brokerage-based cash management accounts is that they make it easier to buy and sell securities. The stockbroker can take funds out of the account when an investor buys a security and put the money into the account when the investor sells securities.

Full-Service Versus Discount Brokers Before the mid-1970s, virtually all brokerage houses charged the same commissions on trades. Brokerage houses distinguished themselves primarily on the basis of their research and customer relations. Regulators determined that fixed commissions were anticompetitive and made amendments to each province's securities act, which abolished fixed commissions. Now brokerage houses may charge whatever fees they choose. This has resulted in two distinct types of brokerage firms: full-service and discount.

Full-service brokers provide research and investment advice to their customers. Full-service brokers will often mail weekly and monthly market reports and recommendations to their customers in an effort to encourage them to invest in certain securities. For example, when the investment banking department of the brokerage house has an initial public offering available, brokers will contact customers they feel may be interested and offer to send a prospectus. Full-service brokers attempt to establish long-term relationships with their customers and to help them assemble portfolios that are consistent with their financial needs and risk preferences. Of course, this extra attention is costly and must be paid for by requiring higher fees for initiating trades. RBC Dominion Securities is the biggest of the full-service brokers in Canada, and Merrill Lynch is the biggest in the United States.

Discount brokers simply execute trades on request. If you want to buy a particular security, you call the discount broker and place your request. No advice or research is typically provided. Because the cost of operating a discount brokerage firm is significantly less than the cost of operating a full-service firm, lower transaction costs are charged. These fees may be as little as half the fees charged by a full-service broker. TD Waterhouse is the largest discount broker in Canada; Charles Schwab & Company is the best-known discount broker in the United States. Many discount brokerage firms are owned by large commercial banks, which have historically been prohibited from offering full-service brokerage services.

Regardless of which type of brokerage firm you choose, it will have access to the automated trading system of the Toronto Stock Exchange and computer links to the Canadian Dealing Network Inc. (CDN), the Canadian equivalent of Nasdaq in the United States. Suppose that you place an order for 100 shares of IBM with your local CIBC World Markets office. Your broker will send an electronic message to the CIBC World Markets headquarters in Toronto to buy 100 shares of IBM in your name. The firm's order (or desk) trader will enter it into the trading system, and the order will be executed immediately at the current ask price. Confirmation of the purchase will then be communicated back to your local broker, who will inform you that the trade has been completed.

Securities Dealers

Securities dealers hold inventories of securities, which they sell to customers who want to buy. They also hold securities purchased from customers who want to sell.

It is impossible to overemphasize the importance of dealers to the smooth functioning of the Canadian financial markets. Consider what an investor demands before buying a security. In addition to requiring a fair return, the investor wants to know that the investment is *liquid*—that it can be sold quickly if it no longer fits into the investor's portfolio. Consider a small, relatively unknown firm that is trying to sell securities to the public. An investor may be tempted to buy the firm's securities, but if these securities cannot be resold easily, it is unlikely that the investor will take a chance on them. This is where the dealers become crucial. They stand ready to make a market in the security at any time—that is, they make sure that an investor can always sell or buy a security. For this reason, dealers are also called **market makers**. When an investor wants to sell a thinly traded stock (one without an active secondary market), it is unlikely that another investor is simultaneously seeking to buy that security. This nonsynchronous trading problem is solved when the dealer buys the security from the investor and holds it in inventory until another investor is ready to buy it. The knowledge that dealers will provide this service encourages investors to buy securities that would be otherwise unacceptable. In countries with less well developed financial markets, where dealers will not make a market for less popular securities, it is extremely difficult for small, new, or regional firms to raise funds. Securities market dealers are largely responsible for the health and growth of small businesses in Canada.

REGULATION OF SECURITIES FIRMS

Many financial firms engage in all three securities market activities, acting as brokers, dealers, and investment bankers. The largest in Canada is RBC Dominion Secirities; other well-known firms include ScotiaMcLoad, TD Securities, and Merrilll Lynch HSBC. The provincial securities commissions not only regulate the firms' investment banking operations but also restrict brokers and dealers from misrepresenting securities and from trading on *insider information,* unpublicized facts known only to the management of a corporation.

When discussing regulation, it is important to recognize that the public's confidence in the integrity of the financial markets is critical to the growth of our economy and the ability of firms to continue using the markets to raise new capital. If the public believes that there are other powerful players with superior information who can take advantage of smaller investors, the market will be unable to attract funds from these smaller investors. Ultimately, the markets could fail entirely.

The lemons problem introduced in Chapter 14 also applies to the securities markets. Due to asymmetric information, investors will not know as much about securities being offered for sale by firms as firm insiders will. If an average price is set for all securities based on this lack of information, good securities would be withdrawn and only poor and overpriced securities would remain for sale. With only these securities offered, the average price would fall. Now any securities worth more than this new average would be withdrawn. Eventually, the market would fail as the average security offered drops in quality and market prices fall as a result. One solution to the lemons problem is for the government to regulate full disclosure so that asymmetric information is reduced.

The Canadian Securities Administrators (CSA) Website, www.csa-acum.ca, provides information on how to choose a financial adviser, how to invest in mutual funds, and how to use the Internet for investment purposes

The Websites of some of the available provincial and territorial securities commissions are: www.albertasecurities.com, www.gov.ns.ca, www.bcsc.bc.ca, www.osc.gov.on.ca, www.msc.gov.mb.ca, www.pe.ca, www.nf.ca, and www.cvmq.com

Regulation of the securities industry in Canada is not a federal matter, but falls within the jurisdiction of the 10 provinces and the three territories; each province or territory has its own regulator. This self-regulatory environment, however, has made it necessary for all provincial and territorial securities regulators to form the Canadian Securities Administrators (CSA), an "umbrella" organization that coordinates and synchronizes various policies across the country with the objective of increasing market efficiency. For example, recently the CSA adopted a system of "mutual reliance," choosing the lead securities regulator to review the various applications and disclosure files of firms that carry on securities business in more than one jurisdiction.

Moreover, the CSA maintains the Canadian Securities Regulatory System (CSRS), which offers a national system of directives that each provincial or territorial securities commission must follow. This system of directives was designed with two goals: to protect the integrity of the markets and to restrict competition among securities firms so that they would be less likely to fail. In particular, there are several main objectives that each provincial or territorial securities commission must observe, the most important being the protection of investors from deceptive securities firms. This can be achieved through several mandates including:

- full disclosure of investment information
- licensing of brokers and other investment providers
- the supervision of market intermediaries

Go to www.sedar.com and www.sedi.ca for more information about SEDAR and SEDI.

As already noted, the practice of streamlining the various commissions aims to reduce the failure of investment firms and the subsequent systemic risk to the market system. Another device used by the CSA to provide investors with information is its databases SEDAR and SEDI. SEDAR holds all financial statements, reports on securities holdings, and news releases for companies publicly traded in Canada, while SEDI holds insider-trading reports.

The CSA also works closely with the Investment Dealers Association (IDA), a type of self-regulatory organization (SRO), that promotes competitiveness while still maintaining the protection for investors. Founded in 1916, the IDA has more than 190 member firms, which account for more than 97% of the market's revenue. Members are monitored for liquidity as well as maintaining a business method that is consistent with the rules of the association. In particular, there are four aspects that are involved in the regulations put forth by the IDA: registration, financial compliance, sales compliance, and enforcement.

Visit www.ida.ca, the Website for the Investment Dealers Association.

In particular, each member firm must register with the IDA and must meet a minimum level of capital, which is correlated to the capacity of business that they are involved in. The member firm must also disclose all information to its investors, including advising on investment procedures. Finally, any fraudulent member firm may be penalized, including individual employees. The joint collaboration of the IDA with the CSA encourages competitive growth in each region, while still allowing for the safest and most efficient securities market for the investor.

RELATIONSHIP BETWEEN SECURITIES FIRMS AND COMMERCIAL BANKS

For many years, commercial banks lobbied for legislative relief to enable them to compete with securities firms. This regulatory relief in the 1987 revision of the Bank Act allowed chartered banks to open investment companies within their operations, which started the trend for an investor Cash Management Account (CMA). It was originally introduced in the United States by Merrill Lynch, where it not only provided low-cost chequing but also paid interest that was higher than the law permitted U.S. banks to pay. Securities firms were allowed to make loans, offer credit and debit cards, provide ATM access, and most important, sell securities. Currently, many large investment firms, including BMO Nesbitt Burns, ScotiaMcLeod, and Merrill Lynch HSBC, have the option to open a CMA.

MUTUAL FUNDS

Access the *Mutual Fund Fact Book*, which is published by Investment Company Institute, at www.ici.org./facts_figures/factbook_toc.html to find information about the mutual funds industry's history, regulation, taxation, and shareholders.

The major brokerage houses, independent securities firms, and banks all offer a wide variety of mutual funds. Mutual funds pool the resources of many small investors by selling them shares and using the proceeds to buy securities. Through the asset transformation process of issuing shares in small denominations and buying large blocks of securities, mutual funds can take advantage of volume discounts on brokerage commissions and can purchase diversified portfolios of securities. Mutual funds allow the small investor to obtain the benefits of lower transaction costs in purchasing securities and to take advantage of the reduction of risk by diversifying the portfolio of securities held.

Despite the fact that research discussed in Chapter 10 has consistently demonstrated that mutual funds do not outperform the market, even when fees are not considered, many investors prefer to rely on professional money managers to select their stocks. The failure of mutual funds to post greater-than-average returns should not come as a surprise given our discussion of market efficiency. Still, the financial markets remain something of a mystery to a large number of investors. These investors are willing to pay fees that can often be very high to let someone else choose their stocks. Another reason investors purchase mutual funds is that they provide a low-cost way of diversifying into foreign stocks. It can be difficult and expensive to invest in foreign stocks not listed on Canadian exchanges.

Mutual funds have had a large increase in total proportion of stocks held since 1980. The primary source of this growth has been the booming stock market during the 1990s; another has been the appearance of mutual funds that specialized in debt instruments (which first appeared in the 1970s). Before 1970, mutual funds invested almost solely in common stocks. Funds that purchase common stocks may specialize even further and invest solely in foreign securities or in specialized industries, such as energy or high technology. There are currently over 1800 separate mutual funds available to investors. This means there are more distinct funds than there are stocks listed on the Toronto Stock Exchange.

Mutual fund companies frequently offer a number of separate mutual funds. They are called complexes and are defined as a group of funds under substantially common management (or distributorship), composed of one or more families of funds. The advantage to investors of fund complexes is that investments can usually be transferred among different funds within a family very easily and quickly. Additionally, account information can be summarized by the complex to help investors keep their assets organized. Table 3 reports the total fund assets, number of funds, and number of shareholder accounts since 1980.

Most mutual funds require a minimum investment before an account may be opened. Most funds, however, waive their minimum deposit requirement when an investor is opening an RRSP account.

TABLE 3 Total Industry Assets, Number of Funds, and Shareholder Accounts, 1980–2001

Year	Total Assets ($Billions)	Number of Funds	Number of Accounts (Thousands)
1980	3.6	87	479.6
1981	3.5	91	530.0
1982	4.1	91	577.7
1983	5.8	104	657.2
1984	6.7	115	777.7
1985	10.2	155	952.4
1986	17.5	213	1 700.4
1987	20.4	294	2 444.7
1988	20.8	370	2 370.1
1989	23.5	430	2 349.6
1990	24.9	422	2 587.9
1991	49.9	505	4 533.7
1992	67.3	543	5 514.2
1993	114.6	633	8 928.6
1994	127.3	813	13 486.3
1995	146.2	916	15 295.1
1996	211.8	954	22 297.8
1997	283.2	1 023	32 826.0
1998	326.6	1 030	40 948.7
1999	389.7	1 328	45 752.4
2000	418.9	1 605	50 302.9
2001	426.4	1 831	52 068.7

Source: www.ific.ca

Types of Investment Funds

There are four basic types of mutual funds available to investors. These are (1) stock funds (also called equity funds), (2) fixed income (bond) funds, (3) balanced funds (composed of both stocks and bonds), and (4) money market funds. About 60% of the total investment in mutual funds is invested in stock funds, 15% in money market funds, 9% in bond funds, and the rest in balanced funds.

Founded in 1998, the Investment Funds Standards Committee (IFSC) provides a complete 35 category listing for mutual fund investors. These classes of funds are used to standardize the industry and are summarized in Table 4.

The simplest types of funds to manage are called **index funds**. The managers of index funds simply buy the securities that are included in some popular stock index, such as the S&P/TSX Composite Index. Rebalancing occurs only when a stock enters or leaves the index or when price changes make it necessary. Since no research or aggressive management is required of these funds, lower fees are charged. Research suggests that due to the lower fees, these funds usually outperform the more actively managed funds.

Figure 3 shows the distribution of assets by type of fund in 2001.

Ownership of Mutual Funds

Get more details about the IFIC at www.ific.ca.

An estimated 3 million households in Canada now own mutual funds. In fact, 70% of households who earn above $75 000 annually own mutual funds compared to only 14% of households who earn less than $20 000. According to the Investment Funds Institute of Canada (IFIC), the average mutual fund investor is middle-class, 45 years old, male, and employed with a household income of $64 000.

Generation X (consisting of individuals aged 18 to 30) is also very interested in mutual fund investing. This group has the lowest level of household assets but the second-highest portion of financial assets in mutual funds, after those aged 50 to 70. Among the age groups, Generation X also has the highest tolerance for investment risk. Generation X is also leading the way in Internet access to mutual funds (see Box 2).

TABLE 4 IFSC Mutual Fund Categories

Alternative Strategies	Global Balanced and Asset Allocation
Asia/Pacific Rim Equity	Global Equity
Asia ex-Japan Equity	Healthcare
Canadian Balanced	International Equity
Canadian Bond	Japanese Equity
Canadian Dividend	Labour Sponsored Venture Capital
Canadian Equity	Latin American Equity
Canadian Income Trust	Natural Resources
Canadian Large Cap Equity	North American Equity
Canadian Money Market	Precious Metals
Canadian Mortgage	Real Estate
Canadian Short Term Bond	Science and Technology
Canadian Small Cap	Specialty or Miscellaneous
Canadian Tactical Asset Allocation	High Yield Bond
Emerging Markets Equity	U.S. Equity
European Equity	U.S. Money Market
Financial Services	U.S. Small and Mid Cap Equity
Foreign Bond	

Source: www.cifsc.com/fund_list.htm

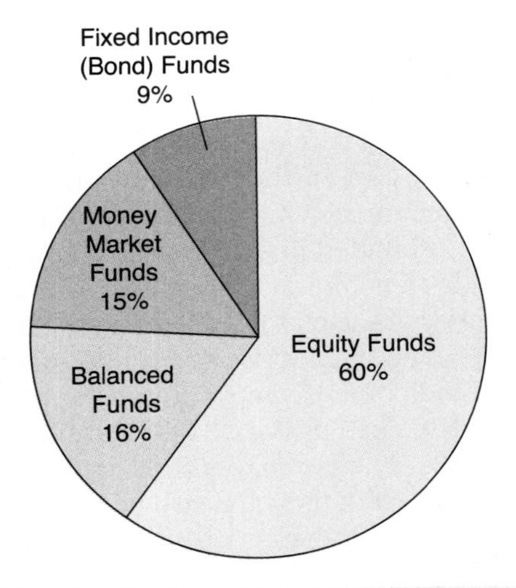

FIGURE 3 Distribution of Mutual Fund Assets, 2001

Source: www.ific.ca

BOX 2: E-FINANCE

Mutual Funds and the Internet

The U.S. Investment Company Institute estimates that as of 2000, 68% of U.S. households owning mutual funds use the Internet, and nearly half of those on-line shareholders visit fund-related Websites. The Internet increases the attractiveness of mutual funds because it enables shareholders to review performance information, share prices and personal account information.

Of all U.S. households that conducted mutual funds transactions between April 1999 and March 2000, 18% bought or sold fund shares on-line. The median number of funds transactions conducted over the Internet during the 12-month period was four, while the average number was eight, indicating that a high volume of on-line transactions were conducted by a small number of shareholders.

On-line shareholders were typically younger, had greater household income, and were better educated than those not using the Internet. The median on-line shareholder was 42 years old, had a household income of $100 900, and was university educated. The median shareholder not using the Internet was 51 years old, had a household income of $41 000, and did not have a university degree.

The use of the Internet to track and trade mutual funds is rapidly increasing. The number of shareholders who visited Websites offering fund shares nearly doubled between April 1999 and March 2000.

Fee Structure of Investment Funds

Mutual funds are structured in two ways. The most common structure is an **open-end fund**, from which shares can be redeemed at any time at a price that is tied to the asset value of the fund. A mutual fund can also be structured as a **closed-end fund**, in which a fixed number of nonredeemable shares are sold at an initial offering and are then traded in the over-the-counter market like common stock. The market price of these shares fluctuates with the value of the assets held by the fund. In contrast to the open-end fund, however, the price of the shares may be above or below the value of the assets held by the fund, depending on factors such as the liquidity of the shares or the quality of the management. The greater popularity of the open-end funds is explained by the greater liquidity of their redeemable shares relative to the nonredeemable shares of closed-end funds.

Application

Calculating a Mutual Fund's Net Asset Value

If you invest in a mutual fund, you will receive periodic statements summarizing the activity in your account. The statement will show funds that were added to your investment balance, funds that were withdrawn, and any earnings that have accrued. One term on the statement that is critical to understanding the investment's performance is the **net asset value (NAV)**. The net asset value is the total value of the mutual fund's stocks, bonds, cash, and other assets minus any liabilities such as accrued fees, divided by the number of shares outstanding. An example will make this clear.

Suppose that a mutual fund has the following assets and liabilities:

Stock (at current market value)	$20 000 000
Bonds (at current market value)	$10 000 000
Cash	$ 500 000
Total value of assets	$30 500 000
Liabilities	–$ 300 000
Net worth	$30 200 000

The net asset value is computed by dividing the net worth by the number of shares outstanding. If 10 million shares are outstanding, the net asset value is $3.02 ($30 200 000/10 000 000 = $3.02).

The net asset value rises and falls as the value of the underlying assets changes. For example, suppose that the value of the stock portfolio held by the mutual fund rises by 10% and the value of the bond portfolio falls by 2% over the course of a year. If the cash and liabilities are unchanged, the new net asset value will be

Stock (at current market value)	$22 000 000
Bonds (at current market value)	$9 800 000
Cash	$ 500 000
Total value of assets	$32 300 000
Liabilities	–$ 300 000
Net worth	$32 000 000

$$NAV = \frac{\$32\ 000\ 000}{10\ 000\ 000} = \$3.20$$

The yield on your investment in the mutual fund is then

$$\text{Yield} = \frac{\$3.20 - \$3.02}{\$3.02} = \frac{\$0.18}{\$3.02} = 5.96\%$$

When you buy and sell shares in the mutual fund, you do so at the current *NAV*.

Originally, shares of most open-end mutual funds were sold by salespeople (usually brokers) who were paid a commission. Because this commission is paid at the time of purchase and is immediately subtracted from the redemption value of the shares, these funds are called **load funds**. Most mutual funds are currently **no-load funds**; the funds sell directly to the public (bypassing brokers) with no sales commissions.

Fees in addition to sales commissions may be charged:

- A *contingent deferred sales charge* imposed at the time of redemption is an alternative way to compensate financial professionals for their services. This fee typically applies for the first few years of ownership and then disappears.
- A *redemption fee* is a back-end charge for redeeming shares. It is expressed as a dollar amount or a percentage of the redemption price.
- An *exchange fee* may be charged when transferring money from one fund to another within the same fund family.
- An *account maintenance fee* is charged by some funds to maintain low-balance accounts.
- *management fees* are deducted from the fund's assets to pay marketing, administrative, and advertising expenses or, more commonly, to compensate sales professionals. This fee is calculated using the "management expense ratio" (MER). If a fund has a value of $100 million, and its cost is $ 2 million, the MER is 2%.

Clearly, there are many opportunities for mutual fund managers to charge investors for the right to invest. Investors should very carefully evaluate a mutual fund's fee structure before investing, since these fees can range from 0.5% to as much as 8% per year. No research supports the argument that investors get better returns by investing in funds that charge higher fees. On the contrary, most high-fee mutual funds fail to do as well, after expenses, as low-fee funds.

Over the last 20 years, competition within the mutual fund industry has produced substantially lower costs. The cost of bond and money market funds dropped substantially due to the requirement by the securities commissions that mutual funds clearly disclose all fees and costs investors will incur. This fee disclosure requirement makes it very easy for investors to compare funds.

Regulation of Mutual Funds

Mutual funds are regulated under the same provincial and territorial securities commissions mentioned earlier. The Canadian Securities Administrators (CSA) enforces three rules that the provincial securities commissions must require of companies in the mutual fund industry. These include

- registration requirements
- prospectus requirements
- fund operations and sales conduct

Mutual fund dealers and advisors must be registered with the securities regulators, which ensures that the basic requirements are met for these employees to act in an investor's best interest.

As part of this regulation, all funds must provide a prospectus initially, as well as financial statements on a regular basis. A mutual fund's prospectus describes the fund's goals, fees and expenses, and investment strategies and risks; it also gives information on how to buy and sell shares. This prospectus must be filed with the individual securities commission as well as with each individual investor.

Annual and semiannual financial statements discuss the fund's recent performance and include other important information. By examining these reports, an investor can learn if a fund has been effective in meeting the goals and investment strategies described in the fund's prospectus.

Finally, each mutual fund must adhere to the laws set forth by each securities commission for the investment industry. This form of regulation refers to the possible fraudulent practices by mutual fund dealers or advisors in regards to capital requirements, false information, or even the misplacement of an investment into undisclosed funds.

Many of the mutual funds are run by brokerage houses; independent investment advisors run others. Because of the volume of stock controlled by these investors, there is tremendous competition for their business. This has led to significant cost cutting and to the proliferation of alternative methods for trading. For example, computerized trading that eliminates the broker from the transaction accounts for a growing percentage of the activity in stocks.

Mutual Funds and the Retirement Market

There is over one trillion dollars worth of assets in the private pension plan market invested in mutual funds, stocks, bonds, or deposits. Accumulations into retirement funds come from two sources: employer pension plans and individual sources such as registered retirement savings plans (RRSP) or registered retirement income funds (RRIF). There is $604 billion in assets in the employer pension plans, with the RRSP and RRIF markets accounting for the other $408 billion. Mutual funds account for 64% of RRSP portfolios and, of those containing mutual funds, comprise over 48% of the portfolio's value.

Hedge Funds

Hedge funds are a special type of mutual fund that have received considerable attention recently due to the near collapse of Long Term Capital Management. In Chapter 22 we discuss how financial markets can use hedges to reduce risk in a wide variety of situations. These risk-reducing strategies should not be confused with hedge funds. Although hedge funds often attempt to be market-neutral, protected from changes in the overall market, they are not riskless.

To illustrate a typical type of transaction conducted by hedge funds, consider a trade made by Long Term Capital Management in 1994. The fund managers noted that $29\frac{1}{2}$-year U.S. Treasury bonds seemed cheap relative to 30-year Treasury securities. The managers figured that the value of the two bonds would converge over time. After all, these securities have nearly identical risk since the maturity risk difference between $29\frac{1}{2}$-year securities and 30-year securities is insignificant. To make money from the temporary divergence of the bond prices, the fund bought US$2 billion of the $29\frac{1}{2}$-year bonds and sold short US$2 billion of the 30-year bonds. (Selling short means that the fund borrowed bonds it did not own and sold them. Later the fund must cover its short position by buying the bonds back, hopefully at a lower price.) The net investment by Long Term Capital was $12 million. Six months later, the fund covered its short position by buying 30-year bonds and sold its $29\frac{1}{2}$-year bonds. This transaction yielded a US$25 million profit.[4]

In the transaction, the managers did not care whether the overall bond market rose or fell. In this sense, the transaction was market-neutral. All that was required for a profit was that the prices of the bonds converge, an event that occurred as predicted. Hedge fund managers scour the world in their search for pricing anomalies between related securities. Figure 4 shows a situation where hedge funds could invest. Securities A and B move in lockstep over time. At some point they diverge, creating an opportunity. The hedge fund would buy security B, because it is expected to increase relative to A, and would sell A short. The fund managers hope that the gain on security B will be greater than the loss on security A. At times, the search for opportunities leads hedge funds to adopt exotic

[4]*Wall Street Journal,* November 16, 1998, p. A18.

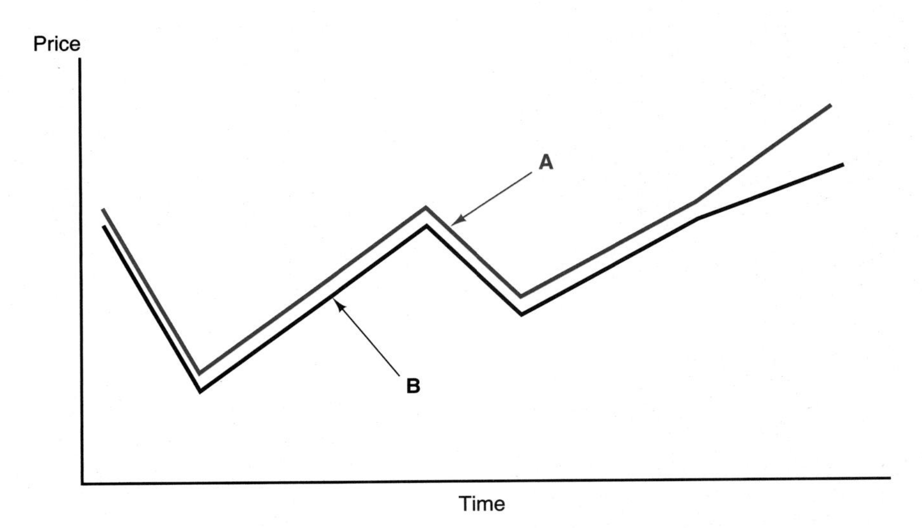

FIGURE 4 The Price of Two Similar Securities

Hedge funds search for related securities that historically move in lockstep but have temporarily diverted. In this example, the hedge fund would sell security A short and buy security B.

approaches that are not easily available elsewhere, from investing in distressed securities to participating in venture-capital financing.

In addition to investing money contributed by individuals and institutions, hedge funds often set up lines of credit to use to leverage their investments. For instance, in our example, Long Term Capital earned $25 million on an investment of $12 million, a 108% return [($25 million – $12 million)/$12 million = 1.08 = 108%]. Suppose that half of the $12 million had been borrowed funds. Ignoring interest cost, the return on invested equity would then be 317% [($25 million – $6 million)/$6 million = 3.17 = 317%]. Long Term Capital advertised that it was leveraged 20 to 1; however, by the time of the crisis, the figure was actually closer to 50 to 1. Box 3 discusses how Long Term Capital eventually required a private rescue plan to prevent its failure.

Hedge funds accumulate money from many people and invest on their behalf, but several features distinguish them from traditional mutual funds. First, hedge funds have a minimum investment requirement of between $100 000 and $20 million, with the typical minimum investment being $1 million. Long Term Capital Management required a $10 million minimum investment. Most hedge funds are set up as limited partnerships. Some managers of hedge funds have restrictions that are aimed at allowing hedge funds to exist largely unregulated, on the theory that the rich can look out for themselves.

Second, hedge funds are unique in that they usually require that investors commit their money for long periods of time, often several years. The purpose of this requirement is to give managers breathing room to attempt long-range strategies.

Hedge funds often charge large fees to investors. The typical fund charges a 1% annual asset management fee plus 20% of profits. Some charge significantly more. For example, Long Term Capital Management charged investors a 2% management fee and took 25% of profits.

BOX 3

The Long Term Capital Debacle

Long Term Capital Management is a U.S. hedge fund managed by a group that included two Nobel Prize winners and 25 other Ph.D.s. It made headlines in September 1998, because it required a private rescue plan organized by the Federal Reserve Bank of New York.

The experience of Long Term Capital Management demonstrates that hedge funds are not risk-free, despite their being market-neutral. Long Term Capital expected that the spread between long-term U.S. Treasury bonds and long-term corporate bonds would narrow. Many stock markets around the world plunged, causing a flight to quality. Investors bid up the price of Treasury securities while the price of corporate securities fell. This is exactly the opposite of what Long Term Capital Management had predicted. As losses mounted, Long Term Capital's lenders required that the fund increase its equity position.

By mid-September, the fund was unable to raise sufficient equity to meet the demands of its creditors. Faced with the potential collapse of the fund, together with its highly leveraged investment portfolio consisting of nearly $80 billion in equities and over $1 trillion of notional value in derivatives, the Federal Reserve stepped in to prevent the fund from failing. The Fed's rationale was that a sudden liquidation of the Long Term Capital Management portfolio would create unacceptable systemic risk. Tens of billions of dollars worth of illiquid securities would be dumped on an already jittery market, causing potentially huge losses to numerous lenders and other institutions. A group consisting of banks and brokerage firms contributed $3.6 billion to a rescue plan that prevented the fund's failure.

The Fed's involvement in organizing the rescue of Long Term Capital is controversial, despite no public funds being expended. Some critics argue that the intervention increases moral hazard by weakening the discipline imposed by the market on fund managers. However, others say that the tremendous economic damage the fund's failure would have caused was unacceptable. This debate is likely to rage for some time.

SUMMARY

1. Investment banks are firms that assist in the initial sale of securities in the primary market and, as securities brokers and dealers, assist in the trading of securities in the secondary markets, some of which are organized into exchanges. The provincial securities commissions regulate the financial institutions in the securities market and ensure that adequate information reaches prospective investors.
2. Underwriting involves the investment banking firm's taking ownership of the stock issue by purchasing all of the shares from the issuer and then reselling them in the market. Issues may be oversubscribed, undersubscribed, or fully subscribed, depending on whether the price is set correctly.
3. Investment bankers assist issuing firms by providing advice, filing documents, and marketing issues. Investment bankers often assist in mergers and acquisitions and in private placements as well.
4. Securities brokers act as go-betweens and do not usually own securities. Securities dealers do buy and sell securities and by doing so make a market. By always having securities to sell and by always being willing to purchase securities, dealers guarantee the liquidity of the market.
5. Investors may place an order, called a *market order*, to buy a security at the current market price. They may also set limits to the lowest price at which they will sell their security or the highest price they will pay for a security. Orders of this type are called *limit orders*.
6. Some brokerage houses provide research and investment advice in addition to conducting trades on behalf of customers. These are called *full-service brokers*. *Discount brokers* simply place orders. Brokerage houses also store securities, advance loans to buy securities, and offer cash management accounts.
7. Investment funds pool the funds of many small investors and purchase large quantities of securities. These funds offer a wide variety of funds designed to appeal to most investment strategies.

KEY TERMS

closed-end fund, *p. 544*
confidential memorandum, *p. 535*
definitive agreement, *p. 535*
due diligence, *p. 535*
fully subscribed, *p. 532*
hedge fund, *p. 547*
index fund, *p. 543*
initial public offering (IPO), *p. 529*
investment banks, *p. 528*
letter of intent, *p. 535*
limit order, *p. 537*
load fund, *p. 545*
margin credit, *p. 537*
market maker, *p. 539*
market order, *p. 537*
mergers and acquisitions market, *p. 535*
net asset value (NAV), *p. 545*
no-load fund, *p. 545*
open-end fund, *p. 544*
oversubscribed, *p. 532*
primary market, *p. 527*
prospectus, *p. 530*
registration statement, *p. 530*
seasoned issues, *p. 529*
secondary market, *p. 527*
short sell, *p. 537*
syndicate, *p. 532*
tombstone, *p. 532*
undersubscribed, *p. 532*

QUESTIONS AND PROBLEMS

***1.** What was the motivation behind legislation separating commercial banking from investment banking?

2. What law separated investment banking from commercial banking?

***3.** What does it mean to say that investment bankers *underwrite* a security offering? How is this different from a best-efforts offering?

4. What are the primary services that an investment banker will provide a firm issuing securities?

***5.** Does the fact that a security has passed a securities commission review mean that investors can buy the security without having to worry about taking a loss on the investment?

6. Why do investment banking firms often form syndicates for selling securities to the public?

***7.** Is it better for a security issue to be fully subscribed or oversubscribed?

8. Why would an investment banker advise a firm to issue a security using best efforts rather than underwriting?

***9.** What is the difference between a hostile takeover and a merger?

10. What valuable service do dealers provide that facilitates transaction trading and keeping the markets liquid?

***11.** What is the difference between a market order and a limit order?

12. How is it possible to make money if you know that the price of a security will *fall* in the future?

***13.** Why do commercial banks object to brokerage houses' being allowed to offer many of the same services traditionally reserved for banks?

14. What is an index fund? Why are index funds increasingly popular?

***15.** What is the difference between a load fund and a no-load fund?

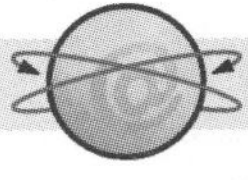

WEB EXERCISES

Investment Banks, Brokerage Firms, and Mutual Funds

1. *The Globe and Mail* is one of the best-known sources that specializes in analysis and review of mutual funds. Go to http://www.globefund.com, under "Tools" choose "Fund Filter." Enter the information you need according to your own preferences for investment. Can you find funds that provide the return you want with the expense ratio you are willing to pay?

2. The U.S. mutual fund industry publishes a fact book containing exhaustive data on the historic and current state of mutual funds. Go to http://www.ici.org/aboutfunds/factbook_toc.html.

a. According to Chapter 3, did the terrorist attack in September 2001 cause an obvious decrease in mutual funds assets?

b. According to Chapter 4, what percentage of mutual funds assets are currently owned by households?

c. According to Chapter 4, what is the average annual income of an investor in mutual funds?

Part 6

The Management of Financial Institutions

Chapter 22 Risk Management in Financial Institutions

Preview

The Website of the Risk Management Association, www.rmahq.org, offers useful information such as annual statement studies, on-line publications, and more.

Managing financial institutions has never been an easy task, but in recent years it has become even more difficult because of greater uncertainty in the economic environment. Interest rates have become much more volatile, resulting in substantial fluctuations in profits and in the value of assets and liabilities held by financial institutions. Furthermore, as we have seen in Chapter 5, defaults on loans and other debt instruments have also climbed dramatically, leading to large losses at financial institutions. In light of these developments, it is not surprising that financial institution managers have become more concerned about managing the risk their institutions face as a result of greater interest-rate fluctuations and defaults by borrowers.

In this chapter we examine how managers of financial institutions cope with credit risk, the risk arising because borrowers may default on their obligations, and with interest-rate risk, the risk arising from fluctuations in interest rates. We will look at the tools that these managers use to measure risk and the strategies that they employ to reduce it.

MANAGING CREDIT RISK

A major part of the business of financial institutions such as banks, insurance companies, pension funds, and finance companies is making loans. In order for these institutions to earn high profits, they must make successful loans that are paid back in full (and so have low credit risk). The concepts of adverse selection and moral hazard (introduced in Chapter 2) provide a framework for understanding the principles that financial institution managers must follow to minimize credit risk and make successful loans.

Adverse selection is problematic in loan markets because bad credit risks (borrowers most likely to default) are the ones who usually line up for loans—in other words, those who are most likely to produce an *adverse* outcome are the most likely to be *selected.* Borrowers with very risky investment projects in mind have much to gain if their projects are successful, and so they are the most eager to obtain loans. Clearly, however, they are the least desirable borrowers because of the greater possibility that they will be unable to pay back their loans.

Moral hazard is a problem in loan markets because borrowers may have incentives to engage in activities that are undesirable from the lender's point of view. In such situations, it is more likely that the lender will be exposed to the *hazard* of default. Once borrowers have obtained a loan, they are more likely to invest in high-risk investment projects—projects that pay high returns to the borrowers if successful. The high risk, however, makes it less likely that the loan will be paid back.

To be profitable, financial institutions must overcome the adverse selection and moral hazard problems that make loan defaults more likely. The attempts of financial institutions to solve these problems help explain a number of principles for managing credit risk: screening and monitoring, establishment of long-term customer relationships, loan commitments, collateral, compensating balance requirements, and credit rationing.

Screening and Monitoring

Asymmetric information is present in loan markets because lenders have less information about the investment opportunities and activities of borrowers than borrowers do. This situation leads to two information-producing activities by financial institutions: screening and monitoring.

Screening Adverse selection in loan markets requires that financial institutions screen out the bad credit risks from the good ones so that loans will be profitable. To accomplish effective screening, financial institutions must collect reliable information from prospective borrowers. Effective screening and information collection together form an important principle of credit risk management.

When you go into a bank or a finance company to apply for a consumer loan (such as a car loan or a mortgage to purchase a house), the first thing you are asked to do is fill out forms that elicit a great deal of information about your personal finances. You are asked about your salary, bank accounts, other assets (such as cars, insurance policies, and furnishings), and outstanding loans; your record of loan, credit card, and charge account repayments; and the number of years you've worked and who your employers have been. You also are asked personal questions such as your age, marital status, and number of children. The bank or finance company uses this information to evaluate how good a credit risk you are by calculating your "credit score," a statistical measure derived from your answers that predicts whether you are likely to have trouble making your loan payments. Deciding on how good a risk you are cannot be entirely scientific, so the bank or finance company must also use judgment. A loan officer, whose job is to decide whether you should be given the loan, might call your employer or talk to some of the personal references you supplied. The officer might even make a judgment based on your demeanor or your appearance.

The process of screening and collecting information is similar when a financial institution makes a business loan. The loan officer needs to collect information about the company's profits and losses (income) and about its assets and liabilities. The officer also has to evaluate the likely future success of the business. So in addition to obtaining information such as sales figures, the loan officer might ask questions about the company's future plans, how the loan will be used, and the competition in the industry and might even visit the company to obtain a firsthand look at its operations. The bottom line is that, be it for personal or business loans, financial institutions need to be nosy.

One puzzling feature of lending by financial institutions is that they often specialize in lending to local firms or to firms in particular industries, such as energy. In one sense, this behaviour appears surprising because it means that the financial institution is not diversifying its portfolio of loans and is therefore exposing itself to more risk. But from another perspective, such specialization makes perfect sense. Recall that the adverse selection problem requires that financial institutions screen out bad credit risks. It is easier for a financial institution to collect information about local firms and determine their creditworthiness than to collect similar information on firms that are far away. Similarly, by specializing in lending to firms in specific industries, the financial institution becomes more knowledgeable about these industries and is therefore better able to predict whether the firms it lends to will be able to make timely payments on their debt.

Monitoring After a loan has been obtained, the borrower may have an incentive to take on risky activities that make it less likely that the loan will be paid off. To reduce this moral hazard, financial institution managers must adhere to the principle for managing credit risk of writing provisions (restrictive covenants) into loan contracts that prevent borrowers from engaging in overly risky activities. By monitoring borrowers' activities to see whether they are complying with the restrictive covenants and by enforcing the covenants if they are not, financial institution managers can make sure that borrowers are not taking on risks at the institution's expense. The need for financial institutions to engage in screening and monitoring explains why successful financial institutions spend so much money on auditing and information-collecting activities.

Long-Term Customer Relationships

An additional way for financial institution managers to obtain information about borrowers is to establish long-term customer relationships, another important principle of credit risk management.

If a prospective borrower has had a chequing or savings account or loans with the financial institution over a long period of time, a loan officer can look at past activity in the accounts and learn quite a bit about the borrower. The balances in the chequing and savings accounts tell the loan officer how liquid the potential borrower is and at what times of the year the borrower has a strong need for cash. A review of the cheques the borrower has written reveals the borrower's suppliers. If the borrower has borrowed previously from the financial institution, the institution has a record of the loan payments. Thus long-term customer relationships reduce the costs of information collection and make it easier to screen out bad credit risks.

The need for monitoring by financial institutions adds to the importance of long-term customer relationships. If the borrower has borrowed from the financial institution before, the institution has already established procedures for monitoring that customer. Therefore, the costs of monitoring long-term customers are lower than those for new customers.

Long-term relationships benefit the customers as well as the financial institution. A firm with a previous relationship will find it easier to obtain a loan at a low interest rate because the financial institution has an easier time determining if the prospective borrower is a good credit risk and incurs fewer costs in monitoring the borrower.

A long-term customer relationship has another advantage for the financial institution. No financial institution manager can think of every contingency when the institution writes restrictive covenants into a loan contract; there will always be risky borrower activities that are not ruled out. However, what if a borrower wants to preserve a long-term relationship with the financial institution to make it easier to get future loans at low interest rates? The borrower then has the incentive to avoid risky activities that would upset the financial institution, even if these risky activities are not specifically addressed in the loan contract. Indeed, if the financial institution manager doesn't like what a borrower is doing even when the borrower isn't violating any restrictive covenants, the manager has some power to discourage the borrower from such activity by threatening to refuse new loans in the future. Long-term customer relationships therefore enable financial institution managers to deal with even unanticipated moral hazard contingencies.

Loan Commitments

Banks have a special vehicle for institutionalizing long-term relationships called a **loan commitment**. A loan commitment is a bank's commitment (for a specified future period of time) to provide a firm with loans up to a given amount at a fixed interest rate or, more commonly, at a rate that is tied to some market interest rate. The majority of commercial and industrial loans from banks are made under the loan commitment arrangement. The advantage for the firm is that it has a source of credit when it needs it. The advantage for the bank is that the loan commitment promotes a long-term relationship, which in turn facilitates information collection. In addition, provisions in the loan commitment agreement require that the firm continually supply the bank with information about the firm's income, asset and liability position, business activities, and so on. A loan commitment arrangement is a powerful method for reducing the bank's costs for screening and information collection.

Collateral

Collateral requirements for loans are important credit risk management tools. Loans with these collateral requirements are often referred to as **secured loans**. Collateral, which is property promised to the lender as compensation if the borrower defaults, lessens the consequences of adverse selection because it reduces the lender's losses in the case of a loan default. If a borrower defaults on a loan with collateral, the lender can sell the collateral and use the proceeds to make up for its losses on the loan. Collateral requirements thus offer important protection for financial institutions making loans, and that is why they are extremely common in loans made by financial institutions.

Compensating Balances

One particular form of collateral required when a bank makes commercial loans is called **compensating balances**: A firm receiving a loan must keep a required minimum amount of funds in a chequing account at the bank. For example, a business getting a $10 million loan may be required to keep compensating balances of at least $1 million in its chequing account at the bank. If the borrower defaults, this $1 million in compensating balances can be taken by the bank to make up some of the losses on the loan.

Besides serving as collateral, compensating balances help increase the likelihood that a loan will be paid off. They do this by helping the bank monitor the borrower and consequently minimize moral hazard. Specifically, by requiring the borrower to use a chequing account at the bank, the bank can observe the firm's cheque payment practices, which may yield a great deal of information about the borrower's financial condition. For example, a sustained drop in the borrower's chequing account balance may signal that the borrower is having financial trouble, or account activity may suggest that the borrower is engaging in risky activities; perhaps a change in suppliers means that the borrower is pursuing new lines of business. Any significant change in the borrower's payment procedures is a signal to the bank that it should make inquiries. Compensating balances therefore make it easier for banks to monitor borrowers more effectively and are consequently another important credit risk management tool.

Credit Rationing

Another way in which successful financial institution managers deal with adverse selection and moral hazard is through **credit rationing**: Lenders refuse to make loans even though borrowers are willing to pay the stated interest rate or even a higher rate. Credit rationing takes two forms. The first occurs when a financial institution refuses to make a loan of *any amount* to a borrower, even if the borrower is willing to pay a higher interest rate. The second occurs when the financial institution is willing to make a loan but restricts the size of the loan to less than the borrower would like.

At first you might be puzzled by the first type of credit rationing. After all, even if the potential borrower is a credit risk, why doesn't the financial institution just extend the loan but at a higher interest rate? The answer is that adverse selection rules out this solution. Individuals and firms with the riskiest investment projects are precisely the ones that are willing to pay the highest interest rates. If a borrower took on a high-risk investment and succeeded, the borrower would become extremely rich. But a financial institution wouldn't want to make such a loan precisely because the investment risk is high; the likely outcome is that the borrower will *not* succeed and the financial institution will not be paid back. Charging a higher interest rate just makes adverse selection worse for the financial institution; that is, it increases the likelihood that the financial institution is lending to a bad credit risk. The financial institution would therefore rather not make any loans at a higher interest rate; instead, it would engage in the first type of credit rationing and would turn down loans.

Financial institutions engage in a second type of credit rationing to guard against moral hazard: They grant loans to borrowers, but not loans as large as the borrowers want. Such credit rationing is necessary because the larger the loan, the greater the benefits from moral hazard. For example, if a financial institution gives you a $1000 loan, you are likely to take actions that enable you to pay it back because you don't want to hurt your credit rating for the future. However, if the financial institution lends you $10 million, you are more likely to fly off to Rio to celebrate. The larger your loan, the greater your incentives to engage in activities that make it less likely that you will repay the loan. Because more borrowers repay their loans if the loan amounts are small, financial institutions ration credit by providing borrowers with smaller loans than they seek.

MANAGING INTEREST-RATE RISK

As the volatility of interest rates increased in the 1980s, financial institution managers became more concerned about their exposure to interest-rate risk, the riskiness of earnings and returns that is associated with changes in interest rates. Indeed, the S&L debacle, described in Chapter 18, made clearer the dangers of interest-rate risk when many S&Ls went out of business because they had not managed interest-rate risk properly. To see what interest-rate risk is all about, let's take a look at the balance sheet of the First Bank:

First Bank

Assets		Liabilities	
Reserves and cash items	$5 million	Chequable deposits	$15 million
Securities		Money market deposit accounts	$5 million
Less than 1 year	$5 million	Savings deposits	$15 million
1 to 2 years	$5 million	CDs	
Greater than 2 years	$10 million	Variable-rate	$10 million
Residential mortgages		Less than 1 year	$15 million
Variable-rate	$10 million	1 to 2 years	$5 million
Fixed-rate (30-year)	$10 million	Greater than 2 years	$5 million
Commercial loans		Overnight funds	$5 million
Less than 1 year	$15 million	Borrowings	
1 to 2 years	$10 million	Less than 1 year	$10 million
Greater than 2 years	$25 million	1 to 2 years	$5 million
Physical capital	$5 million	Greater than 2 years	$5 million
		Bank capital	$5 million
Total	$100 million	Total	$100 million

The first step in assessing interest-rate risk is for the bank manager to decide which assets and liabilities are rate-sensitive, that is, which have interest rates that will be reset (repriced) within the year. Note that rate-sensitive assets or liabilities can have interest rates repriced within the year either because the debt instrument matures within the year or because the repricing is done automatically, as with variable-rate mortgages.

For many assets and liabilities, deciding whether they are rate-sensitive is straightforward. In our example, the obviously rate-sensitive assets are securities with maturities of less than one year ($5 million), variable-rate mortgages ($10 million), and commercial loans with maturities less than one year ($15 million), for a total of $30 million. However, some assets that look like fixed-rate assets whose interest rates are not repriced within the year actually have a component that is rate-sensitive. For example, although fixed-rate residential mortgages may have a maturity of 30 years, homeowners can repay their mortgages early by selling their homes or repaying the mortgage in some other way. This means that within the year, a certain percentage of these fixed-rate mortgages will be paid off, and interest rates on this amount will be repriced. From past experience the bank manager knows that 20% of the fixed-rate residential mortgages are repaid within a year, which means that $2 million of these mortgages (20% of $10 million) must be considered rate-sensitive. The bank manager adds this $2 million to the $30 million of rate-sensitive assets already calculated, for a total of $32 million in rate-sensitive assets.

The bank manager now goes through a similar procedure to determine the total amount of rate-sensitive liabilities. The obviously rate-sensitive liabilities are money market deposit accounts ($5 million), variable-rate CDs and CDs with less than one year to maturity ($25 million), overnight funds ($5 million), and borrowings with maturities of less than one year ($10 million), for a total of $45 million. Chequable deposits and savings deposits often have interest rates that can be changed at any time by the bank, although banks often like to keep their rates fixed for substantial periods. Thus these liabilities are partially but not fully rate-sensitive. The bank manager estimates that 10% of chequable deposits ($1.5 million) and 20% of savings deposits ($3 million) should be considered rate-sensitive. Adding the $1.5 million and $3 million to the $45 million figure yields a total for rate-sensitive liabilities of $49.5 million.

Now the bank manager can analyze what will happen if interest rates rise by 1 percentage point, say, on average from 10% to 11%. The income on the assets rises by \$320 000 (= 1% × \$32 million of rate-sensitive assets), while the payments on the liabilities rise by \$495 000 (= 1% × \$49.5 million of rate-sensitive liabilities). The First Bank's profits now decline by \$175 000 = (\$320 000 – \$495 000). Another way of thinking about this situation is with the net interest margin concept described in Chapter 15, which is interest income minus interest expense divided by bank assets. In this case, the 1% rise in interest rates has resulted in a decline of the net interest margin by 0.175% (= –\$175 000/\$100 million). Conversely, if interest rates fall by 1%, similar reasoning tells us that the First Bank's income rises by \$175,000 and its net interest margin rises by 0.175%. This example illustrates the following point: ***If a financial institution has more rate-sensitive liabilities than assets, a rise in interest rates will reduce the net interest margin and income, and a decline in interest rates will raise the net interest margin and income.***

Income Gap Analysis

One simple and quick approach to measuring the sensitivity of bank income to changes in interest rates is **gap analysis** (also called **income gap analysis**), in which the amount of rate-sensitive liabilities is subtracted from the amount of rate-sensitive assets. This calculation, *GAP*, can be written as

$$GAP = RSA - RSL \qquad (1)$$

where RSA = rate-sensitive assets
RSL = rate-sensitive liabilities

In our example, the bank manager calculates *GAP* to be

$$GAP = \$32 \text{ million} - \$49.5 \text{ million} = -\$17.5 \text{ million}$$

Multiplying *GAP* times the change in the interest rate immediately reveals the effect on bank income:

$$\Delta I = GAP \times \Delta i \qquad (2)$$

where ΔI = change in bank income
Δi = change in interest rates

EXAMPLE 1: Income Gap Analysis

Using the –\$17.5-million gap calculated using Equation 1, what is the change in income if interest rates rise by 1%?

Solution

The change in income is –\$175 000.

$$\Delta I = GAP \times \Delta i$$

where

$GAP = RSA - RSL$ = –\$17.5 million
Δi = change in interest rate = 0.01

Thus

$$\Delta I = -\$17.5 \text{ million} \times 0.01 = -\$175\,000$$

The analysis we just conducted is known as *basic gap analysis,* and it suffers from the problem that many of the assets and liabilities that are not classified as rate-sensitive have different maturities. One refinement to deal with this problem, the *maturity bucket approach,* is to measure the gap for several maturity subintervals, called maturity buckets, so that effects of interest-rate changes over a multiyear period can be calculated.

EXAMPLE 2: Income Gap Analysis

The manager of First Bank notices that the bank balance sheet produces a more refined maturity bucket that allows him to estimate the potential change in income over the next one to two years. Rate-sensitive assets in this period consist of $5 million of securities maturing in one to two years, $10 million of commercial loans maturing in one to two years, and an additional $2 million (20% of fixed-rate mortgages) that the bank expects to be repaid. Rate-sensitive liabilities in this period consist of $5 million of one- to two-year CDs, $5 million of one- to two-year borrowings, $1.5 million of chequable deposits (the 10% of chequable deposits that the bank manager estimates are rate-sensitive in this period), and an additional $3 million of savings deposits (the 20% estimate of savings deposits). For the next one to two years, calculate the gap and the change in income if interest rates rise by 1%.

Solution

The gap calculation for the one- to two-year period is $2.5 million.

$$GAP = RSA - RSL$$

where

$$RSA = \text{rate-sensitive assets} = \$17 \text{ million}$$
$$RSL = \text{rate-sensitive liabilities} = \$14.5 \text{ million}$$

Thus

$$GAP = \$17 \text{ million} - \$14.5 \text{ million} = \$2.5 \text{ million}$$

If interest rates remain 1% higher, then in the second year income will improve by $25 000.

$$\Delta I = GAP \times \Delta i$$

where

$$GAP = RSA - RSL = \$2.5 \text{ million}$$
$$\Delta i = \text{change in interest rate} = 0.01$$

Thus

$$\Delta I = \$2.5 \text{ million} \times 0.01 = \$25\,000$$

By using the more refined maturity bucket approach, the bank manager can figure out what will happen to bank income over the next several years when there is a change in interest rates.

Duration Gap Analysis

The gap analysis we have examined so far focuses only on the effect of interest-rate changes on income. Clearly, owners and managers of financial institutions care not only about the effect of changes in interest rates on income but also about the effect of changes in interest rates on the market value of the net worth of the financial institution.[1]

An alternative method for measuring interest-rate risk, called **duration gap analysis**, examines the sensitivity of the market value of the financial institution's net worth to changes in interest rates. Duration analysis is based on Macaulay's concept of *duration*, which measures the average lifetime of a security's stream of payments (described in Chapter 3). Recall that duration is a useful concept because it provides a good approximation, particularly when interest-rate changes are small, of the sensitivity of a security's market value to a change in its interest rate using the following formula:

$$\%\Delta P = -DUR \times \frac{\Delta i}{1 + i} \tag{3}$$

where

$\%\Delta P = (P_{t+1} - P_t)/P_t$ = percent change in market value of the security
DUR = duration
i = interest rate

After having determined the duration of all assets and liabilities on the bank's balance sheet, the bank manager could use this formula to calculate how the market value of each asset and liability changes when there is a change in interest rates and then calculate the effect on net worth. There is, however, an easier way to go about doing this, derived from the basic fact about duration we learned in Chapter 3: Duration is additive; that is, the duration of a portfolio of securities is the weighted average of the durations of the individual securities, with the weights reflecting the proportion of the portfolio invested in each. What this means is that the bank manager can figure out the effect that interest-rate changes will have on the market value of net worth by calculating the average duration for assets and for liabilities and then using those figures to estimate the effects of interest-rate changes.

To see how a bank manager would do this, let's return to the balance sheet of the First Bank. The bank manager has already used the procedures outlined in Chapter 3 to calculate the duration of each asset and liability, as listed in Table 1. For each asset, the manager then calculates the weighted duration by multiplying the duration times the amount of the asset divided by total assets, which in this case is \$100 million. For example, in the case of securities with maturities less than one year, the manager multiplies the 0.4 year of duration times \$5 million divided by \$100 million to get a weighted duration of 0.02. (Note that physical assets have no cash payments, so they have a duration of zero years.) Doing this for all the assets and adding them up, the bank manager gets a figure for the average duration of the assets of 2.70 years.

The manager follows a similar procedure for the liabilities, noting that total liabilities excluding capital are \$95 million. For example, the weighted duration for chequable deposits is determined by multiplying the 2.0-year duration by \$15 million divided by \$95 million to get 0.32. Adding up these weighted durations, the manager obtains an average duration of liabilities of 1.03 years.

[1]Note that accounting net worth is calculated on a historical-cost (book-value) basis, meaning that the value of assets and liabilities is based on their initial price. However, book-value net worth does not give a complete picture of the true worth of the firm; the market value of net worth provides a more accurate measure. This is why duration gap analysis focuses on what happens to the market value of net worth, and not on book value, when interest rates change.

TABLE 1 Duration of the First Bank's Assets and Liabilities

	Amount ($ millions)	Duration (years)	Weighted Duration (years)
Assets			
Reserves and cash items	5	0.0	0.00
Securities			
Less than 1 year	5	0.4	0.02
1 to 2 years	5	1.6	0.08
Greater than 2 years	10	7.0	0.70
Residential mortgages			
Variable-rate	10	0.5	0.05
Fixed-rate (30-year)	10	6.0	0.60
Commercial loans			
Less than 1 year	15	0.7	0.11
1 to 2 years	10	1.4	0.14
Greater than 2 years	25	4.0	1.00
Physical capital	5	0.0	0.00
Average duration			2.70
Liabilities			
Chequable deposits	15	2.0	0.32
Money market deposit accounts	5	0.1	0.01
Savings deposits	15	1.0	0.16
CDs			
Variable-rate	10	0.5	0.05
Less than 1 year	15	0.2	0.03
1 to 2 years	5	1.2	0.06
Greater than 2 years	5	2.7	0.14
Overnight funds	5	0.0	0.00
Borrowings			
Less than 1 year	10	0.3	0.03
1 to 2 years	5	1.3	0.07
Greater than 2 years	5	3.1	0.16
Average duration			1.03

EXAMPLE 3: Duration Gap Analysis

The bank manager wants to know what happens when interest rates rise from 10% to 11%. The total asset value is $100 million, and the total liability value is $95 million. Use Equation 3 to calculate the change in the market value of the assets and liabilities.

Solution

With a total asset value of $100 million, the market value of assets falls by $2.5 million ($100 million × 0.025 = $2.5 million).

$$\%\Delta P = -DUR \times \frac{\Delta i}{1 + i}$$

where

$$DUR = \text{duration} = 2.70$$

$$\Delta i = \text{change in interest rate} = 0.11 - 0.10 = 0.01$$

$$i = \text{interest rate} = 0.10$$

Thus

$$\%\Delta P \approx -2.70 \times \frac{0.01}{1 + 0.10} = -0.025 = -2.5\%$$

With total liabilities of \$95 million, the market value of liabilities falls by \$0.9 million (\$95 million × 0.009 = –\$0.9 million).

$$\%\Delta P \approx -DUR \times \frac{\Delta i}{1+i}$$

where

DUR = duration = 1.03

Δi = change in interest rate = 0.11 – 0.10 = 0.01

i = interest rate = 0.10

Thus

$$\%\Delta P \approx -1.03 \times \frac{0.01}{1+0.10} = -0.009 = -0.9\%$$

The result is that the net worth of the bank would decline by \$1.6 million (–\$2.5 million – (–\$0.9 million) = –\$2.5 million + \$0.9 million = –\$1.6 million).

The bank manager could have gotten to the answer even more quickly by calculating what is called a *duration gap,* which is defined as follows:

$$DUR_{gap} = DUR_a - \left(\frac{L}{A} \times DUR_l\right) \tag{4}$$

where

DUR_a = average duration of assets
DUR_l = average duration of liabilities
L = market value of liabilities
A = market value of assets

EXAMPLE 4: Duration Gap Analysis

Based on the information provided in Example 3, use Equation 4 to determine the duration gap for First Bank.

Solution

The duration gap for First Bank is 1.72 years.

$$DUR_{gap} = DUR_a - \left(\frac{L}{A} \times DUR_l\right)$$

where

DUR_a = average duration of assets = 2.70

L = market value of liabilities = 95

A = market value of assets = 100

DUR_l = average duration of liabilities = 1.03

Thus

$$DUR_{gap} = 2.70 - \left(\frac{95}{100} \times 1.03\right) = 1.72 \text{ years}$$

To estimate what will happen if interest rates change, the bank manager uses the DUR_{gap} calculation in Equation 3 to obtain the change in the market value of net worth as a percentage of total assets. In other words, the change in the market value of net worth as a percentage of assets is calculated as

$$\frac{\Delta NW}{A} \approx -DUR_{gap} \times \frac{\Delta i}{1+i} \tag{5}$$

EXAMPLE 5: Duration Gap Analysis

What is the change in the market value of net worth as a percentage of assets if interest rates rise from 10% to 11%? (Use Equation 5.)

Solution

A rise in interest rates from 10% to 11% would lead to a change in the market value of net worth as a percentage of assets of −1.6%

$$\frac{\Delta NW}{A} = -DUR_{gap} \times \frac{\Delta i}{1+i}$$

where

DUR_{gap} = duration gap = 1.72

Δi = change in interest rate = 0.11 − 0.10 = 0.01

i = interest rate = 0.10

Thus

$$\frac{\Delta NW}{A} = -1.72 \times \frac{0.01}{1+0.10} = -0.016 = -1.6\%$$

With assets totaling $100 million, Example 5 indicates a fall in the market value of net worth of $1.6 million, which is the same figure that we found in Example 3.

As our examples make clear, both income gap analysis and duration gap analysis indicate that the First Bank will suffer from a rise in interest rates. Indeed, in this example, we have seen that a rise in interest rates from 10% to 11% will cause the market value of net worth to fall by $1.6 million, which is one-third the initial amount of bank capital. Thus the bank manager realizes that the bank faces substantial interest-rate risk because a rise in interest rates could cause it to lose a lot of its capital. Clearly, income gap analysis and duration gap analysis are useful tools for telling a financial institution manager the institution's degree of exposure to interest-rate risk.

Study Guide To make sure that you understand income gap and duration gap analysis, you should be able to verify that if interest rates fall from 10% to 5%, the First Bank will find its income increasing and the market value of its net worth rising. For even more practice with these concepts, do some of the problems at the end of this chapter.

Example of a Nonbanking Financial Institution

So far we have focused on an example involving a banking institution that has borrowed short and lent long so that when interest rates rise, both income and the net worth of the institution fall. It is important to recognize that income and duration gap analysis applies equally to other financial institutions. Furthermore, it is important for you to see that some financial institutions have income and duration gaps that are opposite in sign to those of banks, so that when interest rates rise, both income and net worth rise rather than fall. To get a more complete picture of income and duration gap analysis, let us look at a nonbank financial institution, the Friendly Finance Company, which specializes in making consumer loans.

The Friendly Finance Company has the following balance sheet:

Friendly Finance Company

Assets		Liabilities	
Cash and deposits	$3 million	Commercial paper	$40 million
Securities		Bank loans	
Less than 1 year	$5 million	Less than 1 year	$3 million
1 to 2 years	$1 million	1 to 2 years	$2 million
Greater than 2 years	$1 million	Greater than 2 years	$5 million
Consumer loans		Long-term bonds and	
Less than 1 year	$50 million	other long-term debt	$40 million
1 to 2 years	$20 million	Capital	$10 million
Greater than 2 years	$15 million		
Physical capital	$5 million		
Total	$100 million	Total	$100 million

The manager of the Friendly Finance Company calculates the rate-sensitive assets to be equal to the $5 million of securities with maturities less than one year plus the $50 million of consumer loans with maturities of less than one year, for a total of $55 million of rate-sensitive assets. The manager then calculates the rate-sensitive liabilities to be equal to the $40 million of commercial paper, all of which has a maturity of less than one year, plus the $3 million of bank loans maturing in less than a year, for a total of $43 million. The calculation of the income gap is then

$$GAP = RSA - RSL = \$55 \text{ million} - \$43 \text{ million} = \$12 \text{ million}$$

To calculate the effect on income if interest rates rise by 1%, the manager multiplies the GAP of $12 million times the change in the interest rate to get the following:

$$\Delta I = GAP \times \Delta i = \$12 \text{ million} \times 1\% = \$120\ 000$$

Thus the manager finds that the finance company's income will rise by $120 000 when interest rates rise by 1%. The reason that the company has benefited from the interest-rate rise, in contrast to the First Bank, whose profits suffer from the rise in interest rates, is that the Friendly Finance Company has a positive income gap because it has more rate-sensitive assets than liabilities.

Like the bank manager, the manager of the Friendly Finance Company is also interested in what happens to the market value of the net worth of the company when interest rates rise by 1%. So the manager calculates the weighted duration of each item in the balance sheet, adds them up as in Table 2, and obtains a duration for the assets of 1.16 years and for the liabilities, 2.77 years. The duration gap is then calculated to be

$$DUR_{gap} = DUR_a - \left(\frac{L}{A} \times DUR_l\right) = 1.16 - \left(\frac{90}{100} \times 2.77\right) = -1.33 \text{ years}$$

Since the Friendly Finance Company has a negative duration gap, the manager realizes that a rise in interest rates by 1 percentage point from 10% to 11% will increase the market value of net worth of the firm. The manager checks this by calculating the change in the market value of net worth as a percentage of assets:

TABLE 2 Duration of the Friendly Finance Company's Assets and Liabilities

	Amount ($ millions)	Duration (years)	Weighted Duration (years)
Assets			
Cash and deposits	3	0.0	0.00
Securities			
Less than 1 year	5	0.5	0.05
1 to 2 years	1	1.7	0.02
Greater than 2 years	1	9.0	0.09
Consumer loans			
Less than 1 year	50	0.5	0.25
1 to 2 years	20	1.5	0.30
Greater than 2 years	15	3.0	0.45
Physical capital	5	0.0	0.00
Average duration			1.16
Liabilities			
Commercial paper	40	0.2	0.09
Bank loans			
Less than 1 year	3	0.3	0.01
1 to 2 years	2	1.6	0.04
Greater than 2 years	5	3.5	0.19
Long-term bonds and other long-term debt	40	5.5	2.44
Average duration			2.77

$$\Delta NW = -DUR_{gap} \times \frac{\Delta i}{1+i} = -(-1.33) \times \frac{0.01}{1+0.10} = 0.012 = 1.2\%$$

With assets of $100 million, this calculation indicates that net worth will rise in market value by $1.2 million.

Even though the income and duration gap analysis indicates that the Friendly Finance Company gains from a rise in interest rates, the manager realizes that if interest rates go in the other direction, the company will suffer a fall in income and market value of net worth. Thus the finance company manager, like the bank manager, realizes that the institution is subject to substantial interest-rate risk.

Some Problems with Income and Duration Gap Analysis

Although you might think that income and duration gap analysis is complicated enough, further complications make a financial institution manager's job even harder.

One assumption that we have been using in our discussion of income and duration gap analysis is that when the level of interest rates changes, interest rates on all maturities change by exactly the same amount. That is the same as saying that we conducted our analysis under the assumption that the slope of the yield curve remains unchanged. Indeed, the situation is even worse for duration gap analysis because the duration gap is calculated assuming that interest rates for all maturities are the same—in other words, the yield curve is assumed to be flat. As our discussion of the term structure of interest rates in Chapter 5 indicated, however, the yield curve is not flat, and the slope of the yield curve fluctuates and has a tendency to change when the level of the interest rate changes. Thus to get a truly accurate assessment of interest-rate risk, a financial institution manager has to assess what might happen to the slope of the yield curve when the level of the interest rate changes and then take this information into account when assessing interest-rate risk. In addition, duration gap analysis is based on the approximation in Equation 3 and thus only works well for small changes in interest rates.

A problem with income gap analysis is that as we have seen, the financial institution manager must make estimates of the proportion of supposedly fixed-rate assets and liabilities that may be rate-sensitive. This involves estimates of the likelihood of prepayment of loans or customer shifts out of deposits when interest rates change. Such guesses are not easy to make, and as a result, the financial institution manager's estimates of income gaps may not be very accurate. A similar problem occurs in calculating durations of assets and liabilities because many of the cash payments are uncertain. Thus the estimate of the duration gap might not be accurate either.

Do these problems mean that managers of banks and other financial institutions should give up on gap analysis as a tool for measuring interest-rate risk? Financial institutions do use more sophisticated approaches to measuring interest-rate risk, such as scenario analysis and value-at-risk analysis, which make greater use of computers to more accurately measure changes in prices of assets when interest rates change. Income and duration gap analyses, however, still provide simple frameworks to help financial institution managers to get a first assessment of interest-rate risk, and they are thus useful tools in the financial institution managers' toolkit.

THE PRACTISING FINANCIAL INSTITUTION MANAGER

Strategies for Managing Interest-Rate Risk

Once financial institution managers have done the duration and income gap analysis for their institutions, they must decide which alternative strategies to pursue. If the manager of the First Bank firmly believes that interest rates will fall in the future, he or she may be willing to take no action knowing that the bank has more rate-sensitive liabilities than rate-sensitive assets and so will benefit from the expected interest-rate decline. However, the bank manager also realizes that the First Bank is subject to substantial interest-rate risk because there is always a possibility that interest rates will rise rather than fall, and as we have seen, this outcome could bankrupt the bank. The manager might try to shorten the duration of the bank's assets to increase their rate sensitivity either by purchasing assets of shorter maturity or by converting fixed-rate loans into adjustable-rate loans. Alternatively, the bank manager could lengthen the duration of the liabilities. With these adjustments to the bank's assets and liabilities, the bank would be less affected by interest-rate swings.

For example, the bank manager might decide to eliminate the income gap by increasing the amount of rate-sensitive assets to \$49.5 million to equal the \$49.5 million of rate-sensitive liabilities. Or the manager could reduce rate-sensitive liabilities to \$32 million so that they equal rate-sensitive assets. In either case, the income gap would now be zero, so a change in interest rates would have no effect on bank profits in the coming year.

Alternatively, the bank manager might decide to immunize the market value of the bank's net worth completely from interest-rate risk by adjusting assets and liabilities so that the duration gap is equal to zero. To do this, the manager can set DUR_{gap} equal to zero in Equation 4 and solve for DUR_a:

$$DUR_a = \frac{L}{A} \times DUR_l = \frac{95}{100} \times 1.03 = 0.98$$

These calculations reveal that the manager should reduce the average duration of the bank's assets to 0.98 year. To check that the duration gap is set equal to zero, the calculation is

$$DUR_{gap} = 0.98 - \left(\frac{95}{100} \times 1.03\right) = 0$$

In this case, as in Equation 5, the market value of net worth would remain unchanged when interest rates change. Alternatively, the bank manager could calculate the value of the duration of the liabilities that would produce a duration gap of zero. To do this would involve setting DUR_{gap} equal to zero in Equation 4 and solving for DUR_l:

$$DUR_l = DUR_a \times \frac{A}{L} = 2.70 \times \frac{100}{95} = 2.84$$

This calculation reveals that the interest-rate risk could also be eliminated by increasing the average duration of the bank's liabilities to 2.84 years. The manager again checks that the duration gap is set equal to zero by calculating

$$DUR_{gap} = 2.70 - \left(\frac{95}{100} \times 2.84\right) = 0$$

Study Guide To see if you understand how a financial institution manager can protect income and net worth from interest-rate risk, first calculate how the Friendly Finance Company might change the amount of its rate-sensitive assets or its rate-sensitive liabilities to eliminate the income gap. You should find that the income gap can be eliminated either by reducing the amount of rate-sensitive assets to $43 million or by raising the amount of rate-sensitive liabilities to $55 million. Also do the calculations to determine what modifications to the duration of the assets or liabilities would immunize the market value of Friendly Finance's net worth from interest-rate risk. You should find that interest-rate risk would be eliminated if the duration of the assets were set to 2.49 years or if the duration of the liabilities were set to 1.29 years.

One problem with eliminating a financial institution's interest-rate risk by altering the balance sheet is that doing so might be very costly in the short run. The financial institution may be locked into assets and liabilities of particular durations because of its field of expertise. Fortunately, recently developed financial instruments, such as financial futures, options, and interest-rate swaps, help financial institutions manage their interest-rate risk without requiring them to rearrange their balance sheets. We discuss these instruments and how they can be used to manage interest-rate risk in the next chapter.

SUMMARY

1. The concepts of adverse selection and moral hazard explain the origin of many credit risk management principles involving loan activities, including screening and monitoring, development of long-term customer relationships, loan commitments, collateral, compensating balances, and credit rationing.
2. With the increased volatility of interest rates that occurred in recent years, financial institutions became more concerned about their exposure to interest-rate risk. Income gap and duration gap analyses tell a financial institution if it has fewer rate-sensitive assets than liabilities (in which case a rise in interest rates will reduce income and a fall in interest rates will raise it) or more rate-sensitive assets than liabilities (in which case a rise in interest rates will raise income and a fall in interest rates will reduce it). Financial institutions can manage interest-rate risk by modifying their balance sheets and by making use of new financial instruments.

KEY TERMS

compensating balance, *p. 554*
credit rationing, *p. 555*
duration gap analysis, *p. 559*
gap analysis (income gap analysis), *p. 557*
loan commitment, *p. 554*
secured loan, *p. 554*

QUESTIONS AND PROBLEMS

1. Can a financial institution keep borrowers from engaging in risky activities if there are no restrictive covenants written into the loan agreement?

***2.** Why are secured loans an important method of lending for financial institutions?

3. "If more customers want to borrow funds at the prevailing interest rate, a financial institution can increase its profits by raising interest rates on its loans." Is this statement true, false, or uncertain? Explain your answer.

***4.** Why is being nosy a desirable trait for a banker?

5. A bank almost always insists that the firms it lends to keep compensating balances at the bank. Why?

***6.** "Because diversification is a desirable strategy for avoiding risk, it never makes sense for a financial institution to specialize in making specific types of loans." Is this statement true, false, or uncertain? Explain your answer.

For Problems 7–14, assume that the First Bank initially has the balance sheet shown on page 556 and that interest rates are initially at 10%.

7. If the First Bank sells $10 million of its securities with maturities greater than two years and replaces them with securities maturing in less than one year, what is the income gap for the bank? What will happen to profits next year if interest rates fall by 3 percentage points?

***8.** If the First Bank decides to convert $5 million of its fixed-rate mortgages into variable-rate mortgages, what happens to its interest-rate risk? Explain with gap analysis.

9. If the manager of the First Bank revises the estimate of the percentage of fixed-rate mortgages that are repaid within a year from 20% to 10%, what will be the revised estimate of the interest-rate risk the bank faces? What will happen to profits next year if interest rates fall by 2 percentage points?

***10.** If the manager of the First Bank revises the estimate of the percentage of chequable deposits that are rate-sensitive from 10% to 25%, what will be the revised estimate of the interest-rate risk the bank faces? What will happen to profits next year if interest rates rise by 5 percentage points?

11. Given the estimates of duration in Table 1 on page 560, what will happen to the bank's net worth if interest rates rise by 10 percentage points? Will the bank stay in business? Why or why not?

***12.** If the manager of the First Bank revises the estimates of the duration of the bank's assets to four years and liabilities to two years, what is the effect on net worth if interest rates rise by 2 percentage points?

13. Given the estimates of duration in Problem 12, how should the bank alter the duration of its assets to immunize its net worth from interest-rate risk?

***14.** Given the estimates of duration in Problem 12, how should the bank alter the duration of its liabilities to immunize its net worth from interest-rate risk?

For Problems 15–20, assume that the Friendly Finance Company initially has the balance sheet shown on page 563 and that interest rates are initially at 8%.

15. If the manager of the Friendly Finance Company decides to sell off $10 million of the company's consumer loans, half maturing within one year and half maturing in greater than two years, and uses the resulting funds to buy $10 million of treasury bills, what is the income gap for the company? What will happen to profits next year if interest rates fall by 5 percentage points? How could the Friendly Finance Company alter its balance sheet to immunize its income from this change in interest rates?

***16.** If the Friendly Finance Company raises an additional $20 million with commercial paper and uses the funds to make $20 million of consumer loans that mature in less than one year, what happens to its interest-rate risk? In this situation, what additional changes could it make in its balance sheet to eliminate the income gap?

17. Given the estimates of duration in Table 2 on page 564, what will happen to the Friendly Finance Company's net worth if interest rates rise by 3 percentage points? Will the company stay in business? Why or why not?

***18.** If the manager of the Friendly Finance Company revises the estimates of the duration of the company's assets to two years and liabilities to four years, what is the effect on net worth if interest rates rise by 3 percentage points?

19. Given the estimates of duration in Problem 18, how should the Friendly Finance Company alter the duration of its assets to immunize its net worth from interest-rate risk?

***20.** Given the estimates of duration in Problem 18, how should the Friendly Finance Company alter the duration of its liabilities to immunize its net worth from interest-rate risk?

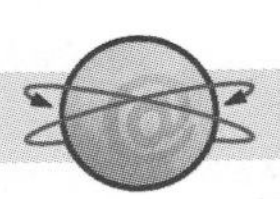

WEB EXERCISES

Risk Management in Financial Institutions

1. This chapter discussed the need financial institutions have to control credit risk by lending to creditworthy borrowers. If you allow your credit to deteriorate, you may find yourself unable to borrow when you need to. Go to http://www.quicken.com/cms/viewers/article/banking/39654 and assess your own creditworthiness. What can you do to improve your appeal to lenders?

2. The CDIC is extremely concerned with risk management in banks. High-risk banks are more likely to fail and cost the CDIC money. The CDIC regularly examines banks and rates them using a system called CAMELS. Go to http://www.fdic.gov/regulations/safety/manual/index.html. What does the acronym CAMELS stand for? Go to Part VII. 7.1 and review the discussion of Market Risk. Summarize the interest-rate risk-measurement methods.

Chapter 23 Hedging with Financial Derivatives

Preview

Starting in the 1970s and increasingly in the 1980s and 1990s, the world became a riskier place for financial institutions. Swings in interest rates widened, and the bond and stock markets went through some episodes of increased volatility. As a result of these developments, managers of financial institutions have become more concerned with reducing the risk their institutions face. Given the greater demand for risk reduction, the process of financial innovation described in Chapter 15 came to the rescue by producing new financial instruments that help financial institution managers manage risk better. These instruments, called **financial derivatives**, have payoffs that are linked to previously issued securities and are extremely useful risk reduction tools.

In this chapter we look at the most important financial derivatives that managers of financial institutions use to reduce risk: forward contracts, financial futures, options, and swaps. We examine not only how markets for each of these financial derivatives work but also how each can be used by financial institution managers to reduce risk.

HEDGING

Financial derivatives are so effective in reducing risk because they enable financial institutions to **hedge**, that is, engage in a financial transaction that reduces or eliminates risk. When a financial institution has bought an asset, it is said to have taken a **long position**, and this exposes the institution to risk if the returns on the asset are uncertain. On the other hand, if it has sold an asset that it has agreed to deliver to another party at a future date, it is said to have taken a **short position**, and this can also expose the institution to risk. Financial derivatives can be used to reduce risk by invoking the following basic principle of hedging: ***Hedging risk involves engaging in a financial transaction that offsets a long position by taking an additional short position, or offsets a short position by taking an additional long position.*** In other words, if a financial institution has *bought* a security and has therefore taken a long position, it conducts a hedge by contracting to *sell* that security (take a short position) at some future date. Alternatively, if it has taken a short position by *selling* a security that it needs to deliver at a future date, then it conducts a hedge by contracting to *buy* that security (take a long position) at a future date. We first look at how this principle can be applied using forward contracts.

FORWARD MARKETS

Forward contracts are agreements by two parties to engage in a financial transaction at a future (forward) point in time. Here we focus on forward contracts that are linked to debt instruments, called **interest-rate forward contracts**; later in the chapter we discuss forward contracts for foreign currencies.

Interest-Rate Forward Contracts

Interest-rate forward contracts involve the future sale of a debt instrument and have several dimensions: (1) specification of the actual debt instrument that will be delivered at a future date, (2) amount of the debt instrument to be delivered, (3) price (interest rate) on the debt instrument when it is delivered, and (4) date on which delivery will take place. An example of an interest-rate forward contract might be an agreement for the First Bank to sell to the Rock Solid Insurance Company, one year from today, $5 million face value of the 8s of 2023 Canada bonds (coupon bonds with an 8% coupon rate that mature in 2023) at a price that yields the same interest rate on these bonds as today's, say, 8%. Because Rock Solid will buy the securities at a future date, it has taken a long position, while the First Bank, which will sell the securities, has taken a short position.

THE PRACTISING FINANCIAL INSTITUTION MANAGER

Hedging Interest-Rate Risk with Forward Contracts

To understand why the First Bank might want to enter into this forward contract, suppose that you are the manager of the First Bank and have previously bought $5 million of the 8s of 2023 Canada bonds, which currently sell at par value and so their yield to maturity is also 8%. Because these are long-term bonds, you recognize that you are exposed to substantial interest-rate risk and worry that if interest rates rise in the future, the price of these bonds will fall, resulting in a substantial capital loss that may cost you your job. How do you hedge this risk?

Knowing the basic principle of hedging, you see that your long position in these bonds must be offset by a short position with a forward contract. That is, you need to contract to sell these bonds at a future date at the current par value price. As a result you agree with another party, in this case, Rock Solid Insurance Company, to sell them the $5 million of the 8s of 2023 Canada bonds at par one year from today. By entering into this forward contract, you have locked in the future price and so have eliminated the price risk First Bank faces from interest-rate changes. In other words, you have successfully hedged against interest-rate risk.

Why would the Rock Solid Insurance Company want to enter into the forward contract with the First Bank? Rock Solid expects to receive premiums of $5 million in one year's time that it will want to invest in the 8s of 2023 but worries that interest rates on these bonds will decline between now and next year. By using the forward contract, it is able to lock in the 8% interest rate on the Canada bonds (which will be sold to it by the First Bank).

Pros and Cons of Forward Contracts

The advantage of forward contracts is that they can be as flexible as the parties involved want them to be. This means that an institution like the First Bank may be able to hedge completely the interest-rate risk for the exact security it is holding in its portfolio, just as it has in our example.

However, forward contracts suffer from two problems that severely limit their usefulness. The first is that it may be very hard for an institution like the First Bank to find another party (called a *counterparty*) to make the contract with. There are brokers to facilitate the matching up of parties like the First Bank with the Rock Solid Insurance Company, but there may be few institutions that want to engage in a forward contract specifically for the 8s of 2023. This means that it may prove impossible to find a counterparty when a financial institution like the First Bank wants to make a specific type of forward contract. Furthermore, even if the First Bank finds a counterparty, it may not get as high a price as it wants because there may not be anyone else to make the deal with. A serious problem for the market in interest-rate forward contracts, then, is that it may be difficult to make the financial transaction or that it will have to be made at a disadvantageous price; in the parlance of the financial world, this market suffers from a *lack of liquidity*. (Note that this use of the term *liquidity* when it is applied to a market is somewhat broader than its use when it is applied to an asset. For an asset, liquidity refers to the ease with which the asset can be turned into cash, whereas for a market, liquidity refers to the ease of carrying out financial transactions.)

The second problem with forward contracts is that they are subject to default risk. Suppose that in one year's time, interest rates rise so that the price of the 8s of 2023 falls. The Rock Solid Insurance Company might then decide that it would like to default on the forward contract with the First Bank because it can now buy the bonds at a price lower than the agreed price in the forward contract. Or perhaps Rock Solid may not have been rock solid and will have gone bust during the year and so is no longer available to complete the terms of the forward contract. Because there is no outside organization guaranteeing the contract, the only recourse is for the First Bank to go to the courts to sue Rock Solid, but this process will be costly. Furthermore, if Rock Solid is already bankrupt, the First Bank will suffer a loss; the bank can no longer sell the 8s of 2023 at the price it had agreed with Rock Solid but instead will have to sell at a price well below that because the price of these bonds has fallen.

The presence of default risk in forward contracts means that parties to these contracts must check each other out to be sure that the counterparty is both financially sound and likely to be honest and live up to its contractual obligations. Because this is a costly process and because all the adverse selection and moral hazard problems discussed in earlier chapters apply, default risk is a major barrier to the use of interest-rate forward contracts. When the default risk problem is combined with a lack of liquidity, we see that these contracts may be of limited usefulness to financial institutions. Although there is a market for interest-rate forward contracts, particularly in mortgage-backed and Canada securities, it is not nearly as large as the financial futures market, to which we turn next.

FINANCIAL FUTURES MARKETS

Given the default risk and liquidity problems in the interest-rate forward market, another solution to hedging interest-rate, stock market, and foreign exchange risks was needed. This solution was provided by the development of financial futures contracts by the Chicago Board of Trade starting in 1975.

Financial futures are classified as (1) interest-rate futures, (2) stock index futures, and (3) currency futures. In Canada, such contracts are traded in the Montreal Exchange that maintains active markets in short- and long-term Canada bond futures and stock indexes futures. In what follows, we discuss interest-rate and stock index futures. Later in the chapter we also discuss currency futures.

Interest-Rate Futures Contracts

An **interest-rate futures contract** is similar to an interest-rate forward contract in that it specifies that a financial instrument must be delivered by one party to another on a stated future date. However, it differs from an interest-rate forward contract in several ways that overcome some of the liquidity and default problems of forward markets.

To understand what interest rate futures contracts are all about, let's look at one of the most widely traded futures contracts, that for 10-year Canada bonds, which are traded on the Montreal Exchange (ME). (An illustration of how prices on these contracts are quoted can be found in the "Following the Financial News" box.) The contract value is for $100 000 face value of bonds. Prices are quoted in points, with each point equal to $1000, and the smallest change in price is one hundredth of a point ($10). This contract specifies that the bonds to be delivered must have at least 10 years to maturity at the delivery date. If the Canada bonds delivered to settle the futures contract have a coupon rate different from the 8% specified in the futures contract, the amount of bonds to be delivered is adjusted to reflect the difference in value between the delivered bonds and the 8% coupon bond. In line with the terminology used for forward contracts, parties who have bought a futures contract and thereby agreed to buy (take delivery of) the bonds are said to have

FOLLOWING THE FINANCIAL NEWS

Interest-Rate Futures

The prices for interest-rate futures contracts are published daily. In the *National Post: Financial Post*, these prices are found in the "Futures Prices" columns under the "Interest Rate" heading. An excerpt is reproduced here.

Lifetime High	Lifetime Low	Mth	Open	Daily High	Daily Low	Settle	Chg	Prev. op. int
Interest Rate								
Canadian Govt. Bonds 5 Year (ME)								
$100,000, points of 100%; 0.01=$10 per contract								
Vol.	0		Prev. vol. 0		Prev. open int.		0	
Canadian Govt. Bonds 10 Year (ME)								
$100,000, points of 100%; 0.01=$10 per contract								
104.05	99.55	June02	102.58	102.67	102.01	102.03	−0.83	63,102
Vol.	6,675		Prev. vol. 6,619		Prev. open int. 63,102			

The following information is included in each column. The Montreal Exchange's contract for delivery of 10-year Canadian government bonds in June 2002 is used as an example.

Lifetime High: Highest price ever; each point corresponds to $1000 of face value—104.05 is $104 050 (for $100 000 face value) for the June 2002 contract.

Lifetime Low: Lowest price ever—99.55 is $99 550 for the June contract.

Mth: Maturity month of the futures contract.

Open: Opening price—102.58 is $102 580 for the June contract.

High: Highest traded price that day—102.67 is $102 670 for the June contract.

Low: Lowest traded price that day—102.01 is $102 010 for the June contract.

Settle: Settlement price, the closing price that day—102.03 is $102 030 for the June contract.

Chg: Change in the settlement price from the previous day; -0.83 is -$830 for the June contract.

Prev. op. int.: Number of contracts outstanding—63 102 for the June contract, with a face value of $6.3 billion (63 102 × $100 000)

Source: *The National Post: Financial Post*, May 10, 2002, p. *FP14*

taken a *long position*, and parties who have sold a futures contract and thereby agreed to sell (deliver) the bonds have taken a *short position*.

To make our understanding of this contract more concrete, let's consider what happens when you buy or sell one of these Canada bond futures contracts. Let's say that on February 1, you sell one $100 000 June contract at a price of 115 (that is, $115 000). By selling this contract, you agree to deliver $100 000 face value of the long-term Canada bonds to the contract's counterparty at the end of June for $115 000. By buying the contract at a price of 115, the buyer has agreed to pay $115 000 for the $100 000 face value of bonds when you deliver them at the end of June. If interest rates on long-term bonds rise so that when the contract matures at the end of June the price of these bonds has fallen to 110 ($110 000 per $100 000 of face value), the buyer of the contract will have lost $5000 because he or she paid $115 000 for the bonds but can sell them only for the market price of $110 000. But you, the seller of the contract, will have gained $5000 because you can now sell the bonds to the buyer for $115 000 but have to pay only $110 000 for them in the market.

It is even easier to describe what happens to the parties who have purchased futures contracts and those who have sold futures contracts if we recognize the following fact: ***At the expiration date of a futures contract, the price of the contract is the same as the price of the underlying asset to be delivered.*** To see why this is the case, consider what happens on the expiration date of the June contract at the end of June when the price of the underlying $100 000 face value Canada bond is 110 ($110 000). If the futures contract is selling below 110, say, at 109, a trader can buy the contract for $109 000, take delivery of the bond, and immediately sell it for $110 000, thereby earning a quick profit of $1000. Because earning this profit involves no risk, it is a great deal that everyone would like to get in on. That means that everyone will try to buy the contract, and as a result, its price will rise. Only when the price rises to 110 will the profit opportunity cease to exist and the buying pressure disappear. Conversely, if the price of the futures contract is above 110, say, at 111, everyone will want to sell the contract. Now the sellers get $111 000 from selling the futures contract but have to pay only $110 000 for the Canada bonds that they must deliver to the buyer of the contract, and the $1000 difference is their profit. Because this profit involves no risk, traders will continue to sell the futures contract until its price falls back down to 110, at which price there are no longer any profits to be made. The elimination of riskless profit opportunities in the futures market is referred to as **arbitrage**, and it guarantees that the price of a futures contract at expiration equals the price of the underlying asset to be delivered.[1]

Armed with the fact that a futures contract at expiration equals the price of the underlying asset makes it even easier to see who profits and loses from such a contract when interest rates change. When interest rates have risen so that the price of the Canada bond is 110 on the expiration day at the end of June, the June Canada bond futures contract will also have a price of 110. Thus if you bought the contract for 115 in February, you have a loss of 5 points, or $5000 (5% of $100 000). But if you sold the futures contract at 115 in February, the decline in price to 110 means that you have a profit of 5 points, or $5000.

[1]In actuality, futures contracts sometimes set conditions for delivery of the underlying assets that cause the price of the contract at expiration to differ slightly from the price of the underlying assets. Because the difference in price is extremely small, we ignore it in this chapter.

THE PRACTISING FINANCIAL INSTITUTION MANAGER

Hedging with Interest-Rate Futures

As the manager of the First Bank, you can also use interest rate futures to hedge the interest-rate risk on its holdings of $5 million of the 8s of 2023 (Canada bonds with an 8% coupon rate that mature in 2023).

To see how to do this, suppose that in March 2003, the 8s of 2023 are the long-term bonds that would be delivered in the Montreal Exchange's Canada bond futures contract expiring one year in the future, in March 2004. Also suppose that the interest rate on these bonds is expected to remain at 8% over the next year so that both the 8s of 2023 and the futures contract are selling at par (i.e., the $5 million of bonds is selling for $5 million and the $100 000 futures contract is selling for $100 000). The basic principle of hedging indicates that you need to offset the long position in these bonds with a short position, so you have to sell the futures contract. But how many contracts should you sell? The number of contracts required to hedge the interest-rate risk is found by dividing the amount of the asset to be hedged by the dollar value of each contract, as is shown in Equation 1 below.

$$NC = VA/VC \tag{1}$$

where

NC = number of contracts for the hedge
VA = value of the asset
VC = value of each contract

EXAMPLE 1: Hedging with Interest-Rate Futures

The 8s of 2023 are the long-term bonds that would be delivered in the Montreal Exchange's Canada bond futures contract expiring one year in the future in March 2004. The interest rate on these bonds is expected to remain at 8% over the next year so that both the 8s of 2023 and the futures contract are selling at par. How many contracts must First Bank sell to remove its interest-rate exposure from its $5 million holdings of the 8s of 2023?[2]

Solution

$$VA = \$5 \text{ million}$$
$$VC = \$100\ 000$$

Thus

$$NC = \$5 \text{ million}/\$100\ 000 = 50$$

You therefore hedge the interest-rate risk by selling 50 of the Canada bond futures contracts.

[2] In the real world, designing a hedge is somewhat more complicated than the example here because the bond that is most likely to be delivered might not be an 8s of 2023.

Now suppose that over the next year, interest rates increase to 10% due to an increased threat of inflation. The value of the 8s of 2023 the First Bank is holding will then fall to $4 163 508 in March 2004.[3] Thus, the loss from the long position in these bonds is $836 492 as shown below:

Value on March 2004 @10% interest rate	$4 163 508
Value on March 2003 @8% interest rate	−$5 000 000
Loss	−$ 836 492

However, the short position in the 50 futures contracts that obligate you to deliver $5 million of the 8s of 2023 on March 2004 has a value equal to the $5 million of these bonds on that date, after the interest rate has risen to 10%. This value is $4 163 568, as we have seen above. Yet when you sold the futures contract, the buyer was obligated to pay you $5 million on the maturity date. Thus the gain from the short position on these contracts is also $836 492, as shown below:

Amount paid to you on March 2004, agreed in March 2003	$5 000 000
Cost of bonds delivered on March 2004 @10% interest rate	−$4 163 508
Gain	$ 836 492

Therefore the net gain for the First Bank is zero, showing that the hedge has been conducted successfully.

The hedge just described is called a **micro hedge** because the financial institution is hedging the interest-rate risk for a specific asset it is holding. A second type of hedge that financial institutions engage in is called a **macro hedge**, in which the hedge is for the institution's entire portfolio. For example, if a bank has more rate-sensitive liabilities than assets, we have seen in Chapter 22 that a rise in interest rates will cause the value of the bank to decline. By selling interest-rate future contracts that will yield a profit when interest rates rise, the bank can offset the losses on its overall portfolio from an interest-rate rise and thereby hedge its interest-rate risk.

Organization of Trading in Financial Futures Markets

Visit www.cme.com, the Website for the Chicago Mercantile Exchange.

Financial futures contracts are traded on organized exchanges such as the Chicago Board of Trade, the Chicago Mercantile Exchange, the Montreal Exchange, the London International Financial Futures Exchange, and the Marché à Terme International de France. These futures exchanges are highly competitive with one another, and each organization tries to design contracts and set rules that will increase the amount of futures trading on its exchange. The exchanges are also regulated to ensure that prices in the market are not being manipulated. The most widely traded financial futures contracts listed in the *Wall Street Journal* and the exchanges where they are traded (along with the number of contracts outstanding, called **open interest**, on January 2, 2002) are listed in Table 1 (interest-rate futures), Table 2 (stock-index futures), and Table 3 (currency futures).[4]

Given the globalization of other financial markets in recent years, it is not surprising that increased international competition has been occurring in financial futures markets as well.

[3]The value of the bonds can be calculated using a financial calculator as follows: FV = $5 000 000, PMT = $400 000, I = 10%, N = 19, PV = $4 163 508.

[4]For a more detailed treatment of financial futures and option markets, see Franklin R. Edwards and Cindy W. Ma, *Futures and Options* (New York: McGraw-Hill, 1992).

TABLE 1 Widely Traded Interest-Rate Futures Contracts

Type of Contract	Contract Size	Exchange*	Open Interest Jan. 2, 2002
A. Short-term debt contracts			
U.S. Treasury bills	$1 million	CME	533
30-day Federal funds	$5 million	CBT	31 714
1-month LIBOR	$3 million	CME	14 497
Eurodollar	$1 million	CME	4 229 780
Euroyen	100 million	CME	30 207
Sterling	£500 000	LIFFE	732 345
3-month Euribar	€1 million	LIFFE	1 714 847
Euroswiss franc	SF1 million	LIFFE	141 856
Canadian banker's acceptance	C$1 000 000	ME	504 056
B. Long-term debt contracts			
U.S. Treasury bonds	$100 000	CBT	418 017
U.S. Treasury notes	$100 000	CBT	538 391
5-year U.S. Treasury notes	$100 000	CBT	447 337
2-year U.S. Treasury notes	$200 000	CBT	69 559
Municipal Bond Index	$1000	CBT	7 736
Long Gilt	£50 000	LIFFE	58 147
10-year Euronational bonds	€100 000	MATIF	12 316
10-year German Euro bonds	€100 000	ME	54 300

Source: *Wall Street Journal*, January 2, 2002, p. C11.

*Exchange abbreviations: CME, Chicago Mercantile Exchange; CBT, Chicago Board of Trade; LIFFE, London International Financial Futures Exchange; ME, Montreal Exchange; MATIF, Marché à Terme International de France.

TABLE 2 Widely Traded Stock Index Futures Contracts

Type of Contract	Contract Size	Exchange*	Open Interest Jan. 2, 2002
Standard & Poor's 500 Index	$250 × index	CME	482 048
Standard & Poor's MIDCAP 400	$500 × index	CME	14 780
Nasdaq 100	$100 × index	CME	47 412
Nikkei 225 Stock Average	$5 × index	CME	12 587
Financial Times — Stock Exchange 100	£10 per point	LIFFE	356 840

Source: *Wall Street Journal*, January 2, 2002, p. C11.

*Exchange abbreviations: CME, Chicago Mercantile Exchange; LIFFE, London International Financial Futures Exchange.

TABLE 3 Widely Traded Currency Futures Contracts

Type of Contract	Contract Size	Exchange*	Open Interest Jan. 2, 2002
Yen	12 500 000 yen	CME	111 232
Euro	€125 000	CME	93 058
Canadian dollar	C$100 000	CME	58 305
British pound	£62 500	CME	23 591
Swiss franc	SF125 000	CME	35 097
Mexican peso	N$500 000	CME	26 902

Source: *Wall Street Journal*, January 2, 2002, p. C11.

*Exchange abbreviations: CME, Chicago Mercantile Exchange.

Globalization of Financial Futures Markets

At www.liffe.com, www.tse.or.jp, www.matif.fr, and www.ose.or.jp, you can learn more about futures exchanges.

Because futures exchanges in the United States were the first to develop financial futures, they dominated the trading of financial futures in the early 1980s. For example, in 1985, all of the top ten futures contracts were traded on exchanges in the United States. With the rapid growth of financial futures markets and the resulting high profits made by the American exchanges, exchanges in other countries saw a profit opportunity and began to enter this business. By the 1990s, Eurodollar contracts traded on the London International Financial Futures Exchange, Japanese government bond contracts and Euroyen contracts traded on the Tokyo Stock Exchange, French government bond contracts traded on the Marché à Terme International de France, and Nikkei 225 contracts traded on the Osaka Securities Exchange. All became among the most widely traded futures contracts in the world. Even developing countries are getting into the act. In 1996, seven developing countries (also referred to as *emerging-market countries*) established futures exchanges, and this number is expected to double within a few years.

International competition has also spurred knockoffs of the most popular financial futures contracts initially developed in the United States. These contracts traded on financial futures exchanges in other countries are virtually identical to those traded in the United States and have the advantage that they can be traded when the American exchanges are closed. The movement to 24-hour-a-day trading in financial futures has been further stimulated by the development of the Globex electronic trading system, which allows traders throughout the world to trade futures even when the exchanges are not officially open. Financial futures trading is thus well on the way to being completely internationalized, and competition between financial futures exchanges in the United States and other countries will continue to be intense in the future.

Explaining the Success of Futures Markets

There are several differences between financial futures and forward contracts and in the organization of their markets that help explain why financial futures markets, like those for Canada bonds have been so successful.

Several features of futures contracts were designed to overcome the liquidity problem inherent in forward contracts. The first feature is that, in contrast to forward contracts, the quantities delivered and the delivery dates of futures contracts are standardized, making it more likely that different parties can be matched up in the futures market, thereby increasing the liquidity of the market. In the case of the 10-year Canada bond futures contract, the quantity delivered is $100 000 face value of bonds, and the delivery dates are set to be the last business day of March, June, September, and December. The second feature is that after the futures contract has been bought or sold, it can be traded (bought or sold) again at any time until the delivery date. In contrast, once a forward contract is agreed on, it typically cannot be traded. The third feature is that in a futures contract, not just one specific type of Canada bond is deliverable on the delivery date, as in a forward contract. Instead, any Canada bond that matures in more than 10 years and is not callable for 10 years is eligible for delivery. Allowing continuous trading also increases the liquidity of the futures market, as does the ability to deliver a range of Canada bonds rather than one specific bond.

Another reason why futures contracts specify that more than one bond is eligible for delivery is to limit the possibility that someone might corner the market and "squeeze" traders who have sold contracts. To corner the market, someone buys up all the deliverable securities so that investors with a short position cannot obtain from anyone else the securities that they contractually must deliver on the delivery date. As a result, the person who has cornered the market can set exorbitant prices for the securities that investors with a short position must buy to fulfill their obligations under the futures contract. The person who has cornered the market makes a fortune, but investors with a short position take a terrific loss. Clearly, the possibility that corners might occur in the market will discourage people from taking a short position and might therefore decrease the size of the market. By allowing many different securities to be delivered, the futures contract makes it harder for anyone to corner the market because a much larger amount of securities would have to be purchased to establish the corner. Corners are more than a theoretical possibility, as Box 1 indicates, and are a concern to both regulators and the organized exchanges that design futures contracts.

Trading in the futures market has been organized differently from trading in forward markets to overcome the default risk problems arising in forward contracts. In both types, for every contract there must be a buyer who is taking a long position and a seller who is taking a short position. However, the buyer and seller of a futures contract make their contract not with each other but with the clearinghouse associated with the futures exchange. This setup means that the buyer of the futures contract does not need to worry about the financial health or trustworthiness of the seller, or vice versa, as in the forward market. As long as the clearinghouse is financially solid, buyers and sellers of futures contracts do not have to worry about default risk.

To make sure that the clearinghouse is financially sound and does not run into financial difficulties that might jeopardize its contracts, buyers or sellers of futures contracts must put an initial deposit, called a **margin requirement**, of perhaps $2000 per Canada bond contract into a margin account kept at their brokerage firm. Futures contracts are then **marked to market** every day. What this means is that at the end of every trading day, the change in the value of the futures contract is added to or subtracted from the margin account. Suppose that after buying the Canada bond contract at a price of 115 on Wednesday morning, its closing

BOX 1

The Hunt Brothers and the Silver Crash

In early 1979, two Texas billionaires, W. Herbert Hunt and his brother, Nelson Bunker Hunt, decided that they were going to get into the silver market in a big way. Herbert stated his reasoning for purchasing silver as follows: "I became convinced that the economy of the United States was in a weakening condition. This reinforced my belief that investment in precious metals was wise . . . because of rampant inflation." Although the Hunts' stated reason for purchasing silver was that it was a good investment, others felt that their real motive was to establish a corner in the silver market. Along with other associates, several of them from the Saudi royal family, the Hunts purchased close to 300 million ounces of silver in the form of either actual bullion or silver futures contracts. The result was that the price of silver rose from $6 an ounce to over $50 an ounce by January 1980.

Once the regulators and the futures exchanges got wind of what the Hunts were up to, they decided to take action to eliminate the possibility of a corner by limiting to 2000 the number of contracts that any single trader could hold. This limit, which was equivalent to 10 million ounces, was only a small fraction of what the Hunts were holding, and so they were forced to sell. The silver market collapsed soon afterward, with the price of silver declining back to below $10 an ounce. The losses to the Hunts were estimated to be in excess of $1 billion, and they soon found themselves in financial difficulty. They had to go into debt to the tune of $1.1 billion, mortgaging not only the family's holdings in the Placid Oil Company but also 75 000 head of cattle, a stable of thoroughbred horses, paintings, jewellery, and even such mundane items as irrigation pumps and lawn mowers. Eventually both Hunt brothers were forced into declaring personal bankruptcy, earning them the dubious distinction of declaring the largest personal bankruptcies ever in the United States.

Nelson and Herbert Hunt paid a heavy price for their excursion into the silver market, but at least Nelson retained his sense of humour. When asked right after the collapse of the silver market how he felt about his losses, he said, "A billion dollars isn't what it used to be."

Source: G. Christian Hill, "Dynasty's Decline: The Current Question About the Hunts of Dallas: How Poor Are They?" *Wall Street Journal,* November 14, 1984, p. C28. Republished by permission of Dow Jones, Inc. via Copyright Clearance Center, Inc.

price at the end of the day, the *settlement price*, falls to 114. You now have a loss of 1 point, or $1000, on the contract, and the seller who sold you the contract has a gain of 1 point, or $1000. The $1000 gain is added to the seller's margin account, making a total of $3000 in that account, and the $1000 loss is subtracted from your account, so you now only have $1000 in your account. If the amount in this margin account falls below the maintenance margin requirement (which can be the same as the initial requirement but is usually a little less), the trader is required to add money to the account. For example, if the maintenance margin requirement is also $2000, you would have to add $1000 to your account to bring it up to $2000. Margin requirements and marking to market make it far less likely that a trader will default on a contract, thus protecting the futures exchange from losses.

A final advantage that futures markets have over forward markets is that most futures contracts do not result in delivery of the underlying asset on the expiration date, whereas forward contracts do. A trader who sold a futures contract is allowed to avoid delivery on the expiration date by making an offsetting purchase of a futures contract. Because the simultaneous holding of the long and short positions means that the trader would in effect be delivering the bonds to itself, under the exchange rules the trader is allowed to cancel both contracts. Allowing traders to cancel their contracts in this way lowers the cost of conducting trades in the futures market relative to the forward market in that a futures trader can avoid the costs of physical delivery, which is not so easy with forward contracts.

THE PRACTISING FINANCIAL INSTITUTION MANAGER

Hedging Foreign Exchange Risk with Forward and Futures Contracts

As we discussed in Chapter 12, foreign exchange rates have been highly volatile in recent years. The large fluctuations in exchange rates subject financial institutions and other businesses to significant foreign exchange risk because they generate substantial gains and losses. Luckily for financial institution managers, the financial derivatives discussed in this chapter—forward and financial futures contracts—can be used to hedge foreign exchange risk.

To understand how financial institution managers manage foreign exchange risk, let's suppose that in January, the First Bank's customer Frivolous Luxuries, Inc., is due a payment of 10 million euros in two months for $14 million worth of goods it has just sold in Germany. Frivolous Luxuries is concerned that if the value of the euro falls substantially from its current value of $1.40, the company might suffer a large loss because the 10 million euro payment will no longer be worth $14 million. So Sam, the CEO of Frivolous Luxuries, calls up his friend Mona, the manager of the First Bank, and asks her to hedge this foreign exchange risk for his company. Let's see how the bank manager does this using forward and financial futures contracts.

Hedging Foreign Exchange Risk with Forward Contracts

Forward markets in foreign exchange have been highly developed by commercial banks and investment banking operations that engage in extensive foreign exchange trading and so are widely used to hedge foreign exchange risk. Mona knows that she can use this market to hedge the foreign exchange risk for Frivolous Luxuries. Such a hedge is quite straightforward for her to execute. Because the payment of euros in two months means that at that time Sam would hold a long position in euros, Mona knows that the basic principle of hedging indicates that she should offset this long position by a short position.

Thus, she just enters a forward contract that obligates her to sell 10 million euros two months from now in exchange for dollars at the current forward rate of $1.40 per euro.[5]

In two months, when her customer receives the 14 million euros, the forward contract ensures that it is exchanged for dollars at an exchange rate of $1.40 per euro, thus yielding $14 million. No matter what happens to future exchange rates, Frivolous Luxuries will be guaranteed $14 million for the goods it sold in Germany. Mona calls up her friend Sam to let him know that his company is now protected from any foreign exchange movements, and he thanks her for her help.

Hedging Foreign Exchange Risk with Futures Contracts

As an alternative, Mona could have used the currency futures market to hedge the foreign exchange risk. In this case, she would see that the Chicago Mercantile Exchange has a euro contract with a contract amount of 125 000 euros and a price of $1.40 per euro. To do the hedge, Mona must sell euros as with the forward contract, to the tune of 14 million euros of the March futures.

EXAMPLE 2: Hedging with Foreign Exchange Futures Contracts

How many of the Chicago Mercantile Exchange March euro contracts must Mona sell in order to hedge the 10 million euro payment due in March?

Solution

Using Equation 1:

$$VA = 10 \text{ million euros}$$

$$VC = 125\,000 \text{ euros}$$

Thus

$$NC = 10 \text{ million}/125\,000 = 80$$

Mona does the hedge by selling 80 of the CME euro contracts.

Given the $1.40 per euro price, the sale of the contract yields 80 × 125 000 euros = $10 million. The futures hedge thus again enables her to lock in the exchange rate for Frivolous Luxuries so that it gets its payment of $14 million.

One advantage of using the futures market is that the contract size of 125 000 euros, worth $175 000, is quite a bit smaller than the minimum size of a forward contract, which is usually $1 million or more. However, in this case, the bank manager is making a large enough transaction that she can use either the forward or the futures market. Her choice depends on whether the transaction costs are lower in one market than in the other. If the First Bank is active in the forward mar-

[5]The forward exchange rate will probably differ slightly from the current spot rate of $1.40 per euro because the interest rates in Europe and Canada may not be equal. In that case, as we saw in Equation 2 in Chapter 12, the future expected exchange rate will not equal the current spot rate and neither will the forward rate. However, since interest differentials have typically been less than 6% at an annual rate (1% bimonthly), the expected appreciation or depreciation of the euro over a two-month period has always been less than 1%. Thus the forward rate is always close to the current spot rate, and so our assumption in the example that the forward rate and the spot rate are the same is a reasonable one.

ket, that market would probably have the lower transaction costs, but if First Bank rarely deals in foreign exchange forward contracts, the bank manager may do better by sticking with the futures market.

STOCK INDEX FUTURES

More detailed information about stock index futures is available at www.usafutures.com/stockindexfutures.htm

As we have seen, interest rate futures markets can be useful in hedging interest-rate risk. However, financial institution managers, particularly those who manage mutual funds, pension funds, and insurance companies, also worry about **stock market risk**, the risk that occurs because stock prices fluctuate. Stock index futures were developed in 1982 to meet the need to manage stock market risk, and they have become among the most widely traded of all futures contracts. The futures trading in stock price indexes is now controversial (see Box 2) because critics assert that it has led to substantial increases in market volatility, especially in such episodes as 1987's stock market crash.

Stock Index Futures Contracts

To understand stock index futures contracts, let's look at the Standard & Poor's 500 Index futures contract (shown in the "Following the Financial News" box), the most widely traded stock index futures contract in North America. (The S&P 500 Index measures the value of 500 of the most widely traded stocks in the United States.) Stock index futures contracts differ from most other financial futures contracts in that they are settled with a cash delivery rather than with the delivery of a security. Cash settlement gives these contracts the advantage of a high degree of liquidity and also rules out the possibility of anyone's cornering the market. In the case of the S&P 500 Index contract, at the final settlement date, the cash delivery due is $250 times the index, so if the index is at 1000 on the final settlement date, $250 000

BOX 2

Program Trading and Portfolio Insurance: Were They to Blame for the Stock Market Crash of 1987?

In the aftermath of the Black Monday crash on October 19, 1987, in which the U.S. stock market declined by over 20% and the Canadian market by 11% in one day, trading strategies involving stock price index futures markets have been accused of being culprits in the market collapse. One such strategy, called program trading, involves computer-directed trading between the stock index futures and the stocks whose prices are reflected in the stock price index. Program trading is a form of arbitrage conducted to keep stock index futures and stock prices in line with each other. For example, when the price of the stock index futures contract is far below the prices of the underlying stocks in the index, program traders buy index futures, thereby increasing their price, and sell the stocks, thereby lowering their price. Critics of program trading assert that the sharp fall in stock index futures prices on Black Monday led to massive selling in the stock market to keep stock prices in line with the stock index futures prices.

Some experts also blame portfolio insurance for amplifying the crash because they feel that when the stock market started to fall, uncertainty in the market increased, and the resulting increased desire to hedge stocks led to massive selling of stock index futures. The resulting large price declines in stock index futures contracts then led to massive selling of stocks by program traders to keep prices in line.

Because they view program trading and portfolio insurance as causes of the October 1987 market collapse, critics of stock index futures have advocated restrictions on their trading. In response, certain brokerage firms, as well as organized exchanges, have placed limits on program trading. For example, the New York Stock Exchange has curbed computerized program trading when the Dow Jones Industrial Average moves by more than 50 points in one day. However, some prominent finance scholars (among them Nobel laureate Merton Miller of the University of Chicago) do not accept the hypothesis that program trading and portfolio insurance provoked the stock market crash. They believe that the prices of stock index futures primarily reflect the same economic forces that move stock prices—changes in the market's underlying assessment of the value of stocks.

FOLLOWING THE FINANCIAL NEWS

Stock Index Futures

The prices for stock index futures contracts are published daily. In the *Wall Street Journal,* these prices are found in the section "Futures Prices" under the "Index" heading. An excerpt from this listing is reproduced here.

Index

S&P 500 INDEX (CME) $250 times index

						LIFETIME		OPEN
	OPEN	HIGH	LOW	SETTLE	CHANGE	HIGH	LOW	INTEREST
Mar	115950	116250	114100	114920	−10.10	134960	94100	479,906
June	....	....	....	115140	−10.40	170550	95030	12,645
Sept	115000	116950	115000	115470	−10.80	165670	95530	2,114

Est vol 31,660; vol Fri 35,552; open int 496,439, −2,076.
Idx prl: High 1161.16; Low 1148.04; Close 1148.08, −12.94.

Information for each contract is given in columns, as follows. (The March S&P 500 Index contract is used as an example.)

Open: Opening price; each point corresponds to $250 times the index—1159.50; that is, 1159.50 × $250 = $289 875 per contract

High: Highest traded price that day—1162.50, or $290 625 per contract

Low: Lowest traded price that day—1141.00, or $285 250 per contract

Settle: Settlement price, the closing price that day—1149.20, or $287 300 per contract

Chg: Change in the settlement price from the previous trading day— −10.10 points, or $2525 per contract

High: High price for the year—1349.60, or $337 400 per contract

Low: Low price for the year—941.00, or $235 250 per contract

Open Interest: Number of contracts outstanding—479 906, or a total value of $137 billion (= 479 906 × $287 300).

Source: Wall Street Journal, January 2, 2002, p. C11. Republished by permission of Dow Jones, Inc. via Copyright Clearance Center, Inc.

would be the amount due. The price quotes for this contract are also quoted in terms of index points, so a change of 1 point represents a change of $250 in the contract's value.

To understand what all this means, let's look at what happens when you buy or sell this futures contract. Suppose that on February 1, you sell one June contract at a price of 1000 (that is, $250 000). By selling the contract, you agree to a delivery amount due of $250 times the S&P 500 Index on the expiration date at the end of June. By buying the contract at a price of 1000, the buyer has agreed to pay $250 000 for the delivery amount due of $250 times the S&P 500 Index at the expiration date at the end of June. If the stock market falls so that the S&P 500 Index declines to 900 on the expiration date, the buyer of the contract will have lost $25 000 because he or she has agreed to pay $250 000 for the contract but has a delivery amount due of the $225 000 (900 × $250). But you, the seller of the contract, will have a profit of $25 000 because you agreed to receive a $250 000 purchase price for the contract but have a delivery amount due of only $225 000. Because the amount payable and due are netted out, only $25 000 will change hands; you, the seller of the contract, receive $25 000 from the buyer.

THE PRACTISING FINANCIAL INSTITUTION MANAGER
Hedging with Stock Index Futures

Financial institution managers can use stock index futures contracts to reduce stock market risk.

EXAMPLE 3: Hedging with Stock Index Futures

Suppose that in March 2004, Mort, the portfolio manager of the Rock Solid Insurance Company, has a portfolio of stocks valued at $100 million that moves percentagewise one-for-one with the S&P Index. Suppose also that the March 2005 S&P 500 Index contracts are currently selling at a price of 1000. How many of these contracts should Mort sell so that he hedges the stock market risk of this portfolio over the next year?

Solution

Because Mort is holding a long position, using the basic principle of hedging, he must offset it by taking a short position in which he sells S&P futures. To calculate the number of contracts he needs to sell, he uses Equation 1.

$$VA = \$100 \text{ million}$$

$$VC = \$250 \times 1000 = \$250\,000$$

Thus

$$NC = \$100 \text{ million}/\$250\,000 = 400$$

Mort's hedge therefore involves selling 400 S&P March 2005 futures contracts.

If the S&P Index falls 10% to 900, the $100 million portfolio will suffer a $10 million loss. At the same time, however, Mort makes a profit of 100 × $250 = $25 000 per contract because he agreed to be paid $250 000 for each contract at a price of 1000, but at a price of 900 on the expiration date he has a delivery amount of only $225 000 (900 × $250). Multiplied by 400 contracts, the $25 000 profit per contract yields a total profit of $10 million. The $10 million profit on the futures contract exactly offsets the loss on Rock Solid's stock portfolio, so Mort has been successful in hedging the stock market risk.

Why would Mort be willing to forgo profits when the stock market rises? One reason is that he might be worried that a bear market was imminent, so he wants to protect Rock Solid's portfolio from the coming decline (and so protect his job).

OPTIONS

Another vehicle for hedging interest-rate, foreign exchange, and stock market risk involves the use of options on financial instruments. **Options** are contracts that give the purchaser the option, or *right,* to buy or sell the underlying financial instrument at a specified price, called the **exercise price** or **strike price**, within a specific period of time (the *term to expiration*). The seller (sometimes called the *writer*) of the option is *obligated* to buy or sell the financial instrument to the purchaser if the owner of the option exercises the right to sell or buy. These option contract features are important enough to be emphasized: The *owner* or buyer of an option does not have to exercise the option; he or she can let the option expire without using it. Hence the *owner* of an option is *not obligated* to take any action but rather has the *right* to exercise the contract if he or she so chooses. The *seller* of an option, by contrast, has no choice in the matter; he or she *must* buy or sell the financial instrument if the owner exercises the option.

Because the right to buy or sell a financial instrument at a specified price has value, the owner of an option is willing to pay an amount for it called a **premium**. There are two types of option contracts: **American options** can be exercised *at any time up to* the expiration date of the contract, and **European options** can be exercised only *on* the expiration date.

Option contracts are written on a number of financial instruments (an example of which is shown in the "Following the Financial News" box). Options on individual stocks are called **stock options**, and such options have existed for a long time. Option contracts on financial futures called **financial futures options**, or, more commonly, **futures options**, were developed in 1982 and have become the most widely traded option contracts.

You might wonder why option contracts are more likely to be written on financial futures than on underlying financial instruments such as bonds. As you saw earlier in the chapter, at the expiration date, the price of the futures contract and of the deliverable debt instrument will be the same because of arbitrage. So it would seem that investors should be indifferent about having the option written on the financial instrument or on the futures contract. However, financial futures contracts have been so well designed that their markets are often more liquid than the markets in the underlying financial instruments. Investors would rather have the option contract written on the more liquid instrument, in this case the futures contract. That explains why the most popular futures options are written on many of the same futures contracts listed in Tables 1 to 3.

In Canada, the regulation of option markets is the responsibility of the Canadian Derivatives Clearing Corp. Inc. (CDCC), a firm that is jointly owned by Canada's stock exchanges: the Toronto Stock Exchange, the TSX Venture Exchange, and the Montreal Exchange. The regulation of U.S. option markets is

FOLLOWING THE FINANCIAL NEWS

Futures Options

The prices for financial futures options are published daily. In the *National Post: Financial Post*, they are found in the section "Futures Options." An excerpt from this listing is reproduced here.

Information for each contract is reported in columns, as follows. (The Montreal Exchange's option on its 3-month banker's acceptances futures contract is used as an example.)

Strike Price: Strike (exercise) price of each contract, which runs from 96.5 to 97

Calls-Settle: Premium (price) at settlement for call options on 3-month banker's acceptances futures expiring in the month listed, with each full point representing $1000; at a strike price of 96.75, the March call option's premium is 0.300, or $300 per contract

Puts-Settle: Premium (price) at settlement for put options on 3-month banker's acceptances futures expiring in the month listed, with each full point representing $1000; at a strike price of 96.75, the June put option's premium is 0.160, or $160 per contract

Interest Rate

Cdn. 3 Mth. Banker's Accept. (ME)
$1 000 000, points of 100%

	CALLS-SETTLE			PUTS-SETTLE		
Strike	Mar	June	Sept	Mar	June	Sept
96.500	0.535	0.520	0.540	0.005	0.090	0.280
96.625	0.415	0.425	0.460	0.005	0.120	0.325
96.750	0.300	0.340	0.385	0.015	0.160	0.375
96.875	0.200	0.260	0.320	0.040	0.205	0.435
97	0.115	0.195	0.260	0.080	0.265	0.500
	Prev. open int. 12 300			Prev. open int. 10 400		

Source: The *National Post: Financial Post*, January 18, 2003, p. *IN14*.

split between the Securities and Exchange Commission (SEC), which regulates stock options, and the Commodity Futures Trading Commission (CFTC), which regulates futures options. Regulation focuses on ensuring that writers of options have enough capital to make good on their contractual obligations and on overseeing traders and exchanges to prevent fraud and ensure that the market is not being manipulated.

Option Contracts

A **call option** is a contract that gives the owner the right to *buy* a financial instrument at the exercise price within a specific period of time. A **put option** is a contract that gives the owner the right to *sell* a financial instrument at the exercise price within a specific period of time.

Study Guide Remembering which is a call option and which is a put option is not always easy. To keep them straight, just remember that having a *call* option to *buy* a financial instrument is the same as having the option to *call in* the instrument for delivery at a specified price. Having a *put* option to *sell* a financial instrument is the same as having the option to *put up* an instrument for the other party to buy.

Profits and Losses on Option and Futures Contracts

To understand option contracts more fully, let's first examine the option on the June Canada bond futures contract. If you buy this futures contract at a price of 115 (that is, $115 000), you have agreed to pay $115 000 for $100 000 face value of long-term Canada bonds when they are delivered to you at the end of June. If you sold this futures contract at a price of 115, you agreed, in exchange for $115 000, to deliver $100 000 face value of the long-term Canada bonds at the end of June. An option contract on the Canada bond futures contract has several key features: (1) It has the same expiration date as the underlying futures contract, (2) it is an American option and so can be exercised at any time before the expiration date, and (3) the premium (price) of the option is quoted in points that are the same as in the futures contract, so each point corresponds to $1000. If, for a premium of $2000, you buy one call option contract on the June Canada bond contract with an exercise price of 115, you have purchased the right to buy (call in) the June Canada bond futures contract for a price of 115 ($115 000 per contract) at any time through the expiration date of this contract at the end of June. Similarly, when for $2000 you buy a put option on the June Canada bond contract with an exercise price of 115, you have the right to sell (put up) the June Canada bond futures contract for a price of 115 ($115 000 per contract) at any time until the end of June.

Futures option contracts are somewhat complicated, so to explore how they work and how they can be used to hedge risk, let's first examine how profits and losses on the call option on the June Canada bond futures contract occur. In February, our old friend Irving the Investor buys, for a $2000 premium, a call option on the $100 000 June Canada bond futures contract with a strike price of 115. (We assume that if Irving exercises the option, it is on the expiration date at the end of June and not before.) On the expiration date at the end of June, suppose that the underlying Canada bond for the futures contract has a price of 110. Recall that on the expiration date, arbitrage forces the price of the futures contract to be the same as the price of the underlying bond, so it too has a price of 110 on the expiration date at the end of June. If Irving exercises the call option and buys the futures contract at an exercise price of 115, he will lose money by buying at 115 and selling at the lower market price of 110. Because Irving is smart, he will not exercise the option, but he will be out the $2000 premium he paid. In such a situation, in which the price of the underlying financial instrument is below the exercise price, a call option is said to be "out of the money." At the price of 110 (less than the exercise price), Irving thus suffers a loss on the option contract of the $2000 premium he paid. This loss is plotted as point A in panel (a) of Figure 1.

On the expiration date, if the price of the futures contract is 115, the call option is "at the money," and Irving is indifferent whether he exercises his option to buy the futures contract or not, since exercising the option at 115 when the market price is also at 115 produces no gain or loss. Because he has paid the $2000 premium, at the price of 115 his contract again has a net loss of $2000, plotted as point B.

If the futures contract instead has a price of 120 on the expiration day, the option is "in the money," and Irving benefits from exercising the option: He would buy the futures contract at the exercise price of 115 and then sell it for 120, thereby earning a 5% gain ($5000 profit) on the $100 000 Canada bond contract. Because Irving paid a $2000 premium for the option contract, however, his net profit is $3000 ($5000 – $2000). The $3000 profit at a price of 120 is plotted as point C. Similarly, if the price of the futures contract rose to 125, the option

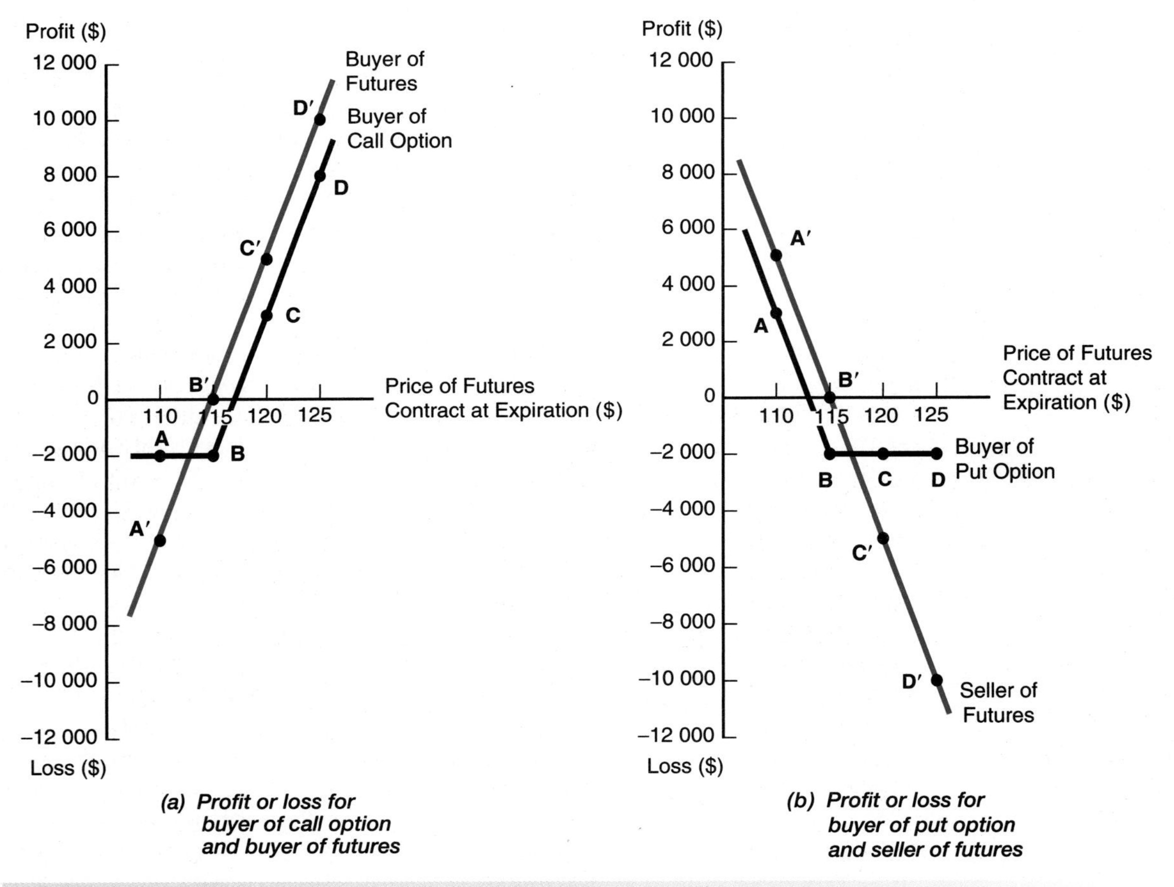

FIGURE 1 Profits and Losses on Options Versus Futures Contracts

The futures contract is the $100 000 June Canada bond contract, and the option contracts are written on this futures contract with an exercise price of 115. Panel (a) shows the profits and losses for the buyer of the call option and the buyer of the futures contract, and panel (b) shows the profits and losses for the buyer of the put option and the seller of the futures contract.

contract would yield a net profit of $8000 ($10 000 from exercising the option minus the $2000 premium), plotted as point D. Plotting these points, we get the kinked profit curve for the call option that we see in panel (a).

Suppose that instead of purchasing the futures *option* contract in February, Irving decides instead to buy the $100 000 June Canada bond *futures* contract at the price of 115. If the price of the bond on the expiration day at the end of June declines to 110, meaning that the price of the futures contract also falls to 110, Irving suffers a loss of 5 percentage points, or $5000. The loss of $5000 on the futures contract at a price of 110 is plotted as point A′ in panel (a). At a price of 115 on the expiration date, Irving would have a zero profit on the futures contract, plotted as point B′. At a price of 120, Irving would have a profit on the contract of 5 percentage points, or $5000 (point C′), and at a price of 125, the profit would be 10 percentage points, or $10 000 (point D′). Plotting these points, we get the linear (straight-line) profit curve for the futures contract that appears in panel (a).

Now we can see the major difference between a futures contract and an option contract. As the profit curve for the futures contract in panel (a) indicates, the futures contract has a linear profit function: Profits grow by an equal dollar amount for every point increase in the price of the underlying financial instrument. By contrast, the kinked profit curve for the option contract is highly nonlinear, meaning that profits do not always grow by the same amount for a given change in the price of the underlying financial instrument. The reason for this nonlinearity is that the call option protects Irving from having losses that are greater than the amount of the $2000 premium. In contrast, Irving's loss on the futures contract is $5000 if the price on the expiration day falls to 110, and if the price falls even further, Irving's loss will be even greater. This insurance-like feature of option contracts explains why their purchase price is referred to as a premium. Once the underlying financial instrument's price rises above the exercise price, however, Irving's profits grow linearly. Irving has given up something by buying an option rather than a futures contract. As we see in panel (a), when the price of the underlying financial instrument rises above the exercise price, Irving's profits are always less than that on the futures contract by exactly the $2000 premium he paid.

Panel (b) plots the results of the same profit calculations if Irving buys not a call but a put option (an option to sell) with an exercise price of 115 for a premium of $2000 and if he sells the futures contract rather than buying one. In this case, if on the expiration date the Canada bond futures have a price above the 115 exercise price, the put option is "out of the money." Irving would not want to exercise the put option and then have to sell the futures contract he owns as a result of exercising the put option at a price below the market price and lose money. He would not exercise his option, and he would be out only the $2000 premium he paid. Once the price of the futures contract falls below the 115 exercise price, Irving benefits from exercising the put option because he can sell the futures contract at a price of 115 but can buy it at a price below this. In such a situation, in which the price of the underlying instrument is below the exercise price, the put option is "in the money," and profits rise linearly as the price of the futures contract falls. The profit function for the put option illustrated in panel (b) of Figure 1 is kinked, indicating that Irving is protected from losses greater than the amount of the premium he paid. The profit curve for the sale of the futures contract is just the negative of the profit for the futures contract in panel (a) and is therefore linear.

Panel (b) of Figure 1 confirms the conclusion from panel (a) that profits on option contracts are nonlinear but profits on futures contracts are linear.

Study Guide To make sure you understand how profits and losses on option and futures contracts are generated, calculate the net profits on the put option and the short position in the futures contract at prices on the expiration day of 110, 115, 120, and 125. Then verify that your calculations correspond to the points plotted in panel (b) of Figure 1.

Two other differences between futures and option contracts must be mentioned. The first is that the initial investment on the contracts differs. As we saw earlier in the chapter, when a futures contract is purchased, the investor must put up a fixed amount, the margin requirement, in a margin account. But when an option contract is purchased, the initial investment is the premium that must be paid for the contract. The second important difference between the contracts is that the futures contract requires money to change hands daily when the contract is marked to market, whereas the option contract requires money to change hands only when it is exercised.

Factors Affecting the Prices of Option Premiums

If we again look closely at the *National Post: Financial Post* entry for 3-month Canadian banker's acceptances futures options in the "Following the Financial News" box (page 584), we learn several interesting facts about how the premiums on option contracts are priced. The first thing you might have noticed is that when the strike (exercise) price for a contract is set at a higher level, the premium for the call option is lower and the premium for the put option is higher. For example, in going from a contract with a strike price of 96.5 to one with 97, the premium for the June call option falls from 0.520 to 0.195, and the premium for the June put option rises from 0.090 to 0.265.

Our understanding of the profit function for option contracts illustrated in Figure 1 helps explain this fact. As we saw in panel (a), a higher price for the underlying financial instrument (in this case a Canada bond futures contract) relative to the option's exercise price results in higher profits on the call (buy) option. Thus the lower the strike price, the higher the profits on the call option contract and the greater the call premium that investors like Irving are willing to pay. Similarly, we saw in panel (b) that a higher price for the underlying financial instrument relative to the exercise price lowers profits on the put (sell) option, so that a higher strike price increases profits and thus causes the put premium to increase.

The second thing you might have noticed in the *National Post: Financial Post* entry is that as the period of time over which the option can be exercised (the term to expiration) gets longer, the premiums for both call and put options rise. For example, at a strike price of 96.75, the premium on the call option increases from 0.300 in March to 0.340 in June and to 0.385 in September. Similarly, the premium on the put option increases from 0.015 in March to 0.160 in June and to 0.375 in September. The fact that premiums increase with the term to expiration is also explained by the nonlinear profit function for option contracts. As the term to expiration lengthens, there is a greater chance that the price of the underlying financial instrument will be very high or very low by the expiration date. If the price becomes very high and goes well above the exercise price, the call (buy) option will yield a high profit, but if the price becomes very low and goes well below the exercise price, the losses will be small because the owner of the call option will simply decide not to exercise the option. The possibility of greater variability of the underlying financial instrument as the term to expiration lengthens raises profits on average for the call option.

Similar reasoning tells us that the put (sell) option will become more valuable as the term to expiration increases because the possibility of greater price variability of the underlying financial instrument increases as the term to expiration increases. The greater chance of a low price increases the chance that profits on the put option will be very high. But the greater chance of a high price does not produce substantial losses for the put option because the owner will again just decide not to exercise the option.

Another way of thinking about this reasoning is to recognize that option contracts have an element of "heads, I win; tails, I don't lose too badly." The greater variability of where the prices might be by the expiration date increases the value of both kinds of options. Since a longer term to the expiration date leads to greater variability of where the prices might be by the expiration date, a longer term to expiration raises the value of the option contract.

The reasoning that we have just developed also explains another important fact about option premiums. When the volatility of the price of the underlying instrument is great, the premiums for both call and put options will be higher. Higher volatility of prices means that for a given expiration date, there will again be greater variability of where the prices might be by the expiration date. The "heads, I win; tails, I don't lose too badly" property of options then means that the greater variability of possible prices by the expiration date increases average profits for the option and thus increases the premium that investors are willing to pay.

Summary

Our analysis of how profits on options are affected by price movements for the underlying financial instrument leads to the following conclusions about the factors that determine the premium on an option contract:

1. The higher the strike price, everything else being equal, the lower the premium on call (buy) options and the higher the premium on put (sell) options.
2. The greater the term to expiration, everything else being equal, the higher the premiums for both call and put options.
3. The greater the volatility of prices of the underlying financial instrument, everything else being equal, the higher the premiums for both call and put options.

The results we have derived here appear in more formal models, such as the Black-Scholes model, which analyze how the premiums on options are priced. You might study such models in other finance courses.

THE PRACTISING FINANCIAL INSTITUTION MANAGER

Hedging with Futures Options

Earlier in the chapter, we saw how a financial institution manager like Mona, the manager of the First Bank, could hedge the interest-rate risk on its $5 million holdings of 8s of 2023 by selling $5 million of Canada bond futures (50 contracts). A rise in interest rates and the resulting fall in bond prices and bond futures contracts would lead to profits on the bank's sale of the futures contracts that would exactly offset the losses on the 8s of 2023 the bank is holding.

As panel (b) of Figure 1 suggests, an alternative way for the manager to protect against a rise in interest rates and hence a decline in bond prices is to buy $5 million of put options written on the same Canada bond futures. Because the size of the options contract is the same as the futures contract ($100 000 of bonds), the number of put options contracts bought is the same as the number of futures contracts sold, that is, 50. As long as the exercise price is not too far from the current price as in panel (b), the rise in interest rates and decline in bond prices will lead to profits on the futures and the futures put options, profits that will offset any losses on the $5 million of Canada bonds.

The one problem with using options rather than futures is that the First Bank will have to pay premiums on the options contracts, thereby lowering the bank's profits in order to hedge the interest-rate risk. Why might the bank manager be willing to use options rather than futures to conduct the hedge? The answer is that the option contract, unlike the futures contract, allows the First Bank to gain if interest rates decline and bond prices rise. With the hedge using futures contracts, the First Bank does not gain from increases in bond prices because the profits on the bonds it is holding are offset by the losses from the futures contracts it has sold. However, as panel (b) of Figure 1 indicates, the situation when the hedge is conducted with put options is quite different: Once bond prices rise above the exercise price, the bank does not suffer additional losses on the option contracts. At the same time, the value of the Canada bonds the bank is holding will increase, thereby leading to a profit for the bank. Thus using options rather than futures to conduct the micro hedge allows the bank to protect itself from rises in interest rates but still allows the bank to benefit from interest-rate declines (although the profit is reduced by the amount of the premium).

Similar reasoning indicates that the bank manager might prefer to use options to conduct the macro hedge to immunize the entire bank portfolio from interest-rate risk. Again, the strategy of using options rather than futures has the disadvantage that the First Bank has to pay the premiums on these contracts up front. By contrast, using options allows the bank to keep the gains from a decline in interest rates (which will raise the value of the bank's assets relative to its liabilities) because these gains will not be offset by large losses on the option contracts.

In the case of a macro hedge, there is another reason why the bank might prefer option contracts to futures contracts. Profits and losses on futures contracts can cause accounting problems for banks because such profits and losses are not allowed to be offset by unrealized changes in the value of the rest of the bank's portfolio. Consider the case when interest rates fall. If First Bank sells futures contracts to conduct the macro hedge, then when interest rates fall and the prices of the Canada bond futures contracts rise, it will have large losses on these contracts. Of course, these losses are offset by unrealized profits in the rest of the bank's portfolio, but the bank is not allowed to offset these losses in its accounting statements. So even though the macro hedge is serving its intended purpose of immunizing the bank's portfolio from interest-rate risk, the bank would experience large accounting losses when interest rates fall. Indeed, bank managers have lost their jobs when perfectly sound hedges with interest-rate futures have led to large accounting losses. Not surprisingly, bank managers might shrink from using financial futures to conduct macro hedges for this reason.

Futures options, however, can come to the rescue of the managers of banks and other financial institutions. Suppose that First Bank conducted the macro hedge by buying put options instead of selling Canada bond futures. Now if interest rates fall and bond prices rise well above the exercise price, the bank will not have large losses on the option contracts because it will just decide not to exercise its options. The bank will not suffer the accounting problems produced by hedging with financial futures. Because of the accounting advantages of using futures options to conduct macro hedges, option contracts have become important to financial institution managers as tools for hedging interest-rate risk.

INTEREST-RATE SWAPS

In addition to forwards, futures, and options, financial institutions use one other important financial derivative to manage risk. **Swaps** are financial contracts that obligate each party to the contract to exchange (swap) a set of payments it owns for another set of payments owned by another party. There are two basic kinds of swaps: **Currency swaps** involve the exchange of a set of payments in one currency for a set of payments in another currency. **Interest-rate swaps** involve the exchange of one set of interest payments for another set of interest payments, all denominated in the same currency. We focus on interest-rate swaps.

Interest-Rate Swap Contracts

Interest-rate swaps are an important tool for managing interest-rate risk, and they first appeared in the United States in 1982 when there was an increase in the demand for financial instruments that could be used to reduce interest-rate risk. The most common type of interest-rate swap (called the *plain vanilla swap*) specifies (1) the interest rate on the payments that are being exchanged; (2) the type of interest payments (variable or fixed-rate); (3) the amount of **notional principal**, which is the amount on which the interest is being paid; and (4) the time period over which the exchanges continue to be made. There are many other more complicated versions of swaps, including forward swaps and swap options (called *swaptions*), but here we will look only at the plain vanilla swap. Figure 2 illustrates an interest-rate swap between First Trust and the Friendly Finance Company. First Trust agrees to pay Friendly Finance a fixed rate of 7% on $1 million of notional principal for the next ten years, and Friendly Finance agrees to pay First Trust the one-year treasury bill rate plus 1% on $1 million of notional principal for the same period. Thus as shown in Figure 2, every year, First Trust would be paying the Friendly Finance Company 7% on $1 million while Friendly Finance would be paying First Trust the one-year T-bill rate plus 1% on $1 million.

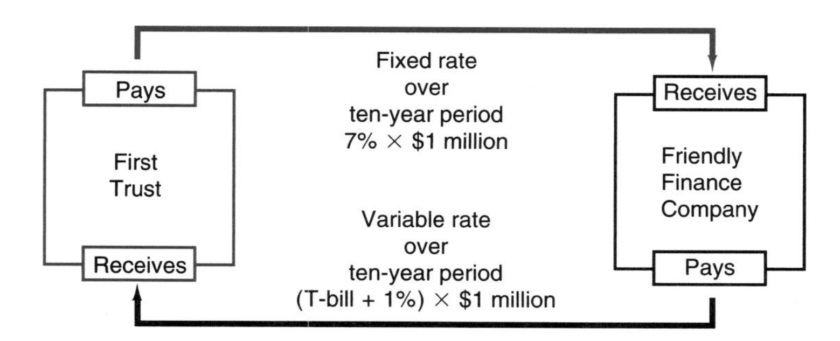

FIGURE 2 Interest-Rate Swap Payments

In this swap arrangement, with a notional principal of $1 million and a term of ten years, First Trust pays a fixed rate of 7% × $1 million to the Friendly Finance Company, which in turn agrees to pay the one-year treasury bill rate plus 1% × $1 million to First Trust.

THE PRACTISING FINANCIAL INSTITUTION MANAGER

Hedging with Interest-Rate Swaps

You might wonder why the managers of the two financial institutions find it advantageous to enter into this swap agreement. The answer is that it may help both of them hedge interest-rate risk.

Suppose that First Trust, which tends to borrow short-term and then lend long-term in the mortgage market, has $1 million less of rate-sensitive assets than it has of rate-sensitive liabilities. As we learned in Chapter 22, this situation means that as interest rates rise, the rise in the cost of funds (liabilities) is greater than the rise in interest payments it receives on its assets, many of which are fixed-rate. The result of rising interest rates is thus a shrinking of First Trust's net interest margin and a decline in its profitability. As we saw in Chapter 22, to avoid this interest-rate risk, the manager of First Trust would like to convert $1 million of its fixed-rate assets into $1 million of rate-sensitive assets, in effect making rate-sensitive assets equal to rate-sensitive liabilities, thereby eliminating the gap. This is exactly what happens when she engages in the interest-rate swap. By taking $1 million of its fixed-rate income and exchanging it for $1 million of rate-sensitive treasury bill income, she has converted income on $1 million of fixed-rate assets into income on $1 million of rate-sensitive assets. Now when interest rates increase, the rise in rate-sensitive income on its assets exactly matches the rise in the rate-sensitive cost of funds on its liabilities, leaving the net interest margin and bank profitability unchanged.

The manager of the Friendly Finance Company, which issues long-term bonds to raise funds and uses them to make short-term loans, finds that he is in exactly the opposite situation to First Trust: He has $1 million more of rate-sensitive assets than of rate-sensitive liabilities. He is therefore concerned that a fall in interest rates, which will result in a larger drop in income from its assets than the decline in the cost of funds on its liabilities, will cause a decline in profits. By doing the interest-rate swap, the manager eliminates this interest-rate risk because he has converted $1 million of rate-sensitive income into $1 million of fixed-rate income. Now the manager of the Friendly Finance Company finds that when interest rates fall, the decline in rate-sensitive income is smaller and so is matched by the decline in the rate-sensitive cost of funds on its liabilities, leaving profitability unchanged.

Advantages of Interest-Rate Swaps

To eliminate interest-rate risk, both First Trust and the Friendly Finance Company could have rearranged their balance sheets by converting fixed-rate assets into rate-sensitive assets, and vice versa, instead of engaging in an interest-rate swap. However, this strategy would have been costly for both financial institutions for several reasons. The first is that financial institutions incur substantial transaction costs when they rearrange their balance sheets. Second, different financial institutions have informational advantages in making loans to certain customers who may prefer certain maturities. Thus, adjusting the balance sheet to eliminate interest-rate risk may result in a loss of these informational advantages, which the financial institution is unwilling to give up. Interest-rate swaps solve these problems for financial institutions because in effect they allow the institutions to convert fixed-rate assets into rate-sensitive assets without affecting the balance sheet. Large transaction costs are avoided, and the financial institutions can continue to make loans where they have an informational advantage.

We have seen that financial institutions can also hedge interest-rate risk with other financial derivatives such as futures contracts and futures options. Interest-rate swaps have one big advantage over hedging with these other derivatives: They can be written for very long horizons, sometimes as long as 20 years, whereas financial futures and futures options typically have much shorter horizons, not much more than a year. If a financial institution needs to hedge interest-rate risk for a long horizon, financial futures and option markets may not do it much good. Instead it can turn to the swap market.

Disadvantages of Interest-Rate Swaps

Although interest-rate swaps have important advantages that make them very popular with financial institutions, they also have disadvantages that limit their usefulness. Swap markets, like forward markets, can suffer from a lack of liquidity. Let's return to looking at the swap between First Trust and the Friendly Finance Company. As with a forward contract, it might be difficult for First Trust to link up with the Friendly Finance Company to arrange the swap. In addition, even if First Trust could find a counterparty like the Friendly Finance Company, it might not be able to negotiate a good deal because it couldn't find any other institution to negotiate with.

Swap contracts also are subject to the same default risk that we encountered for forward contracts. If interest rates rise, the Friendly Finance Company would love to get out of the swap contract because the fixed-rate interest payments it receives are less than it could get in the open market. It might then default on the contract, exposing First Trust to a loss. Alternatively, the Friendly Finance Company could go bust, meaning that the terms of the swap contract would not be fulfilled.

It is important to note that the default risk of swaps is not the same as the default risk on the full amount of the notional principal because the notional principal is never exchanged. If the Friendly Finance Company goes broke because $1 million of its one-year loans default and it cannot make its interest payment to First Trust, First Trust will stop sending its payment to Friendly Finance. If interest rates have declined, this will suit First Trust just fine because it would rather keep the 7% fixed-rate interest payment, which is at a higher rate, than receive the rate-sensitive payment, which has declined. Thus a default on a swap contract does not necessarily mean that there is a loss to the other party. First Trust will suffer losses from a default only if interest rates have risen when the default occurs. Even then, the loss will be far smaller than the amount of the notional principal because interest payments are far smaller than the amount of the notional principal.[6]

Financial Intermediaries in Interest-Rate Swaps

As we have just seen, financial institutions do have to be aware of the possibility of losses from a default on swaps. As with a forward contract, each party to a swap must have a lot of information about the other party to make sure that the contract is likely to be fulfilled. The need for information about counterparties and the liquidity problems in swap markets could limit the usefulness of these markets. However, as we saw in Chapter 14, when informational and liquidity problems crop up in a market, financial intermediaries come to the rescue. That is exactly what happens in swap markets. Intermediaries such as investment banks and especially large banks have the ability to acquire information cheaply about the creditworthiness and reliability of parties to swap contracts and are also able to match up

[6]The actual loss will equal the present value of the difference in the interest payments that the bank would have received if the swap were still in force as compared to interest payments it receives otherwise.

parties to a swap. Hence large banks and investment banks have set up swap markets in which they act as intermediaries.

Application Are Financial Derivatives a Worldwide Time Bomb?

With the bankruptcy of the Barings Bank in 1995 (discussed in Chapter 15)—which involved trades in financial derivatives—politicians, the media, and regulators have become very concerned about the dangers of derivatives. This concern is international and has spawned a slew of reports issued by such organizations as the Bank for International Settlements (BIS), the Bank of England, the Group of Thirty, and the U.S. Commodity Futures Trading Commission. Particularly scary are the notional amounts of derivatives contracts—tens of trillions of dollars worldwide—and the fact that banks, which are subject to bank panics, are major players in the derivatives markets. As a result of these fears, some politicians have called for restrictions on banks' involvement in the derivatives markets. Are financial derivatives a time bomb that could bring down the world financial system?

Go to www.bankofengland.co.uk and www.cftc.gov for details about the Bank of England and the Commodity Futures Trading Commission.

There are three major concerns about financial derivatives. First is that financial derivatives allow financial institutions to increase their leverage; that is, they can in effect hold an amount of the underlying asset that is many times greater than the amount of money they have had to put up. Increasing their leverage enables them to take huge bets on currency and interest-rate movements, which if they are wrong can bring down the bank, as was the case for Barings in 1995. This concern is valid. As we saw earlier in the chapter, the amount of money placed in margin accounts is only a small fraction of the price of the futures contract, meaning that small movements in the price of a contract can produce losses that are many times the size of the initial amount put in the margin account. Thus although financial derivatives can be used to hedge risk, they can also be used by financial institutions to take on excessive risk.

The second concern is that financial derivatives are too sophisticated for managers of financial institutions because they are so complicated. Although it is true that some financial derivatives can be so complex that some financial managers are not sophisticated enough to use them, this seems unlikely to apply to the big international financial institutions that are the major players in the derivatives markets. Indeed, in the Barings case, the bank was brought down not by trades in complex derivatives but rather by trades in one of the simplest of derivatives, stock index futures. (Recall from Chapter 15 that Barings's problem was more a lack of internal controls at the bank than a problem with derivatives per se.)

A third concern is that banks have holdings of huge notional amounts of financial derivatives, particularly swaps, that greatly exceed the amount of bank capital, and so these derivatives expose the banks to serious risk of failure. Banks are indeed major players in the financial derivatives markets, particularly the swaps market, where our earlier analysis has shown that they are the natural market-makers because they can act as intermediaries between two counterparties who would not make the swap without their involvement. However, looking at the notional amount of swaps at banks gives a very misleading picture of their risk exposure. First is that because banks act as intermediaries in the swap markets, they are typically exposed only to credit risk—a default by one of their counterparties. Furthermore, swaps, unlike loans, do not involve payments of the notional amount but rather the much smaller interest payments based on the notional amounts. For example, in the case of a 7% interest rate, the payment is only $70 000 for the $1 million swap. Estimates of the credit exposure from swap contracts indicate that they are on the order of only 1% of the notional value of the contracts and that credit exposure at banks from derivatives is generally less than a quarter of their total credit exposure from loans. Banks' credit exposure from their derivatives activities are thus not out of line with other credit exposures they face.

The conclusion is that financial derivatives do have their dangers for financial institutions, but some of these dangers have been overplayed. The biggest danger occurs in trading activities of financial institutions, and as discussed in Chapter 18, regulators have been paying increased attention to this danger and have issued new disclosure requirements and regulatory guidelines for how derivatives trading should be done. The credit risk exposure posed by derivatives, by contrast, seems to be manageable with standard methods of dealing with credit risk, both by managers of financial institutions and their regulators.

SUMMARY

1. Interest-rate forward contracts, which are agreements to sell a debt instrument at a future (forward) point in time, can be used to hedge interest-rate risk. The advantage of forward contracts is that they are flexible, but the disadvantages are that they are subject to default risk and their market is illiquid.

2. A financial futures contract is similar to an interest-rate forward contract in that it specifies that a debt instrument must be delivered by one party to another on a stated future date. However, it has advantages over a forward contract in that it is not subject to default risk and is more liquid. Forward and futures contracts can be used by financial institutions to hedge against (protect) interest-rate risk.

3. Stock index futures are financial futures whose underlying financial instrument is a stock market index. Stock index futures can be used to hedge stock market risk by reducing systematic risk in portfolios or by locking in stock prices.

4. An option contract gives the purchaser the right to buy (call option) or sell (put option) a security at the exercise (strike) price within a specific period of time. The profit function for options is nonlinear—profits do not always grow by the same amount for a given change in the price of the underlying financial instrument. The nonlinear profit function for options explains why their value (as reflected by the premium paid for them) is negatively related to the exercise price for call options, positively related to the exercise price for put options, positively related to the term to expiration for both call and put options, and positively related to the volatility of the prices of the underlying financial instrument for both call and put options. Financial institutions use futures options to hedge interest-rate risk in a similar fashion to the way they use financial futures and forward contracts. Futures options may be preferred for macro hedges because they suffer from fewer accounting problems than financial futures.

5. Interest-rate swaps involve the exchange of one set of interest payments for another set of interest payments and have default risk and liquidity problems similar to those of forward contracts. As a result, interest-rate swaps often involve intermediaries such as large banks and investment banks that make a market in swaps. Financial institutions find that interest-rate swaps are useful ways to hedge interest-rate risk. Interest-rate swaps have one big advantage over financial futures and options: They can be written for very long horizons.

6. There are three concerns about the dangers of derivatives: They allow financial institutions to more easily increase their leverage and take big bets (by effectively enabling them to hold a larger amount of the underlying assets than the amount of money put down), they are too complex for managers of financial institutions to understand, and they expose financial institutions to large credit risks because the huge notional amounts of derivative contracts greatly exceed the capital of these institutions. The second two dangers seem to be overplayed, but the danger from increased leverage using derivatives is real.

KEY TERMS

American option, *p. 584*
arbitrage, *p. 573*
call option, *p. 585*
currency swap, *p. 591*
European option, *p. 584*
exercise price (strike price), *p. 583*
financial derivatives, *p. 569*
financial futures, *p. 571*
financial futures option (futures option), *p. 584*
forward contracts, *p. 570*
hedge, *p. 569*
interest-rate forward contract, *p. 570*
interest-rate futures contract, *p. 572*
interest-rate swap, *p. 591*
long position, *p. 569*
macro hedge, *p. 575*
margin requirement, *p. 578*
marked to market, *p. 578*
micro hedge, *p. 575*
notional principal, *p. 591*
open interest, *p. 575*
option, *p. 583*
premium, *p. 584*
put option, *p. 585*
short position, *p. 569*
stock market risk, *p. 581*
stock option, *p. 584*
swap, *p. 591*

QUESTIONS AND PROBLEMS

1. If the pension fund you manage expects to have an inflow of $120 million six months from now, what forward contract would you seek to enter into to lock in current interest rates?

***2.** If the portfolio you manage is holding $25 million of 8s of 2023 Canada bonds with a price of 110, what forward contract would you enter into to hedge the interest-rate risk on these bonds over the coming year?

3. If at the expiration date, the deliverable Canada bond is selling for 101 but the Canada bond futures contract is selling for 102, what will happen to the futures price? Explain your answer.

***4.** If you buy a $100 000 June Canada bond contract for 108 and the price of the deliverable Canada bond at the expiration date is 102, what is your profit or loss on the contract?

5. Suppose that the pension you are managing is expecting an inflow of funds of $100 million next year and you want to make sure that you will earn the current interest rate of 8% when you invest the incoming funds in long-term bonds. How would you use the futures market to do this?

***6.** How would you use the options market to accomplish the same thing as in Problem 5? What are the advantages and disadvantages of using an options contract rather than a futures contract?

7. If you buy a put option on a $100 000 Canada bond futures contract with an exercise price of 95 and the price of the Canada bond is 120 at expiration, is the contract in the money, out of the money, or at the money? What is your profit or loss on the contract if the premium was $4000?

***8.** Suppose that you buy a call option on a $100 000 Canada bond futures contract with an exercise price of 110 for a premium of $1500. If on expiration the futures contract has a price of 111, what is your profit or loss on the contract?

9. Explain why greater volatility or a longer term to maturity leads to a higher premium on both call and put options.

***10.** Why does a lower strike price imply that a call option will have a higher premium and a put option a lower premium?

11. If the finance company you manage has a gap of +$5 million (rate-sensitive assets greater than rate-sensitive liabilities by $5 million), describe an interest-rate swap that would eliminate the company's income gap.

***12.** If the bank you manage has a gap of −$42 million, describe an interest-rate swap that would eliminate the bank's income risk from changes in interest rates.

13. If your company has a payment of 200 million euros due one year from now, how would you hedge the foreign exchange risk in this payment with a 125 000 euros futures contracts?

***14.** If your company has to make a 10 million euros payment to a German company in June, three months from now, how would you hedge the foreign exchange risk in this payment with a 125 000 euros futures contract?

15. Suppose that your company will be receiving 30 million euros six months from now and the euro is currently selling for 1.6 Canadian dollars. If you want to hedge the foreign exchange risk in this payment, what kind of forward contract would you want to enter into?

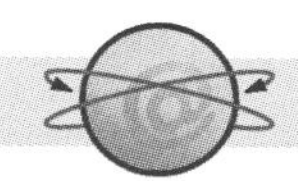

WEB EXERCISES

Hedging with Financial Derivatives

1. We have discussed various stock markets in detail throughout this text. Another market that is less well known is the Canadian Venture Exchange. Here contracts on a wide variety of commodities are traded on a daily basis. Go to http://www.tse-cdnx.com to find some information about the origin and purpose of this exchange. Write a one-page summary discussing the information you obtained.

2. We leave the details of pricing option contracts to another course. However, the following site can be used to demonstrate how the features of an option affect the option's prices. Go to http://www.intrepid.com/~robertl/option-pricer4.html. Indicate what happens to the price of an option under each of the following situations:
   - **a.** The strike price increases.
   - **b.** Interest rates increase.
   - **c.** Volatility increases.
   - **d.** The time until the option matures increases.

Glossary

advances: See *discount loans.*
adverse selection: The problem created by asymmetric information before a transaction occurs: the people who are the most undesirable from the other party's point of view are the ones who are most likely to want to engage in the financial transaction. 21
American depository receipts (ADR): A receipt for foreign stocks held by a trustee. The receipts trade on U.S. stock exchanges instead of the actual stock. 244
American option: An option that can be exercised at any time up to the expiration date of the contract. 584
amortized: Paid off in stages over a period of time. Each payment on a loan consists of the accrued interest and an amount that is applied to repay the principal. When all of the payments have been made, the loan is paid off (fully amortized). 274
annual percentage rate: The actual rate of return. 47
annuity: An insurance product that provides a fixed stream of payments. 491
appreciation: Increase in a currency's value. 4, 295
arbitrage: Elimination of a riskless profit opportunity in a market. 573
asset: A financial claim or piece of property that is a store of value. 2, 67
asset management: The acquisition of assets that have a low rate of default and diversification of asset holdings to increase profits. 383
asset market approach: Determining asset prices using stocks of assets rather than flows. 77
asymmetric information: The inequality of knowledge that each party to a transaction has about the other party. 21
automated banking machine (ABM): An electronic machine that combines in one location an ATM, an Internet connection to the bank's website, and a telephone link to customer service. 400
automated teller machine (ATM): An electronic machine that allows customers to get cash, make deposits, transfer funds from one account to another, and check balances. 399
balance of payments: A bookkeeping system for recording all payments that have a direct bearing on the movement of funds between a country and all other countries. 323
balance-of-payments crisis: A foreign exchange crisis stemming from problems in a country's balance of payments. 334
balance sheet: A list of the assets and liabilities of a bank (or firm) that balances: total assets equal total liabilities plus capital. 375
balloon loan: A loan on which the payments do not fully pay off the principal balance, meaning that the final payment must be larger than the rest. 274, 514
bank panic: The simultaneous failure of many banks, as during a financial crisis. 366
bank rate The interest rate the Bank of Canada charges to members of the Canadian Payments Association. 159, 385
bank supervision: Overseeing who operates banks and how they are operated. 458
banker's risk The risk of not holding enough reserves to make immediate and larger than normal cash payments to liability holders. 379
banks: Financial institutions that accept deposits and make loans (such as commercial banks, savings and loan associations, and credit unions). 6
base money: The sum of the Bank of Canada's monetary liabilities (notes outstanding and bank settlement balances) and coins outstanding. 138
Basel Accord: An agreement by the Basel Committee on Banking Supervision to implement risk-based capital requirements. 458
Basel Committee on Banking Supervision: A committee that meets under the auspices of the Bank for International Settlements in Basel, Switzerland and that sets bank regulatory standards. 458
basis point: One one-hundredth of a percentage point. 49
bearer deposit notes: CDs and GICs that can be traded and are in bearer form. This means that whoever holds the instrument at maturity receives the principal and interest. 212
Big Six: The six largest commercial banks in Canada (Royal Bank of Canada, Canadian Imperial Bank of Commerce, Bank of

Montreal, Bank of Nova Scotia, TD Canada Trust, and the National Bank of Canada). Together they hold over 92% of the assets in the industry. 205, 414

Board of Directors of the Bank of Canada: A board with fifteen members (including the governor) that is responsible for the business affairs of the Bank. 151

Board of Governors of the Federal Reserve System: A board with seven governors (including the chairman) that plays an essential role in decision making within the Federal Reserve System. 145

bond: A debt security that promises to make payments periodically for a specified period of time. 2

bond indenture: Document accompanying a bond that spells out the details of the bond issue, such as covenants and sinking fund provisions. It states the lender's rights and privileges and the borrower's obligations. 236

Bretton Woods system: The international monetary system in use from 1945 to 1971 in which exchange rates were fixed and the U.S. dollar was freely convertible into gold (by foreign governments and central banks only). 327

brokered deposits: Deposits that enable depositors to circumvent the $100,000 limit at each bank so that the total amount deposited is fully insured. 479

brokers: Agents for investors who match buyers with sellers. 16

bubble: A situation in which the price of an asset differs from its fundamental market value. 269

call: A redemption feature allowing issues to be 'called' on specified notice. 231

call option: An option contract that provides the right to buy a security at a specified price. 585

Canadas: The securities issued by the federal government. 234

capital account: An account that describes the flow of capital between the United States and other countries. 325

capital adequacy management: Managing the amount of capital the bank should maintain and then acquiring the needed capital. 383

capital market: A financial market in which longer-term debt (maturity of greater than one year) and equity instruments are traded. 17

capital mobility: A situation in which foreigners can easily purchase a country's assets and the country's residents can easily purchase foreign assets. 322

captive finance company: A finance company that is owned by a retailer and makes loans to finance the purchase of goods from the retailer. 520

cash flow: The difference between cash receipts and cash expenditures. 249, 366

cash setting: The management of participants' settlement balances by means of shifting government deposits between the government's account at the Bank of Canada and the government's accounts at the participating financial institutions. 172

casualty (liability) insurance: Protection against financial losses because of a claim of negligence. 495

central bank: The government agency that oversees the banking system and is responsible for the amount of money and credit supplied in the economy; in Canada it is the Bank of Canada. 5, 410

Central Liquidity Facility (CLF): The lender of last resort for credit unions, created in 1978 by the Financial Institutions Reform Act. 447

Central Payor and Transfer Agent (CPTA): The agent that maintains the registry of NHA MBS investors, issues ownership certificates, replaces sold or lost certificates, collects payments of principal and interest form the MBS issuers, and makes payments to the registered NHA MBS investors. Also assists CMHC in monitoring the performance of MBS issuers and maintains information useful in supporting secondary market pricing. 289

certainty equivalent: An amount that will be received or spent with certainty. An insurance payment is a certainty equivalent since it removes the risk that unexpected amounts will need to be spent. 486

chaos: A nonlinear deterministic process that looks random. 265

chartered banks: Another term for commercial banks in Canada. So called because they used to be established only by charter granted either in a special Act of Parliament or by the minister of finance. 409

closed-end fund: A fund that sells a fixed number of shares of stock and does not continue to accept investments. 544

coinsurance: An insurance policy under which the policyholder bears a percentage of the loss along with the insurance company. 470, 500

collateral: Property that is pledged to the lender to guarantee payment in the event that the borrower should be unable to make debt payments. 350

collateralized mortgage obligation (CMO): Securities classified by when prepayment is likely to occur. Investors may buy a group of CMOs that are likely to mature at a time that meets the investors' needs. 289

common bond membership: A requirement that all members of credit unions share some common bond, such as working for the same employer. 440

common stock: A security that gives the holder an ownership interest in the issuing firm. This ownership interest includes the right to any residual cash flows and the right to vote on major corporate issues. 241

compensating balance: A required minimum amount of funds that a firm receiving a loan must keep in a checking account at the bank. 554

competitive bidding: Competing in an auction against other potential buyers of Treasury securities. 208

confidential memorandum: A document that presents detailed financial information required by prospective buyers prior to making an offer to acquire a firm. 535

conventional mortgages: Mortgage contracts originated by banks and other mortgage lenders that are not guaranteed by the FHA or the VA. They are often insured by private mortgage insurance. 282

cooperative bank: A financial institution that focuses on servicing the banking and lending needs of its members. 439

costly state verification: Monitoring a firm's activities, an expensive process in both time and money. 359

coupon bond: A credit market instrument that pays the owner a fixed interest payment every year until the maturity date, when a specified final amount is paid. 34

coupon rate: The dollar amount of the yearly coupon payment expressed as a percentage of the face value of a coupon bond. 34

credit rationing: A lender's refusing to make loans even though borrowers are willing to pay the stated interest rate or even a higher rate or restricting the size of loans to less than the amount being sought. 555

credit risk: The risk arising from the possibility that the borrower will default. 383

Credit Union Central of Canada (CUCC) or **Canadian Central:** The central bank for the provincial credit unions. The Canadian Central serves as the third tier for the credit union movement; it coordinates various functions and provides cheque-clearing services for all provincial Centrals. 441

Credit Union National Association (CUNA): A central credit union facility that encourages establishing credit unions and provides information to its members. 446

Credit Union National Extension Bureau (CUNEB): A central credit union facility established in 1921 that was later replaced by the Credit Union National Association. 446

creditor: A holder of debt. 363

currency swap: A swap that involves the exchange of a set of payments in another currency. 591

current account: An account that shows international transactions involving currently produced goods and services. 323

currency: The sum of the Bank of Canada's notes and the Canadian Mint's coins. 154

currency union: A group of countries that share a common currency. 339

current yield: An approximation of the yield to maturity that equals the yearly coupon payment divided by the price of a coupon bond. 45

dealers: People who link buyers with sellers by buying and selling securities at stated prices. 16

debt-currency swaps: The debt denominated in foreign currency is converted into domestic currency. 423

debt deflation: A situation in which a substantial decline in the price level sets in, leading to a further deterioration in firms' net worth because of the increased burden of indebtedness. 368

debt-debt swaps: Banks holding the debt of one LDC exchange it for the debt of another LDC. 423

debt-equity swaps: The debt is converted into the equity of public and private domestic enterprises. 423

deductible: An amount of any loss that must be paid by the insured before the insurance company will pay anything. 488

deep markets: Markets where there are many participants and a great deal of activity, thus ensuring that securities can be sold rapidly at fair prices. 207

default: A situation in which the party issuing a debt instrument is unable to make interest payments or pay off the amount owed when the instrument matures. 110

default-free bonds: Bonds with no default risk, such as Canada bonds. 110

default risk: The risk that a loan customer may fail to repay a loan as promised. 110, 516

defensive open market operations: intended to offset movements in other factors that affect bank reserves, such as changes in government deposits with the central bank. 167

defined-benefit plan: A pension plan in which the benefits are stated up front and are paid regardless how the investments perform. 502

defined-contribution plan: A pension plan in which the contributions are stated up front but the benefits paid depend on the performance of the investments. 502

definitive agreement: A legally binding contract that details the terms and conditions for an acquisition of one firm by another. 535

demand curve: A curve depicting the relationship between quantity demanded and price when all other economic variables are held constant. 72

demand deposit: A deposit held by a bank that must be paid to the depositor on demand. Demand deposits are more commonly called *checking accounts*. 212

demutualization: The process by which mutual life insurance companies convert to stock companies. 489

deposit outflows: Losses of deposits when depositors make withdrawals or demand payment. 383

deposit rate ceilings: Restrictions on the maximum interest rates payable on deposits. 403

depreciation: Decrease in a currency's value. 4, 295

desired reserves: Reserves that are held to meet the banks' desire that for every dollar of deposits, a certain fraction should be kept as reserves. 154, 379

desired reserve ratio: The fraction of deposits that banks desire to keep as reserves. 155, 379

devaluation: Resetting of the par value of a currency at a lower level. 329

direct clearers: Members of the Canadian Payments Association who participate directly in the Automated Clearing Settlement System (ACSS) and maintain a settlement account at the Bank of Canada. 158

direct placement: An issuer's bypassing the dealer and selling the security directly to the investor. 214

discount bond: A credit market instrument that is bought at a price below its face value and whose face value is repaid at the maturity date; it does not make any interest payments. Also known as a *zero-coupon bond*. 34

discount yield: See *yield on a discount basis*.

discounting: Reduction in the value of a security at purchase such that when it matures at full value, the investor receives a fair return. 206

disintermediation: A reduction in the flow of funds into the banking system that causes the amount of financial intermediation to decline. 403

diversification: The holding of many risky assets. 71

dividends: Periodic payments made by equities to shareholders. 16, 249

dollar duration: The change in a bond's price in units of money. 64

dollarization: A monetary strategy in which a country abandons its currency altogether and adopts that of another country, typically the U.S. dollar. 330

down payment: A portion of the original purchase price that is paid by the borrower so that the borrower will have equity (ownership interest) in the asset pledged as collateral. 277

drawdowns: Transfers of government deposits from the government's accounts with the direct clearers to the government's account with the Bank of Canada. 172

dual-banking system: The system in the United States in which banks supervised by the federal government and banks supervised by the states operate side by side. 411

due diligence period: A 20–40 day period used by the buyer of a firm to verify the accuracy of the information contained in the confidential memorandum. 535

duration: The average lifetime of a debt security's stream of payments. 58

duration gap analysis: A measurement of the sensitivity of the market value of a bank's assets and liabilities to changes in interest rates. 559

dynamic open market operations: A type of open market operation intended to change the level of bank reserves and the monetary base. 167

e-cash: A second form of electronic money used on the Internet to pay for goods and services. 401

econometric model: A model whose equations are estimated using statistical procedures. 99

economies of scale: Savings that can be achieved through increased size. 21, 524

economies of scope: Increased business that can be achieved by offering many products in one easy-to-reach location. 524

effective interest rate: The interest rate as if it were compounded once per period rather than several times per period. 276

efficient market hypothesis: The hypothesis that prices of securities in financial markets fully reflect all available information. 256

electronic money (or e-money): Money that exists only in electronic form and substitutes for cash as well. 401

equities: Claims to share in the net income and assets of a corporation (such as common stock). 16

equity capital: See *net worth.*

equity multiplier: The amount of assets per dollar of equity capital. 389

Eurobonds: Bonds denominated in a currency other than that of the country in which they are sold. 18

Eurocurrencies: Foreign currencies deposited in banks outside the home country. 18

Eurodollars: U.S. dollars that are deposited in foreign banks outside of the United States or in foreign branches of U.S. banks. 18

European option: An option that can be exercised only at the expiration date of the contract. 584

excess demand: A situation in which quantity demanded is greater than quantity supplied. 75

excess reserves: Reserves in excess of required reserves. 155

excess supply: A situation in which quantity supplied is greater than quantity demanded. 75

Exchange Fund Account: The fund that holds Canada's official foreign exchange assets. The Bank of Canada manages it, on behalf of the government. 138, 173

exchange rate: The price of one currency in terms of another. 293

exchange rate overshooting: A phenomenon whereby the exchange rate changes by more in the short run than it does in the long run when the money supply changes. 313

exchange rate union: A group of countries that agree to fix exchange rates among themselves while floating jointly against the currencies of countries outside the union. 333

exchanges: Secondary markets in which buyers and sellers of securities (or their agents or brokers) meet in one central location to conduct trades. 17

exercise price: The price at which the purchaser of an option has the right to buy or sell the underlying financial instrument. Also known as the *strike price.* 583

expected return: The return on an asset expected over the next period. 67

face value (or **par value):** Specified final amount of a debt market instrument. 34

factoring: The sale of accounts receivable to another firm, which takes responsibility for collections. 517

fallen angels: Investment-grade securities whose rating has fallen to junk levels. 112

Federal Credit Union Act: Law passed in 1934 that allowed federal chartering of credit unions in all states. 446

Federal Open Market Committee (FOMC): The committee that makes decisions regarding the conduct of open market operations; composed of the seven members of the Board of Governors of the Federal Reserve System, the president of the Federal Reserve Bank of New York, and the presidents of four other Federal Reserve banks on a rotating basis. 145

Federal Reserve banks: The 12 district banks in the Federal Reserve system. 145

Federal Reserve System (the Fed): The central banking authority responsible for monetary policy in the United States. 145

Federal Savings and Loan Insurance Corporation (FSLIC): An agency that provided deposit insurance to savings and loan similar to the Federal Deposit Insurance Corporation which insured banks. FSLIC was eliminated in 1989. 450

financial conglomerate: A firm that owns and manages a number of different types of financial intermediaries. 523

financial crisis: A major disruption in financial markets, characterized by sharp declines in asset prices and the failures of many financial and non-financial firms. 364

financial derivatives: Instruments that have payoffs that are linked to previously issued securities and are extremely useful risk reduction tools. 569

financial engineering: The process of researching and developing new financial products and services that would meet customer needs and prove profitable. 397

financial futures contract: A futures contract in which the standardized commodity is a particular type of financial instrument. 571

financial futures options: Options in which the underlying instrument is a futures contract. Also called *futures options*. 584

financial guarantee: A contract that guarantees that bond purchasers will be paid both principal and interest in the event the issuer defaults on the obligation. 240

Financial Institutions Reform Act: Law passed in 1978 that created the Central Liquidity Facility as the lender of last resort for credit unions. 447

Financial Institutions Reform, Recovery, and Enforcement Act: Law passed in 1989 to stop losses in the savings and loan industry. It reversed much of the deregulation included in the Garn–St Germain Act of 1982. 448

financial instrument: See *security*.

financial intermediaries: Institutions (such as banks, insurance companies, mutual funds, pension funds, and finance companies) that borrow funds from people who have saved and then make loans to others. 6

financial intermediation: The process of indirect finance whereby financial intermediaries link lender-savers and borrower-spenders. 19

financial markets: Markets in which funds are transferred from people who have an excess of available funds to people who have a shortage of available funds. 1

financial panic: The widespread collapse of financial markets and intermediaries in an economy. 28

Fisher effect: The outcome that when expected inflation occurs, interest rates will rise; named after economist Irving Fisher. 83

fixed exchange rate regime: Policy under which central banks buy and sell their own currencies to keep their exchange rates fixed at a certain level. 327

fixed-payment loan: A credit market instrument that provides a borrower with an amount of money that is repaid by making a fixed payment periodically (usually monthly) for a set number of years. 34

fixed-rate mortgage: A mortgage for which the interest rate does not change with changes in market conditions. 282

floor plan: A type of loan for which inventory is pledged as security and a portion of the loan is repaid each time an item of inventory is sold. 518

foreign bonds: Bonds sold in a foreign country and denominated in that country's currency. 18

foreign exchange intervention: An international financial transaction in which a central bank buys or sells currency to influence foreign exchange rates. 319

foreign exchange market: The market in which exchange rates are determined. 4, 293

foreign exchange rate: See *exchange rate*.

forward contract: An agreement by two parties to engage in a financial transaction at a future (forward) point in time. 570

forward exchange rate: The exchange rate for a forward transaction. 295

forward rate: The interest rate predicted by pure expectations theory of the term structure of interest rates to prevail in the future. 129

forward transaction: An exchange rate transaction that involves the exchange of bank deposits denominated in different currencies at some specified future date. 295

four-pillar approach: Regulation by institution that enforces the separation of institutions according to their core financial service. Four distinct types of financial services are identified: banking, brokerage, trusts, and insurance. 416

fractal: A complex geometric figure characterized by self-similarity. 265

free banking: A system that permitted the organization of a bank by any group that met certain established criteria concerning the amount of equity capital and maintenance of reserves. 411

free-rider problem: The problem that occurs when people who do not pay for information take advantage of the information that other people have paid for. 354

fully funded: Describing a pension plan in which the contributions to the plan and their earnings over the years are sufficient to pay out the defined benefits when they come due. 502

fully subscribed: Describing a security issue for which all of the securities available have been spoken for before the issue date. 532

futures options: See *financial futures options*.

gap analysis: A measurement of the sensitivity of bank profits to changes in interest rates, calculated by subtracting the amount of rate-sensitive assets. Also called *income gap analysis*. 557

general obligation bonds: Bonds that are secured by the full faith and credit of the issuer, which includes the taxing authority of municipalities. 235

globalization: The growing integration and interdependence of national economies. 187

gold standard: A regime under which a currency is directly convertible into gold. 326, 412

governing Council of the Bank of Canada: A council with six members (including the governor) that is responsible for the management of the Bank. 137

government deposit transfers: The transfer (by the Bank of Canada) of government deposits between the government's deposit account with the Bank of Canada and the government's deposit accounts with the direct clearers. 172

gross debt service ratio: The percentage of total income needed to cover the mortgage loan payment, including taxes, insurance, and heating costs. Generally, it should not exceed 32%. 278

Guaranteed Investment Certificates (GICs): Term deposits issued by trust and mortgage loan companies. 212

hedge: To protect oneself against risk. 547, 569

incentive-compatible: Aligning the incentives of both parties to a contract. 361

income gap analysis: See *gap analysis*.

indebtedness: The total amount countries have borrowed from banks. 423

index fund: A mutual fund that is composed only of securities that are included in some popular stock index, such as the S&P 500. The fund is designed to mimic the returns generated by the underlying index. 543

indexed bonds: Bonds whose interest and principal payments are adjusted for changes in the price level and whose interest rate thus provides a direct measure of a real interest rate. 52

indirect clearers: Members of the Canadian Payments Association who do not maintain a settlement account at the Bank of Canada, but retain a direct clearer to represent then in the clearing and settlement process. 158

initial public offering (IPO): A corporation's first sale of securities to the public. 226, 529

insolvent: In a situation in which the value of a firm's or bank's assets have fallen below its liabilities; bankrupt. 367

installment credit: A loan that requires the borrower to make a series of equal payments over some fixed length of time. 514

insured mortgage: Mortgages guaranteed by either the Federal Housing Administration or the Veterans Administration. These agencies guarantee that the bank making the loan will not suffer any losses if the borrower defaults. 282

interest parity condition: The observation that the domestic interest rate equals the foreign interest rate plus the expected appreciation in the foreign currency. 304

interest rate: The cost of borrowing or the price paid for the rental of funds (usually expressed as a percentage per year). 2

interest-rate forward contracts: Forward contracts that are linked to debt instruments. 570

interest-rate futures contract: A futures contract that is linked to a debt instrument. It is similar to an interest-rate forward contract. 572

interest-rate risk: The possible reduction in returns that is associated with changes in interest rates. 56, 383

interest-rate swap: A financial contract that allows one party to exchange (swap) a set of interest payments for another set of interest payments owned by another party. 591

intermediate target: Any number of variables, such as monetary aggregates or interest rates, that have a direct effect on employment and the price level and that the Fed seeks to influence. 178

intermediate term: With reference to a debt instrument, having a maturity of between one and ten years. 16

International Monetary Fund (IMF): The international organization created by the Bretton Woods agreement whose objective is to promote the growth of world trade by making loans to countries experiencing balance-of-payments difficulties. 327

international policy coordination: Agreements among countries to enact policies cooperatively. 188

international reserves: Central bank holdings of assets denominated in foreign currencies. 319

inverted yield curve: A yield curve that is downward-sloping. 116

investment banks: Firms that assist in the initial sale of securities in the primary market. 16, 528

January effect: An abnormal rise in stock prices from December to January. 263

junk bonds: Bonds rated lower than BBB by bond-rating agencies. Junk bonds are not investment grade and are considered speculative. They usually have a high yield to compensate investors for their high risk. 112, 239

Large Value Transfer System (LVTS): An electronic, net settlement system for the transfer of large-value payments. 157

law of large numbers: The observation that when many people are insured, the probability distribution of the losses will assume a normal probability distribution. 491

law of one price: The principle that if two or more countries produce an identical good, the price of this good should be the same no matter which country produces it. 297

leasing: An arrangement whereby one party obtains the right to use an asset for a fee paid to another party for a predetermined length of time. 518

lender of last resort: A lender that provides reserves to solvent banks in order to prevent bank failures from spinning out of control; in Canada, the Bank of Canada acts in this capacity. 169, 414

letter of intent: A document issued by a prospective buyer that signals a desire to go forward with a purchase and that outlines the preliminary terms of the purchase. 535

leverage ratio: A bank's capital divided by its assets. 458

liabilities: IOUs or debts. 14

liability management: The acquisition of funds at low cost to increase profits. 383

lien: A legal claim against a piece of property that gives a lender the right to foreclose or seize the property if a loan on the property is not repaid as promised. 277

limit order: An order placed by a customer to buy stock that specifies a maximum price or an order to sell stock that places a minimum acceptable price. 537

liquid: Easily converted into cash. 17

liquid market: A market in which securities can be bought and sold quickly and with low transaction costs. 207

liquidity: The relative ease and speed with which an asset can be converted into cash. 67

liquidity management: The decision made by a bank to maintain sufficient liquid assets to meet the bank's obligations to depositors. 383

liquidity preference framework: A model developed by John Maynard Keynes that predicts the equilibrium interest rate on the basis of the supply of and demand for money. 89

liquidity premium theory: The theory that the interest rate on a long-term bond will equal an average of short-term interest rates expected to occur over the life of the long-term bond plus a positive term (liquidity) premium. 123

liquidity risk: The risk that a firm may run out of cash needed to pay bills and to keep the firm operating. 516

load fund: A mutual fund that charges a fee when money is added to or withdrawn from the fund. 545

loan commitment: A bank's commitment (for a specified future period of time) to provide a firm with loans up to a given amount at an interest rate that is tied to some market interest rate. 391, 554

loan sale: The sale under a contract (also called a *secondary loan participation*) of all or part of the cash stream from a specific loan, thereby removing the loan from the bank's balance sheet. 391

loanable funds: The quantity of loans. 76

loanable funds framework: Determining the equilibrium interest rate by analyzing the supply of and demand for bonds (loanable funds). 76

London interbank bid rate (LIBID): The rate of interest large international banks charge on overnight loans among themselves. 217

London interbank offer rate (LIBOR): The interest rate charged on short-term funds bought or sold between large international banks. 217

long position: A contractual obligation to take delivery of an underlying financial instrument. 569

long term: With reference to a debt instrument, having a maturity of ten years or more. 16

LVTS participants: Members of the Canadian Payments Association (CPA) who participate in the LVTS and maintain a settlement account at the Bank of Canada. 157

macro hedge: A hedge of interest-rate risk for a financial institution's entire portfolio. 575

managed float regime: The current international financial environment in which exchange rates fluctuate from day to day, but central banks attempt to influence their countries' exchange rates by buying and selling currencies. Also known as a *dirty float*. 319

margin credit: Loans advanced by a brokerage house to help investors buy securities. 537

margin requirement: A sum of money that must be kept in an account (the margin account) at a brokerage firm. 578

marked to market: Repriced and settled in the margin account at the end of every trading day to reflect any change in the value of the futures contract. 578

market equilibrium: A situation occurring when the quantity that people are willing to buy (demand) equals the quantity that people are willing to sell (supply). 74

market fundamentals: Items that have a direct impact on future income streams of the security. 259

market maker: Dealers who buy or sell securities from their own inventories, thereby ensuring that there is always a market in which investors can buy or sell their securities. 539

market order: An order placed by a customer to buy stock at the current market price. 537

market segmentation theory: A theory of the term structure that sees markets for different-maturity bonds as completely separated and segmented such that the interest rate for bonds of a given maturity is determined solely by supply and demand for bonds of that maturity. 112

maturity: Time to the expiration date (maturity date) of a debt instrument. 15

mean reversion: The phenomenon that stocks with low returns today tend to have high returns in the future, and vice versa. 264

mergers and acquisitions market: An informal and unorganized market where firms are bought, sold, or merged with other firms. 535

micro hedge: A hedge for a specific asset. 575

modified duration: The Macaulay duration divided by 1+ i. 63

monetarism: A theory that emphasizes a steady, predictable rate of growth in the monetary aggregates. 184

monetary base: See *base money*.

monetary conditions: The level of short-term interest rates and the exchange rate of the Canadian dollar. 165

monetary neutrality: A proposition that in the long run, a percentage rise in the money supply is matched by the same percentage rise in the price level, leaving unchanged the real money supply and all other economic variables such as interest rates. 313

monetary policy: The management of the money supply and interest rates. 5

money: Anything that is generally accepted in payment for goods or services or in the repayment of debts. Also called *money supply*. 5

money centre banks: Large banks in key financial centers. 387

money market: A financial market in which only short-term debt instruments (maturity of less than one year) are traded. 17

money supply: See *money*.

moral hazard: The risk that one party to a transaction will engage in behavior that is undesirable from the other party's point of view. 21

mortgage: A long-term loan secured by real estate. 273

mortgage-backed security: A security that is collateralized by a pool of mortgage loans. Also called a *securitized mortgage*. 287

mortgage default insurance: Insurance that protects the lender against losses from defaults on mortgage loans. 277

mortgage pass-through: A security that has the multiple borrower's mortgage payments pass through a trustee before being disbursed to the investors. 287

multilateral netting: When only the net amounts of each LVTS participant vis-à-vis all other participants are calculated in order to effect settlement. 158

municipal bonds: Bonds issued by municipal governments. 234

municipals: See *municipal bonds*.

mutual insurance company: An insurance company that is owned by the policyholders and has the objective of providing insurance for the lowest possible price. 488

named-peril policy: Insurance policy that protects against loss from perils that are specifically named in the policy. 496

National Association of Securities Dealers Automated Quotation System (Nasdaq): A computerized network that links dealers around the country together and provides price quotes on over-the-counter securities. 229

National Credit Union Act of 1970: Law that established the National Credit Union Administration (NCUA), an independent agency charged with the task of regulating and supervising federally chartered credit unions and state-chartered credit unions that receive federal deposit insurance. 447

National Credit Union Administration (NCUA) An independent federal agency charged with regulating and supervising federally chartered credit unions and state-chartered credit unions that receive federal deposit insurance. 447

National Credit Union Share Insusrance Fund (NCUSIF): Agency established by the National Credit Union Act of 1970 that is controlled by the National Credit Union Administration and insures the deposits in credit unions for $100,000 per account. 447

natural rate of employment: The rate of employment consistent with full employment at which the demand for labour equals the supply of labor. 175

near banks The collection of trust and mortgage loan companies and credit unions and *caisses populaires* that are primarily concerned with lending to individuals and households. 23, 435

net asset value: The total value of a mutual fund's assets minus any liabilities, divided by the number of shares outstanding. 545

net interest margin (NIM): The difference between interest income and interest expense as a percentage of assets. 396

net worth: The difference between a firm's assets (what it owns or is owed) and its liabilities (what it owes). Also called *equity capital*. 357

no-load fund: A mutual fund that does not charge a fee when funds are added to or withdrawn from the fund. 545

nominal interest rate: An interest rate that does not take inflation into account. 50

nonbank banks: Limited-service banks that either do not make commercial loans or do not take in deposits. 420

noncompetitive bidding: Offering to buy Treasury securities without specifying a price; the securities are ultimately sold at the weighted average of the competitive bids accepted at the same auction. 208

notional principal: The amount on which interest is being paid in a swap arrangement. 591

off-balance-sheet activities: Bank activities that involve trading financial instruments and the generation of income from fees and loan sales, all of which affect bank profits but are not visible on bank balance sheets. 391, 458

official reserve transactions balance: The current account balance plus items in the capital account. 325

open-end fund: A mutual fund that accepts investments and allows investors to redeem shares at any time. The value of the shares is tied to the value of investment assets of the fund. 544

open interest: The number of contracts outstanding. 575

open market operations The Bank of Canada's buying or selling of bonds in the open market. 139, 155

open market purchase A purchase of bonds by the Bank of Canada. 167

open market sale A sale of bonds by the Bank of Canada. 167

open-peril policy Insurance policy that insures against all perils except those specifically excluded from the policy. 496

operating band The Bank of Canada's range of 50 basis points for the overnight interest rate. 158

operating expenses: The expenses incurred from a bank's ongoing operations. 394

operating income: The income earned on bank's ongoing operations. 394

operating target: Any of a set of variables, such as reserve aggregates or interest rates, that the Fed seeks to influence and that are responsive to its policy tools. 178

opportunity cost: The amount of interest (expected return) sacrificed by not holding an alternative asset. 96

options: Contracts that give the purchaser the option (right) to buy or sell the underlying financial instrument at a specified price, called the *exercise price* or *strike price*, within a specific period of time (the *term to expiration*). 583

overfunded: Describing a pension plan that has assets greater than needed to make the projected benefit payments owed by the plan. 502

oversubscribed: Having received more offers to buy than there are securities available for sale. 532

over-the-counter (OTC) market: A secondary market in which dealers at different locations who have an inventory of securities stand ready to buy and sell securities to anyone who comes to them and is willing to accept their prices. 17

overdraft loans: A bank's borrowings from the Bank of Canada. Also known as *advances*. 377

overnight interest rate The interest rate financial institutions borrow and lend overnight funds to each other in the overnight market. 158, 211

passbook savings account: An interest-bearing savings account held at a commercial bank. 449

personal pension plans: Registered Retirement Savings Plans that provide tax shelter and are self-financed. 505

pension plan: An asset pool that accumulates over an individual's working years and is paid out during the nonworking years. 501

perpetuity: A perpetual bond with no maturity date and no repayment of principal that makes periodic fixed payments forever. 42

political business cycle: A business cycle caused by expansion policies before an election. 148

preferred stock: Stock on which a fixed dividend must be paid before common dividends are distributed. It often does not mature and usually does not give the holder voting rights in the company. 241

premium: The amount paid for an option contract. 584

present discounted value: See *present value*.

present value: Today's value of a payment to be received in the future when the interest rate is i. Also called *present discounted value*. 34

price earnings ratio: Measure of how much the market is willing to pay for $1 of earnings from a firm. 253

primary dealers: The Big Six and the major investment dealers the Bank of Canada deals with when it conducts its open-market buyback operations. 168

primary market: A financial market in which new issues of a security are sold to initial buyers. 16, 527

principal-agent problem: A moral hazard problem that occurs when the managers in control (the agents) act in their own interest rather than in the interest of the owners (the principals) due to differing sets of incentives. 358

private pension plan: A pension plan sponsored by an employer, group, or individual. 503

property insurance: Insurance that protects against losses from fire, theft, storm, explosion, and neglect. 495

prospectus: A portion of a security registration statement that is filed with the Securities and Exchange Commission and made available to potential purchasers of the security. 530

provincial bonds: The securities issued by provincial governments. 234

provincials: See *provincial bonds*.

public pension plan: A pension plan sponsored by a government body. 503

pure expectations theory: The theory that the interest rate on a long-term bond will equal the average of the short-term interest rates that people expect to occur over the life of the bond. 118

put option: An option contract that provides the right to sell a security at a specified price. 585

quotas: Restrictions on the quantity of foreign goods that can be imported. 300

random walk: The movements of a variable whose future changes cannot be predicted because, given today's value, the variable is just as likely to fall as to rise. 260

rate of capital gain: The change in a security's price relative to the initial purchase price. 55

rate of return: See *return*.

real interest rate: The interest rate adjusted for expected changes in the price level (inflation) so that it more accurately reflects the true cost of borrowing. 50

real terms: Terms reflecting actual goods and services one can buy. 51

redemption: See *call*.

redeposits: Transfers of government deposits from the government's account with the Bank of Canada to the government's accounts with the direct clearers. 172

refinance: To pay in full the loan and arrange for a new loan not necessarily with the same lender. 282

registered bonds: Bonds requiring that their owners register with the company to receive interest payments. Registered bonds have largely replaced bearer bonds, which did not require registration. 231

registration statement: Information about a firm's financial condition, management, competition, industry, and experience that must be filed with the Securities and Exchange Commission prior to the sale to the public of any security with a maturity of more than 270 days. 530

Regulation Q: The regulation under which the Federal Reserve System has the power to set maximum interest rates that banks can pay on savings and time deposits. 403

regulatory arbitrate: An attempt to avoid regulatory capital requirements by keeping assets on banks' books that have the same risk-based capital requirement but are relatively risky, while taking off their books low-risk assets. 458

regulatory capital: The amount of capital that regulatory authorities require financial institutions to maintain. 30

regulatory forbearance: Refraining from exercising a regulatory right to put insolvent savings and loans out of business. 467

reinsurance: Allocating a portion of the risk to another company in exchange for a portion of the premium. 497

reinvestment risk: The interest-rate risk associated with the fact that the proceeds of short-term investments must be reinvested at a future interest rate that is uncertain. 57

repos: A tool to reduce undesired upward pressure on the overnight interest rate; known as Special Purchase and Resale Agreements (SPRAs) in Canada. 167

repossession: The taking of an asset that has been pledged as collateral for a loan when the borrower defaults. 518

reserve account: An account used to make insurance and tax payments due on property securing a mortgage loan. A portion of each monthly loan payment goes into the reserve account. 286

reserve currency: A currency such as the U.S. dollar that is used by other countries to denominate the assets they hold as international reserves. 328

reserve for loan losses: An account that offsets the loan accounts on a lender's books that reflects the lender's projected losses due to default. 521

reserves: Settlement balances plus currency that is physically held by banks. 154, 179

Resolution Trust Corporation (RTC): A temporary agency created by FIRREA that was responsible for liquidating the assets of failed savings and loans. 448

restrictive covenants: Provisions that specify certain activities that a borrower can and cannot engage in. 237, 350

return: The payments to the owner of a security plus the change in the security's value, expressed as a fraction of its purchase price; more precisely called the *rate of return*. 53

return on assets (ROA): Net profit after taxes per dollar of assets. 388

return on equity (ROE): Net profit after taxes per dollar of equity capital. 388

revaluation: Resetting of the par value of a currency at a higher level. 329

revenue bonds: Bonds for which the source of income that is used to pay the interest and to retire the bonds is from a specific source, such as a toll road or an electric plant. If this revenue source is unable to make the payments, the bonds can default, despite the issuing municipality's being otherwise healthy. 235

reverse mortgage: A mortgage for which the bank advances funds as a cash lump-sum, or a guaranteed monthly schedule, or a combination of the two. The increasing-balance loan is secured by the real estate. The borrower does not make any payments against the loan and continues to own the property and therefore benefit from any future appreciation in its value. 283

reverse repos: A tool to reduce undesired downward pressure on the overnight rate; known in Canada as Sale and Repurchase Agreements (SRAs). 167

risk: The degree of uncertainty associated with the return on an asset. 67

risk premium: The spread between the interest rate on bonds with default risk and the interest rate on default-free bonds. 110

risk structure of interest rates: The relationship among the various interest rates on bonds with the same term to maturity. 109

roll over: To renew a debt when it matures. 516

Sale and Repurchase Agreements (SRAs): The Bank of Canada's sale of government securities to primary dealers with an agreement to repurchase them one business day later. 168

Schedule I banks: The Big Six, the Laurentian Bank of Canada, and the Canadian Western Bank. 414

Schedule II banks: Three domestic Schedule II banks (Citizen Bank, First Nations Bank, and Manulife Bank) and 36 subsidiaries (i.e., separate Canadian legal entities) of foreign banks. 414

Schedule III banks: A foreign bank allowed to branch directly into Canada, under certain restrictions 416

seasoned issues: Securities that have been trading publicly long enough to have let the market clearly establish their value. 529

secondary market: A financial market in which securities that have previously been issued can be resold. 16, 527

secured debt: Debt guaranteed by collateral. 350

secured loan: A loan guaranteed by collateral. 554

securitization: The process of transforming illiquid financial assets into marketable capital market instruments. 428

securitized mortgage: See *mortgage-backed security*. 290

security: A claim on the borrower's future income that is sold by the borrower to the lender. Also called a *financial instrument*. 2

seigniorage: The government receives a share of the profits from the issuance of money. 412

Separate Trading of Registered Interest and Principal Securities (STRIPS): Securities that have their periodic interest payments separated from the final maturity payment and the two cash flows are sold to different investors. 233

settlement balances: Deposits held by directly clearing members of the Canadian Payments Association at the Bank of Canada. They are also known as clearing balances. 29, 154, 378

short position: A contractual obligation to deliver an underlying financial instrument. 569

short sale: An arrangement with a broker to borrow and sell securities. The borrowed securities are replaced with securities purchased later. Short sells let investors earn profits from falling securities prices. 537

short term: With reference to a debt instrument, having a maturity of one year or less. 16

simple loan: A credit market instrument providing the borrower with an amount of funds that must be repaid to the lender at the maturity date along with an additional payment (interest). 34

sinking fund: Fund created by a provision in many bond contracts that requires the issuer to set aside each year a portion of the final maturity payment so that investors can be certain that the funds will be available at maturity. 237

smart card: A more sophisticated stored-value card that contains its own computer chip so that it can be loaded with digital cash from the owner's bank account whenever needed. 401

sovereign loans: Loans to foreign governments and their agencies in the less developed countries. 423

special drawing rights (SDRs): A paper substitute for gold issued by the International Monetary Fund that functions as international reserves. 332

Special Purchase and Resale Agreements (SPRAs): The Bank of Canada's purchase of government securities from primary dealers with an agreement to resell them one business day later. 168

spot exchange rate: The exchange rate at a given moment. 129, 295

spot transaction: The immediate exchange of bank deposits denominated in different currencies. 294

standing facilities: The Bank of Canada's framework to influence the overnight interest rate, by making one-business-day loans at the upper limit of the operating band for the overnight interest rate (bank rate) and paying the lower limit of the operating band (bank rate less 50 basis points) on deposits to LVTS participants. 160

state banks: Banks chartered by the state. 411

sterilized foreign exchange intervention: A foreign exchange intervention with an offsetting open market operation that leaves the monetary base unchanged. 321

stock: A security that is a claim on the earnings and assets of a corporation. 3

stock company: A firm that issues stock and has the objective of making a profit for its shareholders. 488

stock market risk: The risk associated with fluctuations in stock prices. 581

stock option: An option on an individual stock. 584

strike price: See *exercise price*.

supply curve: A curve depicting the relationship between quantity supplied and price when all other economic variables are held constant. 74

swap: A financial contract that obligates one party to exchange (swap) a set of payments it owns for a set of payments owned by another party. 591

syndicate: A group of investment banks that come together for the purpose of issuing a security. The syndicate spreads the risk of the issue among the members. Each participant attempts to market the security and shares in losses. 532

systematic risk: The component of an asset's risk that cannot be eliminated by diversification. 157

T-account: A simplified balance sheet with lines in the form of a T that lists only the exchanges that occur in balance sheet times starting from some initial balance sheet position. 319

tariffs: Taxes on imported goods. 300

term deposit receipts (term notes): Non-negotiable CDs, i.e. those that cannot be sold to someone else and cannot be redeemed from the bank before maturity without paying a substantial penalty. 212

term security: A security with a specified maturity date. 212

term structure of interest rates: The relationship among interest rates on bonds with different terms to maturity. 109

theory of efficient capital markets: The theory that prices of securities in financial markets fully reflect all available information. 256

theory of purchasing power parity (PPP): The theory that exchange rates between any two currencies will adjust to reflect changes in the price levels of the two countries. 298

tombstone: A large notice placed in financial newspapers announcing that a security will be offered for sale by an underwriter or group of underwriters. 532

total debt service ratio: The percentage of total income needed to cover the sum of all monthly payments. Generally, it should not exceed 40%. 278

trade balance: The difference between merchandise exports and imports. 323

transaction costs: The time and money spent trying to exchange financial assets, goods, or services. 20

Treasury bills (T-bills): Securities sold by the federal government with initial maturities of less than one year. They are often considered the lowest-risk security available. 206

trustees: Groups or people appointed to manage the affairs of an institution. 436

underfunded: Describing a pension plan in which the contributions and their earnings are insufficient to pay out the defined benefits when they come due. 502

undersubscribed: Having received fewer offers to buy than there are securities available for sale. 532

underwriters: Investment banks that guarantee prices on securities to corporations and then sell the securities to the public. 488

underwriting: Guaranteeing prices on securities to corporations and then selling the securities to the public. 16, 245

unexploited profit opportunity: A situation in which an investor can earn a higher-than-normal return. 258

unsecured debt: Debt not guaranteed by collateral. 350

unsterilized foreign exchange intervention: A foreign exchange intervention in which a central bank allows the purchase or sale of domestic currency to affect the monetary base. 320

U.S. Central Credit Union: A central bank for credit unions that was organized in 1974 and provides banking services to the state central credit unions. 447

usury: Charging an excessive or inordinate interest rate on a loan. 521

variable-rate mortgage: A mortgage for which the interest rate changes with changes in market conditions. 282

vault cash: Currency that is physically held by banks and stored in vaults overnight. 379

venture capital firm: A financial intermediary that pools the resources of its partners and uses the funds to help entrepreneurs start up new businesses. 360

wealth: All resources owned by an individual, including all assets. 67

wholesale market: Market where extremely large transactions occur, as for money market funds or foreign currency. 202

World Bank: The International Bank for Reconstruction and Redevelopment, an international organization that provides long-term loans to assist developing countries in building dams, roads, and other physical capital that would contribute to their economic development. 327

yield curve: A plot of the interest rates for particular types of bonds with different terms to maturity. 116

yield on a discount basis: The measure of interest rates by which dealers in bill markets quote the interest rate on U.S. Treasury bills. Also known as the *discount yield*. 46

yield to maturity: The interest rate that equates the present value of payments received from a credit market instrument with its value today. 37

zero-coupon bond: See *discount bond*.

Answers to Selected Questions and Problems

Chapter 1

2. Businesses would cut investment spending because the cost of financing this spending is now higher, and consumers would be less likely to purchase a house or a car because the cost of financing their purchase is higher.

4. No. People who borrow to purchase a house or a car are worse off because it costs them more to finance their purchase; however, savers benefit because they can earn higher interest rates on their savings.

6. Higher stock prices mean that consumers' wealth is higher and so they will be more likely to increase their spending.

8. It makes British goods more expensive relative to Canadian goods. Canadian businesses will find it easier to sell their goods in Canada and abroad, and the demand for their products will rise.

10. In the mid- to late 1970s and in the early 1980s and 1990s, the value of the dollar was low, making travel abroad relatively more expensive; that would have been a good time to vacation in Canada and see the Canadian Rockies. As the dollar's value rose in the late 1980s, travel abroad became relatively cheaper, making it a good time to visit the Tower of London.

12. Trust and mortgage loan companies, credit unions and *caisses populaires*, insurance companies, mutual funds, pension funds, and finance companies.

14. The profitability of financial institutions is affected by changes in interest rates, stock prices, and foreign exchange rates; fluctuations in these variables expose these institutions to risk.

Chapter 2

1. The share of IBM stock is an asset for its owner because it entitles the owner to a share of the earnings and assets of IBM. The share is a liability for IBM because it is a claim on its earnings and assets by the owner of the share.

3. Yes, because the absence of financial markets means that funds cannot be channeled to people who have the most productive use for them. Entrepreneurs then cannot acquire funds to set up businesses that would help the economy grow rapidly.

5. This statement is false. Prices in secondary markets determine the prices that firms issuing securities receive in primary markets. In addition, secondary markets make securities more liquid and thus easier to sell in the primary markets. Therefore, secondary markets are, if anything, more important than primary markets.

7. Because you know your family member better than a stranger, you know more about the borrower's honesty, propensity for risk taking, and other traits. There is less asymmetric information than with a stranger and less likelihood of an adverse selection problem, with the result that you are more likely to lend to the family member.

9. Loan sharks can threaten their borrowers with bodily harm if borrowers take actions that might jeopardize paying off the loan. Hence borrowers from a loan shark are less likely to engage in moral hazard.

11. Yes, because even if you know that a borrower is taking actions that might jeopardize paying off the loan, you must still stop the borrower from doing so. Because that may be costly, you may not spend the time and effort to reduce moral hazard, and so moral hazard remains a problem.

13. Because the costs of making the loan to your neighbour are high (legal fees, fees for a credit check, and so on), you will probably not be able to earn 5% on the loan after your expenses even though it has a 10% interest rate. You are better off depositing your savings with a financial intermediary and earning 5% interest. In addition, you are likely to bear less risk by depositing your savings at the bank rather than lending them to your neighbour.

15. Increased discussion of foreign financial markets in the press and the growth in markets for international financial instruments such as Eurodollars and Eurobonds.

Chapter 3

1. Less. It would be worth $1/(1 + 0.20) = \$0.83$ when the interest rate is 20%, rather than $1/(1 + 0.10) = \$0.91$ when the interest rate is 10%.

3. $\$1100/(1 + 0.10) + \$1210/(1 + 0.10)^2 + \$1331/(1 + 0.10)^3 = \$3000$.

5. $\$2000 = \$100/(1 + i) + \$100/(1 + i)^2 + \ldots + \$100/(1 + i)^{20} + \$1000/(1 + i)^{20}$.

7. 14.9%, derived as follows: The present value of the \$2 million payment five years from now is $\$2/(1 + i)^5$ million, which equals the \$1 million loan. Thus $1 = 2/(1 + i)^5$. Solving for i $(1 + i)^5 = 2$, so that $i = \sqrt[5]{2} - 1 = 0.149 = 14.9\%$.

9. If the one-year bond did not have a coupon payment, its yield to maturity would be $(\$1000 - \$800)/\$800 = \$200/\$800 = 0.25 = 25\%$. Since it does have a coupon payment, its yield to maturity must be greater than 25%. But because the current yield is a good approximation of the yield to maturity for a 20-year bond, we know that the yield to maturity on this bond is approximately 15%. Therefore, the one-year bond has a higher yield to maturity.

11. You would rather own the treasury bill because it has a higher yield to maturity. As the example in the text indicates, the discount yield's understatement of the yield to maturity for a one-year bond is substantial, exceeding 1 percentage point. Thus the yield to maturity on the one-year bill would be greater than 9%, the yield to maturity on the one-year Treasury bond.

13. No. If interest rates rise sharply in the future, long-term bonds may suffer such a sharp fall in price that their return might be quite low, possibly even negative.

15. The observers are right. They reason that nominal interest rates were below expected rates of inflation in the late 1970s, making real interest rates negative. The expected inflation rate, however, fell much faster than nominal interest rates in the mid–1980s, so nominal interest rates were above the expected inflation rate and real rates became positive.

17. The present value of the five \$80 coupon payments plus the \$1000 face value of the bond are, respectively, \$77.67, \$75.41, \$73.21, \$71.08, \$69.01, and \$862.61, which sum to a total present value of \$1228.99. The weights for these payments are, respectively, 0.0631982, 0.0613593, 0.0595692, 0.0578361, 0.0561518, and 0.7018853. The duration is then the sum of the weighted maturities: $(1 \times 0.0631982) + (2 \times 0.0613593) + (3 \times 0.0595692) + (4 \times 0.0578361) + (5 \times 0.0561518 + (5 \times 0.7018853) = 4.3861543$ years.

19. The approximate percentage change in the price is $-DUR \times \Delta i/(1 + i) = -8 \times 0.01/1.07 = -0.075 = -7.5\%$.

Chapter 4

2. (a) More, because your wealth has increased; (b) more, because it has become more liquid; (c) less, because its expected return has fallen relative to Air Canada stock; (d) more, because it has become less risky relative to stocks; (e) less, because its expected return has fallen.

4. Purchasing shares in the pharmaceutical company is more likely to reduce my overall risk because the correlation of returns on my investment in a football team with the returns on the pharmaceutical company shares should be low. By contrast, the correlation of returns on an investment in a football team and an investment in a basketball team are probably pretty high, so in this case there would be little risk reduction if I invested in both.

6. When the Bank of Canada sells bonds to the public, it increases the supply of bonds, thus shifting the supply curve B^s to the right. The result is that the intersection of the supply and demand curves B^s and B^d occurs at a higher equilibrium interest rate, and the interest rate rises. With the liquidity preference framework, the decrease in the money supply shifts the money supply curve M^s to the left, and the equilibrium interest rate rises. The answer from the loanable funds framework is consistent with the answer from the liquidity preference framework.

8. When the price level rises, the quantity of money in real terms falls (holding the nominal supply of money constant); to restore their holdings of money in real terms to their former level, people will want to hold a greater nominal quantity of money. Thus the money demand curve M^d shifts to the right, and the interest rate rises.

11. Interest rates would rise. A sudden increase in people's expectations of future real estate prices raises the expected return on real estate relative to bonds, so the demand for bonds falls. The demand curve B^d shifts to the left, and the equilibrium interest rate rises.

13. In the loanable funds framework, the increased riskiness of bonds lowers the demand for bonds. The demand curve B^d shifts to the left, and the equilibrium interest rate rises. The same answer is found in the liquidity preference framework. The increased riskiness of bonds relative to money increases the demand for money. The money demand curve M^d shifts to the right, and the equilibrium interest rate rises.

15. Yes, interest rates will rise. The lower commission on stocks makes them more liquid than bonds, and the demand for bonds will fall. The demand curve B^d will therefore shift to the left, and the equilibrium interest rate will rise.

17. The interest rate on long-term bonds will rise. Because people now expect interest rates to rise, the expected return on long-term bond and the demand for these bonds will decline. The demand curve B^d will therefore shift to the left, and the equilibrium interest rate will rise.

19. Interest rates will rise. When bond prices become volatile and bonds become riskier, the demand for bonds will fall. The demand curve B^d will shift to the left, and the equilibrium interest rate will rise.

Chapter 5

2. Canada treasury bills have lower default risk and more liquidity than negotiable CDs. Consequently, the demand for treasury bills is higher, and they have a lower interest rate.

4. True. When bonds of different maturities are close substitutes, a rise in interest rates for one bond causes the interest rates for others to rise because the expected returns on bonds of different maturities cannot get too far out of line.

6. (a) The yield to maturity would be 5% for a one-year bond, 6% for a two-year bond, 6.33% for a three-year bond, 6.5% for a four-year bond, and 6.6% for a five-year bond. (b) The yield to maturity would be 5% for a one-year bond, 4.5% for a two-year bond, 4.33% for a three-year bond, 4.25% for a four-year bond, and 4.2% for a five-year bond. The upward-sloping yield curve in (a) would be even steeper if people preferred short-term bonds over long-term bonds because long-term bonds would then have a positive risk premium. The downward-sloping yield curve in (b) would be less steep and might even have a slight positive upward slope if the long-term bonds have a positive risk premium.

8. The flat yield curve at shorter maturities suggests that short-term interest rates are expected to fall moderately in the near future, while the steep upward slope of the yield curve at longer maturities indicates that interest rates further into the future are expected to rise. Because interest rates and expected inflation move together, the yield curve suggests that the market expects inflation to fall moderately in the near future but to rise later on.

10. The cost of borrowing increases, since the return demanded by investors rises to compensate them for the greater probability of default.

12. Lower brokerage commissions for corporate bonds would make them more liquid and thus increase their demand, which would lower their risk premium.

14. The expected one-year interest rate two years from now is $i^e_{t+2} = [(1 + i_{3t} - k_{3t})^3/(1 + i_{2t} - k_{2t})^2] - 1 = [(1 + 0.06 - 0.0035)^3/(1 + 0.05 - 0.0025)^2] - 1 = 0.075 = 7.5\%$.

Chapter 6

1. The primary motivation for the formation of the Bank of Canada was political. As the Great Depression undermined faith in the existing market economy and inflation blamed on the concentrated banking industry, support was given to the idea of a central bank.

3. The Bank Act was amended in 1967 to give the ultimate responsibility for monetary policy to the government. In practice, however, the Bank of Canada does essentially control monetary policy. In the event of a disagreement between the Bank and the government, the minister of finance can issue a directive that the Bank must follow.

5. After governor Coyne tendered his resignation in 1961 and Louis Rasminsky became the third governor of the Bank of Canada, upon assuming office he issued a public statement making clear his views regarding the division of responsibility between the Bank and the government. The matter rested until 1967 when the Bank of Canada Act was amended to confirm that the minister of finance and the governor of the Bank of Canada should consult regularly on monetary policy.

7. True. Assuming that politicians are driven by the need to win the next election, they are likely to seek short-run solutions to problems like high unemployment and interest rates. For example, they are likely to increase money growth in order to reduce unemployment and interest rates in the short run. In the long run, however, such policies will lead to more inflation.

9. By not renewing the governor's appointment when it expires.

11. False. Maximizing one's welfare does not rule out altruism. Operating in the public interest is clearly one objective of the Bank of Canada. The theory of bureaucratic behaviour only points out that other objectives, such as maximizing power, also influence Bank of Canada decision making.

13. False. The Bank is still subject to political pressure because the government can pass legislation limiting the Bank's power. If the Bank is performing badly, the government can therefore make the Bank accountable by passing legislation that the Bank does not like.

15. During the first 60 or so years of Confederation there was little need for a central bank in what was a scattered and mainly rural economy. The branch bank network, influenced by the British tradition, was sufficient to serve the banking needs of the small, scattered, rural settlements.

Chapter 7

1. Disagree. Some unemployment is beneficial to the economy because the availability of vacant jobs makes it more likely that a worker will find the right job and that the employer will find the right worker for the job.

3. True. In such a world, hitting a monetary target would mean that the Bank would also hit its interest target, or vice versa. Thus the Bank could pursue both a monetary target and an interest-rate target at the same time.

5. The Bank can control the interest rate on three-month treasury bills by buying and selling them in the open market. When the bill rate rises above the target level, the Bank would buy bills, which would bid up their price and lower the interest rate to its target level. Similarly, when the bill rate falls below the target level, the Bank would sell bills to raise the interest rate to the target level. The resulting open market operations would of course affect the money supply and cause it to change. The Bank would be giving up control of the money supply to pursue an interest-rate target.

7. Disagree. Although nominal interest rates are measured more accurately and more quickly than the money supply, the interest rate variable that is of more concern to policymakers is the *real* interest rate. Because the measurement of real interest rates requires estimates of inflation, it is not true that real interest rates are necessarily measured more accurately and more quickly than the money supply. Interest-rate targets are therefore not necessarily better than money supply targets.

9. An inflation-targeting framework increases the transparency of monetary policy and reduces the likelihood that the Bank of Canada will fall into the time-inconsistency trap (trying to expand output and employment by pursuing overly expansionary monetary policy). The transparency of policy associated with inflation targeting tends to make the Bank of Canada highly accountable to the public and the government.

11. When the Bank of Canada raises the operating band for the overnight interest rate the monetary base declines and this reduces the money supply. In the opposite case, when the Bank lowers the operating band, it encourages banks to borrow reserves. The increase in reserves increases the monetary base and ultimately leads to an increase in the money supply.

13. In a repo, the Bank of Canada buys government of Canada securities from participants with an agreement to resell them on the next business day. The Bank pays for the repos by crediting the participant's account at the Bank, thereby increasing settlement balances. This increase in settlement balances puts downward pressure on the overnight interest rate, as banks would have to borrow less to meet their settlement requirements. In a reverse repo, the Bank of Canada sells government of Canada securities with an agreement to buy them back on the next day. When the Bank sells these securities, it debits the participant's account at the Bank, thereby reducing settlement balances. This reduction in settlement balances puts upward pressure on the overnight rate, as banks would have to borrow more to meet their settlement requirements.

15. When the Bank was concerned that the dollar had risen too much, it pursued expansionary monetary policy to bring the value of the dollar back down again. When it felt that the dollar had fallen far enough, it pursued more contractionary policy to keep the dollar from falling further.

17. When the economy enters a recession, interest rates usually fall. If the Bank is targeting interest rates, it tries to prevent a decline in interest rates by selling bonds, thereby lowering their prices and raising interest rates to the target level. The open market sale would then lead to a decline in the monetary base and in the money supply. The decline in interest rates would also cause excess reserves to rise, thereby raising reserves. With a reserve target, the Bank would find monetary policy easy and would pursue contractionary policy. Therefore, neither interest-rate nor reserve targets are very satisfactory because both can lead to a slower rate of money supply growth during a recession, just when the Bank would not want to slow money supply growth.

19. The Bank of Canada may prefer to control interest rates rather than the money supply because it wishes to avoid the conflict with the government that occurs when interest rates rise. The Bank might also believe that interest rates are actually a better guide to future economic activity.

Chapter 8

1. The money markets can be characterized as having securities that trade in one year or less, are of large denomination, and are very liquid.

3. Banks have higher costs than the money markets owing to the need to maintain reserve requirements. The lower cost structure of the money markets, coupled with the economies of scale resulting from high volume and large-denomination securities, allows for higher interest rates.

5. Following the Great Depression, regulators were primarily concerned with stopping banks from failing. By removing interest-rate competition, bank risk was substantially reduced. The problem with these regulations was that when market interest rates rose above the established interest-rate ceiling, investors withdrew their funds from banks.

7. Businesses both invest and borrow in the money markets. They borrow to meet short-term cash flow needs, often by issuing commercial paper. They invest in all types of money market securities as an alternative to holding idle cash balances.

9. Life insurance companies can invest for the long term because the timing for their liabilities is known with reasonable accuracy. Property and casualty insurance companies cannot predict the natural disasters that cause large payouts on policies.

11. In competitive bidding for securities, buyers submit bids. A noncompetitive bidder accepts the average of the rate paid by the competitive bidders.

13. The Bank of Canada cannot directly set the rate of interest. It sets the operating band for the overnight interest rate, but the overnight rate can be anywhere within the operating band, although the Bank uses repos and reverses to target the overnight rate at the midpoint of the band.

15. Banker's acceptances substitute the creditworthiness of a bank for that of a business. When a company sells a product to a company it is unfamiliar with, it often prefers to have the promise of a bank that payment will be made.

Chapter 9

1. Investors use capital markets for long-term investment purposes. They use money markets, which have lower yields, primarily for temporary or transaction purposes.

3. The primary market is for securities being issued for the very first time, and the issuer receives the funds paid for the security. The secondary market is for securities that have been issued previously but are being traded among investors.

5. NASDAQ is a computer network in the United States that allows traders to monitor stocks traded on the over-the-counter market. It provides current bid and ask prices on about 4000 actively traded securities.

7. Treasury bills mature in less than 1 year and Canada bonds mature in 1 to 30 years.

9. Agencies that issue securities include the Canada Mortgage and Housing Corporation (CMHC), the Ontario Municipal Improvements Corporation, Hydro Quebec, the Alberta Municipal Financing Corporation, and the New Brunswick Electric Power Commission.

11. A sinking fund contains funds set aside by the issuer of a bond to pay for the redemption of the bond when it matures. Because a sinking fund increases the likelihood that a firm will have the funds to pay off the bonds as required, investors like the feature. As a result, interest rates are lower on securities with sinking funds.

13. Stocks do not mature, do not pay a fixed amount every period, and often give holders the right to vote on management issues.

15. At least 7 of the 30 firms are involved in high-technology products or services. This has increased the volatility of the Dow index in recent years as these firms were added.

Chapter 10

2. There are two cash flows from stock, periodic dividends, and a future sales price. Dividents are frequently changed when firm earnings either rise or fall. The future sales price is also difficult to estimate, since it depends on the dividends that will be paid at some date even farther in the future. Bond cash flows also consist of two parts, periodic interest payments and a final maturity payment. These payments are established in writing at the time the bonds are issued and cannot be changed without the firm defaulting and being subject to bankruptcy. Stock prices tend to be more volatile, since their cash flows are more subject to change.

4. $P_0 = \dfrac{\$3 \times (1.07)}{.18 - .07} = \$29.18$

6. False. Expectations can be highly inaccurate and still be rational because optimal forecasts are not necessarily accurate: A forecast is optimal if it is the best possible even if the forecast errors are large.

8. No, because he could improve the accuracy of his forecasts by predicting that tomorrow's interest rates will be identical to today's. His forecasts are therefore not optimal, and he does not have rational expectations.

10. No, you shouldn't buy stocks because the rise in the money supply is publicly available information that will be already incorporated into stock prices. Hence you cannot expect to earn more than the equilibrium return on stocks by acting on the money supply information.

12. No, because this is publicly available information and is already reflected in stock prices. The optimal forecast of stock returns will equal the equilibrium return, so there is no benefit from selling your stocks.

14. No, if the person has no better information than the rest of the market. An expected price rise of 10% over the next month implies over a 100% annual return on IBM stock, which certainly exceeds its equilibrium return. This would mean that there is an unexploited profit opportunity in the market, which would have been eliminated in an efficient market. The only time that the person's expectations could be rational is if the person had information unavailable to the market that allowed him or her to beat the market.

16. False. The people with better information are exactly those who make the market more efficient by eliminating unexploited profit opportunities. These people can profit from their better information.

18. True in principle. Foreign exchange rates are a random walk over a short interval such as a week because changes in the exchange rate are unpredictable. If a change were predictable, large unexploited profit opportunities would exist in the foreign exchange market. If the foreign exchange market is efficient, these unexploited profit opportunities cannot exist and so the foreign exchange rate will approximately follow a random walk.

20. False. Although human fear may be the source of stock market crashes, that does not imply that there are unexploited profit opportunities in the market. Nothing in rational expectations theory rules out large changes in stock prices as a result of fears on the part of the investing public.

Chapter 11

1. Securities in the mortgage markets are collateralized by real estate.

3. The global market for loans results in competition that keeps the rates low.

5. A lien is a publicly recorded claim on a piece of real property that has been pledged as collateral. Mortgage lenders file liens to secure loans.

7. Lenders may require mortgage default insurance.

9. Insured mortgages guarantee lenders against losses from loans insured by them. Conventional loans do not have this guarantee, so the lender usually requires private mortgage insurance.

11. The goal of the graduated-payment loan is to let the borrower qualify by reducing the first few years' payments, whereas the goal of the growing-equity loan is to let the borrower pay off early.

13. The bank accepts the home as security and advances money each month. When the borrower dies, the borrower's estate sells the property to retire the debt.

15. The payments on a pool of mortgages are sent by the borrowers to a trustee, who then passes the payments through to holders of securities that are backed by the pass-through.

Chapter 12

2. False. Although a weak currency has the negative effect of making it more expensive to buy foreign goods or to travel abroad, it may help domestic industry. Domestic goods become cheaper relative to foreign goods, and the demand for domestically produced goods increases. The resulting higher sales of domestic products may lead to higher employment, a beneficial effect on the economy.

4. It predicts that the value of the euro will fall 5% in terms of dollars.

6. Even though the Japanese price level rose relative to the American, the yen appreciated because the increase in Japanese productivity relative to American productivity made it possible for the Japanese to continue to sell their goods at a profit at a high value of the yen.

8. The pound depreciates but overshoots, declining by more in the short run than in the long run. Consider Britain the domestic country. The rise in the money supply leads to a higher domestic price level in the long run, which leads to a lower expected future exchange rate. The resulting expected depreciation of the pound raises the expected return on foreign deposits, shifting R^F to the right. The rise in the money supply lowers the interest rate on pound deposits in the short run, which shifts R^D to the left. The short-run outcome is a lower equilibrium exchange rate. However, in the long run, the domestic interest rate returns to its previous value, and R^D shifts back to its original position. The exchange rate rises to some extent, although it still remains below its initial position.

10. The dollar will depreciate. A rise in nominal interest rates but a decline in real interest rates implies a rise in expected inflation that produces an expected depreciation of the dollar that is larger than the increase in the domestic interest rate. As a result, the expected return on foreign deposits rises by more than the expected return on domestic deposits. R^F shifts rightward more than R^D, so the equilibrium exchange rate falls.

12. The dollar will depreciate. An increased demand for imports would lower the expected future exchange rate and result in an expected appreciation of the foreign currency. The higher resulting expected return on foreign deposits shifts the R^F schedule to the right, and the equilibrium exchange rate falls.

14. The contraction of the European money supply will increase European interest rates and raise the future value of the euro, both of which will shift R^F (with Europe as the foreign country) to the right. The result is a decline in the value of the dollar.

Chapter 13

2. The purchase of dollars involves a sale of foreign assets, which means that international reserves fall and the monetary base falls. The resulting fall in the money supply causes interest rates to rise and R^D to shift to the right while it lowers the future price level, thereby raising the future expected exchange rate, causing R^F to shift to the left. The result is a rise in the exchange rate. However, in the long run, the R^D curve returns to its original position, and so there is overshooting.

4. Because other countries often intervene in the foreign exchange market when the United States has a deficit so that U.S. holdings of international reserves do not change. By contrast, when Canada has a deficit, it must intervene in the foreign exchange market and buy Canadian dollars, which results in a reduction of international reserves for Canada.

6. Two euros per dollar.

8. A large balance-of-payments surplus may require a country to finance the surplus by selling its currency in the foreign exchange market, thereby gaining international reserves. The result is that the central bank will have supplied more of its currency to the public, and the monetary base will rise. The resulting rise in the money supply can cause the price level to rise, leading to a higher inflation rate.

10. Countries may implement a contractionary monetary policy when they decide to intervene in the foreign exchange market and buy domestic currency to finance the deficit. The result is that they sell off international reserves and their monetary base falls, leading to a decline in the money supply.

12. When other countries buy U.S. dollars to keep their exchange rates from changing vis-à-vis the dollar because of the U.S. deficits, they gain international reserves and their monetary base increases. The outcome is that the money supply in these countries grows faster and leads to higher inflation throughout the world.

14. There are no direct effects on the money supply because there is no central bank intervention in a pure flexible exchange rate regime; therefore, changes in international reserves that affect the monetary base do not occur. However, monetary policy can be affected by the foreign exchange market because monetary authorities may want to manipulate exchange rates by changing the money supply and interest rates.

16. Although capital outflows can harm a country when they lead to a devaluation of the domestic currency, controls in capital outflows are generally not thought to be a good idea. They are seldom effective in a crisis because the private sector figures out ways to get around them; they may even stimulate further capital outflows because they weaken confidence in the government. They also can lead to corruption and may also encourage governments to procrastinate and not take the steps necessary to reform their financial systems.

18. Engaging in a lender-of-last resort operation is likely to weaken the credibility of the central bank and lead to inflation and an even larger depreciation of the domestic currency. Because debt is short-term and denominated in foreign currency in emerging-market countries, the depreciation would lead to a deterioration of balance sheets; thus, the lender-of-last resort operation is likely to make the financial crisis even worse.

20. The international lender of last resort needs to make it clear that it will extend liquidity only to governments that take measures to prevent excessive risk taking. It can also reduce moral hazard by restricting the ability of governments to bail out stockholders and large uninsured creditors of domestic financial institutions.

Chapter 14

2. Financial intermediaries develop expertise in such areas as computer technology so that they can inexpensively provide liquidity services such as checking accounts that lower transaction costs for depositors. Financial intermediaries can also take advantage of economies of scale and engage in large transactions that have a lower cost per dollar of investment.

4. Standard accounting principles make profit verification easier, thereby reducing adverse selection and moral hazard problems in financial markets and hence making them operate better. Standard accounting principles make it easier for investors to screen out good firms from bad firms, thereby reducing the adverse selection problem in financial markets. In addition, they make it harder for managers to understate profits, thereby reducing the principal-agent (moral hazard) problem.

6. Smaller firms that are not well known are the most likely to use bank financing. Since it is harder for investors to acquire information about these firms, it will be hard for the firms to sell securities in the financial markets. Banks that specialize in collecting information about smaller firms will then be the only outlet these firms have for financing their activities.

8. Yes. The person who is putting her life savings into her business has more to lose if she takes on too much risk or engages in personally beneficial activities that don't lead to higher profits. So she will act more in the interest of the lender, making it more likely that the loan will be paid off.

10. True. If the borrower turns out to be a bad credit risk and goes broke, the lender loses less because the collateral can be sold to make up any losses on the loan. Thus adverse selection is not as severe a problem.

12. The separation of ownership and control creates a principal-agent problem. The managers (the agents) do not have as strong an incentive to maximize profits as the owners (the principals). Thus the managers might not work hard, might engage in wasteful spending on personal perks, or might pursue business strategies that enhance their personal power but do not increase profits.

14. A stock market crash reduces the net worth of firms and so increases the moral hazard problem. With less of an equity stake, owners have a greater incentive to take on risky projects and spend corporate funds on items that benefit them personally. A stock market crash, which increases the moral hazard problem, thus makes it less likely that lenders will be paid back. So lending and investment will decline, creating a financial crisis in which financial markets do not work well and the economy suffers.

Chapter 15

2. The rank from most to least liquid is (c), (b), (a), (d).

4. Reserves drop by $500. The T-account for the First Bank is as follows:

First Bank			
Assets		Liabilities	
Reserves	−$500	Chequable deposits	−$500

6. The bank would rather have the balance sheet shown in this problem because after it loses $50 million due to deposit outflow, the bank would still have excess reserves of $5 million: $50 million in reserves minus desired reserves of $45 million (10% of the $450 million of deposits). Thus the bank would not have to alter its balance sheet further and would not incur any costs as a result of the deposit outflow. By contrast, with the balance sheet in Problem 5, the bank would have a shortfall of reserves of $20 million ($25 million in reserves minus the desired reserves of $45 million). In this case the bank will incur costs when it raises the necessary reserves through the methods described in the text.
8. No. When you turn a customer down, you may lose that customer's business forever, which is extremely costly. Instead, you might go out and borrow from other banks, corporations, or the Bank of Canada to obtain funds so that you can make the customer's loan. Alternatively, you might sell negotiable CDs or some of your securities to acquire the necessary funds.
10. You would want to make short-term loans. Then, when these loans mature, you will be able to make loans at higher interest rates, which will generate more income for the bank.
12. True. Banks can now pursue new loan business much more aggressively than in the past because when they see profitable loan opportunities, they can use liability management to acquire new funds and expand the bank's business.
14. Interest expenses have large fluctuations because interest rates fluctuate so much; provisions for loan losses fluctuate a lot because when the economy turns down or a particular sector of the economy deteriorates, the potential for loan losses rises dramatically.
16. The net interest margin measures the difference between interest income and expenses. It is important because it indicates whether asset and liability management is being done properly so that the bank earns substantial income on its assets and has low costs on its liabilities.
18. To lower capital and raise *ROE,* holding its assets constant, it can pay out more dividends or buy back some of its shares. Alternatively, it can keep its capital constant but increase the amount of its assets by acquiring new funds and then seeking out new loan business or purchasing more securities with these new funds.
20. It can raise $1 million of capital by issuing new stock. It can cut its dividend payments by $1 million, thereby increasing its retained earnings by $1 million. It can decrease the amount of its assets so that the amount of its capital relative to its assets increases, thereby meeting the capital requirements.

Chapter 16

2. (a) The Office of the Superintendent of Financial Institutions (OSFI), the Bank of Canada, and the CDIC; (b) the OSFI and provincial banking authorities; (c) provincial banking authorities.
4. Improvements in technology made it easier for investors to screen out bad from good credit risks. This made it easier for corporations to issue long-term debt securities as in the junk bond market, and also to raise funds by issuing short-term debt securities like commercial paper.
6. The Big Six were severely punished in the early 1980s when the recession hit hard the less developed countries. When Argentina, Brazil, Mexico, and Peru threatened to default on their loans, the banks chose to make more loans to enable them to service their debts, instead of declaring these countries in default and acknowledging losses. This increased the indebtedness of these countries and led to a number of debt conversion schemes (such as debt-debt swaps, debt-currency swaps, and debt-equity swaps) to alleviate their debt service obligations.
8. No, because the Saudi-owned bank is subject to the same regulations as the Canadian-owned bank.
10. The rise of inflation and the resulting higher interest rates on alternatives to chequable deposits meant that banks had a big shrinkage in this low-cost way of raising funds. Foreign banks were also able to tap a large pool of domestic savings, thereby lowering their cost of funds relative to Canadian banks.
12. The growth of the commercial paper market and the development of the junk bond market meant that corporations were now able to issue securities rather than borrow from banks, thus eroding the competitive advantage of banks on the lending side. Securitization has enabled other financial institutions to originate

loans, again taking away some of the banks' loan business.

14. To introduce more competition into the Canadian financial services industry.

Chapter 17

1. All of the depositors at a mutual bank are owners of the firm. Instead of receiving interest payments, they receive dividend income.

3. The primary assets of TMLs are loans, for the most part mortgage loans.

5. They increased from $3 billion to about $134 billion.

7. The net worth ratio is the most common measure of capital adequacy.

9. Credit unions are mandated to provide financial services to consumers rather than corporate customers.

11. Only people living in a certain geographic area or employed in a specific business or by a particular employer are eligible for membership in a credit union.

13. The common bond membership rule restricts membership in any particular credit union so that the average size of credit unions is substantially lower than for commercial banks.

15. The main advantages of credit unions are employer support and strong trade associations.

Chapter 18

2. There would be adverse selection because people who might want to burn their property for some personal gain would actively try to obtain substantial fire insurance policies. Moral hazard could also be a problem because a person with a fire insurance policy has less incentive to take measures to prevent a fire.

4. Regulations that restrict banks from holding risky assets directly decrease the moral hazard of risk taking by the bank. Requirements that force banks to have a large amount of capital also decrease the banks' incentives for risk taking because banks now have more to lose if they fail. Such regulations will not completely eliminate the moral hazard problem because bankers have incentives to hide their holdings of risky assets from the regulators and to overstate the amount of their capital.

6. Because off-balance-sheet activities do not appear on bank balance sheets, they cannot be dealt with by simple bank capital requirements, which are based on bank assets, such as a leverage ratio. Banking regulators have dealt with this problem by imposing an additional risk-based bank capital requirement that requires banks to set aside additional bank capital for different kinds of off-balance-sheet activities.

8. Bank supervision involves bank examinations in which bank examiners assess six areas of the bank represented in the CAMELS rating (capital adequacy, asset quality, management, earnings, liquidity, and sensitivity to market risk). A low score on the CAMELS rating allows the supervisors to declare a bank to be a "problem bank," making it more subject to frequent examinations and to sanctions to reduce the amount of risk taking it is engaged in. Bank examiners also check that the bank is following the rules and regulations and is not holding securities or loans that are too risky. All of these measures help ensure that banks are not taking on too much risk, and thus promote a safer and sounder banking system.

10. With the advent of new financial instruments, a bank that is quite healthy at a particular point in time can be driven into insolvency extremely rapidly from risky trading in these instruments. Thus, a focus on bank capital at a point in time may not be effective in indicating whether a bank will be taking on excessive risk in the near future. Therefore, to make sure that banks are not taking on too much risk, bank supervisors now are focusing more on whether the risk-management procedures in banks keep them from excessive risk taking that might make a future bank failure more likely.

12. Eliminating or limiting the amount of deposit insurance would help reduce the moral hazard of excessive risk taking on the part of banks. It would, however, make bank failures and panics more likely, so it might not be a very good idea.

14. The economy would benefit from reduced moral hazard; that is, banks would not want to take on too much risk because doing so would increase their deposit insurance premiums. The problem is, however, that it is difficult to monitor the degree of risk in bank assets because often only the bank making the loans knows how risky they are.

Chapter 19

1. People carry insurance because they are risk-averse and prefer to know their wealth with certainty.

3. Information asymmetry exists when one party to a transaction knows more about the situation than the other does. Often the person buying insurance knows more about the risk than the insurance company knows.

5. Insurance companies protect themselves by requiring inspections and medical examinations, insuring groups rather than individuals, and insisting on a deductible.
7. Most are stock companies.
9. Term life insurance pays a death benefit if the policyholder dies; no other benefit is paid. Whole policies pay a death benefit but also include a savings program that pays out if the policyholder lives.
11. Reinsurance allocates a portion of the risk to another company in exchange for a portion of the premium.
13. A more sophisticated public, greater awareness of providing for retirement, and a lack of confidence in Social Security have led to growth in private pension plans.
15. The demographics suggest that more people will be retiring than will be entering the workforce in the future. With fewer people paying into the plan and more taking out, it could go bankrupt.

Chapter 20

2. Venture financing is long-term. Pension funds hold long-term funds and can predict very accurately when the funds will be needed. The illiquidity of the investment is not a problem for them. Property and casualty insurance companies need access to their funds if there are a large number of claims, say from a hurricane. They could not tolerate the illiquidity of the investment.
4. Ventures firms provide screening of potential investments. They monitor firm activities and participate in management decision making. They also require firms to demonstrate progress in order to obtain continuing funding.
6. A balloon loan requires that a single large payment be made when the loan matures, whereas on an installment loan, the borrower makes a series of small, equal payments.
8. They often have poor credit records, low incomes, or inferior security. All of these factors make them unacceptable to banks.
10. Yes, because there is no well-established secondary market for their loans.
12. Factoring is selling accounts receivable to a finance company. The selling firm gets immediate cash for its sales and avoids having to go after its customers for collections.
14. Under a floor plan, the finance company holds the inventory as security and releases its lien on the inventory only when the items are sold and the loan is paid.
16. The tax code in the United States allows the interest paid on loans secured by homes to be deducted from taxes. This lowers the effective cost of the debt.
18. No, consumers did not perceive any great benefit to dealing with a single firm for all of their financial needs.

Chapter 21

1. Regulators felt that investment banking was riskier.
3. When an offering is underwritten, the investment banker purchases the issue at a prespecified price. In a best-efforts issue, the investment banker does not take ownership.
5. No, a securities commission review simply determines if the proper documents have been filed.
7. It is better to be fully subscribed because oversubscription indicates that the investment bankers priced the security too low.
9. In a hostile takeover, the target firm does not want control to pass to the acquiring firm, and so its management makes every effort to prevent the takeover from happening. In a merger, both sides work together to expedite the union of the firms.
11. A market order has the broker buy or sell the security at the current market price. A limit order sets a maximum price for buying the security and a minimum price for selling the security.
13. Banks object because legislation prevents banks from entering the brokerage business but does not prevent brokers from entering the banking business.
15. Load funds charge sales commissions; no-load funds do not.

Chapter 22

2. Secured loans are an important method of lending for financial institutions because if the borrower defaults, the financial institution can take title to the collateral, sell it off, and use the proceeds to offset any losses on the loan. Thus the financial institution can worry less about the adverse selection problem because it has some protection even if the borrower was a bad credit risk.

4. To reduce adverse selection, a banker needs to screen out bad credit risks by learning as much as possible about potential borrowers. Similarly, to minimize moral hazard, the banker must continually monitor borrowers to see that they are complying with restrictive loan covenants. Hence it pays for the banker to be nosy.

6. False. Although diversification is a desirable strategy for a bank, it may still make sense for a bank to specialize in certain types of lending. For example, a bank may have developed expertise in screening and monitoring a particular kind of loan, thereby improving its ability to handle problems of adverse selection and moral hazard.

8. Rate-sensitive assets increase by $4 million, so *GAP* goes from –$17.5 million to –$13.5 million. (Of the $5 million of fixed-rate mortgages, $1 million is rate-sensitive because 20% are repaid within a year, so converting the $5 million of fixed-rate mortgages into variable-rate mortgages produces a net increase of rate-sensitive assets of $4 million.) Because *GAP* falls in absolute value, the effect of changes in interest rates on its profits and hence on its interest-rate risk is smaller.

10. The manager raises the estimate of rate-sensitive liabilities by $2.25 million so that *GAP* goes from –$17.5 million to –$19.75 million. Because *GAP* rises in absolute value, the effect of changes in interest rates on its profits and hence its interest-rate risk is larger. If interest rates rise by 5 percentage points, profits next year change by $\Delta I = GAP \times \Delta i = -\$19.75$ million $\times 0.05 = -\$0.9875$ million.

12. The duration gap is now $DUR_{gap} = DUR_A - (L/A \times DUR_L) = 4 - (95/100 \times 2) = 2.1$ years. The change in net worth as a percentage of assets is $\%\Delta NW = -DUR_{GAP} \times \Delta i/(1 + i) = -2.1 \times 0.02/(1 + 0.10) = -0.038 = -3.8\%$. With $100 million of assets, net worth declines by $3.8 million, from $5 million to $1.2 million.

14. It should solve the following equation: $0 = 4 - (95/100 \times DUR_L)$. This yields a duration of liabilities DUR_L of 4.2 years.

16. Interest-rate risk stays the same because rate-sensitive assets and rate-sensitive liabilities increase by an equal amount, leaving the income gap the same. The Friendly Finance Company still has an income gap of $12 million, and to eliminate it, it could either reduce its rate-sensitive assets to $43 million or increase its rate-sensitive liabilities to $55 million.

18. The duration gap is now $DUR_{GAP} = DUR_A - (L/A \times DUR_L) = 2 - (90/100 \times 4) = -1.6$ years. The change in net worth as a percentage of assets is $\%\Delta NW = -DUR_{GAP} \times \Delta i/(1 + i) = -(-1.6) \times 0.03/(1 + 0.08) = 0.044 = 4.4\%$. With $100 million of assets, net worth increases by $4.4 million, from $10 million to $14.4 million.

20. It should solve the following equation: $0 = 2 - (90/100 \times DUR_L)$. This yields a duration of liabilities DUR_L of 2.22 years.

Chapter 23

2. You would enter into a contract that specifies that you will sell the $25 million of 8s of 2015 at a price of 110 one year from now.

4. You have a loss of 6 points, or $6000, per contract.

6. You would buy $100 million worth (1000 contracts) of the call long-term bond option with a delivery date of one year in the future and with a strike price that corresponds to a yield of 8%. This means that you would have the option to buy the long bond with the 8% interest rate, thereby making sure that you can earn the 8%. The disadvantage of the options contract is that you have to pay a premium that you would not have to pay with a futures contract. The advantage of the options contract is that if the interest rate rises and the bond price falls during the next year, you do not have to exercise the option and so will be able to earn a higher rate than 8% when the funds come in next year, whereas with the futures contract, you have to take delivery of the bond and will only earn 8%.

8. You have a profit of 1 point ($1000) when you exercise the contract, but you have paid a premium of $1500 for the call option, so your net profit is –$500, a loss of $500.

10. Because for any given price at expiration, a lower strike price means a higher profit for a call option and a lower profit for a put option. A lower strike price makes a call option more desirable and raises its premium and makes a put option less desirable and lowers its premium.

12. It would swap interest on $42 million of fixed-rate assets for the interest on $42 million of variable-rate assets, thereby eliminating its income gap.

14. You would hedge the risk by buying 80 euro futures contracts that mature 3 months from now.

Index

Note: Page numbers followed by letters *f*, *n*, and *t* refer to figures, notes and tables, respectively.

G

H